International Directory of
COMPANY
HISTORIES

International Directory of

COMPANY HISTORIES

VOLUME 51

Editor

Tina Grant

ST. JAMES PRESS®

Detroit • New York • San Diego • San Francisco • Cleveland • New Haven, Conn. • Waterville, Maine • London • Munich

THOMSON

GALE

International Directory of Company Histories, Volume 51

Tina Grant, Editor

Project Editor
Miranda H. Ferrara

Editorial
Erin Bealmear, Joann Cerrito, Jim Craddock,
Stephen Cusack, Peter M. Gareffa,
Kristin Hart, Melissa Hill,
Margaret Mazurkiewicz, Carol A. Schwartz,
Christine Tomassini, Michael J. Tyrkus

Imaging and Multimedia
Randy Bassett, Dean Dauphinais, Robert
Duncan, Lezlie Light

Manufacturing
Rhonda Williams

LIBRARY OF CONGRESS CATALOG NUMBER 89-190943

ISBN: 1-55862-481-3

BRITISH LIBRARY CATALOGUING IN PUBLICATION DATA

International directory of company histories. Vol. 51
I. Tina Grant
33.87409

Printed in the United States of America
10 9 8 7 6 5 4 3 2 1

CONTENTS

Company Histories

PREFACE

The St. James Press series *The International Directory of Company Histories (IDCH)* is intended for reference use by students, business people, librarians, historians, economists, investors, job candidates, and others who seek to learn more about the historical development of the world's most important companies. To date, *IDCH* has covered over 5,850 companies in 51 volumes.

Inclusion Criteria

Most companies chosen for inclusion in *IDCH* have achieved a minimum of US$25 million in annual sales and are leading influences in their industries or geographical locations. Companies may be publicly held, private, or nonprofit. State-owned companies that are important in their industries and that may operate much like public or private companies also are included. Wholly owned subsidiaries and divisions are profiled if they meet the requirements for inclusion. Entries on companies that have had major changes since they were last profiled may be selected for updating.

The *IDCH* series highlights 10% private and nonprofit companies, and features updated entries on approximately 45 companies per volume.

Entry Format

Each entry begins with the company's legal name, the address of its headquarters, its telephone, toll-free, and fax numbers, and its web site. A statement of public, private, state, or parent ownership follows. A company with a legal name in both English and the language of its headquarters country is listed by the English name, with the native-language name in parentheses.

The company's founding or earliest incorporation date, the number of employees, and the most recent available sales figures follow. Sales figures are given in local currencies with equivalents in U.S. dollars. For some private companies, sales figures are estimates and indicated by the abbreviation *est.* The entry lists the exchanges on which a company's stock is traded and its ticker symbol, as well as the company's NAIC codes.

Entries generally contain a *Company Perspectives* box which provides a short summary of the company's mission, goals, and ideals, a *Key Dates* box highlighting milestones in the company's history, lists of *Principal Subsidiaries, Principal Divisions, Principal Operating Units, Principal Competitors,* and articles for *Further Reading.*

American spelling is used throughout *IDCH*, and the word ''billion'' is used in its U.S. sense of one thousand million.

Sources

Entries have been compiled from publicly accessible sources both in print and on the Internet such as general and academic periodicals, books, annual reports, and material supplied by the companies themselves.

Cumulative Indexes

IDCH contains three indexes: the **Index to Companies**, which provides an alphabetical index to companies discussed in the text as well as to companies profiled, the **Index to Industries**, which allows researchers to locate companies by their principal industry, and the **Geographic Index**, which lists companies alphabetically by the country of their headquarters. The indexes are cumulative and specific instructions for using them are found immediately preceding each index.

Suggestions Welcome

Comments and suggestions from users of *IDCH* on any aspect of the product as well as suggestions for companies to be included or updated are cordially invited. Please write:

The Editor
International Directory of Company Histories
St. James Press
27500 Drake Rd.
Farmington Hills, Michigan 48331-3535

ABBREVIATIONS FOR FORMS OF COMPANY INCORPORATION

A.B.	Aktiebolaget (Sweden)
A.G.	Aktiengesellschaft (Germany, Switzerland)
A.S.	Aksjeselskap (Denmark, Norway)
A.S.	Atieselskab (Denmark)
A.Ş.	Anomin Şirket (Turkey)
B.V.	Besloten Vennootschap met beperkte, Aansprakelijkheid (The Netherlands)
Co.	Company (United Kingdom, United States)
Corp.	Corporation (United States)
G.I.E.	Groupement d'Intérêt Economique (France)
GmbH	Gesellschaft mit beschränkter Haftung (Germany)
H.B.	Handelsbolaget (Sweden)
Inc.	Incorporated (United States)
KGaA	Kommanditgesellschaft auf Aktien (Germany)
K.K.	Kabushiki Kaisha (Japan)
LLC	Limited Liability Company (Middle East)
Ltd.	Limited (Canada, Japan, United Kingdom, United States)
N.V.	Naamloze Vennootschap (The Netherlands)
OY	Osakeyhtiöt (Finland)
OAO	Otkrytoe Aktsionernoe Obshchestve (Russia)
OOO	Obshchestvo s Ogranichennoi Otvetstvennostiu (Russia)
PLC	Public Limited Company (United Kingdom)
PTY.	Proprietary (Australia, Hong Kong, South Africa)
S.A.	Société Anonyme (Belgium, France, Switzerland)
SpA	Società per Azioni (Italy)
ZAO	Zakrytoe Aktsionernoe Obshchestve (Russia)

ABBREVIATIONS FOR CURRENCY

$	United States dollar	KD	Kuwaiti dinar
£	United Kingdom pound	L	Italian lira
¥	Japanese yen	LuxFr	Luxembourgian franc
A$	Australian dollar	M$	Malaysian ringgit
AED	United Arab Emirates dirham	N	Nigerian naira
B	Thai baht	Nfl	Netherlands florin
B	Venezuelan bolivar	NIS	Israeli new shekel
BFr	Belgian franc	NKr	Norwegian krone
C$	Canadian dollar	NT$	Taiwanese dollar
CHF	Switzerland franc	NZ$	New Zealand dollar
COL	Colombian peso	P	Philippine peso
Cr	Brazilian cruzado	PLN	Polish zloty
CZK	Czech Republic koruny	PkR	Pakistan Rupee
DA	Algerian dinar	Pta	Spanish peseta
Dfl	Netherlands florin	R	Brazilian real
DKr	Danish krone	R	South African rand
DM	German mark	RMB	Chinese renminbi
E£	Egyptian pound	RO	Omani rial
Esc	Portuguese escudo	Rp	Indonesian rupiah
EUR	Euro dollars	Rs	Indian rupee
FFr	French franc	Ru	Russian ruble
Fmk	Finnish markka	S$	Singapore dollar
GRD	Greek drachma	Sch	Austrian schilling
HK$	Hong Kong dollar	SFr	Swiss franc
HUF	Hungarian forint	SKr	Swedish krona
IR£	Irish pound	SRls	Saudi Arabian riyal
ISK	Icelandic Króna	TD	Tunisian dinar
K	Zambian kwacha	W	Korean won

International Directory of

COMPANY HISTORIES

A.W. Faber-Castell Unternehmensverwaltung GmbH & Co.

Nuernberger Strasse 2
D-90546 Stein
Germany
Telephone: (49) 911 9965-0
Fax: (49) 911 9965-856
Web site: http://www.faber-castell.com

Private Company
Incorporated: 1784 as A.W. Faber
Employees: 5,550
Sales: EUR 369 million ($278 million) (2001)
NAIC: 339942 Lead Pencil and Art Good Manufacturing;
    339941 Pen and Mechanical Pencil Manufacturing;
    339943 Marking Device Manufacturing

A.W. Faber-Castell Unternehmensverwaltung GmbH & Co. is the organizational umbrella for the Faber-Castell Group, the world's largest and oldest manufacturer of lead and coloring pencils. Based in Stein near Nuremberg in Germany, the group manufactures lead, coloring, and mechanical pencils; erasers and rules; a variety of pens, colored markers, and highlighters; and chalk, charcoals, oil, and soft pastels and paints for a broad range of customers—from children and students to professional artists and CEO's. The group's industrial activities are organized under the management holding Faber-Castell AG; its service arm, Faber-Castell-Consulting, offers IT and management consulting services; and Faber-Castell Projetos Imobiliarios is the group's Brazilian real estate development arm, founded in 1994. Faber-Castell AG generates 85 percent of total sales abroad and operates 15 production plants and 19 distribution subsidiaries in 19 countries around the globe. The largest among the company's subsidiaries is located near Sao Paulo in Brazil, where every year some 3,000 employees produce 1.5 million wooden pencils as well as about 1,500 other items, including decorative cosmetics products such as eye and lip liners, lipsticks, and eye shadow pencils under its own brand name and for other cosmetics companies. Faber-Castell Brazil also grows its own wood in a sustainable forestry project. CEO Count Anton Wolfgang Graf von Faber-Castell owns 85 percent of the company that was founded by his ancestors.

Foundation for Pencil Dynasty Set Up in 1761

The history of Faber-Castell began in Stein, a small town south of Nuremberg. Joiner Kaspar Faber had settled in Stein and after a few years decided to make lead pencils. He made the square wooden shafts, drilled a groove in them, inserted graphite sticks, closed the gap with a small piece of wood and glued it all together. Finally, he gave the pencil a rectangular or oval form. Since stationary stores did not yet exist in pre-industrial Germany, Kaspar Faber's wife frequently stashed the pencils her husband made in a basket and sold them at the market in Nuremberg. There he competed with pencil maker Guttknecht who was also based in Stein. Guttknecht tried to sue Faber out of his territory. This action failed because at that time pencil making was an unregulated trade.

In 1784, Kaspar's son Anton Wilhelm took over the small workshop and incorporated the family business as A.W. Faber. From his father's savings he was able to acquire a larger property in Stein where the company's headquarters was still located 228 years later. In 1795, a new law issued by the traditionally bureaucratic German craft guilds imposed strict rules on every aspect of the pencil making trade. However, Anton Wilhelm carried on the family enterprise with much success and left his son Georg Leonhard a good-sized inheritance.

Georg Leonhard Faber expanded the family property but struggled against unfortunate events. The reign of Napoleon that followed the French Revolution of 1789 brought more than 20 years of war and political unrest to Europe. Moreover, the progressive exhaustion of the world's foremost source for graphite in England made the raw material for pencils more and more expensive, then unaffordable, and finally unavailable. Consequently, German pencil makers were pushed to use graphite of bad quality, which consequently earned a bad name for pencils made in Germany. In 1806, Stein and Nuremberg became part of the newly founded Kingdom of Bavaria. The new government lifted some of the obstacles to free trade and allowed pencil makers from outside the city to sell their mer-

Company Perspectives:

The lead pencil keeps writing history in the 21st century. The pencil's unmistakable profile continues to evolve and supplements every modern means of communication, be it a mobile phone, Laptop or PC. Uncomplicated, robust, non-perishable, and environmentally friendly as it is, as a natural product, it is ultimately closer to the writing human and his hand than cold keyboards. Unlike any other means of writing, mistakes made with it are correctable; it bears this provisional character to great advantage.

chandise at the Nuremberg market. The old rule of the craft guild was ended in 1808. The new, more liberal trade law gave way to increasing competition among pencil makers. In 1839, Georg Leonhard Faber died at age 51.

Success for A.W. Faber in the 19th Century

Georg Leonhard Faber's son Lothar was 22 years old when he took over the family business after his father's sudden death. By that time, the enterprise had grown into a small factory with 20 employees. After his apprenticeship as a merchant, the young man had spent three years working in Paris. His witnessing of a thriving pencil-making trade in one of the world's major centers of free trade deeply impressed Lothar Faber. When he returned to Nuremberg, the city was just making its first steps into the industrial age, led by a new generation of business people, engineers, and bankers. One of their first accomplishments was the first railroad in Germany which started operations between Nuremberg and Fürth in 1835.

There was much that needed improvement when Lothar Faber took over the family business. In addition, the market for pencils made in Germany was very limited, mainly because of their bad reputation. Middlemen dictated a price level that barely enabled pencil manufacturers to prosper. Nevertheless, Lothar Faber rolled up his sleeves and started making fundamental changes to the business that led to his success.

First of all, Faber significantly improved the quality of his pencils. He introduced and refined the so-called clay-graphite process, a new technology that had been invented at the end of the eighteenth century. The graphite was ground and mixed with clay, formed into strips, and baked. This technology enabled Faber to offer pencils of varying hardness or softness. Next, Faber modernized his manufacturing plant to ensure a steady quality and to increase the output and efficiency of his operation. Soon, a water-powered steam engine was driving the mechanized saws and planes. Faber's factory was now outfitted for mass production.

In another step, Faber focused on boosting the sales of his pencils. To distinguish his products from those of other manufacturers, he printed ''A.W. Faber'' on his pencils—a novelty at the time. Also, unlike any other pencil manufacturer, Faber—equipped with a beautifully carved wooden sample case—traveled through Germany and Europe, personally promoting his merchandise. Confident about the high quality of his pencils, he demanded prices as high as top quality pencils from England.

Surprised by Faber's high prices, a Nuremberg businessman is said to have asked him sarcastically if his pencil mines were made from silver. But the young entrepreneur stuck to his guns and got plenty of orders on his promotional trips through Germany, Austria, Belgium, the Netherlands, France, England, Italy, and Russia. Within ten years, Faber had created a network of trade partners in many countries. In 1849, he sent his youngest brother, Eberhard, to the United States, where he established the company's first foreign subsidiary in New York. Soon after, A.W. Faber set up sales offices in Vienna, London, Paris and St. Petersburg in Russia and expanded its market as far as Africa, Australia, India, the Middle East, and China.

In the second half of the nineteenth century, the world's major supplier of high-quality graphite—the ore that looked like lead and therefore gave the lead pencil its name—the English Cumberland mines ran out of the material. Geologists started searching for new deposits in many parts of the world and one of them, Johann Peter Alibert, spotted a rich graphite deposit of high quality in Siberia, Russia, in 1847. Nine years later, Alibert sold Faber the exclusive rights to exploit the mine. This deal secured the company's raw material base for many years to come and gave it an independence and competitive advantage that ultimately led to Faber's market leadership.

Becoming the Market Leader

Lothar Faber's efforts paid off. His company was flooded with orders, so production capacity had to be expanded. With A.W. Faber's growth, its host community grew as well. Lothar Faber initiated and sponsored the construction of housing for his workers, a kindergarten, and even a church in Stein. In 1862, Bavarian King Maximilian II made Lothar Faber a peer by giving him the inheritable title of ''Freiherr'' and three years later appointed him Imperial Counselor to the Bavarian Crown. The entrepreneur who was now called Lothar *von* Faber as a sign of his nobility, stayed actively involved in local and regional politics for the rest of his life. His main focus, however, was on becoming the world's number one pencil maker.

Two of A.W. Faber's emerging competitors came from his own family—Lothar von Faber's two brothers, Johann and Eberhard. Eberhard, who managed A.W. Faber's New York office, started his own pencil company, Eberhard Faber, Inc., on the side. In 1876, Lothar's brother Johann, who had been sent to South America to explore the unknown market for A.W. Faber, left the family business to set up a pencil company of his own.

To stay on top of the market and to further enhance product quality, Faber established a number of standards for his pencils. He distinguished them by length, grades of hardness and other criteria, and gave them a hexagonal shape. His Siberian graphite, which was transported long distances on the backs of reindeer through undeveloped wilderness to the closest sea port, was of the best quality available at the time. Lothar von Faber also attempted to gain independence from middlemen for his second crucial raw material—cedar wood, which he obtained from California because his cedar plantation in Stein yielded wood that was too hard for use in pencils.

Another of Faber's strategies to grow the company was the expansion of his range of products. One of the new markets he developed was colored pencils for artists' use. Over time, Faber's catalogues grew to over 70 pages. Designed to emphasize the company's high-quality image, they were available in German, English, Spanish, and Russian.

By the late nineteenth century, Nuremberg had become the world's center of pencil manufacturing, with 25 factories putting out 250 million lead pencils a year. A.W. Faber, the largest of them, employed a workforce of 1,000 and an additional 300 home workers in 1890. Faber's success, however, attracted competition. The company's brand name "A.W. Faber"—a synonym for top quality—was frequently imitated. To protect himself from this practice, Lothar von Faber drafted and promoted a petition in 1874 demanding that the German Imperial parliament recognize and protect brand names. A law based on Faber's suggestions passed the governing body a year later and paved the way for a unified German trademark law. By the 1890s, the tensions between Eberhard Faber, Inc. and A.W. Faber had grown and escalated in a law suit over the trademark.

Getting Ahead Between World Wars

When Lothar von Faber's era ended with his death in 1896, the company was left without a male heir. Since Lothar's only son, Wilhelm, had died before him at age 41, he was succeeded by his wife and later by his granddaughter Ottilie von Faber. In 1898, Ottilie married Count Alexander zu Castell-Rüdenhausen, a descendant of one of Bavaria's oldest noble families. Alexander became a new shareholder in the family business.

Count Alexander, who had no experience in doing business as a pencil manufacturer, made strategic decisions but left the day-to-day operations to the company's experienced directors. However, under his leadership the company introduced CASTELL 9000, a new lead pencil line with a green coating that became a huge success. CASTELL 9000 emerged as A.W. Faber's single best-selling article and remained a flagship product for almost 100 years after it was launched in 1905. In the same year, the company introduced an advertising poster showing a "pencil tournament"—two knights on horses fighting with huge pencils instead of lances—that was used to publicize

the new "noble" image. The popular motive also became part of the company's stationery. Between 1903 and 1906, a castle was erected in Stein that became the company's new headquarters. From his huge study on the first floor, overlooking the production plants, Count Alexander steered the family operation with a global reach.

World War I, which broke out in 1914 and ended with Germany's defeat in late 1918, suddenly interrupted the company's growth. Moreover, with the United States entering the war in 1917, A.W. Faber was cut off from this major market, where the company lost its production facilities and sales offices. When the German economy entered a short growth period in the second half of the 1920s, Faber-Castell's production facilities were once more expanded. After Count Alexander died in 1928, his son Roland took over the enterprise at age 23, and the company was transformed into A.W. Faber, Castell-Bleistiftfabrik AG.

The early 1930s turned out to be a crucial time for A.W. Faber. In 1931, the company entered a cooperation agreement with Nuremberg-based Johann Faber AG, the company that was founded by Lothar von Faber's brother Johann in 1878. Since then, Johann Faber AG had become a fierce competitor of A.W. Faber. In the following years Johann Faber's manufacturing operations were moved to Stein and integrated into A.W. Faber's. Another action that insured the company's continued world market leadership was the acquisition of an interest in Johann Faber's production subsidiary in Sao Carlos, Brazil, which was the largest of its kind in South America, in 1937. The outbreak of Word War II two years later once more interrupted the company's development. Throughout the conflict, Faber-Castell, which by that time had been transformed into the legal form of a public stock company, was put under the leadership of an out-of-family CEO appointed by the Nazis, while Count Roland von Faber-Castell was drafted into the German army, leaving him with no influence over his company. During the war, however, his wife Nina managed to transform the company back into a sole proprietorship, which was renamed A.W. Faber-Castell in 1942.

Changes in the Second Half of the 20th Century

The bombing raids on Nuremberg had left Faber-Castell's premises almost untouched, and in 1946 the company resumed operations. The period after World War II saw Germany recover in record time. Throughout this period of enormous economic upswing, interrupted only by short recessions, Faber-Castell profited from the country's double-digit growth rates. In 1949, the company ventured into manufacturing ball point pens and afterwards kept expanding its product range, workforce, production capacity, and distribution network. Faber-Castell's product range grew to about 5,000 articles, including technical drawing instruments. In 1967, the company was able to acquire a majority stake in Lapis Johann Faber, the world's largest factory for lead and colored pencils in Sao Carlos, Brazil. The "economic miracle" years of the 1950s and 1960s were followed by the oil crises of the 1970s, which brought about a flood of technological innovations. One of them was the electronic pocket calculator that within a short time period replaced the slide rule, a product area in which Faber-Castell had achieved world market leadership.

Two years before he died in 1978, Count Roland had chosen his son Anton Wolfgang as his successor among his ten children. The 35-year-old attorney, who had attended Swiss business schools and gathered practical experience working at investment bank Credit Suisse First Boston, seemed to be the best choice to become the new Faber-Castell CEO. After his father's death, Count Anton Wolfgang put a renewed emphasis on profitable, environmentally friendly products of top quality. First, he streamlined the company's operations. The production of unprofitable articles was ceased and the product range slimmed down. To replace the lost business from slide rules, Faber-Castell started producing make-up pencils for international cosmetics companies. During the 1980s, the company expanded its product range to felt tip pens, such as markers and highlighters. Early in the decade, Faber-Castell initiated a pioneering sustainable forestry project for its subsidiary in Brazil. To be independent of other suppliers, the company established its own growth of Caribbean pine trees about 240 miles away from its Sao Carlos production plant in the Brazilian savanna. On 27,000 acres, Faber-Castell grows its own wood, which can be harvested after ten to fourteen years and used for making lead and colored pencils. The plantation, which was set up in the Minas Gerias province on former grazing land with dry, sandy soil, also includes a nursery that plants about two million pine trees a year.

The 1990s saw the company once more reinvent itself. While its Brazilian subsidiary was profitable, the German production slipped into the red in 1992 and 1993. Faber-Castell laid off about 30 percent of its German workforce and worked on improving the company's image. Marketing research had shown that the Faber-Castell brand name was well known but not necessarily associated with "exclusivity." The company redefined its core competence in a handful of product categories and gave its products a more upscale look. Faber-Castell communicated its focus on tradition and high value with a new image campaign. The company's redesigned logo included the "pencil tournament" motive that had boosted Faber-Castell's popularity at the beginning of the century. Along the same lines, the company also introduced the "Count von Faber-Castell Collection," a luxury set of five pencils with a silver grip and sharpener in a wooden box made from rare wood and a silver cover which sold for over $100. The "noble collection" was later extended to include mechanical pencils, fountain pens, and blotters. In 1994, Faber-Castell re-acquired the trademark rights the company had lost in the United States as a result of World War I. In exchange, A.W. Faber-Castell sold the 25 percent stake Roland Count von Faber-Castell had acquired in its former U.S.-subsidiary Faber-Castell Co. after World War II. Faber-Castell Co.—in the meantime under independent U.S. management—had taken over Eberhard Faber Inc. in 1987.

In the second half of the 1990s, the company established new production plants and sales subsidiaries in countries around the globe, including the Czech Republic, Colombia, India, and Costa Rica. A new distribution center for the Asian-Pacific region was set up in Singapore in 2000. In the same year, a new management holding company for the company's industrial activities, Faber-Castell AG, was established. The new century saw another Faber-Castell innovation—the silver-colored triangular-shaped lead pencil Grip 2000, which featured lacquer bumps for a firm grip. In the summer of 2001, the company celebrated its 240th anniversary and launched a limited edition of its premium sets, including a pencil with an extender made from massive white gold and a cap with three embedded diamonds. For the cost of a small car, the sets sold out within a short time.

After a first experiment to sell Faber-Castell products over the Internet failed, Count von Faber-Castell was looking for new distribution channels to expand the company's markets. At age 60, he had not decided yet if his 21-year-old son Alexander, who was studying in the United States, might take over his global family enterprise, or if taking Faber-Castell public was the better choice.

Principal Subsidiaries

Faber-Castell AG (Germany); A.W. Faber-Castell Produktion GmbH (Germany); A.W. Faber-Castell Vertrieb GmbH (Germany); Faber-Castell COSMETICS GmbH (Germany); A.W. Faber-Castell Brasil S.A.; A.W. Faber-Castell Argentina S.A.; A.W. Faber-Castell (India) Pvt. Ltd.; A.W. Faber-Castell (Aust.) Pty. Ltd. (Australia); Maderin ECO S.A. (Costa Rica); A.W. Faber-Castell (Guangzhou) Stationery Co. Ltd. (China); A.W. Faber-Castell Peruana S.A. (Peru); Tecnacril Ltda (Colombia); PT. A.W. Faber-Castell Indonesia; A.W. Faber-Castell (M) Sdn. Bhd. (Malaysia); Faber-Castell Projetos Imobiliarios (Brazil); A.W. Faber-Castell USA, Inc.

Principal Competitors

Schwan-Stabilo Schwanhäußer GmbH & Co.; STAEDTLER Group; LYRA Bleistift-Fabrik GmbH & Co.; Dixon Ticonderoga Company; Newell Rubbermaid Inc.; Caran d'Ache SA; Parker Pen Co; Montblanc International GmbH.

Further Reading

Dunsch, Juergen, "Ein Familienmitglied im Unternehmen reicht," *Frankfurter Allgemeine Zeitung*, July 8, 1995, p. 17.

"Faber-Castell will auf chinesischen Markt," *dpa*, July 26, 2001.

Im Galopp durch die Bleistiftgeschichte, Stein/Nuremberg, Germany: Faber-Castell AG, 2000, 11 p.

"Internetpartner bringen Faber-Castell Verluste," *Frankfurter Allgemeine Zeitung*, July 28, 2001, p. 18.

Mangelsdorf, Martha E., "I'm my own grandpa," *Inc.*, May 1988, p. 13.

Muehleisen, Stefan, "Gemessen wird die Qualität der Idee," *Lebensmittel Zeitung,* December 21, 2001, p. 29.

Nobbe, Marion, "Ein wohlmeinender Diktator," *Süddeutsche Zeitung*, June 7, 2001, p. 26.

—Evelyn Hauser

ACCO World Corporation

300 Tower Parkway
Lincolnshire, Illinois 60069-3640
U.S.A.
Telephone: (847) 419-4100
Toll Free: (800) 222-6462
Fax: (847) 419-4110
Web site: http://www.accobrands.com

Wholly Owned Subsidiary of Fortune Brands Inc.
Incorporated: 1970
Employees: 6,967
Sales: $1.25 billion (2001 est.)
NAIC: 339942 Lead Pencil and Art Good Manufacturing;
    333313 Office Machinery Manufacturing; 323118
    Blankbook, Looseleaf Binders, and Devices
    Manufacturing

ACCO World Corporation manufactures a wide variety of office supplies, ranging from paper clips and staplers to personal organizers, computer peripherals, and software. As a subsidiary of Fortune Brands Inc., ACCO World has operations in 60 locations across the globe. Its major brands include Wilson Jones, the number one leader in ring binders in North America; Swingline, the leading brand in stapling, punches, paper clips, and fasteners in North America; Day-Timer, the second-largest market share holder in the North American paper-based organizer industry; Kensington, the leading computer security products brand in North America; Gravis, a joystick and game pad brand; Maco, a printer label brand; and Apollo and Boone, two leading presentation products brands. During 2000, Fortune Brands set plans in motion to divest its office supply business segment. Due to unfavorable market conditions, Fortune Brands instead opted to restructure ACCO World, focusing on improving its financial record.

The Birth of the ACCO Brand Name

ACCO World has several predecessor companies but the core organization that gave it its name was the Clipper Manufacturing Company. Clipper was founded in 1903 by Fred J. Kline. Originally located in Long Island City, New York, Clip-

per had one product: paper clips. Seemingly insignificant at only a fraction of a cent per piece, Clipper eventually turned out billions of the little wire contraptions.

In 1910, Kline changed the name of his firm to the grander sounding American Clip Company. Two years later he invented a new paper fastener that he dubbed the "ACCO Fastener" after his company's acronym. This two-pronged locking paper compressor proved highly successful and cleared the way for several new products, including folders, binders, punches, and clamps. Also marketed under the ACCO brand name, these items became better known than the company that made them. This prompted Kline to change the name of the company again in 1922, this time to ACCO Products, Inc.

Operating under the claim "ACCO originates and develops," the company prospered from the proliferation of paperwork in consumers' business and personal affairs. ACCO Products grew tremendously in this expanding market. In 1924, Kline established an English subsidiary and three years later added another in Canada. The company also established a new product line, pressboard binders, in 1928. Available in five colors, these binders became common office supplies and represented the company's continuing effort to broaden its product line.

In 1933, ACCO Products changed its distribution channels. Rather than serving as the exclusive distributor of its own products, the company established a network of commercial vendors and later began printing mail order catalogs. Within one year, the distribution network grew dramatically and a much greater demand for the company's products was created. This led to another company tagline, "We're easy and profitable to do business with."

Swingline Is Established: 1925

During this time, another ACCO World company got its start. Swingline Inc., a manufacturer of staplers, was established in 1925 by Jack Linsky. From its factory on the lower east side of New York City, Swingline made a name for itself by developing more efficient stapler designs.

Swingline was one of the first companies to package staples in glued rows. Prior to this, staples had to be loaded individually

Company Perspectives:

Our vision is to be a sought-after company delivering exceptional value to our investors, our customers, our suppliers, and our people. At ACCO World, business leaders need to create simple, reality-based, customer-focused, actionable plans and communicate them straightforwardly to all constituencies. We can only achieve sought-after status through the strengths of our people, their ability to execute, and their commitment to a core set of operating principles—Focus, Simplicity, and Agility.

or came attached to overly sturdy sheets of metal that did not break away cleanly. The glued staples, called frozen wire staples, allowed Swingline to introduce another innovation during the 1930s, the open channel stapler, in which rows of 50 or more staples could be dropped in at once. Swingline also developed a stroke control that almost eliminated the common problem of staples jamming.

ACCO and Swingline were deeply affected by the outbreak of World War II. With government controls on production, rationing, and the diverting of metal stocks to the defense industry, both companies had to find a new way to do business. Far from being pressed into action as war material suppliers, the companies' products proved to be essential because of the increased need for government record keeping.

ACCO Products fared better, having developed a paperclip made of pressed paper fiber as an alternative to metal clips and staples. In addition, the company reduced the meal content of its product line, manufacturing paper punches out of wood but with metal hole punchers. It also introduced laced binders and lace ties for envelope binders. On the strength of wartime demand, ACCO Products had become a large company; in fact, after the war it was forced to relocate to a larger facility in Ogdensburg, New York in 1947. This plant had been requisitioned during World War II to handle production for the government.

ACCO Products continued to prosper after the war as a steady business expansion occurred in all industries. As the nation's commerce grew, so did the need for record keeping. In fact, by the mid-1950s ACCO Products had become an attractive takeover target.

Gary Industries, a private holding company based in Chicago, acquired ACCO Products in 1956. Meanwhile, ACCO Products continued its growth by expansion and by this time was a major office supply manufacturer offering a complete line of products. Gary Industries did not become actively involved in ACCO Products' affairs until 1966, when the parent moved the operation from Ogdensburg to Chicago. At that time, Gary brought in Douglas K. Chapman, formerly head of ACCO Products' Canadian operations to run the company, which was now known as the ACCO Division of Gary Industries.

Swingline Acquires Wilson Jones Company: 1960

Swingline, Inc., achieved its own recovery from World War II on the strength of the same postwar business boom that

had catapulted ACCO Products to a leading position in the industry. The company was still limited to the manufacture of staplers and sought to diversify. In 1960, Swingline took over the operations of the Wilson Jones Company.

Wilson Jones was founded in 1893 as the Chicago Shipping and Receipt Book Company. The company's original proprietor was a Chicago jeweler who invented and began manufacturing a simple aluminum paper clasp. Six years later, the small company was taken over by Ralph B. Wilson. In 1904, the company developed the first three-ring binder, an invention that greatly contributed to its growth. Also that year, Wilson merged his company with the Jones Improved Loose Leaf Specialty Company run by W. Gifford Jones and his two brothers. As the Wilson Jones Company, the enterprise benefited from a wider product line and a more efficient combined sales force.

ACCO Products intensified its international sales efforts in the 1960s and 1970s. In 1964, the company established a subsidiary in Holland and entered into a joint venture in Mexico. These were followed by a joint venture in Jamaica in 1970 and a venture in Venezuela two years later. To standardize the company's identity, a new corporate design was introduced in 1968 that featured distinctive red and black bars. Two years later, ACCO Products was reorganized under a new parent company, ACCO World Corporation. This holding company assumed centralized ownership of the United States and European operations.

Chapman Leads an LBO of ACCO World: 1971

In 1971, however, Chapman and a group of senior executives launched a leveraged buyout (LBO) of ACCO World. They succeeded and, having won their autonomy from Gary Industries, began several efforts to boost sales. The increase in product demand caused a need to move to larger, more modern quarters. At the time, however, the nation was in the grips of a serious recession, exacerbated by an oil embargo perpetrated by Middle Eastern countries. In spite of the adverse conditions, Chapman pressed on with plans to build a new headquarters facility in Wheeling, Illinois. After the move was completed in 1976, Chapman remarked that the decision to erect the new building was ''one of the most positive things we could tell our employees, customers, and suppliers about our optimism for the future.''

Meanwhile, ACCO World continued its international expansion with the establishment of a French subsidiary in 1975, another in West Germany in 1977, and joint ventures in New Zealand, Nigeria, Brazil, and Australia. At this time, ACCO Products, which was renamed ACCO International, started a new company, the Polyblend Corporation, based in St. Charles, Illinois. Polyblend was established specifically to extrude polyethylene, a plastic used in the manufacture of ACCO binders.

In 1982, the company's Toronto-based ACCO Canada Ltd. subsidiary acquired Plymouth Tool and Stamping, Ltd. Plymouth, which had been an important supplier to ACCO International, was one of the most sophisticated tool and die manufacturers in Canada.

In February 1983, senior management took ACCO International—the American side of the business—public and gained

Key Dates:

1903: Clipper Manufacturing Co. is founded by Fred J. Kline.
1912: Kline invents a new paper fastener, dubbing it the ACCO Fastener.
1922: The company changes its name to ACCO Products Inc.
1925: Swingline Inc. is established by Jack Linsky.
1956: Gary Industries acquires ACCO Products.
1960: Swingline acquires Wilson Jones Company.
1970: ACCO Products is reorganized under a new parent company, ACCO World Corporation.
1971: Company executives launch a leveraged buyout of ACCO World.
1987: American Brands acquires ACCO World.
1990: The firm launches the Worldmark logo to unify its brands.
1997: American Brands changes its name to Fortune Brands Inc.
2001: ACCO World launches a major restructuring effort.

a listing on the New York Stock Exchange. In May of that year, the company purchased the Systems Furniture Company and in 1984 acquired Twinlock PLC, a British office products manufacturer, through its European subsidiary. In 1986, ACCO International also took over Kensington Microware, which produced computer workstation products. These acquisitions were intended to shore up ACCO's position in the broader office market by adding furniture and other products to the line.

The Twinlock acquisition resulted in European wholesalers offering two competing product lines from the same company to their customers. In order to avoid confusion, the ACCO International logo was incorporated into individual brand names in 1986.

American Brands Acquires ACCO: 1987

In 1987, American Brands—a tobacco, food, consumer products and financial services conglomerate—announced a bid to acquire ACCO World for $603 million. American Brands had acquired Swingline in 1970 and Wilson Jones in 1972. This caused the U.S. Justice Department to oppose the transaction on the grounds that American Brands would enjoy excessive control over the fastener market.

In August 1987, American Brands allowed the transaction to proceed by agreeing to divest itself of a substantial portion of its fastener business. The company sold its Swingline punch and two-hole fastener operations to Bates Manufacturing, and ACCO International sold its stapler business to Hunt Manufacturing.

The following year, ACCO International and Swingline coordinated their manufacturing and marketing operations, resulting in the expansion of ACCO's Wheeling plant. American Brands, meanwhile, acquired Vogel Peterson Furniture Company, another office products and furniture manufacturer, and

Day-Timers, Inc., which made diaries and time planners. Vogel Peterson was consolidated with Systems Furniture in 1990, and its headquarters were relocated to Garden Grove, California.

In 1990, ACCO World introduced a new "Worldmark" logo for its American companies, which now included ACCO, Swingline, Wilson Jones, Vogel Peterson, Kensington, and, through an earlier acquisition, Perma Products. The following year, ACCO International, Swingline, and Wilson Jones were merged into one company—ACCO USA. The individual brand names, however, were retained. ACCO North America was also formed and included the operations of ACCO USA, ACCO Canada, and ACCO North America.

ACCO World spend the latter half of the 1990s restructuring and streamlining its operations. In 1996, its Australian business unit officially became ACCO Australia, and its operations fell under the ACCO World corporate umbrella. The following year, Marbig-Rexcel, a company acquired in 1989, became part of ACCO Australia. The company also moved Swingline's manufacturing operations from New York to Mexico. Company headquarters were then moved from Wheeling, Illinois, to Lincolnshire.

In 1997, Day-Timer Concepts Inc. and Kensington Microware Ltd. were merged into ACCO USA. After the integration, ACCO USA changed its name to ACCO Brands Inc. That year, NOBO of Europe and U.S.-based MACO were acquired. Two years later, Boone International was purchased.

Battling an Industry Slowdown: Late 1990s and Beyond

While ACCO was occupied with strategic realignment, its parent company, who in 1997 changed its name to Fortune Brands Inc., was becoming increasingly concerned about its office product division's overall operating contribution—operating company contribution equals net sales less costs and expenses. While sales had increased from $1.2 billion in 1996 to $1.4 billion in 1998, the business segment's operating contribution to Fortune Brands had been falling significantly since 1998. By 2000, it had fallen from $134 million to $79.5 million.

During this time period, the office supply industry was plagued by weakening demand as a result of slowing economies. At the same time, both competitors and customers in the industry were consolidating, which resulted in pricing pressures. Fortune Brands' chairman and CEO commented on ACCO's operating environment in an October 2000 press release, remarking that "ACCO competes in an industry that will likely benefit from consolidation and we don't see ourselves making that kind of commitment to office products." Fortune Brands itself was launching a cost cutting effort and began a strategic review of its brand portfolio. Eyeing its home products, spirits and wine, and golf products divisions as key to securing maximum shareholder value, Fortune Brands announced its intention to sell its ACCO World unit.

The office supply industry continued to feel the negative effects of a weakening economy into 2001. That year, ACCO World sales fell by 12 percent and operating company contribution fell by 37 percent over the previous year. Fortune Brands received many offers for ACCO, but each bid was deemed unacceptable. As a result of the unfavorable conditions, Fortune Brands took ACCO off the market and instead began a thorough reorganization of the firm in order to bolster its financial record and increase the long-term value of the company.

As part of the initiative, ACCO's North American operations were revamped and streamlined, the company focused on profitable core product lines, under-performing assets were sold, and significant cost cutting measures were taken. While Fortune Brands' management felt confident that the restructuring would bolster ACCO World's value, the company remained highly dependent on the turnaround in both the United States and European economies. Even as ACCO World's future remained up in the air, its major brands—including Wilson Jones and Swingline—would no doubt continue as leaders in many market segments for years to come.

Principal Subsidiaries

ACCO Brands Inc.; ACCO Canada; ACCO Mexico; ACCO Europe; ACCO Australia; ACCO Asia.

Principal Competitors

Avery Dennison Corp.; Esselte AB; Fellowes Inc.

Further Reading

''Fortune Brands Reports First Quarter Results,'' *Business Wire*, April 19, 2001.
''Justice Department Approves Plan to Acquire Acco World,'' *Wall Street Journal*, August 10, 1987.
''Staplers in Living Color,'' *Machine Design*, October 21, 1999.

—John Simley
—update: Christina M. Stansell

Albany International Corporation

P.O. Box 1907
Albany, New York 12201
U.S.A.
Telephone: (518) 445-2200
Fax: (518) 445-2264
Web site: http://www.albint.com

Public Company
Incorporated: 1895 as Albany Felt Company
Employees: 6,769
Sales: $836.7 million (2001)
Stock Exchanges: New York
Ticker Symbol: AIN
NAIC: 313210 Broadwoven Fabric Mills

Albany International Corporation plays a key role in paper-making as the world's leading designer and producer of paper machine clothing (PMC)—large, continuous belts of custom designed and engineered fabrics that are installed on paper machines to carry paper stock through the three primary stages of the paper production process. With facilities in 15 countries, the company controls 30 percent of the global PMC market. Through its Engineered Fabrics business segment, which includes its PMC operations, the company provides custom engineered wires, belts, and fabrics to the nonwovens, pulp, and building industries. The firm also manufactures industrial doors through its Albany Door Systems division and a host of patented materials through its Applied Technologies unit.

Company Origins: Understanding PMC

PMC comes in fabric sizes more than 30 feet wide and 200 feet long and has a useful life of one to 15 months, depending on the type of clothing and its use. A paper machine may require one million dollars of clothing a year and is needed for making all paper, from the finest writing paper to tissue to containerboard.

Demand for PMC is dependent on the health of the papermaking industry. According to *Fortune* magazine, U.S. paper manufacturing grew by only about 3 percent a year in the 1990s. To maintain healthy growth, Albany International spends as much as 3 percent of sales on research and development of new products, a very high rate for the industry. Because of its technological advances and its reputation for producing quality materials, it has grown to become the world leader in market share.

Albany International has been an innovator in PMC technology, developing many specialty materials and even licensing competitors to produce them. To follow the history of Albany International, it is helpful to understand more about the role of Albany's products in the production of paper. There are three major phases to paper production—forming, pressing, and drying—and each phase requires different clothing for the gigantic papermaking machines, some of which are as long as a football field.

During the forming stage, a thin mixture of 1 percent cellulose fiber and 99 percent water is sent through the machine, riding on the machine clothing. As the clothing moves, it works almost like a strainer, with water draining out and pulp fibers remaining on top of the clothing. This phase reduces the water content to about 83 percent, and it is at this phase that the paper's characteristics are set. The forming fabrics last from two to four months.

During the pressing stage, the paper is carried on the press fabric through rollers that, like a wringer washer, squeeze water out until the paper is 60 percent water. The pressing fabric must be capable of absorbing large amounts of water, then quickly getting rid of that water through pressure, centrifugal force, or vacuum. The pressing paper also influences the finish of the paper because the paper is still mostly water when it enters this phase and the rollers exert great pressure. A press fabric lasts only one to three months. Ideally, as much water as possible is removed at this stage, as the last phase requires high energy usage.

In the drying stage, the paper rides the drying clothing around huge heated cylinders so that most of the remaining water evaporates. Drying fabric can last nine to 15 months. According to Albany International, the use of paper machine clothing worldwide was about 35 percent forming clothing, 45 percent pressing clothing, and 20 percent dryer clothing in the 1990s. The company estimated that 85 percent of the fabrics it produced in the 1990s had not even existed ten years before. Of course, the technology had changed quite a bit since the company's early days, when its name was Albany Felt Company and it was producing only press felts made from wool.

Incorporation of Albany Felt Company in 1895

Albany Felt Company was incorporated in 1895 by Parker Corning, James W. Cox, Jr., and Selden E. Marvin, with a total investment of $40,000. Corning's father, Erastus, who was a banker and industrialist, may have been the person who thought of starting the company because of a variety of circumstances: the feltmaker from the nearby F.C. Huyck & Sons had been released from employment and was available for hire; the Huyck mill had burned down in 1894; and Parker's father thought the paper machine felt business might be just the project his son needed after his graduation from Yale in 1895.

Parker Corning became vice-president of Albany Felt Company, and partner James Cox served as president from 1895 to 1918, when Corning succeeded him. Two years later, Corning bought Cox's shares, thus securing control of 72 percent of the company shares. Marvin, president of Albany Savings Institution and Corning's uncle by marriage, died in 1899.

Cox managed a 30-person staff the first year. Within six years, Albany Felt had outgrown its original site and the company built a new plant on a six-acre lot in Menands, a town near Albany. A staff of 150 worked at this new building, constructed to withstand the tremendous vibrations of the felt-making machines. By 1907 the president's salary had been raised to $5,000 a year, and the vice-president's to $4,000.

In 1908 the Albany Company expanded its markets to Europe, Canada, Japan, and Mexico. The company continued to prosper in the 1920s and even during the Depression of the 1930s. Its facilities did not expand beyond the Albany area, however, until 1945, when it acquired a mill in North Monmouth, Maine. This plant was used to expand the company's production of flannel for baseball uniforms. Albany Felt also produced felts for other purposes. It became the leading producer in the United States and the world of Sanforized Blankets; Sanforizing is a patented process invented by Sanford Cluett for preshrinking cloth.

In 1952 Albany Felt became an international company when it established Albany Felt Company of Canada. This led to growth in its worldwide market. The firm's president, Lewis R. Parker, also saw great opportunity in the South. During his tenure Albany Felt built a new mill in St. Stephen, South Carolina.

Growth and Diversification During the 1960s

Parker died in 1957, and John C. Standish, who had been hired in 1921 as a feltmaker, became president. Under his leadership, Albany Felt became the pacesetter in the design and manufacture of needled press felts and moved into dryer fabric manufacture and development. In 1961 Standish became chairman of the board. Under the presidency of Everett C. Reed, Standish's successor at that position, the 1960s proved to be a decade of growth, diversification, and innovation for Albany International. It developed an innovative forming fabric that was actually multilayered and more efficient than the woven metal wire cloth that papermakers had been using prior to the 1960s. This became the standard for the industry. During the 1990s, Albany International maintained forming fabrics plants in the United States, Canada, Mexico, Australia, Norway, Sweden, Finland, Germany, The Netherlands, and France.

Albany International produced dryer fabrics in the 1960s, with its introduction of an open-mesh synthetic fabric for the third section of the paper machine. Heavy canvas cotton and asbestos had been the standard drying clothing until Albany introduced a monofilament fabric from which water evaporated more quickly, lowering energy costs and allowing the machine to be operated at higher speeds.

That same decade, it acquired Woven Belting Co. of Buffalo, as well as wire and plastics companies. It also acquired a felt company in France to gain entrance to the felt market there. By 1966 Albany Felt employed 2,500 people and had 19 plants in six countries. In 1969 the company bought Nordiskafilt in Sweden, as well as mills in England and Brazil. It also built new mills in Holland, Finland, and Australia.

The company successfully defended itself from a hostile takeover in the late 1960s. In 1944 Clark Estates Inc., an investment company, had purchased a large block—32 percent—of Albany stock. In 1967 Clark sold its shares to Deering Milliken. That company's head, Roger Milliken, soon informed Albany Felt that it was sending tender offers to stockholders in order to acquire a 51 percent share of the company. Six Albany directors, however, owned 42 percent of the shares, and they informed shareholders that they did not think purchase by Deering Milliken was in the company's best interests. A syndicate of directors and a local businessman offered stockholders the option of selling their shares to this syndicate at whatever price Deering Milliken offered. Deering Milliken tendered at $27 per share, then $37, and finally $50. Most shares that were tendered were purchased by this syndicate.

In 1968 the company, still under control of the management syndicate, engineered the purchases of Appleton Wire Works Corp., International Wire Works Corp., and Crellin Plastics in exchange for shares of Albany stock. Under state law, however, the company needed shareholder permission to increase the number of capital shares. Deering Milliken was unable to muster enough votes to block approval, and with the increased shares created, Milliken's stake dropped from 32 percent ownership to 20 percent. In 1972 Milliken sold its Albany International shares in a public offering.

Key Dates:

1895: Albany Felt Company is incorporated.
1908: The company expands its markets to Europe, Canada, Japan, and Mexico.
1945: A mill in North Monmouth, Maine, is acquired.
1952: Albany Felt of Canada is established.
1969: The company is renamed Albany International.
1972: Milliken sells its shares of Albany in a public offering.
1983: The company is taken private through a leveraged buyout.
1988: Albany lists on the New York Stock Exchange.
1990: The company cuts costs during an economic slowdown.
1999: Albany acquires the Geschmay Group.
2001: The company launches a $25 million cost reduction program.

Adopting a New Name in 1969

In 1969 Albany Felt was renamed Albany International to reflect its new identity with facilities and markets around the world. In the 1970s Albany International moved its offices from the plant it had occupied since 1902 to Fernbrook, a former estate. During this decade, Albany also launched a new division called Albany Engineered Systems to produce auxiliary equipment to maintain and improve clothing performance. Albany Engineered Systems manufactured high-pressure showers for keeping the clothing clean, drainage elements such as vacuum foils blades, doctor blades for removing the paper sheet from the roll on the machine, and vacuum systems for improving water removal.

In the 1980s Albany developed and patented an on-machine seamed press fabric that was safer, quicker, and easier to install than previous press fabrics. This saved paper companies time and money since it substantially reduced the length of time that the machine had to be shut down for installation of a new pressing cloth.

In 1983 Albany International became a private company through a leveraged buyout by a group of its managers. They sold all of the businesses that were not related to papermaking, including a division that produced tennis ball covers and another that made plastic tubes. Albany International's status as a private company was short-lived, though. Four years later, with record sales of $402 million, it once again was listed on the New York Stock Exchange.

New Product Development in the Late 1980s

By the late 1980s, the company had begun to diversify again as research into new fabrics for its core business led to the production of synthetic fabrics for other applications. Company researchers developed a synthetic goose down that the company called Primaloft, which they claimed had all the advantages of goose down and none of the disadvantages. Goose down provides great protection against frigid temperatures but when wet absorbs 160 percent of its weight, while some other synthetics absorb as much as 1000 percent of their weight. According to Albany International, Primaloft, which it developed for the U.S. Army, maintains its warmth even when damp and absorbed only 30 percent of its weight after being submerged for half an hour. Leading manufacturers of winterwear, sleeping bags, and clothing for mountaineering began using Primaloft in their products.

Albany International had supplied material for America's space shuttle program since the 1970s. In 1989 Albany International further expanded its involvement in such high technology manufacturing, selling a lightweight, noncombustible insulation material used in automotive, plastics, and aerospace applications.

Using technology developed while engineering fabrics, the company also came out with a high-speed industrial door that rolled up and down like a window shade and was used in airports and carwashes. The subsidiary, Nomafa Door Division, had factories in four countries.

In late 1989 Albany International moved its headquarters back to its roots—the 450,000-square-foot factory complex with its various additions—that Albany Felt had occupied almost 90 years before in Menands. Four million dollars later, it had been transformed into contemporary, efficient office space. A new, multimillion-dollar press fabric facility was erected in 1988 across the river in East Greenbush.

Battling Turbulent Economic Times in the Early 1990s

The company reported a relatively unsuccessful year in 1990, citing the poor state of the world economy and its own high overhead costs. It initiated a cost reduction program, reducing its salaried workforce by about 10 percent and cutting other operational costs. That same year, it started up a new fabrics plant in Sondrum, Sweden, replacing the Nordiskafilt plant three miles away. It also built new plants in Finland and The Netherlands. In addition, the company acquired Wallbergs Fabriks A.B., a paper machine clothing maker founded in 1823 in Halmstad, Sweden.

During the 1990s the papermaking industry was consolidating globally, increasing the competition and consolidation within the paper machine clothing industry as well. As the largest clothing supplier, however, Albany International said that it would benefit from consolidation in both industries, reasoning that large papermaking concerns would find it more efficient to work with one company that could supply clothing for all three phases.

The world's papermaking industry remained depressed in 1991 and 1992, and Albany International's sales reflected this, as they rose only slightly. The company continued to put substantial resources into research and development. The American paper industry had a goal of manufacturing 40 percent of all U.S. paper from recycled fibers by 1995, and to achieve this goal, Albany International worked closely with its customers in the paper industry as well as with makers of paper machines.

In 1993 Albany International strengthened its position in the market for dryer clothing by acquiring Mount Vernon Group for $51 million. This company, with plants in North Carolina and

South Carolina, produced clothing for forming, pressing, and drying; by acquiring it, Albany moved from third place to second in the dryer cloth market.

Albany International's operating environment picked up in the mid-1990s. Sales in 1993 increased to $546 million, and then to $567 million and $652 million in 1994 and 1995, respectively. Net income also rebounded, a sure sign that the firm had weathered the economic downturn of the early 1990s effectively.

Remaining a Leader in a Consolidating Industry in the Late 1990s and Beyond

Indeed, Albany International had taken advantage of the industry's consolidation trend by making key acquisitions and creating new products that left it a step ahead of its competitors. With six international research and development facilities, the company's dedication to new product development remained a crucial part of the firm's long-term strategy. In fact, company CEO Frank Schmeler claimed in a 2000 *PIMA's North American Papermaker* article that the firm "expected that tomorrow's paper machine clothing will be decidedly different than the products offered today. It is our objective to bring these opportunities to our customers as soon as possible."

By 2000, the number of major PMC suppliers had shrunk from eight to just four. Instead of consolidating along with the industry, however, Albany International had expanded its operations. In 1999, the firm completed its $250 million acquisition of the Geschmay Group, a PMC firm with operations in both the United States and Europe. The firm also purchased Jansen Tortechnik, a Germany-based manufacturer of overhead doors. During this external growth spurt, Albany International began a $50 million internal restructuring effort in 1998 that included job cuts, changes in marketing and selling, and the disposal of certain assets. The efforts appeared to pay off. Sales increased from $722 million in 1998 to $852 million in 2000.

During the fall of 2000, company management—led by chairman and CEO Schmeler—adopted a new growth plan that focused on revenue enhancement, capital management, cost reductions and process improvements, information systems implementation, and R&D project management—specifically new product development. The firm also was focused on paying down debt that it had incurred during the Geschmay purchase.

The global economy weakened once again in 2001. This forced the company to launch another cost-cutting restructuring effort, this time to the tune of $25 million. The firm discontinued production of PMC at its plants in Italy and also reduced its manufacturing capacity in Mexico and the United States. Sales in 2001 fell to $836.6 million while net income fell by 15.5 percent over the previous year.

Sales continued to slide during the first half of 2002, mostly due to weakening demand brought on by the sluggish economy. As such, the firm continued to analyze its operations, cut costs, and focus on debt reduction. Although the economic climate remained uncertain, company management remained confident that the firm would achieve future success. As the world's largest PMC manufacturer, Albany International did indeed stand well positioned for growth in the years to come.

Principal Subsidiaries

Albany International Corp.; Albany International Holdings One, Inc.; Albany International Holdings Two, Inc.; Albany International Research Co.; Albany International Techniweave Inc.; Geschmay Corp.; Albany International Pty., Ltd. (Australia); Nomafa Gesellschaft GmbH (Austria); Albany Nordiskafilt GmbH (Austria); Albany International Feltros E Telas Industrials Ltds. (Brazil); Albany Engenharia de Sisternas Industria e Com. Ltda. (Brazil); AI Finance Canada, Inc.; Albany International Canada Inc.; Geschmay Canada, Ltd.; M&I Door Systems, Ltd. (Canada); Albany International (China) Co., Ltd.; Schieffer Skandinavien A/S (Denmark; 67%); Albany Fennofelt OY (Finland); Metco Form OY (Finland); Albany International France, S.A.S.; Albany International S.A.S. (France); Cofpa S.A. (France); Nomafa S.A.R.L. (France); Nomafa GmbH (Germany); Albany Door Systems GmbH (Germany); Albany Germany GmbH & Co. KG; Albany International Verwaltungs GmbH (Germany); AI Financial Services Company (Ireland); Albany International Italia S.p.A.; Albany International S.p.A. (Italy); Albany Nordiskafilt Kabushiki Kaisha (Japan); Albany International Korea, Inc.; Telas Industriales de Mexico, S.A. de C.V.; Albany International de Mexico S.A. de C.V.; Martel Wire S.A. de C.V. (Mexico); Albany International B.V. (Netherlands); Nomafa B.V. (Netherlands); Albany Nordiskafilt AS (Norway); Schieffer Polska Sp. zo.o. (Poland; 65%); Nevo-Cloth Ltd. (Russia; 50%); Geschmay Asia Private Limited (Singapore); Nordiskafilt S.A. (Proprietary) Ltd. (South Africa); Beier Albany and Company (Proprietary Limited) (South Africa; 50%); Albany Nordiska S.A. (Spain); Albany International AB (Sweden); Albany Door Systems AB (Sweden); Portsam AB (Sweden); Nomafa AG (Switzerland); Loading Bay Specialists Limited (U.K.; 50%); Albany International Ltd. (U.K.; 28%).

Principal Competitors

Cardo AB; J.M. Voith AG; Tamfelt Corp.

Further Reading

"Albany International," *Pulp & Paper,* August 1999, p. 62.
Albany International: A History, Albany, N.Y.: Albany International Corporation.
"Albany International Adapts with Innovation," *PIMA's North American Papermaker,* October 2000, p. 56.
"Albany International Corp.," *Pulp & Paper,* August 1998, p. 25.
"Albany International Restructures," *Nonwovens Industry,* February 2002, p. 19.
Nulty, Peter, "Growing Fast on the 500s Fringe," *Fortune,* April 24, 1989, p. 72.

—Wendy J. Stein
—updated by Christina M. Stansell

Altran Technologies

251 Boulevard Pereire
75017 Paris
France
Telephone: (+33) 01 44 09 64 00
Fax: (+33) 01 44 09 64 89
Web site: http://www.altran-group.com

Public Company
Incorporated: 1982
Employees: 12,823
Sales: EUR 1.28 billion ($1.02 billion) (2001)
Stock Exchanges: Euronext Paris
Ticker Symbol: ALT
NAIC: 541511 Custom Computer Programming Services;
    541512 Computer Systems Design Services; 541330
    Engineering Services

France's Altran Technologies is Europe's leading high technology consulting company—Altran prefers to call itself "Innovation Consultants"—and is aiming for worldwide leadership in this fast-growing consulting sector. Altran's army of more than 15,000 consultants, the majority of whom are engineers, enable it to provide consulting support services across a wide variety of industries and technologies, ranging from the physical sciences to electronics, chemistry, automation, information technology, financial mathematics, and modeling. Most of Altran's work is for major corporations unable or unwilling to gain in-house expertise for specific projects. As such, Altran has placed consultants with automaker Renault to assist in its development of a next-generation Formula 1 racer. The company was also responsible for the design and development for a hydraulic system for the Airbus A350-600 aircraft. Altran has also long been involved in the aerospace industry, completing such projects as the design and development of the Node2 project for the Alpha international space station program. The company's multi-discipline approach has helped shield it from individual industry downturns, as does its position at the innovation end of the high-technology arena.

As a company, Altran is one of France's success stories, seeing its revenues grow from about EUR 50 million at the beginning of the 1990s to more than EUR 1.2 billion in 2001. The company is aiming still higher—notably with plans to expand into the United States and Asia in the early years of the new century—and forecasts growth in sales to more than EUR 2 billion by 2003 and a leap in its number of consultants to more than 40,000 by 2005. A unique feature of Altran is its extensive, yet highly independent network of more than 130 subsidiaries across 14 countries, which cooperate through technology sharing and other support services guided through central management but otherwise operate more or less autonomously. Unlike its competitors, Altran is able to go further than simply consulting on a project, but can offer complete design and development services. Architects of this network are chairman Alexis Kniazeff and co-chairman Hubert Martigny, the company's founders, and CEO Michel Friedlander. Altran's shares are traded on the Euronext Paris Stock Exchange, as part of its prestigious CAC 40.

Management Innovators in the 1980s

Alexis Kniazeff and Hubert Martigny met while working as consultants at Peat Marwick, later known as KMPG. At Peat Marwick, Kniazeff, a civil engineer with a master's degree in business, and Martigny developed their own vision of how a company should be organized—notably by adopting a highly decentralized management, which in turn would enable the creation of independent profit centers. The future partners became knowledgeable in the rapidly expanding technology sector, and in 1970 launched their own consulting agency. However, since few of their clients were willing to convert to their decentralized ideal, Kniazeff and Martigny decided to launch their own company, Altran, in 1982.

From the start, Altran targeted the high-technology segment of the aerospace industry, providing engineering consulting on various space program and military hardware projects. The company's strong engineering background enabled it to position itself as a full-service consultancy—Altran's engineers did not merely provide consulting services but also participated in actual design and development as well. Altran grew rapidly

---

Company Perspectives:

ALTRAN, founded in 1982, represents a unique endeavour. Today, we are Europe's leading technology consultancy, with 15,000 engineers in 14 countries worldwide providing high value-added support for innovation. Our commitment is to help clients in industry and services gain a new competitive edge and enhance their performance with innovative products and processes. This support spans every stage from preliminary studies, strategic planning, and technology watch to design, implementation, and inspection. ALTRAN stands out from other consultancies in that we are active in sectors from aerospace and telecoms to banking, with expertise covering all areas of engineering. This unique knowhow enables us to make a key contribution to innovations shaping our daily lives, now and in the years ahead.

through the first half of the decade and by 1985 counted a staff of 50 engineers, including future CEO Michel Friedlander, who joined the company that year.

Altran had already put into place the management theories touted by Kniazeff and Martigny, organizing its operations into a number of small business units that would later generally range from 10 to 200 employees. Each business unit was then operated more or less as an independent company that identified its own growth strategy and controlled its own investment program while at the same time receiving support from central management. Business units supported each other mutually, creating what the company referred to as a ''cross-fertilization'' of expertise. Managers' salaries were based on their business units' performance, further stimulating the entrepreneurial nature of Altran's operations.

Altran went public in 1987, listing on the Secondary Market of the Paris Stock Exchange. By 1989, Altran's sales had neared the equivalent of EUR 48 million. The number of the company's employees grew as well, nearing 1,000 by 1990. Along the way, Altran continued to expand its range of expertise, moving into the transportation, telecommunications, and energy sectors, as well as developing a strong information technology component. This multi-disciplinary approach had a number of benefits, helping to protect the company during cyclical downturns, but, more importantly, by allowing it to share expertise across a variety of fields. In this way, Altran was able to take on highly complex projects for its major clients.

The early 1990s marked a turning point for Altran as the company adopted a new business model. While much of the company's work during the 1980s had been performed in-house, at the beginning of the 1990s the company developed a new operational concept, that of a temp agency for the high-technology sector. Altran began placing its staff of highly-skilled engineers with its clients, where the Altran employees worked alongside the client's staff, adding their specialized expertise to a project.

Altran's growth picked up in the early 1990s, and the company quickly established a network of subsidiaries and offices

throughout France, in part through a series of acquisitions. By the end of the decade, the company had more than 50 subsidiaries in France, and had taken the lead of that market's technology consulting sector. The company was helped by the long-lasting recession affecting France and much of Europe at the beginning of the decade, as companies began outsourcing parts of their research and development operations. Altran was also expanding by acquisition, buying up a number of similarly operating consultancies in France, such as the 1992 acquisition of GERPI, based in Rennes. By the end of that year, Altran's revenues had swelled to the equivalent of EUR 76.5 million.

International Expansion in the 1990s

The elimination of border controls within the European Community in 1992 inaugurated a new era of transnational activity as European companies began expanding into the newly opened markets. As more of its clients began operations in other European countries, Altran found itself confronted with the need to follow them. At first Altran turned to foreign partnerships in order to accommodate its clients. Yet this approach quickly proved unsatisfactory, and Altran put into place an aggressive acquisition plan in order to establish its own foreign operations.

Altran targeted the Benelux countries—the first to lower their trade barriers—acquiring a Belgian company in 1992. Those markets remained a company target over the next several years as Altran built up a network of some 12 companies and 1,000 consultants by the end of the decade. Altran's takeovers were always friendly—part of the company's acquisition criteria was that existing management remain in place—and in general the acquired firms retained their names. At the same time, Altran shrewdly protected itself from taking on a heavy debt load in order to fund its acquisition moves, establishing a policy of paying a set initial fee for an acquisition, then basing subsequent annual payments on the acquired unit's performance.

Spain became the company's next target in 1993. Starting with the acquisition of SDB Espan, a leading telecommunications consultant in that country, Altran's Spanish operations later grew into a group of nine companies with more than 2,000 consultants. Spain was to remain one of the company's top three markets into the new century, with a total of six companies, including new acquisitions Norma, STE, and Inser, and then Strategy Consultors, based in Barcelona, in 2000.

By 1995, Altran's sales had topped EUR 155 million, and its total number of employees had grown to nearly 2,400. At this point, Altran was already becoming known for its highly active recruiting program, since its business depended on attracting large numbers of high-caliber engineers. However, Altran also recognized that the majority of engineers lacked a background in management. Thus, the company launched its own accelerated management training program, which was capable of training 200 candidates per year.

The United Kingdom became Altran's next international growth market in 1995. In that year, the company acquired High Integrity Systems, a consulting firm that specialized in the information technology (IT) market, with a focus on assisting com-

<table>
<tr><td colspan="2" align="center">**Key Dates:**</td></tr>
<tr><td>**1982:**</td><td>Altran Technologies is founded by Alexis Kniazeff and Hubert Martigny.</td></tr>
<tr><td>**1987:**</td><td>Altran Technologies goes public.</td></tr>
<tr><td>**1990:**</td><td>Altran shifts its business model, becoming a high-technology temporary agency.</td></tr>
<tr><td>**1992:**</td><td>Altran acquires a Belgian company, initiating its international expansion throughout Europe and eventually to the United States.</td></tr>
<tr><td>**1993:**</td><td>The company acquires SDB Espan.</td></tr>
<tr><td>**2002:**</td><td>Altran acquires the international brand and trademark of Arthur D. Little, Inc.</td></tr>
</table>

panies that were transitioning into new-generation computer and network systems. Other acquisitions in the United Kingdom included IT consulting specialist DCE Consultants, which operated from offices in Oxford and Manchester, and, in 1997, Praxis Critical Systems, founded in Bath in 1983 to provide software and safety-engineering services. Not all of Altran's expansion moves came through acquisitions. In order to supplement the activities of its acquisitions, the company also opened new subsidiary offices, such as Altran Technologies UK, founded in 1997 as a multi-disciplinary and cross-industry engineering consultancy.

Altran stepped up its expansion in the second half of the 1990s. Acquisitions continued to provide the bulk of its international growth as the company began acquiring an average of 15 companies per year. Italy became a target for growth in 1996, when Altran established subsidiary Altran Italy, as well as CE Consulting, before making its first acquisition in that country in 1997. In 1998, Altran added four new Italian acquisitions, EKAR, RSI Sistemi, CCS and Pool. In 1999, the company added an office in Turin as well as two new companies, ASP and O&I. Then, in 2000, the company's Italian branch expanded to 10 subsidiaries with the opening of offices in Lombardy and Lazio and the acquisition of CEDATI.

Germany was also a primary target for Altran during this period, starting with the 1997 establishment of Altran Technologies GmbH and the acquisition of Europspace Technische Entwicklungen, a company that had been formed in 1993 and specialized in aeronautics. In 1998, the company added consulting group Berata; the following year, Askon Consulting joined the group, which then expanded with a second component, Askon Beratung. In 2000, Altran acquired I&K Beratung. In 2002, Askon Beratung was spun off from Askon consulting as a separate, independently operating company within Altran.

Similar progress was made in Switzerland, a market Altran entered in 1997 with the purchase of D1B2. The Berate Germany purchase brought Altran that company's Swiss office as well in 1998; that same year, Altran launched its own Swiss startup, Altran Technologies Switzerland. In 1999, the company added three new Swiss companies, Net@rchitects, Innovatica, and Cerri. Then, in 2000, Altran's presence in Switzerland grew with two new subsidiaries, Infolearn and De Simone &

Osswald. By 2002, the company's Swiss network had added a new component with the purchase of Sigma.

Other European countries joined the Altran network in the late 1990s as well, including Portugal and Luxembourg in 1998 and Austria in 1999. By the end of 1999, the company's sales had climbed to EUR 614 million; significantly, international sales already accounted for more than one-third of the company's total revenues.

In 1998, Altran moved up to the Paris main board's monthly settlement market. Altran nonetheless remained largely unknown outside its industry; in the late 1990s, however, the company began to take a number of public relations initiatives. One of the most successful of these was the establishment of the Altran Foundation, which began offering an annual Innovation Award for projects based on a set theme—the development of desalination systems, for example. In another public relations move, in 1999 the company joined the Proust racing team as sponsor and technology contributor.

With its European network largely in place at the turn of the century, Altran turned its sights on building up its global network. The United States became a primary target for the company's expansion with the acquisition in 2000 of a company that was renamed Altran Corporation. Altran began building its operations in South America as well, especially in Brazil. By the end of 2001, Altran's revenues had jumped to more than EUR 1.2 billion, while its ranks of consultants now topped 15,000.

In 2002, Altran appeared to be preparing for a full-scale entry into the United States. After providing $56 million to back a management buyout of the European, Asian, and Latin American operations of bankrupt Arthur D. Little—the technology consultants spun off from the Massachusetts Institute of Technology in 1982—Altran itself acquired the Arthur D. Little brand and trademark. This acquisition was seen as an important step in achieving the company's next growth target, becoming the world's leading high-technology consultancy firm with sales of EUR 2 billion by 2003 and more than 40,000 engineers by 2005.

Principal Subsidiaries

Alplog; Altior; Altran Esp; Altran Europe; Altran Gmbh; Altran Italia; Altran Scandinavia; Altran Switzerland; Altran Systèmes D'information; Altran Uk; Axiem; Ciriel; Dp Consulting; Atlantide Gerpi Ouest; Orthodrome; Altran Netherlands; Netarchitects Communication; Adena; Altaïr Technologies; Altran Technologies Gmbh; Altran Informatique Technologies; Altran Technologies UK; Altran Critical Systems; Dp Consulting UK; Altran Luxembourg; Altran Technologies Luxembourg: Berata Gmbh; Altran Technologies Netherlands; Altran Technologies Switzerland; Altran Belgium; Altran Usa Inc; Ag Technology.

Principal Competitors

Cap Gemini Ernst & Young; Alten SA; Transiciel SA; Atos Origin; GFI Informatique SA; SRI International.

Further Reading

"Altran Climbs on Strong Results," *Reuters*, April 10, 2002.

"Un Bill Gates en version française," *Challenges*, December 1999.

Bremer, Catherine, "Altran Sees 30 Pct Sales Growth in H1 2002," *Reuters*, December 10, 2001.

Dufrene, Catherine, "Altran Technologies fait l'unanimité," *Le Figaro Economic*, October 14, 2001.

Hirst, Clayton, "Altran Defies Downturn in Drive to Recruit 500 Staff in the UK," *Independent on Sunday*, April 22, 2001, p. 2.

Rap, Carole, "Altran carbure à la technologie," *Nouvel Economiste*, May 3, 2002.

Toby, Geraldine, "Nous aimerions realiser un chiffre d'affaires de 2 milliards d'euros en 2003," *Investir*, February 17, 2001.

—M. L. Cohen

AMB GENERALI
Holding AG

AMB Generali Holding AG

Aachener und Münchener Allee 9
D-52074 Aachen
Germany
Telephone: (49) (241) 461-01
Fax: (49) (241) 461-1805
Web site: http://www.amb.de

Public Company
Incorporated: 1825 as Aachener Feuerversicherungs-
Aktiengesellschaft
Employees: 21,189
Sales: EUR 11.2 billion ($8.42 billion) (2001)
Stock Exchanges: Frankfurt am Main
Ticker Symbol: AMB
NAIC: 524113 Direct Life Insurance Carriers; 524114
Direct Health and Medical Insurance Carriers; 524126
Direct Property and Casualty Insurance Carriers;
524128 Other Direct Insurance (Except Life, Health,
and Medical) Carriers; 524130 Reinsurance Carriers

AMB Generali Holding AG is the management holding company of Germany's third largest direct insurance group. Life insurance is the company's strongest business segment, which generates 60 percent of its annual premium income. AMB is Germany's second biggest life as well as property and casualty insurer and has a 5.5 percent market share in the country's health insurance market. The AMB group consists of 14 insurance companies, a subsidiary that provides financial services for would-be homeowners called *Bausparkasse,* which has a 6.8 percent market share, an investment arm and several service units. In addition to the company's own sales force of 6,560 (5,204 full-time and 92,000 part-time agents), AMB has exclusive strategic distribution partnerships with Deutsche Vermögensberatung AG, a firm that gives financial advice to individuals and sells selected financial products through network marketing; and with Commerzbank, one of Germany's leading banks, whose service personnel offer AMB policies and financial services for homeowners at the bank's branch offices. About one-fifth of new business by AMB's direct insurance arm

COSMOS is generated over the Internet. AMB is controlled by Italian insurance group Assicurazioni Generali S.p.A., which holds about 65 percent of the company's share capital. The company is headquartered in Aachen, the westernmost German city on the border of Belgium and France.

A "Charitable Insurer" with the Approval of German Kings in the Early 1800s

In the early 19th century the old imperial city Aachen was occupied by Napoleon. Its merchants, especially in the textile trade, greatly benefited from their direct connection to Paris. After Napoleon's defeat at Waterloo in 1815 Aachen became part of Prussia, the largest and most powerful German kingdom. Business slowed for the city's textile merchants and they were looking for new growth opportunities. One of them was David Hansemann, the owner of a wool shop. The store had earned the young man financial success and a reputation among the city's textile merchants. To make some extra money on the side, he became an investor in and agent for Germany's third fire insurer, Vaterländische Feuerversicherung, in 1923. When his request to raise the company's capital base was rejected, he decided to found his own fire insurance company.

The German insurance industry was still in its infancy at a time when the country was fragmented into more than 20 independent kingdoms, duchies, and independent cities. Whereas public fire insurers offered coverage exclusively for buildings, their content could only be covered by one of the 18 or so French, English, and Dutch fire insurers dominating the market in the Rhineland. Fraud on both the customers' and insurers' side was widespread. While some people tried to enrich themselves by over-insuring and then burning down their property, a number of insurance agents skimmed insurance premiums from their clients or did not pay anything in case of a casualty.

Hansemann wanted to clearly distinguish his insurance company from all others and came up with the idea to dedicate half of all profits to charitable causes. That was quite a revolutionary idea at a time when the emerging capitalist society brought about by industrialization created mass poverty and starvation for the lower classes, causing whole German villages to emi-

Company Perspectives:

Fehler! Textmarke nicht definiert. Security on the basis of success: AMB Group, which more than 175 years ago was founded as a regional fire insurance company, has grown to be the third largest German direct insurance group today. That success is substantially attributable to a strategic approach based on a partnership cooperation between insurance companies, building society and bank. The client obtains all services at one stop: detailed advice in all questions concerning financial services and all-round solutions tailored to his or her individual needs. By using the slogan of "accumulated efficiency" AMB Group has dedicated itself entirely to the idea of integrated financial services. The companies working today under the head of the AMB holding company offer the complete financial services range. Starting from life, health, property and casualty as well as legal expenses insurance over tailor-made housing finance to attractive banking products and other services, such as asset management for third parties. Up-to-date products in line with clients' needs and qualified advice on a solid and secure basis made the Group one of the leading providers of integrated financial services in the German market. The coherence of this Group of companies, its conception and its being part of the worldwide operations of Generali Group are perfectly illustrated by the Lion of St. Mark. The Winged Lion symbolizes confidence, strength and dynamics. The success and the growth of the group are self-explanatory and provide clients with the security they have a right to expect.

grate to America. In August 1824, 23 local investors and sponsors signed the bylaws of the newly founded Aachener Feuerversicherungs-Aktiengesellschaft, most of whom were from the city's textile industry. After Hansemann had overcome some resistance from the Prussian government, Prussian King Wilhelm III approved the enterprise in June 1825. While Ludwig von Seyffardt, the former general agent of a leading French insurance company in Aachen, became the company's "general agent" (comparable with today's CEO), Hansemann steered his enterprise from his post as director.

On September 1, 1825, Aachener started operations and the 300 or so agents Hansemann had hired started selling fire insurance policies in the Rhineland as well as in Hamburg, Königsberg, and Danzig. Among the company's agents were a mayor and a liquor manufacturer who—as was common at the time—sold insurance on the side. Seyffardt organized the business according to his know-how from the French insurer he had worked for and laid the groundwork for an efficient administration. Aachener's agents, however, were given more responsibility than was common elsewhere at the time, which enabled them to regulate their cases without consulting company headquarters, thereby keeping central administration slim. One of the first big fish caught by the company was the city of Aachen, which insured all furniture in the city's public buildings. Within one year Aachener's capital exceeded that of its three main competitors. The company came a long way until in 1934 it was able for the first time to contribute funds to the charitable organization it had set up. It took another five years until Aachener's shareholders saw their first regular dividend.

One of the agents Hansemann had hired for Aachener in 1825 was Friedrich Adolph Brüggemann, a city clerk in Magdeburg. It soon became apparent that he had a natural talent for this business. His territory was expanded more and more until he finally quit his job at city hall to become a full-time insurance agent. In 1831 Brüggemann took over Aachener's main agency in Berlin where his experience in dealing with city government officials worked to his advantage. He finally convinced the Prussian Ministry of the Interior to lift the limiting condition that Aachener was obliged to spend all its charitable contributions within the Prussian kingdom—a major step for further expansion.

Aachener's next target was the Kingdom of Bavaria where the bad state of affairs in fire insurance made headlines. In 1834 Bavaria's King Ludwig I approved Aachener as a "domestic" insurer—under the precondition that the firm change its name to Münchener und Aachener in the state and contribute its charitable funds directly to the kingdom's treasury. In the rest of Germany the company now called itself Aachener und Münchener. Riding on a wave of success, Aachener managed to gain approval in many other German kingdoms and grand duchies between 1834 and 1840, and its cash flow soared.

Becoming a Leading German Insurer and Conquering the World in the Second Half of the 19th Century

In May 1842 a fire destroyed large parts of Hamburg, one of Germany's biggest and wealthiest cities. Brüggemann did not hesitate to travel to the northern German trade capital to administer his cases in person within two weeks. The disaster cost the young insurance company a considerable sum: about one-third of its share capital of one million *Taler.* The incident confirmed Aachener's reputation, however, for quickly paying in cases of fire damage and the insurance company was overwhelmed by a run of new customers. Aachener's premium income almost doubled between 1841 and 1850 when the company reached a market share of 25 percent among fire insurers in Germany. When company founder Hansemann left the company to become Prussia's finance minister, Brüggemann was elected Aachener's new director. In 1853 the company founded a reinsurance subsidiary, Aachener Rückversicherung, Germany's second reinsurer.

During the next two decades Aachener established itself firmly in the marketplace. The company's main clientele were private households, small businesses, and farm cooperatives that received part of Aachener's charitable funds in exchange for their members' insurance. The steady flow of premium income allowed the company to build large financial reserves that made Aachener one of Germany's richest insurance companies. Aachener's capital was tripled and dividends rose from 10 percent in 1845 to 70 percent in 1878.

One of the company's major successes was its commitment to not only insure, but also to prevent fires. Part of its charitable funds were used to help organize municipal fire brigades and equip them with state-of-the-art water pumps. Not only did this practice lower the number of fires; it also gave the company lots of free publicity. Many city officials thanked Aachener publicly in newspaper ads for its generosity. About 120 such public endorsements were published in German newspapers in 1853

Key Dates:

1825: Prussian King Wilhelm III approves the foundation of fire insurance company Aachener Feuerversicherungs-Aktiengesellschaft.

1840: The company is licensed in all of Germany.

1893: General agencies are established in San Francisco, New York, and Chicago.

1924: The company takes over insurers Thuringia, Aachen-Potsdamer Life Insurance, and Oldenburger.

1944: The company's headquarters are moved temporarily to Erfurt during World War II.

1970: Aachener acquires a stake in building society Badenia Bausparkasse AG; the company is renamed Aachener und Münchener Versicherung Aktiengesellschaft.

1972: The German business of insurance company Cosmos Allgemeine Versicherung-AG is taken over.

1979: A management holding company is created and named AMB Aachener und Münchener Beteiligungs-AG.

1983: A distribution partnership with financial service provider Deutsche Vermögensberatung is initiated.

1989: AMB acquires a 25 percent share in life insurer Volksfürsorge Deutsche Lebensversicherung AG.

1992: French insurer AGF announces ownership of 25 percent plus one share in AMB.

1993: AMB takes over control of Volksfürsorge Holding AG.

1995: The company sells its non-group reinsurance business.

1998: Italian insurance group Assicurazioni Generali S.p.A. becomes AMB's majority shareholder.

2001: The company is renamed AMB Generali Holding AG.

alone. Up until 1900 Aachener spent the large sum of 9.4 million marks, almost one-third of its charitable funds, on promoting fire fighting. In 1870 Aachener helped with a substantial donation to establish Aachen Technical College. After the new German Empire was formed in 1871, Aachener also gave a considerable amount of money to charities that cared for the many injured and invalids the French-German war caused. Another part of the company's charitable funds was donated to the victims of floods, fires, and other disasters.

In the middle of the 1860s, however, the company's fat years came to an end. Due to growing competition Aachener's revenues from insurance premiums grew only slightly between 1860 and 1870. Profits were shrinking. At the company's 50th anniversary in 1875 shareholders demanded that Aachener's charitable contributions be limited to 50 percent of income from premiums. Profits from capital investments were excluded from this policy. Until 1892 the policy was changed again twice, allowing a charitable contribution to be made only if the insurer's profits reached a certain limit. Some disgruntled shareholders who were still unhappy with this policy left Aachener and founded their own insurance company, Aachen-Leipziger Versicherungs-Aktiengesellschaft. In 1878, after working for Aachener for more than 50 years, director Brüggemann died at age 81.

By the late 1870s Aachener was one of Germany's best-known insurance companies. One of its prominent customers was Chancellor Otto von Bismark, the founder of Germany's public health insurance. He was skeptical about private insurance companies, but insured his farm, Gut Varzin in Pomerania, with Aachener. The company's success, however, led to self-satisfaction and inner stagnation. While competition grew stronger in the farm sector, the beginning industrialization opened up a potential new market. But Aachener's agents resisted the challenge of building new relationships with the growing industrial clientele and starting from scratch in a market where they had not much experience in insuring industrial risks. Under the leadership of former Kölnische Rück director Fritz Schröder, who joined Aachener in 1896, the company intensified its marketing efforts and introduced a number of new policies that covered burglary, damaged water pipelines, and the interruption of the production process in manufacturing plants. Schröder, who was experienced in international reinsurance business, also initiated the company's international expansion. Aachener's first subsidiary overseas was set up in San Francisco in 1893. By 1900 the company was represented in 56 foreign offices on all continents, including two more offices in the United States in New York and Chicago, and some 25 in Asia, including Bangkok, Bombay, and Singapore. As a result, Aachener's premium income tripled between 1893 and 1913, with about half of the total generated abroad.

San Francisco Earthquake and World War I

On April 18, 1906, San Francisco was shaken by a strong earthquake and the resulting fires destroyed big parts of the city. Aachener's San Francisco branch had signed numerous fire policies in the city and paid approximately $3.5 million in damages—a huge sum at the time. All cases were regulated by the end of the same year and ate up Aachener's profits of two years.

In the following four decades, however, man-made disasters shook the company. When World War I broke out in August 1914, Aachener's international expansion—with the exception of North and South America—came to a sudden halt. In October 1914 Adolf Harbers replaced deceased director Fritz Schröder. In the first war year Aachener had to cover enormous damages from burned cities and villages in Eastern Prussia after Russian attacks. In 1915 the company added coverage of fire damages caused by explosions of bombs to its fire policies to retain its customers. The company's burglary insurance branch wrote huge losses in the later war years, when food became scarce and crime rose. When the United States entered the war in 1917 Aachener transferred its American business to Japanese insurer Tokyo Marine. The government put increasing pressure on the company to insure ammunition factories at unprofitable premiums, while the number of large damages to be covered rose substantially in 1917 and 1918. The forced takeover of industrial risks changed the company's insurance portfolio. The percentage of industry coverage rose from about one-third in 1913 to 50 percent in 1918, while premium income decreased by 20 percent between 1913 and 1917. At the same time the company's female workforce grew from almost zero in 1914 to 60 percent four years later, due to the rising number of men drafted to fight in the war.

Hyperinflation and Depression in the 1920s

In November 1918 Germany and its allies were defeated. The German *Kaiserreich* ceased to exist and was replaced by the first German republic, established in the city of Weimar. According to the Versailles Treaty, Aachener not only lost its business in large parts of former Prussia and in the areas bordering France, Belgium, and Luxembourg, but suddenly found itself ''abroad'' under French administration. Business travel and communication with the company's branch offices in Germany were difficult. It took until 1930 before the last soldiers left the Rhineland and the Saar. After lengthy negotiations Aachener managed to retain parts of its confiscated capital holdings in the United States. The toughest test for the company, though, was the rallying inflation that overtook Germany in the early 1920s. Aachener's 99th year in business was its craziest to date. Due to hyperinflation, a building's worth in 1914 had climbed to 1,800 billion its worth in November 1923. While the company's employees had to carry their salaries home in baskets, the calculation of insurance premiums became impossible with damage cost jumping hundredfold in the course of a day. And while the worth of the company's capital base lessened, Aachener's employees made space in their offices to store food. At the end of 1923 the German government replaced 500 trillion *Papiermark* with one *Rentenmark*. Despite huge losses, Aachener survived the chaos, due to its large reserves, partly in Swiss francs, and its considerable real estate.

The mid-1920s marked the beginning of a period of bankruptcies, mergers and acquisitions, and partnerships in Germany's insurance industry. Aachener took over the insurers Thuringia, Aachen-Potsdamer Life Insurance, and Oldenburger, which comprised the new Aachener und Münchener Group. Aachener also joined the Rheinische Gruppe, a group of insurers that founded the reinsurance company Unitas in 1920. During the decade the automobile became increasingly popular in Germany and Aachener added auto insurance to its services. Other novelties included the movie theater and broken-glass insurance.

The worldwide economic depression that followed the New York Stock Exchange crash of October 1929 hit the German insurance industry with some delay in 1931. During the following four years Aachener's premium revenues dropped by one-fifth. While many businesses went bankrupt and unemployment soared, violent fights between radicals from the political left and right erupted in the streets. In January 1933 Adolf Hitler was appointed Germany's new chancellor and his National Socialist party eventually drove the country into another devastating war.

The Nazi Years and World War II

In 1935 Walter Schmidt, the former CEO of Cologne Re, resumed Aachener's leadership and steered the company through the Nazi years, World War II, and the postwar reconstruction period. To combat mass unemployment the National Socialist government required businesses to create more jobs. Hence, despite decreasing premium income caused by the ongoing depression, the company offered 100 new positions. The Nazis also demanded that auto insurance premiums be cut to encourage demand for cars and pressed fire insurers to jointly insure important industries at no profit. When thousands of Jewish stores and synagogues were burned down by violent Nazis on November 9,

1938, the government forbid insurers to pay damages to Jewish customers (with the exception of Jews living abroad). Shortly after that, Jews were no longer allowed to drive in Germany and some insurers withheld auto insurance premiums that had already been paid. In 1997 Aachener and other German insurance companies were sued by survivors of the Holocaust, for withholding payments. The company's remaining files from that period, however, did not indicate any fraud.

During the first years of World War II Aachener's business soared. In 1939 the company took over the German business of British insurer Liverpool and—following the German troops— gradually expanded its business activities into the occupied territories, including Poland, Czechoslovakia, The Netherlands, Belgium, and France. To finance its war effort, the German government required insurance companies in 1939 to invest two-thirds of their capital investments into government bonds. In 1942 the percentage was raised to 75 percent. As had happened in World War I, however, the bonds became worthless with the end of the Nazi rule.

By summer 1944 half of Aachener's employees were women who, again, replaced the men fighting in the war. When the war returned to Germany in 1943, Aachener suffered large damages of its office buildings in many cities. After several bombs had destroyed most of the company's headquarters, and after the Western allies started marching toward Germany's western border, Aachener moved headquarters to Erfurt, where the company's subsidiary Thuringia was located, in September 1944. In March 1945 Aachener's management moved once again, to Bad Kissingen in Bavaria.

PostWar Boom and Globalization in the Second Half of the 20th Century

With Germany's defeat in World War II Aachener's fire insurance business decreased by about 40 percent. Many of its farm clients were located in the eastern part of the country, which was occupied by Soviet troops. A few years after the war the whole insurance industry was nationalized in the Soviet sector. This development drove many insurers from eastern Germany to the West, where competition for the smaller insurance pie became more intense. After the currency reform of 1948 in the three western zones, however, West Germany entered its legendary postwar ''economic miracle'' years. In the following decade Aachener's premium income tripled, and doubled again between 1960 and 1970. As the Volkswagen ''Bug'' conquered West Germany's streets, auto insurance replaced fire insurance as Aachener's most important type of property and casualty insurance.

Under Reimer Schmidt, who became Aachener's CEO in 1968, the company reorganized its shareholdings. As the Rheinische Gruppe was dissolved, Aachener gave up its shares in various property insurers in exchange for a 25 percent share in Cologne Re. The company also acquired a majority share in life insurer Volkshilfe Lebensversicherung, which was merged with its own life insurance division to form Aachener und Münchener Leben. In 1970 the company abandoned its traditional name in Bavaria and started using its new name Aachener und Münchener Versicherung AG in all of West Germany. In the same year the company acquired private insurer Central

Krankenversicherung and a share in Badenia Bausparkasse, a financial service provider for homeowners. The 1970s were characterized by increasing prices caused by the first oil price shock in 1973. A rising number of damages and a fear of inflation drove insurance premiums and cost up during the decade. Aachener, which for the first time since 1906 reported a loss from insurance business in 1970, reorganized its operative business and introduced electronic data processing to cut cost. In the middle of the decade the company started cooperating with Kompass Allgemeine Vermögensberatung, a financial consulting firm that started selling insurance policies for Aachener for a commission. A similar partnership was initiated with Deutsche Vermögensberatung in 1983. The additional sales force of 20,000 financial consultants brought in more than one quarter of Aachener's new business during the 1980s and 1990s, especially in the life insurance segment, and especially in former East Germany after the two German states were reunited in 1990. In 1979 a new holding company, AMB Aachener und Münchener Beteiligungs-Aktiengesellschaft, was founded to head the company's main operations, including Aachener und Münchener Versicherung, Aachener und Münchener Leben, Thuringia, Central Kranken, Cosmos Leben, and Cosmos Allgemeine.

In 1987 AMB took over BfG Bank für Gemeinwirtschaft, a community bank, in order to pursue the so-called *Allfinanz* strategy. The concept that came into fashion in the rapidly consolidating financial markets intended to offer the whole range of financial services, including insurance, asset management, and other traditional banking products, by one institution. This move, however, turned out to be an unfortunate investment that cost AMB a lot of money. In 1992 the company sold a 25 percent share in BfG to French Crédit Lyonnais. In 1999 Swedish bank group SEB acquired AMB's remaining 25 percent.

A more favorable move was the 1993 takeover of Volksfürsorge Holding AG, a major German direct insurer. The combined premium income of the two made AMB Germany's second largest life insurer and number four among the country's property and casualty insurers. While AMB's top management was contemplating a new strategy for the company, an unexpected threat developed quietly, escalated and finally ended in AMB's loss of independence.

The insurance markets of the 1990s were more and more dominated by large international players with immense financial reserves. After the member countries of the European Union had created a joint market, competition among large European insurers intensified. In 1992 French insurance conglomerate Assurances Générales de France (AGF) announced that it had secretly acquired 25 percent plus one share of AMB shares from various individual shareholders. A group of some bigger AMB shareholders, however, including Allianz, Dresdner Bank, and Munich Re prevented the recognition of AGF's voting rights. Although AGF was denied any influence in AMB, it did not want to give up its shares in the company. Finally, in 1998, the conflict was resolved when AGF itself became the target of a takeover. Germany's insurer Allianz AG and Italian insurer Assicurazioni Generali S.p.A., two of the world's largest direct insurers, were both interested in controlling AGF. In 1998 the two made a deal: Allianz got AGF in exchange for the two companies' combined shares in AMB. Generali also acquired the AMB shares formerly held by Munich Re and Dresdner Bank and thereby gained control over Aachener und Münchener. In 1999 AMB entered a strategic partnership with Germany's Commerzbank, in which Generali also held an interest. The bank agreed to sell AMB insurance policies in its branch offices and the "all round finance" concept finally turned into a success. In 2000 AMB took over Generali's German subsidiary Generali Lloyd and in 2001 changed its name to AMB Generali Holding AG. By that time, AMB had become Germany's third largest direct insurance group.

Principal Subsidiaries

Aachener und Münchener Versicherung AG; Thuringia Versicherung AG; Volksfürsorge Deutsche Sachversicherung AG; AdvoCard Rechtsschutsversicherung AG; COSMOS Versicherung AG; Generali Lloyd Versicherung AG; Aachener und Münchener Lebensversicherung AG; Volksfürsorge Lebensversicherung AG; COSMOS Lebensversicherung-AG; Generali Lloyd Lebensversicherung AG; Dialog Lebensversicherungs-AG; CENTRAL Krankenversicherung AG; COSMOS Krankenversicherung AG; Volksfürsorge Krankenversicherung AG; AMB Generali Finanzanlagen-Management GmbH; AM Generali Invest Kapitalanlagegesellschaft mbH; AMB Generali Immobilien GmbH (Germany); Deutsche Bausparkasse Badenia AG; AMB Generali Informatik Services GmbH; Deutsche Vermögensberatung AG (49.9%).

Principal Competitors

Allianz AG; ERGO Versicherungsgruppe AG; HDI V.a.G.

Further Reading

"AMB baut die Marktposition aus," *Frankfurter Allgemeine Zeitung,* April 4, 2001, p. 20.

"AMB-Tochtergesellschaften verlassen die Börse," *Frankfurter Allgemeine Zeitung,* April 10, 2002, p. 24.

"AMB wechselt den Vorstand aus," *Süddeutsche Zeitung,* October 13, 1992, p. 26.

"AM-Gruppe durch Generali Lloyd gestärkt," *Börsen-Zeitung,* May 11, 2000, p. 8.

"AM-Versicherungen rücken zusammen," *Frankfurter Allgemeine Zeitung,* July 29, 1999, p. 20.

Bartu, Friedemann, "Handschlag zwischen Allianz und Generali," *Neue Zürcher Zeitung,* December 22, 1997, p. 13.

"Das Unternehmergespräch," *Frankfurter Allgemeine Zeitung,* December 28, 1998, p. 20.

"Generali reduziert AMB-Beteiligung," *Börsen-Zeitung,* January 10, 2001, p. 8.

"Kaske übergibt eine gutbestellte AMB," *Börsen-Zeitung,* July 17, 1997, p. 11.

Surminski, Marc, "Von der 'Wohltätigen Gesellschaft zum Versicherungskonzern,'" *Perspektiven* (special edition, "175 Jahre Aachener und Münchener Versicherung Aktiengesellschaft"), May 2000, p. 59.

"Turbulente Hauptversammlung in Aachen," *Süddeutsche Zeitung,* December 31, 1992.

"Wilhelm I., König von Preussen, genehmigte die Gründung," *Frankfurter Allgemeine Zeitung,* September 21, 1993, p. 27.

"Wolfgang Kaske geht in den Ruhestand," *Frankfurter Allgemeine Zeitung,* December 24, 1997, p. 16.

—Evelyn Hauser

Andritz AG

Stattegger Strasse 18
A-8045 Graz
Austria
Telephone: +43 316 6902 0
Fax: +43 316 6902 415
Web site: http://www.andritz.com

Public Company
Incorporated: 1852
Employees: 4,498
Sales: EUR 1.32 billion (US$1.17 billion) (2001)
Stock Exchanges: Vienna OTC
Ticker Symbol: ANDR
NAIC: 333291 Paper Industry Machinery Manufacturing;
  333294 Food Product Machinery Manufacturing;
  333298 All Other Industrial Manufacturing; 333516
  Rolling Mill Machinery and Equipment
  Manufacturing; 333611 Turbine and Turbine
  Generator Set Unit Manufacturing; 333911 Pump and
  Pumping Equipment Manufacturing; 333999 All Other
  General Purpose Machinery Manufacturing; 541330
  Engineering Services

Graz, Austria-based Andritz AG engineers and manufactures high-tech production and processing systems. The company has pursued a targeted acquisition program to become one of the world's leading suppliers of pulp and paper production machinery, as well as other industrial and environmental production machinery and systems. Andritz's operations are grouped under four Strategic Business Areas: Pulp and Paper; Rolling Mills and Strip Processing Lines for the steel industry; Environmental and Process Technologies; and Feed Technology. The company's largest segment is its Pulp and Paper unit, which accounted for 67 percent of Andritz's sales of EUR 1.32 billion in 2001. Andritz manufactures a full range of systems, plants, machinery, and processes covering all types of pulp production, as well as production equipment and systems for specialized tissues. Rolling Mills and Strip Processing Lines accounted for 13 percent of the company's sales in 2001 and

includes the manufacturing and installation of plants for producers of different types of steel, including cold-rolled carbon steel, high-grade steel, and nonferrous metal strip. Environmental and Process Technologies, which includes systems for wastewater and sewage treatment plants, and industrial sludge treatment and drying systems, adds approximately 12 percent of the company's revenues. Andritz is also a leading manufacturer of Feed Technology equipment for the production of animal feeds; the company has captured a 50 percent share of the market for salmon feed equipment. That segment added 8 percent to the company's sales in 2001. Andritz is a globally operating company, with a focus on the European and North American markets, which represent 46 and 38 percent of the company's sales, respectively. Andritz operates 18 manufacturing plants in Austria, Finland, Germany, the United States, France, Canada, China, and Denmark. The company has been listed on the Vienna stock exchange since 2001. In January 2002, the company was added to that exchange's ATX listing. Andritz is led by president and CEO Wolfgang Leitner.

Steel Foundry Founding in the Mid-19th Century

Andritz's roots traced back to the mid-19th century when Josef Körösi established a foundry and machine plant in Graz, Austria. In 1900, the company went public, which led, in 1957, to a takeover by Vienna-based Credietanstalt-Bankverein. By then, Andritz had begun engineering and manufacturing equipment for the forestry industry, which led increasingly to the development of products for the pulp and paper industry. Among Andritz's earliest products were equipment and systems for pulp pumping. The company then went on to develop machinery for paper manufacturing as well as wire presses for removing the water from pulp stock. In 1983, the company formed the basis of its later Environmental and Process Technologies division when it began adapting the dewatering and drying technologies it had been using for its pulp and paper industry systems for use in industrial sludge treatment.

Andritz remained under the control of Credietanstalt-Bankverein until 1987. Under Credietanstalt-Bankverein, much of Andritz's activity involved the production of machinery under license. In the mid-1980s, however, the company adopted a new strategic direction set on redefining the company as a supplier of proprietary, high-technology manufacturing machinery and systems. As such, the company sought to build up its engineering and development component. As part of its strategic change, Andritz found itself under new management, when AGIV AG, an investment company based in Frankfurt, Germany, acquired the company. At that time, the company was placed under the leadership of Wolfgang Leitner, who led the company's transformation.

Through the end of the 1980s, Andritz concentrated on developing its own in-house products. The 1990s, however, were to mark the true start of Andritz's transformation into a globally operating manufacturer. Although the pulp and paper industry was to remain the company's core customer segment—accounting for more than two-thirds of its revenues—Andritz looked to establish itself in other industrial areas. The company's first expansion came in 1990, with the acquisition of Sprout-Bauer, based in Muncy, Pennsylvania.

Sprout-Bauer had been formed in 1986 through the merger of two companies that traced their roots to the late 19th century. The acquisition of Sprout-Bauer by Andritz not only extended Andritz's pulp systems operations, as well as its environmental technologies division, notably with Sprout-Bauer's line of screening and seizing equipment, but also gave Andritz an entry into the mechanical feed production market.

High-Tech Engineering Group for the 21st Century

The Sprout-Bauer acquisition had given Andritz a jump-start in its drive to redefine itself as a diversified yet focused engineering and manufacturing group. The company continued building up its environmental and process technologies division with the acquisitions of TCW in 1991 and a 50 percent stake in France's Guinard Centrifugation, which had started operations in 1950. By then, the company had made another significant purchase, that of Durametal, based in Oregon in the United States. Durametal had originally been founded in 1948 as Brake Drum Supply Company, but had grown to become a major manufacturer of refiner plates and other components for mechanical pulping systems and other industrial applications. The purchase significantly enhanced Andritz's U.S. presence.

Andritz turned to Finland, one of Europe's major forestry markets, in 1994, acquiring the Kone Wood Group. The addition of that company's manufacturing operations, which included wood processing and related equipment, helped strengthen Andritz's position as a major supplier to the European and global pulp industry. The following year, Andritz turned to Denmark, where it bought up Jesma-Matador, a company that had developed a strong position in the Danish market for feed mill machinery and systems, especially for the production of salmon feed.

Jesma-Matador's history dated back to the founding of Jesma in 1895, initially as a transporter of grain and other feed products, before turning to the manufacturing of equipment for the production of animal feed. In 1986, Jesma merged with Matador, also from Denmark, which had been founded in 1931.

The acquisition of Jesma-Matador led Andritz to form a dedicated Feed Technology Division and merge its main operations into a new company in 1995. Called Sprout-Matador, the new subsidiary encompassed the company's feed mill and equipment manufacturing activities in the United States and Denmark.

Andritz took a break from making new acquisitions in the mid-1990s. In 1998, however, the company returned to external expansion with not only a new acquisition, but a new operating division as well. In that year the company purchased a 75 percent stake in Sundwig Eisenhütte Maschinenfabrik GmbH & Co. based in Hemer, Germany. That company's origins reached back to its founding as an ironworks in 1650, before turning to machinery production in the 1850s. By 1920, Sundwig had become a specialist in machinery and plant equipment for the steel industry.

Andritz quickly followed the Sundwig acquisition with those of Thermtec, based in The Netherlands, which specialized in thermal processing applications, and Ruthner, which focused on processing engineering applications. The company then bundled the three companies into a new Rolling Mills and Strip Processing division.

Andritz itself found itself under new ownership in 1999 when AGIV sold the company to a consortium consisting of the Carlyle Group and Unternehmens Invest AG, an Austrian investment group that specialized in acquiring stakes in private companies in order to prepare them for an initial public offering (IPO). Joining the consortium taking control of Andritz was president and CEO Wolfgang Leitner and other members of Andritz's management.

The new financial backing enabled Andritz to set its sights on a new target: in March 2000, the company made its largest acquisition to date, that of a 50 percent stake in Finland's Ahlstrom Machinery Group from the A. Ahlstrom Corporation, a manufacturer of chemical pulp plants and other pulp processing machinery. As part of the purchase agreement, Andritz also received the option of purchasing full control of Ahlstrom Machinery in the event of Andritz going public. In the meantime, Ahlstrom Machinery was renamed Andritz-Ahlstrom and placed under Andritz's Pulp and Paper division.

The Ahlstrom acquisition helped boost Andritz's sales past the EUR 1 billion mark, and also cemented the company's worldwide leadership in a variety of pulp and paper processing machinery categories, including that of chemical pulp plants. Andritz also began preparing a public offering in earnest, in large part in order to complete the Ahlstrom acquisition. Yet the company was forced to postpone its IPO, initially set for October 2000, due to poor market conditions.

Instead, the company made another acquisition, of Universal Milling Technology, which had been the feed technology division of the United Kingdom's Tate & Lyle Plc. The purchase,

Key Dates:

1852: Josef Körösi founds a steel foundry and machine works in Graz, Austria.

1900: Andritz, which has begun producing equipment for the pulp and paper industry, becomes a public company.

1957: Andritz is acquired by Credietanstalt-Bankverein, based in Vienna, and continues expanding its pulp & paper industry operations.

1983: Andritz begins developing its Environmental and Process Technologies Division by extending its dewatering and drying technology to industrial sludge treatment.

1987: Andritz is acquired by AGIV AG, an investment firm based in Frankfurt, Germany, and adopts new strategic direction to become an engineering firm and manufacturer of proprietary systems.

1990: The company acquires Sprout-Bauer, in the United States, adding feed systems manufacturing.

1992: The company acquires Durametal, in the United States, to boost position in North America.

1994: The company acquires Kone Wood Group.

1995: The company acquires Jesma-Matador A/S, of Denmark, which is then combined with Sprout-Bauer to form Sprout-Matador.

1998: The company acquires 75 percent of Sundwig, based in Germany.

1999: AGIV sells Andritz to a consortium, including the Carlyle Group and Andritz management.

2000: Andritz acquires 50 percent of the Ahlstrom Machinery Group, which is renamed Andritz-Ahlstrom.

2001: Andritz lists on the Vienna stock exchange and completes the acquisition of Andritz-Ahlstrom.

2002: Andritz is admitted to the Vienna exchange's ATX blue chip index.

made in November 2000, boosted Andritz as the world's leading manufacturer of systems, processes, and machinery for animal feed production. The company's Feed Technology division now represented nearly 10 percent of the company's annual sales.

Andritz finally went public in July 2001, listing on the Vienna Stock Exchange. The IPO represented somewhat of a disappointment, however, as the company listed on half the number of shares it had originally expected to sell in October of the previous year; meanwhile, the stock failed to meet its initial share price after its first day of trading. Nonetheless, many analysts remained optimistic about the stock and the company. By the beginning of 2002, Andritz had proved them right, when it was added to the Vienna exchange's ATX blue-chip index.

Following the IPO, Andritz made good on completing its acquisition of full control of Andritz-Ahlstrom, buying up the rest of that subsidiary in July 2001. As it turned to the new century, Andritz sought fresh international expansion opportunities. The overwhelming majority of the company's sales, which topped EUR 1.3 billion in 2001, remained focused on Europe (at 46 percent of sales) and the United States (at 38 percent of sales). The company now targeted growth in Asia, specifically in the vast Chinese market, adding two new production facilities in that country to bring its total to 18 manufacturing plants worldwide.

Principal Subsidiaries

Andritz Denmark A/S; Sprout-Matador A/S; Andritz (USA), Inc. ; Andritz Inc. (U.S.); Andritz-Ruthner, Inc. (U.S.); Durametal Corporation (U.S.); Guinard Centrifugation S.A. (France, 50%); Andritz S.A. (France); Andritz Ingenieria S.A. (Spain); Andritz GmbH (Germany); Sundwig GmbH (Germany; 75%); Andritz Ltda. (Brazil); Andritz Oy (Finland); Andritz Ltd. (Canada); Andritz AB (Sweden); Andritz Ltd. (U.K.); Andritz-Kenflo Foshan Pump Co. Ltd. (China; 60%); U.M.T. Limited (U.K.); U.M.T. Deurne B.V. (Netherlands); U.M.T. Boxtel B.V. (Netherlands); Universal Milling Technology S.A. (France); Andritz-Ahlstrom Ltda. (Brazil); Andritz-Ahlstrom Oy (Finland); Andritz-Ahlstrom Holdings USA Inc.; Andritz-Ahlstrom Inc. (U.S.A.); Kamyr Canada Inc. (Canada); Andritz-Ahlstrom AB (Sweden); Andritz-Ahlstrom GmbH (Germany); Andritz-Ahlstrom KK (Japan).

Principal Competitors

Kvarner ASA (KVIB); J.M. Voith GmbH; Stork NV; Thermo Electron Corp.; BTR Inc.; Joy Global Inc.; Kvaerner E and C Plc; Sacmi Cooperativa Meccanici Imola Scrl; Jagenberg AG; Firth Rixson plc; Tetra Pack Italiana SpA; Wanderer-Werke AG; Metso Paper Sundsvall AB; Simon Group PLC; Paper Converting Machine Co.; Windmoller und Holscher; Kadant Inc.; Winkler + Dunnebier AG; Lindauer Dornier Gesellschaft mbH; Black Clawson Company Inc.; Schur International a/s; Brodrene Hartmann A/S.

Further Reading

"Andritz IPO to Raise Up to 108 mln Euros," *Reuters,* June 6, 2001.

"Andritz Takes Full Control of Anditz-Ahlstrom," *Reuters,* July 2, 2002.

"Commission Clears Andritz Takeover by Carlyle and UIAG," *Europe Energy,* November 26, 1999.

Ferguson, Julia, "Andritz—Old Economy and Proud of It," *Reuters,* June 1, 2001.

—M.L. Cohen

Apasco S.A. de C.V.

Campos Eliseos 345
Mexico City, D.F. 11560
Mexico
Telephone: (525) 724-0000
Fax: (525) 724-0280
Web site: http://www.apasco.com.mx

Public Company
Incorporated: 1928 as Compania Mexicana de Cemento
   Portland Apasco S.A.
Employees: 2,900
Sales: 9.12 billion pesos ($995.09 million) (2001)
Stock Exchanges: Mexico City Over The Counter
Ticker Symbols: APASCO; ASSAY; ASSBY
NAIC: 212321 Construction Sand and Gravel Mining;
   32731 Hydraulic Cement Manufacturing; 327320
   Ready-Mix Concrete Manufacturing; 327410 Lime
   Manufacturing; 551112 Offices of Other Holding
   Companies, Not Elsewhere Classified

Apasco S.A. de C.V. is a Mexican holding company for a number of subsidiaries engaged in the production and sale of cement, ready-mix concrete, lime, gravel, and mortar. This low-tech industrial sector is dominated in Mexico by Cemex, S.A. de C.V., a giant Mexican-based multinational firm, but Apasco is its chief competitor. Apasco is majority owned by Holcim, Ltd., a Swiss-based multinational firm, but its stock is publicly traded in Mexico City. In addition to its facilities in Mexico, Apasco holds a minority share in a company that operates plants in all six Hispanic Central American nations: Costa Rica, El Salvador, Guatemala, Honduras, Nicaragua, and Panama. It also offers support services through mobile ready-mix concrete laboratories.

The First 60 Years: 1928–87

The company was founded in 1928 as Compania Mexicana de Cementos Portland Apasco S.A. and was acquired in 1964 by Holderbank Financiere Glaris Ltd., a Swiss company that became the largest producer of building construction supplies in the world. At this time Apasco ranked in the middle of 25 Mexican cement producers. Its annual installed production capacity of 225,000 metric tons in 1966 was 4 percent of the national total. The company's only plant at the time was located in Apaxco in the state of Mexico. In 1970 it acquired Cementos Veracruz, S.A., a firm located in Orizaba, Veracruz. By then Mexican investors held a majority of Apasco's shares, in accordance with government requirements intended to reduce foreign ownership of Mexico's resources. Apasco had sales of 276.1 million pesos ($23 million) in 1975, when it ranked fourth among cement producers. Its net profit came to 21.5 million pesos ($1.72 million). Holderbank held 47 percent of Apasco at this time, while Banco Nacional de Mexico (Banamex) held 21 percent.

In 1979 Apasco began work on a new plant in Macuspana, Tabasco. This tropical, underdeveloped state in southeastern Mexico was undergoing a boom owing to growing output from the petroleum and petrochemical industries in the area. Apasco's new site offered road, rail, and river links and had the advantage of being the first cement plant in the area. Erecting the facility was neither easy nor cheap, however; it involved clearing the site of snakes and ticks and construction on gummy soil exposed to winter torrential rains. Completed in 1981, the plant, which had an initial capacity of 900,000 metric tons a year, required an investment of 2.8 billion pesos (about $122 million).

Apasco also reserved about 750 acres in the area for a project to develop agriculture, animal husbandry, and forestry to aid inhabitants who would otherwise not benefit from the plant. Cattle raising was by far the chief of these activities, but another result was a notable rise in milk production. In 1986 the company created a new agricultural and forestry training center. This center was providing communities with the initial investments, professional advice, and counseling for establishing a self-sufficient enterprise and included training for beekeeping, silkworm raising, and reforestation. There were six such company-sponsored centers in operation by 2000. Apasco also was actively engaged in promoting programs of youth activity, adult literacy, and alcohol and drug treatment.

By 1981 Apasco had tripled its production capacity in a decade and held 18 percent of the Mexican market for cement. That year it began selling shares on the Mexican stock ex-

change. Interviewed for the business magazine *Expansion,* director general Bernard Galley said, ''One of the points that
distinguish us is that we are the only cement company that has a
direct system of distribution, for whose functioning we count
with numerous means of transport (pipelines, cars, trucks, and
two ships, plus terminals in the Federal District [Mexico
City]).'' But the collapse of the peso in 1982 stopped the
company's growth in its tracks as construction ground to a halt.
Apasco's dollar debt, swelled by high interest rates, posed an
immediate threat to the firm and required renegotiation plus an
infusion of investment funds. By 1987 the company's total
liabilities had been reduced by 60 percent, but its foreign debt
still exceeded $100 million.

Apasco demonstrated in 1986 that it was close to recovery. At
the end of the year circulating assets covered 94 percent of short-
term liabilities. Sales for the year reached 75.59 billion pesos
($123.5 million), and the operating profit was 19.81 billion pesos
($32.37 million). The Apasco group now consisted of ten compa-
nies serving almost the entire country. Exportation of its output,
which began in 1983, reached 760,000 metric tons of clinker,
one-fifth of the national total. Among the companies now under
the Apasco group's banner was Concretos Apasco, S.A., established in 1977 from the merger of two firms with combined sales
the previous year of 235 million pesos (about $12 million). Eight
of its 11 plants were in the Federal District; the others were in the
states of Puebla and Mexico, bordering the district. Total capacity
was more than 2,000 cubic meters of concrete per day.

Second Largest Mexican Cement Firm: 1988–99

Apasco still ranked fourth among Mexican cement producers at the start of 1988, but after Cemex acquired Empresas
Tolteca that year, the company moved up to second place.
Taken as a whole, the group of 11 subsidiaries (including one
for paper and cardboard) had sales of 376.85 billion pesos
($165.78 million) and 2,909 employees in 1988. The company
opened a new plant in 1991, in Ramos Arizpe, Coahuila. This
added a million tons of cement capacity a year and enhanced
Apasco's presence in northern Mexico. The company combined
this enhanced capacity with the construction of premixed-concrete plants in the region. That year Apasco also purchased
Decar del Valle, S.A. de C.V., a producer of premixed concrete
based in Mexico City, bringing its number of plants for this
purpose to 44. In 1992 Apasco acquired one of the few remaining independent Mexican cement producers: Cementos de Aca-

pulco, S.A., with annual cement production capacity of 400,000
metric tons a year, at a cost of about $40 million. It also
constructed 11 new premixed-concrete plants.

Apasco also began work on a new plant in the western part
of Mexico, at Tecoman, Colima, with installed annual capacity
of 1.3 million tons of cement. Built at a cost of $130 million and
oriented toward the Guadalajara and central Pacific Coast markets, this facility was opened in late 1993.

To help finance existing and future infrastructure, Apasco
began selling American Depositary Receipts (the equivalent of
shares of common stock) over the counter in the United States.
The company in late 1991 had raised $100 million by selling
bonds to overseas investors and—in part because of its ties to
Holderbank—enjoyed the highest credit rating for such securities available to a company operating in Mexico.

These years constituted a period of headlong expansion and
growing sales and profits for Apasco. By the end of 1994 its
annual productive capacity had reached 7.8 million metric tons
of cement, and its share of the Mexican market for both cement
and ready-mix concrete had reached 22 percent. There were
now 84 ready-mix concrete plants with an annual production
capacity of 7.6 million metric tons, strategically located in 40
cities. The company's workforce swelled to more than 4,000.
Net sales reached 1.98 billion new pesos (about $650 million) in
1993. Sales increased another 15 percent, to 2.36 billion pesos
(about $800 million) in 1994.

Fundamental to Apasco's growth in this period was its strategy of regional diversification, focusing on its principal markets
with the goal of profiting from all types of synergy in order to
overcome Cemex's dominance. This strategy involved the construction—at Ramos Arizpe and Tecoman—of state-of-the-art
cement plants at a reasonable cost of $100 per ton of installed
capacity. Apasco's director general told Javier Martinez Staines
of the Mexican business magazine *Expansion* in 1992 that the
Ramos Arizpe plant ''was the first to reconcile high technology
with an investment much lower than any other plant constructed
before. Not only in Mexico, but in the world.'' Other projects
completed in the early 1990s included the expansion of the
Apaxco and Orizaba cement facilities and the construction of
distribution centers in Guadalajara and Puebla.

The economic crisis that gripped Mexico after the devaluation of the peso in December 1994 meant an end to the many
industrial and housing projects that had fueled Apasco's recent
expansion. Net sales fell nearly 28 percent in 1995 and did not
surpass the 1994 level (discounting inflation) until 1998. The
company remained marginally profitable, however, and was
able to win a higher credit rating than the Mexican government
itself when it marketed $100 million in 12-year notes in July
1995. Although the devaluation of the peso meant that Apasco's
dollar-denominated debt had widened considerably in real
terms, the company had reduced this amount by 44 percent by
the end of 1996. Apasco added marine terminals in Manzanillo,
Colima and Sauzal, Baja California, in 1995 and 1996, respectively. It took a minority stake in a Honduras cement plant in
1996 and an El Salvador plant in 1997.

The remaining years of the century saw continuing gains in
net sales and net profit, which increased 42 percent and 148

Key Dates:

1928: Compania Mexicana de Cemento Portland Apasco S.A. is founded.

1964: The company is acquired by Holderbank, a Swiss-based construction firm.

1975: Apasco reaches fourth place among Mexican cement producers.

1977: Concretos Apasco, S.A. is established from the merger of two firms.

1981: The company begins to offer shares on the Mexico City stock exchange.

1988: Apasco is now Mexico's second-ranking cement producer.

1993: Apasco ADRs (the equivalent of shares) begin to trade in the United States.

2000: The company has 23 percent of the Mexican cement market.

2001: Apasco has holdings in all six Hispanic Central American countries.

percent, respectively, between 1997 and 2000. The results for 2000 were 9.19 billion pesos ((\$956.4 million) and 2.09 billion pesos (\$217.48 million), respectively. Net sales fell by 5 percent, to 9.12 billion pesos (\$995.09 million) in 2001, despite an 8 percent gain for ready-mix concrete. The net profit remained a substantial 1.79 billion pesos (about \$195 million).

Apasco in 2000 and 2001

Apasco's long-term debt was 1.15 billion pesos (\$120 million) at the end of 2000, a reduction of almost 50 percent compared with 1998. In 2001 it received a \$143 million loan from an international bank syndicate. Some \$60 million of this sum was earmarked to pay down debt and another \$50 million to expand the Ramos Arizpe cement plant.

Apasco, in 2001, had six cement plants with combined installed capacity of 8.9 million metric tons of cement. Utilization ranged from 100 percent at Ramos Arizpe to 57 percent at Macuspana. Sales came to 6.8 million tons in 2000, when the company held 23 percent of the Mexican cement market. By 2001 Apasco also had holdings in all six Hispanic Central American countries through its 44 percent stake in Netherlands-based Holcemca B.V. Apasco also had more than 100 plants for the production of premixed concrete. Production came to 2.8 million cubic meters of concrete in 2000, when the company held 25 percent of the national market. Apasco had 25 distribution centers and a technological center. The company maintained five facilities for sand and gravel, but one was inactive and only the ones in Apaxco and Texcoco were being significantly utilized during the year. Holcim, Ltd. (formerly Holderbank) held 65 percent of Apasco's shares.

Apasco's holdings were valued at 6.83 billion pesos (\$745.08 million) at the end of 2001. Of this total, Cementos Apasco accounted for 33 percent, Cementos Veracruz for 17 percent, and Concretos Apasco for 12 percent. The company's stake in Holcemca accounted for 29 percent of its valuation.

Principal Subsidiaries

Cementos Acapulco, S.A. de C.V.; Cementos Apasco, S.A. de C.V.; Cementos Veracruz, S.A. de C.V.; Comindumex, S.A. de C.V.; Concretos Apasco, S.A. de C.V.; Gravasa, S.A. de C.V.

Principal Competitors

Cemex, S.A. de C.V.; Grupo Cementos de Chihuahua, S.A. de C.V.

Further Reading

"Concretos Apasco: fusion en concreto," *Expansion*, February 1, 1978, pp. 38–39.

Flores King, Alejandro, "Del cemento al ejido," *Expansion*, September 2, 1987, pp. 92, 94.

Fretz, Deirdre, "Apasco Relies on the IFC for Concrete Results," *Institutional Investor*, January 1996, pp. 60–62.

Hernandez Martinez, Luis, "Mano a mano," *Expansion*, July 30, 1997, p. 68.

Martinez Staines, Jaime, "Inversiones en concreto," *Expansion*, December 9, 1992, 102, 106–07.

McDermott, Terry, "Laying the Foundation," *Business Mexico*, July 1994, pp. 39–40.

"La nueva planta llena un hueco en el sureste," *Expansion*, July 8, 1981, pp. 58–61, 63, 65, 67.

"Pasos firmes," *Expansion*, June 23, 1992, p. 60.

"Preparing for a Dynamic Future," *Institutional Investor* (Special Supplement), October 1993, pp. 16–17.

—Robert Halasz

Authentic Fitness Corporation

6040 Bandini Boulevard
Commerce, California 90040
U.S.A.
Telephone: (323) 726-1262
Fax: (323) 721-3613
Web site: http://www.speedo.com

Wholly Owned Subsidiary of The Warnaco Group Inc.
Incorporated: 1990
Employees: 1,100
Sales: $311.8 million (2001)
NAIC: 315228 Men's and Boys' Cut and Sew Other
    Outerwear Manufacturing; 315239 Women's and
    Girls' Cut and Sew Other Outerwear Manufacturing;
    448190 Other Clothing Stores

A market leader in the swimwear industry, Authentic Fitness Corporation manufactures and sells swimwear through approximately 75 Speedo Authentic Fitness stores in the United States and Canada via the Speedo Web site and through various other retail outlets. The company markets its products under the Speedo, Speedo Authentic Fitness, Catalina, Anne Cole, Cole of California, Ralph Lauren, Polo Sport, Oscar de la Renta, Sunset Beach, Sandcastle, and Sporting Life brand names. For years, Speedo was owned by women's lingerie maker Warnaco Group, but in 1990 Speedo and the rest of the Warnaco Group's activewear division was sold to Linda J. Wachner and other investors. The result was Authentic Fitness Corp., an offshoot company with Speedo at its core. Wachner, who also served as chief executive officer of Warnaco while she headed Authentic Fitness, transformed Speedo into a retail concept, opening a chain of stores throughout the United States and in selected foreign locations. Authentic Fitness then reunited with Warnaco in 1999 after failed attempts to do so four years earlier. Warnaco, struggling under a huge debt load, declared bankruptcy in 2001. Shortly thereafter, Wachner was ousted from the company.

Wachner and Authentic Fitness's Formation

The formation of Authentic Fitness represented one astute accomplishment in a long series of shrewd business moves ef-

fected by the company's creator, Linda J. Wachner, who made an indelible mark in an area of the business world dominated by male executives. Wachner, in fact, was alone in the upper echelons of corporate America, standing as the only female CEO in the Fortune 500 and the only female to preside over two New York Stock Exchange companies. Not surprisingly, Wachner ascended to such lofty heights by acting aggressively, demonstrating a high degree of determination and decisiveness that sparked her unprecedented rise in the apparel industry. Her singular distinction in an exclusively male domain was her will to win. She was a "savvy negotiator," pundits noted. A "shrewd operator," others remarked. "Wachner," one fashion consultant said, "is like Alexander the Great—she's chosen a very weak marketplace to become the big player."

Wachner, described by a member of the business press as the "diminutive, gray-haired apparel veteran," registered her first major coup in 1986 by taking over the floundering Warnaco Group. It was from this bold move that the foundation for Authentic Fitness's birth was gained. Wachner, who had started her career as an assistant department store buyer during the 1960s, held considerable sway by the 1980s, enough to launch a hostile takeover of the Warnaco Group. Warnaco, which manufactured, among other apparel products, women's lingerie and men's shirts, was in deep trouble at the time, staggering under the suffocating weight of $600 million of debt and sporting a balance sheet that translated into a negative net worth. Despite its myriad problems, Warnaco was Wachner's prize, and she took to her commanding position over the fortunes of the company firmly resolved to turn the struggling enterprise around. This she promptly did, orchestrating a turnaround that earned the accolades of industry analysts. Warnaco's debt was whittled down, and its $425 million in sales were boosted up during the ensuing decade, transforming a beleaguered business into a billion-dollar corporation. Wachner achieved her remarkable results by expanding internationally and significantly broadening the distribution channels of Warnaco's business, thereby freeing the company from its dependence on department stores for sales and opening up avenues of growth in the mass market. As this push overseas and into new distribution channels was underway, Wachner also superintended a massive overhaul of Warnaco's many businesses, shedding those properties that were unprofitable and divesting those that could give

the company much-needed cash. It was during this exodus of
Warnaco businesses that the stage for Authentic Fitness's entrance into the business world was set.

As the 1990s began, the economic climate in the United
States was beginning to display the anemic characteristics that
would pock the early years of the decade as a time of economic
recession. Credit was increasingly hard to come by, and
Warnaco needed cash quickly to meet maturing debts. One by
one, a procession of Warnaco businesses made their exit, but the
company's board of directors and Wachner disagreed on the
fate of one business, Warnaco's money-losing swimwear business. With Speedo swimwear at its core, Warnaco's swimwear
business was grouped within Warnaco's activewear division, a
facet of the overall Warnaco enterprise that the company's
directors deemed dispensable. Wachner disagreed, deciding
that the swimwear business still had enough potential to keep.
Unable to convince Warnaco's directors to retain the swimwear
business, Wachner enlisted the financial support of General
Electric Credit Corp. and venture capitalists Pentland Ventures
Ltd. and in 1990 purchased Warnaco's entire activewear division for $85 million.

The activewear division, which included Speedo and White
Stag skiwear, was christened Authentic Fitness Corporation in
1990. Wachner served as CEO of both the newly formed
Authentic Fitness and its former parent Warnaco, guiding each
toward recovery in distinct directions. For Warnaco, Wachner's
panacea was geographic expansion and a headlong move into
the mass market; for Authentic Fitness, Wachner's prescription
was different, its essence revealed when she took the activewear
manufacturer public one year after taking Warnaco public. Authentic Fitness debuted on the New York Stock Exchange at $7
per share in June 1992, when Wachner announced her plans to
transform the widely recognized Speedo label into a retail concept. Initially, Wachner's plans for opening Speedo retail outlets were relatively modest. Five stores were to be opened
during a six-month span that began in November 1992 when the
first Speedo store opened. Wachner's plans quickly escalated
after initial success, however, and the ensuing years would
witness a prodigious spate of Speedo store openings throughout
the United States and on foreign soil.

Speedo Retail Begins in 1992

The first Speedo outlet opened in Los Angeles, an 1,800-
square-foot store that featured a complete line of Speedo swimwear and Speedo Authentic Fitness, a new line of activewear
designed to be worn in or out of water. Inside, diving manne-
quins, a seven-foot cascading waterfall, and ceiling decor that
replicated an upside-down swimming pool—complete with
pool markings, ladders, and tile—lent an aquatic theme to the
store. Patrons quickly lined up in front of the Los Angeles

Speedo store, the first of five units to be opened by June 1993.
Each of these five units were to serve as, in the company's
words, "merchandising laboratories" for Authentic Fitness's
wholesale division, providing executives with up-to-date information on the buying patterns of the public.

As work was underway to establish five Speedo stores during
the first half of 1993, Wachner displayed her talents as a
dealmaker by adding important new lines of apparel to dilute
Authentic Fitness's overwhelming dependence on the Speedo
label to drive sales. The company by this point derived roughly
80 percent of its sales from the sale of Speedo swimwear through
its handful of retail outlets and to department stores, but by the
end of 1993 the company could also look to other well-known
labels for sales support. In August 1993, Wachner signed a licensing agreement with Oscar de la Renta Ltd. for a line of swimwear
bearing the designer's label. The following month, Wachner
added three strong properties, acquiring the Cole, Catalina, and
Anne Cole swimwear labels, each at bargain prices obtained out
of bankruptcy court. Also in September, Wachner signed an
exclusive licensing agreement to be the official sponsor at the
1996 Summer Olympics in Atlanta, rounding out a highly productive month for the 46-year-old CEO.

The string of momentous events in September 1993 did not
end with the announcement of the Summer Olympics deal,
however. While new labels were being added to Authentic
Fitness's portfolio during the month, Wachner developed decidedly more ambitious expansion plans for Speedo specialty
shops, resolving to open 100 mall-based retail stores during the
ensuing two years. The expansion plans called for ten new
stores by the end of October 1993, 40 more stores by the end of
1994, and another 50 stores by the end of 1995, which was
expected to provide additional sales of more than $100 million
on top of the $133 million collected in 1993.

Month by month, new Speedo stores opened, each adorned
with the same decor as the company's first store in Los Angeles.
As planned, the increased exposure of the Speedo name through
store openings breathed new life into the venerable yet
struggling Speedo brand Wachner took charge of in 1990. By
the spring of 1994, when there were 15 Speedo stores in
operation, the Speedo swimwear line held a hefty 50 percent
share of the market for competitive swimwear, and its men's
water shorts garments held 30 percent of the department store
market, up from the 20 percent market share held in 1990.
Wachner's strategy was working. She was gaining a dominant
position in what characteristically had been a weak marketplace
through resolute expansion, and Authentic Fitness was the
instrument she used to establish jurisdiction. As the company
entered the mid-1990s, it was growing by leaps and bounds.

Between 1993 and 1995, when the frenzied rush to open 100
Speedo stores was underway, Authentic Fitness's revenues doubled as Wachner displayed the qualities that elicited her comparison to Alexander the Great. She was stealing market share
from smaller competitors in the fragmented swimwear market
by assembling a broad collection of brands that covered nearly
every segment of the market. By early 1996, there were 100
Speedo stores in operation, fulfilling the objective Wachner had
laid out in late 1993, but she did not stop there. The expansion
of Speedo stores continued after the 100th unit was opened.
Meanwhile, Wachner set herself to the task of completing her

next bold maneuver, and that was the reunion of Warnaco and Authentic Fitness into one corporation.

Failed 1996 Merger

Separated since 1990, Warnaco and Authentic Fitness had each recorded meaningful growth under the stewardship of Wachner, blossoming into vibrant enterprises that were textbook examples of the strength of astute marketing. By early 1996, Wachner wanted to reunite her two success projects under one corporate banner, declaring that the merger would put together "two powerful growth stories and provide the benefits to shareholders." In June 1996, the first step toward the merger was taken when Warnaco proposed an exchange of stock worth an estimated $500 million for Authentic Fitness. The following month, the board of directors of each company agreed to the proposal and a merger agreement was signed that designated Authentic Fitness as a future wholly-owned subsidiary of Warnaco. Before the month of July was through, however, the merger was terminated, shelved indefinitely as Authentic Fitness was forced to deal with an unexpected problem.

The merger agreement was terminated because of financial difficulties experienced by Authentic Fitness during the summer of 1996. The company's largest customer, Herman's Sporting Goods, had declared bankruptcy in May 1996 and consequently tarnished the luster Authentic Fitness exuded. As the merger grew imminent, it became clear that Authentic fitness was headed for a financial loss for the fourth fiscal quarter, and the merger was aborted as a result. Although the loss of the company's largest customer was sufficient to scrub the plans for the merger, the financial loss was only a hitch in Authentic Fitness's otherwise glowing record of growth. The company plotted its course for the late 1990s with Wachner at the helm. Authentic Fitness executives were focused on moving past the temporary setback caused by Herman's Sporting Goods' failure.

A Reunion in 1999

Indeed, the company recovered well from the 1996 blunder. By 1999, it had grown at a compounded annual growth rate of 21.7 percent over the past nine years and there were over 145 Speedo retail locations. The firm also operated and sold swimwear and accessories through the Speedo Web site. That year, company sales reached $410.8 million while net income was

$21.9 million. With Authentic Fitness performing solidly, Wachner once again set plans in motion to join with Warnaco.

Unlike Authentic Fitness, however, Warnaco's financial situation was showing signs of weakness. During the previous year, the company had posted a lost of $32.2 million. Despite the warning signals—including slowing sales at department stores—Wachner and company shareholders rallied behind the merger efforts. Finally in December 1999, Warnaco and Authentic Fitness were reunited in a $540 million deal.

Warnaco's faltering financial position continued to worsen as the company entered the new millennium. During 2000, Warnaco secured revenues of $2.2 billion but also shored up losses to the tune of $338 million. Its debt load had increased to $1.84 billion, while company filings indicated that it had just $11 million in cash reserves. Speculation rose that the firm's major business units—its Calvin Klein line, the Authentic Fitness unit, and its Warner's and Olga bra line—would be sold in order to fend off bankruptcy.

By June 2001, however, Warnaco was forced to declare Chapter 11 bankruptcy. The firm maintained that its Authentic Fitness unit would stay intact but that expansion would be curtailed and various store locations closed. Wachner's future, on the other hand, was a different story. In November, the industry veteran was relieved from her duties.

Roger Williams was named president of Authentic Fitness in December 2001. While Warnaco's original reorganization plans included the possible sale of the swimwear business, Williams and Warnaco's new CEO Tony Alvarez instead eyed the company for its potential to pull Warnaco out of bankruptcy. As such, Authentic Fitness launched an intense branding campaign. The company revamped its junior swimwear division and began forming strategic partnerships, including one with cosmetics firm Hard Candy to manufacture the Hard Candy Bikini. Authentic Fitness also began manufacturing swimsuits under a private label for Victoria's Secret.

Authentic Fitness, which had posted losses in 2001, appeared to be back on track during 2002. Warnaco continued to struggle financially, however, and had yet to emerge from Chapter 11 by mid-2002. Because of Warnaco's financial instability, the swimwear company's future was indeed up in the air. Nevertheless, as the sole licensee for the Speedo brand in North America, it held tight to its market position in competitive swimwear and would no doubt continue to do so despite its parent company's woes.

Principal Competitors

NIKE Inc.; Quiksilver Inc.; VF Corporation.

Further Reading

Barman, Sharon, "Wachner Takes on the World," *Working Woman*, February 1995, p. 11.
Belgum, Deborah, "Bathing Suit Manufacturer Back in Swim with Speedo Pact," *Los Angeles Business Journal*, July 15, 2002, p. 7.
Berman, Phyllis, "End Game for Linda Wachner," *Forbes*, May 14, 2001, p. 96.

Brown, Christie, ''The Body-Bending Business,'' *Forbes*, September 11, 1995, p. 196.

Curan, Catherine, ''Sales Seem Only Way Out for Desperate Warnaco CEO,'' *Crain's New York Business*, May 21, 2001, p. 4.

Feitelberg, Rosemary, ''Treading to Stay Afloat,'' *WWD*, December 12, 2001, p. 43S.

Fiedelholtz, Sara, ''Authentic Braves the Waters,'' *WWD*, November 3, 1993, p. 10.

Kellin, Dana, ''Speedo's First Fitness Store to Open in Los Angeles,'' WWD, December 2, 1992, p. 13.

Lee, Georgia, ''Wachner Talks Swim, Mum on Bankruptcy,'' *WWD*, July 17, 2001, p. 2.

Monget, Karyn, ''Speedo Means Speed at Retail,'' *WWD*, May 25, 1994, p. 11.

——, ''The Consensus on Wachner: She's Doing OK,'' *WWD*, December 16, 1996, p. 8.

Rutberg, Sidney, ''Warnaco, Authentic Fitness Eye Becoming One Again,'' WWD, June 7, 1996, p. 2.

Ryan, Thomas J., ''Wachner Sees New Growth for Warnaco, Authentic Fitness,'' *WWD*, April 20, 1994, p. 18.

Seckler, Valerie, ''Warnaco Sweetens Offer, Authentic's Board OK's It,'' *WWD*, July 15, 1996, p. 2.

——, ''Warnaco-Authentic: What Went Wrong with Wachner's Deal,'' *WWD*, July 31, 1996, p. 1.

Serwer, Andrew E., ''A Wachnerian Soap Opera: Linda W. Hunts for CEO, Loses Accountant: What Gives?,'' *Fortune*, May 12, 1997, p. 22.

Siegel, Jeff, ''Authentic Fitness Sets Big Retail Expansion Plans,'' *Daily News Record*, September 24, 1993, p. 3.

''Warnaco Group Agrees to Purchase Authentic,'' *WWD*, November 17, 1999, p. 18.

—Jeffrey L. Covell
—update: Christina M. Stansell

Autocam Corporation

4070 East Paris Avenue, SE
Kentwood, Michigan 49512
U.S.A.
Telephone: (616) 698-0707
Toll Free: (800) 747-6978
Fax: (616) 698-6876
Web site: http://www.autocam.com

Majority Owned Subsidiary of Titan Acquisition
  Corporation
Incorporated: 1988
Employees: 2,100
Sales: $250 million (2002 est.)
NAIC: 332116 Metal Stamping

Autocam Corporation manufactures high-precision automotive fuel injection and brake parts, as well as computer components and medical devices, at its home base near Grand Rapids, Michigan, and in several other parts of the United States and at locations in Brazil and France. The company's largest customers include General Motors Corporation (GM) unit Delphi Automotive Systems, TRW, and Bosch. Autocam has been headed by James C. Kennedy since he bought the firm from Autodie, Inc. in a leveraged buyout in 1988. Controlling interest in Autocam was acquired by Titan Acquisition Corporation in 2000, but Kennedy retains a sizable stake.

Beginnings

Autocam began its existence as a subsidiary of a Grand Rapids, Michigan-based automotive die and mold manufacturing company named Autodie, which was founded in 1963 by Joseph N. Spruit. Autodie supplied the automakers of Detroit, slightly more than two hours' drive away, as well as other companies that used dies and molds in the manufacturing process. Spruit was a believer in keeping up with technology and was one of the first in his industry to embrace computer-aided design and manufacturing in the late 1970s. The successful company formed a subsidiary called Autocam in 1982, which manufactured small, high-precision metal-alloy parts such as automotive fuel injectors using turning, grinding, and

milling processes. Autodie subsequently enjoyed a successful public offering in 1985. A slowdown in orders caused business to fall off in 1987, however, at which point Spruit decided to sell off the ailing Autocam division. A ready buyer was found in Autodie's chief financial officer John C. Kennedy, who had graduated from the University of Detroit at the age of 20 and had been hired as Autodie's CFO in 1982 at the age of 23. Kennedy borrowed heavily to finance the leveraged $6.5 million deal, which was completed in February of 1988.

Autocam's first year saw the newly independent company tally sales of $23.3 million, slightly less than a third of its former parent firm's annual figure. This amount was more than double what Autocam had taken in a year before, and profits reached $1.6 million, well up from the previous year's loss of $1.9 million.

Kennedy soon moved the firm to a new location in the Grand Rapids suburb of Kentwood and invested $20 million in computerized manufacturing equipment to facilitate production of large quantities of the firm's high-precision parts. GM was Autocam's largest customer, with some 15 different fuel injector components made for the carmaker accounting for 64 percent of sales. Fuel injectors were rapidly replacing carburetors in vehicles because they yielded greater gas mileage and reduced emissions. Precision parts produced for computer disc drive maker Hutchinson Corporation made up another 30 percent of Autocam's business.

In 1990 the company formed a joint venture called Emerald Compressor Systems with ROVAC Corporation of Rochdale, Massachusetts, to manufacture an automotive air conditioning system that was free of chlorofluorocarbons (CFCs), which were considered harmful to the earth's ozone layer. ROVAC would handle the design, and Autocam the manufacturing, with both sharing in the profits. Emerald began by targeting consumers in environmentally conscious areas with so-called ''aftermarket'' air conditioners, hoping later to make sales to the major automakers themselves.

Initial Public Offering in 1991

Seeking to pay down the company's heavy debt load, in 1991 Autocam went public. A total of 29 percent of the firm's stock was offered, with Kennedy retaining more than 60 percent, and

Company Perspectives:
Our customers answer to the global marketplace. We give them a stronger voice.

Edward W. Hekman, head of product development, holding 6 percent. A total of 800,000 shares of stock were offered at $10 each; the price rose to $13 a share by the end of the first day on the market and kept climbing over the next few months.

During this period Autocam was seeking ways to diversify so it could reduce its heavy reliance on GM for business. The company began making parts for anti-lock brakes and airbags, although these as well were sold mostly to GM at first. The emphasis on new types of components, which were much in demand because of the industry's renewed focus on making safer, more efficient vehicles, helped Autocam avoid, for the most part, the U.S. economic slowdown taking place in the early 1990s. During the summer of 1992 the company began construction on a 30,000-square-foot expansion to its Kentwood manufacturing facility, at a cost of $1 million. An additional $7.7 million was earmarked for purchasing manufacturing equipment to use in the new space.

Another diversification move took place in the fall of 1992 when Autocam purchased a Fremont, California-based maker of precision medical and electronic components, Rehrig Manufacturing, for $2.9 million. The acquisition gave the firm access to the medical market, which Autocam had been unable to penetrate on its own, through Rehrig's production of small precision metal-alloy parts used in surgery and related applications. Rehrig had annual sales of $5 million.

Autocam's growth continued in 1993, with annual sales hitting $36 million. Profits were down slightly, however, due to pricing pressure from GM, which now accounted for 76 percent of the company's revenues. Rehrig-produced medical components constituted a small but growing portion, accounting for 8 percent.

In 1994 Autocam signed an agreement with GM to supply the automaker with a specific fuel injector part for the "life of the product"—a move that decreased the firm's vulnerability to GM changing suppliers if it found a cheaper source for the item. The year was another good one, with sales increasing to $47.2 million and profits to $4.76 million.

CEO Kennedy, who also owned Conway Products Corporation, a maker of spas located next door to Autocam's headquarters, was an active participant in his local community. He oversaw the donation of Autocam money to fund a Waste Water Reduction and Management Program at Grand Valley State University and also served on the boards of several healthcare agencies, the Grand Rapids Urban League, and the state of Michigan Transportation Commission. He later took part in efforts to improve Michigan's business tax laws.

Seeking Ways to Expand at the End of the 20th Century

The company's growth continued during 1995 and 1996, with sales to the medical sector, particularly overseas, increas-

ing at a steady rate. The year 1996 saw Autocam invest $9.2 million in new production equipment to enable it to meet the increased demand for its products. The company's growth also was highlighting the need for more manufacturing capacity, and Kennedy began looking for new sites on which to build. After initially considering the southeastern United States, in particular South Carolina, the focus shifted back to Grand Rapids, where a tax-free "Renaissance Zone" had been designated to offer companies incentive to build. After buying two acres there for a new facility, Autocam backed out of the plan upon discovering that there were too few skilled machinists available in the area to staff the operation. Deciding to stay in Michigan, the company subsequently began construction of a plant in Marshall, located halfway between Grand Rapids and Detroit. Twenty-one workers who commuted to Kentwood from that area would be shifted to the new facility, with a number of recently laid-off machinists discovered in nearby Jackson helping round out the staff. The state of Michigan contributed $8.8 million in tax credits to cement the deal.

Although sales were up for 1997, profits were again reduced, a result that was attributed to late deliveries of new manufacturing equipment, some of which had proven faulty. The company subsequently had been forced to use alternate methods to fulfill orders, which raised the production cost per unit. Autocam's diligent efforts to satisfy its customers did not go unrecognized, and the firm was named a GM "Supplier of the Year" for several years running.

The year 1997 also saw Autocam purchase The Hamilton Group, Inc., a maker of anti-lock brake parts for the auto industry, which had factories in Gaffney, South Carolina and Dowagiac, Michigan. The $18 million acquisition gave the company a firm with approximately $15 million in annual revenues and 110 employees. At the end of the year another purchase was made, the company's first one outside of the United States. For $10.2 million Autocam bought a controlling interest in Qualipart Industria E Comercio Ltda., a Brazilian maker of fuel injection components with annual sales of approximately $15 million. Commenting on the purchase, CEO Kennedy stated: "This acquisition is consistent with one of our strategic objectives—becoming a dominant, world-wide manufacturer of fuel systems components."

That intention was reinforced in October of 1998 when a French company, Frank & Pignard, was acquired for $53 million plus $20 million in debt. Frank & Pignard was a manufacturer of braking, fuel injection, and steering components for the auto industry, with annual sales of $82 million. Following the purchase the company upgraded the French firm's manufacturing facility, which resulted in greater production efficiency. After the improvements, Frank & Pignard's staff was reduced by 10 percent. Autocam's income was continuing to show growth at this time from the addition of the new acquisitions' earnings, but sales were impacted negatively by a strike at GM, which caused a slowdown in orders.

In early 1999 Autocam announced that it would be closing its South Carolina plant and moving its operations to Dowagiac, Michigan. The move was expected to save $750,000 annually. The company's bank account had nearly been depleted by the Frank & Pignard acquisition, and in the fall rumors began to float that Autocam was seeking a deep-pocketed buyer who could help fund further growth. The rumors were verified in

November when it was announced that Titan Acquisition Corporation, a unit of Aurora Capital Group of Los Angeles, would pay $18.75 a share for a majority interest in the company. CEO Kennedy, who would remain on the job, kept about two-thirds of his holdings. The deal cost Titan approximately $230 million, with Kennedy pocketing $27 million of that amount. Aurora specialized in investing in well-run manufacturing companies, which were typically allowed to retain their autonomy. Commenting on the sale, Kennedy stated, "Consolidation is occurring in the industry at a very rapid rate right now. Today, Autocam is a leader. What we want to do is make sure Autocam remains a leader." In early 2001 Autocam acquired another French precision auto parts maker, Bouverat Industries.

As part of Titan Acquisitions, Autocam remained one of the top makers of precision automotive and medical components in the United States, South America, and Europe. Demand for the company's parts continued to be strong as automakers increasingly focused on safety and fuel efficiency, both of which were aided by items made by Autocam.

Principal Subsidiaries

Autocam International Sales Corporation; Autocam Foreign Sales Corporation (Barbados); Autocam International, Ltd.; Autocam Acquisition, Inc.; Autocam Laser Technologies, Inc.; Autocam-Pax, Inc.; Autocam South Carolina, Inc.; Autocam do Brasil Usinagem Ltda. (Brazil); Autocam Europe B.V. (Netherlands); Autocam France SARL (France); Frank & Pignard SA (France); Bouverat Industries (France).

Principal Competitors

Dana Corporation; Delco Remy International, Inc.; Hilite Industries, Inc.; Metaldyne Corporation; Dura Automotive Systems, Inc.

Further Reading

"Autocam Develops New Air Conditioner for Cars," *Grand Rapids Press,* May 30, 1990, p. E9.
Calabrese, Dan, "Autocam Positions for Growth," *Grand Rapids Business Journal,* December 13, 1993, p. 3.
——, "Kennedy Moving Autocam into Expansion Position," *Grand Rapids Business Journal,* April 25, 1994, p. 3.
Hampton, William J., "A Tool-and-Die Maker Goes Full Tilt into High Tech," *Business Week,* September 28, 1987, p. 102F.
Harger, Jim, "Autocam's Initial Offering Is Success as the Stock Quickly Moved Up in Price," *Grand Rapids Press,* October 30, 1991, p. F3.
——, "Stock Offering Will Test Faith in Autocam Team," *Grand Rapids Press,* October 6, 1991, p. D1.
Leith, Scott, "Big Difference for Autocam in Deal Will be Cash," *Grand Rapids Press,* November 9, 1999, p. B5.
McCarthy, Tom, "Autocam's Initial Year as Public Firm a Good One," *Grand Rapids Press,* October 30, 1992, p. C6.
Murphy, Chris, "Diversification, New Markets Pay Off for Autocam," *Grand Rapids Press,* November 4, 1993, p. B7.
Rivers, Anne, "Autodie Is Tops for Auto Makers," *Grand Rapids Business Journal,* April 21, 1986, p. 1.
Sabo, Mary Ann, "Autocam Hopes for a Rebound," *Grand Rapids Press,* October 12, 1997, p. G1.
Sullivan, Elizabeth, "Autocam Cuts Air Conditioner Deal," *Grand Rapids Business Journal,* June 4, 1990, p. B10.
Weiker, Jim, "Auto Supplier Decides Not to Build in GR," *Grand Rapids Press,* June 11, 1997, p. B5.
Well, Garrison, "Autocam Merges with Investment Group," *Grand Rapids Press,* February 5, 2000, p. D6.

—Frank Uhle

Baldwin & Lyons, Inc.

1099 North Meridian Street
Indianapolis, Indiana 46204
U.S.A.
Telephone: (317) 636-9800
Toll Free: (800) 644-5501
Fax: (317) 632-9444
Web site: http://www.baldwinandlyons.com

Public Company
Incorporated: 1930 as H.C. Baldwin Agency, Inc.
Employees: 267
Sales: $109.89 million (2001)
Stock Exchanges: NASDAQ
Ticker Symbol: BWINB
NAIC: 524126 Direct Property and Casualty Insurance
 Carriers

Baldwin & Lyons, Inc. sells and underwrites casualty insurance for the trucking industry. The company provides insurance coverage through two main subsidiaries: Protective Insurance Company and Sagamore Insurance Company. Protective Insurance, which is licensed in all 50 states and Canada, insures large and medium-sized trucking fleets. Sagamore, which is licensed in 37 states, provides personal insurance coverage to higher risk drivers and fleet coverage to smaller trucking fleets. Sagamore also sells workers' compensation insurance to small businesses. The company sells its policies through its own agency and through other independent agents.

1940s–60s: Industry Pioneers

The forerunner to Baldwin & Lyons, the H.C. Baldwin Agency, Inc., was formed in 1930 by Harry C. Baldwin, a 37-year-old insurance agent. In 1944, Harry was joined by Voris Lyons, a 40-year-old fellow insurance agent. Lyons was to be the driving force behind the company's growth and the direction in which it grew. Believing that there was great potential in the trucking market, Lyons carved a niche for the company by designing a self-insurance program for small trucking fleets.

Within a few years, it was apparent that Lyons's plan was a solid one, and Baldwin's course was set. In 1954, the company formed a wholly owned subsidiary—Protective Insurance Company—to focus solely on the trucking insurance market. The new subsidiary began insuring small trucking companies, many of which consisted of owner-operated vehicles.

More growth followed, with the company acquiring and establishing agencies located in Michigan, Illinois, and Pennsylvania. In 1962, Baldwin acquired Mitchell & Company, of San Francisco, and in 1965, Woodsmall Agency. The following year, the company was renamed Baldwin & Lyons, Inc. (B & L) reflecting the importance of Voris Lyons's role in the business.

In 1969, B & L went public, making an initial offering of 200,000 shares. Two years later, the company made a second offering of 187,500 shares. Together, the two offerings generated $9.8 million, more than doubling the net worth of the company.

1970s: Growing Pains

In 1970, H.C. Baldwin, the company's founder and chairman of the board, retired, becoming an honorary chairman. Voris Lyons, who had served previously as president, assumed the role of chairman; the office of president was filled by Merritt Smith. That same year, Protective Insurance, which had until that time insured almost exclusively single units or very small fleets of trucks, broadened its scope, writing for some of the country's largest trucking companies. Also in the early 1970s, Protective began writing policies for sports, fishing, and excursion boats on the West Coast.

The early 1970s saw aggressive price cuts in the insurance industry. Because many insurance companies had realized higher-than-normal profits in the first few years of the decade, they had an excess of underwriting capacity. They took advantage of this surplus by reducing their rates to bring in new business, as well as insuring classes of risks they had previously rejected. While many of its competitors were reducing their rates, B & L did not do so. This meant that although the price decreases hurt the company's agency side, which placed business with other insurers, they did little damage to Protective's business.

Key Dates:

1930: Harry Baldwin forms the H.C. Baldwin Agency.

1944: Voris Lyons joins Baldwin.

1954: Baldwin forms Protective Insurance Company as a subsidiary to write insurance for small trucking fleets.

1966: The H.C. Baldwin Agency is renamed Baldwin & Lyons, Inc.

1969: Baldwin & Lyons makes its first public offering of stock.

1970: Protective Insurance begins writing for larger trucking fleets.

1971: Baldwin & Lyons makes a second stock offering.

1980: The U.S. trucking industry is deregulated; B & L introduces a small fleet insurance plan.

1981: Baldwin & Lyons forms two new subsidiaries: Sagamore Insurance Company and B & L Insurance, Ltd.

1986: Baldwin & Lyons makes a third stock offering; Hoosier Insurance Company is formed as a subsidiary.

1995: Hoosier Insurance is sold; the remaining businesses are restructured; the company enters the private passenger auto insurance market.

1997: Sagamore Insurance begins offering a line of small business workers compensation insurance products.

Meanwhile, Protective was growing at an incredible rate. Between 1974 and 1977, the company's premium volume almost tripled, and its number of claims settled per year had increased by almost 40 percent. At the same time, the company's exposure increased. Whereas in 1974, Protective's maximum exposure on any single occurrence was $100,000, by 1977, it was $192,500. This increase in business, multiplied by the increase in exposure, left Protective in a somewhat vulnerable position. This situation was only exacerbated by general trends in the insurance industry. Nationwide, both the number of claims filed and the settlement cost per claim were increasing sharply. Whereas the high inflation of the period was quickly pushing up insurance companies' settlement costs, industry regulation prevented the companies from immediately passing those increases on to their policyholders by increasing their rates.

As a result of these factors, Protective suffered its first underwriting loss in 16 years in 1975. The following two years also saw losses in underwriting, although B & L's investment and agency income was high enough to maintain profitability for the company overall. Protective took rapid steps to reverse the unfavorable trend in underwriting. The company slowed down its rate of increase in new policies, thereby limiting its exposure. For existing policies, it increased the amount of risk its customers were responsible for themselves, which also served to reduce its exposure. It also implemented tighter screening processes to better eliminate high-risk drivers and, as the regulators allowed, increased its rates. Consequently, Protective returned to profitability in 1978.

The late 1970s saw the departure of the second of B & L's founders. In 1977, Voris Lyons retired from his post as chair-

man. The company's president, Merritt Smith, moved into the position of chairman, and Fred Peoples, the president of Protective Insurance became president of the parent company.

1980s: Changes in the Trucking Industry

In 1980, the United States deregulated its trucking industry. As is always the case, this opening up of the market meant increased competition and a downward pressure on prices. In addition to struggling with the chaos of a newly deregulated market, trucking companies also had to contend with a general downturn in the U.S. economy. The combination of these factors led to a sharp decrease in trucking revenues and, as the slump wore on, many transportation companies were forced out of business.

One result of deregulation and the relaxing of ICC requirements was the entrance of many smaller, independent carriers into the market. To take advantage of this growing market segment, B & L initiated a small fleet plan, which was structured similarly to private passenger auto insurance. By the end of 1980, the company had received licensure in Indiana and Illinois for its small fleet program; by the end of 1981, it was licensed in 27 other states.

In 1981, B & L formed two new subsidiaries—Sagamore Insurance Company, an Indiana company, and B & L Insurance, Ltd., which was incorporated in Bermuda. Sagamore was engaged in reinsurance and excess and surplus lines insurance on a non-admitted basis—that is, it insured risks that could not be covered in a particular state's insurance market by companies licensed in that state. B & L Insurance functioned as an offshore reinsurer, accepting business from Protective Insurance and other firms. The company also was experimenting with a new field of business. In 1980, it had begun offering an excess workers' compensation program to small businesses.

Despite its efforts to keep pace with the changing markets, B & L, like its competitors, felt the impact of the trucking industry slowdown. Because insurance rates for trucking companies were typically based on a percent of the company's revenues or payroll, the decline in customer revenues meant a decline in B & L's premium revenues. By 1982, the problematic business environment was starting to show in the company's bottom line. For that year, net income fell by almost 30 percent, on revenues that were down by 27 percent from 1981.

The year 1983 was even worse for B & L. Although revenues increased a bit, the company posted a net loss of $1.2 million. Part of the problem was the company's new small fleet insurer, Sagamore. The company had generated a large amount of new business since its inception in 1981. Due to weaknesses in Sagamore's selection and rating system, some of these new customers were paying rates that were too low to compensate for the amount of risk they presented. Another problem was that the casualty insurance industry, as a whole, was in a period of price-cutting. Although B & L refused to make radical rate cuts, it did have to reduce its prices somewhat just to stay competitive. Ultimately, it found that its premiums were not sufficient to offset underwriting losses and keep the company profitable.

B & L's fortunes soon turned around, however. The overly optimistic price cutting of the previous two years had caused many of the company's competitors to falter. By 1984 and 1985, many insurance companies realized their mistake and began increasing their rates, while others stopped writing trucking insurance altogether. Still others went out of business completely. The result of this market contraction was positive for B & L. Not only did it scoop up many refugee customers from the companies that had failed or stopped writing trucking insurance, but it also was able to comfortably raise its rates. By mid-1985, these factors had propelled the company into such aggressive growth that its existing personnel and processing infrastructure were taxed. B & L's directors took steps to slow down the pace, placing a moratorium on writing new fleet business and discontinuing its small fleet program. Even with these braking mechanisms, however, the company's revenues almost tripled from 1984 to 1985.

In 1986, the company again made a stock offering. The capital generated—almost $43 million—allowed B & L to expand once again. It removed its self-imposed moratorium on new business and began writing new policies. It also formed a new subsidiary, Hoosier Insurance Company, to write general, nontrucking policies—such as personal and smaller commercial property and casualty insurance. Hoosier Insurance began marketing its products in Indiana and also insured an existing collection of businesses in Florida. The company hoped that this expansion into nontrucking lines would produce a relatively stable stream of revenue, thereby helping to reduce the impact of downturns in the more volatile trucking market. Early results from these general lines were disappointing, however. In 1988, B & L decided to stop insuring its business clients in Florida, but continued to pursue new business in Indiana.

1990s: Exploring New Avenues

Although the insurance market as a whole softened in the early 1990s, B & L turned in a consistently stable performance, with revenues hovering around the $100 million mark and net income between $20 and $25 million. In 1995, the company sold its general insurance subsidiary, Hoosier Insurance, to General Casualty Company of Wisconsin. Although Hoosier had shown good growth, it had failed to produce the hoped-for returns. That same year, B & L restructured its remaining businesses. Under the new structure, Protective sold all fleet trucking insurance, and Sagamore served as an "incubator" for developing new lines and products. Included in this incubator environment were a new line of small fleet products and a line of nonstandard private passenger auto products, introduced in 1994 and 1995, respectively. In early 1997, Sagamore added a third new line to its developing collection: small business workers' compensation products.

Sagamore's experimental lines proved beneficial to B & L in the latter part of the 1990s. The nonstandard auto line, particularly, showed tremendous growth; by the end of 1998, it was being marketed in seven states and had posted a 75 percent increase in earned premium over the previous year. The growth in Sagamore's business helped to offset difficulties experienced by B & L's other subsidiary, Protective, which was suffering from a combination of increasing loss costs and overcapacity in the trucking insurance market.

Moving into a New Century

As B & L left the 20th century behind, it appeared that conditions in the ever-fluctuating commercial insurance industry had taken a favorable turn. After close to a decade of intense competition that kept rates unprofitably low, the market began to contract and rates began to creep up. As a result, Protective Insurance was able to emerge from its slump, posting a 22 percent increase in large fleet trucking premiums over the previous year. Unfortunately, Sagamore did not fare as well; the company posted a large underwriting loss in its nonstandard personal auto division. The subsidiary responded by increasing rates in all of its personal auto and small fleet products and implementing stricter screening terms.

In the September 11, 2001 attacks on the World Trade Center, B & L, like so many other insurers, incurred an enormous loss—approximately $20 million. As a result, the company finished the year with a net income of just $5.4 million, barely a quarter of the previous year's profit. Aside from the disaster, however, B & L was on solid ground. The trucking insurance market continued to harden, allowing Protective to charge both higher rates and attract new business. At the same time, Sagamore's rate and terms modifications in its personal auto line allowed it to return to profitability.

With industry conditions in its favor, then, B & L approached the future optimistically. In a February 2002 letter to shareholders, Gary Miller, the company's CEO, said that while the September 11 losses were a significant setback, the company's "positive expectations" were higher than ever. "Our prospects for top line and bottom line growth appear excellent," he said.

Principal Subsidiaries

Protective Insurance Company; Sagamore Insurance Company; B & L Insurance, Ltd.

Principal Competitors

Acceptance Insurance Companies Inc.; Fairfax Financial Holdings Limited; HCC Insurance Holdings, Inc.

Further Reading

Andrews, Greg, "Baldwin & Lyons Puts Growth on Hold," *Indianapolis Business Journal,* March 2, 1992, p. 1.

Fullam, Peter, "Baldwin & Lyons, Inc.," *Indianapolis Business Journal,* January 5, 1987, p. 19.

—Shawna Brynildssen

Barton Malow

Barton Malow Company

26500 American Drive
Southfield, Michigan 48034
U.S.A.
Telephone: (248) 436-5000
Fax: (248) 436-5001
Web site: http://www.bartonmalow.com

Private Company
Incorporated: 1924 as the C.O. Barton Company
Employees: 1,550
Sales: $1.25 billion (2002)
NAIC: 233310 Manufacturing and Industrial Building
   Construction; 233320 Commercial and Institutional
   Building Construction

Barton Malow Company is one of the 20 largest construction firms in the United States. The company handles general construction projects that include hospitals, educational buildings, stadiums, and corporate and industrial facilities. In addition to erecting structures, Barton Malow also offers construction management services to assist clients with their needs from pre-construction through final close-out. Headquartered in Southfield, Michigan, Barton Malow has regional offices in Maryland, Virginia, Arizona, Ohio, and Georgia. The family of president Ben Maibach III owns controlling interest in the firm.

Roots

Barton Malow's origins date to 1924 when Carl Oscar Barton founded the C.O. Barton Company in Detroit, Michigan. The Canada-born Barton, age 26, had studied engineering at the University of Michigan, and after a brief stint at the Detroit Water Board had begun working for the J.A. Utley Company, a general contractor. While at Utley, he hatched plans to start a new construction firm with a coworker, Peter Darin, and borrowed $500 to start the business. Shortly afterwards, Darin left on a honeymoon vacation, during which his new wife talked him out of the venture. When the news reached Barton, he decided to go it alone and opened the doors of the C.O. Barton Co. on August 4, 1924. Barton held 998 of the 1,000 shares of

stock, with his sister Margaret and Kins Collins, his auditor, receiving one share each.

Business was slow at first, and the firm was soon forced to relocate from an office on Washington Boulevard to the Detroit Free Press Building. The company's first work came from Michigan Bell Telephone, performing interior renovations, and from the Hudson Motor Car Company, doing alterations and repairs. Revenues for the first year totaled $521,000, with net income of $1,247. The next several years saw the firm receive other assignments from Detroit-area auto makers, including Hudson, Ford, Chrysler, and Packard, but it began to record a growing deficit.

In 1927, Carl Barton, who had been putting in long hours and enduring significant stress over the company's financial woes, suffered a nervous breakdown. After being advised to declare bankruptcy, he decided to persevere and eventually paid his debts in full. Immediate assistance came in the form of a $25,000 investment from Arnold Malow, whose father had been involved in several prominent local construction companies. Malow borrowed the money from his father-in-law, George Fink, who was the president of Michigan Steel Company. That firm, later renamed National Steel Corp., would become Barton's largest client over the next few years. After buying in, Malow was named vice-president and treasurer.

By 1929, the revived Barton Co. was doing nearly $1 million in annual sales. The Great Depression was starting to hit Americans hard, but the company was able to withstand it due to an investment that had been made in National Steel Corp., which was sold to pay debts and use for working capital. Barton Co. recorded a profit of $20,000 in 1930 and over $14,000 in 1931. In May 1932, the firm changed its name to the Barton Malow Company.

The Depression Hits Home

The year 1932 saw the bleak economy finally impact the firm as gross sales declined to $119,000 and a loss of $3,553 was recorded. A new contract to build the Great Lakes Steel Corporation's Ecorse plant helped Barton Malow through the next several years, however, and led to further work for that

Company Perspectives:

We live by the credo that we are a local broadcaster, serving the needs of people and advertisers in large and small communities. However, by our sheer size, we acknowledge that BBGI is also a national broadcaster involved with important issues, trends and developments across the country.

helped Beasley make the transition to working in radio full-time in the fall of 1969. Despite having devoted many years of his life to the education field, earning a master's and other advanced degrees, Beasley decided that for monetary reasons he should quit his chosen profession.

Major Stepping Stone: 1971 Purchase of Fayetteville Station

Beasley's goals in broadcasting were modest at this point in his career. He considered ownership of three radio stations to be a lofty, and perhaps unattainable, lifelong goal. He was also content to operate in smaller markets well outside the top 100. Very quickly, however, he acquired a pair of smaller stations and his 1971 acquisition of a Fayetteville station proved to be a major stepping stone to larger markets. FCC rules at this time required stations to be owned for at least three years, and for tax reasons most sellers preferred only 29 percent of the purchase price to be paid in cash. The rest came in the form of a ten-year note. This practice proved beneficial to Beasley as he built up his business with the limited financial backing of three minority investors. He explained the advantages to *Radio and Records* in a 2001 profile: "If you do a good job operating the station, you can create some pretty good cash flow. It doesn't take long when you have very low capital payments. That's what we were able to do; then we moved on to other markets. Each time we sold a station, we'd sell it for 29% down and take a note."

Following his move into the Fayetteville market, the company bought a station in Augusta, Georgia, then Mobile, Alabama. With success in these and other mid-sized markets, Beasley began to gain confidence that he could operate in larger cities, too. During this time his children began to become involved in running the business, which was already known as the Beasley Broadcast Group, a name it would formally adopt when taken public in 2000. Bruce G. Beasley started working for the company in 1975, and after filling a variety of posts rose to the rank of chief operating officer in 1997. Brian E. Beasley became involved in broadcasting in high school and went to work for the company full-time in 1982, initially serving as general manager of the company's short-lived venture in cable television before ultimately becoming vice-president of operations in 1997. Caroline Beasley joined the company in 1983 and like her brothers held a number of positions before joining the ranks of senior management. She became vice-president and chief financial officer in 1994. Another son, Brad Beasley, became the market manager of five radio stations in Fort Myers, Florida.

Beasley Broadcast's entry into a major market came with the 1976 purchase of a Cleveland station, WDMT-FM. The acquisition also reflected a greater commitment to FM radio. Until the early 1970s the company shied away from FM stations, which despite the strength of their signal had difficulty competing with smaller AM stations for local advertising dollars. As FM receivers became more common and the format began to reach a critical mass in listeners, Beasley Broadcast began to acquire smaller FM operations in the early 1970s. The addition of Cleveland's WDMT-FM was also the quintessential Beasley Broadcast acquisition of an underperforming property at a bargain price. Eschewing offers to buy FM stations in such markets as San Diego and Rochester, New York, as well as another Cleveland station, all priced in the $1 million range, the company paid $200,000 for WDMT-FM, an amount in keeping with some of its smaller-market AM purchases. Although licensed to serve Cleveland, the station and its broadcast tower were separated from the city by a mountain, which resulted in almost nonexistent ratings and cash flow. According to Beasley, people in Detroit had a better chance of receiving the signal than people in downtown Cleveland. He had the tower raised to reach his target audience and an urban format installed. Cash flow grew to $1 million a year, and ultimately Beasley Broadcast was able to sell the station for $4 million, realizing a tidy profit on the venture.

Continuing Growth Through Acquisition: 1980s–90s

The company continued to buy and sell radio stations in the 1980s. It also upgraded stations in order to enter into markets from out-of-town locations; such as a move-in with a Conway, South Carolina, station to enter Myrtle Beach. A station in Lumberton was able to become the number one station in Fayetteville, North Carolina. As the company expanded its operations across the country, Beasley Broadcast picked up WRXK-FM in Fort Myers, Florida, which also served the Naples market. Not only did George Beasley like the area, Florida offered tax advantages over North Carolina, prompting him to move the corporate headquarters of Beasley Broadcast to Naples in 1988. The most important acquisition of the decade also came in 1988 when Beasley Broadcast purchased the Los Angeles AM and FM stations of KRTH for $87 million, thereby cracking the top ten markets. By now Beasley Broadcast was comprised of nine AM and 11 FM stations. In order to finance the KRTH-AM/FM deal four of those stations were sold. Los Angeles at first proved to be a tough market for the company and it soon sold off the AM station for $23 million. Not only was the growth in advertising revenues slow during the first year of ownership, the FM station faced a direct challenge on its format from a CBS FM station. With KRTH-FM's ratings on the decline by 1990 the company brought in a new program director and was able to reverse the trend. With the economy in recession during this period, Beasley Broadcast faced difficulties on another front. Many banks decided to reduce the number of broadcast loans in their portfolios, which brought tremendous pressure on radio operators. As a result, the value of radio stations collapsed and many owners, forced to sell, were left with little from their original investments. One of the fortunate ones, Beasley was able to work with his bankers to ride out this period, which he called "probably the toughest time I recall in broadcasting."

In 1993 Beasley Broadcast sold its Los Angeles station for $117 million, a record at the time for the purchase of a stand-alone FM station. With the proceeds the company paid $26 million for WDAS-FM Philadelphia, an urban-formatted station

---

Key Dates:

1961: High school principal George Beasley launches WPYB-AM in Benson, North Carolina.

1969: Beasley quits the education field for a full-time career in radio.

1976: The company enters its first major market with the purchase of Cleveland station.

1988: Beasley cracks top ten markets with the purchase of a Los Angeles AM & FM station.

1996: The Telecommunications Act permits ownership of several stations, clusters, in a single market.

2000: Beasley goes public.

---

that it hoped would complement a country music station it already owned, WXTU-FM. Although the two stations never developed the kind of synergy that it envisioned, the company was still able to sell WDAS-FM three years later for $103 million. The high price was due in large part to the 1996 Telecommunications Act, which allowed ownership of a greater number of stations across the country and several in a single market. With ownership rules loosened, the stage was set for radio station operators like Beasley Broadcast to acquire several radio stations in a single market, so-called clusters, which offered a number of advantages. Broadcast companies could run a number of radio stations more economically than one, and they could also better compete with other media for advertising dollars. With their stations offering a variety of formats, owners of clusters were able to deliver the demographics advertisers desired. Conversely, the new rules also resulted in the decline of local ownership and the kind of family-run stations that produced the likes of George Beasley.

Going Public in 2000

Beasley Broadcast Group pursued the cluster strategy during the rest of the 1990s, with multiple stations in such top 50 markets as Philadelphia and Miami. By the end of 1999 Beasley owned 32 radio stations in seven eastern markets, comprising the 16th largest radio broadcasting company in the United States in terms of revenue, according to BIA Financial Network. To sustain the company's growth, which was becoming a virtual necessity in the rapidly consolidating radio industry, Beasley Broadcast went public in 2000, netting the company approximately $97.7 million. Proceeds were used to reduce borrowings under the company's credit facility and to repay other indebtedness. Three AM operations were acquired in the Miami and West Palm Beach markets, and by February 2001 the company closed on the purchase of Centennial Broadcasting, a $113.5 million transaction that added clusters in Las Vegas and New Orleans. Moreover, by going

public BBGI was able to reward key managers by granting stock options in the company.

Throughout its history BBGI was generally quick to adopt to changing landscapes and new technologies. George Beasley took advantage of the availability of low-powered radio stations to enter the business. Although cautious about committing the company to the FM format too soon, he eventually took advantage of FM opportunities as well. In the 1970s Beasley Broadcast stations began using syndicated network programming, delivered by several evolving technologies. Records and tapes that originally provided such programs as Casey Kasem's "American Top 40" and commentaries by Paul Harvey gave way to CD and satellite transmissions. Beasley Broadcast stations also pursued systems that allowed on-air personalities to pre-record programming. Starting in the late 1980s the computerized Scott System was adopted, allowing announcers to record an entire show in a fraction of its running time. With the rise of the Internet in the 1990s, a large number of Beasley Broadcast stations began to stream their signals over the Internet, although copyright and royalty issues eventually forced non-talk streams to be switched off. As a public company, BBGI began to plan for the future of radio and the eventuality of digital AM radio, which would allow AM stations to offer the same quality as FM. In anticipation of this change, BBGI began acquiring AM stations in large markets such as Atlanta and Boston.

Beasley topped the $100 million revenue mark in 2000. Facing a recessionary economy soon thereafter, the radio broadcasting industry and BBGI adjusted accordingly. Cost reduction efforts were initiated and in March 2002 two FM radio stations in the New Orleans market were divested with proceeds used to reduce debt. When asked what he saw on the horizon for BBGI, Beasley told *Radio Ink* magazine in a May 2002 interview, "We're going to do what we think is in the best interests of all the shareholders."

Principal Competitors

Cox Radio Inc.; Clear Channel Communications Inc.; Cumulus Media Inc.; Infinity Broadcasting Corporation.

Further Reading

Bunzel, Reed, "40 Years and One to Grow On!," *Radio Ink,* May 13, 2002.

Farber, Erica, "George Beasley," *Radio & Records, Inc.,* December 7, 2001, p. 104.

Rathbun, Elizabeth A., "Success Is the Family Way," *Broadcasting & Cable,* October 16, 2000, p. 68.

Workman, Jennifer, "Like the Dew Covers Dixie," *Southwest Florida Business,* September 2000, p. 30.

—Ed Dinger

Beech-Nut Nutrition Corporation

100 South Fourth Street
Suite 1010
St. Louis, Missouri 63102
U.S.A.
Telephone: (314) 436-7667
Toll Free: (800) 233-2468
Fax: (314) 436-7679
Web site: http://www.beech-nut.com

Wholly Owned Subsidiary of Milnot Company
Incorporated: 1890 as Imperial Packing Co.
Employees: 350
Sales: $139 million (2001)
NAIC: 311422 Specialty Canning; 311421 Fruit and
Vegetable Canning

Beech-Nut Nutrition Corporation, a subsidiary of the Milnot Company, is the third largest baby food manufacturer in the United States, behind Gerber and Heinz. In the past, this century-old company produced foodstuffs ranging from bacon to chewing gum, but it has been exclusively engaged in the baby food business since 1972. Having overcome a highly publicized adulterated apple juice scandal and numerous changes of ownership, Beech-Nut has remained a major force in the baby food industry by introducing innovative products, including Beech-Nut First Advantage, a line of baby food that contains DHA and ARA. Docosahexaenoic acid and arachidonic acid, or DHA and ARA, are fatty acids found naturally in breast milk and are considered to be an important building block in central nervous system development. In 2001, Milnot and H.J. Heinz Co. abandoned merger plans after antitrust delays.

Company Origins in the 1890s

Beech-Nut was founded in 1890 by five residents of Canajoharie, New York: Raymond and Walter Lipe, John and David Zieley, and Bartlett Arkell. Company lore has it that the home-smoked hams of Raymond and Walter's father, Ephraim, were renowned in the small Mohawk Valley farming community for their unique nutty flavor. Ephraim, a wealthy miller, had no thought of marketing his curing process, but his two sons, and their friends the Zieley brothers, were looking to set up a business, and they managed to convince their father to lend them both the recipe and the $10,000 capital needed to get started. The elder Lipe, unsure of the business acumen of his sons, made one stipulation. The boys must bring in Bartlett Arkell, the 28-year-old son of a successful local businessman and already a budding entrepreneur himself with a partnership in a rug importing firm. Arkell agreed to join the new venture as president and suggested they call the company the Imperial Packing Co. after the Imperial Hotel where he had stayed on a visit to New York City.

Operating out of a rented room in a local store, the Imperial Packing Co. got off to a less than imperial start. By 1899, the Zieleys and Raymond Lipe had bailed out of the foundering firm, which owed the local bank some $60,000. Bartlett Arkell came to the company's rescue by selling his share of the rug business. In exchange for paying off the debt, Arkell took $60,000 worth of stock in the company that was reorganized with a capitalization of $150,000. On the advice of a friend, who said that ''Imperial'' was an undemocratic name for an American ham, Arkell renamed the firm Beech-Nut, evoking the beech trees that grew around Canajoharie as well as the smoky, nutty flavor of the company's hams.

Beech-Nut's first success came, not from the hams that inspired its founding, but from the unlikely development of vacuum-packed jars of sliced bacon. One of Arkell's first moves upon taking full control of the company was to hire engineers to perfect a vacuum seal for glass jars in which to pack the company's meat products. Against the advice of his friend and mentor, ham baron Philip Armour, who thought the fat content in sliced meats should be hidden inside cans, Arkell introduced transparent jars of bacon, sliced to ''micrometer thinness to insure a crisp fry.'' Whether it was the thin slices or the novelty of bacon in jars, Beech-Nut's bacon was an immediate success, and by 1905 the company was grossing $1 million a year.

New Products in the 1920s and 1930s

The popularity of Beech-Nut's jarred bacon was short-lived as the invention of cellophane wrap, refrigeration, and inexpensive mechanical slicers took their toll. Nevertheless, by the

---

1920s the company had enough other food products on grocers' shelves to more than fill the void. Throughout the first two decades of the century, Beech-Nut manufactured a dizzying array of foodstuffs, including sliced meats, peanut butter, baked beans, jam, tomato sauce, coffee, mustard, ginger ale, spaghetti, biscuits, candy, gum, and canned fish bait. Many of these offerings, such as the ginger ale, spaghetti, and fish bait, had a limited appeal and were quickly dropped, but the peanut butter, tomato products, coffee, and candy had more enduring success.

It was Beech-Nut chewing gum, however, that would prove the company's second major product breakthrough. The idea of manufacturing gum came in 1910 from Arkell's brother-in-law, Frank Barbour, whose own brother had been involved with the founding of the American Chicle Co., the originator of Chiclets. Competition was limited in the gum business, in large part because of the difficulties involved in obtaining chicle, the rubbery sap of the sapota tree that grew only in the rain forests of Central America and was the key ingredient in chewing gum. Barbour made annual trips to Guatemala and Yucatan to ensure Beech-Nut's supply of the chewy sap, which was soon the life-blood of Beech-Nut's business. During the Great Depression, when Beech-Nut's higher priced products were passed over in the grocery stores, Beech-Nut chewing gum kept the company afloat, providing $11 million of the company's $18 million in sales in 1935.

The Baby Boom and Baby Food in the 1950s

Like most U.S. companies, Beech-Nut entered into war production during the early 1940s, earning the dubious distinction of becoming the country's largest producer of ''K'' rations. Rationing and controlled prices during World War II caused the company to drop production of a number of items, including candy, bacon, and tomato products. With the return to peace, Beech-Nut's line of products was limited to gum, peanut butter, coffee, and baby food. It was the last that would become the prime money maker for the company through the next half century.

Strained foods for babies were introduced in 1931 by Clark Arkell, who had succeeded his father Bartlett to the presidency of the company. According to his own account, Clark Arkell decided to enter the baby food market after a grocer, questioned about the sales of Beech-Nut products, held up a can of Gerber baby food and said, ''We sell more of this stuff than all your line put together.'' Beech-Nut differentiated its baby food by packing the strained fruits, vegetables, and meat exclusively in glass jars rather than the cans used by most manufacturers. The company's jarred baby food did well from the start, but it was in the late 1940s with the advent of the postwar baby boom that

sales took off, doubling between 1948 and 1950. By 1950, the 48 different types of jarred baby foods—produced in Beech-Nut plants in Canajoharie; Rochester, New York; and San Jose, California—provided more than a quarter of the company's $70 million sales volume.

In the Boat with Life Savers in the 1960s

In 1956, Beech-Nut reentered the hard candy market through a merger with Life Savers Corp. The merged company, called Beech-Nut Life Savers, sold coffee, tea, gum, baby food, and Life Savers candy. The famous multicolored candies with the hole in the middle had been perennial market leaders since their introduction at the beginning of the century. Although Life Savers Corp. was only one quarter the size of Beech-Nut when the companies merged, the candy's 25 percent profit margins offered an attractive addition to the Beech-Nut mix. By 1960, Beech-Nut Life Savers sales had climbed to almost $120 million. Providing about one-third of these sales was Beech-Nut baby food, which had become the second best-selling brand in the nation, behind industry founder and perennial leader, Gerber.

In 1962 the death of Clark Arkell marked the end of an era for Beech-Nut, which had been controlled by the Arkell family since its founding. Under the new directorship of chairman Alger Chapman, a former tax lawyer and Republican politician, Beech-Nut Life Savers began to look for growth through acquisitions outside the food processing industry. In 1964, the company acquired two cosmetics companies, Lander Company and Carlova, Inc., followed, in 1966, by a food service company, Dobbs House.

Merger with Squibb in the Late 1960s

In 1968, Beech-Nut Life Savers took a new direction when the company merged with pharmaceutical giant ER Squibb & Sons. The new company, called Squibb Beech-Nut, manufactured a huge array of products, including prescription drugs, cosmetics, tooth brushes, vitamins, Martinson brand coffee, Tetley brand tea, Life Savers candy, and Beech-Nut gum and baby food. Initially, Beech-Nut baby food provided the bulk of Squibb Beech-Nut's consumer products division, which in total delivered about one-quarter of the company's $578 million in sales in 1968. The baby boom of the 1950s and early 1960s had dropped off precipitously by the late 1960s, however, and a falling birth rate was disastrous for an industry that could hold its consumers for only a brief two years. Sales of Beech-Nut baby foods stagnated and, with their attention and capital absorbed by many more promising products, Squibb Beech-Nut management was unwilling to invest in the kind of marketing required to steal market share away from other baby food manufacturers. By 1970, management had become so disenchanted with the brand that it had halted distribution in the central United States and the company's archrival, H.J. Heinz & Co., slipped into second place behind Gerber in the baby food market, leaving Beech-Nut a distant third.

Control by Nicholas and Nestlé in the 1970s and 1980s

In 1973, Squibb sold the underperforming Beech-Nut baby food line for $16 million to a three-man partnership led by entrepreneur Frank Nicholas. With Beech-Nut gum left behind

Key Dates:

1890: The Imperial Packing Co.—the predecessor to Beech-Nut—is founded by five residents of Canajoharie, New York.

1899: The company incorporates as Beech-Nut Packing Company.

1905: The company grosses $1 million per year upon the success of its jarred bacon.

1910: Beech-Nut enters the gum business.

1931: Strained baby foods are launched.

1956: The company merges with Life Savers Corp.

1968: The firm merges with pharmaceutical giant ER Squibb & Sons.

1973: Squibb sells the Beech-Nut baby food line to a three-man partnership.

1979: Beech-Nut is sold to Nestlé S.A.

1982: The firm recalls its apple juice.

1986: The company and two of its executives are indicted on 470 counts of violating the Federal Food, Drug, and Cosmetic Act for selling adulterated apple products.

1989: Ralston Purina Co. purchases Beech-Nut.

1994: Ralston spins off its human food businesses as Ralcorp Holdings Inc.

1998: The Milnot Company acquires Beech-Nut.

2001: H.J. Heinz Co. and Milnot abandon merger plans.

at Squibb, the 75-year-old firm was reduced for the first time to a single product manufacturer. Nicholas had planned to cross-market Beech-Nut strained foods with the infant formula of a company he had purchased the previous year, but when that company withdrew from the U.S. market he was left with an unprofitable company controlling a shrinking share of a stagnant market. Beech-Nut sales dropped from $70 million in 1973 to $54 million the following year and, for the first time since its founding, the company finished the year with a net loss. Nicholas scrambled to keep the company in business. During the early 1970s, nutritionists had begun to complain loudly about the amount of salt, sugar, and modified starch baby food manufacturers were putting into their products. Nicholas saw a potential opening for Beech-Nut products to gain market share if they could capitalize on these concerns. In the mid-1970s Beech-Nut announced that it was purging salt from all of its products and eliminating sugar from all but those clearly intended as desserts. Nicholas began touring the country promoting the "all natural" Beech-Nut baby food on radio and television talk shows by quoting nutritionists and playing up his own role as a father of three young children. Ironically, given the scandal that followed, it was during this nutrition-oriented promotion that Beech-Nut also introduced apple juice in single-serving glass jars. A parent could avoid filling a separate bottle by screwing a nipple directly onto the jar. Beech-Nut's apple juice sales quadrupled as the result of the new packaging and Nicholas's "Mr. Natural" promotional campaign saw total sales climbing back up to $65 million. In spite of sales increases, a lack of capital prevented Nicholas from extending his marketing and advertising program and the company could not recoup its losses. In 1979, Nicholas sold the struggling company to Swiss food giant

Nestlé S.A. for $35 million, more than twice what he had paid Squibb for the company in 1973.

With $15 billion in sales and the leading position in the worldwide baby food market, Nestlé could afford to invest the kind of marketing and advertising budget that was needed to turn Beech-Nut around. Nestlé appointed Niels Hoyvald to serve as president of its new subsidiary, now renamed Beech-Nut Nutrition Corp. Hoyvald, a native of Denmark who had relocated to the United States in the early 1960s, already had a reputation for his ability to turn around troubled food companies. Under Hoyvald, Beech-Nut undertook an intensive push into new geographic markets and invested a hefty $60 million in advertising and promotion. In 1984, the company launched a new line of baby foods called "Stages," which used color-coded packaging to identify the age at which babies could start eating each type of food. The introduction of Stages, backed with a $22 million advertising campaign, appeared to be a huge success. By 1986, Beech-Nut had regained its second place position with a 20 percent market share, and analysts estimated that sales had risen to about $125 million.

Scandal in the Mid-1980s

Although appearances suggested that Beech-Nut had turned the corner on its lean years, the company in fact was deeply embroiled in one of the worst scandals in American business history. Back in 1977, when Frank Nicholas had been touring the country promoting the nutritional quality of the Beech-Nut brands and apple juice sales had quadrupled, the company signed a contract with a new apple concentrate supplier called Universal Juice Co., which sold its product at up to 25 percent below the market. Initial tests of the concentrate by Beech-Nut research scientists raised the possibility that it might be adulterated with corn syrup, but company executives, including head of operations John F. Lavery, chose to turn a blind eye to the possibility of a problem with the product's quality. With up to 30 percent of Beech-Nut's sales accounted for by products containing the concentrate, the already struggling company was saving millions of dollars by using Universal and a switch to another supplier could well have tipped the scales toward insolvency.

When Nicholas sold the company to Nestlé, Beech-Nut's director of research and development, Jerome LiCari, went once more to senior management to warn of problems with the concentrate, which further testing had again shown to be suspect. Lacking a definitive test for the purity of apple juice, however, LiCari could not prove absolutely that the juice was tainted, and without this proof Lavery and company president Hoyvald refused to take action.

In April 1982, that proof came in the form of a private investigator, Andrew Rosenzweig, who had been hired by the Apple Processors Trade Association to investigate claims of adulterated concentrate. Rosenzweig had staked out the processing plant where Universal claimed to produce their concentrate and found that the company was not just adding sweeteners to their mix, they were failing to add the apples altogether. Documents found in the plant's dumpsters revealed that the so-called apple juice was in fact nothing but water, sugars, flavoring, and coloring. According to the New York Times, Rosenzweig tracked a trailer truck full of the bogus concentrate from the Universal plant to Beech-Nut's facilities in Canajoharie and confronted Beech-Nut management with his findings.

It was at this point that Beech-Nut committed ''a grave tactical error,'' as an attorney close to the case was later to tell *Business Week*. Instead of immediately recalling all of the products made from the synthetic concentrate, a recall that would have involved some 700,000 cases of inventory and might possibly have bankrupted the company, Beech-Nut began shipping the tainted juice out of the country clandestinely. Meanwhile, Beech-Nut lawyers stalled U.S. Food and Drug Administration investigators, who were asking for samples of the suspect product. It was October before fed-up FDA officials threatened a seizure unless the company issued a voluntary recall. Beech-Nut finally issued the recall in November 1982, but by that time all but 20,000 cases of the juice had been distributed overseas.

FDA investigators initiated an investigation into Beech-Nut's role in the sale of the phony juice and of the cover-up. In November 1986, a federal grand jury found that there was sufficient evidence to indict both Beech-Nut as a corporate entity as well as its two top executives, John Lavery and Neils Hoyvald, on 470 counts of violating the Federal Food, Drug, and Cosmetic Act for selling adulterated apple products. Beech-Nut pleaded guilty to 215 counts of the indictment and was fined a record $2 million. Lavery and Hoyvald both pleaded not guilty but were convicted for their involvement in what the judge in the case would call ''the largest consumer fraud case ever.'' Both men were sentenced initially to a year and a day in prison and fined $100,000, but these convictions would later be overturned on a technicality and the sentences reduced in a retrial to probation and community service.

Ironically, the recall of the phony apple juice in 1982 never created the bad press for Beech-Nut that Hoyvald had so feared. Apple juice sales continued to grow during the four years of the FDA investigation. It was only after the indictments of the company in 1986, long after all bogus juice had been removed from grocery store shelves, that the scandal began to impact sales. The intense publicity that surrounded the trial and sentencing, however, was disastrous for the company. Market share dropped from more than 20 percent in early 1986 to 16 percent in 1987. Most of this drop was the result of plummeting apple juice sales, which fell about 20 percent within a few months of the indictment. Although Nestlé did not release sales figures for its subsidiaries, company sources told *Business Week* that Beech-Nut racked up near-record losses in 1987.

Beech-Nut quickly undertook a new promotional campaign that stressed the quality of the Stages line of baby food and was designed to appeal to the increasing number of older first-time mothers. All baby food manufacturers had long since followed Beech-Nut's lead in removing salt and artificial flavors from their products. Now Beech-Nut became the first major firm to purge their food of the modified starch that had long been responsible for the creamy consistency of most baby food. The company spent millions trying to recapture consumer confidence, urging mothers to read the labels of their products and compare them with their competitors. By 1989, Beech-Nut had succeeded in regaining some of its lost market share, but the cost of the campaign virtually wiped out profit margins, according to industry analysts.

Renewal with Ralston Purina in the 1990s

In September 1989, Ralston Purina Co. purchased Beech-Nut from Nestlé for an estimated $85 million, about half of the baby food's $150 million annual sales. Ralston Purina, better known as a pet food manufacturer, had a small but growing line of human food products, including Chex and Cookie Crisp cereals, and felt it was getting a bargain with the tarnished but still viable Beech-Nut. Ralston Purina continued to promote the Beech-Nut brand for its purity and in 1991 became the first major manufacturer to launch an organic line of products. Called Special Harvest, the new line was made entirely of food grown without synthetic fertilizers or pesticides. The concept of pesticide-free baby food was originally promoted by a small specialty firm called Earth's Best, which had quickly captured three percent of the baby food market. Beech-Nut was faced with a major problem in promoting its new line, however. Unlike Earth's Best, Beech-Nut could not play up the potential dangers of chemical residues without risking damage to its primary product line. Consumer interest in organic products failed to grow as expected and after a couple of years the Special Harvest line was dropped.

In 1994, Ralston Purina spun off its human food businesses as Ralcorp Holdings, Inc. Ralcorp continued to advertise the nutritious quality of Beech-Nut baby food, which received a boost in 1995 when an independent report conducted by the Center for Science in the Public Interest found Beech-Nut foods to be ''nutritionally superior to Gerber and Heinz, using more whole foods, fewer fillers, and less added salt and sugar.'' During the mid-1990s, Ralcorp also undertook an aggressive campaign to widen distribution, including a price-cutting strategy that had some analysts speculating about the possibility of the century-old firm once more changing hands.

A Milnot Company in the Late 1990s and Beyond

That speculation rang true in 1998 when the Milnot Company purchased the baby food concern for $68 million. Privately held by Madison Dearborn Partners Inc., Milnot more than doubled its revenue with the purchase, which added the Beech-Nut brand to its arsenal of private-label food products. Milnot then looked to secure a stronger position in the U.S. baby food market. In 2000, it announced that it would team up with competitor H.J. Heinz Co. Upon completion of the deal, the Beech-Nut and Heinz baby food lines would be linked and would give the combined company up to a 30 percent market share. At the time, Gerber controlled the U.S. baby food market with a 70 percent share.

The proposed $185 million merger was met with opposition from the Federal Trade Commission. Antitrust regulators set plans in motion to block the deal, claiming it would create a duopoly, which in turn, could lead to future price fixing by the two firms. Beech-Nut and Heinz on the other hand, argued that Gerber was currently operating in a monopolistic state, and with the competition so far behind in terms of market share, the company was not forced to develop new products. Milnot's president Scott Meader claimed in a 2000 *CNN Money* article that ''the combination of Heinz and Beech-Nut is in the best interest of American consumers because it is pro-competitive and will result in more innovation to reinvigorate the baby food industry.'' In April 2001—after a U.S. Court of Appeals put a temporary block on completion of the deal—Heinz and Milnot abandoned their plans to merge.

The failed attempt to link up with Heinz did little to curtail Beech-Nut's new product development. In 2002, the company was the first to launch a product that contained both DHA and ARA, nutrients found in breast milk that aid in the development of the central nervous system, specifically vision and mental development. The product line, Beech-Nut First Advantage, hit store shelves in 2002 in 13 different varieties. The company also began a new marketing program entitled the Beech-Nut Baby Club, which gave customers incentives for shopping at certain retail locations.

Having successfully emerged from scandal, changes in ownership, and a failed merger attempt, Beech-Nut stood in third place in the U.S. baby food market in the early years of the new century. With over 150 different baby foods to its name, Beech-Nut remained dedicated to infant nutrition and new product development. Whether or not Beech-Nut would remain a Milnot company in the years to come however, remained to be seen.

Principal Competitors

The Hain Celestial Group Inc.; H.J. Heinz Co.; Novartis AG.

Further Reading

''Beech-Nut Is Acquired by Milnot,'' *Supermarket News*, August 10, 1998, p. 51.

''Beech-Nut Life Savers Recipe,'' *Investor's Reader*, March 1, 1961, pp. 1–3.

Bernstein, Peter W., ''Who Buys Corporate Losers,'' *Fortune*, January 26, 1981, pp. 60–6.

Chamberlain, John, ''Beech-Nut,'' *Fortune*, November 1936, pp. 85–93.

Dagnoli, Judann, ''Beech-Nut Ready to Fight Back,'' *Advertising Age*, November 14, 1988, p. 6.

Fannin, Rebecca, ''High Stakes at the High Chair,'' *Marketing and Media Decisions*, October 1986, pp. 62–69.

Fierman, Jaclyn, ''Beech-Nut Bounces Up in the Baby Market,'' *Fortune*, December 24, 1984, p. 56.

''FTC Nixes Baby Food Deal,'' *CNN Money*, July 7, 2000. Available from http://money.cnn.com/2000/07/07/deals/heinz.

''Heinz to Buy Beech-Nut Baby Foods,'' *The Food Institute Report*, March 6, 2000.

Hughes, Lawrence M., ''Beech-Nut Keeps the Kettle Boiling,'' *Sales Management*, July 15, 1950, pp. 37–39, 104–111.

Johnson, Robert, ''Ralston to Buy Beech-Nut, Gambling It Can Overcome Apple Juice Scandal,'' *Wall Street Journal*, September 18, 1989, p. 3A.

Kindel, Stephen, ''Bad Apple for Baby,'' *Financial World*, June 27, 1989, p. 48.

Murray, Barbara, ''Milnot, Heinz Abandon Baby Food Merger Bid,'' *Supermarket News*, May 7, 2001, p. 119.

Pawlosky, Mark, ''Health Food for Babies Is Slow to Grow,'' *Wall Street Journal*, June 14, 1995, p. 1B.

Spethmann, Betsy, ''Baby Foods Digest a New Idea: Growing Up,'' *Brandweek*, May 2, 1994, pp. 38–39.

''The Sound Beech-Nut Life Savers Recipe,'' *Investor's Reader*, September 23, 1964, pp. 17–19.

''Squibb Beech-Nut—Strong Combination,'' *Financial World*, September 2, 1970, p. 7.

Traub, James, ''Into the Mouths,'' *New York Times Magazine*, July 24, 1988, pp. 18–20, 37–38, 52–53.

Urbanski, Al, ''Beech-Nut Reborn,'' *Sales & Marketing Management*, December 6, 1982, pp. 26–29.

Welles, Chris, ''What Led Beech-Nut Down the Road to Disgrace,'' *Business Week*, February 22, 1988, pp. 124–28.

—Hilary Gopnik
—update: Christina M. Stansell

Bonduelle SA

rue Nicolas Appert, BP 173
Villeneuve d'Ascq Cedex
F-59653
France
Telephone: (+33) 3 20 43 60 60
Fax: (+33) 3 20 43 60 00
Web site: http://www.bonduelle.com

Public Company
Incorporated: 1853
Employees: 4508
Sales: EUR 1.25 billion ($1.10 billion)(2002)
Stock Exchanges: Euronext Paris
Ticker Symbol: BON
NAIC: 311421 Fruit and Vegetable Canning; 311411
    Frozen Fruit, Juice, and Vegetable Processing

Based near Lille, France, Bonduelle SA is Europe's leading producer of prepared vegetables. The company operates in three primary markets: Canned Vegetables, Frozen Vegetables, and Fresh Vegetables. Canned Vegetables is Bonduelle's historic activity and accounts for 57 percent of its revenues; the company is European leader in this category, with 30 percent of the market. The company markets its canned vegetables under the brands Bonduelle, Cassegrain, and, in Belgium, Marie Thumas. Frozen Vegetables represents 29 percent of the company sales, giving it the position as number two European producer in this market. The company's frozen vegetable offering includes "classic" vegetables as well as prepared, ready-to-heat meals. Fresh Vegetables—such as salads and prepared, ready-to-eat vegetables—accounts for 17 percent of the company's sales and is also Bonduelle's fastest-growing market. Despite entering this market only in the late 1990s, Bonduelle has quickly captured the European lead, notably through an aggressive acquisition program. Nearly half of the company's sales, which topped EUR 1.25 billion at the end of its 2002 year (in July 2002), came from outside of France. While Europe represents the company's primary market, Bonduelle has been present in North and South America since the late 1990s. Bonduelle is listed on the Euronext Paris Stock Exchange's secondary market but remains majority owned by the founding Bonduelle family.

Canning Success Begins in the 1920s

Bonduelle began as an offshoot of the Bonduelle family grain and food oil farm in France's Nord Region. In 1853, two members of the Bonduelle family, Louis Bonduelle and Louis Lesaffre joined together to open a grain alcohol distillery in Marquette-sur-Lille. That business prospered, and the family added a second distillery nearby, in Renescure. By the end of the century, the family's business included seven distilleries. At that time, the family decided to divide up the assets among its three main branches.

The Bonduelle branch continued to run a family farm. In the 1920s, the family spotted a new opportunity in the development of new canning equipment. The Bonduelles purchased sterilizing and other equipment and planted their first crop for canning: peas in 1926. The original crop was based on a 20-hectare plot, yielding some 120 tons of canned peas.

Demand for canned vegetables soared in the 1930s, and in 1936 the Bonduelle company increased planting to 230 hectares. Bonduelle expanded its canning facilities as well. Yet the company restricted itself to producing and canning, turning over marketing and distribution to another company.

The German invasion of France in 1940 put an end to the company's activity. Production did not begin again until the end of the war. Soon after, instead of turning to its former distributor, Bonduelle decided to place its own name on its products, launching the Bonduelle brand in 1947. Bonduelle quickly became a widely recognized brand name for canned peas. The growth of the Bonduelle brand soon outpaced the company's own farm production, and Bonduelle began putting into place a network of farmer suppliers in the Nord region.

The mid-1950s saw the company's breakthrough. In 1957, Bonduelle introduced a new product, canned peas and carrots, which established the Bonduelle brand as one of the leading names in the French canned vegetables market. Bonduelle continued to build on its success, putting into place quality standards that contributed to boosting the brand's reputation.

Bonduelle continued to expand during the 1960s, adding a new production facility in Estrées-en-Chaussée, in the Picardie region, in 1963. The company then moved into other prime agricultural areas in France. At the end of that decade, Bonduelle expanded its operations, adding an entirely new component—that of frozen vegetables. The new product line proved a success on the French market, confirming Bonduelle's reputation as a vegetable specialist.

International Expansion in the Late 1960s

Bonduelle also expanded beyond France, opening its first foreign subsidiary in Germany in 1969. That was followed in 1972 by the opening of a subsidiary in Italy, then in the United Kingdom in 1973. The export market quickly became a crucial one for Bonduelle. By the mid-1970s, half of the company's sales came from outside of France.

Bonduelle's expansion had brought it into new contact with a number of new crops, including corn and mushrooms, both added at the end of the 1970s. While mushrooms remained a more limited category for the company, the growth in sales of canned corn sales led the company to establish a dedicated facility for that product in Labenne, in the French southwest, in 1978.

Bonduelle's international expansion continued into the next decade. In 1980, the company turned to Belgium, acquiring Marie Thumas, a major supplier of canned vegetables in that country. A move into the Netherlands followed in 1982. The company next turned to Spain, acquiring Malagro as the basis of a new subsidiary for that country in 1986.

By then, Bonduelle's leadership had been taken over by Bruno Bonduelle. The new generation of the Bonduelle family proved highly ambitious, launching the company toward a new goal: that of becoming the European leader by the early 1990s. For this, Bonduelle stepped up its acquisition drive, acquiring a new corn canning facility in southwest France and launching a new subsidiary and factory, Primeurop, in 1987. The following

year, the company purchased Talpe, based in Belgium, adding that company's factory in Kortemark. Bonduelle also moved into Portugal, building a new production plant there.

By the end of the 1980s, Bonduelle had already captured the lead in several individual European markets, including Germany, the Netherlands, and Belgium. It had also gained the position of Europe's leading canned and frozen vegetable producer. In 1989, the company cemented that lead through the acquisition of Cassegrain, a producer of high-end canned vegetable products. That acquisition gave Bonduelle the lead position in the French market as well. Meanwhile, Bonduelle had stepped up its marketing campaign, launching the successful slogan, ''Quand c'est bon, c'est Bonduelle'' (''When it's good, it's Bonduelle'').

Global Expansion Effort for the New Century

By the beginning of the 1990s, Bonduelle's sales had topped FFr 4.3 billion (approximately EUR 655 million). Bonduelle had also expanded into a number of new markets, including Denmark in 1989. The company was quick to seize on the opportunity presented by the end of the Cold War, entering East Germany in 1990, then launching new subsidiaries in the Czech Republic, Poland, and Hungary in 1991 and 1992. These were followed by entries in Russia and Slovenia in 1994.

Bonduelle, by then led by Christophe Bonduelle and Daniel Bracquart—the first non-family member to head the company—also turned to South America, launching a joint-venture with Iansa in Chile in 1992, then opening a subsidiary in Brazil in 1994. In 1996, the company added another Latin American subsidiary, in Argentina.

By the mid-1990s, Bonduelle's sales neared FFr 5 billion. Yet the company's core product markets, canned and frozen vegetables, had matured, and the company's growth slowed. In response, Bonduelle sought entry into a new and promising market: that of prepared fresh vegetables. Bonduelle found its entry point in 1997 with the acquisition of French fresh vegetables specialist Salade Minute. The purchase, which gave Bonduelle four new factories and business of more than FFr 400 million, enabled the company to launch a new brand, Bonduelle en Frais. Targeting at first the restaurant sector, the new brand was rolled out to the consumer market in 1998.

The move into the fresh vegetables sector completed Bonduelle's prepared vegetables offering. The company, which, in addition to its European lead in canned vegetables, held the second place spot in the frozen vegetables segment, now sought to build a leadership position in fresh vegetables as well. In order to fund this effort and the company's further expansion, Bonduelle went public in 1998, listing on the Paris Stock Exchange's secondary market. The Bonduelle family nonetheless maintained majority control of the company.

Following the stock listing, Bonduelle opened new subsidiaries, entering the United States for the first time, as well as launching its first subsidiary in Africa, in Zimbabwe. In 1999, the company returned to external growth with the acquisition of Avril, also based in the north of France, with operations in Italy as well. That acquisition strengthened the company's position as a private-label producer for supermarket groups. The com-

---

Key Dates:

1853: Louis Bonduelle and Louis Leaffre-Roussel found a grain and juniper distillery near Lille, France.
1926: The Bonduelle family begins a pea canning operation.
1968: The Bonduelles begin producing frozen vegetables.
1969: The company establishes its first foreign subsidiary in Germany.
1980: Marie-Thumas of Belgium is acquired and Bonduelle becomes the leading canned vegetable company in that country.
1989: Bonduelle acquires Cassegrain to become the leading producer of canned vegetables in France.
1998: The company begins production of chilled vegetables and makes a public offering on the Euronext Paris Stock Exchange's secondary market.
1999: Bonduelle acquires Avril/Cirio France, producers of private label canned vegetables.
2000: The company restructures into five autonomous subsidiaries; Cielo e Campo of Italy is acquired.
2002: Bonduelle acquires Inter Champ, in Poland, and adds canned and frozen mushrooms to its line of products.

---

pany then reorganized its operating structure, separating its activities into five independently operating divisions.

After launching the Bonduelle en Frais brand in Italy in 1999 and in Germany in 2000, the company made a new acquisition, of Italy's Cielo e Campo, the number two Italian producer of fresh prepared vegetable products. The company also deepened its position in Spain, acquiring former Unilever subsidiary Frudesa, a specialist in frozen vegetables, at the end of 2000. Then, at the beginning of 2001, Bonduelle acquired Ortobell, the Italian leader of the fresh vegetable segment, giving Bonduelle not only the lead in Italy but also a leading position in that category across Europe. The company then merged its Italy holdings into a single subsidiary.

Bonduelle continued to target new expansion opportunities in 2002. In June of that year, the company agreed to acquire Inter Champ, a Polish subsidiary of struggling France Champignon. The acquisition added mushrooms, long a weak link in Bonduelle's chain of more than 240 vegetables. The acquisition agreement also called for an eventual Bonduelle takeover of all canned and frozen production for France Champignon in Europe. Bonduelle looked back on more than

75 years as a vegetable specialist, and forward to a future as a continued leader in its core markets.

Principal Subsidiaries

Agrilusa, Agro-Industria; Agrologica; Appetifrais S.A.; Avril Alimentaire SNC; Bonduelle Belgium; Bonduelle Ceskoslovensko; Bonduelle Espagnola; Bonduelle Espana; Bonduelle Frais Investissements; Bonduelle GmbH; Bonduelle Great-Britain; Bonduelle Iberica; Bonduelle Incorporated; Bonduelle Investment Company; Bonduelle Italia; Bonduelle Moscou; Bonduelle Nagykoros; Bonduelle Nederland; Bonduelle Nord Europa; Bonduelle Nordic; Bonduelle Osterreich; Bonduelle Polska; Bonduelle Portugal; Bonduelle Slovensko; Bonduelle Sud Europe; Bonduelle Zimbabwe; Bonmais; Bouclet Zunequin; Duvet; Iansa Bonduelle; Nieuwe Marie-Thumas; Primeurop; SCI Revoisson; Salade Minute; Salade Minute Traiteur; Sud Ouest Legumes; Vinet Bernard et Louis SCEA.

Principal Competitors

Unilever PLC; PepsiCo Inc.; Diageo PLC; Groupe Danone; H.J. Heinz Co; Dean Foods Co.; Tomkins PLC; McCain Foods Ltd.; Orkla ASA; Quaker Oats Co.; Parmalat SpA; Reckitt Benckiser plc; Dole Food Company Inc.; Sudzucker AG; Clorox Co.; Koninklijke Wessanen nv; COPEC ; Danisco A/S; Kikkoman Corp; Nestle Holdings UK PLC; CSM NV; Kerry Group plc; Chiquita Brands International Inc.; Ebro Puleva SA; Unilever Bestfoods Inc.; Golden State Foods Corp.; Borden Inc.; Del Monte Foods Co.; Cumberland Farms Inc.; Diversified Food Products; Coopagri Bretagne; Agrilink Foods Inc.; Royal Cosun.

Further Reading

Besses-Boumard, Pascale, "Bonduelle va mettre de 15 à 20 % de son capital en Bourse," *Les Echos*, May 28, 1998, p. 12.
"Bonduelle Acquires Unilever's Frozen Vegetables Activities in Spain," *European Report*, December 6, 2000.
"Bonduelle prêt à des acquisitions," *Les Echos*, October 19, 2000, p. 17.
"Bonduelle to Acquire Italian Fresh Vegetables Group," *European Report*, February 21, 2001.
"Bonduelle to Buy France Champignon Subsidiary," *Eurofood*, June 20, 2002, p. 6.
Flallo, Laurent, "Bonduelle en quête d'opportunités en Europe," *Les Echos*, May, 4, 2001, p. 15.
Le Cocq, François, "Un terrien bien implanté chez Bonduelle," *Nouvel Economiste*, December 12, 1997.
"Strong Growth at Bonduelle," *Eurofood*, February 14, 2002 p. 5.

—M. L. Cohen

BRAUN

designed to make a difference

Braun GmbH

Frankfurter Strasse 145
D-61476 Kronberg im Taunus
Germany
Telephone: (49) (6173) 30-0
Fax: (49) (6173) 30-2875
Web site: http://www.braun.com

Private Company
Incorporated: 1921 as Firma Max Braun, Maschinen-
   und Apparatebau
Employees: 8,300
Sales: $1.03 billion (2001)
NAIC: 335211 Electric Housewares and Household Fan
   Manufacturing; 339112 Surgical and Medical
   Instrument Manufacturing; 334518 Watch, Clock, and
   Part Manufacturing

Braun GmbH is one of the world's leading manufacturers of small electric appliances. Headquartered in the small German town of Kronberg near Frankfurt am Main, the company sees itself as the world market leader for electric foil shavers, electric toothbrushes, kitchen appliances, and electric hair removers. They also make electric water kettles, coffee makers, juicers, irons, hair dryers, stylers and curlers, infrared ear thermometers, blood pressure monitors, clocks, and calculators. Braun's product range includes about 200 products which are manufactured at its ten production plants in Germany, Ireland, France, Spain, China, Mexico, and the United States. Braun products are distributed worldwide by Boston-based Gillette Group, which has owned the company since 1967. Braun's widely acclaimed reputation for innovative product design goes back to German engineer and inventor Max Braun.

Company Origins in the Early 1920s

Max Braun, the sixth of seven sons of sailor and farmer Friedrich August Braun, grew up in a small town in eastern Prussia. At age 14 he started an apprenticeship at a nearby machine building company. His entrepreneurial spirit first emerged when, after finishing his four-year professional education as a machinist, he invented a steam-powered thresher and made his living leasing out himself and his machine to local farmers around harvest time. In 1910, Max Braun left eastern Prussia for Hamburg, where he worked at precision mechanics and machine-building company Wilhelm Fette. However, only a few months later he was drafted to serve in the German army in Berlin. After finishing the required six months of army service, Braun decided to stay in Berlin and started working for engineering firm and electrical equipment manufacturer AEG as a machinist. Later he worked for Siemens as a technical drawer and at yet another machine building firm, Storck & Co., where he became a tool designer. Besides working, Braun took evening classes at a private technical school and began studying English. In 1914, he graduated from technical school. In the same year, World War I began, and Braun was drafted again into the German army, where he served in the engineering corps. However, after only a few months he was lucky enough to be "reclaimed" by AEG to work at their turbine plant. In November 1920, following Germany's defeat in the war, Braun married and moved to Frankfurt am Main.

In 1921, Braun set up his own workshop in a space rented in Frankfurt. Starting out with one apprentice, he invented a small apparatus to fix, expand, or cut belts for machinery that he was building at the time. When he showed his invention, which he called "Trumpf," at the Frankfurt Fair in 1921, he stirred the interest of English businessmen, who started selling it in England.

One year later, a new era began in Germany, when the first regular radio shows were broadcast. The new medium inspired Max Braun. To learn about the new technology, he started taking evening classes organized by the *Gesellschaft der Freunde der Radio-Phonie und -Telegraphie*, a society of the friends of radio broadcasting and telegraphy, in Frankfurt. The first element of radio technology that caught Braun's attention was the so-called detector, a crystal connected to a needle that listeners used to tune in to different stations. This technology was neither easy to handle nor precise. For months Braun, together with a pharmacist friend, conducted experiments in the laundry room of the house where he lived, until he came up with a better solution. Instead of using unevenly shaped crystals, he heated crystal powder and formed it into a cylinder which he then connected to the contact point. By means of this device, listeners could tune in the radio stations much easier by turning the crystal cylinder. A trade journal hailed Braun's new detector, which he had exhibited at Germany's second radio trade show, as the most functional and best model on the market. In 1925, after Braun passed the examination at the evening course in radio technology, the German post office granted him admission to set up and run a radio receiver for private use.

Growth and Destruction: 1925–45

The quickly emerging market for radios became Braun's mainstay for the following two decades. In 1925, Braun became interested in the plastic powders he had seen at a trade show in Frankfurt. He designed machines that processed these powders to mold them into parts used in radio receivers, such as tube sockets, dials, knobs, and plugs. Braun also pioneered the existing technology for radios with new high-frequency transformer sets for two wavelengths, improved condensers, and a new scale for fine tuning radio stations. Braun's business grew so quickly that he had to find a new location for his 20 employees in 1926. Two years later, the company's workforce had swollen to 400, necessitating the construction of a new factory. In 1929, the company expanded its product range to include speaker amplifiers. Braun was now also manufacturing whole appliances in addition to individual components. It was mainly the good reputation of Braun radios and turntables that helped the company through the Great Depression.

The 1930s marked Braun's first massive expansion abroad. Max Braun's experience with independent salespeople encouraged him to set up his own distribution network outside of Germany. The company's English salesman in London had imitated the Braun's plastic molding machines and made and sold similar products on the side. Another German representative followed suit when he exported Braun products to Belgium, Switzerland, and the Netherlands, keeping the profits for himself. It was only natural that Max Braun decided to take over control of the export end of his operations, and he established sales offices in France, Switzerland, Spain, Tunisia, Morocco, and the Netherlands in the early 1930s. To avoid the usually high customs costs at the time, he also established manufacturing sites in England and France and an assembly workshop in Belgium.

The rise of the sound recording industry created another related market that Braun started catering to. His company

became a vendor of motors and pickups for turntables. The combination of the two technologies was only a matter of time. In 1932, Braun was among the first manufacturers to launch a radio and turntable in one unit, the "Cosmophon 777." The first radios Braun made were sold under the name Sevecke. The Frankfurt-based firm Sevecke owned a license for a technology patented by German radio manufacturer Telefunken that Braun used in its radios. In 1935, Braun acquired Sevecke's license and launched the "Braun" trademark used from that time on. In 1936, the company launched its first battery-powered portable radio. Two years later, the company's growth—Braun employed about 1,000 people at that time—made it necessary to rent additional production space.

In 1933, the National Socialists under the leadership of Adolf Hitler took over political power in Germany. To spread their propaganda, they promoted the distribution of a cheap radio called the "Volksempfänger"—the people's receiver. However, the receiver the Volksempfänger was equipped with was so weak that only the German Reichsrundfunk could be received and not radio stations from other European countries. Braun was among the firms that built the Volksempfänger. But the company also offered an add-on appliance that made it possible to listen to radio stations of other European countries.

It was almost inevitable that Max Braun's liberal spirit collided with the narrow-minded Nazi ideology. Denounced by one of his employees in 1934 for secretly putting aside earnings in foreign currency, the Nazis put Max Braun under home arrest for several days and searched his offices for evidence, which was not found. Four years later, the Gestapo tried to take away Max Braun's company leadership position by claiming that Braun, who admittedly had an easily excitable temperament, was not mature enough as a person to head a corporation. Braun demanded that a lawsuit against him be brought by the German authorities. After five hearings, they concluded that Braun was a rebel but a harmless one. After Braun had initially refused to take in orders for war goods, his company made two-way radios, radio control devices, and land mine searching equipment during World War II. When accusations were brought against Max Braun again in 1943—including charges that he had an anti-Nazi mindset, connections with non-Aryans abroad, listened to enemy radio stations, and refused to follow the Nazi's economic guidelines—his company's importance for the German war industry rescued him. In 1944, both Braun factories in Germany were almost completely destroyed during bombing raids.

New Beginnings after World War II

After Germany's defeat, it seemed almost certain that Braun's factories would be dismantled. But Max Braun threw all of his energy into doing everything possible to save his company from that fate. After lengthy negotiations, he succeeded. In October 1945, Braun started out with 150 employees to rebuild his enterprise. The company's first postwar product was actually a product of the war: a pocket flashlight powered by a hand-dynamo. Braun also started making chassis for phonographs again and in 1947 resumed the production of radios. By 1948, the year when a new currency was introduced in the western German sectors, the company's workforce was up to

Key Dates:

1921: German inventor Max Braun starts his own company.
1929: Braun starts manufacturing radios and turntables.
1935: The Braun brand name and logo are invented.
1944: Braun's factories are destroyed during bombing raids.
1950: The company's "S 50" dry foil shaver and "Multimix" blender are patented.
1951: Max Braun's sons Artur and Erwin take over company leadership.
1962: Braun becomes a public stock company.
1967: The company is acquired by Boston-based Gillette Group.
1988: Braun acquires French hair remover manufacturer Silk-Epil.
1996: The company buys U.S. manufacturer of infrared thermometers ThermoScan.
1998: Braun AG is transformed into a private company.

almost 400. One year later, the reconstruction of Braun's second plant in Frankfurt am Main was finalized.

Max Braun had used the slack period right after the war to think about possible areas of innovation for his firm. His vision was to make articles for the world market that required little material input. He finally decided to venture into two new product categories: electric dry shavers and kitchen appliances. During the war, Max Braun had already started thinking about making dry shavers. After inspecting the ten or so models of electric dry shavers available in 1947 in terms of cost and performance, Braun, together with a few other people, developed a new technology. During this time—so the story goes—all of Baun's male staff was shaved by the boss personally at least once. The result of this effort was Braun's first dry shaver, the "S 50," which was composed of a small universal motor powering an oscillating block of sharp round blades covered by a perforated metal plate. This device was patented in 1950. The company's first electric kitchen appliance, a blender called "Multimix," was also patented in 1950. In the following year, Braun Commercial GmbH, a new subsidiary for marketing Braun's blender and dry shaver, was established. Sales from household appliances went up quickly, especially abroad, and soon surpassed the company's revenues generated by radios and turntables. However, Max Braun was not to witness the overwhelming commercial success of his innovations. On November 6, 1951, he died suddenly while at work in his office.

Braun's Sons Take Over in 1951

Max Braun's sons Artur and Erwin, who had both joined the company in 1950, took over its leadership after their father's death. Artur Braun, 26 years old at the time, took over the technical side of the enterprise. He had a degree in engineering and had also helped his father develop Braun's first electric shaver. Thirty-year-old Erwin Braun had earned a degree in business administration and assumed responsibility for marketing and finances. He oversaw a market research project that

involved an undercover interviewer who traveled throughout Germany during 1953 to find out which retailers carried Braun products and how they perceived, presented, and sold them to consumers. As a result, Braun decided to invest in an ongoing informational campaign, hiring representatives who traveled around Germany to educate specialized retailers about the company's products and to build a closer relationship with them.

Thorough market research was used not only to improve Braun's relationship with customers but also as a basis for the company's design strategy. In 1953, the company co-sponsored research conducted by Germany's Allensbach Institute relating to consumer trends in interior design. Based on that study, Braun products became a synonym for simplicity and longevity. With a new vision in mind to clearly distinguish itself from other manufacturers, Braun's whole product range was given a brand-new design between 1954 and 1958. In 1954, New York's Museum of Modern Art included a number of Braun products in its design collection. Ten years later, the museum opened a new design exhibition with the entire Braun product range.

In the 1950s and 1960s, Braun introduced a great variety of new products. The 1950s saw the company launch an electronic flash for cameras, a juicer, a hand-held mixer, a television set, an automatic slide projector, and a hot-air heater. Novelties of the 1960s included a table-top heater, a toaster, an electric water kettle, a coffee grinder, a battery-powered dry shaver, a reel-to-reel tape recorder, a table-top cigarette lighter, a citrus press, and a hi-fi system with headphones. Braun also acquired two German companies, one that made 35-mm film and one that manufactured electronic thermostats. In 1963, the company started distributing microphones by U.S. manufacturer Shure in Germany.

In addition to expanding its product range, Braun extended the company's international reach. In 1954, the company sold a license for its shaver line to U.S. firm Ronson. Between 1958 and 1962, Braun established subsidiaries in Canada, Finland, the Netherlands, Denmark, France, Spain, and Japan which were organized under the umbrella of Switzerland-based holding company Braun Electric International S.A. Subsidiaries in other countries were later established.

Reorganization and Renewal after Takeover in 1967

Braun got its share of the postwar consumer boom in West Germany. To finance further growth, the company had been transformed into a public stock company in 1962. Two years later, Braun shares were publicly traded on the Frankfurt Stock Exchange for the first time. By 1967, Braun AG employed about 5,700 people, and the company started moving its headquarters to its current location in Kronberg. At the end of 1967, the Boston-based Gillette Company bought a majority share in Braun.

In the 1970s, 1980s, and 1990s Braun kept developing and launching new products for which it was awarded many design prizes. In fact, Braun's high rate of innovation—new products continuously contributed between 50 and 70 percent of total revenues—secured the company a leading position among the world's electric appliance makers. However, there were also disadvantages. First, many of Braun's competitors tried to take a shortcut to commercial success by copying Braun designs without delivering the same performance. The lawsuits Braun launched to limit the damage done by this practice to the company's image cost millions. Second, diversification had reached a point where Braun's broad product range got in its own way. While the company had successfully ventured into stereo sound systems and semi-professional and professional photo equipment, including video cameras, these areas demanded high-level investments on a constant basis. Kitchen appliances, electric shavers, and oral care products had become the company's mainstay, and Braun's managers realized that consumers might hesitate to buy a high-tech stereo system from a company that made razors and juicers. Therefore, in the early 1980s, Braun initiated two decades of strategic refocusing, cost consolidation, and reorganization.

In 1981, the company's hi-fi division, which grew out of Braun's former core business of radios and turntables, was spun off into Braun Electronic GmbH. The legally independent Gillette subsidiary put out its last hi-fi set in 1990 before the business was discontinued. Also in the early 1980s, Braun sold its photo division to Robert Bosch GmbH. In 1982, Gillette tied Braun closer to the parent company by taking full control over its operations. In 1984, Braun ceased the production of cigarette lighters. By the late 1980s, the company made over 70 percent of its sales outside of Germany. The United States and Japan had become the company's two major markets abroad. New production plants were established in Ireland, Spain, Mexico, and China, while staff in Germany was reduced.

By the mid-1990s, almost half of Braun's workforce was located outside of Germany, where about 40 percent of the company's appliances were made. Oral care products such as electric toothbrushes had become the company's main market besides electric shavers and kitchen appliances. In 1996, Braun added infrared thermometers to its product range with the acquisition of the U.S. firm ThermoScan. Two years later, Gillette decided to transform Braun AG into a private company before it bought back a 19.9 percent share in its subsidiary The Gillette Company Inc., which Braun had acquired in 1988, to avoid taxes it would have to pay in a public stock transaction. In 1999, Braun's sales organization was merged with those of Gillette's other business divisions to cut cost and to simplify the ordering process for customers. At the end of the 1990s, Braun and Gillette suffered losses in several areas, partly caused by the Asian financial crisis. Looking for ways to attain the high level of financial performance it had experienced in the past, the razor blade maker was considering the disposal of some of Braun's less profitable divisions, such as electric toothbrushes, kitchen

appliances, and thermometers, but abandoned the idea a few months later when finding a buyer turned out to be difficult, and Braun's sales in those areas started picking up again. However, many of the company's kitchen appliances, such as coffee makers, water kettles, irons, and hair dryers, were offered in selected markets only, mainly in Europe, while Braun's design strategy became more open to incorporating consumer trends, such as popular colors, without compromising the company's product philosophy of longevity and high technical standards. In 2000, the readers of *markt intern,* a German trade journal for retailers of electric appliances, voted Braun Germany's number one ''Electro Retail Partner'' ahead of three of its competitors. Apparently, the company's image for superior design and cutting-edge technology was strong enough to carry Braun's success of eighty years over into a new century.

Principal Subsidiaries

Consul GmbH (Germany); Braun Beteiligungsverwaltung GmbH (Germany); Braun Ireland Ltd.; Braun Espanola, S.A. (Spain); Silk-Epil S.A. (France).

Principal Competitors

Remington Products Company, L.L.C.; Conair Corporation; Koninklijke Philips Electronics N.V.; Sunbeam Corporation.

Further Reading

''Bei Braun beginnt die farbige Zeit,'' *HORIZONT*, April 20, 2000, p. 86.

''Braun bleibt bei Gillette,'' *Frankfurter Allgemeine Zeitung*, July 23, 2000, p. 33.

Braun im Rückblick 1921–1989, Frankfurt am Main, Germany: Braun AG, 1990, 73 p.

''Braun macht auch am Standort Deutschland hohe Gewinne,'' *Frankfurter Allgemeine Zeitung*, February 21, 1996, p. 19.

''Braun sieht bei Kopien rot,'' *Süddeutsche Zeitung*, March 1, 1997.

''Die Braun AG firmiert zur GmbH um,'' *Frankfurter Allgemeine Zeitung*, September 24, 1998, p. 26.

''Gillette-Ertrag leidet unter Schwierigkeiten bei Braun,'' *Frankfurter Allgemeine Zeitung*, July 17, 1999, p. 22.

''Gillette sucht Käufer für Teile von Braun,'' February 24, 2000, p. 28.

Max Braun-Unternehmer, Frankfurt am Main, Germany: Max Braun Kreis e.V., 1990, 20 p.

Wurm, Fabian, ''Strategien; Bernhard Wild, Vorstandsvorsitzender von Braun, über Markenpflege, Werbung und die Förderung von Designernachwuchs,'' *HORIZONT*, November 8, 2001, p. 70.

—Evelyn Hauser

Calloway's Nursery, Inc.

4200 Airport Freeway, Suite 200
Fort Worth, Texas 76117
U.S.A.
Telephone: (817) 222-1122
Fax: (817) 302-0031
Web site: http://www.calloways.com

Public Company
Incorporated: 1986
Employees: 300
Sales: $43.5 million (2001)
Stock Exchanges: NASDAQ
Ticker Symbol: CLWY
NAIC: 444220 Nursery and Garden Centers

Calloway's Nursery, Inc. is the largest lawn and garden retailer in Texas, the third-largest retail market in the United States. Calloway's Nursery operates 17 stores in the Dallas-Fort Worth area and three Cornelius Nurseries stores in Houston. Supported by two growing operations, Miller Plant Farms and Turkey Creek Farms, the company positions itself to attract mid- to uppper-income customers, differentiating itself from discount chains by presenting an upscale image to consumers. The typical Calloway's Nursery store consists of a 10,000-square-foot building, a 12,000-square-foot greenhouse, and a 40,000-square-foot outdoor nursery. Although configured somewhat differently, Cornelius Nurseries stores are roughly the same size as Calloway's Nursery stores.

Origins

The garden center industry in Texas underwent significant change during the 1990s as competitors fought for market supremacy—or, at the very least, for survival. Some market participants buckled under the pressure exerted by mass-merchandise, discount chains such as Wal-Mart and Kmart, while other garden center firms consolidated their operations to improve their odds for survival. Caught in the midst of the pitched battle for the garden business of Texas was relative newcomer, Calloway's Nursery.

Calloway's Nursery was founded in 1986 by three former senior executives at Sunbelt Nursery Group. Formed in 1984, Sunbelt Nursery was created to help expand Pier 1 Imports' Wolfe Nursery Inc. concept. Selected to lead the company toward such an objective were Jim Estill, Sunbelt Nursery's president and chief executive officer; John Cosby, the company's vice-president of corporate development; and John Peters, its vice-president of operations. Together, the three executives helped develop the company into a regional force with more than 100 stores in a five-state area. After a change in ownership at Sunbelt Nursery, the trio disagreed with the new owners about the future direction of the company. In March 1986, they formed Estill/Cosby Enterprises to facilitate the creation of their entry in the garden center market, Calloway's Nursery.

Although Estill, Cosby, and Peters were veterans of the industry, they consulted the patriarch of the garden center industry in the Southwest, 65-year-old Sterling Cornelius, before starting out on their own. Sterling Cornelius' father, Frank Cornelius, started the family nursery business in 1937, initially occupying a portable building that measured only slightly larger than 100 square feet. Except for a four-year stint in the U.S. Navy during World War II, Sterling Cornelius was employed by his father's company from its start, witnessing the addition of Turkey Creek Farms, a nursery operation, in 1951 and the company's development into a favorite among Houston's lawn and garden enthusiasts. Estill, Cosby, and Peters solicited the help of Sterling Cornelius because, by their own admission, they wished to copy the operating strategy used by Cornelius Nurseries. "We saw an opportunity to create a different kind of nursery in Dallas-Fort Worth, and quite honestly, Cornelius was our pattern," Estill remarked in a November 26, 1999 interview with *Dallas Business Journal*. "Cornelius was always the group in Houston that went after the upper-income customer, and there wasn't anything like that in the Dallas-Fort Worth area."

After Sterling Cornelius helped Estill, Cosby, and Peters develop a business plan, the effort to build a new chain of garden centers in the Dallas-Fort Worth area began in earnest. Cosby assumed responsibility for developing the company's retail locations, including site selection and development, and lease and acquisition negotiations. Estill served as the com-

---

Company Perspectives:

Our objective is to provide an unmatched level of retail excellence in the quality and variety of living plants and garden products we offer. We strive to consistently and dependably furnish quality products, information, presentation, and service. Our commitment to providing an exciting retail experience is grounded in the proven principles of traditional retail. We combine these principles with advanced technologies specially developed to ensure the success of our products. Our customers seek us out because of our demonstrated ability to dependably provide them with an unequaled shopping experience. We believe that gardening is a creative process, that landscaping adds value to a home and that gardening provides both pleasant diversion and environmental benefit.

---

pany's chief strategist, while Peters took responsibility for operations, distribution, administration, and human resources. In April 1987, the first Calloway's Nursery store, located in Richardson, Texas, opened for business. Before the end of the month, two more stores opened, and before the end of the year the fledgling company opened its fourth store.

General Host Encourages 1991 IPO

Capital was scarce during the company's first years in business, which led to the intervention of a financial partner in 1988. Stamford, Connecticut-based General Host Corp. invested $2 million in the Forth Worth company, obtaining an 80 percent stake in Calloway's Nursery in return. After the infusion of cash, the company expanded, adding an average of nearly three new stores a year. General Host, meanwhile, waited for the right time to recoup its investment. In 1989, the company recorded a loss of $1.9 million, which was trimmed to a $545,000 loss the following year. Calloway's Nursery posted its first annual profit in 1991, registering a $2 million gain that convinced executives at General Host the time was right for the Connecticut company to cash out.

At the urging of General Host, Estill and his colleagues filed with the Securities and Exchange Commission in May 1991 for an initial public offering (IPO) of stock. The company planned to sell 3.2 million at an expected price of $6.50 per share. At the time of the stock offering, Calloway's Nursery was generating $22 million in annual sales, a total derived from the company's 11 retail stores, all of which were located in the Dallas-Fort Worth area. The company had been able to secure a place for itself in a fiercely competitive market, successfully competing against industry veterans such as Wolfe Nursery and the "big-box" discount chains by putting an emphasis on quality rather than price. The completion of the IPO gave Estill $6 million, proceeds he intended to use to pay off $1.7 million in long-term debt owed to General Host and to fund the company's continued expansion. Following the IPO, Estill, with Cosby as his lieutenant, planned to open two new garden centers a year for the next five years. From its $2 million investment in 1988, General Host received a substantial profit, walking away from the IPO and its affiliation with Calloway's Nursery with $24 million.

The years immediately following the company's IPO were difficult ones. Calloway's Nursery failed to deliver consistent financial growth after registering its first annual profit in 1991, although considering the recessive economic climate of the early 1990s it was not surprising that the company failed to impress. After posting a $2 million profit in 1991, the company recorded a $825,000 gain the following year before suffering a nearly $500,000 loss in 1993. Sales slipped as well, dropping from $28.8 million in 1992 to $28.2 million in 1993. "Nineteen-ninety-three was a difficult year for the nursery industry," Estill explained in a December 3, 1993 interview with *PR Newswire*. "Calloway's Nursery did not achieve the sales increases or profitable operating results that we would have liked," he added. Despite the company's anemic financial performance during the early 1990s, it did achieve great strides through expansion. In late 1993, the company opened its 17th store, the sixth new store opening since the company's IPO. The opening of the new store in a north Dallas suburb marked the end of the company's internal expansion during the 1990s. Physical growth in the future would be achieved solely through acquisition.

Acquisitions in the Late 1990s

One major problem challenging the company from 1993 forward was maintaining its stock of plants. National retailers such as Wal-Mart, Kmart, and The Home Depot flocked to the Dallas area, hoping to wrest control of the lucrative market away from independent chains. The massive stores purchased large amounts of plants and flowers, causing a drain on the supply that had previously fed Calloway's Nursery's demand. To ameliorate what potentially could put the company in a precarious position, Estill looked to secure his own supply of garden products. In mid-1997, Estill made his move, acquiring a nursery production facility near Tyler, Texas. Comprising more than 80 acres and more than 100 greenhouses, Miller Plant Farms was expected to provide Calloway's Nursery with one-fifth of the living plants its chain of stores required.

Calloway's Nursery's next big move on the acquisition front occurred two years after Miller Plant Farms joined the company's fold. In a bold proposition, Estill announced his intention to acquire two familiar garden center retailers. One of the companies was Wolfe Nursery, the concept he, Cosby, and Peters had presided over during the early 1980s. Sunbelt Nursery had filed for bankruptcy protection and was looking to liquidate its assets. The other company on Estill's list was the Houston-based chain controlled by his mentor, Sterling Cornelius. By 1999, Cornelius was 77 years old and ready to retire. "I am up in the senior-citizen bracket now," Cornelius explained in an August 14, 1999 interview with *The Houston Chronicle*. "We've had several offers before," he continued, "but this seemed like the right time. These people [Calloway's Nursery] have a good track record. They walk the high moral road. They are good people, and that's why we are doing this."

Estill's ambitious plan promised to triple the size of Calloway's Nursery and to expand the company's geographic scope considerably, adding properties in Austin, San Antonio, and Houston to its established presence in the Dallas-Fort Worth area. The acquisitions did not go ahead as planned, however. In July 1999, one month after the acquisitions were announced, Calloway's Nursery terminated its plan to acquire the Wolfe Nursery

---

Key Dates:

1986: Three former executives at Sunbelt Nursery Group form Calloway's Nursery.

1987: The first Calloway's Nursery store opens in Richardson, Texas.

1988: General Host Corp. invests $2 million in Calloway's Nursery, gaining an 80 percent stake in the company.

1991: Calloway's Nursery converts to public ownership.

1997: Miller Plant Farms, a nursery production operation, is acquired.

1999: Calloway's Nursery acquires Cornelius Nurseries.

2001: Calloway's Nursery divests its wholesale business.

---

chain, explaining that it lacked the financial resources to complete both acquisitions. Forced to chose only one of the candidates, Estill opted for Cornelius Nurseries. In late 1999, the acquisition, valued at between $15 million and $20 million, was completed, giving Calloway's Nursery control of four Cornelius Nurseries garden centers in Houston, a 160-acre nursery production operation named Turkey Creek Farms, and two wholesale distribution centers, one in Houston, the other in Austin.

Calloway's Nursery exited the 1990s as the largest garden center retailer in Texas. The Texas market, ranked as the third largest in the country, generated an estimated $1.6 billion in sales in 1999, a total that excluded the sales recorded by mass merchandisers, who did not separately report nursery product sales. As they had for more than a decade, retailers such as Lowe's, The Home Depot, and Wal-Mart represented a formidable force in the market, presenting Estill and Calloway's Nursery's management team with a perennial threat. To distinguish itself from the discount retailers, the company unveiled a prototype store before the end of the 1990s. The store's design was expected to be the model for the future, as the company sought to strengthen its image as an upscale retailer.

Calloway's Nursery's new flagship store, located in southwest Fort Worth, was designed to replicate a historic Texas homestead. Measuring 100,000 square feet, the Stonegate store featured a greenhouse decorated with garden benches and pottery, wandering landscaped paths, and a courtyard with a fountain. The merchandise differed from the traditional selection found at a discount retailer as well, including items such as pots imported from Vietnam, China, and Malaysia. The store also sold potting soil with added sulfur and iron, which the soil found in the Dallas-Fort Worth area required. The Stonegate store did not offer a precise blueprint for future store design—a store in McKinney, Texas, for example, featured a scaled-down replica of Monticello in the nursery—but its essence as an upscale, specialty retail location provided a direction the company opted to pursue in the 21st century.

As Estill and his team planned for the future, there was cause for celebration and concern. In August 2000, the company reported the most profitable fiscal quarter in its history, posting $3.2 million in the third quarter. During the first nine months of 2001, however, the company reported a loss of $1.15 million, partly because of losses stemming from its wholesale business. In response, Calloway's Nursery sold its wholesale operation, comprising distribution centers in Austin and Houston, to Coppell, Texas-based Landmark Nurseries. The divestiture was completed in October 2001. With the drag on its profits removed, Calloway's Nursery looked forward to consistent financial growth in the years ahead and to maintaining its lead in the lucrative Texas market.

Principal Subsidiaries

Miller Plant Farms, Inc.; Calloway's Nursery of Texas, Inc.; Cornelius Nurseries, Inc.

Principal Competitors

Wal-Mart Stores, Inc.; Kmart Corporation; The Home Depot, Inc.

Further Reading

Bond, Helen, "Metroplex's Fertile Market Has Calloway's Eyeing IPO; Upscale Nursery Chain Plans More Growth Around," *Dallas Business Journal,* May 31, 1991, p. 2.

"Calloway's Nursery Announces Acquisition of Nursery Production Facility," *Business Wire,* July 28, 1997.

Elder, Laura, "Calloway's Closes on Cornelius Nurseries Purchase," *Houston Business Joournal,* September 24, 1999, p. 10A.

Gordon, Frances, "Growing Pains," *Dallas Business Joiurnal,* August 17, 2001, p. 56.

Halkias, Maria, "Calloway's Won't Buy Wolfs," *Dallas Morning News,* July 20, 1999, p. 12D.

Hassell, Greg, "Calloway's Prunes Its Acquisition List; Firm Won't Buy Wolfe, but Cornelius Deal Still Expected to Blossom," *The Houston Chronicle,* August 14, 1999, p. 2.

"In the South," *National Home Center News NewsFax,* November 5, 2001, p. 1.

Taylor, Lisa, "Making Calloway's Garden Grow," *Dallas Business Journal,* November 26, 1999, p. 43.

—Jeffrey L. Covell

Campbell Scientific, Inc.

815 West 1800 North
Logan, Utah 84321-1784
U.S.A.
Telephone: (435) 753-2342
Fax: (435) 750-9540
Web site: http://www.campbellsci.com

Private Company
Incorporated: 1974
Employees: 200
Sales: $50 million (2002 est.)
NAIC: 334511 Search, Detection, Navigation, Guidance,
Aeronautical, and Nautical System and Instrument
Manufacturing; 334519 Other Measuring and
Controlling Device Manufacturing

Campbell Scientific, Inc., headquartered in Logan, Utah, designs and manufactures dataloggers, data acquisition systems, and measurement and control products used worldwide in both industrial applications and in research. The company enjoys an excellent reputation for making instruments that are both very accurate and dependable as well as flexible enough for use in climactically harsh or remote environments. It specializes in developing systems for a wide range of applications, including the unattended long-term monitoring of air quality. Industrially, its equipment is used at smelters, refineries, tailings, mines, landfills, construction sites, manufacturing and processing plants, and industrial and hazardous waste sites. It is also used in such special applications as atmospheric monitoring at historical preservation sites and museums and libraries. The company is private and is owned by the families of its founders, Eric and Evan Campbell.

1974–78: Manufacturing Dataloggers

CSI appeared on the corporate radar in 1974 when two brothers, Eric and Evan Campbell, using family funds, began building it into a successful developer and manufacturer of special-purpose electronic measurement and control equipment,

principally a line of dataloggers. Eric and Evan brought separate but complimentary skills to the undertaking. While a student of Utah State University, where he majored in physics and minored in electrical engineering, Eric developed his own company, Logan Scientific Instruments, which produced soil psychrometers. He then sold the company to pay for his university training and help bankroll his next business, CSI. Evan, who was studying manufacturing engineering, brought an expertise in mechanical design and systems to the enterprise.

In addition to their own funds, the two Campbell brothers had the financial support of their six brothers and their father, Sanford Campbell. They also had the help of Professor Gaylon Campbell of Washington State University, who directed them in product definition and conceptual design.

The Campbell brothers started out producing a product for the U.S. Army, the Model CA9 Path Averaging Laser S Anemometer, for application at the White Sands Missile Range in New Mexico. The Campbell's modeled their anemometer on an earlier, larger instrument experimentally developed at the NOAA Wave Propagation Laboratory in Boulder, Colorado. The new company sold about 60 CA9s to military facilities and other installations involved in atmospheric research.

In the next year, CSI began marketing its Model CR5 Digital Recorder, a portable, battery-run datalogger employing CMOS (complementary metal oxide semiconductor) logic technology. According to Campbell, it was the first battery-operated system capable of taking time-averaged measurements from thermocouples, solar radiation sensors, and wind sensors demanding vector averaging.

Spurred by the sale of about 500 CR5s, by 1978 the company had expanded to 20 employees and close to $1 million in annual revenue. In that year, it also established its presence outside the United States, when Claude Labine obtained the exclusive right to distribute Campbell instruments in Canada. His business quickly expanded as the Canadian demand for CSI's products increased, and within two years he incorporated his company under the laws of Canada, forming Campbell Scientific (Canada) Corp. It was the first company in what would become CSI's international network.

In 1979, CSI introduced another product, its Model CR21 Micrologger, which would eventually reach 3,600 sold worldwide. This system was widely adapted for use in weather station applications that required reliability, minimal power consumption, and unattended operation.

1981–90: Growth Spurs New Products and Overseas Expansion

CSI moved its operations to a building on the outskirts of Logan, Utah, in 1981. A solar energy efficiency facility, the building conserved energy and used natural lighting to keep its utility expenses below those of more conventional buildings of similar size. The company, which used one of its own CR21 units to control heating, air conditioning, and ventilation, found the building agreeable enough to continue to call it home through the end of the century.

A major technological advance was achieved by CSI in the beginning of 1983, when it introduced its Model CR7 Measurement and Control System. It was first developed to expand the channel range of the CR5, but improvements made in integrated circuitry and new thinking about analog measurement placed the CR7 ahead of much field measurement technology. Many of the 180 CR7 units sold in 1983 were employed in new applications for CSI, including, for example, the monitoring of experimental car performance. At the same time, CSI continued to expand the sale of its systems for use in more traditional applications, including agricultural research and meteorology. Thanks to the wide application of the CR7, in just over a decade, the company sold close to 1600 systems.

In 1984, in a move to adapt some of the CR7 capability to a highly integrated, lower cost system, CSI developed the Model 21X Micrologger. It was achieved at a cost only slightly higher than that of the original CR21. Like the CR7, the 21X was a successful seller, and by 1994 SCI had sold 12,256 units of the micrologger. Also like the CR7, the 21X was adapted to new markets, including oceanography and automotive engineering.

With its development of new products and the need to interface with products of other manufacturers, in the 1980s CSI worked on further development of efficient and reliable communication and data transfer. It would eventually have the ability to transfer data using a variety of systems: switched network phone lines; cellular phones; dedicated lines; VHF, UHF, and spread-spectrum radios; meteor burst transmissions; and satellites. Among other things, it developed an RF modem for assuring fail-safe, two-way communication employing UHF or VHF radios. The new system was first tested with a 21X micrologger in mountains near Logan over a four-month period at the end of 1984 and the start of 1985. It would become a major component in a system of 140 portable weather stations operated by the Atmospheric Sciences Laboratory at the White Sands Missile Range in New Mexico.

Increasing sales in overseas markets led Campbell to establish a UK subsidiary in 1985. Named Campbell Scientific Limited (CSL), its main purpose was to combine the technology created by CSI with peripheral equipment then manufactured in the United Kingdom and to provide the end products and support services to customers within the European market area.

In 1987, Campbell introduced a new datalogger, its CR10 Measurement and Control Module. It very quickly became the datalogger of choice at many weather stations. The unit held the promise of greater efficiency, cost effectiveness, and reliability than other dataloggers, and it featured better shielding from radio frequency and electromagnetic interference and a tighter environmental seal. Over the next seven years, Campbell would sell 27,310 CR10s.

Throughout the 1980s, CSI collaborated with outside researchers in the development of sensors for measuring heat and water vapor released from crop and soil surfaces into the atmosphere. Using eddy covariance techniques, the method required the use of fast response sensors that could measure vertical wind, temperature, and water vapor changes. As part of this project, Campbell developed a fast-response humidity sensor capable of measuring ultraviolet light emitted from a krypton gas source tube. Also, from 1987 to 1991, CSI engineers engaged in a project to detect and monitor leakage from underground fuel-storage tanks, a study that led to an important breakthrough in the detection of changes in liquid levels by using ultrasonic transducers and digital signals. Campbell would later license the resulting technology to the Marley Pump Company.

1991–95: Development of Other New Products and Continued Expansion

In the 1990s, CSI placed increasing emphasis on developing software tools to aid data reduction and develop system program documentation. The work, first designed in the 1980s for the IBM PC, centered on microcomputers. In 1993, Campbell completed RTMS, a software package for datalogger networks. Its purpose was to support mutli-tasking, real-time monitoring. A major customer for the company was the state of Oklahoma, which installed over 120 remote weather stations that communicated with computers using RTMS. These computers then fed data to a mainframe computer at Oklahoma's Climatology Office.

The company was also developing other new products in the early 1990s. In 1991, for example, it introduced products designed to extend the utility of its dataloggers, particularly for the recording of volumetric water content through the use of time-domain reflectometry (TDR). Other new products included probes and interface products that would allow CR10 dataloggers to communicate with a reflectometer. In conjunction

```
┌─────────────────────────────────────────────┐
│               Key Dates:                    │
│                                             │
│ 1974:  Eric and Evan Campbell found Campbell│
│        Scientific, Inc. (CSI) and market    │
│        their first product, the Model CA9   │
│        Path Averaging Laser Anemometer.     │
│ 1975:  CSI begins making the Model CR5      │
│        Digital Recorder.                    │
│ 1978:  Company reaches $1 million in annual │
│        sales.                               │
│ 1979:  CSI introduces its Model CR21        │
│        Micrologger.                         │
│ 1981:  The company relocates to an energy   │
│        efficient building located on the    │
│        outskirts of Logan, Utah.            │
│ 1983:  CSI reaches a milestone technological│
│        achievement with the introduction of │
│        its Model CR7 Measurement and        │
│        Control System.                      │
│ 1985:  The company establishes a subsidiary │
│        in England, Campbell Scientific      │
│        Limited (CSL).                       │
│ 1993:  CSI establishes a subsidiary in      │
│        Australia.                           │
│ 2001:  The company acquires Irrisoft.       │
└─────────────────────────────────────────────┘
```

with other researchers, CSI developed and implemented software for use in dataloggers that would allow automated, remote-site measurement and recording of such information. Also in 1991, CSI began marketing its BDR320 for hydrological use. The unit was designed for use in harsh and remote environments that imposed a need for low power use and automated equipment. The BDR320, using simple sensors, took reliable measurements of temperature, pressure, force, or position and was perfectly suited to taking water-stage measurements and use in well draw-down tests.

Campbell Scientific further expanded through the 1990s. In 1993 it established a second subsidiary located outside North America, in Australia, with a similar purpose to that of CSL in the United Kingdom but covering the Southeast Asia and South Pacific regions. Also in 1993, CSI sold its first Trace Gas Analyzer, a sophisticated and highly sensitive instrument able to measure nearly infinitesimal amounts of CH_4 (methane) or N_2O (nitrous oxide, or ''laughing gas'').

In the middle 1990s, CSI also expanded and upgraded its assembly and work areas. Among other things, it incorporated the use of CAD (computer aided design) equipment for mechanical and printed circuit board designs and improved its computer-based MRP (manufacturing recourse planning) capability for improving its manufacturing efficiency and product control. In 1995, the company shipped its first CR9000, a new data logger with a much greater measurement and processing speed than any of its earlier models. The instrument's sensitivity and speed allowed its use in such demanding applications as noise and vibration measurement and turbulence studies.

1996–99: Keeping Pace with Changing Technology and Developing New Markets

The next year, 1996, the company's UK subsidiary, CSL, moved into a new 17,000-square-foot facility specifically designed to accommodate the company's manufacturing, service, and support activities. CSI also started delivering its CR10X, an

upgrade of its CR10. It provided the same kind of functions as its predecessor, but it expanded the data storage ability, had a larger program capacity, and included such other features as non-volatile flash memory, an expanded instruction set, and a battery-backed RAM and clock. It was also the company's first datalogger to employ surface-mount technology, an improvement over through-hole technology because it allowed for, among other things, smaller components, a faster signal speed, and lowered RF emission.

Expansion abroad also continued after 1996. First, in 1997, Campbell established a subsidiary branch, Campbell Scientific Africa (Pty.) Ltd., in Stellenbosch, South Africa; then, in 1999, it established Campbell Scientific do Brasil in Sao Paulo, Brazil. Also, on the domestic scene, in August 1999 CSI made a $3.75 million investment in Kent, Washington-based Meteor Communications Corporation (MCC), one of the world's first designers and builders of wireless, packet switched networks using meteor burst communications (MBC) and extended-line-of-sight (ELOS) technologies. That company had begun providing these networks to various customers worldwide in 1975 for use in a variety of applications, including environmental monitoring. The investment was a strategic step for CSI, which made instruments and systems suited to Meteor's technology and had a big stake in seeing the messaging costs in data networking made economically feasible for it own customers, something it was convinced MCC could achieve.

2000–02: New Growth and Product Development in the 21st Century

Campbell Scientific's growth, diversification, and new product development continued apace at the beginning of the new century. In June 2001, the company acquired Irrisoft, Inc., a software development firm that Travis Barney and Steven Moore started up in 1998. Campbell bought the company in order to provide a variety of integrated software solutions, particularly programs designed to meet its product distribution needs. In addition, the company expanded its CR200 line of wireless sensors and dataloggers with the introduction of CR205. In the same period, it also developed, produced, and began marketing other products, including its CR5000 and CR9052 dataloggers, RF400 spectrum radio, and TDR100 time domain reflectometer (a device to measure the water content and electrical conductivity in soil and other porous media). Campbell's robust research and development and recent acquisitions argued a secure corporate future in its highly specialized field.

Principal Subsidiaries

Campbell Scientific Corp. (Canada); Campbell Scientific Ltd. (United Kingdom.); Campbell Scientific Australia Pty. Ltd.; Campbell Scientific Africa (Pty.) Ltd.; Campbell Scientific do Brasil.

Principal Competitors

Dickson Monitoring Solutions; Grant Instruments; Logic Beach Incorporated; Omega Engineering, Inc.; Omni Controls, Inc.; Onset Computer Corporation.

Further Reading

Baker, M. Sharon, ''Meteor Lands Millions to Spread Its Telecom System,'' *Puget Sound Business Journal*, August 13, 1999, p. 12.

McDermott, Kevin, ''Selling High Technology: If You Have the Best Product, Isn't That Enough,'' *D & B Reports*, September-October 1987, p. 34.

Valenti, Michael, ''Precision Logger Sent into Space,'' *Mechanical Engineering*, September 1995, p. 34.

—John W. Fiero

America's Oldest Chemists and Perfumers

ESTABLISHED 1752

Caswell-Massey Co. Ltd.

121 Fieldcrest Avenue
Edison, New Jersey 08837
U.S.A.
Telephone: (908) 225-2181
Toll Free: (800) 326-0500
Fax: (908) 225-2385
Web site: http://www.caswellmassey.com

Private Company
Incorporated: 1752 as Dr. Hunters' Dispensary
Employees: 87
Sales: $20 million (2001 est.)
NAIC: 325611 Soap and Other Detergent Manufacturing;
    325620 Toilet Preparation Manufacturing; 446120
    Cosmetics, Beauty Supplies, and Perfume Stores

Originally an apothecary shop, Caswell-Massey Co. Ltd. has been creating America's most enduring scents since well before the specialty bath segment exploded in the 1980s and 1990s. Founded in 1752, the same year as Benjamin Franklin's shocking kite incident, the firm is considered the fourth oldest business in the United States. At the time of Caswell-Massey's 250th anniversary, "America's oldest chemists and perfumers" had 15 retail stores in the United States and several licensed outlets overseas. The firm also sold products through a web site and a catalog reaching more than two million people. Three-quarters of Caswell-Massey's 450 products have been around at least 25 years, and some, like Number Six Cologne, date from the 18th century.

Colonial Origins

William Hunter, a Scottish-born doctor, founded what would become Caswell-Massey in Newport, Rhode Island on March 26, 1752. Originally called Dr. Hunters' Dispensary, the shop's first specialty was providing medicine for midwives. Dr. Hunter is known as the inventor of orange soda, which people imbibed to take the edge off the dispensary's bitter medicines.

The resort town of Newport attracted the Colonies' social elite, who sought European-style luxuries. Dr. Hunter imported fragrances from the Old World and blended some himself. One enduring concoction was Number Six Cologne, based on an English blend of nearly 30 botanicals, including cloves, orange peel, rosemary, bergamot, orange blossoms, and pine. In those days, it was used for washing face and hands in place of water, which was considered unhealthful. George Washington bought two cases of Number Six for the Marquis de Lafayette. John Adams was another early customer, and Dolly Madison adored White Rose.

In spite of his products' popularity among Patriots, Dr. Hunter himself was a Loyalist, and was forced to leave the area after the war. Before he did, he handed the key to his assistant—a mode of succession that would continue for 150 years.

Still Prominent in the 1800s

John Quincy Adams brought Number Six Cologne back to the White House upon taking office in 1824. In another 175 years, one of his descendants, Anne Robinson, would buy the company.

A Manhattan branch of the shop opened in 1833. In that year, the firm's name was registered as Caswell & Hazard Company. The firm became known as Caswell-Massey in 1876, when then-owner John Rose Caswell formed a partnership with New York businessman William Massey. The firm then had one store in Newport and one in New York City, at 25th Street and Fifth Avenue. In the next 30 years, Caswell-Massey grew to ten stores in New York City, but closed its Newport store in 1906.

During this time, the company continued to be associated with eminent clients and enduring products. Before George Armstrong Custer made his Last Stand at the Battle of the Little Bighorn, he brushed his teeth with a Caswell-Massey Tilbury toothbrush. Annie Oakley and Edgar Allen Poe were other famous customers of the day. The legendary actress Sarah Bernhardt had the firm's cucumber night cream, dating from 1887, shipped to her in Paris. Jockey Club, introduced in 1840, would later become a favorite of President John F. Kennedy.

20th-Century Glamour

The store launched a soft, intoxicating fragrance called Casma (a contraction of the company name), in 1922. Casma had notes of rose, jasmine, magnolia, vanilla, musk, ginger, and bergamot, and was a favorite of Carole Lombard. It would be re-released in 2001, in time for the 75th anniversary of Caswell-Massey's flagship Manhattan shop. The store has been located in the Barclay New York Hotel at 48th Street and Lexington Avenue since its opening in 1926.

Although it was considered one of the country's leading perfumers, Caswell-Massey was forced to scale back during the Great Depression. From ten New York City stores in the Roaring Twenties, by 1932, it was down to just one store.

In 1936, Milton and Ralph Taylor bought the company, the first time a change of ownership was accompanied by payment of money. In keeping with the apprentice's tradition, however, it was noted that new chairman Ralph Taylor had once swept the shop floor. He and his brother, who served as company president, would own Caswell-Massey for 50 years.

The store continued to attract a stellar clientele, including musicians like Cole Porter and George Gershwin, and film stars John Barrymore, Errol Flynn, Judy Garland, Katharine Hepburn, and Greta Garbo. Lauren Bacall chose the Manhattan store for her first meeting with Humphrey Bogart prior to the filming of *To Have and Have Not* in 1945. She apparently felt the proverbial soda fountain, which closed a few years later, provided the appropriate atmosphere for a budding starlet. President and Mrs. Dwight Eisenhower brought almond cold cream soap to the White House. It would remain the company's best-selling soap for 50 years.

Caswell-Massey's catalog, last seen in 1904, was reintroduced in 1963. The catalog business was said to be the third oldest in the United States, after that of Sears Roebuck and Montgomery Ward.

New Competition in the 1970s–80s

In the 1970s, a wholesale customer formed a new company that would become a serious competitor. Before founding Crabtree & Evelyn Ltd. in 1972, Cyrus I. Harvey, Jr., had offered to update Caswell-Massey's packaging, reported *Business Week.*

In 1984, Caswell-Massey rolled out its first new scent in 43 years, Greenbriar. In the next few years, the company expanded its almond and aloe line of products and brought out a line of "old school" shaving products for men. Sales were about $10 million a year in the mid-1980s. The company had half a dozen company-owned stores, and about the same number of franchised stores. Its products were also sold in another 2,400 specialty stores. Two of Milton Taylor's sons were being groomed for leadership positions: Adam Taylor served as vice-president while brother Joshua studied the perfumer's craft.

High rents from an expansion into the nation's malls resulted in near-insolvency for the company. In a bid to compete with Crabtree & Evelyn, which had grown enormously since 1979, the Taylors expanded to 100 franchised stores—more than they could reliably supply. The category of specialty bath stores was becoming crowded with old competitors like Crabtree & Evelyn and New Age-inspired, London-bred Body Shop International. Sales were about $15 million a year by the end of the decade.

New Owners in the 1990s

Two wealthy Hong Kong entrepreneurs, Peter Hsu and Sally Aw Sian, acquired Caswell-Massey in 1989. Sian's family had developed Tiger Balm ointment. The pharmacy in the Barclay Store closed in 1990. Company headquarters were relocated from Manhattan to more modern facilities in Edison, New Jersey in April of the year. The decade soon brought other changes, marking the end of an era. Ralph Taylor died in 1993 and his brother Milton Taylor died the next year.

In 1992, W.R. Grace & Co. acquired a 40 percent holding in Caswell-Massey. The next fall, the company began a mass-market misadventure, selling to drugstore chains. This left a huge stockpile of unsold merchandise.

Beauty Nectar, $37.50 for 8.5 ounces, a face and body alpha hydroxy treatment, rolled out in 1994. The next year, the company introduced its complex Elixir of Love No. 1, a mix of passionflower, jasmine, lavender, musk, and wormwood. This reversed an emphasis on single-note floral fragrances begun in the early 1970s. Beauty Nectar and Elixir represented Caswell-Massey's first use of national advertising.

Caswell-Massey opened its fifth Manhattan store, in Soho, in 1995. By this time, the company was again on the verge of liquidation. Caswell-Massey had annual sales of $13 million, reported *Forbes,* and was losing $3 million a year. W.R. Grace sold its holding to then-CEO Edward Hung. Anne Robinson was placed in charge of Caswell-Massey's wholesale division in July 1995. She had an M.B.A. from another venerable Yankee institution, Harvard University, and experience with retailers like Filene's Basement, Lord & Taylor, and Excell Home Fashions.

Robinson's involvement with Caswell-Massey had begun in 1991, when she was marketing head for Aphrodisia, Caswell-Massey's Brooklyn-based supplier of potpourri and other supplies. After taking a marketing job with Caswell-Massey, she was soon named executive director after presenting a plan for saving the company.

Key Dates:

1752: Dr. Hunter's Dispensary opens in Newport, Rhode Island.
1833: The firm is registered as Caswell & Hazard Co.; a New York City branch is opened.
1876: John Rose Caswell and William Massey form a partnership.
1906: The Newport store closes.
1922: Casma is introduced.
1926: The Barclay Hotel opens with a Caswell-Massey shop inside.
1932: Caswell-Massey is down from ten stores to one during the Great Depression.
1936: Milton and Ralph Taylor buy the company; Red Jasmin is introduced.
1945: Bogie and Bacall choose the Manhattan store for their first meeting.
1963: Catalog sales are reintroduced.
1989: The company is acquired by Hong Kong entrepreneurs.
1993: A disastrous mass market adventure begins.
1995: Anne Robinson is brought on board.
1999: Robinson leads a management buyout of Caswell & Massey.
2002: Caswell-Massey celebrates its 250th anniversary by reintroducing historic scents.

The company had 28 stores and 113 employees when Robinson took over. After adding two high-end boutiques, she shut more than half the stores, trimmed the product line by a third, and released a quarter of the employees. She also refined inventory management and streamlined the organization structure to a single business instead of five divisions.

The catalog was redesigned in the fall of 1997 to give it a more old-fashioned feel. This helped make it profitable for the first time in eight years. The company catalog, with a circulation of 2.5 million, was important both for its contribution to earnings as well as serving as an introduction to the firm's products for many people.

Repackaging also made a big difference. After putting a view of an English country cottage on the lavender soap wrapper, and using a cheaper bottle for the Beauty Nectar and knocking $12.50 off the price, both items became bestsellers.

1999 Management Buyout

Caswell-Massey returned to profitability in the last quarter of 1998. Robinson assembled a pool of investors to buy the company, a deal completed on September 17, 1999. American Capital Strategies, a NASDAQ-listed firm specializing in management buyouts, joined her in the deal, acquiring a 24 percent holding while investing $4.2 million.

Soon, Robinson was on QVC pitching the company's wares. Her first visit to the television-shopping channel, in October 1999, was a success. Eight of the ten Caswell-Massey products presented sold out—Robinson logged $11,000 in sales per minute during the show.

Annual revenues were a profitable $20 million as Caswell-Massey entered the 21st century. While new channels such as QVC and the Internet were being exploited, the company also was paying careful attention to its retail stores. The flagship unit on Manhattan's Lexington Avenue was remodeled. A 12-foot-long ''perfume bar'' encouraged shoppers to test 15 different fragrances. Other brands like Mustela, Claus Porto, and Avaha also were sold there and at Caswell-Massey's ten other stores, scattered in upscale locations ranging from Washington, DC to Newport Beach, California.

There were also licensing agreements with overseas retailers in Italy, Egypt, Saudi Arabia, and the Philippines. A Tokyo store opened in 2000, in collaboration with the Tashiro Co., Ltd. beauty products retailer. This brought the total number of Caswell-Massey stores worldwide to 18. In addition to its overseas licensees, Caswell-Massey had 15 U.S. stores in 2002. The company planned to add two stores per year through 2007.

The reintroduction of Casma as Casma Stepping Out was accompanied by the company's first use of nontraditional packaging. An ornate rhinestone, gold, and enamel shoe symbolic of the flapper era held the perfume. A new product, Bathtub Gin bubble bath, followed the jazzy 1920s theme.

250th Anniversary in 2002

One of America's oldest companies, Caswell-Massey had a keen sense of history. As it celebrated its 250th anniversary it brought out limited editions of nearly all of the 33 fragrances it had ever sold. They were packaged in apothecary-style glass-stopper bottles with pewter labels. Number Six Cologne, George Washington's favorite, was still number one among the company's men's fragrances.

Ever immersed in history, Caswell-Massey supplied the unique PBS reality series *Frontier House* with the types of toiletries the pioneers used. The series placed three families in a rural setting, and limited them to what would have been available to homesteaders in 1883. Caswell-Massey supplied such products as toothbrushes, 3½-pound blocks of Castile soap, and straightedge razors.

Principal Competitors

Bath & Body Works; The Body Shop; Compagnie de Provence; Crabtree & Evelyn Ltd.; Origins (Estée Lauder Cos.).

Further Reading

Chiacchio, Cassandra, ''Caswell-Massey Gets a Leg Up on Fragrance,'' *WWD,* May 4, 2001, p. 8.

Cohen, Edith, ''Revolutionary Ventures: Surviving and Profiting Through the Centuries,'' *New York Times,* Sec. 3, June 30, 1985, p. 4.

Collins, Glen, ''Milton Taylor, 86, Co-Owner of Caswell-Massey Pharmacies,'' *New York Times Current Events Edition,* November 9, 1994, p. D27.

Davis, Donald A., ''Cosmetics: The Demarcation Lines Begin to Unravel,'' *DCI,* June 1994, pp. 28ff.

Del Franco, Mark, "Synergies 250 Years in the Making," *Catalog Age,* March 15, 2001, pp. 47–48.

Drake, Diana Lasseter, "Has Caswell-Massey Found Its Elixir for Survival?," *Business News New Jersey,* October 11, 1999, pp. 22f.

Ehlert, Athena, and Mary Forsell, "The Fragrant World of Caswell-Massey," *Victoria,* July 1996, pp. 34f.

Grossman, Andrea M., "Caswell-Massey Turns 250," *WWD,* February 8, 2002, p. 10.

——, "A 21st-Century Look for Historic Caswell-Massey," *Women's Wear Daily,* Best Beauty Retailers Supp., October 2000, p. 12.

Hoppe, Karen, "Caswell-Massey: America's Oldest Drugstore," *Drug & Cosmetic Industry,* November 1991, pp. 50ff.

Howe, Marvine, "Ralph Taylor, 89, 50-Year Co-Owner of Pharmacy Chain," *New York Times Current Events Edition,* June 26, 1993, p. A27.

Jones, Lamont, "Sweet Smell of Success; Caswell-Massey Marks 250 Years of Pleasing Customers Who Have Included U.S. Presidents," *Pittsburgh Post-Gazette,* May 12, 2002, p. G11.

Kagan, Cara, "Caswell-Massey Tries Its First Love Potion," *WWD,* June 2, 1995, p. 6.

McCue, Janet, "Lathering in Luxury," *Plain Dealer* (Cleveland), June 30, 1994, p. 1F.

MacDonald, Veronica, "Caswell-Massey Thrives on History: History Abounds in Caswell-Massey's Manhattan Store," *happi-Household & Personal Products Industry,* December 2001, pp. 48f.

Marchie, Melanie, "Lasting Luxury: Fine Fragrance Update," *happi-Household & Personal Products Industry,* November 2001, pp. 63ff.

Messina, Joseph R., "Everything Old Is New Again," *DCI,* November 1995, pp. 82f.

"Ms. Robinson, Mr. Hamilton," *New York Times,* October 10, 1999.

Murphy, Victoria, "Will It Stay Afloat?," *Forbes,* August 12, 2002, pp. 104f.

Naughton, Julie, "Caswell-Massey's New Direction," *WWD,* October 1, 1999, p. 10.

"Package of the Month: Caswell-Massey's Rosewater & Glycerine Hand Creme," *Drug & Cosmetic Industry,* January 1998, p. 44.

Puente, Maria, "Caswell-Massey: 250 Fragrant Years in the Beauty Biz," *USA Today,* February 8, 2002.

Rigg, Cynthia, "New Owners Repowder Image of Struggling Firm," *Crain's New York Business,* May 14, 1990, p. 15.

Robinson, Anne, "How I Think of New Products," *Star-Ledger* (Newark, N.J.), March 19, 2002, p. 16.

Roman, Monica, "Peter Hsu: Will America's Oldest Soapmaker Get Bubbling?," *Business Week,* May 6, 1991, p. 70.

"Rub-a-Dub-Dub, What Tales of the Tub!," *Plain Dealer* (Cleveland), December 26, 1991.

Shaw, Anita, "The New Age of Gift Giving," *Soap & Cosmetics,* March 2000, p. 36.

Simon, Ellen, "Sweet Smell of Success; Caswell-Massey Gets Back to Its Roots," *Star-Ledger* (Newark, N.J.), March 17, 2000, p. 53.

——, "You, Too, Can Smell Like a Pioneer," *Star-Ledger* (Newark, N.J.), March 13, 2002, p. 45.

Sparks, Debra, "Saving a Troubled Brand," *Business Week,* September 11, 2000, p. F22.

Tode, Chantal, "Bathroom Chic Goes Mail Order," *WWD,* January 9, 1998, p. 10.

Werner, Ray O., "Legal Developments in Marketing," *Journal of Marketing,* April 1990, pp. 95f.

Winegar, Karin, "Clean Shaving: Traditional Gear Makes a Comeback," *Minneapolis Star and Tribune,* December 21, 1986.

—Frederick C. Ingram

Chi-Chi's Inc.

10200 Linn Station Road
Louisville, Kentucky 40223
U.S.A.
Telephone: (502) 426-3900
Fax: (502) 339-4204
Web site: http://www.chi-chis.com

Wholly Owned Subsidiary of Prandium Inc.
Incorporated: 1975
Employees: 8,900
Sales: $205.8 million (2000)
NAIC: 722110 Full-Service Restaurants

Chi-Chi's Inc., owned by Prandium Inc., is a chain of 130 Mexican full-service restaurants that can be found in Illinois, Indiana, Maryland, Michigan, Ohio, Pennsylvania, Virginia, and Wisconsin. In addition to company-owned stores, there is also a handful of Chi-Chi's franchise locations. After a booming start in the late 1970s and a growth spurt in the early 1980s, Chi-Chi's sales and store count declined. In the late 1990s and into 2000, the company embarked on a new marketing campaign designed to revitalize the Chi-Chi's image. While the firm remains a well-known player on the Mexican restaurant scene, it continues to face staunch competition in the industry.

Origins

Established in 1975 by Mexican restaurant magnate Marno McDermott and investor Max McGee, Chi-Chi's specialty was Sonoran-style Mexican food. McDermott, a long-time fan of Mexican food, had previously created a fast food concept entitled Zapata Foods after graduating from the University of Minnesota. Believing that there was indeed a demand for a full-service Mexican restaurant in the Midwest, McDermott sought out the help of McGee, a former professional football player who owned the Left Guard Bar/Restaurant in Minneapolis, Minnesota. Together, the pair opened Chi-Chi's Mexican Restaurante in a section of the downtown bar. Chi-Chi's, which took its name from the nickname of McDermott's wife, was an

instant success. First year sales surpassed the planned $400,000, climbing to $2 million.

McDermott's good fortune caught the eye of John Stephens, a Minnesota-based stockbroker. Stephens convinced McDermott to sell him the rights to operate and franchise Chi-Chi's restaurants. Shelly Frank, the vice-president of concept development at the Kentucky Fried Chicken fast food chain, was then called upon to run the new restaurant business. In 1977, Frank was named president and CEO, and company headquarters were moved to Louisville, Kentucky—Frank's hometown.

Starting in the early 1980s, Frank drove rapid expansion of company-owned stores. Spurred on by stores which frequently opened to sales of $70,000 or $80,000 a week, Chi-Chi's spread throughout the Midwest, where they had virtually no competition. From 1981 to 1983, company-owned restaurants soared from one to 46, and profits multiplied eleven-fold from the beginning of the decade to $9.1 million in 1983. In 1985 alone, 42 new Chi-Chi's opened, with 27 company-owned and 15 franchised. This increased total units by more than one-third, and company-owned units by 50 percent. In 1984, Chi-Chi's net income peaked at 16.7 million. By 1986, Chi-Chi's operated 200 restaurants.

Problems Arise: Mid- to Late 1980s

From 1984 to 1987, however, the chain's profitability began to slide. This coincided with an overall decline in the industry due to lowered alcohol consumption, saturated restaurant markets, maturing baby boomers, and the growing popularity of at-home food and entertainment options. Chi-Chi's was also showing weakness created by the stress of rapid expansion.

During its growth spurt, the chain had built 10,000 to 12,000 square foot restaurants, which were too large to operate profitably as the economy flattened out in the mid-1980s. In addition, Chi-Chi's had clustered restaurants in order to seize high market share in a given area, cutting average sales for individual units. There were also several failed attempts to penetrate new markets: nine company-owned units choked in New York City, as did three in New England. Franchises in Atlanta, Texas, New Mexico, and San Diego also failed to take root.

Company Perspectives:

At Chi-Chi's, Salsafication is more than a word. It's an attitude. It's a spirit. It's a way of life. Salsafication to us is ensuring that our guests are greeted with a smile and that they leave with one. During the Salsafication experience, our guests will enjoy fast friendly service and delicious food and drink served in a fun, festive atmosphere. It's what we're all about.

While Chi-Chi's had grown, it had neglected to create an effective corporate communication network. The corporate management was not in touch with the needs of field managers and franchisees, so that team spirit and confidence in the company was ebbing low. Franchisees were feeling uneasy, particularly after the Chapter 11 bankruptcy of Chi-Chi's Food Services Inc., an Oklahoma City-based franchise that was a subsidiary of Kelly Johnston Enterprises. But even in company-owned stores, management turnover had reached as high as 80 percent. Inconsistency in management translated to the customer as unreliable service and food. After their peak year in 1984, sales began to decline, and by 1986 total revenues had dropped from $269.3 million to $206 million, while net income bottomed at $9.1 million from $15.6 million.

When Shelly Frank retired in 1986, Hal Smith came on board as Chi-Chi's new leader, leaving his position as president and CEO of the Chili's restaurant chain. Smith identified three major problems in the company: declining store sales, poor unit profitability, and high management turnover. His recovery strategy focused on opening the lines of corporate communication and streamlining the bureaucracy. Smith gained the support of the corporate officers, all of whom had been hired by Frank, by having a face-to-face meeting with every middle and upper-level manager in order to get the lay of the land. He reduced corporate staff by 18 percent and redefined certain jobs.

Chi-Chi's held its first management conference in September 1987, bringing together over 200 general managers, area supervisors, regional directors, and executives to galvanize the team. Further, Smith encouraged direct communication between field managers and the home offices in Louisville. Franchisees were pleased to find Smith, who would personally return phone calls, far more accessible than his predecessor.

A former franchise owner was brought on as vice-president of franchise relations in 1987, and the independent operators were encouraged to develop and share ideas with the company. Consul Corp., which operated 40 restaurants, had pioneered the idea of the El Pronto walk-up units, which featured selections from the full Chi-Chi's menu. The company tested two small El-Prontos in Midwest malls. In turn, the company helped smaller franchisees cover the $45,000 costs of refurbishing units and stepped up communications and visits.

In company-owned stores, Smith cut paper work for store managers so that they could turn their attention to the customers. Managers' schedules, which had frequently ballooned to 80 hours and six days a week, were cut back to 50 to 55 hours a week with two consecutive days off. Managers' salaries were

also made more competitive. New bonus plans, health and life insurance plans, and a stock ownership program were instituted. Training was improved for managers, and employees and servers were encouraged to show their personality within the parameters of quality service. Inside of a year, management turnover was reduced to 35 percent.

Within two years, Smith had created a team of employees—from executives to managers and wait staff—that felt committed to working at Chi-Chi's. Financial benefits began to appear early in 1987, when same-store average volumes were up slightly for the first time in more than a year, and the second time in four years. Instead of expansion, Chi-Chi's had disposed of 21 marginal stores by April of 1988, taking a $20 million write-off against earnings. The chain planned to build only eight to ten new restaurants in fiscal 1988, down from the previous rate of 20 to 30 a year. Only five new stores were franchised.

Chi-Chi's also opened three new conceptual restaurants in the winter of 1987–88: Papanda's Border Café, Chajita's Mexican Café, and G.W. Sharkey's. Papanda's was a Mexican restaurant aimed at the southeastern and south central United States, where Chi-Chi's had previously failed; Chajita's was a fast food restaurant with touches of dining house atmosphere; and G.W. Sharkey's Oyster Bar and Grill was a fresh seafood restaurant. All three restaurants featured display mesquite grilling, informality, and a good price/value ratio.

Foodmaker Acquires Chi-Chi's: 1988

By 1988, all the refurbishment attracted an unwanted takeover bid from the Carlyle Group, a limited partnership that had recently become Chi-Chi's largest stockholder with 7.5 percent outstanding shares. Chi-Chi's commissioned First Boston Corp. to locate an investor to outbid Carlyle's offer of $200 million. Carlyle removed its bid in February of 1988, but in April the company was purchased by San Diego-based Foodmaker, Inc., the owner of Jack in the Box restaurants, then the country's fifth largest fast food chain. It purchased the 129 company-operated Chi-Chi's (there were also 77 franchises) for about $235 million in April of 1988. Chi-Chi's retained its own corporate staff while Hal Smith continued to head the company as a division of Foodmaker.

The chain did well for a period, hitting its best year in 1990 with sales of $450 million; things held steady in fiscal 1991, with pretax profits of $57.3 million on about the same amount of sales. Despite continued good management, the tight economy began taking a toll on the chain once again. In 1992, Chi-Chi's was still second in its segment, but sales had dropped to $445 million and guest counts were on the decline yet again throughout the 160 company-owned and 65 franchised restaurants. Segment leader Taco Bell threatened Chi-Chi's with its cheap eats and 4,000 outlets racking up sales of $3.3 billion. The competition proliferated as McDonald's restaurants offered a breakfast burrito, and restaurants of every stripe added Mexican food to their menus. In addition, non-Mexican restaurants were outstripping Chi-Chi's at the low-cost, fun atmosphere game. Dinner house chains like the Olive Garden, Cookers, and Macaroni Grills were stealing customers from Chi-Chi's with their appealing image of fresh food and hospitality.

To combat the slump in sales, Chi-Chi's introduced value-priced entrees at $3.99 and $4.99 and freshly prepared rice, beans, and beef. Smith felt that customers were not aware of the amount of "scratch" cooking that went on in Chi-Chi's kitchens, and the chain began emphasizing the fresh food in their advertising. Tortilla making machines were brought into the lobbies of company-owned stores to give customers an immediate message of freshness.

The restaurant's original menu of Sonoran cuisine was all but replaced by Tex-Mex and grilled items. The menu thrust was to take popular American foods and "mexicanize" them; the chain was experimenting with items such as Mexican pasta with blue-corn fettucine, Mexican pizza as an entree, and Mexican stir fry.

In June 1992, Smith quit Chi-Chi's unexpectedly, citing personal reasons. A year earlier, Mike Fiori, Smith's vice-president, had left the chain. Thus, with Smith's departure, only two senior executives remained who had extensive Chi-Chi's experience. Kenneth R. Williams, executive vice-president of Jack in the Box, was named to replace Smith.

In the summer of 1992, Chi-Chi's and its parent, Foodmaker, took over Consul Restaurant Corp., a major franchisee operating in Chapter 11 bankruptcy. Although Consul aligned with a group of unsecured creditors to counter the takeover bid, Chi-Chi's was able to purchase the publicly traded Consul's assets for $8.7 million in cash, taking over its operations and debt.

Consul was burdened with $17 million in debt, most of which stemmed from the company's failed expansion into Texas and the western markets in the mid-1980s, when fourteen units went under. Chi-Chi's kept 22 of the 26 Chi-Chi's units Consul operated, liquidating the remaining assets in order to pay Consul's creditors at 80 cents on the dollar. The Consul units, located in Minnesota, Wisconsin, Nebraska, and North and South Dakota were refurbished and upgraded, and new menu items were introduced, along with new uniforms, table wear, and Tortilla machines. Most of the field employees were retained, although CEO William D. Etter and chief financial officer Bob Lamp were replaced. Williams was tapped to be senior vice-president of Foodmaker just six months after taking the presidency of Chi-Chi's and was succeeded by long-time Chi-Chi's employee Joe Micatrotto.

In 1993, the chain continued to see same-store sales slip. Store makeovers that ran to $200,000 per unit and featured a festive color scheme with banners, striped neon lighting, new tiling and wood, a sun room and a display cart featuring an array of fresh fruit were continued. Spinach quesadillas were introduced, while advertising featured "Fiesta for Two," a complete dinner package for $14.99.

Family Restaurants Takes Control: 1994

Early in 1994, Chi-Chi's was acquired by Family Restaurants Inc. Family Restaurants was formed after the Chapter 11 bankruptcy reorganization of Restaurant Enterprises Group, which already owned Chi-Chi's top competitor El Torito. The chains were brought together under one parent, newly named Family Restaurants. Although each retained its individual name and style, the marriage created the first coast-to-coast chain of full-service Mexican restaurants, comprising 315 units, including some Casa Gallardo establishments as well as other divisions. The merger also made Family Restaurants one of the five or six largest operators of full-service restaurants, with a total of 680 units in all.

Foodmaker exchanged the 237-unit chain for a 40 percent stake in the new venture and approximately $200 million in cash. They shared ownership of Family Restaurants with Apollo Advisers L.P., and Green Equity Investors L.P. Micatrotto was brought in to lead the restructured Family Restaurants. Barry Krantz assumed leadership of Family's Mexican division in February of 1995. By the mid-1990s, Chi-Chi's was strengthened by its merger with El Torito, but the chain continued to face the stiff competition that characterized the food service business in the early 1990s.

In fact, Chi-Chi's remained plagued by problems related to both image and competition throughout the remaining years of the 1990s and into the new century. By 1996, sales had fallen off to $278 million. Even as the firm continued to revamp its menu and advertising, it came under fire for its high-fat menu by the consumer advocacy group Center for the Science in the Public Interest. In dire need of drastic changes, Chi-Chi's hired a new advertising company and adopted the slogan, "Life Always Needs a Little Salsa." Its menu was updated with fresher, healthier selections while old favorites were given new plate presentations. Stores were also remodeled to compete with the new modern looks of chains such as Don Pablo's, whose restaurants had open floor plans with high ceilings, water fountains, and plants.

Chi-Chi's also attempted to stay ahead of competition by offering a line of takeout products that could be ordered online through the Chi-Chi's Web site and then picked up at a local restaurant. In 1999, the firm unveiled its "Get Salsafied" advertising campaign, which was followed by traveling Volkswagen Beetles that were adorned with Chi-Chi's advertising and sombreros. The "Bug Tour" was initially launched in 1999 in Philadelphia and New Jersey and moved into its major market areas during 2001 when the restaurants began touting their "Sizzlin New Menu."

Despite the company's efforts, sales dropped from $227.7 million in 1999 to $205.8 million in 2001. Store count also fell from 150 company-owned and 15 franchised locations in 1999 to 137 company-owned and seven franchises in 2001. In order to better position itself for future growth, Chi-Chi's parent company, Prandium Inc.—the new name was adopted in 1999—began a restructuring program in 2001 at its headquarters in California and at Chi-Chi's headquarters in Louisville. Kevin S. Relyea took over as chairman, president, and CEO of Prandium and also remained at the helm at Chi-Chi's. Overburdened by debt, Prandium declared Chapter 11 bankruptcy in May 2002. Its reorganization plan was approved by the U.S. Bankruptcy Court in July of that year.

While Chi-Chi's had yet to regain the momentum of its early years, the company forged ahead with its advertising and remodeling efforts. With nearly 20 million customers under its belt, management felt certain its reorganization would pay off. Whether or not Chi-Chi's would be able to combat its harsh competition in the years to come, however, remained to be seen.

Principal Competitors

Applebee's International Inc.; El Chico Restaurants Inc.; Mexican Restaurants Inc.; Avado Brands Inc.

Further Reading

Beirne, Mike, "What Does It Take to Stop Traffic? Ask Chi-Chi's," *Brandweek*, February 5, 2001, p. 40.

Carlino, Bill, "Chi-Chi's, El Torito Preen for Marriage," *Nation's Restaurant News*, August 9, 1993, pp. 3, 73.

——, "Micatrotto Steps Up, Fills Chi-Chi's Top Spot," *Nation's Restaurant News*, January 4, 1993, pp. 3, 80.

Cebrzynski, Gregg, "Chi-Chi's Revamps Menu to Start Mexican Food Revolution," *Nation's Restaurant News*, May 15, 2000, p. 14.

"The Changing Face of Chi-Chi's," *Restaurant Business*, March 1, 1988, pp. 146–63.

"Chi-Chi's: The Newest Challenge," *Restaurant Business*, August 10, 1988, pp. 116–17.

Krummert, Bob, "Hot Stuff Coming Through," *Restaurant Hospitality*, May 2002, p. 15.

Martin, Richard, "REGI Finalizes Deal to Acquire Chi-Chi's," *Nation's Restaurant News*, November 8, 1993, pp. 1+.

O'Keegan, Peter O., "Chi-Chi's Prexy Smith Quits," *Nation's Restaurant News*, June 8, 1992, pp. 1, 49.

——, "Consul, Creditors Team Up to Oppose Chi-Chi's Takeover," *Nation's Restaurant News*, April 27, 1992, pp. 1, 58.

"Prandium Gets Court OK for Ch. 11 Reorganization," *Nation's Restaurant News*, July 8, 2002, p. 8.

Van Houten, Ben, "Spicing it Up; The Once Mighty Chi-Chi's Has Lost Its Zing," *Restaurant Business*, May 15, 1997, p. 49.

—Elaine Belsito
—update: Christina M. Stansell

Cintas Corporation

6800 Cintas Boulevard
Cincinnati, Ohio 45262
U.S.A.
Telephone: (513) 459-1200
Fax: (513) 573-4130
Web site: http://www.cintas-corp.com

Public Company
Incorporated: 1929 as Acme Overall & Rag Laundry
Employees: 23,000
Sales: $2.3 billion (2002)
Stock Exchanges: NASDAQ
Ticker Symbol: CTAS
NAIC: 812331 Linen Supply; 561499 All Other Business
  Support Services; 315225 Men's and Boys' Cut and
  Sew Work Clothing Manufacturing; 315239 Women's
  and Girls' Cut and Sew Other Outerwear
  Manufacturing

Cintas Corporation is the leading supplier of rental uniforms in the United States, with a market share of around 25 percent. It serves some 500,000 customers in North America. Cintas primarily rents its uniforms, and then provides laundry service, pick up and delivery, and related services. The company also provides entrance mats, sanitation supplies, and cleanroom supplies. Through its Xpect First Aid division, the company also delivers first aid kits and safety devices and trains workers in first aid and in Occupational Health and Safety Administration (OSHA) compliance. Cintas also sells its uniforms, as well as accessories such as hats and belts. The company runs 13 garment manufacturing plants and hundreds of laundry facilities and owns a fleet of approximately 3,000 delivery trucks. The company is highly automated, with state-of-the-art manufacturing and distribution facilities allowing for rapid order turnaround. Cintas grew quickly through acquisitions in the 1990s and absorbed a large competitor, Omni Services, Inc., in 2002. The company is publicly traded, with over 20 percent of the shares in the hands of chairman Richard Farmer.

Depression-era Origins

The Cintas saga is a literal rags-to-riches story. Patriarch Richard Farmer started out as a rag man who, with his son Herschell, built up a thriving industrial linen business in the 1930s and 1940s. But it was third-generation leader Richard T. Farmer who would guide the company into uniform rental in the late 1950s and lead a trend-setting consolidation of that industry in the 1980s and 1990s. Called a ''visionary'' by his second-in-command, Farmer pioneered new fabrics, instituted modern management and control systems, and expanded his target market from industrial to service businesses, among other innovations. In the process, he became one of Cincinnati's wealthiest and most influential businessmen.

The foundations of the family enterprise date to the 1930s, when Richard ''Doc'' Farmer started a rag business. Born in 1884, Farmer joined the John Robinson traveling circus as an animal trainer at the age of 14. There he met and married a trapeze artist named Amelia Boven. According to a 1962 article in the *Post & Times-Star* (Cincinnati), a tragic accident ended both performers' careers in 1908. A more recent account of these early days notes that this phase in the family history ended when the circus closed due to the Great Depression.

Forced from his profession, Farmer dabbled in amateur boxing, blacksmithing, and railroading before turning to junk collecting in 1929. He soon concentrated his efforts on salvaging household rags, which he would launder and sell to factories as clean-up cloths. It was not long before this business evolved into a rag rental service, with Farmer completing the recycling loop by picking up dirty rags at the plants, washing them, and returning them to the customer. Farmer moved his business and family from northern Kentucky across the Ohio River to Cincinnati in 1936. By this time, the Acme Overall & Rag Laundry had grown enough to warrant conversion of a local bath house into a laundry. Joined by his adopted son Herschell, Farmer and his family painstakingly refurbished the building at night and on weekends. Unfortunately, tragedy struck the Farmers a second time when the business suffered heavy damage from a major flood in 1937. The family quickly rebuilt, resuming business by the end of the following year. Herschell assumed leadership of the company upon his father's death in 1952 and carried on much as his father had.

Expansion into Uniform Rentals

Rapid growth at the family company began in the late 1950s, following the arrival of Richard T. Farmer, son of Herschell. Born in 1934, young Richard graduated from Miami University of Ohio in 1956 and joined the U.S. Marines. His stint as an officer was cut short, however, and Richard was discharged for medical reasons in 1957. He returned home that year and joined the family business. The young graduate was brimming with new ideas, chief among them an urge to expand into uniform rental. Scarred by the financial struggles of the Great Depression, Herschell strongly resisted his son's notion that the company should borrow to finance growth. However, Richard's youthful enthusiasm soon won him over; in 1957, Herschell relinquished day-to-day management of the business to his 23-year-old son.

The company immediately began to experiment with uniform rental. Within two years, this line of business had grown to such an extent that the firm changed its name to the more inclusive Acme Uniform & Shop Towel Supply Co. According to a 1962 profile of the father-son team in the *Post & Times-Star*, revenues multiplied six-fold in just five years. During this period Acme rented uniforms to individual, mostly blue-collar, businesses ranging from large industrial plants to corner auto repair shops. In the 1960s, Richard hit on the first of several innovations that would help make his company an industry leader. Up to this time, most industrial uniforms were fashioned from all-cotton fabric, which required a great deal of ironing and could only be expected to last a year. The development of easy-care poly-cotton blends in the mid-1960s presented a unique opportunity for the company. Made of 65 percent cotton and 35 percent polyester, the fabric resisted wrinkling but held a crease. Uniforms made from the new blend could last at least twice as long as cotton ones. Richard Farmer drew up exclusive contracts with the developers of this new material and made major investments in the conversion of his plant from soap-and-water laundering to the dry-cleaning that was then the ideal care for the new blend. By 1966, Acme was laundering about 80 tons of uniforms a week and making annual revenues of $1.8 million.

Richard soon proved himself a forward-looking businessman. With a view to taking the family company public in the future, he formed what was essentially a holding company, Satellite Corp., in the late 1960s. Funded with $400,000 in equity raised by Farmer and his 23-year-old controller, Robert Kohlhepp, Satellite established new uniform plants throughout the Midwest's major cities, starting with Cleveland, in 1968. Satellite and Acme merged two years later, and the unified company's name was changed to Cintas in 1972. Farmer had originally hoped to raise additional growth funds by taking the company public in 1973 but found equity markets inhospitable to initial public offerings at that time.

Cintas tapped the "corporate identity" segment of the uniform market in the late 1960s and early 1970s. Richard Farmer broke into this market by convincing companies of the benefits uniformed employees bring to the workplace. As Susan Avery of the trade magazine *Purchasing* noted in 1994, "Employees in uniform are perceived to be trained, competent, and dependable. . . . [They] also help convey images of cleanliness, safety, and security." Acme designed uniforms especially for each segment, incorporating corporate logos and signature colors in highly functional clothing tailored for each particular work environment. Working with national companies compelled Cintas to grow geographically in order to service its new customers; by 1972, it had established offices throughout Ohio and in Chicago, Detroit, and Washington, D.C. Sales surpassed the $10 million mark in 1973. Within two years, Cintas boasted operations in 13 states.

IPO Presages Acquisition Spree in 1980s

Richard Farmer finally took his company public in 1983, selling a minority stake on the over-the-counter market at $17 per share. The equity sale signaled the beginning of a string of acquisitions that would catapult Cintas to the highest ranks of the uniform rental industry. Though some regional mergers and acquisitions had occurred before this time, the 1980s witnessed an unprecedented consolidation of this service industry, which shrunk from about 1,600 mom-and-pop companies in 1981 to less than 800 by the early 1990s. Cintas was one of a handful of trend-setting companies, among them Unitog Co.; UniFirst Corp.; G & K Services, Inc.; and the leader, Aramark Uniform Services Inc. (formerly Aratex, Inc.), a subsidiary of Aramark Corporation.

Over the course of the 1980s, Cintas expanded into 17 new geographic markets via savvy—and often small—acquisitions. Revenues doubled from $63 million in 1983 to $123.7 million in 1987, then doubled again by 1989, to $285 million. By the early 1990s, the company had a presence in three-fourths of the nation's 100 largest markets, and its market share had more than doubled from about 3.5 percent in 1983 to ten percent. Significantly, only about one-third of Cintas' growth during this period was generated by acquisitions, with the remainder coming from organic growth.

In the latter years of the decade, Cintas spearheaded the uniform industry's expansion from a blue-collar base into more tailored uniforms for hotel and motel employees, restaurant workers, and even bank employees. Within its core airline constituency, for example, the company moved from coveralls for baggage handlers and mechanics to uniforms for pilots, flight attendants, and other customer service workers. By the mid-1990s, major national clients included Wal-Mart, Delta, Coca-Cola, Pepsi, Northwest Airlines, Chevron, Jiffy Lube, Sunoco, Aamco, Safety Kleen, and Chemlawn.

Growth Continues in Early 1990s

From 1992 to 1997, Cintas added 70 new cities to its roster of service areas. As it grew, the company also focused on improving its productivity, committing millions to research and development each year. For example, it brought in automated manufacturing systems featuring computerized design, cutting,

Key Dates:

1929: Richard Farmer begins a rag salvage business.
1952: Farmer dies, and the business passes to his son Herschell.
1957: Herschell's son Richard takes over the business and begins to expand into uniform rental.
1972: The company's name is changed to Cintas.
1983: Cintas goes public.
1997: The company moves into the first aid market.
1999: Cintas acquires Unitog.
2002: Omni Services, Inc. is acquired.

and embroidery machines, while electronic data interchange systems used bar-coding to manage inventory, processing, and distribution. Mechanization of laundering facilities cut staffing in those operations in half.

Cintas went international with the 1995 acquisition of Toronto's Cadet Uniform Services Ltd. While geographic diversification such as this continued to be key to growth, the company also experimented with new product lines during this period. In 1997, Cintas acquired two businesses that supplied OSHA-required first-aid kits to companies. With only $18 million in sales that year, this new business segment was little more than an interesting sideline at first. The company quickly assembled four major brands through acquisition, and over the next three years picked up over 100 small first aid companies.

In the mid-1990s, Richard Farmer initiated a management transition that would culminate in his exit from Cintas. In 1995, he turned over the chief executive office and presidency to his longtime right-hand man, Robert Kohlhepp. In 1997, Richard's son Scott Farmer was promoted to president, setting up the fourth generation of Farmers to lead the company. Meanwhile, the elder Farmer concentrated on broad strategic initiatives with a view to capturing an ever-larger share of the latent market for uniforms.

Leading the Market in the Late 1990s

Growth continued through acquisitions during the late 1990s and into the 2000s, while the uniform rental industry as a whole also continued to expand. Census Bureau statistics showed the uniform rental industry growing at a rate of over eight percent a year over the late 1990s, and Cintas management believed that there were many more business sectors left that would benefit from uniforms. The company had an impressive record of rising sales and profits, with growth in the double digits through the late 1990s. This served to boost Cintas's stock price, and the company was able to make many acquisitions by swapping its valuable shares. Between 1997 and 1999, the company acquired 65 companies. Most were small companies in the uniform rental business, with some providing first aid supplies and services, a growing segment for Cintas. Some were larger companies, such as Uniforms to You, which Cintas bought in 1998. Uniforms to You was a private company based in Chicago, with sales of around $150 million. Sales for Cintas in 1998 were over $1 billion. Then, in 1999, Cintas made its largest acquisition yet,

taking up one of its prime rivals, Kansas City-based Unitog Co. The transaction, which was paid for in Cintas stock, was valued at roughly $357 million. Unitog ran a uniform rental operation in 24 states and in Canada, and it had close to 60 plants. With this new purchase under its belt, Cintas increased its market share to about 25 percent. It became the largest company in the uniform rental industry, surpassing Aramark for the first time. Integration of the new company, however, was not altogether smooth. Within six months, three-quarters of Unitog's sales force had resigned.

By 1999, Cintas's operations had grown to over 200 uniform rental facilities across the United States. It had expanded its manufacturing facilities from four to 13; it had six distribution centers; its cleanroom business had grown to six facilities; and its first aid business now had 32 business centers. About 4 million people put on a Cintas uniform every day, yet the company still saw room in the market for more penetration. The uniform rental market in total was worth about $10 billion annually in the late 1990s, but Cintas management thought that figure could still grow to around $31 billion. The company's research showed that some 37 million people worked in occupations where uniforms could or should be used. The company seemed successful in expanding into the ancillary area of first aid, too, assembling an array of small companies and unifying them into one brand, which it debuted in 2000 as Xpect First Aid. The first aid division and other services outside of uniform rental still accounted for less than a quarter of the firm's revenue, however.

As the industry leader, Cintas was nevertheless still intent on growing and consolidating. In 2002, the company spent $22 million to acquire certain portions of the uniform manufacturing and marketing division of the Missouri-based laundry company Angelica Corp. One month after the Angelica sale was completed, Cintas announced it had bought out Omni Services, Inc., in what was its largest acquisition, surpassing the Unitog deal of two years earlier. Omni Services, of Culpepper, Virginia, was owned by the French company Filuxel, S.A., and it had apparently suggested the merger. Omni had annual sales of around $300 million, with 90,000 customers in over 30 states. The merger was expected to bump Cintas's sales to around $2.5 billion, and it would clearly continue to lead the industry over the next several years.

Principal Subsidiaries

Respond Industries, Inc.; Xpect First Aid Corp.

Principal Competitors

Aramark Corp.; G&K Services, Inc.; UniFirst Corp.

Further Reading

Bosquez, Kristina D'Aun, "Clothing Supplier Finds Success by Keeping Things Uniform," *Business Press* (Dallas), July 23, 1999, p. 1.
"Cintas," *Fortune*, July 26, 1993, p. 105.
Epatko, Elena, "Suppliers Can Help Meet Customer Desires," *Purchasing*, November 24, 1994, pp. 9–11.
Fasig, Lisa Biank, "Growth Plan Fits Farmer," *Cincinnati Enquirer*, July 8, 1996, p. 1D.

Fields, Gregg, "Cintas Is Uniformly Successful," *Cincinnati Enquirer*, October 23, 1985, p. E1.

Frazier, Mya, "Cintas Seeing Fruits of Last Year's Unitog Buyout," *Business Courier Serving Cincinnati-Northern Kentucky*, December 8, 2000, p. 16.

Giese, William, "Unappetizing Suggestions for Tasty Stock Profits," *Kiplinger's Personal Finance Magazine*, October 1991, pp. 73–6.

Head, Lauren Lawley, "Cintas Takes First-Aid Business Nationwide," *Business Courier Serving Cincinnati-Northern Kentucky*, October 13, 2000, p. 6.

Jaffe, Thomas, "The Uniform Fits," *Forbes*, November 12, 1990, p. 368.

Jankowski, David, "Cintas Expanding Locally To Meet Demand," *Cincinnati Business Courier*, December 15, 1986, pp. 3–4.

McLean, Bethany, "An Urge to Merge," *Fortune*, January 13, 1997, pp. 158–59.

Paul, Gail L., "Cintas Tailors Steady Growth Into Tradition," *Cincinnati Business Courier*, January 18, 1988, pp. 8–9.

Peale, Cliff, "The Next Carl Lindner," *Cincinnati Business Courier*, December 14, 1992, pp. 1–3.

Pettibon, Sula, "Cincinnati-Based Uniform Firm Cintas Corp. Buys Rock Hill, S.C. Company," *Knight-Ridder/Tribune Business News*, May 22, 2002.

Rodda, Kelly, "Cintas to Break Ground on $2.4M, 57,000sf Plant," *Business Press* (Fort Worth), March 20, 1998, p. 1.

Schifrin, Matthew, "Overdressed," *Forbes*, November 15, 1999, p. 302.

Sheets, Ken, "When Boring Stocks Are Beautiful," *Kiplinger's Personal Finance Magazine*, February 1995, pp. 81–3.

Smith, Sarah, "Cintas Corp.," *Fortune*, August 1, 1988, p. 72.

The Spirit Is the Difference: The Explanation of the Corporate Culture of Cintas Corporation, Cincinnati: Cintas Corporation, 1991.

—April D. Gasbarre
—update: A. Woodward

CompuDyne Corporation

7249 National Drive
Hanover, Maryland 21076
U.S.A.
Telephone: (410) 712-0275
Fax: (410) 712-0677
Web site: http://www.compudyne.com

Public Company
Incorporated: 1952
Employees: 950
Sales: $127.39 million
Stock Exchanges: NASDAQ
Ticker Symbol: CDCY
NAIC: 334511 Search, Detection, Navigation, Guidance, Aeronautical, and Nautical System and Instrument Manufacturing; 56162 Security Systems Services; 54171 Research and Development in the Physical, Engineering, and Life Sciences; 541512 Computer Systems Design Services

CompuDyne Corporation is the leading U.S. manufacturer of physical security systems, corrections and emergency dispatch software, and blast- and attack-resistant building materials, all of which are produced by subsidiaries that include Norment Security Group, Norshield Security Products, Quanta Systems, Data Control Systems, CorrLogic, Fiber SenSys, and Tiburon. The company's primary customers are federal and state government agencies in the United States. CompuDyne head Marty Roenigk owns 25 percent of the firm's stock.

Early Years

CompuDyne Corporation was formed in Pennsylvania in 1952 to serve as a contractor for the U.S. Defense department through a subsidiary called CompuDyne Controls. In 1967, the firm started making acquisitions by buying a majority stake in American Custom Metals Co., Inc. of Cincinnati, Ohio. The next year, General Indicator Corporation of Pardeeville, Wisconsin, a sign manufacturer, and Hydra-Tool Company of Topeka, Kansas, were purchased.

In 1969, CompuDyne bought Melweb Signs, Inc. of Daytona Beach, Florida, and merged York-Shipley, Inc. of York, Pennsylvania, into the company. A deal to buy the Frimberger Group of companies backfired, however, and after a few months of ownership it was returned to the sellers, with CompuDyne keeping the outstanding shares of Sportsman's World of Bay City, Michigan, in compensation.

The company sold part of CompuDyne Controls in 1970 and transferred the remainder of that unit's operations to General Indicator Corp. the following year. Further acquisitions were made during the 1970s, including purchases of the Kolux Division of VLN Corporation in 1973, the NPI Illuminated Signs Division of Essex International, Inc. in 1974, the Republic Electric and Development Co. (REDCO) in 1976, and the Ocean Applied Research Corporation (OAR) in 1978. Along the way, 75 percent of Ovitron Corporation was acquired, and the American Custom Metals Co. was sold.

In 1981, CompuDyne purchased controlling interest in another defense-related company, Quanta Systems Corp. of Rockville, Maryland, as a first step toward acquisition of the entire firm. Three years later, General Indicator Corp., York-Shipley, and Melweb Signs, Inc., were merged into Robintech, Inc. in exchange for 80 percent of Robintech's stock. The move completed a Chapter 11 reorganization of Robintech, which was a maker of polyvinyl-chloride (PVC) pipe. For fiscal 1984, the company reported sales of $90.1 million, with net earnings of $218,000.

1985: Lydall Buys In

In the fall of 1985, company head Frank Kelley and his wife sold most of their stake in CompuDyne to Lydall, Inc., which consisted of 37 percent of the company's stock. Kelley also resigned from the firm and was replaced by two Lydall executives, David Stevens (as president and CEO) and David Clark, Jr. (as board chairman). Lydall was a maker of industrial materials, including fiber and elastomeric components.

Several months after these changes, CompuDyne undertook a major restructuring that included selling the billboard operations of Melweb Signs for $16 million. The following summer, the company bought Advanced Navigation, Inc., a maker of air

Company Perspectives:

CompuDyne is an industry leader in sophisticated security products, integration, and technology for the public security markets. CompuDyne operates within four business segments, each with leading positions in physical and electronic security and technology-based solutions.

and marine navigation systems, for $1.2 million. In the fall, CompuDyne's Robintech subsidiary sold its REDCO division to Jetronic Industries, Inc. for $4 million, and discontinued manufacture of PVC pipe. Another acquisition took place in early 1987, when Vega-Cantley Instrument Co. of London was purchased. Vega-Cantley, with annual sales of $3 million, made airborne transponders and ground-based radar systems for the British Ministry of Defense.

CompuDyne was now organized into two divisions: the Defense Electronics group, which provided electronic equipment and systems and related services for American and foreign military intelligence and industrial customers, and the General Indicator group, which manufactured signs for the petroleum, fast food, and convenience store industries, as well as electronic scoreboards and other custom electric signs. In the fall of 1988, the two divisions were reduced to one when CompuDyne sold General Indicator to Everbrite Electric Signs for $7 million.

More changes took place in the spring of 1989 when chairman David Clark took on the roles of president and CEO from David Stevens, who stayed aboard as president of the Vega operation. That unit was subsequently sold, along with CompuDyne's Ocean Applied Research subsidiary. Both were purchased by Carlton Industries, Inc. of Vienna, Virginia, the home base of Vega. This was a difficult period for CompuDyne, which was experiencing financial stress due to reduced revenues and a sizable debt load. In March of 1991, the company's stock was delisted by the AMEX and moved to the over-the-counter market. Two years later, in an effort to diversify, Quanta Systems formed a division called QDI to market home improvement products and security systems in the Baltimore-Washington area.

1995: Enter Marty Roenigk

By 1995, CompuDyne's annual revenues had dropped to just $12.3 million from upwards of $95 million a decade earlier. The firm was in dire straits, and bankruptcy appeared imminent. Fortunately for the company, a white knight appeared in the form of Martin "Marty" Roenigk, chairman and majority owner of MicroAssembly Systems, which made devices that were used in manufacturing processes involving tiny screws. A reverse merger was effected in which MicroAssembly was acquired by CompuDyne in exchange for 1.25 million shares of preferred stock, with Roenigk appointed chairman and CEO. CompuDyne's outgoing head, Norman Silberdick, bought the company's home-improvement unit upon his departure.

The Cleveland-born Roenigk had gotten his MBA from the University of Chicago in 1967, then earned a CPA while working for Arthur Andersen in the late 1960s. After a stint with the

U.S. Army's Finance Corps in Vietnam, he joined the Travelers Corporation, where he remained for the next 23 years. During the latter part of his tenure there he served as Vice-President for Corporate Strategy and Research, a position in which he gained much experience in corporate planning, operations research, and acquisitions and divestitures while working with small companies around the United States. In addition, he acquired controlling interest in MicroAssembly Systems, along with partner Alan Markowitz.

Following its merger with MicroAssembly, CompuDyne was reorganized to focus upon its strengths—the Quanta Services and Data Control Systems units. Quanta provided engineering and security-related services, largely to U.S. government agencies, while Data Control produced telemetry and telecommunications products for military, aeronautic, and satellite use.

By the summer of 1996, the firm had rebounded enough to acquire Shorrock Electronic Systems, a U.S. subsidiary of the British Rentokil PLC. Shorrock designed and installed physical security and surveillance systems for courthouses and prisons and had recently begun to emphasize maintenance services, which provided a good fit with CompuDyne's long-term strategy of developing recurrent business. After the purchase, Shorrock was renamed Quanta SecurSystems. An agreement to distribute the products of sister unit Shorrock Integrated Systems led to the creation of another CompuDyne entity, SYSCO Security Systems.

The year 1996 also saw CompuDyne's Quanta Systems unit designated the sole worldwide warranty repair and maintenance facility for the IriScan biometric identification system, a deal which gave Quanta the job of performing most major IriScan installations. Sales for 1996 were up dramatically over 1995, at $22.1 million compared to $10.3 million. During the year, and continuing into 1997, the company continued to strengthen its operations, which resulted in the development of a healthy backlog of orders.

Norment and Norshield Acquired in 1998

In late 1998, CompuDyne bought Norment Industries, Inc. and Norshield Corporation from Apogee Enterprises for $22.5 million, funding for which was obtained through William Blair & Co. The two new acquisitions, along with Norment's subsidiaries Airteq, Trentech, SESCO, and EMSS (Engineered Maximum Security Systems), had annual sales of approximately $80 million. Norment was a leading designer and builder of prison and courthouse security systems worldwide, while Norshield made bullet resistant building products such as doors and windows, which were sold to U.S. embassies and other government and commercial clients. The acquisition of the two Montgomery, Alabama-based firms made CompuDyne the largest supplier of security products and systems integration services to prisons and courthouses in the United States. Roenigk had reportedly spent two years working out the deal.

Following these acquisitions, the company announced plans to expand the regional office system of Quanta SecurSystems to help market Norment products and maintenance services around the United States and to expand by 50 percent Norshield's manufacturing facility in Montgomery. New contracts for Norment were soon announced that included provision of electronic and pneumatic locking systems, closed circuit television, intercommunications and perimeter detection systems for a new 1400-bed prison in Lexington, Kentucky, and for a 900-bed Federal Correctional Institution in Petersburg, Virginia. These and other deals put Norment's work backlog at $80 million, a record for the firm. Terrorist attacks on two U.S. embassies in Africa during the year had also precipitated a huge surge in government orders for Norshield blast and attack-resistant building materials.

In the spring of 1999, CompuDyne completed acquisition of the Corrections Information Systems division of BI, Inc., a maker of inmate management software. After the $3.2 million deal was finalized, CompuDyne renamed the unit CorrLogic, Inc. At the same time, the firm was selling its MicroAssembly Systems business, which was purchased for $1.4 million by Penn Engineering & Manufacturing. CompuDyne subsequently moved its headquarters from MicroAssembly's home base of Willimantic, Connecticut, to Hanover, Maryland, and its stock began trading on the NASDAQ exchange. Although the company was headquartered on the East Coast, Roenigk himself lived in Eureka Springs, Arkansas, where he was restoring two National Historic Register-listed hotels. He also maintained a large collection of antique mechanical musical instruments.

November 1999 saw CompuDyne buy Ackley-Dornbach, a Milwaukee-based detention equipment contractor. After the purchase, the company announced plans to add electronic security products and maintenance services to Ackley-Dornbach's offerings. The acquisition was another step in the ongoing expansion of CompuDyne's regional office system.

During 2000, the company logged a number of new orders, including $22 million worth of equipment for a prison in New Jersey and $9 million worth for one in Maine. In the fall, Norment announced the availability of its MaxWall Modular Cell System, a prefabricated steel and concrete prison cell unit complete with doors, hardware, furniture, windows, plumbing,

and electrical systems. The company expected the product to generate $12 million in sales in its first year. CompuDyne also began offering the CorrMedica Institutional Health Care System, a medical records software program designed for use in prison hospitals.

In October 2000, the company reached an agreement to purchase Fiber SenSys, Inc., a maker of fiber-optic sensors for use in security systems, for $1.8 million. At year's end, CompuDyne reported record sales of $130.6 million and net earnings of $4.1 million.

2001: Further Expansion and Increased Profits

In May 2001, the company invested $6 million to buy 19.7 percent of Tiburon, Inc., the largest American maker of software used by fire and police department emergency-dispatch centers, as the first step in an acquisition of the entire company. After September's terrorist attacks on the World Trade Center and Washington, D.C., CompuDyne's stock price nearly doubled as investors sought out companies that offered security products. The firm's Norshield unit was already in the process of upgrading the doors and windows of U.S. embassies in 50 countries, work which had begun following the terrorist bombings of embassies in Africa. Norshield products had also been used in seven of the last eight Federal Reserve buildings, many federal courthouses, and at the White House.

A short time after the stock value rose, CompuDyne sold 1.1 million newly issued shares for $12 each to a group led by 14 institutional investors. William Blair Mezzanine Capital Partners II simultaneously sold 1.37 million shares in the company, and CompuDyne retired $9 million in debt owed to Blair.

In November, the company announced it was expanding its Bullet, Blast, and Attack Protection Division by purchasing a new 75,000-square-foot factory in Montgomery, Alabama. The $3 million facility would incorporate a $650,000 laser cutting machine and would increase production capacity by 40 percent. Since the 9/11 attacks, inquiries had been pouring in, and the company's order backlog was increasing at a rapid rate for work that included providing strengthened enclosures for nuclear power plants.

CompuDyne also introduced a new package of airport security products and services, including video badging and access control; bullet, blast, and attack-resistant products for entrance protection; fiber-optic perimeter sensing systems; shoreline attack detection systems; and emergency services dispatch and record management software. Orders for several of these systems were soon received from the U.S. Air Force for use in Southeast Asia, Europe, and at Cape Canaveral in Florida. Though sales for 2001 were down slightly from 2000, largely due to delays in a prison-construction project in New Jersey, newly received orders were expected to boost income to the $180 million mark during the next fiscal year.

In the spring of 2002, after several delays, the acquisition of Tiburon was completed. The company also announced the signing of several new multi-million dollar contracts with the state of California for installation of prison locking and inmate tracking software systems during the year.

CompuDyne Corporation's expertise in the blast- and attack-resistant building materials category made it a first choice for many government agencies and companies seeking greater protection in the post–9/11 world. When combined with its emergency services software and detection systems offerings, the firm covered a wide range of territory in the security and anti-terrorism fields. CompuDyne's largest business by volume, the manufacturing and servicing of detention and corrections equipment, was also one for which there remained strong demand.

Principal Subsidiaries

SYSCO Security Systems, Inc.; CompuDyne Corp. of Maryland; Quanta Systems Corp.; CompuDyne, Inc.; CorrLogic, Inc.; Norment Security Group, Inc.; Norshield Corp.; Norment Industries S.A. (Pty) Ltd. (South Africa); Fiber SenSys, Inc.; New Tiburon, Inc.

Principal Competitors

Armor Holdings, Inc.; ASSA ABLOY AB; Ingersoll-Rand Security and Safety; Wackenhut Corrections Corporation.

Further Reading

Adler, Carlye, "Safe and Sound," *Fortune Small Business*, July 1, 2002, p. 46.

Allen, Frank, "CompuDyne Sees Yr. Slightly in Black, '88 Shr. Net Over $1.67," *Dow Jones News Service*, December 23, 1987.

"Apogee to Sell Unit to CompuDyne for $22.5 Million," *Reuters News*, November 10, 1998.

Bruno, Michael P., "CompuDyne Secures Fiber SenSys for $1.8M," *Newsbytes News Network*, October 19, 2000.

Gladwell, Malcolm, "CompuDyne to Sell Large Part of its Defense Operations," *The Washington Post*, July 22, 1988, p. B2.

Glanz, William, "Security Products Firm Sees a Future Clear as Glass; The Threat of Terrorism Is Creating New Markets," *The Washington Times*, October 15, 2001, p. D8.

McCarthy, Ellen, "In a Dismal Week, CompuDyne Stock Posts Gain of 96%," *The Washington Post*, September 24, 2001, p. E3.

Woods, Bob, "CompuDyne Profit Up; Well Positioned for Acquisitions," *Newsbytes News Network*, March 1, 2000.

—Frank Uhle

COOKER

Cooker Restaurant Corporation

2609 West End Avenue, Suite 500
Nashville, Tennessee 37203
U.S.A.
Telephone: (615) 301-2665
Fax: (615) 301-2666
Web site: http://www.the-cooker.com

Public Company
Incorporated: 1986 as Cooker Bar and Grille
Employees: 2,984
Sales: $112.9 million (2001)
Stock Exchanges: OTC-Bulletin Board
Ticker Symbol: CGRT
NAIC: 722110 Full-Service Restaurants

Cooker Restaurant Corporation is a 37-unit casual dining restaurant chain, with locations in Florida, Michigan, Ohio, Tennessee, and Virginia. During the mid-1990s, revenues per restaurant averaged almost $3 million annually, which were among the highest for casual full-service restaurants. In 1996 alone, the company served over ten million meals. Slowing sales during the late 1990s, however, halted the firm's expansion efforts. Burdened by a heavy debt load, Cooker was forced to declare Chapter 11 bankruptcy in 2001. As part of its restructuring effort, the company closed 26 restaurants in Florida, Georgia, Indiana, Kentucky, Ohio, North Carolina, and Tennessee during 2001 and the first part of 2002.

Traditional Fare in the Mid-1980s

In 1984, The Cooker Restaurant Corporation was founded in Nashville, Tennessee, by G. Arthur Seelbinder, a former Wendy's franchisee, along with three others—Phil Hickey, Jerry Hornbeck, and trained chef Glenn Cockburn. Cockburn, a graduate of the Culinary Institute of America, who became director and senior vice-president of operations for the company, created most of the items on the Cooker menu. Cockburn developed the home-style recipes that included pot roast, lasagna, soups, meatloaf, fish, steaks, sandwiches, hamburgers, ribs, and chicken—all made from scratch—for their restaurants.

Cooker varied its menu with a wide assortment of salads and vegetables but originally set its sites on offering heartier fare with the intention of competing with the leaner menus served in trendier restaurants. They began by offering traditional dining at a moderate price, averaging $8.75 per meal, with items on the children's menu for $2.50.

In the spring of 1989, an initial public offering (IPO) raised over $12 million, which was earmarked for paying off bank debt, with the balance intended for expansion costs. Within months of the offering, Seelbinder assumed the duties Cooker's president after a failed buyout attempt by then-president Philip J. Hickey, Jr. (who held a five percent stake in the company) and an outside group. Rajan Chaudhry reported in *Restaurant News* that "the buy-out proposal called for the resignations of Seelbinder and all other company directors, except Hickey. . . . In June, Cooker [had begun] trading over the counter, and analysts [were] puzzled by the timing of the bid." The *Wall Street Journal* quoted Seelbinder (who owned 16 percent of the company) as stating that there were "differences over control of the company" and long-term strategy. Hickey resigned from the company's board after a severance agreement was completed wherein Cooker's employee stock ownership plan bought out 1.1 million shares of the company's stock at $3.25 per share. Half of the shares were purchased from Hickey, with the remaining shares purchased from Gerald A. Hornbeck, who then resigned as Cooker vice-president of development and became a company consultant. Both agreed to a five-year relinquishment of interest in Cooker and entered into non-competition agreements, including the stipulation that they not participate in any proxy fight for the company. Speculation over the "management void" led to uncertainty concerning the future of the company, and analysts downgraded investment opinions. Cooker argued that despite the loss of its operations director, they maintained a strong management team capable of competent leadership.

New Leadership in the Early 1990s

New restaurant openings and lower pricing accounted for a 17 percent increase in 1991 sales, attracting notice from Wall Street. The company's stock price increased more than 300 percent, followed by two splits. Management attributed accelerated earn-

Company Perspectives:

100% Satisfaction Guaranteed. Yes, that's exactly what we mean. Your satisfaction is guaranteed by all of us at Cooker. That means a quality meal, friendly and efficient service in a comfortable, clean environment. If you find we haven't delivered on any of these, please let us know. If we fail to make you happy, then we don't expect you to pay. It's that simple. We value you as a guest, and providing you with a pleasant dining experience is our only goal.

ings to the trimming of labor expenses and the savings gained in efficiency afforded by the chain's expansion. Cooker experimented with scheduling and profit margins and concluded that service was not compromised by cutting labor in non-peak hours. With labor costs at 34 percent of profits, which are considered high for the industry, Cooker remained committed to its strategy of providing exemplary service. At the administrative level, they found that with new stores opening, no new corporate staffers were needed to handle the higher percentage of sales.

In an effort to increase customer frequency, several value-priced items were added to the menu, including Caesar salad, grilled tuna Caesar salad, and an assortment of sandwiches. Obtaining a full liquor license resulted in boosted earnings that accounted for 14 percent of sales. Cooker's policy was to offer a money-back, satisfaction guarantee, or to give away free meals if customers were dissatisfied. In 1992, Cooker gave away $750,000 in free meals to back up the guarantee and justified that expense as a positive advertising strategy.

By 1993, despite sluggish same-store sales trends, the company optimistically moved ahead with its restaurant expansion drive, concentrating six new locations in its already established regions, with plans for an additional 25 to 35 openings within the following five years. Eight to ten new restaurants were scheduled to open the next year in the cities of Ann Arbor, Michigan, and Cincinnati and Columbus, Ohio. Cooker decided that it needed to aggressively compete with other casual dining restaurants such as Applebee's, Chili's, and Lone Star Steakhouse that were moving into the upper midwestern region. By the fourth quarter, however, company officials admitted that the timing of the new stores was off and the corporation had stretched itself too thin. In its haste to expand, Cooker purchased some unprofitable real estate. Officials admitted that the goal of 50 percent growth was overly ambitious, determining that 20 to 25 percent would have been more realistic.

The company completed a $23 million convertible debenture offering to finance the openings and to make improvements in existing locations. A company official told Rebecca Walters of Business First that "the combined effects of lower sales and higher operating expense related to Cooker's expansion program caused the decline in earnings." But another official told Walters that the new units were placed in new market areas that were not performing to expectations. Walters reported that also affecting earnings was the "one-time, non-cash charge of between $800,000 and $900,000 to cover operating expenses for new store openings from 1991 through 1993." With approximately

$200,000 needed to open a new store, the company planned to pay off future store openings in 12 rather than 36 months. Walters explained that costs that remained from 1991 and 1992 would be paid off concurrently with 1993's pre-opening costs, effecting a write-off that would help future earnings.

The short-term effect of the company's too-rapid expansion into untried regions was reflected in decreased earnings, causing its stock to sink to a new low. The company then began buying back Cooker stock, paying about $6 million for 500,000 common shares, feeling that the lower stock price did not reflect the company's actual value. Officials reasoned that by decreasing the available stock, earnings per share would increase as profits were spread over a smaller number of shares and confidence would be restored. The company also blamed the decline in earnings on higher labor costs and severe weather in the majority of its markets, which caused several units to close due to power outages.

Glen Cockburn explained to Marjorie Coeyman of *Restaurant Business* that the company "started as a mom-and-pop kind of place. It was casual and homey, but it wasn't attracting the kind of clientele we wanted. It wasn't profitable enough." Pricing was too low, management thought, and its valued servers were leaving because their tips were based on checks averaging less than $9. The company instituted a more upscale menu and interior appearance. Explained Cockburn, "Low-voltage lighting replaced the warmer, pink lights of earlier units. Old-fashioned black-and-white photos aimed at evoking a cheerful, nostalgic tone gave way to starker art photos of, for instance, a lone tomato. Customers didn't like it. They looked at it and said, 'That looks too expensive.'" As a result Cooker got burned by going too upscale, which alienated former customers.

New Recipes For Mid-1990s Growth

The company made changes in its 1994 development schedule following a 52 percent plunge in profits and targeted only six new sites for the year from its previous target of 12 stores. Cooker began a retraining effort for management and serving staff in an attempt to restore service standards and levels of ambiance which had faltered following cost cuts. "We've had to retool a bit," Glenn Cockburn told Bill Carlino of *Nation's Restaurant News*. He continued, "But we've had tough times before. You can say we've recommitted ourselves to the basics." The marketing team spent more than $100,000 on a radio and print campaign, deviating from the previous word-of-mouth promotional strategy, and introduced a new menu. Then, in November, Cooker began organizing a new management team beginning with the selection of General Mills's China Coast Division operations vice-president Philip L. Pritchard as the new company president, a newly created position. He had been a Darden's Red Lobster Restaurant executive vice-president from 1986 to 1992 and was credited with successfully implementing their rapid growth before moving to General Mills, where he worked until taking the Cooker position. His strengths earned him a reputation as a manager who could handle aggressive expansion. A new human resources director, Jeff Karla, was recruited from McDonald's, and Dave Sevig became CFO, leaving his controller's post at Red Lobster. A new director of real estate was also hired to seek out new Cooker sites, relieving Seelbinder from that additional responsi-

```
┌─────────────────────────────────────────────────┐
│                   Key Dates:                    │
│                                                 │
│  1984:  Arthur Seelbinder establishes Cooker    │
│         Restaurant Corporation.                 │
│  1989:  Cooker goes public.                     │
│  1993:  The company launches an aggressive      │
│         expansion plan.                         │
│  1994:  Profits tumble and force Cooker to      │
│         pare back new store openings.           │
│  1996:  The firm acquires six former China      │
│         Coast Restaurants from Darden           │
│         Restaurants Inc.                        │
│  1999:  Henry Hillenmeyer is named chairman     │
│         and CEO.                                │
│  2001:  Cooker declares Chapter 11 bankruptcy;  │
│         company headquarters are moved to       │
│         Nashville, Tennessee.                   │
│                                                 │
└─────────────────────────────────────────────────┘
```

bility. The year 1995 also marked Cooker's move from Ohio to its new headquarters in Palm Beach, Florida, home to many of Cooker's executives and a region targeted for new expansion. At the time, the company operated its headquarters in the areas it wished to penetrate. Cooker bought the 32,000-square-foot building out of foreclosure for $1.9 million, a considerable bargain price for the area.

The company continued its efforts to refinance its debt in order to strengthen existing operations. Finally, by the second quarter of 1995, Cooker managed to increase net revenues 8.9 percent over that earned in the previous comparable quarter, despite rising general and administrative costs. The company's reliance on attentive service and fresh ingredients came at a high price and Pritchard trimmed food costs through pre-portioning with vendors and encouraged servers to promote appetizers and desserts, which provided healthier profit margins. He maintained that Cooker should still set itself apart from other casual dining restaurants by staffing for heavier traffic than the competition might employ, justifying the tactic of one-on-one advertising to increase the customer base by impressing diners with heightened service and quality levels. Cooker cut managers, who can earn over $85,000 including bonuses, from 8.3 per store down to 5.8, basing numbers of managers on store volume, which led to an average reduction of three managers per unit.

Cooker concentrated efforts on selecting sites in close proximity to office and retail centers. The company's expansion plans also continued to involve the opening of new restaurants in regions where Cooker restaurants already existed. The new operational strategy soon paid off. In 1996, the company acquired six former China Coast Restaurants from Darden Restaurants, Inc. (owners of Olive Garden Italian Restaurants) with the intention of converting them to the Cooker concept in the areas of Saginaw and Grand Rapids, Michigan; Cincinnati, Ohio; Chesapeake, Virginia; and Tampa, Florida. Eleven new Cooker restaurants opened in 1996—showing strong performance— and plans were implemented for the opening of another dozen or so by the end of fiscal 1997. According to an interview in *Financial News* with Nashville analyst Jonathan Ruykhaver, "Not only have they [Cooker] gotten preopening expenses and labor costs down, but they're continuing to improve unit volumes, and every extra sales dollar on top helps those margins."

Net income for 1995 rose 49 percent from the previous year's performance and grew another 52 percent in 1996. That performance attracted investors to Cooker's secondary offering, which raised $34.7 million for the chain. After paying off its $29 million credit line (leaving approximately $15 million in outstanding debt), the remainder would fund further unit development, along with another $10 million or so from cash flow. The company also entered two new markets: Johnson City, Tennessee, and Boardman Township (Youngstown), Ohio, and closed one underperforming unit. For a time, Cooker Restaurants still felt the impact of decreased sales, which were blamed in part on consumer focus on the 1996 Olympics. Dinner-oriented businesses were mainly affected, although successes at new Cooker unit openings offset its losses.

In July 1996, with restaurant stocks again slipping, Cooker president Pritchard increased his stock holdings to approximately two percent of Cooker's outstanding stock, indicating an insider vote of confidence in the company, a move inconsistent with the trend away from investing in the consumer product sector. Pritchard told a *Wall Street Journal* reporter: "I put my money where my mouth is." With Cooker's steady growth commitment, and gains of over 20 percent in sales over 1995 figures, his confidence appeared more than justified.

Bankruptcy in the Late 1990s and Beyond

Unfortunately, Cooker faced problems in the late 1990s and was once again forced to pare back its expansion efforts. While sales reached an all time high of $160.5 million in 1998, net income remained flat. Cooker's finances began to feel the pains of mounting debt, slowing sales growth, and falling customer traffic brought on by increased competition. In attempt to give its menu new life, Cooker added new items that included bruschetta, oriental chicken salad, and roasted portobello grill to its offerings. The company also decided to update its menu three times per year.

Hoping that some new blood would bolster Cooker's operations, the company named Henry Hillenmeyer chairman and CEO in August 1999. The new leader faced challenges, however, as the first years of the new century proved to be a financial challenge. Sales fell to $147 million in 2000 and then dropped to $112.9 million in 2001. Under his leadership, the firm began selling off its stores in the south. Company headquarters were then moved from Florida—an unprofitable region for Cooker—to Nashville, Tennessee. Store count fell from 66 in ten states in 2000 to 50 in five states by mid-2001. In May of that year, Cooker was forced to declare Chapter 11 bankruptcy.

"The thing that pushed us to this point was a battle with the banks," claimed Hillenmeyer in a June 2001 *Business First* article. He went on to explain that Cooker had borrowed $42 million in 1998—as part of a stock buyback program—which pushed its debt up to $70 million. By mid-1999, sales had fallen off, leaving the company unable to meet its debt load. By the time the company filed for bankruptcy protection, its debt had grown to $115 million.

As part of its reorganization efforts, Cooker began to focus on strengthening its relationship with its customers. As such, it revitalized its "100% Satisfaction Guarantee" and also focused on friendly and fast service, along with serving its customary large portions. The company also brought in industry veteran Dan Clay as vice-president and chief operating officer and co-founder Jerry Hornbeck, whose responsibility included revamping the menu.

Cooker filed its reorganization plan in July 2002. If approved by the Bankruptcy Court, the company would emerge as a private entity owned by a group of investors. While sales continued their downward trend, Hillenmeyer and his management team remained optimistic about Cooker's future. Whether or not the restaurant chain would be able to weather this financial storm, however, remained to be seen.

Principal Subsidiaries

CGR Management Corporation; Florida Cooker LP, Inc.; Southern Cooker Limited Partnership.

Principal Competitors

CBRL Group Inc.; Darden Restaurants Inc.; Metromedia Company.

Further Reading

"Bankrupt Cooker Reports 9-month Loss of $23 Million," *Nation's Restaurant News*, January 7, 2002, p. 12.

Boldt, Ethan, "Cooking Up Some Changes: Casual Chain Set to Roll New Menu," *Restaurant Business*, August 1, 2000, p. 15.

Carlino, Bill, "Cooker Targets Unit-Level Basics to Rejuvenate Sales," *Nation's Restaurant News*, August 29, 1994, p. 3.

Chaudhry, Rajan, "Cooker President Exists After Failed Buyout Try," *Nation's Restaurant News*, October 2, 1989, p. 4.

Coeyman, Marjorie, "Slow Down," *Restaurant Business*, November 1, 1995, p. 28.

"Cooker Restaurant Corporation," *Business First—Columbus*, July 13, 1992, p. 27.

"Cooker Restaurant's President Is Replaced After Fight for Control," *The Wall Street Journal*, September 19, 1989, p. B18.

Hayes, Jack, "Cooker Uses Backfilling Strategy to Step Up Expansion," *Financial News*, June 3, 1996, p. 11.

——, "Retrenched Cooker Chain Plots Ch. 11 Comeback," *Nation's Restaurant News*, August 6, 2001, p. 4.

Keegan, Peter O., "Cooker Trims the Fat, Boosts Earnings Growth," *Nation's Restaurant News*, August 12, 1991, p. 14.

Klara, Robert, "Stirring the Pot; Cooker Spices Up a Tired Menu," *Restaurant Business*, June 1, 1998, p. 16.

Labate, John, "Cooker Restaurants," *Fortune*, June 28, 1993, p. 107.

Newpoff, Laura, "Debt-hurt Cooker Seeks New Future," *Business First—Columbus*, June 22, 2001, p. A1.

Tippett, Karen L., "This Time Around, Cooker's Plans for Growth Look More Palatable," *The Wall Street Journal*, September 4, 1996.

Walkup, Carolyn, "Cooker Eyes Regional Push After Strong Second Quarter," *Nation's Restaurant News*, September 20, 1993, p. 18.

Walters, Rebecca, "Cooker Will Keep Growing, But More Cautiously," *Business First—Columbus*, January 24, 1994, p. 12.

Waresh, Julie, "Cooking Up Expansion," *Palm Beach Post*, April 6, 1997, p. F1.

"When More Is More," *Restaurant Business*, March 1, 1997, p. 10.

—Terri Mozzone-Burgman
—update: Christina M. Stansell

Co-operative Group (CWS) Ltd.

Manchester M60 4ES
United Kingdom
Telephone: (+44) 161-834-1212
Fax: (+44) 161-834-4507
Web site: http://www.co-op.co.uk

Cooperative
Incorporated: 1863 as the North of England Co-operative
Society
Employees: 60,000
Sales: £5.4 billion ($8.64 billion)(2001)
NAIC: 445110 Supermarkets and Other Grocery (Except
Convenience) Stores; 445120 Convenience Stores;
447110 Gasoline Stations with Convenience Stores;
522110 Commercial Banking; 522120 Savings
Institutions; 524128 Other Direct Insurance (Except
Life, Health, and Medical) Carriers; 812210 Funeral
Homes and Funeral Services

Co-operative Group (CWS) Ltd. is the world's largest retail cooperative, with sales of more than £5.5 billion and a network that embraces activities including food retailing, department stores, banking and insurance, automotive sales, and building services. Despite stiff competition, CWS remains one of the United Kingdom's largest food retailers, with 1,000 shops ranging from small-scale convenience stores to full-range supermarket, as well as some 39 "superstore" department stores. Co-operative Bank remains one of the country's top full-service banks and also operates the smile.co online bank, the first of its kind in the United Kingdom. Another strong area for CWS is its CIS insurance wing. In 2002, CWS created a new entity, Co-operative Financial Services, combining the Co-operative Bank with CIS in order to create greater cross-selling potential between the two groups. CWS also operates the United Kingdom's largest chain of funeral homes, providing burial services to more than 80,000 people per year through a network of 580 funeral homes. Farmcare is the company's farming subsidiary, which is the United Kingdom's largest commercial farmer, working more than 85,000 acres of farmland through 34 agri-

cultural businesses. CWS's Priority Motor Group sells more than 12,000 new and used cars each year, including BMW, Ford, Rover, Mazda, and Alfa Romeo models through a network of 27 dealerships; the subsidiary also operates service centers and filling stations. Synchro is CWS's building services arm, formed in 2001 to group its activities in design and project management, facilities management, equipment services, and energy management and procurement services. ACC Milk operates as CWS's milk processing and distribution arm, with five creameries and a milk distribution facilities across much of the United Kingdom. ACC also operates two manufacturing dairies to provide a line of food ingredients products. CWS represents the spearhead for the more than 150-year-old co-operative movement in the United Kingdom; created from the merger of Co-operative Wholesale Society with Co-operative Retail Services in 2000, the company adopted its present name in 2001.

Founding the Co-operative Movement in the mid-19th Century

The forerunner to CWS, Co-operative Wholesale Society, as its name implied, was not originally set up as a retailer but instead provided wholesale provisions buying and other services to the growing number of cooperative societies being founded in the middle of the nineteenth century in the United Kingdom. The cooperative movement was born in 1844 in the town of Rochdale, Lancashire, when a group of 28 workers from a local weaving manufacturer joined together to form the Rochdale Equitable Pioneers' Society.

The aim of the new group was to provide a different type of retail outlet to the United Kingdom's hard-pressed Industrial Revolution-era workers. British shoppers had long been subjected to often unscrupulous business practices—such as adulterated food stuffs and short-changing on weights—of the country's retailers, many of which were operated as retail outlets by manufacturers for their own products. Meanwhile, much of the nation's working class struggled with poverty, barring them from the country's traditional shops, which catered to the wealthier classes. The Rochdale Pioneers instead founded a business based on honesty and respect for their customers. At the same time, customers were given a financial stake in the company, as members of the cooperative, as well as given a vote in its operation, through a one-person, one-vote organization that granted women equal voting status with men. Profits were then returned to customers in the form of semi-annual dividends. For many people, these "divis" became their only means of savings, providing additional cash for such purchases as clothing and gifts.

The Rochdale shop opened in 1844 on Toad Lane, selling basic foodstuffs at first but later expanding its assortment. The Rochdale experiment caught on quickly and soon spread throughout the United Kingdom and then throughout much of the world. By the middle of the nineteenth century, food cooperatives had become an established retail force in the United Kingdom; cooperatives tended, however, to operate on a local basis. Their small size left them vulnerable to their retail competitors. Many of these were operated by manufacturers and wholesalers, and the cooperative movement found itself the subject of various attempts at sabotage and other dishonest business practices.

In response, a group of 300 cooperatives in the Lancashire and Yorkshire regions banded together to create their own wholesaling group, the North of England Co-operative Society. Founded in 1863, the new body was able to use the combined purchasing power of its retail members to obtain fairer prices for its bulk goods purchases. The North of England Co-operative Society operated according to the same code of honesty and shared profits of its retail cooperative members. All profits were passed back to the retail cooperatives, which helped them to reduce their business costs still further. North of England soon expanded beyond its initial wholesaling base to begin manufacturing a range of goods, such as shoes and clothing, sold in the retail cooperatives.

In 1872, as the cooperative movement spread across the United Kingdom, the North of England Co-operative Society changed its name to Co-operative Wholesale Society (CWS). At that time, CWS branched out into providing financial services through the Co-operative Bank. Another diversification of the same period brought the group into the insurance industry, with the founding of its Co-operative Insurance Society subsidiary. CWS continued to expand its manufacturing operations, adding items such as soap, biscuits, and jam. The cooperative movement began operating farms, providing dairy and meat products, and also began operating plantations in India to supply its retail members with tea. The growing range of CWS's import activities led it to launch its own shipping fleet.

The cooperative movement in the United Kingdom counted more than 1,000 cooperative societies at the turn of the century. While a number of these societies consisted of a single shop in a remote rural location, other societies had grown into large-scale operations with dozens of stores operating in many towns and cities. CWS remained the central body supplying wholesale purchasing services, as well as banking and insurance products, and an increasing number of its own manufactured goods.

The cooperative movement and CWS played an increasingly prominent role in its members' lives and in British society in general. In 1893, the cooperative movement joined in the creation of the Independent Labour Party. In 1904, CWS inaugurated its first convalescent home; the society had also begun to offer funeral and burial services, becoming one of the largest providers of these services in the United Kingdom, and also added life insurance policies to its insurance arm. CWS also founded the Co-operative Permanent Building Society to provide affordable housing to cooperative movement members. CWS's growing manufacturing operations were to play a prominent role in clothing the British army during World War I, as the group converted its clothing operation to uniform production at the outbreak of hostilities. At the end of the war, the cooperative movement became a leader of social change when it began reducing work hours, increasing wages, improving working conditions, and providing paid vacations and pensions as well as paid sick leave. The "divi" had by then become a British institution, with pay-outs provided twice a year.

Merging Movements in the 1970s

The financial chaos that accompanied the Great Depression in the 1930s threatened the existence of growing numbers of retail cooperative societies. In response, the movement set up a new body in 1934, Co-operative Retail Services (CRS), which had as its purpose to operate as an "ambulance" for failing retail societies. CRS quickly grew to become a dominant force in the cooperative movement, becoming not only the largest single retail cooperative society, but also one of the United Kingdom's top five department store groups.

Until the end of World War II, the United Kingdom's food shops retained their traditional approach, where customers were served by shopkeepers and staff. In 1948, however, a store in London became the first cooperative to introduce the self-service supermarket concept that had been pioneered in the United States. Over the next two decades, more and more cooperatives followed suit. By the 1960s, however, the cooperative movement found itself under pressure from a new type of competitor, as a small number of large-scale supermarket groups began to dominate the UK retail scene.

In 1973, CWS itself became an ambulance group for the cooperative movement when it agreed to merge with failing Scottish Co-operative Wholesale Society, which controlled several hundred retail stores. Over the following decades, CWS was called on to rescue a growing number of societies, becoming in the process one of the largest retailers in the United Kingdom. Already by the middle of the 1970s, CWS held some 20 percent of the UK's retail food market.

By this time, however, CWS and the cooperative movement in general were under heavy pressure. Falling profits had forced most of the movement to abandon the "divi," which had been paid in cash since the 1960s; these dividends were replaced with

---

Key Dates:

1844: The Rochdale Equitable Pioneers' Society is founded, launching a worldwide cooperative retail movement.

1863: North of England Co-operative Society is created to provide wholesale purchasing operations for a group of 300 cooperative societies in Lancashire and Yorkshire.

1872: North of England Co-operative Society changes its name to Co-operative Wholesale Society (CWS) and begins manufacturing and banking operations.

1934: Formation of Co-operative Retail Services (CRS) to serve as ''ambulance'' to struggling cooperative societies.

1948: London cooperative store becomes first to open an American-style supermarket.

1973: Co-operative Wholesale Society takes over Scottish Co-operative Wholesale Society, which brings CWS into the retail sector for the first time.

1994: CWS sells off its manufacturing arm.

1997: CWS fights off hostile takeover attempt, then conducts strategic review.

1998: CWS launches Travelcare travel services subsidiary and acquires Broadoak Farming.

2000: CWS and CRW announce their agreement to merge, creating the world's largest retail cooperative group.

2001: CWS changes its name to Co-operative Group (CWS) to reflect its status as a diversified retailer.

2002: CWS creates new financial services unit, grouping together its banking and insurance subsidiaries.

---

redeemable stamps. Yet these too were phased out by the early 1980s. Meanwhile, the cooperative movement was finding it more difficult to attract and retain members, who fled the movements' many small and cramped stores for the larger stores being opened by such growing supermarket groups as Tesco and Sainsbury.

CWS continued to act as the cooperative movement's ambulance, rescuing a number of failing societies despite the financial pressure these acquisitions placed on the group. By the early 1990s, CWS itself was posting losses as it absorbed two recent acquisitions. At this point, the cooperative movement, which at one time had counted more than 11 million members of more than 2,000 cooperative societies, had dwindled to just 60 societies. CWS had become the single largest cooperative group. Second place position was held by Co-operative Retail Services.

Revitalized for the New Century

A merger of the two groups had long been considered an inevitability, and talks between CWS and CRS had been held since 1981. Yet the two sides had not been able to agree upon a mutually acceptable arrangement. Meanwhile, CWS found itself outclassed by the rising strength of Tesco, Sainsbury, and other growing retail rivals. In 1994, CWS sold off most of its manufacturing operations to entrepreneur Andrew Regan for

£111 million. Regan shut down a number of the CWS factories, restored the remainder to profitability, then sold them again for £120 million.

Regan returned to CWS in 1996 with an offer to buy out its non-foods operations for £500 million. CWS refused the offer, and in 1997 Regan announced his intention to launch a hostile takeover of CWS worth more than £1.2 billion with the intention of breaking up the group and selling its components to the takeover's financial backers. CWS braced itself for battle—yet the takeover attempt quickly fizzled when it was revealed that Regan had induced a number of high-ranking CWS executives to steal confidential financial documents.

Embarrassed by the incident, which if nothing else had revealed the poor financial position of the UK's cooperative movement, CWS used the remainder of 1997 to conduct an extensive review of its operations in order to define a new strategy to enable it to regain its former prominence on the UK retail scene. At that time the company determined that its future lay especially with the convenience store format; the company's superstores were put up for reviews, with a number sold off to its competitors. At the same time, CWS began a program of renovating its supermarkets. Another initiative taken was the launch of a new breed of dividend, a customer loyalty card. Unlike its competitors, which linked their loyalty card purchases to name-brand products, CWS's Dividend Card instead gave points on purchases of its own-label products.

In 1998, CWS entered a new retail arena when it launched a new travel services subsidiary, Travelcare. Its CWS Farms subsidiary grew into the UK's largest commercial farmer with the acquisition of Broadoak Farming that same year. The new group was renamed Farmcare, representing 34 businesses operating more than 85,000 acres of farmland, much of which was owned by the CWS group.

Meanwhile, CWS and CRS once again began merger talks as CRS struggled with losses at the end of the 1990s. The first move toward a merger was taken in 1999 when CRS at last joined the CWS-led purchasing group, Cooperative Retail Trade Group (CRTG). In 2000, the sides at last agreed to merge their operations, and CWS took over CRS, creating a company with more than 1,100 food stores and annual sales of more than £5 billion.

Following the merger, CWS took steps to revitalize its image. In 2001, the company adopted a new name, Co-operative Group (CWS) Ltd., reflecting not only the diversity of its activities but also its intention to lead the co-operative movement as a whole into a new era. The group also began an extensive modernization program, revamping some 400 of its stores along a more modern, ''market town'' concept. The group also stepped up the rollout of its line of own-label products.

CWS continued to build its other operations as well. In 2001, the group bundled together its various and growing building services subsidiaries into a single entity, dubbed Synchro, which became one of the UK's leading full-service building services and facilities management companies. In April 2002, CWS turned toward its Co-operative Bank and CIS insurance subsidiaries, creating a new Co-operative Financial Services to bring the two operations under a single management in order to encourage cross-selling of both entities products among their banking and insurance customers. The company also announced plans to revive the twice-yearly dividend beginning in 2004. CWS was able to look back on more than 150 years as both the pioneer in the worldwide cooperative movement and its leading light for the new century.

Principal Subsidiaries

Co-operative Insurance Society Ltd.; CIS Mortgage Maker Ltd.; Hornby Road Investments Ltd.; CIS Unit Managers Ltd.; CIS Policyholder Services Ltd.; The Co-operative Bank plc; Unity Trust Bank plc (27%); Co-operative Bank Financial Advisers Ltd.; Northern Ireland Co-operative Society Ltd.; (Northern Ireland); Millgate Insurance Brokers Ltd.; Associated Co-operative Creameries Ltd.; Syncro Ltd.; Goliath Footwear Ltd.; Farmcare Ltd.; Herbert Robinson Ltd.; Manx Co-operative (CWS) Ltd. (Isle of Man); CRS (Properties) Ltd.; National Co-Operative Chemists Ltd. (74%); Shoefayre Ltd. (76%); Gilsland Spa Ltd. (98%).

Principal Competitors

ALDI Group; ASDA Group Ltd.; Bongrain SA; Booker Cash & Carry Ltd.; The Boots Company; Friesland Coberco Dairy Foods Holding N.V.; J Sainsbury plc; John Lewis Partnership plc; Marks and Spencer p.l.c.; Safeway plc; Somerfield plc; Tesco PLC; Koninklijke Wessanen nv.

Further Reading

Amerlang, Soren, "Co-op to Focus on Convenience Stores, Acquisitions," *Reuters*, June 7, 2000.

Dutter, Barbie, "Co-op Returns to the Days of the 'divi' '', *Daily Telegraph*, February 2, 1998.

Farrelly, Paul, "Counter-attack from the Man at the Co-op," *Independent on Sunday*, February 16, 1997, p. 5.

Griffin, Jon, "Modern Move for the Co-op," *Evening Mail*, September 7, 2000, p. 39.

Hardcastle, Elaine, "UK's Coop Unveils Modernisation Plan," *Reuters*, February 8, 2001.

Potter, Ben, "Superstores to Go in Co-op Shake-up," *The Daily Telegraph*, December 12, 1997, p.1.

—M.L. Cohen

Cost-U-Less, Inc.

8160 304th Avenue SE, Building 3, Suite A
Preston, Washington 98050
U.S.A.
Telephone: (425) 222-5022
Fax: (425) 222-0044
Web site: http://www.costuless.com

Public Company
Incorporated: 1989
Employees: 500
Sales: $186.3 million (2000)
Stock Exchanges: NASDAQ
Ticker Symbol: CULS
NAIC: 452910 Warehouse Clubs and Superstores

Cost-U-Less, Inc., owns and operates warehouse-style retail stores in remote island locations on Pacific islands, in Hawaii, Guam, American Samoa, and Fiji, and in the Caribbean, in the U.S. Virgin Islands and the Netherlands Antilles. Cost-U-Less stores, including one mainland store, average 31,000 square feet and offer merchandise in a plain, no-frills environment, with goods being displayed in their cases, on shipping pallets, or on steel shelves. The stores offer groceries, housewares, consumer electronics, lawn and garden supplies, and other merchandise at discount or bulk rate prices. Although Cost-U-Less operates as a mid-sized warehouse club, the company does not charge membership fees.

Origins

At the time that he conceived of the Cost-U-Less warehouse store, Jim Rose owned and operated Rose-Chamberlin, the in-house buyer for Costco Wholesale stores. That experience gave Rose the idea for a smaller version of the warehouse store located in markets considered insufficient for the large format warehouse clubs, such as Costco and Sam's Club, as well as discount retailers, such as Kmart and Wal-Mart. Rose designed the Cost-U-Less concept for remote, island locations where such competition did not exist. Locating stores on resort islands insured a ready market for bulk purchases from hotels and restaurants serving tourists; thus, Cost-U-Less did not depend solely on the local population for its consumer base. While the large format stores carried inventory for over 100,000 square feet of space, Rose planned Cost-U-Less stores to be 20,000 to 40,000 square feet. Rose reduced the size of the stores by avoiding products and services generally available in warehouse clubs. Products included apparel, automotive tires, and fresh baked goods; services included a photo finishing center, a pharmacy, and an optical service. Initially, Cost-U-Less did not offer produce or meats. By selling brands and merchandise with proven success at Costco stores, Rose lowered operating overhead by minimizing the need for buyers.

Rose formed Cost-U-Less with funds from a group of 35 investors and opened the first Cost-U-Less store on the island of Maui, Hawaii, in July 1989. The 22,000-square-foot store stocked $500,000 in inventory, 90 percent of which Rose purchased from the Costco in Honolulu. Though Cost-U-Less paid retail prices, the merchandise still sold at prices lower than that available on the island and yielded a profit margin of 17 to 18 percent. The Maui store began to earn a profit six months after it opened. In 1991, its second full year in operation, the store sold $13.5 million in goods.

Early Expansion of Company

In 1992, Rose sold his interest in the wholesale brokerage firm and prepared to open new Cost-U-Less stores. The company opened two stores on Pacific islands in 1992, a 31,000-square-foot store in Dededo, Guam, and a 22,000-square-foot store in Hilo, on the big island of Hawaii. In Guam, the low priced merchandise actually decreased the cost of living, causing the government to halt consumer price index measurements. Also, Cost-U-Less began to experiment with the mid-sized warehouse concept in small towns on the mainland, seeking markets underserved by mass merchandisers. The first mainland store opened in Walla Walla, Washington, in late 1992. Cost-U-Less supplied most of the merchandise in the stores in the Pacific islands through the Costco in Honolulu, while most of the merchandise at the Walla Walla store came from Costco in Kennewick, Washington. Other mainland stores followed, but closed rather quickly due to unsatisfactory performance.

Cost-U-Less opened four stores in 1993 and 1994. In 1993, the company opened a store in Hawaii; in Kapaa, Kauai; and its first store in the Caribbean, on St. Thomas in the U.S. Virgin Islands. In 1994, the company opened another store in the U.S. Virgin Islands on St. Croix. The company also opened several new stores on the mainland, including a 23,000-square-foot unit in Sonora, California, but closed two of them. At the end of 1994, Cost-U-less recorded $117.2 million in revenues and $1.2 million in profit from eight units.

As Cost-U-Less opened and prepared to open new stores, the company began to buy all of its merchandise direct from manufacturers. Since Cost-U-Less no longer needed to purchase goods at retail prices, the company diverted the savings on inventory to hiring buyers. The company began to tailor its product mix to accommodate local tastes and preferences and to market higher margin goods and more of the popular U.S. brands.

In February 1995, Cost-U-Less opened a distribution center in Union City, California, serving stores in the Pacific islands and mainland stores in the Pacific Northwest. Shipments across the sea involved consolidation of merchandise from various vendors at a cross-dock facility in Union City. Each store was designated a lane where goods were loaded into a freight container until it was full; then the container was shipped to the designated store. The logistics of shipping perishable goods, such as frozen foods and fresh meats and produce, proved to be more complicated, as shipping took from seven to fourteen days. In order to avoid excess inventory, the company gave its vendors an estimate of goods required. When the final order was determined, goods were drawn from the suppliers' consignment depot near the cross-dock. The goods were considered purchased at the time of delivery to the cross-dock for shipment. A distribution facility in Port Everglades served the Caribbean stores in a similar manner, but an independent company operated that facility. Cost-U-Less paid fees for the service on a volume, per pallet basis.

The distribution facilities supported expansion as Cost-U-Less opened four new stores in 1995. New operations in the Pacific islands involved a 32,000-square-foot store in Pago Pago, American Samoa, and a 35,000-square-foot store in Tamanig, Guam. A recession and new competition in Maui prompted the company to close that store in December 1995 when the lease expired. Cost-U-Less opened two more stores on the mainland, including a store in San Jose, California, its first in a major metropolitan location. The 31,000-square-foot store operated in an area where warehouse clubs had not saturated the market; Cost-U-Less hoped to attract customers interested in bulk rate goods without the additional cost of a membership fee. Some mainland stores did not meet expectations, resulting in

closing and lease buy-out expenses. At the end of 1995, Cost-U-Less recorded revenues of $139.7 million and profits of $250,000 from 11 units.

Cost-U-Less Returns Focus to Island Markets in 1995

The company's experiment in mainland markets failed for several reasons, including a low volume of merchandise turnover, low profit margins, at 14 to 15 percent, and the entry of major discount retailers into these markets at this time. Also, Cost-U-Less underestimated the competition from warehouse clubs that required customers to drive some distance. By June 1997, Cost-U-Less closed five of the six mainland stores, keeping the profitable Sonora unit open to test new merchandising and operating methods. In 1997, revenues dropped to $124.9 million, from $134.8 million in 1996, while net earnings remained steady at $363,000 from eight units.

Cost-U-Less decided to return its focus of business to remote, island markets. Rose determined that to operate successfully a store locale required a minimum population of 40,000 people and Gross Domestic Product of $125 million. Before continuing expansion, Cost-U-Less sought to improve operations, applying specially designed management information systems to inventory control and the logistics of delivery. Communication by electronic mail, facsimile, and the Internet helped to link management in distant places to headquarters in Bellevue, Washington. Also, Cost-U-Less began to develop a prototype store easily replicated at low cost. A new store required an investment of $2.5 million to $3 million for construction of a 28,000- to 48,000-square-foot facility, plus $2 million for inventory and fixtures.

One aspect of operating businesses in exotic, island locations involved the risks and unpredictable economic consequences due to tropical storms. Facilities must be built to withstand hurricanes in the Caribbean and typhoons in the Pacific Ocean to minimize the cost of insurance deductibles to pay for damage. In summer 1998, Cost-U-Less relocated its St. Thomas operations to a larger store, the first prototype unit, because the original store had been damaged during a hurricane in 1995 and the landlord had not repaired the building properly. Another unpredictable consequence of tropical storms was the possibility of store closures. In September 1998, Hurricane Georges instigated very high sales before and after the storm, but required stores to close. The St. Thomas store closed one day, while the harder hit island of St. Croix required that Cost-U-Less store to close for four days. Despite losses related to minor property damage, demand for goods nearly tripled normal sales and resulted in an overall profit; however, this has not always been the case with other storms.

Initial Public Offering Funds Expansion: Late 1990s

In July 1998 Cost-U-Less became a public company in an initial offering of 1.5 million shares of stock at $7.00 per share. Ironically, the share value of the stock closed at $6.875 per share at the end of the first day of trading. Nevertheless, the company raised almost $10 million in capital funds to pay short-term debt and to use for working capital and for expansion. Cost-U-Less hoped to open 26 new stores by the end of 2002,

Key Dates:

1989: The first Cost-U-Less store opens on the island of Maui, Hawaii.

1992: Cost-U-Less expands with new stores in Hawaii and Guam.

1993: The company opens its first store in the Caribbean, on St. Thomas.

1995: Failure of stores on mainland causes company to refocus on island locations.

1998: Initial public offering of stock provides funds for expansion.

2000: After less than one year in operation, Cost-U-Less closes its two stores in New Zealand.

including two in Fiji in 1998 and six stores in 1999. After a two-year hiatus of new store openings, Cost-U-Less commenced operations of two stores in Fiji during 1998, in the resort town of Nadi and the capital city of Suva. With two new stores and a 10 percent increase in sales at existing stores, the company rebounded financially in 1998, recording $134.9 million in revenue and $1.2 million in profit.

Cost-U-Less had determined that 30 Pacific and Caribbean islands met its minimum market requirements, with 90 potential store sites. In the Pacific Cost-U-Less considered Tahiti, Papua New Guinea, and New Zealand as viable possibilities. In the Caribbean Cost-U-Less explored opportunities on Aruba, St. Maarten, Barbados, and Grand Cayman. Cost-U-Less opened a store on Curacao, a Caribbean island in the Netherlands Antilles, in summer 1999. Finding employees on the islands has been difficult, as the local people prefer outdoor work. Hourly pay ranged from $14 per hour in Guam and $8 to $9 per hour in American Samoa to $3 per hour in Fiji.

In June 1999 Cost-U-Less announced its intention to open two stores on the North Island of New Zealand. The company planned a 36,000 square-foot store in Rotorua, a tourist center, and a 30,000 square-foot store in Porirua, suburb of the capital city of Wellington. The stores opened in November and December 1999, respectively. The stores stocked a mix of New Zealand, Australian, and American brands of goods. Buying offices in Aukland, New Zealand, and Sydney, Australia, supported store operations. Also, Cost-U-Less relocated its cross-dock distribution facility from Union City to a larger, 81,000-square-foot facility in San Leandro to ease distribution from the United States.

In September Cost-U-Less installed a new management team led by Jefferey Meder, founder of Western Drug Distributors, owner and operator of 20 Drug Emporium franchises in the Pacific Northwest. Meder had sold the company in 1998 and became CEO and president of Cost-U-Less after the board asked Rose to relinquish involvement in daily operations; the board then elected Rose chairman. Meder restructured the executive management staff and began development of a three-year business plan to open new stores and to improve operations and profits at existing stores. Relocation of company headquarters to Preston, Washington, in June 2000, allowed Cost-U-Less to double its office space and save on overhead expenses.

By May 2000, it became clear that Cost-U-Less could not succeed in New Zealand and the company decided to close the stores there. Company officials had not anticipated the high level of loyalty to local brands among residents of New Zealand or the lack of familiarity with American brands and with the concept of bulk purchase. Also, the environment was more competitive than Cost-U-Less had expected. The company had planned to open 18 stores in New Zealand, but withdrew completely. The company lost $3.4 million in closing costs and $1.5 million from operating and development losses. The failure of the New Zealand experiment, as well as economic decline in Guam and Curacao resulted in a net loss of $4.9 million on revenues of $186.3 million in 2000.

Cost-U-Less opened a store on St. Maarten in July 2000 and encountered the opposite result. In this instance the new business surpassed expectations as the awareness and popularity of brand merchandise from the United States led to a high level of merchandise turnover and high revenues. Company management realized it needed to focus its efforts in areas similar to St. Maarten, where brand awareness and understanding of the warehouse concept attracted customers; they needed to build on the success of this experience. Cost-U-Less sought to improve store operations by sending a management team to all of the stores to examine operations. In early 2001, the company became profitable again. The company was forced to consolidate the two Fiji stores into one, however, as political turmoil hampered tourism. Cost-U-Less closed the store in the resort town of Nadi.

Principal Competitors

Costco Wholesale Corporation; Kmart Corporation; Wal-Mart Stores, Inc.

Further Reading

"Bellevue Retailer Increases Its Sales Due to Hurricane," *Seattle Post-Intelligencer*, September 26, 1998, p. B3.

"Cost-U-Less," *Warehouse Club Focus*, August 28, 2000, p. 1.

"Cost-U-Less Announces Management Changes," *Business Wire*, August 11, 2000.

"Cost-U-Less Announces Opening of Second Fiji Store, Suva Locations Is the Largest Store in All of Fiji," *Business Wire*, November 11, 1998.

"Cost-U-Less Announces Same Store Sales Increase; Caribbean Stores Weather Hurricane Georges," *Business Wire*, October 8, 1998.

"Cost-U-Less Consolidates Fiji Store Operations," *Business Wire*, January 18, 2000.

"Cost-U-Less Inc. Completes Initial Public Offering of Common Stock," *Business Wire*, July 24, 1998.

"Cost-U-Less Opens St. Maarten Store," *Business Wire*, July 5, 2000.

"Cost-U-Less Shares Down on First Day of Trading," *Seattle Times*, July 23, 1998, p. D3.

"Cost-U-Less to Open Stores in New Zealand; Bellevue, Wash.—Retailer to Expand International Presence," *Business Wire*, June 4, 1999.

Hartnett, Michael, "Advanced Systems Help Cost-U-Less Run Far-Flung Store Network," *Stores*, June 1998, p. 84.

Healea, Tim, "Niche Clubs Find Ways to Adapt and Grow," *Discount Store News*, August 7, 1995, p. 4.

Johnson, Jay, "Searching for Paradise," *Discount Merchandiser*, January 1999, p. 23.

Kontzer, Tony, "Cost-U-Less Comes to San Jose; First Metropolitan Outlet," *Business Journal*, March 27, 1995, p. 5.

''Lockhart Turns Over Prepared Sites to Cost-U-Less and Caribbean Cinemas,'' *Business Wire,* March 13, 1998.

Morrison, Tina-Marie, ''Cost-U-Less NZ foray an $11.8m loss,'' *Dominion,* August 9, 2000, p. 20.

''Moving to Preston Will Cost Less for Cost-U-Less,'' *Puget Sound Business Journal,* April 14, 2000, p. 18.

Riordan, Daniel, ''Warehouse Joint Venture Declined,'' *Sunday Star Times,* August 1, 1999, p. 1.

Sather, Jeanne, ''Cost-U-Less, a Small-Town Costco Clone, Goes Urban,'' *Puget Sound Business Journal,* March 31, 1995, p. 3.

Tice, Carol, ''Cost-U-Less Inc.,'' *Puget Sound Business Journal*, February 16, 2001, p. 17.

——, ''Cost-U-Less Plans Island-hopping Growth,'' *Puget Sound Business Journal*, August 11, 2000, p. 7.

—Mary Tradii

Denver Nuggets

1000 Chopper Circle
Denver, Colorado 80204
U.S.A.
Telephone: (303) 405-1100
Fax: (303) 575-1920
Website: http://www.nba.com/nuggets

Private Company
Founded: 1967
Sales: $72 million (2001)
NAIC: 711211 Sports Teams and Clubs

The Denver Nuggets is a professional basketball franchise based in Denver, Colorado, that operates under the auspices of Kroenke Sports Enterprises, which also owns the Colorado Avalanche, a professional hockey franchise, and the Pepsi Center arena.

Company Beginnings

The Nuggests franchise was born in 1967 as one of the original members of the new American Basketball Association (ABA). Denver's first owner was James B. Trindle, a partner in a large southern California engineering firm who put up $35,000 as one of the initial investors in an ABA franchise. Trindle and several of his business associates originally pooled their money to establish a franchise in Kansas City. When it proved difficult to secure a guarantee for scheduled playing dates at a large enough venue in Kansas City, ABA Commissioner George Mikan recommended locating the franchise in Denver, where his friend Vince Boryla lived. Boryla was a Denver business man who had played for the New York Knicks and had served as coach and general manager of the Knicks after finishing his career. After several meetings with Boryla, Trindle and his partners agreed to relocate the franchise to Denver and to hire Boryla as the team's general manager. The team's original name was to be the Larks after Colorado's state bird. Nonetheless, when the team soon ran into financial difficulty, Trindle sold two-thirds of the franchise to local trucking executive Bill Ringsby and his son Don for $170,000 before the team even played its first game. Ringsby named the team the Rockets, after the nickname of his trucking company's long-haul vehicles, the Ringsby Rockets, and put his company's logo on the team uniforms. In addition, he subsequently hired Dick Eicher, chairman of the board of the Ringsby System Trucking company, as the franchise's executive vice-president and new general manager. The franchise then recruited Bob Blass, who coached Oklahoma Baptist College to a national small-college championship in 1966, as head coach at a salary of $20,000.

In the Rocket's first season (1967–68), the team's roster was composed largely of unknowns, including forwards Julian Hammond and Willie Murrell, center Byron Beck, and guards Larry Jones and Willis "Lefty" Thomas. Nonetheless, the team played winning basketball and compiled a 45–33 record, third best in its Western Division. The Rockets, however, were eliminated early from the 1968 playoffs, a pattern that nearly all Denver teams have followed ever since. The club's early popularity drew nearly 4,000 a game to the Auditorium Arena. The team also led the league in ticket sales. To further increase attendance and revenue, Eicher negotiated radio and television deals to broadcast some of the games.

The team's second season was marked by controversy when Bass left for Texas Tech University over a contract dispute, and Eicher departed for undisclosed reasons. Ringsby hired his son Don as the new general manager and John McClendon was recruited to replace Bass as head coach. McClendon, a highly regarded coach within the AAU club circuit, became the first black coach in the ABA. Ringsby also signed McClendon with the aim of recruiting the highly touted Spencer Haywood, a young power forward who achieved national acclaim for leading the U.S. team to the gold medal in the 1968 Olympic games in Mexico City. As an influential member of the Olympic basketball selection committee, McClendon played a critical role in getting Haywood a spot on the U.S. Olympic team. In addition, the Olympic star figured prominently in the ABA's rivalry with the National Basketball Association (NBA) for star players and credibility. As a result, the ABA decided to pursue Haywood, handing the signing rights to the Rockets since Ringsby was the only franchise owner with the cash to recruit Haywood. Ringsby offered Haywood, then a 19-year-old sophomore at the

Key Dates:

1967: A sports franchise is founded by James B. Trindle as one of the original members of the American Basketball Association (ABA).

1972: San Diego investors Frank M. Goldberg and A.G. ''Bud'' Fisher purchase the team.

1975: The team's general manager, Carl Scheer, and a group of investors buy the Nuggets.

1976: The Denver Nuggets become one of four ABA teams that merge with the National Basketball Association for an entrance fee of $4.5 million.

1979: B.J. ''Red'' McCombs purchases the Nuggets for almost $2 million.

1985: McCombs sells the franchise to a group of investors headed by Sidney L. Shlenker for $20 million.

1989: Comsat Video Enterprises, a subsidiary of telecommunications company Comsat Corporation, purchases a majority 67.5 percent stake in the Nuggets, with the remaining 32.5 percent held by two African American businessmen.

1992: Comsat Video assumes 100 percent ownership of the franchise.

1995: Comsat Corporation organizes its Denver sports assets, including the Denver Nuggets, the Colorado Avalanche, a hockey franchise, and the Pepsi Sports Arena, as well as its video entertainment business, under a separate subsidiary, Ascent Entertainment Group, which goes public in 1995.

1997: Comsat Corporation sells Ascent Entertainment Group to AT&T's Liberty Media Group of Englewood, Colorado, for $755 million.

2000: Liberty Media sells Ascent's sports assets—the Denver Nuggets, the Colorado Avalanche, and the Pepsi Center—to Wal-Mart heir and real estate developer Stan Kroenke in a deal valued at $450 million.

University of Detroit, a lucrative deal of $450,000 over three years plus such perquisites as a penthouse apartment in the exclusive Brooks Towers, a high-rise apartment building in downtown Denver. By breaking the unwritten rule that professional teams would not recruit college players until they had finished school, the Haywood contract outraged the NCAA and the NBA, both of which subsequently sued the Rockets and the league to block the deal. Nonetheless, the courts allowed Haywood to turn pro and his signing led the way for other highly talented college players to enter the ABA.

The Haywood deal also had an immediate impact on the Rockets. In his one season with Denver, Haywood led the ABA in scoring and rebounding, was named Rookie of the Year and Most Valuable Player, and sparked the Rockets to their first Western Division crown with a 51–33 record. His prowess on the court also considerably helped the Rockets financially at a time when most ABA franchises were struggling to make money. Nevertheless, the Rockets rise to the top was short-lived as Haywood left Denver after one season for a better contract with the Seattle Supersonics of the NBA. Without their star player, the Rockets became a mediocre club. Their record sank

to 30–54 in the 1970–71 season, causing the team to fall from first to last place in its division. At the same time, the Ringsbys were growing weary of owning a basketball team in a struggling league that by 1971 was plagued by numerous law suits. With attendance lagging and burdened with a money-losing team, in the summer of 1972 the Ringsbys sold the franchise to Frank M. Goldberg and A.G. ''Bud'' Fisher, both of San Diego.

The 1970s and 1980s:
Financial Struggles and Turmoil

The new owners aimed to base the future prospects of the franchise on a proposed new arena that could seat 18,500 for basketball. Planned to host figure skating and hockey as part of Denver's successful bid for the 1976 Winter Olympic Games, the new venue was scheduled for completion in time for the 1975 ABA season. In 1974, Goldberg and Fisher hired a new general manager, Carl Scheer, the former NBA deputy commissioner who had also been president and general manager of the successful Carolina Cougars. In turn, Scheer hired a new coach, Larry Brown, also from the Carolina Cougars. Together they worked to save the Denver franchise, which was suffering from poor attendance, declining revenues, and no broadcasting contracts. Denver's precarious state differed little from other ABA franchises, which existed in a league on the verge of extinction. When the founders organized the ABA league in 1967, they hoped to merge it with the NBA within three years. The ABA's lack of viable television deals increasingly proved highly detrimental to the league's continued survival.

After the 1974–75 season, the league continued to struggle financially more than ever. Nonetheless, in Scheer's first year, the Denver franchise compiled a remarkable 65–19 record, setting a club benchmark for success and achieving the finest season in ABA history. Scheer also made two other changes in his first year. First, he announced that the team would play the next season in the larger McNichols Sports Arena; second, he renamed the team the Denver Nuggets after an earlier Denver club that played one year in the NBA during the 1949–50 season. With Denver's winning season, ticket sales and attendance soared. Fans packed the old Auditorium Arena nearly every night, and the Nuggets' sold out the house twenty-nine times.

Despite the Nuggets' turnaround, Fisher and Goldberg were concerned about the league's losing prospects and their own investment in the franchise. When the owners proposed to Scheer that he find additional local investors to shore up the franchise, he decided to buy them out altogether. He made a stock offering at $35,000 a share and purchased the team in the summer of 1975. Ownership of the team came under the newly formed Nuggets Management, Inc., which comprised five general partners, including Scheer, and 18 limited partners. The purchase price was just under $1 million.

By the end of the 1975–76 season, the financial circumstances surrounding the ABA compelled the league's owners to seek a merger with the NBA. Several of the franchises had already disbanded or were in serious financial trouble, game attendance was poor, and the league failed to secure a national television contract. The league had dropped to only six teams and the prospects for another season appeared bleak. The ABA nevertheless held the rights to highly talented players and the NBA expressed interest in a merger with some of the stronger ABA franchises. Under the agreement, four ABA teams, including the Denver Nuggets, New York Nets, San Antonio Spurs, and Indiana Pacers, merged with the older league at an entrance cost of $4.5 million each. The merger agreement also provided that the four ABA franchises compensate the two franchise owners who were not accepted into the NBA. The Denver Nuggets were required to pay an additional price when, at the demand of the NBA, they had to unsign three college stars—Marquis Johnson and Richard Washington of UCLA and Quinn Buckner of Indiana University—before merger talks could proceed.

Following the Nugget's entry into the NBA, the team captured first place in the Midwest Division with a 50–32 record in the 1976–77 season. Nevertheless, the team continued its unbroken tradition of losing early in the playoffs. By the end of the 1980–81 season, the team sank to a losing record of 37–45, missing the playoffs altogether. The next season (1981–82) proved pivotal for the franchise. Although the Nuggets compiled a winning season record of 43–31, the team was again ousted early in the playoffs. The Phoenix Suns upset the Nuggets 124–119 before a sellout crowd of 17,443 at McNichols Arena in game three of the series. The early defeat was devastating for Scheer's ownership group, which needed the cash that would have come from the best-of-seven series in the conference semi-finals. Scheer needed to raise additional capital from his owners and outside interests to keep the franchise running. Many of the owners, however, preferred to sell the team. At the recommendation of Denver's coach Doug Moe, who replaced Larry Brown starting with the 1978–79 season, Scheer approached B.J. ''Red'' McCombs, a Texas businessman who had made a considerable fortune selling cars. McCombs agreed to assume Denver's debt and pay the shareholders limited cash. McCombs later negotiated steep discounts on the team's debt service, making the total purchase price slightly less than $2 million. After the 1983–84 season, McCombs replaced Scheer as president and general manager with Vince Boryla, whose association with the team dated to the very first days of its existence. In the 1984–85 season, the Nuggets again won the Midwest Division and made a post-season run all the way to the conference finals before losing to the Los Angeles Lakers.

On May 30, 1985, just days after Denver's defeat, McCombs announced that he had sold the franchise to a group of investors headed by Sidney L. Shlenker, a friend and business associate from Houston, for $20 million. Shlenker's tenure as owner, however, was marked by numerous failures. In his first year, Shlenker negotiated a new 15-year lease at McNichols Arena that tied the team to the venue until 2001. He also planned on spending $7.5 million in renovations, including the construction of luxury boxes, an elaborate VIP lounge and dinner club, three themed restaurants, and a futuristic scoreboard that would feature instant replays. By the time the renovations were completed, Shlenker had paid $12.5 million in construction costs with a heavy debt service, more than the original $10 million that it cost to build McNichols ten years earlier. The restaurants also proved failures as did his investments in other sports prospects, including an arena football league team and a major indoor soccer league franchise that folded even before he could field a team. He also tried to make a public offering of Nuggets stock, but his prospectus revealed that his broadcasting company had gone broke.

Shortly before the 1987–88 season, which proved to be the best in the team's NBA history, Shlenker put the franchise up as collateral on a $25 million loan from Heller Financial Services of New York, a specialist in leveraged buyouts. Finally, in November 1989, Comsat Video Enterprises (a subsidiary of Comsat Corporation, a publicly held satellite and telecommunications company) bought a majority 67.5 percent stake in the franchise. Two African American businessmen, Peter C.B. Bynoe of Chicago and Bertram A. Lee of Boston, held the remaining 32.5 percent stake. Under Robert Wussler, a former president of the CBS television network, Comsat Video financed nearly the entire deal, approximately $45 million plus assuming the debt service for the renovations made to McNichols Sports Arena in 1987 and 1988. The buyout agreement also provided that Bynoe and Lee would serve as managing general partners, with Bynoe in charge of the day-to-day operations. Soon after assuming ownership of the team, tensions emerged between Bynoe and Wussler over the franchise's operations. At the same time, there was frequent turnover among top personnel in the front office. In the corporate suite, an acrimonious split occurred between Bynoe and Lee, the latter of whom had failed to provide his ten percent of the cash needed to purchase the franchise in 1989. With the aim of keeping his group's investment alive, Bynoe recruited other partners, including real estate developer Jerold Wexler and hotel owner Jay Pritzker. In addition, Bynoe mortgaged a 12 percent share of the team to Drexel, Burnham, Lambert, the junk bond investment house. When Lee missed calls for additional capital for the money-losing franchise, he was forced out of the organization. The continuing friction between Wussler and Bynoe concerning the team's day-to-day operations also took a heavy toll on staff morale. The team fared little better on the court in 1990–91, losing 62 of 82 games, the league's worst record. As losses were anticipated to reach $10 million for the year, speculation arose that the franchise would again be up for sale.

The 1990s: Ownership Turnover Continues

The franchise soon made a turnaround, however, due to a series of fortuitous events. In May 1991, Tim Leiweke, a 34-year-old marketing star who had helped launch the Minnesota Timberwolves expansion franchise, was hired as senior vice-president of the Nuggets in charge of reversing the team's business fortunes. Together with Bernie Bickerstaff, a former NBA coach who had been brought in as general manager, Leiweke worked to rebuild the credibility of the franchise with the Denver public. In January 1992, the new chief executive officer of Comsat ousted Wussler from Comsat Video, replacing him with Charlie Lyons, a business executive with experience in the ski and hotel industries in Colorado. Under Lyons, Comsat Video bought out both Drexel, Burnham, Lambert and Bynoe and his partners, assuming 100 percent ownership of the team by the end of summer 1992. Lyons also created a new entity—Comsat Denver, Inc. to manage the franchise's business operations.

With a new management team in place, the franchise began rebuilding the team. Bickerstaff fired Nuggets coach Paul Westhead after his second season produced only 24 wins, four more than his first. In his place, he hired former Nuggets forward Dan Issel. By recruiting new players, including center Dikembo

Mutombo and point guard Mahmoud Abdul-Rauf, the Nuggets scored one of its most notable moments in the 1994 playoffs. After earning the last playoff spot in the Western Conference, the Nuggets faced the Seattle Supersonics, holders of the NBA's best record. Seattle won the first two games, but Motombo's dominating play in the next three games led Denver to produce one of the greatest upsets in NBA history. With its impressive winning season, the team also boasted increased revenue and publicity.

By 1997, however, the Nuggets ranked among the NBA's worst teams after losing several of its leading players, including Motombo, who went to the Atlanta Hawks. Comsat's diversification into sports franchises and entertainment also proved to be significant money losers. The $850 billion communications company had entered the media production and distribution business with the aim of producing content for distribution and broadcast by satellite. In addition to the Nuggets, Comsat bought the Avalanche, winners of the 1996 Stanley Cup, movie maker Beacon Communications, and in November 1997 broke ground on a new multi-million dollar sports arena to replace the aging McNichols venue. The company organized its Denver franchises and entertainment businesses under a separate subsidiary, Ascent Entertainment Group Inc., which went public in 1995. Comsat bought 80 percent of the stock and the remaining 20 percent became available on the NASDAQ exchange. Nonetheless, in the first quarter of 1997 alone, Comsat lost $18 million due exclusively to the lackluster Nuggets and its companion team the Colorado Avalanche, which lost its bid for a second Stanley Cub. In addition, construction costs for the new sports arena, the Pepsi Center, were climbing precipitously, adding to the company's financial woes and helping to spark a shareholder revolt.

The Late 1990s and Beyond

As a result, in 1997 Comsat sold Ascent Entertainment to AT&T's Liberty Media Group of Englewood, Colorado, for $755 million. Liberty immediately put Ascent's sports assets—the Nuggets, the Avalanche, and the Pepsi Center—up for sale while retaining control of the video movie component. In July 2000, after considerable intrigue, false bidders, and failed negotiations by other bidders, St. Louis real estate developer and Wal-Mart heir Stan Kroenke purchased the Denver Nuggets, the Colorado Avalanche, and the Pepsi Center in a deal valued at $450 million. The agreement included $268 million in cash to buy 93.5 percent of the teams and arena, plus $136 million for the assumption of debt on the Pepsi Center. In addition, Kroenke paid $27.3 million in advance ticket sales that had been earmarked for the next season's operations. Liberty retained a 6.5 percent stake worth $18.7 million. Kroenke's bid for the teams and arena came after failed talks with Denver billionaire Donald Strum, who offered $461 for the sports assets but could not reach agreement with the city over whether the teams would remain in Denver for 25 years if he died before that term expired. Other bidders included Kroenke's brother-in-law, Bill Laurie, who offered $400 million for the sports assets, and a three-way partnership that comprised investor John McMullen, Denver Bronco's owner Pat Bowlen, and Bronco's quarterback John Elway. Alan Cohen, owner of the NBA's Boston Celtics, and David McDavid, a Texas auto dealer who sold his share of the NBA's Dallas Mavericks with the aim of buying the Nuggets and the Avalanche, also bid for the sports franchises and sports arena. Nonetheless, Kroenke's winning bid stemmed in part from his willingness to open his books to Liberty executives, plenty of cash, no financing, and a guarantee to the city of Denver that he would not relocate the team for 25 years. After the deal was consummated, Kroenke organized the sports assets under Kroenke Sports Enterprises. With Kroenke's enormous fortune, the Denver Nuggets appeared for the first time to have gained a semblance of long-term stability.

Further Reading

Blevins, Jason, "Game Over as Kroenke Closes Deal for Teams: Nuggets, Avs, Pepsi Center Sale Complete," *Denver Post*, July 7, 2000.

Caulk, Steve, "Pepsi Center Deal Comes As A Shock After Months of Delays, Sudden Sale to Wal-Mart Heir Stuns Other Bidders," *Rocky Mountain News*, April 30, 2000.

——, "Playing to Win: Hard-Driving Kroenke Turns His Energy to Nuggets, Avalanche," *Rocky Mountain News*, August 27, 2000.

——, "Sale of Teams Completed: Kroenke Praised for Easy Purchase of Avs, Nuggets, Arena," *Rocky Mountain News*, July 7, 2000.

Frisch, Aaron, *The History of the Denver Nuggets*, Mankato, MN: Creative Education, 2002.

Monroe, Mike, "Ascent Assets for Sale? Nuggets, Avs Seen as Attractive," *BusDateline*, 1999.

——, *The Rise and Fall . . . and Rise of the Denver Nuggets*, Dallas, TX: Taylor Publishing Company, 1994.

Sachare, Alex, ed., *The Official NBA Basketball Encyclopedia*, second edition, New York: Villard Books, 1994.

—by Bruce P. Montgomery

DiamondCluster International, Inc.

Suite 3000
John Hancock Center
875 N. Michigan Avenue
Chicago, Illinois 60611
U.S.A.
Telephone: (312) 255-5000
Fax: (312) 255-6000
Web site: http://www.diamondcluster.com

Public Company
Incorporated: 1994 as Diamond Technology Partners, Inc.
Employees: 1,478
Sales: $259.34 million (2001)
Stock Exchanges: NASDAQ
Ticker Symbol: DTPI
NAIC: 541611 Administrative Management and General Management Consulting Services; 541618 Telecommunications Management Consulting Services

DiamondCluster International, Inc. is a consulting firm that helps companies develop their Internet-based business and tele-communications strategies. The company, which was created in 2000 with the merger of American firm Diamond Technology Partners, Inc. and Cluster Consulting of Spain, is headquartered in Chicago and has offices in Europe, the United States, and Brazil. The public firm is headed by Diamond Technology Partners co-founder Melvyn Bergstein.

Beginnings

DiamondCluster traces its beginnings to February 1994, when former Technology Solutions Corp. co-chief executive Melvyn E. Bergstein decided to start his own consultancy business. Bergstein, who had lost his job in a recent management shakeup, joined with Christopher Moffitt, Michael Mikolajczyk and eleven others to come up with $7 million in startup funds, also securing $5 million from venture capital firm Safeguard Scientifics, Inc. The new company, Diamond Tech-nology Partners, Inc., was chartered to operate as a consulting firm that would help design and implement computer system integration projects for Fortune 100 companies in the financial services and healthcare industries.

Diamond chose to deploy smaller, more experienced consulting teams than the industry norm, with its recruitment efforts focused on people with 8 to 15 years consulting experience, in addition to an M.B.A. degree. The company required that each new partner would have to be elected by 80 percent of the existing ones, and if a pay offer was rejected by two thirds of the group the chief executive would have to resign. Bergstein, who had also worked for 21 years at the accounting firm of Arthur Andersen, took the jobs of president and CEO. Many of Diamond's 29 original employees came from Technology Solutions, who later sued the firm for damages. During its first months of operation Diamond established relationships with nine clients.

The company's first year was a good one, with $13 million in revenues and expansion to 70 employees. In 1996, Diamond formed a strategic alliance with B. Joseph Pine II and James H. Gilmore of Strategic Horizons LLP to offer ''Mass Customization'' consulting services. The pair's theory laid out ways of managing that could enable businesses to provide customized products to customers while relying on mass production. By this time Diamond had opened a second office in Cleveland, the home base of Strategic Horizons. For fiscal 1996 Diamond's income doubled to $26 million, though the company posted a deficit because it had lost two of its largest customers. The firm now had 145 employees and was doing business with 29 clients.

In 1997, Diamond went public when Safeguard Scientific offered its shareholders the right to purchase one share of Diamond for every ten they owned of Safeguard. A total of 3.2 million shares were offered on the NASDAQ. The firm also formed the Diamond Network during the year, which utilized the expertise of top outside experts like Joseph H. Pine, Microsoft's Gordon Bell, and Disney's Alan Kay to help the company keep on top of developing technology trends. Network members who worked on Diamond projects shared in the proceeds with the firm.

Developing Contacts

The Diamond Network was one element of the firm's public relations strategy, which included sending key staffers on speaking engagements, publishing articles and surveys in journals such as the *Harvard Business Review,* and pitching the firm's services directly to top executives. Keeping its employees happy was another important part of Diamond's business plan, and the firm had a lower-than-average turnover rate for the industry. Among other perks, Diamond paid 100 percent of medical expenses, and allowed partners, who were frequently on the road, to live anywhere they chose to. To keep in touch, the company sent frequent email and voice mail messages and developed a proprietary software system that helped compile the consultants' knowledge so it was available to everyone in the firm. Diamond also held several face-to-face group meetings in Chicago each year.

The company's efforts to keep its name in front of potential clients led to the creation of the Diamond Exchange, a thrice-yearly forum for invited senior executives intended to help them learn about the potential value of digital technology to their businesses. In the fall of 1997, the company also began publishing *Context,* a quarterly magazine that covered technological change in the world of business. *Context,* which was put together by former *Wall Street Journal* editor Paul Carroll, was distributed to 35,000 senior U.S. executives. The magazine's debut issue featured an interview with Microsoft CEO Bill Gates. *Context* was a slick, newsstand-friendly publication with ads from the likes of BMW, Microsoft, and American Airlines. The company had reportedly spent $250,000 on the first issue, with Carroll made a full partner in the firm. *Context* vied for executives' attention with several similar publications already on the market.

By the end of Diamond's fourth fiscal year, in April 1998, sales had grown to $58.4 million, with income of $6 million. An additional offering of three million shares of stock was made just before the accounting period ended. In June, the firm celebrated the release of *Unleashing the Killer App: Digital Strategies for Market Dominance* by Diamond Partner Chunka Mui and company fellow Larry Downes. The book gained a great deal of attention in the media and went on to sell 100,000 copies. It was described by Diamond CEO Bergstein as "a how-to book for CEO's trying to figure out how to compete in a world transformed by technology [that also] provides a guide for investors who want to understand who the winners and losers will be in the digital future." June also saw Bergstein give up the role of president to

Michael E. Mikolajczyk, the firm's chief financial officer. He retained the jobs of CEO and chairman.

In April 1999, Diamond made its first acquisition, purchasing OmniTech Consulting Group of Chicago for approximately $7.5 million. OmniTech, a management consulting firm that specialized in web-based and multimedia corporate training, had been founded in 1985 and employed 43 at offices in Chicago, Boston, and Bridgewater, New Jersey. Its clients included AT&T, Xerox, and Microsoft.

Zeroing in on E-Commerce

By this time, Diamond's practice had become heavily focused on Internet-based business consulting and the now rapidly growing company began ramping up its hiring of support staff to design Web pages and help with so-called "e-commerce" businesses. A new unit, Diamond Marketplace Solutions, was formed to handle work from the many established "bricks and mortar" firms that wanted to get their businesses quickly online, as the rush to get in on the anticipated Internet bonanza became a flood tide. The company's stock price was emulating that of the market's tech stocks, rising 300 percent during 1999. The year also saw the firm open a San Francisco office and acquire the Leverage Group, another consulting firm.

In early 2000, to help deal with its explosive growth, Diamond announced it was creating a new structure and dividing its business into East, Central, West, and European sectors, with a new office also established in London. The firm now had more than 450 employees, and the latest fiscal year ended with a record $136 million in revenues.

Diamond was working with some of the largest corporations in the world on major projects like the Internet-based business-to-business exchange Covisint, formed as a joint venture by Ford, General Motors, and DiamlerChrysler to help the automakers reduce costs in purchasing parts. Diamond was also involved with development of Enron Corp.'s bandwidth trading unit, Enron Broadband Service. Other major clients included Goldman, Sachs; First Data Corp.; Clayton, Dubilier & Rice; and Simon Property Group. Diamond preferred to work with established firms rather than new dot-com startups which had no immediate revenue prospects, a move that brought the company one of the industry's best records for paid-up accounts. Rather than simply establishing a generic online presence for its clients, Diamond consultants worked directly with the companies' CEO's to develop a so-called "killer app" strategy which would utilize the possibilities of the Internet in a way unique to the medium.

In April 2000, Diamond formed a joint venture with Silgan Holdings and Morgan Stanley Dean Whitter Private Equity to form Packtion, a new business-to-business packaging service intended to improve efficiency in the $400 billion global packaging industry. The three firms invested a total of $53 million in the project. The same month Diamond acquired Momentus Group Ltd. of London, which was renamed Diamond Technology Partners Ltd. and merged with Diamond's London office. The three-year old Momentus, acquired for $10 million, was a consulting firm with 21 employees that focused on Web-based business. April also saw Diamond invest in Participate.com, a

---

Key Dates:

1994: Diamond Technology Partners, Inc. is formed by Melvyn E. Bergstein and others.
1997: Diamond Technology goes public on the NAS-DAQ.
1999: The company is acquired by OmniTech Consulting Group.
2000: Diamond Technology merges with Cluster Consulting, and the company's name is changed to DiamondCluster International.
2001: Amid mounting losses the company cuts salaries, lays off staff.

---

new firm that was formed to manage Web communities for other companies. At the same time, the company promoted 13 executives to partner status, raising the total to 74.

In the summer of 2000, Diamond created a formal partnering program to work with outside firms to deliver services. The first to be signed up was iSyndicate, an Internet content creator. Others soon followed, including chipmaking giant Intel, who came aboard in August. By this time Diamond was ranked by Fortune as the ninth fastest growing company in the United States.

Merger with Cluster

September 2000 brought news that Diamond would merge with Cluster Consulting, a Spanish firm that offered consulting services primarily for wireless telecommunications providers. Cluster was the leading telecom advising firm in Europe, with 370 consultants, and clients throughout Europe and in the United States and Brazil. The deal gave Cluster $44 million in cash and 6 million shares of Diamond stock, which was then worth more than $430 million. Cluster was also given options on another seven million shares of the combined company. After the merger, the firm, which changed its name to DiamondCluster International, Inc., would have offices in Chicago, Barcelona, Boston, Dusseldorf, Lisbon, London, Madrid, Munich, New York, Paris, San Francisco, and Sao Paulo. Mel Bergstein continued to head the operation, with Javier Rubio, Cluster's CEO, placed in charge of the company's European and Latin American operations. Cluster had been formed in 1993 and had grown rapidly. Its client list included the likes of Sprint PCS, Ericsson, and Deutsche Telekom. Privately held Cluster's revenues were an estimated $80 million, just under two-thirds of Diamond's total. The move was a necessary one for Diamond according to CEO Bergstein, who told the Chicago Tribune, ''We'd been called to the carpet recently. Unless we have a meaningful presence in Europe, we will not be able to compete for that core transformation work.'' Diamond had also become highly dependent on a few major clients like Goldman, Sachs, which accounted for ten percent of the firm's annual revenues, and Cluster brought an entirely different set of customers to the table.

Analysts were now predicting an imminent shakedown in the Internet consultancy field, as the rush to the Web slowed

down and many promising dot-com's began to show serious signs of trouble. DiamondCluster's share price, which had hit a peak of $98 in July 2000, dropped to $7.50 by the following April, though it began to rebound slightly. As firms began to question their commitment to e-commerce, business began to fall off drastically, and in May the company's partners voted to take a ten percent pay cut, with the rest of the employees urged to take voluntary cuts in exchange for stock options. CEO Bergstein, who pledged no consultants would be laid off, halved his own salary. Several months later, cuts of ten percent were made mandatory for all employees earning more than $50,000 a year, and 200 consultants were placed on furloughs of six months at one-third salary, with everyone at the firm required to take a two-week unpaid vacation. DiamondCluster's 107 partners also agreed to increase their pay cuts to 15 percent, and Bergstein gave his entire paycheck back to the firm. Despite the firm's troubles, 2001 saw DiamondCluster form The Center for Market Leadership, a think tank based at the firm's Boston office, and the Center for Technology Innovation, another research center based at its Chicago headquarters.

All of the cutbacks were not enough to prevent layoffs, however, and with the company counting losses of over $112 million for the first three quarters of the fiscal year on revenues of $145 million, DiamondCluster began to let some consultants go, as well as telling recent M.B.A.'s it had promised jobs to look for work elsewhere. At the end of December, the company was down to 958 consultants, 100 less than a year before, and the size of the firm's support staff had also dropped. DiamondCluster had cash reserves of $113 million available to help ride out the downturn in business, and at the start of 2002 CEO Bergstein voiced his take on the company's outlook, which mirrored that of most firms in its field, commenting, ''We think we have seen the bottom.''

With the most prolonged crisis in years hitting the consulting field, DiamondCluster International was doing its best to hang tough and weather the storm. When the U.S. economy made it back to solid footing, the firm would hopefully be ready to resume its work helping build the still-young Internet and telecommunications industries.

Principal Subsidiaries

Leverage Information Systems, Inc.; OmniTech Consulting Group, Inc.; Momentus Group Limited (U.K.).

Principal Competitors

Andersen Consulting; McKinsey & Co.; Bain & Co.; Braun Consulting, Inc.; The Boston Consulting Group.

Further Reading

Borden, Jeff, ''Consultant Launches Magazine,'' *Crain's Chicago Business*, November 24, 1997, p. 28.
Crockett, Roger O., ''Diamond Technology: Attack of the Killer Apps,'' *Business Week*, May 29, 2000, p. 188.
''Diamond Technology Shuffles Top Management, Names New President,'' *Dow Jones News Service*, February 18, 2000.
Geller, Adam, ''Employers Push Workers to Stay Home in Bid to Cut Costs,'' *Associated Press Newswires*, September 18, 2001.

''Going Public: Locking in, Not Cashing Out,'' *Consultants News*, June 1, 1997, p. 4.

Grace, Tim, ''Diamond Technology Against Giants,'' *Computer Reseller News*, August 22, 1994, p. 168.

Kaiser, Rob, ''Chicago-Based Technology Consulting Company to Cut More Costs,'' *Knight Ridder Tribune Business News*, July 20, 2001.

——, ''Partners of Chicago-Based Internet Consultant Agree to Take Pay Cuts,'' *Knight Ridder Tribune Business News*, May 15, 2001.

Keeton, Ann, ''Diamond Technology CEO Banks On 'Killer' Strategies,'' *Dow Jones News Service*, April 7, 2000.

Lingblom, Marie, ''Economic Ripple Effect Travels Across the Pond,'' *Computer Reseller News*, July 16, 2001, p. 31.

Murphy, H. Lee, ''Diamond Tech Shifts Focus to Internet,'' *Crain's Chicago Business*, August 23, 1999, p. 20.

''Shining a Diamond for Public Consumption,'' *Consultants News*, March 1, 1997, p. 4.

Upbin, Bruce, ''Consulting Silicon in the Snowbelt,'' *Forbes*, December 13, 1999, p. 330.

Wolinsky, Howard, ''Consultants Feel the Heat,'' *Chicago Sun-Times*, November 5, 2001, p. 53.

Zacks, Mitchell, ''Diamond's Unique Strategy Makes It Wall Street Gem,'' Chicago Sun-Times, July 2, 2000, p. 43.

—Frank Uhle

Dr. August Oetker KG

Lutterstrasse 14
D-33617 Bielefeld
Germany
Telephone: (49) (521) 155-0
Fax: (49) (521) 155-2995
Web site: http://www.oetker.de

Private Company
Incorporated: 1902 as Dr. August Oetker, Apotheker,
    Bielefeld
Employees: 18,993
Sales: EUR 5.26 billion ($3.95 billion) (2001)
NAIC: 311822 Flour Mixes and Dough Manufacturing
    from Purchased Flour; 31123 Breakfast Cereal
    Manufacturing; 311412 Frozen Specialty Food
    Manufacturing; 31152 Ice Cream and Frozen Dessert
    Manufacturing; 311813 Frozen Cakes, Pies, and Other
    Pastries Manufacturing; 311812 Commercial Bakeries;
    311999 All Other Miscellaneous Food Manufacturing;
    42249 Other Grocery and Related Products Whole-
    salers; 483111 Deep Sea Freight Transportation;
    31212 Breweries; 31213 Wineries; 31214 Distilleries;
    312112 Bottled Water Manufacturing; 51113 Book
    Publishers; 52211 Commercial Banking; 325312
    Phosphatic Fertilizer Manufacturing; 32532 Pesticide
    and Other Agricultural Chemical Manufacturing;
    721110 Hotels (Except Casino Hotels) and Motels;
    524113 Direct Life Insurance Carriers; 524126 Direct
    Property and Casualty Insurance Carriers; 551112
    Offices of Other Holding Companies

Dr. August Oetker KG is the management holding company for one of the largest players in Germany's food industry, with a leading position in the markets for frozen pizza, baking mixes, products for home canning, breakfast cereals, honey, and cream products. Headquartered in Bielefeld, the company supplies the country's supermarkets with about 370 products carrying the "Dr. Oetker" brand name. Dr. Oetker's four German produc-tion plants manufacture a great variety of processed food products, from baking powder to bake mixes, breakfast cereal, and honey, to frozen desserts, pizza, and seafood specialties. Although Germany is the company's major market, Dr. Oetker's food division Oetker International operates factories and markets products in most western and eastern European countries as well as in Canada and Brazil. Although best known for its "Dr. Oetker" line of products, the group holds a diverse portfolio of interests in other industries. Oetker's food division includes baked goods manufacturers Martin Braun KG and Swiss Agrano AG, as well as catering wholesaler "Frische Paradies," which serves upscale eateries in large German cities.

Oetker's sparkling wine, wine, and spirits division Henkell & Söhnlein is Germany's number-one seller of sparkling wine. Its best known German brands are premium sparkling wines "Fürst von Metternich," "Henkell Trocken," "Söhnlein Brilliant," and "Deinhard;" wines include the German brand "Deinhard Trocken," Hungarian labels "Csárdás" and "Dél Balatoni," and Italian brand "Prosecco Yello"; the division's most famous liquor is "Wodka Gorbatschow." Henkell & Söhnlein also owns leading sparkling wine manufacturers in the Czech Republic, Slovakia, Poland, Hungary, Austria, and France and distributes alcohol-free energy drinks such as "Red Bull."

Although Oetker's food and wine divisions generate about 43 percent of total sales, the company's less well known deep sea shipping division Hamburg Süd alone accounted for another 44 percent. The company, which owns 19 ships, operates scheduled container freight services around the globe, with a strong market position on the Europe-South America route. Hamburg Süd also charters ships on demand for its customers, which accounts for about one quarter of the division's revenues. Oetker's fourth consolidated business division is called "other interests" and includes such diverse holdings as five luxury hotels in Germany, Switzerland, and France; food retailer Meyer & Beck in Berlin; German specialty chemicals manufacturer Budenheim with U.S. subsidiary Gallard Schlesinger; the company's cookbook publishing house Dr. Oetker Verlag; as well as real estate management and construction subsidiaries.

In addition to Dr. Oetker's four consolidated business divisions, the group has major interests in other companies, which are organized in two nonconsolidated divisions. The group's beer and nonalcoholic beverage division is organized under the umbrella of the Radeberger group and includes national beer brands such as ''Radeberger'' and ''Schöfferhofer,'' the nonalcoholic beer ''Clausthaler,'' premium sparkling mineral water ''Selters,'' as well as a number of regional beer brands in Germany, Poland, and the Czech Republic and beverage retail chain Getränke Hoffmann with 200 outlets in and around Berlin. Oetker's financial services division includes shareholdings in German bank Bankhaus Lampe, as well as in German life and property and casualty insurer Condor and auto insurer Optima. Dr. August Oetker is the fourth-generation CEO who heads the family-owned group consisting of more than 200 companies.

Baking Powder with Guarantee a Success in the 1890s

Dr. August Oetker's great-grandfather, who bore the same name, built the foundation of the Oetker empire in the last decade of the 19th century. Oetker did not invent baking powder, as some Germans believe. But in many hours of trial and error—the 29-year-old experimented late at night at the pharmacy he had taken over in 1891—he developed one that, according to his promise to German housewives, would always do the perfect job. That was not necessarily the case with other baking powders on the market at that time. Making sure that he used only top-quality raw ingredients and that they were mixed in the same ratio all the time, he called his baking powder ''Backin,'' put a ''Dr. Oetker'' label on the packet, and started selling it on the side in Bielefeld. Dr. August Oetker's success was mainly due to his clever marketing ideas. To promote his baking powder, he published booklets with recipes and printed some of them on the packaging. In newspaper ads Oetker stressed ''Backin's'' high quality and reliability—''just the right amount for one pound of flour.''

Oetker soon added new products that carried the ''Dr. Oetker'' brand, including vanilla-flavored sugar and pudding mix. To keep up with the ever-growing demand, his ''side business'' expanded to industrial proportions. In May 1900 a brand-new ''Dr. Oetker'' factory started operations. To better distinguish his merchandise, Oetker introduced a trademark—a woman's head in profile on a red background—which he started printing on all of his packages in 1900. Around the same time he established the company's own trial kitchen where all ''Dr. Oetker'' products were rigorously tested by baking-savvy women. The company's product range expanded further to include powder for dessert sauces, gelatin, pancake mix, ice cream powder, and other dessert specialties in different flavors.

In 1908 August Oetker established his first foreign subsidiary in Vienna, Austria, which also became a success.

Surviving Two World Wars: 1914–45

The outbreak of World War I in 1914 suddenly interrupted Oetker's successful growth. August Oetker's son Rudolf was drafted to serve in the German army and lost his life in the Battle of Verdun in 1916. The company founder himself died two years later. His legacy, however, was the creation of one of Germany's first brand name products.

The widow of the company founder's son remarried Richard Kaselowsky, who took over the company's management. Under his leadership Oetker further expanded internationally after World War I had ended. By 1920 the company employed 600 people and produced about 300 million packages with the ''Dr. Oetker'' brand name on them. New subsidiaries sprang up abroad, extending the company's reach to The Netherlands, Belgium, Luxembourg, Denmark, Norway, and Italy. Kaselowsky was no less imaginative than his predecessor when it came to advertising his products. In the late 1920s the company promoted the ''Dr. Oetker'' brand with 20-minute-long commercials in movie theaters. A promotional truck pulling a giant Bundt pan traveled all over the country, educating German housewives about the latest ''Dr. Oetker'' products and baking tips.

Whereas Germany's lower and middle classes had lost their savings in the hyperinflation of the early 1920s, many of them lost their jobs in the early 1930s. The mass unemployment caused by the worldwide economic depression led to mass poverty and political and social unrest. In those times of hardship and food scarcity for many, Dr. Oetker published ''lean'' recipes that showed housewives how to make delicious baked goods with less ingredients. Adolf Hitler's National Socialist party, which resumed political power in Germany in 1933, eased the suffering by sponsoring job programs, but drove the country into another devastating war. Richard Kaselowsky, his wife, and two half-sisters were killed in a bombing raid during World War II in 1944.

Building a Diversified International Group After 1945

Rudolf August Oetker, the founder's grandson, took on the leadership of the family business after World War II. Born just six months after his father had lost his life in the battlefield, Rudolf August had no formal education but a bank apprenticeship. In 1941 he had been introduced into the family enterprise and rolled up his sleeves after the war to revive the shrunken organization. A number of foreign subsidiaries that had been expropriated during the war were re-purchased. Soon it became obvious that ''Dr. Oetker's'' popularity was unbroken. Only the Holy Bible was sold more often in Germany than the company's cookbooks. Demand for ''Dr. Oetker'' products grew fast after the currency reform in June 1948. In the 1950s the company established 15 foreign production and distribution subsidiaries and grew significantly during the ''economic miracle'' years. In the 1960s Oetker ventured into the frozen food market and expanded its product range to include ready-made frozen entrees and cooled desserts, ice cream, and Créme fraîche, a French specialty made from cream, followed in the 1970s by frozen pizza.

Key Dates:

1891: Pharmacist Dr. August Oetker invents the baking powder ''Backin.''
1900: The Dr. Oetker trial kitchen is established.
1908: The company's first subsidiary is set up in Austria.
1922: The cookbook, ''The Joy of Baking,'' is published.
1945: Rudolf August Oetker takes over as CEO.
1958: Rudolf August Oetker acquires Henkell & Söhnlein Rheingold AG.
1961: Oetker takes over control of Hamburg-Südamerikanische Dampfschiffahrts-AG.
1981: Rudolf August Oetker's son Dr. August Oetker takes over leadership.
1990: Oetker acquires the ''Radeberger Pilsner'' brewery and frozen seafood specialty manufacturer Copa Bade.
1993: New business division Oetker International East is established.
2002: The company launches the frozen pizza line ''Culinaria.''

Rudolf August Oetker also opened a new chapter of the company's history, however, as he began to diversify the group through acquisitions. In 1955 he became the personally liable partner in Hamburg-Südamerikanische Dampfschiffahrts-AG (for short, Hamburg-Süd), one of Germany's largest deep sea shipping companies in which the Oetker family had acquired a stake in 1934. Founded in 1871 by prominent entrepreneurs in Hamburg, the company had grown to its size through the ever-expanding trade and the streams of emigrants and migrant workers between Europe and South America in the late 19th and early 20th centuries. During that time, tens of thousands of seasonal farm workers from eastern and southern Europe crossed over to South America on container ships to harvest coffee and wheat. After World War I Hamburg-Süd offered passenger service for tourists for the first time, cruising the seas around Scandinavia and the Mediterranean. The company's flagship luxury cruise liner ''Cap Arcona'' became infamous when the ship brought more than 26,000 refugees from besieged Eastern Prussia to the West in the last months of World War II. Then Hitler's SS took over the ship and converted it into a floating prison. On May 3, 1945, a British dive bomber sank the ship anchored in Lübeck's harbor—and more than 4,500 prisoners, some transferred there from concentration camps, drowned.

With a federal low-interest loan for the postwar reconstruction of Germany's destroyed harbor and fleet Oetker rebuilt the company. In 1951 Hamburg-Süd was transformed into a private company in which OHG Dr. August Oetker held 49.4 percent. Oetker added another old German shipping firm, Deutsche Levante Linie, to Hamburg-Süd, which within only a few years outgrew all of his German competitors. In 1961 Rudolf August Oetker became the company's sole owner. Container freight shipping replaced the piece-good transportation in the following decades and the emerging airline industry took away most passengers from passenger lines. Despite some crises, however, Hamburg-Süd managed to stay on top of the business.

Aside from Hamburg-Süd, Oetker acquired major stakes in several breweries, wineries, and distilleries; luxury hotels in Germany, Switzerland, and France; Bankhaus Lampe, a bank; and direct life and casualty insurer Condor. In 1981 Rudolf August Oetker retired and was succeeded by his eldest son Dr. August Oetker. He remained actively involved in the business, however, as an advisor and shareholder.

Fourth Family Generation Taking Over in the 1980s

August Oetker was chosen by his father from among his seven brothers and sisters to lead the company into the 1980s. After graduating from high school he felt drawn to the sea and started working as an apprentice at deep sea shipping company Knoehr & Burchard in Hamburg. For another three years Oetker worked at other shipping companies and agencies in Germany and abroad, and studied business administration at Münster University from 1968 until 1972. After graduating from college Oetker worked at investment banks in London and New York. In 1978 he was thrust involuntarily into the spotlight of the German media when his brother Richard was kidnapped. The then-34-year-old August delivered the DM 21 million that the kidnapper had blackmailed from his father. In 1979 August Oetker joined the family business and two years later he took the leading position.

In the 1980s August Oetker streamlined the group's organization, introduced new products, and launched programs for making the company's operations more environmentally friendly. Several legally independent subsidiaries in the food sector were reorganized under the umbrella of Dr. August Oetker Nahrungsmittel KG, the new management holding company for the group's domestic activities. One of the company's successful new product launches was a line of breakfast cereals. In 1987 Oetker hired his first full-time environmental manager, who in the following years introduced environmental programs in several areas. For example, Oetker started using organically grown grains in its breakfast cereals. In 1995 the company published its first environmental report based on audits that were conducted in cooperation with the *Umweltbundesamt,* the German federal environmental protection agency. In the same year August Oetker was awarded the title ''Eco-manager 1995'' by the WWF and the German magazine *Capital.* In 1988, Oetker expanded into Turkey, where a joint venture was set up with the Piyale family enterprise to market ''Dr. Oetker'' products.

Taking Risks and Sticking with Family Tradition in the 1990s and Beyond

After the fall of the Berlin Wall and the disintegration of the Soviet Union August Oetker initiated an expansion program into Eastern Europe. Despite the obvious risks, he saw mainly opportunities. In 1990 the company acquired three East German breweries in Potsdam, Leipzig, and near Dresden and later built a brand-new factory for frozen entrees and baked goods in Wittenburg, located in the Eastern German state of Mecklenburg-Vorpommern. In the following years the company established subsidiaries in Hungary and Slovakia, took over food manufacturer Oliwa and pizza maker Rigga in Poland, and set up a joint venture with a food manufacturer in Moscow, Russia, to produce breakfast cereals. In 1993 the company's holding for its international business, Oetker International GmbH, was split into two subgroups, one for Western Europe and the Americas, and one for Eastern Europe. August Oetker's brother Richard took over the management of Oetker International East. Later in the decade Oetker's food division expanded into Croatia, Slovenia, Macedonia, Bulgaria, and Malaysia. Oetker's sparkling wine division acquired German competitor Deinhard AG and Polish wine maker Vinpol. The national beer brands ''Radeberger Pilsener'' and ''Schoefferhofer Weizen'' grew in the two-digit range, while sales of ''Binding'' and other regional brands declined. In summer 2002 Oetker decided to merge the existing seven sales organizations for beer into two and to rename the company's beer division Radeberger.

In the West the food sector went through a phase of stagnating growth. New competitors, shrinking consumer demand, and the consolidation of retail chains contributed to the declining prices in some segments. Instead of giving in to the pressure to lower prices, Oetker kept investing in advertising its brand name and stuck with its quality standards. The company increasingly focused on strategically important market segments, invested in new product development, and unified the packaging design scheme for its baking ingredients. With sales of ice cream declining sharply, Oetker sold off this part of the food division, closed its Austrian subsidiary, but invested heavily in penetrating Europe, including Turkey, with its frozen pizza lines ''Ristorante'' and ''Culinaria.''

In the early 1990s the weak dollar after the Persian Golf crisis and recessions in South America, Australia, New Zealand, and the United States took their toll on Hamburg Süd. Later in the decade overcapacities put pressure on freight rates, which declined constantly. Oetker decided to cooperate with other shipping companies and focused on promoting Hamburg Süd's capacities for refrigerated shipping services. In 1996, however, the shipping company slipped into the red. A merger with major competitor Hapag-Lloyd was considered, but abandoned. Instead, Oetker invested in rationalizing Hamburg Süd's operations and sold off a few ships to boost the company's cash flow. The financial crises in Asia and South America in the late 1990s kept the shipping company in the red. Despite the unfavorable conditions, Hamburg Süd took over several competitors during the decade, including Furness Withy & Co., Laser Lines, Alianca, and Transroll. Finally, in 2000 the deep sea shipping market recovered and Hamburg Süd, which by then had become one of Germany's two leading players, turned up profits again.

Some of Oetker's five luxury hotels, which were organized under the umbrella of Oetker AG—Brenner's Parkhotel & Spa in Baden-Baden, Park Hotel Vitznau at Vierwaldstädter See in Switzerland, the Bristol in Paris, the Hotel du Cap Eden Roc in the French Cap d'Antibes, and Chateau du Domaine St-Martin in Vence in the French Provence—were struggling with low occupancy rates and high cost. Frankfurter Bankgesellschaft von 1899 AG, in which Oetker had acquired a majority stake, merged its banking operations with Bankhaus Lampe KG, after Frankfurter had lost DM 42 million in the mid-1990s when two of the private bank's corporate clients went bankrupt. In 2001 Bankhaus Lampe's business amounted to EUR 3.7 billion.

By the beginning of the 21st century, 98 out of 100 Germans knew the ''Dr. Oetker'' brand. Despite intensifying international consolidation in the food manufacturing and retail markets, there were no signs that the Oetker group would abandon its family tradition when the company entered its 111th year. At the beginning of the 1990s Rudolf August Oetker had distributed shares in the group's various operations among his eight children. He kept the company's stakes in luxury hotels and banks for himself, in which he had a personal interest. Two of Rudolf August Oetker's children other than August and Richard Oetker were actively involved in the family enterprise. Christian Oetker was responsible for market research in the group's food division. Daughter Rosely Schweizer was the personally liable shareholder for Henkell & Söhnlein. August Oetker was not concerned about not being able to find a successor among his family, including his own six children. The 58-year old Oetker told *Frankfurter Allgemeine Zeitung* reporter Svenja Wilke in the spring of 2002, however, that he found it more important for his successor to have the skills needed to successfully carry on the company than to bear the name Oetker.

Principal Subsidiaries

Oetker International GmbH; Langnese Honig KG; Agrano AG (Switzerland); Henkell & Söhnlein Sektkellereien KG; Hamburg-Südamerikanische Dampfschiffahrtsgesellschaft KG; Binding-Brauerei AG; Bankhaus Hermann Lampe KG (70%); Meyer & Beck Handels-Kommanditgesellschaft; Brenner's Park Hotel GmbH; Dr. Oetker Verlag KG; Chemische Fabrik Budenheim Rudolf A. Oetker KG; Gallard Schlesinger Industries Inc. (United States); Douglas Holding AG (11.5%).

Principal Competitors

RUF Lebensmittelwerk GmbH & Co.; Maggi GmbH; C.H. Knorr GmbH; Wagner Tiefkühlprodukte GmbH; Freiberger Lebensmittel GmbH & Co.; Hapag Lloyd AG.

Further Reading

Balzer-Drohner, Heike, ''Oetker gibt Backzutaten weltweit gleiches Gesicht,'' *Lebensmittel Zeitung,* November 30, 2001, p. 50.

Chwallek, Andreas, ''August Oetker sieht den Konzern gut gewappnet,'' *Lebensmittel Zeitung,* July 12, 2002, p. 12.

——, ''Oetker verbucht solide Entwicklung,'' *Lebensmittel Zeitung,* July 14, 2000, p. 14.

''Die Gruppe der Oetker-Hotels kann noch größer werden,'' *Frankfurter Allgemeine Zeitung,* November 4, 1994, p. 24.

''Die Oetker-Gruppe profitiert von wirksamer Markenpflege,'' *Frankfurter Allgemeine Zeitung,* September 2, 1993, p. 16.

''Dr. Oetker: Der Konzern dämpft die Erwartungen,'' *Der Tagesspiegel* (online edition), July 11, 2001.

Drohner, Klaus, ''Oetker wächst über dem Durchschnitt,'' *Lebensmittel Zeitung,* March 29, 1996, p. 12.

''From Germany to Istanbul, Oetker Markets Frozen Pizza,'' *Quick Frozen Foods International,* April 2001, p. 64.

''From Greek to Chinese Toppings, Dr. Oetker Debuts Culinaria Line,'' *Quick Frozen Foods International,* April 2002, p. 76.

Helmer, Wolfgang, ''Die Oetker-Gruppe trägt bis heute die Handschrift der Familie,'' *Frankfurter Allgemeine Zeitung,* February 2, 1995, p. 16.

Helmer, Wolfgang, ''Glaubt an die Marke,'' *Frankfurter Allgemeine Zeitung,* July 10, 2002, p. 15.

Hoffmann, Thomas, ''Westfälischer Puddingprinz auf Öko-Kurs,'' *HORIZONT,* October 13, 1995, p. 81.

Kurze Unternehmensgeschichte, Bielefeld, Germany: Dr. August Oetker Nahrungsmittel KG, 1996.

"Mehr Chancen als Risiken im Osten," *Werben und Verkaufen,* November 12, 1993, p. 72.

Meyer-Larsen, Werner, "Legenden des Wirtschaftswunders," *DER SPIEGEL,* May 17, 1999, p. 140.

"Oetker beklagt Preisrutsch bei Pizzen," *Süddeutsche Zeitung,* August 31, 1994.

"Oetker: Hamburg-Süd auch künftig tragende Säule des Konzerns," *Frankfurter Allgemeine Zeitung,* October 24, 1996, p. 22.

"Oetker legt Bankentöchter zusammen," *Börsen-Zeitung,* March 19, 1998, p. 5.

"Oetker legt eine Verschnaufpause ein," *Süddeutsche Zeitung,* September 3, 1992.

"Oetker wächst vor allem bei Nahrungsmitteln," *Börsen-Zeitung,* September 3, 1997, p. 8.

"Oetker wieder in ruhigeren Bahnen," *Süddeutsche Zeitung,* September 5, 1991.

"Oetker will sich die Ostmärkte rechtzeitig vornehmen," *Frankfurter Allgemeine Zeitung,* March 11, 1993, p. 19.

"Rudolf August Oetker 80," *Frankfurter Allgemeine Zeitung,* September 18, 1996, p. 25.

"Schiffahrt bleibt Sorgenkind bei Oetker," *Börsen-Zeitung,* July 16, 1999, p. 27.

Wilke, Svenja, "Im Porträt: Dr. August Oetker," *Frankfurter Allgemeine Zeitung,* May 19, 2002, p. 44.

—Evelyn Hauser

DVI, Inc.

2500 York Road
Jamison, Pennsylvania 18929
U.S.A.
Telephone: (215) 488-5000
Toll Free: (800) 665-4384
Fax: (215) 488-5010
Web site: http://www.dvi-inc.com

Public Company
Incorporated: 1985 as Delta Health, Inc.
Employees: 375
Sales: $139.62 million (2001)
Stock Exchanges: New York
Ticker Symbol: DVI
NAIC: 522298 All Other Non-Depository Credit
    Intermediation

DVI, Inc. is a finance company serving the healthcare industry. The company provides medical equipment financing and medical receivables financing, enabling mid-sized healthcare providers such as outpatient healthcare centers, physician group practices, and medical imaging centers to acquire costly medical equipment. DVI provides financing for equipment ranging between $5,000 and $3 million, including high-cost items such as magnetic resonance imaging equipment and less expensive purchases such as X-ray systems. The company's medical receivables business helps its customers meet cash flow problems or fund expansion, enabling healthcare providers to use money they are owed by insurance companies or government agencies as collateral to obtain working capital. DVI maintains operations in 15 U.S. cities and is expanding internationally, where its services are offered in Latin America, South Africa, Asia, Australia, Europe, and the United Kingdom.

Origins

DVI's predecessor, Delta Health, Inc., was founded by David L. Higgins in 1985. Before starting Delta Health, Higgins had spearheaded North American sales and service operations

for Elscint, Inc., an Israel-based manufacturer of diagnostic imaging equipment. Higgins created Delta Health to serve as a healthcare services provider, originally forming the company to manage healthcare facilities. The company's name and its nature of business would change, however, transforming into a type of company that financed the purchase of equipment produced by Higgins' former employer and other manufacturers. The transformation was engendered by Higgins' response to dramatic changes in the healthcare industry, changes that began to occur during the mid-1980s.

During the mid-1980s, the need for the services provided by DVI was born. When the federal government replaced ''cost-plus'' reimbursement for Medicare with a fixed fee reimbursement system, hospitals were forced to justify the acquisition of costly medical equipment by meeting a standard of utilization for the equipment. If a sufficient level of utilization was not met for a particular piece of equipment, the hospital could not obtain the particular item. Insurance companies followed the federal government's lead and limited the amount they would pay for medical services, which forced groups of physicians and non-hospital medical providers to acquire equipment for medical services such as magnetic resonance imaging (MRI), radiation therapy, and lithotripsy (the pulverization of kidney stones or gallstones). Because many hospitals cut back on purchasing high-cost medical equipment, non-hospital healthcare providers, for the first time, became major users of such equipment. There was a problem, however. Generally, the non-hospital healthcare providers did not possess the clout to obtain financing from traditional lending sources. A new market niche was created to meet this need, providing a new source of revenue for commercial finance companies and for companies like DVI, which specialized in providing financing for medical equipment.

Although medical equipment financing came to serve as DVI's core business in the twenty-first century, its original business of managing healthcare facilities occupied much of the company's attention during the early 1990s. Renamed Diagnostic Ventures Inc. (the source of the initials ''DVI'' that later became the company's corporate title) in 1988, the company fleshed out its diagnostic imaging services business through a series of acquisitions. In October 1991, the company purchased

Company Perspectives:

Our singular understanding of the industry allows us to enjoy a special relationship with healthcare providers to whom we extend credit. More than merely lenders, we become partners to our borrowers, because experience teaches us this is the surest guarantee for their success and, ultimately, our own. In evaluating the creditworthiness of a potential customer, we don't stop with a cursory examination of financial statements. We take an entrepreneurial ''we want to do business with you'' approach and explore ways to structure deals that work. Then, we roll up our sleeves and do exactly that. We talk to the physicians who will refer patients to utilize the medical equipment we finance. We study local demographics, utilization patterns, patient volumes, and the competitive environment. We don't just review a borrower's business plan for the equipment; we help them refine one. If the plan calls for a new facility, we discuss site selection, facility design, and layout. A ribbon cutting is just an intermediate step in what we view as a long-term relationship. We stay involved for the long haul. If the business encounters problems, we can help clients adjust the business plan. Our competitors foreclose on problems. We work to solve them. This attitude, combined with our knowledge and experience, helps explain why DVI enjoys a below average loss rate. In fact, since our first full year of operations in 1987, the Company has incurred losses of only 0.5%, while underwriting $5.2 billion of loans and credit commitments.

a stake in Healthcare Imaging Services, Inc., a provider of diagnostic imaging and lithotripsy services to outpatient healthcare providers in the northeastern United States. In February 1992, DVI purchased an equity interest in SMT Health Services, Inc., a provider of diagnostic imaging services and radiation therapy services in the state of Washington and in the mid-Atlantic area. Later in the year, in September, the company acquired another stake in a diagnostic imaging services company, purchasing an equity interest in IPS Health Care, Inc., which operated in southern California.

New Corporate Strategy: 1993

Less than a year after investing in diagnostic imaging services companies, DVI's management team altered the company's strategic course. In June 1993, the company announced its decision to dispose of the seven outpatient facilities it operated. Within a year, the company had either divested or entered into definitive agreements to sell five of the facilities; the investment and assets of the remaining two facilities were written off. Along with the disposition of its original business, the company divested its interests in Healthcare Imaging Service, SMT, and IPS. Once these transactions were completed, DVI was left to operate exclusively as a financial services company.

When the dynamics of the healthcare industry changed during the mid-1980s, the new market niche created to cater to non-hospital healthcare providers became quickly populated. Commercial finance companies and general equipment lessors flocked to the new market niche during the mid- and late 1980s, but by the early 1990s most of these competitors had exited the market. DVI, unique in its position as an experienced healthcare provider newly cast as a financial services company, bolstered its market presence as the number of competitors diminished. At roughly the same time the company was shedding its role as a medical services provider, it expanded its financial services capabilities.

In 1993, the company acquired Concord Leasing, Inc., a provider of medical, aircraft, shipping, and industrial equipment financing. Concord's subsidiary, U.S. Concord, Inc., provided equipment financing for the medical imaging industry. The acquisition was significant not only because it was involved in DVI's new, exclusive line of business but also because it marked the arrival of Michael A. O'Hanlon, Concord Leasing's president and chief executive officer. O'Hanlon, a former senior executive at Pitney Bowes Credit Corporation, joined DVI in March 1993 as the company's executive vice-president. Promotions soon followed, making O'Hanlon the company's president and chief operating officer in September 1994 and its chief executive officer in November 1995.

The addition of Concord Leasing and O'Hanlon occurred at approximately the same time DVI completed another important acquisition. In January 1993, the company purchased Medical Equipment Finance Corporation (MEF). MEF was well established in the medical equipment finance arena, possessing numerous long-term relationships with equipment purchasers and many of the largest manufacturers of diagnostic imaging equipment. Equally as important, MEF had cultivated strong ties with funding sources, credit rating agencies, and others in the financial market. The acquisition of MEF marked the beginning of DVI's explosive rise in the medical equipment financing market. In 1992, the company completed $46.4 million worth of financing transactions, a figure that increased to $58.6 million in 1993 before leaping to $163 million in 1994.

By the mid-1990s, DVI was touting itself as one of the leading independent sources of financing for diagnostic imaging and radiation therapy equipment. Nearly all of the company's fixed-interest financing transactions were structured so that the full cost of the equipment and all financing costs were recouped during the financing term, which generally lasted five years. The equipment financed ranged in cost from $100,000 to $2 million, including high-cost MRI equipment, radiation therapy systems, and less expensive equipment such as ultrasound and X-ray systems. Aside from financing medical equipment, DVI, beginning in 1993, also operated a medical receivables business through which the company provided loans to healthcare providers who used their receivables from payors such as insurance companies and Medicare as collateral. During the years immediately following O'Hanlon's arrival and the acquisition of MEF, DVI enjoyed robust growth in both its business segments. After the substantial gain recorded in 1994, DVI's volume of equipment financing loans grew stridently, swelling to $238 million in 1995 and $316 million in 1996. The volume of medical receivables funded by the company increased from roughly $22 million in 1995 to $38 million in 1996.

Further Expansion in the Late 1990s

As DVI entered the latter half of the 1990s, the company stepped up its efforts to tailor itself into an international firm

Key Dates:

1985: David L. Higgins founds DVI's predecessor, Delta Health, Inc.
1993: DVI announces its decision to focus exclusively on healthcare financing.
1995: Michael A. O'Hanlon is named DVI's chief executive officer.
1999: The pace of international expansion accelerates.
2001: After underwriting $5.2 billion of loans and credit commitments, DVI reports it has incurred losses of only 0.5 percent.

with a global reach. In November 1995, DVI formed a joint venture with a subsidiary of CoreStates Financial Corp. and Philips Medical Systems, a major manufacturer of medical equipment. The company created through the joint venture, Medical Equipment Credit Pte. Ltd. (MEC), was established in Singapore, its mission to garner a share of the expanding diagnostic imaging market in the Asia-Pacific region. DVI invested $2 million for a 40 percent stake in MEC. DVI also joined forces with Philips Medical to enter markets in Latin America, part of the company's overseas expansion efforts that would see it establish a presence in Australia, Thailand, and Europe.

DVI's progress during the late 1990s delivered continued financial growth as the company assumed a posture of considerable influence in the medical equipment finance industry. By the end of the company's fiscal year in June 1998, its volume of equipment financing loans had eclipsed the half-billion-dollar mark, reaching $524 million, exponentially higher than the $46 million recorded six years earlier. DVI's medical receivables business grew substantially as well, maturing into a meaningful contributor to the company's financial vitality. After increasing to $75 million in 1997, the medical receivables funded by the company grew to $137 million in 1998.

Following the disclosure of its financial results in June 1998, DVI pursued expansion in earnest, completing a series of acquisitions that injected growth both domestically and abroad. In September 1998, the company paid $77.5 million for Affiliated Capital, a Chicago-based medical equipment financing business. Also in September, DVI acquired Healthcare Technology Solutions, a 20 year-old firm that designed accounts receivable analysis software for financial services companies and accounts receivable collections software for healthcare providers. In June 1999, DVI bolstered its foreign interests by opening DVI Italia, S.r.l. in Milan. Through its Italian subsidiary, DVI, in October 1999, purchased certain assets of Leasing Medica Europa S.p.A., a company that specialized in providing financing to healthcare providers.

DVI's expansion in Italy paved the way for further overseas growth as the company entered the twenty-first century. In March 2000, the company opened DVI Finance SA (Pty) Ltd., a South African subsidiary based in suburban Johannesburg. Through DVI Finance, the company provided medical equipment financing and other financial services to healthcare providers, including clinics, medical centers, and physicians groups. In June 2000, DVI acquired a joint venture interest in Medi Lease B.V., a Dutch company based in Helvoirt. Medi Lease offered financing services to hospitals and other healthcare organizations.

DVI's efforts to become the dominant healthcare financing firm earned the company national recognition in late 2000. *Forbes* magazine selected DVI as one of the ''200 Best Small Companies in America,'' praising the company for 30 percent sales growth for the previous five years and for nearly tripling its earnings from the $8 million posted in 1996 to the $23.5 million recorded in 2000. On the heels of the plaudits handed out by *Forbes* magazine, DVI lined up $150 million in funding for its foreign expansion, with roughly half of the total earmarked for the Far East and Latin America. DVI derived approximately 15 percent of its business from overseas operations at this point, a total the company's management hoped to increase to 20 percent within the first several years of the new century. In December 2001, the company made good on its pledge for further international growth when it announced a joint venture with Diamond Lease Co. Ltd., a major leasing company based in Japan. The joint venture company created through agreement was named Diamond Medical Finance Company Ltd., of which DVI owned 50 percent. Based in Tokyo, Diamond Medical provided financing services for diagnostic and other medical equipment in Japan.

As DVI progressed toward its 20th anniversary, its position as one of the dominant healthcare financing concerns appeared secure. In the years ahead, the company anticipated continued expansion, particularly in international markets. In April 2002, DVI announced an agreement with Captiva Finance Ltd., a finance company based in Toronto, Canada, to establish DVI Canada. Through DVI Canada, the company intended to penetrate the market for financing diagnostic and other therapeutic medical equipment in Canada. Another signal of the company's future strength became apparent in May 2002, when DVI announced the completion of a $441 million equipment lease asset-backed securitization. It was the 30th such transaction the company had completed, representing the largest dollar amount in its history.

Principal Subsidiaries

DVI Financial Services, Inc.; DVI Strategic Partner Group, Inc.; DVI Business Credit, Inc.; Third Coast Capital, Inc.; DVI Equipment Finance; DVI International, Inc.

Principal Competitors

GE Commercial Finance; The FINOVA Group, Inc.; CIT Group Inc.

Further Reading

Geiger, Mia, ''CEO Portrait,'' *Philadelphia Business Journal,* February 9, 2001, p. 14.
Gotlieb, Andy, ''Firm Makes Mark in Health-Care Financing,'' *Philadelphia Business Journal,* June 15, 2001, p. 6.

—Jeffrey L. Covell

Egyptian General Petroleum Corporation

Palestine Street part 4
New Maadi
Cairo
Egypt
Telephone: (2) 706-5956
Fax: (2) 702-8813
Web site: http://www.egpc.com.eg

State-Owned Company
Incorporated: 1956 as General Petroleum Authority
Sales: E£2.66 billion ($1.04 billion) (1986)
NAIC: 211111 Crude Petroleum and Natural Gas
    Extraction; 213112 Support Activities for Oil and Gas
    Field Exploration; 324110 Petroleum Refineries;
    486990 All Other Pipeline Transportation

The Egyptian General Petroleum Corporation (EGPC) operates as a state-owned concern overseeing the petroleum industry in Egypt. Egypt's government, through EGPC, owns or partially owns a large group of companies, including the Gulf of Suez Petroleum Co. (Gupco), Petrobel, General Petroleum Co. (GPC), Badr el-Din Petroleum Company, Suez Oil Company, and El Zaafarana Oil Company. All of Egypt's refineries are run by EGPC subsidiaries. Starting in the early 1990s, Egypt began reforming its fiscal policy and launched incentives to promote foreign investment and exploration. The country is privatizing many of its industry sectors but keeping tight reins over EGPC. Although Egypt is not among the most important players on the international oil scene, oil is a vital element of the Egyptian economy. Oil exports are a major source of scarce foreign currency, accounting for 40 percent of export earnings and ten percent of gross domestic product (GDP) in the late 1990s. The country currently operates as an oil exporter, but increases in demand and declining oil production have raised concern that by 2010 Egypt will become a net importer of oil. This increase in demand coupled with high international oil prices forced the country to report its first oil trade deficit in nearly 25 years in 1999. As such, EGPC and its subsidiaries are focused on exploration activities and growth in the natural gas sector.

History of Egyptian Oil Production

Egypt's oil was not always as firmly under the control of its government. As early as the 1860s, the government began drilling for oil. In 1869, the Gemsa field came to light, but it was left to overseas interests to develop the find after a delay of over 40 years. Anglo-Egyptian Oilfields, a joint venture between Shell and British Petroleum, began to produce oil from the Gemsa field in 1910. Three years later, another field at Hurghada was brought onstream by Anglo-Egyptian, which mapped the west coast of the Gulf of Suez in the course of its explorations.

Five more oil fields were found between the world wars. By the time exploration resumed after World War II, other foreign companies were becoming involved. However, Anglo-Egyptian was still the dominant player until 1964, when it was nationalized.

In 1956, the General Petroleum Authority (GPA) had been created by the Egyptian government to safeguard the country's interests in the development of its valuable mineral resources. In the same year the General Petroleum Company (GPC), Egypt's first oil company, was formed and was granted licenses to prospect in the Gulf of Suez and in Egypt's Eastern Desert. GPC was later to acquire licenses in Sinai also, and to become the most important operating company owned by EGPC.

EGPC Begins Joint Venture Exploration: 1960s

Egyptian General Petroleum Corporation was the new name given in 1962 to the GPA. The following year, it entered into the first of a series of joint ventures with international companies for oil exploration and production. Among EGPC's earliest partners was Amoco, then known as Standard Oil Company (Indiana), with whom EGPC formed the Gulf of Suez Petroleum Company (Gupco), soon to become Egypt's largest oil producer. The largest company after Gupco, Petrobel, dates from 1963 and was the progeny of EGPC's union with the International Egyptian Oil Company (IEOC), the latter itself a joint venture between the Italian company ENI and an Egyptian firm. Phillips Petroleum was another important EGPC partner.

EGPC soon gained a solid reputation; the *Financial Times,* June 5, 1985, credited it with ''an independence and efficiency not normally associated with public sector entities.'' EGPC's joint venture arrangements stimulated an upsurge in drilling, and in 1965 Gupco made a major find, the Morgan field in the Gulf of Suez, followed by the July and Ramadan fields in the same region. Petrobel found the first of Egypt's gas fields, Abu Madi, in 1967, though its major activity was the operation of the Belayim field in Sinai and Belayim Marine in the Gulf of Suez, oil fields which had been discovered in 1955 and 1961 respectively. Phillips Petroleum's explorations in the Western Desert led to the discovery of the El-Alamein oil field in 1966 and the Abu Gharadiq field, with both oil and gas, two years later.

Key Developments: 1970s to Mid-1980s

In 1973, the Arab Petroleum Pipeline Company was created, in which EGPC took a 50 percent share. The co-owners included Saudi Arabia, Abu Dhabi, and other Gulf states. Four years later, the Suez-Mediterranean (Sumed) pipeline opened, serving as an alternative to the Suez Canal as a means of transporting oil. In the first ten years of its life, the pipeline brought Egypt $632 million in royalties and investment dividends, even though it was not being used to full capacity.

Also in 1973, EGPC switched from joint explorations to its present policy of issuing exploration licenses to foreign contractors with subsequent sharing of any finds. Instead of EGPC and the contractor sharing the cost and the risk of explorations that might prove abortive, the contractor now footed the bill, recouping costs out of any resultant products. No more of the old-style joint ventures were set up after 1973, and existing joint ventures were either converted to the new system—as were Gupco and Petrobel—or phased out. Besides its agreements with overseas companies, EGPC continued to prospect in its own right through its subsidiary, the GPC.

In 1976, Egypt became a net exporter of crude oil for the first time. From then on, oil played a progressively greater part in the Egyptian economy, rising from less than five percent of GDP—differing from gross national product in that GDP excludes income from investment abroad—in 1974 to nearly 20 percent ten years later. The Gulf of Suez continued to yield important new discoveries through the late 1970s, including a string of successes for Suez Oil Company (Suco), another of EGPC's cooperative ventures, this time between EGPC, Royal Dutch/Shell, BP, and the operator, Deminex of West Germany. Ras Budran, discovered in 1978, came onstream in 1983, as did Ras Fanar. Zeit Bay, which came onstream two years later, was the last major Suco discovery.

A series of moderately productive Gulf of Suez explorations took place throughout the 1980s; at the end of the decade this was still Egypt's largest oil-producing area with 90 percent of total output. Sinai, handed back to Egypt in 1979 after a period

under Israeli occupation, was the next most fruitful area of exploration, progressively growing in importance through the 1980s. The most dramatic change of the 1980s was the increase in exploration and production activity in the Western Desert, where Khalda Petroleum Company, a joint venture between Conoco, Texas International, and EGPC, was a major player. Improvements to the pipeline networks there, in addition to optimism about its resources, contributed to the attractions which the Western Desert held out to oil companies.

The Oil Slump Leads to Policy Changes: Mid-1980s

EGPC had always enjoyed a close relationship with the Egyptian Ministry of Oil. When Abul Hadi Qandil, EGPC's chairman, became oil minister in July 1984, he continued to hold both positions for three years, a demanding double commitment which was blamed for some of the operational difficulties that EGPC encountered in the mid-1980s.

EGPC had set Egypt an output target of one million barrels of oil, gas, and condensate per day, to be reached by 1985–86, but the oil slump of the mid-1980s put paid to this plan. In 1984, EGPC restricted output to 900,000 barrels, in line with OPEC (Organization of Petroleum Exporting Companies) price stabilization policies, even though Egypt was not a member of OPEC. Crude output was pegged at less than 900,000 barrels per day for the five years from 1987.

The effects of the oil upsets of the mid-1980s on the Egyptian economy were severe. By then, only agriculture constituted a larger element in the domestic economy, and oil was the largest foreign-currency earner. Between 1986 and 1987, the drop in oil prices reduced the oil sector's share of export earnings from 81 percent to 47 percent. This crisis brought about several important policy changes.

The slump had a particularly severe effect on Egypt because its wholesale prices were often set too high relative to other exporters. This experience prompted EGPC to introduce a system of reviewing prices every two weeks instead of monthly as before, reducing the lag in adjustments. The biweekly reviews have continued to be held ever since.

In 1987, in the aftermath of the 1986 oil slump, Egypt and the International Monetary Fund (IMF) agreed on a rescheduling of the country's burdensome foreign debts together with an IMF facility for $175 million in loans at a favorable rate. However, the agreement collapsed when Egypt was unable to implement the economic reforms on which the IMF's loan was dependent. In the light of Egypt's wider economic problems, its management of its oil industry came under scrutiny.

Egypt needed to make as much of its oil as possible available for export, but until 1985 the annual growth in production had been more or less matched by the growth in domestic demand. Since subsidized prices for domestic consumers were doing little to improve matters, in 1985 the Egyptian government had begun to reduce these subsidies, resulting in massive price increases.

Focus on Natural Gas and Diversification: Late 1980s

The World Bank was urging Egypt to capitalize on its natural gas, concluding that ''the more natural gas is used for

Key Dates:

1910: Anglo-Egyptian Oilfields begins to produce oil from the Gemsa field.

1956: The General Petroleum Authority (GPA) is created by the Egyptian government; General Petroleum Company is formed.

1962: GPA's name is changed to Egyptian General Petroleum Corporation (EGPC).

1964: Anglo-Egyptian is nationalized.

1973: EGPC takes a 50 percent interest in The Arab Petroleum Pipeline Company; EGPC switches from joint explorations to issuing exploration licenses to foreign contractors.

1976: Egypt becomes a net exporter of crude oil for the first time.

1977: The Sumed Pipeline opens.

1986: A drop in oil prices leads to policy changes in EGPC.

1991: Egypt begins to offer incentives for foreign investment and exploration as part of its fiscal reform.

1996: Oil production reaches its peak at 922,000 barrels per day.

2000: The Egyptian government allows for the export of natural gas.

domestic needs the more Egypt's petroleum—in the form of crude or refined products—can be used to earn or save foreign exchange,'' as reported in the *Financial Times,* June 29, 1987. Aware of this opportunity, EGPC encouraged the substitution of gas for oil, particularly in power stations.

Egypt had a considerable amount of undiscovered natural gas, but EGPC realized that it had been doing little to encourage foreign companies to bring these valuable resources to light. Egypt had originally taken the view that gas should be exploited only by Egyptian organizations, and early exploration licenses had laid down that gas discovered in the course of drilling and not exported would become government property. This arrangement acted as a disincentive for foreign companies to look for gas or to exploit any gas resources discovered in the course of oil prospecting.

A ''gas clause'' to remunerate foreign companies for gas discoveries was introduced into concessions in 1980, but it was not until 1986 that a model agreement that actively encouraged investment in gas was devised. The Shell Winning agreement for the Western Desert Bed-3 was used as a basis for subsequent agreements, and the ''gas clause'' under which profit on gas was divided, typically on a basis of approximately 80 percent-20 percent in favor of EGPC, was inserted retrospectively into some licenses.

Meanwhile, EGPC's interests were diversifying. In the late 1970s, EGPC had become interested in the petrochemicals industry. After an abortive joint venture with the Italian petrochemical specialist Montedison, EGPC undertook the construction of a plant at Ameriyah for the production of polyvinyl chloride (PVC), vinyl choride monomer (VCM), chlorine, and

caustic soda. The plant went into production during 1986 and 1987. Further units for ethylene and polyethylene were added, and other petrochemical activities were planned, some of them joint ventures between EGPC's Egyptian Petrochemicals Company and the Italian EniChem. The ultimate aim was vertical integration, but pending completion of the whole Ameriyah petrochemical complex some of the raw materials had to be imported. For this purpose, an innovative offshore terminal with facilities for the unloading and storage of ethylene was constructed off Alexandria.

Since 1979, the Abu Qir Fertilizer and Chemical Industries Company, one-fifth owned by EGPC, had run the largest fertilizer manufacturing operation in Egypt, obtaining some of its raw material from the Abu Qir gas field. A project that would more than double the company's output of ammonia and urea and permit the production of ammonia nitrate was begun in the late 1980s with completion due in 1991.

In 1987, Abul Hadi Qandil was succeeded as EGPC chairman by Muhammed Maabed, who had already served EGPC as deputy chairman for production. The following year Hamdi al-Banbi, Gupco's president, took over the chairmanship of EGPC.

Encouraging Exploration:
Late 1980s and Early 1990s

Entering the 1990s, EGPC could point to some encouraging strikes on the part of its companies and licensees. The Gulf of Suez looked set to remain the most important area for oil. Shell Winning and Gupco both announced important new finds in the Gulf during 1990, Gupco calling one of it's the best discovery since 1983. Suco too was reportedly planning to increase expansion of its three Suez Gulf fields by the sinking of new wells. In the Western Desert, Phillips had made a promising discovery in its South Umbarka block. Preliminary studies indicated the existence of oil in Upper Egypt, a previously unexplored region, and prospecting was expected to begin there shortly.

The oil ministry and EGPC were encouraging licensees to exploit fields more rapidly and improve their delivery by investing in the construction of new pipelines. The licensees were also being urged to step up production by such measures as water injection to recover previously inaccessible reserves, a process undertaken, for instance, by Agiba Petroleum in the Western Desert.

During the period of Egypt's Five-Year Plan (1987–92), natural gas output was expected to double. Much of the gas found to date was in the Western Desert, which was believed to contain more gas than oil, but by 1990 the Nile delta was the richest gas-producing area. It was also thought that gas resources were to be found off Egypt's Mediterranean coast and perhaps in the Red Sea.

EGPC continued to be energetic in promoting exploration for all types of hydrocarbons, and according to the *Financial Times,* April 4, 1990, Egypt was among the countries with the highest concentrations of foreign exploration activities. Over 1,200 wells came onstream during the 1980s alone.

In the late 1980s, aside from exploration and production, EGPC assigned a high priority to downstream activities. According to the Five-Year Plan, the refinery capacity was to increase by almost 40 percent by 1992. To illustrate the importance given to this work, 42 percent of the Egyptian public sector investment in the oil and gas sector was concerned with refinery and refined products in 1987–88. Refinery construction work was commissioned mainly from EGPC subsidiaries Engineering for the Petroleum and Process Industries and Petroleum Projects Company, since the government wanted to use local resources. In 1990, Egypt had seven refineries, all of them controlled by EGPC subsidiaries; the oldest, built by Anglo-Egyptian, dated back to 1913. Further refinery expansion was planned, even amidst doubt as to how it would be financed. Some observers expected that private investment would be necessary. Although this procedure had been the norm for upstream activities, it would be a new departure for EGPC in the refinery area. The construction of pipelines to deliver oil, gas, and refined products to industrial and domestic users in Cairo and Alexandria was also among EGPC's planned projects for the 1990s.

By this time, there had been important advances in Egypt in the substitution of gas for oil. In 1990, around 60 percent of Egypt's gas was being used for electricity generation. Many of Egypt's power stations were being converted to use gas instead of fuel oil and new stations were being designed to use gas from the start. The remainder of the gas was used in industry for the manufacture of fertilizers, iron, steel, and cement, with a mere one percent being bottled for domestic use.

Despite these advances in resource management, and despite Egypt's ongoing oil and gas explorations and reasonable flow of new finds, there was no scope for EGPC to rest on its laurels. Some observers feared that without major new discoveries, Egypt would eventually revert to being a net importer of oil. Total output was restricted for conservation reasons, but new discoveries were still equaled or outweighed by reductions in reserves from the fields currently operating, so that in 1990 recoverable oil reserves seemed to be stuck at around four billion barrels. An additional problem was that because the finds tended to be smaller than in Egypt's more fortunate neighbors around the Persian Gulf, unit production costs were higher than average.

EGPC continued to grapple with the problem of mounting domestic demand detracting from exports. Despite the reduction of subsidies, the *Petroleum Economist* reported in March 1990 that domestic demand was still rising by ten to 15 percent per annum. As such, gas presented the brightest prospect for the future, with the assurance of rapidly increasing reserves. According to one estimate, the one to two trillion cubic feet reserves established up to 1990 was scheduled to triple in two years' time.

Egyptian Reform: 1990s and Beyond

Shocks to the oil market arising from the 1991 conflict in Iraq also presented EGPC with both challenges and opportunities. During that time period, Egypt—by the prompting of the IMF—began to reform is fiscal policies and set plans in motion to privatize many of its major industries. It began to offer incentives for foreign investment and exploration, including offering larger exploration regions and longer exploration contracts. Under the leadership of President Hosni Mubarak, Egypt underwent a large-scale economic reform, and while privatization began in the

mid-1990s in the Egyptian telecommunications and utilities industries, EGPC was deemed off limits for such action.

The country's fears about reverting to a net importer continued into the late 1990s and beyond. Oil production reached a peak of 922,000 barrels per day in 1996 and then fell to 834,000 in 1998 and 640,000 barrels per day in 2001. Increases in demand and high international oil prices forced Egypt to report an oil trade deficit—the first in nearly 25 years—in 1999. That year, imports of petroleum products reached $1.945 billion, while exports were $1.821 billion. EGPC claimed the $124 million deficit was brought on by a 14 percent increase in demand for refined products over the previous year. That demand continued to increase, reaching 585,000 barrels per day in 2001.

Proven oil reserves were estimated at just three billion barrels, while probable crude oil reserves hovered around 8.2 billion barrels. Natural gas resources, however, included 55 trillion cubic feet of proven reserves and considerable probable reserves. As such, EGPC eyed natural gas as key to future export growth—production was expected to double between 1999 and 2002. In 1998, EGPC signed a 25-year franchise agreement with a consortium led by British Gas International to extend the Cairo natural gas grid pipeline in four phases. In 2000, Egypt allowed natural gas to be exported for the first time, signaling the country's commitment to this growing sector of the industry.

EGPC also continued to focus heavily on exploration activity, hoping to increase oil recovery and perhaps even find new sources. In the early years of the new century, Egypt's oil production stemmed from operations in four main areas, including the Gulf of Suez, the Western Desert, the Eastern Desert, and the Sinai Peninsula. Companies that produced oil from these regions including Gupco and Petrobel, began restructuring operations and making key investments in both oil development and exploration.

The company also began offshore exploration efforts, awarding deepwater contracts in the Mediterranean to Shell, BP Amoco, and Elf Aquitaine. While initial discoveries were mostly natural gas, EGPC was confident that with further exploration, large oil reserves would be discovered. To encourage increased exploration, EGPC announced that it would make 38 regions available for exploration to foreign investors. Eight of those included were offshore sites in the Mediterranean.

EGPC's future, and the future of Egypt's export status, hinged on its ability to develop and exploit natural gas while maintaining crude oil operations. By 2002, EGPC was exploring liquefied natural gas projects and had also sketched out plans to construct a gas pipeline through the Mediterranean coast to Lebanon and Turkey. The latter was put on hold, however, due to the unrest in the Middle East.

Principal Subsidiaries

General Petroleum Co.; Suez Oil Processing Co.; Cairo Petroleum Refining Co.; El Nasr Petroleum Co.; Alexandria Petroleum Co.; The Egyptian Petrochemical Co.; Amerya Petroleum Refining Co.; Assuit Petroleum Refining Co.; Petroleum Cooperative Societies; Misr Petroleum Co.; Petroleum Gases Co.; Gulf of Suez Petroleum Co.; Petrozeit Co.; Offshore Shukeir

Oil Co.; Western Desert Petroleum Co.; Belayim Petroleum Co.; Suez Oil Co.; Geisum Oil Co.; Agiba Petroleum Co.; Badr El Deen Petroleum Co.; El Amal Petroleum Co.; Sea Gull; The Arab Petroleum Pipelines Co.; The Egyptian Drilling Co. Petroleum Projects and Technical Consultations Co.; Egyptian Natural Gases Co.

Further Reading

"British Gas Signs First Egyptian Private Sector Franchise," *Petroleum Times Energy Report*, May 8, 1998, p. 5.

"Egyptian General Petroleum Corporation," *Petroleum Economist*, October 2000, p. 50.

"Egyptian Oil Output Rises," *The Oil Daily*, March 6, 2002.

"Egypt Signs Deal for Nile Valley Gas Grid," *The Oil and Gas Journal*, April 27, 1998, p. 28.

"El Paso Global LNG to Explore Opportunities in Egypt," *Pipeline & Gas Journal*, May 2000, p. 4.

"Gas: The Upstream Future," *Petroleum Economist*, August 2001, p. 6.

"Shell, Egypt Report Gas Deal," *The Oil Daily*, February 1, 2001.

"World Companies Compete to Prospect For Oil in 32 New Regions," *Arabic News*, March 12, 2002. Available at http://www.arabic news.com.

—Alison Classe
—updated by Christina M. Stansell

Elamex, S.A. de C.V.

4171 North Mesa, Building D
El Paso, Texas 79902
U.S.A.
Telephone: (915) 351-2382
Fax: (915) 351-3895
Web site: http://www.elamex.com

Public Company
Incorporated: 1972 as Elamex International
Employees: 1,860
Sales: $131.98 million (2001)
Stock Exchanges: NASDAQ
Ticker Symbol: ELAM
NAIC: 332116 Metal Stamping; 339999 All Other
    Miscellaneous Manufacturing; 561499 All Other
    Business Support Services

Elamex, S.A. de C.V. provides manufacturing services in Mexico and the United States to original-equipment manufacturers—primarily U.S. companies, mainly in the appliance, telecommunications, automotive, confectionery, and medical industries. It focuses on the effective management of assembly processes, ranging from assembly-only services managed by the customer or by Elamex, to full materials procurement and assembly contracts. It also operates a metal-stamping subsidiary in Louisville, Kentucky, and takes part with General Electric Co. in a joint venture for plastics and metal stamping in Mexico. Elamex is majority owned by Accel, S.A. de C.V., a Mexican holding company. Although it is incorporated in Mexico, its common stock is traded in the United States, and it moved its headquarters from Ciudad Juarez, Chihuahua, across the Rio Grande to El Paso, Texas, in 2001.

Fledgling Contract Manufacturer: 1972–90

Elamex International was founded in 1972 and was owned for 17 years by Charles Dodson, who was its chairman of the board and chief executive officer throughout this period. Elamex was a pioneer in the maquiladora concept, in which, starting in 1965, real estate, originally, and later also labor, were provided to foreign original-equipment manufacturers. Under this Mexican program raw materials could be imported into Mexico in-bond, transformed into a finished component or product, and exported without duty. To take advantage of Mexico's cheap labor, manufacturers would design or partly manufacture a product in the United States, then send it to Mexico for further assembly, usually labor-intensive, before shipping it back to the United States.

The first maquiladora law was passed in 1971. It allowed plants in Mexican cities along the U.S. border and along the coasts to be totally owned by foreigners, to employ foreign technicians, and to import raw materials, supplies, and machinery duty-free. A 1972 law extended these provisions to the entire country. As a result Mexican entrepreneurs began to build large industrial parks, stimulating the growth of maquiladora factories and employment. U.S. and other foreign firms began to move the labor-intensive aspects of their manufacturing operations to Mexico. The dominant businesses were apparel and electrical assembly plants.

By 1979 the maquiladora industry was employing 106,000 people on the Mexican side of the U.S. border. The major site was Ciudad Juarez, just across the Rio Grande from El Paso. Half of the economically active population was working, directly or indirectly, for a maquiladora enterprise. Prominent among the entrepreneurs there was Jaime Bermudez Cuaron, a former president of the local government. Grupo Bermudez, S.A. established several large industrial parks in Ciudad Juarez. Its director general was Francisco Barrio, who worked closely with Elamex and, from 1983, ran his own construction company, Constructora Lintel. During the 1980s the maquiladora industry continued to grow, in part because of the sizable depreciation of the peso, which resulted in Mexican wages falling below those in Asia and the arrival of such large non-U.S. employers as Sony Corp., Matsushita Electric Industrial Co., Ltd.,, and Samsung Corp. A single new factory now might employ 3,000 or more workers.

Expansion in the 1990s

A majority interest in Elamex International was acquired in 1990 by a subsidiary of Accel, S.A. de C.V., a Mexican holding

Company Perspectives:

In business for over 28 years, Elamex understands Mexico and has facilities throughout the country. The company provides shelter, assembly, injection molding, and metal stamping services to a wide variety of industries. Elamex is ISO 9002 and FDA registered. Its management and technical staff are fluent in English and projects are managed through a formal program management system.

company. In the early 1990s Elamex increasingly changed from being a contract manufacturer supplying manufacturing services for a client who retained responsibility for parts procurement, to a so-called shelter operator that performed most tasks required to operate a manufacturing facility in Mexico. It provided the industrial space, hired all workers and administered payroll, coordinated labor relations, obtained all permits and paid all utility fees, imported the foreign manufacturer's raw materials, equipment, and machinery, and exported the finished products. Net sales came to $50.9 million in 1991.

Elamex International, in 1992, reached 33rd place among Mexican exporters and 201st among reporting Mexican firms in terms of sales. Its exportations were principally electronic and electromechanical products. In 1993 Elamex was also 12th among Mexican importers, indicating the high volume of raw materials, equipment, and machinery being obtained for its shelter operations. The company was employing more than 4,000 workers in 1994. Elamex reached its zenith in 1995, when it was the fifth largest maquiladora in Mexico and the largest shelter operator, since the four maquiladoras that ranked above it were subsidiaries of foreign companies such as Sony and Motorola, Inc. Elamex was the world's fourth largest contract manufacturer in terms of square footage. Assembly of electronic products accounted for 82 percent of its revenue.

Elamex International became Elamex in 1995. The following year Accel sold 49 percent of the shares of Elamex's common stock on the NASDAQ exchange. Elamex was operating or directing operations at 17 manufacturing facilities. The company's headquarters and many of its manufacturing facilities were located within nine miles of the U.S. border and the international airport, rail, and truck depots in El Paso, Texas. Eight of these plants were in Ciudad Juarez. Two were in Nuevo Laredo and two in Tijuana. The plants in the interior included one each in Guadalajara, Monterrey, and Torreon.

Elamex's operations were primarily the assembly of electronic equipment and of electromechanical, avionics, and medical products. Some 28.5 percent of Elamex's net sales came from contract manufacturing, but the remainder was from shelter operations in which the company was responsible for delivering the completed product. Some 77 percent of net sales was derived from electronic products. The company specialized in assembling high-quality, technologically advanced printed circuit boards with computer-automated equipment using surface-mount and pin-through-hole interconnection technologies. Elamex customized its assembly lines for each client by assigning a separate workforce, team leaders, supervisors,

production engineers, managers, and quality-control personnel to each project.

Elamex dropped to eighth place among maquiladoras in 1996 but was still first among shelter operators. Its net sales came to $118.92 million (compared with $60.22 million in 1992) and its net income to $7.93 million (compared with a $45,000 loss in 1992). Both figures were records and seemed to indicate that the investors who bought company stock at $9 a share in the initial public offering had made a wise decision. Thomas N. Cochrane of *Barron's* warned, however, that in spite of "the company's fine growth over recent years, it's well to remember that Elamex is primarily an assembler of electronic devices, not a manufacturer with a producer's potentially large margins. ... The Mexican government has decreed a 21% increase in the minimum wage, and a 26% boost in utility charges, but the effects of these added expenses aren't yet reflected in Elamex earnings." In 1997 Elamex raised its sales by 11 percent, but its net income began to decline, and company shares rarely traded as high as the initial $9 in ensuing years.

Elamex acquired Eurotec S.A. de C.V. in 1997 for about $3.9 million. This company owned a plant in Ciudad Juarez dedicated to plastic molding and metal stamping, with revenues of $7.9 million in 1996. The purchase expanded Elamex's capacity for plastic molding injection and added metal stamping and powder-coat painting to its capabilities. In 1998 General Electric International Mexico, S.A. de C.V. acquired a 49 percent interest in Elamex's plastic molding and stamped metal operations in Ciudad Juarez for about $3.5 million. This became a joint venture known as Qualcore, S. de R.L. de C.V., which added a 116,000-square-foot facility in Celaya, Guanajuato, and was offering plastics injection molding, metal stamping, powder-coat painting, and pad-printing services in 1999. Elamex, in 1999, acquired a Louisville, Kentucky, metal-stamping company, Precision Tool, Die & Machine Co., for $20.3 million in cash. The acquisition of this privately held company, with sales that amounted to $54.6 million in fiscal 1998, expanded the company's customer base in the automotive, appliance, and industrial controls industry and added welding, orbital riveting, and machining to its in-house portfolio of capabilities. Elamex also began packaging food products in 1999.

Elamex got out of its chief business—turnkey contract manufacturing of electronic components—in 2000, when it sold these operations, housed in two leased Ciudad Juarez plants, to Plexus Corp. for about $53.7 million in cash. The sold activities accounted for about $82 million of Elamex's $160 million in net sales in 1999. In 2000 Elamex recorded by far its highest net income ($17.38 million). The company actually suffered an operating deficit, however, with its profit resulting from $21.8 million collected from the sale of subsidiaries.

Elamex in 2001–02

Elamex was operating 19 facilities in 2001 with a combined total of 1.22 million square feet of manufacturing space. Eight of these were in Ciudad Juarez, turning out medical, electromechanical, telecommunications, military, and confectionery products, plus industrial bags. The Torreon factory was assembling shotgun parts and a facility in Ramos Arizpe, Coahuila, was assembling ceiling air conditioners. Three plants—in

Key Dates:

1972: Elamex International is founded to assemble U.S. goods in Mexico for re-export.
1990: Accel, S.A. de C.V., a Mexican holding company, acquires a majority interest.
1995: Now offering more than assembly, Elamex is the largest shelter operator in Mexico.
1996: The company's common stock is now being publicly traded in the United States.
1998: Company employment peaks at 5,431.
1999: Elamex acquires a metal-stamping company in Louisville, Kentucky.
2000: Elamex sells its main business—making electronic components in Mexico for export.
2001: Its Mexican operations in decline, Elamex moves its headquarters to El Paso, Texas.

spring 2002 as demand from the United States contracted sharply after the September 11, 2001 terrorist destruction of New York City's World Trade Center. In addition, the strong performance of the Mexican peso in relation to the U.S. dollar in 2001 had caused production costs on the Mexican side of the border to rise. Elamex's number of employees had fallen, in 2001, by two-thirds from its peak of 5,431 in 1998. The company again lost money in the first quarter of 2002 as its Mexican contract manufacturing operations continued to decline.

Elamex, in March 2002, acquired Mt. Franklin Holdings LLC, owner of a general-line candy manufacturer located in El Paso, and also Franklin Inmobiliarios, S.A. de C.V., owner of the candy-manufacturing plant used by Franklin Holdings' operating subsidiary—Franklin Connections LP—in Ciudad Juarez. The purchase was made for about $1.15 million in cash and the issuance of about 1.85 million shares of restricted Elamex stock. Franklin Holdings was 33 percent owned by Accel.

Principal Subsidiaries

Elamex de Torreon, S.A. de C.V.; Precision Tool, Die & Machine Company Inc. (U.S.); Servicios Administrativos, S.A. de C.V.

Principal Operating Units

Contract Manufacturing; Metal Stamping.

Principal Competitors

Manufacturers' Services Ltd.

Further Reading

Bergsman, Steven, "Bright Spot in Texas: El Paso Exploits Global Trends," *Barron's,* January 29, 1970, p. 72.
Broutles, Lance Eliot, John P. McCray, and Timothy J. Wilkinson, "Maquiladoras: Entrepreneurial Experimentation to Global Competitiveness," *Business Horizons,* March/April 1999, pp. 37–44.
Cochrane, Thomas N., "Offerings in the Offering: Elamex," *Barron's,* March 18, 1996, p. 52.
Eaton, David W., "Taking Shelter," *Business Mexico,* April 1999, pp. 22–23.
Gori, Graham, "Latest Data Dampens Mexico's Hopes," *New York Times,* April 12, 2002, pp. W1, W7.
"Maquiladoras: Entrepreneurial Experimentation to Global Competitiveness," *Business Horizons,* March/April 1999, pp. 37–44.
"La respuesta esta en el otro lado," *Expansion,* September 19, 1979, pp. 102, 104, 106.
Sklair, Leslie, *Assembling for Development,* San Diego: University of California at San Diego, 1993.

—Robert Halasz

Chihuahua, Ciudad Juarez, and Nuevo Laredo—were vacant. There were three metal stamping and assembly plants in Louisville and Jefferson Town, Kentucky. The company headquarters and warehouse were in El Paso. In April 2001 Richard Spencer became president and chief executive officer of Elamex, replacing Hector Raynal, who remained with the company as its chief operating officer.

Elamex's Mexican manufacturing services accounted for 41 percent of total sales in 2001. This included Qualcore's operations during the first six months of the year, which came to $8.6 million. Qualcore was selling primarily to a single manufacturer of home appliances, and disappointing results were putting its future into doubt. The Precision operations accounted for the remaining 59 percent of sales and were predominantly for the appliance, automotive, and consumer electronics industries. Capabilities in this area included tooling design and repair, fabrication or procurement of tooling, injection-molded plastics, metal stamping, powder-coat painting, pad printing, and plating. Both the contract manufacturing and metal-stamping segments of Elamex's business were profitable, but the company sustained a net loss of $11 million on sales of $131.98 million in 2001 because it lost $7.8 million on the Qualcore joint venture and also took a $2.6 restructuring charge. Accel owned 59 percent of Elamex's common stock at the end of 2001.

Elamex's trend away from maquiladora manufacturing in the late 1990s continued into the next century. Companies that focused primarily on hiring cheap labor had been leaving Mexico to employ even cheaper labor in countries such as Guatemala and China. Maquiladoras employed some 1.2 million workers in mid 2001, but one-fifth of these jobs had been lost by

eram·

Eram SA

49111 Saint Pierre Montlimart Cedex
France
Telephone: (+33) 241 75 32 00
Fax: (+33) 241 75 32 38
Web site: http://www.eram.fr

Private Company
Incorporated: 1927
Employees: 10,199
Sales: EUR 1.28 billion ($1.25 billion) (2001)
NAIC: 316214 Women's Footwear (Except Athletic)
Manufacturing; 316213 Men's Footwear (Except
Athletic) Manufacturing; 316214 Women's Footwear
(Except Athletic) Manufacturing; 316219 Other
Footwear Manufacturing; 448210 Shoe Stores

Eram SA is the leading manufacturer of shoes in France, producing more than 11 million pairs of shoes per year. The company operates ten manufacturing facilities, including nine in its Vendée region home base; the remaining plant is located in Portugal. The company's shoe production ranges from discount shoe styles to high-end (just below luxury) fashions under brand names that include Bocage (high-end fashion), Anne Flavie (fashion comfort), TBS (sports and leisure), Buggy (children and juniors) and Parade (safety, including hiking). Yet shoe production accounted for just EUR 200 million of the company's EUR 1.28 billion in sales in 2001. The largest part of the company's revenues are generated through its internationally operating portfolio of retail distribution networks. In total, the company owns and operates 1,300 stores and supports an additional 240 franchise stores in France, Belgium, Luxembourg, and Germany. The company's flagship retail chain is its Eram stores, with more than 650 stores selling youth-oriented shoe fashions in a downtown store format. Other chains operated by Eram include Bocage, Franc Arno (157 stores), Taneo (153 stores), Heyraud (50 stores), and Divergence (38 stores). While these stores are typically found in city center locations, Eram has also implanted itself in the ex-urban shopping center circuit with the deep-discount retail

format L'Hyper aux Chaussures and with 260 Gemo stores, a low-to-mid-range format that also includes clothing fashions. Sales of more than 38 million pairs of shoes per year generated revenues of more than EUR 720 million in 2001, while clothing sales, of nearly 32 million garment pieces, raised revenues of EUR 360 million. Eram is led by Xavier Biotteau, president, and Luc Biotteau, vice-president, both of whom are grandsons of the company's founder. The Biotteau family, including longtime Chairman Gérard Biotteau, continues to own the private company.

Shoemaker's Apprentice in the 1920s

Albert-René Biotteau-Guery began his professional life at the age of 13 as a shoemaker's apprentice. In the 1920s, Biotteau became determined to go into business on his own. In 1927, he founded a workshop in Saint Pierre Montlimart, near Angers, in France's Vendée region. That business was to flourish, becoming not only the region's largest single employer but also the nation's leading shoe manufacturer.

Biotteau's shop grew quickly and by the beginning of the 1930s had reached production levels of more than 600 pairs of shoes per day. Throughout the decade, Biotteau continued to build up his company, adding two new production plants in the area surrounding Saint Pierre Montlimart, where the company remained centered into the next century. By the mid-1930s, production had risen to more than 2,400 pairs of shoes per day.

It was around that time that Biotteau developed a new name for the company—and a new brand name for the company's shoes. Taking the first two letters from his second name, René, and the first two letters from his wife's name, Marie, Biotteau formed the anagram "Eram."

Development of the new brand name was temporarily put on hold at the end of the 1930s with the outbreak of World War II. By 1942, however, Eram was once again in production. In that year, the company made a strategic move that was to form the backbone of its future success—the opening of its first retail stores. For this, the company purchased a store in Paris, giving it the Eram name. The company quickly added more stores in the Paris area before expanding throughout France.

118

Company Perspectives:

"A company . . . must keep in mind that it has never reached the top and that it can never be allowed to contemplate its own success. Its achievements are always being called into question. Stimulated by this risk, its directors and staff have to find among themselves the experience, the enthusiasm, and the energy which will ensure its future by continuing to respond profitably to the needs of the market."
                                    —*Gérard Biotteau, chairman*

Eram's development continued into the 1950s. The company also became noted for its technological development and included among its patents a method for producing shoes featuring injection-molded plastic soles in 1955. By the end of that decade, Eram had also begun its first expansion beyond France, creating sales subsidiaries in Belgium and Germany in 1958. The company soon added retail sales to its growing international operations, opening its first foreign retail store in Belgium in 1961.

Supporting Eram's growth was the addition of new manufacturing plants—by the beginning of the 1970s, the company operated nine production plants, all located in communities near its Saint Pierre Montlimart headquarters. By then, the company had opened its first store in Germany. Eram had also begun to put into place a franchise network through the establishment of Club Eram, launched in 1969. The company's franchise network was later to grow to more than 400 stores, with Eram owning the majority of them.

Expanding Brands in the 1970s

Gérard Biotteau, son of the company's founder, took over as CEO and chairman in 1970. Throughout his nearly 30 years at the head of the company, the younger Biotteau remained true to his father's vision, especially the company's insistence on developing its own distribution network, a strategy that in part served as a means for maintaining the viability of its manufacturing operations. The company by then found itself faced with a new breed of competitor—the hypermarket, a fast-rising store format combining supermarket and department store offerings, including shoe departments. Eram long remained hostile to what became known as the "large-scale" distribution channel in France, which threatened to dominate the French retail scene. In part to counter the threat presented by the country's growing number of hypermarkets, Eram launched its first national advertising campaign in 1970.

Eram's industrial park grew during the 1970s to include a new facility for the production of polyurethane-based soles. In 1974, the company opened a production plant in Portugal, its first such venture outside of France, and the following year extended its manufacturing operations with the opening of a plant in Spain.

In the late 1970s, the company began expanding its catalogue of shoe brands. Erman acquired the high-end women's fashion brand Bocage in 1977 and introduced its first winter collection under that label. That same year, Eram launched a new brand name, Mi-Temps, featuring sports-and leisure-ori-

ented shoes, clothing, and accessories. The company then purchased the brand TBS and began production of synthetic soles specifically for the sports shoe market. This purchase led the company to launch its own line of sports shoes under the TBS brand name.

Eram continued to add new brands through the end of the 1970s, including Parade, a line of safety shoes and boots, launched in 1978, and Buggy, featuring sportswear shoe designs, launched in 1979. These brands helped extend Eram's line of footwear across most of the major shoe and boot categories. The company also began importing shoes, creating a dedicated subsidiary, Interco, in order to complete its retail footwear offering.

New Retail Formats in the 1980s

By the beginning of the 1980s, more than 600 Eram stores had been opened. The company next turned its attention to developing other retail store formats. An early move in this direction came with the development of the Mi-Temps brand into a separate retail concept dedicated to sportswear, with the first Mi-Temps stores opening in 1982. The following year, Eram began developing a new retail concept for the German market as well. Meanwhile, the company continued to expand its Eram network, notably with the launch of a franchise network in Belgium in 1982. Investment in manufacturing operations also continued, most prominently with the development of automated, laser-based leather cutting equipment. Eram also began automating other parts of its industrial operation, beginning with its leather-punching workshops in 1981.

Eram added other new retail formats during the 1980s. In 1986, the company launched the Divergence chain of shoe stores, which was to grow to nearly 40 stores by the end of the 1990s. The arrival of the deep-discount trend, imported from Germany, and itself a reaction to the growing strength of the hypermarket distribution channel, encouraged Eram to develop its own deep-discount formula in the mid-1980s. Until then, the company had focused primarily on the urban and downtown markets, developing its stores under a city center format. In 1987, however, the company launched a new store format, L'Hyper aux Chaussures. The new stores were located in the growing number of ex-urban shopping centers springing up throughout France during the 1980s and featured shoes at discount prices. At the same time, Eram ventured into new territory, that of clothing and textile sales, launching a companion store format, L'Hyper aux Vetements that same year.

The success of the Hyper format led the company to combine shoes and clothing into a new store format at the beginning of the new decade. Launched in 1991, the Gemo network, which adopted the same ex-urban location policy as the Hyper stores, targeted the mid-priced market, offering shoes and clothing for men, women, teenagers, and children. With the French economy in turmoil at the beginning of the decade, the Gemo format became a strong success for Eram and grew into the company's second-largest retail chain, trailing only the company's flagship Eram chain. The Gemo network was boosted in 1993 with the purchase of the Tenir retail group, giving Eram that company's existing portfolio of ex-urban shopping center-based locations.

Key Dates:

1927: A shoe manufacturing company is founded by Albert-René Biotteau-Guery.
1942: Eram opens its first retail store in Paris under the Eram name.
1958: The company opens sales subsidiaries in Belgium and Germany.
1961: Eram opens its first foreign retail store in Belgium.
1969: The company opens its first retail store in Germany and begins development of a franchise network.
1974: Production facilities in Portugal, and the following year in Spain, begin operation.
1977: Eram acquires upscale Bocage shoe brand, introduces Mi-Temps sportswear brand, acquires TBS sports shoes brand, and launches Interco import subsidiary.
1987: The company launches L'Hyper aux Chaussures and L'Hyper aux Vetements, deep-discount shoe and clothing retail stores.
1991: Gemo, a chain of mid-priced stores featuring both shoes and clothing, is launched.
1995: The company acquires Heyraud, an upscale retail shoe chain.
2002: Eram acquires children shoe store retail chain NA!

Meanwhile, Eram had continued to add to its brand portfolio through acquisitions. An important move came in 1989 with the purchase of the France Arno retail group. That acquisition strengthened the company's position in France's downtown shopping districts. By the beginning of the new century, the company featured nearly 160 France Arno stores.

European Shoe Leader in the 21st Century

By the early 1990s, Eram was posting nearly FFr 3.7 billion in sales (approximately EUR 560 million), including some 23 percent in foreign sales. By then, its retail empire had become its strongest revenue generator, with more than 780 company-owned stores and some 450 franchised stores. In 1993, the company undertook a vast upgrade of its retail network, spending some FFr 33 million to refit nearly all of its stores in France and abroad.

Into the mid-1990s, Eram continued to expand its retail holdings, launching a new mid-range clothing and shoe format, Tandem, in 1995. The following year, the company developed another shoe format, dubbed Taneo, as a bridge format between its downtown and ex-urban store formats. Meanwhile, Eram had extended its portfolio with the acquisition of the Heyraud retail chain in 1996. That chain had grown to 47 stores by the mid-1990s, with sales of more than FFr 190 million, complementing the company's existing operations with its focus on upscale shoe fashions for men and women.

Eram's industrial park had grown to 13 plants by the mid-1990s. By the turn of the century, however, the company had eliminated four locations, including its facility in Spain. The prevailing trend in both the shoe and clothing industries had long been that of moving production to lower-cost facilities in Asia and other regions. Nonetheless, Eram maintained its commitment to manufacturing in Europe, and particularly in France, noting that its proximity to the market enabled it to react more quickly to changes in fashions. Such reactivity enabled the company to continue to build on its leading position in France.

Gérard Biotteau turned over leadership of the company to his sons, Xavier and Luc, as the company entered the new century under a third generation of family leadership. The company's new president and vice-president moved to take on the hypermarket sector by acquiring the wholesale company Dresco in 1999, adding that company's expertise in distributing to the country's powerful hypermarket groups.

By 2001, Eram had boosted its sales to EUR 1.28 billion. Its store network, which expanded into Luxembourg, Belgium, and Germany, helped it claim a position as one of the leading European shoe producers and retailers. The company had also begun trimming back its franchise operations, boosting the number of company-owned stores to more than 1,200, while cutting back its franchise network to just 240 stores. Yet Eram showed no sign of resting on its laurels—in 2002, the company acquired yet another retail store format, the ten-store NA! chain of children's shoe specialists.

Principal Subsidiaries

Interco; Desco.

Principal Competitors

Continental AG; Nike Inc.; Orkla ASA; adidas-Salomon AG; Foot Locker Inc.: Freudenberg und Co.; Reebok International Ltd.; Ansell Ltd.; Brown Shoe Company Inc.; Phillips-Van Heusen Corp.; C and J Clark Ltd.; Vasque Outdoor Footwear Div.; Timberland Co.; New Balance Athletic Shoe Inc.; Salamander AG; Skechers U.S.A. Inc.; C and J Clark International Ltd.; Acushnet Co.; Columbia Sportswear Co.; Genesco Inc.; Wolverine World Wide Inc.

Further Reading

''En rachetant Heyraud, Eram veut maîtriser ses circuits de distribution,'' Les Echos, January 15, 1996 p. 17.
''Eram: A Shoe Champion's Reinvigorating Lessons,'' Anjou Economique, November 29, 1999.
''Eram relooke ses boutiques en Europe,'' Les Echos, September 14, 1993, p. 20.
''Le PDG d'Eram passe la main à ses deux fils,'' Les Echos, February 2, 1998, p. 36.

—M. L. Cohen

EVA Airways Corporation

EVA Air Building
376 Hsin-Nan Road, Section 1
Luchu Hsiang, Taoyuan Hsien
Taiwan
Telephone: (+886) 3 351-5151
Fax: (+886) 2 2501-2099
Web site: http://www.evaair.com

Public Company
Incorporated: 1989
Employees: 4,552
Sales: NT$52.45 billion ($1.53 billion) (2001)
Stock Exchanges: Taiwan
Ticker Symbol: 2618
NAIC: 481111 Scheduled Passenger Air Transportation;
481112 Scheduled Freight Air Transportation; 481212
Nonscheduled Chartered Freight Air Transportation;
481211 Nonscheduled Chartered Passenger Air
Transportation

EVA Airways Corporation, or EVA Air, is Taiwan's second largest airline. It was founded by the Evergreen shipping group. (There is no relation to Oregon's Evergreen International Aviation.) EVA flies passengers and freight as far as Milan, Italy, on a fleet of mostly widebody aircraft. EVA also owns an interest in domestic carrier UNI Air. The company had about a 60/40 mix of passenger and cargo revenues in 2001, a ratio that, in contrast to other airlines, it hoped to reverse. EVA was also unique in eschewing global airline alliances in favor of making its own way through the world's skies.

Launched in 1991

It was not enough for Chang Yung-fa to build Evergreen Marine Corporation, one of the largest container shipping lines in the world. He looked to the skies to build another empire. The name of choice was already being used by Oregon's Evergreen International Airlines, so the new airline was called EVA Airways Corporation, or EVA Air. It was incorporated on March 8,

1989; start-up capital was $400 million. Chang spent two years laying the groundwork for the first flight, including placing orders and options for 28 aircraft worth $3.6 billion.

Company president Frank Hsu had been in charge of Evergreen's U.S. container business for eleven years. Alitalia, the Italian flag carrier, was contracted to initially handle pilot training and aircraft maintenance.

EVA Air began flying on July 1, 1991. The airline's first destinations were Singapore, Bangkok, Kuala Lumpur, Jakarta, Penang, and Seoul; by the end of the year, the company had added a few other stops in east Asia and as well as Vienna, Austria. First year revenues were $40 million.

Growth was brisk in EVA's early years, as EVA expanded the market through unique offerings such as the world's first four-class service. The Evergreen Deluxe class, introduced in 1991, was a step up from economy, with personal seatback video screens.

EVA Enters the U.S. Market in 1992

EVA entered the U.S. market in December 1992 with a nonstop route between Taipei and Los Angeles. A Taipei-Seattle-Newark service was added in June. This was the only direct service connecting Seattle to Taiwan; EVA was the first Asian carrier to serve the Newark Airport, which had recently lured Federal Express Corp. from John F. Kennedy International. EVA was carrying cargo in the bellies of the Boeing 747s used on these flights.

EVA began flying to London's Heathrow Airport via Vienna and Bangkok in March 1993. At the same time, complicated negotiations with mainland China allowed a specially created subsidiary of British Airways called British Asia Airways to begin flying to Taiwan via Hong Kong. In order for the service to begin, Britain's aviation minister had to publicly acknowledge the People's Republic as ''the sole legal government of China,'' including Taiwan.

Y.F. Chang relinquished the chairmanship of EVA Airways to former vice-chairman Cheng Shen-Chih in autumn 1995,

---

Company Perspectives:

Like a majestic bird, the Evergreen Group has taken flight. It stepped from the seas to land. Then, with EVA Air as the embodiment of the best of this great transportation heritage, it soared into the wide-open skies. The Evergreen Group steadily transformed itself as a transportation giant on the world stage. From the wellspring of its Taiwanese heritage, it built on strengths of its culture and created "EVA Air-the Wings of Taiwan."

Key Dates:

1991: Evergreen Marine founder Chang Yung-fa launches EVA Air.
1992: EVA begins service to Los Angeles, Seattle, and Newark.
1995: EVA Air posts its first annual profit and begins cargo operations.
1999: The company goes public.

---

while company president Frank Hsu became the new vice-chairman. Richard Huang, head of the U.S. operations, became EVA's new president.

By 1995, the company was operating 20 aircraft with an average age of less than a year—an impressive fleet for a carrier that began flying only four years earlier. Its route network now stretched to London and Paris. The airline carried more than three million passengers a year, and cargo was accounting for 30 percent of revenues.

Profitable in 1995

Revenues were $800 million in 1994. In 1995, EVA posted its first profit, $7.2 million, on revenues of $1.05 billion, up 45 percent from the previous year. The company broke even a year ahead of schedule. Another important milestone was the start of cargo operations. The company's new MD-11 freighter connected Taipei, Singapore, Penang, San Francisco, New York, and Los Angeles on a weekly run beginning in April. Four more cargo aircraft were added to the line in June 1995. Cargo traffic would grow at a rate of 50 percent a year for the next five years, accounting for $665 million in revenues in 1999. Deliveries of three Boeing 747 freighters began in 2000.

EVA Air had begun investing in domestic airlines. It acquired 20 percent of Great China Airlines and Makung Airlines in 1995. It also bought shares in Taiwan Airlines, raising its stake from 30 to 40 percent in 1996. Unlike its rival China Airlines, EVA preferred not to get heavily involved in the management of its regional affiliates.

Though most of these small airlines were profitable, by 1997 overcapacity in the domestic market was becoming apparent. Taiwan had gone from four to 17 carriers in ten years. A series of crashes at China Airlines and its domestic unit hurt Taiwan's air travel market as a whole. In July 1998, EVA merged Great China Airlines and Taiwan Airways into another holding, UNI Air. The domestic market would continue to get more difficult in the next three years as passenger counts dropped.

EVA continued to expand its cargo operations in the late 1990s in spite of the Asian financial crisis. The demand for time-sensitive freight, such as computer and telecommunications components, remained high on both sides of the Pacific, though the demand for U.S.-made consumer goods did fall about 20 percent. Taiwan's economy was among the least affected in the region. The instability of South Korea's currency

prompted buyers in the west to shift orders to Taiwanese manufacturers.

A new combination passenger/freight service from Kaohsiung to Los Angeles was launched in April 1998 via Boeing 747. However, this route was temporarily suspended seven months later due to the regional slowdown. Profits were down sharply in 1998, and EVA posted a loss in the first half of the year. Plans to buy a dozen Airbus passenger jets were also scrapped.

By the end of 1999, EVA had all-cargo flights extending as far as the Persian Gulf and Atlanta, Georgia. Other cargo destinations included Amsterdam, Brussels, London, Mumbai (Bombay), and Manila. Like rival China Airlines, it was expanding its cargo fleet in anticipation of a boom in freight upon the Asian economy's recovery. By this time, EVA had invested $4 billion in new aircraft since its founding.

A complex diplomatic and economic clash between Taiwan and the Philippines had consequences for EVA. Manila scrapped its aviation agreement with Taipei in September 1999, claiming EVA and China Airlines exceeded pre-determined passenger quotas to the detriment of Philippine Airlines (PAL).

Public in 1999

In the same month, earthquakes knocked out power to some Taiwanese electronics firms, disrupting shipments. This may not have been the best introduction to an initial public offering, but EVA pressed on with plans to go public on October 27, 1999. One percent of EVA's shares were designated for this over-the-counter offering. The parent company, Evergreen Marine Corporation, owned a quarter of the airline's shares and EVA employees owned another 25 percent. The company's listing moved to the Taiwan Stock Exchange in September 2001.

EVA placed $3 billion worth of orders and options for fifteen new long-range Boeing 777 aircraft worth $3 billion in June 2000. Delivery of three Boeing 747 super freighters, each with a capacity of 100 tons, began in August 2000. A slowdown in Taiwan's high-tech economy soon hurt cargo volume, however, while the same recession, plus the aftermath of the September 11 attacks on the United States, cut into passenger traffic.

EVA posted a net loss of NT$3.17 billion ($91 million) for 2001, its first full-year loss in several years. Layoffs and other cost-cutting measures followed. Transpacific routes were the hardest hit, while European and Asian routes rebounded fairly quickly. UNI Air, in which EVA held an 18 percent shareholding, was also losing money, burdened by high interest rates.

Kitty Yen, a 25-year veteran of the Evergreen shipping group, was made president of EVA in January 2002. She had been president of Evergreen Sky Catering since 1999; before that, she held a variety of posts at Evergreen International and Evergreen Marine.

EVA forecast a NT$1.25 billion ($36 million) profit for the year 2002, with revenues rising ten percent to NT$57.7 billion. A bright spot on the horizon for EVA and other local carriers was the possibility of direct flights between Taiwan and Mainland China, as both countries were joining the World Trade Organization.

Principal Subsidiaries

Evergreen Air Cargo Service Co. (55.8%); Evergreen Airline Services Corp (56.33%); Evergreen Airways Service (Macau) Ltd. (99%); Evergreen Aviation Technologies Co., Ltd. (79.8%); Evergreen Security Co., Ltd. (31.25%); Evergreen Sky Catering Corp. (49.8%); Evervoyage Transport Corp. (43.67%); Green Siam Air Services Co., Ltd. (Thailand; 51%); Hsiang-Li Investment Corp. (99.99%); RTW Air Service(s) Pte. Ltd. (Singapore; 51%); UNI Airways Corp. (18.43%).

Principal Competitors

Cathay Pacific Airways Ltd.; China Airlines; Delta Air Lines; Far East Air Transport; Singapore Airlines Ltd.; TransAsia Airways; United Airlines Inc.

Further Reading

Armbruster, William, ''Crossing the Strait; China Market Lures Taiwan's Air Carriers; EVA Considers Sea-Truck-Air Route,'' *Journal of Commerce,* July 2, 2001, p. 18.

——, ''EVA Airways' Cargo Outlook Has Analysts Optimistic,'' *Journal of Commerce,* March 29, 1993, p. 2B.

——, ''Flying High,'' *Journal of Commerce,* October 9, 2000, p. 38.

Bangsberg, P.T., ''EVA Airways Sees Profit Dive in 1998,'' *Journal of Commerce,* February 24, 1999, p. 13A.

——, ''Local Carriers Add Planes as Business Rebounds,'' *Journal of Commerce,* August 24, 1999, p. 8.

——, ''Taiwan Carrier Expands Service to Atlanta,'' *Journal of Commerce,* August 11, 1999, p. 4.

Brown, Chris, ''Taiwan's EVA Begins Service to Central Europe,'' *Journal of Commerce,* November 13, 1991, p. 2B.

Burstiner, Marcy, ''Cargo Pays the Freight,'' *San Francisco Business Times,* April 14, 1995, p. 3.

Dannhorn, Robin, ''EVA Profits from Being Different,'' *Bangkok Post,* April 5, 2001, p. 1.

Davies, R.E.G., ''Airline Transfer to an Offshore Island,'' *Airlines of Asia Since 1920,* London: Putnam, 1997, pp. 362–82.

''Despite RP Carrot, Taipei Plays Hardball,'' *Manila Standard,* November 5, 1999.

Dickie, Mure, and Tony Tassell, ''Taiwan-Philippines Air Dispute Flares,'' *Financial Times* (London), Asia-Pacific Sec., August 4, 1999, p. 4.

Elliott, Harvey, ''On a Fast Flight to Taipei,'' *The Times* (London), April 1, 1993.

Engardio, Pete and Dirk Bennett, ''Look, Up in the Sky—It's Taiwan's Shipping Tycoon,'' *Business Week,* July 8, 1991, p. 45.

Engbarth, Dennis, ''EVA Confident of Riding Out Crisis; Taiwanese Airline Navigates a Safe Passage Through the Fallout from Asia's Financial Turbulence,'' *South China Morning Post,* Freight and Shipping Post, May 6, 1998, p. 6.

——, ''Evergreen, EVA Work Together, Keep Cargo Network in the Family,'' *Journal of Commerce,* April 28, 1998, p. 7C.

''EVA Air in Profit Zone One Year Ahead of Schedule,'' *Business Times* (Kuala Lumpur), Shipping Times, February 28, 1996, p. 1.

''EVA Airways Expects Revenue to Expand 10% to NT$57.7B in 2002,'' *Taiwan Economic News,* January 4, 2002.

''EVA Orders Boeing 777 Jets in US$3b Deal,'' *Business Times* (Singapore), Shipping Times, June 28, 2000, p. 16.

''EVA Share Offering Unaffected by Cargo Slump,'' *China News,* October 19, 1999.

''EVA's Profits,'' *Air Cargo World,* March 2000, p. 16.

Flynn, Matthew, ''Taiwan—Evergreen Feels Draught from Airline,'' *Lloyd's List,* Bus. & Ins. Sec., September 5, 2001, p. 2.

''Founder of Evergreen Quits Chairman Post,'' *Business Times* (Malaysia), September 15, 1995, p. 2.

Hannon, Brent, ''Local Carriers Face Gray Skies,'' *Taipei Times,* March 22, 2001.

Ionides, Nicholas, ''Evergreen Optimism,'' *Airline Business,* May 2002, pp. 76ff.

Jones, Dominic, ''Competition Intensifies in Taiwan's Air Transport Market,'' *Airfinance Journal,* April 1997, pp. 34–35.

Kelly, Emma, ''Taiwan's EVA Air Finds Itself in Favour as CAL Struggles,'' *Flight International,* September 12, 2000, p. 29.

Lo, Joseph, ''Golden Route Deal Hopes Improve,'' *South China Morning Post,* May 25, 2002, p. 1.

Lugo, Leotes Marie T. and Czarina A. Baetiong, ''Estrada Orders Representative in Taiwan to Sign New Air Pact,'' *Businessworld* (Manila), September 25, 2000, p. 1.

Mayer, Christopher, ''EVA to Begin Operations Next Year,'' *Lloyd's List,* December 7, 1990, p. 2.

Moore, Jonathan, and Mark L. Clifford, ''The Feathers Are Flying in Taiwan's Skies,'' *Business Week,* Asian Business: Taiwan ed., April 21, 1997, p. 19.

''Super Freighter Joins EVA Air Fleet,'' *New Straits Times* (Kuala Lumpur), August 1, 2000, p. 25.

''Taiwan Regionals Forced to Merge,'' *Aviation Week & Space Technology,* April 20, 1998, p. 36.

Taylor, Paul, ''Softly Singing the Praises of Eva Air,'' *The European,* November 18, 1994, p. 28.

Toh, Eddie, ''Malaysia Welcomes More Flights by Evergreen Aviation Arm,'' *Business Times Singapore,* April 5, 2002.

Tyson, Laura, ''Asian Smog Hits Taiwan Airline,'' *Financial Times* (London), October 3, 1997, p. 7.

Wu, Sofia, ''Taiwan Carriers Competitive in World Air Cargo Market,'' *Central News Agency* (Taiwan), October 11, 1999.

Yeow, Jimmy, ''EVA Air Continues to 'Sell' Malaysia,'' *Business Times* (Kuala Lumpur), Shipping Times, July 8, 1996, p. 1.

—Frederick C. Ingram

Exel plc

Ocean House, The Ring
Bracknell, Berkshire RG12 1AN
United Kingdom
Telephone: (1344) 302000
Fax: (1344) 710031
Web site: http://www.exel.com

Public Company
Incorporated: 1865 as the Ocean Steam Ship Company;
   1981 as National Freight Consortium PLC
Employees: 61,700
Sales: £4.5 billion ($6.5 billion) (2001)
Stock Exchanges: London
Ticker Symbol: EXL
NAIC: 541614 Process, Physical Distribution, and
   Logistics Consulting Services; 488510 Freight
   Transportation Arrangement

Exel plc was formed from the 2000 merger of Ocean Group plc and NFC plc. Both Ocean and NFC had started out as simple cargo service providers and grew into major logistics and supply chain management concerns by the late 1990s. Their union formed a global logistics powerhouse with operations in over 120 countries. Exel's core services include e-commerce fulfillment, home delivery, manufacturing and retailer inbound services, regional and global freight management, supply chain management and design, transportation, and warehousing and distribution services. The firm caters to the automotive, chemical, consumer, healthcare, retail, and technology industries. Subsidiary Cory Environmental also provides environmental services throughout the United Kingdom.

Ocean Group History

The history of Ocean Group begins in 1865, when two brothers, Alfred and Philip Holt of Liverpool, set up the Ocean Steam Ship Company. Its purpose was to provide a regular steamship cargo service from England to China, at first via the Cape of Good Hope. At that time the steamship was not consid-

ered an economical long distance cargo carrier, but the Holt brothers planned to use a new type of steamer that they were convinced could compete effectively with sail on this route.

This was an ambitious project requiring a large investment. It involved building three ships, each of 2,280 tons, iron-hulled, and powered by a new type of compound steam engine designed by Alfred Holt, who was an engineer. He and his brother were the sons of a wealthy Liverpool cotton broker, and they had already proven the potential of this type of ship in West Indian trade. By selling the five ships they had owned in that trade they were able to put up almost half the capital needed for the new enterprise. The rest of the money came from other members of the family and their business friends in Liverpool. The company was founded before the days of limited liability, so all the shareholders were taking a considerable risk. The two Holt brothers, then aged 37 and 36, took on the management of the ships.

Their gamble paid off. The ships performed well and the cargoes followed: in the early days the chief goods transported were cotton textiles, which went from England to China, and tea, which went from China back to England. The Holts' ships became well known for their classical names (Agamemnon, Ajax, and Achilles were the first three) and their trademark blue funnels. Although the company was officially called Ocean it was much more often referred to as ''Holts'' or the ''Blue Funnel Line.''

Selecting Key Agents

The commercial success of the line was due partly to the Holts' high standing in the Liverpool business world and partly to their shrewd choice of agents. In some cases their agents were also shareholders in the company and therefore had a double incentive to bring business to the line. A prime example was the firm of John Swire & Sons. The Swire brothers, who built up this eastern trading business, were also from Liverpool and were contemporaries and friends of the Holt brothers. They invested in each other's businesses, and when the Swires set up shop in Shanghai (as Butterfield & Swire) it was partly to act as agents for the Holts. This partnership was so successful that Swires later became agents for Holts in other Far Eastern ports as well as in London.

Another fruitful agency appointment, and one which owed nothing to the Liverpool connection, was that of Mansfields in Singapore. The enterprise of this firm in developing trade with neighboring territories made Singapore a rich source of business for the line.

Only three years after the Holts started their China service, Far Eastern trade was transformed by the opening of the Suez Canal. By dramatically shortening the route to China, this greatly stimulated business. On the downside, however, it also attracted new competitors. In the next 20 years, the Blue Funnel Line grew to 30 ships, all financed out of profits. The main route from Liverpool to Shanghai was extended to Nagasaki as trade with Japan grew, and the volume of traffic all along the route was increased by feeder services. The Swires operated services along the Yangtze River and around the coast of China, while the Holts and Mansfields started feeder services centering on Singapore. Another profitable sideline was the carrying of passengers, particularly Chinese emigrants and Moslem pilgrims en route to and from Mecca in Saudi Arabia.

Fleet Expansion, Takeovers, and Joint Enterprises: 1890s–Early 1900s

Despite all this expansion, Ocean's profits began to decline in the 1880s. Competition from other steamship owners was driving freight rates down and the Blue Funnel ships were being overtaken in carrying capacity and speed by more modern ships. It became necessary to replace virtually the whole fleet if the company was to survive.

A decisive move was made in 1892, when four new ships were ordered and ten old ones transferred to feeder services. In the course of the 1890s, 23 new ships were added to the fleet and its total tonnage almost tripled. Ocean had to dig deep into its reserves and borrow from its bankers to make this investment, but it laid the foundations for another surge of growth in the next two decades.

Takeovers and joint enterprises played an important role in this second phase of growth. In 1902, Ocean became a limited company and bought one of its main competitors on the Liverpool-Far East route, the China Mutual Steam Navigation Company Ltd. This added another 13 modern ships to the Blue Funnel fleet. A few years earlier, Ocean had become the majority shareholder in an Amsterdam-based company Nederlandsche Stoomvart Maatschappij Oceaan (NSMO), which came to control the bulk of the tobacco trade from the Dutch East Indies to Europe. Other purchases and joint ventures enabled Ocean to extend its routes to Australia and, after the opening of the Panama Canal, to New York.

However, it was internally generated growth that made these investments possible. World trade was growing fast, and the Holts and their agents were very active in developing new types of business. Tin and rubber from the Malay states, tobacco from the East Indies, and refrigerated fruit and meat from Australia all became important inward cargoes, while machinery and manufactured goods of all kinds filled the outward-bound ships.

Two World Wars and the Great Depression

By 1913, the Blue Funnel fleet numbered 77 ships, and its total tonnage had nearly tripled again from its 1901 level. The years immediately before World War I brought record profits to Ocean, and the war pushed them still higher. Some of the company's ships were commandeered by the government at good rates, and freight rates also rose. The Far East trade was not affected much by the war, and Ocean was fortunate to lose relatively few of its ships before the fighting ended in 1918.

In retrospect, the end of the war and the short postwar boom proved to be the high watermark of the company's expansion. From then on, Ocean, along with other British shipowners, had to struggle to maintain business. In most of the interwar years, world trade was below its 1913 level and later suffered a severe decline during the first four years of the Great Depression, from 1929 to 1933. At the same time, Britain's share of the traffic was being eroded as other countries built up their merchant fleets. Existing shipping lines were able to protect themselves to some extent by the conference system, a form of cartel, but were under constant pressure from nonconference companies. In these circumstances, Ocean did well to keep the bulk of its business and to continue paying dividends throughout the period.

The depression brought about the collapse of one British shipping combine, the Royal Mail Group, and Ocean was in a strong enough position to be able to acquire parts of that business at bargain prices. It bought the Glen Line in 1935, gaining ten ships serving the Far East from London, as opposed to Liverpool. The year after, it acquired a large holding in the Elder Dempster Line, which was strong in the West African trade.

Then came World War II, which had a devastating effect on Ocean's business. The Japanese occupation of China and much of Southeast Asia completely destroyed the Europe-Far East trade from 1941 to 1945. Half the Blue Funnel fleet was sunk by enemy action, and its Liverpool headquarters was destroyed by bombs.

When the war ended, the company—still headed by a member of the Holt family—courageously set about rebuilding the business. Its urgent need for more ships was met by buying some secondhand and by having others built abroad. Rebuilding the company's trading connections, however, was not so easy. Trade with China never recovered after the civil war and Communist takeover, but trade with Australia was buoyant and that with other territories was gradually restored.

By the late 1950s, the Blue Funnel fleet again numbered almost 70 ships still pursuing traditional liner trade. Ocean was not at this stage interested in oil tankers or bulk carriers, and the day of the container had not yet arrived. As a company, Ocean was perhaps a shade too conservative at this time. It was still a family business, owned and managed mainly by descendants of the founders. All the directors sat in one room at the Liverpool head office, just as their predecessors had for almost a hundred years. Their standards in ship safety and efficiency were high, and the company was universally respected. In 1965, *Investors Chronicle*, a financial paper, characterized Ocean as "one of the largest British shipping companies, with a sound, steady profits record."

By then, however, it was clear that things had to change. The success of containerization in the United States was forcing the company to contemplate radical business strategies, and to facilitate these it was decided that its shares should be traded on the stock exchange. (It was already a public company, but an unquoted one.) This change went into effect in March 1965.

Investing in Containerization

Later the same year, two other far-reaching decisions were made. The first was to start investing in containerization. This meant merging Ocean's main business into a larger grouping to finance the massive investment required. The other decision, linked to the first, was to start diversifying into other branches of the shipping business to provide new opportunities for Ocean's own organization.

The company was spurred into action by reports that the Australian government was keen to containerize and was negotiating with SeaLand, an American company. Neither Ocean nor its competitors in the Europe-Australia trade could risk losing this business, so four of the British companies, including Peninsular & Oriental Steam Navigation Company (P&O) and Ocean, jointly set up Overseas Containers Ltd. (OCL) to provide a container service on this route.

OCL began operations in 1969. Within a few years its Australian service was showing a profit, and it had joined a still larger international consortium to containerize the Europe-Far East route. At this point in the early 1970s, Ocean's stake in OCL grew to 49 percent, and its Blue Funnel fleet became largely superfluous.

In anticipation of this, Ocean had been investing in other shipping businesses since 1965. That year it took over a company called Liner Holdings. This included the Elder Dempster Line, in which Ocean had held shares since 1936, and other subsidiaries. Over the next few years, Ocean also acquired interests in tankers, bulk carriers, and cargo handling services, laying the foundations of much of the company's business through the 1980s. For example, MSAS Cargo International began in 1968 as McGregor Swire Air Services, a joint venture between Ocean and its long-time partner, Swire. Panocean Storage & Transport was set up a year later in cooperation with P&O.

Continued Acquisition and Expansion

Another important move—because it put Ocean into land transport for the first time—was the purchase of William Cory & Son Ltd. in 1972. Cory was a long-established company that had first made its name carrying coal by sea from northeast England to London. From this it moved into the transport of fuel oil by sea and land and later again into food distribution. Cory also had offshoots in towage and waste disposal. The acquisition of this business increased Ocean's assets by over 40 percent.

It cannot be said that all Ocean's diversifications in the 1960s and 1970s were successful. There were a few expensive failures, and there were bad times when the company was itself threatened with takeover. Nevertheless, enough of the new ventures succeeded to provide a strong basis for future growth. The company's remaining shipowning interests, apart from OCL and Elder Dempster, were sold off in the late 1970s and early 1980s, and in 1986 a decision was made to withdraw from OCL. Ocean's then 33 percent holding was sold to P&O, and, in a partial exchange, Ocean acquired P&O's holding in Panocean. Elder Dempster was sold in 1989.

After the sale of the OCL holding, Ocean was in possession of a large amount of cash in 1986, and this attracted an unwelcome takeover bid from New Zealand entrepreneur Ron Brierley. The company successfully resisted this and focused on investing all its resources in building up its core businesses: sea freight, air freight, logistics, marine services, and waste management. In particular, it invested in overseas companies, with the result that its business was very widely spread around the world by the late 1980s.

The company's name changed twice in the latter half of the twentieth century to reflect its changing activities. In 1973, after the Cory takeover, it became Ocean Transport & Trading Ltd., and in 1990 it adopted the Ocean Group name. The last director with a family connection retired in 1976, and the company's head office moved from Liverpool to London in 1980, and then to Berkshire in 1992. Nicholas Barber, who joined Ocean in 1964, took over as chief executive in 1987.

By the early 1990s, Ocean Group's main business was international freight management. Its largest subsidiary, MSAS Cargo International, was one of the world's leading freight forwarders and was among the top five companies in air freight forwarding, with over 220 offices in 30 countries.

Ocean's other businesses also centered on transport. Its distribution services sector included McGregor Cory, which undertook contract distribution and warehousing in half a dozen

European countries, and Panocean Storage & Transport, which specialized in moving and storing bulk liquids in Europe and the United States. Its marine services sector included O.I.L. Ltd., which provided support services for the offshore oil industry worldwide and was the second largest in the world, while Cory Towage provided towage services in certain parts of the world.

By this time, the company had also built up a stake in the environmental services industry. In the United Kingdom, it disposed of a fifth of London's refuse, among other contracts, and in the United States it operated a chain of 20 environmental testing laboratories.

Changing Direction

Despite its restructuring efforts, Ocean's lackluster performance of the early 1990s left it repositioning once again. Prompted by investor disinterest in the company, Ocean management began looking for a new leader to revamp the company. "We needed someone to reshape the headquarters and the operating units with a modern set of solutions, not the concepts of the 1950s and 1960s, which were still evident," claimed former chairman Peter Marshall in a 1998 *Management Today* article. Management decided on business executive John Allan, who was named CEO in 1994.

Under Allan's leadership, Ocean began to shift its focus to global logistics. The strategy appeared to pay off. In 1998, revenues increased by nearly 20 percent over the previous year while operating profit grew by 32 percent. That year, the company created MSAS Global Logistics, uniting all of its logistics businesses, including MSAS Cargo International, under the new name.

The company was also involved in strategic ventures and key acquisitions during this time period. In 1996, the company established a joint venture in China and subsidiaries in Finland and Korea. The following year, Intexo and Marken were acquired, and ventures were set up in Brazil, India, and Chile. Acquisitions in 1998 included Oslo Havnelager, Mercury, Laker Cargo, Skyking, A.W. Fenton, and Dutch Air. Additional purchases followed in 1999, including Mark VII, Malenstein, Parkhill Reclamation, and Aerocar Spedition AB. Then, in 2000, Ocean set its sights on NFC, which had recently restructured into a supply chain management firm.

NFC History

A very distinctive feature of NFC plc was that it was largely owned by its employees, their families, and pensioners. During the early 1990s, employees held around 18 percent of the equity and their shares carried two votes each. New employees were helped to buy shares, and management kept all employees informed about the company's progress. It also invited their views on major issues. Employee ownership, the company said, was "the essence of NFC's culture."

The reason for this lay in the circumstances of the company's birth. The letters "NFC" originally stood for National Freight Corporation, which was a collection of road transport businesses owned by the British government. The Thatcher administration, when it took power in 1979, was determined to

return it to the private sector, and in 1982 agreed to a unique employee buy out. At that point, employees, their families, and pensioners owned 82.5 percent of the equity. The company became extremely successful in its new form, and it was only because of its rapid expansion that the employees' percentage dropped.

It is debatable at what point a history of this company should begin. Legally, it began life in November 1981, when the buy out consortium was formed. However, the assets it acquired two months later had been brought together as the National Freight Corporation in 1968 and had been owned by the state under other names since about 1948. Furthermore, many of the businesses that were taken over at that time had existed for generations in private ownership.

Pickford's Wagon, Barge, and Rail Service: 1700s–1800s

It is obviously impractical to trace all these companies back to their beginnings, but one exception must be made. This is Pickfords, a well-known name in England that was used by NFC until 1999. It was almost certainly the oldest road haulage business in the United Kingdom and was the largest at the time the industry was nationalized.

It is said that the firm was founded in the seventeenth century, but the earliest documentary evidence of its existence is an advertisement from 1756 in the name of "James Pickford, the London and Manchester Waggoner." He offered a regular wagon service for goods between Manchester and London. To cope with the rough roads of those days, his wagons had wheels with rims nine inches wide, and they were pulled by teams of as many as eight horses. They covered the 200 miles or so in eight or nine days, which at the time must have been good going for a heavy load.

James Pickford and his sons developed a flourishing business on this important route and gradually extended their service to other towns in the midlands. By the end of the eighteenth century, canals formed an alternative means of transportation, and Pickfords were quick to use them too. By 1835, the firm was said to be "the greatest carrier on the canals," with over 100 barges and 800 horses in use.

Then came the railways. Pickfords tried to persuade the railway companies to let them run their own goods wagons on the railways. Failing in this, they became agents to the London and North Western Railway, which ran the best service between London and Manchester. In this capacity, Pickfords carried goods by horse and cart to the stations and, at the end of the rail journey, on to their ultimate destinations. As railway traffic grew, this became a very profitable business. Pickfords made similar arrangements with other railway companies, operated their own road services where there were no railways and all over London, and by the end of the nineteenth century had a countrywide business and reputation.

Changes in Ownership and Nationalization

The Pickford family lost control of the business around 1850, but another family, the Baxendales, operated it under the old name for another two generations. It then suffered from bad luck in the early 1900s and was bought first by one company, then another, until in 1933 it was bought jointly by the four railway companies that at that time owned Britain's entire rail network. Under their ownership, Pickfords again flourished and grew, used by the railway companies as a means of recouping some of the business they lost to road transport services with the coming of gasoline-powered trucks.

During the 1920s and 1930s, Pickfords branched out into household moving and, with its national network of offices and depots, became the leading firm in that business. By the end of World War II, Pickfords offered a unique range of road transport services, from heavy loads and bulk liquids to furniture-moving and parcel delivery service.

At this point, Britain's postwar Labor government decided to nationalize the road transport industry, along with the railways, the docks, and other major utilities and industries. The rationale was that with railways and road haulers under common ownership, wasteful competition would be eliminated and a more efficient transport system would emerge.

The fragmented road transport business was a formidable challenge to government bureaucrats. Ultimately, the state took over only those companies whose major business was the carriage of goods for 40 miles and upwards, but even so it took the government agency five years—from 1948 until 1952—to buy the 3,744 firms in this category. Most of them lost their old identities and became part of a new corporation, British Road Services (BRS), but Pickfords and a few other large operators were allowed to keep their old names within BRS.

Even before this process was complete, the Conservatives were back in power, intent on reversing nationalization. In the early 1950s, much of the BRS fleet was sold back to private operators. However, BRS was retained, still in the public sector, to provide a single nationally coordinated road haulage service on trunk routes.

Over the years, and through various reorganizations, BRS expanded to take in a whole range of road transport services. Certain specialized services, including household moving, were carried on under the name of Pickfords, and a parcel delivery service operated under the name Roadline. At the same time, British Railways developed its own rail and road parcel delivery service. The advent of the container in the 1960s increased the railways' involvement in road transport still further.

The Government Forms NFC

Because of these overlaps in the public sector, the government decided in 1968 to bring BRS/Pickfords' and British Railways' parcel delivery business (renamed National Carriers) and container operation (Freightliner) under the control of one organization, the National Freight Corporation (NFC). In the same piece of legislation, the licensing system, which had restricted the number of new entrants into the road haulage business, was relaxed.

These measures committed NFC to running several services in competition with each other, while exposing it to still more competition from the private sector. The NFC's services had to be comprehensive and therefore had higher overhead costs than the small private operators, and were inevitably undercut in price.

Despite these inherent weaknesses, NFC got off to a good start. Its workforce, which numbered 66,000 at its inception, was gradually reduced, and profitability improved so that the initial government subsidy granted to NFC became unnecessary. Encouraged by this, the corporation decided to expand into continental Europe and bought businesses in France, Germany, and elsewhere.

The oil crisis of 1974 hit all NFC markets simultaneously, and its modest profits gave way to serious losses. In 1976, NFC's top management underwent change—curbs on spending were set and the Freightliner business was returned to British Railways.

NFC's new chief executive was Peter Thompson, who later led the buy out. His career had been mainly in the private sector of the transport business until he became managing director of BRS in 1972. Once at the head of NFC, he began to apply private sector criteria to all its operations. Its European ventures, which had proved to be liabilities, were sold and other loss-makers severely pruned. The workforce was reduced still further, to 34,000 by 1979. The organization was decentralized, many senior managers were retired, and younger employees who had proved their worth were promoted. Not least important, the government was persuaded to write off much of the corporation's accumulated debt. By 1979, NFC was beginning to look more like a shareholder-owned company.

In that year, the Thatcher government came into office and NFC was at the top of its list of state-owned businesses to be privatized. In 1980, a merchant bank was appointed by the government to advise on how this should be done. It soon found that there were snags. NFC's pension arrangements had not been properly funded, business was again suffering from a recession, and NFC had just lost a lucrative contract with British Railways as a result of pressure on the latter to cut its losses. The bank advised that NFC should not be brought to market for two or three years, and even then set a relatively low value on it.

Thompson and his team believed that NFC was worth more, or soon would be under their management, and began to think about a buy out. Realizing that they could not raise sufficient capital themselves, even with loans, they decided to propose the idea to employees. The response was favorable, and this solution also appealed to the government because it would speed up the privatization process. After much negotiation, a deal emerged whereby a consortium of banks would lend the money to make good the pension deficit in return for 17.5 percent of the equity, while employees and pensioners of NFC and their families would put up the rest (about £7 million).

NFC Becomes Employee Owned

NFC became a public company, owned by its employees, in February 1982. Thompson remained chief executive, and the board had full authority to run the business. At the same time, employees were encouraged to contribute to a new definition of the company's aims. The first of these was of course to increase profits for its existing shareholders. More unusually, it was also agreed that the company should allocate a portion of each year's profits to making more employees shareholders and that it should aim to increase employment opportunities.

The company was therefore committed to expansion, as well as improving profits, almost from the start. To achieve this, the management set itself some very specific growth objectives and some equally specific cost reduction requirements. One obvious way of cutting costs was to make better use of the company's properties. Because BRS, Pickfords, Roadline, National Carriers, and other subsidiaries had all developed their own branch networks, there were many towns where NFC had four or more depots. Once these subsidiaries saw that they had a common interest in cutting costs, it was not difficult to persuade them to share premises, and large savings were made in this way. The surplus properties were then sold or redeveloped, boosting profits.

More controversially, the management decided that its two parcel delivery services, Roadline and National Carriers, must either merge or be reduced by one. The two companies were merged as National Carriers Roadline and then relaunched under the name of Lynx Express Delivery.

International Expansion

The most important growth objectives the new company set itself was to expand overseas until at least a quarter of its profits were coming from abroad. This time, acquisitions would be more selective than in the 1970s. NFC resolved to concentrate first on building an international household moving service, to meet the needs of executives being moved around the world, and second on acquiring businesses in the growing field of contract distribution.

In the moving market, Pickfords provided a strong base for expansion. It first bought an Australian company, then set up branches in Hong Kong, New Zealand, and elsewhere. In 1988, it acquired the roughly 500 independent firms comprising Allied Van Lines, one of the leading moving companies in the United States. This link-up established the Allied Pickfords group in more countries than any other moving company. Another United States acquisition was that of Merchants Home Delivery Service of California, which specializes in deliveries to private homes from furniture and appliance retailers.

On the contract distribution side, NFC was again building from a position of strength in its home market. It undertook distribution for Marks & Spencer and other big retailers in the 1970s, and in the recession of 1981–83 found many more companies receptive to the idea of sub-contracting delivery and warehousing to a specialist in this area. NFC took over an increasing number of transport fleets and storage facilities, especially from food manufacturers and retailers. Later in the 1980s, newspaper groups became customers too.

In the United States, NFC was able to acquire two important businesses in the same field: Dauphin Distribution Services of Pennsylvania in 1986 and Distribution Centers Incorporated of Ohio three years later. These and other companies in North America and Europe were then grouped together by NFC to form the Exel Logistics division in 1989.

In the United Kingdom, NFC improved profitability chiefly by continuing to move away from general haulage and into more specialized services. BRS became the market leader in contract hire and developed truck rental, tank freight, and waste management subsidiaries. The travel side of Pickfords was also expanded, becoming a leading British travel agency.

NFC had seen some failures as well, notably an attempt to sell its computer software to a wider market, but they have been few. The company's turnover had grown solidly since the early 1980s, and its pre-tax profit increased almost tenfold from £11.8 million in 1983 to £114.4 million in 1989. It began to decline slightly in the face of a long recession, but was still a very respectable £102 million in 1991. In keeping with its employment objective, the company's workforce rose from 23,000 in 1982 to 33,000 in 1992.

Growth aside, the most important change in the company since 1982 was the wider spread of its ownership. To provide a more efficient market in its shares, NFC applied for a Stock Exchange quotation in February 1989. As such, institutions held a significant proportion of its shares, although control continued to rest with the company's employees families, pensioners, and former employees. Peter Thompson was honored with a knighthood for his part in creating NFC and was succeeded as chief executive by James Watson in 1991.

By the early 1990s, NFC plc was the largest road transport, household moving, and contract distribution business in the United Kingdom. It was also a significant contender in these markets in North America, Europe, and Australia, with about a third of its total business overseas. Worldwide, NFC had over 20,000 vehicles on the road. The company had four divisions. The transportation division operated chiefly in the United Kingdom under the names of BRS and Lynx Express Delivery. The logistics division undertook distribution and warehousing for retailers and manufacturers, mainly under the name Exel, and was particularly strong in North America. The home services division carried out household moving under the names Pickfords and Allied Van Lines. NFC also had a property division.

Before its merger with Ocean, NFC made several key moves to broaden its global reach. In 1993, it entered the Mexican market and, two years later, announced its intention to enter the entire Latin American market as well. The firm also established Tradeteam, a joint venture that served the UK beverage industry. By 1996, the company had restructured into five distinct business units: automotive, electronics, retail, consumer, and petroleum and chemicals.

NFC continued to revamp its operations, streamlining internal business processes in 1997 and creating a global board of officers in 1998. That year, its Exel Logistics unit acquired the logistics division of Walsh Western Group and Monros Logistica of Spain. Perhaps its most significant move, however, was the decision to sell its Allied Pickford Moving Services division in an effort to focus on its supply chain management businesses. It was this focus that made NFC attractive to its merger partner.

The 2000 Merger

Upon entering the new century, Ocean—whose focus had shifted to global logistics in the late 1990s—was searching for a merger partner that would solidify its position in the industry. Having undergone a restructuring effort itself, NFC seemed to fit the bill with its strong supply chain management structure. Both companies agreed that a union would be beneficial and in February 2000, Ocean Group announced its £1.64 merger with NFC. The deal was completed in May of that year and created one of the world's largest global logistics concerns. A May 2000 Logistics Management and Distribution Report claimed that the merger was prompted by the "need to provide customers with integrated supply chain management and information technology on a global basis." The article also pointed to four trends—increased globalization, the growth of logistics outsourcing, worldwide consolidation throughout many industries, and the increase in e-commerce—that made the merger attractive to both companies.

The newly merged company adopted the Exel plc name and was headed by Allan. Under his continued leadership, Exel made several key acquisitions including Total Logistics Co., whose operations were based in the Asia Pacific region, U.S.-based FX Coughlin, and Werthmann Koster, a German automotive logistics provider. In 2002, United States Consolidation Limited, All Cargo Logistics, and Power Logistics and Power Europe were purchased. Exel also disposed of several non-core assets, including Exel Froid, a French chilled food distribution business, and its German frozen food distribution business.

Demand for Exel's services in both the technology and automotive sectors began to fall off as global economies weakened during the early years of the new century. At the same time, however, the trend to outsource logistical needs continued to grow, placing Exel in a prime position. While only time would tell if the 2000 merger would pay off, Exel management was confident that the company would continue to rank among the world's leading logistics concerns for years to come.

Principal Subsidiaries

Exel Logistics Belgium NV; Exel Logistics France SA; Exel Logistics GmbH (Germany); Exel Europe Ltd.; Exel Freight Management UK Ltd.; Higgs International Ltd.; Mercury International Ltd.; Tradeteam Ltd. (50.1%); Exel Walsh Western Holdings Ltd. (Ireland); Exel Italy SpA; Exel Services Holdings BV (The Netherlands); Exel SL (Spain); Exel Freight Management AB (Sweden); Exel Global Logistics Canada Inc.; Exel Logistics de Mexico SA de CV; Exel Inc. (U.S.); Exel Direct Inc. (U.S.); Exel Global Logistics Inc. (U.S.); Exel North American Logistics Inc. (U.S.); Exel Transportation Services Inc. (U.S.); FX Coughlin Inc. (U.S.); Exel Hong Kong Ltd.; Exel Japan KK; Exel Logistics Korea Ltd.; Exel Singapore Pte Ltd.; Cory Environmental Ltd.

Principal Competitors

CNF Inc.; Deutsche Post AG; Stinnes AG.

Further Reading

Davidson, Andrew, "John Allan," *Management Today*, April 1998, p. 76.
"Exel Confident Despite 6% Fall in Full-Year Pretax Profit," *Futures World News*, June 8, 2001.
"Exel Reorganizes," *Chemical Week*, November 3, 1999, p. 45.
Falkus, Malcolm, *The Blue Funnel Legend: A History of the Ocean Steam Ship Company, 1865–1973*, London: Macmillan, 1990.
Hobsbawm, E. J., *Industry and Empire: From 1750 to the Present Day*, London: Penguin Books, 1969.
Hyde, Francis E., *Blue Funnel: A History of Alfred Holt and Company of Liverpool from 1865 to 1914*, Liverpool: Liverpool University Press, 1956.
McLachlan, Sandy, *The National Freight Buy-Out*, London: Macmillan, 1983.
"NFC, Ocean Group Agree to Combine for 2.66 Billion Euros," *Wall Street Journal Europe*, February 22, 2000, p. 4.
"Ocean, NFC Merger Focuses on Growth," *Logistics Management & Distribution Report*, May 1, 2000, p. 24.
Roskill, S. W., *A Merchant Fleet in War: Alfred Holt & Co. 1939–1945*, London: Collins, 1962.
Thompson, Peter, *Sharing the Success: The Story of NFC*, London: Collins, 1990.
Turnbull, Gerard L., *Traffic and Transport: An Economic History of Pickfords*, London: George Allen & Unwin, 1979.
Turney, Roger, "MSAS Grows," *Air Cargo World*, April 1999, p. 13.

—John Swan
—update: Christina M. Stansell

CHRISTIAN STORES
Helping to Strengthen Hearts, Minds & Souls

Family Christian Stores, Inc.

5300 Patterson Avenue SE
Grand Rapids, Michigan 49530
U.S.A.
Telephone: (616) 554-8700
Fax: (616) 554-8608
Web sites: http://www.familychristian.com

Private Company
Incorporated: 1994
Employees: 5,000
Sales: $325.0 million (2001 est.)
NAIC: 451211 Book Stores

Family Christian Stores, Inc., based in Grand Rapids, Michigan, is the nation's largest retailer of Christian-themed products. The company owns and operates over 340 stores in 39 states. It sells a wide range of merchandise, including books, music, greeting cards, videos, clothing, toys, and church supplies. It also sells through its widely circulated catalog and via its Web site, familychristian.com. The venture capital firm of Madison Dearborn Partners owns about 70 percent of the private company. In 2002, the company, headed by Leslie E. Dietsman, celebrated its 70th anniversary.

1931–70: Christian Bookstore and Publishing House Is Founded and Expands

The company that would eventually give corporate birth to Family Christian Stores was founded in 1931 in Grandville, Michigan, by brothers Peter J. (Pat) and Bernard (Bernie) Zondervan. The pair opened shop in their mother's farm house, starting what eventually would emerge as The Zondervan Corporation, specializing in the publication of Christian books, including Bibles, but with no affiliation with Family Christian Stores.

In 1932, the brothers opened their first bookstore in Grand Rapids and in the next year began publishing books under the Zondervan imprint. Through the next two decades, the company slowly expanded, taking significant steps in 1959, when it bought a religious music company, Singspiration, and in 1960,

when it took over the publication of *Halley's Bible Handbook*, buying the rights from a private concern. Over the next few years it sold over four million copies of that work.

By the 1960s, Zondervan had started opening outlets in shopping malls and met with considerable success, encouraging the company to restrict its new openings to such locations. In 1966, the company acquired Harper Row Publishing Company's Bible department, which transferred to Zondervan the publication rights to a number of Bibles and Bible textbooks, including the widely adopted *Harper Study Bible*.

1971–83: Rapid Growth for Zondervan Corporation

In 1971, Zondervan invested capital in the financially troubled International Bible Society and its translation of the New International Version (NIV) of the Bible, an investment that paid off handsomely when that publication, completed in 1978, became a best-selling Bible, ranking second only to the King James Version. Adopted as the Bible of choice by many churches, the work catapulted Zondervan into the top tier of publishers of religious works.

The company thrived through the first part of the 1980s, growing significantly via the acquisition of other companies, including, in 1980, the John T. Benson Company, a religious music publisher, several book publishers, and Tapley-Rutter Co., a specialty bindery. It also acquired a foreign subsidiary, Marshall Pickering Holdings Ltd., a UK-based printer and publisher of religious books and music. Although it logged unexpected losses in 1979, over the next four years its sales and profits more than doubled, with annual revenues reaching $93 million by 1983. However, trouble loomed just ahead.

1984–94: Buyout of Zondervan

In 1984, it was revealed that for several years the company's books had been incorrectly kept, masking losses of several million dollars. Since the company had gone public in 1976, the disclosure brought both lawsuits and SEC sanctions. Straightening matters out became the major task of James Buick, who had become Zondervan's CEO just prior to the debacle, a task made difficult by the bottom-line losses that

---

Company Perspectives:

Vision: Family Christian Stores' vision is to provide high-quality Christian products that impact the lives of people everywhere and to achieve exceptional business performance. Mission: Family Christian Stores' mission is to serve Jesus Christ as a growing national retailer that is Christ-centered, offering exceptional value, products, and services for our customers.

---

followed it. In 1988, to thwart a hostile buyout attempt, Zondervan's directors sold the company to Harper Row for $56.7 million, a figure that left some investors unhappy enough to bring new suits against the directors. However, most were mollified when Harper Row merged with Collins Publishing to form HarperCollins.

In 1989, while a division of HarperCollins, Zondervan created a New Media division and became the first in the industry to publish books and Bibles in an electronic format. However, despite is successes, Zondervan did not fit readily into the HarperCollins mode. The result was a major change that came towards the end of 1994, when the management of the Zondervan's Family Bookstores chain purchased it from HarperCollins in an amicable buyout. The buyout group was headed by Zondervan's Family Bookstores president and CEO, Leslie Dietzman, with the additional financial backing of a group of private individuals who were not affiliated with any other corporation or company. The Zondervan group had actually started mounting its buyout effort as early as 1992, when Buick, its former president, confided in the *Grand Rapids Press* that the move was designed to ''return the direction and control of the company into the Christian community.'' The management buyout effort was also being encouraged by George Craig, president and CEO of Harper-Collins, who, rather than put Zondervan up for sale, gave its managers time to get the necessary financial backing. Meanwhile, in September 1993, the Zondervan division split into two distinct parts, the publishing operation, which retained the Zondervan name, and the Family Bookstores operation. The split, engineered by Buick, put him out of his job. The top post of the publishing operation passed to Bruce Ryskam, while that of book sales went to Dietzman.

The private company that broke apart from HarperCollins was named Family Bookstores Co. It was totally divorced from the Zondervan name, which remained with HarperCollins as part of its publishing empire. Zondervan continued its own evolution as The Zondervan Corporation, which continued to publish Christian books under the Zondervan imprint, including its world renowned NIV Bible.

The executive team of Family Bookstores remained in place under Dietzman. He had joined the Zondervan chain in 1992, two years before the buyout from HarperCollins. His experience before 1990 had been in secular retailing, but he was the son of a pastor and had assisted his father in church while growing up in Loyal, Wisconsin. His career in merchandising took him to Wal-Mart Stores in 1990, where he became vice-president in that giant's toy and automotive divisions. Both his family his-

tory and retail sales experience led to his recruitment to head the Zondervan bookstore chain at HarperCollins.

When the sale was made, there were 148 renamed Family Bookstore outlets, but soon after the closing of the sale the newly independent company acquired five more stores when it bought The Quest chain in Seattle, Washington. Plans called for the addition of more, larger stores. Many of the existing stores were mall-based outlets averaging 2,200 square feet, but, in a strategy change that called for moving out of the malls, new units were being added with an average size of between 5,000 and 6,000 square feet.

1995–97: Growth Through Acquisition and a New Company Name

By the summer of 1995, with the acquisition of Religious Book & Supply, with its 12-unit chain located exclusively in Florida, Family Bookstores had a 171 locations in 32 states. The company had earlier bought out some smaller operations, including Christ's Corner Bookstore, with outlets in Plainsfield and Brownsburg, Indiana; two Christian Armory stores in Atlanta; and the Password in Pennsylvania. In 1994, it had also bought the 35,000-square-foot Living Vine store in Irving, Texas. The great majority of the established and newly purchased stores were located in the nation's principal Christian sales areas in the Southeast and Midwest, including ten in Atlanta, ten in Chicago, four in Cincinnati, seven in Dallas, three in Indianapolis, five in the Raleigh/Durham and Greensboro, North Carolina areas, five in Nashville, and six in Washington, D.C. These cities were promising market sites because they attracted tourists to their many fine churches. Still, Family Bookstores was expanding into other markets, and also had stores in Boise, Idaho, as well as Denver and, with the acquisition of Quest, in Seattle. At the time, as reported in *Billboard*, Family Bookstore's CEO Dietzman indicated that ''eventually we will be nationwide.''

Family Bookstores sold more than books, and from the outset started a further diversification of its inventory. In 1995, it estimated that at least 25 percent of its annual revenues were generated from the sale of music recordings and videos, including items in its stores' children's departments. In fact, tapes, CDs, and videos were growing product lines, and the company indicated that they had the potential to comprise over a third of the company's business.

For its 1997 fiscal year, Family Bookstores had net sales of $168.1 million, up by an annual growth rate of about 15.4% from 1995, when its net sales were $126.1 million. Its operating income over that two-year period also grew from a deficit of $2.5 million to a profit of $5.5 million. The growth encouraged expansion and a refurbishing of its image, starting with a change of name. Partly to reflect its mission and partly to indicate that it was selling a more diverse product line than books alone, the company was restyled Family Christian Stores, Inc. (FCS).

1998–99: Major Expansion

Under its new name, the company took a major step in 1998, when it acquired a Forth Worth, Texas-based chain, Joshua's Christian Stores, from that company's parent, Tandycraft Inc.

Key Dates:

1931: FCS starts out as Zondervan.
1966: The company acquires Harper & Row's Bible department.
1971: Zondervan invests in NIV Bible, a key to its spurt in growth.
1984: The company is beset with difficulties when its faulty bookkeeping is disclosed.
1988: Zondervan is bought by Harper & Row.
1994: FCS is acquired from HarperCollins through a leveraged buyout.
1995: The company acquires Religious Book & Supply Chain
1998: FCS acquires Joshua's Christian Stores from Tandycrafts.
1999: The company launches its iBelieve.com Internet site.
2000: FCS buys eight stores of Shepherd Shoppe chain.

Under Tandycraft, Joshua's, dating back to 1982, had been a fast-growing chain, expanding to 76 stores from its single outlet before being scaled back to 56 stores at the time of its buyout by FCS. In its fiscal year ending in June 1997, the company grossed $32 million in sales but logged an operating loss of $7.7 million; however, for first six months of fiscal 1998, Joshua's had reported an operating profit of $846,000 on sales of $18 million.

Before purchasing Joshua's, the FCS chain itself had grown to 210 stores located in 34 states. The Joshua outlets added 56, and new openings in 1998 brought the total to 280 by May. At that time, Dietzman indicated that the company also had plans to expand by about 30 new stores by the end of 1998. FCS was already far and away the largest Christian bookstore chain in the country, having almost twice the number of outlets as the next two largest chains combined. These, the Baptist Bookstores and Lifeway Christian Stores operating 74 stores through the Southern Baptist Convention, and Lemstone Books operating 73 stores, together had a total of 147. Clearly, in 1998 FCS dominated the $4.3 billion specialty, Christian-theme retail market. The company generated $227 million in revenue, with about 20 percent of being accounted for by music sales.

In order to finance further expansion, FCS put in motion plans to go public and float an issue of common stock. In August 1998, it filed an S-1 registration form with the SEC, and although it did not indicate how many shares of common stock it was planning to issue and at what price, it hoped to raise about $45 million. It intended to use around $12 million of the IPO's proceeds for financing new store openings and making acquisitions over the next year or year and a half. The filing also indicated that control of FCS would remain with the existing shareholders and management. At the same time, the company took the unusual step of looking for a large infusion of capital from other sources.

The company was then operating 276 stores in 36 states. Its sale of Bibles, other books, audio tapes, and videos accounted for about 39 percent of its sales, gifts and cards for about 26 percent, music for around 20 percent, children's items for 10 percent, and church supplies for 4 percent. At the start of the 1998, to help vary its product mix, FCS had also established its own publishing imprint, the Family Christian Press. The company also had begun marketing is product line on the Internet at its www.familychristian.com site.

As matters turned out, the planned IPO was put on hold. The IPO market weakened soon after FCS filed its intention to float a stock issue. Then, in October 1998, the company filed its notice of suspending its plans. It would remain private into at least the start of the new century. In 1999, it also got the needed financial backing it sought when Madison Dearborn Partners began investing in FCS. The funds provided by that firm allowed the company to stay on its expansion track. Projected to end up owning as much as 80 percent of FCS, Madison Dearborn was also able to provide a wealth of experience in specialty retailing, in which it had a rich history of investment.

2000–02: Company Launches iBelieve.com Web Site and Slows Expansion

FCS took a major step at the beginning of 2000 when it launched iBelieve.com, described in a *PR Newswire* as "a comprehensive Christian lifestyle site aimed at satisfying the spiritual, social, and resources needs of the nation's 90 million committed, active Christians." Originally set up as a stand-alone sister company to FCS, iBelieve.com was supported by a $30 million private equity infusion from Madison Dearborn Partners. The site was designed by Andersen Consulting's Global Retail/E-commerce Practice to meet various needs of the Christian community. It was launched with an on-line catalog of over 70,000 e-commerce products covering a wide variety of merchandise, from books and Bibles to music, gifts, and clothing. The site also offered a range of services, including entertainment and financial, family, and parenting consulting.

Rumors claiming that it was heading for bankruptcy plagued the company through the close of the twentieth century and the start of the twenty-first. Although dismissing such claims out of hand, in the spring of 2001, FCS did slow down its expansion rate, holding back both new acquisitions and new store openings. Although it had once been on schedule to grow to 500 locations by the end of 2000, it decided to step back to concentrate its investment in remodeling and relocating some of its existing outlets. The slowdown did not warrant speculation that the company would soon be on the auction block. It was, insisted CEO Dietzman, merely a cyclical adjustment of the sort all such retail chains faced as they adjusted to marketplace realities. Adjustments included the closing of 14 stores between Christmas of 2000 and March 2001, but, according to the company, these were largely marginal units whose leases had expired.

Principal Competitors

Amazon.com, Inc.; Barnes & Noble, Inc.; Books-A-Million, Inc.; Borders Group, Inc.; Crosswalk.com, Inc.; Deseret Management Corp.; Hobby Lobby Stores, Inc.; The Musicland Group, Inc.; Parable Group, Inc.; Powell's Books, Inc.; Standex International Corporation; Wal-Mart Stores, Inc.

Further Reading

Bates, Patricia, ''Family Bookstores Rapidly Multiplying,'' *Billboard* (August 26, 1995), p. 90.

Bates, Patricia, ''FCS to Acquire Joshua's Stores: Chain Is Becoming Force to Reckon with in Christian Retail,'' *Billboard* (May 9, 1998), p. 61.

Calabrese, Dan, ''Family Bookstores Gets New Ownership in Zondervan Break,'' *Grand Rapids Business Journal*, December 12, 19994, p. 3.

''Christian Lifestyle, Commerce Website iBelieve.com Launches Today,'' PR Newswire, January 26, 2000, http://www.findarticles.com.

Crosby, Cindy, ''Family Christian Slows Store Growth,'' *Publishers Weekly* (March 12, 2001), p 12.

McAlpine, John, ''Praying for Business,'' *Everett Business Journal* (September 2001), p. A16.

Milliot, Jim, ''Family Christian Stores to Acquire Joshua's Stores,'' *Publishers Weekly* (April 27, 1998), p. 11.

Ruark, James E., and Theodore W. Engstrom, *The House of Zondervan*. Grand Rapids, MI: Zondervan Publishing House, 1981.

—John W. Fiero

George Wimpey plc

Manning House
22 Carlisle Place
London SW1P 1JA
United Kingdom
Telephone: (020) 7802 9888
Fax: (020) 7963 6355
Web site: http://www.wimpey.co.uk/

Public Company
Incorporated: 1919 as George Wimpey & Co. Ltd.
Employees: 11,590
Sales: £1.9 billion ($1.7 billion) (2001)
Stock Exchanges: London
Ticker Symbol: WMPY
NAIC: 233320 Commercial and Institutional Building
    Construction; 233210 Single Family Housing
    Construction

George Wimpey plc ranks among the world's oldest and largest private construction concerns, with operations in the United Kingdom and the United States. Over the course of its history, the company has built over 850,000 homes, more than any other company in the world. In 2002, George Wimpey expected to complete 13,000 housing projects in the United Kingdom, where its operations included inner-city as well as suburban developments. U.S. operations rank among that nation's top 30 homebuilders, spanning five Sunbelt states under the Morrison Homes brand. In an industry marked by stiff competition and rapid consolidation, Wimpey has held its own, completing an internal consolidation of its UK homebuilding operations as well as major acquisitions in its two key markets. In the early twenty-first century, the company built accommodations ranging from modest one-bedroom apartments to mammoth five-bedroom showplaces.

Late 19th Century Origins

The firm was established by Walter Tomes and George Wimpey as a stone-working partnership in 1880. The young entrepreneurs initially took contracts for structural and decorative residential masonry, but by the late 1890s they had expanded into paving, specializing in laying the foundations for the horse-drawn streetcars of that era. Tomes sold out in 1893, leaving Wimpey with a sole proprietorship. Winning local public works contracts boosted the contractor's reputation in the 1890s. The company built the local town hall in 1896 and was contracted to lay the foundations for London's first "electric tramway" in the latter years of the decade. After the turn of the century, Wimpey won a prestigious contract to build the 140-acre White City complex. This series of pavilions and gardens built for the Franco-British Exhibition of 1908 featured an 80,000-seat stadium that also served as the site of that year's Olympic Games.

Four years of progressive illness culminated in George Wimpey's death in 1913 at the age of 58. Owing partly to the distractions and labor shortages of World War I, the founder's family put the business up for sale in 1919. With £500 for goodwill, £2,500 stock-in-trade, and an extra £100 to help the Wimpey heirs meet their last payroll, Godfrey Way Mitchell bought the firm and registered it as a private enterprise. In recognition of the fine reputation built during the company's first four decades, Mitchell retained the Wimpey name.

With £3,000 in working capital borrowed from his father, the 27-year-old Mitchell took his company back to its roots: paving. Mitchell built up a fleet of eleven steam rollers and took contracts for public and private paving jobs. In spite of severe economic recession in Britain in the early 1920s, Wimpey's annual revenues topped £137,000 by 1925. The company subcontracted for several housing developers during this period. Mitchell astutely observed that Wimpey stood to make higher profits (albeit at an increased risk) if it bought the land and built and sold homes itself instead of just contracting for the projects. The company's first residential development, Greenford Park Estate, was completed in 1928.

It seemed an inauspicious time to expand operations into such a capital-intensive venture: unemployment ran high in the 1920s, and in 1931 Britain followed the United States into the most serious economic depression in modern history. Although unemployment in the United Kingdom neared three million by

1933, Wimpey and its housing venture boomed. The company concentrated its early efforts on construction of inexpensive, accessible homes. Those in the Greenford Park development, for example, sold for £550. Buyers needed less than five percent (£25) down and received a £50 government subsidy as further incentive. Wimpey's emphasis on the low end of the residential market, with its high and relatively stable demand, would characterize its housing business for decades to come. The construction bonanza was credited with fueling one-third of Britain's re-employment from 1932 to 1935. In the decade before World War II, Wimpey built an average of 1,200 houses annually. The company continued to build roads throughout southern England during this period.

When Mitchell took Wimpey public in 1934, he set up a unique ownership scheme wherein the charitable Tudor Trust (later renamed Grove Charity Management) held about half of the firm's shares. By that time, the company's annual revenues neared £2 million, over 13 times its turnover of a decade before. In 1936, Wimpey won its first major civil engineering contract, an £800,000 government agreement to build the Team Valley Trading Estate in northeast England. The comprehensive job called for diverting a river as well as building railways, a viaduct, and other accouterments of an industrial park. By this time, the company was able to provide a full range of contracting services, from planning to marketing.

Wartime Contracts Boost Sales, Reputation

After Germany's 1938 invasion of Austria, the British government began issuing defense contracts in cautious preparation for a conflict that British diplomats tried in vain to avert. Wimpey's war-related government contracts started that year with immense underground concrete tanks used to store aviation fuel reserves. A second £4 million contract called for the construction of a Royal Ordnance Factory near Glasgow, but even this extensive project paled in comparison to Wimpey's later contributions to the war effort. In 1938, Wimpey began bidding on contracts to build airfields or "aerodromes," as they are known in the United Kingdom. By the war's end, Wimpey had built nearly 100 of the facilities for the burgeoning Royal Air Force (RAF), which proved key to Britain's defense. Wimpey received so many government contracts during this time that some in the media speculated that the company was receiving preferential treatment and that Winston Churchill had a financial stake in it. In response, Mitchell himself requested a government investigation, which cleared the company of all charges and noted that Wimpey's efficiency won it the contracts. The company also built fortifications along Britain's

eastern coastline in case of a German invasion. Although the RAF averted a ground invasion of Great Britain, intensive bombing forced Wimpey from its headquarters to a suburban, bomb-proof outpost on land owned by Mitchell. The Hammersmith complex was bombed shortly thereafter, and the company stayed in its "temporary" headquarters until a new office building was completed in 1949. In 1948, Mitchell was knighted "in recognition of his public services."

Global Expansion and Diversification: The Postwar Era

Mitchell laid the foundation for postwar growth by establishing local offices throughout Great Britain in the years immediately following the war. These satellites helped absorb the deluge of veteran workers and prompted diversification into coal mining, among other activities.

Demand for housing was especially high in the postwar era; nearly one-third of Britain's housing had been damaged in the bombing and practically no new homes had been built since 1939. A shortage of bricks drove Mitchell to seek out an economical, reliable, and efficient alternative method of construction. Wimpey architects and engineers based their "No-Fines" technique on a Norwegian idea. The concept employed concrete containing no fine aggregate (sand or stone), hence the name. Poured concrete walls formed the main structure upon which conventional interior and exterior finishes were then applied. Government housing contracts propelled the construction of tens of thousands of residences annually in the early 1950s, and after the government lifted restrictions on private home-building in 1954, Wimpey re-entered that market as well. The proliferation of automobiles brought many road building contracts. Other major projects in the immediate postwar era included a factory for Pirelli General Cable Works, the Queen Elizabeth II grandstand at Ascot, London Bridge House, and Heathrow Airport.

Wimpey became one of Britain's first contractors to expand overseas in 1946, when the company added offices in Cairo, Baghdad, and Singapore. Early international projects concentrated on roads and airfields, but the rapid expansion of the global automotive industry in the postwar era drove burgeoning demand for oil and petroleum products. Wimpey "mutually developed" with the oil industry, both at home and abroad. The company built oil fields, refineries, pipelines, and support systems in Kuwait, Borneo, Iraq, Syria, and New Guinea. Many of these early projects required the contractor to build its own roads out to the chosen sites. In Borneo, Wimpey built an entire town, complete with over 2,200 residences, a shopping center, swimming pools, hotels, and a power station. At first the company shipped laborers from the United Kingdom to its often-remote sites, but it gradually started training indigenous labor, subcontracting locally, and using local materials.

Wimpey naturally moved "downstream" in the petroleum industry, building numerous plants for the world's largest petrochemical firms. Contracts with chemical giant Union Carbide Corporation alone called for the construction of 15 plants in Sweden, Belgium, India, and Australia. Other major clients included Imperial Chemical Industries plc (ICI), Shell Oil Company, Conoco Inc., and, of course, British Petroleum Company PLC.

Key Dates:

1880: The firm is established by Walter Tomes and George Wimpey as a stone-working partnership.
1893: Tome sells his share of the partnership to Wimpey.
1908: The company is contracted to build a series of pavilions and gardens for the Franco-British Exhibition.
1913: George Wimpey dies.
1919: Godfrey Way Mitchell buys the company from the Wimpey family.
1928: The company completes its first residential development.
1934: The company goes public, with annual revenues near £2 million.
1938: Wimpey begins landing extensive government contracts in connection with the British war effort.
1946: The company expands its operations overseas, soon establishing itself as a major contractor in the Middle and Far East, Australia, and Canada.
1954: Wimpey re-enters the private-home market.
1979: After a reorganization, the presidency of Wimpey is assumed by Reginald B. Smith, who is succeeded shortly thereafter by Sir Clifford Chetwood.
1984: Wimpey expands into the United States with the acquisition of Morrison Homes, Inc.
1992: Joe Dwyer assumes the leadership position at Wimpey.
2001: The company charts £1.9 billion in sales.
2002: The company projects completion of 13,000 housing projects in the United Kingdom.

Oil industry projects often offered the foothold that Wimpey leveraged into other overseas contracts. For example, the company's expertise in petroleum took it to Jamaica in the mid-1950s, but construction of sugar processing plants, hotels, highways, schools, and offices soon established it as one of the biggest contractors in the Caribbean. Political upheaval forced the closure of Wimpey's Cairo and Baghdad offices in the late 1950s, but by that time the company had launched operations in Canada and Australia that would prove vital contributors to overseas revenues. Wimpey's open-cast coal mine, launched in Australia in 1950, produced more than 1.5 million tons of coal in its first year alone. Over the years, operations ''down under'' expanded to three offices with the capacity to provide infrastructure, private and public housing, and general contracting.

Expansion into Canada was precipitated by a survey that indicated a ''desperate need for construction and housing development expertise.'' Accordingly, Wimpey established an office in Toronto in 1955. The rapid pace of postwar suburbanization supported the company's expansion from residential construction into roads and highways as well as support systems like water mains and sewers. By 1970, Wimpey was building nearly 2,000 homes each year in the province of Ontario alone. Its high concentration of work in this region ranked Canada as the largest contributor to Wimpey's overseas revenues, at more than 30 percent.

Mitchell remained Wimpey's executive chairman until 1973. Geoffrey Foster's 1994 examination of Wimpey for *Man-*

agement Today noted the deep and lasting effects of Mitchell's tenure, characterizing him as a visionary, ''patriarchal'' leader whose influence was felt through the 1980s. Dick Gane, formerly chair of Canadian operations, led Wimpey from 1973 to 1976, when Reginald B. Smith advanced to the executive chair. A ''life-long Wimpey man'' and former chief estimator, Smith essentially carried on Mitchell's ideals as the company slogged through the difficult 1970s.

Boom and Bust: 1970s and 1980s

Wimpey's internationalization gave it something of a ''split personality'' during this decade. When the Organization of Petroleum Exporting Countries (OPEC) more than tripled oil prices after 1973's Yom Kippur War between Egypt and Israel, construction in the Middle East boomed, while most of the rest of the industrialized world went bust. Wimpey's activities there centered on Amman, the capital of Jordan, where the contractor built government offices, roads, and a stadium. Wimpey's overseas expansion earned it a Queen's Award for Export Achievement in 1977.

Although high oil prices meant a bonanza in the Middle East, they sparked astounding rates of inflation in the rest of the developed world. In the United Kingdom, wage freezes, strikes and 50 percent inflation characterized the middle years of the decade. When both the government and commercial interests lowered their capital expansion budgets, the company added remodeling of homes and historic buildings to take up the slack. In spite of the dramatic reduction in home-building, Wimpey was able to remain Britain's biggest private house-builder, building over 106,000 homes throughout the decade. The company also looked to joint ventures in continental Europe for new housing business.

A 1979 restructuring made Smith president and nominally reorganized the company's numerous departments into four primary divisions: U.K. Construction, International and Engineering, Specialist Holdings, and Group Services. Wimpey had grown exponentially in the postwar era: By 1980, the company had 40,000 employees, and its annual revenues exceeded £1 billion. However, some critics noted that the company's management techniques had not developed to accommodate the company's expansion. Sir Clifford Chetwood, who took the Wimpey reins in the early 1980s, worked to create divisional autonomy and responsibility by transforming over a dozen British subsidiaries into three divisions: homes, construction or contracting, and minerals.

In 1984, Wimpey expanded into the United States with the acquisition of San Francisco-based Morrison Homes. Morrison had been established in Seattle in 1905 by C.G. Morrison and moved to northern California in 1946. By the mid-1980s, the company had shifted focus from apartment buildings and shopping centers to single-family homes and subdivisions.

Wimpey's UK housing and public works markets remained depressed through the 1980s, but the middle years of the decade saw another ''boom'' that helped mask any organizational shortcomings. The global recession of the late 1980s and early 1990s saw Wimpey slide from a pre-tax profit of nearly £145 million at a 1988 peak to £43 million (after exceptional items) in 1990. The company registered consecutive annual losses of £16 million in 1991 and £112 million in 1992. From 1989 to 1992, Chetwood had divested some nonessential businesses, cut employment rolls in the United Kingdom by 30 percent, and reduced debt by 40 percent. The chief executive relinquished his office to a hand-picked successor, Joe Dwyer, at the end of 1992.

New Leadership, New Ideas: The 1990s

Dwyer intensified Chetwood's reorganization, coordinating all activities around business areas. Perhaps more importantly, Dwyer purged the top executive offices, bringing in a completely new, significantly younger, board of directors, some from outside Wimpey's ranks. These new managers brought new techniques to the somewhat dated company. For example, Richard Andrew, Wimpey's recently appointed director of the homes division, instituted market research to help guide that department's activities.

Dwyer also worked to change Wimpey's ownership structure. In 1993, he convinced the trustees of Grove Charity Management to reduce its stake in the contractor from over one-third to about five percent. Within a few months, Wimpey raised capital vital to fuel its continued growth with its first rights issue since going public in 1934. As Geoffrey Foster's 1994 article in *Management Today* observed, "after three horrendous years, Wimpey found itself towards the close of 1993 with a strong balance sheet and a range of options such as it had not had in 50 years." The firm recorded a £25.5 million profit before taxes that year on revenues of £1.59 billion and had reduced its debt another 80 percent, from £136.1 million in 1992 to £27.9 million.

This strengthened financial position enabled the company to acquire McLean Homes from Tarmac in 1996, at which time Wimpey divested its other construction and quarry businesses to devoted itself exclusively to house construction.

In the early years of the twenty-first century, Wimpey embraced new design concepts and experimented with modular construction. Modular homebuilding held out the possibility of vast improvements in efficiency; a home could be built in one-fourth the time of a conventionally-built house. However, it remained an experimental building method for Wimpey. As one company official told *Building Design* magazine, "If it improves the quality, decreases cost, and gains better customer satisfaction then it's a no-brainer that people will want to use it. The jury's out in terms of being able to say 'yes' to all of these questions." The company also invested £400,000 in its website, creating 300 "microsites," each devoted to a specific development.

In 2001, the company invested £29 million in the merger and reorganization of its two UK divisions, Wimpey Homes and McLean Homes, as George Wimpey. Later that same year, Wimpey acquired Alfred McAlpine plc for £461 million ($659 million). Although some analysts questioned the wisdom of the acquisition—Wimpey paid a high premium to book value and took on additional debt to do so—the new business increased Wimpey's penetration of southeast England, an area that was expected to grow rapidly in the years to come. The acquisition also moved Wimpey into a slightly higher-margin segment of the homebuilding business.

Up to this time, the UK homebuilding industry had been very fragmented, with Wimpey the dominant player. Three key rivals—Taylor Woodrow plc, Persimmon plc, and Wilson Connolly Holdings plc—emerged from the merger frenzy. In fact, Persimmon's acquisition of Beazer Group plc in March 2001 vaulted it past Wimpey to the top of the UK homebuilding heap.

Wimpey was able to maintain growth in both revenues and profits throughout the late 1990s and early 2000s, with sales increasing from £1.2 billion in 1997 to nearly £1.9 billion in 2001. Pre-tax profits more than doubled during that period, from £63 million to £152 million. The company's interim results for the first half of 2002 showed revenues up 44 percent over 2001, positioning Wimpey to break the £2 billion mark. Profit before tax more than doubled during the first half, from £38.9 million to £86.3 million.

Principal Subsidiaries

George Wimpey UK Ltd.; Morrison Homes, Inc.

Principal Competitors

Taylor Woodrow plc; Persimmon plc; Wilson Connolly Holdings plc.

Further Reading

Almond, Siobhan, "U.K. Homebuilders Close to Deal," *The Daily Deal*, August 2, 2001.
——, "George Wimpey Buys Alfred McAlpine Unit," *The Daily Deal*, August 14, 2001.
Du Bois, Peter C., "U.K. Earnings Point to Mixed Revival," *Barron's*, September 13, 1993, pp. 54–55.
Fairs, Marcus," Wimpey Goes Modular," *Building Design*, February 25, 2002, p. 2.
Foster, Geoffrey, "Why the Whimpering Stopped," *Management Today*, February 1994, pp. 40–44.
Sweney, Mark, "Wimpey UK Invests L400k in Overhaul," *Revolution*, November 28, 2001, p. 5.
White, Valerie, *Wimpey: The First Hundred Years*, London: Wimpey News, 1980.

—April Dougal Gasbarre

GERLING

Gerling-Konzern Versicherungs-Beteiligungs-Aktiengesellschaft

Gereonshof
D-50670 Cologne
Germany
Telephone: (49) (221) 144-1
Fax: (49) (221) 144-3319
Web site: http://www.gerling.com

Private Company
Incorporated: 1904 as Bureau für Versicherungswesen Robert Gerling & Co. Ges. m.b.H.
Employees: 13,432
Total Assets: EUR 10.4 billion ($9.3 billion) (2001)
NAIC: 524126 Direct Property and Casualty Insurance Carriers (pt); 524128 Other Direct Insurance (except Life, Health, and Medical) Carriers; 524130 Reinsurance Carriers (pt); 524113 Direct Life Insurance Carriers; 524114 Direct Health and Medical Insurance Carriers (pt)

Gerling-Konzern Versicherungs-Beteiligungs-Aktiengesellschaft (GKB) is the holding company for the family-owned Gerling group of insurance companies based in Cologne, Germany. The Gerling group is Germany's fifth largest insurance company and the country's second largest insurer for business and industry. Gerling's credit insurance subsidiary, Gerling NCM Credit and Finance AG, is the second largest credit insurer worldwide. Its reinsurance arm, Gerling Global Re, operates around the globe, but was hit hard by a number of natural and man-made disasters in 2001, resulting in large operating losses. Other Gerling subsidiaries offer health, life, property, and casualty insurance, mainly in Germany, where almost half of the company's revenues derive. After one of the founder's grandsons, Rolf Gerling, had shelved a planned initial public offering (IPO) in the late 1990s, he announced he would sell his majority share in the Gerling group in the spring of 2002.

Company Origins: 1904

Rolf Gerling's grandfather, Robert Gerling, Jr., was 26 years old when he decided to take a chance and put an idea into practice that would soon change Germany's insurance industry. It all began twelve years earlier, in 1892, when one spring day insurance agent Conrad Mihr, an acquaintance of Robert Gerling, Sr., persuaded the Gerlings to take their highly intelligent teenager out of school early and—instead of sending him to law school as they had intended—allow their son to go into the insurance business. As an apprentice, then 14-year-old Robert Gerling, Jr., began to learn the ins and outs of selling insurance hands on. Later, he worked for two insurance companies, Mannheimer and Prussian National. More and more he began to specialize in signing general coverage contracts for large industrial clients.

When Robert Gerling, Jr., set out on his own in 1904, he did not possess any of the assets that might help an aspiring entrepreneur to carve out a niche for himself: he had no money, no formal education, and no protection by an established business community. He called his insurance brokerage Bureau für Versicherungswesen Robert Gerling & Co. Ges. m.b.H., which was located at Cologne's Hohenzollernring 27. Underwear maker Wilhelm Marum gave Gerling the missing 4,000 Reichsmark he needed to open up shop. Three well-known entrepreneurs—Arnold von Guilleaume, Hans-Rudolf von Langen, and Adolf Lindgens—opened many doors for the young man in Cologne's industrial circles. Gerling wanted to break out of the traditional general-agent system that dominated Germany's insurance industry. General agents, who were paid a provision by insurance companies for ready-to-sign insurance contracts they brokered, kept costs for insurers and premiums for customers high. Gerling wanted to give the insurance trade a better image and regulate claims faster and in a more equitable way than was common. The time and place were right for him. Heavy and manufacturing industries were booming in Westphalia and the Rhineland around the turn of the century.

Company Perspectives:

Our mission is: *to provide the best possible comprehensive risk management and insurance protection in dialogue with our clients, to form and shape an exceptional and responsible company, and to be in harmony with creation for the benefit of man and nature.*

Since 1900, 78 of Germany's large fire insurers were organized as a cartel, the Vereinigung der in Deutschland arbeitenden Privat- Feuerversicherungsgesellschaften. The Fire Syndicate, as it was referred to—or, for short, the Syndicate—kept fire insurance premiums high at a time of economic downturn. As a response, a number of nonprofit organizations emerged that helped insurance clients with their legal issues, the so-called *Schutzverbände*.

Only a few months after opening his insurance bureau, Gerling, together with six investor-friends, founded their own such organization, the Rheinische Versicherten-Verband. For a small annual membership fee, Rheinische offered legal advice regarding insurance at no extra cost. Rheinische also acted as an insurance brokerage, picking the best and cheapest plans for its members in all types of insurance. Gerling offered his members significant savings for their insurance coverage if they gave him all of their business, which was then channeled through his bureau. This new service soon became popular in the Rhineland region. By 1908, Rheinische included almost 3,000 members.

In 1907, Gerling founded another private company, the Gesellschaft für Versicherungs-Vermittlung m.b.H. (G.f.V.V.). To attract large industrial clients, Gerling offered to share the provisions he received as an insurance broker from insurance companies if they became shareholders in his company. In turn, for their insurance business, they received part of those provisions as dividends, according to the volume of their insurance coverage. The company's capital base grew rapidly, from 100,000 Marks in 1908 to five times as much three years later. The 30 percent dividend Gerling offered attracted more and more shareholders.

Gerling's enterprise would not have been possible without help from his family and friends. His brother Richard soon took over management of the Rheinische Versicherten-Verband, while, until 1909, Robert, Jr., brokered policies for various German insurance companies. Due to his natural talent for assessing risks and his communicative and persuasive personality, Gerling had collected a good number of mid-sized and large companies from industry and trade on his client roster. However, more and more insurance companies refused to cooperate with Gerling because they saw how his system slowly undermined their own business. Consequently, in 1909 Gerling founded his own fire insurance company, Rheinische Feuer-Versicherungs-Aktiengesellschaft—in short, Rheinfeuer. Gerling's insurance customers once again became shareholders—this time in their own insurance company. By providing their own insurance coverage, Gerling's "client-shareholders" were able to further reduce their cost. The successful establishment of this enterprise, however, came with a grain of salt for Gerling, who was not elected to the executive board and had little control over his creation. Run by two bureaucrats of the old school, the company soon drifted into traditional patterns, setting up expensive general agencies all over the country. Although Gerling's bureau, G.f.V.V. and Versicherten-Verband generated half of Rheinfeuer's premium income, they refused to make a binding contract with Gerling and to pay him fixed provisions. Contrary to his original idea, Rheinfeuer began turning into one of his competitors. However, the company's high costs were eating up most of its working capital, and Gerling carried out an attack to rescue his creation. In December 1910, he established the "Kronprinz" Versicherungs-AG, his own reinsurance company. Then Gerling canceled his contracts with Rheinfeuer and channeled the insurance business he acquired to Kronprinz. Finally, in December 1911, he succeeded and became Rheinfeuer's new CEO.

Press Wars and Economic Crises in the 1920s

While the Fire Syndicate let loose a massive press war of many years to discredit Gerling's reputation, more and more companies voted with their feet. Fed up with high premiums, inflexible insurance plans, and less-than-sufficient service of the Fire Syndicate insurers, they chose the only existing alternative: Gerling. In 1915, the cost in relation to premium income was around 40 percent in Rheinfeuer's general agency system but only around 20 percent in Gerling's G.f.V.V. and Bureau.

When the Fire Syndicate realized that Gerling's system was successful, they decided to deny him reinsurance protection. When World War I cut Gerling off from his reinsurers abroad, he founded a second reinsurance company, Rheinische Versicherungsbank A.G., in 1917. It was followed by the establishment of Allgemeine Versicherungs-AG, another direct insurer that did not limit itself to fire insurance, in 1918. The Syndicate declared a total boycott against Gerling. However, the small number of his large industrial clients, among them steel giant Krupp AG and chemicals manufacturer Bayer AG, was easily administered from his Cologne headquarters at low cost, and Gerling was fortunate enough not to be struck by big disasters.

In 1920, Robert Gerling's brother Richard, who had a significant share in getting the business off the ground, left the enterprise to found one of his own. In the same year, Gerling organized his companies under the umbrella of Rheinische Versicherungs-Gruppe AG and introduced the term "solidarity liability." This meant that if any of Gerling's companies had to cover a loss, all the other companies would help out if necessary—a novelty in the industry. In the early 1920s, Gerling established four dozen smaller insurance companies; these functioned as regional branch offices that brought in the business for the main Gerling insurance concern. Instead of the agent-broker system, Gerling employed his own sales staff who worked with clients to design custom-tailored insurance coverage. The number of Gerling's large insurance clients climbed to 300. In 1922 and 1923, Gerling reorganized his group of companies and renamed it Gerling-Konzern. He established his own life insurance company, Gerling-Konzern Lebensversicherungs-AG; another reinsurance company, Gerling-Konzern Rückversicherungs-AG; as well as other subsidiaries. In the same year, Gerling took over Berlin-based Friedrich Wilhelm, one of Germany's older insurers whose life insurance arm

Key Dates:

1904: Robert Gerling opens an insurance brokerage in Cologne.

1909: Rheinische Feuer-Versicherungs-Aktiengesellschaft is founded.

1919: Regional subsidiaries are established all over Germany.

1922: Gerling's enterprise is renamed Gerling-Konzern and starts its own life insurance company.

1935: The company founder dies and non-family member Walter Forstreuter becomes CEO.

1945: Robert Gerling's son Hans is granted an insurer's license.

1954: An international reinsurance holding company and a new credit insurance division are established.

1974: Hans Gerling gives up control in his company to compensate for financial liabilities.

1986: German industrial magnate Friedrich Karl Flick sells the company back to Hans Gerling.

1992: Rolf Gerling becomes chairman of the supervisory board after his father's death.

1992: Deutsche Bank acquires a 30 percent share in Gerling.

1998: Gerling takes over American reinsurer Constitution Re.

2001: The company's credit insurance subsidiary merges with Dutch credit insurer NCM.

2002: Gerling is put up for sale after the founder's grandson agrees to give up his majority share in the company.

administered every fourth German life insurance contract. One year later, he acquired life insurer Magdeburger Leben. The Gerling companies now offered a wide range of insurance coverage, including property and casualty insurance, life insurance, and reinsurance coverage for the group.

With the value of the German currency declining in the early 1920s, Gerling started offering life insurance coverage on a stable currency basis, at first Goldmark, later dollars. When Gerling sensed that inflation in Germany could get out of control—with devastating effects on the insurance industry—he established two foreign subsidiaries to provide access to foreign currencies. In March 1923, Rheinische Rückversicherungs-Gruppe AG was established in Basel, Switzerland, and equipped with three million Swiss francs in capital. About a year later, the Gerling-Konzern Nederlandsch-Duitsche Verzekering Maatschappij was set up in Amsterdam, the Netherlands. However, Gerling's "crisis-save" policies became a real risk when the German government passed a crisis law that required that foreign currencies be handed over to the treasury. After that, premiums were paid in worthless paper money while they had to be covered by hard currencies. A big enough number of claims could have driven Gerling into a difficult financial situation. However, only when Germany introduced total control over hard currencies in 1932 was Gerling required to take his offer from the market.

When the German government set an end to hyperinflation by introducing a new currency, the Rentenmark, in November 1923,

Gerling's financial assets had shrunk considerably. However, unlike many other insurance companies that went bankrupt, Gerling-Konzern met the challenge, not least due to the real estate holdings of its subsidiary, Friedrich Wilhelm. To boost the company's business, Gerling-Konzern introduced several pioneering insurance products. Among them were a foreign travel insurance for traveling businessmen, a lifetime renter's insurance for a one-time premium, a standardized all-round insurance coverage from raw material to finished product for textile companies, and group life insurance for large organizations.

By 1924, the year when the Syndicate dissolved, Gerling-Konzern had reached a strong foothold in the German insurance market that put the company on the track toward growth for many decades to come. The conglomerate consisted of 70 subsidiaries and branch offices. In the second half of the 1920s, Gerling's competitors utilized any measure at hand, including defamation through press campaigns and the initiation of rumors designed to undermine his client's trust in Gerling's liquidity. Consequently, the Reichsaufsichtsamt, the government agency that regulated the insurance industry, inundated him with ever new requests for changing the structure of his group to make it more transparent and for boosting its capital base. Gerling complied as much as he needed to, since his enterprise depended on the agency's goodwill.

By the end of the 1920s, the superiority of Gerling's system was obvious. Administrative costs were about 30 percent of premium income. Competitor Allianz had to take off about 44 percent from its premium income for administrative costs, and Colonia, another leading German insurer, as much as 50 percent.

In 1929, Gerling contracted an incurable disease of the kidneys. The following year, as he began to think about who would succeed him as head of his insurance empire, he continued to run his business in between time-consuming medical regimens. After he traveled to Berlin to oversee his succession by his sons with the Reichsaufsichtsamt, Gerling died in January 1935, at age 56.

Leadership Change Before World War II

When the company founder died, his three sons were too young to take over responsible management positions. He had appointed his oldest son—also named Robert Gerling, Jr.—who at that time was 21 years old, to inherit his shareholdings in Gerling-Konzern. His second oldest son, Hans, was 19 years old and studied business administration. Gerling's youngest son, Walter, was 16 years old at the time. For the time being, one of the company's executive directors, Walter Forstreuter, took over the leading position and steered Gerling-Konzern through the rough waters of the Nazi era that ended with World War II. Neither the Gerling family nor Forstreuter were members of Hitler's party NSDAP. The Gerling companies did not closely cooperate with the Nazis but did not oppose to doing business with them either. In 1937, after he had finished his studies, Hans Gerling joined the family business. For two years he learned the trade from scratch in one of Gerling's branch offices. For five years, Hans Gerling left the corporate realm when he was drafted into the German army. In 1939, his older brother Robert left the country for the United States and, in 1940, gave up his mandate as an executive director.

Only four weeks after the war had ended in May 1945, the American military government granted Hans Gerling an insurer's license. Four years later, he became the new CEO of Gerling-Konzern, while his younger brother Walter worked in management of some of the group's operations up until the 1960s. Gerling greatly participated in the country's postwar reconstruction boom as the German economy recovered and industrial enterprises rebuilt their production facilities, which needed insurance coverage. By 1953, the Gerling-Konzern had branch offices and subsidiaries in more than two dozen big cities and over 3,500 employees.

During the 1950s, Hans Gerling opened up the chapter of the company's international expansion. In 1954, he established Gerling-Konzern Globale Rückversicherungs-AG, an international reinsurance holding company. Following its industrial customers abroad, Gerling Globale became the first German insurance company to expand overseas. In 1957, branch offices opened in Toronto, Canada, and Johannesburg, South Africa, followed by an office in Stockholm, Sweden, two years later. During the 1960s, new Gerling subsidiaries were established in Paris, London, New York, Milan, and Bombay. In the early 1980s, Gerling gained a foothold in Australia and later in the decade the company conquered Japan through a cooperation agreement with Sumitomo, the country's largest insurer. From a new office in Kuala Lumpur, Gerling served its Southeast Asian customers in surrounding countries such as Malaysia, Singapore, Thailand, Indonesia, and the Philippines.

Also in the 1950s, Hans Gerling established a new credit insurance division, Gerling Speziale Kreditversicherung AG, which expanded abroad in the following decades. The company's international network enabled Gerling to offer insurance coverage across borders since the mid-1950s.

New Focus and Loss of Independence in the 1970s

In the 1970s, risk prevention became a new focus of industrial insurance. Gerling's new research institute, the Institut für technische Schadenforschung, founded in 1969, assessed damage-causing events in industrial settings. At the end of the decade, the Gerling Institute for Risk Management and Risk Consulting started advising industrial clients on how to improve the security of technical facilities. Preventing technical disasters before they occurred were in the interest of both the insured and the insurer. Beginning in 1987, risk consulting and security management were offered through Gerling's Consulting Group, which assessed environmental risks and developed technical maintenance and crisis management systems as well as recycling schemes.

In 1974, Cologne-based bank I.D. Herstatt, in which Hans Gerling held 80 percent of the share capital, got into a financial crisis when it was discovered that the bank's chief foreign currency trader had lost about DM700 million in currency speculation, almost ten times the bank's capital. To generate the money necessary to pay the bank's creditors, Hans Gerling sold a 51 percent share in Gerling-Konzern to Swiss insurer Zürich Versicherungsgesellschaft and Versicherungs-Holding der Deutschen Industrie (VHDI), a group of German industrialists that were also Gerling clients, seeking influence over their insurer's business policies. Gerling also gave up his executive management positions and became a member of Gerling-Konzern's advisory board. In 1976, the new owners reorganized

Gerling-Konzern under the roof of Gerling-Konzern Versicherungs-Beteiligungs-AG, a new holding company. In spring 1978, the insurance group changed hands again. Zurich Versicherungsgesellschaft sold its share to VHDI, while industrial magnate Friedrich-Karl Flick acquired a majority share in VHDI and thereby gained control over Gerling-Konzern. In November of the same year, Flick allowed Gerling to return to his position as the company's CEO. For the next eight years, Hans Gerling worked relentlessly to regain control over his company. Finally, effective January 1, 1986, he achieved his goal after Friedrich-Karl Flick—exhausted from years of bad press as a result of his involvement in illegal donations to political parties—had sold his 88.83 percent share in VHDI back to Gerling.

When the insurance outsider that outsmarted its competitors and grew strong in the early storms of the twentieth century had became part of the "establishment" and was finally back in the hands of the Gerling family, its fortunes declined during the following decade. Disregarding the two principles that had once put Robert Gerling's company on the road to success—keeping cost down and carefully selecting the risks taken on—turned into Gerling-Konzern's stumbling stone.

Losing Momentum in the 1990s

Rolf Gerling, Hans Gerling's only son, was 36 years old when his father died in August 1991. After Hans Gerling's death, his close friend Adolf Kracht, an experienced bank manager who had helped Gerling through the financial crisis when the Herstatt bank collapsed, became the company's new CEO. Rolf Gerling did not have a strong interest in business management but felt an obligation to carry on the family tradition. After he had finished his studies in business administration and psychology at Zurich University, his father introduced him to Gerling-Konzern's executive management board in 1989. In 1992, Rolf Gerling was appointed chairman of Gerling-Konzern's supervisory board. He wanted to have a say in Gerling-Konzern's strategic direction but left the day-to-day business to Kracht. He preferred to work at his Gerling Akademie für Risikoforschung AG, which he had established in Zurich, Switzerland. There he conducted research and put out publications on ecological risk management and trained Gerling-Konzern's managers in sustainable business practices and leadership.

Hans Gerling had made Gerling-Konzern a top address among Germany's insurers and greatly extended the company's global reach. However, international expansion and regaining control over the family business came with a price tag. The buyback of Flick's shares was mainly financed through loans. On the other hand, much of the international growth of Gerling-Konzern's reinsurance division derived from insuring higher risks of small and mid-sized businesses. As a result, Hans Gerling had left Gerling-Konzern on a weak financial basis burdened with high-risk insurance contracts.

In 1992, Deutsche Bank agreed to acquire a 30 percent share in Gerling-Konzern. The estimated DM1.5 billion in cash flow allowed Rolf Gerling to pay his inheritance tax, pay off some loans, and to strengthen the company's capital base. However, when Deutsche Bank wanted to take over control in summer 1998, Rolf Gerling refused to cooperate. He briefed his managers to adhere to the company's family tradition. Deutsche Bank in turn wanted to sell its share, but plans to prepare Gerling-Konzern for an IPO were postponed and finally fell through because of the company's mounting problems.

New CEO Jürgen Zech, a former McKinsey partner who headed Gerling's non-life insurance division, succeeded Kracht after his retirement in December 1995. He launched a restructuring program in 1998 aimed at cutting costs and streamlining operations. But the reorganization did not yield the result Gerling's top management hoped for and could not prevent the company from falling behind its competitors. The pressure for low insurance premiums from large industrial clients increased even more during the 1990s. In addition, a growing number of natural and man-made disasters ate up more and more of the reinsurance premiums that contributed to almost half of the company's revenues. Gerling-Konzern tried to counteract by diversifying its portfolio and launched insurance plans for entrepreneurs and the self-employed. But it lacked the experience and marketing power of its competitors. One of the company's more promising markets were retirement plans for large German firms with which Gerling-Konzern traditionally maintained close contact. In summer 1998, Gerling acquired American reinsurer Constitution Re for $700 million to strengthen its capital base in the United States. However, the deal was less beneficial than expected. Some of Constitution Re's old risks turned out to be quite expensive for Gerling.

By 2001, it had become clear that mid-sized Gerling-Konzern lacked the financial power to compete with the handful of global reinsurers dominating the world market. To strengthen its leading position in this market, Gerling's credit insurance subsidiary merged with Dutch credit insurer NCM in 2001. However, the year ended with a EUR 563 million loss for Gerling-Konzern, mainly due to the terror attacks on September 11 and other high claims in the United States that had to be covered by its reinsurance arm. Deutsche Bank bailed Gerling-Konzern out with two major capital boosts of combined EUR 422 million, which raised the bank's share in Gerling-Konzern to 34.5 percent. In fall 2001, CEO Zech was replaced by insurance insider Heinrich Focke. In spring 2002, Rolf Gerling agreed to give up his majority share, since he did not have the financial resources necessary to provide the company with the capital needed. Gerling-Konzern was put up for sale and was hoping to find a strategic partner that guaranteed the endurance of the Gerling brand. Almost 100 years after its foundation, Gerling's fate was up in the air. In the worst case, Germany's industrialists could be left again with just another quasi-monopoly, Allianz AG, to cover their business risks.

Principal Subsidiaries

Gerling-Konzern Allgemeine Versicherungs-AG (89.99%); Gerling-Konzern Speziale Kreditversicherungs-AG (99.9%); Gerling-Konzern Lebensversicherungs-AG (99.86%); Gerling E & L Lebensversicherungs-AG; Gerling-Konzern Globale Rückversicherungs-AG; Gerling G & A Versicherungs-AG; Gerling Globale Rückversicherung AG (Switzerland); Namur Re S.A. (Luxemburg; 99.97%); Gerling Namur-Assurances du Crédit S.A. (Belgium); Étoile Commerciale S.A. (France; 99.58 %); Étoile Caution S.A. (France; 97.88%); Gerling Corporate Capital Ltd. (U.K.); Gerling Global Life Reassurance Company (U.K.) Ltd.; Gerling Global GenerL and Reinsurance Company Ltd. (U.K.); Gerling Global Reinsurance Company (Ireland); Gerling Nordic Kredittforsikring AS (Norway); Gerling Global Sweden Reinsurance Company Ltd.; Gerling Polska Towarzystwo Ubezpieczen' S.A. (Poland); Gerling Polska Towarzystwo Ubezpieczen' na Zycie S.A. (Poland); Poistovna Gerling Slovensko A.S. (Slovakia); Constitution Insurance Company (U.S.A.); Gerling Slovensko A.S. (Slovakia); Gerling America Insurance Company (U.S.A.); Gerling Global Reinsurance Corporation of America (U.S.A.); Gerling Global Life Reinsurance Company (U.S.A.); Gerling de México Seguros S.A.; Gerling Comesec S.A. (Mexico); Gerling Canada Insurance Company (99.99%); Gerling Global Life Insurance Company (Canada; 99.96%); Gerling Global Reinsurance Company (Canada; 99.98%); Gerling Australia Insurance Company Pty. Ltd.; Gerling Global Life Reinsurance Company of Australia Pty. Ltd.; Gerling Global Reinsurance Company of Australia Pty. Ltd.; Gerling General Insurance of South Africa Ltd.; Gerling Global Reinsurance Company of South Africa Ltd.; Gerling Global Life Reinsurance International Company Ltd. (Barbados); Gerling Global International Reinsurance Company Ltd. (Barbados); Rex Re Insurance Ltd. (Bermudas).

Principal Competitors

Allianz AG; ERGO Versicherungsgruppe AG; HDI V.a.G.; AMB Generali Holding AG; AXA Konzern AG; Munich Re; GeneralCologne Re; Hannover Re.

Further Reading

Balzer, Arno, and Dietmar Palan, "Die Abrechnung," *manager magazin,* June 1, 2002, p. 17.

"Börsengang soll Signal zum Aufbruch sein," *Süddeutsche Zeitung* December 14, 1998.

"Der Gerling-Clan zieht aus," *Frankfurter Allgemeine Zeitung*, March 24, 2002, p. 45.

"Deutsche Bank steigt bei Gerling ein," *Süddeutsche Zeitung,* July 11, 1992.

Gerling, Rolf, ed., *Hans Gerling. Reden eines außergewöhnlichen Unternehmers,* Munich, Germany: Gerling Akademie Verlag GmbH, 1999, 224 p.

"Gerling's Kronprinz Kracht übernimmt das Kommando," *Süddeutsche Zeitung*, August 19, 1991.

"Herstatt auch 25 Jahre nach der Krise aktuell," *Börsen-Zeitung,* June 30, 1999, p. 21.

"Konzernchef aus Pflichtgefühl," *Frankfurter Allgemeine Zeitung*, March 16, 2002, p. 15.

"Neue Leitlinien sollen Gerling auf sicheren Ertragspfad führen," *Frankfurter Allgemeine Zeitung*, March 16, 1993, p. 21.

"Noch kein Gerling-Grossaktionär in Sicht," *Frankfurter Allgemeine Zeitung*, June 7, 2002, p. 19.

Noonan, Brendan, "Gerling Realigns as It Seeks a Buyer," *A.M. Best Newswire,* June 7, 2002.

Palan, Dietmar, "Eine Frage der Ehre," *manager magazin,* June 1, 2001, p. 136.

"Reinsurers Consolidate: Gerling Buys Constitution Re," *Business Insurance,* August 3, 1998.

Sturbeck, Werner, "Der Gerling-Konzern musste schon zahlreiche Klippen umschiffen," *Frankfurter Allgemeine Zeitung*, February 24, 1995, p. 23.

Von Niebelschütz, Wolf, *Robert Gerling,* Tübingen, Germany: Rainer Wunderlich Verlag Hermann Leins, 1954, 333 p.

—Evelyn Hauser

The Goldman Sachs Group Inc.

85 Broad Street
New York, New York 10004
U.S.A.
Telephone: (212) 902-1000
Fax: (212) 902-3000
Web site: http://www.gs.com

Public Company
Founded: 1885
Employees: 22,627
Total Assets: $312.21 billion (2001)
Stock Exchanges: New York
Ticker Symbol: GS
NAIC: 523110 Investment Banking and Securities Dealing

The Goldman Sachs Group Inc.—the company changed its name from Goldman, Sachs & Co. after it went public in 1999—has been a respected player in world finance for more than 100 years. The company operates as a leading global investment banking and securities firm with two main divisions. The first division is Global Capital Markets, which includes investment banking, financial advisory services, trading, and principal investments. The second division is Asset Management and Securities Services, a business unit responsible for investment advisory services. Goldman Sachs's clients include corporations, financial institutions, governments, and wealthy individuals. The company operates over 40 offices across the globe.

Early History: Late 1880s

The company was founded by Marcus Goldman, a Bavarian school teacher who immigrated to the United States in 1848. After supporting himself for some years as a salesman in New Jersey, Goldman moved to Philadelphia, where he operated a small clothing store. After the Civil War he moved to New York City, where he began trading in promissory notes in 1869. In the morning, Goldman would purchase customers' promissory notes from jewelers on Maiden Lane, in lower Manhattan, and from leather merchants in an area of the city called "the

swamp." Then, in the afternoon, Goldman visited commercial banks, where he sold the notes at a small profit.

Goldman's son-in-law, Samuel Sachs, joined the business in 1882. The firm expanded into a general partnership in 1885 as Goldman, Sachs & Co. when Goldman's son Henry and son-in-law Ludwig Dreyfus joined the group.

Henry Goldman led the firm in new directions by soliciting business from a broader range of interests located in Providence, Hartford, Boston, and Philadelphia. In 1887, Goldman, Sachs began a relationship with the British merchant bank Kleinwort Sons, which provided an entry into international commercial finance, foreign-exchange services, and currency arbitrage.

On the strength of this growing exposure, Goldman, Sachs won business from several midwestern companies, including Sears Roebuck, Cluett Peabody, and Rice-Stix Dry Goods. With the establishment of Goldman, Sachs offices in St. Louis and Chicago, Henry Goldman became responsible for the firm's domestic expansion.

Railroads—indispensable to the opening of the American West—were the preferred investment of financiers in the eastern United States at this time. But Goldman, Sachs, committed to a diversified portfolio, saw great potential in a number of other developing industries. At first difficult to market, these investments became profitable ventures only after Goldman, Sachs persuaded companies to adopt stricter accounting and auditing procedures.

In 1896, soon after Samuel Sachs's brother Harry joined the company, Goldman, Sachs joined the New York Stock Exchange. With Harry Sachs in the company, and with the New York operations firmly under control, Samuel Sachs took special responsibility for Goldman, Sachs's overseas expansion. Through Kleinwort, he gained important new contacts within the British and European banking establishments.

The Company Co-Manages Its First IPO in 1906

In 1906, one of the firm's clients, United Cigar Manufacturers, announced its intention to expand. Goldman, Sachs, which

Company Perspectives:

At Goldman Sachs our culture is very much in evidence, helping us attract and retain the best employees and clients. Goldman Sachs's commitment to its clients, teamwork, integrity, professional excellence, and entrepreneurial spirit has its beginnings in 1869 with Marcus Goldman. At the core of our business remains our commitment to our clients, which is embodied in our fourteen business principles. Our business principles are a consistent measure for evaluating recruits and employees. To maintain our competitive edge and meet the high expectations of our clients, our culture continues to evolve. Goldman Sachs has made a commitment to creating an environment that values diversity and promotes inclusion. The Goldman Sachs culture is what sets our company apart from other firms and helps to make us a magnet for talent.

had previously provided the company with short-term financing to maintain inventories, advised United Cigar that its capital requirements could best be met by selling shares to the public. Although Goldman, Sachs had never before managed a share offering, it succeeded in marketing $4.5 million worth of United Cigar stock; within one year United Cigar qualified for trading on the New York Stock Exchange.

On the strength of this success, Goldman, Sachs next co-managed Sears Roebuck's initial public offering (IPO) that same year. Henry Goldman was subsequently invited to join the boards of directors of both United Cigar and Sears. The practice of maintaining a Goldman partner on the boards of major clients became a tradition that continues today.

During the 1910s, a time of feverish industrial activity, Goldman, Sachs instituted a number of innovative financial practices that today are common, including share buyback and retirement options. The firm managed public offerings for a number of small companies which, in part due to Goldman, Sachs's activities, later grew into large corporations. Some of the firm's clients at this time included May Department Stores, F.W. Woolworth, Continental Can, B.F. Goodrich, and Merck.

Henry Goldman retired in 1917, and shortly afterward Samuel and Harry Sachs became limited partners. The company was still a family business, and a third generation consisting of Arthur, Henry E., and Howard J. Sachs were promoted to directorships.

World War I depressed financial activity until 1919. In its aftermath, however, came a strong economic expansion. Built primarily on large war-related capital investments, the expansion led many of the firm's clients—H.J. Heinz, Pillsbury, and General Foods among them—to return to Goldman, Sachs for additional financing.

Opportunities in the Post-Depression Era

The company's expansion continued well into the 1920s. Goldman, Sachs, eager to take advantage of the promising economic climate at that time, formed an investment subsidiary

called the Goldman Sachs Trading Corporation. The new company expanded rapidly. But in the fall of 1929, Goldman Sachs Trading, like many other companies, fell victim to a crisis of confidence that forced the stock market into a devastating crash. By 1933, the investment subsidiary was worth only a fraction of its initial $10 million capitalization.

The company's recovery from the Depression was slow, but by the mid-1930s, the commercial-paper and securities businesses again were highly profitable. During this period, Sidney J. Weinberg, an "outsider" in the family business, assumed a leading position within the firm. Starting out in 1907 as a porter's assistant making $2 per week, Weinberg rose quickly at Goldman, Sachs. In 1927, at the age of 35, Weinberg became only the second outsider to be made a partner. Weinberg was known for his diligence and for his attention to detail.

In the aftermath of the 1929 stock market crash, Congress passed the Securities Act of 1933. This act created the Securities and Exchange Commission, which required that every investment be accompanied by a detailed prospectus. These often contained confusing small-print passages. As a conservative and practical securities dealer, Goldman, Sachs worked to reduce investor confusion by providing concise information in common language.

Goldman, Sachs also began a securities-arbitrage business in the 1930s under the direction of Edgar Baruch and, later, Gustave Levy. Meanwhile, the firm continued to expand by taking over other commercial-paper firms in New York, Boston, Chicago, and St. Louis. The firm subsequently engaged in a broad variety of investment activities, including new domestic and international share offerings, private securities sales, corporate mergers and acquisitions, real estate financing and sales, municipal finance, investment research, block trading, equity and fixed-rate investment portfolios, and options trading.

During World War II, Sidney Weinberg was placed on leave to serve on the government's War Production Board. With virtually all U.S. industry under special government supervision, many of Goldman, Sachs's activities were supplanted by government agencies; investment capital was raised through instruments such as war bonds, which were sold to individuals.

Goldman, Sachs did not fully regain its prewar momentum until several years after the war ended, which was a time when American industry and the economy in general experienced unprecedented growth. Intimately involved in this economic expansion, Goldman, Sachs recruited hundreds of new employees from leading business schools and launched many new activities in finance and investment.

Sidney Weinberg was called into government service again during the Korean War, serving with the Office of Defense Mobilization. His absence, in part, precipitated the creation of a management committee intended to decentralize the decision-making process. Gus Levy, who later became president of the New York Stock Exchange, was its first chairman.

Postwar Investment Strategies

Goldman, Sachs's most important management of a new share issue occurred in November 1956, when shares of the Ford

Key Dates:

1869: Marcus Goldman moves to New York City and begins trading promissory notes.

1882: Goldman's son-in-law, Samuel Sachs, joins the business.

1885: The firm expands into a general partnership, Goldman Sachs & Company.

1896: The company lists on the New York Stock Exchange.

1906: Goldman Sachs co-manages its initial public offering (IPO).

1929: The Goldman Sachs Trading subsidiary falters after the stock market crashes.

1956: The firm co-manages the IPO of Ford Motor Company.

1967: The company handles the floor trade of a block of Alcan Aluminum stock—the largest block trade ever made at the time.

1981: Goldman Sachs absorbs the commodities-trading firm of J. Aron & Company.

1982: London-based First Dallas Ltd. is acquired.

1993: A federal appeals court rules that Goldman Sachs can no longer advise corporate clients in bankruptcy organization.

1999: The company goes public and adopts the name The Goldman Sachs Group Inc.; Henry Paulson, Jr., becomes sole chairman and CEO.

2002: Subsidiary Goldman, Sachs & Co. becomes one of the largest market makers in the industry.

Motor Company were sold to the public for the first time. As co-manager, Goldman, Sachs helped market 10.2 million shares, worth $700 million. The firm set another record in October 1967, when it handled the floor trade of a single block of Alcan Aluminum stock consisting of 1.15 million shares, worth $26.5 million, at the time the largest block trade ever made.

Sidney Weinberg died in November 1969 and was succeeded as senior partner by Gus Levy. Goldman, Sachs began to attain its current position as a highly influential financial institution during the 1960s, and that position was solidified during the 1970s, as commodities such as oil grew to dominate the economy. Large new investments in domestic petroleum projects placed the company at a critical juncture. To some degree it was able to determine the complexion of the industry by channeling investment funds. Goldman, Sachs's expertise in this area resulted in its management of several large energy-industry share offerings.

John L. Weinberg and John Whitehead were promoted to senior partners upon the death of Gus Levy in 1976. Some years later, Whitehead left the firm to become Assistant Secretary of State in the Reagan administration, and Weinberg became chief partner and chairman of the management committee.

Goldman, Sachs diversified late in 1981 by absorbing the commodities-trading firm of J. Aron & Company, which dealt mainly in precious metals, coffee, and foreign exchange. The

company's acquisition of Aron would give it a strong footing in South American markets, an area of later growth for the firm. In May 1982, under the leadership of co-partner John Weinberg—son of Sidney Weinberg—the firm took over the London-based merchant bank First Dallas, Ltd., which it later renamed Goldman, Sachs, Ltd.

Beginning in 1984, a new craze erupted on Wall Street in which investment companies engineered leveraged buyouts (LBOs) of entire firms. These buyouts were financed with junk bond debt, which was paid off with operating profits from the purchased firm or from the piecemeal break-up and sale of the firm's assets. At the time, the practice could be highly profitable for firms willing to assume the associated risks.

Goldman, Sachs, however, preferred to stress its transaction work rather than to undertake higher risk LBOs. But the market crash of October 1987 reduced the profitability of transaction work. In addition, Goldman, Sachs began to lose clients to more aggressive investment firms, forcing it to begin efforts at downsizing and reducing overhead. Several hundred employees would be laid off through the end of the decade.

In early 1989, in an effort to retain its partnership status in the face of growing corporate competition, Goldman, Sachs elected to seek capital to expand its merchant-banking activities. With seven insurance companies, it formed a ten-year consortium that infused the firm with $225 million in new capital. Structured like a preferred stock, the expanded partnership was similar to that undertaken in 1986 with Japan's Sumitomo Bank when the bank purchased a 12.5 percent share of the brokerage house for upwards of $500 million. While entitled to 12.5 percent of Goldman, Sachs's profits, Sumitomo, like the newer partners, would be prevented by federal law from having voting rights within the firm. Goldman, Sachs would continue to accept such equity investments into the next decade.

The company also created a holding company, Goldman Sachs Group, which, technically, was not subject to the capital requirements of the New York Stock Exchange. The firm also began to spin off several subsidiaries. Engaging in bridge loans, mortgage insurance, and LBOs—as well as the creation of the Water Street Corporate Recovery Funds, a $500 million fund dedicated to investing in financially troubled companies—the firm's subsidiaries bolstered the company's profits but also caused lower bond ratings from Moody's and Standard & Poor's. Other changes in the company included the 1990 introduction of the GS Capital Growth Fund, a mutual fund targeted for the moderate-income investor through a minimum investment of $1,200. The introduction of this fund signaled the company's efforts to stretch its market beyond the rich client base to which it had previously catered.

International Expansion in the 1990s

Goldman, Sachs began the 1990s with a boom, reporting a record pre-tax profit of $1.1 billion in 1991 and paying out end-of-1992 bonuses of 25 percent annual salaries to employees. By 1993, the company had become one of the most profitable in the world, with pre-tax earnings of $2.7 billion. Some of this gain could be attributed to its successful offering of Japanese securities to U.S. investors as other than foreign exchange instruments, as well as the investment banking firm's expansion of its markets overseas. The firm experienced rapid growth by participating in several overseas investment projects, acting, for example, as a global coordinator in Finland's Neste Oy oil company in 1992. However, some markets, such as China, remained volatile due to differing political and cultural climates. And in a venture in the former U.S.S.R., the company worked with a government official who unfortunately lost his political influence during the changes in the Russian government at that time. The company closed its Russian office in 1995, although interest in rekindling its involvement in that country's fluctuating financial markets would resume in mid-1997.

While Goldman, Sachs's charted record profits between 1991 and 1993, there were setbacks for the company later in the decade. In 1993, a federal appeals court ruled that an investment banking firm could no longer advise a company with whom it had a business relationship in bankruptcy proceedings. This decision, issued as a result of Goldman, Sachs's representation of client Eagle-Picher Industries in Chapter 11 proceedings, signaled the end to a lucrative area for large investment banking—the advising of corporate clients in bankruptcy reorganization—that netted Goldman and similar firms over $100 million a year.

The crash in the market price of Treasury and other bonds in 1994, as well as the drop of the U.S. dollar in foreign markets, found Goldman, Sachs laying off more employees by mid-decade. More serious, however, was a mass wave of "retirements" by almost 50 of the firm's veteran partners, including firm chairman Stephen Friedman. Due to Goldman, Sachs's rapid expansion in the early 1990s, partner relationships had become strained. As discontented partners left the company, they were expected to take their much-needed equity with them, forcing the firm to find $250 million worth of new capital. By mid-1994, the company had named 58 new general partners, a record for the company; announcements of a new wave of layoffs quickly followed.

Fortunately, the bull market that had been in place on Wall Street since August 1982, as well as a stronger bond market, helped to stabilize the firm, growing its profits to replace the capital lost due to departing partners. Cost cuts and an internal restructuring further buoyed the firm.

Firm Pursues a More Aggressive Strategy

By 1996, the company was back on track, posting a pre-tax profit of $565 million for the first quarter. By mid-March, Goldman, Sachs had led an investor group in the successful but much-contested purchase of New York City's Rockefeller Center—dubbed the "greatest urban complex of the 20th century"—for $306 million. In further efforts to expand its roster of small-scale investors, the firm also began to aggressively acquire other firms, including Liberty Investment Management, the United Kingdom-based pension fund manager CIN Management from British Coal, and Stockton Holdings' Commodities Corp., located in New Jersey. The acquisition of such fee-based asset management firms helped to stabilize the company's unpredictable trading business both in the United States and on international markets, allowing Goldman, Sachs to retain its leadership role in the securities and banking industry.

The year 1996 was also notable for several internal changes. A new class of "junior partners" was created in September—dubbed "partnership extension" by the company—in the hopes that such promotions would stem the tide of partner defections and retirements that characterized the beginning of the decade. The firm also voted to adopt a limited liability structure, effective in November. The conversion, while significant in that it changed the company's 127-year structure as a partnership, was expected to have little impact on the way the company conducted its business. This prediction was borne out by the company's year-end pre-tax profits of $2.7 billion—the second highest in company history.

Going Public in 1999

Then, in 1998, the company began toying with the idea of going public. After ditching its initial plans in September 1998—due to faltering global markets—Goldman, Sachs launched one of the largest financial services IPOs in U.S. history. In early May 1999, the company listed on the New York Stock Exchange, raising $3.6 billion. The firm sold off approximately 69 million shares, just under 12.5 percent of the company. It then officially adopted the name The Goldman Sachs Group Inc. and named Henry Paulson, Jr., as sole chairman and CEO.

Goldman Sachs entered the new century on solid ground. After the IPO, Paulson immediately set plans in motion to secure the company's position as a major independent player in its industry. Goldman Sachs nearly tripled its employee count before making a series of job cuts in 2001. It also spent over $7 billion in acquisitions. Its most significant purchase was that of Spear, Leeds & Kellogg L.P., a leading market making firm. In 2002, this firm's NASDAQ trading and market making businesses were integrated into subsidiary Goldman, Sachs & Co., making it one of the largest market makers in the industry.

During 2000, Goldman Sachs secured net earnings of $3 billion. The following year proved to be more challenging as both earnings and revenues fell due to weakening market conditions and the economic uncertainty caused by the September 11th terrorist attacks. During 2001, the company stood as the leading advisor in merger activity and was involved in eight out of the ten largest deals completed that year. The firm advised 46 percent of Japan's merger activity and secured a position as Germany's leading merger and equity offering advisor. It also was the top underwriter of all IPOs and common stock offerings throughout the year.

The company's reliance on such activity, however, left it vulnerable to slowdowns. Indeed, in 2002 both IPO and merger activity faltered. In March, overall merger activity was down 42 percent over the previous year and just four IPOs had been launched in the United States from December 2001 to March 2002. As Goldman Sachs prepared for one of its most challenging years, its independent status came into question. The industry had seen a wave of merger and acquisition activity in past years that had created financial powerhouses that included Citibank, whose assets were triple that of Goldman Sachs, and J.P. Morgan Chase & Co., whose assets were twice as large. Rumors surfaced that unless the economy recovered, Goldman Sachs itself may be forced into a merger.

Paulson, however, maintained that Goldman Sachs would thrive on its own. He laid out the company's strategy in a 2002 *Business Week* article, claiming, "We want to be the premier global investment bank, securities, and investment management firm. We want to have a disproportionate share of the business of the most important clients in the most important markets." The article went on to report that in order to accomplish this, the company "must gain a lock on providing financial advice to marquee corporations, government authorities, and superrich individuals in the world's major economies—the U.S., Germany, Britain, Japan, and China." With its long-standing history of success and solid reputation behind it, Goldman Sachs may prove to do just that.

Principal Subsidiaries

Goldman, Sachs & Co.; Goldman Sachs (Asia) Finance Holdings L.L.C.; Goldman Sachs (Asia) Finance (Mauritius); Goldman Sachs (United Kingdom) L.L.C.; Goldman Sachs Group Holdings (United Kingdom); Goldman Sachs Holdings (United Kingdom); Goldman Sachs International (United Kingdom); GS Financial Services L.P.; Goldman Sachs Capital Markets, L.P.; Goldman Sachs (Japan) Ltd.; J. Aron Holdings, L.P.; J. Aron & Company; Goldman Sachs Mortgage Company; Goldman Sachs Credit Partners L.P.; Goldman Sachs Holdings (Netherlands) B.V.; Goldman Sachs Mitsui Marine Derivative Products, L.P.; Goldman Sachs (Cayman) Holding Company; Goldman, Sachs & Co. oHG (Germany); Goldman Sachs Financial Markets, L.P.; GS Hull Holding, Inc.; The Hull Group, L.L.C.; SLK LLC; Spear, Leeds & Kellogg, L.P.; SLK Holdings Inc.; First Options of Chicago, Inc.

Principal Competitors

Credit Suisse First Boston Corp.; Merrill Lynch & Co. Inc.; Morgan Stanley.

Further Reading

Creswell, Julie, "Goldman Goes Shopping," *Fortune*, May 10, 1999, p. 120.

"Goldman Sachs: After the Fall," *Fortune*, November 9, 1998, p. 128.

"IPO Again," *Crain's New York Business*, March 15 1999, p. 34.

Lowenstein, Roger, "Goldman Sets Fund for Firms in Distress," *Wall Street Journal*, April 16, 1990.

Raghavan, Anita, "Goldman Sachs Moves to Stem Staff Defections," *Wall Street Journal*, September 24, 1996.

Serwer, Andy, "Will Goldman Go Pulic—Finally?," *Fortune*, June 22, 1998, p. 188.

Spiro, Leah Nathans, "How Public Is This IPO?," *Business Week*, May 17, 1999.

Swartz, Steve, "Goldman Sachs Gets $225 Million as an Investment from 7 Insurers," *Wall Street Journal*, March 30, 1989.

Tarquino, J. Alex, "In Brief: Goldman Sachs Group Sells 69M Shares," *American Banker*, May 4, 1999, p. 28.

"Wall Street's Lone Ranger," *Business Week*, March 4, 2002.

Weinberg, Neil, "Short-Term Greedy?," *Forbes*, May 15, 2000, p. 170.

—updates: Pamela Shelton, Christina M. Stansell

Grupo Financiero Banorte, S.A. de C.V.

359 Paseo de la Reforma
Mexico City, D.F. 06500
Mexico
Telephone: (525) 625-4800
Toll Free: (01) (800) BANORTE
Web site: http://www.gfnorte.com.mx

Public Company
Incorporated: 1899 as Banco Mercantil de Monterrey
   S.A.
Employees: 11,284
Sales: 8.19 billion pesos ($893.62 million) (2001)
Stock Exchanges: Mexico City
Ticker Symbol: GFNORTE
NAIC: 493110 Warehousing and Storage Activities;
   522110 Commercial Banking; 523110 Investment
   Banking and Securities Dealing; 523120 Securities
   Brokerage; 523920 Portfolio Management; 524113
   Direct Life Insurance Carriers; 524126 Direct
   Property and Casualty Insurance Carriers; 525110
   Pension Funds; 551111 Offices of Bank Holding
   Companies

Grupo Financiero Banorte, S.A. de C.V., once a regional bank mostly concerned with serving commercial and industrial accounts, has grown to become a full-service financial conglomerate—the fourth largest in Mexico in terms of capitalization (and third largest in portfolio value) and the largest one still controlled by Mexican shareholders. It is a holding company whose units include not only the bank but allied subsidiaries for brokerage, life, and property/casualty insurance, pension funds and annuities, leasing, factoring, and warehousing. Careful, conservative management enabled GFNorte (usually still called Banorte) to survive the currency crisis of 1994 and its aftermath. While many other banks its size went under, Banorte took advantage of the crisis to acquire other banks and to expand from Mexico's north into all areas of the country.

From Regional Bank to Full-Service Financial Group: 1899–1993

Banco Mercantil de Monterrey S.A. was founded in 1899 in Monterrey, capital of the state of Nuevo Leon and home of many of Mexico's largest and most dynamic industrial enterprises. In 1913, during the revolution that swept across the country, bank officers sent millions of dollars worth of gold bullion to the United States to keep it from falling into the hands of the warlords who roamed the countryside. The bank later expanded into the other states of northeastern Mexico. By 1976 it ranked 14th among Mexican banks in total assets, and in 1978 it had 53 offices. Still, Banco Mercantil de Monterrey did not receive much attention in a city where there were 13 banks of deposit, 18 lending houses, and six mortgage banks, all but six headquartered in Monterrey.

Banco Mercantil de Monterrey subsequently grew to become the largest of Mexico's five regional banks, with 125 branches in northern Mexico. When world oil prices dropped in 1982, however, the value of Mexico's peso collapsed and the government nationalized the nation's banks in order to restructure the financial system. Banco Mercantil de Monterrey was merged with Banco Regional del Norte in 1986 and took the name Banco Mercantil del Norte, or Banorte for short. Capably administered by Eugenio Clariond Reyes Retana, Banorte was found in a 1990 survey to be the most profitable of the 15 biggest banks in Mexico. Total assets had reached more than 4 billion pesos.

Banorte was one of the last nationalized banks to be reprivatized in the early 1990s. In 1992 the government sold 66 percent of the bank for 1.78 billion pesos ($567 million), to a group headed by Monterrey-based tycoon Roberto Gonzalez Barrera, chairman of Gruma, S.A. de C.V., Mexico's largest producer of cornmeal and tortillas. The new owners intended to increase service along the border with the United States, buy or establish a brokerage house, and create an integrated financial group. Banorte's chief executive, Francisco Patino Leal, kept his job. Speaking of his bosses, he later told Joel Millman of the *Wall Street Journal,* ''None live from the bank, so they don't need dividends. That gives us freedom to manage soundly.'' In 1993 the bank acquired Grupo Financiero Afin, whose holdings in-

Company Perspectives:

The company's mission is to satisfy our clients' financial needs through the most up to date means of delivery to ensure that quality service is provided with cordiality and efficiency; maintain the integrity and quality of all our operations, particularly in the handling of the Group's deposits and capital; adopt profitability and the generation of value as the work approach that will serve as an endorsement for depositors and shareholders, and will be a base for the Group's reinvestment as well; be responsible both as citizens and as an institution, seeking to hold a position of leadership in the communities we serve, promoting development through a philosophy of "Pensar en Grande" (Thinking Big); be, as a company, a source of serious and fair employment, with the objective of treating each of our employees with the highest sense of equality and fairness.

cluded a brokerage, and became Grupo Financiero Banorte. In addition to the bank and brokerage house, its subsidiaries now included a currency exchange, warehouser, equipment lessor, and guarantor of bonds and sureties.

Profiting in Hard Times: 1994–99

The reprivatized banking system quickly ran into trouble when—in late 1994—investors and depositors concerned over Mexico's growing payments deficit converted their pesos into dollars, resulting in a severe depreciation of the currency and an ensuing recession. Nine of the nation's 16 domestic banks either were taken over by a government agency or, like Banorte, were bailed out in the form of ten-year notes from a public fund for the bad loans on their books. The situation had been made more severe by an unchecked expansion of credit in the year preceding the crisis; during this period loans grew by 36 percent—nine times the rate of growth in the economy as a whole. Banorte's own market capitalization fell to $350 million from its peak of $1.2 billion. Even so, it emerged as Mexico's least hard-hit bank (with net income down only 13.5 percent in 1994 and 12.4 percent in 1995) because it had, in large part, confined its loan portfolio to commercial customers rather than extending consumer loans freely to the less creditworthy general public.

Consumers who had amassed debts to Banorte that they could not pay in full were offered discounts. In this way the group collected something from credit card holders and lessees, for example. Those who had taken out auto loans had the option of returning the car or paying only its current worth, which because of depreciation was less than when purchased. For its part, Banorte negotiated discounts from its own creditors. Banorte ranked first among banks in capitalization ratio in 1995 and 1996. It did not lay off any employees during this period and even added a few hundred. The number of Banorte branches grew to 154 in 11 states in 1995.

In 1996 Banorte acquired Banco del Centro S.A. (Bancen), a regional bank with 111 branches that was about to fail, paying 729.97 million pesos (about $94 million). "The government put two and two together and saw they were about to take over a

bank," Patino Leal explained to Millman. "They didn't want to manage the bank, so they offered it to us." The acquisition brought Banorte a presence in three more states and made it the seventh largest Mexican bank. It was handling payroll for some 350,000 employees, each receiving cash in individual envelopes twice a month. Another 44,000 workers could withdraw their salaries using debit cards good at Banorte's ATMs.

A much bigger acquisition for Banorte was the 1997 purchase of 81 percent of Grupo Financiero Asemex-Banpais S.A. for 678.1 million pesos ($87.4 million). Banpais, which was not formerly merged with Banorte until 2000, had been owned by the big glassmaker Vitro S.A. before it was nationalized in 1982. Like Banorte, it was reprivatized in the early 1990s, but in 1995 the government seized control again, citing irregularities in the bank's operations. It was considered by analysts to be in the worst shape of any of Mexico's banks. A federal official said 80 percent of its loans were approved with no more than a signature as guarantee, creating a loan portfolio of which half eventually had to be written off as worthless. Charged with embezzling $4 million, the bank's former president fled to Spain before being apprehended and extradited. (Banpais's holdings, however, included Aseguradora Mexicana, the country's largest insurance company.) Also in 1997, Banorte sold 49 percent of its annuities and insurance subsidiaries to the Italian-based Generali group of insurance companies.

Banorte's leasing subsidiary, Arrendadora del Norte, S.A. de C.V., was rated the most profitable financial institution in Mexico in 1997. Among banks, Banorte was rated number one in this category. By the fall of 1998 Banorte was one of only four of the 18 Mexican banks privatized in the early 1990s still under the same ownership. In early 1999 it ranked fifth in size, with 461 branches covering every Mexican state. During the last six years the bank also had increased its number of automated teller machines from 12 to 1,000, installed 7,000 point-of-sale terminals, mounted 3,600 corporate computer worksites, and added more than 600,000 electronic payment accounts. "This is one of the best banking stories in Latin America," an investment analyst told James R. Kraus of *American Banker.* "They dominate the Monterrey market, they've successfully acquired and integrated other banks seized by regulators, and their basic asset quality remains good." Another analyst called Banorte the lowest-risk bank in Mexico. One of its strengths was collecting the bad loans made by other banks. In 1999, for example, it bought the bad-loan portfolio of Banca Serfin S.A. from the government, paying only about 11 percent of the value of the loans and earning a $60 million net profit from the portfolio, according to Othon Ruiz Montemayor, Banorte's CEO.

Becoming the Biggest Mexican-Owned Financial Group: 2000–01

Banorte formed a joint venture in 2000 with Hewlett-Packard Co. to establish a business-to-business web trading site for Latin American companies and their global trading partners. Banorte and Hewlett-Packard were planning to connect corporate customers and suppliers in various industries, including automakers, supermarkets, and secondary chemical providers. "We see this as a natural extension of our corporate banking business," Banorte director Robert Chandler told Jessica

Key Dates:

1899: The group is founded as Banco Mercantil de Monterrey S.A.

1976: Banco Mercantil de Monterrey ranks 14th in assets among Mexico's banks.

1986: Banco Mercantil de Monterrey merges with Banco Regional del Norte to become Banco Mercantil del Norte (Banorte).

1990: A survey finds Banorte to be the most profitable of Mexico's 15 largest banks.

1992: A two-thirds stake in Banorte is sold to a group headed by Roberto Gonzalez Barrera.

1993: The bank becomes part of Grupo Financiero Norte, an integrated financial group.

1996: Banorte acquires Banco del Centro S.A. (Bancen), a failing regional bank.

1997: Banorte acquires Grupo Financiero Asemex-Banpais S.A. for $87.4 million.

1999: Now truly national, Banorte has 461 branches, located in every Mexican state.

2001: Banorte buys Banco de Credito y Servicio (Bancrecer) for $174 million.

Toonkel of *American Banker*. About this time the company moved its headquarters from Monterrey to Mexico City.

Banorte rose to fourth largest bank in Mexico in 2001, when the government body charged with selling off the last banks and bank assets taken over after the 1994 crisis sold Banco de Credito y Servicio (Bancrecer) for 1.65 million pesos ($174 million). Bancrecer had been Mexico's fourth most important bank in 1982 but fared poorly under government administration in the 1980s. "Bancrecer is ideal for banks that already have a presence here and want to expand," the government agency's chief executive officer, Vicente Corta, had told Karina Robinson of *The Banker* in 2000. "It has good technological systems and 800 branches but small, bad-quality assets." Before selling Bancrecer, the government spent $10 billion to bail out the institution. Corta called Bancrecer "the most clear-cut case of lack of market discipline, continuing to grow its assets when it was already in trouble."

The Bancrecer acquisition more than doubled Banorte's branches, to 1,207, and increased its assets by about 70 percent to $17.5 billion. In particular, the purchase gave it a more substantial presence in Mexico City and the southeast and northwest of Mexico. Banorte estimated the cost of merging the two institutions at $110 million but described the merger as a quicker and cheaper alternative to opening hundreds more branches on its own. Banorte also assumed Bancrecer's $587 million portfolio of mainly government bonds that were issued in exchange for the bad loans the government took off

Bancrecer's books. Interviewed by Jennifer Galloway for *LatinFinance*, Jorge Colin, Banorte's director of investor relations, conceded, "On a stand-alone basis, Bancrecer was not a good acquisition." However, he added, "But it will become profitable if we can make use of existing synergies and reduce costs. We know there are negatives, but we also know that we can obtain enough benefits to outweigh the negatives."

Grupo Financiero Banorte recorded a net profit of 1.5 billion pesos ($164.1 million) on net revenues of 8.19 billion pesos ($893.62 million) in 2001. The banking sector accounted for 85 percent of the total. These figures did not include results for Bancrecer, since its shares were not transferred to Banorte until the beginning of 2002.

Principal Subsidiaries

Afionsadora Banorte, S.A. de C.V.; Almacenadora Banorte, S.A. de C.V.; Arrendedora del Norte, S.A. de C.V.; Banco del Centro, S.A.; Banco Mercantil del Norte, S.A.; Banpais, S.A. (81%); Casa de Bolsa Banorte, S.A. de C.V.; Factor Banorte, S.A. de C.V.; Pensiones Banorte, S.A. de C.V. (51%); Seguros Banorte Generali, S.A. de C.V. (51%).

Principal Competitors

Grupo Financiero Banamex-Accival, S.A. de C.V.; Grupo Financiero BBVA-Bancomer, S.A. de C.V.; Grupo Financiera Serfin, S.A.

Further Reading

Crawford, Leslie, "Harsh World for Mexican Banks," *Financial Times,* March 6, 1995, p. 6.

Fraser, Damien, "Banorte Sale Brings in 1,776bn Pesos," *Financial Times,* June 16, 1992, p. 28.

Galloway, Jennifer, "Going Big, Going Wide," *LatinFinance,* October 2001, p. 47.

Kraus, James R., "A Jewel of Mexico Banking Seen Growing Fast, Solidly," *American Banker,* February 18, 1999, p. 14.

Leal Garcia, Alba, "Bancos si; casa de bolsa, no," *Expansion,* November 20, 1996, pp. 120, 123–24.

"Los banqueros mas prominente de Mexico," *Expansion,* September 26, 1990, pp. 90–162.

"Mexico's Banpais, Now Restructured, Goes Up for Sale," *Wall Street Journal,* August 9, 1996, p. A5A.

"Mexico's Regional Bank Banorte Wins Stake in Banpais," *Wall Street Journal,* September 2, 1997, p. A15.

Millman, Joel, "Banorte Thrives Despite Near Collapse of Mexican Banking System, Recession," *Wall Street Journal,* April 1, 1996, pp. A10.

Sedelnik, Lisa, "Banking on Banorte," *LatinFinance,* October 1996, pp. 28–30, 32.

Toonkel, Jessica, "Banorte, HP to Start Site for Latin Business," *American Banker,* March 10, 2000, p. 12.

—Robert Halasz

Gunite Corporation

302 Peoples Avenue
Rockford, Illinois 61104
U.S.A.
Telephone: (815) 964-7124
Toll Free: (800) 677-3786
Fax: (815) 965-9197
Web site: http://www.gunite.com

Division of Transportation Technologies Industries Inc.
Incorporated: 1854
Employees: 263
Sales: $100 million (2002 est.)
NAIC: 336340 Motor Vehicle Brake System
    Manufacturing; 336399 All Other Motor Vehicle Parts
    Manufacturing

Gunite Corporation manufactures wheel-end components for medium- and heavy-duty trucks. The company's products—which include automatic slack adjusters, brake drums, disc brake rotors, disc wheel hubs, spoke wheels, and disc and spoke wheel assemblies for trailers—come as standard equipment on many North American-made trucks.

Origins in the 19th Century

Gunite is based in Rockford, Illinois, where it is believed to be the city's oldest manufacturing operation. The company originated from the efforts of Duncan Forbes, who was born in Scotland. Duncan came to Troy, New York, with his son Alexander Duncan Forbes in 1842, and the two became involved in the foundry business. By 1854, the men had migrated to Rockford and established a partnership called Duncan Forbes & Son on Forbes Street. Their foundry was located in the city's Water Power District, where a dam had been constructed across the Rock River to provide power for industry. According to an early historical profile of the company from the mid-1950s, "The operators had to be content with high water in the spring and shallow water in the summer. At times the foundry had to shut down and everyone went hunting and fishing. The diary of

Alexander Forbes is filled with notations of going fishing or hunting at almost any time of the year."

According to the same historical profile, father and son arrived in Rockford during the month of March. Within six months, "they had leased a building, constructed a cupola, connected water power for the blast fans and drawn up a partnership agreement and were advertising in local newspapers the products they were making." The partnership produced a variety of products from gray iron, including small cast iron stoves, kettles, branding irons, water and steam pipes, fireplace grates, chain pump wheels, railing, wagon wheel axel hubs, plow castings, and sled runners. During the mid-1850s and 1860s, production shifted from gray iron to malleable iron, which the company sold in large quantities to farm implement manufacturers.

During these early years, the Forbes partnership operated under several different business names. According to different sources, the enterprise was called Forest City Foundry, D. Forbes & Son, Proprietors; Eagle Foundry; and Forbes Malleable Iron Works. Duncan Forbes died in April of 1871, but his descendants carried on in his footsteps. That year, Alexander Forbes established a new partnership called A.D. Forbes & Co., which existed until the company was finally incorporated as Rockford Malleable Iron Works in 1890.

Continued Growth in the 20th Century

By the dawn of the twentieth century, the foundry had grown to employ about 150 people. In 1906, it relocated to a 38-acre tract of land on Peoples Avenue. It was around this time when the company began to benefit from the burgeoning U.S. transportation sector. In only a few short years, the railroads became its top market for malleable iron, which was used in the manufacture of freight cars. A period of rapid growth followed, and the foundry's workforce grew to about 550 by the spring of 1917. At that time, Rockford Malleable Iron established a bureau of employment and welfare to look after the interests of its growing employee base, in the event employees were hurt or became ill.

The railroads provided a steady stream of business until approximately 1920, by which time the foundry had been serving the emerging automobile market for five or six years. In addition to the passenger transportation industry, the company found a niche in the commercial sector and began marketing cast iron brake drums for trucks in 1924. By this time, five generations of the Forbes family had been involved with the company.

When Ford Motor Co. ceased production of the Model T in 1927, the decision had a grave impact on Rockford Malleable Iron, significantly reducing business. However, the Forbes family did not give up. It was amidst these disappointing and challenging conditions that Duncan Patterson Forbes, great-grandson of founder Duncan Forbes, defined the enterprise's future. According to an early newspaper account, after experimenting with the properties of gun iron in a college metallurgy class, Duncan inspired the company's engineers to conduct further research into the high-strength metal, which had been used mainly in the production of large field artillery. This ultimately led to the birth of a new product called Gunite—a variety of processed gray iron—and the establishment of a new subsidiary called Gunite Corp.

Following the development of Gunite, the parent company consolidated its operations with Northwestern Malleable of Milwaukee in 1928 and adopted the name Rockford Northwestern Malleable Corp. In 1931, John A. Forbes was promoted from vice-president and general manager to president, replacing Duncan P. Forbes, who became chairman. The following year, the Gunite subsidiary was assimilated into the parent company, which then changed its name to Gunite Foundries Corp. In addition to products made of malleable iron, the newly named company offered a variety of products made from Gunite and a metal known as Z-ron. These included heavy-duty truck wheels made from cast iron, along with bolts, clutch pressure plates, wrenches, connecting rods, and brake drums.

When the 1940s arrived, rising freight costs prompted Gunite to stop casting production for the automobile industry. World War II followed, and the company's resources were devoted to wartime production. Specifically, Gunite began making steel castings, as well as gray iron castings, that were needed for the production of machine tools. After the war ended, Gunite's capabilities with steel were used to make truck wheels that complemented the iron brake drums it began manufacturing in the mid-1920s.

By the mid-1950s, Gunite had achieved steady growth through 100 years of operation. It employed roughly 700 workers with an annual payroll of about $4 million. The company's production workers were unionized. As an early historical profile of Gunite explains, the company weathered more than one rough period during its first 100 years, including a number of nationwide financial panics and periods of economic depression.

According to the August 17, 1955 *Rockford Morning Star*, at this time various types of commercial castings constituted approximately one-third of Gunite's production. The remainder of the foundry's output was devoted to truck brake drums, as well as truck wheels that included brake drums. Gunite shipped anywhere from 16,000 to 18,000 of the latter item every month. The article called Gunite ''a classic example of private initiative, courage and freedom of enterprise'' and said its strong, lightweight wheel had ''an enviable reputation'' because it allowed trucks to carry heavier loads on roads and highways with weight restrictions.

Changes and Challenges: Mid-1950s to Late 1980s

After 91 years, Gunite ceased to make malleable iron castings in August of 1955. High labor costs made this type of casting non-profitable. The company continued to make castings from its namesake Gunite, as well as from steel and gray iron. By spring of the following year, a $1 million expansion program had been announced. The program included planned facilities upgrades like a new electric furnace that would enable Gunite to double its production of steel. In November of 1956, President Duncan P. Forbes succeeded John A. Forbes as Gunite's chairman, while E.C. Fales was named president and general manager. Together, all of these changes may have seen somewhat drastic. However, they paled in comparison to those that were around the corner.

In July 1960, Noble J. Schmidt replaced Fales at the helm of Gunite and was named president and CEO. A long-time employee, Schmidt had served Gunite in a variety of capacities since 1906. A little more than two months later, the company announced that it had agreed to be purchased by Kelsey-Hayes Co. of Detroit, which at the time was the nation's largest automobile brake drum manufacturer. Kelsey-Hayes saw Gunite as a strong complement to its existing automobile operations, since Gunite attributed 75 percent of its business to truck manufacturers like Chrysler, Diamond T., Dodge, Ford, General Motors, and White, and the remainder to companies like Baldwin Locomotive and Caterpillar.

By November 1960, Gunite Foundries Corp. officially became the Gunite Foundries Division of Kelsey-Hayes Co., and Noble Schmidt announced that he would retire in December. Responsibility for the division was given to William H. Shinn, who had been with Gunite for nearly 20 years. Gunite's new owner increased the foundry's size and introduced new products for trucks and trailers including aluminum spoke wheels and a skid control system modeled after one found in the aircraft industry. Sales climbed more then 300 percent between 1960 and 1968, when the company announced a $1.8 million addition that included a new iron melt shop and systems for environmental regulation compliance.

In 1972, Kelsey-Hayes turned Gunite into a manufacturing plant and removed the element of local control. At this time, president and general manager William Shinn left the company. In November of the following year, Kelsey-Hayes became a subsidiary of truck trailer manufacturer Fruehauf Corp. At the same time, the gradual physical expansion of Gunite that had been underway since the early 1960s received a big boost. The foundry revealed $20 million plans to increase its 500,000-

square-foot facility by approximately 25 percent. In the November 1, 1973 *Rockford Register Republic*, Gunite general manager Kenneth Schroeder described some of the planned improvements, which included a new iron foundry with the capacity to melt 35 tons, an expanded machine shop and steel melt department, and an additional steel automated molding line.

In late 1978, reorganization at Kelsey-Hayes returned local control to Gunite, and William Shinn returned to manage the foundry. By November 1979, Gunite's workforce had grown from 700 employees to 1,100, and the foundry had grown to occupy 1 million square feet. The company continued to invest in the future. It ordered $4 million in new equipment, some of which was devoted to produce a new line of wheel hubs for customers like General Motors, which signed a contract with Gunite worth $3 million per year. However, bad times loomed on the horizon. In 1982 an economic recession, coupled with a sluggish trucking industry, resulted in large-scale layoffs.

Conditions started to improve in 1983, when federal weight restrictions on trucks were reduced. By 1984, Gunite was benefiting from the development of new products at Kelsey-Hayes, including a new disc brake system. However, by this time a mere 500 workers remained in Rockford. In addition, Gunite announced plans to move some 200 machinists jobs from Rockford to Elkhart, Indiana, by 1986. In September 1987, a new Oak Brook, Illinois-based firm called Truck Components Inc. purchased Gunite, as well as Fabco Automotive Corp., from Kelsey-Hayes. At this time, Gunite was officially named Gunite Corp.

A major win for Gunite came in 1988, when Navistar International named the foundry as its only supplier of wheel-end components on medium- and heavy-duty trucks. Another important contract came from Ford Motor Co. As reported in the May 17, 1988 *Rockford Register Star*, Ford opted to include Gunite's automatic slack adjusters, which helped breaks to wear in a more even fashion, as standard equipment on all of the automaker's "medium- and heavy-duty chassis with air brakes starting with the 1989 model year."

Labor Troubles and a New Parent Company: 1990s and Beyond

Gunite started the 1990s under new leadership. Thomas Cook was named the foundry's president in April 1991. Cook had previously served as president and CEO of automotive part manufacturer Redlaw Industries, and came to Gunite with more than 30 years of experience in the metals industry. By 1993, the company's employee base had returned to previous levels, totaling approximately 724 workers. Of these, 263 employees worked at the Rockford plant. That year, the U.S. Department of Labor's Occupational Health and Safety Administration proposed that Gunite be fined $216,000 after an investigation revealed it had violated 62 safety regulations. The proposed fines came in the wake of two employee deaths that happened between 1991 and 1993.

In May 1994, Gunite's parent company, Truck Components Inc., was purchased by New York-based Castle Harlan Inc. for $170 million. As part of the deal, Cook became CEO of Truck Components. The following year, company ownership changed once again when Truck Components was acquired by Chicago-based Johnstown America Industries Inc.

In 1998, union workers at Gunite's Rockford plant went on strike in an effort to obtain better pay and more agreeable working conditions. In the April 29, 1998 *Rockford Register Star*, a representative for the United Auto Workers explained, "It's not your normal strike, where it just amounts to pure economics. It's hard to say how long the strike will last because the membership was upset with the morale in the plant. It's pretty low. They have to work long hours, . . . and it's a hot, dirty job." After approximately two weeks, the workers reached an agreement with Gunite that required them to work fewer hours on weekends. In addition, Gunite agreed to bring in a third-party consultant to improve relations between the foundry and its workers.

By the late 1990s, Gunite continued to struggle with safety issues. From 1990 through 1998, the November 24, 1998 *Rockford Register Star* revealed the foundry had paid actual fines of $88,125 for various safety violations. However, these paled in comparison to proposed OSHA fines that totaled $407,000 in late 1998. Of this large sum, $140,000 was related to charges that Gunite exposed its workers to silica dust, which causes a condition called silicosis. The remainder was "for 35 other alleged violations, including the company's failure to provide annual hearing tests, to inspect respirators, and to properly maintain a clean work environment."

In June 1999, Johnstown America Industries Inc. was re-named Transportation Technologies Industries Inc. (TTI) as the company sharpened its focus on the transportation industry. By 2002, Gunite remained one of several key TTI companies, which together resulted in annual revenues of more than $500 million. Despite challenges in the areas of safety and labor relations, Gunite has been recognized for excellence within its industry. According to the company, in addition to receiving QS-9000 certification, Gunite has received the Q-1 award from Ford Motor Co. and Freightliner's Masters of Quality award. However, perhaps its most remarkable achievement of all is surviving and thriving after more than 150 years of continuous operation.

Principal Competitors

ArvinMeritor Inc.; Citation; INTERMET.

Further Reading

"Company Background," Transportation Technologies Industries Inc., October 22, 2002. Available from http://www.tti-inc.com.

"Firm Founded 100 Years Ago," *Rockford Morning Star*, August 9, 1954.

"A Gentleman Who Talked Sense," *Rockford Morning Star*, March 21, 1954.

"Gunite. Tracking Changes at Firm with Deep Rockford Roots," *Rockford Register Star*, December 1, 1993.

"Gunite Corporation History," Gunite Corp., October 3, 2002. Available from http://www.gunite.com/history.asp.

"Gunite Foundries Names New Chairman, President," *Rockford Morning Star*, November 8, 1956.

"Gunite Workers Strike Over Wages, Hours," *Rockford Register Star*, April 29, 1998.

"Merger of Two Local Firms Announced. Gunite, Northwestern Malleable Headed by Duncan Forbes," *Rockford Morning Star*, February 5, 1932.

"Noble Schmidt is Elected President of Gunite Firm," *Rockford Morning Star*, July 16, 1960.

"Oak Brook Firm Buys Gunite," *Rockford Register Star*, September 9, 1987.

"Oldest Business Gets New Owner," *Rockford Register Star*, May 10, 1994.

"OSHA Fines Gunite $407,000," *Rockford Register Star*, November 24, 1998.

"They Came to Town a Century Ago," *Rockford Morning Star*, March 7, 1954.

—Paul R. Greenland

HERSHEY'S

Hershey Foods Corporation

100 Crystal A Drive
Hershey, Pennsylvania 17033-0810
U.S.A.
Telephone: (717) 534-6799
Toll Free: (800) 539-0261
Fax: (717) 534-6760
Web site: http://www.hersheys.com

Public Company
Incorporated: 1927 as Hershey Chocolate Corporation
Employees: 14,000
Sales: $4.5 billion (2001)
Stock Exchanges: New York
Ticker Symbol: HSY
NAIC: 311330 Confectionery Manufacturing from
   Purchased Chocolate; 311340 Nonchocolatc
   Confectionery Manufacturing; 311320 Chocolate and
   Confectionery Manufacturing from Cacao Beans

Hershey Foods Corporation holds the top position in the U.S. confectionery market. The name Hershey is synonymous with chocolate, yet the company's founder made his first fortune by manufacturing caramel. While famous for its major candy brands—Hershey's, Reese's, Kit Kat, Kisses, Twizzlers, Jolly Rancher, Ice Breakers, Carefree, and Breath Savers—the company also markets grocery products including Hershey's baking chocolate, chocolate milk, ice cream toppings, cocoa, chocolate syrup, peanut butter, and Reese's and Heath baking pieces. Hershey operates with two main divisions, Hershey Chocolate North America and Hershey International, the latter of which exports the firm's products to over 90 countries. The Milton Hershey School Trust controls 77 percent of Hershey's voting power. In 2002, the Trust planned to diversify its holdings and, in a controversial move, announced that it was putting Hershey Foods up for sale.

Company Origins

Milton S. Hershey was born in 1857 in central Pennsylvania. As a young boy Hershey was apprenticed to a Lancaster, Pennsyl-vania, candymaker for four years. When he finished this apprenticeship in 1876, at age 19, Hershey went to Philadelphia to open his own candy shop. After six years, however, the shop failed, and Hershey moved to Denver, Colorado. There he went to work for a caramel manufacturer, where he discovered that caramel made with fresh milk was a decided improvement on the standard recipe. In 1883, Hershey left Denver for Chicago, then New Orleans, and later New York, until in 1886 he finally returned to Lancaster. There he established the Lancaster Caramel Company to produce "Hershey's Crystal A" caramels that would "melt in your mouth." Hershey had a successful business at last.

Hershey Makes His First Chocolate Sale: 1895

In 1893, Hershey went to the Chicago International Exposition, where he was fascinated by some German chocolate-making machinery on display. He soon installed the chocolate equipment in Lancaster and in 1895 began to sell chocolate-covered caramels and other chocolate novelties. At that time, Hershey also began to develop the chocolate bars and other cocoa products that were to make him famous.

In 1900, Hershey decided to concentrate on chocolate, which he felt sure would become a big business. That year, he sold his caramel company for $1 million, retaining the chocolate equipment and the rights to manufacture chocolate. He decided to locate his new company in Derry Church, the central Pennsylvania village where he had been born, and where there would be a plentiful milk supply. In 1903, Hershey broke ground for the Hershey chocolate factory, which would remain the largest chocolate-manufacturing plant in the world through the twentieth century.

Before this factory was completed, in 1905 Hershey produced a variety of fancy chocolates. But with the new factory, Hershey decided to mass-produce a limited number of products that he could sell at a low price. The famous Hershey's Milk Chocolate Bar, the first mass-produced chocolate product, was born.

In 1906, the village of Derry Church was renamed Hershey. The town was not simply named after the man or the company: it was Milton Hershey's creation, the beneficiary of and heir to his energy and his fortune. Hershey had begun planning a whole community that would fulfill all the needs of its inhabitants at the same time that he planned his factory. A bank, school, recreational park, churches, trolley system, and even a zoo soon followed, and the town was firmly established by its tenth anniversary. One of Hershey's most enduring contributions was the Hershey Industrial School for orphans, which he established in 1909 with his wife Catherine. After Catherine's death in 1915, the childless Hershey in 1918 gave the school Hershey company stock valued at about $60 million. In 2002, the school, which became the Milton Hershey School in 1951, continued to control 77 percent of the company's voting stock.

In 1907, Hershey's Kisses were first produced, and the next year, in 1908, the Hershey Chocolate Company was formally chartered. In 1911, its sales of $5 million were more than eight times the $600,000 made ten years earlier at the company's start.

Continued Success: 1920s–1940s

The Hershey company continued to prosper, producing its milk chocolate bars (with and without almonds), Kisses, cocoa, and baking chocolate. In 1921, sales reached $20 million, and in 1925 Hershey introduced the Mr. Goodbar Chocolate Bar, a chocolate bar with peanuts. In 1927, the company was incorporated as the Hershey Chocolate Company and its stock was listed on the New York Stock Exchange.

By 1931, 30 years after the company was established, Hershey was selling $30 million worth of chocolate a year. As the Great Depression cast its shadow on the town of Hershey, Milton Hershey initiated a ''grand building campaign'' in the 1930s to provide employment in the area. Between 1933 and 1940, Hershey's projects included a 150-room resort hotel, a museum, a cultural center, a sports arena (where the Ice Capades was founded), a stadium, an exotic rose garden, and a modern, windowless, air-conditioned factory and office building. Hershey liked to boast that no one was laid off from the company during the Depression.

Though Hershey's intentions seem to have been wholly sincere, there was always some suspicion about his ''company town.'' Labor strife came to the company in 1937, when it suffered its first strike. Though bitter, the strike was soon settled, and by 1940 the chocolate plant was unionized.

In 1938, another famous chocolate product was introduced: the Krackel Chocolate Bar, a chocolate bar with crisped rice. The next year Hershey's Miniatures, bite-sized chocolate bars in several varieties, were introduced.

During World War II, Hershey helped by creating the Field Ration D—a four-ounce bar that provided 600 calories and would not melt—for soldiers to carry to sustain them when no other food was available. The chocolate factory was turned over to the war effort and produced 500,000 bars a day. Hershey received the Army-Navy E award from the quartermaster general at the war's end. Hershey died soon after, on October 13, 1945.

Hershey Begins Expansion: 1960s

After Milton Hershey's death, the chocolate company continued to prosper and maintain its strong position in the chocolate market. By the 1960s, Hershey was recognized as the number one chocolate producer in America.

With the company's growth came expansion. In 1963, Hershey broke ground for the construction of two new chocolate factories, in Oakdale, California, and Smiths Falls, Ontario. Expansion for Hershey also meant looking for acquisitions, the first of which was the H.B. Reese Candy Company that same year. Also in 1963, the company's president and chairman, Samuel Hinkle, arranged for the founding of the Milton S. Hershey Medical Center of the Pennsylvania State University in Hershey, Pennsylvania.

While the company played a hand in many developments within Pennsylvania, its main endeavor continued to be the food industry, including, for the first time, non-confectionery food. Among its acquisitions were two pasta manufacturers, San Giorgio Macaroni Inc., in Lebanon, Pennsylvania, and Delmonico Foods Inc., in Louisville, Kentucky, in 1966. In 1967, the Cory Corporation, a Chicago-based food-service company, was acquired. Due to its expansions beyond chocolate, the company changed its name in 1968 to the Hershey Foods Corporation. The name change also marked the passing of an era when in 1969 it raised the price of Hershey's candy bars, which had been five cents since 1921, to ten cents.

As the 1970s unfolded, changes in American culture forced Hershey Foods Corporation to change also. Before the 1970s, the company, heeding the words of its founder that a quality product was the best advertisement, had refused to advertise. Thousands of people who came to tour the chocolate factory each year had spread the world about Milton Hershey and his chocolate. A visitors bureau had been established as early as 1915 to handle tours of the facilities, and by 1970 almost a million people a year visited Hershey.

Word of mouth had served as a valuable source of advertising for Hershey during most of its existence. But as people became more health conscious and the consumption of candy declined, the influence of advertising became a greater factor in the candy business. By 1970, Mars had deposed Hershey as the leader in candy sales, provoking Hershey to launch a national advertising campaign. On July 19, 1970, Hershey's first consumer advertisement, a full-page ad for Hershey's Syrup, appeared in 114 newspapers. Within months, the corporation was running ads on radio and television as well. Also that year, under an agreement with British candymaker Rowntree Mackintosh, Hershey became the American distributor of the Kit Kat Wafer Bar. Hershey introduced a second Rowntree candy, Rolo Caramels, the next year.

In 1973, Hershey's Chocolate World Visitors Center was opened to educate people about chocolate-making, with exhibits about tropical cocoa-tree plantations, Pennsylvania Dutch milk farms, and the various stages of the manufacturing process. The facility was established to replace tours of the actual plant, which were discontinued in 1973 due to an overload of traffic.

Under the direction of its chief executive officer, William E. Dearden, Hershey adopted an aggressive marketing plan in 1976 to offset its shrinking market share. Dearden, who had grown up in Milton Hershey's orphanage, joined forces with his chief operating officer, Richard A. Zimmerman, to implement a campaign aimed at customers in grocery stores, where half of all candy was sold. Specialty items such as a wide line of miniatures, holiday assortments, and family packs were marketed. A national ad campaign promoting Hershey's Kisses, and the introduction of the Giant Hershey's Kiss in 1978 tripled sales of the product between 1977 and 1984. The Big Block line of 2.2-ounce bars and premium candies such as the Golden Almond Chocolate Bar were also introduced, as were Reese's Pieces Candy and Whatchamacallit and Skor Candy Bars.

Growth Through Acquisition: Late 1970s and 1980s

Hershey also made plans to diversify, to lessen the company's vulnerability to unstable cocoa-bean and sugar prices. In 1977, Hershey acquired a 16 percent interest in A.B. Marabou, a Swedish confectionery company, and bought Y&S Candies Inc., the nation's leading manufacturer of licorice. The following year, it bought the Procino-Rossi Corporation (P&R), and in 1979 it acquired the Skinner Macaroni Company to add to its stable of brand-name pastas. In 1984, Hershey purchased American Beauty, another pasta brand, from Pillsbury and formed the Hershey Pasta Group.

Another 1979 acquisition, the Friendly Ice Cream Corporation, a 750-restaurant chain based in New England, tripled the number of employees on Hershey's payroll. After experiencing major structural changes owing to its 1970s expansion, the company

implemented an intensive values study to pinpoint and communicate the principles inherent in its corporate culture and history.

In 1982, Hershey opened another plant, in Stuarts Draft, Virginia. The next year it introduced its own brand of chocolate milk, and in 1984 it introduced Golden Almond Solitaires (chocolate-covered almonds). In 1986, in addition to introducing two new products, the Golden III Chocolate Bar and the Bar None Wafer Bar, Hershey acquired the Dietrich Corporation, the maker of the 5th Avenue Candy Bar, Luden's throat drops, and Mello Mints. Not content with such a year—the first to top $2 billion in sales—in December Hershey purchased G&R Pasta Company, Inc., whose Pastamania brand became the eighth in Hershey's pasta group.

However, the acquisitions did not stop there. In June 1987, Hershey acquired the Canadian candy and nut operations of Nabisco Brands for its subsidiary Hershey Canada Inc. The three main businesses Hershey acquired were Lowney/Moirs, a Canadian chocolate-manufacturing concern; the Canadian chocolate manufacturer of Life Savers and Breath Savers hard candy; and the Planters snack nut business in Canada.

The biggest acquisition of all came in August 1988, when Hershey made a $300 million deal for Peter Paul/Cadbury, an American subsidiary of the British candy and beverage company Cadbury Schweppes plc. Hershey purchased the operating assets of the company and the rights to manufacture the company's brands, including Peter Paul Mounds and Almond Joy Candy Bars and York Peppermint Patties, and Cadbury products including Cadbury chocolate bars and Cadbury's Creme Eggs, an Easter specialty candy. Observers predicted that Hershey's economies of scale and clout with retailers would bring increased profitability to the newly acquired Cadbury lines. This purchase pushed Hershey's share of the candy market from 35 percent to 44 percent, and helped Hershey back to the top of the American candy business. At the same time, Hershey decided to sell the Friendly Ice Cream Corporation to concentrate on its core confectionery businesses. The company was sold to Tennessee Restaurant in September for $374 million.

The decline in candy consumption that began after World War II, as a prosperous America found its waistline expanding uncomfortably, accelerated during the 1970s as the fitness craze began. However, in the 1980s this trend reversed. Candy consumption reportedly increased from 16 pounds per capita in 1980 to 19.5 pounds in 1988, coincidentally the same period during which Hershey regained the top spot in U.S. candy through its acquisitions of Dietrich Corporation and Peter Paul/Cadbury. In the early 1990s, Hershey maintained its confectionery position in the United States through several successful introductions: Hershey's Kisses with Almonds chocolates in 1990; Hershey's Cookies 'n' Mint chocolate bars in 1992; Hershey Hugs white chocolate-covered kisses in 1993 (which had become a $100 million brand by 1995); and Reese's NutRageous bar in 1994, which quickly moved into the top 20 candy-bar list.

Diversification and International Expansion: Early 1990s

Outside of its chocolate realm, Hershey continued to bolster its pasta business while also attempting to capture more of the nonchocolate confectionery market. In 1990, it acquired the Ronzoni Foods Corp., yet another regional pasta brand, and in 1993 the Hershey Pasta Group opened a new plant in Winchester, Virginia. Through such moves, Hershey became the leader in dry pasta in the United States by 1995. Meanwhile, continuing fierce competition with Mars and the low inflation of the period—both of which made increasing prices untenable—put pressure on Hershey's chocolate earnings. One of the company's responses to this pressure was to increase its offerings in nonchocolate confections. Among the 1990s introductions were Amazin' Fruit gummy bears in 1992, Twizzlers Pull-n-Peel candy in 1994, and Amazin' Fruit Super Fruits in 1995. By going after the nonchocolate confectionery business, Hershey aimed to capture more market share among youthful shoppers, who generally preferred nonchocolate candy. It also made sense in the overall U.S. market, where nonchocolate candy sales were increasing faster than chocolate candy sales.

In the early 1990s, Hershey attempted to lessen its dependence on the North American market by cautiously moving into overseas markets. In 1990, the company introduced the Hershey brand to the Japanese market through a joint venture with Fujiya. The European market, a difficult market for foreign firms to penetrate given differing European tastes and such entrenched firms as Nestle, was targeted next. This venture was less than successful than Hershey's move into Japan, at least at first. In 1991, Hershey acquired the German chocolate maker Gubor Schokoladen, which in the first few years after the takeover failed to meet Hershey's expectations. In 1992, the firm purchased an 18.6 percent interest in the Norwegian confectionery firm Freia Marabou, but then promptly sold the stake the following year after it was outbid for majority control by Philip Morris. Later, in 1993, Hershey acquired the Italian confectionery business of Heinz Italia S.p.A. for $130 million, which primarily gave it the Sperlari brand, a leader in nonchocolate confectionery products in Italy. Shortly thereafter, Hershey acquired the Dutch confectionery firm Oversprecht B.V. for $20.2 million, which under the Jamin brand manufactured confectionery products, cookies, and ice cream. Although primarily distributed in the Netherlands and Belgium, Jamin gave Hershey its first penetration of the potentially lucrative Russian market when it began to distribute chocolate there after the Hershey takeover.

Strategic Changes: Mid- to Late 1990s

Meanwhile, back in North America, Hershey was being hurt by results in Canada, where too many competitors were chasing too few customers, and in Mexico, where political and economic turmoil slowed Hershey's growth. In response, Hershey announced a restructuring in late 1994, taking a $106.1 million aftertax charge. Over the next 15 months, the company cut its staff by more than 400 and consolidated its operations in the United States, Canada, and Mexico into a Hershey Chocolate North America division. Earlier in 1994, Hershey had formed a Hershey Grocery division to give special attention to the company's various baking and grocery products. These two divisions, along with Hershey International and Hershey Pasta Group, comprised the four main areas in which Hershey operated. The company also raised its prices for the second time in ten years and launched a stock repurchase program to bolster its stock price.

In the mid-1990s, Hershey added partnering to its arsenal of corporate strategies. In 1994, Hershey partnered with General Mills to introduce Reese's Peanut Butter Puff's Cereal. In 1995, a partnership with Good Humor-Breyers resulted in Reese's Peanut Butter Ice Cream Cups. That same year a cross-marketing deal with MCI offered free long-distance telephone calls to purchasers of selected Hershey's chocolate products. Having celebrated its 100th anniversary in 1994, Hershey looked forward to a bright future in its second century. By that time, Hershey had increased its share of the U.S. confectionery market to 34.5 percent, while Mars had seen its share fall to 26 percent, and Hershey's nonchocolate confectionery and pasta operations were growing.

Under the leadership of Kenneth Wolfe—named chairman and CEO in 1994—Hershey's success continued into the latter half of the 1990s. During 1996, the company launched its first hard candy product, TasteTations, and the reduced-fat Sweet Escapes product line. That year, the company acquired Leaf North America in a $440 million deal that added Jolly Rancher, Good & Plenty, Whoppers, and Milk Duds to its product arsenal.

Hershey continued its dominance of the U.S. market by continuing to introduce new, successful products, including the Reese's Crunchy Cookie Cups, Classic Caramels, and the Mini Kisses Semi-Sweet Baking Pieces. The company also revamped its business operations once again, divesting its European operations in 1996, and then selling its pasta division in 1999 to New World Pasta LLC for $450 million in cash. Wolfe commented on the sale in a 1999 *Prepared Foods* article claiming that "after a thorough review of our strategic direction, we have concluded that we can generate a better return for our shareholders by focusing on our confection, related grocery, and foodservice businesses."

Hershey continued to add to product line in 2000 with the purchase of RJR Nabisco Inc.'s mints and gum business. The acquisition included the Ice Breakers and Breath Savers Cool Blast mints, and the Ice Breakers, Carefree, Stickfree, Bubble Yum, and Fruit Stripe gums. Wolfe retired in 2001, leaving industry veteran Rick Lenny at the helm. That year, the company sold its Luden's throat drop business and began a $275 million restructuring effort that included 400 job cuts, closure of three Hershey plants, and the outsourcing of cocoa powder production. While net income fell during 2001, sales increased by eight percent to $4.5 billion.

A Surprise Announcement: 2002

During 2002, Hershey dealt with a labor strike—the first one since 1980. Just as the labor issues were resolved, Hershey faced yet another blow. In July 2002, the Milton Hershey School Trust, which controlled 77 percent of Hershey's voting power, announced that it wished to diversify its holdings and that a sale of the company would be beneficial to the school. At the time, over half of the Trust's $5.4 billion portfolio consisted of Hershey stock. While Hershey's board was opposed to a sale, it agreed to work with the Trust on viable options. The announcement however, left the citizens of Hershey, Pennsylvania, in an uproar. Nearly half of the city's residents were employed by Hershey and feared a sale of the company, especially to a foreign firm, would negatively impact their jobs as well as the city. As such, the state's attorney general and potential governor filed a petition against the Trust that would call for court approval of any offers made for Hershey. The possible sale received negative reviews throughout the business world. In fact, an August 2002 article in *The Economist* went as far to say that "Milton Hershey must be turning in his grave."

In September, Wm. Wrigley Jr. Co. offered $12.5 billion bid for the company, outbidding Nestlé and Cadbury Schweppes, who had teamed up to make a $10.5 billion play for the company. Both offers were turned down, leaving Hershey independent for the time being. While Hershey's future remained up in the air, one thing was certain. With well over 100 years of history behind it, the Hershey name would remain a favorite among chocolate lovers around the world for years to come.

Principal Subsidiaries

Hershey Chocolate & Confectionery Corporation; Hershey Chocolate of Virginia, Inc.; Hershey Canada, Inc.

Principal Divisions

Hershey Chocolate North America; Hershey International.

Principal Competitors

Cadbury Schweppes plc; Mars Incorporated; Nestlé S.A.

Further Reading

Barrett, Amy, "How Hershey Made a Big Chocolate Mess," *Business Week*, September 9, 2002.
"Bitter Times for a Sweet Town," *Economist*, August 31, 2002.
Byrne, Harlan S., "Hershey Foods Corp.: It Aims to Sweeten Its Prospects with Acquisitions," *Barron's*, May 6, 1991, p. 41.
Castner, Charles Schuyler, *One of a Kind: Milton Snavely Hershey, 1857–1945*, Hershey, PA.: Dairy Literary Guild, 1983, 356 p.
Gold, Jackey, "How Sweet It Is," *Financial World*, November 13, 1990, p. 17.
Halpert, Hedy, "Face to Face: Hershey's Next Century," *U.S. Distribution Journal*, September 15, 1993, p. 43.
"Hershey Foods—Packaging Leader of the Year," *Packaging Digest*, October 1997, p. 91.
"Hershey Foods Sells Pasta Business," *Prepared Foods*, January 1999, p. 26.
"Hershey Foods' Wolfe to Retire," *Candy Industry*, October 21, 2001, p. 12.
Hershey's 100 Years: The Ingredients of Our Success, Hershey, PA: Hershey Chocolate Corporation, 1994, 24 p.
Heuslein, William, "Timid No More," *Forbes*, January 13, 1997, p. 98.
Koselka, Rita, "Candy Wars," *Forbes*, August 17, 1992, p. 76.
Kuhn, Mary Ellen, "Sweet Times in the Hershey Candy Kingdom," *Food Processing*, January 1995, p. 22.
A Profile of Hershey Foods Corporation, Hershey, Pa.: Hershey Chocolate Corporation, 1995, 24 p.
The Story of Chocolate and Cocoa, Hershey, PA: Hershey Chocolate Corporation, 1926, 30 p.
"Workers Strike at Nation's Largest Candy Maker," *Food Institute Report*, April 29, 2002, p. 1.

—updates: David E. Salamie and Christina M. Stansell

Hillerich & Bradsby Company, Inc.

800 West Main Street
Louisville, Kentucky 40202
U.S.A.
Telephone: (502) 585-5226
Toll Free: (800) 282-BATS
Fax: (502) 585-1179
Web sites: http://www.slugger.com;
          http://www.powerbilt.com;
          http://www.louisville-hockey.com

Private Company
Incorporated: 1897 as J.F. Hillerich & Son
Employees: 400
Sales: $100 million (2001 est.)
NAIC: 339920 Sporting and Athletic Goods
    Manufacturing

Hillerich & Bradsby Company, Inc. is a privately owned sporting goods manufacturer best known as the producer of the Louisville Slugger baseball bats. In addition to its traditional wooden Sluggers, which are still made in Louisville, the company manufactures more than 100 models of aluminum bats for baseball and softball in an Ontario, California manufacturing plant, and a line of baseball and softball gloves. Hillerich & Bradsby also manufactures and markets a line of golf equipment—including clubs, bags, and gloves—under the trade name ''PowerBilt,'' and a line of hockey equipment under the trade name TPS Louisville Hockey. The company also owns some 5,000 acres of forest in Pennsylvania and New York, from which it harvests the wood to produce its bats.

1800s: A Budding Bat Maker

The company that would come to be one of the biggest names in American baseball traces its roots to a young German immigrant named J. Michael Hillerich. In 1842, Hillerich—a ''cooper,'' or craftsman who made wooden casks and barrels—left his home in Baden-Baden and moved his family to Baltimore, Maryland. Baltimore was only a temporary stop, how-

ever, and the Hillerichs soon settled permanently in Louisville, Kentucky. There, J. Michael's son, J. Frederic, opened his own cooperage. The business, J.F. Hillerich, Job Turning, was located in a two-story building in downtown Louisville. Hillerich made a variety of rounded wooden objects, including handrails, porch columns, bed posts, bowling pins, and bowling balls.

In 1880, a third Hillerich entered the woodworking business when 14-year-old John (''Bud''), J. Frederic's son, became an apprentice at his father's shop. It was Bud's entry into the family business that would ultimately result in the Hillerichs' most famous product. A baseball fan, Bud skipped out of work one day in 1884 to watch a Louisville Eclipse game. The Eclipse played in the American Association (the forerunner of the National League), and one of its most prominent players was Pete Browning. During the game Bud Hillerich attended, Browning broke his favorite bat—a fairly significant setback in a day when bats were expensive to make, and most players owned only one.

After the game, Bud Hillerich approached Browning and offered to make him a new bat. The two men went back to Hillerich's shop and worked through the night to turn a stick of white ash wood into a bat custom-designed to Browning's preferences. As Hillerich turned the wood on his lathe, Browning watched over his shoulder, periodically testing it for weight and swing. The next day, Browning hit three-for-three with his new, Hillerich-made bat.

As the word about Hillerich's craftsmanship spread, other Louisville players began approaching him with their own bat orders. His father, however, was unenthusiastic. Perceiving his son's new product as a trivial sideline, he preferred to focus on the business's original goods. Even so, Bud continued producing his bats, which came to be known as ''Falls City Sluggers.'' Soon, there was a demand for Hillerich's bats even outside the professional leagues, and in 1890, a hardware company in St. Louis agreed to handle all bat sales except those to professional players.

In 1894, Hillerich changed the name of his bats from Falls City Slugger to Louisville Slugger, registering the new name as an official trademark. Continuing to turn out bats that were

---

Company Perspectives:

It takes a special place to craft the Official Bat of Major League Baseball. Since 1884, Louisville Slugger has put prime lumber in the hands of the greatest players of the game. A visit to the museum shows you how the sport has changed a bit between then and now, but the "crack of the bat" remains one of the sporting world's most thrilling moments.

---

customized to each individual player's preferences, he also began branding the player's name on his bat. This allowed the player to readily distinguish his own bat from others.

In 1897, the 31-year-old Bud Hillerich became a partner in his father's business, and the company's name was changed to J.F. Hillerich & Son to reflect the new ownership structure. Business continued to thrive, and in 1901 the Hillerichs had to move to a larger facility. Sales of baseball bats got an additional boost in 1905, when Honus Wagner, a well-known shortstop for the Pittsburgh Pirates, gave Hillerich & Son the right to use his autograph on their bats. This proved to be the start of a long tradition of product endorsements by professional athletes—both for Hillerich and for endless other companies. Shortly after signing Wagner, Hillerich got the rights to use another baseball superstar's signature: Ty Cobb signed an agreement with the company in 1908.

Early 1900s: Hardships and Changes

The Hillerichs faced a serious setback in 1910, when their bat factory caught fire. During the rebuilding process, the two men hired Frank Bradsby to oversee the company's sales policy. Bradsby was a buyer for the St. Louis hardware company that had earlier agreed to handle the non-pro athlete segment of Hillerich's bat sales. A skilled salesman, it did not take Bradsby long to make his mark within the growing business. In 1916, his efforts won him a partnership, and the company's name was changed to Hillerich & Bradsby Company.

The addition of Bradsby resulted in further changes at the company. Bradsby was a golf lover, who believed that the sport would soon become popular in the United States. Under his influence, in 1816 Hillerich & Bradsby (H & B) entered the golf equipment market. Its first golf clubs did not carry the company's brand; rather they were privately branded for the stores in which they were sold. Within a few years, however, H & B began branding its own clubs. Adopting the strategy that had proven successful with baseball bats, the company's golf division soon began producing clubs that carried the signature of famous golfers. The first such model was autographed by Stewart Maiden, a pro golfer from Scotland, who settled in the United States and gained fame as the teacher of golf legend Bobby Jones.

In 1924, Hillerich & Bradsby lost its founder when J. Frederick Hillerich died from a fall on an icy street. Meanwhile, the company's foray into the golf market was proving advantageous. In 1925, demand for its clubs had grown to such an extent that H & B was forced to expand. It purchased a large

warehouse in downtown Louisville and moved its golf club manufacturing operation and its offices into the new space. In 1933, H & B first used the name that was to become the permanent brand for its clubs: PowerBilt.

Hillerich & Bradsby suffered, as did many others, during the Louisville flood of 1937, when weeks of unusually heavy winter rains caused the Ohio River to overrun its banks and flood much of the city. Both the company's offices and its factory were damaged. But more significant was the effect of the catastrophe on Frank Bradsby who, weakened by the strain and the extra work, died later that year.

Mid-1900s: New Facilities, New Products

The war years caused Hillerich & Bradsby to turn its focus temporarily from the making of sporting goods to the making of M1 carbine stocks and tank pins. Bud Hillerich died in 1946 at the age of 80, and his son, Ward, assumed the presidency of Hillerich & Bradsby. Ward's tenure as the company's leader was brief, however. He died just three years later and was succeeded by his younger brother, John Hillerich, Jr. John served as Hillerich & Bradsby's leader for two decades—during which the company continued to thrive. The Louisville Slugger continued to be the bat of choice in the Major Leagues, and H & B produced models that were graced by the signatures of such baseball luminaries as Mickey Mantle, Babe Ruth, and Hank Aaron. The golf equipment division also expanded during John Hillerich's leadership. This was due, in part, to a surge in the game's popularity during the 1960s, when the U.S. public became enamored with such players as Arnold Palmer and Jack Nicklaus.

In 1966, Hillerich & Bradsby expanded into yet another sport when they acquired Wally Enterprises in Ontario, Canada. Wally Enterprises produced croquet sets, pool tables, and—of more importance—hockey sticks. H & B changed the brand on the hockey equipment to Louisville TPS (Tournament Players Series) and began selling its sticks through sporting goods distributors in the United States and Canada.

In 1969, John Hillerich, Jr., died, and his son, John "Jack" Hillerich III took the reins at Hillerich & Bradsby. It was around this time that an important change began taking place in baseball. Although the professional players were still using wooden bats, larger and larger numbers of amateur players were turning to aluminum—a material that was thought to be not only safer, but more durable and thus more economical. The new material had another advantage as well. Because aluminum bats were hollow, they weighed less than the traditional wooden ones. This meant that the batter could swing the bat faster, thereby hitting the ball with more force and making it travel further.

In 1971, the aluminum bat was approved for Little League play and, four years later, it was approved for college play. Hillerich & Bradsby did not immediately jump on the aluminum bandwagon. Although the company contracted with an outside aluminum company to manufacture the first H & B aluminum bat as early as 1970, it felt that replacing wood with aluminum would detract from the game of baseball. Therefore, it remained focused on the traditional wooden Sluggers.

By the early years of the 1970s, Hillerich & Bradsby was growing out of its facilities in downtown Louisville. Needing

Key Dates:

1842: J. Michael Hillerich and his family immigrate to America.

1859: J. Frederic Hillerich opens a cooperage in Louisville.

1880: J. Frederic's son Bud joins his father's business.

1884: Bud Hillerich makes a baseball bat for Pete Browning, player for the Louisville Eclipse.

1894: Hillerich's growing bat business begins using the name "Louisville Slugger."

1897: The Hillerichs' company changes its name to J.F. Hillerich & Son.

1905: The Hillerichs create the first autographed Louisville Slugger model, with the signature of Honus Wagner.

1911: Frank Bradsby joins the company.

1916: The company's name is changed to Hillerich & Bradsby Company; the company begins manufacturing golf clubs.

1933: H & B starts using the brand name "PowerBilt" on its golf clubs.

1966: The company acquires Wally Enterprises, making an entry into the hockey stick market.

1970: H & B contracts with a California company to produce its first aluminum bat.

1973: H & B moves from its Louisville facilities to Slugger Park in Jeffersonville, Indiana.

1978: The company purchases the California aluminum bat company with whom it had originally contracted.

1996: H & B moves its headquarters and bat factory back to Louisville.

more space, the company acquired a 56-acre facility just across the Ohio River in Jeffersonville, Indiana. In 1973, the company moved its golf products operation to the new complex—named "Slugger Park." The following year, the baseball bat production also was moved to Jeffersonville.

Continuing to churn out literally millions of wooden bats each year in its new facility, H & B further penetrated the baseball market when it introduced a line of Louisville Slugger baseball and softball gloves in 1975. The company's large, 13-inch softball glove, "The Big Daddy," became one of the best-selling gloves in softball history.

As the 1970s wound down, the demand for wooden bats began to decrease significantly. Although the bulk of major league players still used Louisville Sluggers, their use outside the majors had dwindled. There was simply no fighting the popularity of aluminum—and in 1978, Hillerich & Bradsby made peace with the inevitable, buying the California manufacturer that had previously produced its aluminum bats on contract.

Late 1900s: Catching Up in the Aluminum Bat Market

Even so, the company's delay in getting serious about aluminum left it playing catch-up to its competitors. Easton Sports, of California, had leapt into the aluminum bat market early on,

using the same technology it used to make metal arrows; by the early 1980s, it held the lion's share of the market. Between 1980 and 1985, H & B's sales stagnated, and its profits plunged by approximately 90 percent. Jack Hillerich knew he had to move fast to turn the business around.

His answer was to develop a better aluminum bat. The company started talking to players who used aluminum, obtaining feedback they could use in the design process. Then, pouring money into research and development, it began to improve the original product, making important innovations. One early innovation involved changing the grip surface to make it "tackier," thereby giving the batter more control over the bat. Others included weighted-end designs, pressurized air chambers inside the bat barrels, and thinner bat walls made out of super-strong alloys.

By the start of the 1990s, H & B's aluminum bat business had greatly picked up and was generating approximately 30 percent of the company's revenue. In fact, its aluminum bat facility in Santa Fe Springs, California was having trouble making enough product to meet the market demand. So in August of 1991, H & B moved its aluminum division into a larger facility in nearby Ontario, California. It also increased the staffing at that facility by some 35 percent. That same year, H & B supplemented its aluminum production capabilities by opening a smaller bat and hockey stick manufacturing facility in Florence, Kentucky.

While the aluminum bat division was growing out of its space, however, the wooden bat plant was in just the opposite situation. Not only had the demand for wooden bats dwindled, but the company's improvements in technology and delivery systems had reduced the amount of space needed. In 1996, H & B left Slugger Park and moved back across the river to Louisville, locating just a few blocks from where J. Michael Hillerich had opened his original cooperage back in 1975. The company's new complex included a Louisville Slugger Museum, complete with a 120-foot-tall bat.

The Future of H & B

As the 21st century got under way, Hillerich & Bradsby installed its sixth Hillerich as CEO. In November of 2001, Jack Hillerich resigned, leaving the company's operations to his son, John A. Hillerich, IV, who had previously served as president of H & B's PowerBilt division.

Aside from the leadership change, it appeared to be business as usual at Hillerich & Bradsby. Baseball and softball equipment sales accounted for around 60 percent of the company's revenues, with the fastest-growing segment of that market being women's fast-pitch softball. Hockey equipment sales generated some 20 percent of the total revenue, and the company was optimistic about the future of that division.

If any part of H & B had a questionable future, it was its golf division. Although the PowerBilt brand was well thought-of among golfers, it was not widely used among the game's pros. Since pro athlete endorsements were the most common form of sports equipment marketing, PowerBilt was at a disadvantage. In addition, the entire golf equipment industry was suffering from a flatness in the game's growth. The stagnant demand for equipment meant that many companies had to merge to stay afloat; others simply folded up.

In a 1998 interview with the *Seattle Times,* Jack Hillerich had hinted that the company might get out of the golf equipment business altogether. Although there is no indication of that happening soon, H & B has taken a different marketing approach in recent years. It has stopped pursuing equipment contracts with the tour pros and begun focusing instead on the concept of quality at an affordable price, with the slogan, "They only play expensive." Whether PowerBilt can weather the difficult times still besetting the golf industry, however, remains to be seen.

Principal Divisions

Louisville Slugger; PowerBilt; TPS Louisville Hockey; Louisville Slugger Museum.

Principal Competitors

Easton Sports, Inc.; Rawlings Sporting Goods Company, Inc.

Further Reading

Bernstein, Andy, "Jack Hillerich: Chairman and CEO, Hillerich & Bradsby," *Sporting Goods Business,* October 14, 1997, p. 24.

Bowman, John, "Slugging It Out," *Business First of Louisville,* July 22, 1991, p. 1.

Helyar, John, "The Ball and Glove May Be Important; The Bat Is American," *Wall Street Journal,* October 9, 1984.

Johnson, Chuck, "Still Swinging at 100: Louisville Slugger Shows Staying Power," *USA Today,* November 10, 1994, p. 6C.

"Kentucky Bat Maker Changes As Game Changes," *Seattle Times,* April 26, 1998, p. D6.

Oldham, Scott, "Louisville Slugger," *Popular Mechanics,* September 1999, p. 66.

Patton, Phil, "Wooden Bats Still Reign Supreme at the Old Ball Game," *Smithsonian,* October 1984, p. 152.

Summers, Lisa, "An American Icon," *Lane Report,* April 1999.

—Shawna Brynildssen

Horsehead Industries, Inc.

110 East 59th Street
New York, New York 10022
U.S.A.
Telephone: (212) 527-3000
Fax: (212) 527-3008
Web site: http://www.horseheadinc.com

Private Company
Incorporated: 1981
Employees: 2,925
Sales: $765 million (2001)
NAIC: 551112 Offices of Holding Companies

Horsehead Industries, Inc. is one of the largest privately held companies in the United States. Based in New York City, it operates through four subsidiaries. Zinc Corporation of America sells the company's zinc products and is the direct link to Horsehead's most significant ancestor, the New Jersey Zinc Company, which established the zinc industry in the United States and operated independently for more than 100 years. ZCA Mines provides the Zinc Corporation with much of its raw materials from a mine operation in Balmat, New York. Further zinc is produced through the recovery and recycling efforts of Horsehead Resource Development Corporation, out of which developed Sterling Resources, the fourth Horsehead subsidiary, which is dedicated to providing environmental management and remedial services. Horsehead is run by chairman and CEO William Flaherty, a former Gulf + Western executive who led a management group that bought certain New Jersey Zinc assets from the conglomerate in 1981.

Early Origins of Horsehead Industries

Horsehead's name and horse head logo is its most tangible link to the New Jersey Zinc Company. The horse head was actually an allusion to the state of New Jersey. In 1786, the Colony of New Jersey minted its first penny with a horse head and plow, both of which would become part of the Great Seal of the State of New Jersey. In 1848, the company first used the horse head crest, casting it in the doors of an experimental furnace located near the present-day site of Newark's Pennsylvania Railroad Station. By 1855, New Jersey Zinc was using the horse head as a trade mark, which appeared on labels or was imprinted in metal products. It would become a recognized symbol around the world.

The basis of New Jersey Zinc's business was a zinc-iron-manganese ore body formed by geological processes that took place over one billion years ago in the northwestern corner of the state. The area is unique, containing over 150 minerals, of which 25 are found nowhere else in the world. Moreover, the ore body became commercially viable through an accident of nature. Erosion exposed the deposits in the pre-Cambrian period, which were then covered by Paleozoic sediment and later eroded by glacial activity. The result was that deposits were readily visible to European settlers. By 1640, not long after the establishment of the Nieuw Amsterdam settlement, the natural outcrops had been discovered and were being explored. The Franklin mine, according to the Franklin Mineral Museum, passed through a number of owners, including King Charles II of England and William Penn and a group of investors. In 1760, the Earl of Stirling made failed attempts to extract zinc from the ore body, although he did produce iron, which would become a mainstay of the local economy late into the 1800s.

A number of parties worked the Franklin-Sterling deposits from 1765 to 1848, but no one was able to successfully separate the zinc. In 1848 the Sussex Zinc & Copper Mining & Manufacturing Company was formed. Four years later it developed the first commercially viable way to smelt the ore to produce zinc oxide. Also in that year, Sussex Zinc changed its name to the New Jersey Zinc Company. It began selling zinc oxide to the paint industry as a non-toxic substitute for lead, leading to the rise of ready-mixed paints. Zinc oxide also became an important compound in the rubber industry, not only serving as a reinforcing agent but as a way to cut the curing time of rubber. With the birth of the automobile and the need for tires and the increased need for other rubber goods, zinc oxide would take on an even greater significance. Starting in 1870, zinc oxide would also play an important role in the cosmetics industry.

New Jersey Zinc also attempted to recover metallic zinc from the Franklin-Sterling deposits, but it wasn't until 1865 that the

Company Perspectives:

Since 1981, Horsehead has successfully completed numerous transactions totaling over $3 billion, including acquisitions, divestitures, and corporate financings, and has provided a superlative return on investment to our shareholders.

company was able to produce commercial slab zinc. Some ten years earlier, because of these efforts, the company had been able to create a second product, spiegeleisen (German for "mirror iron"), an iron-manganese alloy used in the manufacture of manganese steel. The company was not alone, however, in working the Franklin-Sterling outcrop, and conflicting deeds of ownership caused considerable legal wrangling. Finally in 1897, New Jersey Zinc was able to consolidate the area's mining and smelting operations and begin to build a world-class business.

New Jersey Zinc Expands in a New Century

Under the leadership of its president, Stephen S. Palmer, New Jersey Zinc began a program of rapid expansion. Looking for a place to build larger, modern manufacturing facilities, the company selected a site in Pennsylvania that was close to both anthracite fields and the New Jersey mines. It was also situated along the Lehigh River and featured good rail connections. The resulting plant and company town would become Palmerton, Pennsylvania. In 1899, the new plant would begin to ship its first product, zinc oxide. In 1904, Palmerton would begin producing spiegeleisen, taking advantage of the residuum from the zinc oxide furnaces. Because of rising demand for zinc oxide, the company built a second plant in 1912. The engineering department, which had been located at the company's New York headquarters, also moved to Palmerton in 1912, permitting New Jersey Zinc to steadily build more facilities, including a major research laboratory and a rolling mill that allowed the company in 1917 to enter the zinc rolling business.

In the meantime, New Jersey Zinc expanded its operations well beyond the Franklin-Sterling area. In 1901 a mine in Austinville, Virginia, was acquired to produce high grade zinc. Two years later the company acquired another mine in Hanover, New Mexico. To take advantage of the zinc available from the production of lead concentrates at Leadville, Colorado, in 1902 New Jersey Zinc built a plant at Canon City, Colorado. Magnetic separation was used to work zinc-iron middlings, then in 1920 a zinc oxide plant was added to the facility. Because of rising demand for zinc products in the Midwest, New Jersey Zinc opened a plant in Depue, Illinois in 1905.

After 100 years of operation, New Jersey Zinc was producing chemicals in addition to its zinc products. It was a well respected corporation, known for its sound management and consistent earnings. In the 1950s the company would begin a transition to a new era. The Franklin mine closed in 1954. The Sterling mine would close in 1958, then reopen in 1961 and continue in operation until 1986 before closing completely. In 1961 Bush Terminal Co., which operated warehouse, piers, and railroad facilities in Brooklyn, New York, bought a major stake

in the company. Four years later Bush Terminal would sell its shares, and New Jersey would lose its independence, becoming part of Gulf + Western Industries.

Although the assets of Gulf + Western were swallowed by Viacom in a 1993 mega-merger, it was the acquisition of New Jersey Zinc in 1965 that was the first step in making Gulf + Western a conglomerate that would accumulate a number of marquee businesses, including Paramount Pictures, the Simon & Schuster publishing house, Madison Square Garden, and the New York Knicks and New York Rangers sports franchises. Gulf + Western was created by Charles George Bluhdorn who emigrated to the United States from Austria in 1942. He created an auto parts business that in 1958 he renamed Gulf + Western. By 1965 he wanted to diversify and was looking to acquire a company with large enough cash reserves to fuel his plans for expansion. One of Gulf + Western's new board members, Harold U. Zerbe, recommended New Jersey Zinc, on whose board he also sat. Not only did the company have available cash, management and ownership were at odds over what to do with it. The managers wanted to grow the business, while the dominant shareholders wanted to expand the company's investment portfolio. In the fall of 1965, Gulf + Western purchased approximately 55 percent of New Jersey Zinc's common shares at $40 a share. The major sellers in the transaction were Bush Terminal Co., Hamilton Watch Co. (a 51 percent-owned Bush Terminal subsidiary), Jacob L. Hain (chairman of Bush Terminal), as well as some of Hain's associates. Some months later Gulf + Western bought Paramount Pictures and began to move away from the manufacturing sector.

Gulf + Western Sell New Jersey Zinc Assets in 1981

Although the New Jersey Zinc acquisition served a purpose for Gulf + Western at the time, market conditions eventually made it a disappointment for the rising conglomerate. New Jersey Zinc was now saddled with outdated facilities that were expensive to operate, and the industry in general suffered from excess capacity, as well as rising labor costs and expensive new pollution control regulations. Moreover, U.S. producers found it increasingly difficult to compete against government subsidized European zinc. New Jersey Zinc closed many of its long-time plants in the 1970s and drastically cut its work force. In 1978 Gulf + Western consolidated a number of assets into a Natural Resources Unit centered around New Jersey Zinc. The unit's chief operating officer, William E. Flaherty, was charged with selling the business. He lobbied management to allow him to cherry pick some of the New Jersey Zinc assets, including the Palmerton facility and Sterling Mine, but more important to his strategy was the company's valuable zinc-based patents and other technologies. By 1981 his efforts paid off. As the head of a group of investors, Flaherty raised approximately $60 million to buy the assets that would form the basis for Horsehead Industries as a holding company.

As the CEO and chairman of Horsehead, Flaherty was quick to make changes with the remnants of New Jersey Zinc. He slashed the workforce significantly and closed 80 of the mines, opting instead to buy cheap zinc from Zaire and Mexico. He also trimmed the product line. Even as the industry continued to suffer, New Jersey Zinc was able to realize a profit by 1983 and, two years ahead of schedule, repay $15 million borrowed from

---

Key Dates:

1848: Sussex Zinc & Copper is formed.
1852: Sussex Zinc changes its name to New Jersey Zinc Company.
1897: Franklin-Sterling zinc operations consolidated into New Jersey Zinc.
1954: Franklin mine closes.
1965: Gulf + Western Industries acquires company.
1981: Management-led groups buys New Jersey Zinc assets to form Horsehead Industries.
1986: Sterling mine is closed.
1987: New Jersey Zinc combined with acquisition to form Zinc Corporation of America.

Gulf + Western in the buyout. Flaherty also looked for similar businesses to acquire and turn around. Horsehead's second major acquisition came in 1985 when the company acquired Great Lakes Carbon Corporation, a maker of carbon and graphite products founded in 1919. Like New Jersey Zinc, Great Lakes was established in its market but had become a high-cost producer. As he had done before, Flaherty restructured the operation, soon making it one of the lowest-cost producers in its sector.

Horsehead created a new business in 1986, Horsehead Resource Development Co. (HRD) when it combined waste recovery technology and assets of New Jersey Zinc and Great Lakes Carbon to become involved in the environmental cleanup business that resulted from the government Superfund legislation of the 1980s. With an emphasis on the recovery of zinc and other metals from electric arc furnace dust, HRD would become a major recycler of hazardous industrial waste, as well as expanding to provide other environmental services.

Also in 1986, Horsehead formed Pony Industries to acquire eight businesses from the Atlantic Richfield Company, including building products, specialty-chemical, and high-technology materials operations. Each business was set up as a stand-alone division, but Horsehead soon realized that in order to thrive they each needed to be combined with larger operations. Beginning in 1988 Horsehead began to divest itself of its individual divisions, a process that was completed in 1990 and resulted in what management described as an extremely attractive return on its investment.

In 1987, Horsehead would acquire the zinc business of the Fluor Corp., which had been part of the St. Joe Minerals Corp, acquired by Fluor in 1981. Looking to focus its natural resources holdings in coal and lead, Fluor sold the St. Joe business to Horsehead for approximately $62 million. Horsehead subse-

quently combined the assets with New Jersey Zinc to form the Zinc Corporation of America (ZCA), becoming the country's largest producer of zinc, as well as the world leader in the production of zinc from recycled sources and value-added zinc products. It also established itself as a major global provider of zinc for use in the increasingly important alkaline battery industry. In addition, Horsehead created ZCA Mines, Inc., to operate the Balmat, New York, mine it acquired in the St. Joe transaction.

Horsehead combined the graphite electrode business of Great Lakes with the Sigri Gmbh unit of Germany's SGL Carbon AG in 1992, forming SGL Carbon AG. The business then made an initial public offering of stock in 1995 and Horsehead was able to sell off its interest. The remaining Great Lakes' assets were also subsequently divested. Horsehead created yet another business in 1998 when it formed Sterling Resources, Inc. to further the company's interest in environmental work. Sterling focused on environmental business management and consulting services for the industrial sector. It assisted companies in remediation programs, engineering and project management, and regulatory compliance.

In some twenty years Flaherty grew Horsehead into a company with annual revenues estimated to be $815 million, large enough to be listed by *Forbes* magazine as number 310 on its list of the top 500 private companies. Horsehead boasted a solid record of acquiring, turning around businesses, and divesting them at a profit. The company appeared well suited to continue that successful formula for some time to come.

Principal Subsidiaries

Zinc Corporation of America; Horsehead Resources Development Co.; ZCA Mines; Sterling Resources

Principal Competitors

Mitsui Mining & Smelting; Noranda; Teck

Further Reading

Bergson, Lisa, "Good-bye Gulf + Western, Hello Independence," *International Management,* February 1984, p. 38.
Burne, Malcolm, "Inside Story of a Bumper Success," *International Management,* June 1979, p. 20.
"The New Jersey Zinc Story," *Mining Engineering,* December 1953.
"New Jersey Zinc Control Sought by Gulf-Western," *Wall Street Journal,* September 14, 1965, p. 5.
"G&W Unit to Close Colorado Zinc Mine Dec. 31, Idling 200," *Wall Street Journal,* December 22, 1977, p. 16.
"G&W Agrees to Sell Some of the Assets of New Jersey Zinc," *Wall Street Journal*, July 29, 1981, p. 46.

—Ed Dinger

Houchens Industries Inc.

900 Church Street
Bowling Green, Kentucky 42101
U.S.A.
Telephone: (270) 843-3252
Fax: (270) 781-6377

Private Company
Founded: 1917
Employees: 5,200
Sales: $820 million (2001 est.)
NAIC: 445110 Supermarkets and Other Grocery (Except Convenience) Stores; 445120 Convenience Stores

Houchens Industries Inc. is an employee-owned company based in Bowling Green, Kentucky, and is the fourth largest grocery store operator in Kentucky. Houchens operates 31 Houchens Markets and 199 Save-A-Lot stores, competing with rival megastores by intentionally staying smaller and limiting selection. Houchens also owns seven Foodland/Piggly Wiggly/ IGA stores, 41 Jr. Food Stores, 23 Tobacco Shoppes (located within Save-A-Lot stores), and one The Orchard. Units are spread across 13 states, including Alabama, Georgia, Illinois, Indiana, New York, North Carolina, Ohio, South Carolina, Tennessee, Texas, Virginia, and West Virginia. In addition, Houchens has diversified in recent years, acquiring Southern Recycling Inc., Stewart and Richey Construction Co., Center of Insurance, and the tobacco company Commonwealth Brands.

Ervin G. Houchens Founds Company in 1917

The founding of Houchens Industries by Ervin G. Houchens is a quintessential American success story. One of ten children, Houchens grew up in a three-room log cabin. In 1917, at the age of 19, he opened his first grocery store in rural Barren County, Kentucky, where he grew up. It was a modest enterprise, housed in a 12-foot by 20-foot shed. Less than three years later he was able to relocate his business to Cross Roads, Kentucky, growing into a general merchandise store. The rise of the Houchens' grocery chain began in 1931 when the now-seasoned businessman opened three stores in Glasgow, Kentucky. Despite operat-

ing during the lean years of the Depression, Houchens was able to significantly expand his operations during the 1930s, branching out to other Kentucky communities. After opening stores in Munfordville and Scottsville, he entered Horse Cave, Cave City, Elizabethtown, and Vine Grove in 1937, followed by Bowling Green and Franklin in 1939.

Until the early decades of the twentieth century, grocery stores were full service operations, primarily offering dry goods, with clerks filling customers' orders one by one. Even early chains such as the A&P stores followed this model. Then, in 1916, Clarence Saunders introduced self-service grocery stores when he opened his first Piggly Wiggly in Memphis, Tennessee. The concept proved popular, and by the 1930s grocery chains and independents alike began switching over to self-service, which led to the rise of modern supermarkets offering a wide range of products. The first Houchens' store to follow the new model was one of the Bowling Green outlets in 1939. This store was progressive in other ways as well. It was the first grocery store in the city to host a live radio broadcast, and it also offered frozen food lockers for rent, a concept that proved successful until the introduction of affordable home freezers.

Houchens moved into six new Kentucky communities after World War II: Russellville, Auburn, Fountain Run, Gamaliel, Tompkinsville, and Hodgenville. Following a fire in November 1945 that destroyed the company's Glasgow warehouse and a nearby store, the company relocated its headquarters to Bowling Green, where it took over the wholesale grocery warehouse business of J.D. Reynolds Company, and Houchens reorganized the business as Bowling Green Wholesale, Inc. He later added a slaughter house and meat processing plant to his growing enterprises. To give back to the community, Houchens also established the Houchens Foundation, a non-profit corporation that since 1945 has contributed millions of dollars to civic and religious organizations.

In the 1950s, Houchens further expanded his operations in Kentucky, and in 1952 ventured beyond the state for the first time when he opened a store in Lafayette, Tennessee. Altogether, the company added stores in eight new communities during the decade and another seven in the ten years that followed. In 1960, the company was active on a number of

Company Perspectives:

Our Values: Listening and reacting to customers; fair and honest dealings with all; operating profitably to enhance our future; innovation and action without fear of failure; open communications with all employee/owners.

fronts. It became involved in investing in real estate used for strip shopping centers. The company also attempted to diversify by moving into the variety store industry. It created a number of Houchens Family Centers and Ben Franklin Family Variety Stores, but the venture never proved overly successful, and 20 years later the company began to close down these operations. Of more long-term importance was the debut of Houchens' first full-service supermarket, located in Bowling Green. All of the company's stores would soon adopt the larger format. Moreover, in 1960 Houchens created an Employee Profit Sharing Plan, which began the process of employees taking a vested interest in the business.

Name Change in 1972

In 1972, the growing company changed its name to Houchens Industries Inc. The 1970s brought even greater growth for the company and represented a high-water mark in terms of profitability for Houchens Markets. Eight new communities were entered during the decade, five in Kentucky and three in Tennessee. At its peak, Houchens had 55 supermarkets in operation. In the following decade, the company adjusted the mix and engaged in remodeling efforts to meet the challenge of a changing environment in the grocery business. In addition to building larger new stores, some older units were sold off in the early 1980s, while others were remodeled and expanded. Of significance during this period was the Schnucks Company's introduction of a super warehouse-style store to the region, prompting a price war with major rival Kroger and adversely affecting about half of Houchens stores as well. The war led to the practice of honoring manufacturer's coupons at twice their stated value.

Now over 80 years old and nearing retirement, Ervin Houchens looked to secure the future of the company and its employees. In 1981, he signed a letter of intent to sell Houchens Industries to the Memphis food distribution company of Malone and Hyde Inc. for $58 million. In addition to ten food distribution centers serving a wide swath of the Southeast, Malone and Hyde also owned 45 supermarkets and 165 drugstores, as well as a number of sporting goods and auto parts stores. In the end, however, both parties backed away from the deal. Houchens retired in September 1983 at the age of 85, remaining on as chairman emeritus but devoting the bulk of his time to the activities of his foundation. Before turning over control of the business, he completed the sale of Houchens' Industries to Red Food of Chattanooga, Tennessee. His nephew, Ruel Houchens, became president of the subsidiary, having worked for the company since 1942 when as a 13-year-old boy he was employed by a Houchens store in Glasgow. Under Ruel Houchens' leadership and new corporate ownership, the company continued to remodel and expand its stores in the mid-1980s. Volume grew

so high for the chain that the company's warehouse was no longer able to adequately supply its stores and an outside supplier had to be contracted.

After five years of operating under Red Food and its French parent company, food wholesaler-retailer Promodes, the employees of Houchens' Industries reached a deal to buy the company. The proceeds would allow Promodes to invest in Red Food and other operations in Chicago. However, according to *Supermarket News,* the corporate parent saw little prospect for growing Houchens, noting that "an industry observer in the region said, 'The speculation is that Houchens turned out to be impervious to being converted to Red Food's methods of operation.'" Another trade source commented, "Since Red Food took over Houchens five years a ago, there has hardly been any change in the way Houchens operates. It was a family-owned business for many years and is still run very much like a mom-and-pop, even with all its stores." Ruel Houchens lined up investors to finance the employee buyout and subsequently became the company's CEO and chairman when the transaction was culminated in November 1988. But it would not be until October 1996 that company made the final payment on the bank note that made an employee buyout possible.

Independent once more, Houchens began to again grow its business. In 1989, after it acquired the Dave and Steve Super-Key stores in the Bowling Green area, the total number in the chain returned to 47. As the economy slowed in the early 1990s, Houchens turned to a discount, limited-selection format to fuel further expansion. In January 1990, the company opened its first Save-A-Lot store in Hardinsburg, Kentucky. Houchens quickly rolled out other stores, and picked up 30 Save-A-Lots in a 1994 acquisition of 30 outlets located in Alabama and Kentucky. Total outlets numbered 86 by the middle of the decade and nearly 140 by the year 2000, spread across 11 states. In the early 1990s, Save-A-Lot became Mor-For-Less, but less than a year later it returned to its original name.

Founder Dies in 1992

Ervin Houchens died on August 17, 1992. The top leadership position then passed out of the hands of the Houchens' family in February 1993 when Jimmie Gipson, who had been with the company since 1965, was elected to the posts of president and chief executive officer. A few months later, he succeeded Ruel Houchens as chairman of the board. During this transition period, the board toyed with the idea of taking the company public, going so far as to draw up a prospectus, but in the end the elected to shelve the idea. Under new management, Houchens now made a concerted effort to expand its private-label line, an industry growth area in which the company lagged behind its competition. Immediate plans were launched to double the number of items it currently offered to 300, with a further goal of increasing to 800 products in five years. Moreover, Houchens initiated plans to offer 300 to 400 health and beauty care products under the Home Best label.

Late in the 1990s, Houchens faced a challenge from well-financed grocery chains that began to open megastores in excess of 200,000 square feet in size. In order to compete, Houchens began to pursue a counter-strategy of opening smaller Save-A-Lot stores, in the 10,000-square-foot range, many of which were

Key Dates:

1917: Ervin G. Houchens opens his first store.
1931: The grocery chain begins with the opening of three stores in Glasgow, Kentucky.
1945: Bowling Green Wholesale, Inc. is formed as a parent corporation.
1960: The first Houchens supermarket opens.
1972: The company's name is changed to Houchens Industries.
1983: Ervin Houchens retires at age 85.
1988: The business becomes employee owned.
1990: Houchens opens its first Save-A-Lot store.
1992: Ervin Houchens dies.
2001: Commonwealth Brands, Inc. is acquired.

located in the shadow of the retail giants. Other Houchens stores, because of their smaller size, were able to open inside neighborhoods rather than in the fringe areas that megastores targeted because of real estate limitations. The company found that no matter where their units were located they were able to find a niche with customers who felt that the megastores were simply too big and preferred shopping at a smaller supermarket for certain everyday products. As a result, Houchens saved money on a number of levels. Fewer employees were needed to run the stores, and real estate costs were lower because the company was often able to take advantage of abandoned retail centers. Houchens also began to diversify beyond its core holdings of Houchens Markets and Save-A-Lot outlets. The Tobacco Shoppe discount cigarette venture, operating out of Save-A-Lot stores, was launched in 1997. In May 1998, Houchens acquired the 42-unit convenience store chain Jr. Food Stores, Inc. Less than a year later, Houchens acquired Southern Recycling, Inc., a Bowling Green company that had a long history with Houchens. Its founder, David Bradford, originally operated a parking lot sweeping business, and one of his major customers was Houchens. Bradford realized he could make extra money from the discarded corrugated boxes he found in the park lots by baling them and selling them to a local paper mill. In 1981, he started Southern Recycling, and over the years expanded his operation to the recycling of iron products and other metals, as well as a curbside recycling operation.

In the year 2000, Houchens became involved in the construction industry when it acquired Stewart and Richey Construction Company, a 200-employee, 14-division full-service business operating in Kentucky and Tennessee. Like Southern Recycling, it too became a wholly owned subsidiary of Houchens, as did Center of Insurance, acquired in September 2000. Center of Insurance, in operation since 1948, was a full-service insurer, offering business, personal, life, and health

insurance, as well as surety bonds to customers in central Kentucky and Tennessee. Furthermore, in 2000, Houchens remained active in growing its main business, acquiring two Foodland Stores in Kentucky, as well as opening two new Save-A-Lot stores in New York and Virginia and acquiring nine other Save-A-Lots in Alabama and Georgia.

Houchens continued to add to its supermarket chains in 2001, when it opened a new Save-A-Lot store in Niagara Falls, New York, and acquired seven existing operations in West Virginia and Georgia. The company also took over a Piggly Wiggly Store in Tompkinsville, Kentucky, and subsequently converted it to the IGA brand. Several months later Houchens' IGA operation expanded to four other Kentucky communities, and additional IGA stores were purchased in 2002. In the meantime, the company acquired another 35 Save-A-Lot stores, adding two new states, Texas and Illinois, to its area of operation. Houchens' effort at diversification also took a major step forward with the August 2001 acquisition of Commonwealth Brands, the fifth largest American cigarette manufacturer in terms of sales volume. It produced cigarettes under such brand names as USA Gold, Montclair, Malibu, Natural Blend, Riveria, and Sonoma. For Houchens, Commonwealth Brands served as an ideal complement to its Tobacco Shoppe operations. A year later, in August 2002, Houchens took a step that might prove a key to future diversification when it entered into a partnership agreement with Remington Capital LLC, a boutique investment banking firm. The two parties agreed to jointly acquire manufacturing businesses which would then be managed by the principals of Remington Capital.

Principal Subsidiaries

Center of Insurance; Commonwealth Brands, Inc.; Houchens Properties; Southern Recycling Inc.; Stewart and Richey Construction Co.

Principal Competitors

The Kroger Co.; K-VA-T Food Stores, Inc.; Winn-Dixie Stores, Inc.

Further Reading

Dowdell, Stephen, "Red Food to Sell Houchens to Employees," *Supermarket News,* August 1, 1988, p. 1.
Fernandez, Jennifer, "Cigarette Company Sold Again," *Greensboro News & Record,* July 21, 2001, p. A1.
Redding, Rick, "A-Lot of Market Expansion," *Business First of Louisville,* February 23, 1998.
Rommel, Stephanie, "Houchens Industries," *Lane Report,* August 2002.

—Ed Dinger

John Laing plc

133 Page Street
London NW7 2ER
United Kingdom
Telephone: (20) 8959-3636
Fax: (20) 8906-5297
Web site: http://www.laing.com

Public Company
Incorporated: 1920
Employees: 5,656
Sales: £1.38 million ($1.58 billion) (2001)
Stock Exchanges: London
Ticker Symbol: LNGO
NAIC: 23321 Single Family Housing Construction

With over 150 years of experience under its belt, John Laing plc operates with two main divisions—the Laing Homes Group and Laing Investments. The Home unit constructs a wide range of residential housing in the United Kingdom as well as in the United States through WL Homes LLC. Laing constructs nearly 1,300 units per year, from simple one-bedroom apartments to £1 million luxury homes. Through its Investments arm, Laing deals with infrastructure projects related to the transportation, health and education, defense, and utilities industries. The company provides development, financing, construction, and service operation through this segment. During the early years of the new century, the company made significant changes to its operations by selling off both its Construction and Property divisions, along with a portion of its stake in WL Homes. In 2002, Sir Martin Laing—fifth-generation descendant of David Laing—retired, leaving Bill Forrester as executive chairman.

Early Beginnings: Mid- to Late 1880s

After building his first house, David Laing worked in the village repairing the church, digging wells, and engaging in other small jobs to maintain his livelihood. His eldest son, James, born in 1816, joined him upon finishing school. It appears that James Laing would have been content to carry on as a repairman and minor builder like his father, but his marriage in 1841 to Ann Graham, who had her eyes on the future, changed

James Laing's life. She convinced him to hire permanent employees and buy a plot of land for £20. In his spare time, Laing built a house on the plot; Ann helped by leading a team of their children in hauling rocks up the hill from a river bed. He finished the house in 1848 and sold it the same year, thus giving birth to the Laing construction firm.

The £150 proceeds from that first sale financed construction of two more houses on the same piece of land. James and Ann raised their family in one of the houses and sold the other. It is uncertain why in 1867 James sold everything and moved the family to Carlisle, where he worked as a laborer until he managed to start another business of his own. Again, the eldest son joined his father in business; John Laing, born in 1842, worked as a stonecarver for his father.

When James Laing died in 1882, John Laing took over the business and began to procure larger contracts for public projects such as the Carlisle electricity works and repairs on the local castle. Under John Laing, the business began to produce its own building materials. Laborers dug clay, made bricks by hand, and fired them in a kiln on the construction site. The business remained relatively small and confined to the Carlisle area until the fourth Laing took over.

John Laing's son John William Laing, born in 1879, was active in the business before he was 20 years old, so active that the firm changed its name to John Laing and Son. Ann Laing, by now quite advanced in age and feeling that her family was suitably established, wanted her grandson to go into a more genteel field than construction. Unaware that the young man was a budding construction tycoon, she tried to keep him out of the business. In a peculiar reversal of the norm, John William Laing rebelled against his grandmother by staying in the family firm.

The construction industry in Great Britain experienced great growth in the first decade of this century. During this period Laing procured many contracts for public works, including the Uldale reservoir and the Barrow sewer.

Expansion Efforts: 1910s–1930s

By 1910, John William Laing was the sole proprietor of the firm and had begun to organize it into the successful interna-

Company Perspectives:

Laing is an innovative company that is embracing the opportunities presented in our rapidly changing world: yet it is one that can do this with the benefit of over 150 years of experience. Our aim is to give our customers a service which spans the entire development, management, and operation of infrastructure, housing, and other accommodation. A service which is second to none. Recognized for the quality of our products and services, we are constantly developing and investing in new skills and systems to support their continuous improvement.

tional business it is today. He hired more employees and started accepting larger and more distant contracts, especially for factory construction. Laing was very concerned about preparing accurate cost estimates, maintaining strict control over the construction workers, and using scientific methods. He wanted to know about every aspect of construction, even at times living on building sites and learning such skills as bricklaying, masonry, and how to inspect each laborer's work.

Laing devised his cost-estimating technique with William Sirey, a clerk in the firm. It consisted of sending trained estimators to the site to prepare a detailed analysis of every phase of the job. As a result, Laing's quotes were more accurate than those of his competitors. The system additionally helped the firm reduce the builder's standard problem of surprise costs surfacing during construction. Estimators remain important in the company that was among the first to apply cost-control procedures systematically.

During World War I, the company received a series of British government contracts for war works. Laing built naval armament testing stations, an armament factory and workers' accommodations in Gretna, an aerodrome, and a riveting school. By the end of the war, John Laing & Son was a substantially larger firm with an intricate and invaluable web of contacts in government departments.

In 1920, the firm became a limited company and opened offices in London. Two years later, the headquarters moved from Carlisle to a 13-acre site in Northwest London at Mill Hill. Now in national competition for construction work, the company won contracts for the Middlesex County Hospital, the Federation of British Industries House, office blocks, pumping stations, power stations, and an army camp.

The postwar housing shortage led to a significant amount of business for the company, which built many public housing blocks for the Local Authorities while also building houses for sale to the public. A subsidiary company, Laing's Properties Ltd., owned and managed large blocks of Laing-built flats. Laing's largest source of work, however, was the Air Ministry, for which the company built aerodromes, airfields, equipment depots, and the underground headquarters for the Bomber Command of World War II. The company began constructing three new aerodromes in October 1939 and 14 more the next year. In the process, Laing developed expertise in runway construction that would prove lucrative during the war years.

World War II brought contracts for a total of 54 aerodromes, including hangars, runways, offices, and housing. Work on ordinance factories, power stations, coal mines, and part of the floating harbor used in the D-Day invasion of France also made significant contributions to Laing profits during the war.

Postwar Growth

The fifth generation of Laings, William Kirby Laing and James Maurice Laing, joined the firm before World War II. In 1950, the company established its first regional center, in Bristol. Two years later the company went public and took the name John Laing & Sons (Holdings) Ltd. The family and its trusts and charities held the bulk of the shares. John Laing became the chairman, and his sons became joint managing directors. By this time, the number of employees was up to 10,000, and every site had a quality supervisor.

Postwar contracts included schools, the Prestwick and Glasgow airports, factories, the Windscale and Berkeley nuclear power stations, and more than 10,000 houses. The firm continued the coal mining it had begun during the war, extracting 12,555 tons in 1947. In 1953, net assets reached £6.6 million, and the company employed 15,000 people at its building sites and offices.

John Laing retired in 1957 and was knighted two years later. Paternalistic and devout, he served as president of the London Bible College; helped establish the Salisbury Bible House in what is now Harare, Zimbabwe; and had his company build the Coventry Cathedral and return the profits to the church. While he was known during his time at the helm of the firm for providing every construction site a welfare officer to look after meals, movies, whist drives, and religious services for the laborers, it was reported that he could also be harsh. He once reportedly fined a man for going to the pub during lunch. He died in 1978 at age 98.

Under William Kirby Laing and James Maurice Laing, the company continued on the successful path the men's father had planned, winning contracts for more power stations and expanding into road construction while continuing to build houses. In 1985, Martin Laing, of the family's sixth generation in construction, became chairman. That year, the company won contracts totaling almost £27 million.

Martin Laing determined that the company, now Britain's largest construction firm, should begin to diversify. With an £84 million cash reserve, Laing had room to experiment. Diversification projects included building supermarkets at airports and creating a new water treatment company, called Water Services, set up as a joint venture with the French company Lyonnaise des Eaux. Martin Laing believed the skills the company gained from the experience of installing its own elaborate computer system could be the basis of a profitable service. Consequently, in 1987 the company established its Energy, Technology, and Environment division, which offered high-technology services, from computer-aided road design to nuclear waste processing.

The company's other divisions continued to be successful as well. Profits rose steadily in the 1980s, from £30.3 million in 1984 to £38.1 in 1986, with each subsidiary doing correspondingly well. Home construction in the United Kingdom, Saudi Arabia, Oman, the United Arab Emirates, Iraq, Spain, and California was now one of the major sources of the company's

Key Dates:

1848: James Laing and his wife Ann build and sell their first house.

1882: Laing's son John takes over the business.

1920: John Laing becomes a limited company and opens offices in London.

1939: The company begins constructing aerodromes as part of the war effort during World War II.

1952: The firm goes public under the name John Laing & Sons (Holdings) Ltd.

1978: John Laing dies.

1987: An Energy, Technology, and Environmental division is established as part of a diversification effort.

1999: The company manages the construction of the Millennium Dome.

2001: John Laing sells its Construction Division.

2002: Laing Property is sold; Sir Martin Laing retires.

growth, although there were some problems with non-payment by clients in Saudi Arabia. This depressed share prices somewhat. Nevertheless, the company's participation in several major projects the British government planned for the late 1980's and early 1990's preserved Laing's leadership of the United Kingdom construction industry into the early 1990s.

Restructuring for the Future: 1990s and Beyond

The remainder of the 1990s and the early years of the new century saw drastic changes for Laing's operations however. By 1997, the company operated with four main divisions—construction, homes, property, and investments. That year, both sales and profits increased over 1996 figures due in part to the completion of the Hong Kong Convention and Exhibition Centre. That year, the company was also awarded the contract for the Millennium Stadium at Cardiff Arms Park, a contract that would prove costly.

As the company celebrated its 150th anniversary in 1998, it faced falling profits due to cost overruns with the Millennium project and continued problems within its construction division related to competition and overcapacity. The company focused on its housing activities and merged its U.S. operations with Watt Residential Partners, which became WL Homes LLC. It also continued to diversify its offerings in the residential housing industry and acquired a 20 percent interest in upscale home builder Octagon Group Ltd. The company was also heavily involved the United Kingdom's Private Finance Initiative (PFI). In fact, the company took part in one of the first PFI projects in the UK when it was contracted to construct and maintain the Second Severn Crossing, a cable bridge connecting England and Wales. The project was completed in 1996.

In 1999, Laing reported positive results as the UK housing market strengthened. That year the company purchased a controlling interest in the Chiltern Rail franchise. The construction division, however, continued to falter. As such, Laing set plans in motion to reposition itself as it entered the new century. During 2000, the company announced it would sell its construction business, which suffered a loss of £88.9 million that year.

The unit was sold to O'Rourke plc in October 2001. Laing also sold its property development division in early 2002 and also began to divest its interest in WL Homes in order to focus on its home building operations in the United Kingdom. Overall, the company divested £122 million in assets in order to reduce debt.

Laing, which by 2002 had transformed itself into two main divisions—homes and investments—underwent yet another change when Sir Martin Laing retired in early 2002. Bill Forrester, a company director, took over as executive chairman. The new leader commented on the company's restructuring actions in a 2002 *The Western Mail* article, stating, "We are now better positioned to take the group forward, building on the trading strength and established market positions of our continuing businesses."

Indeed, the company secured profits in the first half of 2002 after reporting a £24.7 million loss in 2001. Management remained optimistic that its repositioning would pay off in the long term. While there was speculation in the investment world that Laing would sell off its homes division, the company gave no indication that it planned to cut its operations further. With over 150 years of experience behind it, Laing would no doubt remain a player on the UK real estate and construction scene for years to come.

Principal Subsidiaries

John Laing Homes plc; Laing Homes Ltd.; Beechcroft Developments Ltd.; Octagon Group Ltd.; Laing Investment Ltd.; Severn River Crossing plc (35%); Altram LTR Ltd. (33.33%); Altram (Manchester) Ltd. (26.1%); M40 Trains Ltd. (84.36%); Octagon Healthcare Holdings (Norwich) Ltd. (20%); Defence Management Holdings Ltd. (50%); UK Highways Services Ltd. (19%); Hyder Investments Ltd.; Laser Ltd. (50%); UK Highways plc (50%); UK Highways M40 Holdings Ltd. (50%); UK Highways A55 Holdings Ltd. (50%); Countryroute Ltd.; Coastal Clear Water Holdings Ltd. (50%); Services Support Ltd.; Education Support Ltd.; Modus Services Holdings Ltd. (40%); City Greenwich Lewisham Rail plc (40%); Meridan Hospital Company Ltd. (50%); John Laing Services Ltd.

Principal Divisions

Laing Homes Group; Laing Investments.

Principal Competitors

Amey plc; George Wimpey plc; Taylor Woodrow plc.

Further Reading

Coad, Roy, *The Biography of Sir John W. Laing, CBE*, London: Hodder and Stoughton, 1979.

Cook, Andy, "Penalty Time for Laing," *Building*, November 13, 1998, p. 18.

Evans, Graeme, "Construction Arm Pushes Laing Into the Red," *The Western Mail*, March 19, 2002.

Harrison, Godfrey, *Life and Belief in the Experience of John W. Laing CBE*, London: Hodder and Stoughton, 1954.

Sall, Keren, "Laing's Profits Up 41%," *Contract Journal*, September 24, 1997.

—update: Christina M. Stansell

The Judge Group, Inc.

2 Bala Plaza, Suite 800
Bala Cynwyd, Pennsylvania 19004
U.S.A.
Telephone: (610) 667-7700
Fax: (610) 667-1058
Web site: http://www.judge.com

Public Company
Incorporated: 1970
Employees: 307
Sales: $103.06 million (2002)
Stock Exchanges: NASDAQ
Ticker Symbol: JUDG
NAIC: 541512 Computer Systems Design Services
    Company

The Judge Group, Inc. provides staffing services on a contract and permanent placement basis through branch locations located in 14 U.S. cities. The company specializes in supplying professionally trained personnel to companies involved in information technology, engineering, pharmaceutical, biotechnical, and other high-technology fields. The Judge Group augments its staffing services with a range of Web-based software used in the management of personnel.

Origins

The Judge Group was founded by Martin Judge, a Villanova University graduate who earned his Bachelor of Science degree in business administration in 1968. Two years after leaving Villanova, Martin Judge started what would become known as The Judge Group, forming the company in March 1970 and incorporating it in June 1970. The company started as a staffing services company, providing personnel trained in engineering and other high-technology fields to corporations on a permanent basis. The permanent placement of professionally trained personnel gave the company its footing in the business world, but in later years The Judge Group expanded beyond its home state of Pennsylvania and diversified its business activities, creating a more complex, significantly larger firm than The Judge Group

of the 1970s. The story of The Judge Group's development revolves around its efforts to become a larger, more complex company, a process that, as Martin Judge would later concede, was a struggle.

Before Judge and his management team grappled with problems stemming from rapid growth, they enjoyed years of consistent and impressive financial performance. In 1982, the company began recording appreciable sales growth, racking up 30 percent increases in its revenue, compounded annually—a pace it would maintain for 17 years. In 1985, The Judge Group moved into the information technology (IT) sector by providing IT personnel on a contract basis, an important and lasting addition to the company's business scope. In the early 1990s, the company greatly expanded its geographic presence by establishing a national division in 1991 in Foxborough, Massachusetts. Through its national division, The Judge Group provided IT, engineering, and scientific personnel to larger corporations on a contract basis.

As the company was strengthening the range and geographic reach of its contract and permanent placement services, it also added another facet to its business. The Judge Group began providing networking, imaging, and document management services, as well as selling computer hardware and software products. This segment of the company's business was initially created to design networks using the company's private label personal computer products, which were sold to the educational market. The potential of the business was hobbled, however, by low profit margins in the educational market. To increase profitability, The Judge Group entered the document imaging business—an area of particular importance to Martin Judge—in 1988.

A Plan for Growth Formed in 1995

Martin Judge decided in early 1995 to greatly accelerate the growth of his privately-held company. Part of the strategy aimed at expansion included a company reorganization, as well as the addition of new services, the completion of strategic acquisitions, and geographic expansion. Beginning in early 1995, the company added sales, marketing, administrative, and engineering personnel to its four existing regional offices, as well as to its national

Company Perspectives:

The Judge Group's market strategy is focused on creating multiple revenue streams that take advantage of the many service-specific niches within the IT, engineering, and scientific staffing marketplace. These proven revenue streams originate from sources such as temporary contract assignment, permanent staffing placement, Web-based staffing platforms, Web-based recruiting platforms, and proprietary software for on-site staffing management. These niches have been targeted because they represent a combination of an established market, profit growth, and strong profit margins. With over three decades of experience in integrating IT staffing services with forefront technology, the Company has successfully identified and developed these market niches into profitable revenue streams.

division in Foxborough. To further support the expected increase in business, The Judge Group opened a fifth regional office, establishing it in Edison, New Jersey.

Part of Martin Judge's desire to accelerate expansion could be found in encouraging growth projections for the industry segments in which his company operated. Industrywide, the market for technical and computer contract staffing services was growing robustly, with revenues swelling from $5.7 billion in 1993 to $9.2 billion in 1995. Industry analysts were predicting overall revenues to reach $11.4 billion in 1996. From this industry segment, The Judge Group collected its sales in two ways, depending on whether the personnel provided to the corporations were placed permanently or on a contract basis. Temporary placements generally lasted between six and 12 weeks, in which case The Judge Group billed its client on an hourly basis. In 1995, the company had 1.3 million billable hours, which, at an average rate of $38.99 per hour, accounted for nearly 36 percent of the company's total revenues. Clients for The Judge Group's permanent placement services were charged a one-time fee, usually one percent for each thousand dollars of the salary of the person being hired.

The expansion-oriented strategy implemented in 1995 also included a series of acquisitions, which enabled the company to quickly increase its portfolio of services. The company's acquisition campaign was launched in February 1996 with the purchase of DataImage Inc., a Hartford, Connecticut-based provider of imaging and document-management services. In September 1996, the company struck twice, acquiring Berkeley Associates Corp. and Systems Automation. The purchase of Systems Automation enabled The Judge Group to garner imaging and network clients in the Boston area, helping the company to expand beyond its primary base of customers in the mid-Atlantic States. The addition of Berkeley, a provider of IT training services since 1980, gave the company the ability to provide training on a range of computer network and software applications through three offices in Pennsylvania, Virginia, and Maryland.

Following the completion of the three acquisitions of 1996, the company's reorganization was complete, finalized in October 1996. Martin Judge was not finished with his expansion

strategy, however. To help pay for the acquisitions and to develop a national sales force, as well as to obtain additional capital for further expansion, he planned to convert to public ownership. Hoping to raise as much as $35 million, Martin Judge filed with the Securities and Exchange Commission for an initial public offering (IPO) of stock. The Judge Group's IPO was completed in February 1997, raising $21 million. With the proceeds from the IPO, the company was able to retire $12 million of debt incurred from the acquisitions, but its new status as a publicly-traded company exposed The Judge Group to the dangers of falling short of Wall Street's expectations. For Martin Judge, the problems stemming from expanding before the investment community's eyes were about to surface.

Strategic Challenges in 1997

Several years after The Judge Group completed its IPO, Martin Judge conceded he and his management team had ''lost focus when we initially went public,'' according to a March 12, 2001 interview with *Wall Street Transcript*. The company's revenues had jumped from $68 million in 1995 to $100 million in 1997, but profitability was another matter. During the company's first fiscal quarter after its IPO, it failed to meet financial projections for its information management solutions division. The information management solutions division, which contributed nearly 20 percent of The Judge Group's total sales, posted a loss of $900,000. Wall Street, rarely willing to ignore the first indication of financial trouble, reacted quickly, causing the company's stock, which debuted at $7.50 per share, to plummet to $3 within two months. Martin Judge explained what had happened to the *Philadelphia Business Journal* in a May 29, 1998 interview, stating that the company's sales managers ''gave me false numbers.'' He accepted responsibility, however, conceding, ''It was my fault; I was company president,'' before adding, ''but I was out on the road talking to lawyers and investment bankers and when I got back and really looked at things, I saw they were wrong.''

In the wake of the financial loss, Martin Judge turned his attention to curing the problems at the company's information management solutions division. The division's payroll was reduced, ultimately saving the company $100,000 per month, and, in March 1998, new divisional leadership took the helm. The changes assuaged investor fear somewhat, helping the company's stock to rise to $6 per share by May 1998, but the company was far from cleansing its reputation on Wall Street. According to industry pundits, The Judge Group was having a difficult time attracting the investment community to a company with a document management and computer imaging unit tied to a business whose reputation had been made in providing staffing services. The incongruity was exacerbated in some observers' eyes by Martin Judge's reputation as an iconoclast. One analyst, as quoted in the May 29, 1998 issue of the *Philadelphia Business Journal,* explained the perception: ''Mr. Judge is a cowboy. He doesn't follow the normal rules of being a chief executive officer. He thinks outside of the box and he's hardheaded in what he believes. And what he believes is that imaging, or what used to be known as information processing, and document management is the wave of the future.'' The broker continued: ''He believes it's worthwhile in investing in this technology, which so far hasn't produced bottom-line results. It's been rather a drag on the rest of the company.''

In the midst of the misfortune following the IPO, Martin Judge did not waver from his conviction that The Judge Group's involvement in document technologies would ultimately pay off. One market research and consulting firm's examination of the document technologies market supported Martin Judge's visionary stance. Market revenues were expected to increase from $13.9 billion in 1998 to $33.6 billion by 2002, while the document management market niche was expected to triple, jumping from $2.9 billion to $9.5 billion during the same period. Taking every facet of The Judge Group's business scope into consideration, the company—operating in what was categorized as the information technology services sector—was competing in a $230 billion market.

After restructuring the information management solutions division, Martin Judge was ready to resume expansion via acquisition. In March 1998, the company paid $4.3 million to acquire Information Solutions Inc., an information technology staffing and solutions provider with offices in Detroit and the United Kingdom. The following month, The Judge Group purchased Atlanta, Georgia-based Cella Associates, paying $1.3 million for Cella's expertise in supplying executive personnel to the food industry. In May 1998, the company maintained its steady acquisition pace, acquiring On-Site Solutions, an Irvine, California-based provider of integrated work flow solutions. In July 1998, the company acquired computer technology reseller AOP Solutions Inc., a $2.3 million-in-sales company that assisted in the installation of computer networks and digital-imaging equipment. As Martin Judge orchestrated his acquisition spree during the first half of 1998, he also opened four new IT staffing offices, establishing one branch location in New York City and three offices in Southern states.

1999 Divestiture Hints at Recovery

By the end of the 1990s, the time had arrived for Martin Judge to reassess his commitment to Judge Imaging Systems, the information management solutions division that had long been a source of trouble. Roughly a year after attempting to strengthen the division with the acquisition of On-Site Solutions, Martin Judge decided to discontinue operations at the division. The imaging and document management business was dissolved in June 1999, concurrent with the closure of several unprofitable offices. As The Judge Group effected yet another reorganization, branch locations were shuttered in Seattle; Hartford, Connecticut; Needham, Massachusetts; and Melbourne, Florida. The dispositions left the company focused on IT staffing services and, through JUDGE.com, on Internet, Web-based products that assisted in human capital management.

Once The Judge Group's unprofitable assets were divested, the company began to exhibit consistent financial performance. By early 2001, the company had either met or exceeded analysts' growth expectations for six consecutive quarters, helping to improve its tarnished reputation on Wall Street. Looking ahead, Martin Judge remained optimistic, having lost none of his belief in the strength of The Judge Group. Although he intended to expand the company's IT staffing services business, particularly on the West Coast, his faith in the benefits of expanding via acquisition had been shaken. "I think we've learned through experience that acquisitions can hurt you more than they can help you," he remarked in a March 12, 2001 interview with the *Wall Street Transcript*. "With the scars that we have and the scars that our industry has, I think after 31 years the acquisition approach will be one handled very prudently."

Principal Subsidiaries

JUDGE.com.

Principal Competitors

Alternative Resources Corporation; CDI Corp.; Personnel Group of America, Inc.

Further Reading

Croghan, Lore, "Short Bits," *Crain's New York Business,* June 1, 1998, p. 28.

Gotlieb, Andy, "Amid Clouds, Judge Thinks It Has Weathered the Storm," *Philadelphia Business Journal,* May 3, 2002, p. 3.

Hals, Tom, "Judge Group Aims to Raise $35 Million through IPO," *Philadelphia Business Journal,* November 8, 1996, p. 5.

Kasrel, Deni, "Judge Group Is Laboring to Restore Wall St.'s Faith," *Philadelphia Business Journal,* May 29, 1998, p. 1.

Williams, Fred O., "Philadelphia Firm Buys AOP Solutions," *The Buffalo News,* July 10, 1998, p. B9.

—Jeffrey L. Covell

iՈ KAJIMA CORPORATION

Kajima Corporation

2-7, Motoakasaka 1-chrome
Minato-ku, Tokyo 107-8388
Japan
Telephone: (813) 3 404-3311
Fax: (813) 3 470-1444
Web site: http://www.kajima.co.jp

Public Company
Incorporated: February 22, 1930 as the Kajima
    Construction Company
Employees: 11,664
Sales: ¥1.9 trillion ($15.4 billion) (2001)
Stock Exchanges: Tokyo Osaka Nagoya London
Ticker Symbol: 1812
NAIC: 234120 Bridge and Tunnel Construction; 234930
    Industrial Nonbuilding Structure Construction; 234990
    All Other Heavy Construction

The Kajima Corporation is one of the oldest and largest construction companies in Japan. The firm's services include design, engineering, construction, and real estate development. Kajima builds high-rise structures, railways, power plants, dams, and bridges. Its subsidiaries are located throughout Asia, Europe, and North America. A downturn in the construction industry during the latter half of the 1990s prompted Kajima to expand its operations to the environmental sector, specifically waste treatment, water treatment, soil rehabilitation, and environmental consulting.

Early History

Kajima was founded in 1840 by Iwakichi Kajima, an innovative carpenter and designer. Construction remained the family trade of Kajima's sons, who witnessed the transformation of Japan from a isolated nation into a developing regional power after the Meiji Restoration in 1868.

The industrial modernization policies of the Meiji government created a demand for newer and larger factories and buildings as well as railroad lines and tunnels. Kajima built the first European-style commercial building in Japan, an office structure for the Hong Kong-based Jardine Matheson & Company, and entered the field of railroad construction in 1880 under the name Kajima Gumi. The company quickly established a reputation for excellence in railroad bed construction and tunneling. As Japanese industry continued to grow, Kajima Gumi completed a greater number of industrial and infrastructural projects.

Kajima Gumi began construction of hydroelectric dams during the 1920s. Relatively unaffected by the worldwide economic depression, Kajima Gumi became a public company on February 22, 1930, capitalized at three million yen. With the involvement of private stockholders, the company was able to devote more capital to larger projects. With a larger scale of operations, Kajima Gumi became active as an industrial contractor.

Extreme right-wing elements of the Japanese military rose to power during the 1930s, advocating a neo-mercantilist economy and Japanese colonial domination of East Asia and the western Pacific. As part of their "quasi-war economy," large industrial projects were undertaken which were intended to augment Japan's war-making capabilities. Like many other Japanese companies, Kajima Gumi attempted to remain divorced from politics. However, because of the nature of its business, and the overwhelming coercive power of the militarists, the company became an active participant in the Japanese war effort.

Postwar Opportunities

Japan was so completely devastated by the war that it was largely unable to feed or rebuild itself. This created great opportunities for construction companies such as Kajima Gumi, who were needed to build new structures and repair others which had been damaged.

Kajima Gumi was reorganized under the commercial laws imposed by the Allied occupation commander and reestablished in 1947 as the Kajima Construction Company. Two years later, the company established the Kajima Institute of Construction Technology (KICT), where new construction materials and engineering technologies could be developed. The Institute, located in Tokyo's Chuo ward, employed 233 specialists and was the first private research institution of its kind in Japan.

In the early 1950s, Kajima began to design nuclear reactor complexes, which necessitated the expansion of the research institute. In 1956, the Institute was relocated to the Tokyo suburb of Chobu. The following year Kajima built the Number 1 reactor—Japan's first nuclear reactor—at the Japan Atomic Energy Research Institute's Ibarakiken complex.

Kajima completed Japan's first skyscraper, the 36-story Kasumigaseki Mitsui Building in 1956. Part of that building consisted of a Large Structure Testing (LST) laboratory, which helped Kajima to formulate new technologies for other larger, earthquake-resistant skyscrapers, such as the Shinjuku Mitsui Building (55 stories) and the Sunshine 60 Building (60 stories).

International Expansion: 1960s–1970s

During the 1960s, the company undertook an increasing number of projects outside Japan, constructing buildings and dams in Burma, Vietnam, and Indonesia. After establishing its reputation of excellence overseas, Kajima was chosen to complete a variety of projects in Taiwan, South Korea, the Philippines, Malaysia, Thailand, and Hong Kong.

The company's name was changed to the Kajima Corporation in 1970 to better reflect its international character and wide range of engineering services. New technologies developed by KICT were continually applied, particularly in the area of aseismic structures. The Institute built an "earthquake simulator" in 1974. A year later, a hydraulics laboratory was established which placed Kajima in a leading position among Japanese companies in dam, breakwater, and ocean platform construction.

Kajima was given full responsibility by the East German government to build the International Trade Center Building in East Berlin, free of government restrictions or demands that local companies be involved in the project. This project marked Kajima's emergence from East Asia. Projects in the United States, Turkey, Algeria, and Zaire followed.

As early as the 1960s, Kajima used shield tunnel borers, but KICT introduced new processes which improved the safety and efficiency of established tunneling methods, using water jets and concrete-spraying robots. Kajima also developed a shield tunnel borer capable of making sharp turns, and it was one of several companies involved in the construction of the 54 kilometer Seikan Tunnel, linking the Japanese islands of Honshu and Hokkaido. Tunneling work was completed in 1985 and the Seikan Tunnel project was finished three years later.

In 1982, the Kajima Corporation was awarded the Deming Prize for engineering excellence. During the 1980s, it continually received recognition for its achievements. By this time, Kajima held almost 1100 Japanese patents, 72 of which were registered in foreign countries.

In addition to its other major construction activities in the 1980s, Kajima worked on building a floating oil storage facility near Nagasaki capable of holding six million kiloliters (32.4 million barrels) of oil. The company was also working on an integrated method for decommissioning aging nuclear power plants, a service that would become increasingly important as nuclear power plants neared the end of their 40-year life spans.

During the 1980s, Kajima remained under family management. However, when Seiichi Kajima's marriage produced no sons, his daughter Ume married Morino Suke, a career diplomat and scholar who was adopted into the family and given the name Kajima. His first son, Shoichi Kajima, was the company's president until 1990, and a brother-in-law of both the chairman and honorary chairman. Akira Miyazaki was named president in 1990.

By the early 1990s, the Kajima Corporation was extremely competitive in railroad, dam, and other civil engineering projects. It also remained one of the strongest Japanese companies in the overseas markets. Kajima maintained an excellent financial situation with few liabilities and high earnings. The company's research institute and continued strength in the construction of nuclear power plants and earthquake-resistant skyscrapers were indispensable assets that secured the company's place in the Japanese industry.

It was at this time that the Japanese economy as a whole was experiencing strong growth. Kajima made key investments and demand in the construction industry was strong. In 1991, the firm's net income increased by more than 50 percent over the previous year. The positive financial results continued in 1992 as the firm completed construction on Tokyo East 21, a state-of-the-art office tower, hotel, and commercial complex.

Battling Economic Challenges: Late 1990s and Beyond

Japan's economy soon began deteriorating, which lead to a drop in demand for Kajima's services. Overall, the Asian economy was weakening and personal consumption was falling. The Great Hanshin Earthquake prompted an increase in reconstruction services in 1995; however, Kajima's fortunes, along with many large Japanese companies, faltered during the latter half of the 1990s. During this time period, the company focused on increasing the number of new contracts, promoting efficiency, and bolstering profitability. During 1998, revenues and gross profit fell.

The financial hardships continued and in 1999, Kajima was forced to post a $2.6 billion pretax loss due in part to the write off of bad loans and assets that the company had taken on during the early 1990s. That year the firm launched its "New Three Year Plan" that included strategies centered on enhancing marketing efforts, cost cutting, streamlining corporate operations, and improving research and development, along with improving the overall financial position of the company.

Key Dates:

1840: Iwakichi Kajima establishes a construction company.
1880: The company begins railroad construction under the name Kajima Gumi.
1930: Kajima Gumi goes public.
1947: The firm is reestablished as the Kajima Construction Company.
1949: The company establishes the Kajima Institute of Construction Technology—the first of its kind in Japan.
1957: Kajima builds Japan's first nuclear reactor.
1970: The firm changes its name to Kajima Corporation.
1985: The firm completes tunneling work for the Seikan Tunnel.
1991: Net income increases by over 50 percent.
1999: The company reports a loss of approximately $2.6 billion due to debt disposal; management launches the ''New Three Year Plan.''
2000: Kajima establishes an environmental division.

In response to the downturn in the construction industry, Kajima set its sights on diversification in the new century. In October 2000, the firm created an environmental division focused on waste and water treatment, soil rehabilitation, and environmental consulting. Kajima eyed the waste-to-resource industry as key to its future growth. Indeed, Japan's Ministry of Economy, Trade, and Industry believed that the market for waste treatment and recycling in Japan would grow to ¥22 trillion by 2010.

During fiscal 2002, the company launched another management plan entitled the ''Next Three Year Plan.'' Japan's economy and financial condition continued to be problematic and while new government programs and reform promised relief, steady recovery had yet to be seen. As such, Kajima focused on improving its competitiveness by targeting the renovation, housing, and environmental industries. The company also began to develop new business ventures and continued with aggressive research and development activities. Bolstering profits from real estate and international operations and restructur-

ing organizational operations to improve overall profits were also key parts of the firm's strategy. While Kajima did indeed face a challenging future, Kajima management remained confident that the company would remain a leading contractor for years to come.

Principal Subsidiaries

Katabami Kogyo Co. Ltd.; Taiko Trading Co. Ltd.; Kajima Road Co. Ltd.; Nippon Foundation Engineering Co. Ltd.; Kajima Resort Corporation; Chemical Grouting Co. Ltd.; Kajima Institute Publishing Co. Ltd.; Kajimavision Productions Co. Ltd.; Japan Sea Works Co. Ltd.; Yaesu Book Center Co. Ltd.; Kajima Services Co. Ltd.; Kajima Leasing Corporation; Shinrinkohen Golf Club; Ilva Corporation; KOCAMB Co. Ltd.; F.R.C. Corporation; Kajima Mechatro Engineering Co. Ltd.; Kajima Karuizawa Resort Inc.; Kajima Hotel Enterprises Ltd.; Hotel Kajima no Mori; Act Technical Support Inc.; Kajima Aquatech Corporation; Clima-Teq Co. Ltd.; Kobori Research Complex Inc.; Kajima Tenant Planning Co. Ltd.; KRC Co. Ltd.; Armo Architects & Engineers; ARTES Corporation; Kajima Tokyo Kaihatsu Corporation; Nasu Resort Corporation; East Real Estate Co. Ltd.; Creative Life Corporation; Human Life Services Co. Ltd.; Kajima Tourist Co. Ltd.; Plus Alpha Ltd.; Engineer & Risk Services Corporation; Techno-Wave Corporation.

Principal Competitors

Obayashi Corp.; Shimizu Corp.; Taisei Corp.

Further Reading

''Japan's Kajima Books 337 Bln Yen Extra Loss in FY98,'' *AsiaPulse News*, March 31, 1999.
''Japan's Kajima Develops Continuous-Feed Soil Cleaning System,'' *AsiaPulse News*, September, 17, 2002.
''Japan's Kajima Develops Technology to Recycle Waste Concrete,'' *AsiaPulse News*, December 4, 2001.
''Japan's Kajima Yr to March Group Pretax Loss $2.6 Bln,'' *AsiaPulse News*, June 9, 1999.
Reina, Peter, and Gary Tulacz, ''No Keeping Contractors Home After They've Seen the World,'' *ENR*, August 25, 1997, p. 67.

—update: Christina M. Stansell

KANA®

Kana Software, Inc.

181 Constitution Drive
Menlo Park, California 94025
U.S.A.
Telephone: (650) 614-8300
Fax: (650) 614-8301
Web site: http://www.kana.com

Public Company
Incorporated: 1996 as Kana Communications, Inc.
Employees: 450
Sales: $86.9 million (2001)
Stock Exchanges: NASDAQ
Ticker Symbol: KANA
NAIC: 511210 Software Publishers

Kana Software, Inc. provides enterprise-level software solutions for customer relationship management (CRM) and enterprise relationship management (ERM). Initially, Kana's software focused on e-mail management and offered companies a way to automate large amounts of customer e-mail as well as to launch targeted outbound e-mail communications to their customers. Through a series of acquisitions of other software companies, Kana expanded its software to include a broad range of CRM and ERM applications, allowing the company to position itself as a single-source solution.

E-Mail Management Software: 1996–99

Kana Software, Inc. was founded in 1996 as Kana Communications, Inc. by sports enthusiast and entrepreneur Mark Gainey. Gainey had originally intended to launch a sports-themed Web business, but then he realized that there was an opportunity to help companies deal with large amounts of customer e-mail. Many of the sporting goods companies that he dealt with were ignoring e-mail messages because they had no efficient way of responding to them. Instead of developing a Web-based sporting goods business, Gainey founded Kana Communications with $27 million in financing to develop software that would make it easy for businesses to communicate with customers via e-mail and other Web-based communication channels.

Kana released its first e-mail management software in March 1998. In mid-1998 Kana released version 2.0 of its Customer Messaging System (CMS), an enterprise-class e-mail management application. Priced at $79,500 for a server with ten users, the Customer Messaging System enabled businesses to manage and respond to customer e-mail. Version 3.0 was released at the end of 1998 and added an optional module, Kana Direct, that created e-mail lists from specific message categories, thus giving the CMS outbound as well as inbound capabilities. With Kana Direct, companies could build customized lists and send targeted e-mail messages. Other available modules included Kana Classify, which analyzed inbound messages and sorted them, and Kana Link, which let companies connect to other customer databases and exchange information with them. Pricing for version 3.0 started at $39,500.

From 1996 to 1999, Kana's software focused on managing inbound and outbound e-mail and other Web-based communications. Its software facilitated the delivery of specific and personalized messages to each customer. By mid-1999, the company had more than 100 customers, including eBay, eToys, Priceline.com, Ford Motor Company, and Northwest Airlines. Kana went public on September 22, 1999, offering 3.3 million shares at $15 each. The initial public offering (IPO) raised $44.6 million. In the previous two years, Kana reported losses of $1.4 million in 1997 and $7.4 million in 1998. In spite of the company's losses, its stock price rose to a high of $82 by the end of October.

Using 15 percent of its stock valued at $262 million, Kana acquired another e-mail marketing software publisher, Connectify. The acquisition enabled Kana to release version 4.0 of its e-mail management system. The release included an upgrade of Kana Response, which provided automated customer service, as well as Kana Commerce, an application designed to facilitate a range of transactions, and Kana Connect, which incorporated Connectify's technology. Customers could license Kana 4.0 starting at $50,000 or access it as an outsourced service from $5,000 a month.

Before the end of 1999, Kana acquired two more software companies that specialized in providing Web-based customer assistance. They were Princeton, New Jersey-based Business

Evolution, Inc., which was acquired for $140 million in stock, and San Mateo, California-based NetDialog, Inc., which was acquired for $90 million in stock. The acquisitions increased Kana's workforce to approximately 350 employees. Kana announced that the acquisitions would enable it to market two new products: Kana Realtime, which was based on Business Evolution's technology and enabled companies to communicate with customers in real time over the Web, and Kana Assist, an online self-service product based on NetDialog's technology that helped customers obtain information from a company's web site.

Kana also opened regional offices in Munich, Germany, and Sydney, Australia, in December 1999. The company had previously opened a London office in January 1999. Its European customers included Dutch KLM Airways, Iceland Air, and British Airways' Travel Shops. Its Australian office was designed to provide customer support in Australia and New Zealand and serve as a prelude to expansion into Asian markets. While Kana gained more than 300 customers during 1999, it posted much heavier losses. For the year it lost $118.7 million on revenue of $14.1 million.

An Expanded Line of Software: 2000–01

In February 2000, Kana and Silknet Software Inc. of Manchester, New Hampshire, announced they would merge in a stock-for-stock deal valued at $4.2 billion. The two companies offered complementary e-business and CRM software solutions, with Kana offering online customer communications solutions for marketing, sales, and service, and Silknet providing an e-business platform and applications. Silknet's customer-facing applications allowed e-commerce customers as well as customer service representatives to view a customer's complete history, including their order status, previous inquiries, and preferences, among other items. The merger, which was completed in July 2000, increased Kana's workforce to 600 employees in the United States, Europe, and Australia. By mid-2000 Kana had more than 800 employees.

Kana continued to expand internationally by opening an office in Tokyo and selecting a vendor to market and distribute a Japanese version of its CRM software, Kana Response. In October, the company formed a Japanese subsidiary, Kana Japan. In the United States, Kana formed an extensive marketing and development relationship with IBM Corp. that called

for the two companies to integrate their e-business software into an overall enterprise relationship management solution, with IBM also reselling Kana's e-business software system. As a result of its merger with Silknet, Kana expanded its focus from CRM to what it called ERM, or enterprise relationship management. ERM included everything from data analysis to personalization to customer service.

In October 2000, Kana announced the release of Kana 6, which incorporated technologies acquired from Silknet. Kana 6 expanded Kana's e-mail management applications by adding more customer service capabilities for retail Web sites and e-businesses. Kana 6 included marketing and sales modules to manage product offerings to Web shoppers, giving customer service representatives access to customers' marketing preferences and history. It also included a virtual agent that served as an onscreen customer service representative to answer customers' questions. Kana 6 also supported computer-telephony integration. Pricing ranged from $50,000 to $250,000, with implementation for larger Global 2000 companies running to seven figures.

In January 2001 Jay Wood, former chairman and CEO of Silknet Software, became Kana's chairman and CEO when Michael McCloskey resigned for health reasons. It was under McCloskey's direction that Kana embarked on a string of acquisitions in 1999 and 2000 and expanded its CRM and ERM software offerings. At the time McCloskey resigned, Kana's workforce had grown to more than 1,000 employees. For 2000, Kana reported a 748 percent increase in revenue to $119.2 million, due primarily to the acquisition of Silknet. For the year, the company reported a pro forma net loss of $84.8 million, compared to a pro forma net loss of $32 million in 1999.

One of Wood's top priorities was to implement a restructuring plan that would cut expenses by $30 to $40 million annually. In March 2001, Kana cut its workforce across the board by 20 percent, laying off 220 employees. Other aspects of the restructuring included focusing on an integrated ERM software solution, realigning the company's sales force, reorganizing its professional services business, and reducing its real estate commitments. At the time, Kana's stock was trading near its 52-week low at less than $3 a share, well down from its 52-week high of $175.50 a share.

In April 2001, Kana announced it would acquire Broadbase Software, Inc. and change its name to Kana Software, Inc. Broadbase specialized in customer analytics software, something that was missing from Kana's ERM solution. The combined companies would have some 1,300 customers. Jay Wood became chairman, with Broadbase president and CEO Chuck Bay serving as president and CEO of the new company.

At the time of the announcement, both companies were experiencing financial difficulties. Kana anticipated slumping revenue, an increase in net loss per share, and a dwindling cash supply. Broadbase had recently posted a fourth quarter net loss of $87.9 million, and its stock was trading at less than $1 a share. Kana's stock had also plummeted to below $1 a share.

Like Kana, other companies providing CRM and ERM software solutions were anticipating revenue shortfalls for 2001, and analysts were predicting a shakeout in the CRM

Key Dates:

1996: Kana Communications, Inc. is founded to develop e-mail management software.
1999: Kana goes public in September, then acquires three smaller software companies: Connectify; Business Evolution, Inc.; and NetDialog, Inc.
2000: Kana merges with Silknet Software, Inc. in a transaction valued at $4.2 billion.
2001: Kana merges with Broadbase Software, Inc. and changes its name to Kana Software, Inc.

---

sector. The merger with Broadbase gave Kana an additional $130 million in cash, which the company desperately needed after reporting that it was down to its last $20 million in cash before the merger. However, Kana reported first quarter revenue of $24.2 million, operating losses of $38.6 million, and a net loss of $752.9 million, which included restructuring costs, goodwill, and other one-time charges. As part of its cost-cutting efforts, Kana closed down Kana Online, the business unit that hosted its software as an application service provider (ASP).

Kana completed its merger with Broadbase at the end of June 2001. In the second half of 2001, Kana gained some support from IBM. As part of its strategic alliance with IBM, Kana integrated its Web-based products with IBM's Web-Sphere Commerce Suite. Kana also introduced several other new products, including a new call center CRM system that it characterized as the first Web-based, multichannel Java service software. Titled Kana Service 7 EJB, the software enabled call centers to handle complex inquiries and improve their service levels. Kana also introduced Service Analytics to measure and improve customer service operations at all customer touchpoints. It was based on Broadbase technology and was integrated into Kana's other customer service applications.

In the final two months of 2001, Kana gained an additional $55 million in equity financing from Technology Crossover Ventures and funds associated with Amerindo Investment Advisors. The investments served to reassure Kana's customers and enhance the company's long-term prospects. Kana also introduced its iCare Suite, which combined software technology from Kana and Broadbase to create modules for automating e-mail management, developing a knowledge base, generating reports, and saving customer histories.

For 2001, Kana reported revenue of $86.9 million, a net operating loss of $939.6 million, and a net loss of $942.9 million. Through the first half of 2002, many companies in the CRM software sector reported revenue shortfalls as spending on CRM and ERM software softened. In addition to Kana, which reported a second quarter decline in revenue from $23.6 million the previous year to $17.2 million, other CRM software companies with declining revenue included E.piphany Inc., Siebel Systems Inc., AskJeeves Inc., Applix Inc., and Aspect Communications Corp. Kana projected that third quarter revenue would be flat compared to the second quarter, while others in the sector expected things to get worse before they got better. According to some analysts, companies that would succeed in the CRM

and ERM sector would have to provide enhanced solutions that brought a quicker return on investment.

Principal Subsidiaries

Kana Japan.

Principal Competitors

Applix Inc.; AskJeeves Inc.; Aspect Communications Corp.; Blue Martini Software Inc.; E.piphany Inc.; FineGround Networks Inc.; Oracle Corp.; PeopleSoft Inc.; SAS Institute Inc.; Siebel Systems Inc.

Further Reading

Beizer, Doug, "How Can We Help You?" *PC Magazine,* July 1998, p. 40.

Callaghan, Dennis, "Bearish Market Chews up CRM Firms' Profits," *eWeek,* April 16, 2001, p. 37.

Clancy, Heather, "Battling for Share—Kana Enters e-CRM Fray," *Computer Reseller News,* July 10, 2000, p. 44.

——, "IBM, Kana Ink Development Pact," *TechWeb,* August 17, 2000.

Colkin, Eileen, "Integrated Kana Set to Offer Full E-CRM Suite," *InformationWeek,* July 2, 2001, p. 55.

Conlin, Rob, "IBM Helps Struggling Kana Hang On," *CRMDaily.com,* July 10, 2001, available at http://www.crmdaily.com.

——, "Kana and Silknet Announce $4.2B Merger," *E-Commerce Times,* February 7, 2000, available at http://www.ecommerce times.com.

——, "Kana Buys Broadbase for $71M," *E-Commerce Times,* April 10, 2001, available at http://www.ecommercetimes.com.

——, "Kana Expands Customer Support to Europe and Australia," *E-Commerce Times,* December 27, 1999, available at http://www.ecommercetimes.com.

——, "Kana Unwraps Java Call Center App," *CRMDaily.com,* May 30, 2001, available at http://www.crmdaily.com.

Degnan, Christa, "E-mail Tools Focus on Customer Relations," *PC Week,* October 18, 1999, p. 10.

Dembeck, Chet, "Kana Buys BEI and NetDialog," *E-Commerce Times,* December 7, 1999, available at http://www.ecommerce times.com.

Drucker, David, "CRM Coupling Aims to Bridge Customer Data," *InternetWeek,* February 14, 2000, p. 8.

Gareiss, Dawn, "Kana Makes Online Customer Service a Top Priority," *InformationWeek,* May 15, 2000, p. 78.

George, Tischelle, "Kana Deals Bolster Service Offerings," *Information Week,* December 13, 1999, p. 213.

Gollobin, Kelly, "Michael McCloskey–Kana," *Computer Reseller News,* November 6, 2000, p. 96.

Gonsalves, Antone, "Kana Readies New Version of I-CRM Suite," *TechWeb,* October 7, 2000.

Grygo, Eugene, "Kana, Silknet Merger Wares to Remain Viable," *InfoWorld,* February 14, 2000, p. 20.

Hall, Mark, "Emerging to Applause," *Computerworld,* June 12, 2000, p. 40.

Hibbard, Justin, "E-Mail Mining Tools," *Information Week,* December 14, 1998, p. 91.

Kuchinskas, Susan, "Acquisition Begets New Kana Software Offering," *Mediaweek,* October 4, 1999, p. 60.

Leibowitz, Alissa, "Kana Communications Inc.," *Venture Capital Journal,* November 1, 1999.

Morphy, Erika, "Kana Secures $55M in New Funding," *CRMDaily .com,* November 29, 2001, available at http://www.crmdaily.com.

Rodriguez, Karen, ''Software Firms Vying for Dominance,'' *The Business Journal,* April 2000, p. 3.

Songini, Marc L., ''CRM Market Appears Headed for Shakeout,'' *Computerworld,* April 16, 2001, p. 23.

——, ''Struggling CRM Vendor Closing ASP Unit,'' *Computerworld,* June 4, 2001, p. 14.

Sweat, Jeff, ''Kana and IBM Strike CRM Deal,'' *InformationWeek,* August 21, 2000, p. 44.

——, ''Kana Puts on a New Face,'' *InformationWeek,* October 23, 2000, p. 165.

Tillett, L. Scott, ''Kana Integrates E-Mail with Online Service,'' *InternetWeek,* October 16, 2000, p. 12.

Walker, Christy, ''Kana Gets a Handle on Customer Messages,'' *PC Week,* January 4, 1999, p. 45.

—David P. Bianco

PING®

Karsten Manufacturing Corporation

2201 West Desert Cove
Phoenix, Arizona 85029-4912
U.S.A.
Telephone: (602) 687-5000
Toll Free: (800) 474-6434
Fax: (602) 687-4482
Web site: http://www.pinggolf.com

Private Company
Incorporated: 1967
Employees: 750
Sales: $159.5 million (2000)
NAIC: 339920 Sporting and Athletic Goods
Manufacturing

Located in Phoenix, Arizona, Karsten Manufacturing Corporation is famous for its Ping golf clubs. Unlike other equipment makers, Karsten sells its clubs only through golf course pro shops, where customers are custom fitted. Because the privately owned company manufactures only when an order has been placed, it carries no inventory and is able to roll out new models with a minimum of lead time. Founded by engineer Karsten Solheim, the company has been at the forefront of golf innovation since the development of the Ping putter in the late 1950s. Despite its reputation for unsurpassed quality and technical expertise, the company has been eclipsed in recent years by more marketing-savvy competitors. Forced to adapt to changing conditions, a second generation of the Solheim family has taken control of the business, instituting a number of changes to forge a strong comeback. In addition to the design and manufacture of golf clubs, Karsten produces accessories, such as bags and apparel, and owns and operates Moon Valley Country Club in Phoenix. Karsten also owns several subsidiaries involved in the manufacturing process of its golf clubs. Because of their technical expertise these businesses have other commercial applications. Karsten Engineering, for instance, does research for clients such as NASA, IBM, and Motorola. Dolphin Inc., a foundry and brazing operation, not only casts putter and iron heads, but also produces precision parts for a number of airplanes and weapons systems, including the Stealth bomber and the M-A tank.

Karsten Solheim's Immigration to the United States in 1913

Karsten Solheim was born in Bergen, Norway, in 1911 and two years later immigrated to America with his family, which settled in Seattle, Washington. He learned the shoemaking trade from his father but was devoted to the dream of one day becoming a mechanical aeronautical engineer. He enrolled at the University of Washington but after a single year, with the country in the midst of the Depression, he was forced to drop out, unable to pay the tuition. He fell back on the craft his father taught him and for several years ran a shoe repair shop in Seattle. He soon learned a business principle that he would embrace for the rest of his life. When another cobbler opened a shop across the street and undercut the price to repair heels, Solheim followed suit but was surprised by the reaction of his old customers, who wanted to know if the quality of his work would remain the same. He concluded that quality, not price, was the key consideration. As a result he doubled his price, offered higher-quality leather, and ultimately drove away his cut-rate competition.

Solheim continued his engineering studies through college extension courses, but it was not until the advent of World War II and the defense industry's desperate need for engineers that he was able to give up the shoe repair business. He needed only five weeks to complete a ten-week crash course in engineering at the University of California in Berkeley, then moved to San Diego to work at Ryan Aeronautical Corporation, becoming a flight research engineer and working on the Fireball jet fighter plane. He stayed with Ryan until 1951 when he took a job at Convair, serving as a project engineer on the first ground guidance system for the Atlas missile. Two years later he went to work as a mechanical design engineer for General Electric (GE) at its Ithaca, New York plant, becoming involved in radar and guidance systems. In 1953 he was transferred to the GE Electronic Park in Syracuse to work on the development of the company's first portable television and while there invented the rabbit-ears antenna. A Chicago firm manufactured it, after GE proved uninterested in the item, selling millions. Solheim vowed that he would manufacture his next invention himself.

Taking Up Golf in 1953

That Solheim's next invention might involve the game of golf was highly improbable. A tennis player, he never even tried golf until moving to Ithaca, when in 1953 at the age of 42 he played a round with coworkers and became enamoured with the game. Putting was particularly troubling to Solheim, who soon concluded that a large part of his difficulties could be attributed to design flaws in his putter, which no matter how consistently he stroked it would twist just enough to send the ball off course. Knowing that a tennis racket employed perimeter weighting, in which the weight was distributed to the rim to allow the strings to provide greater power, Solheim decided to apply the same principle to the putter. By putting most of the weight at the heel and toe of the putter's blade he would be able to create a forgiving "sweet spot" in the center, allowing the player a much better chance to hit the ball straight. Solheim tested his idea by having a neighbor weld some metal to the back of the heel and toe of a putter, changes that helped the club head to complete a stroke. He then worked out the design of a new putter by gluing two popsicle sticks to the sides of a pair of sugar cubes with a shaft rising from the center. By the time he had constructed a prototype of his new putter, the 1A design, he had been transferred by GE to Palo Alto, California, where he worked with a team that produced the first banking computer system. Years later he recalled trying out the putter for the first time in 1959 in his kitchen in Redwood City, California: "I heard this noise, it startled me so much I dropped the putter on the floor. And then I knew that's what I would call my new putter: Ping."

As he continued to work for GE during the day, Solheim spent his weekends visiting golf course pro shops, giving away free putters to resident professionals to elicit feedback to help him improve the design. He even was known to lay out graph paper on the practice green to provide objective proof that his putter hit the ball straighter. One proshop owner in 1959 urged him to manufacture the Ping putter and sell them through the club professionals. He also warned him not to quit his day job, advice that Solheim followed for several years. To fund the enterprise he took out a $1,100 bank loan, the only financing he would ever need. First in Redwood City and then in Phoenix after GE again transferred him in 1961, Solheim began to produce Ping putters in his garage at night, hand-grinding the heads in his garage and then heating them on the kitchen stove to fit them on shafts. His sons helped out, drilling holes in the putter head to accommodate the shaft and adding the grips. To market his revolutionary putter Solheim began to attend professional tournaments, lingering at the practice green to ask the players to try his putter. Many were reluctant because they considered the Ping to be ugly, a fact to which Solheim was indifferent, insistent that his club should be accepted because of what it could do, not its appearance. Golfers by nature were willing to try almost anything to improve their game, especially their putting, so enough pros gave the Ping a chance to begin to

build word of mouth about the new putter, aided to some degree by Solheim engraving his name and address on the head. Winning tournaments, of course, translated into sales, as casual golfers, hoping the magic would rub off on them, invested in the same equipment as the victor of that weekend's tournament. In the early 1960s the sale of Ping putters was spurred by Gloria Armstong's win in a his-her tournament and John Barnum's win of the 1962 Cajun Classic. A *Sports Illustrated* article on the "musical putter" also helped sell the Pings.

In 1962 Solheim received a patent on the heel-toe weighting design on his putter, but continued to work on improving the design while also beginning to develop irons. Because he lacked access to a wind tunnel, he had a son drive him 100 miles an hour in the desert in order to hold his prototype irons out the window to check the drag caused by a typical swing. In January 1966 an idea for a new putter came to him in a flash of inspiration. Unable to wait to get the concept down on paper he grabbed a record sleeve and sketched the design. His wife Louise thought the new putter should be called "answer," a name that Solheim liked but that possessed too many letters to fit on the club. She then suggested that the "w" be left out. The legendary "Anser" putter, used by countless tournament winners, was born, and Karsten Solheim was on the verge of finally quitting his day job.

Marketing of the Anser was still limited to word of mouth, but those voices would become greatly amplified by the rise of professional golf on television, fueled by the popularity of Arnold Palmer and the rising star of Jack Nicklaus. When Julius Boros won the PGA Tour's Phoenix Open in 1967 using a Ping Anser putter, sales took off. Solheim, not intending to quit his engineering job, continued to meet the demand for his putters through his garage operation, much to the annoyance of his neighbors, but when GE decided to once again transfer him, this time to Oklahoma City, he decided to try the golf business full time. He was 56 when in July 1967 he incorporated Karsten Manufacturing and then bought a 2,200-square-foot building in Phoenix. Years later he told an interviewer, "When I moved into that little room I felt like I was a king." He soon hired his first employee and a year later had 30 people on payroll. Even as a businessman Solheim revealed his innovative spirit. His company had no job descriptions; he simply hired talented people and allowed them to find their most valuable function in the organization. Within two years annual sales grew from $50,000 to $500,000, despite a problem with the United States Golfing Association, which outlawed all but one of the Ping putter designs because of a bend at the base of the grip that helped the head swing square to the ball. A settlement was eventually reached, resulting in some changes to the clubs. This difficulty with the establishment foreshadowed a more contentious battle years later.

Introducing Irons in 1969

Solheim's work on irons came to fruition in the late 1960s. He applied the heel-toe, perimeter weighting principle to fashion a sweet spot on the irons and also employed investment casting, which was far more precise than the popular forging method. Other equipment makers produced shinier clubs, making Karsten irons look almost homemade, and once again Solheim insisted that his clubs be judged by their results. He refused even to add chrome plating in order to please customers.

Key Dates:

1953: Karsten Solheim plays his first round of golf at age 42.
1959: Solheim perfects his first putter design, which he names Ping.
1967: Karsten Manufacturing Corporation is formed.
1969: The first irons are offered for sale.
1995: Solheim's son John replaces him as president of the company.
2000: Karsten Solheim dies at age 88.

Performance eventually converted the reluctant, and that performance was enhanced by other Solheim innovations. He heat-treated the clubheads to resist corrosion and add strength, but it also allowed them to be adjusted for loft and lie, meaning the clubs could be custom fitted to take into account the customer's stance and swing. In the early 1960s Solheim had calibrated loft and lie angles for pro golfers, work that now led to the creation of the Ping Color Code Fitting System. Each set of clubs was then numbered and the specifications kept on file, so that customers in need of a replacement would be able to obtain an exact replacement from the factory. The practice of custom fitting also meant that any Ping clubs found on the shelves were either used or fakes. Combating counterfeiters would become a major area of concern for Karsten over the ensuing years.

Between 1969 and 1976 the company came out with its Karsten I, II, III, and IV irons, followed by the popular Eye series starting in 1979. The company also produced woods but never captured much of the market. Nevertheless, Karsten dominated in putters and irons, making it the top golf equipment manufacturer and allowing Solheim to branch out into other golf products and other business activities, such as Solheim Engineering and Dolphin Inc., as well as the 1984 purchase of Moon Valley Country Club. It was Solheim's success as a golf club designer, in fact, that led to a major distraction in the late 1980s, one that contributed to Karsten's loss of focus in the 1990s.

In 1984 the USGA decided to permit U-shaped grooves in the face of an iron, as opposed to traditional V-shaped grooves. Solheim was quick to take advantage of this rule change with his Ping Eye 2 model, which quickly proved popular, ultimately becoming Karsten's best-selling club in history. Because the grooves were hard on soft-covered balls, Solheim rounded off the edges, which the USGA ruled was a violation and banned from professional play. In essence, the clubs provided extra spin, which made it easier for golfers to execute shots from difficult lies. Solheim insisted that his clubs were consistent with the USGA regulation and eventually took the organization, and later the PGA Tour, to court. Both suits were settled out of court, the USGA in 1990 and the PGA Tour in 1993. Kartsen's older irons were deemed legal but future clubs would have to comply with USGA regulations.

As Karsten emerged from its legal squabble in the 1990s it found itself operating in a new business environment. Other equipment manufacturers had followed Solheim's lead and greatly improved on their technology, but unlike Solheim they were more willing to please their customers and not insist that pure functionality rule the day. Moreover, they effectively advertised their wares, instead of relying on reputation, no matter how strong that reputation might be. Karsten began to lose significant market share, with its top-selling irons falling second to rival Cobra in 1995. It was clear that change was needed and as a result Solheim's son John Solheim took over as president and soon presided over the first layoffs in nearly three decades and instituted a number of changes over the next few years. The company updated its marketing approach, replacing its staid print ads with bolder designs and adding broadcast advertisements; it introduced oversized metal woods that had become popular with players; and instead of merely offering bonus money based on performance to professionals who played with Ping equipment it began to offer a salary to select players.

In the late 1990s Karsten was well on its way to recovery, while at the same time its founder, suffering from Parkinson's disease, began to steadily decline. During his last years he was bound to a wheelchair. He died from complications of the disease on February 16, 2000, at the age of 88. Although a maverick who was never part of the golfing establishment, Karsten Solheim was acknowledged by all as one of the most important influences on golf club development in the modern era. His sons now led the company he created and a third generation was preparing to carry on his commitment to innovation and craftsmanship.

Principal Subsidiaries

Dolphin Inc.; Karsten Engineering; Moon Valley Country Club.

Principal Competitors

Callaway Golf; SHC; TaylorMade Golf.

Further Reading

Brennan, Jody, "The Ping Heard Round the World," *Forbes,* October 26, 1992, p. 248.

Finch, Peter, "The Golf Club with a Handicap All Its Own," *Business Week,* May 1, 1989, p. 126.

Netherton, Martha, "Ping Putts Toward Restructuring," *Business Journal Serving Phoenix & the Valley of the Sun,* May 2, 1997, p. 1.

Newnham, Blaine, "Solheim's Little Ping Makes Big Bang," *Seattle Times,* April 16, 1989, p. C1.

Stewart, Mark, "New Chief at PING is an Old Hand," *Arizona Daily Star,* July 2, 1995, p. 1C.

Stumpf, Diane F., "Stick, Stones and Clubs," *Arizona Trend,* June 1, 1999, p. 62.

—Ed Dinger

Katy Industries, Inc.

765 Straits Turnpike
Middlebury, Connecticut 06762
U.S.A.
Telephone: (203) 598-0397
Fax: (203) 598-0712
Web site: http://www.katyindustries.com

Public Company
Incorporated: 1967
Employees: 2,922
Sales: $506.0 million (2001)
Stock Exchanges: New York
Ticker Symbol: KT
NAIC: 335931 Current-Carrying Wiring Device
   Manufacturing; 335999 All Other Miscellaneous
   Electrical Equipment and Component Manufacturing;
   327910 Abrasive Product Manufacturing

Katy Industries, Inc. operates as a manufacturing company with two main business segments: Maintenance Products and Electrical/Electronics. The company manufacturers a wide variety of products including consumer storage, janitorial supplies, scouring pads, electrical cords, surge protectors, and garden lighting. The firm's customer base includes commercial and consumer retail outlets as well as original equipment manufacturers. Katy Industries has facilities in eleven states and three countries.

Early History

Katy Industries was born out of an acquisition of the Missouri-Kansas-Texas railroad (MKT), a financially troubled operation that was in need of a profitable parent company. Wallace Carroll, whose knowledge of railroads dated back to his job as a section hand that helped pay his way through Boston College became acquainted with MKT many years later when he was persuaded that the ailing railroad had some attractive aspects that outweighed its reputation as a money-loser. In particular, Carroll was attracted by its New York Stock Exchange listing and the $30 million tax loss it would provide for his own company, American Gage.

Katy Industries became the parent holding company of MKT because the railroad company purchased 80% of the stock of Carroll's American Gage. With this purchase, Wallace Carroll became the chairman and majority stock owner of Katy Industries, which listed on the New York Stock Exchange in 1968.

Carroll's experience with company acquisitions and expansions began in 1940 when he established a gauge business in Illinois. He had left New England for Chicago in 1963 after he was hired as a salesman for a Rhode Island precision gauge maker. Four years later, he was selling gauges on his own. However, producing the gauges seemed a more profitable business than selling them, and thus Carroll borrowed $6,000 and took on a partner to start his manufacturing business. Carroll did not regret moving into the manufacturing business, but he did regret going into a partnership. ''I promised myself I'd operate alone from that moment on,'' he stated, and he has held to that promise ever since.

Carroll's entry into the gauge manufacturing business was timely. As with most manufacturing companies during World War II, Carroll's American Gage grew rapidly because of an insatiable wartime demand for products such as gauges. By the end of the war, American Gage was doing so well that Carroll was able to begin purchasing other small manufacturing businesses. Carroll wisely made his acquisitions based on a peacetime economy. In particular, one of the companies that he bought after the war was a manufacturer of pots and pans. By 1948, Carroll's holdings had grown large enough that he established American Gage and Machine Company, of which he became sole owner, as a way in which to contain his holdings.

During this time, Carroll's formula for acquiring companies, as a general rule, was to pay cash. He looked for small, family-owned businesses that produced both a good product and a substantial profit. His preference was to keep the original management, but if the management was comprised of older men then his policy was to make them consultants or honorary officers and hire a younger generation to manage the company.

While Carroll was successfully developing American Gage, the MKT railroad was having its share of problems. Several years before the creation of Katy Industries, MKT was on the

---

Company Perspectives:

We strive to increase the top line, reduce costs, closely manage working capital, and control capital expenditures. Successful execution in these areas will benefit not only our shareholders, but our customers as well, as a stronger company can reinvest more readily into constantly improving its customer service and into more innovative product development.

---

verge of bankruptcy. The "Katy," as the railroad is nicknamed, included 2700 miles of damaged roadbed from Missouri to Texas on which derailments were likely to occur if the cars were moving faster than 25 miles per hour. Shipment of stock would often he damaged, and very few shippers would allow their products to be transported on the Katy. As a result, by March 1965 only 600 cars were moving on a daily basis.

However, by October 1965, 1000 cars were moving daily. The cause for this substantial increase in activity on the Katy lines was a "non-stop talker" name John Barriger, who came on board to save the railroad from its bankrupt condition. Barriger did not expect that the Katy would ever become a prosperous railroad, but he did hope that he could rebuild it so that a larger railroad company would be enticed into a merger.

Barriger had spent many years around the railroads of the country. After his graduation from MIT in 1921, he worked for the Pennsylvania Railroad and then moved on to Calvin Bullock, Limited, a Wall Street firm where he worked as an industry analyst and inspected the nation's railroads. During World War II, he was associate director of the Office of Defense Transportation. After the war, he headed the Monon railroad, which was almost bankrupt. When he left in 1953, Barriger had managed not only to save the railroad from bankruptcy but also to establish a sound financial basis for its future operations.

In 1965, Barriger was nearing retirement age at the Pittsburg & Lake Erie Railroad company when he heard that the Katy was in need of talented management. Preferring the excitement of his work and the challenge of the Katy over retirement, he took on the job. As the new president of MKT, Barriger relied on his friends to help improve the railroad. By repairing the roadbeds as much as he could within the first few weeks of his presidency, and by making deals with his numerous railroad friends to the effect that their use of the Katy would be returned through payment of back damage claims and improved service, Barriger was able to increase the number of cars moving on the Katy lines within a short period of time.

The return to creditable service on the Katy was a difficult task. The poor condition of the roadbed meant spending any profits on the railroad. Still, its reputation as a money-loser had not prevented Barriger from saving it from bankruptcy, and although his hope that a merger with a larger railroad would take place was not realized, the railroad company looked strong enough for a parent company to give it the kind of support it needed. Barriger continued his presidency only long enough to get the Katy in a strong operating position.

Diversification of Katy in the Late 1960s and 1970s

Katy Industries quickly began to diversify after the acquisition of the MKT. Carroll separated the company into four very different groups: the Electrical Equipment and Products Group; the Industrial Machinery, Equipment, and Products Group; the Consumer Products Group; and the Oil Field and other Services Group. By 1972, the company was expanding into European and Canadian markets, particularly within the oil and gas exploration fields.

One of the most important acquisitions for Katy Industries in the late 1960s was that of Bee Gee Shrimp, a collection of companies that operated a 100-trawler fleet off the coast of Georgetown, Guyana, that harvested and sold shrimp. Bee Gee Shrimp was primarily responsible for doubling the sales and earnings of Katy's Consumer Products Group in 1979, and this allowed Katy a degree of comfort during the recession years.

Even the MKT was showing a profit for the first time since 1963. In 1971, the Katy made a $21,000 profit, which proved its ability to operate on a break-even basis. However, the profits were put back into the railroad, particularly in the area of track maintenance, which was a high 16 percent of operating costs that year.

By 1971, another man with a reputation of being able to tackle tough jobs was at the Katy. Reginald Whitman became president and chairman of MKT in 1969 and is credited with keeping the company headed in a profitable direction. Whitman's confidence that the Katy would not only be profitable but that it would also grow was an important aspect of the future earnings of the company. By 1973, neither the railroad's negative book value of $9 million nor its net deficit was consolidated in Katy's annual report. The company did not have to write off the railroad's losses against its consolidated earnings. In addition, Katy no longer had to carry the railroad's large debt on its balance sheet.

For Katy, the railroad provided a shelter that was important to its acquisitions. Between 1970 and 1973, Katy purchased 15 companies for approximately $34 million. Most of the companies were small and privately owned. Once they were put behind the tax shelter of the railroad, their profits increased significantly.

By this time, Katy was considered to be a diversified investment fund, which was different from others of its kind because it usually owned a majority, if not 100 percent, of its affiliate's stock. W.H. Murphy, Treasurer of Katy, regarded this policy as one which allowed a "uniformity of overall corporate policy as well as the exchange of technology, marketing, purchasing, and financial assistance" within the companies.

Katy's formula for acquiring companies did not change significantly over the years. Carroll continued to purchase small companies that had good product lines and presented small risks. As Carroll stated, "If it is profitable or we could make it profitable, we buy it." It was also Carroll's policy to buy companies that already had good management in order to give the division manager a sizable amount of autonomy. In addition, Katy offered incentives to its subsidiaries, which were based on earning increases as a means of keeping the companies productive and efficient.

<table>
<tr><td colspan="2">Key Dates:</td></tr>
<tr><td>1948:</td><td>Wallace Carroll establishes American Gage and Machine Company.</td></tr>
<tr><td>1967:</td><td>Katy Industries incorporates.</td></tr>
<tr><td>1968:</td><td>The company goes public.</td></tr>
<tr><td>1972:</td><td>The firm expands into European and Canadian markets.</td></tr>
<tr><td>1988:</td><td>The company sells MKT to Union Pacific.</td></tr>
<tr><td>1993:</td><td>Katy Industries fends off takeover attempts.</td></tr>
<tr><td>1998:</td><td>Five companies are acquired and six are sold during a restructuring effort.</td></tr>
<tr><td>2001:</td><td>The company completes a recapitalization.</td></tr>
</table>

This formula was a successful one for Katy. Its net growth increased from $2 million in 1971 to $18 million in 1981. Katy managed to increase sales throughout the recession years of the early 1980s. In fact, its earnings were so good that Katy expanded its pump manufacturing company, LaBour Pump, which was located in Ireland.

In 1983, Katy began to expand into the silverware business. Carroll first purchased Wallace Silversmith Inc. in August and then purchased Insilco Corporation's international unit around October of the same year. These new acquisitions and investments in the early 1980s represented some of Katy's efforts to offset the uneven earnings of the company's railroad and machinery operations.

By 1985, plans were in the air to sell MKT. Union Pacific had made an offer that required MKT to obtain 60 percent of the outstanding income certificates on the company. MKT had only purchased 41 percent by mid-1985. Union Pacific then terminated the offer. Chairman Carroll's comment on this turn of events in early 1986 was that Katy would ''keep on running the railroad; it's a good property.''

Katy needed to increase its earnings for 1985. The company had some significant losses, which were blamed on the casualty and property insurance business, Midland Insurance. Midland's problems were caused by difficulties in the market. Katy liquidated the insurance company in the early part of 1986, but net sales dropped from $4.3 million in 1984 to $3.9 million in 1985.

In other areas, however, Katy was experiencing new developments. Early in 1985, Katy announced that its subsidiary, Katy-Seghers Incinco Systems Inc., had been awarded its first contract to build a waste-to-energy plant. It had taken the company six years to win a contract since the start of the business in 1979, and the subsidiary was expected to see some profits in 1985. At the time, Carroll saw the waste-to-energy plants as the ''future direction'' of Katy Industries and expected that there will be great demand, and competition, for these plants because of the increased environmental concerns of the nation. Specifically, state and local governments were considering this form of incineration, and if the trend continued in this area, Katy expected to be in the midst of the development of these plants.

A Transformation Begins: Late 1980s

During the late 1980s and into the 1990s, however, the direction of Katy Industries would change dramatically. Carroll retired, leaving Jacob Saliba as chairman and CEO and William Murphy as president. Under new leadership, Katy began its transformation, which was marked by takeover threats, restructuring, and divestiture.

In 1988, the company finally sold the MKT—which was in financial crisis—to Union Pacific. Katy also divested its seafood business, and by 1990 its main business segments included industrial machinery and components, consumer products, and energy resources. As Katy streamlined its operations, it became attractive as a takeover target. In fact, the Carroll family, which owned approximately 52 percent of the firm in the early 1990s, launched an effort to take the company private. Certain shareholders believed the offer undervalued Katy, and a takeover war began. By 1993, potential suitors included Rosecliff Inc., Pensler Capital Corp., and Steinhardt Enterprises Inc.

During this time, Katy elected a new management team. John Prann was named president while Philip Johnson became chairman. (Saliba was named chairman again in 1997 when Johnson left the firm.) The company also moved headquarters to Englewood, Colorado. In order to maintain its independence, Katy distributed a $14 per share dividend to its shareholders to reduce its available cash and make it less attractive as a target.

The plan worked, and Katy was left to focus on a new restructuring effort that left consumer products, electronics testing equipment, food packaging machinery, and specialty metals as its core business units. The firm continued to sell off unrelated subsidiaries including Panhandle Industrial Co. and also made strategic acquisitions. In 1995, Katy purchased GC Thorsen Inc., a electronic parts distributor. The following year, the firm made a $47 million purchase of Woods Industries Inc., another electronics-related concern.

During 1998 and early 1999, Katy made five acquisitions that included Contico International Inc., a manufacturer of consumer storage, home and automotive products, and janitorial and food service equipment and supplies; specialty abrasives firm Bay State Gritcloth; Wilen Products Inc., a professional cleaning products concern; the consumer electrical division of Noma Industries Ltd.; and Disco Inc., a cleaning products manufacturer catering to the food service industry. By this time, Katy had also divested six companies and its machinery division.

A New Focus for the New Century

As Katy prepared to enter the new century, it adopted yet another focus—maintenance supplies and electrical and electronic products. Revenues jumped from $382 million in 1998 to just under $600 million in 1999 as a result of its aggressive acquisition strategy. In 2000, however, sales fell to $579 million, and the company reported a loss of $5.4 million. Then, in 2001, the firm reported a loss of $63.3 million. That year, the firm took $58.4 million in charges related to restructuring and the write off of certain assets. In addition, sales fell by 12.7 percent in 2001 due to weakening demand and the slowing economy.

As part of the company's cost cutting efforts, it moved headquarters from Colorado to Connecticut and closed an office in Chicago. It also completed a recapitalization with KKTY Holding Company L.L.C. It sold $70 million in stock—700,000 shares—which was mainly used to pay off debt. Saliba retired from his post in 2001 and left C. Michael Jacobi as president and CEO.

In 2002, Jacobi continued to focus on cutting back on expenses, improving profit margins, and new product development. Competition remained fierce, and the recovery of the U.S. economy was crucial to the success of the firm. While Katy had come along way in restructuring itself since the early 1990s, its future held many challenges.

Principal Subsidiaries

American Gage & Machine Company; Contico International, L.L.C.; Contico Manufacturing Limited (U.K.); Contico Manufacturing (Ireland) Limited; CRL Export, Inc. Glit/Disco, Inc.; Hallmark Holdings, Inc.; Duckback Products, Inc.; Primary Coatings, Inc.; GC/Waldom Electronics, Inc.; Katy International, Inc.; Glit/Gemtex, Inc.; Hamilton Precision Metals, Inc.; HPMNC, Inc.; HPM of Pennsylvania, Inc.; Hamilton Metals, L.P.; Wabash Holding Corp.; Wilen Products, Inc.; Katy International, Inc. (British Virgin Islands); Katy Oil Company of Indonesia; Katy-Teweh Petroleum Company; Katy-Seghers, Inc.; Savannah Energy Systems Company Limited Partnership; PTR Machine Corp.; W.J. Smith Wood Preserving Company; Woods Industries, Inc.; Thorsen Tools, Inc.; Woods Industries (Canada), Inc.; Glit/Gemtex, Ltd. (Canada).

Principal Competitors

Ecolab Inc.; The ServiceMaster Company; Unilever.

Further Reading

Aven, Paula, "Katy Industries Buys Five Supply Companies," *Denver Business Journal*, February 26, 1999, p. 21B.

Beaven, Stephen, "Woods Industries Sold Again," *Indianapolis Business Journal*, December 16, 1996, p. 4.

Berenson, Alex, "Katy Industries Regroups," *The Denver Post*, July 21, 1994.

"Katy Industries Completes Sales of Its Seafood Operations," *PR Newswire*, October 15 1987.

"Katy Industries to Consider $252 Million Takeover Bid," *The New York Times*, December 7, 1993, p. D5.

"Katy Industries to Sell Subsidiary to Okla. Firm," *The Denver Post*, September 10, 1994.

"Katy Looking at Buyout," *Denver Business Journal*, November 10. 2000, p. 7A.

"Katy Reports Loss," *Denver Business Journal*, April 6, 2001, p. 6A.

Lewis, Al, "Katy Industries Acquires Contico," *Denver Rocky Mountain News*, January 12, 1999, p. 4B.

——, "Katy Industries Decides Not to Sell Electrical, Electronics Business," *Denver Rocky Mountain News*, December 16, 1999, p. 6B.

—update: Christina M. Stansell

Keolis

Keolis SA

55-57, avenue de Colmar
92846 Rueil Malmaison Cedex
France
Telephone: (+33) 1 41 29 72 00
Fax: (+33) 1 47 32 45 77
Web site: http://www.keolis.com

Private Company
Incorporated: 1919 as Société Générale des Transports
  Departementaux
Employees: 23,500
Operating Revenues: EUR1.4 billion ($1.2 billion)(2001)
NAIC: 485210 Interurban and Rural Bus Transportation;
  485410 School and Employee Bus Transportation;
  485113 Bus and Other Motor Vehicle Transit
  Systems; 482112 Short Line Railroads

Keolis SA is counting on leveraging its position as France's leading private public transportation operator to become a major European intermodal passenger transport group. Created from the merger of the Paribas banking group's VIA GTI and French rail agency SNCF's subsidiary Cariane, Keolis operates the public transportation networks for nearly 90 French cities, as well as the interurban bus networks for more than 65 departments (a French department is equivalent to a county in the United States). As such, the company controls a fleet of more than 10,000 buses. Keolis is also a major operator of tramways and subways in France, excluding Paris, with more than 66 kilometers of automatic, driverless tramways under its control, notably in the cities of Lille, Lyons, Rennes, and Laon, with plans to initiate service in Caen and in Thessalonika in Greece. Keolis also operates more than 14 kilometers of standard tramways. Other Keolis offerings in France include transport-on-demand services, such as a contract to provide transport services for the Paris airport's 55,000 employees; transportation for persons with impaired mobility; airport transportation linkage services, providing airport-to-city and long-distance transportation; airport operations, including passenger ticketing and baggage handling as well as freight handling; and, lastly, shipping services to the Brittany islands. Fifty percent of Keolis' 2001 revenues of EUR1.4 billion came

from its French urban sector operations, while 25 percent was generated in France's interurban sector, chiefly through the company's bus services. Since the late 1990s, however, Keolis has been pushing onto the international public transport scene, notably through the operation of passenger train services, such as the Thameslink line, in conjunction with the Go Ahead Group, the 250-kilometer Bedford-Brighton rail line; the suburban rail network for Stockholm, Sweden; 150 kilometers of local routes in Bielefeld and Freiberg, in Germany; and the Synthus rail network in the Netherlands' Gelderland region. In just five years, Keolis has built up more than 700 kilometers of rail operations in five countries. The company has also extended into North America through a 40 percent stake in busing group Slivia and a 75 percent stake in Quebec's Orléans Express. The company plans to raise its international operations from 25 percent of its sales in 2001 to as much as 50 percent of revenues in the early part of the century. Primary shareholder in privately owned Keolis is SNCF, the group's "reference" shareholder, with nearly 44 percent of the company's shares. Paribas, which holds more than 48 percent of Keolis, has indicated its intention to exit the group's capital by the end of 2002.

Building a Public Transport Leader

Keolis' route to becoming France's leading interurban, multimodal public transport provider started at the beginning of the twentieth century, as automobile makers sought to adapt the internal combustion engine for the needs of public transportation purposes. The first buses appeared in the first decade of the new century, and, by 1908, a new company had been formed, the Société des Transports Automobiles (STA), which, among other activities, began operating bus lines.

In 1919, the STA created a new subsidiary, Société Générale des Transports Départementaux (STGD), which became the forerunner of the later VIA GTI. Initially providing interurban bus connections, STGD added other operations, including a bus tours wing, Transcar, employee transportation services, and school bus services. The company also began operating international bus routes.

Bus transportation rapidly grew into a challenger to France's railroad system. Still reeling from damage inflicted during

World War I, the country's various railroad networks were all operating at a loss. The arrival of new bus lines, and the growth of the bus as a rival public transportation system particularly in the interurban and inter-departmental circuits, continued to depress the country's railroads throughout the 1920s. The onset of the Great Depression dashed any hopes of a return to profitability of the rail lines. With the country's rail system in disarray, the French government decided to nationalize the railroad, merging the various railroad networks into a single body in order to create the government-controlled Société Nationale des Chemins de Fer Français (SNCF) in 1938.

Requisitioned by the German occupation forces during World War II, the SNCF benefited from the disruption of normal bus services. In 1942, the railroad body created a new subsidiary, Société de Contrôle et d'Exploitation de Transports Auxiliares, or SCETA, which began providing linkup bus services with the SNCF's train system, as well as other transportation services. In the postwar years, tourism became a major part of the subsidiary's operations, while the company also developed a strong busing component. Those operations were brought under subsidiary Carianc, created in 1988.

French shipping group Compagnie de Navigation Mixte had diversified its holdings by the late 1960s, stepping into land transport with the acquisitions of STA and then SGTD. In 1971, these two groups were merged to form a new company, Générale de Transport et d'Industrie (GTI). This company then adopted a new brand, VIA, in order to unite its various passenger and freight transportation activities.

Under Compagnie de Navigation Mixte, GTI, which became known as VIA GTI, expanded rapidly. With the purchase of Transexel, a company which specialized in urban passenger transport, in 1981, VIA GTI became France's largest non-rail public transportation provider. The group scored an important first in the early 1980s with the inauguration of the world's first automatic, driver-less tramway system in Lille in 1983. Another important part of the group was its industrial vehicle and truck rental division, VIA Location.

Merging Public Transport Operators in the 1990s

By the beginning of the 1990s, VIA GTI's revenues topped FFr6.5 billion (equivalent to approximately EUR1 billion). Compagnie de Navigation Mixte, by then itself a diversified conglomerate, led VIA GTI on its own diversification run during the 1980s and into the early 1990s, bundling, among other acquisitions, the parcel delivery and messenger service France Express and the security transport services group Brink's France into VIA GTI. Another branch under development was VIA Voyages, which raised itself to the number three rank among France's business travel agents. Yet these moves, particularly the addition of money-losing Brinks, began to weigh heavily on VIA GTI and its parent company into the mid-1990s.

The arrival in the 1980s of the SNCF's new high-speed train system, the TGV, and its full-scale rollout in the 1990s raised a new threat to France's public transportation providers. By the end of the 1980s, the industry was undergoing a massive consolidation, as five major groups, including VIA GTI, emerged as leaders of the French market. For its part, SNCF had joined in the fray with the creation of its dedicated public transport subsidiary Cariane, in 1988, which was placed under SCETA.

Cariane quickly went on its own acquisition drive, growing into a group of more than 30 regionally operating companies—more than 70 percent of Cariane's revenues at the time came from its regional and international bus operations. Cariane was also present in the Convergence consortium, in partnership with rivals Transdev and Verney, which gave it a share in an additional 35 regional bus lines and in the development of a new express bus route to be operated on the country's Autoroute freeway system.

Cariane made a number of significant acquisitions in the early 1990s. The purchase of Athis-Cars in 1991 not only gave it one of the last of the major independent transport groups in France but also boosted its operations in the Parisian perimeter region. The following year, Cariane acquired the Compagnie Française de Transport de Voyageurs, another major provider of urban and interurban bus routes in the Paris region, and boosted the share of urban operations in Cariane's revenues to more than 30 percent. By then, Cariane, with revenues of about FFr1 billion (EUR150 million) in 1992, had largely broken away from its original role as a provider of bus support services for the SNCF rail system, which accounted for less than ten percent of its operations.

Cariane nonetheless lagged behind VIA GTI, which claimed half of the country's urban market (excluding Paris, controlled by the RATP), and as much as 15 percent of France's interurban market. VIA GTI had also made its first, although hesitant, move into the international market, with a modest entry into Spain and the internationally operating bus line Eurolines. Yet the diversification drive of VIA GTI, and parent company Compagnie de Navigation Mixte, turned sour by the mid-1990s.

By 1996, much of VIA GTI's operations, with the exception of its public transport branch, was losing money. In that year, Banque de Paribas took control of Compagnie de Navigation Mixte. By 1997, Paribas had begun cleaning up VIA GTI, disposing of its diversified holdings—including VIA Location, VIA Voyages, and Brinks—and regrouping the subsidiary around its core public transport business, VIA Transport.

The reenergized VIA GTI quickly sought out new expansion targets. Locked out of railroad transport in France, VIT GTI was tempted to extend itself into that transport category by the liberalization of the railroad industry in other European markets. In 1997, the company formed the Go VIA partnership with

Key Dates:

1908: Société des Transports Automobiles (STA) is established.

1919: Société Générale des Transports Departementaux (SGTD) is established.

1938: SNCF, the government-owned French railroad group, is created.

1942: SNCF creates SCETA, an auxiliary transport subsidiary.

1971: STA and SGTD merge to form Générale de Transport et d'Industrie (GTI), a subsidiary of Compagnie de Navigation Mixte; VIA brand is launched.

1981: VIA GTI acquires Transexel and becomes a French urban transport leader.

1988: SCETA creates a new subsidiary, Cariane, for its interurban busing operations.

1991: Cariane acquires Athis-Cars, then Compagnie Française de Transport de Voyageurs the following year.

1996: Paribas takes control of Compagnie de Navigation Mixte and restructures VIA GTI around a core of public transport operations.

1997: VIA GTI, in partnership with the Go Ahead Group, wins a contract for Thameslink rail franchise in England.

1998: VIA GTI forms Eurobahn partnership and wins the first railroad franchise in Germany as well as a suburban rail franchise for Stockholm.

1999: SNCF acquires the "reference" shareholder position in VIA GTI and merges that company with Cariane to form VIA Cariane.

2001: VIA Cariane changes its name to Keolis to emphasize its growing international ambitions.

2002: Keolis acquires Orléans Express, the largest interurban transport provider in Quebec, Canada.

the United Kingdom's Go Ahead Group and won the contract to operate the Thameslink rail line. VIA GTI's rail success continued into 1998, as the company won the contract to operate the suburban rail network outside of Stockholm, Sweden, and then, as majority shareholder in the Eurobahn GmbH partnership, won its bid to operate two regional railroads in Germany.

VIA GTI's growing international rail operations caught the attention of the SNCF in 1999. By the end of that year, SNCF had negotiated a takeover of VIA GTI, acquiring nearly 44 percent of the transport group—and becoming VIA GTI's "reference" shareholder. Paribas, which maintained a 48 percent stake in VIA GTI, planned nonetheless to exit the company's capital entirely.

Following the acquisition of its stake in VIA GTI, SNCF merged that operation with its Cariane subsidiary, forming a new group, VIA Cariane. The new company operated in 85 communities throughout France, with interurban operations in 64 departments, in addition to a growing European rail presence. In addition, the company had by then added operations in the Netherlands, with the Synthus rail network serving that country's Gelderland region.

Via Cariane changed its name to Keolis in April 2001, as part of its plans to position itself for further European expansion. Indeed, further expansion opportunities in France appeared limited, given Keolis' dominant position in that market. Nonetheless, the company continued to look for ways to strengthen its French coverage and in May 2001 acquired Sera, the largest independent bus company in the Aquitaine (Bordeaux) region. Other acquisitions followed, boosting Keolis' operations in the Midi Pyrenees, and in the Parisian region.

Meanwhile, the continued liberalization of the European transport market presented still greater opportunities for Keolis, as that market—that is, transport operations opened to private companies—was expected to be worth nearly EUR30 billion by the end of the decade. Keolis scored a new railroad success in England when the GoVia partnership won the contract to operate that country's South Central line. The partnership also appeared a frontrunner in the race to win the Northern Rail franchise.

While Keolis continued to deploy its European expansion strategy, the company also began looking farther abroad, seeking out "culturally similar" markets. In 2001, the company made a first move into Canada, particularly the French-speaking region, when it launched a new busing subsidiary, Slivia. In 2002, Keolis achieved a still more solid position in that market when it acquired Quebec's interurban transport provider Orléans Express, that market's leading commuter transporter. Back in France, the company's expertise in tramway systems, and especially automated tramways, had helped it acquire the operating contracts for a number of cities, including Rennes, starting in 2002. Yet this activity too presented international possibilities—the company was awarded the contract to run the Thessalonika, Greece, automated metro, slated to become operational in 2005. Keolis' multi-modal strategy had placed the company on the European transport market's fast track.

Principal Subsidiaries

Keolis has more than 170 subsidiaries in France, Germany, the United Kingdom, Sweden, Spain and the Netherlands.

Principal Competitors

Regie Autonome des Transports Parisiens (RATP); Connex; Transdev; Carlson Wagonlit Travel; SLTC; Transports Verney; CGFTE; SEMVAT.

Further Reading

Denis, Anne, "Keolis prend le contrôle du transporteur interurbain canadien Orléans Express," *Les Echos*, April 23, 2002 p. 27.
——, "Le groupe Keolis dispose d'un an de plus pour séduire des partenaires," *Les Echos*, July 31, 2001, p. 16.
Malecot, Dominique, "Via Cariane devient Keolis pour conquérir l'Europe," *Les Echos*, April 5, 2001, p. 19.
Senges, Gilles, "Via GTI sur les bons rails en Angleterre," *Les Echos*, December 2, 1997, p. 15.
Silbert, Nathalie, "Via Cariane, prêt à entrer dans le capital du transporteur britannique Go-Ahead," *Les Echos*, October 17, 2000, p. 25.

—M. L. Cohen

LAUFEN

Keramik Holding AG Laufen

Wahlenstrasse 46
Postfach 4242 Laufen
Switzerland
Telephone: (+41) 61 765 75 75
Fax: (+41) 61 761 57 11
Web site: http://www.laufen.ch

92% Owned Subsidiary of Roca Radiadores SA
Incorporated: 1892 Tonwarenfabrik Laufen AG
Employees: 8,000
Sales: $640 million (2000 est.)
NAIC: 551112 Offices of Other Holding Companies;
327111 Vitreous China Plumbing Fixture and China
and Earthenware Fitting and Bathroom Accessories
Manufacturing; 327122 Ceramic Wall and Floor Tile
Manufacturing; 327123 Other Structural Clay Product
Manufacturing; 531210 Offices of Real Estate Agents
and Brokers

Keramik Holding AG Laufen is one of the world's leading producers of sanitary ware—toilets, bathtubs, sinks, and other bathroom fixtures for private, semi-public, and public markets. Since the late 1990s, Laufen has streamlined its products to focus exclusively on bathroom fixtures. (Previously the company had been a major manufacturer of such diversified ceramics products as roofing tiles and porcelain table service.) The company's products are marketed under a variety of brand names, including Laufen, Jika, Duravit, Inda, MyLife, Swing, Profil, and Moderna, and feature designs by such names as Alessi, frog, Helemont Telefunt, and Phoenix Design. Laufen has been controlled by private Spanish company Roca Radiadores since 1999; the companies' combined operations have given the group the second place position in the world market, after American Standard, and the first place spot in the European market. Despite Roca's controlling share of more than 92 percent, Laufen continues to be operated as an autonomous group. Based in Switzerland, Laufen has long operated internationally, with six production facilities in Switzerland, Austria, Portugal, and the Czech Republic, and sales branches in 28 countries throughout the world. Laufen is also active in South America, in particular through its Brazilian sub-

sidiaries Incepa and Celite, and in Thailand through its stake in partnership UMI-Laufen. In 2000, Laufen's sales were estimated at $640 million.

Turn of the 20th Century Brick Foundations

Laufen began operating at the turn of the century with the founding of the Tonwarenfabrik Laufen AG, in the town of Laufen, near Bern, Switzerland, in 1892. Using the region's clay deposits for raw materials, the company originally concentrated on manufacturing bricks, then added roofing tiles. In 1925, the company expanded its business into the fast-growing market for sanitary ceramics products, forming a new company, AG für Keramische Industrie Laufen. By 1926, the company had a full line of bathroom ceramics products, including sinks, bathtubs, and toilets. Laufen was the first in Switzerland to enter the market and quickly imposed itself as the country's market leader before spreading out across Europe.

Laufen added a new product group in 1932, that of the manufacturing of ceramic tiles for bathrooms, kitchens, and other applications. Part of the company's growth came about when "sanitary" bathrooms—long the privilege of Europe's upper classes—became the norm in new and renovated housing on the continent. Attitudes towards bathrooms in Europe had also evolved: once perceived as a strictly utilitarian facility, they were now viewed as serving an important role in home life.

Beginning of International Expansion: 1950s

Laufen's production remained focused on its domestic market through the end of World War II. By the beginning of the 1950s, however, the company began preparing its international growth. In 1952, Laufen turned to Brazil for its first foreign expansion effort by acquiring Incepa SA, a ceramic tile producer based in Campo Larga. Laufen brought over its technology, and Incepa quickly became a leading producer of both ceramic tiles and sanitary products for the Brazilian market.

Much of Laufen's international growth came through cooperation agreements with local partners. Such was the case with the country's entry into Austria, where by the 1960s the company had been working together with Osterreichische Sanitär-,. Keramik-, und Porzellan-Industria (OSPAG), based in Wil-

Company Perspectives:

We are innovators. Our products are conceived with the common priority of design, quality, functionality, and service, and are there to enhance convenience and quality of life.

helmsburg. In 1967, Laufen acquired OSPAG outright, adding ceramics operations stretching back to the late 1800s, when a workshop was set up in Wilhelmsburg in order to produce stoneware based on technologies being developed by England's Wedgewood.

After being controlled by a series of owners during the nineteenth century, OSPAG came under the proprietorship of the Lichenstern family when brothers Heinrich and Leopold Lichtenstern acquired the factory in 1883. By the turn of the century, however, the Wilhelmsburg works was struggling, as production slowed and debts mounted. When Heinrich Lichtenstern died in 1895, the next generation of Lichtensterns, in the form of Heinrich's son Richard, took over the business. Just 16 years old at the time he inherited the family's ceramics works, Richard Lichtenstern was able to restore the company's business and quickly succeeded in paying off the company's debts.

By the 1930s, a new generation of Lichtensterns prepared to take over the family business. Yet the Austrian *Anschluss* during World War II forced the Lichtensterns to flee the country, and the Wilhemsburg works were taken over by the Austrian government. It was not until 1947 that Kurt Lichtenstern, Richard's son, returned to Austria to reclaim the family business. During the family's stay in the United States, Lichtenstern had become an American citizen and adopted the name Conrad H. Lester.

Lester restructured the ceramics operation and reoriented it toward the production of sanitary ware. In 1955, the company changed its name, to Osterreichische Sanitär-,. Keramik-, und Porzellan-Industria (OSPAG), and introduced a new brand name for its products, Austrovit. By then, the transformation of bathroom fixtures from utilitarian form to more luxurious design was well under way, and in 1959 OSPAG brought bathroom design to the Austrian market with the release of its Ultra series. The company was also credited with being among the first to attach a toilet's bowl to its cistern, creating the semi-WC in 1960.

The merger between Laufen and OSPAG enabled both operations to extend onto a European wide scale. OSPAG was to remain an integral part of Laufen's growing business and was particularly active in launching the company into a new trend in the 1980s, that of hiring external designers to create new and complete bathroom fashions. In 1985, the company turned to designer Helmut Telefunt and debuted the first of Laufen's successful and long-lasting Vienna line. Also in that year, Laufen introduced new manufacturing technology for its sanitary products, using a high-pressure casting production process.

Laufen's operations extended into Germany during the 1980s with the addition of a share in that country's Duravit, which had long been noted for its design-focused bathroom fixtures. That company had originated in 1817 when Georg Freidrich Horn built an earthenware crockery factory in Hornberg, in the Black Forest region. By 1842, Horn's factory had begun producing sanitary fixtures as well. Throughout the remaining half of the century, the Hornberg plant continued to produce both product lines, ending crockery production only in 1912. In the 1950s, the company, which had remained an earthenware specialist, switched its production to porcelain, which it began marketing under the Duraba and Hornbeg brand names beginning in 1956. By 1960, the company had taken on a new name, Duravit GmbH, which later became a brand name as well, especially with the launch of a line of bathroom fixtures and furniture in 1977.

Duravit expanded beyond Germany in the 1980s with the purchase of a stake in France's Ceramique de Bischwiller in 1984. Then, in 1988, Duravit joined up with Laufen, changing its name to Duravit AG. With Laufen as a major shareholder, Duravit continued to grow, taking full control of Ceramique de Bischwiller in 1991 and adding Sanitarporzeltan Dresden GmbH in 1992. A strong success for Duravit came in 1994 with the launch of a new series of bathrooms and fixtures designed by Philippe Starck. Laufen and Duravit also began cooperating together on an international scale, as Laufen took over much of Duravit's international marketing and distribution needs.

International Leader in the 21st Century

The opening of the eastern European markets at the beginning of the 1990s gave Laufen a new opportunity for expansion. In 1991, the company acquired noted Czech ceramics producer Jika. That company's history traced back to 1878, with the construction of a factory in Znojmo, where decorative ceramic objects and utensils were manufactured. In 1920, Jika became the first in the region to launch the production of sanitary ceramics and bathroom fittings with a line of wash basins, tubs, and sinks. By the 1990s, Jika had become the leader in the Czech market.

A public company by the 1990s, with a listing on the Swiss stock exchange, Laufen went on a drive to internationalize its operations, adding subsidiaries in Portugal, the United Kingdom, Germany, and elsewhere. The company also built up a strong presence in Spain through a 35 percent stake acquired in Portuguese company Sanitaria, which brought it in direct competition with another European ceramics heavyweight, Roca Radiadores. The company continued to manufacture a broad line of ceramics-related products, ranging from construction materials to home furnishings, and by the mid-1990s ranked as the world's third-largest producer of ceramics, with more than 14 million pieces per year.

The mid-1990s, however, witnessed the rapid consolidation of the European ceramics sector as companies raced to gain scale for the upcoming single monetary union slated for the end of the decade. Laufen itself joined in the drive for size, turning to Dutch-Swedish counterpart Sphinx Gustavsberg. The two sides agreed to a merger in 1996 but were then forced to call off the agreement as both companies found themselves struggling in the face of an industry-wide slump.

Laufen itself was hard hit into the late 1990s. On the one hand, the ceramics industry's growth was hampered by overproduction; on the other, Laufen found itself too exposed in many of the world's emerging markets, which, after a long period of

Key Dates:

1892: Tonwarenfabrik Laufen AG, a maker of bricks and roofing tiles, is founded in Laufen, Switzerland.
1925: The company adds subsidiary AG für Ceramic Industrie Laufen and begins producing, sinks, tubs, toilets, and other sanitary fixtures.
1932: The company begins producing ceramic tiles.
1952: International expansion begins with the acquisition of Incepa, in Brazil.
1967: A merger takes place with Osterreichische Sanitär-,. Keramik-, und Porzellan-Industria (OSPAG), based in Wilhelmsburg, Austria.
1985: Laufen begins production using high-pressure casting technology.
1998: The company restructures its operations to focus on sanitary ware.
1999: Laufen is acquired by Roca Radiadores of Spain to become part of the world's second-largest sanitary ware manufacturing group.
2002: The company builds on its position in eastern Europe with the acquisition of two Czech companies.

economic growth, had begun to show signs of collapse. Laufen was particularly hurt by its efforts to expand in the Asian markets. Starting in the early 1990s, the company had rapidly built up a presence in Taiwan, Hong Kong, China, Singapore, South Korea, and Indonesia, particularly through the marketing and sales of the Duravit brand. In 1996, the company reinforced its presence in these markets, joining Thailand's United Mosaic Industry Co. to form UMI-Laufen. Yet the cost of setting up operations there, as well as difficulties elsewhere in its network, quickly dragged on the company's profits.

Laufen was also attempting to expand in South America, where its position in Brazil had grown to include Cidamar, a sanitary ware manufacturer acquired in 1976. In 1997, Laufen acquired control of public company Celite S.A. Industria e Comercio, a leading specialist in bathroom fixtures in Brazil. If that purchase made Laufen the clear market leader in Brazil, with a strong position elsewhere in Latin America—the company had gained more than 25 percent of the South American market—it also heightened Laufen's exposure to the troubled economic climate in that region.

By 1998, Laufen had dipped into losses and was forced to undergo a thorough restructuring that included a cut of some 15 percent of its international work force. Laufen also repositioned itself, regrouping its core activity around its profitable bathroom and sanitary ware and selling off its non-core operations, including its crockery and construction materials businesses. By the end of 1998, the company had largely completed its restructuring, enabling it to return to profitability by the beginning of the next year.

In 1999, Laufen announced that it was interested in pursuing strategic partnerships with other major European ceramics producers. The company was reportedly eyeing a merger with rapidly growing Sanitec, of Finland, which went on to buy

Sphinx Gustavsberg that year. Instead, in August 1999, Laufen announced that control of the company had been acquired by privately owned Spanish conglomerate Roca Radiadores. Combining Roca's sanitary ware operations with those of Laufen created an internationally operating sanitary ware heavyweight with sales of more than $1.4 billion, placing it as number two in the world, behind the United State's American Standard, and number one in Europe.

Despite becoming a member of the larger Roca group, Laufen retained its autonomous operations. The company continued to expand, especially in eastern Europe. With operations in the Czech Republic, Slovakia, Poland, Russia, and other countries of the former Soviet Union, Laufen had built up a solid position in the rapidly growing eastern European market. In 2002, Laufen increased its position in the region with the takeover, through its Czech subsidiary Laufen CZ, of two additional Czech companies, Jihoceska Keramika and Keramicke Zavody.

Principal Subsidiaries

AZA Immobilien AG; Bath Plus Inc.; Celite Mineracao do Nordeste Ltda; Celite S.A. Industria e Comercio; Celite do Nordeste Industria e Comercio de Ceramica S.A.; Celite do Parana Industria e Comercio de Ceramica Ltda; Ceramconsult AG; Duravit AG; Fayans Kaspichan AD; Incepa Loucas Sanitarias S.A.; Incepa Metals; Int. American Ceramics Inc.; Jihoceska Keramika a.s.; KWA Immboilien AG; Kera-Immobilien AG; Keramicke Zavody a.s.; Keramik Laufen AG; Laufen Asia Ltd; Laufen Ceramics Inc.; Laufen International Inc.; Laufen Canada Ltd.; Laufen-Duravit Italia S.r.l.; Logasa Industria e Comercio S.A.; Oespag; Reflorestadora Ceramica Parana Ltda; Sanitana S.A.; Sociedade de Mneracao Ceramite Ltda; UMI-Laufen Sanitaryware Ltd.; United States Ceramic Tile Company.

Principal Competitors

American Standard Corp.; Sanitec Corporation; Tostem Inax Holding Corp; TOTO Ltd.; Kohler Co.; Air Water Inc; Takara Standard Co Ltd.; Uralita SA; Villeroy und Boch AG; USI Plumbing Products; Cleanup Corp.; Geberit International AG; Elkay Manufacturing Co.; Coop Costruttori Scarl; Ideal Standard SpA; Homeform Group.

Further Reading

"Globalisation Affects Ceramics Production (Globalizace zasahla vyrobu keramiky)," *Hospodarske Noviny,* January 7, 2000.
"Keramik Laufen Sells Off Ordinary Ceramics (Keramik Laufen trennt sich von der Grobkeramik)," *Neue Zurcher Zeitung,* September 3, 1998, p. 12.
"Laufen CZ Takes Over Two Ceramics Producers," *Czech News Agency,* August 9, 2002.
"Roca Acquires Swiss Laufen and Rises to Second Place Worldwide in the Sector (Roca compra la suiza Laufen y sube al segundo puesto mundial del sector)," *Cinco Dias,* August 31, 1999, p. 4.
"Roca Gains Approval for Laufen Acquisition (Luz verde a la compra de Laufen por Roca)," *Expansion,* March 3, 2001.
White, David, and Hall, William, "Roca Group to Take Over Rival," *Financial Times,* August 31, 1999

—M. L. Cohen

Knowledge Learning Corporation

4340 Redwood Highway, Building B
San Rafael, California 94903-2121
U.S.A.
Telephone: (415) 444-1600
Fax: (415) 444-1664

Wholly-Owned Subsidiary of Knowledge Universe, Inc.
Incorporated: 1983 as Children's Discovery Centers of
    America
Employees: 1,000+
Sales: $93 million (1997)
NAIC: 611110 Elementary and Secondary Schools

Knowledge Learning Corporation is a fast-growing subsidiary of Knowledge Universe, an educational company founded by Michael Milken of Drexel Burnham Lambert fame, his brother Lowell, and Oracle CEO Larry Ellison. Based in San Rafael, California, Knowledge Learning operates more than 350 childcare, preschool, kindergarten, and primary school facilities in 24 states under a variety of names, such as Knowledge Beginnings, Children's Discovery Centers, Magic Years, Learning Universe, and Hildebrandt Learning Centers. In addition, the company provides before- and after-school care, and some of its centers offer camps during the summer months when school is not in session. A large portion of Knowledge Learning's childcare centers are funded by corporate clients for the benefit of their employees, including IBM, Travelers, and the Internal Revenue Service. Underpinning all of the programs developed by Knowledge Learning is an adherence to the educational philosophy of Swiss psychologist Jean Piaget.

Company Origins Date to 1983

Knowledge Learning, originally known as Children's Discovery Centers of America (CDC), was established in the small town of Monroe, Connecticut, in 1983 by an entrepreneur named Tommy Thompson who had been previously involved in a number of successful startups. He was attracted to the industry because of the rising need for day care. With backing from New York venture capitalists, he acquired a small Connecticut chain

of day care centers, operating as Children's Discovery Centers, then used that name to create Children's Discovery Centers of America, Inc. Thompson became the chairman and CEO of CDC, with James DeSanctis serving as his chief financial officer. Within a year they were running 12 facilities, and by 1985 took the company public. Around the same time as the IPO, CDC made a major acquisition, the purchase of Mary Moppets Day Care Schools, an Arizona chain that combined company-owned with franchised units. The timing of both the IPO and the entry into the Arizona market, however, proved disastrous. A change in Arizona regulations mandated a higher ratio of personnel per child in day care facilities, resulting in much higher labor costs and adversely impacting the entire industry in the state.

With the Mary Moppets subsidiary draining the resources of CDC, Thompson resigned and DeSanctis took over as chairman and CEO. Under his leadership, the company continued to struggle, posting a significant loss in 1986. DeSanctis and CDC's backers agreed that a change was needed, and a search was conducted to find a new chief executive with experience in turning around troubled companies. The man chosen was Richard A. Niglio, who was installed as chairman, CEO, and president in March 1987. He had considerable experience in turning around multi-unit operations, albeit in the restaurant field. He served as president and CEO of Mr. Donut of America from 1971 until 1982, then became chairman and CEO of the San Francisco-based Victoria Station restaurant chain after it entered bankruptcy in 1982. In May 1988, Niglio moved CDC's headquarters to San Rafael, California, where he had previously relocated while heading Victoria Station.

Although Niglio planned to maintain CDC's presence in New England, he saw California as an even more promising market. In reality, the childcare industry across the country held great potential. America's birthrate was increasing steadily, an echo effect of the post-World War II baby boom, and with more mothers now entering the workforce, the need for childcare facilities was growing at a fast rate. According to statistics compiled by the National Association for The Education of Young Children, childcare center enrollment increased 400 percent from 1976 to 1990. Moreover, the industry was highly

---

Company Perspectives:

Knowledge Learning Corporation (KLC) is a family of child development centers dedicated to meeting the growing needs of our nation's families. We provide quality early childhood education in several hundred centers nationwide, along with innovative services that help families achieve balance between work and home life.

---

fragmented. Operating just 53 facilities, CDC was already the fifth largest childcare company. The five largest companies combined controlled less than 10 percent of the estimated 40,000 to 50,000 centers operating in the United States. The top two companies, Kinder-Care (with over 1,000 centers) and La Petite Academy, achieved growth by opening new centers. Niglio opted instead to acquire established childcare centers. Further, he focused on providing affordable, quality child care. "Safety, supervision and cleanliness are the minimums," he told the *San Francisco Business Time* in 1988. "Above and beyond those, it gets down to curriculum and program and that can make a substantial difference with children. We've spent a great deal of our resources developing what we think is the greatest curriculum that exists."

Magic Years Acquired in 1990

To support his expansion plans, Niglio raised $4.5 million in a private placement of stock. CDC became profitable in 1988 and 1989 but in 1990, with the economy faltering, it fell into financial difficulties, mostly related to the Mary Moppets operation, which was finally sold off. As a result of a one-time charge against earnings, CDC lost $1.8 million on revenues of $16.5 million in 1990. Nevertheless, the fundamentals of the business remained sound, and by the end of 1990 Niglio was able to complete the company's largest deal, a tax-free stock swap for Magic Years Child Care and Learning Centers Inc. The move also expanded CDC's scope. While most of its 59 facilities were community-based, Magic Years' 32 centers were located at work sites, primarily hospitals and other health care facilities. Eighteen of the units were employer-sponsored centers. CDC now operated in 13 states with a total license capacity of its units standing at 8,000. Niglio was eager to maintain the company's momentum, especially in light of the problems suffered by its chief rivals. Kinder-Care, for instance, was lapsing into bankruptcy after making poor investments in high-yield bonds with Drexel Burnham Lambert, an ironic situation given Milken's eventual purchase of CDC. La Petite Academy would suffer its own problems and ultimately be taken private. As a result of these developments, CDC found itself the only company in the field capable of making sizeable acquisitions.

After completing the Magic Years merger, CDC made another stock offering of $4 million to be used in making further purchases. Niglio's targeted operations with six to ten centers that were on the verge of needing a more sophisticated infrastructure. While they would keep their local names and retain management, the acquisitions would adapt CDC's curriculum and employ its computer management systems. In 1992, the company added 41 facilities, ending the year with a total of 131

in operation and generating revenues of $25.7 million. The company was also on the verge of returning to profitability after posting losses in three consecutive years, due in large measure to CDC's rapid expansion.

CDC continued to add childcare centers in 1993, adding 26 new facilities while closing three. Niglio floated another stock offering, this time selling 1.3 million shares at $10 a share. Just a year earlier CDC's stock traded in the $3 range. The rise in value to $10 was in many ways a reflection of investor recognition that the childcare business was likely to continue to expand for a number of years. CDC picked up the acquisition pace in 1994, adding 42 facilities while closing three. With 193 facilities in operation by the end of 1994, the company grew revenues to $55.3 million, a significant increase over the 1993 total of $38.6 million. Moreover, net profits more than doubled, growing from $1.1 million in 1993 to $2.8 million in 1994. In addition to day care, CDC was also becoming involved in managing before- and after-school programs for older children, ages 6 to 12, as well as operating a few private elementary schools.

In January 1995, CDC completed a major acquisition that began to diversify its interests—the cash and stock purchase of Prodigy Consulting Inc. and its affiliated partnerships. In addition Prodigy added some $6 million in annual revenues to CDC's balance sheet. Founded in 1988, Prodigy operated seven child development centers in suburban Atlanta. It also managed ten employer-sponsored facilities spread across seven states, a segment of the childcare market in which CDC was eager to make inroads. Prodigy concentrated its efforts on such blue chip clients as Amoco, Chrysler, General Motors, IBM, UAW, and Xerox. In the first two months of 1995, CDC won five additional contracts to operate employer-sponsored childcare facilities, including an agreement with the Federal Aviation Administration in Seattle. Moreover, CDC acquired eight community-based childcare facilities during the first quarter of 1995. By the end of the year, the company added 52 units and closed six, for a net increase of 46 and bringing the total operation to 239 facilities. As a result revenues also continued a steady climb, reaching $77.6 million for the year, along with a $2.6 million profit.

Even before the completion of 1995, however, business conditions began to change. The field became more competitive, leading to much higher prices for available acquisitions. Moreover, CDC was having trouble digesting all of its 1995 purchases. Due to these factors, CDC slowed its rate of growth in 1996, adding only nine facilities for the year. Although revenues improved to $87.8 million in 1996, profits fell significantly, dipping below $1 million. One area where CDC remained aggressive was in elementary school programs, adding five operations in 1996, as well as 26 new kindergarten program. The company was also eager to create internal growth by adding grades to some operations, a simple way to boost total enrollment and revenues.

Knowledge Universe Acquires Company in 1998

Although profits rebounded in 1997, improving to $2.5 million, CDC's revenues only grew at a modest rate, reaching $93 million. After a period of retrenchment, CDC was poised to return to a growth mode in 1998. The company was particularly anxious to continue its entry into elementary education, with the

Key Dates:

1983: Children's Discovery Centers of America (CDC) is founded.
1985: CDC goes public and acquires Mary Moppets Day Care School.
1987: Richard Niglio becomes chairman and CEO.
1990: CDC acquires Magic Years Child Care and Learning Centers, Inc.
1996: Knowledge Universe is founded.
1998: Knowledge Universe acquires CDC and renames it Knowledge Learning Corporation.

goal of offering all elementary grades, and possibly higher. With the poor state of the country's education system becoming a salient topic of public discussion, CDC was clearly beginning to position itself as an education company rather than a day care chain. To realize these aspirations, however, required funding, and CDC was not alone in recognizing the potential of the for-profit private education business. One of the new players in the field was Knowledge Universe, and rather than compete against it, CDC decided to join forces when the Milken-led corporation came calling. In May 1998, a subsidiary of Knowledge Universe took CDC private. As part of a transition to a new management team, Miglio agreed to step down and accept a two-year consulting contract.

The driving force behind the creation of Knowledge Universe was Michael Milken, the controversial king of junk bonds who served 22 months in federal prison and paid a $1 billion fine for six counts of felony securities fraud. After his release from prison in 1993, much of his attention was spent on the Milken Family Foundation, which was involved in education through the awards granted to top teachers and minority students. He also came to see for-profit education as a business opportunity, revealing to *Fortune* magazine in 1996 his vision for a "cradle to cane" enterprise, encompassing not only schooling for children but also technical training and continuing education for adults. Even capturing a small percentage of this vast market could mean tens of billions of dollars. To make his vision a reality he contacted Lawrence Ellison, founder and CEO of Oracle. A subsidiary of Oracle was already one of the world's largest computer training companies, making Ellison a likely partner. Milken also enlisted his brother Lowell, and together the three men formed Knowledge Universe with $500 million in financing. The company essentially served as a vehicle for investing in the education industry.

The initial focus of Knowledge Universe was in an area with which Ellison already felt comfortable: IT training. The first acquisition took place in September 1996, a United Kingdom-based IT training company called CRT, followed by similar purchases over the next two years. It was because of Lowell Milken's interest in early childhood education that the company began to look for a suitable investment in the childcare business. They settled on CDC, then paid $80 million to take the company private. It took on the name of the acquiring subsidiary before becoming Knowledge Learning. With the deep

pockets of its corporate parent to back it, and free of shareholder pressure to produce short-term results, the company was again positioned to grow rapidly through acquisitions. Instead of targeting single units or small chains, however, Knowledge Learning was now able to consider buying operations that were larger than itself. Aside from this shift in strategy, the company also began to focus more on children's education, an area that had originally been an offshoot of its childcare operations.

Staking out market share and building a mega-brand were of greater concern than becoming highly profitable in the immediate future. Knowledge Universe was spreading in all directions, quickly becoming a billion-dollar company in annual revenues. Moreover, no other company was attempting to vertically integrate the education market, leaving it virtually unopposed. While Knowledge Universe was very much interested in acquiring more childcare facilities and developing private schools, extending its reach from pre-school through high school, the real opportunity lay with the public schools, which represented about half of America's $665 billion education market. The increasing popularity of charter schools provided a wedge into the public K-12 market. These schools were publicly funded but were operated by foundations or community groups, and in some cases private enterprise. In much the same way that for-profit hospital chains have become a major factor in health care, companies like Knowledge Universe might one day do the same thing with public schools. Regardless, the company was committed to Milken's "cradle to cane" vision, and Knowledge Learning was positioned to play a key role. Through its day care and pre-school operations, the subsidiary would be able to establish the Knowledge Universe brand with both children and parents, who thereafter would be more inclined to turn to affiliated elementary schools, secondary schools, and so on down the line. Such full market coverage of education was an enticing prospect, so much so that it appeared inevitable that major mass-media companies like Disney or AOL-Time Warner would begin to provide some stiff competition. Clearly the real battle for educational dollars had yet to be fully joined, but Knowledge Learning was sure to play a major role in the success of its corporate parent.

Principal Competitors

ARAMARK; Bright Horizon Family Solutions; Childcare Network; Kaplan; KinderCare; La Petite Academy.

Further Reading

Baker, Russ, "The Education of Mike Milken: From Junk-Bond King to Master of the Knowledge Universe," *The Nation,* May 3, 1999, p. 11.

Carlsen, Clifford, "Growing Child-care Chain Poised for Expansion Spurt," *San Francisco Business Times,* October 29, 1993, p. 3.

Galagan, Patricia, "Bullet Train," *Training & Development,* July 1999, p. 22.

Martin, Judith, "Lifelong Learning Spells Earnings," *Fortune,* July 6, 1998, p. 197.

Morris, Kathleen, "Professor Milken's Lesson Plan," *Business Week,* August 4, 1997, p. 32.

—Ed Dinger

Kurzweil Technologies, Inc.

15 Walnut Street
Wellesley Hills, Massachusetts 02481
U.S.A.
Telephone: (781) 263-0000
Toll Free: (877) 263-8263
Fax: (781) 263-9999
Web site: http://www.kurzweiltech.com

Private Company
Incorporated: 1995
NAIC: 511210 Software Publishing; 541511 Custom
    Computer Programming Services; 541990 All Other
    Professional, Scientific, and Technical Services

Kurzweil Technologies, Inc. (KTI) is an umbrella organization for companies dedicated to specific artificial intelligence technologies developed by Ray Kurzweil and his team of scientists. Subsidiary companies include Kurzweil Accelerating Intelligence Network, Inc., providing an online meeting place at www.kurzweilai.com for people interested in the future of artificial intelligence and other advanced technologies. FAT KAT, Inc. is developing a stock market prediction technology using artificial intelligence. Kurzweil CyberArt Technologies applies artificial intelligence to create computer-generated works of original painting and poetry. The Medical Learning Company provides online continuing education to family physicians using the SynPatient case simulator. KTI provides mentoring services for technology asset assessment and management, such as licensing and purchasing patent assets.

A pioneer of intelligent systems, Ray Kurzweil is one of the foremost inventors of the late 20th century and early 21st century. He has received several awards, grants, and prizes, including the National Medal of Technology in 1999, the highest such honor, and the $500,000 Lemelson MIT Prize in 2000. Kurzweil holds honorary doctorates from 11 universities. His numerous published materials include the best-selling books *The Age of Intelligent Machines* (MIT Press, 1990) and *The Age of Spiritual Machines: When Computers Exceed Human Intelligence* (Viking/Penguin, 1999). With 15 technological firsts to

his name, Kurzweil was inducted into the National Inventors Hall of Fame in September 2002.

Technological Firsts: The 1960s–70s

Kurzweil's long history of invention and innovation in computer technology preceded the formation of Kurzweil Technologies in 1995. At the age of 13 he developed the first computerized statistical application, Four Way Analysis of Variance, distributed through IBM. In 1965, at 17 years old, Kurzweil invented a computer with an "expert" system capable of recognizing patterns in classical music compositions; the computer then composed original compositions based on those patterns. For this work Kurzweil won first prize in the International Science Fair for Electronics and Communications and six national prizes; he was one of 40 winners in the Westinghouse Science Talent Search. Kurzweil appeared on the television show, "I've Got a Secret," where he played one of the musical compositions on an upright piano. One of the guest celebrities guessed his secret, that the computer he built had composed the piece.

Kurzweil's first foray into the business world occurred while he was a sophomore at the Massachusetts Institute of Technology (MIT). He input two million facts on 3,000 colleges into a computer program that then matched the preferences of high school students to appropriate colleges. Kurzweil sold the Select College Consulting Program (SELECT) to a New York publisher for $100,000 plus royalties in 1967.

Kurzweil's interest in pattern recognition led to the founding of Kurzweil Computer Products (KCP) in 1974. Kurzweil intended to develop an optical character recognition program capable of reading any font; at that time such programs were capable of recognizing only one or two fonts. By late 1974 Kurzweil succeeded in developing the Omni-Font Optical Character Recognition (OCR), but he did not know what practical applications existed for it. Unexpectedly he met a blind man on an airplane who said the only real disability to his blindness was the inability to read books, magazines, and documents. The encounter prompted Kurzweil to develop the first Print-to-Speech Reading Machine for the Blind. The OCR scanned materials and the program generalized about certain shapes,

Company Perspectives:

The principals of KTI have founded, developed, and sold four successful companies in artificial intelligence technologies. Kurzweil ''firsts'' include the first omni-font optical character recognition (OCR), the first CCD flat-bed scanner, the first text-to-speech synthesizer, the first print-to-speech reading machine for the blind, the first music synthesizer capable of recreating the sounds of the grand piano and other orchestral instruments, the first commercially marketed large vocabulary speech recognition, and others.

identified letters, and then synthesized words into an artificial voice that spoke the words out loud.

Kurzweil had to invent two other technologies first, however. In 1975 KCP completed development of the Text-to-Speech synthesizer and a Charge-Coupled Device flatbed scanner. The combination of these two technologies with the OCR program produced the Kurzweil Reading Machine, introduced in 1976. Not only did the machine incorporate artificial intelligence into a consumer product for the first time, it proved to be the most important tool for the blind since the invention of Braille. When blind musician Stevie Wonder heard about the machine, he contacted Kurzweil, who pushed production forward to provide Wonder with a Reading Machine.

Kurzweil Computer Products sought outside funding to keep the company afloat. The Xerox Corporation invested in 1978, then purchased the company for $6 million in 1980. Kurzweil acted as technology consultant to the company until 1995. Xerox renamed the OCR to TextBridge and the company name to ScanSoft.

Turning Attention to Electronic Music in the Early 1980s

Kurzweil developed a friendship with Stevie Wonder, which led to the formation of Kurzweil Music Systems (KMS) in 1982. Wonder expressed to Kurzweil his desire for a keyboard that created the sounds of acoustic instruments, such as the guitar, violin, and grand piano, yet allowed the ease of composition of an electronic keyboard. Recording multiple layers of sound one layer at a time and editing individual notes are two of the capabilities of electronic music composition. Electronic synthesizers at that time resonated in the tone of an electronic organ. With Wonder as musical advisor, Kurzweil formed KMS to develop an electronic keyboard capable of accurately reproducing acoustic music while providing the flexibility of electronic composition.

When KMS introduced the Kurzweil 250 electronic keyboard in 1983, experienced musicians were unable to discern a difference between the K250 and a grand piano. Priced at $10,700, the K250 provided 60 preset ''voices,'' including violin, guitar, brass, and strings, available for a variety of music styles, such as a symphony orchestra or a rock-n-roll band. Features of the K250 included a digital memory for recording new sounds into the machine and a ''velocity sensitive keyboard'' that produced a sound at the timbre equivalent to the force with which the musician touched the key. The Musical Instrumental Digital Interface allowed the keyboard to be connected to a personal computer that wrote musical notation on a computer monitor.

The high price of the K250 limited KMS customers to recording studios and successful musicians, such as Wonder, Pat Matheny Group, Prince, and Madonna. KMS raised funds through private and public stock offerings and through the issuance of debentures. A lower-priced keyboard, the K1000, introduced in fall 1986, expanded the company's market to amateur musicians with a retail price of $2,000.

Overburdened with debt, the company filed for bankruptcy in April 1990. At this time KMS signed an agreement to sell certain assets to Young Chang Akki Company of Korea, the largest manufacturer of grand pianos worldwide. In exchange for the rights to manufacture Kurzweil instruments under the trade name, Kurzweil received $3 million and royalties for six years. The sale allowed KMS to continue product development. In 1991 Young Chang introduced the K2000, which utilized breakthrough technology, the Variable Architecture Synthesis (VAST), capable of producing three trillion sounds. Kurzweil acted as a consultant for Young Chang until 1994.

Speech Pattern Recognition into the Late 1990s

Although Kurzweil's love of music prompted him to develop an electronic keyboard, his interest in voice pattern recognition inspired much of his inventive abilities. Kurzweil Applied Intelligence (KAI) formed in 1982 to develop a word processor that recognized human speech and responded to its command. Considered the Holy Grail of the computer industry, inventors like Kurzweil sought to create a computer capable of responding to human commands, ultimately to do so in a human voice like HAL in the movie, ''2001: A Space Odyssey.'' Many problems had to be solved first, including inadequate computer speed and computer memory for the level of processing demanded by voice command technology.

Kurzweil pioneered the most complex applications of artificial intelligence for voice command technology. The basic application of artificial intelligence involved teaching the processor to copy the manner in which the human brain recognized language usage and speech patterns. Kurzweil hastened the technological process by utilizing several programs that simultaneously analyzed a word and its role in the sentence, either as pronounced or through prediction. Development involved applying knowledge from the fields of linguistics, signal processing, speech science, and pattern recognition. After exposing the program to thousands of hours of human speech, the team at KAI taught the program to predict word use by looking for common components of sentence structure, such as a noun and its modifier. Kurzweil referred to the multiple testing programs as ''experts'' capable of learning human language usage; these complemented the acoustic phonetic analyzer, the ear of the machine. Investment from Wang Laboratories, at $1.5 million, and the Xerox Corporation, at $2.5 million, supported research at KAI.

The company's work came to fruition in the mid-1980s as KAI introduced a number of speech-to-text systems, each a refinement of the technology and its practical applications. KAI introduced the first speech recognition product in late 1985. The talkwriter employed a vocabulary of 1,000 words; words spoken discretely, with a pause between each word, were displayed as text that could then be edited and printed. A computer user had to train the program to recognize his or her particular speech pattern. This was accomplished by pronouncing a list of more than 200 unusual words into the computer, such as "oof" and "dragon beast"; the words covered every distinctive sound, or phoneme, in the English language.

Also in 1985, KAI introduced the first knowledge-based system, applied to creating medical reports. VoiceMed could be taught language specific to different fields of medicine. Kurzweil Voicesystem was the first knowledge-based speech recognition technology for use with a personal computer. KAI introduced the first commercially marketed, large vocabulary speech recognition system in 1987. VoiceReport utilized a 5,000-word vocabulary for dictation, with the capacity to add new words.

KAI found a market for speech-to-text technology among radiologists, with the vocabulary used by radiologists being taught to the computer program. The technology allowed a radiologist, while analyzing x-rays, to dictate reports into a computer rather than into a tape recorder. Tape recordings took several days to transcribe and radiologists had to proofread the report, perhaps having forgotten what was said. VoiceRAD, introduced in 1988, refined the technology. The system provided at least 75 percent correct word recognition and prompted alternatives to undetermined words; the program user said the number of the word on the list of alternatives and the computer replaced it.

Offshoots of VoiceRAD included VoiceEM, providing instant dictation for emergency rooms, and VoiceMED, developed for other specific medical applications, such as pathology, cardiology, and nephrology. The knowledge-based systems allowed for free text or suggested word phrasing. If the speaker used the term "cardioversion," VoiceMED suggested "Cardioversion was done for . . ." and listed the possible reasons for the test.

KAI sought to develop speech-to-text technology for the personal computer. In 1993 the company introduced KurzweilVoice, a system capable of recognizing 50,000 words without having to be taught an individual's speech pattern. KAI developed systems specifically for government, legal, and financial services as well as for conversion to the Dutch, German, and Italian languages. KurzweilVoice for Windows 1.0 was launched in spring 1994. The speech recognition software allowed voice commands to control Windows and allowed for dictation in various Windows software, such as WordPerfect and Lotus 1-2-3. The user chose a 60,000-word or 30,000-word vocabulary and then taught the system new words for a vocabulary of up to 200,000 words.

To support research and development, KAI made an initial public offering (IPO) of stock in August 1993. An accounting scandal, in which the president, vice-president, and treasurer of the company were found guilty of fraud, required the company to settle with shareholders in 1996. KAI did receive a $1.8 million grant from the U.S. Department of Commerce in 1994 for research in continuous speech recognition technology and its interface with keyboard and pointing devices.

KAI enhanced its voice recognition technologies for the Windows operating system. Kurzweil Voice for Windows 2.0, released in 1996, enabled voice commands to dictate, edit, format, spellcheck, create and send email, input information into spreadsheets, and update databases. In July KAI began shipments of the Kurzweil Clinical Reported, an upgrade of VoiceMed. The Windows-based application interfaced with mouse, pen, and keyboard and allowed faster reporting and greater accuracy than earlier systems.

In the summer of 1997 Kurzweil sold KAI to Lernout and Hauspie (L&H), a speech products company in Belgium, for $53 million. With Kurzweil as chief technologist L&H continued product development. In 1997 KAI introduced the first Continuous Speech Natural Language Command and Control Software, KurzweilVoice Commands. By 1999 personal computer technology accommodated enough speed to allow for program recognition of continuous speech. Kurzweil's Voice Xpress Plus led the market. KAI later became part of ScanSoft.

Formation of Kurzweil Technologies to Oversee New Ventures in the Late 1990s, Early 2000s

Kurzweil Technologies, Inc. (KTI) was founded in 1995 to handle advising and mentoring services, being offered to other advanced technology companies since 1993. KTI arranged for the purchasing or licensing of patents assets and advised companies on possible utilization of new technology. Clients included Wang Laboratories, Kendall Square Research, and Tech Online. KTI also acted as an umbrella organization for companies that would be formed to develop new technologies.

Kurzweil Educational Systems (KES), formed in 1996, continued Kurzweil's interest in print-to-speech technology. KES developed the Kurzweil 3000 Reading System for Persons with Reading Disabilities. The machine displayed an image of text while it read the text aloud, allowing a student with learning disabilities to read along. Thousands of schools worldwide purchased the Kurzweil 3000. KTI sold KES to Lernout & Hauspie for $20 million in 1998.

Kurzweil's interest in medical applications for technology led to a joint venture between KTI and the American Board of Family Practice (ABFP). The Medical Learning Company (MLC) formed to design and offer online continuing education options for family physicians. In January 2000 MLC launched FamilyMed.com, an interactive medical patient simulation education system designed by KTI to improve diagnostic skills. For instance, HeartLab, a cardiac auscultation simulator, reproduced the sounds of a heart to teach doctors to learn to hear and diagnose unknown sounds in a "virtual patient encounter." The "Case of the Week" presented a complete case file, including patient history, test results, and other information, for diagnosis and treatment recommendations. The site incorporated reference and resource materials from ABFP to the multimedia environment and provided access to clinical and research journals and medical and general news. For patients the site included a National Registry of family physicians.

MLC refined and added to the content of the FamilyMed web site, renamed FamilyPractice.com. The Family Practice Virtual Lecture Series provided doctors with an opportunity to fulfill Continuing Medical Education (CME) credit requirements. Topics in the series covered geriatric agitation, pain management, drug abuse, posttraumatic stress disorder, and other contemporary medical concerns. Doctors could send questions to the presenting doctor by electronic mail for one month after each lecture was introduced. Through an alliance with Moore Medical Corporation in early 2001, MLC offered a hyperlink to that company's web site, where member doctors could order medical, surgical, and pharmaceutical products at a discounted rate. FamilyMed.com expanded its patient services in June 2001 with the introduction of the Patient Information Center. The site provided a medical dictionary, a symptom checker, and an upgraded physician search.

In 2002 new education applications included the Peripheral Arterial Disease (PAD) Information Resources. This included the latest information on PAD and a monthly interactive patient case to aid doctors in learning diagnosis and treatment. In cooperation with the Medical Management Group and Advance PCS, health improvement services, MLC introduced the Bioterrorism Practical Readiness Network (Bio-PRN) to assist doctors in recognizing symptoms and treating simulated cases.

Another project in the application of artificial intelligence concerned the 1999 founding of FAT KAT, Inc., short for Financial Accelerating Transactions from Kurzweil Adaptive Technologies. FAT KAT utilized self-organizing principles and statistical analysis of minute data to create an intelligent system for making predictions on stock market behavior and to assist in making decisions on stock market transactions. The sets of rules on buying and selling stock provided the basis for the system to learn from successful decisions and to eliminate those rules that

contributed to poor decisions. Kurzweil sought to create a self-sustaining quantitative investment system (known as a Quant). Still in the early stages of development, FAT KAT obtained $6 million in funding for research through two private stock offerings in 2000 and 2001.

In 2000 Kurzweil founded Kurzweil CyberArt Technologies (KCAT) to offer intelligent interactive art creation programs. Ray Kurzweil's Cybernetic Poet provided assistance for the process of creating poetry and song lyrics, and "AARON" the Cybernetic Artist created original paintings, a process that can be watched with each stroke. Artist Harold Cohen developed the software over 30 years' time. Cohen taught the software his theory of color and composition and how to draw. Paintings by AARON have sold for thousands of dollars and have been displayed in renowned museums worldwide. KTI obtained an exclusive license to the AARON software. With the formation of KCAT, Kurzweil's team of programmers developed a Windows application, including a screensaver, which generated a continuous stream of original paintings, displayed a stroke at a time.

In 2001 Kurzweil founded Kurzweil Accelerating Intelligence Network. Inc., an online resource for people interested in artificial intelligence and other advanced technologies. In addition to a daily electronic newsletter, the site offered an archive of more than 500 articles by 70 authors, including Kurzweil. The web site emphasized artificial intelligence, virtual reality, and avatar technologies and their potential impact on society.

To demonstrate the possibilities of new technologies Kurzweil developed Ramona, a lifelike, animated character—and his alter ego. The project required a team of 50 engineers and artists, from several companies. The project combined several state-of-the-art technologies, including 3-D human scanning, computer graphics, and audio processing. A 25-year-old woman on the team was digitally scanned, including several different facial expressions; the pictures were transformed into animation. Ramona had the capacity for real-time conversation through the implementation of natural language processing technology. Under the persona of a rock star, Ramona debuted at an exclusive technology conference in February 2001. Kurzweil acted as virtual reality puppeteer behind the scenes. Kurzweil employed Ramona as an interactive "virtual hostess" at the web site, with Ramona guiding visitors through the web site and explaining technological concepts. Kurzweil expects that a "virtual personality" like Ramona will be used as a personal information assistant. By 2020, he predicts, interaction with computers will occur only through voice and gestures.

Principal Subsidiaries

FAT KAT, Inc.; Medical Learning Company (50%); Kurzweil Accelerating Intelligence Network, Inc.; Kurzweil CyberArt, Inc.; Kurzweil Educational Systems, Inc.

Principal Competitors

Southwest Research Institute; SRI International; Voicenet, Inc.

Further Reading

Altman, June, "Hospital Utilizes Voice Recognition," *MIS Week*, July 11, 1988, p. 1.

Buckler, Grant, "Kurzweil Applied Intelligence in Public Offering," *Newsbytes,* August 18, 1993, p. NEW08180024.

Davis, Bob, "Xerox, Wang Invest $4 Million for Stakes in Inventor's Firm—Companies Eager to Develop Computers That Respond to Voice, Use Microphone," *Wall Street Journal,* October 11, 1984, p. 1.

Dyszel, Bill, "Talking to Kurzweil Voice 2.5," *Windows Sources,* March 1997, p. 58.

Emigh, Jacqueline, "Speech/Pen Apps from KAI & IBM Deal," *Newsbytes,* December 21, 1993, p. NEW12210007.

Fraser, Jay, "Raymond Kurzweil and the Second Industrial Revolution," *EDN,* November 9, 1989, p. 356.

Henry, Gordon M., "Can We Talk?," *Time,* April 28, 1986, p. 54.

Johnson, R. Colin, "Era of Smart People Is Dawning," *Electronic Engineering Times,* December 28, 1998, p. 62.

Kozlov, Alex, "Wolf! Wolf! The Final Ignominy for a Notorious Technology Booster Is to Be Ignored When the Payoff Hits," *Financial World,* October 3, 1989, p. 54.

"Kurzweil Completes First Year with Young Chang," *Music Trades,* August 1991, p. 78.

Kurzweil, Raymond, "Merging Human and Machine," *Computer Graphics World,* August 2000, p. 23.

"Lernout and Hauspie Acquires Second Kurzweil Firm," *Computergram International,* September 3, 1998.

Panos, Gregory Peter, "Digital Diva," *Computer Graphics World,* August 2001, p. 72.

Patton, Carol, "Better Speech Recognition Means That Computers Must Mimic the Human Brain," *Electronic Design,* November 15, 1984, p. 83.

Pethokoukis, James M., "Robotrading 101," *U.S. News & World Report,* January 28, 2002, p. 23.

Petre, Peter, "Speak, Master: Typewriters That Take Dictation," *Fortune,* January 7, 1985, p. 74.

Pfeiffer, Eric W., "Start Up: Ray Kurzweil: The Ultimate Thinking Machine," *Forbes,* April 6, 1998, p. S17.

Porter, Martin, "The Impact of the Kurzweil 250," *Computers & Electronics,* July 1984, p. 42.

Rosch, Winn L., "Kurzweil Voicesystem," *PC Magazine,* October 27, 1987, p. 288.

Schroeder, Erica, "Kurzweil Voice Dictation Meets Windows Applications," *PC Week,* May 9, 1994, p. 39.

Stecklow, Steve, "Kurzweil Restates Fiscal '93 Results, Reporting a Loss," *Wall Street Journal,* September 8, 1994, p. B5.

"Young Chang to Buy Kurzweil Assets for $5.7 mil; Kurzweil Files Chapter 11; Sales Agreement Requires Court Approval," *Music Trades,* June 1990, p. 33.

—Mary Tradii

Lakes Entertainment, Inc.

130 Cheshire Lane
Minnetonka, Minnesota 55305
U.S.A.
Telephone: (952) 449-9092
Toll Free: (800) 946-9464
Fax: (952) 449-9353
Web site: http://www.lakesgaming.com

Public Company
Incorporated: 1998 as Lakes Gaming, Inc.
Employees: 30
Sales: $34.9 million (2001)
Stock Exchanges: NASDAQ
Ticker Symbol: LACOE
NAIC: 541611 Administrative Management and General
   Management Consulting Services; 713210 Casinos;
   713290 Other Gambling Industries

Lakes Entertainment, Inc. (formerly Lakes Gaming, Inc.) has experience managing two casinos on Indian-owned land in Louisiana. When its contracts to manage those casinos ended in 2000 and 2002, the company lost its revenue sources and found itself without a casino to manage. The company has agreements in place with other Indian groups to manage potential future casinos, but it was faced with a slowly moving regulatory climate in which approvals were taking longer than expected. Hoping to generate new revenue sources, the company changed its name to Lakes Entertainment, Inc. in 2002 and invested in developing the World Poker Tour, a televised series of poker tournaments. It also invested in a joint venture to develop a time-share project on property it owned in Las Vegas.

Managing Two Casinos and Entering
New Partnerships in 1999

Lakes Gaming, Inc. was formed on December 31, 1998, through a distribution of common shares to the shareholders of Grand Casinos, Inc., as part of the break-up of Grand Casinos' business. Grand Casinos separated its Mississippi casinos in

Tunica, Gulfport, and Biloxi, from its Indian casino management business. The Mississippi casinos were acquired by Park Place Entertainment Corp., a new gaming company formed by Hilton Hotels Corp. Lakes Gaming was formed to take over the former Grand Casinos' Indian casino management business.

Lyle Berman, former chairman of Grand Casinos, became the chairman and CEO of Lakes Gaming. Berman, a serial entrepreneur, formed Grand Casinos, Inc. to manage Indian casinos in Minnesota following passage of the Indian Gaming Regulatory Act in 1988. Grand Casinos went public in 1991. Other senior executives also joined Lakes Gaming from Grand Casinos, including Thomas Brosig, former president of Grand Casinos, who became president of Lakes Gaming, and Timothy Cope, former chief financial officer of Grand Casinos, who became CFO of Lakes Gaming. In addition, Lakes' board of directors was the same as that of Grand Casinos.

Lakes Gaming began by managing two Indian-owned casinos in Louisiana, Grand Casino Avoyelles and Grand Casino Coushatta. They were the two largest casino resorts in Louisiana. Grand Casino Avoyelles first opened in June 1994 and was located in the central part of the state in Marksville, about 80 miles northwest of Baton Rouge. Grand Casino Coushatta opened in January 1995 and was located in southwestern Louisiana.

Both casinos were land-based and had hotels with more than 200 rooms each. Grand Casino Avoyelles had a 50,000-square-foot gaming floor with some 1,700 slot machines, 50 table games, and an 11-table poker room. It also featured a 1,700-seat entertainment center, three restaurants, and a nightclub with live entertainment. Other amenities included a full-service RV resort and a child care activity center. Grand Casino Coushatta offered similar nongaming amenities. It had 98,000 square feet of gaming space with more than 3,000 slot machines, more than 75 table games, and a 12-table poker room.

Grand Casino Avoyelles was owned by the Tunica-Biloxi Indians of Louisiana, and Grand Casino Coushatta was owned by the Coushatta Tribe of Louisiana. The management contracts with each casino were of a seven-year duration, with the Grand Casino Avoyelles management contract set to expire in June 2001 and the Grand Casino Coushatta contract expiring in

---

Company Perspectives:

Lakes Entertainment, Inc. currently has development and management agreements with four separate tribes for four new casino operations, one in Michigan, two in California and one with the Nipmuc Nation on the East Coast. The company also has agreements for the development of one additional casino on Indian-owned land in California through a joint venture with MRD Gaming. The company also has an approximate 80 percent ownership in the World Poker Tour, LLC, a joint venture with an experienced producer of televised poker tournaments. The purpose of this joint venture is to launch the World Poker Tour and establish poker as the next significant televised mainstream sport. In addition, the company offers years of expertise in all casino disciplines for consulting projects large and small.

January 2002. When the contracts expired, the casino owners would have the option of renewing the contract, seeking a new company to manage the casinos, or managing the casinos themselves.

For the rest of 1999 Lakes Gaming sought new partners and agreements for the development and management of yet-to-be-built, Indian-owned casinos. In March the company entered into an agreement with Casino Resource Corporation to form a joint venture intended to approach the Pokagon Band of Potawatomi Indians, a Michigan-based tribe, and submit a proposal to oversee the development, construction, and management of a casino gaming resort facility. Lakes owned 80 percent of the joint venture and was the managing partner.

In June Lakes' proposal to the Band was accepted, although various regulatory approvals were needed before development could begin. At the same time Lakes announced that it would not form the previously announced joint venture with Casino Resource Corporation. In August the development and management agreements were ratified by the Pokagon Band, thus finalizing the selection process.

Later in 1999 Lakes set its sights on managing Indian casinos in California, even though California voters had not yet approved a gaming amendment. In May the company agreed to form a limited liability corporation (LLC) with Kean Argovitz Resorts (KAR), based in Houston, Texas, to develop a casino on Indian-owned land near San Diego. In July Lakes announced that it would develop and manage a second proposed Indian gaming facility with KAR near Sacramento.

In November Thomas Brosig resigned as president of Lakes Gaming to concentrate on his duties as president of the mid-South region of Park Place Entertainment Corp. In December Lakes announced a proposed merger with Rainforest Cafe, Inc., which was another venture of Lyle Berman's. The merger was called off the next month, however, reportedly due to negative reactions from Rainforest's shareholders.

For 1999 Lakes Gaming reported income of $54.7 million, all of which came from management fees. Net income for the year was $28.8 million. The company's balance sheet showed $160 million in equity, which consisted almost entirely of cash, assets convertible to cash, and land held for sale or development.

Focusing on New Casino Projects in 2000

In the first half of 2000 Lakes Gaming announced a new five-year management contract with the Coushatta Tribe of Louisiana. Under the terms of the contract, Lakes' management fees would be reduced. Nevertheless, Lakes felt that the new formula was fair to both parties. If approved by the Tribe, the contract would become effective January 2002 and continue until January 2007.

On the other hand, the Tunica-Biloxi Tribe of Louisiana elected to exercise its option for an early buyout of Lakes' management contract for Grand Casino Avoyelles. The contract, which was scheduled to expire on June 3, 2001, was concluded on March 31, 2000. Under the terms of the original management agreement, Lakes would be compensated for the management fees it would have received through the original expiration date.

Lakes received good news in California in March when voters there overwhelmingly approved a state constitutional amendment that would allow California tribes to operate Nevada-style casinos on Indian land. At the time Lakes had agreements in place for the development and management of casino resort operations with the Jamul Indian Village near San Diego and the Shingle Springs Band of Miwok Indians near Sacramento, both in partnership with Kean Argovitz Resorts. By August Lakes had agreed to form another partnership with MRD Gaming, a Las Vegas-based company that had successfully developed Indian casinos in Arizona and Kansas. The partnership with MRD would form two separate LLCs to develop two new casinos on Indian-owned land in California.

In July Lakes formed a joint venture with Metroplex, LLC to develop Las Vegas real estate that was controlled by Lakes. The property consisted of about 16 acres at the corner of Harmon Avenue and Las Vegas Boulevard (also known as ''The Strip''). The joint venture, called Metroplex-Lakes, LLC, planned to develop an upscale retail, commercial, hotel, and entertainment complex on the site. Metroplex, LLC was owned by Las Vegas-based real estate developer Brett Torino, who had a 20-year history of developing and managing award-winning residential and commercial communities in the Southwest.

During the second half of 2000 Lakes also was exploring other business opportunities, including life insurance and international Internet gaming. These investments, however, were subsequently written off over the next two years. By the end of the year Lakes was fully focused on the continued success of Grand Casino Coushatta in Louisiana and the five new casino projects slated for future development.

For 2000 Lakes reported revenue of $59.0 million and net income of $15.7 million. The company's revenue for the year included compensation from the early buyout of its management agreement with Grand Casino Avoyelles. Net income was negatively affected by the company's share of losses from unconsolidated affiliates and the write-off of investments in unconsolidated affiliates, which totaled $15.6 million.

<table>
<tr><td colspan="2">Key Dates:</td></tr>
</table>

1998:	Lakes Gaming, Inc. is formed on December 31 through a distribution of common shares to the shareholders of Grand Casinos, Inc.
1999:	Lakes Gaming operates the Indian casino management business formerly owned by Grand Casinos, consisting of two Indian-owned casinos in Louisiana.
2000:	The contract to manage Grand Casino Avoyelles in Louisiana is terminated.
2001:	The contract to manage Grand Casino Coushatta in Louisiana is not renewed.
2002:	Lakes Gaming invests in the World Poker Tour and changes its name to Lakes Entertainment, Inc.

Continuing to Pursue Management of Native American Casino Sites in 2001

In February Lakes and the Paskenta Band of Nomlaki Indians in California agreed to terminate Lakes' involvement in Band's planned casino development in northern California. The project was one of two joint ventures with MRD Gaming that Lakes had previously announced for the development of casinos on Indian-owned land in California.

In mid-2001 Lakes announced that its management contract with the Coushatta Tribe of Louisiana for the management of Grand Casino Coushatta would expire in January 2002 and not be renewed. The Tribe decided that it would place its casino operations under its direct control. Lakes' chairman and CEO Lyle Berman noted that ''the Coushatta contract is currently our only significant source of revenue.'' He expected, however, that the company's current cash resources and financing for specific projects would be sufficient to fund operations until new casino projects began operation.

In July Lakes signed development and management agreements with the Nipmuc Nation of Massachusetts for a potential future casino resort on the East Coast. The Nipmuc Nation was in the process of obtaining federal recognition and had recently received a positive finding from the Bureau of Indian Affairs (BIA). The Nipmuc Nation had more than 1,600 enrolled members, most of whom lived in central Massachusetts. As part of the agreement, Lakes would help finance the Nipmuc Nation's bid for federal recognition. In September 2001 the BIA reversed its position and issued a negative finding relating to the Nipmuc Nation's bid for federal recognition.

Before the end of the year Lakes sold property that it owned in Las Vegas to Metroflag Polo, LLC, and leased adjacent property to a related company, Metroflag BP, LLC. Lakes would receive $31.8 million for the combined transaction, while incurring a one-time pre-tax charge of $26.5 million and receiving a tax benefit of some $10 million. The company continued to own a 3.4-acre undeveloped site known as the Shark Club property, which was adjacent to the property it sold. The Shark Club property was the subject of ongoing negotiations for the development of an upscale time-share project.

In reporting revenue of $34.9 million for 2001, Lakes' management noted that regulatory and development approvals were moving more slowly than expected. The company began no new construction during the year. Several nonrecurring charges resulted in a net loss of $321,000 for the year.

Expansion into Related Businesses and a Name Change to Lakes Entertainment, Inc. in 2002

In March Lakes announced that it would enter into a joint venture with Steven Lipscomb, an experienced producer of televised poker tournaments. The venture, known as the World Poker Tour, LLC, was launched at the end of May and premiered its made-for-television poker tournament in June. Lakes made an initial investment of $100,000 in the World Poker Tour, which gave it a 78 percent ownership position, and committed to lend up to $3.2 million as needed. Lakes' announcement of the venture also noted that its CEO, Lyle Berman, was a world-renowned poker player.

The World Poker Tour intended to produce 13 nationally televised poker events to be filmed in casinos around the world, with finalists competing for multimillion-dollar prize pools. The concept was premiered in June in Las Vegas at the Bellagio Five Diamond World Poker Classic. The event was filmed, with television broadcast to be arranged later. The second event was The Legend of Poker No-limit Texas Hold'em Championship, held on August 31 at The Bicycle Casino in Bell Gardens, California, where poker was legal.

On June 5, 2002, Lakes shareholders approved a change in the company's name to Lakes Entertainment, Inc. The name change reflected the company's involvement in the World Poker Tour and the potential for other gaming and nongaming entertainment-related business opportunities. In August the company announced that it had formed a joint venture with Diamond Resorts, LLC, to develop an upscale time-share project on its Shark Club property in Las Vegas, with construction of a 33-story, four-tower, 850-unit complex to begin in 2004. Although the company reported no new casino developments through the end of the third quarter, it remained committed to pursuing new business opportunities.

Principal Subsidiaries

World Poker Tour, LLC (78%).

Principal Competitors

Harrah's Entertainment, Inc.; Mandalay Resort Group; MGM Mirage; Park Place Entertainment Corporation.

Further Reading

''Gambling Company to Finance Indians' Push for Tribal Status,'' *Knight-Ridder/Tribune Business News,* July 10, 2001.

''Minnetonka, Minn.-Based Gambling Firm May Be Left Without Casino,'' *Knight-Ridder/Tribune Business News,* June 27, 2001.

Palmeri, Christopher, ''Now the Public Takes the Risk,'' *Forbes,* August 17, 1992, p. 108.

—David P. Bianco

LANDAUER®

Landauer, Inc.

2 Science Road
Glenwood, Illinois 60425-1586
U.S.A.
Telephone: (708) 755-7000
Toll Free: (800) 323-8830
Fax: (708) 755-7016
Web site: http://www.landauerinc.com

Public Company
Incorporated: 1987 as Tech/Ops Landauer, Inc.; 1956 as
R.S. Landauer, Jr. and Company.
Employees: 400
Sales: $58.6 million (2002)
Stock Exchanges: New York
Ticker Symbol: LDR
NAIC: 541380 Testing Laboratories; 334513 Instruments
and Related Product Manufacturing for Measuring,
Displaying, and Controlling Industrial Process Variables

Since 1954, Laudauer, Inc. has provided radiation dosimetry services to hospitals, medical and dental offices, university and national laboratories, nuclear power plants, and other industries. The company has more than two hundred employees devoted to services that include the manufacture of various types of radiation detection monitors for measuring dosages of x-ray, gamma radiation, and other penetrating ion radiations by means of optically stimulated luminescent, film, and thermoluminescent badges worn by its clients' personnel; the distribution and collection of monitors to and from clients; and the analysis, reporting, and record keeping of exposure findings. Laundauer's subsidiary, HomeBuyers Preferred, Inc. provides a radon monitoring service and radon remediation.

Getting Started As a One-Man Laboratory: 1954–68

In 1954, Robert Landauer began R.S. Landauer, Jr. and Company to provide radiation monitoring, or dosimetry, services. Landauer's interest in dosimetry began as a child in the 1930s, when he had on occasion accompanied his father as the Landauer,

Sr. made his rounds calibrating radiology equipment used in medical x-ray therapy. After serving in World War II, the younger Landauer worked part-time with his father while earning a degree at the University of Chicago. He then worked for two and a half years in the commercial radiation instrumentation field before starting his own dosimetry company out of his home in Park Forest, Illinois, in 1954. According to company literature, he began ''with a few borrowed dollars and a prayer.'' Landauer incorporated R.S. Landauer, Jr. and Company in 1956.

At first, Landauer did most of the work himself, which included marking film, processing badges, and preparing reports for clients. Purdue University, General Electric, and Michael Reese Hospital were his early customers, lending credibility to his business, and Landauer's venture expanded steadily. In 1959, the company introduced the practice of cumulative total reporting to the marketplace. By 1965, the company processed more than a million dosimeters. It permanently archived the results of its monitoring.

In 1968, Landauer and Company merged with Tech/Ops, Inc. and became the R.S. Landauer Division of Tech/Ops. The combined company pioneered a number of innovations that made their services more user-oriented: an 8mm film system; a smaller, more convenient badge for clients' employees to wear to monitor radiation exposure; and an automated film reading system. Badges used film emulsion, which darkened with exposure, to record the wearer's exposure to radiation. In 1973, Tech/Ops expanded its offerings to provide Laudauer's Thermo Luminescent Dosimetry (TLD) service as a means of improving its finger badges. In 1978, it introduced neutron track etch technology, which it called Neutrak, and, in 1982, nitrous oxide dosimetry, called Nitrox. The company leased rather than sold its detection badges to customers, who returned the badges to Tech/Ops for processing. The company also took its first major step toward doing business internationally with the Nagase-Landauer Ltd. joint venture, an undertaking that provided dosimetry service in Japan in 1973.

Capitalizing on Home Radon Monitoring: 1987–90

In 1987, Landauer and Tech/Ops incorporated as Tech/Ops Landauer, Inc. to carry on the radiation business previously

Company Perspectives:

Landauer's leadership is the result of superior technical competence, advance data management, and, most importantly, a results oriented customer commitment.

handled by Tech/Ops. This business included the activities of Terradex Corp., a pioneer in the field of radon gas detection and measurement that had been purchased by Tech/Ops in 1986. It also included Landauer-Nagase Ltd. and Tech/Ops Sevcon Inc., Tech/Ops' solid-state electronic speed controller business. The move to incorporate followed Tech/Ops decision to divest itself of its businesses, a decision it implemented in 1988 when it transferred its radiation monitoring business to Tech Ops/ Landauer, Inc. in exchange for shares of common stock. After it began to operate independently in 1988, Tech/Ops Landauer purchased Terradex Corp. Tech/Ops Landauer began trading on the American Stock Exchange under the symbol TOV.

Tech/Ops Landauer received a boost in 1988 when the Environmental Protection Agency (EPA) and the Surgeon General issued a public health advisory concerning radon gas. The gas, a naturally occurring radioactive element found as a result of uranium decay in soil and rock formations, can infiltrate into basements of homes. It was presumed that exposure to radon gas could cause significant health risks.

The ensuing radon scare created business opportunities for Tech/Ops, the industry leader in radon detection. With more than 50 percent of the $12 to $15 billion market nationwide, its share price shot upward in anticipation of further growth. Thomas M. Fulton, Tech/Ops Landauer's president and CEO, speaking of the $20 million company's opportunity for expansion, was quoted in a 1988 article in *Crain's Chicago Business* as saying, "We're ready to ride it as far as it's gonna take us."

Detecting radon gas in homes was simple. Most detection services at the time sold inexpensive canisters containing charcoal to absorb the gas. These were placed in homes through one heating season—a time when most households were closed tight, cutting off natural escape routes for the gas—and, at the end of the season, the canisters were removed and sent off for processing to assess radon level of a particular house. Tech/Ops offered somewhat more sophisticated measuring devices in home testing kits, which it also had the capability of monitoring.

Tech/Ops Landauer's revenues for fiscal 1989 reflected growth directly attributable to its radon test kits: a 31 percent increase to $25.9 million overall, of which approximately 25 percent was brought in by its radon detection business. By 1990, however, public concern about household radon had abated and demand for radon detectors had slowed. The downturn in the first quarter of fiscal 1990 for the company was sudden and steep. By the end of the year, the company's sales had fallen five percent to $24.7 million.

Fortunately for Tech/Ops Landauer, the demand for dosimeters remained strong. The basic dosimetry business continued to post unit growth of 4 to 5 percent a year. In addition, while retail demand for radon testing kits fell, institutional demand re-

mained strong. Tech/Ops Landauer had contracts to provide kits for the U.S. Department of Agriculture, the U.S. Army, and school districts in Wisconsin, Virginia, and Minnesota. In addition, other industries were facing the need for dosimeters, among them airports, whose baggage handlers were exposed to x-rays, and airlines, whose pilots were exposed to cosmic radiation at high altitudes. Between 1990 and 1995, the company grew at a steady 15 percent rate per year. In 1993, it renovated and expanded its facilities at a cost of $2.2 million.

New Dosimetry Technologies: 1990s and Beyond

In 1991, the company changed its name to Landauer, Inc. and formulated plans for expanding its services into Europe. In 1992, Landauer, Inc. took a major step toward overseas expansion when it opened an office in the United Kingdom. It also began collaborating with Pacific Northwest Laboratory to develop new dosimetry technology, which it called optically stimulated luminescence (OSL) Technology. This technology used materials that luminesced when stimulated with beams of light to determine levels of radiation exposure. Until that time, traditional dosimetry methods relied upon heat exposure and were less precise. In 1994, Landauer acquired the exclusive worldwide license for use of the new technology, which it introduced shortly thereafter. That year radon gas detector kits sales were down to less than $1 million from more than $6 million in 1989. Still, overall sales for fiscal 1994 at Landauer rose 8 percent to $31.7 million.

In 1995, Landauer became the first U.S. company whose products were certified by Canada's Atomic Energy Commission. It was also the leading company in its market niche in the United States, providing radiation monitoring for corporate clients such as the Fermi National Laboratory, the Mayo Clinic, and Columbia/HCA Healthcare Corp. It controlled nearly half of the domestic $75-million market for radiation monitoring and was the number two company in its market niche in Japan. In fiscal 1995, revenues were up 8 percent to $34 million.

In 1998, Brent A. Latta replaced Fulton upon the latter's retirement after 21 years as president and chief executive officer of Landauer. Latta had joined Landauer in 1987 and had been vice-president of marketing and executive vice-president. Also in 1998, Landauer acquired a 75 percent interest in the radiation dosimetry business of Servico de Assessoria e Rotecao Radiologica S/C Ltda. (SAPRA) of Brazil.

By mid-1999, about 40 percent of Landauer's customers in the United States had been converted to OSL, which it called Luxel; the rest were converted by the end of 1999. The company began to introduce film strips, which had to be replaced monthly, to crystals, which lasted a year or longer, toward the end of 1998. This change drove income down temporarily due to a $3 million write-off of film-based radiation measurement technology. However, 1998 revenues were still up 7 percent to $42.7 million.

With Landauer's cutting-edge technology, there was optimism that the company would experience growth of 8 to 12 percent yearly in the first years of the twenty-first century. There was also hope that its new technology would give Landauer the means to penetrate European and other markets in

Key Dates:

1954: Robert Landauer founds R.S. Landauer, Jr. and Company.
1956: Landauer incorporates his business.
1968: Landauer merges with Tech/Ops, Inc.
1987: The combined company incorporates as Tech/Ops Landauer, Inc.
1991: Tech/Ops Landauer, Inc. changes its name to Laudauer, Inc.
1992: Landauer, Inc. opens an office in the United Kingdom.
1995: Landauer becomes the first U.S. company certified by Canada's Atomic Energy Commission.
2001: Landauer enters into a collaborative agreement with Matsushita Industrial Electric Company.
2002: The company's common stock begins trading on the New York Stock Exchange.

the years to come. (Despite operations in Japan and Brazil and an office in United Kingdom, only a small percentage of Landauer's sales came from overseas.) Landauer entered into a collaborative agreement with Matsushita Industrial Electric Company to develop a series of instruments and radiation detec-tors based on OSL technology in 2001. It also began offering service to customers in China that year. In 2002, there was further optimism when the company's common stock began trading on the New York Stock Exchange; Latta and Landauer's chairman of the board were there for the ringing of the opening bell on the day the company made the switch from the American Stock Exchange.

Principal Subsidiaries

HomeBuyers Preferred, Inc.; SAPRA-Landauer Ltd.; Beijing-Landauer, Ltd.; Nagase-Landauer, Ltd.

Principal Competitors

Abatix Corp.; AFA Technology; First Alert, Inc.; ICN Pharma-ceuticals Inc.; Siemens Gammasonics; Teledyne Inc.

Further Reading

Murphy, Lee, ''New Radiation Meter Fuels Landauer Gain,'' *Crain's Chicago Business*, February, 19, 2001, p. 45.
Stazewski, Len, ''Firm's Fortunes Ride Radon Scare,'' *Crain's Chicago Business*, February 26, 1990, p. 11.
Strahler, Steven R., ''Profits Detected in Radon Gas Scare,'' *Crain's Chicago Business*, September 26, 1988, p. 1.

—Carrie Rothburd

⋀ LEATHERMAN®

Leatherman Tool Group, Inc.

12106 NE Ainsworth Circle
Portland, Oregon 97220
U.S.A.
Telephone: (503) 253-7826
Toll Free: (800) 847-8665
Fax: (503) 253-7830
Web site: http://www.leatherman.com

Private Company
Incorporated: 1983
Employees: 450
Sales: $100 million (2000 est.)
NAIC: 332212 Hand and Edge Tool Manufacturing;
339920 Sporting and Athletic Goods Manufacturing;
421710 Hardware Wholesalers; 332999 All Other Miscellaneous Fabricated Metal Product Manufacturing

Leatherman Tool Group, Inc. originated the multipurpose tool and a new market niche when it began catalog sales of its Pocket Survival Tool in 1983. Since that time, the company has expanded its offerings to include nearly two dozen different hand-held multi-tools that sell in 70 countries around the world.

Marketing a Multipurpose Tool: 1976–83

The idea that led to the formation of the Leatherman Tool Group occurred to Tim Leatherman during his honeymoon. After leaving Saigon, where he married in 1975, Leatherman and his wife spent ten months touring Europe in a used 1968 Fiat that they bought for three hundred dollars. Staying in ramshackle lodgings and working on his sometimes temperamental car, Leatherman conceived of what later became the Pocket Survival Tool and, in a Tehran hotel, he made his first cardboard model. "At times the faucets didn't have handles and there was no way to turn the water on with the Boy Scout knife I carried," Leatherman was quoted in a 1985 *Oregonian* article.

A native of Oregon, Leatherman had received a bachelors degree in mechanical engineering from Oregon State University in 1970, after which he held a variety of jobs, including positions as an English teacher and a helicopter mechanic. He returned to

Portland, Oregon, with his wife in June 1976 after researching how to develop, patent, and market a new product at the Library of Congress. The two agreed that he would spend the next three months designing the tool and calling on potential customers.

Instead of months, it took Leatherman until late 1978 to develop the tool he wanted, a five-ounce, four-inch stainless steel tool that came with large and small screwdrivers, a file, scissors, a can opener, punch, ruler, knife blades, and pliers that popped out when the tool was opened. He began by modifying pliers, working with basic hand tools in his garage. In 1980, he received a patent on his "Mr. Crunch." Leatherman took a job selling welding supplies by day while he wrote and visited companies all over the United States, introducing them to his tool. He even pitched his idea to 23 of the largest purchasing organizations in the country, from the U.S. Army to AT&T. No one was interested. "Unfortunately, nobody wanted to buy my invention. The knife companies thought it was a tool; the tool companies thought it was a knife," he is quoted as saying on the company's Web site.

Leatherman continued to refine his design with the help of Steve Berliner, a college friend whose father owned and operated a machine shop, Simplicity Tool Co. The two originally saw their invention as an industrial product to be sold directly to large companies—standard equipment to be carried by telephone technicians, for example. That vision changed during a sales call to Early Winters catalogue, where someone advised Leatherman fortuitously to simplify and refine the tool to emphasize only its most widely useful features.

Berliner and Leatherman reduced the tool's complexity, cutting its wholesale cost from $40 to $20. They incorporated as the Leatherman Tool Group and set up production in Simplicity's plant, shipping their first tools right before Christmas 1983. Early Winters Ltd. of Seattle, Washington, placed an order for 500 of Leatherman's tools; so, too, did Cabela's of Sidney, Nebraska.

Creating a New Market Niche: Mid-1980s to the Mid-1990s

Three days after its catalog was out, Early Winters had sold 250 of Leatherman's tools and asked for more. Two weeks later, they came back with a request for another 1,000. The new

---

Company Perspectives:

To lead the high-quality compact multi-purpose tool market by providing the best value for our customers, being the most innovative, and continuously improving while meeting our financial goals, providing a rewarding work environment and operating legally and ethically.

Key Dates:

1980: Tim Leatherman receives a patent for his ''Mr. Crunch.''
1983: Early Winters and Cabela's catalogs begin selling Leatherman's Pocket Survival Tool.
1991: Leatherman wins the first of many trademark infringement cases.
1999: The U.S. Circuit Court of Appeals rules that competitors can faithfully copy Leatherman's tool without violating trademark laws.

---

company now faced a problem: it did not have the capacity to keep up with the orders that kept pouring in. By June 1984, Leatherman had shipped 4,000, but was about three months behind on deliveries. By Christmas 1984, close to 30,000 knives had been shipped. All knives came with a 25-year, no-questions-asked warranty.

Growth continued at a rapid pace. In late 1985, ten U.S. catalog companies sold the knife, including Spiegel, Neiman-Marcus, and L.L. Bean. In 1992, the 100-employee company moved into a new building with 24,000 square feet of production space—more than twice the size of its former factory. By 1993, Leatherman Tool Group dominated one of the hottest and newest niches in the cutlery business—that of the multi-purpose folding pocket tool—selling more than one million of its Pocket Survival Tools and generating upwards of $30 million in revenue. By 1994, sales had increased 45 percent since the debut of the Pocket Survival Tool. The $45 million company employed 200 people and sold more than a million tools for the second year in a row. Still, Leatherman continued to face issues of product backlog; as late as 1993, the year Berliner left the company to join Simplicity Tool, the company had been unable to reduce its five-month backlog.

Through the remainder of the 1980s, the Pocket Survival Tool was alone in the multipurpose tool market. Then, in the early 1990s, Leatherman began to face competition. Portland-based Gerber Legendary Blades, one of the companies that had shown no interest in Tim Leatherman's prototype, introduced its own pocket tool, the Multi-Plier. So did SOG Specialty Knives of Edmonds, Washington, with its Paratool. Coast Cutlery of Portland brought out the Pocket Mechanic. Buck Knives of El Cajon, California, teamed up with the manufacturer of the Swiss Army knife, Wegner, to make the Swissbuck. Competition brought lawsuits. In 1991, Leatherman won a $50,000 judgment—the first of many—in a trademark infringement case against Starcrest Products of California. By 1993, the company had successfully sued 13 companies for trademark infringement—among them Sears, Roebuck & Co. and JC Penney. By 1996, it had initiated 20 lawsuits and won 17 of them.

Competition drove Leatherman to shift away from being a ''limited-product'' company and to reevaluate its marketing strategy. It attempted to stay ahead of newcomers by producing a larger product with more features and locking blades, its Super Tool, which it added to its offerings in fall 1994. It also attempted to broaden its potential market base. Into the mid-1990s, the Pocket Survival Tool appealed mostly to outdoors enthusiasts. Then Keanu Reeves used a Leatherman to pry open elevator doors in the 1994 film *Speed*. The Leatherman tool also began to make appearances on shows such as NBC's *The Profiler*, where

a character used it to defuse a bomb, and *Mad About You*, where characters came across a Leatherman in a hardware store. In 1996, the company began a series of full-page ads in magazines such as *Outside*, *Outdoor Life*, and *Men's Journal*. In these ads, users described how their Leatherman had gotten them out of trouble at home and in the field. The company also its increased distribution to large consumer chains, including Wal-Mart, Home Depot, and Sports Authority.

Appealing to a Broader Market: Late 1990s and Beyond

Leatherman posted sales of about $91 million in 1996. It had 11 consecutive years of annual sales growth of 50 percent or more to its name. Still, as popular as the new tools were—by 1996, their total market was between $100 million and $150 million—the number of American households with a multipurpose tool was fewer than one in ten. In 1997, with sales in 50 countries, Leatherman addressed the challenge of potential sales by attempting to broaden the appeal of its tools. ''We looked at how people use these tools and decided that concept-driven tools were the right direction,'' according to the company's marketing vice-president in a 1997 *Brandweek* article.

Leatherman continued to introduce newly designed tools to keep ahead of competitors: a miniature model, the Micra, which was brought out in 1997, was named editor's choice by *Backpacker Magazine*. In 1998, the company introduced another new addition, the Wave, a tool designed with more features than any other Leatherman. This product was recognized by *Workbench* magazine in 1999 and *Technical Rescue* in 2000. While the Wave was a success, sales of multipurpose tools had flattened by this time. From 1993 to 1998, Leatherman sales had increased 35 to 45 percent a year; by 1999, however, the growth rate had stabilized at around 10 to 12 percent. Also in that year, the U.S. Circuit Court of Appeals dealt Leatherman a blow when it ruled that competitors could faithfully copy Leatherman's tool without violating trademark laws because its appearance was a function of use rather than an element of style.

In 2001, Leatherman brought out the Juice in five versions and colors, bringing its total product offering to about two dozen. As Leatherman's designer, Ben Rivera, was quoted in a 2001 *Design News* article: ''With the Juice, an appealing appearance was one of our top design priorities.'' So, too, was maximum portability. The more streamlined, less industrial looking Juice was 3.25 inches in length and contoured in shape to fit in a pocket. The Juice, which was the editor's pick of *Backcountry Magazine* in 2001, was followed by its miniaturized version, the Squirt, in 2002.

By the end of 2001, the company had sold more than 20 million tools. It had a computerized drawing program in-house to design new tools, 450 workers, and sales of $100 million annually, with some of this income deriving from Leatherman fans who faithfully bought updates to the traditional models. The company's success notwithstanding, Tim Leatherman continued to pursue his goal: to get a Leatherman-brand tool into the hands of 20 percent of world's population. He also held to his four business fundamentals: provide on-time delivery, meet specs, increase value, and provide a pleasant work environment.

Principal Competitors

Buck Knives Inc.; Coast Cutlery Co.; Gerber Legendary Blades; Gutmann Cutlery Inc.; Swiss Army Brands, Inc.; Wenger North America.

Further Reading

Dworkin, Andy, "Bring on the Juice," *Oregonian*, January 12, 2001, p. B1.

Ogando, Joseph, "Pocket Tool Gets a Makeover," *Design News*, November 19, 2001, p. 52.

Welsh, Jonathan, "This Gismo Grips, Clips, Cuts, Folds, Bends—And Sells," *Wall Street Journal*, March 11, 1997, p. B1.

—Carrie Rothburd

LG&EENERGY

LG&E Energy Corporation

220 West Main Street
P.O. Box 32030
Louisville, Kentucky 40232
U.S.A.
Telephone: (502) 627-2000
Fax: (502) 627-2579
Web site: http://www.lgeenergy.com

Wholly Owned Subsidiary of PowerGen plc
Incorporated: 1913 as Louisville Gas and Electric
    Company
Employees: 4,000
Sales: $2.3 billion (2001)
NAIC: 221111 Hydroelectric Power Generation; 221112
    Fossil Fuel Electric Power Generation; 221119 Other
    Electric Power Generation; 221121 Electric Bulk
    Power Transmission and Control; 221122 Electric
    Power Distribution

LG&E Energy Corporation is a diversified energy services company formed in 1990 as a holding company for the Louisville Gas and Electric Company. Its operations include two regulated businesses in Kentucky, including Louisville Gas and Electric and Kentucky Utilities Company. Together, these companies provide service to 840,000 electricity and 290,000 natural gas customers. Both firms are considered to be among the lowest-cost energy providers in the United States. LG&E's unregulated business operations include 50 percent stakes in facilities in Texas and Georgia, interests in three Argentina-based gas distribution companies, and a wind turbine in Spain. LG&E holdings also include Western Kentucky Energy, LG&E Operating Services, Enertech, and CRC-Evans, an equipment and service provider catering to the gas and oil pipeline industry on an international level. LG&E became a subsidiary of UK-based Powergen plc in 2000. Two years later, German utilities giant E.ON Energie AG acquired Powergen, creating the world's second-largest utility.

Early History: 1800s

Louisville Gas and Electric Company traces its roots to the formation of the Louisville Gas and Water Company in 1838. City fathers needed a solution to a growing crime problem in the young and bustling town that was fast becoming a jumping-off point for westward expansion. Recognizing the deterring effects of city lighting on crime, they called for a company to provide a gas-manufacturing plant and lighting system. A group of investors responded, and Louisville Gas and Water was formed with Leven Shreve as its first president.

The fledgling company sold gas manufactured from coal at a plant on Jackson Street; it made Louisville the fifth city in the United States to have gaslights in streets and homes. In 1842, the company's charter was amended to repeal a provision calling for it to establish a city waterworks, and the firm's name was shortened to the Louisville Gas Company. The company kept pace with the city's rapid expansion and growing importance as a commerce center and the "Gateway to the South." By 1859, the company boasted 35 miles of gas mains and 925 street lamps.

The next year, the United States found its attention diverted from growth to Civil War. The war itself left Louisville relatively unscathed, but economic shifts after the war, notably the rise of rail travel, sent much of the region's commerce to Cincinnati. The postwar years also brought changes to Louisville Gas—some of them unwelcome. A competitor, the Citizens Gas Light Company, built a gas plant in the city in 1871. Louisville Gas claimed that this violated its rights as the sole provider of gas in the city, but the courts ruled against Louisville Gas. The decision brought a swarm of competitors into the gas business in the city.

Another competitor, the Kentucky Heating and Lighting Gas Company, founded in 1891, was able to offer lower rates because it supplied natural gas from a well in Meade County. However, this company failed to exploit its advantage and survived only by a succession of mergers with companies that sold the more reliable manufactured gas, which was produced by roasting coal at very high temperatures.

In the 1880s, a new competitor came on the scene: electricity. Its greatest asset was the bright, concentrated light it generated that literally outshone gaslight. Louisville residents gaped at the first commercial electric lights in the city in 1881, which were installed by the Brush Electric Light Company of Louisville. Another company, the Louisville Electric Light Company, began service in 1882. But early electric systems were awkward and accident-prone, and it was not until the Great Southern Exposition of Art, Industry, and Agriculture in 1883 that the city found a new electric system, the one perfected by Thomas Edison. The inventor had designed not only the light bulb but also an entire system of wires, switches, fuses, generators, and other apparatus that were needed to make the thin glass bulbs glow.

Private power plants sprang up in the city during the 1880s. Officials at Louisville Gas watched the progress of the wires, saw the illuminated writing on the wall, and prepared to enter the new business. The key move came in 1890, when the company obtained an amendment to its new charter that allowed it to manufacture, distribute, and sell electricity and to buy stock in electric companies. Louisville Gas quickly acquired a controlling interest in the Louisville Electric Light Company and began replacing gas street lamps with electric arc lights.

The Birth of Louisville Gas and Electric: 1913

The Louisville Lighting Company was formed in 1903, and the city council authorized only underground wiring in the city's central business district. Colonel Henry M. Byllesby, an electrical expert whose company, H.M. Byllesby & Company Inc., managed utilities in a number of states, had been watching the developments in Louisville. Byllesby succeeded in streamlining the city's utility operations into a single company in 1913. This was the birth of Louisville Gas and Electric, which consolidated the old Louisville Gas Company, the Louisville Lighting Company, and the Kentucky Heating Company. Three other companies were later added, and the new giant was soon serving 37,000 gas customers and 19,000 electric customers.

Most of the city's larger businesses soon switched from individual steam (electricity) plants to LG&E's service. The city used its stock in the Louisville Gas Company as leverage to require Byllesby to agree to construct a gas pipeline from West Virginia that would shore up the city's dwindling gas supply. The line was completed in March, 1914, at a cost of about $3 million, remaining in service until 1962. The new gas burned brighter, allowed customers to use less, and became cheaper as usage soared.

The low cost of gas in the growing city brought steady increases in demand: from 1914 to 1924, Louisville's appetite for gas doubled every four years. From 1920 to 1923, for example, 192 new industries came to the city. LG&E expanded to meet these growing needs but at times was forced to urge conservation because of the skyrocketing demand. In late 1920, the company bought 51 percent of the stock in the Ivyton Oil &

Gas Company, which had 18 gas wells in Magoffin County, Kentucky. In 1923, the company began work on a new manufactured-gas plant that would provide a long-term solution to the gas shortage. The company also turned to hydroelectric power in the 1920s, and received permission from the Federal Power Commission to build a generating station on the Ohio River as part of a power and navigational dam project on the river. Ohio Falls station, completed in 1927 at a cost of about $8 million, met much of the city's power needs through the 1930s.

Louisville's swelling demand for gas was reined in sharply by the Great Depression. LG&E made it through the hard times better than many firms, with only one pay cut for employees that lasted just three months. The tobacco and distillery industries, areas that tend to prosper during hard times, helped keep Louisville's industrial base afloat. But changes were in store: Franklin D. Roosevelt's New Deal brought a host of new regulations and legislation designed to affect the way public utility companies did business. In 1934, the Kentucky legislature created the Public Service Commission to oversee rate regulation and approve public-construction projects.

Key Decisions Lead to Postwar Growth

In 1939, LG&E made a key decision that would influence Louisville's emergence as a post-World War II industrial center. The company ordered two 25,000-kilowatt, steam-powered electrical generating units just a few months before the government's growing mobilization for war halted utility-expansion projects. Beating that deadline left the city in much better shape than many others when the fighting was over. The new electrical capacity also enabled the utility to be a supplier of energy for government and defense needs. That brought new industry to Louisville during the war and attracted peacetime industries to the city even into the 1960s, including LG&E's biggest customer, General Electric's Appliance Park. The company also developed new underground natural gas storage facilities to meet the postwar boom in gas heating and cooking appliances, and the construction of interstate gas pipelines brought in new supplies of gas to fill those storage facilities.

A challenge to the company's future came in 1944 and 1945, when Mayor Wilson Wyatt, with the support of the city's Board of Aldermen, sought to have the city acquire all LG&E's physical properties. LG&E employees fought the takeover attempt and worked to turn public opinion against it. Democratic alderman candidates in the November 1945 election supported the move, but the Republicans won the election, and their victory effectively quashed the attempt.

The 1950s and 1960s saw LG&E's diversification into new opportunities. In 1952, the company was one of 15 investor-owned utilities that formed the Ohio Valley Electric Corporation to meet most of the power requirements of an Atomic Energy Commission plant in Ohio. In 1967, LG&E became a charter member of the East Central Area Reliability Coordination group, a network of utilities whose interconnections have been used to supplement local power output during emergencies and peak demand periods.

A different sort of company milestone came in 1957: the first general increase in electric rates in LG&E history. In 1972, the company applied to the Public Service Commission of Kentucky for a second general rate increase following reductions in 1964 and 1965. The 1972 increase marked the beginning of a tough decade for utilities and energy providers nationwide. LG&E was forced in 1973 to seek a moratorium on new and additional gas loads by its customers.

The problem of declining natural gas supplies was compounded by the extremely cold winters of 1976–77 and 1977–78 and the oil shortage that occurred at the same time, forcing the company to curtail its industrial and commercial gas customers. Fortunately, the supply picked up again in 1979, when the company began hooking up new residential and small commercial and industrial customers who could be served from existing mains.

LG&E began construction of a massive new project, the Trimble County electric generating station, in 1979. The 495-megawatt, coal-fired power plant began commercial operation in December 1990. Early in 1991, the company sold about 12 percent ownership interest in the Trimble County plant to the Illinois Municipal Electric Agency. LG&E also entered a long-term agreement with the Indiana Municipal Power Agency for the remaining 12.88 percent of Trimble County's capacity. The two sales were important because they ensured a market for the portion of the plant's capacity that was not covered by customer rates.

Litigation over the plant had been troublesome, however. In February 1991, the Franklin Circuit Court overturned a 1989 settlement agreement approved by the Public Service Commission of Kentucky. The agreement had excluded one-fourth of the plant's capacity from the rate base, but some intervenors argued that even 75 percent left the utility with an overcapacity. LG&E vigorously contested this challenge, arguing before the courts that no further rate action was justified. The issue was resolved the following year.

LG&E Energy Corp. Is Formed: 1990

In 1990, the company began aggressively expanding into the increasingly competitive field of energy services, forming LG&E Energy Corp. as a holding company. In 1991, the company reorganized into three distinct operating units: retail electric, wholesale electric, and retail gas.

Crucial to success in the energy field were the increasing concerns over protecting the environment. The company appeared in a good position to meet that challenge: LG&E was one of the first utilities in the nation to equip its coal-fired boilers with "scrubbers." Scrubbers were designed to enable plants to reduce sulfur-dioxide emissions to levels required by the year 2000 under the Clean Air Act.

However, there were some problems. Costs of reducing sulfur dioxide emissions at LG&E's Mill Creek and Cane Run plants, cited in 1991 by the Air Pollution Control District of Jefferson County, were expected to run about $52 million to $70 million. Also, residents near the Mill Creek plant reported damage to unprotected metal surfaces and spotting of paint on automobiles caused by plant emissions. The company worked with regulatory officials to solve the problems and surveyed residents to identify potential property damage claims. The utility has traditionally sought to recover the costs of complying with environmental regulations and settling property damage claims through future rate-making proceedings.

Anticipating that by the year 2000 half of all the new electricity generating capacity in the country would be provided by unregulated, independent suppliers, the company formed LG&E Energy Systems Inc. in 1991 to spearhead the expansion into the unregulated marketplace. In December 1991, this subsidiary acquired Hadson Power Systems, Incorporated, of Irvine, California, for about $50 million. The move was considered crucial to the company's goals of expanding into unregulated power supply. Hadson, which employed about 1,000 people, was renamed LG&E Power Systems Inc. The company designed, built, and operated electric generation plants that sold energy to local utilities. LG&E Power Systems has developed numerous power plants across the United States.

In 1992, LG&E Energy Systems, through a subsidiary, acquired a one-third general partnership interest in Natural Gas Clearinghouse (NGC). An indirect, wholly owned subsidiary of British Gas plc also acquired a one-third interest in NGC. LG&E Energy Systems' subsidiary paid approximately $52 million plus fees and expenses for its one-third partnership interests in NGC. Based in Houston, NGC was the largest independent natural gas marketer in the United States. This move, like the acquisition of Hadson, seemed designed to strengthen the company's ability to continue to meet new challenges and offer new opportunities for energy providers outside the field of regulated utilities. This interest was sold in 1994 however, for $170 million.

In 1993, the firm realigned its business, creating retail gas, retail electric, and wholesale generation divisions. The following year it restructured further, segmenting its operations into utility and non-utility business units. LG&E Power Marketing was then established in 1994 as a trading subsidiary. It received the go-ahead from the Federal Energy Regulatory Commission to market and trade power, making it the first U.S. company with ties to a regulated utility allowed to do so. In 1995, the company acquired Hadson Corp., a natural gas concern based in Dallas, Texas. It was renamed LG&E Natural Inc. the following year. The firm also made strides in international expansion when it completed development of a natural gas-fired plant in Argentina. In 1997, it increased its stake in Argentina's gas market by purchasing interests in two Argentine gas distribution companies. This was followed by the 1999 acquisition of a 19.6 percent share of Argentine gas distribution firm Gas Natural BAN.

Strategic Changes: Late 1990s and Beyond

LG&E made several key moves in 1998. It purchased KU Energy Corp. in a deal that added Kentucky Utilities Company to its regulated business arsenal. The firm also signed a 25-year lease agreement with Big Rivers Electric Corp., which gave LG&E access to the company's generation assets. As a result of both transactions, LG&E's assets grew from $3.6 billion to $4.7 billion. The company opted to exit the merchant trading and sales arena that year. Turbulent prices in the highly competitive U.S. wholesale electricity market had forced LG&E to rethink its strategy in that sector. Chairman and CEO Roger W. Hale commented on the firm's rationale behind the decision in a 1998 *Electric Light & Power* article, claiming that the firm ''lacked the size and scale necessary to manage the existing portfolio of contracts, and simultaneously grow our energy marketing business in other areas.'' The company's focus on its physical assets also became apparent when it began construction of a merchant plant in Georgia in 1999 and acquired CRC Holdings Corp., the parent company of CRC-Evans Pipeline International Inc., a company that provided equipment and services related to gas and oil pipelines.

LG&E entered the new century on solid ground. Both net income and revenues had increased during 1999, and the company had been ranked number one among electric service providers in customer satisfaction by J.D. Power and Associates. The year 2000, however, brought significant change to the company. In February, LG&E announced that it would be acquired by London, England-based Powergen plc in a $3.2 billion cash deal, which also included the assumption of $2 billion in debt. The purchase, which gave Powergen a foothold in the U.S. market, was completed in December and strengthened LG&E's position in the energy services industry. In 2002, Powergen was acquired by German utility E.ON Energie AG in a union that created the world's second-largest utility concern. E.ON planned to utilize LG&E for future growth in the U.S. utilities market. While LG&E's ownership had changed hands, its reputation remained constant. In 2002, it was ranked number one in customer satisfaction in a J.D. Power & Associates survey for the second time in four years. The Edison Electric Institute also found that Kentucky Utilities' average electricity rates were the lowest in the nation in July 2001. With a utilities powerhouse as a parent, LG&E appeared to be well positioned for future growth in both its regulated and unregulated businesses.

Principal Subsidiaries

Louisville Gas and Electric Company; Kentucky Utilities Company; LG&E Operating Services; CRC Holdings Corp.

Principal Competitors

American Electric Power Company Inc.; Cinergy Corp.; NiSource Inc.

Further Reading

Burr, Michael T., ''Not for the Faint Hearted,'' *Electric Light & Power*, September 1998, p. 3.
''FERC Approves Utility Merger,'' *Oil Daily*, June 29, 2000.
Fuhrmans, Vanessa, and Marc Champion, ''E.ON and Powergen Form a Superpower,'' *Wall Street Journal Europe*, April 10, 2001, p. 1.
''LG&E, KU Energy Close Merger,'' *Oil Daily*, May 5 1998.
''Powergen,'' *Power Engineering*, August 2002, p 20.
Shook, Barbara, ''Powergen to Buy LG&E in $5.2 Billion Deal,'' *Oil Daily*, February 29, 2000.
Zipser, Andy, ''Power Trip,'' *Barron's*, February 18, 1991.

—Steven Drummond
—update: Christina M. Stansell

Lifetime Entertainment Services

309 West 49th Street
New York, New York 10019
U.S.A.
Telephone: (212) 424-7000
Fax: (212) 957-4110
Web site: http://www.lifetimetv.com

Wholly Owned Subsidiary of The Walt Disney Company and The Hearst Corporation
Incorporated: 1984 as Hearst/ABC-Viacom Entertainment Services
Employees: 700
Sales: $715 million (2001 est.)
NAIC: 513210 Cable Television Networks; 512110 Video Production; 511120 Magazine Publishers; 514191 On-Line Information Services

Lifetime Entertainment Services is a joint venture owned by The Walt Disney Company and The Hearst Corporation. It operates the Lifetime Television Network, a basic cable network focusing on women viewers, launched in 1984. As of 2002 Lifetime TV was the top-rated cable network in prime time. Lifetime Entertainment Services also owns and operates the Lifetime Movie Network and Lifetime Real Women, two related networks that feature programming for women. The company also has an in-house production studio and an online division.

Providing Talk Show Programs for Women: 1984–87

The joint venture that has operated the Lifetime Television Network since its debut in February 1984 originally had three partners with equal shares: Hearst Corp., ABC Inc., and Viacom. Prior to the launch of Lifetime Television, Hearst and ABC operated Daytime, a four-hour per day weekday cable service that featured alternative programming for women. Daytime began broadcasting in March 1982. Meanwhile, Viacom launched its Cable Health Network in June 1982 as a 24-hour service offering a wide range of health-related programming. The Cable Health Network was renamed Lifetime Medical Television in November 1983 and ran until July 1993.

In 1984 the three companies formed Hearst/ABC-Viacom Entertainment Services to operate Lifetime Television, which was created through a merger of Daytime and the Cable Health Network. Thomas F. Burchill was named president and CEO; he would serve in that capacity until February 1993. Lifetime's programming was initially designed to capitalize on Daytime's primarily female audience and, to a lesser degree, the audience of Lifetime Medical Television. At first programming consisted of a wide range of talk shows targeted to women, including "Good Sex with Dr. Ruth" and "Regis Philbin's Lifestyles," as well as medically related programming such as "Cardiology Update." Following her debut on Lifetime, Dr. Ruth Westheimer became something of a media celebrity, appearing regularly on NBC's "The Letterman Show" and churning out books, newspaper columns, home videotapes, and even a sex-oriented board game.

Lifetime had committed $25 million to its talk show programming. Although Dr. Ruth's show was quite popular, the other shows did not catch on, and the network was $16 million in debt by the end of 1985. Burchill decided to add more original programming and diversify Lifetime's audience. He also consolidated the network's medical shows into Sunday-only blocks called "Doctor's Sunday." The Sunday medical programs attracted pharmaceutical advertisers, which contributed about one-fourth of Lifetime's advertising revenue. By 1986 the all-talk shows were eliminated, having failed to attract viewers, and Lifetime was $36 million in debt.

Obtaining Off-Network Programming and Developing the Lifetime Brand for Women: 1987–92

Lifetime quickly refocused on women as its primary audience and branded itself as "Television for Women." In 1988 Pat Fili was hired as senior vice-president of programming and production. She began acquiring the rights to syndicated shows that had run on the broadcast networks, starting with "The Days and Nights of Molly Dodd," which had developed a cultlike following during its prime time run on NBC. Lifetime paid $14 million for 26 existing episodes and then produced 39 more episodes of the series. Other shows acquired by the network included "Cagney and Lacey" at $100,000 per episode and "L.A. Law," for which it paid a reported $210,000 per episode.

The completion of Lifetime Astoria Studios in Queens, New York, enabled the network to produce more original programming. These included series such as "The Parent Survival Guide," produced by Scholastic Productions, and "What Every Baby Knows: The First Three Years." In 1990 Lifetime announced that it would produce 15 original movies for its female audience over the next three years. It also acquired movies from the major studios, including a package of 23 films from Orion Pictures that included *Bull Durham* and *Married to the Mob* and ten films from Warner Bros. including *The Accidental Tourist* and *Tequila Sunrise*. Both film packages bypassed syndication and aired exclusively on Lifetime.

On the medical front, Lifetime launched Healthlink Television in June 1990 to provide programming for physicians' offices. It planned to be in 12,000 offices by the end of 1990 and 20,000 by June 1991. As part of its service, Healthlink provided participating physicians with a large-screen television, videocassette player, and free programming.

By 1991 Lifetime found that original movies boosted the network's ratings; ratings were three times higher than for acquired movies. Broadcast networks became interested in Lifetime's original movies, and ABC aired Lifetime's original movie "Stop at Nothing" following its Lifetime premiere. Lifetime aired six original movies in the 1991–92 season and planned to offer nine for 1992–93.

During 1991 Lifetime continued to acquire films and off-network rights to syndicated series. It paid $25 million for 38 movies from Orion, including *Dances with Wolves* and *Silence of the Lambs*. It also acquired the "China Beach" series from Warner Bros. and the rights to the 85-episode series, "thirtysomething," from MGM.

The production of a two-hour political special, "Seize the Power: A Lifetime Challenge," in 1992 marked a first for Lifetime. The special was produced by ABC News, marking the first time in Lifetime's history that a broadcast news division produced a premiere special for the network. The two-hour special was broadcast live from Sarah Lawrence College and looked at issues important to women.

New Management: 1993–99

When President and CEO Thomas Burchill announced in 1993 that he would resign to join Petry, Inc., a broadcast sales rep firm, longtime Lifetime executive Douglas W. McCormick was named to replace him. McCormick wanted Lifetime to begin producing more news and information shows aimed at women, and he stepped up the network's branding efforts by launching a major consumer ad campaign.

Shortly after McCormick was appointed president and chief operating officer (COO), Pat Fili left to take charge of ABC's daytime programming. She was replaced by Judy Girard of WNBC in New York as senior vice-president of programming and production. By April 1993 Lifetime was reaching 57.2 million homes and broadcasting seven hours of original programming daily. The network's original programming budget increased by 50 percent between 1992 and 1993, and in 1994 Lifetime announced that it would spend between $50 and $60 million on original movie productions.

Lifetime also made a major programming change in mid-1993 when it dropped its Sunday-only block of medical programming. The move freed up Sundays for more popular programming, allowing the network to counter-program the sports events and shows that dominated that day. Lifetime's new Sunday programming focused on events and was anchored by movies at 6:00 p.m. and 8:00 p.m. "Lifetime Magazine," the network's news show produced by ABC News and hosted by ABC News correspondent Lisa McRee, aired at 10:00 p.m. on Sunday.

By 1994 it was clear that Lifetime Television was a leading cable network. It ranked eighth among basic cable networks in prime time viewing and was first among basic cable networks in total daytime viewing among 18- to 49-year-old women. In April Viacom sold its one-third interest in Lifetime to its partners, Hearst and CapCities/ABC, for $317.6 million. By mid-1994 Lifetime was reaching 59 million households, and in August it achieved its highest ratings in prime time with a 1.4 rating.

At the beginning of the 1994–95 season, Lifetime resurrected the tag line, "Television for Women," and began using it extensively. Among newly acquired programs were 162 episodes of "Designing Women" from Columbia. The network also debuted a new hour-long series, "Barbara Walters: Interviews of a Lifetime," which offered two celebrity interviews per show from ABC News' library of Walters specials. In addition Lifetime committed to 52 weeks of "Good Housekeeping" programming to be produced by Hearst Corp. In March 1995 Lifetime debuted "Intimate Portraits," a series of one-hour profiles of accomplished women.

For 1995–96 Lifetime committed $100 million to original programming. The network had four dramas and a reality series in development for the coming year. It also announced that it would co-sponsor the USA Basketball Women's National Team and air more than 100 vignettes to be underwritten by other sponsors of the team. In mid-1996 ESPN and Lifetime announced that they would both carry the inaugural season of the National Basketball Association's new WNBA during the summer of 1997. As a result of its involvement with women's sports, Lifetime created a new sports division in April 1997.

During 1996 Lifetime continued to acquire the off-network rights to network series. It paid more than $450,000 per episode for the rights to the CBS series "Chicago Hope," and in August 1996 the network paid $600,000 per episode for the ABC series "Ellen." The acquisition of "Ellen" marked the first time that a cable network purchased a top-20 sitcom directly off its network run. "Ellen" was set to run on Lifetime starting in the fall of 1998.

In the second half of 1996 Dawn Tarnofsky was named Lifetime's new head of programming, replacing Judy Girard. Tarnofsky was formerly senior vice-president of creative affairs at 20th Century Fox Television. Her goal at Lifetime was to boost original programming from 50 percent of the network's schedule to 80 percent. For 1996 Lifetime aired about 1,500 hours of original programming. One of the first new programs launched under Tarnofsky was a two-hour original programming block called "The Place." Aimed at the 18 to 34-year-old female audience, "The Place" was dropped after a year for not reaching the older members of the 18 to 34-year-old segment. Tarnofsky also had the go-ahead to develop five series pilots.

Toward the end of 1997 Lifetime announced plans to launch its first spinoff network, Lifetime Movie Network, in the fall of 1998. The ad-supported network would be launched in both analog and digital formats and feature contemporary made-for-television films and miniseries from the network's library. The network also would run select theatrical films.

In February 1998 Lifetime won a heated bidding contest for the off-network rights to "Party of Five." The network paid $550,000–$650,000 per episode to Columbia TriStar Television Distribution, with the series set to run on Lifetime in the fall. Later in the year Lifetime acquired the second-cycle rights to another sitcom, "Caroline in the City," for about $300,000 per episode. Lifetime could air the series after its first cycle of syndication on TV stations and cable superstation WGN, starting in September 2002. Lifetime President Doug McCormick commented, "We've had a tremendous degree of success with sitcoms on Lifetime."

For the 1998–99 season, Lifetime selected Tuesday nights to showcase its new original series, consisting of one drama and two sitcoms. The hour-long drama, "Any Day Now," was produced by Spelling Entertainment Group and followed the relationship of a successful female African-American lawyer and her white homemaker friend in the South. Debuting in August, "Any Day Now" achieved a 1.9 rating, which represented a 21 percent increase over the same time period of the previous year. It was followed by two sitcoms: "Maggie," starring Ann Cusack, and "Oh Baby," featuring Cynthia Stevenson and Joanna Gleason.

Becoming Top-Rated Cable Network Under Carole Black's Leadership: 1999–2002

When it was announced at the end of 1998 that President and CEO Douglas McCormick would be leaving Lifetime, there was a great deal of discussion about whether the network would select a woman to replace him. Despite achieving strong ratings and increasing ad revenue for Lifetime, McCormick's five-year contract was not renewed by Lifetime's owners, The Walt Disney Co. and Hearst Corp. In February 1998 Carole Black, a local broadcaster who was relatively unknown to the cable community and Madison Avenue, was selected to head Lifetime Entertainment Services. Prior to joining Lifetime Black was president and general manager of KNBC, the NBC-owned and -operated station in the Los Angeles market.

When Black took over, Lifetime was rated the number one cable network among women aged 18 to 49 in both prime time and total-day viewing. For the 1999–2000 season, Lifetime introduced two new reality-based shows: "How Could It Happen," hosted by Melissa Etheridge, and "The Ruby Wax Show," which featured the British talk show host. Two other original series, "Any Day Now" and "Oh Baby," were renewed for second seasons of 22 episodes each, while another original series, "Maggie," was canceled. In mid-1999 Lifetime paid about $58 million, or $360,000 per episode, for 160 episodes of "Mad About You," which would begin airing on Lifetime in March 2002. The network also reached an agreement with ABC to rerun "Once and Again" episodes just three days after the new drama was shown on ABC. Other key aspects of Lifetime's 1999–2000 programming included 12 original movies and four documentaries. The network also announced the start-up of its own in-house production unit, which would produce primarily daytime shows.

Beginning in February 2000, Lifetime faced a new competitor for female viewers from Oxygen Media, a new network with the backing of Geraldine Laybourne and Oprah Winfrey, among others. New programming introduced by Lifetime included a game show, "Who Knows You Best," which was hosted by Gina St. John of "E! News Daily," and a reality-based series, "Love and Life," which followed real-life relationships. For the noon hour, Lifetime introduced "Lifetime Live," a news show produced by ABC News and co-hosted by ABC correspondent Deborah Roberts and Dana Reeve, the wife of actor Christopher Reeve. The network also relaunched its web site, www.lifetimetv.com.

Lifetime also continued to acquire off-network rights to such popular sitcoms as "Will and Grace," which would begin airing on Lifetime in the fall of 2005, and "The Nanny," which would start being shown on Lifetime in November 2002. In May 2000 Lifetime introduced a new public awareness campaign called "Our Lifetime Commitment: Strong Women." The series of public service announcements (PSAs) were designed to build self-esteem in teenage girls and to support their mothers and mentors.

In mid-2000 Lifetime's ratings showed significant strength. The network had the biggest prime time increase of the ten top-rated cable networks, and overall it ranked fifth for prime time behind USA, TBS, TNT, and Nickelodeon. Lifetime's prime time audience increased by 21 percent, from a 1.4 rating with one million households in 1999 to a 1.7 rating with 1.3 million households.

"Strong Medicine," a drama featuring women doctors serving women patients, debuted in July 2000. The Sunday night drama was the highest-rated new series launched in 2000 in prime time on ad-supported cable, averaging 2.0 after its first seven episodes. Overall, Lifetime ranked fourth among cable networks in prime time viewing for the fourth quarter of 2000, tied with USA Network and the Cartoon Network at a 1.7 rating. In total-day Nielsen ratings, Lifetime tied for second place. For 2000 the network's estimated annual ad revenue reached $570 million, fourth among cable networks behind ESPN, MTV, and Nickelodeon.

In January 2001 Lifetime finally unseated perennial winner USA Networks and became the top-rated cable network in prime time. The network achieved a 2.1 rating in large part on the strength of nightly movies and a trio of original Sunday series: "Strong Medicine," "The Division," and "Any Day Now." "The Division" debuted in January and focused on the lives of female detectives in San Francisco; it pulled a 3.1 rating and drew the largest audience of any basic cable original series premiere in 2000. The network also aired the original movie, "What Makes a Family," produced by Whoopi Goldberg and Barbra Streisand and starring Brooke Shields as a lesbian parent, in January.

Lifetime maintained its top-ranked position among cable networks throughout 2001, averaging a 2.0 rating for the year. Its original series, "Strong Medicine," was the highest-rated original drama on basic cable in 2001 with a 2.5 average household rating. During the year Lifetime extended its brand by publishing the first books under the Lifetime imprint and launching Lifetime Real Women, a digital network that featured reality-based programming. Ad revenue reached an estimated $715 million. Carole Black received numerous awards in 2001, including *Fortune's* Top 50 Women in Business, *Business Week's* Top 25 Managers of the Year, and *People's* 50 Most Beautiful People. She also was recognized by the National Organization of Women for Lifetime's "unmatched public affairs advocacy work."

At the end of the 2001–02 season Lifetime's popular series, "Any Day Now," completed its fourth season. The show's run came to an end after 88 original episodes, with new episodes averaging 1.6, 2.0, and 2.2 ratings during the first three seasons. In its fourth and final season the show averaged 2.8 through 12 installments. Lifetime planned to air reruns of the series starting in summer 2002.

For 2002 Carole Black increased Lifetime's programming budget to a record $300 million, and she doubled the marketing budget. A minor setback was encountered early in the year when executive vice-president of entertainment Dawn

Tartofsky-Ostroff left the network to become president of UPN Entertainment. She was replaced later in the year by Barbara Fisher, who was formerly president of network programming for Universal Studios. New programming introduced in 2002 included the hour-long dramatic series "For the People," which debuted on the network's Sunday night block of dramas that also included "The Division" and "Strong Medicine," and an original movie starring Mia Farrow.

The network maintained its top ranking among cable networks for the first two quarters of 2002 and was available in 85 million households. It announced plans to extend its brand by publishing a *Lifetime* magazine and promised a new series for 2003 called "Final Justice," starring Erin Brockovich.

Principal Operating Units

Lifetime Television Network; Lifetime Movie Network; Lifetime Real Women; Lifetime Astoria Studios; Lifetime Online.

Principal Competitors

Oxygen Media Inc.; Rainbow Media Holdings Inc.

Further Reading

Brown, Rich, "Original Ideas from Lifetime," *Broadcasting & Cable,* December 4, 1995, p. 58.
——, "Ownership Change Doesn't Cut Lifetime's Lifeline," *Broadcasting & Cable,* April 4, 1994, p. 6.
Dempsey, John, "Femme Niche a Lifetime Club," *Variety,* January 29, 2001, p. 27.
Donohue, Steve, "Lifetime Is Aglow After January Win," *Multichannel News,* February 5, 2001, p. 8.
"Douglas Walter McCormick," *Broadcasting & Cable,* November 29, 1993, p. 102.
Freeman, Michael, "Falling Under a Spell(ing)," *Mediaweek,* September 28, 1998, p. 9.
Furman, Phyllis, "Having the Time of Her Life," *Crain's New York Business,* November 11, 1996, p. 37.
Hundley, Heather, "The Evolution of Gendercasting: The Lifetime Television Network—'Television for Women'," *Journal of Popular Film and Television,* Winter 2002, p. 174.
"Lifetime," *Mediaweek,* March 7, 1994, p. 29.
Littlejohn, Janice Rhoshalle, "Lifetime's Rise Lifts Bar in Women's Sector," *Multichannel News,* November 26, 2001, p. 80.
McAdams, Deborah, "Lifetime Zooms," *Broadcasting & Cable,* July 3, 2000, p. 31.
——, "Opportunity of a Lifetime," *Broadcasting & Cable,* October 18, 1999, p. 22.
McConville, Jim, "Black's Chance of a Lifetime," *Electronic Media,* July 5, 1999, p. 1.
——, "Lifetime Job Search Spurs Hot Debate," *Electronic Media,* December 7, 1998, p. 1A.
——, "Women's Network War Begins," *Crain's New York Business,* November 15, 1999, p. 51.
Moshavi, Sharon D., "Original Movies Boosting Lifetime's Fortunes," *Broadcasting,* September 2, 1991, p. 27.
Moss, Linda, "Lifetime: We Need Better Branding," *Multichannel News,* March 1, 1993, p. 46.
Oei, Lily, "More 'Medicine' at Lifetime," *Daily Variety,* February 1, 2002, p. 25.
Offman, Craig, "Femme Cabler Bows Mag," *Daily Variety,* June 28, 2002, p. 1.

Reynolds, Mike, ''High-Riding Lifetime Plans New Diginet,'' *Multi-channel News,* April 16, 2001, p. 24.

Richmond, Ray, ''It's a Woman Thing, and Getting More So,'' *Variety,* January 13, 1997, p. 73.

Romano, Allison, ''Lifetime's Quiet Threepeat,'' *Broadcasting & Cable,* October 8, 2001, p. 22.

Schlosser, Joe, ''Lifetime Jumps into the Game,'' *Broadcasting & Cable,* April 14, 1997, p. 64.

——, ''Lifetime of the 'Party','' *Broadcasting & Cable,* February 2, 1998, p. 70.

'' 'Television for Women': No One's Laughing Now,'' *Business Week,* December 24, 2001, p. 56.

Zahradnik, Rich, ''It's All in the Attitude,'' *Marketing & Media Decisions,* June 1987, p. 36.

—David P. Bianco

あしたに、あなたに

LION

Lion Corporation

3-7, Honjo 1-chome
Sumida-ku, Tokyo 130-8644
Japan
Telephone: 81-3-3621-6211
Fax: 81-3-3621-6048
Web site: http://www.lion.co.jp

Public Company
Incorporated: 1891 as Kobayashi Tomijiro Shoten
Employees: 3,074
Sales: ¥309 billion ($2.35 billion) (2001)
Stock Exchanges: Tokyo
Ticker Symbol: 4912
NAIC: 325412 Pharmaceutical Preparation Manufacturing; 325611 Soap and Other Detergents Manufacturing; 325620 Toilet Preparation Manufacturing; 325990 All Other Chemical Product and Preparation Manufacturing

Lion Corporation is Japan's biggest seller of toothpastes and a major producer of other toiletries and consumer items for household use. Three-quarters of its sales come from its health and beauty lines, including toothpaste, toothbrushes, mouthwash, and other oral care items, hair products such as shampoos and conditioners, laundry detergents and bleaches, household cleansers, and cooking aids such as plastic wrap and baking parchment. Lion's pharmaceutical division markets the aspirin brand Bufferin in Japan through a licensing agreement with drugmaker Bristol-Myers Squibb. The division also makes so-called ''medical toiletries'' designed to alleviate minor ailments. These products include foot compresses, a cooling compress for fevers, and a brand of eye drops, among others. Lion operates in several Asian countries outside of Japan, marketing unified brands throughout the region. Some of the company's manufacturing operations are based abroad, and the company also runs joint ventures with other firms in Asia. Lion also runs a joint venture with the German firm Henkel. Operated by the same family, the Kobayashis, throughout its entire history, the company has earned a prominent place in its domestic market, while maintaining successful overseas ventures.

19th-Century Roots

Kobayashi Tomijiro Shoten was founded in 1891 by Tomijiro Kobayashi, to produce soap. In 1902 Japan concluded an alliance with Great Britain, and just three years later, in 1905, Kobayashi first exported its products to the United Kingdom and the United States. In 1919 Kobayashi split into two entities. Lion Soap Co., Ltd. consisted of Kobayashi's soap division and T. Kobayashi & Co., Ltd. consisted of the remainder of Kobayashi Tomijiro Shoten, which at the time made tooth powders. The Kobayashi family retained control of both companies. In 1940 Lion Soap Company became Lion Fat & Oil Co., Ltd., reflecting a shift in its activities in conjunction with Japan's military buildup. T. Kobayashi became the Lion Dentifrice Co., Ltd. in 1949. During the first part of its history, both portions of the Kobayashi enterprise flourished. Starting in the 1960s, however, substantial changes were made in the operations of the companies.

Postwar Changes

In the mid-1960s Lion Fat & Oil found itself in heated competition with the Kao Soap Company, which, in Japan, held the lead in sales of synthetic detergents. With the generous use of public relations and advertising, Lion challenged that lead, accomplishing a strong rise in sales in the first half of 1968. Later that year, the company aggressively confronted Kao in its area of greatest strength, western Japan, by building a new plant in Sakai, Osaka. This new factory, capable of producing both powder and liquid detergents, increased Lion's production capacity by about 30 percent, from 14,500 tons to 19,000 tons monthly. Lion benefited from its substitution of petrochemical products for agricultural oils. The use of alcohol-rich petrochemicals enabled the company to cut production costs.

Lion's growth during this period was based on the development of new technology and the expansion of its foreign connections. By 1972 sales reached $27 million. In 1973 Lion Fat & Oil entered into a cooperative arrangement with Akzo, a Dutch chemical company, with the expectation of benefiting its chemical and household products operations.

By the mid-1970s Lion Dentifrice was running second to Kao in the field of toiletries, but the forecast was for sinking profits for the next term as a consequence of rising costs for raw materials and stiff competition, from Japanese companies and from U.S. giant Procter & Gamble, which had recently entered the market in a joint venture with another Japanese firm. Lion Dentifrice sales began to grow, however, in the first half of 1976, increasing 12 percent over the same period a year earlier. Demand for its traditional dental products increased, and sales of new lines, such as products for the eye and for hair, grew as well. Throughout this period, both Lion companies enjoyed strong financial positions and relative lack of debt.

Reorganization in the 1980s

By this time it was clear that separate corporate structures for Lion Fat & Oil and Lion Dentifrice were inefficient. Both companies faced intense competition, and they needed to control costs for high-volume, low-priced products. The similarity in the companies' names caused confusion among wholesalers and business partners. In late 1977 Lion executives announced that the two companies would merge into one, on an equal basis, with the aim of creating one sales force to market all Lion products. Facing a stagnant market and subject to cutthroat competition, Lion leaders expected the reunited company, with a solidified corporate image, to expand in old areas, initiate new products, and enter into new markets.

In 1978 Lion Products Co., Ltd. was created, and in 1980 this sales organization joined with the two older Lion companies to form Lion Corporation. The newly unified company moved to increase the efficiency of its product distribution by implementing a retail information system for its wholesalers, which in turn led to the 1985 creation of a management company for the entire toiletries industry.

Throughout the 1980s Lion continued its research-and-development activities, leading to new products that were keyed to new niches in a crowded market. Responding to environmental concerns, the company marketed Top, a nonphosphorous detergent, in 1980. In 1981 the company introduced Clinica, a plaque-fighting toothpaste that used enzymes to clean the teeth. Other new products, such as Look bathroom cleaner and Soft in 1, a combination shampoo and rinse, made strong contributions to the company's sales for the late 1980s.

In 1983 Lion laid out its goals for the next eight years, in a program designed to coincide with the arrival of the company's centennial. The campaign involved strengthening existing fields, improving global business, and exploiting new business sectors. To facilitate the plan, a companywide restructuring was implemented. In an attempt to meet these goals, Lion developed new techniques in production and distribution. In conjunction with Akzo the company had finished construction of a plant for the refinement of raw materials in 1981 that used a new, low-pressure process to produce ingredients for household detergents. In 1983 in an effort to reduce production costs, essential in an industry where retail price-slashing was rampant and profit margins were low, Lion installed computer surveillance of the manufacturing process in its Kawasaki plant as a test, and ultimately scheduled controlled production to be implemented in all seven of the company's plants by 1989.

Expanding Markets and Product Lines: Late 1980s and Early 1990s

Throughout the 1980s the company continued to work with foreign partners. In conjunction with Henkel, of Düsseldorf, Lion operated joint ventures in Taiwan, Hong Kong, and Germany as well as in Japan. In 1987 the company entered into a joint venture with the U.S. firm S.C. Johnson & Son to buy the previously unprofitable line of plaque-fighting dental products, Check-Up. S.C. Johnson already was marketing Lion's Zact toothpaste for smokers in the United States. In June 1989 the company bought out S.C. Johnson's 50 percent interest in Rydelle-Lion to form a wholly owned subsidiary, Lion Corporation (America), in an effort to establish a base for further entries into the U.S. oral-care and hair-care markets. Lion subsequently turned over the marketing of its Zact and Check-Up products to Schering-Plough, another U.S. firm, under a licensing agreement.

In July 1989 Lion announced a joint venture with Akzo and two other entities to build a plant for the production of silica in Map Ta Phud, Thailand. Lion further expanded its Thai operations later that year, when it announced plans to build another plant in Rayong, Thailand, with five other partners for the production of a chemical used to make detergents. Construction of the plant, with economic incentives granted by the Thai government, began in May 1990. This overseas expansion, though aggressive, was not enough to prevent a 1988 decline in Lion's sales and profits. Although by this time 10 percent of the company's sales came from outside Japan, ''we are a little bit behind our main competitors in Japan in globalizing our operations,'' a Lion representative admitted to *Advertising Age* on October 2, 1989.

Lion lagged behind its competitors in introducing a compact, highly concentrated detergent, a big market-winner in crowded Japan, where smaller is inevitably better. It was not until 1989 that Lion introduced Hi-Top, its compact product with fat-dissolving enzymes, in answer to Kao's Attack. Attack had enabled Kao to grab better than half the detergent market when it hit the stores in 1987. In 1990 compact detergents made up 70 percent of the Japanese detergent market, with Lion's overall share rising to around 25 percent after the introduction of its compact product.

Lion's development of new products was not without problems, however. In mid-1989 the Health and Welfare Ministry of Japan closed a Lion factory after discovering that the company in 1986 had misrepresented certain qualities of its Pentadecan hair-growth product while attempting to get it approved. As a penalty, the company was forced to withdraw Pentadecan, the market leader, from Japanese and Southeast Asian distribution and to cease the manufacture for 20 days of all products made by the same division, a move that cost Lion $14 million. More important, the resulting negative publicity damaged the company's reputation, leading to fears about its overall image and sales.

Given these factors, it became clear by the end of 1989 that the company would not meet its goals on schedule. Shaken by its failure to beat Kao to market with an innovative compact detergent and facing a detergent price war and an overall lower market share, Lion set out to shore up profits by the end of 1989 by holding prices firm on its other products. In addition, the company planned to open a new fat-and-oil plant in Kagawa Prefecture, enabling it to launch a new product to vanquish Kao's lead.

Faced with a very competitive and maturing market for household products in Japan, Lion increasingly turned to overseas sales. The company's nondomestic sales grew 7 percent over 1990, while sales at home dipped slightly. Lion emphasized this good news, and worked on reorganizing its overseas marketing, dividing its main Asian market into three regions. Lion set up new joint ventures in Thailand, Indonesia, and Malaysia that year, and entered what it termed a "technological collaboration" with a Korean firm as well. Yet market conditions remained difficult, particularly in Japan itself. In 1991 Lion embarked on another three-year plan, this time to make its management structure more efficient. The company reduced its number of products from almost 500 to 422, and scheduled fewer new products for introduction. Although the company had a vast array of goods on store shelves, it had a core list of 37 longstanding products that accounted for about 70 percent of sales. Lion hoped to hold on to its lead with these well-known items and reduce inventory in its more marginal product lines.

Difficult Conditions in the Late 1990s and After

By the mid-1990s, Lion Corporation's sales were still flat. Japan's economy was in a long slump, and recovery always seemed just around the corner. Health and beauty products accounted for 77 percent of the company's sales by 1995, and the slowdown in Japanese consumer spending made growth quite difficult for Lion. The company posted a small uptick in domestic sales over 1995, only .4 percent, but the company's foreign subsidiaries and various joint ventures did better, with overall sales up more than 20 percent. Lion braced for continu-

ing declines in its home market if the economy did not come back to life. The company made investments in information technology to make its operations more efficient, looked for other ways to cut costs, and concentrated on bringing out new products that would capture consumer attention. Lion ceased its operations in the United States in the mid-1990s, while continuing to build its relationship with the German firm Henkel. Henkel developed a highly concentrated tablet form laundry detergent for Lion, and the two companies cooperated in research and development, marketing, contract manufacturing, and other areas in their respective countries. But the Japanese economy continued to stagnate over the 1990s, and the Japanese consumer products market became locked in competition for what little growth remained. Lion had worked with more than 1,100 wholesalers to distribute its health and beauty products in the 1980s. By 1999, Lion's network had dropped to only 834. Domestic sales drooped, and rival companies cut away at Lion's hold. Lion had a longstanding agreement with U.S. drugmaker Bristol-Myers Squibb Company to sell Bufferin in Japan. The brand had held sway as the leading over-the-counter painkiller in Japan. But in 2000 Takeda Chemical Industries made an arrangement with another U.S. drug company, Johnson & Johnson, for the right to market its pain reliever Tylenol. Tylenol was the most widely used pain reliever in the world, and Takeda hoped to take the lead in the Japanese market within five years.

In 2001, the company reported another poor year, with sales falling more than 7 percent and Lion taking a loss. All of its main household product lines had flat or shrinking sales. Shampoos, toothpaste, laundry soap, and toothbrushes all did slightly worse or only held steady with figures from the year previous. Although Lion had some individual products that did well, the outlook was still poor. The company sold its tampon business in 2002 and shut down the Japanese plant that had manufactured this product. Lion predicted moderate sales growth of less than half of one percent for the following year. The company's long-term plan called for focusing renewed efforts on core brands and shedding areas in which it did not excel.

Principal Subsidiaries

Lion Fat & Oil (Taiwan) Co., Ltd.; Lionboy Trading Co., Ltd. (Taiwan); Taiwan Lion Chemistry Co., Ltd.; Taiwan Lion Trading Co., Ltd.; Lion Corporation (Thailand) Ltd.; Lion Home Products (International) Ltd.; Southern Lion Sdn. Bhd. (Malaysia); Lion Home Products (M) Sdn. Bhd. (Malaysia); Lion Corporation (Singapore) Pte., Ltd; Qingdao Lion Daily Necessities Chemicals Co., Ltd. (China; 50%); Henkel Lion Cosmetics Co. Ltd.

Principal Divisions

Lion Household Products Division; Lion Pharmaceutical Products Division; Lion International Division.

Principal Competitors

Takeda Chemical Industries Ltd.; Kao Corporation; Kanebo, Ltd.

Further Reading

"Henkel and Lion in Consumer Alliance," *Soap, Perfumery & Cosmetics,* January 2000, p. 3.

"Japanese Lion Showing a Recovery," *Cosmetics International,* September 25, 1996, p. 14.

"Japan's Unclear Future," *Cosmetics International,* July 10, 2000, p. 2.

"Lion Corporation Survives Difficult Market Conditions," *Cosmetics International,* September 10, 1992, p. 11.

"Lion Corporation's Overseas Sales Rise by 7%," *Cosmetics International,* September 10, 1991, p. 13.

"Lion Price Restructuring Among Factors Pulling Sales Down 7.3%, Profits 30.6%," *Cosmetics & Toiletries & Household Products Marketing News in Japan,* June 25, 2002.

"The Lion Share of the Market Gets VIP Treatment," *Cosmetics International,* July 10, 2001, p. 4.

—Elizabeth Rourke
—update: A. Woodward

Lone Star Steakhouse & Saloon, Inc.

224 East Douglas Avenue, Suite 700
Wichita, Kansas 67202
U.S.A.
Telephone: (316) 264-8899
Fax: (316) 264-5988
Web site: http://www.lonestarsteakhouse.com

Public Company
Incorporated: 1992
Employees: 18,425
Sales: $598.01 million (2001)
Stock Exchanges: NASDAQ
Ticker Symbol: STAR
NAIC: 722110 Full-Service Restaurants

Lone Star Steakhouse & Saloon, Inc. is the operator of three restaurant chains: Lone Star Steakhouse & Saloon, Del Frisco's Double Eagle Steak House, and Sullivan's. The company's Lone Star restaurants operate as full-service, casual-dining units positioned in the mid-priced segment of the restaurant industry. The company's Del Frisco's restaurants operate in the upper end of the steak house segment. The menu items at the company's Sullivan's restaurants are priced midway between the selection available at the company's other two restaurant chains.

Origins

Lone Star was founded by Jamie B. Coulter, who graduated from the University of Wichita in 1963. Coulter began his post-college career driving a beer-delivery truck for his father-in-law before entering the food-service industry in 1965, when he contacted Frank Carney, the founder of Pizza Hut, and inquired about becoming a franchisee of the chain. Coulter enlisted the help of several franchise partners and formed CWG Enterprises, which was destined to become the largest U.S. franchisee of Pizza Hut restaurants. Within 15 years, CWG opened more than 170 Pizza Hut units and developed considerable interest in the Kentucky Fried Chicken chain, eventually becoming the company's fifth-largest franchisee. CWG dissolved in 1980, leading Coulter to form his own company, Coulter Enterprises, which

began with 42 Pizza Hut units. During the next ten years, Coulter expanded his business, amassing a 12-state chain of 100 Pizza Hut units by the time he encountered a company called Creative Culinary Concepts.

Based in North Carolina, Creative Culinary had opened the first Lone Star Steakhouse & Saloon prototype in Winston-Salem in October 1989. One of the company's largest share-holders, Lester Rudd, invited Coulter to take a look at the concept, fashioned as a mesquite-grill steakhouse. Coulter was interested, and in 1991 he signed an agreement with Creative Culinary to develop four Lone Star units. Within seven months, Coulter had opened four restaurants that featured a limited menu of mesquite-grilled steaks, chicken, grilled fish, babyback ribs, and a Texas roadhouse ambiance. Seating 200 diners and measuring 6,000 square feet, the Lone Star concept became Coulter's new growth vehicle.

Expansion Begins in 1992

Coulter incorporated Lone Star in January 1992, appointing himself board chairman, chief executive officer, and president. He then began expanding the concept but needed cash to fulfill his ambitious expectations. To raise capital, Coulter turned to Wall Street, completing Lone Star's initial public offering (IPO) of stock on March 12, 1992. When Lone Star's $91 million public offering was completed, the company had eight restaurants in operation, each averaging $2.5 million in sales per year. By November 1992, Coulter had completed a second public offering of stock, raising another $41 million to support expansion plans that called for establishing three more units in 1992 and opening 24 new restaurants in each of the next two years.

As Coulter orchestrated his aggressive expansion campaign, he did so by keeping a close eye on the chain's operating efficiency. The company emphasized reaching monthly performance targets on a restaurant-by-restaurant basis, which was the responsibility of the chain's general managers. The general managers were given substantial bonuses to reach monthly performance targets, earning cash and stock options as incentives to maintain high sales and industry-leading operating profit margins. For a company that operated without district or regional managers, the

Company Perspectives:

Lone Star Steakhouse & Saloon is a unique category of restaurants offering higher-quality service and food than existing chain or independent restaurants. We believe that this niche is a dynamic growth area within the restaurant industry that offers significant growth opportunities for Lone Star. We believe that our restaurants are uniquely positioned as "destination restaurants" that attract a very loyal clientele.

role of the general manager took on heightened importance, serving as the only link from the restaurants in the field to corporate headquarters in Wichita. In an August 1993 interview with *Restaurant Hospitality*, a Lone Star executive vice-president explained: "In other chains, there are people who act as filters for information going from the stores to corporate. That's how we are different. We don't have any filters."

Lone Star's flattened organizational structure and its growing ranks of performance-driven general managers delivered success. In 1993, the company was selected as the best small company in the country by *Forbes* magazine, a distinction it would also be awarded in 1994 and 1995. In 1994, the company was the highest-ranked restaurant company on *Fortune* magazine's list of the country's 100 fastest-growing company's, placing sixth overall. Sales were increasing at an annual rate of 210 percent, while the company's operating profit margins averaged 26 percent, the highest percentage in the industry.

Concept Diversification in 1995

By the end of 1995, three years of frenetic expansion had produced a new formidable force in the casual-dining segment of the restaurant industry. With 182 restaurants in operation, annual sales hit $340 million, up substantially from the $11 million generated in 1991. Coulter was as eager as ever to expand the Lone Star concept further, but he was not averse to exploring new business opportunities. In 1995, as Lone Star was receiving accolades from industry observers, he saw an opportunity for his company in the lower end of the upscale steak market, the niche occupied by restaurants whose checks averaged $35 per patron. As development of a new restaurant concept was underway, the company hired Mike Archer, the former president of Morton's of Chicago. The result of the collaboration among Archer, Coulter, and Lone Star's management team was Sullivan's, a circa-1940s steakhouse named after the early twentieth-century, bare-fisted boxer John L. Sullivan. Featuring more than 200 seats, a limited menu centered on certified Angus beef, mahogany paneled walls, and a decor designed with an 80 percent male clientele in mind, Sullivan's made its debut in May 1996 in Austin, Texas.

Before the first Sullivan's opened its doors, Lone Star made another move to diversify outside the casual-dining segment. The company paid $23 million in cash and stock to acquire Del Frisco's Double Eagle Steak House, a purchase reflective of Coulter's desire to move his company into the upper end of the steak restaurant market, albeit sooner than he had planned. "We

had not intended to go into the prime beef market at this time," Coulter remarked in a July 1, 1996 interview with *Restaurants & Institutions*. "We wanted to launch Sullivan's," he continued, "and get four to six of them under our belts first, but the opportunity presented itself." Although the timing was not perfect, the acquisition of the Del Frisco's concept did represent an important step toward Coulter's goal of developing Lone Star into a $1 billion-in-sales company, an objective he began making public during the mid-1990s. Coulter's chief financial officer, John White, who had been at his side since the inception of Lone Star, greeted the news of the Del Frisco's acquisition without any reservations. "We intend to become *the* steak company," he informed *Nation's Restaurant News* in an October 2, 1995 interview. He likened Lone Star's three-tiered strategy to the seating classifications on a passenger aircraft. With a check average of between $16 and $18, Lone Star represented coach. Sullivan's check average of between $35 and $40 represented business class. Del Frisco's, whose checks averaged $60, served as first-class seating under the corporate umbrella of Lone Star.

Although there were several industry pundits who questioned whether the diversification into two different market niches was prudent, few could question the amazing success story that Lone Star represented. Coulter was named chief executive of the year by *Restaurants & Institutions* in 1996, by which time the company's stock had appreciated 1,037 percent since the March 1992 IPO. Coulter did not intend to slacken the pace of expanding the Lone Star concept, despite the distraction of rolling out two new subsidiary restaurant chains. "This will not slow us down a bit on our Lone Star development," he averred in an October 2, 1995 interview with *Nation's Restaurant News*. Coulter stayed true to his promise but not as long as he would have liked. Lone Star ended the 1990s struggling to regain the form that dazzled Wall Street during the first half of the decade.

Late 1990s Decline

By March 1997, there were 205 Lone Star restaurants in operation, but the company's stock performance was anemic. Shares in Lone Star had traded for $46 in April 1996, but less than a year later the per share price had fallen to $26. Once the company's quarterly rate of growth began to decrease because of market saturation and higher food prices and labor costs, analysts lost their passion for the Wichita-based chain. By mid-1998, the situation had worsened. Performance in same-store sales began to suffer, and a large number of the company's all-important general managers left the company. By Coulter's own admission, Lone Star was slow to react to the operational problems, which hobbled the company's expansion plans. Lone Star's stock value plummeted to $13 per share in July 1998, then fell to $6 per share late in the year. The company opened only two new Lone Star restaurants in 1998. In 1999, the company reversed direction, opening no new restaurants and closing two units that were underperforming. Lone Star ended the 1990s with 265 Lone Star restaurants, 14 Sullivan's restaurants, and three Del Frisco's restaurants.

As the operational difficulties that surfaced during the late 1990s were being dealt with in the early years of the new century, Coulter fought the battle for his survival at the company he had founded. In 2001, a Lone Star shareholder named Guy W. Adams mounted an assault against Coulter, criticizing

<table>
<tr><td colspan="2">Key Dates:</td></tr>
<tr><td>1989:</td><td>A prototype restaurant for Lone Star opens in Winston-Salem, North Carolina.</td></tr>
<tr><td>1992:</td><td>Jamie Coulter incorporates Lone Star.</td></tr>
<tr><td>1995:</td><td>Diversification into the upper end of the restaurant market begins.</td></tr>
<tr><td>2001:</td><td>Dissident shareholder Guy Adams unseats Coulter as chairman.</td></tr>
</table>

the company for more than tripling Coulter's salary as Lone Star's stock value plunged. Adams also disliked one individual holding both the board chairman and chief executive officer positions, so he launched a proxy battle whose aim was to unseat Coulter as chairman, which would make room for Adams to join the company's board of directors. Amazingly, Adams held only 1,100 Lone Star shares, which translated to a 0.005 percent stake in the company. More amazing, Adams won the election when the results were announced in July 2001, becoming the first individual shareholder to unseat a chief executive officer from the board of his own company. Coulter stayed on as chief executive officer, but he was forced to relinquish his seat as board chairman. In July 2001, Clark R. Mandigo, a director of the company since March 1992, was selected as board chairman.

Against the backdrop of Coulter's battle to retain his seat as board chairman, Lone Star opened nine new Lone Star restaurants, its first appreciable expansion in several years. The major news during the company's tenth anniversary year centered on a possible way to avoid the problems that plagued it during the late 1990s. Part of the reason the company's stock value fell during the period was because of its inability to meet the escalating quarterly earnings expectations of Wall Street, forcing it to plan for the short-term, rather than the long-term. One way to avoid the intense public scrutiny was to convert to private ownership, which it appeared the company was going to do. In March 2002, Lone Star signed a letter of intent to be acquired by the investment firm Bruckmann, Rosser, Sherill & Co. LLC (BRS). New York-based BRS agreed to take the company private for roughly $580 million. Lone Star's board approved the letter of intent unanimously, but ultimately the two parties were unable to agree to terms. In May 2002, the deal fell through, leaving Lone Star to plot its future in the public sector.

As Lone Star pressed ahead in its second decade of business, much remained to be accomplished before Coulter could claim victory in his goal of reaching $1 billion in sales. During the first six months of 2002, the company posted a loss of $1.14 million, primarily because of the failed merger and issues related to its stock compensation program. There were no plans to open any new restaurants in 2002.

Principal Subsidiaries

LS Management, Inc.; Lone Star Finance, Inc.; LS Marketing, LLC; L.S. Leasing, Inc.; LS Mail Order, Inc.; Bridgewater Properties, Inc.; Mama's Concept, Inc.; Frankie's Restaurant, Inc.; Big Guns, Inc.; Star Steaks, Inc.; Del Frisco's of Colorado, Inc.; CGB Delaware, Inc.; CWA Delaware, Inc.; Crockett Beverage Corp.; Irwin J. Grossnerr Foundation, Inc.; Sullivan's of Delaware, Inc.; Steak Concepts, Delaware, Inc.; Travis Beverage Corp.; Westheimer Beverage Corp.; Village Beverage Corporation.

Principal Competitors

Metromedia Company; Outback Steakhouse, Inc.; Ruth's Chris Steak House, Inc.

Further Reading

"Coulter, Creative Team to Take Lone Star Chain Public," *Nation's Restaurant News,* February 17, 1992, p. 2.

Dinell, David, "Lone Star Throws Lasso Around Expansion," *The Business Journal—Serving Phoenix & the Valley of the Sun,* November 5, 1999, p. 74.

Farkas, David, "Lone Star's Strong Suits," *Restaurant Hospitality,* August 1993, p. 82.

Grainger, David, "Driving a Stake into Lone Star," *Fortune,* August 13, 2001, p. 32.

Hayes, Jack, "Lone Star Stock Sizzles as Expansion Gathers Steam," *Nation's Restaurant News,* November 16, 1992, p. 3.

"Lone Star Steakhouse 1994 Profit Up 86 percent," *Nation's Restaurant News,* January 23, 1995, p. 16.

"Lone Star Steakhouse Repeats as Best Company on Forbes' List," *Nation's Restaurant News,* November 21, 1994, p. 16.

McDowell, Bill, "Jamie Coulter's Bull Market," *Restaurants & Institutions,* July 1, 1996, p. 26.

Papiernik, Richard, "Lone Star Posts $1.14m Loss after Options," *Nation's Restaurant News,* July 15, 2002, p. 12.

Peters, James, "Rarin' to Go Private," *Nation's Restaurant News,* April 15, 2002, p. 1.

Ruggless, Ron, "Lone Star Launches 3-Tiered Strategy; Opens Second Del Frisco's Unit," *Nation's Restaurant News,* April 29, 1996, p. 7.

Schatz, Amy, "Outsider Ousts CEO from Board; Shareholder Wins Seat in Heated Battle for Spot on Board of Restaurant Chain," *The Austin American-Statesman,* July 12, 2001, p. D1.

Sullivan, R. Lee, "Steakout," *Forbes,* November 6, 1995, p. 365.

Waxler, Caroline, "Falling Star?," *Forbes,* March 24, 1997, p. 188.

—Jeffrey L. Covell

M.A. Gedney Co.

2100 Stoughton Avenue
Chaska, Minnesota 55318
U.S.A.
Telephone: (952) 448-2612
Fax: (952) 448-1790
Web site: http://www.gedneypickle.com

Private Company
Incorporated: 1881
Employees: 250
Sales: $50 million (2001 est.)
NAIC: 311421 Fruit and Vegetable Canning; 111998 All Other Miscellaneous Crop Farming; 311941 Mayonnaise, Dressing, and Other Prepared Sauce Manufacturing

M.A. Gedney Co. is a Minnesota-based manufacturer of pickles, condiments, preserves, salad dressings, and salsas that produces a total of about 200 different products. In addition to its own brands, Gedney also packs private label goods for such major retailers as the Kroger Co. The company's products are distributed in the midwestern United States as well as in New England under the Cains and Oxford brands, which were acquired in 2000. Gedney is the leading pickle maker in the Midwest, accounting for close to 60 percent of total sales there. The privately held company is managed by fifth-generation descendants of its founder.

Early Years

The M.A. Gedney Co. traces its roots to 1881, when the firm was founded in Minneapolis, Minnesota, by Mathias Anderson Gedney. Gedney, who was born in 1822, had already lived a colorful life, having gone to sea at the age of 14 and later participated in the California gold rush. A modest success in the latter endeavor brought him enough money to marry, and he later moved his growing family to Evanston, Illinois, where he began working for Northwestern Pickle Works in 1863.

Taking recipes he learned there, and others gleaned from a stint at S.M. Dingee & Co. in Chicago, Gedney moved to Minneapolis in 1879 and began seeking farmers to grow cucumbers, a vegetable not normally cultivated in northern states. In 1881, Gedney opened his first pickle and condiment production plant at Lowry and Pacific Avenues in Minneapolis, and he began delivering and selling his products directly from horse-driven "cash wagons" the following year.

During its first decade, the new company grew rapidly, with the main plant expanded several times and other facilities opened in St. Paul and Chaska, Minnesota; Mauston, Wisconsin; and Omaha and Kearney, Nebraska. Four of Gedney's sons, Isadore ("I.V."), Henry, Charles, and John, took on key roles at the company during this period.

Mathias Gedney's pickle recipes were popular with the public, and by the mid-1890s annual production had grown to more than 30,000 barrels. The company was producing a number of different varieties, including homemade, sweet, mixed, chowchow, American and English-style, as well as salad dressings, catsup, Worcestershire sauce, horseradish, mustard, olives, and West India and Tabasco pepper sauces.

Continued Growth in the 20th Century

In 1895, Gedney expanded its distribution territory to include North Dakota and Montana, and in 1901 the firm's Chaska plant was enlarged to facilitate production of sauerkraut. The year 1910 saw Gedney replace its horse-drawn cash wagons with motorized trucks.

Control of the company was by this time in the hands of I.V. Gedney, who, as president, continued to guide the firm until his death in 1945. At that time the top job passed to his son-in-law, Harry Tuttle, who had begun working for Gedney in 1928 as a still operator in a vinegar plant.

During the postwar years, the company made improvements in several areas. In 1946, Gedney's cash wagon trucks began selling directly to grocers from orders placed in advance. Five years later, the Chaska plant added equipment to enable production of "fresh pack" pickles, which were becoming increas-

Company Perspectives:

At the M.A. Gedney Company, our true mission is to painstakingly provide products of uncommonly high quality. Whether it's pickles, salsa, or preserves, consumers know that if it's from Gedney it's definitely the best.

ingly popular. In 1958, Gedney's entire operation was consolidated outside Chaska, where a new 50,000-square-foot warehouse, plant, and office facility was built on an 18-acre site.

In 1967, Harry's son Gedney Tuttle was named company president. He had been working for the firm since the late 1940s. At this time, M.A. Gedney was continuing to produce a full line of pickles and condiments, using its founder's original recipes as well as other, more recently created ones.

The beginning of the 1970s saw the company give large customers such as May Brothers and Super Valu the option of picking up their orders directly at the factory in Chaska, thus generating savings on distribution costs. Gedney pickles were now available throughout much of the midwestern United States, from Minnesota down to Arkansas and from Montana across to the Upper Peninsula of Michigan.

Acquisition of Max's Pickles

In 1985, Gedney completed the acquisition of the Flavo Food Company, makers of Max's Pickles. Three years later, the company mothballed its less-profitable food service division to focus solely on retail sales. Gedney products were increasingly being distributed through food brokers to wholesale distributors and chain stores at this time. The company also began identifying itself as the source of "The Minnesota Pickle."

Gedney's pickle making was something that took place largely in the late summer when cucumbers were harvested by about 800 contract growers the company utilized in Minnesota, Wisconsin, Nebraska, and South Dakota. The firm's growers used no pesticides and harvested the cukes by hand for superior quality. Between the end of July and early September about half of Gedney's annual output of pickles would be packed, with the workforce ballooning from 140 to as many as 400 while the plant ran around the clock on three shifts. During the rest of the calendar year, the firm produced its other products, acquiring some pickles as needed from Mexico and North Carolina to pack during the off-season. In contrast to the early days, when most pickles were fermented for a month in brine before they were packed, newly harvested cucumbers were now placed directly into jars with brine and then pasteurized, producing a pickle that was crunchy and tart, rather than soft and sour. This method was known as the "fresh pack" process.

In 1991, Gedney launched its State Fair Pickles line, which featured a pair of prize-winning recipes for kosher dills and bread and butter pickles that had been selected in a company-sponsored competition at the Minnesota State Fair. Photographs of the winning pickle makers were featured on the packaging and in ads, and the company worked with them to ensure that their recipes were faithfully recreated. In addition to a degree of fame, they

each received a small commission for every jar sold. Over the next several years, three more pickle recipes and four State Fair Blue Ribbon varieties of preserves were also introduced, and the popular line continued to grow each year thereafter.

The year 1996 saw introduction of Gedney Pickle Planks, which were long, thinly sliced pickles that were ideal for use in sandwiches. The next year brought Pickle Pick-Ups, small individual-serving packages that contained pickles but no liquid brine. Previous attempts at packaging pickles for individual sale had involved messy brine-filled plastic bags, and the pickles often became discolored through exposure to oxygen, which was absorbed through the plastic. Gedney's proprietary method, which used heat treatment and a preservative, effectively solved these problems. Three company staffers had developed the process, and they later applied for a patent. Gedney had earlier patented a device that gently pushed pickles into jars without smashing them, which replaced the traditional method of having employees who were called "Toppers" tap overflowing pickles into place using a mallet and board.

In 1998, refrigerated Crispy Pickles were introduced to compete with a popular line made by industry giant Claussen, and Gedney began to make salsas under contract for Sparta Foods Inc. This deal took advantage of the company's existing equipment and expertise at making its own Devil's Fire brand of salsa, which had been introduced the previous year.

The same year also saw a change in leadership when Jeff Tuttle, Gedney's son, took over as CEO of the firm. He had been working for the family business since 1995 as head of marketing and advertising, having gotten his MBA from the University of Michigan before putting in time at Miller Brewing in Milwaukee. Other family members employed by the company included his brother Carl and a cousin, Tom Hitch. A short time after Jeff Tuttle's installation, Gedney's distribution area expanded again, growing to include Nebraska, Illinois, Indiana, Michigan, and Wisconsin.

Cains Purchase in 2000 Doubles Company's Size

The year 2000 saw Gedney make its largest acquisition to date, at a time when the pickle industry was becoming increasingly consolidated. In July, the firm bought the pickle, pepper, and relish businesses of Cains Foods LP of Ayer, Massachusetts. Cains had begun making mayonnaise in 1925 and had expanded into pickle production in 1955, marketing its goods under the Cains and Oxford brand names. It produced the number one brand of relish and the number two brand of pickles in New England. The deal, which roughly doubled the company's size, brought Gedney a pickle plant in South Deerfield, Massachusetts, while Cains retained its salad dressing and mayonnaise product lines and manufacturing facilities. Industry analysts estimated that Gedney would control 5 to 6 percent of the U.S. pickle market after adding the Cains brands.

In the spring of 2002, Gedney decided to sell the South Deerfield plant and the food service side of the Cains business and move the Cains retail packing operation to Chaska. The plant was sold to a former Cains executive and four Massachusetts growers. Calling the abandoned food service business an

Key Dates:

1881: Mathias A. Gedney starts a pickle and condiment business in Minneapolis.
1893: Pickle production tops 30,000 barrels per year.
1945: Harry Tuttle takes control of firm from father-in-law I.V. Gedney.
1958: Operations are consolidated at new Chaska, Minnesota, facility.
1967: Harry's son Gedney Tuttle is named president of the firm.
1985: Flavo Food Company and its Max's Pickles brand are acquired.
1988: The company's food service division is closed.
1991: State Fair Pickles line bows; other State Fair products follow.
1998: Gedney Tuttle turns over the CEO post to his son Jeff.
2000: The company acquires the pickle business of Cains Foods of Massachusetts.
2002: Cains food service unit and its Massachusetts packing plant are sold; a deal to pack 500,000 cases of pickles per year is struck with Del Monte.

experiment, CEO Tuttle commented to the *Business Journal of Minneapolis/St. Paul*, "It actually turned out to be more of a drain on our resources. We really would rather focus on retail." Though food service pickle production outstripped that of retail by a significant margin, it was a difficult area to successfully break into. A short time after these changes were finalized, an agreement was reached to pack pickles for canned fruit and vegetable giant Del Monte Foods Co. The five-year deal was expected to involve annual production of 500,000 cases of pickles.

As it neared one and one-quarter centuries in business, the M.A. Gedney Co. was offering a range of food products that included pickles, relishes, sauerkraut, salad dressings, mustard, vinegar, fruit spreads, and salsas, all of which were distributed throughout the company's stronghold of the midwestern United States, as well as in New England under the Cains and Oxford names. National penetration was a possibility for the future, but until it was attained Gedney would no doubt remain one of the leading regional pickle and condiment producers in the United States.

Principal Subsidiaries

Cains Pickles, Inc.

Principal Competitors

Pinnacle Foods Corporation; H.J. Heinz Company; Kraft Foods Inc.

Further Reading

Cruz, Sherri, "Chaska's Pickle Powerhouse," *Star Tribune Newspaper of the Twin Cities Minneapolis–St. Paul*, February 24, 2002, p. 1D.
Egerstrom, Lee, "Chaska, Minn.–Based Pickle Maker to Buy Massachusetts Company," *World Reporter*, July 11, 2000.
——, "Roseville, Minn. Food Firm Signs Pact with Chaska-Based Company for Salsas," *World Reporter*, July 30, 1998.
"History of M.A. Gedney Co." Available at http://www.gedney pickle.com, September 8, 2002.
Jones, Jim, "Public's Relish for Pickles Keeps Gedney Packing," *Star Tribune Newspaper of the Twin Cities Minneapolis–St. Paul*, July 18, 1986, p. 7B.
Kennedy, Tony, "Pickle Packer Pursuing 'Pouch-Pack' Patent," *Star Tribune Newspaper of the Twin Cities Minneapolis–St. Paul*, May 29, 1997, p. 1D.
"M.A. Gedney Buys Cains Pickle Business," *Telegram & Gazette* (Worcester, Massachusetts), September 14, 2000, p. E3.
Merrill, Ann, "Next Generation Takes Over at Gedney," *Star Tribune Newspaper of the Twin Cities Minneapolis–St. Paul*, September 15, 1998, p. 3D.
"Packing a Pickle to Go," *Newsday*, May 30, 1997, p. A65.
St. Anthony, Neal, "Gedney Goes Long With a Cross-Country Pickle Deal," *Star Tribune Newspaper of the Twin Cities Minneapolis–St. Paul*, September 19, 2000, p. 1D.
Sicherman, Al, "It's Not Easy Being Crunchy—Pickle Scientist Jim Cook Tells a Dilly of a Tale," *Star Tribune Newspaper of the Twin Cities Minneapolis–St. Paul*, September 19, 1990, p. 1T.
Tellijohn, Andrew, "Gedney, Del Monte Pen Pickle Pact," *Business Journal of Minneapolis/St. Paul*, June 28, 2002.

—Frank Uhle

Marionnaud
PARFUMERIES

Marionnaud Parfumeries SA

5-7 avenue de Paris
94300 Vincennes
France
Telephone: +33 (0)1 48 08 69 69
Fax: +33 (0)1 48 08 01 51
Web site: http://www.marionnaud.com

Public Company
Incorporated: 1984
Employees: 6,150
Sales: EUR 770.9 million ($747.39 million) (2001)
Stock Exchanges: Euronext Paris
Ticker Symbol: MAR
NAIC: 446120 Cosmetics, Beauty Supplies, and Perfume
    Stores

Marionnaud Parfumeries SA is one of Europe's leading retail perfume specialists. With 1,118 perfume shops in 13 countries, the French company ranks number one in terms of "doors" and lags only Germany's Douglas in terms of sales. Marionnaud's sales topped EUR 770 million in 2001. The company is also number one or two in many of its markets, especially in France, its single largest market, but also in Switzerland, Spain, Italy, Portugal, Austria, and in much of the Eastern European markets. Marionnaud has achieved its position by growing rapidly through a massive acquisition program, typically of smaller retail groups and independent perfume stores—between 2000 and 20002, the company has tripled the number of stores in its network. Marionnaud separates its stores into two categories: the larger "espaces," which reach up to 400 square meters and more and offer more than 16,000 products, including the world's leading perfume and cosmetics brands, and which combine self-service with knowledgeable sales staffs; and the smaller "boutiques," typically found in downtown locations and averaging 100 square feet of sales space, and which offer personalized service. The bulk of Marionnaud's retail network is made up of the smaller boutique stores. Marionnaud is led by Marcel Frydman, backed by his sons Gerald and Jean-Pierre. The Frydman family maintain a major-

ity of the voting rights for the company, which has been listed on the Euronext Paris stock exchange since 1998.

Perfumed Present in the 1980s

Born in Paris in 1931, Marcel Frydman had already built up a successful business specialized in the liquidation of unsold stock. In 1984, Frydman, using his own savings and joined by friends, bought a small perfume shop in the Parisian suburb of Montreuil as a gift for his wife. Frydman quickly showed a flair for retail, cutting prices by some 20 percent to attract more customers in a neighborhood of relatively modest incomes. By the end of that first year, Frydman had succeeded in tripling the store's sales.

The Frydman family's entry into the retail perfume market came at just the right time. In the mid-1980s, the perfume sector was highly fragmented among thousands of small, independent boutiques. Yet these stores were already under heavy pressure from the rise of the hypermarket—large-scale stores combining supermarkets with traditional department store offerings, including perfumes.

Frydman quickly recognized the potential of forming a retail chain dedicated to perfume sales, buying a second store, now in Paris itself, in 1985. By 1986, Frydman decided to leave his stock liquidation business to dedicate himself to his perfume stores. Frydman then began searching for new stores in the Paris area—it was easier and less expensive to acquire existing stores and their often loyal clientele. As his interest moved more and more beyond Paris, Frydman often relied on his suppliers, who informed him of stores that were considering putting themselves up for sale.

Frydman applied the same formula to each new store, cutting prices and insisting on strong customer service. Yet the interior design of the stores was left mostly unchanged, in part so as not to alienate existing clientele. Meanwhile, the company had yet to adopt a unified brand name for its growing number of stores. With four stores in 1988, Frydman prepared to step up his acquisitions. Whereas the company's initial purchases had come from reinvesting its profits, Frydman now turned to outside sources, such as the bank Credit National.

Company Perspectives:

The essence of Marionnaud's success: The Marionnaud spirit; a motivated team in a convivial company; a leading brand backed up by a strong business strategy; balanced growth supported by financial solidity.

By 1992, Frydman's retail group had grown to 16 stores in a market that remained highly fragmented, even hostile to consolidation, as the nation's perfumeries clung to their status as independent shopkeepers. As Frydman told *Nouvel Economiste:* ''It was profession where nothing was happening. When we'd reached eight stores, I prepared a business plan in which we would grow to 30 stores. That seemed enormous to me.''

In the early 1990s, however, Frydman's confidence in his business model continued to grow. The company's ambitions grew as well, and by 1992 the company drafted a new growth target, that of 100 stores and FFr 1 billion (EUR$150 million) in sales.

Yet Frydman was no longer alone in his belief in the consolidation of the retail perfume sector. A number of other groups had begun setting up their own retail networks. Chief among these was Bernard Marionnaud, who had started building a chain of discount perfume shops at the beginning of the decade. By the middle of the 1990s, Marionnaud controlled an empire of 48 stores posting combined sales of more than FFr 550 million (EUR 84 million). Marionnaud had especially become famous throughout France for its discount formula, which offering up to 25 percent off on the major name brands in perfumes and cosmetics.

Marionnaud, however, had run into trouble at the end of 1995, rattled by strikes by its employees and by the refusal of a number of major brands, such as Christian Dior, to supply its stores. The company began losing money, and finally was forced to find a buyer for its network. Twice the size of Frydman's group, Marionnaud was unable to attract an interested buyer among the country's large retail groups. Finally, Marionnaud had no choice but to negotiate with Frydman—and to sell his chain for just EUR 10 million. ''Which wasn't too much,'' Frydman told *Challenges,* ''It was the chance of a lifetime. I was buying the most famous perfumery in France.''

Frydman quickly capitalized on the Marionnaud name, adopting the new name of Marionnaud Parfumeries across his entire retail network. Frydman as quickly brought the acquired group back into profitability, applying his own recipe for success. Meanwhile, Frydman continued buying up stores, adding a further 27 by the end of 1997 and boosting sales to EUR 117 million.

Joined by sons Gerald, who had worked as a consultant at KPMG, and Jean-Pierre, whose interest in IT systems led the company to put into place a sophisticated tracking system linking sales at Marionnaud's stores both to its headquarters and to a growing network of distribution centers, Frydman rolled out the company's two-tiered retail approach of small ''boutiques'' and larger ''espaces.''

By 1998, the company owned and operated 76 boutiques and 14 espaces and began looking for new large-scale acquisitions.

Marionnaud nearly snared one of its main competitors, the Marie-Jeanne Godard retail group. But luxury goods powerhouse LVMH, which had acquired another perfumery rival, Sephora, in 1997, snapped up the Godard chain.

European Perfumery Leader in the 2000s

Marionnaud responded by going public, with a listing on the Paris Stock Exchange's Secondary Market in July 1998. The Frydman family holding was reduced to just two-thirds of the company's stock after the listing. The company now had greater access to capital—until then, Marionnaud had gone to its bankers for financing for each acquisition—and began plans to step up its expansion across France. Frydman once again adjusted the growth target for his company, now forecasting the network's growth to 160 boutiques and 30 espaces by 2001.

Once again, Frydman's targets were to prove too modest. By the end of 1998, the company had already grown to more than 150 stores, including 15 espaces. This was achieved through the acquisition of a number of small independent shops, but also by the acquisition of two more important retail groups, Kleber, with 27 stores, acquired in October 1998, followed by the 24 stores owned by Saresco and operated under the names Silver Moon, Liz Parfums, and Opéra Chic. The company finished the year with sales of more than EUR 145 million.

By the end of 1999, Marionnaud's sales had jumped past EUR 227 as the company continued its aggressive expansion effort. At the end of that year, the company reached an agreement to acquire the 75-store chain of Patchouli stores, boosting the company's totals past 200 stores. That acquisition was soon followed up by two more purchases at the beginning of 2000, those of the Marie Bernard Group, which, with 24 stores, helped extend the company's network into France's Brittany region, and the Annebelle store group, which had 58 stores located primarily in the south of France. Fueling these purchases was the Frydmans' willingness to reduce their own sharcholding in the company, which dropped below 50 percent, and was to sink to below 25 percent by 2002—although the family maintained control of Marionnaud's voting rights.

Marionnaud had succeeded in gaining the lead in France, outpacing Sephora in number of stores. Yet the company had long been reluctant to pursue growth internationally, especially given the difficulties of its major competitors, particularly Sephora, to gain profitability overseas.

In July 2000, Marionnaud made its first international expansion move when it acquired Switzerland's Alrodo, which, with 103 perfumeries operating under the Alrodo and Europarfums names, controlled 16 percent of the Swiss market. This acquisition was quickly joined by a smaller Swiss purchase, that of the five-store Geneva-based chain Parfumerie Principale. Together, these acquisitions added more than EUR 100 million to the company's sales, while making it the leader in the Swiss retail perfume market.

The company's entry into Switzerland was quickly followed by a move into Italy, with the purchase of La Chiocciola, a chain of 35 perfume shops. By the end of 2000, Marionnaud's network had grown to more than 400 stores—including its freshly inaugurated Champs-Elysées flagship store. Revenues topped

Marionnaud was on its way to achieving its newest goal: that of becoming the undisputed European retail perfumery specialist. That goal appeared within reach at the beginning of 2002, as the company entered Eastern Europe with a 51 percent share in a joint venture controlling more than 107 stores.

The company continued to add more stores in 2002, notably with the purchase of the 30-store chain La Maison Blanche, in Spain, which was quickly followed in that country with the acquisition of 43 stores from the Conrado Martin chain, coupled with an agreement to acquire an additional 45 stores from that company by the end of the year. Then in August 2002, Marionnaud cemented its leadership of the Spanish market with the acquisitions of 22 Cusco stores and 12 Mendoza stores. These purchases helped push the company's store total to 1,118 stores.

Marionnaud showed no sign of slowing down, entering Tunisia and Portugal, with plans to enter Greece, among other markets. Meanwhile, arch-rival Sephora's losses continued, giving rise to rumors that LVMH might begin plans to sell off that subsidiary. Marionnaud appeared well placed to snap up its more internationally oriented competitor, should its ambitions take it beyond Europe and onto a global scale.

Key Dates:

1984: Marcel Frydman buys a perfume shop in Montreuil, a Paris suburb, for his wife.

1985: Frydman buys a second store in Paris.

1992: The company opens its 16th store.

1995: The company acquires the Bernard Marionnaud chain of perfume shops and adopts the Marionnaud brand name.

1998: Marionnaud goes public on the Paris stock exchange; the company acquires the Kleber store chain, then Saresco, which operated 24 stores under the Silver Moon, Liz Parfums, and Opéra Chic names.

1999: The company acquires the 75-store Patchouli chain.

2000: The company acquires the 24-store Marie Bernard group in the Brittany region and the Annebelle group, with 58 stores in the south of France; the company acquires Alrodo, with 103 stores in Switzerland, marking its first international expansion, and then acquires La Chiocciola, of Italy, with 35 stores.

2001: The company acquires DSP, of France, with 112 franchised stores; the company acquires more than 60 stores in Italy and enters Austria and Spain.

2002: The company acquires La Maison Blanche, in Spain, with 30 stores and 43 Conrado Martin stores in Spain; the company enters Tunisia and Portugal.

Principal Subsidiaries

Alrodo (Switzerland); Impo (Austria); Marionnaud Parfumeries Italie; Quadrifoglio (Italy); SAS Marionnaud Kleber; Snail (Italy); Xplora (Spain);

Principal Competitors

Bath & Body Works, Inc.; BeautiControl Cosmetics, Inc.; The Body Shop International PLC; The Boots Company PLC; Buth-Na-Bodhaige Inc.; Duane Reade, Inc.; Sephora SA; The Estée Lauder Companies Inc; Galeries Lafayette; Pinault-Printemps-Redoute.

Further Reading

Bouaziz, Franck, ''Marionnaud vend de l'amour,'' *Nouvel Economiste,* May 3, 2002.

Cazenave, Frédéric, ''Marionnaud Parfumeries Le Canada Dry du luxe,'' *Newsbourse,* January 20, 2002.

''French Perfume Group Is Aiming to Take Over Europe,'' *Cosmetics International,* November 25, 2001, p. 6.

Leboucq, Valérie, ''Marionnaud va continuer les acquisitions,'' *Les Echos,* May 22, 2001, p. 12.

Le Hen, Véronique, ''Marionnaud ou . . . le parfum du succes,'' *Dynamique Commercial,* March–April 2002.

''Marionnaud Goes from Strength to Strength,'' *Cosmetics International,* August 15, 2002, p. 6.

''Marionnaud Is Spain's Top Perfumery,'' *Cosmetics International,* July 25, 2002, p. 5.

Rivaud, Francine, ''Le parfumeur des familles,'' *Challenges,* June 2001.

—M.L. Cohen

EUR 500 million, as the company now claimed 20 percent of the French market.

The share grew still greater at the beginning of 2001, with the purchase of DSP, owner of the store brands Bel Espace Parfumerie and Beauté Actuelle, adding 112 stores, for the most part franchised stores. The company decided to maintain these two store brands as the basis for a franchise operation to attract additional storeowners who preferred to maintain their independence while gaining access to Marionnaud's purchasing and marketing strength.

The company celebrated its entry onto the Paris Bourse's Primary Market in May 2001. Marionnaud then stepped up its presence in Italy, buying eight Riviera stores located in and around Venice, then another 36 stores in Piedmont, 22 stores in Milan, and six stores in Tuscany. The company also had entered Austria that year, boosting its number of stores in that country to 85 at the end of the year with the acquisition of 35 stores from the Holzer group. Meanwhile, Marionnaud took its first steps into Spain, buying the eight-store chain Xplora. The company meanwhile continued to build up its portfolio of stores in France, adding the Odylia chain of 12 Parisian stores at the end of 2001.

With sales topping EUR 770 million and a network of stores of nearly 830, including more than 300 stores outside of France,

McClain Industries, Inc.

6200 Elmridge Road
Sterling Heights, Michigan 48313-3706
U.S.A.
Telephone: (810) 264-3611
Fax: (818) 264-3230
Web site: http://www.mcclaingroup.com

Public Company
Incorporated: 1968
Employees: 560
Sales: $91.55 million
Stock Exchanges: NASDAQ
Ticker Symbol: MCCL
NAIC: 336211 Motor Vehicle Body Manufacturing;
    332439 Other Metal Container Manufacturing

McClain Industries, Inc. is a leading manufacturer of waste transport vehicle bodies, containers, and equipment for the waste management industry. McClain brand names include Galion and E-Z Pack. The firm sells its products to resellers and directly to solid waste handling companies like Waste Management, Inc., who account for nearly a fifth of sales. Headquartered in the Detroit, Michigan, suburb of Sterling Heights, the public company remains in the control and majority ownership of members of its founding family.

Beginnings

McClain Industries got its start in the 1950s when Kenneth and Robert McClain's father started an iron and sheet metal fabricating business in the Detroit area that specialized in making trash containers for industrial use. The company was a small one for many years, tallying an estimated $200,000 in annual revenues by the late 1960s. It was at this time that Kenneth and Robert bought their father out and began to run the business themselves. Both already worked for the firm, Kenneth having been trained as a welder.

With Kenneth as president and CEO and Robert as a vice-president, the company began to grow, adding manufacturing of waste compactors to its line of containers. McClain Industries went public in 1973. Its growth continued over the next decade, with revenues reaching $14 million by 1984. The following year, McClain purchased an Oklahoma City-based solid waste handling equipment maker, Custom Metal Industries, Inc. Custom Metal had 51 employees and revenues of $5 million. McClain's customers at this time were principally municipalities, construction contractors, and retail stores that utilized the large trash containers and haulers that the firm made.

During the 1980s, the company's stock price was one of the market's top 100 gainers, as reported in *USA Today*, increasing in value by more than 3,400 percent during the decade. Revenues peaked in 1988 at $33.4 million but began to decline as the U.S. economy started to slow down. The firm reported a loss in 1990 and was later forced to restate earnings from both 1988 and 1989. After a downturn in demand of several years, sales slowly began to increase again, reaching $31.9 million in 1992. A cost control program, instituted at the start of the decade, also helped improve the company's bottom line.

Galion Acquisition Doubles Company's Size

July of 1992 saw McClain make its most significant acquisition when the Peabody Galion division of Peabody Industries was purchased for approximately $18 million. Peabody Galion (later shortened to Galion) had plants in Galion and Winesburg, Ohio, that manufactured front, rear, and side loading truck bodies, recycling truck bodies, dump truck bodies, and other solid waste handing equipment for the construction industry. Peabody Galion's sales actually surpassed those of McClain, having topped $31 million for Fiscal 1991. After the purchase, McClain expanded Galion's manufacturing operation to Oklahoma City and Macon, Georgia.

The company also began ramping up its investment in research and development, an area which hitherto had been given little attention. The efforts soon paid off with the receipt of a U.S. patent for a curbside recycling vehicle, readying McClain to capitalize on a waste management area that was experiencing explosive growth in the United States. The emphasis on research and development served to widen the company's product

Key Dates:

lines, as well as to create products that had a longer life expectancy, bringing McClain in line with the industry's trend toward keeping equipment in service longer and offering more generous warranties, typically five years.

To capitalize on the Galion acquisition, the company began to put an emphasis on marketing and sales, an area which had not been formally organized before. The addition of new manufacturing facilities outside of Michigan also led McClain to set up a computerized communications system to coordinate purchasing and accounting among the various sites.

In 1994, the firm prepared to offer an additional 1.2 million shares of stock to gain funds for additional expansion, but the offer was cancelled when the share price failed to rise to a level deemed adequate by the company. McClain family members held control of the firm with about 70 percent of the stock. At this time, the company had an estimated 16 percent of the $500 million environmental manufacturing market, which constituted four-fifths of McClain's total business. The growing company began operating a mill in the Kalamazoo, Michigan, area to supply its various plants with metal tubing. Among McClain's major customers were WMX Technologies, Inc. and City Management Corp., a Detroit-based trash hauler.

Successful Defense of Patent

In 1995, McClain's Galion subsidiary won a patent infringement suit in federal court against Dempster, Inc. that resulted in Dempster paying restitution for past infringement and licensing the patent for future production of horizontally divided, high capacity waste recycling equipment, which Galion sold under the trademark E-Z Pack. Galion was doing well with sales of E-Z Pack units, having recently sold 50 of them to the city of San Antonio, Texas, for $1.57 million. Also in 1995, a local union in Macon, Georgia, charged McClain with unfair labor practices at the company's plant there. The National Labor Relations Board and U.S Court of Appeals later found for the union, though McClain continued to dispute the result.

May of 1995 saw McClain reach an agreement to acquire EPCO Manufacturing Corp., Inc., a maker of baling equipment for scrap metals and recycled cardboard, paper, and plastics. A year later, the company also acquired a container manufacturing facility in Demopolis, Alabama, from Waste Management of Alabama, Inc.

Fiscal 1997 was a difficult year for McClain. The company closed its EPCO operation and transferred production of balers to one of its Ohio facilities, resulting in a substantial write-off, and production changes at the company's Georgia plant caused additional losses. Revenues for the year reached $90.1 million, but the company reported a loss of $1.7 million, its worst ever, due in part to the manufacturing changes as well as errors in product pricing and an overall slowdown in the market.

During 1998, the firm worked to improve its margins by changing vendors and ordering procedures and purchasing some items in bulk for long-term use. Sales and advertising efforts were also ramped up. The number of its competitors was growing at a rapid clip, and in order to make sales McClain was forced to price its products at a level that yielded relatively little profit. One reason for the heightened competition was the relative ease of entry into the container market. The basic product was essentially a welded steel box, and many small companies across the country possessed equipment to manufacture them. While few had McClain's national distribution or name recognition, this did not deter newcomers from entering the business, though many also left it after a short time.

Despite the crowded field, McClain made it through the year with four quarters of record profits. It was helped in part by consolidation taking place within the waste management industry, which led to more equipment being ordered. McClain was also helped by its policy of selling truck chassis, which it did not manufacture, to go along with its own truck bodies at a small markup, thus allowing customers to acquire the body and chassis from a single source rather than from separate vendors.

Sales leveled off in 1999, however, and the company reduced its workforce by 5 percent to compensate. McClain also authorized a stock buyback program the following year to repurchase 100,000 shares, the second offer of this type it had made in a three-year period. The company's share price continued to hover in the $5 to $7 range, which company officials felt was far too low.

In October 2000, McClain reached an agreement to buy Benlee, Inc. of Romulus, Michigan. Benlee, with annual sales of $12 million in 1999, was a maker of roll-off trailers and containers for the scrap metal industry. The work that Benlee performed was something that McClain often subcontracted out, and the acquisition was expected to save money for the firm.

At this time, McClain's Galion Dump Body unit was having problems in an extremely competitive market, and during the latter part of 2000 the decision was reached to exit the field and liquidate the inventory of dump truck chassis. A loss of $1.75 million was the result, half of the $3.5 million in red ink accumulated by the company's truck group for the year. Sales for 2000 hit a record level of $141 million, with a small loss of $86,000 recorded. However, 2001 saw the tightening U.S. economy hit McClain hard, with revenues dropping by more than a third, to $91.55 million, and losses of nearly $5 million posted. According to CEO Kenneth McClain, ''The loss resulted from decreased sales volume, deep discounting, and increases in bad debt reserves due to the severity of the nationwide economic slowdown. We expect sales to remain depressed during Fiscal 2002 and are continuing our strategy of reviewing and reducing our operating costs and inventories to reflect reduced sales volume.''

Still a leader in its field of waste management equipment manufacturing, McClain Industries was in a business that was suffering from too many competitors and a highly variable demand curve. The company, still under the control of its founding family, had survived other dry periods and would likely do so again.

Principal Subsidiaries

McClain E-Z Pack, Inc.; McClain Galion, Inc.; McClain Southland Company; Shelby Steel Processing Co.; McClain Tube Company; McClain Group Leasing, Inc.; McClain International FSC, Inc. (Virgin Islands).

Principal Competitors

Kann Manufacturing Corporation; Leach Company; Heil Environmental Industries; Waste Technology Corp.; Wastequip, Inc.

Further Reading

''CEO Interview: McClain Industries,'' *The Wall Street Transcript*, November 22, 1993.

Kosdrosky, Terry, ''McClain Turns Around But Faces Challenges,'' *Crain's Detroit Business*, December 21, 1998, p. 3.

——, ''Turning Trash into Cash: McClain Cleaning up on Waste-Hauling Gear,'' *Crain's Detroit Business*, August 16, 1999, p. 2.

''McClain Acquires Peabody Galion Division,'' *American Metal Market*, August 12, 1992, p. 9.

''McClain Sales Down 34% in Third Quarter,'' *Trailer/Body Builders*, September 1, 2001.

''McClain to Buy EPCO,'' *American Metal Market*, May 17, 1995, p. 10.

Raphael, Steve, ''McClain CEO Down After Record High,'' *Crain's Detroit Business*, January 29, 1996, p. 1.

——, ''McClain Industries to Waste No Time on Next Stock Split,'' *Crain's Detroit Business*, May 3, 1995, p. 16.

Snavely, Brent, ''Boss' 65th Gave Birth to McClain Acquisition,'' *Crain's Detroit Business*, October 16, 2000, p. 28.

——, ''McClain Puts Money Where its Stock Is,'' *Crain's Detroit Business*, August 28, 2000, p. 4.

—Frank Uhle

The McGraw-Hill Companies, Inc.

1221 Avenue of the Americas
New York, New York 10020-1095
U.S.A.
Telephone: (212) 512-2000
Fax: (212) 512-4502
Web site: http://www.mcgraw-hill.com

Public Company
Incorporated: 1909 as McGraw-Hill Book Company
Employees: 17,150
Sales: $4.6 billion (2001)
Stock Exchanges: New York Pacific
Ticker Symbol: MHP
NAIC: 511120 Periodical Publishers; 511130 Book Publishers; 511210 Software Publishers; 514191 On-Line Information Services; 513120 Television Broadcasting

Perhaps best known for its textbooks, The McGraw-Hill Companies, Inc. was formed initially from the merger of McGraw Publishing Co. and Hill Publishing Company. The business has always aimed to provide technicians, scientists, and business people complete, accurate, and up-to-date information of both specialized and general interest. The company carried on that tradition in the late 20th and early 21st centuries with mergers and acquisitions that increased market share, reached new markets, and expanded its global reach. Guided by Harold "Terry" McGraw III, great-grandson of founder James H. McGraw, the company employs the latest media technologies to keep its customers in education, business, industrial, professional, and government markets abreast of their disciplines.

Beginnings: 1880s to 1915

Born in 1858, John A. Hill—typesetter, silver prospector, newspaper publisher, and railroad engineer—came to the attention of the publisher of *American Machinist* with his contribution of letters and articles on practical aspects of railroading. When the publisher began *Locomotive Engineering* in 1888,

Hill was his choice for editor. By 1889, Hill had become part owner of both magazines, and in 1897, divesting his interest in *Locomotive Engineering*, he took over full ownership of *American Machinist*, and established the American Machinist Press in 1898. In 1902, he incorporated Hill Publishing Company, going on to acquire *Power, Engineering and Mining Journal*, and *Engineering News*. By 1909, Hill was a leading trade publisher of not just magazines but of books such as Colvin and Stanley's *American Machinist's Handbook* (1908) and Herbert Hoover's *Principles of Mining* (1909).

Hill's chief competitor was onetime teacher and subscription salesman James H. McGraw. McGraw was an advertising salesman for the American Railway Publishing Company in 1884, where he rose to vice-president by 1886. On resigning from American Railway, McGraw began to acquire magazines that reported on technological progress. Titles included the *American Journal of Railway Appliances*; *Electrical Industries* (later retitled *American Electrician*); *Electrical World*; *Electrical Engineer*; *Electrochemical Industry*; and *Engineering Record*. In 1899, McGraw incorporated McGraw Publishing Company; its first engineering handbook, the *Standard Handbook for Electrical Engineers*, was published in 1907.

In the years following the Civil War, the United States evolved from an agrarian to an industrial society. Both McGraw and Hill found a growing market of technicians concerned with the practical applications of science to transportation, lighting, and engineering, among other facets of daily life. In 1909, Edward Caldwell and Martin M. Foss, the respective heads of the book departments of the two firms, agreed that a merger would serve both companies well. After the two men persuaded their bosses, a coin toss decided whose name would come first in naming the new company, the loser becoming president. The McGraw-Hill Book Company, with John A. Hill as president, was thus born, locating itself in McGraw Publishing's building in New York City.

The two companies, however, were still distinct, entities: the magazines that formed the chief interests of both and supplied articles for many of the books remained separate concerns. In 1914, as World War I broke out in Europe, Hill moved his company into an air-conditioned building in New York City, one specially constructed to house his publications and their printing facilities. By 1910, the McGraw-Hill Book Company had established itself with its first publication, *The Art of Engineering*, and its first series, "Electrical Engineering Texts." This series marked the beginning of a company trend toward publishing series of books by multiple authors covering an entire range of knowledge in a specific field.

A New Era: 1916–28

A more complete merger of the McGraw and Hill interests came in 1916 when John A. Hill died at the age of 57. Arthur Baldwin, Hill's attorney, led Hill Publishing for a brief time following Hill's death. McGraw became president of the book company; the two established the McGraw-Hill Publishing Company in 1917, with its offices located in the Hill Building, publishing *Electrical World*, *Electric Railway Journal*, *Electrical Merchandising*, *Engineering Record*, *Metallurgical and Chemical Engineering*, *The Contractor*, *American Machinist*, *Power*, *Engineering and Mining Journal*, *Coal Age*, and *Engineering News*. This concentration of interests, along with the enlargement of the book company, now a subsidiary of McGraw-Hill Publishing, made McGraw-Hill the largest technical publisher in the world at that time.

The United States entered World War I in 1917, and this was a particularly good time for technical publishers. The first McGraw-Hill title to benefit from increased wartime demand was the *American Machinists' Handbook*, originally published before the war. There was also increased demand for engineering books in radio communication, aviation, construction and maintenance, chemical warfare, trench construction, automotive transportation, aerial photography, and antisubmarine tactics. McGraw-Hill responded quickly to this market; an example was its record response to the U.S. Army Educational Commission's order for 150,000 technical books, which were printed, bound, specially packed, and shipped to France in a matter of days.

After World War I, McGraw-Hill expanded rapidly. With Foss in charge of editorial and sales activities and Caldwell heading up finances and production, the book company had grown by establishing close contacts with the faculties of various universities and engineering schools, not only to make sales but also to find new authors. With the addition of a series designed for educational use, McGraw-Hill formed a college department in 1927, thus establishing a lasting emphasis on textbooks. Foss was equally innovative in finding new ways to market the technical books that seldom found space in general bookstores. By both advertising at cost in the parent firm's magazines and sending letters and circulars to subscribers, Foss offered interested parties a chance to examine a book for ten days without payment, an approach that quickly resulted in increased book sales.

The publisher also grew through acquisition during the 1920s, purchasing the Newton Falls Paper Co. in 1920. McGraw-Hill opened offices in Great Britain and California as well. With the purchase of the A.W. Shaw Company of Chicago in 1928, McGraw-Hill extended its reach into the field of business books and magazines. The editorial staff turned one of Shaw's monthlies, the *Magazine of Business*, into a weekly, covering and interpreting news of specific interest to business people. Now named *Business Week*, it would become the best known of all McGraw-Hill publications.

During the 1920s James McGraw began to shift some of his authority in the company to other people. The first shift came when he named himself, his son James McGraw, Jr., and Malcolm Muir to a governing board of trustees. Then, in 1925, McGraw turned over the presidency of the book company to Edward Caldwell, who was succeeded by Martin M. Foss the next year. In 1928, Malcolm Muir became president of the publishing company; James McGraw remained chairman of the board.

New Ventures: 1929–45

McGraw-Hill stock was first traded publicly in 1929. Just after the stock market crash that same year, *The Business Week* (as it was then known) predicted, in its November 2, 1929 issue, that "business will gradually and steadily recover as businessmen regain their perspective and go back to work." Following this optimistic line of thought, McGraw-Hill established four new magazines in 1930, opened a West Coast office and book depository in San Francisco, and, under the imprint of Whittlesey House (named after James McGraw's father-in-law) entered the trade book field for the first time. The first title under the new imprint, selected to distinguish this division from trade publications, was Ernest Minor Patterson's *The World's Economic Dilemma*.

McGraw-Hill commissioned a new office building designed by Raymond Hood and located on West 42nd Street in New York City. Nicknamed "Big Green" because of the blue-green cast of its Art Deco exterior, the new McGraw-Hill building aroused controversy because of the horizontal banding of its windows, now a standard feature of many modern office buildings. When first occupied in 1931, Big Green included a complete production plant taking up four floors. The increasing severity of the economic depression during the early 1930s, however, forced McGraw-Hill not only to make deep cuts in personnel and salaries but to sell its press machinery and equipment in 1933. In 1932, the parent company's deficit ran to $239,137.

That same year, Whittlesey House had its first bestseller, *Life Begins at Forty*, by Walter B. Pitkin. The company's other publications made themselves useful sources of information for business people by providing hard facts and analysis of the economic situation. The vocational-education department of the book company helped those seeking new skills. Established in 1930, it concentrated on mechanical arts, agriculture, and home economics. The 1930s also saw major shifts at the executive level of McGraw-Hill; in 1935 James H. McGraw handed the chairmanship over to James McGraw, Jr. During the next two years, Malcolm Muir failed to get along with the McGraw family; in 1937, he left to run *Newsweek* magazine, and James H. McGraw, Jr., became both president and chairman of the board. By 1937, the company had an annual profit of more than $1 million.

With the coming of World War II in the 1940s, McGraw-Hill was in an advantageous position. Because its technical publications were especially important to the war effort, its paper requirements received special priority. The company's magazines began to cover a range of relevant wartime topics from accelerated training in the use of metalworking power tools to dehydrated foods. The company also added titles in the fields of aviation, health, and atomic energy. In addition, the company began to publish special wartime titles, such as *En Guardia*, a Spanish-language paper promoting Latin American relations, and *Overseas Digest*, excerpting articles from other McGraw-Hill titles for distribution to military personnel posted abroad.

It was in the area of special training manuals, however, that McGraw-Hill was to make a special effort. As untrained men and women poured into industry and the armed services, accelerated technical training became increasingly important to the war effort. By 1943, the book company had published 231 titles for the Engineering and Science Management War Training Program. Of the 304 books published by 1944 to further the war effort, many dealt with radio and electronics, a newly important part of warfare. One title, *Mathematics for Electricians and Radiomen* by Nelson M. Cooke, first published in 1942, continued to be successful after the war, and by 1964, under the new title of *Basic Mathematics for Electronics*, had total sales in excess of 485,000 copies.

Although McGraw-Hill had been present in the United Kingdom and Germany as well as other countries since before World War I, the company made use of the opportunities World War II offered to increase its foreign activities. In 1943, the book company opened a book-export department, which by 1944 had a foreign-language translation office. The same year, McGraw-Hill acquired the Embassy Book Company Ltd. of Toronto, which was renamed the McGraw-Hill Company of Canada, Ltd. and later designated McGraw Ryerson. In 1945, to provide its magazines with international coverage, the company started the World News Service.

After World War II: 1946–59

After the war, the book company prospered under the presidency of Curtis G. Benjamin, who succeeded James S. Thompson, president for only two years. Benjamin developed a text-film department, a venture inspired by the use of educational films during World War II to supplement textbook materials. As teachers discovered the value of motion pictures and film strips in the classroom, the market expanded, and by 1965 McGraw-Hill was the leader in the field. Another wartime dividend for the company was the 13-volume "U.S. Navy Flight Preparation Training" series printed for the Bureau of Aeronautics during the war.

With the growth of commercial aviation in the postwar period, McGraw-Hill found a large market for civilian editions of the series. Building on the close contacts with governmental agencies in research and development made during World War II, the company contracted to publish the "Radiation Laboratory series," 27 volumes concentrating on the results of wartime research into radar. According to Charles A. Madison's

1966 *Book Publishing in America*, this series, published in 1949 and costing more than $1.2 million, "set a precedent for the commercial publication of government-financed projects." Although McGraw-Hill lost money on another project, the "National Nuclear" series, the company made an arrangement with the U.S. Atomic Energy Commission to produce an eight-volume compilation of scientific reference materials that was presented at the first International Conference on the Peaceful Uses of Atomic Energy at Geneva in August 1955.

Another project started in the late 1940s was the publication of James Boswell's manuscripts. Consisting of the voluminous collection of original manuscripts of the eighteenth-century Scottish author collected by Colonel Ralph H. Isham, the project was guided through negotiations with its purchaser, Yale University, by Edward Aswell, Whittlesey House's editor-in-chief since 1947. Publication of a projected 40 volumes began in 1950. It was not to be under the Whittlesey imprint, however, as Yale preferred to have the McGraw-Hill name on the books. Thus began the relegation of Whittlesey House to juvenile titles. Another milestone, this one commercial, proved to be the publication in 1950 of Betty Crocker's *Picture Cook Book*, which achieved sales of more than 235,000 copies in its first two years.

By the time its cofounder, James H. McGraw, died in 1948 at age 87, McGraw-Hill Publishing was well on its way to developing a departmentalized organizational structure. An independent technical-education department had been established in 1941, then a text-film department in 1945. The acquisition of the Gregg Publishing Company, publisher of vocational textbooks, in 1949 transformed the company's business-education department into the Gregg division. In response to the need for training literature during the Korean War, beginning in 1950, the book company established a technical-writing division to produce specialized materials for both government and industry. The next year, following a reorganization of the handbook, technical, and professional publishing department, the industrial- and business-book department was born, and the medical publishing department was formed in 1945. It was not until 1954, when it acquired Blakiston Company from Doubleday, which specialized in medical titles, that McGraw-Hill began to have a major share of the medical market under the newly named Blakiston division.

What proved by far to be the most important division for company progress in the postwar period was the international division, established in 1946. In less than 15 years, book exports trebled, with a profitable business in text-films, filmstrips, and the sale of foreign-language rights. A major force in the international growth of the company was Curtis Benjamin, who proceeded along lines mapped out by James Thompson. Benjamin succeeded, along with B.G. Dandison, head of the international division, in making the company successful in foreign countries: in 1962, McGraw-Hill was presented by President John F. Kennedy with a presidential E-for-Export award, making McGraw-Hill the first commercial publishing firm to be so honored.

James McGraw, Jr., who had headed up the company since 1935, retired in 1950 and was replaced by another son of the first McGraw, Curtis. Curtis led the company for three short years before his sudden death in 1953. He was succeeded by his brother, Donald C. McGraw.

Just before the death of Curtis, the company purchased the National Petroleum Publishing Company, the W.C. Platt Company, and Platt's Price Service, Inc., all from Warren C. Platt. The book company then began three major encyclopedia projects in the late 1950s, each continuing on into the 1960s: *The McGraw-Hill Encyclopedia of Science and Technology*, *The Encyclopedia of World Art*, and *The New Catholic Encyclopedia*. When in 1959 the publishing company commemorated its 50th year, revenues exceeded $100 million.

Growth and Diversification: 1960–79

While Curtis Benjamin remained chairman of the board and CEO of the book company, Edward Booher, who had joined the company in 1936, became president in 1960. They doubled overall sales within five years, contributing 39 percent of the total income of the parent company in 1965. The F.W. Dodge Corporation, information provider to the construction industry, was purchased in 1961. The following year, the general book division was formed by merging the industrial-and-business-book department with the trade department. The purchase of Webster Publishing Company in 1963 marked the company's entry into the elementary school and high school textbook markets.

In 1964, the book company and the F.W. Dodge Corporation merged with McGraw-Hill Publishing Company to form McGraw-Hill, Inc. The reorganization created a single corporation, the parent company, with three operating divisions: book publishing, the Dodge complex, and magazines and news services. The company established an Australian publishing unit the same year. With the acquisition of the California Test Bureau in 1965, McGraw-Hill strengthened its K-12 educational services just in time to benefit from the postwar baby boom. The company moved into two new fields in 1966: one was legal publishing with the purchase of Shepard's Citations, Inc.; the other was financial information services through the acquisition of Standard & Poor's Corporation. Other acquisitions were Schaum Publishing Company, Capitol Radio Engineering Institute, and *Postgraduate Medicine* magazine, all in 1967. The company also expanded into Mexico in 1967 and into Japan in 1969.

A key figure in this expansion was Shelton Fisher. Beginning as promotion manager for *Business Week* in 1940, by 1968 Fisher had succeeded Donald McGraw as president and CEO of McGraw-Hill. His goal was to change the perception of McGraw-Hill as an old-fashioned publisher of trade magazines into that of a dynamic media giant. Fisher further extended the company's reach into Canada, Brazil, and India, bought four television stations from Time Inc., and moved the company out of Big Green and into a new, 50-story international headquarters in 1972. While increasing the company's prestige, the large capital outlay came at a time when a recession caused a loss in revenues for the McGraw-Hill magazines. After a period of uncertainty during which the McGraw family worked out a succession, Harold McGraw, Jr., became president of the parent company and Fisher assumed the chairmanship. This changed within a year when Fisher retired and Harold McGraw, Jr., became chairman in addition to his other positions.

The picture of McGraw-Hill, Inc. at the end of the 1970s, according to John Tebbel's *History of Book Publishing in America*, was of "an extremely healthy, well-managed conglomerate, composed of several operating divisions." Along with the book and publications companies, there was the information system company, composed of the F.W. Dodge division, Sweet's division, and Datapro Research Corporation. Two other divisions were Standard & Poor's Corporation and the McGraw-Hill Broadcasting Company. Total operating revenues amounted to more than $761 million, crossing the $1 billion threshold in 1980.

Its very success made McGraw-Hill the target of a takeover attempt by the American Express Company in 1979. The chairman of American Express, James D. Robinson III, and its president, Roger H. Morley, were shocked by the ferocity with which Harold McGraw fought the attempted stock buyout. Concerted action by the McGraw family, along with various legal actions, defeated the bid for ownership. Although American Express had failed, McGraw-Hill remained a prime target for a takeover. Harold McGraw was planning to retire in four years and, while another generation of McGraws waited in the wings, none were as yet ready to run the corporation. By appointing Joseph L. Dionne, who had been in charge of planning, to the newly created position of vice-president of operations, McGraw sought to improve management organization and put someone in charge who could generate the fast growth needed to discourage further takeover attempts.

Dawn of the Electronic Age: 1980–90

Dionne became president and CEO in 1983, while McGraw remained chairman. A former history teacher, Dionne proved a visionary intent on transforming McGraw-Hill from "a simple publishing company" into an "information turbine" for the digital age. Under this model, McGraw-Hill's content would flow seamlessly throughout the company's vast information-gathering and disseminating "machine." As Suzanne Oliver described it in a 1990 *Forbes* article, "Housing statistics, say, could go into the turbine and come out as a feature story in a magazine and then as a new bond rating on a home builder. Like a packing house of old, McGraw-Hill would turn the same basic raw material into dozens of different products." Under his guidance, the company was reorganized into "market focus groups" as opposed to groupings by media. In 1985, Dionne created 20 market-focused business units.

Although still committed to print publishing, Dionne planned to reduce the 80 percent of the business that was print-oriented in 1983 to 65 percent or 70 percent over several years. The company had made a halting step toward this goal with the acquisition of Data Resources, Inc. in 1979. Dionne was convinced that DRI held not only a vast share of the world's business and economic data but also the expertise required to translate McGraw-Hill's hard copy into malleable electronic information. Although the DRI acquisition would prove to be a misstep—the company actually made most of its money from renting computer space—Dionne pressed on with his plan. During this same period, McGraw-Hill entered the computer publishing field by acquiring *BYTE*, *Unixworld*, and *LAN Times* magazines, as well as Osborne Books, all of which provided support information to computer users. As the company moved into the electronic information marketplace, much of the data supplied by the news service, magazines, Standard & Poor's,

Dodge, Platt, and Shepard's was made available in computerized form and in various configurations.

Despite his reservations, Harold McGraw approved of the direction in which Dionne was taking the company; in 1988, Harold McGraw became chairman emeritus and Dionne added the title of chairman to those of president and CEO. In its attempt to weather the communications revolution, McGraw-Hill had undergone three major reorganizations in four years, resulting in an organization centered around 14 market-focus groups. These reorganizations, the automation of F.W. Dodge, and the shutdown of the general-book division, ending the company's involvement in the trade book market, resulted in a layoff of more then 1,000 workers.

The company expanded globally and had success with the Standard & Poor's Marketscope and with other online, real-time services. Early in 1990, however, two online services, McGraw-Hill News and Standard & Poor's News, were discontinued. Some acquisitions resulted in costly write-offs, notably Numerax Inc., an electronic data and services operation. Yet McGraw Hill continued to invest in strong growth markets and divest itself of publications and units connecting it with its past. *American Machinist & Automated Manufacturing*, *Coal Age*, and *Engineering & Mining Journal* were sold in 1987. Although it took years of acquisitions and divestments, not a few stumbles, and intensive development from within, Dionne's model proved not only successful but prescient.

In 1988, McGraw-Hill celebrated its centennial, acquired Random House's college division for over $200 million and created the Harold W. McGraw Jr. Prize in Education to honor the chairman emeritus's efforts on behalf of education and literacy. Operating revenues for the year were just shy of $1.7 billion. The next year, 1989, McGraw-Hill entered into a 50/50 joint venture with Macmillan, combining the elementary, secondary, and vocational education businesses of both companies. In 1990, a new electronic textbook publishing system known as Primis was implemented, allowing teachers to custom design textbooks with the results printed, bound, and shipped within 48 hours. Primis quickly became America's leading custom publisher.

Keeping the World Up to Speed: The 1990s

The early 1990s found McGraw-Hill growing steadily in its quest to provide information in a wide range of formats for persons of all ages. In 1993, the company bought out Macmillan's half of the Macmillan/McGraw-Hill School Publishing Company for $160.8 million, and by the following year McGraw-Hill's three business segments—Educational and Professional Publishing, Financial Services, and Information and Media Services—helped the company rake in almost $2.8 billion in revenue, a sizeable leap from the previous year's $2.2 billion. The Educational/Professional unit accounted for the most revenue (42 percent) while Financial Services dominated income with over 48 percent (despite the worst bond market since 1927 and rising interest rates).

For McGraw-Hill, Inc., 1995 proved a pivotal year, a year in which the company ceased to exist, at least in its previous form. To reflect its ongoing diversity, the company changed its name from McGraw-Hill, Inc. to The McGraw Hill Companies, Inc.

followed by a broadcast media campaign showcasing how the company was "keeping the world up to speed." Other milestones for 1995 were an all-time high stock price and a two-for-one stock split; additional ratings services and new alliances for Standard & Poor's; a myriad of new CD-ROM products, including Harrison's *Principals of Internal Medicine* (the world's best-selling medical textbook); a joint venture between the company's secondary school publisher, Glencoe/McGraw-Hill, National Geographic, and Capital Cities/ABC; the acquisition of UCB Canada and Hospital Practice; and new offices in Asia, Europe, and the Middle East.

McGraw-Hill's most famous periodical, *Business Week*, experienced a phenomenal year in 1995 with exceptional circulation (one million-plus with a readership of nearly seven million) and pumped up advertising volume and revenue. Additionally, *Business Week Online* gained in popularity and *Business Week Enterprise*, a magazine for small-business executives, published international editions in Asia, Europe, Latin America, and the Middle East. With so many new opportunities swirling about, McGraw-Hill, inevitably, let others go: Shepard's publishing operations and SRA Technology were sold, while Open Computing ceased publication. And despite a disastrous showing in Mexico after the peso's collapse, McGraw-Hill still managed to increase overall earnings by nearly 12 percent to $227.1 million while revenue topped $2.9 billion, a 6.3 percent increase over 1994's stellar performance.

In 1996, McGraw-Hill continued to expand its operations globally, with several high profile acquisitions, including Open Court Publishing Company for its K-8 elementary education division; *Healthcare Informatics* and *InfoCare* magazines from Wiesner Publishing for its Healthcare Information unit; and the Times Mirror Higher Education Group, which prompted the formation of the Higher Education and Consumer Group to house it and McGraw-Hill's well established college division. The Times-Mirror acquisition made McGraw-Hill America's top college publisher, with leading positions in 12 disciplines and a particular strength in business. The college division's emphasis on business and finance meshed well with the corporation's financial services operations. Around that same time, the Financial Information Services unit was renamed to reflect its most important asset, Standard & Poor's, to Standard & Poor's Financial Information Services.

A McGraw at the Helm: Late 1990s and Beyond

When CEO Joe Dionne retired in 1998, he could look back on a 15-year record of innovation and growth. He was succeeded in April 1998 by Harold "Terry" McGraw, a great-grandson of the founder who had logged thirteen years at McGraw-Hill before ascending to president in 1993. Although McGraw's climb to the top spot was viewed by some with skepticism, he quickly proved to be a "big picture" leader for a new era. He focused on enlivening the company's identity through a $4.5 million promotion targeting industry analysts and investors. In-house, he concentrated on cutting costs and investing in growth businesses. He consolidated McGraw-Hill's divisions from 15 down to three and sacked two-thirds of the company's senior managers. A 1998 article in *Crain's New York Business* called Terry McGraw's global expansion of Standard & Poor's "his most meaningful accomplishment."

His efforts paid off in higher returns, for while revenues increased only slightly from 1997 to 1998, earnings increased by 15.6 percent.

In 2000, McGraw-Hill moved to challenge Pearson Education for the top spot in educational publishing with the acquisition of Tribune Education. The nation's top publisher of K-12 supplements, Tribune was one of McGraw-Hill's largest purchases in years, at $635 million. The horserace for leadership of the textbook industry continued, however, when rival Thomson Corp. acquired Harcourt's higher-education and professional/corporate divisions from Reed-Elsevier in 2001.

With sales of $4.6 billion in 2001, McGraw-Hill stood as America's top K-12 education publisher and led the world in financial analyses and risk assessments though its Standard & Poor's financial services. Although the Media and Information services division proved a drag on earnings, it still boasted the powerhouse *Business Week* brand as well as four network television stations. But with a 20 percent decline in net income from 2000 to 2001, the company announced a year-end restructuring that cut 5 percent of the global workforce, or 925 employees. In 2002, McGraw-Hill hoped to increase earnings via an emphasis on business-to-business media as well as growth in its core elementary education group.

Principal Subsidiaries

CM Research Inc.; Calificadora de Valores, S.A. de C.V.; Capitol Radio Engineering Institute, Inc.; Columbia Administration Software Publishing Corporation; Computer and Communications Information Group, Inc.; DRI Europe, Inc.; DRI/McGraw-Hill; Editora McGraw-hill de Portugal, Ltda.; Editorial Interamericana, S.A.; Editoriales Pedagogicals Associadas, S.A.; International Advertising/McGraw-Hill Inc.; J.J. Kenney Company, Inc.; Liberty Brokerage Investment Corp.; MHFSCO, Ltd.; MMS International; McGraw-Hill Broadcasting Company, Inc.; McGraw-Hill Capital Corporation; McGraw-Hill Capital, Inc.; McGraw-Hill Data Services-Ireland, Ltd.; McGraw-Hill Financial Publications, Inc.; McGraw-Hill Holdings (U.K.) Limited; McGraw-Hill Information Systems Company of Canada Limited; McGraw-Hill Interamericana, Inc.; McGraw-Hill/Interamericana de Chile Limitada; McGraw-Hill/Interamericana de Espana, S.A.; McGraw-Hill/Interamericana de Mexico, S.A. de C.V.; McGraw-Hill/Interamericana de Venezuela S.A.; McGraw-Hill/Interamericana, S.A.; Inc.; McGraw-Hill International Enterprises, Inc.; McGraw-Hill Libri Italia; McGraw-Hill News Bureaus, Inc.; McGraw-Hill Publications Overseas, Inc.; McGraw-Hill Ryerson Limited; Medical China Publishing Limited; Money Market Directories, Inc.; Nueva Editorial Interamericana, S.A. de C.V.; Rock/McGraw, Inc.; Standard & Poor's Compustat; S&P's ComStock; Standard & Poor's-ADEF; Standard & Poor's Consumer Investor Network; Standard & Poor's Equity Investor Services; Standard & Poor's Index Services; Standard & Poor's International Ratings, Inc.; Standard & Poor's International, S.A.; Standard & Poor's Investment Advisory Services, Inc.; Standard & Poor's Ltd.; Standard & Poor's-Nordisk Rating AB; Standard & Poor's Securities, Inc.; Tata McGraw-Hill Publishing Company Private Limited; Tower Group International, Inc.

Principal Operating Units

McGraw-Hill Education (School Education Group: SRA/McGraw-Hill, Wright Group/McGraw-Hill, Macmillan/McGraw-Hill, Glencoe/McGraw-Hill, CTB/McGraw-Hill, McGraw-Hill Children's Publishing, Educators' Professional Development, McGraw-Hill Digital Learning; Higher Education); Professional and International Group (McGraw-Hill/Contemporary, McGraw Hill Higher Education, McGraw-Hill Professional, McGraw-Hill International, McGraw-Hill Lifetime Learning); Financial Services (Credit Market Services, Corporate Value Consulting, Investment Services); McGraw-Hill Information and Media Services (*Business Week*, *Broadcast*, *McGraw-Hill Construction*, *Platts*, *Aviation Week*, *Healthcare Information*).

Principal Competitors

Reed Elsevier Group plc; Moody's Corporation; Pearson plc; The Thomson Corporation.

Further Reading

Burlingame, Roger, *Endless Frontiers: The Story of McGraw-Hill*, New York: McGraw-Hill, 1959.

Callahan, Sean, "McGraw-Hill Ready to Bulk Up B-to-B," *B to B*, May 6, 2002, p. 1.

Holt, Donald D., "The Unlikely Hero of McGraw-Hill," *Fortune*, May 21, 1979.

Imprint on an Era: The Story of the McGraw-Hill Book Company, New York: McGraw-Hill.

"Industry Speculation Swirls as Clock Ticks, Thomson Puts Thirty-Eight Titles on the Block," *Educational Marketer*, July 9, 2001.

Kerwin, Ann Marie, McGraw-Hill Ties 'Biz Week' and S&P Together on Web: Financial-Info Site will Raise Brands' Profiles," *Advertising Age*, July 19, 1999, p. 3.

Madison, Charles A., *Book Publishing in America*, New York, McGraw-Hill, 1966.

McGraw, Harold III, "The Global Information Revolution," *Vital Speeches*, August 15, 2000, p. 655.

Milliot, Jim, "New Media Helps Spur Sales at McGraw-Hill Cos.," *Publishers Weekly*, April 15, 1996, p. 20.

——, "MHC-TM-Reed Deal Driven By Need for Heft in Marketplace," *Publishers Weekly*, July 15, 1996, p. 16.

Oliver, Suzanne, "Management by Concept," *Forbes*, November 26, 1990, p. 37.

Picker, Ida, "Joseph Dionne of McGraw-Hill Cos.: A Place in Cyberspace," *Institutional Investor*, December 1996, p. 27.

Schwartz, Matthew, "McGraw-Hill Eyes Growth After Cuts," *B to B*, January 14, 2002, p. 12.

Tebbel, John, *A History of Book Publishing in the United States*, 4 vols., New York: R.R. Bowker Company, 1972–81.

Ward, Sandra, "Brave New World: Searching for Growth, McGraw-Hill Looks-Warily-at the Mutual Fund Business," *Barron's*, October 21, 1996, p. 31.

Waters, Richard, "McGraw Hill Margins Improve," *Financial Times*, February 3, 1995, p. 22.

Young, Alison, "Publisher Gets a Read on Economy's Moods," *Investor's Business Daily*, March 8, 2002.

—Wilson B. Lindauer
—updates: Taryn Benbow-Pfalzgraf, April Gasbarre

Engineering & Energy

Michael Baker Corporation

Airport Office Park
420 Rouser Road, Building 3
Coraopolis, Pennsylvania 15108
U.S.A.
Telephone: (412) 269-6300
Fax: (412) 269-2534
Web site: http://www.mbakercorp.com

Public Company
Incorporated: 1946 as Michael Baker, Jr., Inc.
Employees: 4,200
Operating Revenues: $403.2 million (2001)
Stock Exchanges: American
Ticker Symbol: BKR
NAIC: 213112 Support Activities for Oil and Gas
    Operations; 541330 Engineering Services

Michael Baker Corporation is one of the oldest and largest professional-services companies in the United States, providing engineering and energy services through two main business segments, Engineering and Energy. Its Engineering arm provides a wide array of design services including construction management, consulting, planning, surveying, analysis, and inspection services. The company's Energy business division provides services related to the operation of energy production facilities, and its clients include oil and gas producing firms and domestic and independent utilities. Through this unit, Michael Baker operates in over 12 countries, including Venezuela, Thailand, and Nigeria. As part of a late 1990s restructuring effort, the company divested its building and transportation construction businesses and sold its Baker Support Services Inc. subsidiary.

Origins

Michael Baker, Jr. was born in 1912 in Beaver, Pennsylvania. His mother died when he was only six weeks old and, as one of 12 children, he had, he later observed, ''a constant desire to express myself and get attention . . . and a terrible hunger for

affection.'' His father, a civil engineer, demanded strict dedication to church, duty, and hard work. Baker left home to study engineering at Pennsylvania State University but had to drop out after his freshman year because his father's business collapsed during the Great Depression.

After a year of drifting around the country looking for work, Baker landed a job in Jamestown, Pennsylvania, as timekeeper on the construction of a dam. Soon after, he struck out on his own as a contractor but wound up penniless when he bid too low on a land-clearance project. A $200 loan he solicited from a Beaver benefactor enabled him to return to Penn State, and he graduated at the top of his engineering class. Too restless and ambitious to work for others, he tried contracting again but was bankrupt before the end of 1939.

Undaunted, Baker launched the Michael Baker, Jr. consulting firm in Rochester, Pennsylvania, in 1940. Willing to take any job and backed by six-months' credit on his office rent, he grossed $15,000 by year's end and was employing eight men. In 1941, his billings reached $84,000. Soon after the Japanese attack on Pearl Harbor, Baker won an assignment to conduct surveys of a defense property near Paducah, Kentucky, and complete them in a near-impossible 60 days. Borrowing money for the necessary equipment from the local bank, he assembled 25 survey parties and finished the task in 45 days. By the end of World War II, Baker had provided engineering services to 122 airfields extending from Brazil to Alaska. He also found time to design the eastern part of Pittsburgh's Penn-Lincoln Parkway East.

Postwar Growth

After the war, Baker expanded his focus to community planning, aerial mapping, irrigation, hydroelectric projects, bridge design, and other public works, and he established an architectural association for the design of schools, hospitals, and other public structures, as well as industrial plants. In 1946, he incorporated his firm as Michael Baker, Jr., Inc. Billings exceeded more than $1.5 million in 1948, when net profit came to over $100,000. By the end of 1949, the company had eight divisions offering engineering services ranging from architecture to water control.

Company Perspectives:

Our vision is to perform the biggest and most challenging projects; to be paid for content, not hours; to share knowledge and resources; and to make money. We value safety, customer commitment, people, open and honest communication, innovation, and teamwork.

One of these divisions was earmarked for international assignments. In 1951, Michael Baker was made the consulting engineer and construction administrator for Saudi Arabia. This post entailed the design of harbor facilities, customs buildings, major highway systems, airports, water supply and electrical systems, a private hospital for the royal family, a $30-million air base, and additions to the royal palaces. Baker also acted as purchasing agent for the king, and his firm was responsible for maintenance work in the king's harem, a signal honor.

Baker's billings reached $5.7 million in 1955, when the firm's profits were $200,000. Roughly half of the work came from highways, about one-sixth from defense projects, and about one-tenth from foreign operations. The number of divisions had grown to ten in 1957, when there were a dozen branch offices and four foreign ones. In 1956, the company became consulting engineer to the Pennsylvania Turnpike Commission and the Delaware River Joint Toll Bridge Commission, positions it retained into the 1990s. A colleague of Michael Baker told a *Fortune* reporter in 1957 that he "can smell engineering work like a bird dog smells game. And he's thinking about next year, while you're still thinking about today." He personally reviewed every proposal, project, bill, and billing.

In 1958, when *Engineering News-Record* ranked Baker as the largest architectural-engineering firm in the United States, the firm had 1,009 employees. In 1960, the company was awarded a contract to design Pittsburgh's Three Rivers Stadium. In the same year, the Philippines awarded the firm contracts to design a wharf and marine slipway for the port of Manila and to procure dredging services. Baker surveyed and staked out a 236-mile natural-gas pipeline route from Ohio to Pennsylvania in 1967. Its revenues came to $12.7 million that year, when net income was $543,387.

Baker Goes Public: 1968

Baker became a publicly owned corporation in 1968, with Michael Baker retaining 60 percent of the first-issued common-stock shares. The shares, offered at $12 each, rose to nearly $20 during the year. A year later, Baker had 13 divisions. It had developed a data bank in excess of 300 computer programs used in the location and design of highways and utilities, the analysis and design of structures, soil analysis, population projections, and traffic and revenue studies. About 61 percent of its revenues were coming from state and local governments and agencies, nine percent from the federal government, and the remaining 30 percent from private industry.

By 1972, Baker could boast of having designed more than 7,000 miles of highway, the Pennsylvania Turnpike tunnels, the Squirrel Hill and Fort Pitt tunnels in Pittsburgh, the Mississippi

Memorial Stadium (as well as Three Rivers Stadium), the 44-story Wells Fargo Building in San Francisco, and Seattle's Space Needle. But volume dropped from $21.3 million in 1970 to $19.8 million in 1971, and net income from about $1 million to about $500,000. In 1972, the company lost $473,000 on contract income of $20.1 million. In that year, the firm's name was changed to Euthenics Systems Corp.; it became the Michael Baker Corporation in 1975.

Baker's fortunes were restored by the Trans-Alaska Pipeline. It designed the 360-mile main state road from the Yukon River to the state's North Slope plus more than 200 miles of access road connecting it to the pipeline route. The firm also designed part of the 796-mile-long pipeline itself and a suspension bridge to carry the pipeline over the Tanana River. Between 1969 and 1979, 350 employees spent three million labor hours on the project, which accounted for about 50 percent of the company's revenue and 90 percent of its profit.

Overcoming Hardships: Late 1970s to Mid-1980s

There were other notable accomplishments in the 1970s, including the design of the New River Gorge Bridge in West Virginia, with the world's longest single-span steel arch. When oil began flowing through the Alaska pipeline in 1977, however, there was little more for Baker to do, and the drawbacks of dependency on a single project immediately became obvious. Company president William L. Shaw later explained to a *Management Review* reporter, "We looked around for something else to do, and all those long-time clients whom we had served for many years said, 'Where were you when we needed you?'" Contract income nosedived from $28.3 million in 1977 to $19.8 million in 1978, and the company lost money in both 1978 and 1979.

Michael Baker, Jr. died in 1977 and was succeeded by Michael Baker III as the company's chairman and chief executive officer. A protracted period of instability ensued in which dissatisfied shareholders twice tried to overturn the management. Canadian investors holding nearly 14 percent of the common stock contemplated a takeover in 1982, and Century Engineering Inc. of Towson, Maryland, made an offer in 1983, when the company lost $1 million and was faced with impending bankruptcy. Instead, Baker workers agreed in 1984 to buy nearly 40 percent of the company's outstanding common shares, through an employee stock-ownership plan (ESOP), from Baker family members and a family trust for $8.9 million, or $9 a share. Shaw succeeded Baker as chairman and chief executive officer. Early in 1985 the ESOP raised its stake in the company to 70 percent.

In the last months of Baker's reign, Shaw conceded to *Management Review* that "morale was terrible . . . probably as low as I've ever seen it in this company." About 600 of the 1,000 employees had been laid off, and "Michael III isolated himself from the employees and the clients. . . . Our strategy at that particular point in our life was to be in business for the next year." Baker not only had to attract new customers and lure back old ones but improve its reputation as well. Shaw admitted, "We didn't do anything on time, we didn't meet the schedules, we didn't meet the budgets, and our performance was lousy." Even a client as old as the Pennsylvania Depart-

Key Dates:

1940: Michael Baker launches the Michael Baker, Jr. consulting firm.

1951: Baker is made the consulting engineer and construction administrator for Saudi Arabia.

1968: The company goes public.

1972: The firm changes its name to Euthenics Systems Corp.

1975: The company adopts the Michael Baker Corp. name.

1984: Baker employees buy 40 percent of the company through an employee stock-ownership plan.

1986: Intelcom Support Services Inc. is acquired.

1991: Various assets of Mellon Stuart Co. are acquired.

1995: The firm restructures into five market-focused units as part of its Vision 2000 plan.

1999: Universal Studios fires Baker from an $84 million construction project; company earnings plummet.

2001: Baker reorganizes into two major segments, Engineering and Energy.

ment of Transportation vowed never to give the company another job.

Baker's reputation was also damaged by its dependence on government contracts. A 1991 *Barron's* article described the company founder as "basically a salesman rather [than] an engineer [who] built his business through political links and contributions to politicians, especially those who influenced the awarding of public works contracts." When the U.S. attorney for western Pennsylvania, Richard Thornburgh, a Republican, brought Michael Baker, Jr. before a federal grand jury to question him about contributions to the 1970 campaign of Governor Milton Shapp, a Democrat, Baker took the Fifth Amendment. He said that the company recently had paid the Internal Revenue Service an additional $100,000 in taxes, and that he had paid an additional $27,000 for the years 1970 and 1971 but added that no criminal charges or fraud penalties were involved.

Expansion Through Acquisition: 1986–Early 1990s

Baker's profitability, aided by a $1 million cost-control program and an expanding national economy, soon returned, and in 1986 the company for a second straight year won an award for financial management achievement from the Professional Services Management Association. In 1989, contract revenues passed $100 million and net income reached nearly $2.3 million. One important asset was the acquisition, at the end of 1986, of Intelcom Support Services, Inc., a Texas-based firm providing contract operations and maintenance services to military and other government installations. Expanding Baker's core business to operations and maintenance meant, according to Shaw, "multiyear contracts with excellent cash flows . . . not subject to the fluctuations you experience in the pure engineering design business."

Further acquisitions also expanded Baker's scope. In 1990, the company purchased MO Services, Inc., of Houston, a firm

engaged in providing operations and maintenance services to oil and gas producers, utilities, and industrial customers. The next year it acquired certain assets of the former Mellon Stuart Co., an action that placed Baker in general contracting, construction, and construction management. This closed the gap between design and maintenance in company operations, and by late 1991 Baker was receiving half its revenues from construction. In 1993, Baker completed the acquisition of Overseas Technical Services International, which was providing operations and maintenance services worldwide to major oil and gas producers.

Between 1985 and 1990, Baker averaged annual growth of 20 percent. Employment rose to 2,040 in 1991, compared to only 420 in 1984. Shaw credited much of the company's success to its ESOP, which had a stake in the company valued at $28 million in mid-1991, compared to the initial $3 million in 1984. Employees, he said, rather than expensive consultants, not only identified Baker's acquisition targets but also participated in the ensuing acquisition process. "Previously, we had good engineers and scientists," the president of a Baker subsidiary told a *Wall Street Journal* reporter in 1991. "Now, we have good engineers and scientists who are also good businessmen."

Overcoming Financial Woes: Mid-1990s

Baker's outlook soured again, however, in 1993, when the company lost $15.1 million on revenues of $434.8 million. Shaw attributed Baker's problems to Intelcom, which began losing money in 1991 as a result of a misguided decision to branch into cable installation and housing renovation. Baker lost money again in 1994, more than $7.9 million on contract revenues of $437.2 million. The 1994 deficit arose from a $10 million pretax charge taken not only to deal with Intercom's problems but also projects by Mellon Stuart for government agencies in the Chicago area that became embroiled in claims and disputes. The company's stock lost 60 percent of its value in 1994. Long-term debt, however, fell from $7.7 million to under $4 million during the year. Baker's ESOP held 29 percent of Baker's common stock and 67 percent of the voting power at the end of 1994.

Effective in 1995, Baker converted its three groups—engineering, construction, and operations and maintenance—to five market-focused units—transportation, general buildings, civil, energy, and environmental. The general-buildings sector accounted for 43 percent of contract revenues in 1994; transportation, 22 percent; civil, 18 percent; energy, 10 percent; and environmental, 7 percent. Among the principal markets for the company's services in 1994, some 40 percent came from commercial, industrial, and private clients; 35 percent from various state governmental and quasi-governmental agencies; and 25 percent from the federal government.

Baker's corporate staff in 1995 was being housed in leased office space in Coraopolis, Pennsylvania. The company owned a 75,000-square-foot office building on a 175-acre in Beaver County, Pennsylvania. Office space also was being leased in 13 other states and in Guam, Abu Dhabi, and England.

The company restructuring efforts, dubbed its Vision 2000 plan, appeared to pay off. In 1996, earnings rose by 44 percent on contract revenues of $418.4 million. That year, the company acquired Maquire Associates Inc., a transportation and civil engineering firm based in Virginia, and also created Energy Logistics Inc., a marine transportation joint venture with SEACOR Marine Ltd. Then in 1998, the company purchased GeoResearch Inc., a global positioning software manufacturer.

Restructuring for the Future: Late 1990s and Beyond

However, disaster struck in March 1999 when Baker was fired from an $84 million Orlando, Florida, theme park construction project by Universal Studios due to quality and delay issues. Baker filed suit against Universal but was forced to take a $17 million charge against its earnings in 1999. That year, the company made several strategic changes to its business operations. It set plans in motion to divest its buildings and transportation divisions and also stopped participating in low-bid construction work. Together, these operations accounted for nearly 38 percent of revenues in 1998. Baker was also forced to seek out a new CEO after Charles Homan resigned in September. As such, Donald Fusilli, Jr. was named COO and president, and eventually CEO in April 2001.

A 2000 *Pittsburgh Business Times* article reported that Fusilli believed "all companies experience the good, bad, and ugly, but knowing how to handle negative situations sets long-standing firms apart from those who falter due to unresolved problems." Indeed, Baker focused on securing a successful future by putting its problems behind it. The company reached a conditional settlement with Universal in March 2000. As part of the deal, Baker paid Universal $2 million but remained responsible for settling any disputes with subcontractors and vendors related to the Orlando CityWalk project. With most of its litigation taken care of, Baker set out to rebuild its earnings. In 2000, the company sold its Baker Support Services Inc. subsidiary and continued with its restructuring efforts. That year, company's net income grew to $5.4 million, after reporting a loss of $8.2 million in 1999.

During 2001, the company adopted a new business structure, with Energy and Engineering as its two main business segments. In 2001, the firm secured record earnings, proof that new business alignment was paying off. Net income increased to $11.2 million, while contract revenues were $403 million, up from $391 million in 2000. While the company encountered challenges during early 2002—including delays and cancellations of various civil engineering projects and weakening international results—Baker management remained positive that the company was on the right track. With a history of success behind it, Baker would no doubt continue to hold a significant place in the design and engineering industry in the years to come.

Principal Subsidiaries

Baker Environmental, Inc.; Baker Heavy & Highway, Inc.; Baker Mellon Stuart Construction, Inc.; Mellon Stuart Building Services, Inc.; Mellon Stuart Construction International, Inc.; Michael Baker Global, Inc.; Michael Baker Jr., Inc.; Michael Baker Alaska, Inc.; Baker Construction, Inc.; Baker Global Project Services, Inc.; Baker Holding Corporation; Baker/OTS, Inc.; International Pipeline Services, Inc.; Michael Baker International, Inc.; Baker GeoResearch, Inc.; Baker Engineering, Inc.; Steen Production Services, Inc.; Michael Baker, Jr. Company; Michael Baker Architects/Engineers, P.C.; Baker Engineering NY, Inc.; Baker/MO Services, Inc.; Vermont General Insurance Company; Michael Baker Barbados Ltd.; Baker Energy International, Ltd. (Cayman Islands); Baker O&M International, Ltd. (Cayman Islands); Baker/OTS International, Inc. (Cayman Islands); Overseas Technical Services (Middle East) Ltd. (Cayman Islands); Michael Baker de Mexico S.A. de C.V.; OTS International Training Services Ltd. (UK); Overseas Technical Services (Harrow) Ltd. (UK); Baker/OTS Ltd. (UK); SD Forty-Five Ltd. (UK); Hanseatic Oilfield Services Ltd. (Vanuatu); OTS Finance and Management Ltd. (Vanuatu); Overseas Technical Service International Ltd. (Vanuatu).

Principal Divisions

Energy; Engineering.

Principal Competitors

AECOM Technology Corporation; Tetra Tech Inc.; URS Corporation.

Further Reading

Antonelli, Cesca, "Michael Baker Pursues Growth Goals With Purchase of Maryland-Based Firm," *Pittsburgh Business Times*, October 2, 1998, p. 31.

Carbasho, Tracy, "Staying the Course," *Pittsburgh Business Times*, November 17, 2000, p. 31.

"Consulting Engineer Goes Public," *Engineering News-Record*, June 27, 1968, pp. 67–8.

Gordon, Mitchell, "Blueprint Calls for Sharp Rise in Earnings for Michael Baker," *Barron's*, May 5, 1975, pp. 46–7, 52.

Lott, Ethan, "New Michael Baker COO Fusilli Faces Challenges On Way to CEO Job," *Pittsburgh Business Times*, March 24, 2000, p. 37.

——, "Unamusing Theme Park Debacle a Blow to Baker," *Pittsburgh Business Times*, December 31, 1999, p. 1.

Mason, Julie Cohen, "On the Road to Recovery," *Management Review*, April 1991, pp. 23–4.

Maurer, Herrymon, "Michael Baker of the Turnpikes," *Fortune*, July 1957, pp. 140–41, 145–46, 150, 152.

"Michael Baker CEO Resigns After Unusual $5-Million Loss," *Engineering News-Record*, September 27, 1993, p. 8.

"Michael Baker Corp. Shows Improvement," *Pittsburgh Business Times*, February 23, 2001, p. 35.

"Michael Baker Losses Show Pitfalls of Plans," *Engineering News-Record*, January 2–9, 1995, p. 26.

Narisetti, Raju, "Worker Input Helps an ESOP—and a Company—Work," *Wall Street Journal*, July 12, 1991, p. B2.

Palmer, Jay, "Baker the Moneymaker," *Barron's*, December 16, 1991, pp. 18–19.

—Robert Halasz
—update: Christina M. Stansell

MOLINS

Molins plc

11 Tanners Drive
Blakelands
Milton Keynes, Buckinghamshire MK14 5LU
United Kingdom
Telephone: (+44) 1908-219-000
Fax: (+44) 1908-216-499
Web site: http://www.molins.com

Public Company
Incorporated: 1912 as The Molins Machine Company
Employees: 1,202
Sales: £111.3 million ($161.5 million) (2001)
Stock Exchanges: London
Ticker Symbol: MLIN
NAIC: 333298 All Other Industrial Machinery
   Manufacturing; 541330 Engineering Services

The United Kingdom's Molins plc has been adjusting to the post-tobacco world. One of the leading producers of packaging machinery for the tobacco industry, including cigarette-making machinery, Molins has reoriented itself as a specialist engineering company, including a growing niche packaging component that makes the machinery for such products as pyramid-shaped teabags and toothpaste tubes. Molins also has reacted to the worldwide collapse in sales of tobacco machinery—the company's sales have been slashed by more than half since 1997—by repositioning itself as an aftermarket service provider, particularly for its large installed customer base. The company also has added a new component of scientific measurement devices for the tobacco industry, such as smoke analysis equipment and analytical smoke constituent services. Molins operates through two primary divisions, Tobacco Machinery, which includes subsidiaries Arista, acquired in 2002, and Cerulean; and Food Packaging, which includes subsidiary companies Langen in Canada, Langenpac in The Netherlands, and Rose Forgrove and Sandiacre Packaging Machinery Ltd. in the United Kingdom. Molins, which posted sales of £111 million ($160 million) in 2001, is quoted on the London Stock Exchange and is led by Chairman Peter Byrom.

Cuban Origins in the 19th Century

Molins involvement with the tobacco industry began in the late 19th century. In 1874, Jose Molins set up shop producing hand-rolled cigars and cigarettes in Havana, Cuba. Molins moved to the United States, then to the London. By the turn of the 20th century, cigarette-making machinery had begun to change smoking habits, popularizing that tobacco product. Molins's sons, Harold and Walter, picked up on the packaging potential presented by the machine-rolled cigarette. In 1911 the Molins brothers patented their own packaging machine, capable of producing packaging for a wide variety of items, including tea and cigarettes.

The brothers set up their own company in 1912, The Molins Machine Company, and began production of their packaging machines. By the end of that decade, the company purchased new facilities in Deptford, which became the company's main production and warehouse facility for the next 50 years.

In 1924, the Molins brothers patented a new machine, the Mark 1, the company's first cigarette-rolling machine. Continued improvements on the Mark 1's design enabled the machine to reach production levels of more than 1,000 cigarettes per minute by the end of the 1920s. By the mid-1930s, the company had unveiled its Mark 6 model.

By then, Molins had been expanding, acquiring the Thrissell Engineering Company in 1928, which was later expanded as the Masson Scott Thrissell Company. At the beginning of the 1930s, Molins crossed the Atlantic to set up shop closer to the U.S. tobacco industry. In 1931, the company established its U.S. subsidiary, the Molins Machine Company Inc., in Richmond, Virginia.

The death of Walter Molins left his son Desmond Molins in charge of the company. The younger Desmond quickly followed in his father's inventive footsteps, registering five patents in just one year. One of Desmond Molins's most important patents was filed in 1937, for a hinge-type cigarette box that was to have a major impact on the worldwide cigarette industry. Molins also showed himself to be a shrewd marketer—in 1936, Molins negotiated a supply agreement with U.S. tobacco giant

Reynolds. The deal, which called for Reynolds to buy 278 Mark 6 machines from Molins, was the largest-ever single order for cigarette-rolling machinery. It proved to be the company's breakthrough, establishing Molins as one of the world's major cigarette machinery manufacturers.

Molins converted its production to support the Allied war effort during World War II (which earned Desmond Molins the U.S. Medal of Freedom). Returning to tobacco and packaging machinery production after the war, the company found itself in the midst of a worldwide boom in cigarette consumption, especially as more and more women began to smoke. In 1950, Molins opened a larger facility in Saunderton.

In 1954, Molins achieved a new breakthrough. In that year, Phillip Morris sought to re-introduce one of its discontinued brands. Originally introduced in 1902, the Marlboro had not been a success; re-launched in the 1920s as a "women's" cigarette, the brand had faded out again. The re-launch of Marlboro in the 1950s, and its repositioning as a "men's" cigarette was accompanied by a new package—Desmond Molins's hinged-top lid. The new package helped the brand develop into the world's leading cigarette brand. The Molins Hinge Lid Packer, first sold to Philip Morris in 1954, soon became a standard across the industry, as the hinged-pack became the preferred packaging type throughout the world.

Molins's main product, however, remained its cigarette-making machinery, and in 1959 the company released its newest generation, the Mark 8. The spread of cigarette consumption in other parts of the world led the company to extend its own international presence, and by the beginning of the 1960s the company had opened production facilities in Brazil and India, and a sales office in Hong Kong. In 1964, the company formalized its presence in South America with the creation of its Brazilian subsidiary in 1964. At the same time, the company saw its first sales of machinery to China, which was later to become, if only briefly, one of the company's major markets.

Molins introduced its Mark 9 cigarette-making machine in 1972. By then, however, the company had begun to seek to diversify beyond its core tobacco machinery. Already present in the broader packaging industry, through its Masson Scott Thrissell subsidiary, the company boosted that operation in 1974 with the purchase of the Langston Corporation, based in New Jersey in the United States, for $8.5 million. Founded by Charles Langston in 1880, that company had begun producing corrugated cardboard boxes in 1885, and later grew into an important manufacturer of corrugating and paper converting machinery.

Desmond Molins, who remained at the head of the company, had not lost his inventive spirit, and in the early 1970s the company introduced what it called "System 24," an automated machine tool system. The company succeeded in adapting the system to the production of certain parts for the new Concorde airplane, but was soon forced to abandon the project due to a lack of industry interest.

Reorienting for a New Century

More successful was the company's public offering, made in 1976, which brought Molins to the London Stock Exchange. Yet the decision to go public was to come to haunt the company over the next decade. Nonetheless, the company entered the 1980s riding high as one of the top cigarette machine makers in the world; it was also poised to reap the rewards of patience: by the early 1980s, the technology behind the company's System 24 had led to the creation of what became known as Flexible Manufacturing Systems, or FMS. As the holder of the patents underlying the FMS technology, Molins set out to collect royalties and sell licenses to the technology. It also prepared to extend its expertise by moving into production of FMS systems itself. As part of that effort, the company established a research subsidiary, Molins ITCM, in Coventry in 1985, in order to assist Molins's other businesses in developing new products and technologies.

Yet by the mid-1980s, Molins had become caught up in the hostile takeover craze that marked the decade. By the beginning of the 1990s, the company had been the target of five hostile takeover attempts, including an attack in 1987 by a subsidiary of New Zealand Brierley Group. After the death of Desmond Molins in 1988, Brierley struck again, this time through another holding, Industrial Equity (Pacific), based in Hong Kong, in 1989. Part of the company appeal, in addition to its FMS patents, was its strong position in China, where cigarette consumption was rising rapidly and where Molins had established itself as market leader. By 1990, the company was forced to fight off two new attempts, this time from Leucadia Corporation.

Shaken by these events, Molins had lost a lot of ground and was forced to abandon its plans to enter the factory automation arena. Instead, Molins turned to building up its corrugated paper machinery division, acquiring the Wm. C. Staley Machinery Corporation, in 1990, which was then merged into the company's Langston business as Langston Hunt Valley. Molins also was riding high on the booming Chinese and Asian markets, where demand for the company's cigarette-making machinery rose strongly in the early 1990s. Aiding the company's growth was the launch of a new cigarette machine in 1991.

Molins began new diversification toward the mid-1990s, now targeting the specialty packaging sector. In 1994, the company acquired Sandiacre Packaging Machinery Ltd., which specialized in manufacturing equipment for vertical form fill packaging. In 1996, the company acquired the Langen Group, of Canada, including its subsidiary Langenvac, based in The Netherlands, which extended Molins's packaging arm with carton and related packaging machinery. By then, the Molins ITCM research group had developed its own machinery, for producing pyramid-shaped teabags, which was then purchased by Unilever. That success led the company to establish a new subsidiary, Molins Food Machinery, in 1997, with the aim of developing further innovative packaging products.

Key Dates:

1874: Jose Molins sets up a cigar and cigarette making business in Havana, Cuba.
1912: Molins's sons invent a packaging machine and establish the Molins Machine Company.
1919: The company acquires larger production and warehouse facilities in Deptford.
1924: The company launches the Mark 1 cigarette-making machine.
1931: The company establishes a U.S. subsidiary in Richmond, Virginia.
1936: Reynolds buys 278 Mark 6 cigarette-making machines.
1950: The company opens a new production facility in Saunderton
1959: The company opens a production facility in Calcutta, India, and a sales office in Hong Kong.
1960: A plant in Sao Paulo, Brazil, is established.
1964: The company begins sales to China.
1976: Molins goes public on the London stock exchange.
1985: The company establishes Molins ITCM as a research and development subsidiary in Coventry.
1994: Molins acquires Sandiacre to extend the company into the specialty packaging market.
1996: The company acquires Langen (Canada) and Langenvac (Netherlands), extending into carton packaging.
1997: The company creates Molins Food Machinery to capitalize on successful development of pyramid teabag machinery.
2000: The company moves into providing services to the tobacco industry.
2002: The company acquires Arista Laboratories, a provider of analytical services to the tobacco industry.

Still, Molins once again faced difficulties in the late 1990s. A new wave of anti-tobacco legislation in the United States and Europe, coupled with the collapse of much of the Asian market economies, severely crippled the company's cigarette-making machines. At the same time, the Chinese tobacco monopoly, China Tobacco, had begun a vast restructuring effort, shutting down more than one-third of its factories—putting an end to new orders for cigarette-making machinery, at least temporarily. The company's revenues, which had topped £250 million ($400 million) in 1997, suddenly dropped back to just £170 million in 1998, then to £110 million.

By then, the company had decided to abandon its Langston corrugated cardboard operation, which had been struggling in the face of a depressed market. That business was sold off in 1998 to BancBoston for $40 million. Molins also was forced to cut a large number of its workforce as its tobacco machinery operations continued to dwindle.

Molins's restructuring was to last for nearly three years, enabling the company to raise its profitability by the end of the decade. Molins also had identified a new area for expansion—

that of providing services to the tobacco industry, including aftermarket support for the large installed base of Molins machines. In 2000, the company made a new acquisition, of Filtrona Instruments and Automation (FIA), a maker of analysis and quality control instruments for the tobacco industry, as well as a producer of packaging for niche markets. FIA, purchased from Bunzl, was then renamed Cerulean.

After adding a new factory and subsidiary in the Czech Republic, Molins hit the acquisition trail again, bringing back Rose Forgrove, a manufacturer of horizontal flow wrapping machinery, in 2001. Then, at the beginning of 2002, Molins enhanced its tobacco industry service offerings with the purchase of Arista Laboratories, based in Richmond, Virginia, which had established itself as a provider of smoke constituents analysis services. By then, Molins appeared to have accepted as permanent the change in the worldwide tobacco industry, as anti-smoking efforts were expected to continue to reduce the number of smokers—and the number of cigarette-making machines. At the beginning of 2002, Molins set up its own real estate development company, with the intention of converting the now-unused areas of its Saunderton facility to apartment buildings. While remaining committed to heritage at the center of the tobacco industry, Molins nevertheless showed that it had not lost its spirit of invention.

Principal Subsidiaries

Arista Laboratories Inc. (U.S.); Cerulean; Cerulean Inc. (U.S.); Kunming Molins Tobacco Machinery Company Ltd. (China; 48%); Langen Packaging Inc. (Canada); Langenpac NV (The Netherlands); Molins del Paraguay SA; Molins do Brasil Maquinas Automaticas Ltda; Molmac Engineering Ltd.; Molins Far East Private Ltd. (Singapore); Molins ITCM; Molins Richmond Inc. (U.S.); Molins sro (Czech Republic); Molins Tobacco CIS (Russia; 69%); Molins Tobacco Machinery Ltd.; Rose Forgrove Ltd.; Sandiacre Packaging Machinery Ltd.; Sandiacre Packaging NA (U.S.).

Principal Competitors

Sasib Tobacco Group (Compagnia Finanzaria de Benedetti); Gibraltar Packaging Group, Inc.; Metso Corporation; Robert Bosch Corporation; Shorewood Packaging Corporation.

Further Reading

Anderson, Simon, "Molins Closes Factory Due to Tobacco Crisis," *Daily Telegraph,* June 30, 1998.
Arzoumanian, Mark, "Anatomy of Langston's Collapse," *Paperboard Packaging,* October 2001 p. 24
Clark, Andrew, "I'm Your Cigarette Pack, Can We Have a Little Chat?," *The Guardian,* March 8, 2001.
Coyle, Diane, "Chinese Smokers Light Up Molins," *Independent,* March 19, 1994.
Grimond, Magnus, "Molins Packs a Mighty Punch," *Independent,* September 6, 1996, p. 20.
"Molins Acquires Rose Forgrove Operations," *Candy Business,* September 2001, p. 8.
Tuinstra, Taco, "Molins' Comeback," *Tobacco Reporter,* November 2000.

—M.L. Cohen

Moss Bros Group plc

8 Saint Johns Hill, Clapham Junction
London SW11 1SA
United Kingdom
Telephone: (+44) 20 7447 7200
Fax: (+44) 20 7350 0112
Web site: http://www.mossbros.com

Public Company
Founded: 1851
Employees: 1,587
Sales: £141.3 million ($227 million) (2001)
Stock Exchanges: London
Ticker Symbol: MOSB
NAIC: 448110 Men's Clothing Stores; 532220 Formal
   Wear and Costume Rental

After more than 120 years in business, Moss Bros Group plc remains one of the preeminent names in the United Kingdom's men's fashions retail sector. The company owns and operates a retail network of more than 165 stores across the United Kingdom, selling its own Moss Bros and Cecil Gee brands as well as others, including Hugo Boss, for which it holds the exclusive UK license. Moss Bros' specialty has long been men's suits, especially premium suits—the company is the United Kingdom's leader in the high-end suit segment, with about 30 percent of the market. At the end of the 1990s, Moss Bros made an unsuccessful to extend into the popular casual clothing segment, and in 2002 the company began a restructuring and re-branding program, placing its stores into three primary cateogries: Premium, with nine Hugo Boss stores and 23 Cecil Gee stores; Moss, with 95 stores; and Value, with 37 stores operating primarily as factory outlet stores in out-of-town locations. In addition to its retail sales, Moss Bros is also well-known for its Moss Bros Hire operations, which has long been the leading formalwear rental company in the United Kingdom. Moss Bros Hire operates primarily through the company's retail network, primarily its Moss chain, and hires out more than one million clothing items a year, including military uniforms. Moss is listed on the London Stock Exchange. At the end of 2001 and

through much of 2002, Moss Bros faced additional pressure as it became the target of two hostile takeover attempts. However, with 38 percent of the company's shares—and 70 percent of voting rights—held by the Moss and Gee families, the company was able to resist both attempts.

Renting Success in the 19th Century

Moss Bros had its start in 1851 when Moses Moses opened a second-hand clothing shop owned in London. Moses' shop prospered, and he opened a number of other stores in London, assisted by his four sons and added tailor services. In 1881, two of Moses' sons, Alfred and George, opened a new shop in London's Covent Gardens on what was later to become one of the city's main shopping streets, Kings Street. Alfred and George Moses inherited the family business in 1894.

The Moses store might have remained a tiny retail business if not for the predicament of a family friend. Charles Pond had been a stockbroker in London but had lost all of his money and had turned to entertaining at parties in order to survive. Pond needed a dress suit for his engagements and turned to the Moss brothers, who agreed to lend him one of the store's suits on the condition that he pay a small nightly fee and that he return the suit to the store each day for cleaning and pressing.

The idea quickly caught on among London's entertainment world, and the Moses brothers soon found itself with a thriving formalwear rental business. The company quickly built up a reputation not only for its rentals but also for its expertise—particularly in navigating the various dress requirements of British society at the time. In 1898, Alfred and George Moses anglicized their name to Moss and expanded the Kings Street store to include a new rental section. The store then became known as Moss Bros.

At the turn of the century, Moss Bros began collecting military uniforms, and in 1910 added a new military rental and tailoring department. With the outbreak of World War I, the company came under strong demand for new uniforms, especially from the class of commissioned officers being sent up to fight. By then, the brothers had formally incorporated the company, as Moss Bros plc, in 1914.

Company Perspectives:

The company's mission it to be Britain's No. 1 authority in menswear.

At the end of the war, Moss Bros continued to expand. The return to peacetime had created a surge in demand for civilian clothing, particularly formalwear. British society was also undergoing vast changes in the social structure, with the rise of a true middle class in the interwar years and the extension of formal occasions beyond the upper classes. By the outbreak of World War II, ceremonial and social occasions requiring formalwear had become common not only for the middle class but also for the working class as well. Moss Bros was by then the country's leading name in formalwear rentals. The company also built up a position as a leading name in the men's suits retails sector.

During World War II, Moss Bros once again became a major provider of military uniforms, including to such noted personalities as the General Montgomery and General Patton. During the postwar boom years, Moss Bros expanded onto a national scale, opening shops throughout the United Kingdom and developing a reputation across the country, to the point where the Moss Bros name became synonymous with formal attire and dress suits.

Merging As a Retail Men's Fashions Group in the 1980s

By the 1980s, Moss Bros had begun a new phase in its growth when it began making a series of acquisitions, starting with the purchase of textiles and clothing specialist Fairdale. In 1987, Moss Bros added another strong brand name when it acquired The Suit Company, which, as its name implied, targeted the retail market for suits and accessories.

Moss Bros next expansion move came in 1988, when the company agreed to merge with another well-known name in British men's fashions, Cecil Gee. That company had been founded in London's Charring Cross Road in 1929 by Cecil Gee, who had quickly revealed himself to be one of the country's most innovative men's clothing specialists, starting with his introduction of the ''jacket-shirt'' in the 1930s. The return of the British forces after World War II gave the store new success with its ''demob'' suit, and Cecil Gee opened two new stores to meet the demand.

Another Cecil Gee success came in the 1950s when he began importing Italian-made suits made from lightweight, more comfortable and more versatile fabrics. Among the brand names brought back by Cecil Gee were Canali and Brioni—the latter was the maker of the soon to be famous ''James Bond'' suit. The success of that suit helped Cecil Gee become a noted leader of men's fashions, attracting such customers as the Beatles to its stores. Cecil Gee also began its own expansion, opening new stores—including a store on Kings Road—and adding such noted men's clothing stores as Savoy Taylors Guild and Beale & Inman.

The merger of Moss Bros and Cecil Gee, by then run by Gee's son Rowland Gee, created the Moss Bros Group, with the Moss and Gee families sharing ownership of the new enterprise. After going public, the two families continued to control the group, with more than 38 percent of its shares and more than 70 percent of the company's voting rights. Rowland Gee was put into place as the group's managing director. Under Gee, the company began developing its strong portfolio of store brands. While Moss Bros was reserved for its formalwear rental operation, retail was segmented among its Cecil Gee, Suit Company, and Savoy Taylors Guild formats, the latter taking over as the company's high-end men's fashions format. The company had also gained the exclusive license to market the Hugo Boss brand in the United Kingdom. By the beginning of the new century, the company operated 17 Hugo Boss stores.

Comeback from Casual in the 2000s

By the mid-1990s, Moss Bros Group had more than 100 stores, more than three-quarters of which also featured Moss Bros Hire shops. The company had begun acquiring more retail brands, including Dormie in 1992. Part of the motivation behind Moss Bros' acquisition drive was the company's desire to extend its retail operations beyond its core of men's suits and into the larger men's fashion sector, particularly into casual fashions. In 1996, the company took a step toward achieving that goal with the acquisition of the 28-store Blazer chain. That company had been founded in the early 1980s, then taken over by the Storehouse group, which also owned the BhS and Mothercare stores.

With its sales rising strongly, along with its market share, Moss Bros began to hone its ambitions, targeting a 15 percent share of the men's suit market in Britain by the end of the decade. The company continued to make gains on the competition, such as Marks & Spencers and the Burton Group, by offering a wide range of high-quality labels. The company added a new label when it acquired the British retail rights to Yves Saint Laurent's men's fashions line. Moss Bros opened its first YSL retail store in June of 1997. Moss Bros was buoyed by what appeared to be a new interest in suits purchases, particularly among the younger men's market segment, as sales rose to £122 million for that year.

By 1999, Moss Bros's retail network had grown to 190 stores, including a growing number of out-of-town discount clothing stores operated under the Brand Centre name. The company was also helped by difficulties at Marks & Spencer's, which controlled 15 percent of the men's suits market as Moss Bros' own share climbed to 13.5 percent. By the end of 1999, the company's sales had risen to nearly £154 million.

Yet Moss Bros' reliance on suits and more formal fashions placed it in an awkward position as the men's fashion market embraced the casual fashion trend. The company found itself all the more hard-pressed as increasing numbers of corporations adopted casual dress codes. Moss Bros scrambled to catch up, restructuring its holdings in 2000 to create a new clothing brand. Called Code, from ''Casualwear, Office, Dressing up, and Essentials,'' the new retail format took over Moss Bros' Savoy Taylors, Blazer, and Suit Company locations. The company ultimately planned to open as many as 80 to 100 Code stores, including the conversion of 50 of its stores existing under other formats. As part of the restructuring, the company

Key Dates:

1851: Moses Moses sets up a second-hand clothing shop in London.
1894: Moses' sons Albert and George take over the business.
1898: The company becomes the first to offer formalwear rentals; the Moses' brothers changes their name to Moss, and the company adopts Moss Bros signage.
1914: The firm incorporates as Moss Bros plc.
1929: Cecil Gee opens a men's clothing store in London.
1982: Moss Bros acquires Fairdale clothing company.
1987: The company acquires The Suit Company retail chain.
1988: Moss Bros merges with Cecil Gee to form Moss Bros Group.
1996: The firm acquires Blazer retail group.
1997: Moss Bros launches Yves Saint Laurent men's clothing retail store branch.
2001: The company converts The Suit Company, Blazer, and Savoy Taylors Guild retail formats into new casual format, Code.
2002: Moss Bros abandons Code format and restructures most of its stores into new Moss format.

also sought to sell off nearly 60 of its under-performing store locations.

Yet the restructuring dragged the company into the red, with losses mounting to £2.7 million on sales of just under £156 million for the 2000 year. Moss Bros turned to a new chairman, Keith Hammill, to help steer the company back into profits. Hammill quickly put an end to the company's casualwear experiment, dropping the Code retail format. The company also named a new CEO, Adrian Wright. By the beginning of 2002, the company had once again focused its operations on its formalwear specialty, realigning its retail network into three main categories: Premium, which included the company's Cecil Gee and Hugo Boss stores; Value, which took over the company's out-of-town locations; and a new store format, Moss, which took over more than 95 of the company's stores and included the Moss Bros Hire rental service.

Moss Bros' difficulties at the turn of the century had caused severe cuts in its stock price, which in turn made the company a takeover target. First up to bat was Shami Ahmed, who had built up a fortune with the Joe Bloggs jeans label. Yet the unified weight of the Gee and Moss families, which continued to control the company's voting rights, enabled the company to resist Ahmed's repeated takeover offers. Soon after Ahmed gave up, in April 2002, a new suitor knocked on Moss Bros' door in the form of Harold Tillman, who had acquired Baird Menswear Brands, which manufactured suits under the Jasper Conran and Pierre Cardin labels, in 2000, and who sought access to Moss Bros' retail network.

Moss Bros fought off Tillman's offer for discussions in June 2002, leading observers to suggest that Tillman would return with a full-fledged takeover bid by the end of the year. Meanwhile, Moss Bros continued its restructuring. By the end of the year, the company had reason for optimism, as men's fashions—and corporate cultures—appeared to swing back toward more conservative clothing. After more than 150 years in business, Moss Bros remained one of the United Kingdom's leading names in suits.

Principal Competitors

Marks and Spencer Group PLC; Arcadia Group plc; Next plc; JJB Sports plc; Burberry Ltd.; Lewis Trust Group Ltd.; Alexon Group PLC; Blacks Leisure Group plc; Sears Ltd.; River Island Clothing Co Ltd.; Peacock Group plc; William Baird PLC; French Connection Group PLC; H and M Hennes Ltd.; Mackays Stores Ltd.; Austin Reed Group PLC; GPS Great Britain Ltd.; Be Wise Group Ltd.; WEW Group plc; Alexandra plc; Gold Group International Ltd.; Liberty PLC; Speciality Retail Group Ltd.

Further Reading

Banniester, Nicolas, "Years of Overnight Success," *Guardian*, June 10, 2000.
Cole, Cheryl, "Why Moss Bros Got a Good Dressing Down," *Birmingham Post*, April 12, 2002, p. 19.
Cope, Nigel, "The Monday Interview: Keith Hamill," *Independent*, December 17, 2001, p. 15.
Foley, Stephen, "Moss Bros Braced for New Bid Approach from Tillman," *Independent*, June 24, 2002, p. 16.
Mesure, Susie, "Moss Bros Finds Casual Wear No Longer Suits," *Independent*, April 12, 2002, p. 25.
"Rolling Moss Gathers No Moans in Push Back to Black," *Birmingham Post*, April 3, 2001, p. 23.
Slingsby, Helen, "Gee Fights to Retain Moss Bros Helm," *Guardian*, November 29, 2001.

—M. L. Cohen

Mothers Against Drunk Driving (MADD)

511 East John Carpenter Freeway
Suite 700
Irving, Texas 75062-8187
U.S.A.
Telephone: (214) 744-6233
Toll Free: (800) GET-MADD
Web site: http://www.madd.org

Nonprofit Organization
Incorporated: 1980
Employees: 350
Operating Revenues: $50.22 million (2001)
NAIC: 813319 Other Social Advocacy Organizations;
    813940 Political Organizations

Mothers Against Drunk Driving (MADD) has been called America's most-liked charity, though its familiar acronym suggests the rage that prompted its formation in 1980. The group's traditional mission has been to fight what MADD national president Millie Webb has called "the most frequently committed violent crime in the nation"—drunk driving injuries and deaths. In its first two decades, the organization has been credited with fostering a profound reduction in the number of alcohol-related fatalities. Along the way, it changed an entire society's attitude towards driving under the influence (DUI) and introduced terms like "designated driver" into the lexicon. MADD continues to work to lower number of drunk driving deaths, and it has expanded its mission to include prevention of underage drinking.

Origins

In May 1980, 13-year-old Cari Lightner was killed by a drunk driver as she walked on the sidewalk in her suburban Sacramento neighborhood. The driver, Clarence William Busch, did not stop, but when he was apprehended he was found to have a blood alcohol level of 0.20 percent—and previous drunk-driving convictions. He was, in fact, out on bail for a similar hit-and-run.

Cari Lightner left behind two sisters, one of them her twin. The Lightners' story was horrifying but not unique—there were 27,000 alcohol-related traffic fatalities in the United States that year, 2,500 of them in California. However, in this case, the girl's mother, Candace Lightner, a real estate agent, used her grief to fuel a new grassroots organization dedicated to reshaping the public's perception of drunk driving.

The name of the new group and the date of incorporation were borrowed from family members. Her sister suggested calling the group Mothers Against Drunk Drivers, or MADD. *The Guardian* of Manchester, England, among others, noted the gender implications. The feminine aspect of the title was an entirely accurate statement of feminine anger against the chiefly male perpetrators, who included the lawyers and judges that coddled this behavior. MADD's mission was to convince society that driving under the influence was a serious crime, and the devastating results of the decision to drive under the influence were not "accidents."

As for the date of incorporation, September 5, 1980—that would have been Cari Lightner's 14th birthday. *The Guardian* also noted the political implications of the word "Mother"—as American as apple pie. Still, the first couple of months were slow going. Later that fall, Lightner persuaded California governor Jerry Brown to set up a task force. Two years later, a presidential commission was formed which recommended raising the minimum drinking age to 21 and revoking the license of drunk drivers.

MADD was not the first organization of its kind in the United States—RID (Remove Intoxicated Drivers) had been formed in 1978—but it soon proved to be the most influential. It had chapters in 31 states by 1982. MADD's members, typically parents who had lost children to drunk driving accidents, testified before lawmakers. MADD's pitch focused on these innocent children, and the media was sympathetic. In fact, Lightner's own story was told in a made-for-TV movie on NBC in 1983. The same year, MADD forged an alliance with Anheuser-Busch to promote the then-novel concept of responsible drinking. The group was clearly making big waves in the beverage industry.

Drinking Age Raised to 21 in 1984

MADD relocated its national headquarters to a suburb of Dallas, Texas, in 1983. An important name change took place in

---

Company Perspectives:

The mission of Mothers Against Drunk Driving (MADD) is to stop drunk driving, support the victims of this violent crime, and prevent underage drinking.

1984, when the group began calling itself Mothers Against Drunk Driving. That year, the group saw passage of a new federal law that raised the drinking age to 21.

In 1985, Lon G. von Hurwitz produced the public-service video "Don't Drive Drunk" starring Stevie Wonder. A follow-up featured Aretha Franklin. Hurwitz would become the organization's chairman in 1993. Also in 1985, founder Candace Lightner and the organization she founded parted ways due to disagreements with the MADD board.

By this time, MADD had 650,000 members in 47 states. About the same time as the U.S. organization was gathering steam, a number of anti-drunk driving groups were springing up in Canada, including PRIDE (People to Reduce Impaired Driving Everywhere) in Ontario, PAID in Alberta, and CAID in Manitoba. PRIDE became MADD Canada in 1990.

Fighting for 0.08 in the 1990s

Revenues, largely achieved through telemarketing, were about $50 million in 1990. The group set up a 900 number to support its "Strike Against Drunk Driving" program for league bowlers. Probably the most visible effort was the Red Ribbon campaign, which asked motorists to show support for responsible drinking behavior during the holidays by tying ribbons to their car antennas.

In the early 1990s, MADD began a long campaign to lower the nation's blood alcohol level (BAC) from 0.10 to 0.08, or 80 milligrams of alcohol in 100 milliliters of blood. This was the difference between four or five drinks in an hour for the average-sized person, according to a MADD spokesman.

By 1992, 41 states and the District of Columbia had adopted a BAC of 0.10 as the legal measure of intoxication. Five states had already adopted the lower 0.08 limit; MADD lobbyists had persuaded Congress to link federal highway grants to states' acceptance of the lower limit.

The lower limit met with resistance from the National Restaurant Association (NRA), which quoted statistics from Maine that suggested most drunk driving deaths occurred above the 0.10 standard and that only a tiny fraction of heavy drinkers on the road were arrested, reported *Restaurant Hospitality*. Naturally, the restaurant industry worried about the implications of a lower BAC for highly profitable wine sales.

MADD president Milo Kirk countered that the state of California had reduced alcohol-related deaths 15 percent in one year after going to a 0.08 BAC and implementing a few other measures such as high publicity and strict enforcement.

In 1993, MADD financed an infomercial that brought together some of Hollywood's top talents in a retrospective

chronicling the depiction of drunk driving in film. In *It's a Wonderful Life,* Jimmy Stewart's drunken character wrecked into a tree without censure. By the early 1990s, attitudes had matured; designated drivers were appearing in movies, and the MADD tagline "Friends don't let friends drive drunk" was uttered in the Bill Murray movie *Groundhog Day.* The well-known film critic team Siskel & Ebert hosted the program.

In early 1994, MADD founder Candace Lightner began working for the Berman & Co. lobbying firm in Washington, D.C., on behalf of the American Beverage Institute. Her mission: persuading states not to lower their legal drunk driving standard to 0.08 percent blood-alcohol content. Both Lightner and MADD's then-president Beckie Brown downplayed the apparent conflict of interest, saying they merely disagreed on the 0.08 issue. Others, however, saw her as a traitor to the cause.

By the mid-1990s, MADD was considered America's most-loved charity by one survey. Alcohol-related traffic deaths had fallen 40 percent in the 15 years since MADD was founded. However, there was trouble in Texas, as local chapters battled the national office over the way money was raised and spent. The national office lost $1 million on a botched grocery store coupon book giveaway in 1991, reported the *Wall Street Journal.* The Las Vegas chapter disbanded to form a rival group, Stop DUI, after a disastrous $50,000 telemarketing campaign that netted the unit just one dollar and some change.

Nationwide revenues fell 22 percent, to $40 million, in fiscal 1993, leading to a desperate shortfall for the head office. A telemarketing blitz raised revenues to $47.7 million in fiscal 1994, but the $1 million deficit nearly tripled. MADD's national office responded by cutting costs and also garnishing $1.3 million in future telemarketing earnings from several states. The Michigan office filed a lawsuit to prevent this in February 1995.

Taking On Teens in 1996

In 1996, MADD claimed 3.2 million members and 500 chapters. Towards the end of the year, it reported a depressing statistic: after ten years of decreases, the number of alcohol-related highway deaths in the United States rose by 4 percent in 1995, to 17,274.

MADD shifted its focus to fighting underage drinking. The group produced a $250,000 video and slide show called "Take the Lead" that it presented in high schools. U.S. Fidelity & Guaranty Co.'s USF&G Foundation footed the bill for the production.

MADD and other child advocates pressured Anheuser-Busch to take its talking frog commercials off the air, claiming they appealed to children. The organization had launched its first major attack on alcohol advertising three years earlier, when national president Becky Brown warned industry advertisers against using "celebrities, music stars, athletes, animals, cartoon characters, or other language or images that have special appeal to youth."

Tie maker Stonehenge Limited teamed with MADD in 1997 to produce a range of neckties intended to serve as alcohol awareness reminders. They were decorated with reproductions

Key Dates:

1980: Candy Lightner starts MADD after her daughter is killed in a motor vehicle accident involving a drunk driver.
1983: MADD relocates its headquarters to Texas.
1984: The legal drinking age is raised to 21 in the United States.
1985: Lightner leaves MADD.
1996: MADD expands its mission to take on underage drinking.
2000: A blood alcohol level (BAC) of 0.08 percent is adopted as the federal drunk driving standard.
2002: MADD updates its logo.

of the molecular structures of various cocktails as seen under a microscope.

The National Restaurant Association (NRA), MADD's longtime lobbying opponent, was its partner in a 1997 designated driver effort. Another sponsor of the campaign was AAMCO Transmissions, which placed promotions inside restaurants using such taglines as "Designate a Driver, Not a Beneficiary." The NRA continued to oppose MADD's efforts to lower the legal intoxication limit to 0.08 percent, however.

The Labor Day weekend was traditionally the most deadly time of year relating to drunk driving incidents in the United States. During this period in 1997, 250 people were killed by drunk drivers; these were mourned in national advertising that also noted a high-profile loss overseas: the death of Diana, Princess of Wales, whose driver had been profoundly intoxicated.

20 in 2000

At the time of MADD's 20th anniversary in 2000, alcohol-related traffic fatalities had dropped 40 percent in two decades. That was still 16,000 too many needless deaths for the group, which set a goal of lowering the number to 11,000 by 2005. MADD won a major victory when, late in 2000, the Clinton administration passed a law tying federal highway funds to states' adoption of the 0.08 blood alcohol content standard. States with the toughest drunk driving laws were beginning to treat drunk driving accidents as murder—even first-degree murder, in one North Carolina case.

In 2001, MADD found new support for its decade-long fight to persuade states to lower the drunk driving standard to 0.08 blood alcohol content. The Distilled Spirits Council of the United States (DISCUS) pledged its support, despite objections from operators who believed the measure would criminalize more of their patrons without affecting the number of problem drinkers. At the time, 19 states were using the 0.08 standard.

MADD rolled out its "Pasa Las Llaves" ("Pass the Keys") program in California in late 2001 to promote responsible driving concepts among Latinos, a group with a disproportionate rate of alcohol consumption. Around the same time, the organization was signing up MADD chapters, known as UMADD, at universities around the country. Underage drinking and binge drinking

were problems on campus. Another group, Students Against Driving Drunk (SADD), was not affiliated with MADD.

The MADD logo was updated for the first time in August 2002. The words "Mothers Against Drunk Driving" were dropped from the logo due to name recognition for the MADD acronym, which a Gallup survey pegged at 97 percent.

Further Reading

Blumenthal, Karen, "Philanthropy: Chapters Fight MADD Over Control of Money," *Wall Street Journal,* March 13, 1995, p. B1.

Deam, Jenny, "MADD Milestone: California Mom Changed Nation's Drinking Habits," *Denver Post,* September 5, 2000, p. E1.

"Diana's Death Invoked in MADD Ad Campaign," *Record* (Bergen County, N.J.), September 14, 1997, p. A10.

"Drunken-Driving Fight Slipping, MADD Reports; Alcohol-Related Deaths Increasing Again After Falling for a Decade," *Milwaukee Journal Sentinel,* November 27, 1996, p. 6.

Griffin, Katherine, "MADD Again," *Health,* July/August 1994, pp. 62+.

Houghton, Jennifer, "Neckties Bring Attention to DUI Dangers," *Parkersburg (West Virginia) News,* May 22, 1997, p. C1.

Humphrey, Tom, "Stiffer Law Pleases MADD; Legal Limit 0.08 Starting in 2003," *News Sentinel* (Knoxville, Tenn.), July 11, 2002, p. B1.

Jonsson, Patrik, "State May Give Drunk Drivers Death Penalty; N. Carolina Is at Front of Trend that Treats Vehicular Homicide as Just Plain Murder," *Christian Science Monitor,* April 3, 2000, p. 2.

Koltnow, Barry, "MADD Sees Something to Be Glad About," *Orange County Register,* November 5, 1993, p. P41.

Lowe, Kimberly, "Has MADD Gone Mad?," *Restaurants & Institutions,* March 15, 1997, p. 14.

"MADD Founder Switches Sides," *Oregonian,* January 15, 1994, p. A17.

"MADD Hopes Drivers Will 'Tie One On' to Save Lives," *Oregonian,* November 26, 1991, p. B4.

"MADD's Attorney Accused of Using Link to Get Clients—And Minnesota President Is Trying to Oust Director," *Star Tribune* (Minneapolis), February 19, 1991, p. 1B.

Marshall, Mac, and Alice Oleson, "MADDer Than Hell," *Qualitative Health Research,* February 1996, pp. 6+.

Martin, Hugo, "Drunk-Driving Foes Launch Effort to Reach State's Latinos," *Los Angeles Times,* December 15, 2001, p. B1.

Mathews, Jay, "MADD Against Ads: Widening a Crusade, Group Opposes Pitches Appealing to Youth," *Washington Post,* December 14, 1994, p. F1.

Nichols, Hans S., "Getting Drunk on Rebellion," *Insight on the News,* July 16, 2001, pp. 18f.

Peters, Eric, "MADD House," *National Review,* September 28, 1998, pp. 36f.

Pianin, Eric, "How Pressure Politics Bottled Up a Tougher Drunk-Driving Rule," *Washington Post,* May 22, 1998, p. A20.

Prewitt, Milford, "Operators Angry Over Liquor Industry's Support of MADD," *Nation's Restaurant News,* April 30, 2001, pp. 1, 79.

Robison, Clay, and R.G. Ratcliffe, "Bill to Cut DWI Level Likely Killed; MADD Criticizes Senator's Maneuver," *Houston Chronicle,* May 19, 1997, p. A1.

Rudavsky, Shari, "After Car Crash at UMass, Students Turn to MADD; Chapter Is Among First in the Nation," *Boston Globe,* December 2, 2001, p. C9.

Santana, Arthur, "MADD Marks 20th Anniversary with New Appeal to Congress," *Seattle Times,* September 7, 2000, p. A17.

Sealey, Geraldine, "Drunken-Driving Foes Face a New Enemy: Their Own Success," *St. Louis Post-Dispatch,* October 18, 1998, p. A1.

Smith, Lynn, "MADD at 20: Still a Force for Change," *Los Angeles Times,* April 2, 2000, p. E1.

Somerville, Sylvia, ''MADD About Money,'' *Restaurant Hospitality,* February 1992, p. 48.

Stamborski, Al, ''Wise-Er? Under Pressure, A-B Drops Frog Commercials,'' *St. Louis Post-Dispatch,* January 15, 1997, p. C1.

Sutherland, John, ''How America's Roads Became Safer Thanks to a Bunch of Madd Women—and Where the US Goes, We Follow,'' *Guardian,* March 19, 2001.

Teinowitz, Ira, ''MADD's Demands for Equal Ad Time Fall on Deaf Ears,'' *Advertising Age,* June 14, 1999, p. 16.

Valentine, Paul W., ''MADD Turns Its Message to Teenagers; Young Drivers to Be Focus of Anti-Drinking Initiatives,'' *Washington Post,* October 24, 1996, p. B1.

''Volunteering For and Working With Your Local MADD Chapter,'' *Journal of American Insurance,* Fourth Quarter 1990, pp. 9+.

Walker, Theresa, ''O.C. Resident Takes Over MADD Leadership,'' *Orange County Register*, December 31, 1993, p. B2.

Ward, Kyle, ''MADD's Telemarketing: Successes and Cautions,'' *Fund Raising Management,* March 1992, pp. 26+.

Weed, F.J., ''The MADD Queen: Charisma and the Founder of Mothers Against Drunk Driving,'' *Leadership Quarterly,* 1993, pp. 329–46.

Zuber, Amy, ''NRA and MADD Unite to Combat Drunk Driving,'' *Nation's Restaurant News,* June 16, 1997, pp. 1, 99.

—Frederick C. Ingram

Mullen Advertising Inc.

36 Essex Street
Wenham, Massachusetts 01984-1799
U.S.A.
Telephone: (978) 468-1155
Fax: (978) 468-1133
Web site: http://www.mullen.com

Division of Interpublic Group of Companies
Founded: 1970
Employees: 544
Gross Billings: $95.9 million (2001)
NAIC: 541810 Advertising Agencies

Mullen Advertising Inc., a division of advertising conglomerate Interpublic Group, is a $640 million, full-service agency that in addition to advertising offers its clients such services as design, public relations, direct marketing, interactive marketing, field marketing, and strategic planning. Despite having its headquarters in Wenham, Massachusetts, Mullen has long resisted the idea that it is a regional shop. Since joining Interpublic in 1999, Mullen has merged its operations with other agencies owned by the parent corporation, in the process adding offices in Massachusetts, Michigan, Pennsylvania, and North Carolina, and becoming the 24th largest agency in America. Since the departure of founder Jim Mullen, the agency has struggled to retain the iconoclastic, innovative spirit that brought a small Boston-area firm to national prominence.

Mullen Advertising Established in 1970

James Xavier Mullen never intended to become involved in advertising. After graduating from college in the early 1960s, he planned on going to medical school, changed his mind, and attended art school instead. A painting career never materialized, forcing Mullen seek employment in another field. He worked several years at the Harvard Biophysics Research Laboratory before growing restless and turning his attention to the sea. He sailed across the Atlantic in a small sailboat, became the skipper of a Caribbean charter boat, and learned the craft of sail making. Mullen, entering his 30s with no clear career path,

finally took stock of his career possibilities. "Unburdened by either money or commercial experience, I considered my skill set," he reflected in a 1990 *Inc.* self-profile. "I could write; I had once drawn pictures; I owned a dictionary; I was adventuresome. What was there to do but start an advertising agency?" In 1970, Mullen started his new business, which at first he called Superfine Productions, out of his two-room apartment in the coastal town of Marblehead, Massachusetts. For the first few years, the agency was a one-man shop, doing the bulk of its business with area marinas and boating suppliers.

The prospects for the tiny agency improved significantly with the 1974 addition of Paul Silverman, who would become Mullen's long-time creative director. Like Jim Mullen, Silverman had taken a less conventional route to the advertising industry. He grew up in Boston, the son of a deli owner, and attended the University of Massachusetts and Boston University, studying history and government as an undergraduate student. He went on to earn a master's degree in the history of ideas from Brandeis University. Deciding to become a literary writer, he supported himself as a waiter in Boston while working on poetry and short stories. He published several of his stories as well as a short novel, but to make money with his pen he turned to news writing. He worked as a local reporter for the *Beverly Times* and the *Quincy Patriot-Ledger*, then moved to New York to work two years for trade publications *Chain Store Age* and *Discount Store News*. Returning to Massachusetts, Silverman renewed his fiction writing, paying the bills by doing freelance work for *Chain Store Age* publisher Lebhar-Friedman. He wrote trade publication "advertorials" for major companies like DuPont and Armour and began to shift his focus to advertising. It was then that a space salesman for Lebhar-Friedman introduced him to Jim Mullen. The two advertising amateurs hit it off and Silverman joined the agency. They pitched clients together and slowly built up the business. Unfamiliar with the ways of other advertising firms, they followed their instincts, becoming unconventional almost by default. According to Silverman, "There might have been a lack of knowledge but never of energy, so things were done, even when it meant working all night, all weekend."

Mullen Advertising's first major break occurred in 1978 when it helped launched *Inc.*, a magazine devoted to small businesses. With the shop now well established in the New England market, Jim Mullen was still the chief copywriter, but as Silverman began to win area advertising awards he began to rethink his role, a process he detailed in his *Inc.* profile. "Each passing year saw the talent pool grow and my substantive contributions erode," he wrote. "In short order, everything I ever did even passably well was being done better by someone smarter, more skilled, and damnably younger. . . . As inexpert as I was at making and managing advertising, I still had the unique opportunity to influence the quality of every piece of work that came out of our company, as well as the quality of every client relationship we formed. While my business card describes me as Mullen's president, in fact it lies. What it really should say is 'Director of Environment and Standards.' "

While rival agencies worked in urban office towers, Jim Mullen opted for a more bucolic setting and located his offices on the grounds of a former estate. The choice set Mullen Advertising apart, but to a large degree it simply satisfied Jim Mullen's preference for nice property. He was difficult to pigeonhole, a man of varied interests who just happened to run one of the hottest ad agencies in New England. Not only an accomplished sailor, he also became a world class professional endurance race car driver. In 1983, at the age of 43, he and his co-driver won the prestigious 12 Hours of Sebring. This hobby worked to Mullen's advantage in growing his business: clients could follow his exploits in the sports pages, and potential clients were impressed by his competitive spirit.

Mullen Advertising Almost Devastated by 1987 Fire

No matter what title Jim Mullen cared to adopt or how he chose to spend his spare time, the agency he founded was on an upward swing in the 1980s. A 26-person firm in 1983, Mullen Advertising grew to become a 65-person agency by the end of 1986. The following year, however, the company was almost put out of business when an early morning fire ravaged the Beverly, Massachusetts, mansion that housed its offices, destroying all the furniture and equipment, as well as every file. Mullen had purchased the 90-acre Loeb Estate just 16 months earlier at the cost of $2.2 million and spent another $2 million in renovations. Within hours, Mullen summoned his top managers, Silverman and director of client services Joseph Grimaldi, to map a strategy for keeping the agency operational. Early that afternoon, employees set up makeshift work stations in another home located on the estate and went back to work, aided by donations of office supplies and equipment from rival ad agencies. Clients were quickly informed of the fire and assured that Mullen Advertising would meet its commitments. In some cases, Mullen staff worked out of clients' offices, but more importantly the clients provided copies of all records so the agency could reconstruct its files. Fortunately, much of the creative materials were at the printers, separaters, or engravers. The agency appeared to have suffered its most critical loss when photographs for one of its clients, boat builder Boston Whaler Inc., were destroyed in the fire. However, by sheer chance, a Mullen art director and photographer were in the process of re-shooting the company's catalog and simply stayed on in Florida to reproduce the file photographs. Mullen Advertising lost no clients because of the fire.

To replace the Loeb mansion, Mullen purchased a larger manor house in Wenham to serve as the agency's new headquarters. While the cause of the blaze was under investigation, a second fire occurred seven months later at the new location, causing extensive damage. Because both fires exhibited signs of multiple points of origin, state investigators concluded that each was an act of arson. According to *Adweek,* "Suspicion was cast upon Mullen himself, for he is majority stockholder. Mullen says that his own private investigators found both fires to be accidental, adding that he and other company officers passed lie detector tests ordered by his insurance companies. . . . Employees had no choice but to question whether Mullen himself set the fires in order to claim the insurance, or whether an unknown enemy was out to destroy the company. 'It was the worst time in my life,' says Mullen, 'worse than my divorce.' "

Despite the turmoil, Mullen Advertising began to make its mark on the national scene during this period. Especially important was the campaign it created for Timberland, a company that had been focusing its advertising on work boots despite also offering a wide range of upscale apparel. Rather than directly sell the wares, Silverman tried to establish Timberland as a place rather than a product. Print ads were shot in Scotland, scenic vistas and Timberland items complementing one another. This campaign and another for Smartfood established Mullen Advertising as a creative and versatile agency. Although Mullen and his staff disliked the label, Mullen Advertising was still considered a regional agency, one with a strong print portfolio but lacking in broadcast work. To meet the challenge of the 1990s, it had no choice but to broaden its scope. The agency scored a major win in 1993 when it landed a $30 million BMW account, especially satisfying to Jim Mullen who because of his racing experience probably knew more about cars than any advertising executive in the world. However, two years later it lost the account as well as the $20 million Timberland account. With potential New England clients looking to national ad agencies, Mullen Advertising expanded into integrated services in a diversification effort. The shop also began to focus on adding broadcast work, which proved to be a key element in raising Mullen Advertising's national profile.

Jim Mullen Sells Business in 1999

An agency with less than $100 million in billings at the start of the 1990s, Mullen Advertising topped the $250 million mark by 1999, making it the largest independent shop in the Boston area. It was responsible for a number of successful, memorable campaigns and as a result was courted by a number of larger suitors. Knowing that his agency was one of the last midsize independents in the industry, Mullen freely admitted that it was inevitable he would sell the business to one of the larger holding companies. In addition to the personal financial benefits of such a transaction, the backing of a parent corporation would allow the agency to broaden its international reach, an important consideration when so many of its clients had international scope as well. Mullen's search for a suitable buyer of the business came to an end in April 1999 when he agreed to an estimate $40–50 million stock and cash sale to London-based Lowe Group, part of the international stable of advertising agencies owned by Interpublic Group of Companies. According to the terms of the deal, the shop would be able to keep its name, management team, and estate headquarters.

Mullen agreed to head the agency for another year or two, but by October 1999 he turned over the CEO position to Grimaldi, electing to direct his attentions to his new duties as vice-chairman of Lowe and its North American operations. As part of a succession plan, Silverman also turned stepped down as chief creative officer in favor of his long-time associate Edward Boches. Despite a smooth transition at the top, the agency soon faced difficulties when it lost a pair of top clients, Monster.com and L.L. Bean, and was unsuccessful in landing the business of Goldman Sachs and General Motors' Hummer. Grimaldi dismissed the setbacks as the normal ebb and flow of the advertising business. There were no staff cuts as a result of this rough patch, although the new hire list was trimmed. To bolster the operation, Interpublic merged Mullen with another agency, Long Haymes Carr, with Grimaldi tabbed as CEO of the combined business. The move was intended to strengthen both companies, LHC's retail advertising work complementing Mullen's strength in creative and public relations. As a result of the merger, Mullen grew to be a 500-employee agency with multiple offices and annual billings of $620 million.

Mullen's slump lasted well into 2001. In particular, the LHC Winston-Salem, North Carolina, office suffered a significant blow when it lost the Winston tobacco account, as well as such important clients as Hanes and Thomasville Furniture. The office was forced to cut staff, and a new president was installed. In the meantime, Interpublic underwent some changes of its own, reorganizing into four divisions. As part of this restructuring, some of the operations of another ad agency, Bozell Kamstra, were folded into Mullen, which inherited staff and clients from Bozell Kamstra's Danvers, Massachusetts, office as well as adding the shop's Pittsburgh office.

By the autumn of 2001, Mullen regained its footing and began to win important new accounts, including wireless company Nextel Communications, eyeglass manufacturer FosterGrant, and clothier Eddie Bauer. The agency was especially optimistic about generating new business from a new consulting unit, Frank About Women, created in March 2002 by two of its Winston-Salem executives, Jennifer Ganshirt and Carrie McCament. The concept, developed over the previous year, was to create a specialty-marketing service to help clients target women. In the early months of 2002, the new unit was responsible for most of Mullen's major wins. The creation of Frank About Women reaffirmed Mullen's reputation for innovation even as the shop continued to find its place as part of a corporate giant.

Principal Competitors

BBDO Worldwide; GSD&M Advertising; Havas.

Further Reading

Bottorff, Dana, ''Fire Claims Mullen Advertising's Home, but Mansion Living Seems to Fuel Production,'' *New England Business,* September 7, 1987, p. 29.

Gianatasio, David, ''Paul Silverman; Deli Man's Son Puts Mullen at the Fore in Award Shows,'' *Adweek–Eastern Edition,* June 3, 1991, p. 16.

Jones, Sarah, ''Mullen: 'A Dream Fulfilled,' '' *Adweek New England Advertising Week,* May 3, 1999, p. 2.

McMains, Andrew, ''Challenge for Mullen,'' *Adweek New England Advertising Week,* July 17, 2000, p. 8.

Mullen, Jim, ''Owners Needs Not Apply,'' *Inc.,* August 1990, p. 76.

Thomsen, Ian, ''Inside Mullen,'' *Adweek,* September 16, 1991, p. 24.

—Ed Dinger

National Grid USA

25 Research Drive
Westborough, Massachusetts 01582
U.S.A.
Telephone: (508) 389-2000
Fax: (508) 389-3198
Web site: http://www.nationalgrid.com/usa

Wholly Owned Subsidiary of National Grid Transco plc
Incorporated: 1926 as New England Power Association
Employees: 3,836
Sales: $2.97 billion (2001)
NAIC: 221122 Electric Power Distribution

National Grid USA was formed when London-based National Grid Group plc acquired New England Electric System (NEES) in 2000. The company's main operations include the transmission and distribution of electricity—National Grid USA maintains 84,000 miles of overhead and underground transmission and distribution lines. Through its subsidiaries, the company provides electrical services to approximately 3.2 million customers in upstate New York, Massachusetts, Rhode Island, and New Hampshire. Its Niagara Mohawk subsidiary, which was acquired in 2002, provides natural gas delivery. The company also builds high-speed fiber optic telecommunications networks through its NEES Communications Inc. subsidiary and provides consulting services through Wayfinder Group Inc.

Early History

The company traces its origins back to 1906, when Malcolm Chace and Henry Harriman obtained charters from Vermont and New Hampshire to construct a dam and hydroelectric generating plant at Vernon, Vermont. Even in 1910, when the Vernon plant began to transmit electric power to industries in central Massachusetts, the structure of the Chace-Harriman operations was complex. There was a company formed under the more liberal corporation laws of Maine, the Connecticut River Power Company of Maine, and a holding company, the Massachusetts Company, as well as two operating companies,

the Connecticut River Power Company of New Hampshire and the Connecticut River Transmission Company. The Massachusetts Company, not subject to the regulations on public utilities, was able to issue and hold securities and therefore had greater flexibility in financing. Within a few years, Chace and Harriman expanded their hydroelectric operations to include one plant on the Connecticut River at Bellows Falls, Vermont, and several plants along the Deerfield River in Massachusetts. The New England Power Company was established to develop the Deerfield projects and to manage the electricity transmission lines in Massachusetts. The combined operations of the companies became known as New England Power System during this period.

As neither the Connecticut River nor the Deerfield River had a sufficiently large flow of water, especially during the summer months, to serve as a single, reliable source of electricity, Chace and Harriman decided to secure additional sources from thermal units, in which steam-driven turbines rather than falling water produced electricity. In the early years, they did this through sharing arrangements with the thermal plants of local lighting companies in Massachusetts and Rhode Island. Later, they purchased or constructed their own steam-generating plants.

In 1926, the New England Power System, the Northeastern Power Corporation, Stone & Webster, and International Paper Company formed New England Power Association (NEPA). This Massachusetts voluntary association had sufficient funds to purchase a number of smaller electric and gas companies in New England. By the 1930s, NEPA controlled 26 hydroelectric stations, 17 steam-generating plants, and more than 2,000 miles of transmission lines.

The Great Depression and the World War II years were difficult for NEPA financially. Annual earnings from 1933 through 1937 were lower than those of 1932, although sales rose, and full preferred dividend amounts were paid only three times between 1935 and 1946. Part of the problem lay in the fact that state authorities would not allow the retail companies to increase their charges for electricity, and the complicated network of holding companies prevented operating company mergers that could have resulted in economies of scale in production and distribution.

NEPA Emerges As the New England Electric System: 1947

In 1942, the Securities and Exchange Commission (SEC) ordered NEPA to simplify its corporate structure. An acceptable reorganization was not worked out until 1947, when NEPA emerged as New England Electric System, a new holding company that replaced five former holding companies and reduced 18 different classes of securities to two. NEES at this time was the largest electric utility system in New England, with 10,000 employees serving a population of 2.5 million.

The postwar years, and especially the 1960s, were a period of prosperity and reorganization for NEES. Electricity demand increased at an annual average of 7.7 percent in New England, and NEES revenues from electricity sales, and from the distribution and sale of manufactured and natural gas in Massachusetts, rose from $160 million in 1961 to $251 million in 1969. During this period the company gradually sold off a number of its generating units. In 1960, it operated 22 hydroelectric plants and 13 steam-generating plants, and, in 1970, only 13 hydroelectric plants and eight steam-generating plants. The number of employees in 1970 had fallen to 7,000. The main change in its retail operations involved the merger of a number of small electric companies to form the Massachusetts Electric Company in 1961. Some of this reorganization resulted from federal regulation. In 1957, the SEC ordered NEES to divest its minority interest in a number of small electricity subsidiaries and, in 1958, opened hearings regarding the company's natural gas distribution and sales outlets. NEES appealed the commission's 1964 order that it dispose of these up to the U.S. Supreme Court, which upheld the SEC ruling in 1968. The company subsequently sold off its eight gas companies gradually over the next few years.

In 1967, the three major electric utilities in New England—NEES, Boston Edison Company, and Northeast Utilities—began merger talks; Northeast Utilities later withdrew from these negotiations and was replaced by Eastern Utilities Associates. A corporate affiliation plan was drawn up in mid-1968 and presented to the SEC. The Justice Department opposed the merger, but an SEC hearing officer approved it in 1972, subject to certain conditions; the three utilities objected to these and the proposal was referred to the full SEC, which denied the application early in 1975.

Reducing Dependence on Foreign Oil: Late 1970s–Early 1980s

In the 1960s, electricity generating plants burning oil were fairly inexpensive to build and run and had cleaner emissions than those burning coal. By 1969, all NEES steam-generating plants were burning oil, including several that had previously burned coal, and, in 1971, the company announced the construction of a new large oil-fired power plant in Salem, Massachusetts. By the mid-1970s, oil was providing 78 percent of NEES's energy requirements, and the company ranked third among U.S. electric utilities in its dependence on oil. It was therefore very vulnerable to the effects of the oil price and supply crises of this period and concerned about government proposals to levy import fees on foreign oil.

In 1979, to counter this threat, NEES President Guy Nichols, later credited with building NEES into one of the region's strongest utilities, announced a 15-year plan to reduce the company's use of foreign oil and to keep customers' electricity costs to a minimum through conservation measures and load growth management. To lower the share of oil in its energy requirements to less than ten percent by 1996, the company decided to convert some of its oil-fired generating plants to coal burning. The Environmental Protection Agency (EPA) granted a temporary waiver of pollution-control rules in 1979 to permit the conversion of NEES's biggest generating station at Brayton Point in Somerset, Massachusetts. The conversion of three of its Brayton Point units to coal burning, which was completed in the early 1980s, was the first large-scale conversion of an oil-burning generating plant by a U.S. electric utility. NEES then proceeded with a second major conversion of three of its oil-burning units at Salem. To ensure coal supplies for its plants, NEES contracted for the construction of its own coal-carrying ship in 1980. *Energy Independence*, the first coalfired ship built in the United States since 1929, began carrying coal up the eastern seaboard to Brayton Point in 1983.

NEES also reduced its dependency on oil by using, on a small scale, alternative energy sources for electricity generation, such as wood, windmills, solid waste, and small hydroelectric projects. To secure oil for the steam-generating units it could not convert to coal burning, NEES established a partnership with Noble Affiliates, an independent oil producer, to drill and develop domestic oil wells. By 1984, the percentage of oil used for NEES energy requirements had fallen to around 25 percent, and by 1990 the company's fuel mix was 22 percent oil, 42 percent coal, 19 percent nuclear, 8 percent hydroelectricity, 3 percent natural gas, and 6 percent alternative energy sources. The latter included 32 lowhead hydroelectric plants, 79 wind or solar generators, four trash-burning plants, and 24 cogenerators—facilities producing thermal energy and electricity from the same source.

To meet the second goal of keeping customers' electricity bills to a minimum, NEES focused on slow growth. Peak load capacity—the amount of generating capacity that an electric utility needs to satisfy residential and commercial demand at its highest point in the day—determines the amount of generating capacity that the utility must have. The NEES slow-growth strategy involved an extensive conservation and load management (C&LM) program designed to reduce the annual peak load growth for the mid-1990s from the previous forecast of 3.1 percent to 1.9 percent. Achieving this would reduce the need for constructing additional generating capacity by the 1990s; it would also eliminate the need for rate increases for customers to pay for plant construction. The C&LM program included rate discounts to large industrial, commercial, and residential users for off-peak—9 P.M. to 8 A.M.—use of electricity; the dispatch of energy audit teams to customers to give them free energy-saving tips; the promotion, through rate incentives, of the installation of heat and/or cooling storage systems; the holding of large public programs on energy conservation; and the initiation of a solar project.

Problems with Nuclear Power

For additional generating capacity to meet the lower peak load growth, NEES intended to rely on nuclear power, hydroelectric projects, and natural gas-burning plants. Nuclear power was a significant source of energy in New England in the 1970s, and its seven nuclear power plants supplied about 28 percent of the region's power, more than double the national figure of 12 percent. New England Power, the NEES generating company subsidiary, was a stockholder in the Massachusetts-based Yankee Rowe, Vermont Yankee, Connecticut Yankee, and Maine Yankee nuclear power plants completed between 1961 and 1972. Its ownership in these varied between 30 percent and 15 percent, and it purchased electricity in accordance with these ownership percentages.

In 1974, NEES announced plans to build a nuclear power station in Charlestown, Rhode Island. The Three Mile Island accident in March 1979, however, resulted in new safety requirements for nuclear plants, making them much more expensive to build and operate. Late in 1979, NEES canceled plans for the Charlestown plant. At the time, it still had a stake in three nuclear projects scheduled for completion in the 1980s: the Millstone 3 plant in Waterford, Connecticut; the Pilgrim II plant

in Plymouth, Massachusetts; and the two Seabrook plants in New Hampshire. Construction of Pilgrim II was canceled in 1981, but Millstone 3, in which NEES had a 12.2 percent share, became operational in 1986. The Seabrook project, however, had serious problems, with estimates of construction costs for Seabrook 2, some 17 percent complete, having risen from $900 million in 1972 to $5.24 billion by the early 1980s.

In 1983, NEES announced that it wanted to sell its ten percent interest in Seabrook 2 but to retain its interest in Seabrook 1, then 70 percent complete. If it could not sell its share of Seabrook 2, it proposed that the project be canceled, and eventually it was. In 1985, the Federal Energy Regulatory Commission (FERC) ruled that NEES could charge its customers for construction costs on Pilgrim II and, in 1986, for the construction costs of Seabrook 2. The main investor in Seabrook 2, Public Service Company of New Hampshire (PSNH), however, did not fall under FERC jurisdiction, and its rates were regulated entirely by the state public utility commission. PSNH filed for bankruptcy in 1988 after the courts barred it from passing along the Seabrook 2 costs to its customers. NEES then submitted a bid to buy PSNH, exclusive of its shares in Seabrook 2, but dropped its offer when other utilities submitted higher bids.

The Seabrook 1 nuclear plant was completed in late 1986, but the Chernobyl accident in April of that year led the Nuclear Regulatory Commission to refuse to license the plant for commercial operation until emergency response measures were in place. These measures were subject to review by the states. Seabrook is located two miles from the Massachusetts border, and for four years Massachusetts refused to submit the evacuation plan the commission required. Seabrook I finally started commercial operations in June 1990.

NEES continued to follow its slow-growth program through the 1980s even though growth in electricity demand in New England between 1982 and 1988 generally was more than five percent per year, considerably higher than the NEES forecast. In 1985, Samuel Huntington, who had succeeded Guy Nichols as chief executive officer, announced further measures to provide an adequate supply of electricity at the lowest possible cost and to encourage customers to use electricity efficiently and economically. The company's subsidiary, NEES Energy, began to provide energy conservation services under contracts that provided for sharing of resultant energy savings between the company and customers. In 1989, the SEC approved the application of NEES Energy to expand its business and to participate in cogeneration projects.

When high electricity demand in New England resulted in voltage reductions during the summers of 1987 and 1988, the wisdom of a slow-growth program was questioned by a rival utility, Northeast Utilities, which noted that NEES then had no spare generating capacity. The recession, however, lessened the pressure on NEES as the annual increase in electricity demand in the region fell to 2 percent in 1989, down from 5.4 percent in 1988.

In July 1988, CEO Samuel Huntington was killed during a lightning storm. A successor, John Rowe, was not selected until December of that year. In the interim, Chairman Joan T. Bok, long the highest woman executive in the electric utility industry, assumed CEO responsibility.

Adding Natural Gas as a Fuel Source: Late 1980s–Early 1990s

In the late 1980s, NEES decided to include natural gas as a fuel source and announced plans to expand and convert its Providence, Rhode Island, oil-fired plant to natural gas by 1995. It also planned to add the capability of burning natural gas at its oil-fired Brayton unit in Somerset, Massachusetts. In addition, in 1988 it formed the Narragansett Energy Resources Company to take a 20 percent interest in Ocean State Power, a general partnership established to build, own, and operate a gas-fired electric power plant in Burrillville, Rhode Island. The first unit of the Ocean State Power plant was operational in late 1990; the second was scheduled for completion in 1991.

For additional hydroelectric power, NEES tapped Canadian sources through arrangements with the New England Power Pool (NEPOOL), a consortium of New England utilities that coordinated the generation and transmission facilities of its members. In 1983, NEPOOL had made an agreement with Hydro-Quebec, the electric utility owned by the province of Quebec, to purchase sufficient surplus power generated by hydroelectric stations in the James Bay region to meet 3 percent to 4 percent of the region's energy needs. NEES had been heavily involved in the building of many of the direct-current transmission lines and terminals required to link the Canadian and New England electric systems. The first stage in the Hydro-Quebec project went into operation in 1987; the second, in late 1990.

At the start of the 1990s, NEES was doing well. The two new nuclear plants in which it had a share, Millstone Unit 3 and Seabrook 1, the Hydro-Quebec hydroelectric project, and the Ocean State Power gas plant were all in operation. Its oil and gas exploration subsidiary, which had been operating at a loss, was being wound down, and the coal-carrying ship, which it owned, had been sold to Keystone Shipping Co. but continued to transport coal to NEES's generating stations. Revenues were also up.

Deregulation Leads to New Ownership: Late 1990s and Beyond

The landscape of the electricity industry began to change dramatically during the mid- to late 1990s. Deregulation and restructuring in the industry had long since been topics of discussion among consumers, government officials, and company executives. Indeed, deregulation became a reality with the passing of the Rhode Island Utility Restructuring Act in January 1998, which was the first act in the U.S. that enabled customers to choose their power supplier. Massachusetts became the second state to pass similar legislation in March 1998.

As deregulation promised to increase competition, and thus stimulate competitive pricing for consumers, NEES began to restructure to position itself as a leading electricity distributor. NEES was the first U.S. utility to set plans in motion to sell its non-nuclear generation business. In 1997, the company sold its 15 hydroelectric and three fossil fuel plants to U.S. Generating Company, a subsidiary of PG&E Co., for $1.6 billion. A September 1997 *Electric Light & Power* article commented on

the deal, claiming it was the first "major move in the power plant trend that is hitting the U.S. investor-owned electric utilities." The article went on to report that "so far, the trend is concentrated in New England and California, but it promises to spread to other regions. It is driven by the desire to make electricity markets more competitive. That requires the elimination, or at least the reduction, of generation market domination by a few large companies."

NEES continued to strengthen its position in the distribution market and in late 1998 announced that it agreed to be acquired by London-based National Grid Group plc, an electricity concern with operations in England and Wales. At the time, National Grid was looking to gain a foothold in the U.S. electricity market—a market it deemed crucial to its expansion efforts. The $4.1 billion union was completed in 2000. NEES adopted the National Grid USA name.

By focusing on distribution, National Grid USA had its work cut out for it. Demand for electricity in the U.S. grew by 14 percent from 1995 to 2000. Capacity, however, grew by just 13 percent during the same time period. National Grid USA used cutting-edge technology, including lasers and software, to avoid problems as well as track electricity usage.

During 2000, Eastern Utilities Associates was merged into National Grid USA's operations. That year, National Grid Group also announced its purchase of New York-based Niagara Mohawk Holdings Inc. That purchase, completed in January 2002, doubled the size of National's Grid U.S. business and catapulted National Grid USA into the top echelon of U.S. power distributors, securing it as the ninth-largest in the nation.

National Grid USA proved to be highly successful for its parent. During 2001, the U.S. concern accounted for 60 percent of National Grid's revenues and 43 percent of its profits. During 2002, its parent merged with Lattice Group plc to form National Grid Transco plc. As a subsidiary of what was now the largest energy utility in the United Kingdom, National Grid USA stood well positioned for future growth. In fact, Transco planned to make additional purchases in the United States, which would leave National Grid USA a step ahead of many of its competitors.

Principal Subsidiaries

Niagara Mohawk Power Corp.; Massachusetts Electric Company; Narragansett Electric Company; Granite State Electric Company; Nantucket Electric Company; National Grid Transmission USA; New England Power Company; National Grid Transmission Services Corp.; New England Electric Transmission Corp.; New England Hydro-Transmission Corp.; New England Hydro-Transmission Electric Co.; National Grid USA Service Company Inc.; NEES Communications Inc.; Wayfinder Group Inc.

Principal Competitors

Energy East Corporation; Northeast Utilities; NSTAR.

Further Reading

Blankinship, Steve, "Mergers and Acquisitions," *Power Engineering*, January 2002, p. 19.

Boschee, Pam, ''National Grid Weighs In On U.S. Transmission Market,'' *Electric Light & Power*, September 2002.

''Lattice and National Grid to Merge,'' *Modern Power Systems*, May 2002, p. 5.

''London Firm Buys NEES,'' *The Oil Daily*, December 16, 1998.

''New England Electric System Thrives on Slower Growth,'' *Electric Light and Power*, November 1979.

Smock, Robert W., ''USGen Buys NEES Power Plants for $1.59 Billion,'' *Electric Light & Power*, September 1997, p. 1.

Wherry, Rob, ''Electricity in the Air,'' *Forbes*, October 14, 2002, p. 104.

—Judith Gurney
—update: Christina M. Stansell

New York City Off-Track Betting Corporation

1501 Broadway
New York, New York 10036
U.S.A.
Telephone: (212) 221-5200
Web site: http://www.nycotb.net

Government-Owned Corporation
Incorporated: 1971
Employees: 1,500 (est.)
Operating Revenues: $1 billion (2000)
NAIC: 713290 Other Gambling Industries

The New York City Off-Track Betting Corporation is a quasi-government operation run for the benefit of the city. Each year more than $1 billion is wagered on horse races at 68 OTB parlors, three teletheaters, restaurant locations, as well as via telephone accounts, which have become more popular with the introduction of OTB telecasts on a local public access cable television channel. In addition to races run at area tracks, both thoroughbred and harness, OTB also provides wagering on out-of-town locations. Long criticized as a bloated, wasteful bureaucracy, OTB has come close to being sold off in recent years. Improvements to the operations, however, have helped to stave off the transfer to private interests.

Calls for Off-Track Betting in the 1950s

While horse racing takes place at numerous facilities throughout the United States, New York City has long been the wagering capital of the sport, as well as the place where the business of off-track betting has been the center of much political debate. Early in the twentieth century, the horse racing was briefly banned in New York state, but this prohibition did little to suppress gambling. While some began advocating for the legalization of off-track betting, arguing that people would always feel compelled to wager, before the 1950s it remained a challenging position to hold for politicians. In 1944, for instance, New York City Mayor Fiorello LaGuardia denounced the idea in one of his weekly radio addresses, maintaining that off-track betting would pave the way for legalized roulette, faro,

dice, and other gambling. Moreover, he stated that the city could balance its budget without "one cent of this dirty or blood money." The truth was that the state of New York was already very much dependent on its share of gambling at the local tracks, taking 5 percent of the handle (the amount bet on a race). Race tracks themselves accounted for another 5 percent of the "takeout." LaGuardia's successor, Mayor William O'Dwyer, was able to get an extra 5 percent share for the New York City in 1946, the "O'Dwyer bite," which raised the total takeout to 15 percent. Over the next several years, however, the city was unable to fend off politicians at the state level who managed to wrest away the 5 percent, thereby doubling the state's share to 10 percent. Starting in the 1950s, New York City mayors began to actively lobby for an off-track betting operation that could benefit the city coffers, which were beginning to increasingly feel a financial strain. Not only would the city not have to ask for more state funding, they argued, off-track betting would drive out illegal bookmakers and decrease the burden on the police.

The battle lines for off-track betting were essentially drawn between city Democrats and upstate Republicans. Also involved were a pair of unlikely allies: church groups opposed to gambling and the race tracks opposed to giving up a share of the takeout. The tracks simply did not believe that off-track betting would increase the betting market, as advocates argued. In 1963, Mayor Robert Wagner placed an off-track betting referendum question on the ballot for city voters. Although it held no legal effect, its support by a three-to-one-margin exerted pressure on upstate politicians, especially after Senator Jacob Javits, a leading Republican and the state's senior senator in the U.S. Congress, called for the legislature to accede to the voters' wishes. Nevertheless, over the next several years off-track betting bills died in committee or were defeated by the legislature. All the while, city officials prepared to create a corporation to run the off-track betting operations and as early as 1964 were envisioning a computerized wagering system. They also dreamed of realizing $200 million a year from the enterprise.

The breakthrough came suddenly, at the end of the 1970 legislative session, when the city projected a $630 million budget shortfall. City-backed legislation was passed permitting the creation of the New York City Off-Track Betting Corporation, a public-benefit corporation to be run by a board of directors to be appointed by the mayor. The OTB takeout would be 17 percent, with .5 percent of the handle going to the state, 1.5 percent to the tracks and horsemen, and the remaining 15 percent retained by the corporation to cover costs and generate a profit, which would then be split between the city and the state. In an attempt to lessen the impact on the tracks, OTB facilities were mandated to be uncomfortable: no food, no drink, no chairs, no bathrooms. The racing industry, taking no solace in the knowledge that OTB patrons would be made to suffer, was still outraged by the development and turned to the courts to have OTB declared unconstitutional, an effort that ultimately failed. A long-term conflict between OTB and the industry ensued, resulting, at the best of times, in an uneasy coexistence. Labor unions representing track employees were also hostile to the new venture, afraid that a long-term slide in track attendance would only be aggravated by OTB and cost them jobs.

OTB Begins Operations in 1971

To establish OTB, Mayor John Lindsay chose Howard Samuels, a former state senator who fell short in his 1970 bid for the Democratic nomination for governor. Samuels had considerable business experience, having co-founded Kordite Company, best known for the creation of Baggies. Samuels made several million dollars when the company was sold to Mobil Oil. Billed as the ''New Game in Town,'' OTB began operations on April 8, 1971, less than a year after the passage of off-track betting legislation, becoming the first legalized off-track betting operation in the United States. The start was modest, with only two betting facilities available to take wagers on that night's harness races at Roosevelt Raceway: several windows at Grand Central Terminal and an OTB shop in Forest Hills, Queens. Mayor Lindsay held the honor of placing the first off-track bet, $2 on a pacer by the name of Moneywise at four-to-one odds. Other patrons, lacking the privileges of rank, waited in line as long as two hours to place their bets. Because OTB's computer system was not yet deemed reliable, they used three-part betting slips that took time to fill out and were then manually checked. Moveover, it was evident that the slips could easily be altered to create winning tickets.

After the first day's handle of $66,091, OTB began to ramp up its operations. By the end of its first year in operation, OTB boasted more than 50 parlors located in all five boroughs, with a daily handle of $1.2 million. It remained a controversial venture, however, with its computer system proving to be slow and unreliable and attendance at local tracks falling, thereby cutting into the takeout of both the state and tracks. Parimutuel clerks went on strike at Aqueduct to protest job cuts that the tracks attributed to the loss of patrons cause by OTB. Critics also contended that OTB was trying to dress the books. According to

a March 1972 *New York Times* article, ''By scrimping on services (no security guards or cleaners in the shops), hiring part-timers for four-hour shifts and deferring payments on such obligations as a $5 million fee for computer installation, OTB has sought to make itself appear more profitable at an earlier date than it really is.''

OTB also faced a continue challenge from the New York Racing Authority (NYRA), a non-profit corporation which represented the interests of the three state thoroughbred tracks: Aqueduct, Belmont, and Saratoga. Samuels attempted to negotiate with NYRA and the harness tracks about a more equitable split in the OTB takeout, and it appeared that the two sides were on the verge of an agreement. However, relations quickly deteriorated when a racing industry-supported bill was presented in the New York legislature calling for the creation of a board, dominated by racing officials, which would consolidate all of the state's track and off-track betting commissions. Samuels vowed to fight the obvious attempt to take over OTB, suggesting that the tracks would be better served by cooperating with OTB in order to stimulate bettor interest, especially by permitting televised races.

During his tenure as the head of OTB, Samuels was able to fend off attempts to gain control of the organization. He was unsuccessful, however, in expanding the scope of the corporation to include the taking of bets on other sporting events, such as football, baseball, basketball, and hockey. His successor at OTB, Paul Scevane, who took over in March 1974, floated the idea of a betting card format, in which bettors attempted to pick the highest number of winners on a slate of games, but this concept failed to gain backing, and OTB's quest to become an all-purpose bookie gradually faded. The corporation was having enough trouble fulfilling its stated mission of generating large revenues for the city's coffers. The dream of gaining $200 million a year from OTB was dismissed from the outset of operations. In fact, annual profits peaked in 1974 when $43 million was turned over to the city. Despite the disappointment of declining profits, the city continued to collect its 5 percent share of the takeout. Even that amount would begin to fall off as OTB's annual handle peaked in fiscal 1988, totaling $1.03 billion, then began a steady slide.

OTB received mounting criticism over the years: its parlors were shabby, technology antiquated, management inept, and work force inefficient. Like so many city institutions, it had become a source for political patronage, providing high-paying, high-sounding, do-little jobs to supporters. In the early 1980s, the comptroller's office began urging OTB to cut costs, including the consolidation of branch offices, but little progress was made. OTB attempted to improve its finances by upgrading its product to spur revenues. Live calls from the race tracks were piped into OTB parlors. In 1986, OTB opened its first Teletheater, the Inside Track, in Manhattan. These changes did little to offset increased competition over gaming dollars from the state lottery and casinos in Atlantic City and on the lands of Native Americans. Illegal bookmaking operations, featuring satellite-televised races and comfortable accommodations, as well as credit, were also flourishing in the city. Moreover, the demographics of the typical OTB bettor were troubling. A survey conducted in 1991 indicated that almost 70 percent of patrons were over 45 years old. An OTB spokesman was quoted in a 1994 *Forbes* article as saying: "The average bettor is a 55-year-old white man who's overweight and a chain smoker. How long will that customer base be around before you don't have any customers at all?"

OTB Becomes A Political Issue in 1993 Mayoral Race

By cutting the number of OTB shops from 157 to 90, it came as no surprise that OTB's annual handle slipped from $959.2 million in 1990 to $742 million in fiscal 1994, and despite cost-savings measures, the corporation actually lost over $7.4 million that year. During Rudolph Guiliani's run for mayor in 1993, the state of OTB became a salient campaign issue when he questioned how a bookie operation could possibly lose money. In addition, Guiliani's opponent, David Dinkins, the city's first minority mayor, was troubled by his appointment to head OTB, Hazel Dukes. According to a 1994 *Forbes* profile of OTB, "She might have cost the mayor the election, as OTB became a symbol of ineptitude. She clearly regarded OTB as a candy jar: She fired older white managers and replaced them with nonwhites, saddling OTB with big lawsuits from the fired whites and thus adding to OTB's deficit."

Although mayoral candidate Guiliani vowed to sell OTB to private interests, after his election he allowed the corporation a chance to redeem itself. Under the leadership of Robert Palumbo, who was soon succeeded by former New York Giants football coach Allie Sherman, OTB began to show improvement. A first step was to simply clean the OTB parlors, which were notoriously dingy and marred by graffiti. Sherman also lowered OTB's overhead by closing twelve poorly performing parlors, cutting back on the number of parlors opened on Sunday to reduce double overtime for labor and eliminating staff through buy-out packages. More important to revitalizing the fortunes of OTB was a new law that allowed OTB to simulcast out-of-state races in its parlors and the March 1995 introduction of experimental in-home simulcasting of races on the city's public access cable channel, which spurred growth in new telephone accounts for both OTB and NYRA. As a result of these developments, OTB posted a $4.6 million profit for fiscal 1995 while improving the handle to $821 million.

OTB outlets featuring simulcasts were added to several restaurant locations in 1997. Although it appeared that the simulcasts mutually benefited OTB and NYRA, especially in light of

the rise of Internet wagering on horse races, the two sides soon fell out over the arrangement. NYRA blamed in-home signals for a significant drop in track attendance, which OTB officials pointed out was a nationwide trend unconnected to the telecasts. After an agreement covering the pricing of track signals expired in July 1997, OTB and NYRA engaged in protracted and sometimes heated negotiations. In July 1998, NYRA pulled the plug on the home telecasts, followed in October by cutting off the feed to OTB parlors and teletheaters as well as affiliated bars and restaurants. The impasse was not settled until November 1998 when the parties finally agreed on a four-year contract.

For fiscal 2000, OTB's annual handle topped the $1 billion mark, and the corporation contributed $39.2 million to New York City. As he entered the final year of his administration, unable to run again because of imposed term limits, Mayor Guiliani sought to fulfill a long-term pledge to sell the enterprise to commercial interests, while retaining a minority interest for the city. With a minimum offer of $250 million, two bidders ultimately emerged: Magna Entertainment Corporation of Ontario, Canada, and Churchill Downs Inc. of Louisville, Kentucky, in partnership with NYRA. The sale faced several obstacles, including a lawsuit from labor unions representing 1,700 OTB employees, which maintained that the city had not properly evaluated the impact of the sale on city employees as required by law. Any deal would also require approval from the state legislature, which was far from certain. In addition, both suitors for OTB were under somewhat of an ethical cloud. NYRA was under investigation by the state attorney general's office as well as federal authorities for possible tax evasion and money laundering at its three thoroughbred tracks. One of Magna's partners, Robert W, Green, a British bookmaker and track owner, was tainted by his close association with a New Jersey businessman who had just been convicted of money laundering and bank fraud.

A deal to sell OTB to Magna twice fell apart before Mayor Guiliani was able to announce in August 2001 that a $262 million deal had been struck. Critics claimed that the sale was shortsighted, and opponents, which included NYRA and the OTB union, vowed to stop the transaction in the state legislature. The matter would be put on hold following the September 11, 2002, terrorists attacks that destroyed Manhattan's World Trade Center. It was still pending when Michael Bloomberg took over as New York's mayor in 2002. He floated the novel alternative idea of selling OTB's future revenues for a single, up-front payment, but in the end decided to delay the sale for at least a year, saying that it was uncertain whether OTB would be sold or not. In the meantime, OTB continued to conduct its wagering business and implemented measures to broaden its appeal to a wider and younger audience.

Principal Subsidiaries

NYC OTB Racing Network.

Principal Competitors

New York Racing Authority; www.youbet.com.

Further Reading

Cady, Steve, "OTB: 11 Months Later," *New York Times,* March 15, 1972, p. 59.

Clines, Francis X., "OTB: A Sure Bet Now Falling Behind," *New York Times,* May 7, 1993, p. B1.

Flint, Jerry, "Horsefeathers," *Forbes,* October 24, 1994, p. 169.

Lentz, Philip, "A New Parlay For OTB," *Crain's New York Business,* May 1, 1995, p. 3.

Lipton, Eric, "Conglomerates in Horse Racing Compete to Buy OTB Parlors," *New York Times,* June 4, 2001, p. B1.

Marriott, Michel, "Hoping to Run With a Younger Crowd at OTB," *New York Times,* September 18, 1992, p. B1.

McDonald, John, "How the Horseplayers Got Involved With the Urban Crisis," *Fortune,* April 1972, p. 94.

Tierney, John, "For New York City's OTB, A Sure Bet Ends Up a Loser," *New York Times,* November 14, 1994, p. A1.

Unger, Howard Z., "Track Marks: The Death of New York Horse Racing," *Village Voice,* January 20, 1998, p. 150.

Viuker, Steven J., "High Stakes," *Barron's,* June 10, 1996, p. 20.

—Ed Dinger

Nippon Telegraph and Telephone Corporation

3-1 Otemachi 2-chrome
Chiyoda-ku
Tokyo 100-8116
Japan
Telephone: (03) 5205-5111
Fax: (03) 5205-5589
Web site: http://www.ntt.co.jp

Public Company
Incorporated: 1985
Employees: 213,000
Sales: $86.7 billion (2002)
Stock Exchanges: Tokyo New York London
Ticker Symbol: NTT
NAIC: 513322 Cellular and Other Wireless
   Telecommunications; 51331 Wired
   Telecommunications Carriers

Nippon Telegraph and Telephone Corporation (NTT) is the largest telecommunications firm in the world. In 1999, NTT was reorganized as part of Japan's telecommunications reform and became a holding company for regional phone companies, NTT East and NTT West, and long-distance carrier NTT Communications. Along with traditional telephone services, NTT offers Internet access, broadband services, and mobile communication services. The company owns 64 percent of Japan's leading cellular provider, NTT DoCoMo Inc. Japan's telecommunications sector continues to face increased competition from foreign entrants, leaving NTT heavily focused on international investments—including the $5.1 billion purchase of U.S.-based Verio Inc.—and restructuring business operations. In 2002, Japan's government owned 46 percent of NTT.

Origins

In 1877, one year after its invention by Alexander Graham Bell, the telephone became available in Japan. At first its use was reserved for the government, public affairs organizations such as the police, and a few businesses. It was not until 1890 that telephone services became available to the general public. Lines were laid between Tokyo and Yokohama, connecting 155 Tokyo subscribers to 42 in Yokohama. The first long-distance service became available in 1899 between Tokyo and Osaka, and discussions began as to how the telephone industry could best be developed. In 1889, the government approved a state-run telephone system. Although there were calls for a privately run company to be established, the Sino-Japanese War of 1894 to 1895 and the Depression of the 1930s meant that calls for privatization went unheeded. In the 1930s, the Ministry of Communications created a special telegraph and telephone system research committee, which discussed the establishment of a half-government, half-private company. Initial plans were made for the formation of Nippon Telegraph and Telephone Corporation but were abandoned again due to an economic downturn and a sudden decline in the number of telephone subscribers. The outbreak of World War II led to another drop in telephone subscribers, to 468,000. It was not until 1952, after a bill for a public telephone company was passed, that the Nippon Telegraph and Telephone Public Corporation (NTTPC) was formed, based on recommendations issued in a report by the government-run Telegraph and Telephone Restoration Council. In 1953, KDD Ltd. was established to facilitate international telecommunications, and international telegraph and telephone business was transferred to this company.

Postwar Demand for Telecommunication Services

As Japan began to recover after World War II, the demand for telecommunication services increased. In 1953, NTTPC's first five-year expansion project of telegraph and telephone started, leading to an increase in the number of subscribers from 1.55 million to 2.64 million. Fueled by consumers' needs and advances in telecommunications technology, by 1963 the number of subscribers had increased to 9.89 million. As NTTPC's domestic market grew rapidly, NTTPC began to expand into the international market, although at this time technical cooperation was the extent of NTTPC's international involvement.

Within Japan, the demand for telecommunication services continued to grow. By 1972, the number of telephone subscribers had reached 20 million, and despite the demand caused by such enormous growth, NTTPC saw two of its aims realized in 1977: telephone services became available nationwide and the company was able to install services as soon as they were required. Automatic dialing also became nationally available, and with the goal of international involvement, an international office was opened in 1979.

NTT Is Partially Privatized: 1985

Moves towards privatization came slowly. Meanwhile, NTTPC began to examine its infrastructure. The second ad hoc commission on privatization in 1981 examined the "public" corporate side of NTTPC and saw privatization as a way of improving efficiency. A third report detailed plans for privatization, reorganizing the company's structure and making independent the data communications systems sector; in May to July 1988, the latter was established as NTT Data Communication Systems Corporation (NTT Data), a wholly owned NTT subsidiary. NTT's corporation law went into effect on December 20, 1984. Nippon Telegraph and Telephone Corporation was newly launched as a privatized joint stock corporation on April 1, 1985, with the provision that the Nippon Telegraph and Telephone Law be subject to revision within five years. On an international level, similar events were taking place in the United States and the United Kingdom. In 1984, the British Telecommunications Bill came into force, allowing the privatization of British Telecom and liberalizing the British telecommunications industry, as competitors such as Mercury were issued licenses to operate. The United States followed a similar pattern in 1984, when American Telephone & Telegraph Company's Bell System was broken up and restructured into seven regional holding companies.

After privatization, the market opened to new carriers to start operations in competition with NTT. In April 1985, three carriers—Daini-Denden, Nippon Telecom, and Teleway Japan—applied for approval to operate as telecommunications companies. One effect of direct competition was that NTT was obliged to make a reduction in long-distance rates and upgrade its services. In July 1985, several new services were launched. A further measure to enhance performance was the restructuring of NTT's business into divisional organizations and the reorganization of the research and development headquarters from four to nine laboratories. NTT's first subsidiary company was launched in April 1985 and marked the opening of a chapter in NTT's history that would lead to the establishment of over 80 subsidiaries. The first was NTT Lease Co. Ltd.; its activities included the leasing and installment sales of terminal equipment.

Privatization Leads to Changes in International Growth

In terms of international activities, privatization allowed NTT slightly more room to maneuver through the creation of subsidiaries that had greater powers abroad. Prior to privatization,

NTTPC's overseas operations on the whole had been restricted to participating in international exchanges, sending experts abroad and forming agreements with a number of countries. As early as 1954, NTTPC had accepted trainees from Taiwan, and up to the early 1990s accepted approximately 160 trainees from 60 countries a year. The expert dispatch scheme that started in 1960 has resulted in more than 500 specialists being sent to 54 countries. During the 1960s and 1970s, a whole series of technical assistance programs were arranged between participating countries and NTTPC. Projects as diverse as assisting with the establishment of a training center in Thailand in 1961 or setting up a microwave radio system in Paraguay characterized NTTPC's activities abroad at this time. Kuwait, in particular, was involved in a whole series of projects. A contract was signed in June 1965 between Kuwait's Minister of Communications and NTTPC that led to the launch of a ten-year project.

The setting up of representative offices was another method whereby NTTPC extended its operations overseas. NTTPC's first overseas office opened in Bangkok in 1958, offering technical assistance, and a European base was established in 1965 with the opening of the Geneva representative office. This was followed in 1973 with the opening of NTTPC's London representative office. Prior to NTTPC's privatization, the London office had concentrated on issuing bonds and collecting information. NTT Europe Ltd. was formally incorporated in the United Kingdom in 1989 to encourage cooperation with that country's own telecommunications industry and to help extend global networks for Japanese business users. In similar fashion, the representative office in Brasilia, Brazil, became an officially registered overseas subsidiary company in November 1987. NTT do Brasil Comercio e Representacoes Lomita provides technical assistance and supports international exchange programs to countries in South America, in particular Brazil and Argentina, as well as Mexico. Representative offices also opened in Jakarta, Indonesia, in 1972; in Kuala Lumpur, the Malaysian capital, in 1986; and in Singapore in 1990. After the restoring of diplomatic relations between China and Japan in 1972, NTTPC made a technical exchange agreement with China in 1980, leading to the opening of an office in Beijing in 1985.

NTT had a presence in the United States as early as 1966, when NTTPC employees were sent to New York. In 1970, a branch office was established with the primary objective of forming connections with U.S. carriers, and that went on to play an important role in international procurement. Due to an increase in business, NTT's California representative office was established, and after privatization NTT expanded its U.S. operations, incorporating the two U.S. offices into NTT America Inc. NTT also established exchange programs with several U.S. companies, including NYNEX and Pacific Bell, and a number of equipment purchase agreements were made. In May 1986, a purchase agreement was set up with Northern Telecom in a $250 million deal.

NTT International Corporation (NTTI) was established in the year of NTT's privatization. Starting with ¥3 billion and 150 employees, it had become one of NTT's largest subsidiaries by the late 1980s. Originally established with the aim of providing consulting services related to the telecommunications industry and providing products to overseas buyers, NTTI was able to carry out a number of functions overseas that the NTT Corporation was unable to do because of Japanese regulations. Marketing NTT's products overseas and carrying out market research to see which products would be profitable were two important functions of NTTI. A third was to provide services related to the establishment of telecommunications infrastructures. An example of such work was a development project funded through NTTI by the World Bank in Indonesia. Australia was another country in which NTTI was active, helping to develop a facsimile mail service in 1987. In Finland, NTTI sold large numbers of hand-held computer terminals to a Finnish bank.

The Recruit Scandal: 1988

NTT's fluctuating fortunes since privatization tended to be reflected in the company's share price. In October 1986, the minister of finance invited tender for the initial price of NTT stock before flotation. The initial price decided on was ¥1.97 million. By February 9, 1987, NTT was listed on the Tokyo, Nagoya, and Osaka stock exchanges and was soon to be extended to other Japanese stock exchanges. After shares were floated, they reached a high of ¥3.18 million in 1987 but then collapsed to ¥1 million by the end of 1990. Another contributing factor to NTT's struggles during this time was the infamous "recruit scandal" that hit Japan in 1988, when a number of senior officials were accused of accepting bribes. Scandal hit NTT when its former chairman Hisashi Shinto received a heavy fine and a suspended jail sentence for his part in the illegal activities. The post of NTT chairman was left open until Haruo Yamaguchi was appointed to the post in the middle of 1990. Although NTT corporation law originally obliged the government to hold one-third or more of the total number of outstanding shares at all times and stated that "no foreign nationals or foreign judicial persons" were allowed to possess NTT shares, after some deliberation in October 1990 NTT announced a plan overturning this law. In December 1990, the Japanese government declared that it would start selling 500,000 shares a year beginning in April 1991. In 1992, foreign investors were allowed to purchase NTT stock for the first time.

Launching New Services: Late 1980s

Privatization also forced NTT to examine its operational efficiency and to provide better customer services. On May 23,

1988, NTT Data Communications Systems Corporations was established as a wholly owned subsidiary. Aimed at designing data communications that link hardware with software for financial institutions, private companies, and government organizations, NTT Data also provided training seminars and consultation facilities. It proved to be a profitable part of the NTT group. In 1990, operating revenues from NTT Data increased to ¥306.1 billion. One of NTT Data's major achievements was helping to set up the Tokyo International Financial Futures Exchange System in June 1989. Further recognition came to NTT Data when its IC Card, a card that allowed Nissan car owners to store car history information, won the 1989 Nikkei Annual Products Award. Another significant move was the introduction in April 1988 of INS-NET 64, described as the world's first wide-area commercial integrated services digital network (ISDN). NTT, KDD, and AT&T put together a three-day presentation simultaneously at sites in Japan and New York. Following this, NTT sponsored a global ISDN exhibition, NTT Collection '90. Approximately 40,000 visitors attended this exhibition that demonstrated the capability of ISDN and featured an actual ISDN link-up between NTT, AT&T, British Telecom, France Telecom, and Singapore Telecom.

In the area of international equipment procurement, NTT began to play a greater role. In accordance with the General Agreement on Tariffs and Trade (GATT), by 1990 orders had grown by nine percent to $352 million and included purchases as diverse as digital transmission equipment from AT&T, digital switching systems from Northern Telecom, and pocket bell pagers and cellular telephone equipment from Motorola. Procurement seminars were held at various European sites to encourage European suppliers, as well as in various cities in the United States.

By March 1989, NTT's performance was suffering because of increased competition from other common carriers, the cost of launching NTT Data, and the enforced reduction in long-distance telephone rates. In order to bring about recovery, NTT re-examined its administrative structure and in April 1989 reduced its four-tiered administrative structure to three levels. Another cost-cutting reform was the reduction in staff numbers. At its peak in 1979, NTT had 330,000 staff, but by 1989 the company had managed to reduce this number to 276,000. Not satisfied with this, however, there were further plans for greater reductions in staff.

In an interview with the *Financial Times* in January 1991, the president of NTT, Masashi Kojima, spoke of some of the problems NTT was facing. Enforced cuts in rates, because of increased competition from other carriers, and a scheme whereby competitors were connected to the network at a rate that reduced NTT's profitability, led to some resentment. President Kojima favored the introduction of a new kind of access charge or fee system to create a fairer market.

In terms of long-term international strategy, Kojima did not have ambitious plans for NTT to play a full international role but favored a specific international strategy that meant installing a network in a country with less developed telecommunication systems. In March 1991, however, discussions were under way for a joint venture between three of the most powerful telephone companies: NTT, the British telecommunications group, and the

German telecommunications group Deutsche Bundespost Telecom. This joint venture, called Pathfinder, offered a telecommunications network to large international companies. This presented NTT with the problem of operating internationally while still abiding with NTT corporation law. In an effort to exploit the potential of the European market as it moved towards greater unity, and the markets of Eastern Europe and the countries of the former Soviet Union as they become more accessible, NTT announced in June 1991 the establishment of a new subsidiary in Düsseldorf, Germany: NTT Deutschland GmbH.

In the early 1990s, NTT's plans centered on streamlining its operations in a cost-effective fashion and offering high-quality service to its customers. In an attempt to promote a fair and open market, NTT opened the Fair Competition Promotion Office in 1990. In the long term, NTT stressed the need to develop ISDN technology and to realize the importance of the cellular mobile market.

Indeed, the focus on ISDN and new broadband technologies, as well as mobile phone services, would prove to be cornerstones to NTT's growth strategy. Throughout the 1990s, NTT increased its research and development efforts related to cutting edge technologies. In 1992, it created subsidiary NTT Mobile Communications Network Inc.—now known as NTT DoCoMo—to oversee the sales of its mobile phones. By 1997, NTT controlled nearly half of Japan's cellular market, which was deregulated in 1994.

Deregulation Leads to Reorganization: Late 1990s and Beyond

During the late 1990s, Japan's telecommunications sector was changing rapidly. Foreign companies were allowed into the Asian market, which brought on a wave of increased competition. In December 1996, NTT lost its monopoly on local service. In return, however, the firm received approval to offer international services for the first time. By 1997, it had operating licenses in the United Kingdom, France, Germany, Hong Kong, and Singapore.

As deregulation knocked on NTT's door, company management struck a deal with the Japanese government to reorganize the company while at the same time keeping it largely intact. Reorganization plans were set in motion in 1997 and finalized two years later. NTT became a holding company for three major subsidiaries: NTT East Corp., NTT West Corp., and NTT Communications Corp. Its local phone operations were divided into NTT East and NTT West, while its long distance and international telecommunications operations became part of NTT Communications. As NTT management eyed the reorganization as a rebirth of sorts—an opportunity to make key strategic changes, cut costs, and revamp corporate culture—NTT's competitors viewed the new company just as it had the old one. In fact, a 1999 *Economist* article claimed that "as rivals see it, NTT continues to dominate local calls, long-distance, leased lines, cellular and data communications, just as it did before the break-up." The same article pointed out that NTT's reorganization in Japan was "nothing like the break-up of AT&T in America during the 1980s, nor the busting of most national telephone monopolies in the 1990s."

Even after its restructuring, NTT held on to nearly a 90 percent share of Japan's telecommunications market. By this time, its cellular subsidiary, NTT DoCoMo also controlled a 57 percent share of Japan's cellular market. Because of its long-standing control over Japan's infrastructure, Internet users in Japan paid an estimated five times more than Americans or Europeans for access. A July 1999 *Forbes* article claimed that a telephone line installation cost nearly 11 times more in Japan than in New York.

The Japanese government slowly put pressure on NTT to lower its prices. In late 1999, both NTT East and NTT West began offering flat-rate Internet service with an approximate monthly fee of $75. As Japan's Ministry of Public Management, Home Affairs, Posts, and Telecommunications became even more focused on increasing competition in Japan's information technology sector, NTT's close relationship with the government, which brought it many benefits, appeared to be diminishing.

As such, NTT entered the new century intent on maintaining its market share. In 2000, it made a $5.1 billion purchase of Verio Inc., a U.S.-based Internet solutions provider. Meanwhile, NTT DoCoMo had invested nearly $16 billion in global cellular companies that included AT&T Wireless and KPN Mobile in Europe. That plan backfired, however, when shares of many wireless firms in the United States and around the world began falling off. By October 2002, DoCoMo was forced to write off over $13 billion of its investments.

Overall, NTT was suffering due to Japanese deflation, increased competition, and a general slump in the information technology sector. During 2001, the company launched a three-year business plan aimed at restructuring its regional phone companies and shifting focus to integrated cellular and Internet services along with various broadband offerings, including an asymmetric digital subscriber line (ADSL). The company also nixed much of its spending related to its fixed lines and planned to cut back on capital spending by 15 percent through 2003.

In 2002, Norio Wada was named president of NTT. During that fiscal year, the company posted a $6.35 billion loss, the largest ever reported by a non-financial firm in Japan. The company claimed restructuring charges and investment losses were to blame, in addition to continued deterioration of the economy and falling personal consumption. NTT's new leader pledged to position the company favorably in order to benefit from changing demand and new technologies. As competition in the global telecommunications industry continued to heighten, NTT indeed faced a challenging future.

Principal Subsidiaries

Nippon Telegraph and Telephone East Corporation; Nippon Telegraph and Telephone West Corporation; NTT Communications Corporation; NTT DoCoMo Inc. (64.1%); NTT Data Corporation (54.2%).

Principal Competitors

AT&T Corp.; Japan Telecom Holdings Co. Ltd.; KDDI Corporation.

Further Reading

"Foreign Adventures; Japanese Telecoms," *The Economist U.S.*, May 11, 2002.

Fulford, Benjamin, "The Last Empire," *Forbes*, July 26, 1999, p. 51.

Guth, Robert A., "NTT Posts Loss of $6.35 Billion for Fiscal Year," *Wall Street Journal*, May 15, 2002, p. B6.

"Japanese Telecoms: Who Needs NTT?," *The Economist U.S.*, December 18, 1999, p. 115.

Kunii, Irene M., "NTT Com's Parent May Be Too Big," *Business Week*, July 17, 2000.

"Nippon Telegraph and Telephone," *The Economist U.S.*, July 3, 1999, p. 55.

"NTT Must Change in Accordance with Market," *AsiaPulse News*, June 28, 2002.

"There's No End to DoCoMo's Wireless Hangover," *Business Week*, October 14, 2002.

Think Global, Challenge Global (International Activities of NTT), Tokyo: Nippon Telegraph and Telephone Corp., 1990.

Wasserman, Elizabeth, "Clinton Approves NTT-Verio Deal," *Network World*, August 28, 2000.

Weinberg, Neil, "This Gorilla Wants to Dance," *Forbes*, September 22, 1997, p. 97.

Williams, Martyn, "U.S. Group Criticizes Japan's Telecom Deregulation Plans," *InfoWorld*, April 23, 2001, p. 75.

—Clare Doran
—update: Christina M. Stansell

Oregon Dental Service Health Plan, Inc.

601 Southwest Second Avenue
Portland, Oregon 97204
U.S.A.
Telephone: (503) 228-6554
Toll Free: (800) 852-5195
Fax: (503) 948-5557
Web site: http://www.odshealthplans.com

Private Company
Incorporated: 1955 as Oregon Dental Service
Employees: 800
Sales: $573 million (2001)
NAIC: 524114 Direct Health and Medical Insurance
Carriers; 524210 Insurance Agencies and Brokerages;
524292 Third Party Administration of Insurance and
Pension Funds

With offices in Portland, Milwaukie, and La Grande, Oregon, Oregon Dental Service Health Plan, Inc. (ODS Health Plan) is one of the few remaining insurance carriers based in and focused on providing service in Oregon. Founded in 1955 as Oregon Dental Service, ODS Health Plan works with more than 6,000 Oregon physicians and specialists and more than 1,800 dentists to provide a full range of medical and dental plans to more than 650,000 members. ODS Health Plan, Inc., a subsidiary of Oregon Dental Service, founded in 1985, provides traditional indemnity plans, managed care plans, preferred provider organization plans, and point of service plans. The company has three other subsidiaries—BestChoice Administrators, Inc., which provides third-party administrator coverage for self-insured businesses; Dental Benefits Insurance Company, a property and casualty insurance company serving the needs of dentists; and Dentists Management Corporation, which pioneered the development, marketing, and support of integrated dental practice management software and hardware.

A Statewide Nonprofit Branching Out: Mid-1950s Through 1989

The Oregon Dental Association, a dentists' trade association, founded Oregon Dental Service (ODS) in 1955 in response to a direct request by the Longshoreman's Union to provide dental care to union members' children. ODS, a nonprofit provider of group dental plans, one of the first dental insurers in the nation, from the start had a board of directors, half of whom were non-dentists appointed by the Oregon Dental Association. ODS prided itself on distinguishing its plan from other plans in two ways: Claims came directly to ODS from the dentist, whom ODS reimbursed, and the customer received a bill from ODS for any amount he or she owed after the deductible. The insurer began to grow significantly in 1972 when some schools in Portland picked up the plan and, in 1976, when state employees joined, giving the insurance company statewide standing. In 1974, Bud Lindstrand assumed the role of CEO of the company, a post he retained until 1998.

By the mid-1980s, ODS felt that it had exhausted the possibility of much new client growth in Oregon and turned its attention to expanding its services, diversifying into fee-for-service medical coverage in 1985 with the founding of Oregon Dental Service Health Plan, Inc. The company also launched three other subsidiaries. When Oregon dentists began to experience difficulty purchasing malpractice insurance, ODS founded a wholly owned for-profit subsidiary of Oregon Dental Service, which provided all classes of dental property, casualty, and liability insurance in 1985. Dental Benefits Insurance Company also began offering workers' compensation policies in 1990 when dentists and their employees began having difficulty getting workers' compensation policies written. BestChoice Administrators, Inc. started to provide third-party administrator coverage for self-insured businesses. Dentists Management Corporation, a for-profit company owned by Oregon Dental Association, pioneered the development, marketing, and support of integrated dental practice management software and hardware that tied into a mainframe at ODS.

ODS also faced significant challenges in response to changes in Oregon's health insurance market beginning in the second half of the 1980s. Competition between insurance companies turned fierce; at each bid for a new contract, ODS vied with 10 to 15 other companies, such as Blue Cross/Blue Shield, United Benefit, Aetna, and others. In addition, expensive medical technology, rising labor costs, an aging population, and a growing number of uninsured patients led insurance companies

Company Perspectives:

ODS Health Plans will be the premier carrier in the fields of dental and medical health insurance by focusing on its customers, the brokers who facilitate our ability to win business, the employers who buy our products, the insureds who use our products and services, and the health care professionals who provide these services. We will provide the highest value products supported by the best possible service. We will keep our promises, and meet all of the reasonable expectations of our customers.

to introduce double-digit premium hikes to compensate for the increased costs of doing business. As a result, employers began turning to managed healthcare plans, or health maintenance organizations, otherwise known as HMOs, to provide health and dental coverage for their employees.

The Second Largest Indemnity Plan in the State: Early 1990s

By the early 1990s, ODS contracted with close to 2,000, or 95 percent, of dentists in the state of Oregon. The second largest indemnity plan in the state—still one-eighth the size of Blue Cross/Blue Shield—it had 592,614 enrollees in its dental plan and 94,640 enrollees in its medical plan. ODS's dental business made up about 55 percent of its earned premiums and accounted for about 20 percent of all dental business in the state.

But trouble arose in 1991 when dentists, who were also members of a preferred provider organization (PPO) run by Dental Registry Inc. of Portland, resigned from that PPO after ODS reminded them of its policy that dentists who were part of ODS were not allowed to charge fees to other groups lower than those charged to ODS members. Although such a contract clause—called "most favored nation"—was common among insurers, sources at the time insisted that the impact of ODS's "Rule 3" was to thwart the formation of managed care dental products for dentists. The Willamette Dental Group, in association with Dental Registry Inc., filed an unsuccessful lawsuit against ODS, claiming that ODS had interfered with their ability to offer discounted fees to competing insurance plans. Although Willamette Dental lost its suit, it took its case to the Oregon Court of Appeals, and in 1994 the U.S. Department of Justice began investigating potential antitrust violations by ODS.

The year 1991 also saw the passage of new state law in Oregon, which required that all insurers offer a basic benefits package to small businesses—those with from 3 to 25 employees—at lower rates than traditional packages, that is, with limitations on premiums and exclusions. ODS began to offer small group health insurance in 1992, positioning itself well to capitalize on the mandate, which became mandatory for all small businesses in 1998.

Developments After the Institution of the Oregon Health Plan: Late 1990s

Another new law, adopted by the legislature in 1994, created the Oregon Health Plan, which spearheaded a shift within healthcare to HMO-style coverage in Oregon and expanded the

Medicaid market. In response to these changes, in 1993 ODS entered the managed care business, teaming up with Oregon Health Sciences University to launch head-to-head competition with Blue Cross/Blue Shield of Oregon. ODS and OHSU linked up with an estimated 2,500 physicians in all but two Oregon counties and forged a relationship with most of the hospitals outside the Portland metropolitan area. One of 22 applicants seeking contracts with the state, the joint venture initially went after the newly growing Medicaid business. It gave ODS an entrée with rural physicians who sought more Medicaid and private business.

The combined ODS businesses had 500,000 policyholders and revenues of $185.5 million in 1994, $101.5 million of which came from the company's dental plans. Although dropped by the state's Bargaining Units Benefits Board for 1994, the new HMO, ODS Health Plan, was added to the list of plans offered by the State Employees Benefits Board, giving it a shot at some of the $80 million worth of insurance purchased by the state in 1994.

At about this time, many on ODS's board began to lobby to get the Oregon Dental Association out of those businesses that it had developed, which they considered tangential to its mission. In 1995, top managers at ODS, led by Lindstrand, the company's CEO, offered to buy the ODS Health Plan, Inc. and the Association's three for-profit subsidiaries from the Oregon Dental Association. The offer, however, which was originally well received, created divisions among board membership of the $240 million company. It was rejected by board vote.

The following year, the company had outgrown its headquarters, and ODS began construction on a new $65 million building, the ODS tower, in downtown Portland. As the majority owner and occupant of the tower, which was completed in 1999, ODS leased 40 percent of the office space. Also in 1999, ODS opened a satellite office in LaGrande, Oregon when it could not find enough skilled workers to process its claims in Portland. More building was completed in 2001 when ODS opened the ODS Plaza in the converted Pendleton Woolen Mills shirt factory in Milwaukie, Oregon. This building housed offices for ODS Health Plan's claims, printing, and mailing divisions and for the company's BestChoice Administrators, Inc. and Dentists Management Corporation

Under the leadership of Robert Gootee, a longtime board member, who assumed the positions of president and chief executive of the company in 1998, ODS now faced the shortcomings of the Oregon Health Plan. According to a *Wall Street Journal* article published in 1999, many HMOs began to pull out of the plan shortly after it was inaugurated, finding that they could not make it work without a "sophisticated provider network and a critical mass of patients." In 1997, ODS Health Plans offered the state plan in 15 counties; by 1999, it offered it in only six, five of those in the more densely populated Willamette Valley in which Portland is located.

With solid dental membership of more than 600,000, health plan membership of about 200,000 in 2001, and total revenues of approximately $573 million, management under Gootee fixed its attention on expanding ODS's subsidiary businesses. Several of the company's subsidiaries experienced significant advances in 2001: BestChoice Administrators added 60 new

Key Dates:

1955: Oregon Dental Association founds Oregon Dental Service.
1972: Schools in Portland pick up ODS's dental insurance benefits.
1974: Bud Lindstrand becomes president and CEO of ODS.
1976: State employees begin to use the ODS dental plan.
1985: ODS Health Plan, Inc. is founded; Dental Benefits Insurance Company subsidiary begins operation.
1993: ODS begins a joint venture with Oregon Health Sciences University to offer HMO coverage.
1998: Robert Gootee becomes president and chief executive.
1999: ODS opens a satellite office in LaGrande and moves into new offices in the ODS Tower.
2000: ODS acquires additional office space in the old Pendleton Woolen Mills factory in Milwaukie.

accounts, including the Portland metro area's transportation provider, Tri-Met, and Rite Aid Corporation; it added these to a wide range of public and private sector clients. The sales arm of Dental Benefits Insurance Company, the leading malpractice dental insurer in Oregon, received certificates necessary to expand operations in Montana, Utah, and Arizona. Dentists Management Corporation added an online version of its software services.

Principal Subsidiaries

Health Services Group: ODS Health Plan, Inc.; BestChoice Administrators, Inc.; Dental Benefits Insurance Company; Dentists Benefits Corporation; Dentists Management Corporation.

Principal Competitors

Blue Cross/Blue Shield of Oregon; Foundation Health Plan; Greater Oregon Health Service Inc.; Kaiser Permanente; Pacific Health & Life Insurance Co.; PACC Health Plans Inc.; Pacificare of Oregon; Health Maintenance of Oregon Inc.; Qual-Med Oregon Health Plan; Sisters of Providence.

Further Reading

Brock, Kathy, "ODS, Blues Bidding for Slice of Medicaid," *Portland Business Journal,* May 24, 1993, p. 1.
——, "ODS Braces for Antitrust Probe," *Portland Business Journal,* July 15, 1994, p. 1.
Gauntt, Tom, "Tight Workers' Comp Field Spawns Insurance Venture," *Portland Business Journal,* September 10, 1990, p. 23.
Gordon, Britta, "ODS Dental Plan Casts Long Shadow Over Smaller Rivals," *Portland Business Journal,* October 12, 1992, p. 18.
Holbrook, Susan, "Oregon Dental Service Diversifying Services," *Portland Business Journal,* April 21, 1986, p. 22.
Jones, Steven D., "Oregon Prepares to Revise Its Struggling Health Plan," *Wall Street Journal,* April 28, 1999, p. NW1.
Robbins, Dawn, "They're Out of the Red, But Not in the Pink," *Portland Business Journal,* September 4, 1989, p. 1.
Woodward, Steve, "Open Wide," *Oregonian,* September 7, 1994, p. B16.

—Carrie Rothburd

Overhill Corporation

4800 Broadway, Suite A
Addison, Texas 75001
U.S.A.
Telephone: (972) 386-0101
Fax: (972) 386-8008

Public Company
Incorporated: 1963 as Kappa Networks, Inc.
Employees: 1,200
Sales: $162.2 million (2001)
Stock Exchanges: American
Ticker Symbol: OVH
NAIC: 514200 Packaged Frozen Foods

Overhill Corporation is a Dallas-area holding company in the process of focusing on its core food business, which accounts for nearly 80 percent of sales. Formerly known as Polyphase Corporation, the company in 2001 changed its name to Overhill, an allusion to its Overhill Farms subsidiary, which is a manufacturer of value-added quality frozen foods products. Its customers include major airlines, such as American, United, and Delta. Overhill Farms also produces frozen entrees for weight loss company Jenny Craig, as well as supplying major restaurant chains, including Carl's Jr., Denny's, Jack-in-the-Box, and Panda Express. The subsidiary's six manufacturing operations are located in southern California, with three each in the Los Angeles area and San Diego area. Overhill's other business segment is devoted to the forestry industry and conducted through Texas Timberjack, Inc. and its majority-owned subsidiaries. Struggling in recent years, the forestry segment is a distributor of industrial and logging equipment. It also invests in logging and sawmill ventures. Overhill expected to complete its transition by spinning off Overhill Farms, leaving the forestry business as the sole surviving operation. Overhill then expected to again change its name and sell off the company, thus freeing management to concentrate on the growing food business of Overhill Farms.

Corporate Lineage Dating Back to 1963

The corporate entity that would become Overhill was founded in 1963 as Kappa Networks, an electronics firm located in Rahway, New Jersey. Its founder was Stanley L. Pearl, who had served as chief engineer of Columbia Technical Corporation, manufacturer of delay lines. He also had gained experience with delay lines during his five years at ESC Electronics Corp. Striking out on his own, Pearl established Kappa to produce his own delay lines, which were important in synchronizing signals in electronics products. In the beginning Kappa sold delay lines to makers of television broadcast equipment, mostly the RCA Corporation. It also produced custom delay lines for use in aircraft control and communications systems, sonar systems, shipboard systems, military countermeasure devices, radar ranging, and guided missiles. In 1966 Kappa became involved in the design and manufacture of communications filters, for use in commercial as well as military applications. These frequency-selective filters permitted communications devices to accept frequencies that carried desired information while eliminating or attenuating other frequencies. Kappa sold its filter business to a former employee in 1973 and under terms of the deal was not allowed to engage in the business for four years. Kappa returned to the communications filter business from 1978 through 1980.

The rise of the personal computer industry in the early 1980s promised to enhance greatly the demand for Kappa's delay lines. Starting in 1981 the company began a concerted effort to tap into this market. After generating $1.7 million in revenues and a $34,000 profit in 1982, Kappa increased sales to $6.68 million in 1984 while earning nearly $325,000. Close to 80 percent of its delay lines were sold to the computer industry. Shortly after completing its fiscal year on September 30, 1984, Kappa drew on its resources to make a major acquisition, paying $4.5 million in cash and notes for Polyphase Instruments Company, located in Fort Washington, Pennsylvania. In business since 1956, Polyphase designed, manufactured, and marketed transformers and filters, primarily for the military. Kappa then went public in 1985 and began trading on the American Stock Exchange in March 1986. Later in the year, Kappa expanded further, acquiring the test equipment division of VIZ Manufacturing.

Losses and Reorganization in the 1980s and Early 1990s

The fortunes of Kappa peaked in the mid-1980s. In 1985 the company earned more than $600,000, followed in 1986 by record

---

Key Dates:

1963: Kappa Networks is incorporated.
1985: Polyphase Instrument Co. is acquired.
1991: The name is changed to Polyphase Corp.
1992: Paul Tanner and James Rudis are named directors.
1995: Overhill Farms subsidiary is formed to acquire IBM Foods.
1998: Rudis replaces Tanner as chairman and CEO.
2001: The company changes its name to Overhill Corporation.

---

revenues of $13.8 million. Business then soured for the rest of the 1980s, as revenues fell and losses increased—nearly $900,000 in 1987, more than $1 million in 1988, and close to $2.4 million in 1989. In July 1989 Pearl, nearing 70 years of age, stepped down as CEO in favor of Paul Stevens, who had joined the company earlier in the year to serve as the general manager of the Polyphase division. Stevens initiated a reorganizing effort to concentrate on Kappa's core business, which by now had become the Polyphase products. In January 1990 he closed down the struggling Kappa/Viz Test Equipment Division. Then in April 1990 he unloaded the Delay Line Division, which had been unprofitable in recent years, selling it to a former controlling shareholder group, including Pearl's son, Michael.

Because the primary business of the Kappa Networks corporation was now its Polyphase Instruments business, Stevens changed the name of the company to Polyphase Corporation in June 1991, and changed its state of incorporation from New Jersey to Pennsylvania. Although Polyphase returned to profitability in 1991, earning $1.64 million, the company was not well positioned for continued growth. Nearly 95 percent of its business was connected to equipment and systems used by the military. With the end of the Cold War, as well as a downturn in the economy, defense budgets were cut, resulting in a significant decrease in sales. After generating sales of $7.6 million in 1991, Polyphase saw its revenues fall to $5.56 million in 1992 while losing more than $800,000.

With its stock worth about 25 cents per share, Polyphase was in dire condition when it was approached by Dallas businessman Paul Tanner and his partner James Rudis, who were looking for a corporate shell to serve as an investment vehicle. They were attracted to Polyphase because of its Amex listing and depressed stock price. Tanner, a licensed Texas real estate broker, had been involved in a variety of businesses since the mid-1950s. A self-described "big picture" man, Tanner was a dealmaker uninterested in actually operating a company. Rudis, on the other hand, had a much broader business background, having spent 14 years working for CIT Financial Corporation. Although his primary responsibility with Tanner was to help target and complete acquisitions, he was fully capable of fulfilling operational responsibilities. The deal he structured for Polyphase was based on stock options. In essence, Tanner and Rudis offered a no-lose proposition to a desperate Polyphase: if their acquisition investments did not pan out, they would assume the financial risk and Polyphase would be no worse off. The two parties reached an agreement and in December 1992

both men were elected to the board of directors, with Tanner subsequently named chairman and chief executive officer. The headquarters of the company soon moved to Dallas.

Diversification in the Mid-1990s

Using Polyphase stock, Tanner and Rudis wasted little time in making acquisitions and branching out in a number of directions. On January 1, 1993 they bought Computer Systems Concepts, a Long Island City, New York company involved in the computer marketing, service, and networking business. Polyphase's nascent computer segment was then bolstered by the April 1993 acquisition of Network America, a Tulsa, Oklahoma assembler and retailer of computer hardware. In October 1993 Polyphase acquired Taylor-Built Industries, a Dallas automotive aftermarket products business, which was sold off in February 1995. Furthermore, in 1993, Polyphase acquired Dallas Parkway Properties, which owned the office building that housed the company's headquarters.

Polyphase continued to pick up a diversified mix of businesses in 1994. In March it added to its computer segment by acquiring the rights to Register-Mate, a point-of-sale software system. Later in the year the company added PC Repair of Florida, Inc., retailer of computer hardware and networks, followed by the acquisition of Micro Configurations, a Brooklyn, New York company involved in the assembly, sale, and service of computers as well as other electronics products. Furthermore, in 1994 Polyphase acquired Texas Timberjack, creating its forestry segment. Although Polyphase posted a $1 million loss in 1994, after earning more than $1 million in 1993, the company was growing rapidly, with revenues increasing from $7.3 million in 1993 to almost $25 million in 1994.

In 1995 Polyphase entered the food business, making its most significant acquisition. It formed a subsidiary named Overhill Farms to purchase IBM Foods, Inc., a Culver City, California food processor that generated four times as much sales volume as Polyphase had achieved in 1994. In addition, IBM Foods earned $7 million for the year. The purchase price was $31.3 million in cash, plus the assumption of debt. IBM Foods boasted strong enough cash flow, however, that it was expected to have an immediate positive effect on Polyphase's balance sheet. Boasting three state-of-the-art manufacturing plants and 750 employees, it already had steady customers in the airline and hotel industries, as well as the Jenny Craig operation. Because neither Tanner nor Rudis had experience in the food business, they turned to an old hand, Rod Stephens, to serve as president of Overhill Farms, as well as to look for further food acquisitions. The 70-year-old Stephens was the retired chairman and president of Armour Foods and had more than 40 years of experience in all aspects of the food industry. With sales for the new food group added to its transformer group, computer group, and forestry group, Polyphase experienced a dramatic increase in sales and earnings, posting more than $102 million revenues and almost $3.3 million in net profits.

Tanner, ever the ambitious dealmaker, initiated an ill-fated project in 1996 that ultimately led to his departure from Polyphase. He headed a private investment group, PLY Stadium Partners, to build an 85,000-seat indoor stadium to serve as a major sports, entertainment, and convention facility in Las Vegas, Nevada. Polyphase was enlisted to serve as the managing investor for the project, responsible for the design and construction of the stadium, as well as the sale of luxury suites and premium seating, event planning, and operations. With the exception of baseball, the $530 million facility was designed to accommodate any kind of event, with the hope of attracting NCAA, NFL, and NBA games, as well as music performers and trade shows. Unlike in most stadiums, luxury suites would be available for use 24 hours a day with catering. Moreover, the plan called for restaurants and stores, as well as a nongaming hotel with at least 500 rooms on the site. Because the stadium would require only 30 of the 62 acres of the land that PLY Stadium would purchase from Union Pacific Railroad, there was more than enough space for the hotel. It was certainly a daring plan, but financing of the project was dependent on the up-front sale of 300 luxury suites, with an average price of $1.5 million each. Although Tanner would maintain that some suites had been sold and that he was finalizing a wide range of future events for the stadium and talking to major hotel chains about a joint venture for the hotel, the start of construction was continually postponed. Polyphase also became embroiled with a lender over money Overhill Farms transferred to Polyphase accounts, a situation that led the American Stock Exchange to suspend trading of Polyphase stock after litigation prevented the company from making SEC filings. By the time Polyphase was allowed to resume trading, the stadium had lost what little momentum it had, and it began to slowly fade as a viable project.

In addition to becoming involved in stadium development in 1996, Polyphase began to ease out of the computer industry, selling off 51 percent of its interests in the segment. Although revenues for 1996 increased significantly, approaching $150 million, the company lost nearly $400,000. Polyphase suffered an even more disappointing year in 1997. Revenues grew by just one percent, while the company posted a $19.2 million loss, due in large part to the stadium project. In February 1998 Tanner resigned, replaced as chairman and CEO by Rudis, who began to refocus the company. Revenues fell to $141.4 million for fiscal 1998, but the company lost only $329,000. Much of the drop-off in sales was the result of the food group eliminating lower margin business. The following year, the segment rebounded, posting a 21 percent increase in revenues. Moreover, it landed two important new national accounts in Panda Express and Denny's, as well as extending its supply agreement with Jenny Craig. Polyphase's other business groups, however, did not offer as promising a future.

Food and Forestry at the Turn of the Century

In fiscal 1999 Polyphase sold off its Polyphase Instrument subsidiary, severing the company's ties to its past in electronics and leaving the holding company involved in two highly different businesses: food and forestry. The forestry group had proven to be inconsistent, susceptible to weather conditions and other factors that lowered the demand for its products and services. Clearly, Overhill Farms, which was now generating nearly 80 of the company's revenues, had become Polyphase's primary business. In September 2000 the subsidiary grew further by acquiring the operating assets and trademarks of the Chicago Brothers food business, in the process gaining the rights to two trademarked brands: ''Chicago Brothers'' and ''Florence Pasta and Cheese.''

In 2001 Polyphase decided to adopt the name of its subsidiary, becoming Overhill Corporation. Management believed that the move would strengthen the Overhill name with potential customers as well as the investment community. Later in the year the company announced a plan to spin off Overhill Farms, leaving Texas Timberjack as the sole business of Overhill Corporation. Once the spin-off was completed, Overhill Corporation would change its name again, and Rudis would resign to take over Overhill Farms. With the expected completion of these maneuvers in 2002, Overhill Farms would begin a new chapter as an independent food services company. Given Rudis's background and strength in acquisitions, it was likely that the business would begin to pursue an active program of external growth.

Principal Subsidiaries

Overhill Farms, Inc.; Texas Timberjack, Inc.

Principal Competitors

ConAgra, Inc.; Deere & Company; Tyson Foods, Inc.

Further Reading

Armstrong, Michael W., ''Polyphase Seeking to Cut Debt Through Registration,'' *Philadelphia Business Journal,* September 23, 1991, p. 14.

Bounds, Jeff, ''Vegas Stadium Project Still Not Off the Ground,'' *Dallas Business Journal,* June 6, 1997, p. 1.

''Stadium Company Returns to Stock Market,'' *Las Vegas Business Press,* June 23, 1997, p. 31.

Welch, David, ''Polyphase Buys Food Manufacturer,'' *Dallas Business Journal,* June 9, 1995, p. 4.

—Ed Dinger

Packaging Corporation of America

1900 West Field Court
Lake Forest, Illinois 60045
U.S.A.
Telephone: (847) 482-3000
Toll Free: (800) 456-4725
Fax: (847) 482-4738
Web site: http://www.packagingcorp.com

Public Company
Incorporated: 1959
Employees: 7,900
Sales: $1.7 billion (2001)
Stock Exchanges: New York
Ticker Symbol: PKG
NAIC: 322211 Corrugated and Solid Fiber Box
     Manufacturing

Packaging Corporation of America (PCA), once a subsidiary of Tenneco Inc., operates as the sixth largest manufacturer of containerboard and corrugated packing products in the United States. During 2001, PCA produced 2.1 million tons of containerboard and shipped 26.1 billion square feet of corrugated products. The firm has 65 facilities that produce corrugated products, including shipping containers, multicolored boxes and displays used in retail merchandising, and custom boxes used in both the food and agricultural industries. The company converts more than 80 percent of its containerboard into finished corrugated containers for its customers. PCA operated as Tenneco Packaging from 1995 to 1999. During 1999, the containerboard and corrugated packaging business was sold to Madison Dearborn Partners Inc. under the PCA name. During 2000, PCA went public on the New York Stock Exchange.

The Formation of PCA: 1959

PCA was formed in 1959 through the merger of three established packaging companies. Each of those companies, Central Fiber Products Company, American Box Board Company, and Ohio Boxboard Company, was already a major entity in the packaging industry by the time of the merger. Both Ohio Boxboard Company, of Rittman, Ohio, and American Box Board Company (originally called American Paper Box Company), located in Grand Rapids, Michigan, were founded in 1903. Each had enjoyed half a century of steady growth prior to the merger. Central Fiber Products Company, based in Quincy, Illinois, had itself been assembled through the consolidation of several smaller packaging firms. It was formed in 1931 upon the merger of North Star Mill, North Star Egg Case Company, Carey Straw Mill, H.T. Cherry Company, and Indiana Board and Filler Company.

By forming PCA, the merger instantly created a major force in the paperboard and packaging industry. The combined company brought together under one corporate umbrella a network of more than 50 plants and 7,000 employees, with facilities sprawling from the East Coast out to the Rockies. Within the first few years of PCA's existence, it was the sixth largest paperboard producer, the fourth largest maker of cartons or folding boxes, and the tenth largest manufacturer of corrugated containerboard in the United States. One of its facilities, a plant located in Rittman, Ohio, was the largest integrated carton factory in the world.

In the first years after the merger, PCA took steps to cut costs by eliminating redundant operations. Corporate airplanes and other unnecessary assets were sold off, and production was reallocated to take advantage of the company's most efficient facilities. Operations were organized into four divisions: Paperboard, Carton, Container, and Molded Pulp. For 1960 PCA had sales of $138 million. The following year, the company made a move toward self-reliance by purchasing a 52 percent interest in Tennessee River Pulp & Paper Co. Thereafter, Tennessee River provided PCA with most of the kraft linerboard it would need to supply its corrugated container plants. Also in 1961 PCA was listed on the New York Stock Exchange.

Throughout the early 1960s, PCA struggled to improve its profitability as sales remained flat and profits became more elusive, in large part due to depressed prices and stiff competition among container companies. The company was also impaired by a lengthy strike at its Rittman plant. Nevertheless, the company pressed forward with its expansion plans, and in 1962

Company Perspectives:

For over 100 years, we have earned our reputation as an industry leader with a commitment to service that is second to none. Creating the right packaging solution starts with a dynamic, customer-focused operating principal united with a wealth of resources, quality products, and outstanding people. At Packaging Corporation of America, that's precisely what we offer you. We build long-term relationships by doing what's right for our customers instead of what's easy for us. Our approach focuses on strategies that add value and support growth in your business. We maintain your trust by keeping the promises we make. Our commitment to service is supported by a wide range of quality products, a nationwide network of vertically-integrated resources and most importantly, employees who are dedicated to customers.

PCA acquired container plants in Baltimore, San Antonio, and the Dallas-Fort Worth area. In 1963 PCA president U.S. Goodspeed was elected vice-chairman of the company's board of directors. He was replaced as president by J.N. Andrews, who had joined Ohio Boxboard as a salesman in 1936. At the same time, W.D.P. Carey, PCA's chairman and its first president, was named chief executive officer.

Paperboard prices stabilized somewhat in 1964, and PCA was able to gain ground, posting its best earnings in nearly a decade. By this time, the company accounted for about 3 percent of all the paperboard produced in the United States. Of its $145 million in sales that year, 45 percent came from corrugated and solid fiber containers, 24 percent from folding cartons, 22 percent from paperboard mill products, and the rest from molded pulp and molded plastic products. Nearly three-fourths of PCA's paperboard output was converted into containers. The rest was sold to other companies for use in their manufacturing operations.

Becoming a Subsidiary of Tenneco: 1965

In 1965 PCA was acquired in a stock deal by Tennessee Gas Transmission Corporation, now known as Tenneco Inc. As a subsidiary of Tenneco, PCA continued to expand throughout the 1960s. By 1970 the company was operating 55 U.S. facilities. That year, PCA gained full ownership of Tennessee River Pulp & Paper by buying out the interest formerly held by partners Bell Fibre Products, St. Regis Paper Co., and Tennessee River's former president, G.W.E. Nicholson. The purchase gave PCA full access to Tennessee River's cutting rights on 300,000 acres of timberland in Tennessee, Alabama, and Mississippi. PCA also opened its 34th corrugated container plant, located in Burlington, Wisconsin, that year.

By 1972 PCA had annual revenues of $286 million, which represented about 9 percent of Tenneco's total. In early 1973, the company announced that it would begin a $40 million expansion program to boost capacity at its existing paperboard and container plant facilities. The bulk of the spending was to take place at Tennessee River's Counce mill in Counce, Tennessee. Later that year, S.F. Allison, PCA's president and chief

executive officer, announced a reorganization of both the company's product line divisions and its management structure. The number of divisions within the company was reduced from four to the following three: the containerboard products division, including the container plants and the company's Filer City, Michigan, containerboard mill; the paperboard products division, including its carton plants and five paperboard mills; and the general products division, newly formed to include the company's plastics and molded products operations as well as facilities involved in the production of storage units. Each division was led by a senior vice-president reporting to Allison.

The entire boxboard container industry was rocked in 1976 when a federal grand jury indicted 23 companies and 50 of their executives for price-fixing between 1960 and 1974. PCA was one of the companies found to be in violation of antitrust laws. George V. Bayly, senior vice-president of PCA's general products division, and J.A. Neuman, one of the company's plant managers, were among the group of executives to plead no contest and receive short jail terms and fines. Most of the corporations involved, including PCA, also received fines in the case, which was one of the largest of its kind at that time.

Expansion Through Acquisition: 1983 Through the Mid-1990s

From 1983 into the mid-1990s PCA made sizable acquisitions each year, transforming itself into a true powerhouse in the container industry. In 1983 PCA acquired much of Diamond International Corporation's molded fiber products operation. The purchase included both domestic and foreign properties, including plants in Red Bluff, California, and Plattsburgh, New York; a Portland, Maine research and development facility; an idle Ohio factory; Omni-Pac of West Germany; and Hartmann Fibre, a British firm.

The following year, PCA bought Ekco Products Inc., a manufacturer of aluminum and plastic products, many of them for kitchen use. Based in Wheeling, Illinois, Ekco had facilities in New Jersey, California, England, Denmark, Belgium, and Japan. The Ekco purchase, according to PCA president and CEO Monte R. Haymon, enabled the company to fill out its product line with a greater number of specialized items. In 1985 PCA purchased A&E Plastics, a major producer of rigid plastic containers for use in the foodservice industry. The following year PCA formed a new division, the PCA Disposable Packaging Group, as an umbrella for the newly added Ekco and A&E operations.

PCA continued to make the kitchen its favorite room over the next few years. In 1986 the company acquired EZPor Corporation, a company specializing in convenience cookware and disposable baking pans for the retail market. In 1987 PCA acquired Kaiser Packaging, the foodservice foil and foil container operation of Kaiser Aluminum & Chemical Corporation. That acquisition brought with it a manufacturing plant in Wanatah, Indiana; equipment and other assets from a plant in Permanente, California; and a specialty operation in Bensenville, Illinois. More aluminum operations were brought into the fold in 1988. That year, PCA acquired the Ekco Group, Inc.'s Canadian aluminum foil and plastic foodservice container unit, and subsequently renamed it PCA Canada, Inc. The company also bought Revere Foil Containers, Inc., a manufacturer of

Key Dates:

1959: PCA is formed from the merger of Central Fiber Products Company, American Box Board Company, and Ohio Boxboard Company.

1961: The company lists on the New York Stock Exchange.

1965: Tennessee Gas Transmission Corporation—whose name is later changed to Tenneco Inc.—acquires PCA.

1970: PCA gains full ownership of Tennessee River Pulp & Paper Co.

1976: The firm is found guilty of violating antitrust laws by a federal grand jury.

1984: Ekco Products Inc. is purchased.

1991: PCA acquires certain holdings of the Georgia-Pacific firm.

1995: The company changes its name to Tenneco Packaging.

1999: Tenneco Packaging sells its containerboard and corrugated packaging business to Madison Dearborn Partners Inc.; the new firm adopts the name Packaging Corporation of America.

2000: PCA goes public.

aluminum foil containers and clear plastic domes. Middleton Packaging also was purchased that year. Middleton's specialty was molded fiber filler flats for egg packaging. With the addition of these operations, PCA's annual revenue reached $1.3 billion for the year.

In 1989 PCA acquired Carenes, SA, a Spanish molded fiber operation, and Dahlonega Equipment and Supply Company, an East Coast supplier of egg, produce, and seafood packaging. Carenes was renamed Omni-Pac Embalajes, SA, and Dahlonega's name was shortened to Dahlonega Packaging. Among the company's 1990 additions were Polbeth Packaging Limited, a Scottish foodservice thermoformed container firm, and Alupak, A.G., a Swiss company whose products included sterilizable smoothwall aluminum containers. PCA also purchased two important U.S. companies: Pressware International, which was the largest manufacturer of pressed paperboard food containers in the United States, and Dixie Container Corporation, which was the biggest independent corrugated company in the Southeast, producing recycled corrugating medium.

In 1991 PCA made its largest acquisition to date, assuming the operation of 19 corrugated container plants and two containerboard mills and acquiring the cutting rights to about 650,000 acres of timberland from Georgia-Pacific. Some of these properties were purchased outright, and others were operated through lease arrangements. Another 1991 acquisition, the Ellington Recycling Center, supplied secondary fiber to PCA's Counce linerboard mill. In 1992 the company launched a joint venture in partnership with a Hungarian state-owned packaging company. The newly created firm, PCA-Budafok Paperboard Ltd., was formed to operate a recycled paperboard mill and a folding carton plant outside Budapest.

During 1993 PCA focused on improving productivity rather than continuing to expand, returning a profit of $139 million despite a slight drop in revenues. Over the course of the year, 32 new products were introduced by PCA's Domestic Aluminum and Plastics Packaging Group; at the same time, the company's Molded Fibre unit was merged into this group to form a new division called Specialty Packaging.

In 1994 PCA continued to expand both internally and through international development under President Paul Stecko. Plans were announced late in the year for a $73 million project to upgrade the company's Counce, Tennessee, linerboard mill. The project would enable the mill to produce grades of linerboard that were lighter but stronger than had previously been possible. In Europe, the company increased its ownership in the Budapest mill from 30 to 100 percent. The company also began construction of a folding carton plant in Bucharest. That facility, a 50–50 joint venture with a Romanian company, was to operate using paperboard supplied by the Hungarian plant. Negotiations also were under way during 1994 for a joint venture in China.

A Period of Change: Mid-1990s and Beyond

The mid- to late 1990s proved to be a period of change for PCA. The company adopted the name Tenneco Packaging Inc. in 1995 and continued with its expansion efforts under its new name. During the year, the firm acquired Lux Packaging, DeLine Box & Display, the United Group, and a Menasha Corp. facility. Each purchase offered Tenneco a foothold in the graphics segment of the corrugated packaging products market. The company also acquired three corrugated packaging sheet plant operations.

Tenneco Packaging spent the next several years restructuring internally. It launched its "cost of quality" program that cut $80 million in costs related to its mill operations as well as $30 million in converting costs from 1997 to 1999. Meanwhile, parent company Tenneco Inc. had launched similar efforts designed to reposition both its automotive and packaging holdings. During 1999, Tenneco Inc. announced that it would sell its containerboard business to private equity firm Madison Dearborn Partners Inc. (MDP). Meanwhile, Tenneco Packaging's other paperboard businesses were spun off into a new company called Pactiv Corporation. According to an April 1999 *Pulp & Paper* article, the $2.2 billion deal "surprised and captivated various U.S. board industry executives" who believed Georgia-Pacific would gain control of the containerboard business.

Nevertheless, Tenneco Inc. chose MDP as its buyout partner. The purchase was completed in 1999 and included the operations of Tenneco Packaging's four containerboard mills and 67 converting plants. The deal also marked the rebirth of the PCA name, which was adopted for the new company, and the return of Paul Stecko, who was named PCA's chairman and CEO. Stecko had been named chief operating officer of Tenneco Inc. in 1997, and then president the following year. After the MDP deal, he left his post at Tenneco to take over PCA operations. PCA entered the public arena in January 2000 when it listed on the New York Stock Exchange. The following year it acquired Sunbelt Packaging Services Inc. in a deal that strengthened the firm's reach in both Arizona and along the Mexican border.

While PCA entered the new millennium on solid ground, the paper industry as a whole began to suffer. According to the company, industry corrugated shipments in the United States fell by 5.8 percent during 2001—the largest year-over-year decline since 1975. The drop was due in part to the weakening U.S. economy and the strong dollar, which caused demand to fall for U.S. corrugated products. During this time, however, the containerboard segment of the industry remained a lucrative niche. With 96 percent of sales stemming from this product line, PCA benefited from this trend. Both sales and net income fell during 2001 as a result of industry conditions, but management felt that PCA was positioned better than its competitors, whose earnings fell from 28 to 80 percent during the year. The company's focus for the future continued to revolve around securing positive earnings, maintaining strong cash flow, outperforming the industry, and creating overall shareholder value.

Principal Divisions

Containerboard; Shipping Containers; Retail Packaging and Displays; Heavy Duty Packaging; Produce Packaging; Printing Capabilities; Special Packaging; National Account Sales; Graphic Sales; PCA Supply Services; Design Services; Technical Services; Value Improvement; E-Business.

Principal Competitors

Georgia-Pacific Corporation; Smurfit-Stone Container Corporation; Temple-Inland Inc.

Further Reading

"Come-Back for Packager," *Financial World,* September 16, 1964, p. 7.

Facts About Packaging Corporation of America, Evanston, Ill.: Packaging Corporation of America, 1994.

Fales, Gregg, "PCA Offers IPO on NYSE," *PIMA's North American Papermaker,* March 2000, p. 9.

"Packaging Corp. Unfolds a Recovery in Earnings," *Barron's,* March 23, 1964, p. 36.

"PCA Buys Sunbelt Packaging," *Paperboard Packaging,* July 2001, p. 16.

"PCA Is Returning as Stand-Alone Company," *PIMA's North American Papermaker,* March 1999, p. 10.

"PCA Realigns Mgmt. and Product Line Functions," *Paper Trade Journal,* September 17, 1973, p. 32.

Rolland, Louis J., "Packaging by 'PKG'," *Financial World,* April 18, 1962, p. 24.

Shutovich, Christina A., "Tenneco Splits Divisions into Two Stand-Alone Companies," *Aftermarket Business,* July 1999, p. 12.

Solomon, Caleb, "Tenneco Packaging Subsidiary Weighs Making Acquisitions As Big As $1 Billion," *Wall Street Journal,* October 11, 1994, p. B10.

"Tenneco Spins Off Packaging Assets," *Pulp & Paper,* April 1999, p. 23.

"Tennessee Gas Plans to Acquire Packaging Corp.," *Wall Street Journal,* March 29, 1965, p. 26.

Thompson, Morris S., "Aides of Box-Making Concerns Sentenced to Prison, Fined in Price-Fixing Case," *Wall Street Journal,* December 1, 1976, p. 4.

Willoughby, Jack, "Origami: Unfolding the Packaging Corp. IPO," *Barron's,* October 18, 1999, p. 44.

—Robert R. Jacobson
—update: Christina Stansell

Peace Arch Entertainment Group Inc.

56 East 2nd Avenue, Suite 500
Vancouver, British Columbia V5T 1B1
Canada
Telephone: (604) 681-9308
Toll Free: (800) 843-3658
Fax: (604) 681-3299
Web site: http://www.peacearch.com

Public Company
Incorporated: 1981 as Medco Productions Inc.
Employees: 24
Sales: $35.7 million (2001)
Stock Exchanges: Toronto American
Ticker Symbol: PAE
NAIC: 512110 Motion Picture and Video Production

Peace Arch Entertainment Group Inc. is one of Canada's top entertainment companies, developing, financing, and distributing television programming and feature films for worldwide markets. The Vancouver, British Columbia, company also offers production services on a contract basis to Hollywood producers who in recent years have been attracted to Canada because of the exchange range and tax benefits. Because of its diverse geography, temperate climate, and West Coast proximity, Vancouver has become North America's third largest film and television production center, and Peace Arch has grown apace. Its productions have been sold to, or co-produced with, such notable companies as Disney, MGM, Showtime, Hallmark, The Family Channel, and The Learning Channel. In addition, Peace Arch subsidiary The Eyes Multimedia Productions Inc. creates training videos as well as other materials for corporate clients in a variety of formats, including CD-Rom, web-cast streaming media, and narrowcast media for internal electronic distribution. Another subsidiary, StreamScapes Media, is an Internet-based business-to-business operation that provides multimedia and video streaming services and products to industry, government, and entertainment organizations.

Early 1980s Origins

The founder of Peace Arch Entertainment Group, Timothy Gamble, grew up in the Toronto area. Although always interested in pursuing a business career and harboring a secret desire to become involved in the production of television shows and films, he listened to the advice of his mother, a teacher, and studied both Education and Economics at the University of British Columbia in Vancouver. He paid his way through college by giving tennis lessons and by the less glamorous work of "setting chokers" in the forests of the Pacific Northwest, a backbreaking task that required a massive log to be looped by a cable in order to be hauled out to a landing area. Upon graduation from college in 1980 Gamble began to work as a substitute teacher in Vancouver, but a trip to Rio de Janeiro would soon prove pivotal to his entry into the entertainment business. He visited the city because an older brother, Mark, an engineer, was working there for Westinghouse building nuclear power plants. Noting that Westinghouse was now saving money by shipping videos to demonstrate the installation of specialized parts, rather than flying in a trained engineer, Mark suggested that his younger brother consider entering the video business.

Upon returning home, Gamble checked the Vancouver phone book and found there were few video production operations to provide much competition. Never having used a video camera in his life, he turned to a friend named Reg Worthington, a musician whose day job was driving a bus, to help launch the new business. In 1981, with nothing more than an intention, possessing no equipment and no skills, they searched for their first customer. Hoping that an excursion company might be in the market for videos of their vacation destinations, they picked the name of a likely candidate out of the phone book, Silver Wings Holiday, and cold-called owner Wellington Lee to pitch him the idea. Lee was won over and asked the two young men to fly with a group to Reno, Nevada, two days later and start shooting the promotional piece. To raise $50,000 for the necessary video production equipment, Gamble had to mortgage his home, an act that would be repeated more than once in the years to come. Barely familiar with how to operate the equipment, the partners went to work as soon as the Silver Wings group touched down in Reno. Disaster struck immediately. One of the telescopic legs of the tripod was improperly secured and collapsed from the weight of the camera, which was then damaged by the fall and now inoperable. Gamble, revealing an instinct that would serve him well in the film industry, told his partner to set up the camera again and just pretend to be shooting. It was not until the next day, after finding an electronics engineer at the University of Nevada to repair the camera, that the partners actually began to videotape the excursion.

With a successful assignment completed, Gamble and Worthington were joined by a pair of cousins, Craig Sawchuk and Murray Duncan, who were also teachers. The business was named Medco Productions Inc., the result of fusing the words "marketing" and "educational" to emphasize the two major purposes of their service, to produce either promotional or training videos. After generating just $20,000 in sales the first year, Medco over the course of the next two years began to build up a base of local industry customers. But when the North American economy began to falter, resulting in escalating interest rates, corporations were forced to trim expenses, and video work was an easy budget item to cut. Several of Medco's clients canceled projects, forcing the video partners to take a hard look at the future. Rather than simply make videos for clients on a for-hire basis, they decided to become involved in projects in which the client turned into a partner and Medco would have a stake in the final product. They applied these ideas in the summer of 1983, spending around $45,000 to produce a 40-minute video and booklet about a subject they knew well. It was called *Home Video: Shoot Like a Pro.* Once again Gamble displayed boldness, this time cold-calling Eli Stern, president of Sony Corporation's American operation, who was won over by the young Canadian and invited him to New York for a meeting. Gamble was promptly sent to see the head of the Betamax merchandising unit in New Jersey, and while he waited six hours for his meeting managed to charm the man's secretary into helping him put together a proposal and type it into final form. As a result Medco landed a deal with Sony for 3,000 tapes, one for each of its North American dealers. The $21,000 profit on the transaction was welcomed, but it was Craig Sawchuk who provided the sweetener, convincing Sony to package their cameras with a card offering a discount on *Shoot Like a Pro.* The video went on to sell more than 100,000 copies.

Going Public in 1985

Medco changed its name in 1985 to Vidatron Entertainment Group and went public on the Vancouver Stock Exchange, the result of merging the business with a Seattle porcelain-enamel factory owned by a Vancouver promoter. It was an unlikely pairing that would last just two years, at which point both ventures split off and once again went private. The interlude did, however, grant Vidatron the distinction of being the first publicly traded

multimedia company of its kind. In the meantime, Vidatron broadened its scope to include a wide range of products, from corporate training programs and consumer instructional videos to television documentaries and commercials. The company also delved into feature films when it acquired Northern Lights Media, which already had a project under way. The resulting movie, released in 1988, was titled *The Outside Chance of Maximilian Glick,* pleasant family fare that won Best Picture honors at the Toronto Film Festival and the Miami Film Festival. It received limited distribution, however, and did little to forward Vidatron's ambitions in feature films. The terms of the Northern Lights acquisition proved to have a much greater impact than the lack of success of its film, saddling the company with the debt of an original investor. It was during this period that the current chairman of the board of Peace Arch, W.D. Cameron White, became involved with the company, initially helping in 1987 to raise more capital through a secondary public offering, at a time when the Vancouver exchange was booming. The New York stock market crash in October of that year, however, soured all of the North American markets, and when Vidatron's offering was made in January 1988 a smaller crash occurred, resulting in a major disappointment. Only $500,000 was raised for the company.

Undeterred by its introduction to film making, Vidatron soon developed its own project with actor Martin Sheen, backed by the International Movie Group. The co-production, *Cadence,* a film set in an Army prison, was released in 1991. Reviews were mixed, the film only noteworthy because Sheen appeared on screen with sons Charlie Sheen and Ramon Estevez. Strapped for cash after *Cadence,* Vidatron shied away from features for the next few years. In February 1992 the company increased the number of common shares, diluting the stake of the original investors, and in the process changed its name to The Vidatron Group Inc. Money became so tight in the early 1990s that the company's landlord locked them out of their offices. Gamble then traded company stock to receive half-equity in a Yaletown building to set up a new headquarters. Unlike so many transactions of the company during this period the real estate deal panned out. Others strained the company's resources to the breaking point. In 1995 Vidatron acquired Media Services, a major Canadian distributor of educational videos, CD-ROMs, and software, but the business proved too specialized and Vidatron eventually unloaded it. The 1996 purchase of Pilot Software, an educational software distributor, met the same fate. A TV commercial subsidiary, Hot Shots, simply folded.

Vidatron also experienced its share of successes. In 1993 it released *Heartsake,* an informational video about recovering from a heart attack, narrated by Martin Sheen. It was backed by drugmaker Merck Frosst Inc. Vidatron developed other joint venture projects with deep-pocket sponsors, including *ElectroJuice,* an electrical safety video backed by utility B.C. Hydro. The acquisition of film, video, and TV programmer The Eyes Multimedia Productions also proved to be a fruitful acquisition, which resulted in the formation of the Toolshed division, successful producers of music videos.

Acquiring Sugar Entertainment in 1996

As Vidatron struggled through the mid-1990s, three of its original four partners departed. Only Gamble remained, serving

Key Dates:

1981: Medco Productions is formed.
1985: Medco becomes Vidatron and goes public.
1987: Northern Lights Media is acquired.
1996: Sugar Entertainment is acquired.
1999: The company's name is changed to Peace Arch Entertainment Group.
2001: Juliet Jones is named CEO.

as president, with Cam White now the chief executive officer of the company. Both men agreed as early as 1994 about their goal for Vidatron: to become Western Canada's answer to the fully integrated film and television companies of Eastern Canada— Alliance Communications, Atlantis Communications, and Cinar Films. It was not until two years later, however, that they identified a realistic opportunity to make that dream a reality: the acquisition of Sugar Entertainment, the production company of 25-year Hollywood veteran Larry Sugar. A lawyer by training, Sugar worked for Warner Brothers, 20th Century-Fox, and Lorimar International, among other Los Angeles operations. He formed Sugar Entertainment and produced several films before moving to Vancouver in early 1995 to film programming for Showtime. When his marriage ended he decided to stay in Canada, ultimately gaining Landed Immigrant status and becoming a domestic producer, entitled to tax and funding inducements of the federal and provincial governments. At first Gamble and White signed Sugar as a major tenant in a former restaurant supply warehouse they were interested in converting into a production studio. They then arranged for Vidatron to distribute Sugar's films, and finally asked him to become a partner. Because he was new to the area and saw the advantages of having local partners, Sugar in September 1996 sold his production company for 20 percent of Vidatron and $260,000 in cash, becoming president of Vidatron's entertainment division.

In 1997 Vidatron changed its name to Vidatron Entertainment Group, Inc. and raised $6 million in equity financing as well as arranged a $10 million revolving bank line of credit to support its rapidly expanding slate of projects, most of which were due to Sugar's industry connections. Revenues in 1997 grew fivefold over the previous year to $24 million (Canadian). Among the company's projects in the late 1990s were "First Wave," a science fiction television series and "Dead Man's Gun," a Western series. Vidatron's stock began to trade on the Toronto Stock Exchange in 1998, and a year later was listed on the American Stock Exchange. Also in 1999 Vidatron changed its name to Peace Arch Entertainment Group Inc., alluding to the Peace Arch monument that separates Washington State and British Columbia and symbolizes the good relations and cooperative spirit between the United States and Canada. Because the company was working increasingly with Hollywood as well as expanding its international activities the new name was

fitting. Moreover, any lingering confusion with LeGroupe Videtron, a major Quebec cable company, was removed.

In 1999 Peace Arch posted revenues of $51.5 million, a significant improvement over the previous year's $32.5 million, and the third consecutive year of impressive growth. StreamScapes Media was launched in 1999, marking the company's entry into cyber-based products. Of more importance was Peace Arch's expanding slate of television programming. In 2000 "First Wave" entered its third season and "The Immortal" was introduced, as was sitcom "Big Sound." Also in 2000 Peace Arch joined Hallmark Entertainment and Paxson Communications to produce and distribute three new "Christy" movies, based on the exploits of a teacher new to an Appalachian community, circa 1912.

Despite these positive developments, Peace Arch developed funding problems. A lack of financing resulted in the cancellation of "Big Sound." The company also failed to meet certain performance markers in a loan agreement and was forced to fashion a forbearance agreement with its lenders. The company even retained an investment bank in May 2001 to explore its strategic alternatives, although management insisted that there were no plans to sell Peace Arch. Moreover, according to the *Vancouver Sun* in an October 19, 2001 article, "The relationship between Sugar and Peace Arch founder and president Tim Gamble appears to have soured. Last winter Sugar founded a new production company."

Peace Arch underwent a change in management in 2001. In the spring Juliet Jones, who had been with the company for nine years and served as chief financial officer since 1996, replace White as CEO, although he stayed on as chairman of the board. Gamble remained president but by the end of the year, in which revenues fell to $35.7 million and the company lost $9.2 million, he resigned and Jones assumed that position as well.

Principal Subsidiaries

The Eyes Multimedia Productions Inc.; StreamScapes Media.

Principal Competitors

Alliance Atlantis Communications; CanWest Global Communications.

Further Reading

Cecil, Mark, "Peace Arch Doesn't Want to Entertain a Sale," *Mergers & Acquisitions,* May 14, 2001, p. 1.

Grescoe, Paul, "The Entertainer," *BC Business,* July 1998, p. 82.

"Peace Arch Announces Appointment of Juliet Jones as Chief Executive Officer," *123Jump,* April 27, 2001.

Schreiner, John, " 'Heartsafe' Video a Real Risk for Gamble," *Financial Post,* January 16, 1993, p. 15.

"W.D. White—Peace Arch Entertainment," *Wall Street Transcript,* May 1, 2000.

—Ed Dinger

Perstorp AB

SE-284 80
Perstorp
Sweden
Telephone: (46) 435 380 00
Fax: (46) 435 381 00
Web site: http://www.perstorp.com

Private Company
Incorporated: 1881 as Stensmölla Kemiska Tekniska
    Industri
Employees: 2,561
Sales: SKr 3.37 billion ($319.6 million) (2001)
NAIC: 325211 Plastics Material and Resin Manufactur-
    ing; 325131 Inorganic Dye and Pigment Manufacturing;
    325188 All Other Inorganic Chemical Manufacturing

Perstorp AB operates as a specialty chemicals group focusing on polyalcohols, which are used in the production of resins for the coatings industry. Perstorp was acquired by Sydsvenska Kemi AB in 2001. Its operations were merged with Neste Oxo, and in 2002 the entire group reorganized under the Perstorp name. The company operates five divisions: Perstorp Performance Chemicals; Perstorp Coating Intermediates; Perstorp Oxo Intermediates; Perstorp Engineering Materials; and Perstorp Formox. The firm has manufacturing operations in Europe, North America, and Asia. Sydsvenska Kemi is controlled by private investment firm Industri Kapital.

At a small mill on the edge of a beechwood forest in the southern tip of Sweden, Wilhelm Wendt founded Perstorp AB in 1881. Stensmölla Kemiska Tekniska Industri, as it was originally called, was initially dedicated to product development and refinement of its only source of raw materials, the beechwood forest. Today the company is no longer dependent upon wood products; however, it still produces much of its original product line begun over a century ago.

Production of Acetic Acid Begins: 1884

Originally, charcoal was the only commercial product at the Stensmölla Kemiska Tekniska Industri. However, after he had established his own company, Wendt, an engineer, built a purification plant to separate useful products from waste in the fene gases captured during the carbonizing process to produce acetic acid and wood alcohol. The production of acetic acid began in 1884.

Wilhelm convinced skeptical Swedish housewives that this new acetic acid vinegar made from beechwood was better than the alcohol-base vinegar that they had used and trusted for years. The new stock lasted longer, tasted better, was less expensive, and stayed fresh longer than its competitor. The acetic acid won many prizes at exhibitions in Chicago, Lubeck, Copenhagen, and Göteberg. When combined with a winning advertising campaign, this helped Wendt to achieve the first commercial success at his new company.

By 1888, the company grew to employ 16 people in the production of charcoal and acetic acid. During this time, Wendt also shortened the company's name to Skånska Ättiksfabriken. Due to the fact that he did not always have access to the raw materials he needed, Wendt decided that he would have to maximize the refining process to make the company profitable. In 1898, therefore, he built a refinery to separate wood alcohol into pure methanol, chemical acetin, and woodnaphta denaturating methanol.

Financial Difficulties: Early 1900s

From 1900 to 1904, the company was confronted with financial problems. In order to overcome these problems, Wendt constantly reinvested all of the liquid assets back into the company. In 1904, Wendt built a new plant to produce cresote, carbinoleum, and pitch from pine tar, as well as perform other carbonization processes. During the Russo-Japanese War, cresote was issued to Japanese soldiers to prevent dysentery. Wendt sold all of the cresote his company could manufacture to Japan. In 1905, Wendt built a new factory designed to convert methanol to formalin. Formalin, or formaldehyde, was first sold as a disinfectant.

Between the years 1907 and 1914, the company barely met operating costs. Despite the company's dismal financial outlook and Sweden's continuing economic crisis, Wendt continued to heavily fund his product development experiments. At the start of World War I in 1914, however, acetic acid sales were so optimis-

---

Company Perspectives:

It is our objective that Perstorp AB will be a globally oriented specialty chemicals company.

---

tic that Wendt built a glass factory to produce the bottles for the acid. Sales in the new glassworks were supplemented by the production of commercial lighting glass for export to England.

As World War I continued, Wendt realized that he could capitalize on Germany's inability to export products. He began producing acetyl acid, which had previously been imported from Germany. The company's pharmaceutical factory, begun in 1905, expanded its product line to include urotropine, or hexamethylenetetramine, which during those days was considered effective against polio and other diseases.

During this time the sawmill became an integral part of the company's raw materials production. The timber from the mill was now distributed so that the best pieces would go to the newly established furniture factory. Lesser pieces would go to the packaging plant for acetic acid bottles, while others were used to produce butter churns, which had been a product at the mill since Wilhelm Wendt's father started the mill. The worst pieces would be used to fire the burners in the mill.

Developing Isolit: 1910s–20s

During the war years, Wendt employed a well-educated Indian chemist named Das Gupta in the company's pharmaceutical laboratory. Das Gupta's job was to develop a new pharmaceutical product that would compete with the German manufacturers after the war was over. He discovered, after many experiments, a substitute shellac with excellent insulating properties named ''indolac.'' Das Gupta then took the indolac, mixed it with pitch and tar, and created a plastic, or Isolit, as it was called at Skånska Ättiksfabriken. The new raw material was the Swedish version of the German bakelite, which had been on the market for years and was protected by a large number of patents. Fortunately for the company, the Germans decided not to take the matter to court.

In 1917, Skånska began manufacturing its first plastic product, a handle for electrical knife switches. The first products were riddled with problems and were discarded in the stream that ran through the area. When factory officials decided this was not safe, Skånska dumped the defects in a designated area behind the plant. Isolit's production constituted the birth of Scandinavia's first plastic products.

The radio industry soon became the primary customer of Isolit products. In 1923, Skånska Ättiksfabriken began producing laminates, or the strong, brown board in a radio which electrical parts are mounted on. The industrial grade laminate began as the single, largest-selling product for the company. Also, the company's furniture factory became Sweden's largest manufacturer of radio cabinets.

In the early 1920s, Skånska's chemists, after adding a shiny surface to the industrial laminate, discovered decorative lami-

nates. This new product resisted wear and tear, heat and chemicals. In the mid-1930s, Skånska Ättiksfabriken introduced beech parquet. However, because the beech parquet, used as floorboards, had been dried too much, expanded, and subsequently caused a number of household accidents, the company became involved in many lawsuits and was forced to pay substantial damage costs.

During World War II, Skånska refined many tons of charcoal used to manufacture a substitute gas for Sweden's passenger cars. Again, Skånska's production suffered from lack of raw materials. To fuel the modern charcoal plant, Wendt's son, Otto, was forced to cut up millions of parquet boards, which actually turned out to be more economical for the company at this time than selling them on the open market.

Postwar Changes

When World War II ended in 1945, and as the European countries began piecing their industries and economies back together again, Skånska's production was no match for its competitors. Skånska, although no longer the only plastics company in Scandinavia, was the largest, with a product line of more than 10,000 items.

After the war, when Swedish gasoline was placed back on the market, Skånska was faced with disposing of many tons of charcoal. The solution to this problem involved selling the excess charcoal to the carbon bisulphide industry. Thus, in the early 1950s, the company began breaking the dependency link between coal and chemicals. The company did not completely stop operations at the charcoal burning plant until 1970, when environmental controls also became a factor. However, with the purchase of a small barbecue charcoal and industrial coal plant, Skånska never really eliminated coal from its activities.

The company's carefully established chain of raw materials network was finally broken in 1952 when Skånska began using methanol purchased from outside sources to manufacture its formalin. And, in 1967, the saw mill, another important part of the raw materials chain, closed its operation.

After an illness during the early 1950s, Otto Wendt was forced to relinquish some management of the day-to-day operations of the plant. For the first time at Skånska Ättiksfabriken, new methods of planning, budgeting, and market analysis were implemented. The company placed new emphasis on quality and on long-term, low-risk projects rather than on the short-term speculation that had characterized its operations before 1945. Skånska also began making efforts to establish business contacts in export markets. It was during this time that the company established a plant in Brazil for the production of laminates.

The next twenty years became the era of the decorative laminate. It was so successful that Skånska could not produce enough to meet the demand of the Swedish market. Since this lack of production was due largely to a constant labor shortage because of the lack of housing for employees, the company helped solve the problem by collaborating with the town of Perstorp to develop new housing facilities.

Key Dates:

1881: Wilhelm Wendt establishes Stensmölla Kemiska Tekniska Industri.
1884: The company begins production of acetic acid.
1888: The company is operating as Skånska Ättiks-fabriken.
1917: The firm manufactures its first plastic product.
1923: Skånska starts to produce laminates.
1952: The company begins to use purchased methanol to manufacture its formalin.
1956: Skånska turns its attention to the export market.
1970: The firm goes public under the name Perstorp AB.
1984: Perstorp restructures into nine market-oriented business areas; laminate flooring is launched.
1990: Perstorp begins to focus on its core chemical businesses.
2001: Sydsvenska Kemi AB acquires Perstorp.

Polyalcohol Production and Exporting in the 1950s

In 1955, Skånska began producing the polyalcohol tri-methylolopropane, intended primarily for the paint industry. The company's interest in polyalcohols began in the 1940s, when Otto Wendt used profits from the charcoal operations to fund a study at the University of Lund. As a war concession at the end of World War II, the German chemical industry was forced to open up the contents of its patents and process descriptions. Like other chemical companies at the time, Skånska incorporated many of the German ideas into its production methods. Some of these ideas were incorporated into Skånska development of a polyalcohol based on formalin called penta-erythritol.

In 1955, Otto Wendt relinquished the daily management of the company to his brother-in-law, Olle Nauclér. Prior to this appointment, Nauclér served as chairman of the board of directors for ten years. Otto Wendt, however, continued to serve as chairman of Skånska Ättiksfabriken.

By 1956, the company turned its attention to the export market. Despite intense competition, this move was quite successful. Skånska's success was due to three critical factors: first, the company carefully chose its agents abroad; second, it invested funds to maintain a large inventory; and third, the company also instituted a successful marketing strategy aimed directly at the consumer.

Formalin, the primary raw material in Skånska's polyalcohols, was also an important ingredient in several other products. In 1958, in a mutual exchange of information with Reichhold Chemicals, Skånska received valuable information about several products, one being formalin. In 1959, Skånska began using Reichhold's inexpensive method of producing formalin called Formox.

Like Otto Wendt, Olle Nauclér advocated increased research, especially in the field of thermoplastics. During this period, Nauclér established the Perstorp Research Foundation for research projects. During his 15 years as president, he

prepared the company for a larger market. To ensure the company's access to private venture capital and to reduce the chance of a takeover, Nauclér extended ownership of the company and placed its shares on the open market. He also added new members to the board of directors that were outside the circle of family relations. In addition, Skånska Ättiksfabriken A.B. officially changed its name to Perstorp AB.

Perstorp Goes Public: 1970

In 1970, Perstorp's shares went on the open market in Stockholm. More than 700 employees took advantage of Perstorp's special offer and became some of Perstorp's initial shareholders. Olle Nauclér retired in 1970, and Gunnar Wessman took over as president of Perstorp. This marked the first time in the company's 90-year history that a member of the Wendt family was not among the executive management staff. The Wendts were, however, represented on the board of directors. The company then began its program of international expansion first initiated in the 1950s.

Also in 1970, Perstorp acquired one of the largest laminate producers in Great Britain. In addition, Perstorp purchased a polyalcohol plant in the United States. During this time, Gunnar Wessman began a modernization of the company's organizational structure. Under the motto "Security is based on change," Wessman introduced divisionalism, which decentralized Perstorp's decision-making processes.

Karl-Erik Sahlberg became president of Perstorp in 1975. Under his direction, all product development was concentrated in the separate divisions. Perstorp created Pernvo A.B., the company's New Business Development arm, in order to ensure that long-term projects were not neglected for short-term return on investments made by the divisions. In 1984, Perstorp again changed its organizational structure to represent its nine market-oriented business areas. These included: Perstorp additives; Perstorp Chemitec; Perstorp compounds; Perstorp electronics; Perstorp specialty chemicals; Perstorp components; Perstorp plastics systems; Perstorp surface materials; and Pernvo.

Growth Through Acquisition: 1980s

In 1982, Perstorp bought the amino plastics operation of Italy's Resem SpA. With this purchase, Perstorp became the world's leader in the production of amino plastics. In 1983, Perstorp acquired Pispalan Werhoomo Oy and Tunhems Industri A.B. In the fall of 1984, Perstorp entered the biotechnology field. Perstorp Analytical, a division of Perstorp Biotec, acquired Lumac BV of Holland, a manufacturer of analytical systems for industrial microbiology, from 3M Corporation of the United States. In addition, Perstorp acquired the Swedish company ServoChem A.B., which developed analytical instruments for the brewery industry.

In November 1985, Perstorp Chemitec acquired LaBakelite S.A. of France. LaBakelite was one of the largest manufacturers of resins and phenolic molding compounds in Europe. In the same year, Perstorp acquired the seamless flooring and wall covering portion of the Swedish Gunfred Group, which has been incorporated into Perstorp Chemitec. Pernvo Inc. of the United States acquired minority shareholdings in Health Products Inc. (Michigan) and R Cubed Composites Inc. (Utah), while selling all of its shares in Composite Craft Inc.

During its acquisition spree, Perstorp managed to integrate new items into its product line, including Pergo laminate flooring, which was launched in 1984. While many of the companies it acquired during the 1980s specialized in similar fields to Perstorp, the purchases allowed the firm to gain new footholds in the biochemistry and plastics industries.

Specialty Chemicals Operations: 1990s and Beyond

Like many large European chemical companies, Perstorp underwent a series of changes during the 1990s. The company consolidated its operations and renewed its focus on its core businesses. Over the course of the decade, Perstorp revamped its operations in preparation for its boldest move to date, its sale to Sydsvenska Kemi, which would position it as a leading specialty chemicals group.

As part of its reorganization, Perstorp divested and spun off many of its acquisitions from the 1980s. In 1999, its life science operations were spun off as PerBio Science AB. A company executive commented on the move in a March 1999 *Chemical Market Reporter* article, claiming that "by spinning off Perstorp Life Science, we will be able to concentrate more fully on our specialty chemicals operations."

The company continued focusing on its chemical business in the new century. It streamlined its business structure, creating four main divisions: Specialty Chemicals, composed of the firm's polyols business; Chemitec, its resin and molding compound unit; Formox, which included the firm's formalin and catalysts business; and Composites.

Perstorp's new focus made it an attractive takeover target. By 2000, private investment firm Industri Kapital had made a $1.1 billion bid for the company. Industri dropped its offer, however, due to the poor financial results of the company's Pergo unit. During 2001, Perstorp spun off Pergo, sparking Industri's interest in the firm once again.

Perstorp agreed to a deal with Industri, which would solidify the company's position in the chemicals industry. Industri Kapital created Sydsvenska Kemi AB to act as a parent company, and in June 2001 Sydsvenska Kemi purchased Perstorp. It had already acquired Oxo Holding AB and its specialty chemical business Neste Oxo. Originally, Industri planned—along with the Finnish government—to merge the new Sydsvenska Kemi's operations with the chemical businesses of Kemira Oy and Dynea Oy. In December 2001, however, Industri and Finland's government dropped their plans. As such, the operations of Perstorp and Neste Oxo were combined. In early 2002, all operations were integrated under the Perstorp name.

Perstorp, under the leadership of president and CEO Lennart Holm, believed the joining would be beneficial on several fronts. Management expected increased profitability and an upturn in sales and considered the new company's larger customer base and geographical reach as key to future growth opportunities.

The merger was indeed a significant milestone in Perstorp's 119-year history and signaled the company's commitment to its future direction—to become a world-class specialty chemicals company.

Principal Divisions

Perstorp Performance Chemicals; Perstorp Coating Intermediates; Perstorp Oxo Intermediates; Perstorp Engineering Materials; Perstorp Formox.

Principal Competitors

Akzo Nobel N.V.; Clariant Ltd.; Rhodia SA.

Further Reading

Hume, Claudia, "Perstorp Reshuffles to Strengthen Specialties," *Chemical Week*, December 20, 2000, p. 18.
"Industri Kapital Revives Perstorp Plans," *Chemical Market Reporter*, March 12, 2001, p. 8.
Milmo, Sean, "Industri Kapital to Link Perstorp With Its Rivals," *Chemical Market Reporter*, April 17, 2000, p. 8.
——, "Perstorp to Spin Off Life Sciences," *Chemical Market Reporter*, March 29, 1999, p. 6.
"Pergo Spin-Off to Rekindle Industri Kapital Bid for Perstorp," *Chemical Week*, October 25 2000, p. 8.
"Perstorp," *Chemical Week*, August 1, 2001, p. 14.
"U.K. Company Buys Perstorp Flooring Business," *Chemical Week*, June 26, 2002, p. 8.
Wood, Andrew, "Industri Kapital Drops Perstorp Bid," *Chemical Week*, October 4, 2000, p. 9.

—update: Christina M. Stansell

Pinguely-Haulotte ⫽

Pinguely-Haulotte SA

La Péronnière
B.P.9
42152 L'Horme
France
Telephone: (+33) 0 4 77 29 24 24
Fax: (+33) 0 4 77 29 43 95
Web site: http://www.haulotte.com

Public Company
Incorporated: 1995
Employees: 632
Sales: EUR 264.5 million ($258 million) (2001)
Stock Exchanges: Euronext Paris
Ticker Symbol: PIG
NAIC: 333923 Overhead Traveling Crane, Hoist, and
        Monorail System Manufacturing

Fast-rising Pinguely-Haulotte SA has captured the top spots in the market for self-propelled aerial work platforms. The Horme, France-based manufacturer is the European leader, with some 32 percent of the market, and number three in the world, with a market share expected to reach 17 percent by the end of 2002. Pinguely-Haulotte designs, engineers, and markets nearly every category of platform machinery, with 40 models spanning most of the major categories, including articulated booms, telescopic booms, vertical masts, trailer platforms, and, especially, scissor-lifts, the fastest growing category on the market. Led by Pierre Saubot, Pinguely-Haulotte has distinguished itself by concentrating its efforts on research and development, design, engineering, distribution, marketing, and post-sales services. While the company performs assembly of its products, many of the components and even entire machines are manufactured by subcontractor partners. This model has enabled Pinguely-Haulotte to build up production capacity of more than 18,000 machines for 2002. The company expects to produce some 12,000 machines that year, more than four times its production rate just four years earlier. The company has also seen rapid growth, raising revenues from just EUR56 million in 1998 to estimations reaching EUR320 million by the end of 2002. Undisputed leader in France, where

the company has gained a market share of more than 40 percent, Pinguely-Haulotte has nonetheless turned to the international market for its growth, and more than 80 percent of the company's sales came from outside of France in 2001. Europe remains the company's primary market, representing nearly 98 percent of sales. In 2001, however, Pinguely-Haulotte established a U.S. marketing subsidiary in order to begin competing head to head with worldwide industry leaders JLG and Grove, both of the United States.

Rescuing Businesses in the 1980s

In the mid-1980s, both Pinguely and Haulotte remained small-scale, albeit respected manufacturers of construction machinery; yet both appeared slated for oblivion before being acquired by Pierre Saubot. Pinguely, the older of the two, had been formed in 1881 in the town of Chambéry. For many years, Pinguely had been a manufacturer of steam locomotives, producing more than 25 steam locomotives in the years around the turn of the twentieth century. Pinguely later switched its production to machinery for construction and other industries, specializing in producing mechanical shovels and other earthmoving equipment, as well as a line of mobile cranes.

Pinguely eventually came under control of the French steel industry conglomerate Creusot-Loire and was joined with Haulotte, founded in 1924 in L'Horme, which had come to specialize in the manufacture of derricks, mobile cranes, and aerial platforms.

The collapse of Creusot-Loire, which filed for bankruptcy in 1984, nearly spelled the end for both Pinguely and Haulotte. As rescue plans were worked out for the major parts of Creusot-Loire, neither Pinguely nor Haulotte were included in the proposed packages. As future president and CEO Pierre Saubot told *L'Entreprise*, "Just before I bought them, an expert had concluded that the Pinguely and Haulotte companies had no future and should be shut down. But I was convinced of their potential, especially since there was a strong work force and a reputable, 100-year-old brand."

The acquisition of Pinguely and Haulotte was the fulfillment of Saubot's long-time dream. A graduate in engineering from the Ecole Superieure de Paris d'Electricité in 1966, Saubot had gained experience as a salesman for construction machinery, notably lifting equipment, before returning to school to complete a business degree. Saubot then became a engineering consultant. Saubot's specialty was helping companies in financial difficulty. Yet Saubot had long dreamed of heading his own company. In 1985, Saubot gathered his savings and acquired Pinguely and Haulotte. "For ten years, I'd spent my time helping companies on the decline. I felt that it was time that I invested myself personally in one of those companies," Saubot told *L'Enterprise.*

Saubot set to work reorganizing his new businesses, yet Pinguely and Haulotte were kept as separate companies into the 1990s. Both companies faced into a depressed market for construction machinery, a situation worsened by the fact each of the firms shared a specialty in the production of lifting equipment. Saubot and his management team set out to find a new market— and preferably an entirely new product—for the companies' manufacturing and engineering expertise.

Saubot and his team quickly identified two potential growth areas: all-terrain lifting vehicles for the construction site and self-propelled aerial work platforms. Both areas appeared promising, yet the first was already well developed, notably by Manitou of France. The second, however, represented a new market entirely, and, at least in Europe, one with more or less no competition. Developed in the United States in the mid-1980s, the self-propelled aerial work platform had begun to take off in that market by the end of the decade, largely because the new machinery proved more efficient than traditional scaffolding and other methods for working high above ground.

Yet Saubot had recognized the aerial platform's enhanced safety potential. Already in the 1980s, most of the European Community countries had begun drafting work safety regulations governing above ground work. Saubot's team began designing their own aerial work platforms, placing that activity under Haulotte; Pinguely, meanwhile, took over the group's crane manufacturing operations, which geared production largely toward fulfilling contracts for the French army.

Global Top Three in the New Century

Haulotte's work platforms quickly found takers in the French market, where legislation governing above-ground work, initiated in 1985, continued to be tightened. By the mid-1990s, Haulotte's head start had enabled it to capture the leading position in the French market. By 1995, Saubot decided to concentrate his operations entirely on aerial work platforms—despite having won a FFr300-million, five-year contract for 70 bulldozers and 240 heavy-weight tow trucks for the French army in 1995. Saubot was convinced that his future lay in Haulotte's growing line of aerial platforms. As he told *L'Enterprise,* "I had sensed an explosion in demand in the market."

In 1995, Saubot combined his two company's into one, forming Pinguely-Haulotte. With annual sales of just EUR25 million, Pinguely-Haulotte set to work reorganizing its operations, including exiting all its product markets except its new core of self-propelled aerial work platforms. At the same time, Saubot put into place the company's manufacturing model. Rather than committing itself to the heavy investments required to put into place is own manufacturing capacity, Pinguely-Haulotte took a more unusual approach, preferring to concentrate its operations on research and development, engineering, marketing, and distribution, and putting into place a broad network of manufacturing subcontractor partners. This model enabled the company to build up its production more rapidly, and at less cost and risk. As Saubot told *Le Nouvel Economiste,* "Profitability comes first. We have also been attentive to this order of things."

By 1996, Pinguely-Haulotte's revenues had already climbed to EUR40 million and included the sale of some 700 of the company's boom and scissor lifts, compared to just 300 the year before. Yet the company's strongest growth was yet to come. By then, the member countries of the European Community had decided to draft European-wide legislation governing safety for work performed at three meters or more above ground. The new legislation, passed in 1997, encouraged Pinguely-Haulotte to complete its disposal of its former operations, including the delivery of the last of its vehicles for the French army.

The new legislation transformed Pinguely-Haulotte's market. By the end 1997, the company's production was unable to meet the demand. Pinguely-Haulotte was now able to prepare its assault on the larger European market. As part of its international expansion effort, the company began forming sales and marketing subsidiaries, starting in Germany and the United Kingdom in 1997. The move onto the European stage brought the company into direct competition with such market leaders as JGL Industrie and Grove Worldwide. Nonetheless, Pinguely-Haulotte's manufacturing model enabled the company to meet the competition head on with lower pricing. As Saubot told *Le Nouvel Economiste,* "We set the prices on the market, even in the United States, thanks to our original industrial organization."

By the end of 1998, with sales topping EUR56 million, including more than 1,500 machines, Pinguely-Haulotte went public, listing on the Paris Stock Exchange's Secondary Market. The listing, which raised EUR40 million, enabled the company to step up its expansion. By the end of 1999, Pinguely-Haulotte's sales had nearly doubled and production had reached 3,000 units, including the company's latest product innovation of vertical mast lifts, which were ideal for warehouse and retail store environments. Pinguely-Haulotte's share of the European market had already reached 15 percent, representing more than half of the company's total sales.

The year 2000 marked a new turning point for the company, as production topped 5,000 units at the beginning of the year. In

Key Dates:

1881: Pinguely is founded as a constructor of steam locomotives and later specializes in earth-moving and lifting equipment.

1924: Haulotte is founded as a manufacturer of cranes, derricks, and lifting equipment and along Pinguely becomes part of Creusot-Loire conglomerate.

1985: After the collapse of Creusot-Loire, Pinguely and Haulotte are acquired by Pierre Saudot; Haulotte begins production of self-propelled aerial work platforms.

1995: Pinguely and Haulotte are merged into a single company, Pinguely-Haulotte, which focuses its operations on aerial work platforms.

1997: The company establishes sales and distribution subsidiaries in England and Germany.

1998: Pinguely-Haulotte is listed on the Paris Stock Exchange's Secondary Market.

1999: The company becomes European leader in its market and starts subsidiaries in Spain and Australia.

2001: Pinguely-Haulotte launch subsidiaries in the United States, Brazil, Singapore, and Sweden, capturing the world's number three position in its market.

March 2000, Pinguely-Haulotte acquired a new manufacturing plant, in Reims, in partnership with one of its subcontractors, helping to boost production to more than 6,000 units by the end of the year. The company continued to prove itself an innovator in its core market, launching a new 12-meter vertical mast lift that year. Pinguely-Haulotte also began preparing an entry into the U.S. market, which remained three times as large as the European market.

Meanwhile, the company was exploring other international markets, setting up subsidiaries in Spain, Australia, Portugal, and the Netherlands. Pinguely-Haulotte also continued to seek to develop its manufacturing capacity. In November 2000, the company announced its agreement to acquire the European production operations of Terex, of the United States, which included sites in Ireland and the Netherlands. That agreement collapsed the following year, however, as Terex stumbled on a depressed U.S. market. Meanwhile, the strength of the dollar against the new Euro gave Pinguely-Haulotte an edge in Europe. Despite the failure of the Terex acquisition, Pinguely-Haulotte was able to ramp up production to 10,000 machines by the end of 2001.

With sales topping EUR264 million in 2001, Pinguely stepped up its international activity at the end of that year, launching new subsidiaries in Brazil, Singapore, and Sweden. The company also took the leap into the U.S. market, setting up a sales and distribution subsidiary in Baltimore, Maryland. By mid-2002, Pinguely-Haulotte was able to project new record sales: by the end of that year, the company expected its sales to near EUR320 million and its production to top 12,000 units. Pinguely-Haulotte had secured its position as the world's number three maker of self-propelled aerial work platforms, boosting its global share to more than 17 percent. By then, Pierre Saubot had more than succeeded in rescuing Pinguely-Haulotte—he had lifted the company into the world's top ranks.

Principal Subsidiaries

HAULOTTE GmbH; HAULOTTE UK Ltd; HAULOTTE Italia Srl; HAULOTTE Australia Pty Ltd; HAULOTTE Iberica SL; HAULOTTE Netherlands BV; HAULOTTE France Sarl; ABM Industries SA; HAULOTTE US Inc; HAULOTTE Scandinavia AB; HAULOTTE Portugal.

Principal Competitors

JLG Industries, Inc.; Grove Worldwide LLC; Terex Corporation; Komatsu Ltd.; Caterpillar Corporation; Skyjack, Inc; Mobile Tool International, Inc.

Further Reading

"Comment ressuciter une centenaire," *L'Entreprise*, October 2001.

"French Aerial Maker Opens in US," *Rental Equipment Register*, December 1, 2001, p. 76.

Gervais, Louis, "Pinguely-Haulotte, L'equipementier qui monte . . . et qui descend," *Newsbourse*, July 15, 2001.

Jaillard, Laurence, "Pinguely, la rentabilité d'abord," *Nouvel Economiste*, May 3, 2002.

Lebeccq, Valerie, "Pinguely-Haulotte veut lever 85 millions d'euros," *Les Echos*, January 31, 2001, p. 20.

Sall, Keren, "Haulotte to Go It Alone in UK," *Cranes & Access* November-December 2000.

—M. L. Cohen

A personal commitment
to New Mexico

PNM Resources Inc.

Alvarado Square
Albuquerque, New Mexico 87158
U.S.A.
Telephone: (505) 848-2700
Toll Free: (800) 687-7854
Fax: (505) 241-4322
Web site: http://www.pnm.com

Public Company
Incorporated: 1917 as Albuquerque Gas & Electric
    Company
Employees: 2,675
Sales: $2.3 billion (2001)
Stock Exchanges: New York
Ticker Symbol: PNM
NAIC: 221111 Hydroelectric Power Generation; 221112
    Fossil Fuel Electric Power Generation; 221113
    Nuclear Electric Power Generation; 221119 Other
    Electric Power Generation; 221121 Electric Bulk
    Power Transmission and Control; 221122 Electric
    Power Distribution; 486210 Pipeline Transportation of
    Natural Gas; 221210 Natural Gas Distribution

PNM Resources Inc. was created in 2001 to act as a holding company for the Public Service Company of New Mexico and various other energy-related concerns. The company operates as a merchant utility—one involved in both regulated energy service and the competitive sale and trading of energy. PNM is the largest utility concern in New Mexico, providing electricity and natural gas to over 1.3 million customers. The firm owns and maintains 2,282 miles of electric transmission line and 7,594 miles of electrical distribution line. Its natural gas business includes 1,478 miles of pipeline and 10,900 miles of natural gas distribution and service pipe. PNM's holdings also include interests in the San Juan Generating Station and the Palo Verde Nuclear Generating Station. In 2001, PNM's wholesale—generation and trading—operations accounted for nearly 60 percent of company revenues.

Early History: 1880s to Early 1900s

PNM's corporate roots can be traced to the 1880s, when venturesome local entrepreneurs began forming companies to bring electric, gas, and water service to New Mexico's largest communities. Constantly needing additional capital, several of these companies were acquired one by one by Federal Light and Traction, a New York holding company that controlled various public utilities throughout the West and in Arkansas and New Jersey. By the 1920s, Federal dominated the New Mexico market with operating franchises in Albuquerque, Santa Fe, Las Vegas, Deming, and Belen.

The first electric and gas operations in Albuquerque, New Mexico's largest city, began in 1882. Local businessman A.A. Grant obtained a gas manufacturing franchise, incorporated the Albuquerque Gas Company, and secured land to build a plant near the railroad's coal unloading and storage yard. Dr. E.W. Harrison served as president during the company's early years, when it successfully manufactured producer gas—made from nitrogen, carbon monoxide, hydrogen, and coal or coke—for distribution to local businesses and residences. But continuing leaks and pressure problems in the company's underground pipe distribution network restricted service to a half-mile radius from the plant.

Albuquerque businessman and landowner Perfecto Armijo secured the city's first electric franchise in 1882. Immediately after organizing the Albuquerque Electric Company with Dennis Dennison and A.A. Grant, Armijo sold his interest to them, and Dennison became president. In 1883, just one year after Thomas Edison built the world's first generating station in New York City, electricity came to New Mexico. Two years later, a new power plant with a 250-kilowatt generator was constructed. The company was reorganized in 1886 under a new name, the Electric Light Company of Albuquerque, and appointed a new president, A.A. Grant.

In 1895, Grant, who had also served on the board of the Albuquerque Gas Company since its inception, was elected its president as well. Four years later, J.J. Henry, president of the Denver-based United States Light and Traction Company, obtained financial control of the two separate companies. Grant remained president of both organizations until 1902, when Henry sold the assets and franchises of his two recently acquired companies for 99 percent of the capital stock of a new Denver-based corporation, the Albuquerque Gas, Electric Light and Power Company (AGEL&P). Henry briefly served as president of AGEL&P until succeeded by William S. Iliff in 1903.

Albuquerque was a growing town with a new streetcar firm, the Albuquerque Transit Company, which, along with the American Lumber Company and 608 other customers, needed more power than AGEL&P's old plant could furnish. To meet the growing demand, Iliff incorporated and became president of a separate Colorado firm in 1904, the Albuquerque Electric Power Company, created specifically to provide and distribute electric power for AGEL&P. Iliff negotiated a series of agreements with the American Lumber Company whereby it leased land for a new power plant and supplied fuel and water for the boilers. In return, Albuquerque Electric would provide American Lumber with continuous electric service.

Immediate threat of an outside takeover from Kansas City financiers, however, prompted Iliff to propose the merger of Albuquerque Electric, one month after its incorporation, with AGEL&P. Both boards agreed, and in September 1904 AGEL&P secured 60 percent of the financial control of the Albuquerque Electric Power Company. Albuquerque Electric's new power plant, later called Prager Station, opened the following year with a 500-kilowatt generator. The company added a 1,000-kilowatt generator in 1910 and served as AGEL&P's prime power supplier until 1917.

Forming the Albuquerque Gas & Electric Company: 1917

New York City's Federal Light and Traction Company, a public utility holding company, took financial control of AGEL&P and Albuquerque Electric in 1911. Federal's president, Charles C. Chappelle, became president of both New Mexico firms as well, until succeeded by E.N. Sanderson in 1914. Federal merged its two Albuquerque companies into a new organization, the Albuquerque Gas & Electric Company, in 1917. Sanderson continued as president, and in 1919 Arthur Prager was transferred from Federal's Trinidad, Colorado, properties to become agent in residence.

Prager later served as the firm's general manager, became president in 1940, and went on to direct decades of growth in all fields of operation. More powerful generators continued to be

installed at the company's Prager Station, and a new power plant was built in Bernalillo, north of Albuquerque. A 46-kilovolt transmission line connected the two cities in 1926, and three years later another 46-kilovolt line—the first aluminum conductor line west of the Mississippi River—linked Bernalillo to Santa Fe.

The company received its first natural gas in 1930 via a pipeline constructed by the Dallas-based Southern Union Company from the San Juan gas wells in northern New Mexico. AGEL&P began distributing this gas to customers through its retail system and installing generators fueled by natural gas.

Adopting the PNM Name: 1946

On September 12, 1946, with the approval of the Securities and Exchange Commission (SEC), the Albuquerque Gas & Electric Company changed its corporate name to the Public Service Company of New Mexico (PNM) and acquired by statutory merger the properties of utilities in other New Mexico cities, including New Mexico Power Company, Deming Ice and Electric Company, and Las Vegas Light and Power Company. The following year, pursuant to Holding Company Act requirements, Federal liquidated, distributing to its shareholders all company common stock, with approximately 65 percent going to Federal's parent, Cities Service Company. In 1948, Cities Service sold this block to the public, making PNM an independent operating utility.

Arthur Prager, who became the new company's president, began his tenure by standardizing company operations. The subsidiaries in Las Vegas, Santa Fe, Belen, and Deming had been run independently with separate presidents and officers, different operating procedures, and little connection to Federal's other New Mexico utilities. Wide scale changes were made to forge the separate businesses into a single, more efficient operation.

The next step was to unite the widely separated distribution and transmission systems. New Mexico's phenomenal expansion during World War II, spurred by government defense and research installations like Kirtland Air Force Base, Sandia Laboratory, Los Alamos National Laboratory, and White Sands Missile Range, had led to increased power demands. AGEL&P had created a subsidiary, Stonewall Electric Company, in 1941 solely to construct transmission lines. Ten years later, with PNM's statewide power grid completed, Stonewall was dissolved.

Concentrating on expanding electrical operations, PNM sold its retail gas operation to the Southern Union Company in 1949 for $4 million and entered into a long-term contract for delivery of natural gas to its power plants. Southern created a separate division, the Gas Company of New Mexico, to service that state's customers.

Postwar Growth

New Mexico continued growing beyond the national average during the post-World War II years, and most of the growth was concentrated in PNM's service area. The state's population increased 38.6 percent from 1950 to 1960, while the franchised area grew by 53.5 percent. New Mexico's economy—based on farming, livestock, mining, oil, and gas—expanded. In addition, outside manufacturers moved into the state, and new industries that required large amounts of power, including uranium mining and milling, arose. Not only did PNM's customer base increase by 58.2 percent during the decade, but these customers were also using more power. Average residential household electrical use rose 58 percent from 1948 to 1953.

PNM responded by installing new and larger generators on an almost annual basis and constructing two new gas- and oil-fired power plants near Albuquerque. Generators put into service from 1955 to 1962 produced one and a half times more generating capacity than those that had been built in the previous 72 years.

D.W. Reeves became president in 1955, and Prager moved up to chairman. By 1960, all of PNM's generating stations used natural gas purchased from the Gas Company of New Mexico for fuel. Rising fuel costs led Reeves to explore the possibility of substituting coal for gas for better economy. The Public Service Coal Company, a wholly owned subsidiary, was formed that year to explore, acquire, and develop coal properties. It later changed its name to the Western Coal Company.

At the same time, PNM was working to connect its power grid with other regional utilities. A new transmission line to the uranium mines in northwestern New Mexico was completed in 1958. By 1963, that line was extended to the Arizona border and connected with Arizona Public Service's system. The next year, a second interstate tie was completed with Western Colorado Power.

Regional utilities began coordinating future construction plans. In 1964, Reeves became the first president of Western Energy and Supply Transmission Associates (WEST), an organization serving nine western states. The following year, the group announced plans to build a joint power plant, the coal-fired Four Corners Plant in northwestern New Mexico, near PNM's coal leases. PNM acquired a 13 percent ownership in two generating units of the plant, the first step in WEST's ambitious goal of creating 36-million kilowatts of new electrical capacity by 1985 to meet projected demand. Construction began in 1966.

For more than 50 years the cost of electricity had been declining as demand increased. Technological advances and greater demand led to larger and more efficient power plants. The average customer's cost had dropped from 2.66 cents per kilowatt-hour in 1946 to 1.84 cents in 1964. Meanwhile, by 1968, existing homes were using more than twice as much energy as they did in 1953, and new homes consumed up to five times as much.

George Schreiber became PNM's third president in 1966, when Reeves took over as chairman. The next year, Albuquerque, PNM's largest market, gave the company a new 25-year electrical franchise. The Four Corners Plant became operational in 1969, and PNM announced plans to construct with Tucson Gas and Electric Company another coal-fired plant in the same region. Called the San Juan Generating Station, it would have state-of-the-art pollution controls, and PNM would own a 64 percent interest.

Steady Growth: 1970s

New Mexico continued growing in the 1970s. Among the United States, it ranked seventh in total mineral production, first in uranium, third in copper, fourth in natural gas, and sixth in oil, extractive industries that required vast amounts of power. Coal was regaining popularity as a cheaper substitute for more expensive fuels like gas and oil, and the state had known reserves of nearly 300 billion tons. For 15 years, the local uranium industry had been growing steadily; now its electricity use was doubling every year.

PNM took advantage of the growing need for its services. Work began on the San Juan plant in 1970. The company's 1972 construction forecast was astronomical—$252 million would be spent on building new utility plants over the next five years, almost equaling the value of already existing facilities. The Public Service Land Company, a subsidiary of PNM, was created that year to secure land and water rights for future power plants. It was later renamed Paragon Resources.

Rates rose when the New Mexico Public Service Commission (PSC) approved a 10 percent rate increase in 1972, along with a fuel adjustment clause to counter rising energy costs. But since customer rates could not include the cost of unfinished construction projects, PNM sought additional capital on Wall Street, joining the New York Stock Exchange in 1972.

Even though the first unit of San Juan came on line the following year, PNM and four other regional utilities made plans to build Palo Verde, the nation's largest nuclear power plant, in Arizona. Based on PNM's projections for electric power demand, the PSC approved its participation in the project in 1975; construction began the next year.

Rapid cost escalations from this ambitious construction schedule led state regulators to approve PNM's proposed cost-of-service indexing in 1975. The brainchild of executive vice-president Jerry Geist, this controversial method allowed periodic automatic rate adjustments according to company expenditures, providing a guaranteed percentage of return to shareholders.

PNM was the fastest-growing and most profitable electric utility in the country during the late 1970s. From 1974 to 1980 its rates rose 120 percent, while 85 percent of its power came from coal-fired plants, which could be run more cheaply than those using gas or oil, and its coal subsidiary provided much of the fuel.

Diversification Leads to Disaster: Late 1970s–80s

Geist became president in 1976 and began diversifying the company's assets into non-utility businesses, hoping to cash in on the Southwest's booming economy, provide more uses for the increased electric power it would soon be producing, and create profits beyond the reach of regulators. Sunbelt Mining Company was formed in 1979 to provide coal for PNM generating plants. Meadows Resources, created in 1981, became involved in southwestern land development, various telecommunications companies, a Chicago savings and loan, a fiberboard manufacturing plant, and venture capital investments.

For a time all went well. The San Juan plant was completed in 1982, Meadows Resources and the Bellamah Land Company were making money on their joint housing developments, and PNM negotiated the sale and leaseback of its Palo Verde interest, generating additional cash flow. Geist's apparent successes and innovative style made him an industry leader and darling of Wall Street financiers as PNM's stock price soared. He was named chairman of PNM in 1982.

But state lawmakers were wary and passed a 15-month moratorium on further diversification that same year. It was lifted in 1983, when PNM agreed to end its controversial cost-of-service indexing. Two years later, PNM acquired the Gas Company of New Mexico from Southern Union as part of a price-fixing suit settlement by Southern.

As the 1980s wore on, clouds were beginning to appear on PNM's horizon. New Mexico and the entire southwestern economy was slowing down, the regional real estate market began collapsing, and demand for power was nowhere near what had been anticipated. In 1986, the uranium industry actually used less than six percent of its projected power need. Reduced sales meant each kilowatt hour sold had to pay for a greater share of the costs of the company's new generating plants and transmission lines.

In addition, PNM's expenses were running out of control. Pollution control systems at the San Juan plant ended up costing $600 million, nearly half of the facility's total price tag. Construction delays and cost overruns at Palo Verde raised PNM's price tag for its 10.2 percent share from a budgeted $360 million to $1.2 billion. When the plant finally came on line in 1986, it was plagued with safety violations and excessive downtime. Even worse, revised projections showed that New Mexico customers would not need its power until the twenty-first century.

PNM was not alone. The entire Southwest was plagued with an overcapacity of electricity, which then depressed wholesale power prices. PNM proposed to solve some of these problems with a novel restructuring plan, splitting itself into a generating company and a distributing company, each under the control of a holding company that would replace the current PNM. In doing so, PNM hoped to take advantage of tax breaks, less regulation, and increased flexibility on rates to counter rising costs. The proposal was ultimately rejected by the state PSC in 1986. Opponents feared that PNM was trying to skirt state regulatory authority. A revised plan put forth the following year was withdrawn from consideration in 1988 after the company realized it had no chance of receiving approval.

Still, the company logged record profits of $151 million in 1986, and its stock rose to an all-time high of $39.75 a share early the next year. Then the dam broke. PNM's diversification efforts began hemorrhaging money and attempts to pass the Palo Verde costs on to its customers were thwarted. In addition, the company's stock nosedived to $12.63, and its bonds were devalued to junk status. PNM ended 1988 in the red. With losses totaling $241 million, the company cut its dividend to 48 percent and laid off nearly 800 employees, 20 percent of its work force. PNM ended the year by announcing it would begin selling all of its non-utility subsidiaries.

Things did not improve in 1989. Though PNM posted a profit, it suspended its common dividend indefinitely, reorganized to write off $200 million in bad investments, and cut Geist's salary to one dollar for the year. Bellamah Community Development, PNM's largest single non-utility investment, filed for bankruptcy while holding $400 million in real estate in the Southwest. In addition, Albuquerque voters passed an amendment requiring competitive bidding by power suppliers when PNM's electrical franchise expired in 1992. To top the year off, shareholders began suing the company for mismanagement.

Geist resigned in 1990 amid a flurry of news reports highlighting his diversification debacle: $10 million in Bellamah bonuses paid to PNM executives; $4.5 million in PNM payoffs to Bellamah's two partners to prevent a lawsuit; and utility money used to guarantee Meadows Resources' real estate loans, a violation of the Public Utility Act. A PNM special internal committee estimated that $210 million was lost in its diversification efforts. The company sued Geist and two other executives from its diversified subsidiaries the next year, seeking the return of $5 million in bonuses, fees, and retirement benefits. However, 12 months later it dropped the suit due to mounting legal costs, after having already spent $3 million.

Refocusing Under Ackerman: Early to Mid-1990s

John Ackerman, former president of the Gas Company of New Mexico, became PNM's new president and chairman. Charged with restoring its public image, Ackerman stressed the company's rededication to its core business—providing public service. As a show of good will, electric and gas rates were frozen for three years starting in 1991.

Restoring profitability and finding customers to use its excess power were PNM's two biggest problems. Though the company posted a small $13.5 million profit in 1991, excess capacity alone created a financial drain of 86 cents per share. While it cost PNM 4.5 cents per kilowatt hour to produce electricity at its coal plants, and nine cents per kilowatt hour at Palo Verde, it could only sell the excess energy for two cents per kilowatt hour in the saturated southwestern power market. And falling natural gas and oil prices made power generated from such plants cheaper than from PNM's coal and nuclear power facilities.

Despite being called one of the "dismal four" struggling southwestern utilities by Bert Kramer, a utility analyst for Paine Webber who was quoted in the *New York Times*, PNM took some positive steps. Shareholder lawsuits were settled, multi-year contracts were signed to supply power to three regional utilities, and a small interest in its San Juan power plant was sold to the city of Anaheim, California. Electrical sales grew by 1.8 percent in 1991, and its Sangre de Cristo Water Company, which served Santa Fe, received an Environmental Excellence Award from the Environmental Protection Agency (EPA). In August 1992, PNM signed a preliminary 15-year electrical franchise agreement with the city of Albuquerque, whose customers represented 45.4 percent of its total electric operating revenues.

Ackerman was replaced by Ben Montoya as president and CEO in 1994 but remained chairman until 1999. Together, the pair continued to revamp PNM's image. That year, the firm's electric and gas operations were unified under the PNM name. In 1995, the company began expanding its wholesale operations, which sold and traded excess capacity. This portion of PNM's business proved to be highly successful, growing by nearly 30 percent per year between 1995 and 2000. In fact, the company financial position as a whole improved, with both revenues and net earnings increasing each year from 1997 through 2000.

The Formation of PNM Resources: Late 1990s and Beyond

By the late 1990s, the U.S. utilities industry was in the midst of deregulation. New Mexico passed its Restructuring Act of 1999, forcing utility firms to separate regulated and unregulated businesses. As such, PNM revived its holding company plans from the 1980s. Unlike its previous attempts, the formation of a new company would not only gain approval but also serve as a necessary building block in the firm's strategy to compete in both the generation and distribution markets.

Jeff Sterba—named president, CEO, and chairman in 2000—oversaw the creation of PNM Resources Inc., which would act as a holding company for Public Service Company of New Mexico. Shareholders approved the new structure in 2000 and, in June 2001, New Mexico's Public Regulation Commission gave its authorization. Accompanying that authorization, however, were several conditions related to an initial dividend payment and the transfer of various assets that PNM believed to be unfair. Dissatisfied, PNM filed an appeal with the state Supreme Court to overturn the conditions. The company and the Commission finally reached a settlement in December, PNM dropped its appeal, and the new holding company was launched.

Sterba commented on the milestone in a December 2001 *PR Newswire* release, claiming that "activation of PNM Resources marks a significant step toward our goal of creating America's best merchant utility. This new corporate structure allows us the business flexibility to continue our traditional focus on excellent customer service and efficiency in our utility operations, even as we pursue new opportunities in our growing power production and marketing business."

During its first acquisition attempt as PNM Resources, the firm became involved in a legal battle surrounding its proposed purchase of Kansas-based electric utility firm Western Resources Inc. The $4 billion deal was announced in November 2000, but in July 2001 the Kansas Commerce Commission denied Western's rate hike and its reorganization plan, which called for the spin off of non-utility assets. As a result, PNM Resources backed out of the deal and filed suit against Western, claiming it had breached the acquisition agreement. In December of that year, the deal was called off.

Even with acquisition setback, PNM Resources stood well positioned during the early years of the new century. During 2001, the company reported record earnings, and sales had increased by 46 percent over the previous year. PNM's future success, however, was contingent on how well it battled its next round of challenges. New Mexico's retail electricity market was slated to fully deregulate in 2007. Preparation for open competition in this market sector would no doubt bring additional change to PNM Resources. The company also faced staunch competition and price fluctuation in the wholesale market, and there was increased pressure to create and provide renewable or clean energy resources. Despite these obstacles, PNM Resources was confident it would remain New Mexico's largest utility for years to come.

Principal Subsidiaries

Public Service Company of New Mexico.

Principal Competitors

El Paso Electric Company; PG&E Corporation; Xcel Energy Inc.

Further Reading

Boschee, Pam, "PNM: Aggressive Wholesaler Players Eyes Market South of the Border," *Electric Light & Power*, August 2000, p. 16.

Gard, David M., *History of Public Service Company of New Mexico*, Albuquerque: Public Service Company of New Mexico, 1966.

Getschow, George, "PS of New Mexico Generates Controversy With Plan to Sell Power Outside the State," *Wall Street Journal*, October 21, 1980.

"PNM Resolves Remaining Issues Over Holding Company Rules," *PR Newswire*, December 19, 2001.

"PNM's Long-Term Growth Trend Underlies Record-Setting 2001," *Electric Light & Power*, June 2002, p. 14.

Robbins, Cathy, "Utility Earnings Pay for PNM's Diverse Holdings," *Albuquerque Journal*, February 14, 1982.

Sikora, Martin, "A Big Utility Merger Lands in Court," *Mergers & Acquisitions Journal*, December 1, 2001.

Ward, Leah Beth, "Fancy Footwork, Then a Stumble, in New Mexico," *New York Times*, July 17, 1988.

——, "A Reckoning for the Utility High Rollers," *New York Times*, July 29, 1990.

"Western-PNM Deal Terminated," *Oil Daily*, January 10, 2002.

—James J. Podesta
—update: Christina M. Stansell

PROVIGO

Provigo Inc.

400 Sainte-Croix Avenue
Saint-Laurent, Quebec H4N 3L4
Canada
Telephone: (514) 383-3000
Fax: (514) 383-3100
Web site: http://www.provigo.com

Wholly Owned Subsidiary of Loblaw Companies Ltd.
Incorporated: 1961 as Couvrette & Provost Limited
Employees: 30,000
Sales: Not Available.
NAIC: 445110 Supermarkets and Other Grocery (Except
    Convenience) Stores; 422410 General Line Grocery
    Wholesalers

Provigo Inc. is Quebec's largest grocery retailer with over 250 supermarket and discount stores operating under the Loblaws, Provigo, Maxi, and Maxi & Cie names. Along with traditional grocery products, the firm's stores offer over 7,000 items under the President's Choice and "no name" private label brands. Through its wholesale division, Provigo operates 26 Presto cash-and-carry outlets and supplies a network of affiliated outlets under the L'Intermarché, Axep, Proprio, and Atout Prix banners. Provigo was purchased by Loblaw Companies Ltd.—Canada's largest grocery distributor—in 1998.

Operating as Couvrette & Provost: 1960s

Provigo was founded in Montreal when Bernard and Jacques Couvrette and Roland, Ernest, and René Provost decided to link their family businesses. The new wholesale grocer was incorporated in 1961 as Couvrette & Provost Ltd. and dealt mainly in dry goods, tobacco, candy, and toiletries.

Couvrette & Provost's first president, Bernard Couvrette, established a precedent for aggressive acquisition, and over the next eight years the company integrated ten food wholesalers in an effort to diversify its food lines with dairy products, meats, vegetables, and health and beauty aids.

As a wholesaler and distributor, the company depended on independent grocers for its business. At the beginning of the 1960s, a supermarket chain boom consumed much of the smaller grocers' market share, but by 1964, in Quebec at least, these independents had won back most of what had been lost and held 70 percent of the market. Couvrette & Provost was supplying about 800 grocery stores, 300 of them affiliated with the company under various names. The small grocers' success was largely due to their growth in rural Quebec areas, but in some provinces the chains still dominated.

Couvrette & Provost was also diversifying into new areas of the food-service industry. Its subsidiary, Provost & Provost, served restaurants, hotels, schools, and other institutions, and another subsidiary, Les Epiceries Presto Limitée, operated eight cash-and-carry stores. Couvrette & Provost also organized Primes Régal Incorporated, a trading stamp system for retailers to offer their customers. The stamps were redeemable for prizes the shopper could choose from an illustrated catalogue, and the promotion was successful in bringing some of the supermarket glitz to smaller groceries.

In 1965, the company acquired Magasins Régal Stores, a cooperative of several Quebec food retailers that worked through pooled purchases to allow the group to run its own warehouse to keep prices lower. Also that year, Conrad Lajoie Limitée, a small distributor, was acquired as a subsidiary. The company also underwent a five-for-one stock split in 1965, feeling that its C$30 to C$35 unit price was too high for ordinary investors and that the company would benefit from more shareholders and shares outstanding to increase its leverage on the stock market.

During the mid-1960s, profits continued to increase by as much as 29 percent a year, and in 1967 Couvrette & Provost made a change in capital structure. Previously, the company had used the two-class structure of A and B shares that was common for newly incorporated Quebec companies. Only the B shares, which were held by the Couvrette and Provost families, had voting rights. Under the new plan, both classes of shares were converted into no-par-value common shares.

In August 1967, Bernard Couvrette became chairman of the board and René Provost was named president. During the next

Company Perspectives:

Provigo strives to provide high-quality products at the lowest possible price and to provide a healthy work environment where everyone has access to personal growth opportunities through such activities as training programs. We also promote honest business practices, respect free competition, and constantly work towards providing a high return for our shareholders.

two years, the company became a leader in the Quebec market. It acquired P. D'Aoust Limited, a family-owned wholesale grocery business, and then merged with Lamontagne Limited and Denault Limited through an exchange of shares. This was the first merger of its kind in the province, and it expanded the company into new territories—Saguenay, Quebec City, Sherbrooke, and the Eastern Townships. One of the main results of the merger was an overall reduction of operating costs through the integration of management, distribution, advertising, and purchasing, which helped sales to increase at a rapid rate over the next 20 years. *The Financial Post* called the firm's progress in nine years "most impressive," stating that "management appears to be very aggressive and forward looking and has shown sound judgment in the recent mergers."

Supermarket Price Wars: 1970s

In 1969, Antoine Turmel became CEO, while René Provost remained president and general manager. In September of the next year, Couvrette & Provost changed its name to Provigo Inc.

As rural citizens of Quebec began to move to the cities in larger numbers in the early 1970s, their lifestyle changes included patronizing independent grocers less and chain supermarkets more. The chains used modern merchandising techniques and muscular ad campaigns to attract more consumers to their strategically placed sites in shopping centers and suburbs. Because of the volume of their sales and the strength of their purchasing power, the supermarkets could afford to offer lower prices, which soon led to price wars.

In food distribution, often called the "penny business," profit margins are tiny and must be compensated for with a large sales volume. To counteract the supermarket price war, wholesalers began to band together and distributors forged closer links with their independent grocers by affiliating retailers and franchising convenience stores. In 1970, Provigo merged ProviFruit Inc., and, over the next five years, Provigo concentrated on developing its retail sector by establishing a network of 50 supermarkets and 800 affiliated or franchised stores. The company had opened its first warehouse market in 1969; by 1972, it had a dozen warehouse operations. Because of this wise planning during the price wars, Provigo was the only publicly owned food distributor in Canada whose earnings increased rather than declined.

In 1974, Provigo implemented a new approach to retailing by developing a chain of franchised convenience stores under the name Provi-Soir. In 1975, Provigo purchased Jato, a company operating nine supermarkets. In November, 1976 the company moved into the meat sector and created its own subsidiary, Provi-Viande.

Provigo made an audacious move in 1977 when it acquired M. Loeb Limited, a company with larger sales and territories than its own, more than doubling Provigo's size. The company's sales rose from C$500 million to C$2 billion in the next two years. The acquisition was not only shrewd but well timed, since price competition in food retailing lessened during 1977 and sales growth was outrunning inflation. Along with M. Loeb, Provigo acquired Loeb's subsidiaries in Washington, D.C., and northern California, thus gaining a foothold in the United States. Provigo also acquired National Drug Limited, a pharmaceutical distributor.

Provigo's dominance in the food industry so far was mainly due to its wholesale activities, which still earned about 75 percent of the company's sales. In Quebec, the market for independent grocers was growing again as more women were working, families were smaller, and fewer people were shopping in large supermarkets.

Retail Expansion: Early 1980s

Provigo decided to expand its retail operations, extending its Jovi, Provibec, and Provigo stores into all areas of Quebec City. In November 1980, it bought all the shares of Abbatoir St.-Valerien Inc., which operated a large slaughterhouse. In January 1981, the company acquired Sports Experts Inc. and in February bought 87 of Dominion Stores' Quebec operations and distributing facilities. Pierre Lessard, who had become president and general manager in 1976, told *The Wall Street Journal* that "getting a larger presence in Montreal was the key to the transaction."

From the beginning, the Dominion stores had trouble. The managers responsible for integrating the new stores did not always agree with the managers of other Provigo supermarkets, and because of their differences the stores had to be transformed one by one, taking six months longer than expected. As operational losses grew, the acquisition put several other projects on the shelf and cost the company a great deal of money and work. By 1984, Richard Constantineau, who had managed the Dominion stores, had resigned. Several of the Dominion stores were sold to affiliates and about 30 were closed. Others continued to do business until 1986, when the last were closed.

Provigo was involved in another price war in 1983, this time as a retailer. It began when Provigo's competitor, Steinberg Inc., started giving its customers coupons worth 5 percent of their total purchase that were redeemable at the next purchase, a plan that won over shoppers immediately. Two days later, Provigo retaliated by offering a 6 percent discount on most products, which could be applied immediately to the purchase, as well as accepting discount coupons issued by Steinberg. When asked what it would take to end the price war, Turmel told *The Globe and Mail*, "I think it will be over when our competitor sees our results. They'll see we can withstand it better than they can. . . . We don't like it, but we can stand it." Provigo's colorful advertisements drew more customers during the war and attracted wide press coverage.

In October, the company suffered another crisis when 45 of its Montreal-based Provigo stores were shut down by a strike, which followed a one-week strike at Steinberg. About 2,200 workers asked for increased job security and wages. After four weeks, Provigo offered a contract that matched Steinberg's contract with its workers, and the Provigo labor force accepted.

In 1984, Provigo extended its reach in the fast-food area by becoming a majority owner of Restaurants Les Pres Limitée, which operated four restaurants and was set to open eight more. Provigo also planned to focus on the convenience-store industry, which was blossoming in Quebec. That year, the Maxi discount stores were launched. The company also began installing automatic banking machines in its major stores. In July, company stores announced price cuts on many items with a campaign called Permaprix. Between 1980 and 1985, Provigo more than doubled its profits.

In April 1985, Antoine Turmel retired, and the president of the Montreal stock exchange, Pierre Lortie, resigned that post to take control of Provigo as CEO. Later in the year, Pierre Lessard, who many had believed would take Turmel's place, stepped down from his position as president.

Diversification: Mid-1980s

That year was also full of new ventures. Capitalizing on the many young couples who were buying and repairing old houses, Provigo went into the home-renovation business in February, becoming partners with a building supply firm, Val Royal LaSalle, to open a large home-renovation center in Montreal. That month the company also joined with Collegiate-Arlington Sports Inc. in Toronto, merging its Sports Experts division to form a new national business called Sports Experts Inc. In August, Provigo purchased a majority stake in Consumers Distributing Company, a catalogue showroom firm in Ontario. The company also decided to broaden its presence in eastern Quebec by purchasing Alphonse Allard Inc. and Approvisionnement Atlantique, both food wholesalers.

In an effort to increase profits as well as geographical growth, Provigo divided its businesses into five groups: food distribution (still comprising about two-thirds of its business), pharmaceuticals, convenience stores, nonfood distribution, and Provigo U.S.A. Lortie believed this restructuring would enhance Provigo's national presence and help block competition from other firms. Provigo's American subsidiaries had merged under the new restructuring, and sales in the United States increased to account for about 14 percent of the company's annual total.

In 1986, Provigo acquired Pharmacom Systems Limited, a supplier of computer systems to pharmacies. The Sports Experts subsidiary opened five stores, the National Drug subsidiary opened a new distribution center, and several new food-distribution centers and cash-and-carry warehouses were also opened. Provigo undertook a joint venture with McKesson Corporation in San Francisco to distribute health supplies and equipment in Canada. In the supermarket division, the company expanded its fresh-foods and specialty departments.

By 1987, the pharmaceuticals operation was Provigo's fastest-growing business, and in February the company consolidated its C$1 billion operation into one company called Medis Health and Pharmaceuticals Services Inc. The move was viewed by many as a guard against Steinberg, Provigo's fiercest competitor; analysts had predicted that Steinberg would enter the drug-distribution market soon. Provigo also planned to spend C$18 million building drug-distribution warehouses in Montreal and Toronto. In November, the company bought the remaining shares of Consumers Distributing Company.

In 1988, Unigesco Inc., a holding company, and Empire Company, a supermarket concern, raised their joint stake in Provigo stock from about 41 percent to 51 percent, and the president of Unigesco, Bertin Nadeau, who had been a director at Provigo since 1985, gained control of the company as the head of this 51 percent consortium.

Steinberg had been seeking bids for its supermarkets due to a quarrel in the Steinberg family, and in April 1988 Provigo and Metro-Richelieu Inc., another food wholesaler, made a joint bid for its Quebec stores, planning to convert them into their own. Provigo and Metro-Richelieu were very competitive, and the joint bid insured that a bidding war would not occur between them. In the end, however, with a new labor agreement, Steinberg opted not to sell its supermarkets after all.

In June 1988, Provigo began to act on its plans for expansion in the United States, purchasing the Petrini's upscale supermarket chain in San Francisco, ten Alpha Beta stores, and five Lucky Supermarkets throughout northern California. The company was also positioning to establish itself in Europe and Japan by organizing Provigo International to increase exports.

By the late 1980s, Provigo's foundation was in wholesaling. Instead of focusing on vertical expansion into food manufacturing like many similar companies, it chose to test its retail and distribution skills in businesses other than groceries. In a country as large and diverse as Canada, Provigo faced the task of predicting the social, economic, and regional trends that influence shoppers' desires. Provigo's future, therefore, depended largely on its local retailers' sensitivity to the people who walked through their stores.

Focus on Retail and Distribution: 1990s

During the 1990s, Provigo narrowed its focus on two main business groups: Retail and Distribution. In 1992, competitor Steinberg finally conceded, selling 25 of its stores to Provigo. In 1995, 42 Heritage stores were converted into Maxi discount outlets. One year later, the first Maxi & Cie discount outlet store made its debut.

As competition in the industry intensified, customer satisfaction remained a crucial point in Provigo's strategy. In 1997, the company launched a US$144 million campaign that added a new arsenal of prepared foods and fresh products to Provigo store offerings. The move was made in an attempt to attract busy consumers looking for quick and fresh meals. Stores were converted so that 50 percent of floor space was dedicated to fresh products, while hot and cold cooked and prepared foods were placed in the front of each store.

Provigo also began to eye Ontario as a key area for growth. At the time, Loblaw Companies Ltd. was the only major grocery concern in the region, and Provigo believed that with aggressive expansion the firm could boost its 10 percent market share in the area. In 1997, Provigo's net income reached record levels, climbing to US$59.9 million.

Provigo Becomes a Loblaw Company: 1999

By the late 1990s, the Canadian grocery industry was ripe for consolidation. A December 1998 *Canadian Business* article explained that "the mathematics of the grocery business argue strongly for consolidation. If grocers can spread their costs over more stores, they can squeeze out tiny economies of scale that in total add up to millions of dollars of extra profit." Provigo's financial performance had caught the eye of Toronto-based Loblaw, Canada's largest grocer, whose sales had grown at a compounded rate of 6.5 percent per year since 1990. Gaining the leading position in Quebec appealed to the giant, and in 1999 Provigo became a Loblaw subsidiary. The C$1.7 billion deal was met with opposition from some Quebec nationalists; however, a stipulation that Loblaw and Provigo purchase an equal amount of goods and services from Quebec companies over the next seven years satisfied those concerned.

Provigo entered the new century on solid ground. With a powerful parent company in its corner, the firm had the resources to update and expand its stores. The first Loblaw store—this chain was added to Provigo's arsenal after the merger—had opened in Montreal and was quickly followed by six additional locations. Provigo's stores also began carrying the President's Choice and "no name" brand of products. Even as U.S.-based competitors, including Wal-Mart Stores Inc., entered the Canadian grocery scene, Provigo and Loblaw stood well positioned to maintain their leadership in both the Quebec and Canadian markets for years to come.

Principal Competitors

Empire Company Ltd.; Metro Inc.

Further Reading

D'Souza, Patricia, and Sean Silcoff, "On Special This Week: Supermarkets," *Canadian Business*, December 4, 1998, p. 32.
Dunn, Brian, "Grocery Mergers Worry Manufacturers," *Supermarket News*, April 19, 1999, p. 22.
——, "Loblaw Invests in Nonfood Categories to Grow Sales," *Supermarket News*, May 27, 2002, p. 15.
"Loblaw Gets Green Light for Provigo Deal," *Eurofood*, August 26, 1999, p. 9.
Pitt, Françoise, "Ready for the Future," *Food in Canada*, May 2002, p. 26.
"Provigo Costs Loblaw Dear," *Grocer*, December 12, 1998, p. 14.
"Provigo Registers a Record Net Income," *Supermarket News*, March 30, 1998, p. 9.
"Provigo Revamps," *The Food Institute Report*, June 1, 1998.
Provost, René, and Maurice Chartrand, *Provigo: The Story Behind 20 Years of Entrepreneurial Success*, Englewood Cliffs, NJ: Prentice Hall, 1989.

—update: Christina M. Stansell

R&B, Inc.

3400 East Walnut Street
Colmar, Pennsylvania 18915
U.S.A.
Telephone: (215) 997-1800
Fax: (215) 997-7968
Web site: http://www.rbinc.com

Public Company
Incorporated: 1978
Employees: 955
Sales: $201.66 million (2001)
Stock Exchanges: NASDAQ
Ticker Symbol: RBIN
NAIC: 336399 All Other Motor Vehicle Parts
    Manufacturing

R&B, Inc. is one of the largest U.S.-based suppliers of replacement parts and fasteners to the automotive aftermarket. Nearly all of the company's revenues (89 percent) are derived from the design, packaging, and marketing of more than 60 brand names, which are organized into three core brand names. R&B's Motormite products include hard-to-find automotive parts, the company's specialty. Automotive replacement parts within the Motormite master brand include pedal pads, sideview mirror glass, window handles, and interior trim parts. The company's Dorman master brand includes automotive fasteners and traditional replacement parts, such as oil drain plugs, accelerator cables, and flywheels. R&B's Champ master brand includes automotive shop supplies and accessories, including welding supplies, cutting equipment, and safety products. Although the company generally does not manufacture its products, it does spend considerable time and money designing and developing its products. R&B sells more than 60,000 different parts and fasteners, marketing its products in North America, Europe, the Middle East, and the Far East.

Origins

The career of the Berman brothers as entrepreneurs began in a garage. In October 1978, 22-year-old Richard N. Berman and his 19-year-old brother, Steven L. Berman, started a small automotive parts distribution business in their garage, making their start with four employees. The size of their company began to change dramatically after the brothers turned their venture into a supplier of replacement parts for the automotive aftermarket. Specifically, the Bermans occupied a distinct segment of the automotive aftermarket, a segment they helped create. They specialized in automotive parts and fasteners classified as "hard to find," or traditionally available only to consumers from the manufacturers who originally manufactured the products—original equipment manufacturers (OEM's)—or from salvage yards. The Bermans' products, which were manufactured by third-party contractors according to their specifications, included window handles, headlamp aiming screws, power steering filler caps, pedal pads, and carburetor pre-heater hoses. Fasteners marketed by the company included items such as oil drain plugs and wheel lug nuts.

At R&B's inception, Richard Berman served as president and chief executive officer. Steven Berman served as executive vice-president and secretary-treasurer. A significant juncture in the company's maturation occurred on November 3, 1984, when R&B was organized as an S-corporation, which meant that the company's net income and its losses would be devolved to and taxed to individual shareholders. The classification served as a way for the company to obtain capital, with R&B shareholders, in effect, loaning money to the company to promote its growth.

A year after organizing as an S-corporation, R&B posted an annual profit, something the company would accomplish for the remainder of the 1980s. By the end of the decade, the company had grown significantly from its modest start in a garage. Revenues in 1989 reached $32 million. The company's payroll had swelled to nearly 350 employees, while the company's physical presence occupied three locations: office and warehouse space in Colmar, Pennsylvania—R&B's headquarters—a warehouse in Carrollton, Georgia, and a light manufacturing plant in Buffalo, New York.

Going Public: 1991

At this point in the development of their company, the Bermans were ready take the next step in corporate growth. In 1990, they announced their intention to convert to public ownership, filing with the Securities and Exchange Commission for R&B's initial public offering (IPO) of stock. The Berman brothers were hoping to raise more than $11 million from the offering as a way to repay R&B's shareholders a special dividend in recompense for loans made by them to R&B. With the proceeds from the IPO, the company expected to pay $6.58 million in dividends, a figure that represented R&B's accumulated retained earnings since its 1984 organization as an S-corporation. Once the offering was completed, the Berman brothers, their father, Jordan Berman, and their brothers, Fred and Marc Berman, were expected to own roughly three-quarters of R&B's outstanding common stock, more than enough to exercise authority over the selection of the company's board of directors, corporate policies, and most corporate actions requiring shareholder approval. On March 12, 1991, R&B's IPO was completed, raising $11.44 million. The company's stock, traded on the over-the-counter market, debuted at $7.63 per share.

An integral facet of R&B's success hinged on product development, the central reason for the company's robust growth during the years immediately following its IPO. The company developed a broad range of products, focusing on those automotive parts that were not conveniently or economically available. In some cases, the company succeeded in designing parts that were superior to the parts they replaced—the OEM parts. In other cases, the company designed its products to fit a more diverse range of automotive makes and models than the OEM parts they replaced. R&B, for instance, designed a neoprene replacement oil drain plug for Chevrolet models that could also be used on a variety of vehicles, including vehicles made by Ford, Chrysler, and foreign manufacturers.

In the strategic science of product development, R&B demonstrated enviable execution, becoming the dominant supplier of hard-to-find parts. During the fours years after the company's IPO, annual sales more than tripled, reaching $113 million in 1995. The company collected its sales from the larger of the two market segments composing the automotive replacement parts market, the passenger and light truck segment, which accounted for $66 billion in sales in 1995, as opposed to the $26 billion

generated by the market segment for heavy duty trucks. To garner a greater share of the vast market, the Berman brothers began approaching expansion more aggressively during the mid-1990s, a strategy whose implementation was signaled by a significant acquisition. In January 1995, R&B acquired the Dorman Products division of SDI Operating Partners L.P.

Dorman, a well-known manufacturer and marketer of nuts, bolts, and other fasteners, gave R&B a signature brand, one that the company would use to fuel its expansion. In the years ahead, R&B, through its subsidiary Dorman Products of America, Ltd., introduced new product lines that required sizable investments in engineering and manufacturing. As they rolled out, the new products would be brand new, rather than rebuilt parts, incorporating improvements over the OEM parts they replaced. The emphasis was on precise tooling, requiring an unprecedented attention to engineering, primarily because the Dorman product lines would focus on "application-specific" products, that is, parts whose exacting standards of manufacture were required to fit precisely within OEM systems.

By 1997, before embarking on an acquisition spree the following year, R&B's sales had reached $153 million, thanks in large part to the incorporation and cultivation of the Dorman brand name. At this point in the company's development, it designed, packaged, and marketed more than 30,000 different automotive replacement parts and fasteners, approximately half of which were classified as hard-to-find products. Roughly 70 percent of the company's products were marketed under its own brand names, including the recent addition, Dorman, as well as Help!, HPX, Metal Work!, Safety Counts!, Mighty Lift!, Speedi-Boot!, Clutch-In!, and a dozen other trademarks. The remainder of the company's products were sold for resale under customers' private labels, other brands, or in bulk. Primarily all of the company's products were sold through automotive aftermarket retailers, such as AutoZone, The Pep Boys, and Western Auto, or through national, regional, and local warehouse distributors, such as Auto Value, Carquest, and NAPA.

In 1998, the Bermans' bid to make R&B larger and more diverse was on display. The brothers completed three acquisitions during the year, beginning with the January purchase of Scan-Tech USA/Sweden A.B. Based in Stockholm, Sweden, Scan-Tech operated as a distributor of replacement automotive parts for vehicles manufactured by Volvo and Saab. Scan-Tech, which generated roughly $10 million in sales in 1997, distributed its products throughout Europe, the United States, Russia, the Middle East, and the Far East. In September, the Bermans completed a $60 million private placement, earmarking the proceeds for new acquisitions and to repay existing debt. That same month, the Bermans began acquiring certain assets of the Service Line division belonging to Standard Motor Products, Inc. The acquisition, which included the Champ Service Line, Pik-A-Nut, and Everco, was completed in stages, ending with the purchase of Everco in January 1999. R&B's third acquisition of the year occurred in October, when the company purchased Allparts, Inc. from JPE, Inc. Based in Louisiana, Missouri, Allparts supplied automotive hydraulic brake parts to the automotive aftermarket, generating approximately $17 million in sales in 1997.

The Bermans' efforts to deliver an expanding array of new product offerings, both through in-house product development

Key Dates:

1978: The Berman brothers start an automotive parts distribution business in their garage.
1984: The company is organized as an S-corporation.
1991: An initial public offering of stock is completed.
1995: The Dorman Products division is acquired.
1998: Three acquisitions are completed.
1999: R&B restructures for the future.

and via acquisitions, produced robust financial growth. Revenues in 1998 increased $25 million, reaching $178 million during the company's 20th anniversary year. Of the increase, nearly all—$21 million—was attributable to the addition of the three companies acquired during the year. In 1999, the company doubled its rate of sales growth, recording $236 million in revenues for the year. By the time the financial totals were announced for 1999, however, alarm bells had already rung at company headquarters in Colmar, Pennsylvania. In his letter to shareholders in the company's 1999 annual report, Richard Berman referred to 1999 as "the most disappointing year in our 21-year history."

Restructuring: 1999

As R&B entered its third decade of existence, its depth and breadth of product offerings was immense. The company marketed more than 60,000 different automotive replacement parts and fasteners, enough to require its customers to search through 38 catalogs and application guides to survey the entire R&B collection. The diversity of product offerings proved to be burdensome, serving as a drag on the company's earnings. R&B's predicament was exacerbated further by a weakened automotive aftermarket and escalating selling and administrative expenses. Consequently, the 33 percent rise in sales in 1999 was offset by a decline in the company's net income from $7.6 million to $3.9 million.

The Bermans took action in late 1999 to amend the problems, deciding to incur a one-time restructuring charge to ensure that both net income and revenues would increase in the future. The restructuring charge of $9.5 million led to a more than $3 million loss for the year, as the Bermans eliminated thousands of automotive parts from its portfolio of products. The brothers' efforts to create a leaner, more profitable company extended beyond their array of products. A warehouse and production facility was shuttered in Carrollton, Georgia, and the company eliminated 158 employees from its payroll, a reduction equivalent to 12 percent of its national workforce. The Bermans also strengthened the company's marketing efforts to professional installers of automotive replacement parts, as opposed to the do-it-yourself customer that represented R&B's other primary end-user.

Although the automotive aftermarket remained weak after the restructuring changes, the Bermans' achieved improvement with their internal measures. By the end of 2000, the company's debt had been reduced by nearly $30 million, a feat accomplished within the year. Selling and administrative costs were reduced by $8 million. Although the company had weeded out a large number of underperforming products, it continued to focus on new product offerings, aiming to introduce new parts and fasteners every fiscal quarter. The management of the company's product selection, however, had become decidedly easier from the customers' perspective. The 38 catalogs and application guides produced in 2000 had been winnowed down to six publications in 2001. By 2003, the company hoped to simplify the presentation of its products further, intending to publish only four catalogs.

Although the effects of the restructuring changes could not be fully measured as the company competed in 2002, there was some indication that the changes made had engendered a positive result. During the first fiscal quarter of 2002, the company's profitability improved. R&B posted $2.1 million in net income for the quarter, more than quadrupling the $500,000 the company posted during the comparable period for the previous year. Revenues were up as well, increasing nearly 11 percent to $51.1 million for the same period. Richard Berman, though pleased with the results, was somewhat wary of committing to outright celebration. In his letter to shareholders in the company's 2001 annual report, he wrote: "While I am happy with the success of our turnaround, I am disappointed and embarrassed by our 1999 results and my management during that period of growth. The good news is that we have learned as much if not more from failure than we have success. If we don't learn, we can't improve and we'll never have a shot at meaningful growth."

Principal Subsidiaries

RB Distribution, Inc.; RB Management, Inc.; Dorman Products of America, Ltd.; RB Service Supply, L.P.; RBPEACH, Inc.; Cosmos International, Inc.; Cosmos International, Inc.; Scan-Tech USA/Sweden, A.B. (Sweden); Allparts, Inc.

Principal Competitors

Federal-Mogul Corporation; Genuine Parts Company; General Parts, Inc.

Further Reading

"A New Name from Middle Market," *Private Placement Reporter,* September 7, 1998, p. 3.
Armstrong, Michael W., "R&B Attempting to Raise $11 Million from Offering," *Philadelphia Business Journal,* October 22, 1990, p. 4.
"Auto Parts Firm to Cut Jobs," *Philadelphia Business Journal,* January 21, 2000, p. 41.
"Earnings Increase at R&B," *New York Times,* May 4, 2002, p. C4.
Kaufman, Edward, "Find a Need and Fill It," *Automotive Marketing,* July 1999, p. 36.

—Jeffrey L. Covell

Ragdoll Productions Ltd.

11 Chapel Street
Straford-Upon-Avon
Warwickshire, CV37 6EO
United Kingdom
Telephone: +44 1789 404100
Fax: +44 1789 404136
Web site: www.ragdoll.co.uk

Private Company
Incorporated: 1984
Employees: 150 (est.)
Sales: $50 million (2002 est.)
NAIC: 512110 Motion Picture and Video Production

Ragdoll Productions Ltd., is a United Kingdom-based children's media company, best known as the creators of the television show *Teletubbies.* The program, produced in conjunction with the British Broadcasting Corporation, is shown throughout the world, appearing in more than 120 countries in 41 different languages. Ragdoll holds the exclusive rights to *Teletubbies* in the Americas. In addition to video production, the company has also branched into book publishing and audio, music, and theater production.

Ragdoll's Founder Teaches School Until the Mid-1960s

Ragdoll Productions was founded by Anne Wood, who was born in England in 1937. She taught English at a secondary school for several years, then in the mid-1960s quit her post to raise a family with her husband Barrie, ultimately having two children. While teaching, she became dissatisfied with many books that were intended for children but reflected more of an adult sensibility and did little to stimulate a child's imagination. She established the first Children's Book Group in England, which allowed parents and other adults interested in children's literature to share ideas and promote books. To support this effort, in 1965 she founded a magazine, *Books for Your Children,* which recommended books and authors to parents and children, as well as to school librarians and teachers. The

Children's Book Group was also instrumental in the creation of other book groups, which in 1968 led to the foundation of an umbrella organization, the Federation of Children's Book Groups. Long after Wood ceased playing an active role in the book group movement, both the magazine, renamed *Carousel,* and the Federation continued to operate and serve a valuable function in British children's literature.

In 1976, Wood turned to television when she was approached by Yorkshire Television, a regional operation established in 1968, to apply her magazine concept to a weekly program about children's books called *The Book Tower,* which would win a number of major awards. Rather than using television solely to promote children's literature, Wood next became involved in producing children's programming that reflected the storytelling virtues she valued so much in children's books. She produced a television drama for young children based on the book *Ragdolly Anna Stories* by Jean Kenward. The choice was influenced by her daughter's attachment to a special ragdoll, which would also one day provide the inspiration for the name of her own production company. *Ragdolly Anna* proved to be very popular and was an important step in Wood's evolving television career.

In 1982, Wood was named Head of Children's Programs of TV-am, a British "breakfast television" station that generally operated from 6:00 to 9:25 in the morning. The idea for such a service originated in early 1980 when the Independent Broadcasting Authority began taking applications for this previously unfilled airtime. The winning bid, promoting a breezy news format similar to America's *Today Show* or *Good Morning America,* came from TV-am, backed by a group that included David Frost, a television personality well known on both sides of the Atlantic. BBC then announced it would also offer news-oriented programming during the early morning time slot with a show called *Breakfast Time,* which began broadcasting on January 17, 1983. Instead of being a serious news program, as expected, "Breakfast Time" took a lighter approach and offered direct competition to TV-am's proposed *Good Morning Britain.* TV-am planned to debut in May 1983, but moved up it launch date to February 1, 1983. Rushed on the air, TV-am quickly stumbled: ratings floundered and finances became uncertain. Lighter fare was introduced, improving ratings somewhat, but it was Wood who proved to be instrumental in saving TV-am from collapse. In April 1983, she introduced Roland Rat Superstar, the creation of puppeteer David Claridge, as a way to attract children home during vacation breaks. Roland was rude and loud, and although he and his puppet cohorts jarred the nerves of many parents, he became a national phenomenon, resulting in two hit records for Roland and the sale of an untold amount of merchandise, as well as a dramatic increase in ratings for TV-am's *Good Morning Britain.* In addition, Wood produced a popular Sunday morning magazine format show for pre-school children, *Rub a Dub Tub,* an experience that reinforced her desire to provide quality television for young viewers.

Despite Roland's popularity, TV-am was still losing money. An Australian investor brought in Bruce Gyngell to head the service, cut costs, and make it profitable. Gyngell was a longtime veteran of television (in 1957, he was the first person to appear on Australian TV). He was willing to take chances but was also strong-willed and easily fell out with subordinates. One of those with whom he crossed swords was Wood. According to her version of events, she was ''thrown out'' of the company. Gyngell went on to make TV-am a highly profitable venture before its demise at the end of 1992. Roland's star burned bright, but like many another superstar burned out quickly. Subsequently, Anne Wood struck out on her own.

Anne Wood Founds Ragdoll Productions in 1984

Wood accepted a commission from Channel 4 in 1984 to create a children's television program and as a result established Ragdoll Productions in Stratford-upon-Avon. From TV-am she took Robin Stevens, a puppeteer who had collaborated with her on *Rub a Dub Tub.* Together they began to develop a magazine format show, *Pob's Programme,* linked together by a monkey sock puppet character named Pob and featuring celebrity guest stars who participated in the show by following clues left in a garden by the puppet. Pob, according to the show's conceit, interrupted normal transmission, then announced himself by knocking and writing his name on the screen. The latter piece of business was inspired by Wood's observation of a child using his breath to fog a train window then tracing his finger in the condensation. It was a difficult feat to accomplish with a puppet,

so that many parents believed Pob was actually spitting on the television and writing his name in saliva, resulting in a mild controversy when a number of children imitated the character at home. Nevertheless, Pob and his cast of characters, regular features, and animation proved popular with British children. The show premiered in 1985, and over the course of three years Ragdoll produced 52 30-minute episodes of *Pob's Programme.*

Pob established Ragdoll as a viable production company, but Wood was much better prepared to create children's programming than she was to run a small business. To supplement her limited knowledge of business basics, she took a local college course on how to run a shop. Although Ragdoll was not as profitable as it might have been under more seasoned leadership, it made money, and more importantly it continued to make new children's television shows. Wood turned to ragdolls as characters for the next program that her production company developed. *Rosie and Jim,* intended for children two to eight years old, chronicled the adventures of two ragdolls who traveled on a boat with a singer/songwriter in search of inspiration. Unlike the audience, he was unaware that Rosie and Jim had the ability to come to life. Joined by a duck character (named Duck), they invariably fell into mischief. By the end of each episode, order was restored and a new song, inspired by the day's events, capped the program.

Introduced in 1990, *Rosie and Jim,* was more than just a second popular program to the credit of Ragdoll. It was instrumental in broadening the production company's revenue streams. With VCR's now a common household device, Ragdoll began to take full advantage of the growing market for children's videos. Moreover, *Rosie and Jim* offered a wide range or other merchandising opportunities: from ragdolls and toys to apparel. The company ultimately opened its own shop in Stratford where merchandise based on its characters could be sold. Moreover, a play area for children allowed Wood and her colleagues to observe their audience and make notes on their reactions to company products.

Next to be developed by Ragdoll was *Brum,* the adventures of an automobile character. It quickly became a hit in Britain with both viewers and merchandisers. Ragdoll then created *Tots TV,* conceived by Wood and written by Robin Stevens and Andrew Davenport, who also played two of the show's three tot puppets, Tom and Tiny. In essence, the tots lived in a secret house where they could spy on the outside world. It was a live action, 15-minute program filmed on location, and the first mainstream British children's show to expose pre-school children to a second language, French. *Tots TV* first aired in Britain in January 1993, and three years later came to America through the auspices of New York-based The Itsy Bitsy Entertainment Company, whose CEO, Kenn Viselman, was known for the highly successful merchandising of *Thomas the Tank Engine.* Rather than opting for commercial television, he found a home for *Tots TV* on PBS, highly regarded for its lineup of quality children's programming. A number of changes were effected to make the show suitable for American television: episodes were lengthened to 30 minutes, the second language was changed from French to Spanish, and voices were redubbed with American accents rather than British. On the merchandising side, the show launched a Web site, home video sales, and a toy line.

Teletubbies Concept Developed in Mid-1990s

While *Tots TV* made its debut in America in October 1996, Ragdoll was preparing for the British launch of a new program: *Teletubbies*. It originated from an idea of one of the Tots, Andrew Davenport, who was also a trained speech therapist. He had an idea for a sitcom aimed at seven-year-olds that never panned out. Nevertheless, Wood latched onto two of Davenport's characters: spacemen, one more courageous than the other, who try to make sense of everyday household objects. Often surprised, they easily fell down and when worried hugged one another for comfort. As Wood and Davenport developed this germ of an idea into a fully realized program concept, the characters doubled in number to four and went from looking like NASA astronauts to large roly-poly characters with television screens in their tummies on which films would be projected, hence Teletubbies. The target audience was children one to two years of age, and the intent was to create a program about play. In a manner similar to children, the Teletubbies (Po, Laa-Laa, Dipsy, and Tinky Winky) simply lived for play. Unlike many of Wood's earlier low-budget efforts, *Teletubbies* was an expensive proposition, from the outset intended for an international audience and requiring deep-pocketed partners. Wood insisted on a life-size film set for the show, requiring millions of dollars to landscape a six-acre Teletubbyland and construct a Tubbytronic Superdome. To help bankroll and develop the concept, Ragdoll turned to BBC Children's Programming, BBC Education, and BBC Worldwide. Because BBC did not sell advertising, in order to make Teletubbies a successful venture it had to rely on merchandise sales and international licensing of the program. The payoff for Ragdoll was expected to be drawn from the retention of the show's rights in the Americas.

The show's creators had high aspirations for *Teletubbies*. They relied on contemporary theories about how children learn to speak, interviewed nursery school teachers, and observed children in group situations in order to make *Teletubbies* an effective way to prepare its audience for preschool. The characters with the television screens on their tummies were also intended to help young children to accept an increasingly media-saturated world, preparing them for life in the global village. As soon as *Teletubbies* premiered in Britain in the spring of 1997, however, it became the object of criticism by those who challenged the assumptions of the show. Ragdoll was accused of taking part in the on-going "dumbing down" of television and of designing the show more as a merchandising vehicle than a true educational program. Critics focused on the show's infantile dialogue and repetition, maintaining that far from helping children to develop language skills, *Teletubbies* retarded

speech development. Moreover, they suggested that the show helped to make children more dependent on the media, dismissing the idea of the need to make them comfortable with technology.

Despite these very public concerns, the show quickly became a hit in Britain, and the four Teletubbies gained star status, becoming known as the "New Fab Four." Many parents complained about the repetitious nature of the show, yet they also spent millions of dollars buying *Teletubbies'* merchandise for their children. To protect the reputation of the show, the actors playing the four Teletubbies were forbidden to grant interviews, and one, a Shakespearean actor named Dave Thompson who played Tinky Winky, was fired after it was learned he had danced in public wearing only a balloon. Ragdoll and BBC also had to contend with reports that *Teletubbies* was also proving to be popular with the twenty-somethings of the club set, who watched the program while coming down from the drug Ecstasy, and that the gay community adopted purse-carrying Tinky Winky as an icon.

Ragdoll and its U.S. partner Itsy Bitsy sold *Teletubbies* to PBS in a deal reported to be worth $1.6 million. Toymaker Hasbro also geared up to introduce an extensive line of toys, games, and puzzles for the market. In addition, Itsy Bitsy lined up deals for books, videos, and other merchandise. *Teletubbies* premiered in the United States in 1998, backed by a considerable amount of advance billing that resulted in the show becoming an immediate hit. It gained additional publicity, not entirely welcomed by the producers, when the Reverend Jerry Falwell, a nationally known evangelical, maintained that Tinky Winky was championing tolerance of a gay life style. The controversy soon passed, and *Teletubbies* reception in the United States mirrored its success in England: cranky parents tolerated the show and bought large quantities of merchandise. It was a lucrative business for Ragdoll and Itsy Bitsy, and they were very protective of their franchise. In 1999, they sued Wal-Mart Stores, which had been selling four figurines that closely resembled the Teletubbies, called Bubbly Chubbies. The mass merchandiser quickly settled the suit by pulling the items from the shelves and destroying the inventory.

Ragdoll turned its attention to producing its first animation project, *Badjelly the Witch,* a 30-minute program based on a Spike Milligan's 1973 children's book of the same name. After failing to interest the BBC in co-producing, Wood elected to have Ragdoll go it alone, starting pre-production work in 1998. When completed, *Badjelly the Witch* premiered in England on BBC1 on Christmas Day 2000. Subsequent broadcasts and video distribution deals were set up around the world. In the meantime, in February 2001 the company announced that it would stop producing new episodes of *Teletubbies*. Nevertheless, Ragdoll had made enough episodes to ensure than the program would continue to be broadcast for many years to come. The agreement with PBS, for instance, lasted until 2008. Although Ragdoll's profits were reported to have slumped in 2001, Wood maintained that the company was simply investing in new technology and on research and development. Clearly *Teletubbies* had established Ragdoll as a production company to be reckoned with in children's programming. Wood's belief in the future of the company was supported by her decision to sever its ties with Itsy Bitsy in the fall of 2001. Several months later Ragdoll opened an office in New York to handle merchandising and programming in the western hemisphere.

Principal Competitors

AOL Time Warner; News Corp.; Viacom Inc.; The Walt Disney Company.

Further Reading

Ballantyne, Helen, and Lindsay Percival-Straunik, ''Success Is Child's Play,'' *Director,* June 1999, p. 104.

Britt, Ross, Chuck Ross, et al., ''Teletubbies Are Coming: Brit Hit Sets U.S. Invasion,'' *Advertising Age,* January 19, 1998, p. 12.

Brunton, Michael, ''Ga-Ga in Wonderland,'' *Time,* October 6, 1997.

''Ragdoll Facing Threat of Boycott,'' *Coventry Evening Telegraph,* July 24, 2002, p. 15.

Robins, Jane, ''From Ragdoll to Riches Via Tubbyland,'' *Independent,* April 30, 1999, p. 8.

Sweet, Matthew, ''A Mother Who's Always There for Her Tubbies,'' *Independent Sunday,* April 25, 1999, p. 4.

Wolcott, Jennifer, ''Time for Teletubbies,'' *Christian Science Monitor,* April 10, 1998, p. B1.

—Ed Dinger

Recording for the Blind & Dyslexic

20 Roszel Road
Princeton, New Jersey 08540
U.S.A.
Telephone: (609) 452-0606
Toll Free: (800) 221-4792
Fax: (609) 520-7990
Web site: http://www.rfbd.org

Nonprofit Company
Incorporated: 1951 as National Committee for Recording
    for the Blind
Employees: 324
Sales: $45.3 million (2001)
NAIC: 611710 Educational Support Services

Recording for the Blind & Dyslexic (RFB&D) is a national nonprofit organization based in Princeton, New Jersey, dedicated to recording textbooks for people who are unable to read standard text because of visual, learning, or other physical disabilities. Although the organization was originally established to help individuals who are blind, now more than 70 percent of the people it serves are diagnosed as having dyslexia. Students from kindergarten through postgraduate work, as well as professionals, are served by RFB&D, which offers 102,000 members more than 91,000 titles. The organization has especially strong collections on science, medicine, environmental issues, law, women's studies, Jewish studies, literature, and fiction. RFB&D is heavily dependent on its volunteers, numbering more than 5,400, who staff its 32 recording studios located across the United States. Over the last half-century a long list of celebrities as well as experts in every academic field have lent their voices to RFB&D recordings.

Need for Recorded Books Grows Out of World War II

In 1944, in the midst of World War II, Congress passed the GI Bill of Rights, which provided financial assistance to war veterans who wanted to go to college. Many soldiers who lost their sight in the war sought to take advantage of the program but, unlike students who had been blind since birth, they were severely hampered by their inability to read Braille. The clear answer to their needs was the audio recording of textbooks, a task taken up by the Women's Auxiliary of the New York Public Library. One of the women who joined the Auxiliary and became involved in the recording program was Anne T. Macdonald, who would go on to become the driving force behind the creation of RFB&D. The wife of a Wall Street financier, she had served as an Army nurse as well as a Red Cross volunteer and had already worked with wounded veterans. At first she attempted to serve the auxiliary program as a reader, but when her voice proved unsuited for the job she focused her energies on administration. Because the demand for recorded materials grew, in 1948 she established a separate organization, Recording for the Blind, to better carry on the effort. In the beginning the textbooks were recorded in an attic studio of what is now the New York Public Library's Humanities and Social Science Library branch, one of the world's great research libraries, located at 42nd Street and Fifth Avenue. The organization relied on SoundScriber dictating machines to do the original recordings. The material was then transferred to six-inch vinylite disks, which only had a 24-minute capacity. Despite these technical limitations the recorded material proved invaluable to the veterans.

The organization was incorporated as the National Committee for Recording for the Blind, Inc. (RFB) in 1951, expanding its mandate beyond veterans to include everyone with disabilities that make reading challenging or impossible. Although staffed by volunteers and using New York Public Library facilities, RFB still required funding for equipment and supplies. To purchase its first soundproof recording booth it relied on a Wall Street broker to pass the hat on the floor of the New York Stock Exchange, an effort that succeeded in raising $800. A more formal and more important source of funding came from The Fund for Adult Education, which awarded RFB with a three-year $75,000 grant that enabled it to become a national organization. Anne Macdonald served as the chairman of the organization's board of directors from 1951 to 1953 and with approval from The Fund for Adult Education was instrumental in spreading the RFB operation across the country. She traveled extensively, setting up recording studios in Phoenix, Arizona; Denver, Colorado; Oak Ridge, Tennessee; Louisville, Kentucky; Chicago, Illinois; and Los Angeles, California. In 1953 a studio located in Athens, Georgia, opened. Also in 1953 the official name of the organization was shortened to Recording for the Blind and Anne Macdonald ended her term as chair, although she remained active in RFB for the rest of her life.

First Tape in 1957

RFB remained closely allied with the New York Public Library for a number of years. In 1957 a Central Embossing Studio was set up in the 58th Street branch to duplicate and ship the recorded texts. Prior to this time each unit was responsible for mailing tapes to students. The new studio was funded by grants provided by the James Foundation, the New York Foundation, and the American Foundation for the Blind. With the new facilities RFB was able to take advantage of advances in technology. In 1957 it made its first recording tape, which was then embossed on seven-inch vinylite disks capable of holding 60 minutes of recorded material. As a result, production increased by 300 percent. In general it was the ability of the regional studios and national organization to coordinate their activities that allowed a growing number of textbooks to be recorded and distributed to a growing number of disabled students each year. RFB also improved its ability to record new materials in 1957 when The United Nations loaned the use of six soundproof recording booths and some 60 UN staff members became RFB volunteers. Throughout the rest of the 1950s, even as it relied on the New York Public Library, RFB continued its nationwide expansion, mostly by establishing local studios in college communities. In 1957 new facilities opened in Lenox, Massachusetts and Orland Park, Illinois. The following year, additional studios opened in Charlottesville, Virginia; Winnetka, Illinois; Princeton, New Jersey; Detroit, Michigan; and Miami, Florida. In 1959 New Haven, Connecticut, established a recording studio. Affiliation with colleges and universities allowed RFB studios to recruit volunteer readers who were experts on the textbooks they read aloud. Years later an organization senior vice-president, Barbara Vandervolk, explained to the *New York Times*, "I've listened to volunteers read art books. Imagine being able to describe a Renoir to someone who can't see it." RFB also turned to celebrity readers to help raise the profile of the organization. Some of these early volunteers were Walter Cronkite, Loretta Young, and Alistair Cooke. In the years that followed other notable people lent their time and talents to RFB, including Steve Allen, Ed Asner, Anne Bancroft, Mel Brooks, Cher, Rita Hayworth, Gene Kelly, Mary Tyler Moore, Paul Newman, Gregory Peck, Barbara Walters, and Robert Young.

By the early 1960s the national RFB office had outgrown its patchwork network of studios and offices provided by the largesse of the New York Public Library. In 1963 a central operations facility was purchased in New York City, allowing RFB to consolidate its ever-growing library of recordings and to more efficiently duplicate and ship recorded texts to students. Also in 1963 the organization launched a $950,000 national fundraising campaign to finance the establishment of a national headquarters in Manhattan. RFB's new home, located at 215 East 58th Street, opened in 1965. A year later a new master library in the building began to house the book collection as it was converted from vinyl disks to reel-to-reel tapes. In short order, reel-to-reel became supplanted by a newer technology, the cassette tape, each of which was capable of holding as much as four hours of recorded material. Several new regional recording studios were established during the 1960s: Upland, California, in 1963; the University of Chicago in 1966; Palo Alto, California, in 1967; and Williamstown, Massachusetts, in 1968.

In the decade of the 1970s new studios were established in Naperville, Illinois, and Peoria, Arizona, in 1972; Austin, Texas, in 1973; and Santa Barbara, California, and Washington, D.C., in 1976. During this period the demand for textbooks on tape grew even greater, due in large part to the passage of the federal Education for All Handicapped Children Act in 1975, which mandated that a free and appropriate education was a right for all children with disabilities. Over the next decade the number of RFB members and the amount of books in circulation doubled. To help meet the challenge RFB installed a computerized ordering system that by 1980 was able to process 500 book orders a day. By now all of the books were distributed on cassette tape.

With the accumulation of titles and an increase in demand for RFB's services, the organization after less than 20 years in its 58th Street location found that it had once more outgrown its space. With the price of Manhattan real estate prohibitively expensive, RFB's board decided to move out of the city, opting to build a new headquarters in Princeton, New Jersey. The new working facility opened in 1983. It contained administrative offices, duplicating and shipping operations, a master library of all of RFB's titles, and housed a staff of librarians to assist members in finding appropriate titles. Of more importance, it was able to triple the number of books the organization could ship each year. Unlike the prior headquarters in Manhattan, the Princeton facility also had the luxury of available real estate to accommodate future expansion, which in a very short time became a necessity.

Fundraising efforts, as a result, were forced to keep pace. In 1985 RFB received a $1.5 million grant from the W.K. Kellogg Foundation to upgrade the computerized delivery system and establish more studios. A Boston studio opened that year and in 1988 recording facilities were established in Philadelphia, Pennsylvania, and El Segundo, California. Distribution was greatly enhanced by the 1985 purchase of high-speed duplicating machines that were four times faster than the previous models. The math and sciences collections were strengthened by a $750,000 grant from the National Science Foundation in 1988 that funded the recruitment of volunteers with backgrounds in the math and science disciplines. By the end of the decade, however, RFB's financial needs warranted the launch of a five-year $30 million fundraising campaign called "A Vision for the Future." The money was earmarked to help support the growth in the organization's operations and expand the headquarters, as well as contribute to an endowment to provide ongoing funding. With the completion of the successful campaign, RFB was able to add 10,000 square feet in a major addition to the Princeton headquarters. A year later, it purchased ten acres of adjacent land to accommodate even larger expansions in the future.

Testing Digital Technology in the 1990s

Much of RFB's need for increased funding was the result of the organization's need to take advantage of new technologies to better serve its membership. In 1990 RFB established an electronic text operation to make textbooks available on computer disks that could be accessed with adaptive computer equipment. Volunteers soon began coding books for conversion to the new E-Text format. In the mid-1990s the organization took steps to prepare for the rise of multimedia technologies, initiating a pilot program to make digital recordings of textbooks in CD-ROM and other formats. The first of these digital books were demonstrated at the World Blind Union international assembly in Toronto in 1996. A year later the organization became an instrumental part of an international consortium committed to developing the next generation of audio books. For decades users of audiocassette books not only had to deal with a large number of tapes devoted to each book, they could only navigate the text by winding and rewinding and counting beeptones noting page and chapter designations. The new digital books could be contained on a single compact disk and the players offered voice-identifying buttons as well as searching and bookmarking features that were a major advance over cassette technology. Moreover, the players had the ability to speed up the reading without raising the pitch of the voice, an attractive feature for many users who preferred to cut down on the amount of time required to listen to a textbook read aloud.

In 1993 RFB's founder, Anne Macdonald, died at the age of 96. Three years later, to better reflect the large and increasing number of members with learning disabilities it served, the organization to which she devoted so many years of her life changed its name to Recording for the Blind & Dyslexic. By the time of its 50th anniversary in 1998 the changes that had taken place in the organization over the preceding decades were striking.

Membership topped 50,000 and the number of books in circulation exceeded 200,000, and the technologies available to serve its constituency were incredibly advanced over the vinylite disk first relied on. Anne Macdonald always maintained that "Education is a right, not a privilege," and more than ever RFB&D was doing its part to make that belief a reality. She also once said, "The quest for knowledge has no limits, and RFB has a forever expanding future."

In the late 1990s RFB&D continued to grow to meet an ever-increasing need. Improved microphones led to the introduction of boothless studios in 1995, which was also an important factor in allowing volunteers to begin setting up home recording studios to relieve the organization's work load, an initiative launched in 1997. Local studio facilities continued to open as well: West Windsor, New Jersey, in 1993; West Hills, California, in 1995; and Santa Ana, California; and Boca Raton, Florida, in 1998. Moreover, the organization launched a web site and continued its transition from analog to digital recording, which offered the possibility of consolidating all of the textbook files into a single computer archive. As a result RFB&D could decrease its need for storage space and devote freed-up resources for other uses.

To meet these future needs a three-year $35 million fundraising campaign was launched as part of its 50th anniversary in 1998, raising a total of $40.5 million. The move to digital technology was especially costly, and while many nonprofit organizations saw a significant drop in contributions after the events of September 11, 2001, RFB&D's funding remained strong, allowing it to be ever-mindful of its mission to serve the evolving needs of its membership.

Principal Divisions

Program Services; Support Services.

Further Reading

Greenman, Catherine, "Books for the Blind Go Digital," *New York Times,* July 12, 2001, p G4.
The Now and the Future: A Sound Educational Investment for 50 Years, Princeton, N.J.: Recording for the Blind & Dyslexic, 1998.
Sharkey, Joe, "A Quiet Place Where Sounds Becomes Sight," *New York Times,* April 21, 1996, Sec. 13NJ, p. 1.
Taber, George M., "Bringing a Businessman's Eye to Setting Priorities," *Business News New Jersey,* May 13, 2002, p. 11.

—Ed Dinger

Robinson Helicopter Company

2901 Airport Drive
Torrance, California 90505
U.S.A.
Telephone: (310) 539-0508
Fax: (310) 539-5198
Web site: http://www.robinsonhelicopter.com

Private Company
Incorporated: June 1973
Employees: 600
Sales: $100 million (2001 est.)
NAIC: 336411 Aircraft Manufacturing

Robinson Helicopter Company is the leading manufacturer of light piston-engine helicopters. It produces a greater number of civil helicopters per year than any other manufacturer, and 80 percent of those made in the United States. Robinson's two-seat R22 and four-seat R44 helicopters offer public and private users a low-cost alternative to jet turbine helicopters such as the Bell JetRanger. Unique in the multi-tiered aerospace industry, Robinson builds most of its own components.

Uplifting Origins

Frank Robinson was born in 1930 and grew up near Seattle. He financed his education at the University of Washington by working on cargo ships, reports *Forbes*; thus, he did not graduate until he was 27. Robinson began his engineering career working on the CH-1 Skyhook for Cessna Aircraft Company. He later worked on rotorcraft research for manufacturers including McCulloch Motor Company, Kaman Aircraft, Bell Helicopter, and, finally, Hughes Aircraft Company, which he joined in 1969.

Robinson spent 16 years trying to convince his aerospace employers that such a market even existed. Robinson was not the first person who aspired to create an affordable helicopter for personal use. Designer Stanley Hiller had fanned the idea in the late-1940s, and some futurists' vision of the 1950s and 1960s included a helicopter in every driveway. However, it was the military, beginning with the Korean War, which made the most use of helicopters.

Against the advice of colleagues, Robinson struck out on his own in June 1973. Design work on his new lightweight helicopter consumed the living room and garage of Robinson's Palos Verdes residence, which was itself mortgaged to finance the aircraft's development. Robinson would also look close to home for key staff. His wife Barbara became marketing director, and three of the couple's six children would also eventually work for the company. Some dubbed them "Swift Family Robinson."

In 1975, Robinson had a working prototype of the first model, the R22, which had been constructed in a tin hangar at the Torrance Airport in southern California. It would take four years to gain FAA certification. The prototype was then sold to a flight school, a market he told the *Los Angeles Times* he had not even considered when he began to develop the aircraft. The R22 would eventually dominate the world helicopter trainer market. Radio stations, which used helicopters to report on traffic conditions, were another important early market.

Robinson Helicopter soon opened a plant at Torrance Airport. Initial financing was in the $2 to $3 million range. Frank Robinson told *American Metal Market* that $500,000 of this went towards computer-controlled machine tools.

The lightweight piston-engine helicopter could rival the performance of its turbine-powered rivals at a fraction of the cost. Powered by a 160-horsepower Lycoming engine, the R22 had a fiberglass fuselage and sold for a base price of $40,000. Fuel consumption of 20 miles per gallon was claimed for the R22, which was also said to be the quietest chopper around. The R22 would eventually claim world speed and altitude records for its class.

Robinson had projected sales of 500 units a year by 1982, reported *American Metal Markets*, but did not meet the figure due to a recession. After making eight aircraft in 1979, Robin-

Key Dates:

1973: Frank Robinson begins designing his first prototype helicopter.
1975: The R22 helicopter makes its first test flights.
1979: The R22 is certified by the Federal Aviation Administration (FAA) and deliveries begin.
1987: Robinson turns its first profit.
1988: The company is producing more helicopters per year than any other manufacturer.
1989: With 310 units delivered, the R22 is world's best-selling light aircraft for the year.
1991: R22 production peaks at 402 units.
1997: R44 variants for police and TV news crews are introduced.
2001: Robinson promotes lightweight helipads for business sites.

son produced 78 units in 1980 and 176 the next year. The company by then had 150 employees.

Crisis and Recovery in the 1980s

Robinson continued to improve its products. In September 1981, it began offering a more the powerful R22 HP for a base price of $59,850. The Model R22 Alpha, with increased gross weight, was rolled out two years later. In August 1985, the company introduced the Beta model of the R22, featuring advanced avionics. A float-equipped version, dubbed the Mariner, was introduced later in the year and was priced at $94,850.

Besides the recession, product liability was another major factor in slowing sales across the entire U.S. general aviation industry in the early 1980s. Robinson, reported *Forbes*, did not carry liability insurance due to its supreme confidence in his product. Two early R22's were in fatal accidents, however, leading to a redesign of rotor blades. Sales plunged to just 64 units in 1983. Robinson was generally successful in winning lawsuits, having them dismissed, or settling them for reasonable amounts.

Driven by foreign sales, production was soon returning to normal. Robinson was already exporting half of its production in the mid-1980s. The rotorcraft were quite popular with cattle ranchers Down Under. After breaking even for a couple of years, Robinson Helicopter turned its first profit in 1987.

Revenues reached $23.5 million in 1988, when the company sold 204 units. A fully equipped R22 sold for about $105,000 then. A weak dollar was good for exports, which accounted for 80 percent of sales. By this time, Robinson was selling more helicopters than anybody else, including Bell, Sikorsky, Boeing, and McDonnell Douglas. Robinson had 310 employees at the time.

Two More Seats in the 1990s

While California's giant military aerospace firms idled plants after the fall of the Soviet Union, Robinson Helicopter was thriving. The company delivered 384 R22's in 1990; sales were $48 million. The company had sales of $50 million in 1991, when it shipped a record 402 helicopters. Employment would soon pass 400 workers.

Frank Robinson had begun to work on a design for a four-seat helicopter in the mid-1980s. The first prototype took to the

air in March 1990. With its four-seat capacity, the R44 was expected to sell well in the executive aircraft market. Its greater size also opened new possibilities in police work, agriculture, and fish spotting. Robinson began taking orders for the R44 in March 1992 at $235,000 for a fully equipped model. In contrast, the Bell Jet Ranger, a five-seat, turbine-powered helicopter, cost $600,000. The R44 also boasted low operating costs and required less frequent servicing than typical helicopters. In fact, its maintenance schedule was similar to that of light fixed-wing aircraft—an overhaul only every 2,000 hours (later extended to 2,200 hours).

The first production R44 Astro was delivered in February 1993. Robinson was planning to establish a production line for this aircraft in Santa Maria until the city of Torrance offered the company a good rate on a lease of additional land. Santa Maria's purportedly cumbersome licensing process helped seal that decision. Robinson had also looked at locations in the South and Midwest. Robinson moved to a new 260,000-square-foot plant in July 1994.

Sixty workers were soon laid off, however, due to a sales slowdown. The National Transportation Safety Board (NTSB) soon began investigating the R22 after a wave of crashes. These were eventually attributed to pilot error.

The year 1996 saw the introduction of the R22 Beta II, which had a new engine and offered improved hover performance for a base price of $135,000. Robinson brought out a special police-oriented variant of the R44 in mid-1997. Its nose turret could be fitted with infrared sensors or a video camera. The R44 Newscopter debuted around the same time, outfitted for television news coverage.

The company continued to grow in the late 1990s. During this time, the R44—more versatile with its four seats—became the world's top-selling helicopter. (The R44, which featured new hydraulic controls after 1999, was then priced around $300,000.) An overflowing order book called for a major expansion of the Torrance plant. Robinson had 800 employees in 2000.

New Horizions Beyond 2000

Production fell from 390 aircraft in 2000 to 328 in 2001; Robinson still out-produced Eurocopter, its closest volume rival, which saw output rise fifteen percent to 280 units. There was an overall downturn in the U.S. helicopter industry due to a strong dollar, a recession, and the September 11, 2001 terrorist attacks.

Frank Robinson made large donations to two aviation history projects. In 2000, he gave $1 million to the Smithsonian National Air and Space Museum to fund a rotary-wing aircraft display at its new Dulles Airport facility. Two years later, the American Helicopter Museum received another $1 million to purchase its building in West Chester, Pennsylvania.

Like other manufacturers, Robinson had an eye on the emerging Chinese market, which was expected to field 2,000 helicopters by 2010. Russia was another important new territory. In the United States, Robinson was behind an initiative to place lightweight helipads atop business buildings and in industrial parks. In early 2002, a Honda dealer in Santa Ana, California, began installing the first at his auto lot. He planned to commute to work in his R44.

Principal Competitors

Bell Helicopter Textron, Inc.; Enstrom Helicopter Corporation; Eurocopter Group; Schweizer Aircraft Corp.

Further Reading

Brown, David A., "Piston-Powered R44 Offers Low-Cost Flight," *Aviation Week & Space Technology*, March 29, 1993, p. 46.

Del Valle, Christina, and Larry Armstrong, "33 Crashes: Design Flaw or Pilot Error? The FAA Is Under Pressure to Ground Robinson Helicopter," *Business Week*, June 12, 1995, p. 40.

Flint, Jerry, "The Bird Man of Torrance," *Forbes*, April 15, 1991, pp. 64+.

"Foreign Helicopter Giants Vie for Chinese Market," *Xinhua News Agency*, June 12, 2002.

"Frank Robinson Donates $1 Million to Helicopter Museum," *Business & Commercial Aviation*, June 2002, p. 12.

Gray, Peter, "Matching Up," *Flight International*, January 26, 1994, pp. 40+.

Jones, Sam L., "Robinson Maintains Its Niche for Piston-Powered 'Copters," *American Metal Market*, July 1, 1985, p. 8.

Lambert, Mark, "Civil Helicopters; 1984 Is the Year of Change," *Interavia*, January 1984, p. 37.

——, "Hard Times, But Some Hope for the Helicopter Men," *Interavia*, April 1983, p. 297.

Lert, Peter, "Modern Maturity," *Air Progress*, August 1989, pp. 58+.

Lewis, Paul, "Annual Sales: Output Slumps as Economies Slow," *Flight International*, February 5, 2002, p. 25.

Lopez, Ramon, "Nothing to Be Afraid Of," *Flight International*, March 15, 1995, pp. 36+.

Morris, John, "Little Growth Forecast for Helicopter Deliveries," *Business & Commercial Aviation*, March 2002, p. 10.

Norris, Guy, "Around Again," *Flight International*, September 16, 1992, pp. 74+.

Pae, Peter, "Flying High with Modest Venture; Robinson Becomes Top-Selling Maker of Civilian Copters by Sticking to Its Mom-and-Pop Origins," *Los Angeles Times*, September 25, 2000, p. C1.

Parke, Robert B., "FAA Limits Robinson Flight Operations," *Business & Commercial Aviation*, March 1995, pp. 28+.

Phillips, Edward H., "NTSB Urges FAA to Ground R22/R44 Helicopters," *Aviation Week & Space Technology*, January 16, 1995, pp. 29+.

——, "Robinson, Federal Agencies at Odds Over R44, R22 Issues," *Aviation Week & Space Technology*, August 1, 1994, pp. 67+.

——, "R22 Main Rotor Focus of NTSB Report," *Aviation Week & Space Technology*, April 8, 1996, p. 33.

Robinson Helicopter Company, Torrance, CA: Robinson Helicopter Company, c. 2001.

"Robinson Helicopter: The Discipline of the Marketplace," *Financial World* (New York), June 8, 1993, p. 39.

Sarsfield, Kate, "Hydraulic Controls Prove Big Hit for R44 Sales," *Flight International*, January 16, 2001, p. 20.

——, "Order Surge Fuels Robinson's Plans for Expansion," *Flight International*, February 1, 2000, p. 29.

——, "Robinson Considers New Engine for Popular R44," *Flight International*, February 27, 2001, p. 27.

Scott, William B., "Reliability, Low Operating Costs Key to Robinson R-44 Sales," *Aviation Week & Space Technology*, April 13, 1992, p. 57.

Smith, Bruce A., "Robinson Helicopter's R44 to Offer Greater Capacity, Speed Than R22," *Aviation Week & Space Technology*, January 21, 1991, pp. 53+.

Sweetman, Bill, "US Manufacturers Get Their House in Order," *Interavia Business & Technology*, February 2001, p. 24.

Swertlow, Frank, "Choppers on the Cheap," *Los Angeles Business Journal*, July 3, 2000, p. 44.

Vartabedian, Ralph, "Low-Cost Copter Builder Tops Sales of Big-Name Rivals," *Los Angeles Times*, December 15, 1992, p. D1.

——, "Robinson Helicopters Taking Off," *Los Angeles Times*, Sec. 4, April 17, 1989, p. 1.

Wastnage, Justin, "Upgraded Raven Goes on Sale," *Flight International*, July 9, 2002, p. 25.

—Frederick C. Ingram

Salant Corporation

1114 Avenue of the Americas
New York, New York 10036
U.S.A.
Telephone: (212) 221-7500
Fax: (212) 354-3470

Public Company
Incorporated: 1919 as Salant & Salant, Inc.
Employees: 600
Sales: $419.28 million
Stock Exchanges: New York
Ticker Symbol: SLNT
NAIC: 315223 Men's and Boys' Cut and Sew Shirt
    (Except Work Shirt) Manufacturing; 315221 Men's
    and Boys' Cut and Sew Underwear and Nightwear
    Manufacturing; 315224 Men's and Boys' Cut and
    Sew Trouser, Slack and Jean Manufacturing; 315228
    Men's and Boys' Cut and Sew Other Outerwear
    Manufacturing; 315231 Women's and Girls' Cut and
    Sew Lingerie, Loungewear and Nightwear
    Manufacturing; 315291 Infants' Cut and Sew Apparel
    Manufacturing; 315999 Other Apparel Accessories
    and Other Apparel Manufacturing

A leading apparel company in the United States, Salant Corporation designs, manufactures, imports, and markets men's wear under several very well known brand names, including Perry Ellis, Ocean Pacific, and Axis. The company's clothing retails in upscale and mid-range department stores. Salant floundered in and out of bankruptcy court throughout the 1990s, during which time it shed its children's wear, denim, and accessories businesses to focus on Perry Ellis branded men's wear in the early years of the 21st century. Having emerged from Chapter 11 reorganization in 1999, Salant diversified within the better men's wear segment in 2002.

Established 1893

Salant Corporation, incorporated in 1987, is the successor business to Salant & Salant, Incorporated, originally a manufac-turer of work shirts. Solomon Salant founded the original company as a partnership with his son, Gabriel, and a third partner in 1893. The partner soon left the company, leaving no mark on its history. Gabriel stayed and the company became a father and son operation, incorporated in 1919. Although the company first became public in 1959 when it was listed on the NASDAQ supplemental, in 1971 Salant distributed enough shares through a primary and a secondary offering to be listed on the New York Stock Exchange. The Salant family decided to offer company shares publicly to diversify the family investments and reorganize equity.

In the beginning, the company's major business was selling to wholesalers and large customers like Montgomery Ward, which maintained a long and substantial account with the company. When the Spanish-American war broke out in 1898, the company also supplied uniforms for the military. Although the army account dried up upon the war's completion, the company maintained its small customer base of wholesalers and large firms well into the 20th century.

Diversification: 1930–70

The face of the company changed as it began to diversify in the 1930s. The biggest change occurred in 1938 when the company began to manufacture utility pants made out of twill. The pants were predecessors to the khakis of World War II. Utility pants became one of Salant's principal products by the 1950s.

Although the company primarily manufactured slacks, jeans, and utility pants between the 1950s and 1970s, it diversified into many other areas, among them sportswear, with sport shirts in 1949, jackets in 1954, and casual slacks in 1955. It started selling children's wear in 1962 and jeans in 1967. Acquisitions in 1964 and 1966 brought coveralls, men's and boys' outerwear, suits and sport jackets, and a higher priced line of men's and boys' slacks to the company's product mix. In 1964, the company also became one of the first to introduce permanent press apparel, which contributed a substantial amount to company sales until the early 1970s.

As clothing styles changed, the company moved away from the production of chambray work shirts and twill pants, favoring the manufacture of popularly priced jeans and sport and western shirts. This shift in focus by the company's original and largest division allowed it to retain its profitability and position as Salant's mainstay until the demand for jeans slowed and competition, especially from overseas, grew in the mid-1970s.

Retrenchment: The 1970s

These market changes adversely affected the Salant & Salant division's profitability beginning in 1976. The business, which Donald Hamilton of Furman Selz noted in *Forbes* was "barely profitable when the jeans business was booming . . . had to cut prices below breakeven" when the jeans maker Levi Strauss lowered its prices. At the same time, rising interest costs and customer demands strained Salant's ability to provide "mostly low-margin private label goods" to retailers like Sears, Roebuck & Co. and Kmart, according to *Forbes*. Between 1977 and 1980 the division's cumulative losses amounted to $4 a share or about half of Salant's reported earnings during that period. Believing the basic jeans business was no longer a growing market, the company closed the Salant & Salant division in 1981 and began to focus on men's wear, specifically its branded apparel in its large and successful Thomson division. By 1993, the company's product mix was 82 percent men's apparel and accessories, 8 percent women's apparel and accessories, and 10 percent children's apparel and accessories.

As Salant diversified its products it also added to its distribution. In the 1930s and early 1940s, the company might have had 50 customers. In the 1950s, the company continued to sell to national chains and mail-order houses, but gradually wholesalers disappeared by either going out of business or becoming retail chains. As its traditional customer base changed, Salant's management decided to increase volume by selling to smaller retailers and regional chains. By 1972, the company had widened its customer base to about 20,000 accounts, which represented about 37,000 separate stores. At that time, the company sold to most types of retailers, including national chains, mail-order houses, discount stores, regional chains, department stores, smaller independent retailers, and golf pro shops. Wholesalers had become an insignificant part of the company's business.

Although Salant began to broaden its customer base, some of its customers continued to make up significant portions of company sales. Sears, Roebuck & Co. remained one of Salant's largest customers for nearly three decades. Two of Salant's

subsidiaries held agreements (one started in 1960 and the other in 1967) with Sears to buy a set amount of its requirements. In 1971 Sears was the company's biggest customer, accounting for 17 percent of sales. By 1980, Sears accounted for 34 percent of net sales, J.C. Penney Co. Inc. for 16 percent, and Kmart for 12 percent of net sales. In 1985, Sears accounted for 31 percent of sales and J.C. Penney for 18 percent. Salant's efforts to diversify its customer base had succeeded to such a point by 1993, however, that no one customer made up more than 6 percent of the company's net sales.

Financial Difficulties Continuing: The 1980s

Salant's financial difficulties, stemming from the drop in demand for jeans in the mid-1970s, continued into the 1980s. When Salant declared its first bankruptcy in 1985, it reported a net loss of $8.08 million, which compared with a net loss of $21.2 million the previous year. In an effort to return to profitability the company discontinued several of its clothing divisions, including its Salvation sportswear and Thomson women's wear product lines, terminated the operations of its United Pioneer Company outerwear division (which had made ski jackets and parkas part of the company's principal products line for about a decade), closed its retail outlet stores, and closed several production facilities. Also between 1980 and 1985, Salant had reduced the number of its employees from 9,200 to 2,700. Salant emerged from its first bankruptcy in 1987 with its debt almost halved to $4.8 million.

In 1988, Salant acquired Manhattan Industries, an apparel company with three times Salant's annual volume. Manhattan president Nicholas DiPaolo emerged as Salant's president and would be promoted to chairman and CEO in 1991. To finance the acquisition, the company raised its debt to $270 million. Two years later, the company became bankrupt a second time. The company was not alone, however, and joined about 25 other companies who between 1985 and 1994 had fallen into second bankruptcy. Although some of the other companies eventually liquidated, Salant got its balance sheet in order, reducing its debt to a manageable amount.

Salant had help deleveraging from one of the most successful corporate empire builders of the 1990s, Leon Black, and one of his companies, Apollo Apparel Partners, L.P. In 1991, Leon Black bought a significant number of defaulted Salant bonds. When Salant came out of bankruptcy in September 1993, Apollo Apparel traded its Salant bonds for company stock. The swap allowed Salant to discharge claims of $64.8 million in principal of some bonds due in 1995 and gave Apollo Apparel 43.8 percent ownership of Salant. Salant's financial position in 1994 led *Financial World* to use it as an example of a "potential winner," noting that Salant had more than halved its debt.

Focus on Men's Wear: The 1990s

As Salant emerged from its second bankruptcy, it concentrated on its largest business, men's wear. Salant's purchase of Manhattan Industries, which led in part to its second bankruptcy filing, had a silver lining. Manhattan Industries brought a large international sourcing business to Salant and, more important, a license agreement with Perry Ellis. The Perry Ellis business "was so strong it continued to thrive despite Salant Corp.'s bankruptcy filing," according to *Crain's New York Business.*

Key Dates:

1893: Solomon Salant and his son, Gabriel, found Salant & Salant, Incorporated.
1919: The father and son business is incorporated.
1938: The company begins to manufacture one of its principal products, utility pants.
1959: The company is listed on the NASDAQ supplemental.
1964: The company introduces permanent press apparel.
1971: The company is listed on the New York Stock Exchange.
1985: Salant declares bankruptcy, reporting a net loss of $8.08 million.
1987: Salant emerges from bankruptcy, with its debt almost halved to $4.8 million.
1988: Salant acquires Manhattan Industries.
1991: Nicholas DiPaolo becomes chairman and CEO.
1993: The company falls into a second bankruptcy, but is able to reduce its debt to a manageable amount as Apollo Apparel acquires 43.8 percent ownership.
1994: Salant acquires JJ. Farmer Clothing Inc.; through a license agreement with Crystal Brands, Inc., Salant begins to produce dress shirts under the Salty Dog and Gant trademarks.
1997: DiPaolo resigns as CEO and is succeeded by Jerald Politzer.
1998: Again in bankruptcy court, with $110 million in debt, Salant exchanges a controlling ownership to Magten Asset Management Corporation; Michael Setola succeeds Jerald Politzer.
1999: Salant emerges from Chapter 11 reorganization.
2001: Sales continue to decline, to $207.8 million, and the company records a loss of $1.9 million.
2002: Salant acquires Ocean Pacific Apparel Corporation's youth-oriented brand of men's wear.

The *Daily News Record* reported that in 1993 the Perry Ellis name was "three times as strong" as when Salant assumed control in 1988. By 1994, it accounted for 26 percent of Salant's net sales, compared with Salant's Manhattan trademark, which accounted for 12 percent, the John Henry trademark (9 percent), and the Thomson trademark (8 percent of net sales). No other of Salant's more than a dozen trademarks made up more than 5 percent of Salant's 1994 sales.

Salant's 1993 introduction of its Thomson brand wrinkle-free dress shirt also brought the first branded wrinkle-free dress shirt to market and came at a time when men's clothing was the fastest growing segment of the apparel industry. The company appeared to be back on track.

Salant's acquisition of Manhattan had significantly increased its international business. Before the 1970s, Salant owned a Canadian subsidiary that designed, manufactured, and sold slacks, jeans, utility pants, and shirts in Canada, and in 1972, Salant built its first of several production facilities in Mexico. But by the 1990s, more than half of the company's products were produced abroad. Although the company continued to operate its Mexican plants and a Canadian subsidiary (the

first was sold and another purchased in the meantime), much of the company's imported products and materials came from Manhattan's extensive international sourcing business. In 1994, Salant's facilities accounted for 84 percent of its domestic-made products and 28 percent of its foreign-made products.

Diversification: The Mid-1990s

As it had after its first bankruptcy, Salant sought to improve its competitive strength by buying a better product mix. This time, however, the company kept a keener eye on its balance sheet. Although its resources were limited, Salant acquired Canadian-based JJ. Farmer Clothing Inc. in June of 1994. The acquisition was notable, however, because it left Salant's financial position almost unchanged. Salant retained its financial flexibility by making the acquisition on an earnout basis, which linked the purchase price of JJ. Farmer to its performance over a certain period of time. JJ. Farmer quickly helped boost Salant's sales, accounting for approximately one-third of Salant's $13.6 million net sales increase in the third quarter of 1994.

In addition to its acquisition, Salant added to its dress shirt business through a license agreement with Crystal Brands, Inc. in 1994. Salant agreed to produce dress shirts and furnishings under the Salty Dog and Gant trademarks. Salant President Nicholas P. DiPaolo noted the strong consumer following enjoyed by the Gant brand and remarked, "With our marketing and manufacturing expertise we will be able to build on an already solid base. The addition of the Gant and Salty Dog brands to our existing well-known labels insures our continued growth and leadership role in the dress shirt and furnishings categories."

Salant's focus on men's wear in the 1990s was on track with trends in the apparel industry. Men's clothing, which accounted for 36 percent of all apparel sales, outperformed all other apparel categories in 1992, according to Standard & Poor's Industry Surveys. The sale of men's sportswear benefited from wrinkle-resistant textiles, which followed a "trend toward more casual attire in the office." Although Salant's start-up costs for entering the wrinkle-resistant shirt business had lowered operating earnings in 1994, the company was "encouraged by sales of Perry Ellis sportswear and wrinkle resistant dress shirts and slacks," according to the *Daily News Record*.

Throughout its history, Salant's corporate operations remained centered in its New York headquarters. But by the 1990s the company's production had become dispersed, mainly throughout the South. In 1994, Salant owned six U.S. manufacturing facilities located in Alabama, Georgia, New York, Tennessee, and Texas, three manufacturing facilities in Mexico, and five distribution centers located in Georgia, New York, South Carolina, and Texas. The company also leased space for 57 factory outlet stores and one retail store.

Salant looked toward a solid future in 1994. Despite a declining dress shirt market, Salant had increased its sales and market share in that category "to benefit from any improvement in market conditions," according to the company. The company's Manhattan label had become the Wal-Mart chain's best-selling brand of dress shirt while both the Perry Ellis and John Henry brands enjoyed increased sales in department and specialty stores. As Salant took steps to maintain the strength of its position in men's dress wear, it also expanded into the fastest growing area of men's wear, casual apparel. In 1995, the company inked a deal with Sears to make its private-label denim shirts and pants for men and boys under the Canyon River Blues name. Supported by its Children's Apparel Group, which made sleepwear under brands including Dr. Denton, Barney, Disney characters, and Osh Kosh B'Gosh, and sales of its women's wear brands, including Vera and Made in the Shade, Salant's men's wear business seemed capable of maintaining its solid and prosperous position.

Financial Struggles: The Late 1990s

That solidity and prosperity proved fleeting when an anemic market for dress shirts combined with increased competition to negatively impact Salant's profit margins. In fact, the company chalked up a $7.9 million loss on sales of $419.3 million in 1994. After having its debt downgraded by Moody's in 1995, the company restructured twice in 1996, closing two Georgia plants and discontinuing its Liberty of London, Nino Cerruti, and Peanuts lines of dress shirts. Salant also sold off its JJ. Farmer division that year. At that time, the plan was to focus on five business areas: Perry Ellis sportswear, dress shirts, slacks, and accessories; John Henry dress shirts; Manhattan dress shirts; private-label brands like Canyon River Blues; and novelty accessories. DiPaolo told *Daily News Record* in March 1996, "The provision for restructuring reflects our continuing effort to focus our business on those product lines that offer our customers significant value while maintaining higher margins."

DiPaolo resigned in 1997 and was succeeded by Jerald Politzer, who served as CEO for barely a year before the company again found itself in bankruptcy court. Mired in $110 million in debt, Salant was forced to exchange a controlling ownership in the company to Magten Asset Management Corporation. Under the direction of Michael Setola, Salant retrenched to what had become its bedrock: Perry Ellis men's clothing. The company divested its John Henry, Manhattan, Dr. Denton children's wear, and Canyon River Blues jeans, leaving it with more than 80 percent of net sales from Perry Ellis licensed merchandise. Sales declined steadily throughout the late 1990s, from $347.7 million in 1997 to $248.7 million upon Salant's emergence from reorganization in 1999. The company was able to vastly improve the balance sheet, however, from a net loss of $18.1 million to $20.6 million in the period.

It was not long before Salant again began to diversify, this time maintaining a focus on the "better men's wear" category. In 2000, the company licensed the Tallia brand for sportswear and accessories, and in 2002, acquired AXIS Men's wear, maker of better quality clothing sold in pricey department stores and specialty outlets. That same year, Ocean Pacific Apparel Corporation entrusted Salant to take its heretofore youth-oriented brand to the 25 to 50 age group. Michael Setola, who

had succeeded Jerald Politzer in 1998, told *Daily News Record* in January 2002, "The relationship with Ocean Pacific Apparel represents yet another step forward for Salant in diversifying our men's wear distribution." It remained to be seen whether the company's new direction would prove profitable in the long run. Sales continued their multiyear decline to $207.8 million in 2001, and after two consecutive years of profitablilty, the company recorded a loss of $1.9 million that year.

Principal Competitors

Haggar Corporation; Tommy Hilfiger Corporation; Phillips-Van Heusen Corporation; Oxford Industries Inc.

Further Reading

"Aided by Debt Restructuring, Salant Posts Earnings of $22.1 Million," *Daily News Record,* August 23, 1999, p. 110.

"Charges Add Up to a $4.5 M 4th-Period Loss at Salant; Company Back in Black For Year," *Daily News Record,* March 25, 1996, p. 1.

Curan, Catherine M., "Report Salant to Make Private-Label Denim Tops and Bottoms for Sears," *Daily News Record,* March 23, 1995, p. 4.

——, "Salant Discontinues Vera Scarf; May Sell or License Trademark," *WWD,* March 13, 1995, p. 13.

——, "Salant Grabs an Oscar," *Daily News Record,* December 18, 1995, p. 3.

——, "Salant to Sell Farmer Division," *Daily News Record,* August 15, 1996, p. 1.

"DiPaolo to Leave Salant This Year," *Daily News Record,* March 10, 1997, p. 1.

Furman, Phyllis, "Without Its Founder, Perry Ellis Thrives," *Crain's New York Business,* October 26, 1992, p. 3.

Gellers, Annmarie Doddstan, "Hartz Gives Salant License for Tallia Sportswear Line," *Daily News Record,* May 8, 2000, p. 1.

Hart, Elena, "Perry Ellis Men's Stronger Than Ever," *Daily News Record,* February 19, 1993, p. 5.

Light, Larry, "Trouble Outfits That Turn into Two-Time Losers," *Business Week,* April 26, 1993, pp. 81–82.

"Moody's Downgrades Salant's Rating; Points to Poor Financial Showing," *Daily News Record,* May 15, 1995, p. 2.

Romero, Elena, "Ocean Pacific Brand Growing Up," *Daily News Record,* January 14, 2002, p. 8.

"Salant Acquires JJ. Farmer, Canadian Sportswear Maker," *Daily News Record,* June 16, 1994.

"Salant Corp-Acquisition of Axis Clothing Corporation," *Market News Publishing,* January 14, 2002.

"Salant Operating Earnings Plummet 62% in Second Period," *Daily News Record,* August 9, 1994, p. 7.

Schifrin, Matthew, and Riva Atlas, "Hocus-Pocus," *Forbes,* March 14, 1994, pp. 81–83.

Taub, Stephen, "Market Watch: Double-Dippers, Bankruptcy Style," *Financial World,* March 29, 1994, p. 14.

Young, Vicki M., "Debt Restructuring Gives Salant New Lease on Life," *Daily News Record,* March 4, 1998, p. 1A.

—Sara Pendergast
—update: April D. Gasbarre

Sanitec

Sanitec Corporation

Mikonkatu 15 A, 7th floor
00100 Helsinki
Finland
Telephone: (+358) 9 7095 400
Fax: (+358) 9 7731 207
Web site: http://www.sanitec.com

Private Company
Incorporated: 1969
Employees: 8,858
Sales: EUR 994.6 million ($970 million) (2001)
NAIC: 327111 Vitreous China Plumbing Fixture and
    China and Earthenware Fitting and Bathroom
    Accessories Manufacturing

Sanitec Corporation is Europe's leading manufacturer of bathroom ceramics and bath and shower fittings and products. Through its subsidiary Evac International, the company is also the world's leading manufacturer of sewage vacuum systems for boats, trains, aircraft, and buildings. Based in Helsinki, Finland, Sanitec operates primarily through its strong portfolio of brand names, most of which are local market leaders. Sanitec's brands include IDO Bathroom, in Finland; Ifö Sanitär, in Sweden; Allia, in France; Pozzi-Ginori and Domino, which also produces the Albatros and Revita brands, in Italy; Twyford, including the Doulton and Royal Doulton brands, in the United Kingdom; Sphinx, from the Netherlands; Keramag and Koralle, in Germany; Kolo, in Poland; and Lecico, in Egypt. While many of these brands focus largely on their local markets, a number of Sanitec's brands are among Europe's leaders, such as Koralle, which distributes its products throughout much of western and eastern Europe. Bathroom Ceramics is the company's largest business area, accounting for more than 61 percent of Sanitec's 2001 sales of EUR 994.6 million. Bath and Shower Products add nearly 30 percent of the company's revenues. The company's Evac International subsidiary is the only manufacturer in its market supplying to the four major markets of marine, aviation, train, and building sewerage vacuum systems, and represented almost 9 percent of Sanitec's sales in

2001. In that year, Sanitec agreed to be acquired by investment fund group BC Partners, which subsequently delisted the company from the Helsinki Stock Exchange. The company intends to extend its presence globally before returning to the stock market. Sanitec is led by chairman Berndt Brunow and president and CEO Rainser Simon.

Finnish Porcelain Origins in the 19th Century

Sanitec was formed in 1990 when Finnish industrial conglomerate Wartsilä, founded in 1926, grouped together several subsidiaries, all involved in the production of fittings for bathrooms. The following year, when Wartsilä merged with another Finnish conglomerate, becoming known as Metra, Sanitec was spun off as a separate company owned by Metra. The centerpiece of the new Sanitec was the then-named Wartsilä Tammisaaren Posliini, which was renamed IDO Tammisaaren Posliini in 1991, then changed its name again, to IDO Kylpyhuone, or IDO Bathroom. That company's roots traced back to the beginnings of the Finnish ceramics and porcelain industry in the late 1800s.

The first porcelain factory was established in Helsinki in 1878 and became known worldwide for the Arabia brand of porcelain table services and other household ornaments and items. During the 1870s, the Helsinki factory added production of toilets and other items for household sanitary needs. The company also produced sanitary goods for hospitals.

Wartsilä took control of Arabia in 1947. In 1969, the conglomerate transferred most of Arabia's bathroom, shower, and sanitary production to a new, automated facility in Tammisaari, Finland. A new company was established for these operations, called Wartsilä Tammisaaren Posliini. By 1971, the Tammisaari subsidiary had taken over all of Wartsilä's sanitary production activities.

Wartsilä began building up other interests related to the bathroom market in the 1970s, notably with the launch of EVAK Development Project in 1975, a joint venture between Wartsilä Tammisaaren Posliini and Sweden's Ifö Sanitär's Vacuum Systems group. Established in 1887, Ifö Sanitär had captured a leading share of much of the Scandinavian market for

Company Perspectives:

Sanitec's vision is to become a global supplier in bathroom solutions. The company's core purpose is to contribute to the health and well-being of people by providing them with well-designed and ecologically justified bathroom solutions.

sanitary fittings for the bathroom and the kitchen. The partnership with Ifö led to the creation of a full-fledged joint venture company in 1979. Then, in 1982, Wartsilä acquired Ifö Sanitär and full-control of the EVAK joint venture.

During the 1980s, Wartsilä made several more acquisitions involving its sanitary products holdings. The EVAC subsidiary was expanded in 1986 with the purchase of Electrolux's vacuum sewage operations, including subsidiary Envirovac Inc. It was at this time that EVAC adopted the EVAC brand name. Another acquisition came in 1986 with the purchase of sanitary business Porsgrund, of Norway, which had started as a porcelain maker in 1885.

As formed in 1990, Sanitec consisted of IDO, Ifö Sanitär, Porsgrund, and EVAC, and started operations as a leading player in the Scandinavian market. The company then set out to extend its leadership position across Europe. In order to achieve this, Sanitec sought to extend its organic growth with a series of targeted acquisitions through the 1990s.

Acquiring Scale in the 1990s

Sanitec's first major acquisitions came in 1991. In that year, the company picked up Keramag, of Germany. Founded near Düsseldorf in 1903, Keramag had grown to become the leader in Germany in the bathroom ceramics sector. That purchase was accompanied by the acquisition of France's Allia. That company's origins extended back to 1892, when the Lyon-based Compagnie des Cornues et Produits Ceramiques began production of ceramic sanitary fixtures. By 1917, that activity had grown to the extent that the company built a dedicated production facility for its sanitary fixtures in Digoin. Originally specialized in porcelain, Allia later acquired production in other materials, adding a factory in Limoges and then its Polyroc facility in Vendôme, which enabled the company to begin marketing complete bathrooms. By the beginning of the 1990s, Allia had become a leading brand name in the French market.

The addition of Keramag and Allia raised Sanitec's revenues to the equivalent of nearly EUR 275 million. The company next turned to Poland in 1993, acquiring Kolo, a sanitary ceramics specialist founded in 1962. Sanitec then moved to Italy, acquiring another leading brand name, Pozzi-Ginori. Founded in 1735 in Doccia by the Marquis Ginori, the company had merged with Milan's Richard in 1896, becoming Richard-Ginori. In 1956, the company moved its production to Livorno. In 1973, Richard-Ginori merged with another Italian sanitary producer, Pozzi Spa, changing its name to Pozzi-Giorno. The purchase of that company not only helped Sanitec extend its reach into southern Europe, it also helped to boost the company's sales—by the end of 1994, Sanitec's revenues had swelled past EUR 430 million.

By then, Sanitec, through Allia, had acquired another French sanitary ceramics manufacturer, FAS, based in Avranches, boosting Allia to the market leadership in that country. Sanitec continued building on its position in that country, acquiring majority control of Varicor in 1995. That year also saw the acquisition of Poland's Laminex, which specialized in manufacturing acrylic bathtubs. Sanitec also took a 25 percent share in Italian company Domino Spa. Founded in 1982, Domino, originally called Albatros System, had risen quickly in Italy, especially after the launch of the successful Revita brand name. By 1993, Albatros changed its name to Domino, while continuing to distribute its products under its two strong brand names, Albatros and Revita. After Sanitec took over Domino completely in 1998, the company began distributing the Albatros and Revita brands through other parts of its growing European network.

Sanitec was by then a thoroughly international company—more than 96 percent of its sales were from outside of Finland. The company, which already operated worldwide through its EVAC vacuum sewage subsidiary, had successfully expanded throughout much of Europe. In 1997, the company had further broadened its reach when it acquired a 50 percent stake in Lecico. Founded with the assistance of Keramag outside of Beirut in 1959, Lecico had long been the only producer of ceramic sanitary products in Lebanon. In 1975, the company had set up a subsidiary in Egypt, starting sanitary product production in 1978 and adding a second facility for producing ceramic wall tiles in 1983. Following Sanitec's acquisition of 50 percent of the company, Lecico headquarters moved to its Alexandria, Egypt, facility while production at the Lebanon plant continued.

After acquiring Germany's Sanivac, through EVAC, in 1998, Sanitec took control of Johnson Suisse, operating in Malaysia, giving the company a platform for distribution throughout the Asian markets. EVAC grew again the following year with the purchase of Germany's Aquamar, a producer of biologically based sewage treatment plants used in the marine and building sectors.

Sanitec also extended its larger sanitary operations, buying up Koralle, of Germany, which had been founded in 1970 and had built up a strong brand name as a high-end designer and producer of bathroom and other sanitary fixtures, with sales throughout most of Europe. Nonetheless, Sanitec found itself in a battle to maintain its European market lead at the end of the 1990s, as the sanitary products giant American Standard had begun its own acquisition drive in Europe. By mid-1999, however, Sanitec solidified its lead with the announcement of it acquisition of Koninklijke Sphinx, of the Netherlands.

Sphinx's origins reached back to the founding of the Dutch ceramics industry in Maastricht in the 1830s by Petrus Regout. By the 1860s, the Maastricht ceramics community was flourishing; among the new companies joining the Regout works was Société Céramique, formed in 1863 from a merger of two existing companies. Sphinx and Société Céramique then merged nearly a century later, in 1959. Throughout its history, Sphinx had been noted for its porcelain table service and decoration, while also building up a line of sanitary fittings. At the end of 1960s, Sphinx had decided to focus solely on its sanitary production. By the 1990s, the company had grown to

---

Key Dates:

1873: Arabia porcelain factory is established in Helsinki to produce sanitary fixtures.
1947: Wartsilä takes over Arabia's porcelain operations.
1969: Wartsilä builds a new factory in Tammisaari, forming the new company Wartsilä Tammisaaren Posliini.
1975: Wartsilä and Ifö Sanitär create joint-venture development company, EVAK.
1979: The company launches EVAC vacuum sewage operations.
1981: Wartsilä acquires Ifö Sanitär.
1985: The company acquires vacuum sewage systems operations from Electrolux and launches EVAC brand name.
1986: Wartsilä acquires Norway's Porsgrund ceramics operations.
1990: Wartsilä Tammisaaren Posliini, EVAC, Porsgrund and Ifo are bundled into a new company, Sanitec.
1991: Wartsilä and Lohfa merge as Metra; Sanitec is spun off as a separate subsidiary and begins acquisition drive.
1999: Sanitec goes public on the Helsinki Stock Exchange.
2001: BC Partners acquires Sanitec, and the company is delisted from the Helsinki Stock Exchange.

---

become the market leader in the Netherlands, with a strong position in Germany; the company had also become one of the largest sanitary producers in Scandinavia through its subsidiary Gustavsberg.

Sanitec went public in 1999, placing its shares on the Helsinki stock exchange, in part to fund its acquisition of the Dutch company. Yet the purchase was not to be completed until 2000, after Sanitec addressed European Mergers and Monopolies Commission concerns by agreeing to sell off a number of its holdings, including the Gustavsberg operations. The addition of Sphinx helped raised Sanitec's sales to EUR 877 million and helped complete much of its coverage of western Europe. Sphinx, which operated sales offices in the United Kingdom, also gave Sanitec an entry into that county, which had long represented a gap in Sanitec's holdings.

Sanitec continued to look for acquisitions, and in 2001 announced its purchase of UK market leader Caradon Bathrooms—part of the Caradon Plumbing group—and its brands Twyford and Doulton. That company's history stretched back as far as the seventeenth century, when Joshua Twyford set up commercial pottery workshop in Hanley in 1680. Twyford's descendant, Thomas Twyford, set up the modern business with the construction of two factories producing sanitary fixtures, such as wash basins, in 1849. Twyford later became part of Reed Interna-

tional's building products operations in the 1970s, then of Caradon in the 1980s, where it was joined by another strong bathroom products brand, Doulton, founded in 1815. The acquisition of Caradon Bathrooms—which was renamed Twyford Bathroom, helped complete Sanitec's European coverage with more than 20 percent of the UK bathroom fittings market. It was also expected to help boost the company's revenues well beyond the EUR 1 billion market by the end of 2002.

Sanitec's stint as a public company did not last for long. In 2001, Wartsilä, which continued to hold about 50 percent of Sanitec, led a group of investors, worth more than 60 percent of Sanitec's shares, to an agreement to sell Sanitec to investment fund specialist BC Partners. By the end of 2001, BC Partners, which specialized in large-scale public-to-private buyouts, had completed its acquisition of Sanitec, acquiring 100 percent of the company's shares and delisting it from the Helsinki stock exchange. The acquisition, however, quickly revealed itself to be the first step in the next phase of Sanitec's growth, as the company's new owners expressed their intent to expand Sanitec's leadership worldwide.

Principal Subsidiaries

Allia S.A. (France); Domino S.p.A. (Italy); Evac International Ltd; Ido Bathroom Ltd; Ifö Sanitär AB (Sweden); Keramag AG (Germany); Koralle Sanitärprodukte GmbH (Germany); Lecico Egypt S.A.E; Pozzi-Ginori S.p.A. (Italy); Sanitec Kolo Sp. Z o.o. (Poland); Koninklijke Sphinx B.V.(The Netherlands); Twyford Bathrooms Ltd (U.K.).

Principal Competitors

Tostem Inax Holding Corp; TOTO Ltd.; Kohler Co.; Air Water Inc.; Takara Standard Co Ltd.; Uralita SA; Villeroy und Boch AG; USI Plumbing Products; Cleanup Corp.; Geberit International AG; Compania Roca Radiadores SA; Keramik Holding AG; Elkay Manufacturing Co.; Coop Costruttori Scarl; Ideal Standard SpA; Homeform Group.

Further Reading

Archer, John, "Wartsilä Will Use Sanitec Gain to Boost Core Unit," *Reuters*, April 26, 2001.
——, "Sanitec Says to Regain Europe Lead on Sphinx Buy," *Reuters*, June 3, 1999.
"BC Partners Buys Sanitec in 908 Mln Euros Deal," *Reuters*, April 26, 2001.
"Caradon Bathrooms Go to Sanitec," *European Venture Capital Journal*, February 2001, p.30.
"Sanitary Ware: Sanitec's Acquisition of Sphinx Cleared with Conditions," *European Report*, December 4, 1999.
"Sanitec Buys Caradon to Become Europe's Largest Bathroom Ceramics Supplier," *Helsingin Sanomat*, December 1, 2001.

—M. L. Cohen

SanomaWSOY

SanomaWSOY Corporation

Ludviginkatu 6-8
POB 1229
FIN-00101 Helsinki
Finland
Telephone: (+358) 105 1999
Fax (+358) 105 19 5068
Web site: http://www.sanomawsoy.fi

Public Company
Incorporated: 1999
Employees: 18,000
Sales: EUR 1.73 billion ($1.7 billion) (2001)
Stock Exchanges: Helsinki
Ticker Symbol: SWSA
NAIC: 323111 Commercial Gravure Printing; 451211
    Book Stores; 511110 Newspaper Publishers; 511120
    Periodical Publishers; 511130 Book Publishers;
    511140 Database and Directory Publishers; 722110
    Full-Service Restaurants

Finland's SanomaWSOY Corporation leapt onto the broader European media scene with the 2001 acquisition of VNU's Consumer Information Group (CIG) and its 250-strong portfolio of magazine titles. Prior to that acquisition, SanomaWSOY had been Scandinavia's second-largest media group, behind Sweden's Bonnier, as well as the Nordic region's largest publicly listed media company. With the addition of the CIG unit, SanomaWSOY's revenues will climb to EUR 2.4 million in 2002, from EUR 1.73 million in 2001. The acquisition gives the company leading shares in the magazine sector in Finland, the Netherlands, Belgium, Hungary, and the Czech Republic, as well as prominent spots in Croatia, Romania, Slovakia, and Sweden. Prior to the CIG acquisition, more than 92 percent of the company's sales had been restricted to the Scandinavian market; following the acquisition, international sales represented more than 42 percent of SanomaWSOY's total sales. The company's media interests include Newspaper Publishing, including Finland's largest newspaper, *Helsingin Sanomat*, and a range of regional papers; Book Publishing under the imprint of

WSOY, Finland's largest book publisher with more than 600 new titles each year; Retailing and Restaurants, through Rautakirja and its chain of newsstands, bookshops, and betting shops; Television, including Channel Four Finland, cable TV operator Helsinki Television, and commercial broadcaster Nelonen; Film, based primarily around Rautakirja's 15 multiplex movie theaters; and other activities that include printing—the company operates 13 printing plants across Finland—and distribution. SanomaWSOY is listed on the Helsinki Stock Exchange and is led by Hannu Syrjänen, president and chief operating officer. The company remains held at 49 percent by Sanoma's founding Erkko family.

19th-Century Finnish Media Dynasties

The SanomaWSOY entering the twenty-first century was formed through the merger of two of Finland's leading media concerns, Sanoma and WSOY, in 1999. Both companies traced their histories to the late nineteenth century and had become leaders in their respective areas of newspaper publishing (Sanoma) and book publishing (WSOY); the companies had also long been partners in the Rautakirja retail and restaurant group, which had built the largest chain of newsstands in Finland.

WSOY stemmed from 1878, when Werner Söderström published his first book, J.O. Åberg's *Pohjanmaan helmi* (*The Pearl of Ostrobothnia*). The Söderström family had first entered printing when Söderström's father Gustav founded a printing shop in 1860 in the town of Porvoo. The younger Söderström, just 18 at the time he published his first book, soon developed the business into a respected publishing house, extending its title list to including literature, non-fiction, and textbooks by the end of its first decade. In 1904, Söderström incorporated the company as Werner Söderström OY (SOY). Two years later, the company began to publish the first-ever Finnish-language encyclopedia in partnership with another leading Finnish publisher, Otava.

In 1910, WSOY joined with newspaper publisher Sanoma and other Finnish publishers to form Rautakirja, an operator of newsstand kiosks which patterned itself after WH Smith shops in the United Kingdom. By 1911, Rautakirja had opened some

Company Perspectives:

Mission: SanomaWSOY's mission is to be one of Europe's leading media companies in terms of stakeholder value growth. Vision: Our aim is to be the number one media company in our chosen markets, offering the most wanted and valued products and services and the best level of sustainable profitability and growth. Values: Our values are creativity, reliability, and dynamism. Creative work is the essence of communications, and creativity and reliability form the basis of all our activities. Dynamism is essential to our success; our strength lies in our people and working together for common goals.

30 shops, at first targeting Finland's train stations; that company added wholesale book and newspaper distribution in 1913, and by 1920 had expanded its retail network to more than 100 shops across Finland.

WSOY entered the magazine publishing sector in 1922 with the women's title *Kotilesi*. The company quickly added additional titles. In 1934, WSOY and Otava formed the joint-venture Yhtyneet Kuvalehdet, which took over the company's magazine operations. By then, Rautakirja shops had begun appearing on Finland's city streets and had extended their range to a broader convenience offering, including sales of tobacco, film, and candy.

WSOY's partner in Rautakirja, Sanoma, had by then established itself as another major figure in the Finnish publishing market. Sanoma had been founded in 1889 when journalist Eero Erkko launched the daily *Päivälehti*. Erkko was named editor-in-chief of the newspaper, which grew quickly. By the end of the century, however, *Päivälehti* had caught the attention of Finland's governor general, a representative of the Tsar of Russia, which still controlled Finland. *Päivälehti* began running afoul of the official censor, and by 1899 had faced its first three-month suspension. Erkoo was dismissed as editor-in-chief in 1900 but remained on as a journalist until he was deported in 1903. In 1904, *Päivälehti* was banned altogether.

Yet the newspaper was quickly reborn, now as *Helsingin Sanomat*, published by the newly formed Sanoma Corporation. The newspaper began publishing in 1904; the following year, Eero Erkko, who had gone to the United States, came back to Finland, and in 1906 became Sanoma's chairman of the board. Erkko once again took up the editor-in-chief position in 1909.

The growth of the Rautakirja retail network helped stimulate *Helsingin Sanomat*'s sales, and by 1914 the paper, initially published six days a week, added a Sunday edition as well. The Finnish Civil War of 1918 caused a temporary break in the newspaper's publishing schedule, as *Helsingin Sanomat* became a firm backer of Finland's push to break free from Russia, which by then was in the throws of the Russian Revolution. That position helped the newspaper gain stature following the country's independence.

After Eero Erkko died in 1927, Sanoma remained owned by the Erkko family, and son Eljas Erkko took over as the newspa-

per's editor-in-chief. In that year, the newspaper added a new weekly supplement, *Viikkoliite*, which featured illustrations and, from 1929, comic strips. The popularity of the comics soon led the paper to add a dedicated comics supplement. Sanoma launched an afternoon edition of the *Helsingin Sanomat* in 1932, and by the end of the decade the newspaper's circulation had reached 80,000—and rose to 100,000 for the Sunday edition.

Finnish Media Heavyweights in the Postwar Era

At the end of World War II, Sanoma entered the magazine business with the acquisition of *Viikkasanomat*, a weekly news magazine, in 1945. That same year the company launched *Valitut Palat*, the Finnish version of *Reader's Digest* magazine. The growing success of an afternoon edition of *Helsingin Sanomat* led the company to re-launch it as a separate newspaper, under the title *Ilta-Sanomat*, in 1949. Two years later, Sanoma extended its magazine operation into the comic book arena, when the company acquired the Finnish license for Disney's Donald Duck magazine. Called *Aku Ankka* in Finnish, the magazine quickly became popular among Finland's youth and became the company's largest-selling magazine.

Sanoma's operations expanded again in 1951 when the company established a photographic news service, Lehtikuva, in time for Helsinki Olympic Games held in 1952. By then, the company's flagship newspaper had been experiencing strong growth, reaching a circulation of more than 230,000 by the mid-1950s—a figure that established the paper as one of the leading newspapers in the entire Scandinavian region. In 1957, Sanoma had a new success with the launch of a Finnish version of woman's magazine *Me Naiset*. The death of Eljas Erkko in 1965 brought a new generation of the Erkko family, in the form of Aatos Erkko, into Sanoma's leadership. Two years later, the company added a new magazine title, the family-oriented *Kodin Kuvalehti*.

WSOY was posting its own successes in the postwar era. By 1947, the company's new title catalog had topped 400 books for the year. In 1949, the company expanded its printing facilities with the purchase of FG Lönnberg. By the mid-1950s, WSOY had an international success after publishing *Tuntematon sotilas* (*The Unknown Soldier*) by Väin"Linna in 1954.

In the following decade, Rautakirja—which had extended into the bookstore market with a purchase of a single store, Suomalainen Kirjakauppa, in 1924—began to build on its retail holdings and opened its second bookstore in 1965. The success of that branch led the company to roll out Suomalainen Kirjakauppa across Finland, building up a network of more than 60 stores. With a strong retail outlet for its books, WSOY began developing other sales channels, and in 1971 the company launched its own book club, in partnership with fellow publishers Otava and Tammi. WSOY went public in 1976, and in 1977 the company opened a new book production facility in Juva.

Sanoma added color to its newspapers in 1979 after converting the company's printing operations to the new offset printing technology. The company proved eager to expand into other technologies as well, and in 1981 acquired cable television operator Helsinki Television, which had been launched in 1973. That same year, Sanoma made an attempt to expand internationally,

Key Dates:

1878: Werner Söderström starts a publishing business.
1889: Eero Erkko begins publishing daily newspaper *Paivalehti*.
1890: Werner Söderström incorporates as WSOY.
1904: Sanoma Corporation is created.
1922: WSOY enters the magazine publishing sector with the women's title *Kotilesi*.
1945: Sanoma begins magazine publishing with the acquisition of *Viikkasanomat*.
1976: WSOY goes public on the Helsinki Stock Exchange.
1981: Sanoma acquires Helsinki Television.
1984: WSOY acquires audiovisual production company Aveset.
1993: Sanoma forms Helsinki Media Company, combining its book and magazine publishing and new media operations.
1995: WSOY acquires Weilin & Göös publishing group.
1998: WSOY and Sanoma agree to merge, forming SanomaWSOY.
2001: SanomaWSOY acquires Consumer Information Group business from VNU, adding 250 magazine titles to become the fifth-largest magazine publisher in Europe.
2002: SanomaWSOY acquires full control of retail and distribution group Rautakirja.

acquiring the printing operations of American Crafton Graphic Company; Sanoma sold off those operations again in 1988. Meanwhile, the company had created a new division for its book and magazine operations, Sonamaprint. That unit was expanded with the purchase of the over-50 magazine *ET-lehti* in 1983; *Gloria*, a women's magazine, in 1987; and the computer and information technology magazine group Tecnopress in 1984.

WSOY had also begun to diversify in the 1980s, buying up Avest, producer of audiovisual programming in 1984, and launching a calendar publishing division in 1986, which was to go on to become one of Scandinavia's largest calendar publishers. In 1988, WSOY and Sanoma placed Rautakirja on the Helsinki Stock Exchange. The public offering enabled Rautakirja to begin its own diversification drive, starting with the acquisition of a small stake in theater owner Finnkino in 1989 (with full control completed in 1994). In 1990, Rautakirja extended its retail business with the acquisition of the 98-store chain of Tiimari stationery and gift stores, which included a small operation in Sweden as well.

Sanoma had been expanding its printing capacity, opening two new plants into the new decade. The company had also restructured its operations again, creating a new subsidiary, Helsinki Media Company, to combine its Sanomaprint and other media holdings, in 1993. That year, the company began expanding beyond Finland with the acquisition of Sweden's Milvus. The acquisition brought Sanoma Milvus's outdoor sports magazine title and a platform for the launch of a new title, *Sy & Sticka*.

International Media Group for the New Century

In 1995, WSOY acquired Weilin & Göös, a publisher that had been founded in 1872. The two companies had already formed a relationship through a joint venture company, Ajasto, which combined the two company's calendar publishing activities. That company then took the Scandinavian leadership in the calender market when it acquired Esselte Chrono and Emil Mostue in 1997. WSOY continued pursuing other partnerships, such as the formation of Werner Söderström Lakitieto with the Finnish Association of Lawyers in 1996.

Meanwhile, Sanoma had continued pursuing its international expansion, launching a Swedish version of *ET-lehti*, and acquiring ski and outdoor magazine *Aka Skidor*. The company also proved an early entrant to the Internet, launching Web sites for *Ilta-Sanomat* and *Helsingin Sanomat* in 1996. The company then extended its television holdings with the launch of a new television station, Nelonen, also known as Channel Four Finland. Sanoma's publishing wing had also grown with the purchase of Startel and the launch of a daily business-oriented newspaper, *Taloussanomat*.

The year 1998 marked a turning point for the Finnish media market. In that year, Sanoma and WSOY agreed to merge, forming SanomaWSOY in a transaction completed in 1999. The new company, which listed on the Helsinki Exchange in 1999, spanned nearly every media category and took the clear lead in the Finnish market, trailing only privately held Bonnier, of Sweden, in the overall Scandinavian market. The new company, which included control of Rautakirja, began trimming some of its assets, selling off the Tiimari retail chain and the company's book club.

As SanomaWSOY entered the turn of the twenty-first century, it remained almost entirely focused on the Scandinavian market, with some 92 percent of its sales, which had topped EUR 1.3 billion, coming from that region. In 2001, however, the company found what one analyst described as a "once in a lifetime opportunity." The Netherlands' VNU group, which had just acquired the ACNeilson Company, announced that it was selling its Consumer Information Group business unit, with more than 250 magazine titles, a 50 percent share of the Dutch magazine market, a 39 percent share of the Belgian market, and an extensive portfolio of magazine titles across Central Europe. SanomaWSOY leapt at the chance, spending more than EUR 1.25 billion.

The acquisition transformed the group into an internationally operating media company with projected sales of EUR 2.4 billion by the end of 2002, giving it the number five position in the European market. While still small compared to European heavyweights such as Bertelsmann and Pearson, SanomaWSOY had achieved one of its main strategic objectives in a single deal. The company then began putting into place a new long-term strategy, announcing its intention to leverage its magazine division's international presence in order to extend its other areas of operation into the larger European arena as well. As part of that plan, the company moved to take full control of Rautakirja, which by then had extended its own businesses into Estonia and elsewhere, in June 2002.

Principal Subsidiaries

2ndhead Oy; Accres Uitgevers B.V. (Netherlands); Almanacksförlaget AB; Baltic Media Oy (89%); Compad Oy; Emil Moestue as; Esmerk Group; Docendo Finland Oy; Docendo Sverige AB; Etelä-Karjalan Jakelu Oy; Etelä-Saimaan Sanomalehti Oy; Foodstop Oy (99%); Free Ad Production Oy; Geomatic International B.V. (Netherlands); Helsinki Television Ltd; HPR Holding B.V. (75%); ilse Media Group (58.7%); Infosto Oy; Janton Oyj (21.37%); Kymen Lehtimedia Oy; Kymen Sanomalehti Oy; Kymen Viestintä Oy; Lehtikanta Oy; Lehtikuva Oy; Leijonajakelu Oy; Måndag Oy; Nummi-Plast Oy; Oy Ruutunelonen Ab (90.55%); Oy Suomen Medianelonen Ab; RCV Entertainment B.V. (Netherlands); Saimaan Lehtipaino Oy; Sanoma Uitgevers B.V. (Netherlands); Sanoma Magazines Finland Oy; Sanoma Magazines International B.V.; Startel Oy (90%); Tuotantotalo Werne Oy; Uutisvuoksi Oy.

Principal Divisions

Newspaper Publishing; Book Publishing; Electronic Publishing; Television Broadcasting; Retail and Distribution.

Principal Competitors

Bertelsmann AG; Pearson plc; Reed Elsevier plc; United News & Media plc; Wolters Kluwer NV; Gruner Jahr AG & Co.

Druck- und Verlagshaus; Reed International plc; Daily Mail & General Trust plc; Axel Springer Verlag AG; EMAP plc; WH Smith PLC; LOGISTA S.A.; FNAC S.A.; LOGISTA SA; FNAC SA; Reitan Handel ASA; Ingram Industries Inc.; Reitan Narvesen ASA; John Menzies PLC; Ingram Book Group Inc.; Follett Corp.; Timon S.A.; Union INVIVO; Anderson News Co.; Maruzen Company Ltd.; Relais FNAC; Dawson Holdings PLC; Ruch S.A.; Timon SA; Surridge Dawson Ltd.; Ringier AG; Conde Nast and National Magazine Distributors Ltd.; Libro AG.

Further Reading

Braude, Jonathan, "Sanoma Buys Dutch Magazine Group," *The Daily Deal*, July 20, 2001.

Edmunds, Marlene, "Finnish Merger Creates $1.3 Bil Sanoma WSOY," *Variety*, May 3, 1999, p. 73.

"SanomaWSOY Aims for Sharp Rise in Operating Margin," *Reuters*, March 14, 2002.

"Sanoma WSOY, the Helsinki-Based Media Group, Became Europe's Fifth-Largest Publisher," *Europe*, September 2001, p. S4.

Vinha, Laura, "SanomaWSOY Should Focus on Digesting VNU Unit," *Reuters*, July 30, 2001.

"VNU Sells Share in Its Magazines to SanomaWSOY for Euro 1.25 Billion," *European Report*, September 1, 2001, p. 600.

—M. L. Cohen

Service Corporation International

1929 Allen Parkway
P.O. Box 130548
Houston, Texas 77019
U.S.A.
Telephone: (713) 522-5141
Fax: (713) 525-5586
Web site: http://www.sci-corp.com

Public Company
Incorporated: 1962
Employees: 33,430
Sales: $2.51 billion (2001)
Stock Exchanges: New York
Ticker Symbol: SRV
NAIC: 812210 Funeral Homes and Funeral Services

Service Corporation International (SCI) is the largest owner and operator of funeral homes and cemeteries in the world. It operates over 2,500 funeral homes, some 460 cemeteries, and more than 150 crematoria. The company also does some related business in products like funeral urns, flowers, caskets, and burial garments. Most of its business is in the United States and Canada, though the company also maintains a substantial presence in Europe. The company helped consolidate the so-called death care industry, running formerly independent funeral homes in clusters that share personnel and equipment. In 2002, the company was still headed by its founder, Robert Waltrip. Waltrip envisioned the new direction of the formerly fragmented death care industry, and by the early 1990s he had grown his company to three times that of its next nearest competitor. At its peak, SCI owned more than 4,500 funeral homes and cemeteries, spread throughout 20 countries on five continents. As of 1999, the company began to shed acquisitions and focus on internal growth. The company still reaches approximately 75 percent of the population of the United States through its own network and franchised affiliates.

A New Way of Running the Industry in the 1970s

Service Corporation International was founded by Robert L. Waltrip, a Houston funeral director. Waltrip was born in 1931 and grew up in an apartment above his family's funeral parlor. He took over the business at the age of 20, when his father died. By 1962, Waltrip was a licensed funeral director with a chain of three funeral homes in Houston. That year, he founded SCI with the intention of running a larger chain of homes with a standardized business plan, something along the lines of the McDonald's restaurant chain. He soon acquired several prominent funeral homes in major urban markets, including Blake-Lamb in Chicago and Joseph Gawler's Sons in Washington, D.C. SCI kept the original family names on the homes but instituted more efficient business practices. By 1970, SCI began implementing a strategy of more aggressive expansion, when it purchased a total of 30 homes in the United States and Canada. Setting a course that ran contrary to the tradition that funeral homes should be relatively small businesses, the company continued to expand, increasing its ownership to 106 funeral homes in 1972 and 276 by 1982.

In order to acquire privately owned homes, the company employed a team to meet the particular financial needs of each individual seller. Deals often included a tailored combination of common or preferred stock, cash, and secured long-term debt. Where SCI had several homes in one market, it ran them as a "cluster." Using this strategy, no longer did each funeral home need its own hearse. Instead, the cluster operated a fleet of hearses from a central location. The clusters also shared embalming operations and personnel. This eliminated much of the down time in the business, where people had to be kept on the payroll but might have nothing to do between funerals. Under the cluster arrangement, employees worked for whatever SCI funeral home in the area needed them, bringing an efficiency that traditionally family-run businesses could not imitate.

The company began selling shares to the public in 1970, debuting on the American Stock Exchange. SCI's operating income rose almost 40 percent to $2.3 million, or 68 cents a share, in 1971. The growth spurt was principally caused by the acquisition of Kinney Services' 28 funeral homes and related businesses in New York City and Miami. This gave SCI the ability to service about 15 percent of New York's funeral needs. In 1974, SCI moved to the more prestigious New York Stock Exchange. By 1975, the company operated 161 homes with full service hubs to facilitate equipment and personnel sharing in seven major cities in the United States and Canada. SCI had posted increased

Company Perspectives:

In a business that addresses one of life's inevitable occurrences, SCI is committed to service, compassion, and respect. Every day, the Company and its employees around the world work to maintain their position of leadership by creating positive memories of final tribute for families and those they love.

earnings and revenues each year since 1968, with acquisitions accounting for approximately two-thirds of the rise in net income from 1970 to 1975. SCI subsequently built funeral homes from the ground up, though until 1975 the company had never built an entirely new funeral home. Roughly 8 percent of SCI's revenues came from cemetery operations, dropping to $6 million in 1975 from a 1973 high of $8.9 million. The corporation sold seven cemeteries—essentially real estate deals—in 1973 and 1975 because ground maintenance was not as lucrative as the service aspect of the funeral business.

Prosperity for SCI faltered in 1973, however, when the Federal Trade Commission (FTC) began a nonpublic investigation of the funeral service and cemetery industry to determine whether any industry practices were unfair or deceptive. Two years later, the FTC ordered SCI to make refunds to overcharged patrons between 1971 and 1975 for various services and products, including flowers, cremation, and obituary notices. The complaint alleged that several of the company's 139 funeral home subsidiaries overstated the amounts paid to third party providers for their funeral customers. Although SCI did not admit that any deceptive or illegal acts had been committed, the company complied with the consent order so as to avoid costly litigation.

At the same time, the FTC proposed a broad trade rule to redress abuses detected among 22,000 funeral homes operating in the country. The rule restricted funeral directors from picking up or embalming corpses without family consent, requiring a casket for cremation or refusing to provide inexpensive containers, and failing to adequately advertise funeral service prices. The reform also required mortuaries to provide a listing of prices for services, caskets, and other items, making it clear that these were not mandatory sundries.

In February 1976, the FTC dropped the previous complaint and consent order, but it then filed a new complaint that included the previous allegations while also asserting that SCI paid medical examiners to help them generate business. Payment also allegedly went to morgue and hospital employees or police who let the company know when particular deaths occurred. The complaint contended that in certain cases the company had received kickbacks, agent's commissions, volume discounts, or other rebates without sharing the benefits with customers. Furthermore, accusations were made that certain funeral directors misinformed customers that various rubber gaskets or sealing devices on caskets would prevent natural decomposition and that directors were coercing people into purchasing crematory caskets by implying that state law made the funerary boxes requisite. Although the location of these

activities was not specified, an FTC source revealed that the charges occurred in the New York City area and probably in other major cities as well.

SCI refuted each and every allegation, countering—as quoted in a *Wall Street Journal* article—that the FTC's actions were "illegal, unwarranted, malicious, and damaging" to the firm. The company filed suit against the FTC on February 10, 1976, in Washington, D.C. However, the suit was dropped within the year, and in November of 1976 SCI's consent order—regarding the initial allegations—was rendered effective by the FTC. The commission and company were never able to agree about the allegations of the second complaint, but the information within was nonetheless passed on to local law officials. In 1984, the FTC finally required SCI and other funeral homes to provide customers with an itemized list of charges.

Other problems arose for SCI in 1979, when a group of dissident shareholders brought suit against the company, charging that it was conducting suspicious business tactics; the action was dismissed in February 1980. Although their allegations were found to be without merit, a special committee of SCI's board investigated those allegations and did indeed find questionable travel expenses and corporate perquisites, as well as unmonitored advances on company funds. As a result of the investigation, Waltrip and President B.B. Hollingsworth, Jr., repaid $75,716 to SCI, and the company plane and house in Steamboat Springs, Colorado, were sold. The shareholders were dissatisfied, saying not enough was recovered from Waltrip and Hollingsworth, but they agreed to settle the suit because the dubious practices had stopped. The suit cost SCI $50,000 in attorney's fees, which were incurred by the shareholders.

During these difficult years of legal battles with the FTC and others, SCI was headed by Hollingsworth, who stepped into the presidency in 1975 as Sam P. Douglass, president since 1964, moved into both the chairmanship of the executive committee and a position as director. Waltrip remained the chairman and chief executive officer.

New Ventures in the 1980s

Hollingsworth, however, also helped to lead the company's further expansion during his tenure. One major acquisition under Hollingsworth came in 1981, when SCI gained control of IFS Industries—the second largest company in the funeral service industry, with 91 homes and 22 cemeteries in 18 states and three Canadian provinces—in a tax-free swap of stock. After the buyout, SCI stood as an industry giant, yet its 276 homes accounted for only 4 percent of the industry's entire revenues, reflecting the fact that the funeral home industry continued to be dominated by small businesses.

From 1977 to 1982, SCI's earnings rose by 26 percent annually, with 1982 revenues hitting $135 million. SCI's typical home grossed $540,000 each year in 1982—four times the industry average. SCI owned most of the land underlying its funeral homes, and in 1982 it owned about 4,300 acres of cemetery land, most of which was carried on the books at prices typical for the 1950s or 1960s. Because of this, SCI was able to profit through various real estate deals. For example, in 1980 SCI exchanged a five-acre piece of property in Houston's posh

Key Dates:

1962: Robert Waltrip incorporates SCI.
1970: The company goes public.
1974: SCI stock moves to the New York exchange.
1981: The company buys IFS Industries.
1990: Overseas expansion begins.
1996: SCI tries to take over competitor Loewen Group.
1999: The company's stock price declines to its lowest point.

Galleria area for a 20 percent block of its stock owned by American General Life Insurance Company. SCI thus acquired $11 million worth of its own stock in a tax-free exchange for property that on paper was worth a mere $1.6 million.

Although SCI did not buy a single cemetery in 1981, revenues in that area rose 45 percent because 70 percent of those sales came from people purchasing plots for future use. Such cemetery plot sales are not to be confused with SCI's program of "pre-need" sales of funeral services, which started in 1977. In this program, SCI created a trust fund with customer payments accrued over five years. The fund was eventually redeemed for funeral services at the time of the client's death. For a time, the company also issued insurance policies redeemable for funeral services, but by 1990 this sort of pre-payment plan was executed only through a third party and the company itself only issued trusts. SCI began selling the package on two principles: relieving the bereaved of decision-making burdens and reserving future services at present value. Though the company could not access the funds until a funeral was actually performed, all the investment profits earned from those funds were retained by SCI. In 1981, SCI sold nearly $24 million worth of such orders.

While some outsiders hypothesized that rising prices would force SCI to perform the ceremonies at a loss, Waltrip disagreed, since most of the accoutrement costs—like hearses and parlors—were fixed. For the buyer, the program was not necessarily an economical idea, since it was perfectly feasible that the cautious investment of the $1,900 funeral service price could yield a return greater than the relative value of the "pre-need" purchase. Whatever the value for the buyer in cash or peace of mind, pre-sales created internal expansion and a pool of capital that SCI invested in other funeral homes and cemeteries.

During the 1980s, SCI used this money to seek homes in particularly favorable locations such as retirement areas in Florida, where the corporation acquired 41 homes between 1972 and 1982, making Florida the company's largest operating base. SCI also pushed development in Texas, Oklahoma, Colorado, and California. The company initiated a program of placing funeral homes on cemetery grounds, and by 1982 it was operating 18 such combination sites. From 1984 to 1989, sales from prearranged funerals increased 400 percent, becoming a $300 million dollar annual business. Nevertheless, in 1989 the company estimated that after write-offs SCI earned next to nothing on total sales of $450 million.

In an effort to offset such performances, SCI explored several new ventures during the 1980s. For example, the company branched out into flower shops in 1982 and began providing flowers in 15 homes and at 15 free-standing stores. Waltrip had planned to create a fast-flowers chain—again along the lines of McDonald's operation—but the shops were sold in 1986 because of management difficulties.

SCI acquired St. Louis-based Amedco in a $131 million stock deal in 1986. After disposing of Amedco's medical and steel businesses, SCI operated the nation's second largest maker of caskets and a leading supplier of embalming fluids, burial clothing, and mortuary furniture. The company intended not only to supply its own facilities but also to attract outside buyers. By offering volume discounts to private mortuaries on group insurance, auto leasing, and other products, Waltrip hoped to form the "True Value hardware of the funeral-service industry," as he told *Business Week*. The flaw in the plan was that smaller businesses refused to buy anything from their giant competitor. By 1987, the Amedco purchase caused SCI stock to plummet. By 1989, Amedco sales were off by 25 percent, and SCI promptly struck a deal to sell the liability for $62 million in 1990. SCI also put its two insurance agencies up for sale, one of which was sold by 1990.

A less problematic investment was SCI's 1988 founding of Provident Services, Inc., a company designed to provide capital financing to independent funeral homes and cemeteries. Although the new venture was in competition with banks and other loan institutions of greater financial means, SCI believed that Provident would become a substantial competitor in the sector. Provident's analysts would be capable of providing a more accurate assessment of funeral home and industry loans due to the company's close affiliation to the field.

An unusual development in the company's history occurred in 1987, when Marc Feith, an employee of Hillenbrand Industries Inc.—the number one casket maker and a new competitor to SCI in the pre-need funeral business—approached Waltrip with corporate secrets to sell. Waltrip immediately contacted the FBI, who captured Feith, himself a former FBI agent. Feith subsequently confessed to having repeatedly sifted through SCI trash to find information relating to corporate activities. Hillenbrand claimed Feith did the trash searches of his own volition, but Feith asserted that several Hillenbrand executives had assigned him such projects. Interestingly, Hillenbrand's legal council did not dispute the legality of Feith's work. SCI sued Hillenbrand for theft of trade secrets and additionally charged the competitor with fraud because of alleged deceptions during 1983 negotiations in which Hillenbrand considered supplying SCI with funeral equipment. The suit was settled in 1988 under undisclosed terms.

Worldwide Expansion in the 1990s

The 1990s marked the beginning of a new era for SCI. Hollingsworth ended his long tenure as head of SCI in 1990, when L. William Heiligbrodt was named president and chief operating officer. Waltrip remained chairman and chief executive officer. The following year, SCI relocated its cemetery operations headquarters to Houston, so that the two parts of the businesses might operate more closely. The company also absorbed 182 acquired funeral homes, including three large businesses—Pierce Brothers, the Sentinel Group, and the Arlington

Corporation. These were added to a group of 164 prestigious homes—including New York City's Frank E. Campbell and Riverside Memorial Chapel—and 18 cemeteries which have been recognized as among the finest heritage properties in the United States.

The SCI chain included over 1,500 funeral homes and cemeteries by the early 1990s, and the company had revenues of around $1.1 billion. The largest death services company in the United States by far, SCI began to acquire funeral homes abroad. SCI invested approximately $1 billion in the early 1990s for overseas expansion. It quickly snapped up leading funeral homes in France, England, and Australia and made inroads into other markets such as Italy, Singapore, and the Czech Republic. Though funeral customs were different country by country, Waltrip was sure that SCI's methods could work abroad as well. The cost of an American funeral had gone up substantially since the 1970s, tripling in price by the 1990s. Where more inexpensive funerals were the norm in England and France, SCI began offering a more lavish line of urns and caskets, not so much raising prices as making higher-priced options available. By mid-1996, it seemed that its operations abroad were working as planned. The company's overall funeral revenue rose 75 percent for the first quarter of 1996, and SCI's share price was trading at over $50.

Later that year, SCI made a hostile bid for the world's second-largest funeral home operator, the Canadian firm Loewen Group Inc. Loewen had imitated SCI's strategy of buying up North American funeral homes, and competition had driven the price of acquisitions up. There was apparently fierce animosity between Robert Waltrip and Loewen Group's founder Ray Loewen. Loewen, who controlled 15 percent of his company's stock, opposed the deal and began making more acquisitions and offering his top management expensive severance packages in order to drive up the cost of the merger. Several months after making its first offer, SCI withdrew, and Loewen went its own way. But SCI had been forced to dump some of its assets in order to fend off antitrust charges had the deal gone through.

By the late 1990s, it was clear that something had happened in the death services industry, and SCI was no longer the profitable company it had been. The company had had profit margins of around 25 percent since the late 1970s, while the death rate had gone up a steady 1 percent annually. But demographers noted by 1998 that the death rate was actually decreasing as advances in medical treatment allowed people to survive longer. This meant that SCI's market was now shrinking. And the long trend to consolidate in the funeral home industry had brought prices up so much that growth through acquisition was no longer as economical as it had been. In 1998, SCI actually broke up its management group that had spearheaded acquisitions, shifting executives into other areas. The company had lower than expected profits for the fourth quarter of that year. After its stock price dropped by more than 40 percent, SCI's president Heiligbrodt resigned. A string of top executives left the company in the next year, including Robert Waltrip's son. The company was led by Jerald Pullins in 1999, when SCI was named the worst one-year performer out of selected companies tracked by the *Wall Street Journal*. SCI's stock had fallen so low that an investment of $1000 in company stock at the

beginning of 1999 would have been worth only $187 by the end of the year.

Pullins tried to streamline the company, bringing down the number of operating clusters in the United States to only 87, from 200. The company advised its funeral directors to push lower-cost funerals in order to keep consumers who might go elsewhere. SCI brought out a new program in 1999 called Dignity Memorial, which offered customers a one-price package deal at the low end of the price range. Meanwhile, the company had accumulated a load of debt because of its acquisitions. SCI discontinued paying dividends to stockholders in 1999 in order to address the debt problem, and it began selling off assets. In 2001, the company announced plans to sell over 400 funeral homes, as well as more than 100 cemeteries. Pullins articulated a three-part plan to turn the company around, with its first aim to pay down SCI's $3.3 billion debt and to increase cash flow and cut expenses.

Pullins resigned in July, 2002, and chairman Robert Waltrip took over his duties. Several weeks later, the company announced a succession plan, spelling out who would lead the company over the next several years. By that time, SCI had significantly pared its operations. Where it had once been active in 20 countries, it now operated in only eight. Its number of funeral homes had fallen almost by half, to around 2,500. Its nearest competitor, Loewen Group (now known as Alderwoods Group), was in bankruptcy proceedings, possibly having overcommitted itself after the hostile takeover bid. SCI endeavored to weather the hard times, planning future growth to emerge internally, instead of through acquisition. SCI began marketing its Dignity Memorial package as a national corporate brand name, giving its funeral homes a cohesive image they had not hitherto possessed.

Principal Subsidiaries

Equity Corp. International; SCI Financial Services Inc.

Principal Competitors

Stewart Enterprises, Inc.; Carriage Services, Inc.; Alderwoods Group Inc.

Further Reading

"Acquisitions Spur Profits Growth at Service Corp. International," *Barron's*, August 18, 1975.

Barrett, William P., "Lively Death Stock," *Forbes*, March 19, 1990.

"Cemetery Companies Aggressively Market Burial Plots As Costs Soar and Business Falls," *Wall Street Journal*, January 24, 1984.

Conklin, J. C., "Service Corp. Terms Third-Quarter Net Half Expected Level, and Stock Plunges," *Wall Street Journal*, October 4, 1999, p. A19.

——, "Worst 1-Year Performer," *Wall Street Journal*, February 24, 2000, pp. R4, R6.

Davis, Jo Ellen, "Bob Waltrip Is Making Big Noises in a Quiet Industry," *Business Week*, August 25, 1986.

Egodigwe, Laura Saunders, "Service Corp. Insiders Unload Sizable Stake," *Wall Street Journal*, March 25, 1998, p. C1.

Fisher, Daniel, "Buried Trouble," *Forbes*, September 18, 2000, p. 88.

"FTC Proposes to Alter Funeral Practices, Orders Service Corp. to Make Refunds," *Wall Street Journal*, August 29, 1975.

"FTC Accuses Service Corp. International of Paying Bribes to Get Funeral Business," *Wall Street Journal*, February 5, 1976.

"Funeral-Home Chain Says Finance Chief Resigned from Post," *Wall Street Journal*, November 22, 1999, p. B20.

Helliker, Kevin, "Service Corp. Makes Friendly Bid to Buy a Second Big British Funeral Company," *Wall Street Journal*, September 6, 1994, p. B7.

Jacob, Rahul, "Acquisitions Done the Right Way," *Fortune*, November 16, 1992, p. 96.

Johnson, Robert, "The Case of Marc Feith Shows Corporate Spies Aren't Just High-Tech," *Wall Street Journal*, January 9, 1987.

Marcial, Gene G., "This Funeral Stock Is Full of Life," *Business Week*, August 28, 1989.

McWilliams, Gary, "Death Be Not (So) Profitable," *Business Week*, October 5, 1998, pp. 100–01.

McWilliams, Gary, and Symonds, William C., "Dustup in 'Death Services,'" *Business Week*, October 7, 1996, p. 40.

Palmeri, Christopher, "Funereal Prospects," *Forbes*, September 11, 1995, p. 45.

Post, Tom, "Growth Business: Death on the Installment Plan," *Fortune*, April 30, 1984.

"Service Corp. Comes Back to Life," *Business Week*, April 9, 2001, p. 110.

"Service Corp. Expects to Post 1st Period Gain," *Wall Street Journal*, September 14, 1972.

"Service Corp. International: Burying the Troubles That Diversification Brought," *Barron's*, February 13, 1989.

"Service Corp. Is Suing Hillenbrand, Alleges Theft of Trade Secrets," *Wall Street Journal*, March 4, 1987.

"Service Corp. Says FTC Is Studying Funeral Firms," *Wall Street Journal*, August 8, 1973.

"Service Corp. Says FTC Makes Order Effective, Stopping Markups," *Wall Street Journal*, November 3, 1976.

"Service Corp. Says Suit by Dissident Holders Is Dismissed in Texas," *Wall Street Journal*, February 13, 1980.

"Service Corp. to Revise Financing via Warner Communications Plan," *Wall Street Journal*, March 23, 1977.

"Service Corp. to Sue FTC on Complaint, Withdrawn Order," *Wall Street Journal*, February 6, 1976.

Stringer, Kortney, "Service Corp. to Sell Hundreds of Properties," *Wall Street Journal*, January 8, 2001, p. A16.

Tomsho, Robert, "Service Corp. Ends Takeover Offer for Loewen Group," *Wall Street Journal*, January 8, 1997, pp. A2, A8.

——, "Service Corp. Posts 52% Profit Rise, Topping Estimates," *Wall Street Journal*, April 24, 1996, p. A8.

Tomsho, Robert, and Lipin, Steven, "Service Corp. Sweetens Loewen Offer to $2.9 Billion," *Wall Street Journal*, October 3, 1996, p. B4.

Whitford, David, "Funeral Roll-Ups Face a Slow, Painful Death," *Fortune*, February 5, 2001, p. 196.

—Elaine Belsito
—update: A. Woodward

SFI Group plc

SFI House
165 Church Street East
Woking
Surrey GU21 1HJ
United Kingdom
Telephone: (+44) 0 1483 227900
Fax: (+44) 0 1483 227903
Web site: http://www.sfigroup.co.uk

Public Company
Incorporated: 1986 as Surrey Free Inns Plc
Employees: 3,009
Sales: £115.2 million ($221.5 million) (2001)
Stock Exchanges: London
Ticker Symbol: SFI
NAIC: 722410 Drinking Places (Alcoholic Beverages);
722211 Limited-Service Restaurants

Woking-based SFI Group plc is one of the United Kingdom's fastest-growing operators of drinking and eating establishments. The company operates nearly 200 bars across England under four key concepts. The Litten Tree, the company's oldest bar format, are large-scale "chameleon" bars, that is, they change character—from restaurant bar in the daytime to multi-area nightclub at night—in order to attract different groups of patrons. Litten Trees also offer breakfast service, and a number of Litten Trees also feature morning sandwich bar service. In mid-2002, there were 58 Litten Trees in operation. The upscale Slug and Lettuce brand, acquired by SFI in 2000, offers an informal dining and drinking environment. The 52 Slug and Lettuce outlets are typically found in High Street (downtown) locations. Bar Med represents another chameleon bar concept created by the SFI Group, offering Mediterranean-style dining during the day and Ibiza-style dancing at night. The company operated 32 Bar Meds at the end of its 2001 year. The smallest member of the SFI brand group is Fiesta Havana, acquired from Capital Radio 1999. The seven Fiesta Havanas offer dining, music, and dancing with a Latin American theme. In addition to the company's four core brands, SFI Group own

25 other hotels, restaurants, and bars, including five Break for the Border restaurants. The company also has been trying to sell off a number of its For Your Eyes Only lap-dancing bars; that operation was spun off from the company's main business as a separate company. Elsewhere, SFI has adopted an ambitious growth program, acquiring 25 bars, including 24 Paris Café Bars, in 2001, with plans to add up to 30 more in 2002. The company, quoted on the London Stock Exchange, is led by CEO Andrew Latham, who took over the position from founder and Chairman Anthony Hill.

Building on the "Business Expansion Scheme"

Anthony Hill came to the bar business in the mid-1980s after a career that included positions as marketing director for Martini & Rossi and general manager at Seiko's UK branch. In 1985, Hill formed his own company, called Surrey Free Inns plc. Hill intended to take advantage of the new Business Expansion Scheme (BES), which was set up to encourage the creation and growth of small businesses by giving generous tax breaks to investors. The original BES scheme allowed investors to write off the full amount of their investment against their income taxes.

Surrey Free Inns made its first share issue in 1986, raising £5 million. The company then began buying up individual properties, focusing on traditional pubs. The company set to work redeveloping the new businesses, enhancing their profitability. The company's first major acquisition came in 1987, when it took over the Litten Hotel in London. This property, which the company redesigned, became the test ground for the company's first concept bar, the Litten Tree, rolled out in the 1990s. By 1988, the company neared 20 properties.

In 1989, Surrey Free Inns placed a new rights issue, raising £4 million in order to buy 19 pubs from the First Leisure group. The company, now with nearly 40 sites, hoped to accelerate its growth, and in 1990 Surrey Free Inns spent another £4 million to build the 73-room Innlodge, which also featured a restaurant and conference facilities, in what was meant to become a budget-priced hotel offering four-star accommodations. In that year, the company completed two more acquisitions of individual properties.

Yet the company's expansion had proved too rapid for Surrey Free Inns, particularly as the United Kingdom slumped into an economic recession. The difficult climate was further exacerbated by the outbreak of the Persian Gulf War. Surrey Free Inns difficulties continued into the mid-1990s, and by 1995 the company's holdings had shrunk to just 25 sites. Surrey Free was close to going under but was rescued by Canadian brewer John Labatt, which loaned the company £500,000 in exchange for a 4.5 percent stake in the business.

The loan enabled Surrey Free Inns to develop a new strategy of building a chain of bars based on strong concepts. The company's conversion of its Litten Hotel property had led it to develop a new type of bar-restaurant, called The Litten Tree. The company's first chameleon bar, the large-scale Litten Tree was capable of completely changing its character from day to night, offering informal dining at lunchtime and converting to a nightclub featuring music, bands, dancing, karaoke, and other entertainment at night.

The first Litten Tree ''superpub'' opened in 1994 in Sutton and cost the company some £210,000 to develop. It took the company less than a year to realize a return on that investment as the Litten Tree formula proved a popular one. By mid-1995, Surrey Free Inns had decided to peg its future on the success of the concept and began redeveloping other properties in its portfolio to match the new concept—of the company's 25 properties, about 15 met the Litten Tree's large-scale format.

Branding Success for the Turn of the Century

Surrey Free Inns went public in mid-1995, listing on the newly created Alternative Investment Market (AIM) market of the London Stock Exchange. By then, the company had opened its second Litten Tree, in its Woking home, using the loan from Labatt. By mid-1996, the company operated seven Litten Trees. A new share offering, which raised £1.5 million, enabled Surrey Free to open three more Litten Trees before the end of that year. The company by then had caught the attention of the investment community, particularly after being named the first-ever AIM Company of the Year.

Yet Surrey Free nearly lost its independence in 1996 when then-larger Regent Inns acquired a stake in the company and appeared to be attempting to step up its position toward launching a possible takeover. The move fit in with a new period of activity in the United Kingdom's bar scene, following the adoption of the Beer Orders, which required beer brewers to divest their pub holdings—a move set to place 11,000 pubs on the market.

Surrey Free's success with Litten Tree encouraged it to develop a second, smaller bar concept in order to capture a larger percentage of a community's drinking public. At the beginning of 1997, the company launched the pilot of the new brand, called Bar Med, a café concept with a Mediterranean theme, in Bournemouth. Surrey Free then began ramping up for a full-scale rollout of the Bar Med brand across the country.

The company paid more than £11 million in 1997 to acquire Richardsons Inns, a purchase which brought Surrey Free four large-scale venues, plus three small bars, and a side business, For Your Eyes Only, a bar featuring lap-dancing. Surrey Free set to work converting the Richardsons properties to its Litten Tree and Bar Med concepts. It also began developing plans to extend the For Your Eyes Only brand.

During 1998, Surrey Free continued adding new ventures, including the full-fledged rollout of the Bar Med brand. After a four-for-one stock split in August of that year, the company moved its listing to the London Stock Exchange's main board a month later. At that time, Surrey Free Inns changed its name to SFI Group plc. The company continued acquiring individual properties, and by the end of the year had added 12 new bars to its growing network, reaching a total of 55 outlets at the beginning of 1999.

By then, SFI Group revealed that it had been conducting merger talks with Regent Inns, but the two sides were unable to agree on terms for an eventual merger. Instead, SFI Group set out to expand on its own, stepping up its number of new bar openings, with ten new pubs added in the first three months of 1999. Now convinced of the viability of its multi-brand strategy, the company began to search for a new pub brand concept to complement Litten Tree and Bar Med. In May 1999, the company launched a new pilot outlet, an upscale sandwich and coffee bar concept called Café Litten.

SFI continued to seek to diversify its portfolio, and in October 1999 the company acquired seven Fiesta Havana restaurants from Capital Radio for £9.45 million. At the same time, SFI announced its intention to ''de-merge'' the For Your Eyes Only concept, believing the lap-dancing concept to be at odds with its image as a public company. Through 1999, the company opened 20 new bars.

By mid-2000, the company operated 32 Litten Trees and 22 Bar Meds. SFI, however, had begun to seek to reposition its Bar Med brand toward larger venues, with late-night licenses and an Ibiza-style atmosphere, referring to the Spanish island that had become immensely popular with British tourists at the turn of the century for its all-night dance clubs. The acquisition of the upscale pub chain The Slug and Lettuce, for £31.6 million, gave SFI both a new brand and at the same time filled the small-venue niche left behind by Bar Med. In addition, the company's complementary brand strategy enabled the company to rebrand a number of its smaller Bar Med sites, which did not match the new large-scale concept for the chain, under the Slug and Lettuce format.

After announcing its intention to add as many as 25 new sites by the end of 2000, SFI made a new acquisition, buying up a small Ireland-based chain of Break for the Border bars for £4.7 million. By the end of that year, SFI had boosted its total

Key Dates:

1985: Anthony Hill forms Surrey Free Inns Plc and begins acquiring pub and hotel properties.
1987: Surrey Free acquires the Litten Hotel, which will become the basis for company's Litten Tree brand.
1989: Nineteen pubs are acquired from First Leisure.
1994: The first Litten Tree pub is rolled out.
1995: The company goes public on the London Stock Exchange's AIM market.
1998: The company changes its name to SFI Group and switches its listing to London the Stock Exchange's main board.
2002: Anthony Hill retires, and Andrew Latham is named CEO.

number of outlets past 100. The company continued to tout the advantages of its multi-brand offering, which enabled it to establish itself in multiple locations in a single town, and even on the same street. Yet the different target markets for each of its brands shielded the bars from cannibalizing one anothers' sales. In this way, the company was able to raise its future targets as well, with plans to top more than 400 outlets in the years to come.

Acquisitions of other bar groups had clearly become part of the company's strategy at the turn of the century. In 2001, SFI paid CVC Capital Partners and Bridgepoint Capital £15 million to acquire the Parisa Group's Parisa Café Bars, a chain of 24 outlets. SFI began converting those outlets to its portfolio of strong pub brands, with most of the Parisa sites slated to become Slug and Lettuce pubs. Meanwhile, the company, which had opened three additional For Your Eyes Only branches in order to build up that operation to a scale sufficient to sell, had failed to find a buyer for the concept. After an attempt to sell the business in a management buyout fell through because of lack of financing, SFI spun off For Your Eyes Only into a separate, independently operated company.

In 2002, founder Anthony Hill announced his intention to retire from the company at the age of 65, taking the position of chairman and naming Andrew Latham as the new CEO. By then, Hill's company had grown to nearly 186 outlets, with total sales over £144 million. SFI had taken a leading position in the United Kingdom's High Street bar sector. Yet the company showed no signs of slowing down in its ambitions, brandishing a landbank of some 60 new properties lined up for its successful pub brands.

Principal Competitors

Compass Group PLC; Whitbread Holdings PLC; Punch Retail Ltd.; Compass Roadside Ltd; Wolverhampton and Dudley Breweries PLC; Cleveland Place Holdings PLC; Greene King PLC; J D Wetherspoon PLC; Greene King plc; Luminar PLC; Ascot PLC; Enterprise Inns PLC; Punch Pub Company Ltd.; Daniel Thwaites PLC; Pubmaster Ltd.; Young and Co's Brewery PLC; Regent Inns PLC.

Further Reading

Frewin, Angela, "Top-end Focus Puts SFI into Black Again," *Caterer & Hotelkeeper*, August 1, 2002 p. 10.
Horley, Nick, "They're Brazen and They're Coming to a Town Near You," *New Statesman*, November 15, 1999, p. 32.
Michalczyk, Imelda, "Bar Med Goes Chameleon," *Leisure & Hospitality Business*, March 21, 2002 p. 10.
Parry, Caroline, "SFI Group Spins Off For Your Eyes Only from Bar Brands," *Leisure & Hospitality Business*, August 9, 2001 p. 6.
"SFI Makes Steady Progress," *Leisure & Hospitality Business*, February 21, 2002, p. 3.
Walsh, Dominic, "Peaks and Troughs at SFI," *Leisure & Hospitality Business*, August 9, 2001, p. 7.

—M. L. Cohen

Shuffle Master Inc.

1106 Palms Airport Drive
Las Vegas, Nevada 89119-3730
U.S.A.
Telephone: (702) 897-7150
Fax: (702) 270-5161
Web site: http://www.shufflemaster.com

Public Company
Incorporated: 1983
Employees: 224
Sales: $48.0 million (2001)
Stock Exchanges: NASDAQ
Ticker Symbol: SHFL
NAIC: 339999 All Other Miscellaneous Manufacturing;
   541511 Custom Computer Programming Services

Shuffle Master Inc. develops, produces, and sells automatic card shuffling machines (shufflers) and gaming products, including table games, slot machine game software, and slot machine operating system software for the gaming industry. The company's strategy for growth entails the development or acquisition of innovative gaming products and systems—such as productivity enhancing equipment, new table and slot games, and slot game technology—with the intention of marketing these worldwide. The company operates within a gaming industry that is found in 32 states and numerous countries worldwide. Casino gaming has grown dramatically since the early 1990s, and the Shuffle Master believes that the North American and international markets for gaming-related products will continue to expand. The company's shuffler products are suitable for the vast majority of card-based table games, which the company also develops, markets, and licenses to casinos and other lawful gaming establishments. In North, Central, and South America, Shuffle Master sells and services its shuffler, table game, and slot products through its own direct sales force and service department. In selected international jurisdictions, the company markets its products through its international distributor, Technical Casino Supplies, Ltd. Shuffle Master is subject to jurisdic-

tional licensing requirements concerning the marketing of its products and must obtain approval for all of its products.

Company Origins

John Breeding, a former truck driver, founded Shuffle Master in 1983 with the aim of developing and marketing automatic card shufflers. Breeding invented the idea of automatic card shufflers after reading an article in the *Wall Street Journal* about casino card counters. In 1989, the company developed its first single-deck shuffler and sold its first automatic shuffling machine to Bally's Casino in Las Vegas in January 1992. That same year, Shuffle Master also went public. The company's shuffling machines, designed for table card games for the gaming industry, offered several benefits, primarily increased productivity and security. The shufflers provided for more playing time by shuffling one or more card decks while a game was being played. The company's single-deck shuffler worked by automatically shuffling a deck of playing cards and depositing the deck into a holding tray. While the first deck was being dealt, the machine would shuffle a second deck and move it into the holding tray.

Pursuing Product Diversification in the Early 1990s

Soon after the success of its first single-deck card shuffler, the company began producing variations of the system, including a multi-deck system for use with four, six, or eight decks of cards, primarily for blackjack table games. Introduced in 1995, the multi-deck shuffler operated much like the single-deck unit in shuffling a second deck of cards while the first was being played. The company also introduced a model designed for hand-held dealing and another model that shuffled and counted out the cards to be distributed by the dealer while a second deck was being shuffled. The latter model proved especially popular with gaming establishments and was frequently used for well-known card games, including the company's own Let It Ride game.

Shuffle Master received approval for its basic Let It Ride game from the Nevada Gaming Control Board in August 1993 and began licensing it to casinos in October. By 1996, the Let It Ride game had received approval for play in seventeen states

337

Company Perspectives:

Shuffle Master specializes in providing innovative, high-quality products and services to the casino industry. These include card shufflers, table games and table gaming equipment, slot games and operating system software for slot machines. The Company's service, sales, and marketing efforts extend to most of the regulated gaming jurisdictions worldwide.

and five Canadian provinces. The game comprised a patented five card stud poker game in which players were paid according to a fixed payout schedule. Because of its popularity, the company introduced another version called Let It Ride: The Tournament, a five card stud poker table game. The game quickly became an establishment specialty after winning approval from the Nevada Gaming Control Board in June 1995. By the end of October 1996, the company had installed the game in more than 100 casinos in Nevada, Mississippi, and Connecticut. In 1995, the company also signed an agreement with Bally Gaming International, Inc. to produce a video version of Let It Ride, known as Let It Ride Bonus Video. The company introduced the video version in early 1997 after indications that the Let It Ride The Tournament game was declining in popularity due to its high leasing costs to casinos and low returns to players. The company provided the game's video version to casinos at reduced cost and designed it to offer players more liberal paytables for bonus bets.

Marketing Alliances in the Late 1990s

To further position itself in the higher-margin game business, Shuffle Master signed an agreement with master game designer Mark Yoseloff in 1996. Yoseloff was the developer of consumer versions of Pac Man and Donkey Kong. The agreement enabled the company to acquire Yoseloff's personal game library. Yoseloff became a consultant to the company from August 1996 to July 1997. In August 1997, he became Shuffle Master's executive vice-president and head of the New Games Division. The joint venture produced Five Deck Frenzy, a video poker game that the company introduced in 1996. In August 1996, the company also established a joint marketing alliance with International Game Technology (IGT) with the aim of marketing the video version of Let It Ride. Under the terms of the agreement, profits were to be split 50/50. In September 1996, the agreement was modified to include Five Deck Frenzy.

In late 1997, company founder and CEO John Breeding retired for health reasons and was replaced by Joseph Lahti. Under Lahti, the company continued to pursue marketing alliances and product diversification. As a result, in September 1997, the company signed a second development and marketing alliance with IGT. The agreement provided for the company's games to be programmed on IGT's video and slot machines and for both parties to split the profits. In addition, the agreement provided for the company to receive 100 percent of the revenues from casinos that licensed its games using IGT machines. In October 1998, the agreement was cancelled and replaced with a new licensing arrangement. Under the new agreement, IGT received royalties

for Shuffle Master games that ran on IGT machines. IGT also provided the company with software support and training. At the same time, the company signed a separate game marketing agreement with Anchor Gaming to market and service a table game version of Anchor's Double Down Stud. In addition, in April 1998 the company entered into a marketing agreement with Bally Gaming to develop and sell a video slot machine version of *Let's Make a Deal*, the popular and long-running television show hosted by Monty Hall. The agreement was later amended in August 2000 to make the license of intellectual property non-exclusive. The agreement provided that the company receive a preferential share of the game net operating profits and the rights to sell Let's Make A Deal slot machines back to Bally at the company's adjusted net book value.

As a result of pursuing product diversification, by October 1998 the company was marketing several video slot machines, including Let It Ride Bonus Video, Five Deck Frenzy, and Five Deck Poker. The company also had other video products in the market test stage, such as Video Mah Jong, MultiBingo, and Doors to Riches. In December 1998, the company announced that two of its new video slot game software products, Multi-Bingo and Doors to Riches, were approved for installation by the Nevada Gaming Control Board. In December 1998, the company reported revenue of $27.1 million compared to $28.7 million for fiscal 1997. Fiscal 1998 results stemmed primarily from a $2.65 million pre-tax charge resulting from the consolidation of its Minneapolis operations with those of its Las Vegas office and from a write off of part of its older shuffler product inventory due to the development of its next generation shuffler product, the ACE.

In 1999, the company formally introduced its new ACE single deck shuffler system, which substantially replaced the older single deck shufflers in casinos across the country. Unlike the older single deck models, which mechanically mimicked a hand shuffle, the ACE system sorted cards into shelves on a vertically moving elevator in random order according to computer generated instructions. The ACE unit was smaller, had fewer moving parts, required less service, was easily programmable by casino personnel for a variety of single deck games, and could track and display the hands that were played for the casino operator. The company, however, had trouble marketing its new Three Stooges slot machine stemming from concerns that the game lured children. The company also developed its new MD series of multi-deck card shufflers that could simultaneously shuffle two to eight decks of cards primarily for blackjack or mini-baccarat table games. In 2000, the company introduced its next generation of multiple deck card shufflers, the King, which shuffled cards continuously, making card counting virtually impossible. The King was designed primarily for blackjack and other multi-deck table games. In addition, as part of the its aggressive product diversification program, the company introduced three new table games—Bahama Bonus, 3 Way Action, and Wild Hold'em Stud. The new table games joined the company's existing line of successful specialty table games that included Let It Ride Bonus and Three Card Poker.

Growth in the 2000s

In May 2000, the company signed a development and distribution agreement with the Sierra Design Group (SDG) with the

Key Dates:

1983: Shuffle Master Inc. is founded by John Breeding and is incorporated in Minnesota.

1989: The company develops its first automatic single-deck shuffler.

1992: The company goes public, issuing shares of common stock.

1995: Shuffle Master introduces the first multi-deck shuffler.

1996: The company forms its first marketing venture with International Game Technology to market its gaming products

1998: Shuffle Master consolidates its operations in Las Vegas.

2000: The company signs a development agreement with Sierra Design Group to market its gaming rights in the Three Stooges video game for Native American casinos.

2001: The company signs a licensing agreement with Anheuser-Busch to develop video slot machines using images of Anheuser-Busch's flagship brand, Budweiser beer.

2002: Shuffle Master acquires assets of Casino Software and Services LLC of Las Vegas, Nevada.

aim of further commercializing Shuffle Master's gaming rights in The Three Stooges. The revenue sharing agreement provided for the company to develop a Three Stooges themed video game for the Native American casinos in the state of Washington for use on SDG's gaming machines and systems. In addition, the company received approval from the Nevada Gaming Control Board to market its newest video slot game, Press Your Luck. According to Shuffle Master CEO Joseph L. Lahti, the game's approval marked a significant milestone for the company. The control board's approval signified the first time that a stand alone, PC-based operating system useable in multiple gaming machine platforms had been allowed in Nevada. The approval also meant the company could market its own games using the operating system. In July 2000, Shuffle Master signed agreements with IGT to produce video slot games based on three well known television shows—*Let's Make a Deal*, *The Three Stooges*, and *The Honeymooners*. The company's impressive rate of growth cast it into the spotlight as *Forbes Magazine* named Shuffle Master one of America's 200 best small companies for the second year in a row. At the same time, Shuffle Master promoted Mark Yoseloff to the position of president, with Joseph Lahti continuing in the positions of chairman and CEO. For fiscal year 2000, the company reported record revenue of $38.9 million compared to $28.9 million in 1999.

Shuffle Master continued to pursue growth opportunities through licensing and cooperative development, manufacturing, and marketing agreements in 2001. In January, the company entered into a licensing and supply agreement with Recreativos Franco, a Spanish corporation and one of the world's leading manufacturers of slot machines. The agreement granted Shuffle Master rights to use Franco's extensive library of slot machine games in certain casino territories in non-Native American

jurisdictions in the United States and Canada. The agreement provided for the company to use these games on its own proprietary operating system. In April 2001, the company announced its intent to purchase the business and certain assets related to the QuickDraw shuffler product line. The QuickDraw shuffler constituted a multi-deck shuffler that was initially introduced to the casino market in 1996. Shuffle Master also signed licensing agreements for its slot game operating system with Mikohn Gaming Corporation and Fleetwood Manufacturing, Inc. The agreements enabled the licensees to use the company's operating system to program and operate gaming devices in exchange for a fixed share of the profits. In November 2001, the company also signed a licensing agreement with St. Louis-based Anheuser-Busch, Inc. to develop reel and video slot machines using logos and promotional images of Anheuser-Busch's leading brand, Budweiser beer. In addition, the company announced that its board of directors renewed authorization for management to repurchase Shuffle Master's common stock in the open market. As a result, the company repurchased 560,000 shares in the fourth quarter at an average price of $11.45 for $6.4 million. President and new CEO Mark Yoseloff, who replaced Joseph Lahti as chief executive officer, noted the contrast between the recent slide in the company's stock price and Shuffle Master's continued prospects for substantial growth. The company intended to pursue a strategy of using excess cash for share repurchases, especially when the gap between Shuffle Master's current stock price and its long-term appreciation potential widened. Despite the severe economic downturn in 2001, the company again reported record revenues of $48.0 million, an increase of 23 percent over the previous year. The increase in revenue stemmed primarily from the company's aggressive diversification of its table game business and slot games.

In January 2002, the company announced the expansion of the role of Mark Yoseloff, who became the company's chairman of the board of directors in addition to his duties as CEO. In addition, Mark A. Lipparelli, the company's executive vice-president, was promoted to president. Joseph Lathti, who had remained with the company as chair of the board after stepping down as CEO, announced his retirement from the board effective February 2, 2000. Under these new changes, the company continued its strategy of forging joint marketing and supply agreements. In February 2002, Shuffle Master signed another in a series of agreements with Bally Gaming for the supply of mechanical reel slot machines for a Budweiser themed game. Under the provisions of the agreement, the company would develop the game concept and Bally would manufacture and program the slot machine to run the game. The agreement also provided that the company would purchase the Bally machines and assume responsibility for marketing and sales. In addition, in July the company announced that it received approval from Gaming Labs International for its Hollywood and Spider-Man themed games. These approvals allowed Shuffle Master to introduce the new slot games into numerous markets, including California, Connecticut, Illinois, Indiana, Iowa, Louisiana, Minnesota, and Missouri. In August, the company also acquired the assets, technology, and products of Casino Software and Services LLC of Las Vegas, Nevada. As part of the acquisition, Oliver Schubert, CEO of Casino Software and Services, joined Shuffle Master as director of product development.

With continuing strong earnings and revenue growth, the company was informed by Standard & Poors that it would replace Visual Networks, Inc. in the S&P SmallCap 600 Index effective April 24, 2002. The company's addition to the S&P SmallCap 600 Index was reinforced by its record second quarter revenues of $13.4 million, an increase of 8.8 percent over the same period in the previous year. In commenting on the company's performance, Chief Financial Officer Gerald Koslow noted that Shuffle Master ended the quarter with its strongest balance sheet ever. *Fortune Small Business* magazine took notice, naming Shuffle Master the nation's 25th fastest-growing small company in June 2002. The magazine observed that in the previous three years, Shuffle Master's performance included average earnings per share growth of 67.4 percent, revenue growth of 25.3 percent, and total stock return of 77.2 percent. The company's growth appeared especially notable amidst the prolonged slide in the stock market and the continuing weakness in the economy. As a result, the company's business strategy of product diversification and strategic marketing and development alliances seemed to position it well for future growth and profitability.

Principal Competitors

Alliance Gaming Corporation; Innovative Gaming Corporation of America; International Game Technology; Mikohn Gaming Corporation; WMS Industries Inc.

Further Reading

Bhatt, Rob, "Turning the Tables," *Las Vegas Business Wire*, October 5, 1998.

"Buy Recommendation Reiterated on Shuffle Master; Company Also Announces Nevada Gaming Approval of Two Video Slot Products," *PR Newswire*, December 4, 1998.

"*Fortune Magazine* Ranks Shuffle Master as One of America's 1000 Fastest Growing Small Companies," *Business Wire*, June 20, 2002.

"Shuffle Master Acquires Licensing Rights to Develop Budweiser-Themed Gaming Machines," *PR Newswire*, November 27, 2001.

"Shuffle Master Added to S&P SmallCap 600 Index," *Business Wire*, April 23, 2002.

"Shuffle Master Announces Product Acquisition: Oliver Schubert Joins Shuffle Master as Director of Product Development," *Business Wire*, August 12, 2002.

"Shuffle Master's Bahama Bonus Receives Nevada Regulatory Approval," *PR Newswire*, March 30, 1998.

"Shuffle Master Signs Development and Distribution Agreement with Sierra Design Group," *PR Newswire*, May 9, 2000.

"Shuffle Master Signs Reel Slot Game and Slot Machine Component Supply Agreement with Recreativos Franco," *PR Newswire*, February 28, 2001.

—Bruce P. Montgomery

State Farm Mutual Automobile Insurance Company

One State Farm Plaza
Bloomington, Illinois 61710
U.S.A.
Telephone: (309) 766-2311
Fax: (309) 766-3621
Web site: http://www.statefarm.com

Mutual Company
Incorporated: 1922
Employees: 79,300
Total Assets: $71 billion (2001)
NAIC: 524126 Direct Property and Casualty Insurance
  Carriers; 524113 Direct Life Insurance Carriers

State Farm Mutual Automobile Insurance Company, the cornerstone in the State Farm Insurance Companies group, has been the number one automobile insurer in the United States since 1942. Approximately one out of five cars in the United States is insured through State Farm. Through a network of over 16,700 agents, the company and its subsidiaries handle 71 million auto, home, life, and health insurance policies. The State Farm group also offers its customers mutual funds and a variety of banking services, including deposit accounts, CDs, and mortgages via the Internet and telephone.

George Mecherle Enters
the Auto Insurance Business: 1920s

State Farm began in 1922 as one man's plan to offer low-cost automobile insurance to the farmers of Illinois: hence the name State Farm Mutual Automobile Insurance Company. State Farm's early success and strong standing in a volatile marketplace is surely due to the vision of the company's founder, George Mecherle. Mercherle's beginnings are as modest as the company's success is extraordinary. He was a farmer until he was 40, when his wife's failing health forced them to leave their farm and Mecherle started selling insurance with a Bloomington, Illinois, company. Running his own farm had shaped Mecherle into a man who was constantly looking to innovate and improve conditions. When, in his characteristic

outspoken, straightforward manner, he told his boss at the insurance company some of his ideas for improving the business, the boss said, "Well George, if you don't like the way we run things, go start your own company."

Mecherle did just that. He brought to the auto insurance business a fresh perspective and, with the help of a few choice people, began instituting his own ideas, which began with establishing a mutual automobile insurance company. Unlike a capital stock company, which distributes dividends, a mutual company adjusts premium costs and will refund a portion of the company's surplus to policyholders during periods when claims are lower and income higher. At the time, the insurance industry set its own rates and did not distinguish between groups of drivers based on location, driving record, or any other risk criteria. Mecherle decided it was possible to form a mutual insurance company that catered to rural and small town drivers who, as a group, had fewer accidents and cost insurers less in claim payments. Because claim costs for this group tended to be lower, premiums could be lower, and State Farm undercut its competitor's rates significantly.

This innovation of tying insurance rates to risk level established State Farm's legacy as a smart insurer that passed savings on to the customer. The *Wall Street Journal* observed, "Until the late 1950s, the company's competitors were clinging to their traditional insurance rates while State Farm was boasting in ads of savings of 'up to 40%' on its auto insurance."

State Farm was also a pioneer in the practice of charging its customers an initial lifetime membership fee to cover the cost of processing new policyholders and the agent's commission. This one-time, nonrefundable fee allowed State Farm to keep the policy premium low, and it generated essential income that fueled the company's early growth.

Aside from its independent approach to rates, another key element in State Farm's success was its unique agent force. Normally, insurance agents represented a number of different companies, took large commissions, and shouldered a great deal of the paperwork involved in writing and maintaining policies. Mecherle simply tapped into the network of farmer's mutual insurance companies formed to protect members against fire or

---

Company Perspectives:

State Farm's mission is to help people manage the risks of everyday life, recover from the unexpected, and realize their dreams. We are people who make it our business to be like a good neighbor, who built a premier company by selling and keeping promises through our marketing partnership, who bring diverse talents and experiences to our work of serving the State Farm customer. Our success is built on a foundation of shared values—quality service and relationships, mutual trust, integrity, and financial strength. Our vision for the future is to be the customer's first and best choice in the products and services we provide. We will continue to be the leader in the insurance industry and we will become a leader in the financial services arena. Our customers' needs will determine our path. Our values will guide us.

---

lightning damage, as well as farm bureaus and other local institutions established throughout various regions. His first agents were men who were well placed in the community, such as the officials from the local farm bureau or sometimes an area's school principal. These agents worked part-time for State Farm and received less commission than their counterparts selling insurance full-time for other insurance companies. Nevertheless, by selling a sound, affordable insurance package to a population that needed it, State Farm agents were able to make their money on sales volume. Furthermore, State Farm's central office in Bloomington handled most of the paperwork, which freed up its agents to spend the bulk of their time selling.

The strategy worked so well that State Farm outgrew its offices three times in the first seven years. The home-office staff grew from five people in 1925 to 183 in 1927. The company reached a point in the early 1940s where its operations had become so scattered, some employees wore roller skates to speed delivery of interoffice mail.

The beauty of many of State Farm's policies was that they benefited both company and customer. For instance, State Farm followed other companies in offering semiannual—and later monthly—policy payments, which customers found easier to pay and, at the same time, led to accounting advantages for State Farm. State Farm also streamlined operations from the start, simply collecting premiums for a renewed policy on a vehicle, whereas most automobile insurers rewrote the policy each year.

Before long, the company was turning away unsolicited applications for insurance that were coming from prospective customers in urban areas. In 1926, a subsidiary, the City and Village Automobile Insurance Company, was formed. However, because the company lacked economy of scale, it was soon absorbed by State Farm Mutual, which rewrote its bylaws to allow for the extension of services to those urban customers not originally eligible for State Farm insurance.

Growth and Diversification: 1930s–40s

In 1928, just six years after the company's founder told a banker in Bloomington, "I've never had an account here. . . .

I've never cashed a check here, as far as I know. I've never tried to borrow your money. But I'm going to start a little business in this town and, by golly, you're going to lend me the money I need to get started," the company opened its first branch office, in Berkeley, California, and annual income surpassed $1 million. In 1929, the company moved into its own eight-story building, to which it added five floors in 1934. In 1939, State Farm built another eight-story building next door, to which it also added five floors in 1948. In the early 1970s, the company built its present headquarters at a site on the eastern edge of Bloomington.

The company's growth was not just a matter of volume; State Farm continually expanded the services it offered. In January 1929, the company formed a subsidiary, State Farm Life Insurance Company, which, like its parent company, has flourished.

During the banking holiday that brought in the New Deal era, State Farm Mutual operated at a loss, but it continued to operate at a time when many insurance companies folded. The National Recovery Act eliminated discounts on auto parts, and increased wages under this act sent repair costs higher. State Farm tightened in its belt, dropped coverage in its highest risk areas, and continued to attract and satisfy customers.

In 1935, it diversified again with the formation of the subsidiary State Farm Fire Insurance Company, which in 1950 merged with State Farm Casualty Insurance Company to form State Farm Fire and Casualty Company, which quickly became the largest insurer of homes and pleasure boats in the nation. In 1937, George Mecherle became chairman of the board of directors. Ramond Mecherle, who had been with the company for 13 years, was elected president, and G. Ermond Mecherle, who had been acting as director of personnel, was elected secretary.

Under G. Ermond Mecherle's direction, State Farm established a progressive program that addressed employee welfare on several levels, including financial, physical, and educational. He also worked to improve morale. Posture chairs made their appearance as early as 1935.

In 1939, State Farm launched a campaign to reach one million automobile insurance policyholders. The "One million or more by '44" effort relied heavily on advertising, and the company's advertising budget, which amounted to only $16.25 in 1923, swelled to an astonishing $202,000 in 1941.

With the advent of World War II in 1941, car production for civilian use came to a standstill, gasoline was rationed, and rubber for new tires became largely unavailable. State Farm wrote only 607 fewer policies than the year before, which had been a record-breaking year of growth for the industry in general and State Farm in particular. State Farm kept growing, pulling further ahead of its competitors, both mutual and stock. In March of 1944, in spite of the war, State Farm had one million auto insurance policies in effect. This represented a 110 percent increase in five-and-a-half years.

Postwar Difficulties

The postwar years were chaotic and fraught with serious problems for the auto insurance industry. There was a shortage

Key Dates:

1922: George Mecherle establishes the State Farm Mutual Automobile Insurance Co. to offer low-cost auto insurance to Illinois farmers.

1928: The company's income surpasses $1 million; the first branch office is opened in Berkeley, California.

1929: State Farm Life Insurance Company is formed as a subsidiary.

1935: The company launches State Farm Fire Insurance Company.

1944: The company has one million auto insurance policies in effect.

1950: State Farm Fire merges with State Farm Casualty.

1961: State Farm Life and Accident Assurance Company is incorporated to serve New York, Connecticut, and Wisconsin.

1989: Claim payments reach $600 million due to Hurricane Hugo in South Carolina and earthquake damage in California.

1999: State Farm is forced to pay $1.2 billion to policyholders in an auto replacement part lawsuit.

2002: The company launches the "We live where you live" ad campaign.

of dependable, well-educated personnel, as well as a severe lack of sufficient office equipment and office space. This was at a time when Americans were rediscovering their automobiles, driving them farther, and driving them faster. Claims were flooding into insurance companies, their numbers rising 41 percent in 1945, and 57 percent in 1946. The total underwriting loss for the industry during 1945 and 1946 was estimated at $300 million, and for a few months in 1946 State Farm was losing money at a rate of $1 million a month.

It took State Farm several years to regroup and effectively meet the demands of its customers. During this period, State Farm established stricter criteria for accepting new policyholders, setting an age limit on cars and not accepting those policyholders who were very young or very old. State Farm also worked to educate the public in a national automobile-safety campaign. As part of a restructuring plan, branch offices were established in 1947, the first of which opened in Saint Paul, Minnesota, and a committee was appointed to restructure the overcrowded and disorganized Bloomington home office.

George Mecherle exhibited his characteristic leadership during this difficult time. According to Karl Schriftgiesser, author of the *The Farmer From Merna*, Mecherle told the organizational committee, "Let us assume . . . that we are about to start all over, *build a new company*. . . . Remember there is nothing sacred here, nothing that can't be done away with. Be as rough as you want. The only thing I insist upon is that you do not depart from the basic principles on which State Farm has been built—the membership plan, the continuous policy, 6-months premium, and the happiness of our agency force."

The committee restructured the company headquarters along geographical lines—with each department representing a re-

gion of the country and functioning independently on a day-to-day basis—which scaled down and refined operations significantly. When George Mecherle died in 1951, State Farm had over two million auto insurance policies in effect.

Expansion and New Offerings: 1960s–70s

Due to special requirements in state laws, State Farm Life Insurance was unable to do business in New York, Connecticut, and Wisconsin, so to serve these states the subsidiary State Farm Life and Accident Assurance Company was incorporated in 1961. The next year, State Farm General Insurance Company was established to protect low-value property.

In 1962, State Farm offered auto insurance at a 20 percent savings to students who were doing well in school, based on the hope that if they were home studying for their good grades, they would be less likely to be out driving cars. In 1963, the company instituted monthly premium payments, and agents were authorized to make on-the-spot auto claim payments of up to $250, which improved customer service considerably. In 1965, State Farm began offering limited health insurance. The policy offered $15 for every day a policyholder spent in the hospital. This payment was touted as a possible supplement to other health insurance a person may have, perhaps to help pay for a babysitter or a housekeeper while a mother was away from home.

In 1966, an advanced computer system was installed, linking regional offices to headquarters in Bloomington. This investment, and the attention State Farm was paying to customer service earned State Farm praise from consumer groups in 1970.

There were periods when State Farm experienced large underwriting losses, that is, when payments on claims were much higher than income provided by premiums. Through smart investing and the ability to mobilize to cut costs during loss years, however, State Farm has stayed on top. A classic example is underwriting in 1971, in which State Farm's profit was $263 million, compared to $38 million in 1970. State Farm made headlines with its $30 million refund to policyholders as a result of high earnings in 1971.

By this time, the company was known for its independent stands on controversial issues: company executives felt that the insurance industry should not be exempt from federal antitrust laws, as it had been for decades. State Farm also supported federal no-fault-insurance legislation. There was also criticism that the company discriminated against minorities. It divided urban areas up into different risk zones and charged higher rates to those in higher risk zones, which tended to be in the inner city. The company had also been challenged in a number of court cases in the late 1970s and in the 1980s with allegations of sex and racial discrimination in its hiring of agents. To criticism that State Farm has long been "creaming off" the best drivers, Vice-President Thomas C. Morrill once responded, "Every underwriter tries to screen risks, but this isn't to say we go only after the cream. We just try to exclude the dregs."

Battling Industry Challenges: 1980s

During the 1980s, the property and casualty insurance industry was rocked by a number of problems. The industry suffered sharp increases in claims costs, especially natural-disaster claims and environmental-cleanup costs in the commercial arena. The rising cost of car parts, labor, medical treatment, and litigation was also impacting the cost of insurance, and customers were complaining.

In 1988, in reaction to the rising cost of insurance, California voters approved Proposition 103, legislation calling for an overhaul of the state's insurance system, resulting in major rate reductions for auto, homeowners', and business insurance, and a regulatory panel to approve rate increases, replacing the long-standing system in which insurers set their own rates. State Farm was one of the insurers that appealed this ruling and, along with other insurers, was required to justify its rate levels.

In 1989, a policyholder lawsuit was brought against State Farm. The suit alleged that State Farm was holding as its reserve twice as much as the industry standard and led to a court order requiring State Farm to distribute $6.87 billion in refunds to policyholders. State Farm claimed its conservatism was practical and necessary; CEO Edward B. Rust, Jr., told *Business Week*, August 21, 1989, "When it comes to claim time, customers don't want an IOU."

In 1989, disaster-claim payments were more than twice as large as in any other year on record. Between Hurricane Hugo in South Carolina and earthquake damage in California, State Farm paid out nearly $35 million to cover damage to vehicles and $570 million for property damage.

Despite these problems for the property and casualty insurance industries, State Farm continued its strong position relative to its competitors in all of its insurance lines. State Farm's earned premiums on health insurance placed the company third among health insurers. In addition, the outlook for the life insurance industry was one of growth, and State Farm Life affiliates, ranked eighth among life insurers, were in position to capitalize on this growth. As the number of persons with AIDS continued to rise, and more AIDS-related deaths occurred, life insurers feared that the related financial burden could reach unprecedented proportions later in the decade. This situation lead to controversy over life insurers' right to screen applicants for AIDS.

Throughout its history, State Farm built a record on its ability to deliver automobile, other property and casualty, health, and life insurance at competitive prices. This was achieved through innovative marketing strategies, financially sound business practices, lobbying in the political arena, and large-scale public relations campaigns. In the competitive insurance industry, State Farm's ability to keep its customers well-serviced, along with its smart business practices, continued to be key in its future success.

1990s and Beyond

State Farm faced just as many problems in the 1990s, however, as it had during the previous decade. By 1993, natural disasters such as earthquakes and hurricanes had left most in the insurance industry scrambling to get their finances back on track. Meanwhile, State Farm's litigation record left it subject to negative publicity, which began to tarnish its "good neighbor" image. After an earthquake in California in 1994, customers

filed suit against State Farm, claiming that the insurer had cut their coverage in an attempt to forego claims payments. State Farm settled the suit in 1997, paying out $100 million to those involved.

Then, in 1998, the firm was forced to pay $200 million in a class action suit that claimed State Farm life insurance agents had used misleading sales tactics. The firm also had to pay a string of punitive damages related to misconduct, including $25 million for document destruction and $9.5 million related to fraudulent medical claims. To make matters worse, an Illinois state court ruled against State Farm in 1999 after policyholders brought suit against the company for using poor quality replacement auto parts, which was in breach of the policyholder's contract. Throughout the litigation, State Farm maintained its innocence, claiming it had not acted in a fraudulent manner. The Illinois court thought otherwise, and in October the policyholders were awarded $456 million. Later that month, State Farm was forced to pay an additional $730 million in punitive damages for its misconduct. "While the legal judgments aren't an economic threat to State Farm, which has a policyholder surplus of nearly $45 billion, they do raise questions about whether something has gone awry inside the nation's largest property insurer, which has worked hard to become one of America's most trusted companies," claimed a 1999 *Business Week* article.

Despite its legal woes, State Farm went on with a "business as usual" attitude. Even with the negative publicity brought on by its public court battles, State Farm's customer loyalty remained high. In fact, in 1998 it lost just 4 percent of its auto insurance customers, a figure well below the 7.5 percent industry average.

State Farm made a move into the financial services sector in 1998 by creating State Farm Financial Services F.S.B, which offered services that included deposits, residential mortgage loans, home equity loans, and auto loans via the Internet, by mail, and by telephone. As a nontraditional banking concern, the State Farm Bank did not operate any branch offices. The company's focus on financial services continued into the new century. It began offering mutual funds and also started testing a wealth management services program that it created with Phoenix Home Life Insurance Co.

During 2001—the company's third largest catastrophe year in its history—State Farm faced several challenges. The company decided to exit New Jersey's auto insurance market due in part to the state's auto insurance regulations, which drove insurance rates down. The firm's homeowner's insurance sector was also plagued with a flood of claims related to mold, especially from Texas policyholders. In September 2001, State Farm stopped accepting new business in Texas. By 2002, it had dropped new homeowner business in 17 states.

High underwriting losses forced State Farm to report an overall net loss of $5 billion in 2001. As such, the company began positioning itself for financial recovery. It streamlined its 25 regions into 13 zones and began focusing on expense management. The company also launched a new advertising campaign with the tagline "We live where you live," a reference to its presence in the United States, Canada, and on the Internet.

During 2002, State Farm continued to focus on restructuring its operations as well as increasing its reach in the financial services sector. While the company would no doubt face distinct challenges in the future, State Farm stood well positioned to continue its long history of success in the insurance industry.

Principal Subsidiaries

State Farm Life Insurance Company; State Farm Life and Accident Assurance Company; State Farm Fire and Casualty Company; State Farm General Insurance Company; State Farm Federal Savings Bank; State Farm Investment Management Corp.; State Farm County Mutual Insurance Company of Texas; State Farm Florida Insurance Company.

Principal Competitors

The Allstate Corp.; American International Group Inc.; Liberty Mutual Insurance Companies.

Further Reading

Boylan, Anthony Burke, "State Farm Plots Banking Breakout," *Crain's Chicago Business*, December 18, 2000, p. 1.

Daniels, Steve, "State Farm's Homeowner Biz Capped," *Crain's Chicago Business*, July 29, 2002, p. 1.

France, Mike, and Andrew Osterland, "State Farm: What's Happening to the Good Neighbor?," *Business Week*, November 8, 1999.

"Like a Competitor, State Farm Is There," *Mortgage Marketplace*, November 23, 1998.

Reich-Hale, David, "Wealth Management? State Farm Is There Now Too," *American Banker*, April 9, 2001, p. 9.

Schriftgiesser, Karl, *The Farmer from Merna*, New York: Random House, 1955.

Cole, Robert J., "Unorthodox Insurer," *New York Times*, October 28, 1973.

Starr, Mark, "State Farm's Policies Make It Number One But Irk Competitors," *Wall Street Journal*, June 14, 1976.

"State Farm Debuts New Theme," *Brandweek*, April 8, 2002, p. 7.

—Carole Healy
—update: Christina M. Stansell

State Financial Bank

State Financial Services Corporation

10708 West Janesville Road
Hales Corners, Wisconsin 53130
U.S.A.
Telephone: (414) 425-1600
Fax: (414) 425-4231
Web site: http://www.statefinancialbank.com

Public Company
Incorporated: 1910 as State Bank, Hales Corners
Employees: 440
Total Assets: $86.5 million (2001)
Stock Exchanges: NASDAQ
Ticker Symbol: SFSW
NAIC: 522110 Commercial Banking

State Financial Services Corporation is the holding company for State Financial Bank, a growing bank centered in southeastern Wisconsin and reaching into northern Illinois. The bank began by serving the small community of Hales Corners, Wisconsin, and grew through acquisitions, particularly in the late 1990s, into a leading regional financial service provider. State Financial Services has close to 30 branches, offering traditional banking products such as checking and savings accounts as well as home mortgages and commercial loans. The bank also offers trust services and asset management and provides insurance through its subsidiary, State Financial Insurance Agency. Shares in the bank are publicly traded on the NASDAQ exchange.

Early Years in Hales Corners

The town of Hales Corners was founded in 1837 by Seneca Hale, who came to the area from New York. The town was located on an important crossroads for westward pioneers and for people traveling to and from nearby Milwaukee. Though supported mostly by farming, the town boasted a prominent hotel and a mill, was served by a wide plank road, and was a commercial center for outlying areas. The State Bank of Hales Corners was founded in 1910, but at least twenty years before that it operated in a rudimentary manner. In the 1880s, a local businessman, James Smith, ran a real estate and loan office on

Hales Corners' Forest Home Avenue. Smith built a vault into the stone wall of his office and offered casual banking services to area farmers. Farmers brought their cash to Smith, carrying it in milk pails, and Smith stowed it safely in his office vault. Apparently, Smith did no formal bookkeeping. When his customers needed cash, they asked for a withdrawal, and Smith went to the safe and got the money out. Smith died sometime in the late 1890s, and his office was taken over in 1898 by the Hales Corners' school teacher, James Godsell. Godsell continued to sell real estate, offer loans, and act as a bank; he sold insurance as well. The bank operated in this informal way until 1910. That year, Godsell went into partnership with John Meade, who had run the hardware store next door to Godsell's office. They applied for a state charter for the bank, which became State Bank, Hales Corners, on July 20, 1910. The four officers of the new corporation were Godsell and his wife and Meade and his wife. Later Godsell's daughter became the bank's cashier, the first woman in Wisconsin to hold such a position. Though the bank had operated in what seems by today's standards a slap-dash manner, when it incorporated in 1910 it had very respectable assets of $20,000.

During the Great Depression, the bank was hard hit. It had to close for four days in 1932, declaring a special holiday, to prevent a run on deposits which would have forced it out of business. Seven hundred depositors met to work out the fate of the bank. Several community businessmen pooled assets and brought in $38,500, enough to keep the bank from going under. State Bank was then led by Rudolph Holz, who also ran the Hales Corners Chevrolet dealership. Holz was president of the bank through 1972, and his descendent Jerome Holz remains chairman of State Financial Services Corporation's board.

The bank moved out of Godsell's tiny office into its own building in 1910, and it stayed in that location until 1960. That year, it moved into bigger quarters across the street. The original bank was left standing and was still in use by another Hales Corners business in the early 2000s. State Bank opened its first branch in 1968 in nearby Muskego. State Bank was the only bank in Hales Corners until 1970. Through the early 1980s, it still had only the one branch, and it remained very much the prototypical small-town bank.

Company Perspectives:

At State Financial Services Corporation our mission is to be the premier provider of financial services to consumers and businesses, providing a wide range of financial options in the markets we serve. We have positioned ourselves as a one-stop, full-service provider of financial products and services rooted in the tradition of community banking and attentive individualized service. Through our office network, our customers have direct access to professionals to meet their banking, insurance, brokerage, and asset management needs.

A Changing Landscape in the 1980s

The suburbs of Milwaukee expanded to run up against Hales Corners, and by the early 1980s it was no longer the isolated little town it had been. Larger banks in the area began competing for customers, yet State Bank of Hales Corners in many cases had an edge. The bank got a new president in 1983, Michael Falbo, who had previously been a vice-president at Marine Bank in Milwaukee. Falbo's plan was to maintain roots in the community, while growing the bank moderately through acquisitions. State Bank prided itself on customer service, doing face-to-face business where larger competitors would have to refer loan decisions, for example, through layers of distant management. Holz family members maintained voting control of the bank's board through the 1980s, and local control and doing business with the local community were important to the bank. But State Bank began to make strategic acquisitions in the 1980s, expanding into neighboring areas.

In 1984, Michael Falbo became president and CEO of State Financial Services Corporation, which was set up as a holding company for State Bank of Hales Corners, which then became known as State Financial Bank. Falbo was in his early thirties when he became president of the company. He had served in Vietnam as a combat medic, where a harrowing tour of duty gave him valuable lessons in "how you handle situations," according to an interview with the *Business Journal-Milwaukee* (April 30, 1990). Falbo seemed prepared to move the bank beyond its small-town roots, while preserving State Financial from being snapped up itself by consolidating banks in bigger cities. In 1985, the company bought a Milwaukee bank, University National Bank. Two years later, the company made another acquisition, taking over Edgewood Bank in nearby Greenfield, Wisconsin. State Financial began offering its own credit card soon after, finding it was able to offer a more competitive rate to its customers than larger area banks. And it opened more branches, expanding University National Bank into three new locations. The company had a record year in 1989, with net income growing to $1.6 million, compared to $709,000 a year earlier. By 1989, the holding company had assets of $165 million, and 130 employees. In 1990, the company issued stock to the public for the first time, debuting on the NASDAQ exchange. The $2.5 million stock offering was intended to bring the company capital to fund more acquisitions.

Rapid Growth in the Late 1990s

State Financial made more acquisitions of small banks in Wisconsin in the mid-1990s, and by 1997 the company had grown to about $400 million in assets. The bank was still small compared to many banks in the region, and Falbo told the *Milwaukee Journal-Sentinel* (April 18, 1999) that State Financial had received numerous offers to merge with other banks, some in Wisconsin, some from outside the state. State Financial's share price went up sharply, evidently because shareholders expected the bank to be bought for a premium price. But that did not happen. Instead, the bank's board turned down all merger offers and went after more acquisitions itself, doubling the bank's size in the late 1990s.

One of its most significant deals was the company's acquisition of Richmond Bancorp Inc., of Richmond, Illinois, in late 1997. State Financial Services Corp. had never crossed the border into Illinois before, though the Richmond bank was only a fifteen-minute drive from State Financial's branch in Burlington, Wisconsin. State Financial paid $10.7 million for the bank, which had two branches and assets of $90 million. The Richmond bank also had an insurance subsidiary. A bank's ownership of an insurance company had previously been illegal, but laws changed in the 1990s, loosening many of the regulations that had compartmentalized financial services. State Financial took over Richmond's insurance office, making it a separately managed entity of the holding company, incorporated as the State Financial Insurance Group.

Next the company acquired a La Crosse, Wisconsin-based asset management firm called Lokken, Chesnut and Cape. This move in 1998 again expanded the company's role in the financial services market. From being a traditional bank focused mainly on consumer and small business accounts, State Financial now also ran an insurance subsidiary and the asset management company. Then at the end of 1998 State Financial made another large investment, spending $125 million to acquire Home Bancorp of Elgin, Illinois. This was the company's largest acquisition yet, and it doubled the bank's size. Home Bancorp had around $370 million in assets, and it put State Financial's total assets close to $1 billion. Home Bancorp also had a savings and loan subsidiary, Home Federal, with five locations. State Financial's stock price fell as it bought Home Bancorp, with some investors apparently believing the price of the new acquisition was too high. But a banking industry analyst quoted in the *Business Journal-Milwaukee* (June 12, 1998) described the acquisition this way: "They bought the savings and loan from 'It's a Wonderful Life,' and now they can offer a world of new services to those customers who previously had very limited choices," referring to the popular Christmas-time movie about a small town bank. The new owner kept the savings and loan charter and the name Home Federal, while in 1999 it combined the names and charters of its other banks, giving it 16 branches of State Financial Bank. That year State Financial also made another Illinois acquisition, paying $28 million for First Waukegan Corp. This deal brought State Financial's assets over the $1 billion mark for the first time.

First Waukegan Corp. had assets of $212 million, and it was a major purchase, coming on the heels of the acquisition of Home Bancorp. The bank's stock price languished, as investors were apparently skeptical of the bank's ability to integrate all its new business. The bank also had an efficiency ratio which was rather high compared to competitors. The efficiency ratio is a key measure of a bank's performance, showing how much the bank spends for each dollar of revenue. In 1999, State Financial's efficiency ratio was near 70 percent, meaning it spent 70 cents for every dollar it brought in. The national average for commercial banks for the period was just over 60, and some high-performing banks had efficiency ratios in the 40s. CEO Falbo vowed to cut costs and bring the efficiency ratio down. Net income at the bank was also up and down during its period of rapid growth. Profit in 1997, as the buying spree began, was over $7 million, an increase of over 50 percent from the year previous. Net income dropped to $1.2 million for 1998, rebounded to $7.4 the next year, and settled at around $3 million for 2000. The bank's assets had grown solidly between 1995 and 2000, beginning at under $300 million and reaching $1.1 billion by 2000. By 2001, the bank had 23 branches, and it had invested heavily in information technology to link the branches and consolidate operations. It moved all its deposit operations into one Wisconsin location, which was expected to add to the bank's efficiency, and it took other steps to reduce costs throughout its network. The bank continued to build branches and to acquire as well, buying LB Bancorp, holding company for Milwaukee's Liberty Bank, in July 2001, for $12 million.

Nevertheless, State Financial's stock price remained low, and earnings did not improve as fast as management would have liked. By mid-2001, the company's stock price was still around $12 a share, while it had been close to $30 at its peak in 1998. State Financial significantly underperformed the NASDAQ Bank Index. State Financial also had to give up its asset management subsidiary, Lokken Chesnut and Cape, in 2001. The firm had never been profitable for the company, and disagreements with Lokken Chesnut's employees and founding partners meant that many customers took their accounts elsewhere. An industry analyst quoted in the *Milwaukee Journal-Sentinel* (August 5, 2001) called the dissolution of the partnership with Lokken Chesnut "an expensive lesson." State Financial took a $2 million charge against its fourth-quarter earnings to dissolve the relationship. And the bank had to take another $2 million charge at the same time, to write off bad loans that had been made without authority by an employee who later left the firm.

State Financial Bank created a new position of president, chief operating officer, and director in 2002, hiring a man with experience in both banking and in management of a small business to take the post. Michael Falbo remained president and CEO of the holding company, and he admitted in an interview with the *Business Journal-Milwaukee* (January 25, 2002) that the bank needed work on integrating all its new business. "Some things that came on board were not high-performing, and at this point we're not a high-performing bank," Falbo said. But the company was committed to turning this situation around. The bank had changed drastically since the early 1980s, transforming itself from a small-town bank to a relatively large regional player offering a wide variety of financial services. By 2002, management seemed determined to do its best to keep State Financial Services competitive and get the best out of its many recent acquisitions.

Principal Subsidiaries

State Financial Bank; State Financial Insurance Group.

Principal Competitors

U.S. Bancorp; EFC Bancorp; Bank Mutual Corporation.

Further Reading

Causey, James E., "State Financial Facing Show-and-Tell Time," *Milwaukee Journal-Sentinel*, April 18, 1999, pp. 1, 10.

Gallagher, Kathleen, "State Financial's Failed Merger with Money Management Firm a Lesson for Other Banks," *Milwaukee Journal-Sentinel*, August 5, 2001, pp. 1D, 11D.

Hoeschen, Brad, "Banks Continue to Expand with Insurance Subsidiaries," *Business Journal-Milwaukee*, February 6, 1998, p. 4.

——, "State Financial Pursues an Illinois Strategy with Home Bancorp Purchase," *Business Journal-Milwaukee*, June 12, 1998, p. 7.

"Investors Question Loan Problems at Wisconsin-Based State Financial Services," *Knight-Ridder/Tribune Business News*, January 1, 2002.

Schwab, Paul, "A Vision for Banking," *Business Journal-Milwaukee*, January 25, 2002, pp. 3, 42.

——, "Stock Repurchase Plans Meet Mixed Review," *Business Journal-Milwaukee*, March 30, 2001, p. 5.

"Shareholders Give Hales Corners, Wis.-Based Banking Firm an Earful," *Knight-Ridder/Tribune Business News*, May 3, 2001.

Shepherd, Vera, and Ed Weiler, eds., *Hales Corners Wisconsin: A History in Celebration of 150 Years*. Hales Corners, WI: Hales Corners Historical Society, 1988.

Weier, Anita, "Community Banker Falbo Takes Root at State Financial Services," *Business Journal-Milwaukee*, April 30, 1990, p. 10.

—A. Woodward

stelco

Stelco Inc.

P.O. Box 2030
Hamilton, Ontario L8N 3T1
Canada
Telephone: (905) 528-2511
Fax: (905) 577-4575
Web site: http://www.stelco.ca

Public Company
Incorporated: 1910 as Steel Company of Canada Ltd.
Employees: 9,278
Sales: C$2.56 billion ($1.6 billion) (2001)
Stock Exchanges: Toronto
Ticker Symbol: STE
NAIC: 331111 Iron and Steel Mills; 331221 Rolled Steel
   Shape Manufacturing

Stelco Inc. operates as one of Canada's largest steel producers with an annual capacity of 6.2 million tons. The company operates four major steel facilities, including Hilton Works in Hamilton, Ontario; Lake Erie Steel Company in Nanticoke, Ontario; Stelco-McMaster Ltee in Contrecoeur, Quebec; and AltaSteel Ltd. in Edmonton, Alberta. Hot rolled and cold rolled/coated sheet account for the majority of Stelco's sales. The firm's other products include rod and bar products, pipe and tubular products, plate products, and wire. The company's main business segments include integrated steelmaking, mini-mill operations, and manufactured products.

Early History: Mid- to Late 1800s

Like many aspects of the Canadian economy, Stelco's origin reflected both British and U.S. influences. During the 1850s, the Montreal merchant house of Moreland and Watson imported British iron to meet investment needs in the burgeoning Canadian economy. During the following decade, Moreland and Watson established the Montreal Rolling Mills (MRM) to reroll British wrought iron and scrap into nails and other hardware. The MRM managing director was Charles Watson, who in 1873

appointed William McMaster as secretary; McMaster then succeeded Watson in 1888.

The 1880s were a decade of transition for the MRM. This was an era of increasing protectionism by both Canadian and U.S. governments following the devastating trade depression of the 1870s. Tariff increases helped to preserve a role for British metal in the Canadian market, but the advantage was gradually passing to U.S. suppliers whose raw material and transportation costs were falling rapidly. These trends increasingly handicapped the MRM, whose trade relied on the reworking of metal from Great Britain.

MRM sales in the Ontario market were challenged during the 1880s by the Ontario Rolling Mills (ORM), established at Hamilton in 1879 by a group of Ohio businessmen. These U.S. tradesmen and investors were representative of many who migrated north to create industrial enterprises in early Ontario. The ORM used an abandoned mill to reroll scrap iron rails and rework metal for use by local machine shops and hardware manufacturers.

The ORM and other Hamilton-area secondary metal firms created a growing local demand for primary metal. Favorable tariff and transportation changes made it profitable by the early 1890s to establish a blast furnace on Hamilton harbor using U.S. ore and coal. Local foundry owners and the Hamilton municipal council were instrumental in launching the Hamilton Blast Furnace Company (HBFC) in 1894, after U.S. investors withdrew from what seemed a risky prospect. Alexander Wood, a hardware merchant and later a Liberal senator, was the largest HBFC shareholder. By 1899, HBFC had proven its value to the ORM leadership, who agreed to merge the two firms. The resulting company, the Hamilton Steel and Iron Company (HSIC), quickly erected steel furnaces using its capitalization in excess of C$1 million. The company's vice-president and general manager was Robert Hobson, son-in-law to Wood and later president of the Canadian Manufacturers Association.

Mergers Lead to the Creation of Stelco: 1910

The HSIC was Canada's first fully integrated iron and steel company. It flourished during the massive wave of investment that swept over the Canadian economy between 1900 and 1910. In the latter year, William McMaster offered to bring the Montreal Rolling Mills into a larger organization that would provide a secure supply of primary metal. The successful Maritime financier Max Aitken, later Lord Beaverbrook, promptly brokered yet another merger of the HSIC with the MRM and several smaller secondary metal companies, resulting in the Steel Company of Canada, or Stelco as it was soon unofficially labeled.

Stelco's first president was Charles Secord Wilcox, who had arrived in Hamilton by horseback in 1880 to join other family members in the ORM. Wilcox was president of Stelco from 1910 to 1916 and chairman of the board from 1916 to 1938; he began the policy of plowing back as much profit as possible into the company. The firm's location in southern Ontario, which minimized transportation costs on material assembly and product delivery, was the most attractive possible in the fragmented Canadian market. Government tariffs and cash subsidies also augmented company profits and permitted the financing of new investment from retained earnings.

During World War I, Stelco produced large quantities of shell steel, but the production of munitions did not prevent the company from establishing a sheet mill to widen its potential product base, as well as opening ore and coal mines to facilitate raw material supply. Stelco's diversified product base and concentration on light steel products served it well during the Great Depression of the 1930s, as its share of the Canadian steel market rose from 17 percent in 1918 to 45 percent in 1932.

Two presidents served Stelco during this era. Robert Hobson, along with Wilcox from the Hamilton side of the company, presided from 1916 to 1926. Ross McMaster, son of MRM's William McMaster, had stayed to manage the Montreal works after its sale in 1910; he became president from 1926 to 1945.

Postwar Growth

The outbreak of World War II inaugurated a new era for Stelco as it did for the Canadian economy. Stelco expanded its finishing capacity with the erection of plate and hot strip mills in 1941 and cold and tin mills in 1948. The growth of the finishing mills resulted in the use of more primary metal. In 1951, Stelco expanded its primary production facilities by building a 226-foot blast furnace and new open hearth steel furnaces sufficient to increase Canadian ingot capacity by 20 percent.

Hugh Hilton, president from 1945 to 1957 and board chairman from 1957 to 1966, presided over the expansion of the postwar period. Hilton's best-known technical innovation had been a 1928 fuel-saving improvement for the system of distributing waste gas from the furnaces to other applications in the plant. Hilton was the last of the steelmaking engineers to head the company. He was followed by Vincent Scully, an accountant who had come to Stelco as comptroller in 1951. Scully was president from 1957 to 1967 and chairman of the board from 1966 to 1971.

The continued use of open hearth furnaces until the 1980s reflected the slow introduction of basic oxygen furnaces first available during the 1950s. Stelco demonstrated considerable prowess in the development of secondary production technology. In 1959, David McLean, superintendent of Stelco's shapes division, organized a team to improve the cooling and coiling of steel rods in a high speed mill. By 1961, the solution was found in an adaptation of a U.S. patent leading to the Stelmor process for high quality and low cost rod cooling and coiling. During the 1970s, the manager of product design services, Bill Smith, pioneered a coilbox technique used for intermill transfer of hot bars; this technique remained proprietary technology.

The Gordon Era: 1970s

The 1970s comprised the Gordon era of Stelco, named after Peter Gordon, who served as president from 1970 to 1976 and chairman of the board from 1976 to 1985. Gordon guided the company through a major expansion, as the number of Stelco employees mushroomed from 12,500 to 25,000 during the 1970s. Gordon's lasting contribution was the establishment of a new plant on Lake Erie.

Strong market growth before the 1973 oil crisis and subsequent economic slowdown led Stelco in 1974 to begin construction at a new location, the Lake Erie works (LEW). This plant began production during 1980. Annual capacity was 1.7 million tons of semifinished steel. The LEW had large production runs of continuous-cast, low-carbon steel that was cold-rolled into auto sheet and steel used in pipes.

The older and larger Hilton works on Hamilton harbor had an annual capacity of 2.8 million tons. This plant produced diverse and sometimes specialized high- and low-carbon steel in strip, bar, and rod forms. The average production run at Hilton was smaller than at LEW. Between 1985 and 1987, financing and technology from the Japanese firm Mitsui assisted in a major upgrading of the Hilton facilities that included the introduction of basic oxygen technology and continuous casting. The Quebec and Alberta plants had small production runs from mini-mills of a capacity less than one million tons, each from electric arc steel furnaces.

Stelco's four primary plants were part of a production process that was integrated from the mine to a wide array of finished steel, including nails, sheet metal for appliances and vehicles, long-distance gas pipes, springs for vehicles, structural members for bridging and building, steel fencing, and a variety of hardware. During the 1980s, the final destination of output was the construction industry (35 percent), automobile assembly (30 percent), shipbuilding (10 percent), as well as railways, agricultural and other machinery parts, and packag-

Key Dates:

1910: The Steel Company of Canada is created from the merger of HSIC, MRM, and several secondary metal companies.
1932: Stelco's share of the Canadian market climbs to 45 percent.
1941: Plate and hot strip mills are erected.
1951: The firm builds a 226-foot blast furnace.
1961: The company develops the Stelmor process for high quality and low cost rod cooling and coiling.
1974: Stelco begins construction on the Lake Erie works.
1984: The company's market share declines due to slow economic growth.
1992: Stelco lays off over 1,100 workers.
1997: Net sales exceed $3 billion for the first time as Canadian steel consumption reaches a record high.
2001: The company posts a C$178 million loss.

ing. Stelco also undertook secondary processing at Hilton and in more than a dozen subsidiary plants scattered from Montreal to Niagara and in Alberta.

Problems Arise: 1980s

The 1980s proved a difficult decade. Stelco lost its position as Canada's largest steelmaker, and employment declined considerably. Various facilities closed, and the company's long term debt-equity ratio climbed dramatically. In November of 1989, the Canadian Bond Rating Service downgraded its rating of the firm's senior debentures. Revenues in 1990 were 24 percent less than the previous year, as the company posted a C$200 million loss.

In part, Stelco's problems reflected the burden of more than C$2 billion in investments between 1978 and 1988 (just as the demand for steel declined because of slow economic growth from 1973 to 1984), as well as a trend to substitute other materials for steel for a variety of purposes. Lackluster growth in the market for steel and high interest rates during the early 1980s made it possible for Stelco to finance later growth from internal sources, with the hopes that the value of these costly investments during the 1970s and 1980s would positively impact future competitiveness.

Another difficult circumstance for Stelco was the need to reduce emission of suspended particles and sulfur dioxide into the air and various substances into Hamilton harbor. The latter included poisonous coal-tar derivatives and ammonia that deprived the harbor floor of oxygen and hence killed fish. Increasing public concern to minimize environmental damage prompted Stelco to invest in a variety of devices to control pollution. By 1985, the Hilton works alone had 49 facilities to clean waste water and 54 facilities to clean the air. By 1991, there were some signs of improvement in Hamilton-area air and water, although Stelco's emissions remained a concern. In contrast to and perhaps because of the pollution problems at Hilton, the Lake Erie works had been built under careful government scrutiny to minimize environmental concerns.

Difficult relations with organized labor were a traditional Stelco problem. The Hilton workers were represented by Local 1005 of the United Steelworkers of America, which historically had been one of the most militant of Canadian locals. In 1946, violence marred an 85-day strike that is often seen as a turning point in the modern history of Canadian industrial relations. Another strike lasting 86 days in 1958, a violent wildcat strike in 1966, a legal strike in 1969, a 125-day strike in 1981, and a 97-day strike in 1990 continued the record of debilitating labor-management relations.

More significant than resulting wage adjustments was the damage to both workers and investors of a persistently and seriously discordant industrial relations atmosphere. An individual worker needed a very long time to recoup the loss of three months pay. On the other side, Stelco had been disadvantaged by disruption of supply continuity and other costs of bitter collective bargaining.

Challenges Continue: Early 1990s

In 1991, the president and chief operating officer was Robert J. Milbourne, a long-time Stelco engineer. The chairman of the board and chief executive officer was Frederick H. Telmer, a career Stelco employee in marketing. By this time, there were signs that the challenge of competition from east Asia would force labor and management to collaborate in forging a new survival strategy. The union had agreed to set aside traditional job categories in a steel coating mill within the Hilton works. The new mill was a joint venture with Mitsubishi Canada Ltd. to improve the rust-resistance of sheet metal. Hand-picked Hamilton workers visited Japan to acquire technical knowledge and improve their understanding of the Japanese culture of company-worker cooperation.

The new coating mill was one aspect of Stelco's campaign to win contracts from Japanese-owned autfo assembly plants located in southern Ontario. This response to change in secondary markets reflected the same careful attention to customer needs embodied in nineteenth-century mergers with the Montreal Rolling Mills and Ontario Rolling Mills. Stelco policy returned the company to its historically successful strategy of careful integration between primary production and the secondary industry.

By the early 1990s, Stelco—with its new facilities—was well positioned in the competitive North American market. Canada ran a trade surplus with the United States on steel. The introduction of the Canadian-U.S. free trade agreement favored Stelco because it reinforced a tendency to preserve the North American market for North American producers, among whom Stelco with its new facilities was a strong competitor.

This trade agreement, however, received mixed reviews. Even as the company worked diligently to remain competitive in its industry, a recession during the early years of the 1990s forced Stelco to lay off over 1,100 workers at its Hilton Works facility. Leo Gerard, national director of the United Steelworkers union, blamed the favored Canadian-U.S. Free-Trade Agreement for the decline in Canada's steel industry. In a 1992 issue of *Canada Newswire*, Gerard queried, ''How bad does it have to get before the government realizes that the country needs an industrial strategy that allows us to compete in a global economy? Trade deals that take more from the economy than they add, and policies which ignore our basic industries, are ruining the futures of entire communities. The more this kind of thing happens, the more remote recovery becomes.''

The North American economy slowly recovered in the mid-1990s and Stelco's fortunes gradually changed. Sales remained relatively flat between 1994 and 1996 but surpassed the C$3 billion mark for the first time in 1997 due to increased demand. At this time, company management set forth several growth strategies related to improving operational performance, increasing the value of its product mix, and bolstering customer loyalty by providing superior quality. Stelco also completed a $400 million capital investment program that increased output at its facilities by 10 percent and looked to forge strategic alliances to increase market share.

An Industry Downturn in the New Century

The highly competitive nature of the steel industry once again caught up with Stelco in 2000, with steel imports into Canada increasing by 29 percent over 1999, representing a 44 percent share of Canada's market. As a result, Stelco experienced oversupply and a decrease in demand. Sales fell by 9 percent and net income dropped by 96 percent over the previous year.

The slowdown in the North American economy continued in 2001, and the Canadian market was plagued by cheap imported steel—Stelco and other Canadian manufacturers felt this steel was unfairly priced and were working with the Canadian government to rectify the situation. In Stelco's 2001 annual report, the firm reported that North American steel prices fell to their lowest point in over 20 years. The falling prices, coupled with high energy costs and decreasing demand, forced Stelco to report a C$178 million loss that year.

Nevertheless, Stelco management remained optimistic about the future. Over the past five years, it had spent over C$900 million in facility updates and new technology. Its cost cutting measures also began to pay off—by 2001, cost per ton had been reduced by C$35 million over the past three years—and its increased production capabilities had left it well positioned for the eventual economic recovery of the North American market. While low-cost imports remained a thorn in Stelco's side, the Canadian steelmaker remained committed to enhancing shareholder value.

Principal Subsidiaries

Stelco-Mcmaster Ltee; AltaSteel Ltd.; Stelwire Ltd.; Stelfil Ltee; Stelpipe Ltd.; Welland Pipe Ltd.; CHT Steel Company Ltd.; Stelco USA Inc.; Chisholm Coal Company (U.S.).

Principal Competitors

Dofasco Inc.; Ipsco Inc.; Algoma Steel Inc.; United States Steel Corporation; Nucor Corporation.

Further Reading

Alfano, James G., ''A Recipe for Growth at Stelco,'' *American Metal Market*, August 18, 1998, p. 13.

Inwood, Kris, ''The Iron and Steel Industry,'' *Progress without Planning: The Economic History of Ontario from Confederation to the Second World War*, I.M. Drummond, ed., Toronto: University of Toronto Press, 1987.

Jack, Ian, ''Revived Stelco Hopes Demand Will Exceed Capacity,'' *Financial Post*, May 31, 1997, p. 39.

Kilbourn, Williams, *The Elements Combined: A History of the Steel Company of Canada*, Toronto: Clarke Irwin, 1960.

Robertson, Scott, ''Stelco Completes Its Reorganization Move,'' *American Metal Market*, January 7, 1999, p. 3.

''Stelco Layoffs Compounded by Federal Inaction,'' *Canada Newswire*, September 23, 1992.

''Stelco's Profits Slip 13% Despite Slight Sales Gain,'' *American Metal Market*, February 4, 1999, p. 12.

Watson, Thomas, ''The Perfect Storm,'' *Canadian Business*, March 4, 2002, p. 77.

—Kris E. Inwood
—update: Christina M. Stansell

Strix Ltd.

Forrest House
Ronaldsway
Isle Of Man, IM9 2RG
Telephone: +44(0)1624 822991
Fax: +44(0)1624 822918
Web site: http://www.strix.com

Private Company
Incorporated: 1951 as Castletown Thermostats
Employees: 1,000
Sales: £70 million ($112 million)(2001)
NAIC: 335314 Relay and Industrial Control
   Manufacturing; 334512 Automatic Environmental
   Control Manufacturing for Residential, Commercial,
   and Appliance Use

Strix Ltd. is the world's leading designer and manufacturer of temperature controls and cordless interfaces for electric kettles and other fluid-heating and water-boiling appliances. Strix commands a 70 percent share of the worldwide market for controls that turn off an electric kettle once the water has boiled, prevent a kettle from turning on with no water inside, and provide other safeguards to prevent against electrocution and fire hazards. Many of the world's largest manufacturers of kettles, including Rowenta, Tefal, Philips, Morphy Richards, Braun, Bodum, and Russell Hobbs use Strix controls. Strix grew strongly during the 1990s as demand for its products expanded beyond the English-speaking world to include fast-growing Asian markets. As such, sales have leaped from around £5 million at the beginning of the 1990s to more than £70 million ($112 million) in 2001. Strix has followed its international expansion with the development of a strong sales and manufacturing network. The company is based on the Isle of Man, a Dependency of the British Crown but otherwise a politically autonomous state. In addition to its three production facilities on the Isle of Man and a facility in Chester, England, the company operates a manufacturing plant in Guangzhou, China, that accounts for about 60 percent of total production. Strix also operates sales subsidiaries in the United States, Russia, and Belgium, international sales account for some 97 percent of the company's total sales.

At the turn of the century, Strix began extending its technology to include new applications such as under-floor heating and new appliance ranges such as hot pots for the North American market, as well as entering into the coffee maker market. These moves have attracted outside investment interest in the company, and in 2000 Strix sold 40 percent of its shares to HSBC Bank for £50 million. Chairman Edwin Davies and founder and former chairman John Taylor, now retired, retain majority control of the private company. Nonetheless, the HSBC purchase has opened up speculation concerning a possible public offering in the near future.

Thermostat Pioneers in the 1950s

The predecessor to Strix was founded in 1951 by Eric Taylor, a graduate of the Isle of Man's King William's College. Taylor had already proved his inventive skill during World War II when he designed a thermostat based on a bi-metal control design for maintaining the proper temperature of the heated flight suits worn by Royal Air Force bomber pilots. In 1946, Taylor set up Otter Controls Ltd. in Buxton, Derbyshire, in order to exploit his patented control device. The control was quickly adapted as a thermostat for Rover Cars.

In 1951, Taylor and several associates each put up £50 pounds to set up a subsidiary company, Castletown Thermostats. The company originally produced a range of theromostats that were used for a variety of purposes, including Rover Cars and Bendix washing machines.

The company's breakthrough came in 1957 when then managing director Charles Faulkner reached an agreement to supply 500,000 company-designed thermostats to Russell Morphy for use in that company's electric blankets. The large-scale order came as somewhat of a surprise to the company, helping it to establish itself as a major force in the United Kingdom's controls market. Taylor's son, John Taylor, joined Otter Controls in 1959 and soon revealed himself to have inherited his father's inventive genius. By the end of his career, the younger Taylor had been granted some 150 patents in his own name.

Taylor became chairman of Otter Controls in 1971 upon his father's death. In 1973, the Castletown unit, which had been expanding through the 1960s, now built a new extension to its manufacturing plant to produce and test a new "vapourstat" control device for use with a new generation of electric kettles. The Castletown subsidiary continued to produce a variety of thermostat control devices and expanded again in the late 1970s, adding a wing dedicated to production of automotive cooling fan controls.

In 1977, Taylor became a director of Castletown Thermostats. By 1979, he had taken over as chairman the company and separated it from its Otter Controls parent, starting a long feud between the two companies and a long-running legal battle that was not to be resolved until 1995. In 1981, Castleton Thermostats was reincorporated as an independent company, Strix, from the Latin word for "screeching owl." The owl was also incorporated into the new company's logo. With assistance from the Isle of Man government, which helped the company build a new plant in Port Erin, Strix launched a new generation of vapourstats, the C-series, the first integrated control and element system that featured an automatic shutoff switch. The C-series helped the young company get on its feet, and by 1984 Strix was posting sales of £1 million.

New Era of Growth in the 1980s

The year 1984 saw the arrival of Edwin Davies, an Isle of Man native, who was to guide the company to the world leadership of its niche market. Davies quickly identified the C-series kettle thermostat as Strix's core strength. As Davies told the *Financial Times:* "Taylor was an inventor. The opportunity I saw was this mass market for boiling water. Everybody does it. With the increasing use of electrical energy and a global population of 5 billion, it was a growing area."

As Davies, who became part owner of the company and later its chairman, steered Strix's manufacturing and distribution, Taylor continued to improve on the kettle control design, releasing the R-series, which featured an immersed element, in 1985. The safety features of the Strix controls found a ready market in the United Kingdom and other tea-drinking countries that, unlike their North American counterparts, had long used electric kettles for heating water.

The launch of the P-series in 1987 proved a new milestone. Featuring a patented cordless technology, the P-series was not only easier to use but also provided additional safety features— not the least of which was the absence of a cord, the pulling of which had been the cause of a great number of accidents in the past. Growing numbers of kettle manufacturers began to abandon their own controls technology in favor of the Strix control.

By 1988, Strix had sold its ten millionth control and had become the world leader in kettle controls. By 1990, the company's sales had topped £5 million. Supporting this growth was the opening of a new factory, in Ramsey, in 1989, while the company moved to a new headquarters facility to Castletown. In that same year, Strix opened a subsidiary in Hong Kong as an entry into the potentially vast Asian market.

The 1990s, however, were to see the company's strongest growth. One factor behind the company's expansion was the development of new lines of more design-conscious plastic kettles, which incorporated special safety features developed by Strix. Whereas consumers had previously kept the same kettle for many years, the newer designs encouraged consumers to replace their kettles more frequently.

In 1990, Strix acquired Malew Engineering, based on the Isle of Man, adding its production capacity for the development of new products. The company then bought Oak Industries, of South Africa, which was renamed Strix South Africa. In 1992, Strix moved into Australia and New Zealand, creating a new subsidiary, Striz ANZ, based in Melbourne. That year, Strix built itself a new headquarters that doubled as a research and development center, in Ronaldsway. That building was officially opened in 1993; at the same time, Strix celebrated its 50 millionth control.

The continued sales gains made by Strix's kettle controls led the company to expand the Malew plant in 1993. The following year, Strix made its first entry into the North American market, setting up a new subsidiary in Chicago. By then, Strix had succeeded in boosting its share of the worldwide market, capturing some 70 percent of all sales of kettle controls. However, the company was once again straining the limits of its production capacity. Unable to find enough employees on the Isle of Man, Strix opened a new subsidiary and plant in Chester, Derbyshire, in England in 1995, in time to celebrate its 100 millionth control. The company later transferred its head sales office to the Chester site.

International Growth at the Turn of the Century

Strix's sales had been building strongly through the first half of the 1990s, topping £30 million in 1995. A strong factor in the company's growth was its success in reaching Asian markets, where greater numbers of consumers were switching to electric appliances—ranging from tea kettles to rice cookers to cordless irons—all of which required controls technology. In 1997, with its domestic manufacturing facilities straining to meet the rise in demand, Strix opened a new factory in Chuangzhou, China, that was to serve as the base for its growth in the region.

The new facility enabled the company to double its production, and Strix celebrated production of its 200th million control in 1998. Part of the company's success was the launch of a new series of cordless controls, the U-series, released in 1996, which featured under-floor heating technology and an innovative 360-degree connector base. By then, Strix had been officially recognized for its design technology and had received a number of awards, including the Queen's Award for Export Achievement and the Manufacturing Excellence Award.

Strix remained focused on the kettle controls market until the late 1990s, when it began extending its expertise into other potential markets. One of these was the growing market for

Key Dates:

1946: Erik Taylor, inventor of a thermostat control, sets up Otter Controls Ltd. in Buxton, Derbyshire, England.

1951: Taylor opens a subsidiary, Castletown Thermostats, on the Isle of Man.

1957: The company receives its first large-scale order for electric-blanket thermostat controls.

1959: Erik Taylor's son John joins the company.

1971: John Taylor becomes chairman of Otter Controls after his father's death.

1973: Castletown builds a new facility to manufacture and test a new generation of kettle controls, called "vapourstats."

1977: John Taylor becomes the director of Castletown.

1979: Taylor takes over Castletown as chairman and separates from Otter Controls.

1981: The company adopts a new name, Strix Ltd., and launches the first of its C-series electric kettle controls.

1984: Edwin Davies joins the company and later become majority owner and chairman.

1990: The company acquries Malew Engineering on the Isle of Man and Oak Industries in South Africa and sets up Strix AZN in Melbourne, Australia.

1994: Strix sets up a sales office in Chicago.

1997: The company opens a manufacturing plant in Chuangzhou, China and sets up sales subsidiaries in Brussels and Moscow.

2000: HSBC bank buys a 40 percent interest in Strix, and the company prepares to enter coffee-maker control market.

2002: The first electric Moka coffee maker featuring a Strix control system is launched.

heated flooring, which seemed a natural extension of the company's existing technology. Also in 1997, Strix launched its first controls designed for use in thick film heating applications, opening a variety of potential new markets such as water heaters and other large and small appliances. This technology also enabled the company to begin producing covered elements for its kettle controls, thereby opening new markets in France and Germany, which had long avoided electric kettles because of the difficulty cleaning the build-up on exposed elements. Strix opened a new subsidiary, Strix Europe, in Brussels, to support its European growth. Another subsidiary opened in 1997, in Moscow, where the company adapted its controls technology for a range of samovars.

Whereas the North American market continued to prefer stove-top kettles, Strix hoped to find a market there with the release of the U30 series in 1999, designed to be adapted to hot pots in North America and to be used for such products as egg boilers, mini jug kettles, and other appliances in the European markets and elsewhere. Other potential product applications for the company's controls included deep-fat fryers, water distilling systems, and rice cookers.

John Taylor retired in 1999, and Edwin Davies took over as the company's chairman. The following year, Strix agreed to sell 40 percent of its shares—previously Davies had held 60 percent and Taylor 40 percent—to investment bank HSBC, for £50 million. The sale, which included the possible sale of more of Strix's shares at a future date, raised speculation that Strix might be preparing a public offering early in the new century. Davies and Taylor nonetheless retained majority control of the company.

The HSBC purchase was also seen as providing crucial capital for Strix's entry into a new important category—that of coffee makers, a market which could potentially double Strix's sales. As Davies told the *Financial Times* at the time of the HSBC purchase, "We believe we are in a strong position to break into this field because of the holistic approach we take to the business of boiling water."

As Strix celebrated its 50th anniversary in 2001, the company continued to be honored for its growth and product innovation, including winning the Queen's Award for Enterprise: Innovation in 2000. In 2002, Strix was honored yet again, with the Queen's Award for Enterprise: International Trade. By then, too, Strix appeared to be making progress with its plans to enter the market for coffee-maker controls as well. In February 2002, the company joined with Italian manufacturer Bialetti Industries, maker of the famed eight-sided "Moka" coffee pot, to launch an electric Moka pot incorporating a Strix control. Strix hoped to sell as many as three million of the new controls per year by 2005, added some 10 percent to its sales.

Strix had grown into a truly international company—some 97 percent of its sales came from outside of the British Isles, and more than 90 percent from outside of the United Kingdom. The company had successfully implanted itself in the rapidly growing Asian markets and had succeeded in maintaining its worldwide leadership, holding more than 70 percent of the worldwide market for kettle controls. With a firm grip on its patents—and a reputation for fiercely fighting counterfeits—Strix was ready to take on new markets in the new century.

Principal Subsidiaries

Strix Asia (Hong Kong); Strix Russia; Strix Europe (Brussels); Strix South Africa; Strix AZN (Australia); Strix China; Strix (UK) Ltd.

Principal Competitors

Otter Controls Ltd.

Further Reading

Bates, Trevor, "A Business Kept Nicely on the Boil," *Daily Telegraph*, November 7, 1997.

Jones, Sheila, "Sending Temperatures Soaring," *Financial Times*, July 15, 1999.

Marsh, Peter, "Kettle Business on the Boil for Strix," *Financial Times*, January 14, 2002.

——, "Strix and Bialetti Seek Fresh Taste for Coffee," *Financial Times*, January 29, 2002.

——, "Temperature Rising as Strix on Hopes of Floatation," *Financial Times*, September 26, 2000.

—M.L. Cohen

Sumitomo Mitsui Banking Corporation

3-2, Marunouchi 1-Chrome
Chiyoda-ku
Tokyo 100-0005
Japan
Telephone: (03) 3282-5111
Fax: (03) 5512-4429
Web site: http://www.smbc.co.jp/global

Public Company
Incorporated: 1876
Employees: 25,027
Total Assets: ¥102 trillion (2002)
Stock Exchanges: Tokyo Osaka Nagoya Sapporo
    London
Ticker Symbol: 8318
NAIC: 522110 Commercial Banking

Sumitomo Mitsui Banking Corporation (SMBC) was formed from the 2001 merger of Sumitomo Bank and Sakura Bank—Sakura was known as Mitsui Bank until 1990. The merger created Japan's second largest bank with 564 domestic branches and more than 20 international branches. SMBC provides a host of financial services including commercial and investment banking and credit-related services. Through its subsidiaries, SMBC also provides investment advisory and securities services along with research, data processing, and management consulting.

History of Sumitomo Bank

The Sumitomo group of enterprises is one of the oldest surviving business entities in the world, dating to the early 1600s. Sumitomo was originally founded near Kyoto as a medicine and book shop. The discovery by a family member of a new method for copper smelting led the company into the expanding and highly profitable copper trade. The acquisition and development of large copper mines had made Sumitomo one of Japan's largest companies by 1868, when battling clans restored the Meiji emperor to power.

Although Sumitomo supported the losing side in that struggle, the company managed to develop good relations with the new government and later purchased some state enterprises as part of a national modernization campaign. As the company grew, Sumitomo's director general, Teigo Iba, advocated diversification into new fields of business. Flush with money from Sumitomo's copper operation, Iba set up a banking division in 1895 called the Sumitomo Bank.

Acting as the private banker for the ever-expanding Sumitomo enterprises, the Sumitomo Bank experienced smooth and rapid growth. In 1912, in need of further capital, the bank was incorporated and made a share offering. In doing so it became the first Sumitomo division to go public. Between 1916 and 1918 the bank established branch offices in San Francisco, Shanghai, Bombay, New York, and London, and an affiliate, the Sumitomo Bank of Hawaii.

Japan emerged as a major world power following its victory in the Russo-Japanese War in 1905 and, later, after World War I. This new prestige afforded companies like Sumitomo new business opportunities throughout Asia as Japan became a colonial power on par with Great Britain, the United States, The Netherlands, and France. The Sumitomo Bank established an interest everywhere the Sumitomo group went—Korea, Formosa (Taiwan), and China.

The Sumitomo Bank spun off a division of its own in 1923, when its warehousing arm was incorporated as the Sumitomo Warehouse Company. Two years later the Sumitomo group broadened its financial activities by taking over the management of Hinode Life Insurance, which was renamed Sumitomo Life Insurance the following year. Despite the creation of separate Sumitomo corporations—Sumitomo Machinery Works, Sumitomo Fertilizer Works, Sumitomo Mining, and so on—the Sumitomo group remained a closely knit conglomerate called a *zaibatsu* (literally, a "money clique") whose constituent companies owned collective majorities of shares in each other.

The power of the various *zaibatsu* was greatly resented by a quasi-fascist element in the military that rose to power during the 1930s. Advocating Japanese supremacy in Asia as well as a more equitable distribution of wealth, these militarists were bent on the eventual nationalization of the *zaibatsu*. But because the *zaibatsu* made up Japan's military-industrial complex, they were essential to the militarists' plans for conquest.

Company Perspectives:

Our mission is to provide optimum added value to our customers and together with them achieve growth; to create sustainable shareholder value through business growth; and to provide a challenging and professionally rewarding work environment for our dedicated employees.

The *zaibatsu* were uncomfortable in their cooperation with the militarists: they stood to profit from Japan's expansion, but they also faced disintegration if the plan worked. Nonetheless, the Sumitomo Bank helped to finance the military's preparation for combat. Many Japanese considered the war a patriotic cause, seeking to remove western imperialists from Asia. But most Japanese companies, regardless of their reservations, were treated according to their cooperation with the militarists after World War II, and the Sumitomo companies were no exception.

Postwar Reorganization

Despite the militarists' desires, the Sumitomo group, having taken over a number of formerly independent or associated companies, became larger and more concentrated as a result of the war. After the war the Allied occupation authority imposed a series of antimonopoly laws that broke the *zaibatsu* into hundreds and even thousands of smaller companies. Each was forbidden to use its prewar name or to engage in cross-ownership of stock. The Sumitomo Bank was reorganized under this plan in 1948 as the Bank of Osaka.

A relaxation in industrial laws in 1949, and again in 1952, permitted the former Sumitomo companies not only to conduct business with each other, but also to resume use of the Sumitomo name and cross-ownership of stock. The *zaibatsu* re-formed, and the Sumitomo Bank became its coordinating entity.

The man placed in charge of the company after the war was Shozo Hotta, who believed that the bank should differentiate itself from other banks by emphasizing business efficiency. He also personally evaluated business ventures that he felt the Sumitomo Bank should back. As the bank grew during the 1950s, it became better able to support larger industrial ventures such as Matsushita Electric, Toyo Kogyo, and Daishowa Paper. Many of these investments were highly successful, particularly the Matsushita venture. During Japan's first period of export-led growth, from 1955 to 1965, Matsushita grew several times over to become the nation's largest electronics manufacturer.

Adopting the new goal of "quality and quantity," the Sumitomo Bank expanded its corporate business, recognizing the diminishing opportunities for growth from its historical affiliates such as NEC, Matsushita, and other Sumitomo companies. In addition, much of the bank's business was concentrated in the Kansai area around Osaka, leaving Tokyo and Yokohama, both rapidly growing markets, mostly unexploited by Sumitomo.

In a separate effort to expand, the Sumitomo Bank merged with the Kawachi Bank in April 1965. Retaining the Sumitomo name, the banks' combined deposits surpassed those of their competitor, Fuji Bank.

Hotta was named chairman of the bank in 1971, when he was replaced as president by Koji Asai. Asai and his successor, Kyonosuke Ibe, each had a comparatively short tenure, Ibe being replaced by Ichiro Isoda. Although Hotta was removed from the day-to-day administration of the bank, the organization strongly reflected his personality: bureaucratic and authoritarian. Often described as the father of the restoration of the Sumitomo Bank, Hotta had nevertheless created for it a poor public image, which Isoda was determined to change.

Toyo Kogyo and Atake Crises: 1970s

Higher earnings permitted the bank to increase lending to Matsushita, Toyo Kogyo, and Daishowa, as well as to companies outside the Sumitomo group such as Idemitsu Kosan, Uraga Dock Company, Taisho Pharmaceutical, and Ataka & Company. Again, many of these investments were highly profitable. Loans to Ataka, Daishowa, Uraga, and Toyo Kogyo, however, were not. Toyo Kogyo, in particular, was in very serious condition. The manufacturer of Mazda trucks, Toyo Kogyo had bet its future on the success of the Wankel rotary engine, a prewar German design that was supposed to be highly fuel efficient. It proved otherwise, and became a costly problem for Toyo Kogyo, especially in combination with the 1973–74 oil crisis. Sumitomo nevertheless supported Toyo Kogyo during its reorganization.

More serious, however, was the impending failure of Ataka & Company, a major Japanese trading firm. Because it stood to lose substantial amounts of money if Ataka went bankrupt, the Sumitomo Bank pledged to support Ataka until it could again be made solvent. Hotta entrusted Isoda with responsibility for rehabilitating Ataka. Isoda in turn appointed Yasushi Komatsu, managing director of the bank, to head Ataka. A more outgoing, congenial man than Hotta, Isoda enlisted help from the Ministry of Finance, the Bank of Japan, Ataka's customers, and even competitors of the Sumitomo Bank. Under a coordinated effort, Ataka was completely restructured; its unprofitable and underperforming divisions were sold off and cost-cutting procedures were initiated for those that remained. A year after assuming control over Ataka, the bank arranged a merger with C. Itoh, Japan's largest general trading company.

The Sumitomo Bank's handling of the Toyo Kogyo and Ataka affairs greatly enhanced its image among business and government leaders, as well as with the public. The bank's character changed at a crucial time, as the Japanese economy was entering a period of stable growth. A buyer's market emerged in banking, and with little remaining room for growth, each bank was forced to compete vigorously for market share. Had Isoda tried to cut losses by permitting both companies to go bankrupt, the bank would almost certainly have lost major clients to competitors. Instead, Sumitomo demonstrated an unusual degree of dedication to its customers and won more confidence than any advertising campaign could have hoped to generate.

The company's ability to support its clients through hard economic times was tested in the late 1970s when the industrial base in Kansai began to deteriorate. The textile industry, long in a state of decline in Japan, finally felt the effects of cheaper foreign competition. Within the Sumitomo group, business was

Key Dates:

1876: Mitsui Bank incorporates.

1895: Sumitomo Bank is established.

1943: Mitsui Bank merges with Dai-Ichi Bank to form Teikoku Bank.

1948: Sumitomo Bank is reorganized as the Bank of Osaka.

1952: A relaxation in industrial laws allows for the reemergence of the Sumitomo Bank.

1954: Teikoku Bank reverts to its former name, Mitsui Bank.

1965: Kawachi Bank merges with Sumitomo Bank.

1968: Mitsui Bank merges with Toto Bank.

1986: Sumitomo Bank makes a 12.5 percent investment in Goldman, Sachs & Co.

1990: Taiyo Kobe Bank merges with Mitsui to form Mitsui Taiyo Kobe Bank.

1992: Mitsui Bank changes its name to Sakura Bank.

1996: Japan announces a major reform of its financial sector.

2001: Sakura merges with Sumitomo Bank to form Sumitomo Mitsui Banking Corporation.

down for Sumitomo Light Metals, Sumitomo Cement, Sumitomo Metal, and Sumitomo Chemical.

Still, by this time, the Sumitomo Bank had become Japan's largest bank in terms of deposits. That position was later lost, however, not due to a failure in business, but due to the merger of the Dai-Ichi Bank and the Kangyo Bank, forming Dai-Ichi Kangyo Bank. A similar merger between Sumitomo and the Kansai Sogo Bank was canceled in 1978 because the resulting bank would have been too deeply influenced by the Kansai economy.

Reorganization in 1979

In 1979 the Sumitomo Bank carried out a general reorganization on the recommendations of the U.S. consulting firm MacKenzie & Company. The bank was divided into four divisions: business, sales, international, and planning and administration. In addition, greater freedom was given to division heads in order to achieve greater decentralization.

Isoda ordered the expansion of international financial services and the establishment of an in-house securities business. Toward that end, Sumitomo purchased the Swiss Banca de Gottardo in February 1984, and later became the leading Japanese bank in foreign markets. Meanwhile, the bank rescued another troubled company in the early 1980s when it helped turn around Asahi Breweries, Ltd.

Isoda became chairman in 1983, when he was replaced as president by Koh Komatsu, an imaginative manager who had distinguished himself during the 1960s by rehabilitating Sumitomo's operations in California.

In 1986, observing Citicorp's experience with bank competition in the United States, Komatsu decided that Sumitomo needed to diversify its customer base geographically. Having made little progress moving into Tokyo, the bank proposed a merger with an established institution in the region. The partner bank eventually settled upon was the Heiwa Sogo Bank, an institution with about 100 branches that operated until 7:00 p.m.—four hours later than other banks.

1986 Goldman, Sachs & Co. Investment

Sumitomo, already an established leader in international banking and finance, announced in December 1986 that it had made a $430 million, or 12.5 percent, investment in the New York-based investment bank Goldman, Sachs & Co. The investment, which amounted to a controlling interest, greatly alarmed U.S. banks, which charged that a foreign competitor had been permitted to enter a field the Glass-Steagall Act had barred U.S. banks themselves from. The Federal Reserve later ruled that Sumitomo's investment was legal, but that Sumitomo could not increase its interest, exercise management rights, or expand to other countries.

Trouble came for Komatsu the following year, when reports of friction among bank divisions and depressed earnings led the board of directors to replace him as president with Sotoo Tatsumi. The new president pledged to remove excessive layers of bureaucracy that had recently compromised the bank's reputed speed and efficiency. Emphasizing a new competitive spirit, Tatsumi was charged with consolidating the gains made under Komatsu, to rationalize the company's busy expansion of the previous year.

1990s Banking Crisis

From 1985 through 1989, Japan's economy went through a period of extreme speculation as land prices and share prices soared beyond reason. When the ''bubble'' burst in the early 1990s, the banking industry in Japan was hit hard. Sumitomo Bank was no exception, and was one of the first to feel the effects. In October 1990 Isoda resigned as chairman, taking personal responsibility for the bank's involvement in a stock manipulation scandal centering around Itoman & Co., an Osaka-based trading company with longstanding ties to the Sumitomo group. The bank operated without a chairman until early 1993 when Tatsumi took on that post with the appointment of Toshio Morikawa as president. Morikawa had served as vice-president for international operations.

In January 1993, meantime, Sumitomo made the unprecedented move of writing off ¥100 billion ($895 million) in bad loans, a number of them related to the Itoman affair. Another consequence of the 1990s Japanese lending crisis was an increase in violence against the country's bank employees, incidents that were believed to be related to the banks' attempts to collect bad debts from customers. Among the several incidents involving Sumitomo Bank was the September 1994 murder of the director of the bank's Nagoya branch.

As the 1990s proceeded and the Japanese economy continued to stagnate, the banking crisis only deepened. For the fiscal year ending in March 1995, Sumitomo posted a net loss of ¥335 billion ($3.8 billion), the first major Japanese bank since World War II to record a loss. The loss resulted from Sumitomo writing off ¥826 billion ($9.4 billion) in bad loans, a precedent-setting move. Up until this point Japanese regulators had discouraged such writeoffs for fear of weakening confidence in the financial system. Sumitomo, however, wanted to move as quickly as possible to relieve itself of its bad-loan albatross.

In February 1996 Sumitomo Bank took over the U.S. commercial loan portfolio and offices of Daiwa Bank Ltd. in a $3.37 billion asset transfer. The previous December U.S. regulators had ordered Daiwa to discontinue its U.S. operations following the disclosure of the bank's involvement in a $1.1 billion trading scandal. Subsequent discussions between Sumitomo and Daiwa about a full-scale merger were put on hold. Also in 1996 the bank opened a representative office in Shenyang, China, becoming the first Japanese bank to open an office in China. In addition, Sumitomo Bank began preparing for Japan's "Big Bang," which was announced in November 1996 and promised to comprehensively reform the Japanese financial system and open it up to international competition by 2001. Meanwhile, Sumitomo faced a new competitor following the April 1996 merger of The Mitsubishi Bank, Ltd. and Bank of Tokyo, Ltd. to form Bank of Tokyo-Mitsubishi Ltd., which became the new number one Japanese bank. Sumitomo Bank was number two.

In June 1997 Morikawa replaced Tatsumi as chairman, and Yoshifumi Nishikawa was appointed president. Continuing to resolve its bad loans burden, Sumitomo in September 1997 sold ¥40 billion ($330 million) in problem loans to Goldman, Sachs. Unfortunately, that year also brought the beginnings of the Asian financial crisis, which saddled Sumitomo and other Japanese banks with additional bad debt from loans made in such troubled nations as Indonesia and South Korea. Furthermore, new disclosure rules forced Japanese banks to write off more bad loans. For the 1998 fiscal year, therefore, Sumitomo wrote off another ¥1.04 trillion ($7.66 billion), leading to a full-year pretax loss of ¥502.7 billion ($3.7 billion). More bad news came in February 1998 when the bank was one of several named in a scandal involving the bribing of Japanese finance ministry officials.

In anticipation of the "Big Bang," Sumitomo Bank and Daiwa Securities announced in July 1998 a series of alliances in the areas of investment banking, derivatives, and asset management. In October 1998 Sumitomo exited from U.S. retail banking when it sold Sumitomo Bank of California to Zions Bancorp. In late 1998 the Japanese government attempted to mitigate the ongoing banking crisis by passing legislation allowing regulators to inject public money into banks that had depleted their capital through problem loan write-offs. The bailout program eased fears about bank failures and appeared likely to counter the cautious business lending stance adopted by many Japanese banks. In November Sumitomo announced that it would apply for such an injection. In concurrence with its request for public money, Sumitomo considered launching a tough restructuring program through which it would cut staff, close additional overseas branches, and initiate other cost-cutting efforts. Surrounded by intense competition and staggering losses, Sumitomo entered the merger arena in 1999 when it teamed up with Sakura Bank.

History of Sakura Bank

It is commonly believed that the Mitsui *zaibatsu*, or conglomerate, started its business as a bank. In fact, the company began trading in textiles and entered banking only after

Takatoshi Hachirobei, a founder, decided in 1683 that currency would soon replace the barter system. That year Mitsui purchased a money exchange. This exchange began a slow, steady expansion after its appointment as the Tokugawa government's fiscal agent in Osaka. Mitsui's dry goods business, meanwhile, declined steadily due to poor management.

In the mid-1860s, Mitsui switched its allegiance to rebel Meiji forces from the failing Tokugawa government, which had repeatedly levied costly tax assessments against the company. After the restoration of the Meiji emperor, Mitsui lobbied for and won a highly favored status in government. By the early 1870s, Mitsui held so much money for the government that it was basically a state treasury.

Rizaemon Minomura, the Mitsui director who was the architect of the company's rise to power, strongly advocated moving the firm to Tokyo, the new center of government and commerce. Once there, Mitsui began taking a more active role in underwriting industrial ventures. After an initial failure in international trading, Mitsui built up a domestic trading network and secured several government and military contracts. Reentering international trade some years later, Mitsui established numerous foreign offices, and in 1876 the Mitsui Bank was incorporated as a separate entity.

The Mitsui Bank served as the exclusive finance agent for the Mitsui trading company, called the *Bussan,* which had discovered a new and highly profitable trade in cottons and textiles. But, unhappy with its increasingly costly dependence on rival Mitsubishi for shipping and warehousing services, the Mitsui Bussan created its own shipping company. A tremendous bout of competition between the two companies ensued, and Mitsui eventually lost. As the underwriter for the Mitsui Bussan, the Mitsui Bank emerged financially exhausted.

But the bank benefited greatly from its privileged position in government. In addition, the Mitsui companies experienced unprecedented growth after Hikojiro Nakamigawa, a talented businessman and former president of the Sanyo Railway, joined Mitsui Bussan in 1891. As senior director, Nakamigawa dismissed redundant personnel and launched a concerted effort to develop Mitsui's industrial divisions. He also introduced the motto "people make Mitsui," a clever response to its rival's assertion that "organization makes Mitsubishi."

Mitsui again profited from its involvement in a military conflict, this time the Sino-Japanese War of 1894–95. A recession following that war, however, halted the company's growth. Furthermore, Nakamigawa died in 1901, leaving the directorship to his rival and predecessor, Takashi Masuda. Masuda emerged from years of semi-retirement determined to shake Mitsui out of stagnation. He introduced foreign exchange services, secured special trading rights for Mitsui in China, and even proposed purchasing Manchuria in 1911. Two years later he established a Chinese subsidiary, Chogoku Kogyo (China Industries Company).

Although it was a separate company, the Mitsui Bank was broadly influenced by the Mitsui Bussan and its directors; Masuda in many ways retained authority over the bank's director, Shigeaki Ikeda. Ikeda distinguished himself at the bank by providing Masuda and his successor, Takuma Dan, with no surprises.

Mitsui at this time became a focal point for criticism by a right wing military faction that believed the *zaibatsu* should be destroyed because they had become too powerful. As a result of this group's rise to power, Takuma Dan was assassinated in 1932. Masuda designated Ikeda, a more neutral figure, to run the Bussan and Naojiro Kikumoto was named chairman of the bank.

Renaming Mitsui As Teikoku Bank: 1943

When the militarists came to power, a centralization of power took place in industrial as well as government circles. Ikeda, in effect leader of both the Bussan and the bank, was named, in addition, governor of the Bank of Japan in 1937 and minister of finance and minister of trade and industry in 1938. He participated in the government's policy of expansion, supporting the colonization of Manchuria and the war against China and, later, against the United States. The Mitsui Bank, meanwhile, was renamed the Teikoku Bank in 1943, following its merger with the Dai-Ichi Bank. Teruo Akashi was named chairman of the new bank. The following year, Teikoku absorbed the Jugo Bank, at the time about one-tenth the size of Teikoku.

When World War II ended in 1945, Ikeda was designated a "Class A war criminal" and purged from public life by the occupation authority. He died in 1950 at the age of 84.

Chairman Akashi was replaced by Junshiro Mandai in 1945. Mandai and six others, however, resigned in 1946, shortly before the occupation authorities were to purge them as well. Kiichiro Satoh was then elected president of the bank. After the war the occupying authorities imposed a series of new industrial laws that eliminated the *zaibatsu* system by breaking the conglomerates into hundreds of smaller companies. The Dai-Ichi Bank was separated from Teikoku in 1948, and Teikoku was banned from reestablishing ties with former Mitsui companies. Teikoku, however, was designated an authorized foreign exchange dealer in 1949.

Growth Under the Mitsui Name: 1950s–60s

The bank was permitted to establish correspondent agreements with American banks in 1950, which laid the groundwork for the reestablishment of Mitsui's international operations. After reopening offices in London, Bombay, and Bangkok, Mitsui incorporated an IBM punch-card computing system that permitted the bank to centralize more of its operations at its head office.

In 1954, following the relaxation of antimonopoly laws in 1949 and in 1952, Teikoku reverted to its former name, Mitsui Bank. Increasingly the Mitsui Bank began to conduct more business with the former *zaibatsu* companies. With an international network capable of assembling information on foreign markets in place, the *zaibatsu* began to re-form as a more loosely organized *keiretsu*, or banking conglomerate. This recentralization of industry was permitted by the government to encourage faster recovery and industrialization because of a perceived threat from communists on the Asian mainland.

In the meantime, since the bank's ability to grow was restricted by laws that prevented the establishment of more branch offices, Satoh led a campaign to increase deposits at existing branches. Satoh was made chairman in 1959 and was succeeded as president by Masuo Yanagi, a career Mitsui employee, who in 1961 initiated an effort to control the bank's lending activities more efficiently. The rapid growth of the economy resulted in periods of simultaneous demand for loans and deposits; corporations borrowed as consumers spent. The addition of new consumer lending projects and the reestablishment of international banking activities resulted in greater liquidity and mobility and made the bank more competitive.

The Mitsui Bank continued to bring itself closer to the public by marketing financial products specifically for private savers. In 1968 it merged with the Toto Bank, a small, consumer-oriented bank whose 16 branches greatly strengthened Mitsui's presence in Tokyo.

Kyubei Tanaka, who succeeded Yanagi in 1965, was himself succeeded in 1968 by Goro Koyama. Koyama presided over the widespread computerization of Mitsui and ordered the improvement of communications between branches to accommodate people who lived in suburbs but worked in the city.

Also in 1968, Mitsui participated with the Sanwa Bank in the creation of a national credit card company, the Japan Credit Bureau. In an effort to circumvent regulations limiting the number of a bank's branches, Mitsui and the Heiwa Sogo Bank concluded an agreement to service each other's customers, an agreement that was subsequently expanded to include other banks. During the early 1970s, the bank introduced automatic teller machines, which allowed depositors to withdraw money at any hour and greatly reduced labor costs for the bank.

A Decade Marked by Challenges: 1970s

The decision to remove the United States from the gold standard and the subsequent revaluation of the British pound had severe impact on the Japanese banking industry. The Mitsui Bank, which had grown heavily involved in international transactions, was forced to reorganize the following year. Although profits were squeezed, the bank's capital and deposits reached new heights. Despite a second shock created by the OPEC oil embargo of 1974, the bank remained fairly stable, owing to conservative management and successful risk minimization.

Under President Joji Itakura and his successor Kenichi Kamiya, the Mitsui Bank became a much more business-oriented financial institution, participating in the establishment of special capital groups that oversaw the development of emerging companies breaking into expanding markets. One such venture included a 19-company collaboration on new software technologies. Through Bussan-sponsored monthly meetings, the Mitsui Bank coordinated its business with that of the approximately 40 members of the Mitsui Group, including Toshiba, Oji Paper, and Sapporo Breweries.

Restructuring: 1980s

As Japan entered a period of lower, more stable growth in the early 1980s, the Mitsui Bank restructured in order to emphasize its business in the consumer and corporate fields and develop groups of market specialists. As part of the "Century Ten" plan, the restructuring was designed to make Mitsui a more competitive bank for the 1980s. Part of that strategy included a shift away from sheer volume (which was percentage oriented) toward more stable flat-fee business. The bank also introduced CMS, a cash-management system that linked its newly established continental headquarters in New York, London, and Tokyo. In response to the Sumitomo Bank purchase of an interest in the U.S. investment bank Goldman, Sachs—a move that greatly strengthened that bank's position in international securities markets—the Mitsui Bank established closer relationships with Nomura Securities and Yamatame Securities.

Kamiya was promoted to chairman in June of 1988 and was succeeded as president by Ken-ichi Suematsu. The bank repeatedly named like-minded men to the presidency. While that contributed to greater stability and continuity in management policies, critics pointed out that it also created an army of yesmen. Regardless, the Mitsui Bank remained one of Japan's largest financial institutions. In August 1989 Mitsui Bank and the Taiyo Kobe Bank announced that they would merge in April 1990 to form Mitsui Taiyo Kobe Bank, with about ¥40 trillion in assets and 108 overseas offices in 31 countries. The merger, which created Japan's second largest bank, strengthen both banks' positions in the rapidly changing financial world.

The Newly Merged Sakura Facing Challenges: 1990s

The newly merged bank was renamed Sakura Bank in 1992. Sakura, Japanese for ''cherry blossom,'' adopted the new name as part of its strategy to attract more customers. At the time, Japan's banking industry as a whole was marked by intense competition brought on by local deregulation and a weakening domestic economy. To prepare for the challenges of the 1990s and beyond, Sakura adopted the phrase ''ACT 1,'' which stood for an aggressive, creative team effort.

Like Sumitomo, Sakura did indeed face distinct challenges. During 1992, pretax profits fell by 31.5 percent over the previous year, signaling rough times ahead. By this time, the Japanese banking sector faced criticism regarding bank exposure to nonperforming or bad loans. Distrust and uncertainty related to Japanese banking activity and poor investment policies surrounded Sakura, as well as other Japanese ''city'' banks. In 1995, the company posted huge pretax losses related to writing off bad loans. Japan's economy worsened, leaving many companies in the retail, distribution, construction, and real estate industries unable to pay back loans.

In an attempt to get its finances back on track, Sakura turned to the members of its corporate family, the Mitsui *keiretsu*, for a $2.1 billion capital infusion in 1998. Meanwhile, the bank restructured operations and laid out a cost-cutting strategy that included layoffs and the closure of certain branch offices. As changes in the Japanese banking industry brought on consolidation and allowed for major mergers, Sakura elected to team up with competitor Sumitomo Bank.

The Merger: 2001

After forming a strategic alliance in 1999, Sumitomo and Sakura merged in 2001. The union cemented the new bank's position as the second largest financial institution in Japan with US$791.65 billion in assets. Operating under the new name

Sumitomo Mitsui Banking Corporation, the bank's major concern was dealing with updating its business practices to reflect Japan's financial reform.

This reform included revamping the Japanese banking industry to reduce or eliminate bank exposure to bad loans. The initiative was in part overseen by Japan's Financial Services Agency (FSA). Just as the FSA reported that the major banks were financially sound, however, Japan's four largest banks reported a combined loss of $22.7 billion in 2002. In September of that year, Prime Minister Junichiro Koizumi fired his chief bank regulator and named Heizo Takenaka to the post. An October 2002 *Business Week* article claimed that Takenaka felt that the banking system in Japan was ''gravely ill and needing treatment.'' As such, Takenaka immediately set a plan in motion to audit the major banks' loan portfolios. At the time, these banks' bad loans were estimated at US$430 billion, a figure that was considered to be significantly below the actual number.

Amid Japan's bank reform, SMBC worked to integrate both Sakura and Sumitomo into one cohesive unit. Under the leadership of chairman Akishige Okada and President and CEO Yoshifumi Nishikawa, SMBC focused on improving its asset quality by resolving its problem loan issue. The company also looked to increase its earnings by promoting operational efficiency and by revamping certain business practices. While the new SMBC appeared to be on the right path to future success, the bank would no doubt face many challenges related to its nation's banking and financial reform.

Principal Subsidiaries

SMBC Staff Service Co. Ltd.; SMBC Learning Support Co. Ltd.; SMBC Center Service Co. Ltd.; SMBC Total Maintenance Co. Ltd.; Sumitomo Mitsui Card Company Ltd. (46.9%); SMBC Loan Advisor Co. Ltd.; Sakura Card Co. Ltd. (68.5%); The Japan Net Bank (57%); Sansei Guarantee Co. Ltd.; SMBC Leasing Company Ltd. (37.5%); SMBC Capital Co. Ltd. (39.8%); SMBC Mortgage Co. Ltd. (47%); SMBC Business Servicing Co. Ltd.; Sakura Investment Management Co. Ltd.; The Wakashio Bank Ltd.; Manufacturers Bank (U.S.A.); Sumitomo Mitsui Banking Corporation of Canada; Banco Sumitomo Mitsui Brasileiro S.A. (Brazil); PT Bank Sumitomo Mitsui Indonesia; Sumitomo Mitsui Finanz GmbH (Germany); SMBC Financial Services Inc. (U.S.A.); SMBC Capital Markets Ltd. (U.K.); Sakura Finance Australia Ltd.; Sakura Merchant Bank Ltd. (Singapore).

Principal Competitors

Resona Holdings Inc.; Mizuho Holdings Inc.; UFJ Holdings Inc.

Further Reading

Baker, Gerard, ''Sumitomo Bank Posts £1.8bn Loss in Wake of Bad Debts,'' *Financial Times,* January 28, 1995, pp. 1, 18.

Brauchli, Marcus W., and Masayoshi Kanabayashi, ''Exit of Sumitomo Chief Marks End of Era,'' *Wall Street Journal,* October 15, 1990, p. A12.

Brenner, Brian, ''Will This Mr. Fix-It Really Fix Japan's Banks?,'' *Business Week,* October 14, 2002, p. 146.

Chandler, Clay, "The Bank That Broke with Convention," *Financial Times,* May 26, 1995, p. 24.

——, "Sumitomo Bank Selects President in Bid to Surmount Troubled Past," *Wall Street Journal,* April 29, 1993, p. A10.

The Eighty-Year History of the Mitsui Bank, Tokyo: Mitsui Bank, 1957.

"Japan's Sumitomo, Sakura Banks Merge to Form Sumitomo Mitsui," *Asia Pulse News,* April 2, 2001.

Karmin, Craig, "Goldman Gets Jump with Japanese Banks," *Wall Street Journal,* March 26, 1998, p. B13.

The Mitsui Bank: A History of the First 100 Years, Tokyo: Mitsui Bank, 1976.

"Mitsui Taiyo Kobe to Be Renamed Sakura Bank," *Japan Economic Journal,* May 18, 1991, p. 32.

Neff, Robert, and William Glasgall, "An $8 Billion Write-off—And a Celebration," *Business Week,* February 13, 1995, p. 56.

Rowley, Anthony, "Japan Battling to Hold Off Implosion," *Banker,* July 2002, p. 176.

Sapsford, Jathon, "Japan's Banks to Begin Signing Up for an Injection of Public Money," *Wall Street Journal,* November 17, 1998, p. A17.

——, "Japan's Latest Bank Plan Buoys Credit Hopes," *Wall Street Journal,* October 8, 1998, pp. A11, A13.

——, "Sumitomo, Daiwa Venture Looks Abroad," *Wall Street Journal,* July 29, 1998, p. A11.

Shale, Tony, "Sumitomo's Dangerous Liaisons," *Euromoney,* December 1990, pp. 16+.

Shirouzu, Norihiko, "More Banks in Japan Implicated in Scandal," *Wall Street Journal,* February 17, 1998, p. A14.

Shreeve, Gavin, "Asia: Long Wait Till Springtime," *Banker,* March 1, 1992.

"Sumitomo, Sakura to Move up Merger by One Year," *Xinhua News Agency,* April 21, 2000.

Tanzer, Andrew, " 'The Other Banks Feel Threatened,' " *Forbes,* October 2, 1989, pp. 80+.

Tett, Gillian, "Sakura Bank Seeks Y300bn from Partners," *Financial Times* (London), September 1, 1998, p. 25.

—updates: **David E. Salamie and Christina M. Stansell**

SwedishAmerican Health System

1401 East State Street
Rockford, Illinois 61104
U.S.A.
Telephone: (815) 968-4400
Web site: http://www.swedishamerican.org

Private Company
Incorporated: 1911
Employees: 2,900
Sales: $388 million (2002 est.)
NAIC: 622110 General Surgical and Medical Hospitals;
   621111 Offices of Physicians (Except Mental Health
   Specialists); 621112 Offices of Physicians, Mental
   Health Specialists; 621610 Home Health Care
   Services

Located in Rockford, Illinois, SwedishAmerican Health System is a non-profit, locally governed organization serving 12 counties in northern Illinois and southern Wisconsin. Over the past 90 years, SwedishAmerican has evolved from a single hospital into a health system that includes a network of 19 primary care and multi-specialty clinics, a large home care agency and a wide variety of programs devoted to wellness and education.

The Early Years: 1911–39

On March 23, 1911, a mathematician by the name of O.F. Nilson wrote a letter to Carl Hjalmar Lundquist, the editor of the *Svenska Posten,* Rockford's Swedish newspaper, urging the construction of a Swedish hospital in Rockford. Half joking, he challenged every Swedish resident to contribute one dollar per year toward a new hospital, and he enclosed a dollar as a token of his sincerity. Acting on Nilson's request, Lundquist called a meeting of Rockford's Swedish ministers to discuss the matter. He also used Nilson's donation to open a savings account for the hospital at the Swedish-American National Bank. The Swedish-American Hospital Association received its charter of incorporation from the Illinois Secretary of State on June 6, 1911.

Letters went out in Swedish and English asking for financial support, and many fund-raising picnics, bazaars, and concerts followed. By May 1912, more than $4,000 in cash and $8,000 in pledges had been raised toward the construction of Swedish-American Hospital. A three-acre site was purchased on Charles Street for $11,500. On July 17, 1918, a 55-bed hospital was completed at the cost of $175,000. For Rockford's Swedish citizens, a dream had come true.

On July 18, 1918, SwedishAmerican Hospital admitted its first patient, Mrs. J.G. Prowd, whose 11-day stay for surgery amounted to $40. Clarence Pearson was the first baby born at the hospital on August 29, 1918. Healthcare was very different during the early years of SwedishAmerican. It was a time before antibiotics or disposable hypodermic needles, when pneumonia and influenza posed great challenges for caregivers. In fact, two months after SwedishAmerican opened its doors, it was forced to contend with an influenza epidemic that killed almost 2,000 people in Rockford and surrounding areas. At this time, private rooms with bath cost $6 per day. Patients were charged weekly rates of $15 to $42. Top nurse salaries were about $60 per month.

Amid many challenges, SwedishAmerican prospered during the 1920s and 1930s. The hospital opened a nursing school in 1919 that produced its first graduates in 1922. By 1938, Swedish-American had served Rockford for 20 years. To celebrate, an event was held in July on the hospital lawn. Approximately 6,000 people came to see Sweden's Prince Bertil, the 26-year-old son of Prince Gustaf Adolf, who was present for the celebration.

Growing with Rockford: 1940–69

The 1940s marked the beginning of a period of expansion and growth at SwedishAmerican that continued at a strong pace through the 1960s. Between 1938 and 1945, Victor Lindberg and Norman Andrews were among SwedishAmerican's first administrators, before George M. Edblom assumed the role. Edblom was appointed superintendent (administrator) of SwedishAmerican Hospital in 1945 and held the position until his death on July 29, 1964. During Edblom's administration, SwedishAmerican doubled in size. Thanks to his leadership, the hospital evolved into a more modern facility that could meet the

needs of Rockford's rapidly growing community. Edblom's
accomplishments were many, including the establishment and
expansion of pathology services, construction of three large
additions to the hospital, numerous structural improvements,
and positive changes to internal operations.

In 1942, an extension to the west wing of the hospital, which
began in 1940, was completed. The extension comprised five
floors and added 50 beds, expanding the hospital's capacity to
approximately 125 beds. Construction began on the first SwedishAmerican School of Nursing building in 1943 and was
completed the following year. Located north of the main hospital, the building was two stories high and provided housing for
36 students and the school's director, a demonstration room, a
library, as well as classrooms and offices. A third floor was
added approximately three years later, adding housing for 60
additional students.

At the close of the decade, construction began on a new wing
of the hospital, which adjoined the existing structure to the east.
Sweden's Prince Bertil, who had visited SwedishAmerican during the 1930s, was present to turn the first spade of dirt when
construction began. Built in response to Rockford's then critical
shortage of hospital beds, the new wing added five stories and
75 beds to SwedishAmerican Hospital. It also contained new
emergency, delivery, and surgical facilities.

When the new wing was completed in 1953, SwedishAmerican's medical staff numbered almost 200. Of those with privi-
leges, a total of 36 general practitioners and specialists were on
active staff. In addition to caring for the sick, these doctors also
contributed to the hospital's educational programs and provided
assistance and advice to administration, among other duties. By
1955, the Baby Boom was in full effect. A record 200 babies
were born at SwedishAmerican in August 1955, which was then
an all-time record, surpassing the annual total of babies born at
the hospital in all of 1934. At one point, the nursery cared for 46
babies simultaneously.

SwedishAmerican kicked off the 1960s by celebrating the
50th anniversary of the day it was granted a charter to build and
operate a hospital. The backdrop for the 1961 celebration was a
giant, ten-story framework of steel to the east of the existing
hospital. By 1963, this skeletal structure had become a major,
$5.5 million addition to SwedishAmerican Hospital. When the
tower opened, the first five floors were completed for use,

enlarging the hospital's capacity to 330 beds. By 1964, plans
were announced to complete the sixth, seventh, and eighth
floors. A dedication and corner stone ceremony for the new
tower was held on the afternoon of March 26, 1963. Sweden's
Prince Bertil, who had visited SwedishAmerican before in 1938
and 1948, played a central role in the ceremony.

In 1964, Administrator George Edblom died while on duty.
His vacancy was filled by E. Dean Grout, who came to SwedishAmerican from Winfield, Kansas. In his previous position,
he was administrator of William Newton Hospital, a 167-bed,
city-owned general hospital. Grout graduated from Bethany
College in Oklahoma, where he received a Bachelor of Arts
degree in 1955. A year later, he received a Master of Science
degree in hospital administration from Northwestern University. During his tenure as administrator, Grout created several
key positions within the hospital, including comptroller and
directors of personnel, public relations, development, and food
service. In addition, he helped to establish an operating room
technician course for licensed practical nurses and a nursing
program at a local community college.

Many developments unfolded at SwedishAmerican Hospital
during 1967, including the renovation and relocation of many
business offices. In addition, a day nursery for pre-school children of employees was opened, which helped relieve the shortage of nursing personnel. In fiscal year 1968, SwedishAmerican
Hospital admitted 12,677 patients and 1,692 babies were born
there. That year, SwedishAmerican celebrated the 50th anniversary of its hospital building with a festive public event in July.

On February 28, 1969, E. Dean Grout announced he would
resign from SwedishAmerican on April 1 to accept a position at a
New Jersey-based consulting firm. Albert L. Boulenger was
named as SwedishAmerican's administrator on June 23, 1969.
Boulenger had spent the previous five years as director of a three-
county hospital complex of nearly 1,000 beds in Tampa, Florida.
At the time of his appointment, he had 16 years of experience in
hospital administrative posts. Boulenger earned an undergraduate
degree from Bowling Green State University and a master's
degree in hospital administration from Washington University in
St. Louis. Shortly after he became the hospital's administrator,
SwedishAmerican named Boulenger executive vice-president,
and he became the organization's first chief operational officer
and a voting member of the board of trustees.

Expansion and Modernization: 1970s

In 1971, a special radiology and cardiac procedures unit was
constructed in conjunction with the offering of open-heart
surgery at SwedishAmerican Hospital. In 1972, the hospital
established an occupational therapy service and started a pediatric
cardiology unit. SwedishAmerican completed construction on the
ninth and tenth floors of its tower addition in 1973, adding
approximately 100 additional beds. That year, the hospital expanded its outpatient services and achieved an overall increase of
nearly 37 percent more outpatient visits than in 1971.

Progress continued midway through the decade. In 1974,
SwedishAmerican developed the Regional Cancer Center. A
new two-floor surgical pavilion opened in 1975, featuring new
facilities for performing open-heart surgery and a patient trans-

Key Dates:

1911: In response to a great need for healthcare services in Rockford, Illinois, the city's Swedish community decides to build a new hospital.

1918: The 55-bed SwedishAmerican Hospital is completed at a cost of $175,000.

1942: An extension to the west wing is completed, expanding the hospital's capacity to approximately 125 beds.

1947: Construction begins on a new, five-story east wing of the hospital.

1963: A 10-story, $5.5 million addition is completed to the east wing of the existing hospital.

1971: Open-heart surgery is first offered at SwedishAmerican Hospital.

1974: SwedishAmerican develops the Regional Cancer Center.

1975: A new, two-floor surgical pavilion opens featuring facilities for performing open-heart surgery and a patient transportation elevator.

1979: SwedishAmerican opens a large, modern, fully equipped emergency facility with 24 emergency beds and several specialty care areas.

1980: The SwedishAmerican Medical Foundation is established.

1993: SwedishAmerican wins the Rochester Institute of Technology/*USA Today* Quality Cup for its staff's contributions to quality improvement.

2002: SwedishAmerican's main entrance moves to East State Street after being located on Charles Street for more than 90 years.

portation elevator. It was the first of its kind in Illinois. The Outpatient Surgery Center was an important feature of the new pavilion, although SwedishAmerican had offered outpatient surgery since 1971. The hospital concluded the decade by opening a large, modern, fully equipped emergency facility in 1979.

In addition to the expansion and modernization that took place at SwedishAmerican during the 1970s, there also were changes in leadership. Boulenger resigned on September 1, 1971 to accept an administrative post with Samaritan Health Service in Phoenix, Arizona. E. Wynn Presson succeeded Boulenger as executive vice-president.

Presson had served SwedishAmerican as associate administrator (a new position created by Boulenger) since April 27, 1970. Before joining SwedishAmerican, he spent four years with Parkland Memorial Hospital and Woodlawn Hospital in Dallas, where he was assistant administrator. Presson earned an undergraduate degree from the University of Texas in 1963 and a master's degree in hospital administration from Washington University in St. Louis two years later. Presson remained at the helm of SwedishAmerican until October 1977, when he left to assume a similar post with Research Medical Center in Kansas City, Missouri.

In January 1978, Dr. Robert A. Henry, M.D. succeeded Presson and was named president and CEO. Dr. Henry gradu-ated from the University of Rochester Medical School (New York) in 1952. He came to Rockford from Lansing, Michigan, and eventually became director of the hospital's psychiatric unit. Henry was named vice-president of medical affairs in June 1972. His many accomplishments included the formation of a regional pediatric care unit, the creation of the hospital's adolescent psychiatric and chemical dependency unit, as well as joint ventures with other Rockford-area healthcare providers.

People Who Care: 1980s

SwedishAmerican marked the beginning of the 1980s with a new concept in healthcare by establishing an ambulatory care unit. This allowed staff physicians to see their patients on an outpatient basis. On August 6, 1980, the SwedishAmerican Medical Foundation was established. The following year, angioplasty was offered for the first time and a newly expanded pediatric intensive care unit opened. Progress continued to unfold at SwedishAmerican during the mid- to late 1980s. Among many developments were an eight-room guest hotel that opened on the fourth floor and a new nursery for both well and sick newborns.

In June 1989, Dr. Henry retired. Dr. Robert B. Klint, M.D., M.H.A., succeeded him as president and CEO. Klint had been serving as SwedishAmerican's vice-president and chief operating officer since 1983. He received a bachelor's degree in economics from Brown University, a medical degree from Northwestern University, and a master's degree in hospital administration from the University of Minnesota. Klint completed his residency and fellowship at St. Louis Children's Hospital and became board certified in pediatrics and pediatric cardiology. During his tenure with SwedishAmerican, Klint was instrumental in taking a formal approach to total quality management, implementing a strategic planning process and developing an integrated healthcare system with a large primary care base.

The Quality Leader: 1990s and Beyond

During the 1990s, SwedishAmerican carried on its tradition of clinical excellence by becoming the only health system in northern Illinois to receive Accreditation with Commendation from The Joint Commission on Accreditation of Healthcare Organizations (JCAHO). In response to a national push toward healthcare reform, many healthcare systems purchased or pursued partnerships with physician groups in the early 1990s. SwedishAmerican responded by creating SwedishAmerican Medical Group (SAMG). SAMG eventually became the largest primary care group in northern Illinois, spanning from Winnebago County to Lee County 70 miles south. A related strategy was the creation of Benchmark Health Insurance Co.

During the 1990s, there was an industry-wide focus on quality in healthcare, and SwedishAmerican began to receive recognition for its leadership in this area. The accolades began in 1993 with the Rochester Institute of Technology/*USA Today* Quality Cup, which the health system won for its staff's contributions to quality improvement.

In 1995, SwedishAmerican's board of directors announced that the organization would pursue discussions with Oak Brook, Illinois-based Advocate Health Care regarding a possible merger in 1996. However, after many months of discussions, the decision was made to not pursue the merger. Two years later, in April 1997, SwedishAmerican announced its intention to merge into Peoria, Illinois-based OSF Healthcare System, parent of Rockford's OSF Saint Anthony Medical Center. After months of assessment and negotiations to resolve differences about issues that were important to each board, SwedishAmerican decided to withdraw from further discussions in May 1998.

In 1999, SwedishAmerican received further national recognition for its commitment to quality. That year, the organization became the first Illinois healthcare institution to win the Lincoln Award for Excellence—Illinois' equivalent to the Malcolm Baldrige National Quality Award. In addition, SwedishAmerican became the only hospital in northern Illinois to earn a Top 100 Hospital designation. The recognition was sponsored by the Baltimore-based health data firm HCIA.

SwedishAmerican entered the new century by announcing exciting plans for the future. In 2000, the health system unveiled a $32 million campus expansion and renovation project that would benefit northern Illinois residents by providing them with more convenient and expanded service offerings.

In February 2001, Midwest Security Insurance Companies of Onalaska, Wisconsin, announced it would acquire Benchmark Health Insurance Company from SwedishAmerican Health System. In June, Dr. William R. Gorski, M.D. succeeded Dr. Klint as SwedishAmerican's president and CEO. Previously, in addition to maintaining a clinical practice at SwedishAmerican Medical Group/Five Points, Gorski served as president of the SwedishAmerican Primary Care Group and as the organization's chief medical officer. In those roles, Dr. Gorski was responsible for administration and strategic planning of all system-employed physicians and their practices. Dr. Gorski received a bachelor's degree from Kenyon College in Ohio. He earned a medical degree from the University of Cincinnati and completed a family practice residency at the University of Illinois College of Medicine at Rockford. He is board certified in family practice and is a member of the American Academy of Family Physicians and the American College of Physician Executives. Dr. Gorski also serves on the board of directors for SwedishAmerican Health System.

By mid-2002, much of the campus expansion and renovation project announced in 2000 had been completed. In June 2002, SwedishAmerican's main entrance moved to East State Street after being located on Charles Street for more than 90 years. The move gave patients access to a new outpatient care area that included express admissions, spacious waiting areas, a resource center and gift shop, and diagnostic testing and treatment services. In addition to the expansion and renovation of the immediate SwedishAmerican Hospital campus, other changes and improvements took place across the health system. These included construction of the Brookside Specialty Center—which provided treatment in the areas of allergy, audiology, dermatology, and ear-nose-and-throat care—and the SwedishAmerican 9th Street Center, a modern medical office building housing a variety of health system services.

In 1911, SwedishAmerican pledged that it would provide the best healthcare possible to the people of northern Illinois. More than 90 years later, the health system remained focused on this important goal.

Principal Competitors

OSF St. Anthony Medical Center; Rockford Health System.

Further Reading

"Hospital Marks 50th Year Today," *Rockford Morning Star*, July 21, 1968.

"Prince Displays Footwork at Hospital's Dedication," *Rockford Morning Star*, March 27, 1963.

"Swedish-American Hospital Dedication Section," *Rockford Morning Star*, June 27, 1953.

"Swedish-American Hospital Shows History of Progress," *Rockford Morning Star*, June 27, 1953.

"Swedish-American to Double Bed Capacity. Map Plans for Hospital Expansion," *Rockford Register Republic*, September 26, 1967.

"Swedish Hospital to Buy Petritz Site," *Rockford Morning Star*, May 9, 1912.

—Paul R. Greenland

The Testor Corporation

620 Buckbee Street
Rockford, Illinois 61104
U.S.A.
Telephone: (815) 962-6654
Toll Free: (800) 837-8677
Fax: (815) 962-7401
Web site: http://www.testors.com

Wholly Owned Subsidiary of RPM Inc.
Incorporated: 1929
Employees: 300
Sales: 50 million (2001 est.)
NAIC: 325510 Paint and Coating Manufacturing; 325520
    Adhesive Manufacturing; 326199 All Other Plastic s
    Product Manufacturing

Based in Rockford, Illinois, The Testor Corporation manufactures a wide variety of products for plastic and metallic model enthusiasts, model railroaders, craft enthusiasts, artists, and those engaged in various do-it-yourself projects. In addition to actual model kits, the company produces materials hobbyists need to build and assemble them, including model cement, paints, brushes, and assorted tools. Testor's line of paints accounts for a significant share of its business. The company offers customers paints that can be applied with traditional brushes or airbrushes. Beyond its line of enamel paints, Testor also markets non-toxic paints that clean up easily with water.

Early Years: 1928–39

Testor's origins stretch back to the late 1920s and stem from the efforts of two Swedish immigrants named Axel Karlson and Nils F. Testor. When Karlson emigrated from Stockholm to Rockford, Illinois, he brought with him a formula for nitrocellulose-based shoe cement. In 1928 he established a new company, Karlson's Klister, to market his product.

In February 1929, Karlson convinced Testor, then the manager of an F.W. Woolworth store in Rockford's Swedish district, to serve as office manager of his new enterprise. It was a

relatively risky move for Testor, who began his career as a stockroom boy in Woolworth's Chicago store on State Street and had worked his way up over the course of four years.

Karlson's Klister ultimately proved unsuccessful, and Karlson returned home to Sweden. Seeing a new opportunity, Testor borrowed enough money to purchase the firm's assets and found The Testor Chemical Co. After reformulating Karlson's shoe cement, Testor began marketing the adhesive as Testor's Household Cement. Sold in convenient tubes, the new product had a wider range of applications and became especially popular during the Great Depression, when it was necessary to maximize the life and utility of a variety of household items.

Testor began manufacturing its first product in a room on the eight floor of Rockford's Tower Building, located on South Main Street. However, the company later moved to a location on Railroad Avenue. Subsequent locations included the Billstrom Building on 18th Avenue, as well as locations on 7th Street and Charles Street.

Operations at Testor were literally hands-on during the 1930s. According to a *Rockford Register Republic* article published on November 29, 1955, "Even in the mid-thirties, Nils F. Testor, the owner-president, and C. Roderick Stroh, now plant manager of the woodworking division, would come down to the plant at night and mix the batch of cement for packaging the following day. They used a 50-gallon barrel which they turned by hand."

During the 1930s, Testor expanded in size and product offerings. It was during this time that the company began marketing to hobbyists by making cement intended for wooden model airplanes. By 1936, the company offered a line of cements and paints especially for hobby and model airplane enthusiasts.

The War Years and After: 1940s

During the 1930s, Testor established itself as a leading company in the hobby industry. In 1940, the company strengthened its commitment to hobbyists when it became a founding member of the Hobby Industry of America. Although Testor was prepared for continued growth and expansion, a number of roadblocks would slow the pace of progress during much of the decade.

One major challenge was the advent of World War II. Among those affected by the war were U.S. manufacturers, as resources became scarce and large amounts of raw materials were devoted to wartime production. In the wake of this and other challenges, Testor began marketing scale model airplanes made of balsa wood. The popularity of these wooden planes enabled Testor to weather a difficult period in its history.

Following the success of its balsa wood planes, Testor began selling engine-powered balsa planes that hobbyists could control from the ground via an attached line. Working in partnership with model engine manufacturer McCoy Products, Testor marketed kits in four different skill categories—freshman, sophomore, junior, and senior. Each kit contained an airplane, propeller, and fuel (all manufactured by Testor), as well as one of McCoy's engines. These kits were sold until approximately 1952, when Testor turned its attention to making balsa wood hand-gliders.

Testor experienced a setback one month after the company moved into Rockford's Buckbee Building when, on February 1, 1944, a fire completely destroyed the interior of the five-story structure. Several days later Nils Testor—who at the time of the fire was in New York on business—commented on the loss in the *Rockford Morning Star*, proclaiming: "Out of the ashes will come an even better thing." As predicted, the company's fortunes improved, and by the end of the 1940s Testor was able to focus on growth and expansion. It was around this time that Testor unveiled new products, including a line of enamel paints and plastic model cement.

Growth and Expansion: 1950–69

As the 1950s began, Testor prospered in the climate of a thriving American economy. The company added a second factory to its operations in 1951. This enabled the production of a greater number of products, including gloss enamel paints in 48 different colors, new adhesives, and fuel for model airplanes. The following year, Testor began to produce balsa wood hand gliders on a large scale, as well as model airplanes with plastic landing gear and propellers that were powered by rubber bands.

In addition to the company's plants at 2305 Charles Street and 520 Buckbee Street, in January of 1952 Testor leased a third building to increase its manufacturing capacity. With the expansion of both its manufacturing facilities and its line of products, Testor began to grow as an enterprise during the 1950s. Midway through the decade, the firm made its first acquisition, purchasing Duro-Matic Products Co. in 1955. Based in Culver City, California, the company had manufactured the McCoy model airplane engine since 1941. In conjunction with the rapid expansion underway at Testor, Charles D. Miller, who had served as Duro-Matic's president since 1947, was named as Testor's vice-president in charge of manufacturing. He and Nils Testor had enjoyed a close working relationship in previous years. Miller was serving as president of the Hobby Industry Association at the time of his appointment.

In 1955, Testor sold more than 50 million units of merchandise. By this time, the company had evolved into one of the nation's largest buyers of small glass bottles and plastic tubes, respectively used to package its PLA enamel paints and cement. Additionally, Testor had become the world's leading consumer of balsa wood, which it imported from South America. In addition to using balsa wood to manufacture toy airplanes, Testor also sold the wood in board, sheet, and strip form to consumers for hobby use. By the mid-1950s, Testor was also producing approximately 100,000 bottles of its enamel paint each day. In addition to paints and glue, the company sold lighter fluid in cans for 15 cents each.

In spring 1956, Nils Testor announced that his firm had opened a branch in Stockholm, Sweden, called Testor Produkter A.B. In the April 29, 1956 *Rockford Morning* Star, Testor said that the objective of the new office was to capitalize on the Western European market, which then consisted of approximately 275 million people. Two years later, Nils Testor revealed that he would move from Rockford, Illinois, to San Juan, Puerto Rico, where he had established the Testor Balsa Co. for manufacturing toy airplanes, as well as the Testor Adhesive and Paint Co. Inc. These firms handled functions once performed in Rockford. By this time, operations in Rockford consisted of the Testor Corp., which held the primary responsibility of assembling, packaging, and selling the firm's products, and the Testor Chemical Co., which focused on the manufacture of paint, enamel, lacquer, and adhesive. In late 1958, C. Roderick Stroh was president and general manager of Testor Corp., and Forrest K. Elson was president and general manager of the latter company.

Enterprise growth continued in the 1960s. By February 1963, Charles Miller had become president of Testor Corp. In order to serve customers in Canadian and European markets, Testor established a Canadian subsidiary in Weston, Ontario, in 1964. Four years later, Testor bolstered its Duro-Matic line when it acquired Wenmac Corp., a manufacturer of engine-powered cars and planes.

In 1965, the Jupiter Corp., a Chicago-based holding company, acquired Testor. At the time of the sale, Testor employed approximately 450 workers, 200 of whom were based in Rockford, Illinois. Nils Testor, who maintained residences in San Juan and Westport, Connecticut, remained the company's chairman. Miller continued to serve as president and chief operating officer.

In 1969, Testor pioneered sniff-proof glue by adding mustard oil to its formula. The additive, which was intended to protect youth from inhaling harmful fumes, made sniffing glue extremely unpleasant, if not impossible. Testor made its formula available to other glue manufacturers at no charge and supported legislation in several states, including New York and New Jersey, which intended to make such additives mandatory.

The company ended the 1960s with another acquisition. Testor's 1969 purchase of the Hawk Model Co. added plastic

Key Dates:

1928: Swedish immigrant Axel Karlson forms Testor's predecessor, Karlson's Klister.

1929: Nils F. Testor joins Karlson's Klister as office manager, then purchases the firm's assets and founds The Testor Chemical Co.

1936: Testor begins marketing a wide range of cements and paints for hobby and model airplane enthusiasts.

1940: Testor begins marketing scale model airplanes made of balsa wood.

1952: Testor begins making balsa wood hand-gliders.

1955: Testor makes its first acquisition by purchasing Culver City, California-based Duro-Matic Products Co.

1956: Nils Testor announces the opening of a company branch in Stockholm, Sweden, called Testor Produkter A.B.

1964: Testor establishes a Canadian subsidiary in Weston, Ontario.

1965: Chicago, Illinois-based Jupiter Corp. acquires Testor.

1969: By purchasing the Hawk Model Co., Testor adds plastic model kits to its product line.

1978: Annual sales reach $24 million.

1984: RPM Inc. (Republic Powdered Metals) of Medina, Ohio, acquires Testor.

1994: Testor adds the S4 UFO to its lineup of models.

2001: Testor achieves sales of more than $91 million.

model kits to its product line. Hawk reportedly produced the industry's first plastic model.

Progress in Plastic: 1970–79

In 1970, another acquisition followed the purchase of Hawk Model Co. That year, Testor acquired Detroit-based Industro Motive Corp. (IMC) to strengthen its production of plastic model kits at the Rockford plant. By that year, in addition to Duro-Matic and operations in Rockford and Canada, the Testor family had grown to include Testor R-C Corp. and the JTW Corp. In 1970, Forrest Elson was placed in charge of the company's operations in Rockford and was named Testor Corp.'s executive vice-president.

In order to accommodate rapid growth, Testor announced plans to expand its Rockford facilities in January 1973. Specifically, the firm revealed it would build a 50,000-square-foot addition to its warehouse, along with a new manufacturing facility totaling 30,000 square feet. Together, the additional space increased Testor's total warehouse and manufacturing space to 300,000 square feet.

Although fluctuating plastic prices initially had a negative effect on Testor's production of plastic models, by the mid-1970s the company was fully committed to producing them. At that time, the firm also was selling drop cloths, knives, gluing tips, and sandpaper that could be used with its model kits. Testor continued to prosper and by 1978 achieved annual sales of $24 million.

Model Evolution: 1980–2002

Shortly after the 1980s arrived, Testor introduced a new line of high-quality snap-together model kits for intermediate-skilled modelers. Although the kits were relatively simple to assemble and did not require the use of paints or plastic cement, they were designed with great detail so as to satisfy more advanced modelers. Among the models offered in this new line were the Rolls Royce Phantom II and a Peterbilt Conventional semi-truck. At the time, the latter model was the most complex snap-together product ever produced by Testor and was composed of over 50 different parts.

On January 17, 1984, RPM Inc. (Republic Powdered Metals) of Medina, Ohio, acquired Testor. At the time, RPM also operated such well-known companies as Bondex, Bondo, Mohawk, Rustoleum, and Zinser. That same year, Testor extended its international reach even further by forming an Australian subsidiary.

By the mid-1980s, Testor was producing models that were cutting-edge. One such model, the F-117 Stealth fighter plane, sparked a great deal of controversy when it was released. Even though the U.S. Air Force would not acknowledge the plane's existence, Testor was able to paint what it believed to be a realistic representation of the exterior appearance of the top-secret aircraft by speaking to industry experts and reviewing articles and technical drawings. In the May 29, 1986, *Rockford Register Star*, Ernie Petit, then the company's national sales manager, commented: "We do a tremendous amount of research. We accumulate everything we can learn and everything that's already published, and from the information we gather, this is our best guess of what the latest stealth fighter is."

When a real stealth fighter crashed near Bakersfield, California, in August 1986, the event only added to the controversy. With national attention focused on stealth aircraft, Testor was in the media spotlight. Consequently, sales of its stealth fighter climbed to industry record-breaking levels, eventually reaching one million units. Several years later, the Air Force acknowledged it had developed the F-19 Stealth fighter which, in many respects, was similar to the F-117 model produced by Testor.

In the February 1997 issue of *FineScale Modeler*, Testor designer John Andrews recalled: "There were senators holding up our model on television and saying they couldn't get any information on the Stealth and here we had this toy company doing these models. We just happened to be in the correct place at the right time and we had a model."

Although the Department of Defense did not provide Testor with information on the F-19 Stealth fighter, military sources have provided the company with blueprints, photo opportunities, and information related to other military aircraft. Such cooperation allows Testor to produce extremely accurate models. In addition, the company listens to customer feedback when determining which models it will produce.

During the 1990s, Testor acquired English airbrush manufacturer Aztek. During that decade, the company continued to produce a wide array of interesting models in addition to modeling paints and adhesives. By this time, Testor's model kits had evolved considerably from simple hand gliders made of balsa wood to plastic facsimiles of military aircraft like the SR-71 Blackbird Spyplane, the RF-4 Phantom II Spirit of America, and the V-22 Osprey, as well as land vehicles like the Sherman M4 A1 tank.

In 1994, Testor added the S4 UFO to its lineup of models. According to the September 26, 1994 *Rockford Register Star*, the company based the design of its UFO on descriptions from a former government scientist who supposedly worked with such craft at Nellis Air Force Range in Nevada. Based on input from the same man, Testor released a model of Grey—The Extraterrestrial Life Form. In 1997, Testor unveiled its Roswell UFO model, based on the alien craft that supposedly had crashed in the desert near Roswell, New Mexico, 50 years earlier.

By the early 2000s, Testor remained a dominant force in the hobby industry. In addition to its operations in Rockford, Illinois, the company had manufacturing facilities in Europe and the Far East. Almost 50 years before, Nils Testor had commented on the success his company was experiencing in the November 29, 1955 *Rockford Register Republic*, remarking: "Where we are today doesn't mean anything. We hope we never arrive—I hope we keep right on moving." If past performance is any indication, Testor's future will be characterized by continued success.

Principal Competitors

Racing Champions Ertl (AMT); Revell-Monogram.

Further Reading

"55 Years at Testor," *Rockford Register Star*, May 12, 1994.

Boatman, Edie. "How Model Kits Are Produced," *FineScale Modeler*, February 1997.

"Chicago Company Buys Testor Corp.," *Rockford Morning Star*, May 7, 1965.

"Irritating Jolt Awaits Glue Sniffer," *Rockford Morning Star*, July 16, 1969.

"Model Sparks Security Concerns," *Rockford Register Star*, August 10, 1986.

Modeler's Technical Guide, Rockford, Ill.: Testor Corp., 1979.

"RPM Inc. Acquires Testor Corporation," *American Paint & Coatings Journal*, January 30, 1984.

Schiffmann, William, "Testor's Model of Mystery," *Rockford Register Star*, May 29, 1986.

"Stealth Model Takes Off with Publicity," *Rockford Register Star*, August 10, 1986.

"Testor Company Organizes New Branch in Stockholm," *Rockford Morning Star*, April 29, 1956.

"Testor Serves Youth, Hobbyists and 'Do It Yourself' Clientele. 50,000,000 Pieces of Merchandise Carry Testor Name in 1955," *Rockford Register Republic*, November 29, 1955.

"Testor's Terrestrials Launch New Model Toy," *Rockford Register Star*, June 26, 1997.

—Paul R. Greenland

Texas Rangers Baseball

1000 Ballpark Way
Arlington, Texas 76011
U.S.A.
Telephone: (817) 273-5222
Fax: (817) 273-5174
Web site: http://:www.rangers.mlb.com

Private Company
Founded: 1971
Employees: 275
Sales: $134.3 million (2001)
NAIC: 711211 Sports Teams and Clubs

Texas Rangers Baseball is the official company name of the Major League Baseball franchise in Arlington, Texas, situated between the cities of Dallas and Ft. Worth. Because of its state-of-the-art stadium, The Ballpark at Arlington, and a lucrative television rights deal, the Rangers are one of America's most valuable sports franchises, estimated by *Forbes* magazine in 2001 to be worth $342 million. After 30 years of mediocrity on the field, the team has enjoyed recent success, although it has not fared well in the playoffs, winning but a single postseason game. Perhaps the Rangers' most notable achievement has been to serve as a springboard for the political career of George W. Bush, who served as the club's managing general partner before becoming Governor of Texas. The 1998 sale of the Rangers to financier Tom Hicks, whose Southwest Sports Group now runs the team, provided the basis of Bush's personal fortune, granting him the financial freedom that was instrumental in his ability to make a successful bid to become President of the United States.

Awarding Franchise to Washington, D.C. in 1960

Ironically, the Rangers' connection to Washington, D.C., dates back to the foundation of the franchise when it became the second version of the Washington Senators to play in the American League. After 50 years of stability, Major League Baseball saw a number of teams relocate to new cities in the 1950s. In 1958 the Senators' owner, Clark Griffith, expressed interest in moving to Minneapolis, but faced stiff opposition from both President Eisenhower and the Congress, which threatened to strip Major League Baseball of its privileged exemption from the nation's antitrust legislation. The American League fashioned a remedy by allowing Griffith to move the Senators to Minneapolis, where they became the Twins, while granting an expansion franchise to the Capital. The right to own the second Washington Senators baseball team was then awarded to an investment group headed by retired Air Force General Elwood "Pete" Quesada.

Since 1958, Arlington Mayor Tom Vandergriff spearheaded efforts to bring baseball to the Dallas-Ft. Worth area. In 1962 American League officials studied the region and found it a suitable location for a team, although it rejected a bid by the Kansas City A's owner Charley Finley to relocate there. In 1968 Dallas-Ft. Worth would lose out to Montreal and San Diego in gaining a National League expansion team. The reincarnated Senators, in the meantime, proved to be as disappointing as the original version. A variety of partnerships owned the team until 1968 when Robert E. Short bought a majority interest. A Minneapolis lawyer primarily involved in the trucking and hotel industries, Short became involved in professional sports in 1955 when he bought an 80 percent interest in the Minneapolis Lakers for $200,000, then later moved the team to Los Angeles where he sold it for more than $5 million. He hired legendary player Ted Williams to manage the Senators for 1969, and the team enjoyed its only winning record in Washington and saw attendance reach 918,000.

When the Senators reverted to their usual standard of poor play and declining attendance in 1970, American League team owners, tired of their share of slim visiting gate receipts, urged Short to relocate his team. A year earlier, another American League team, the Seattle Pilots, had decided to change cities, and again Vandergriff and Dallas-Ft. Worth lost out. Vandergriff learned about Short's difficulties and began a campaign to urge American League owners to pressure Short to moved to Texas. After a dismal start to the 1971 season, Short failed to sell the team to investors who would keep the Senators in Washington and finally turned to Vandergriff. The mayor offered $7.5 million in low-interest loans provided by a group of ten local banks, as well as $7.5 million from the City of Arlington for the team's broadcast rights. The team also was offered the use of Arlington's 10,000-seat Turnpike Stadium, home of the local Texas League minor league franchise, and Vandergriff pledged to increase seating to 35,000 for the 1972 season. Even after Short agreed to move the Senators, he had to receive approval from nine of the other American League owners. When the league meeting took place, one of Short's supporters, Angels' owner Gene Autry, was hospitalized, resulting in his vote being recorded as abstaining. Finley tried to take advantage of the situation by offering to trade his deciding vote in exchange for the Senators best young player. In the end, American League President Joe Cronin had to visit Autry in the hospital to obtain a proxy allowing him to vote in Autry's absence, and only then did the Dallas-Ft. Worth area finally get its major league baseball team.

Short planned to conduct a contest to name the new Texas team, but with little time to prepare for the first season he simply chose "Rangers," which many fans had suggested in letters sent to him and Vandergriff. There was also interest in re-naming Turnpike Stadium after Vandergriff, an idea with little appeal for the Mayor, who eventually was able to have Turnpike renamed Arlington Stadium.

Sale of Rangers to Brad Corbett in 1974

Baseball in Dallas-Ft. Worth was far from an immediate success. Attendance for the first season was just 662,974, only 7,000 higher than the final season in Washington, and last in the American League. The situation for management was aggravated by the configuration of its new stadium. Significantly more than half the seats were located in the outfield and inexpensively priced. Premium-priced seats were minimal. From the start it was apparent that the limitations of the ballpark would dictate the franchise's finances and ability to field a winning team. A second season brought only a slight increase in attendance, prompting Short to sell the club for $9.5 million and the assumption of more than $1 million in debts to a group of investors headed by area businessman Bradford G. Corbett, who ran the plastic pipe company Robintech Inc. He enjoyed his newfound celebrity and became active in trading players, much to the dismay of his experienced front office. Nevertheless, the Rangers showed significant improvement on the field, posting a winning record and finishing second in their division. As a result attendance soared to nearly 1.2 million.

In 1976 Arlington and the Rangers attempted to address the problem with the stadium by announcing an expansion of the facility that would be completed in two years. Essentially, 7,000 new seats were added by building an upper deck behind home plate. Nevertheless, the bulk of seats remained in the outfield. The team fared relatively well in the late 1970s, posting winning records and seeing attendance rise steadily. Corbett began to have financial problems, however, and early in the 1980 season was forced to sell his majority stake to celebrity Texas businessman Eddie Chiles.

Chiles was almost 70 years old when he bought the Rangers, after making his fortune with the Western Company, which was involved in oil-field services and drilling. He was the quintessential self-made man, who worked his way through college to earn a degree in petroleum engineering. He started Western in 1939, but it was not until the 1960s and 1970s that the company hit its stride, when Chiles became a radio and television pitchman. He drew on the movie "Network" to fashion his signature bit in which he opened his commercials with "I'm Eddie Chiles, and I'm mad." He would then rail on the horrors of big government before ending with his famous pitch, "If you don't own an oil well, get one." As a result, the engineer by training built Western Company into a $500-million-a-year business.

Chiles brought corporate discipline to the Rangers, delegating authority but demanding that his subordinates formulate a clear plan that was then carried out. In 1984 he installed Western Company executive Mike Stone to serve as the team's president. Under Chiles, the franchise bolstered its commitment to scouting and player development. The Rangers were especially aggressive in scouting Latin American players, a region to which other teams had failed to devote significant resources. The Rangers would develop such stars as Juan Gonzalez and Ivan Rodriguez, who would be instrumental in the team's success in the 1990s, as well as a star that got away—Sammy Sosa. Although the team failed in its efforts to land a new ballpark, Arlington Stadium was renovated in 1984. A new scoreboard was added, as well as revenue-generating billboards above the outfield bleachers and 52 luxury suites. In 1987 the team purchased the facility from the City of Arlington. Nevertheless, the ballpark continued to be a drag on the franchise's ability to maximize its potential.

When the bottom fell out of the oil market, Western's revenues, which had peaked in 1981 at $725.7 million, plunged to $176.5 million in 1987, and Chiles was forced out as chief executive and chairman. Although devoted to the Rangers, Chiles could no longer afford to own the team. An effort to sell to Edward Gaylord, however, was denied by the American League because of Gaylord's television interests. In 1984 Gaylord had purchased a one-third stake and television rights, as well as the right of first refusal over any deal to sell the team. He would exercise that prerogative in 1988 when Chiles tried to sell the franchise to a group of Tampa Bay, Florida investors who likely would have relocated the Rangers. Gaylord's matching bid was again rejected by American League owners, but at least the team remained in Texas.

George W. Bush Part of 1989 Buyout Group

In 1989, when his father was President of the United States, George W. Bush began his involvement with the Texas Rangers. At the time, he was long on name recognition and short on cash. His previous oil businesses backed by family connections had folded. Although he never lost his own money on these ventures, he had limited financial resources at his disposal. A former business partner, William DeWitt, whose father had once owned the Cincinnati Reds, first approached Bush about teaming up to buy the team. Bush and his parents were longtime friends of Chiles, who immediately expressed enthusiasm over the prospect of selling the Rangers to Bush, who then assembled a group of investors that included relatives and friends. Because Bush's primary partners were not from Texas, Baseball Commissioner Peter Ueberroth torpedoed the deal. Ueberroth then recruited Texas financier, Richard Rainwater, to buy the team. Rainwater approached a Dallas investor, Rusty Rose, about joining him in the deal, but after talking it over they decided that neither one of them wanted the burden of dealing with the press and as a consequence told Ueberroth that they were uninterested. Ueberroth suggested they contact Bush, who was more than happy to serve as the public face of ownership. Of the $45 million raised by the investors, Bush contributed just $500,000, which he borrowed from the United Bank of Midland, for which he had once served as a director, pledging oil company stock worth more than $900,000. Eventually he would sell the stock to pay off the loan and increase his investment in the Rangers to $606,000, or 1.8 percent.

In March 1989, Bush and his fellow investors purchased a 58 percent controlling interest in the Texas Rangers for $25 million and $9 million in assumed debt. After acquiring Arlington Stadium and surrounding real estate, the price tag reached $80 million. By all accounts, Bush performed his responsibilities well, ingratiating himself with the press as well as the hot dog vendors and ticket takers—on a first name basis with everyone. Rather than sit in a luxury suite, he sat behind the Rangers' dugout and made a point to introduce himself to the fans. Bush was intent on selling tickets and, indeed, in the first year under new ownership the Rangers drew two million fans for the first time. There was already talk that Bush's connection with the Rangers could lead to a run for the office of governor of Texas.

It was little-known Rose, however, who did the heavy lifting with the Rangers. After earning an M.B.A. from Harvard in 1967, he went on to an investment career in which he specialized in uncovering overvalued stocks and shorting them, earning the nickname "the Mortician." He established his Cardinal Investment firm in 1973 with just $25,000 and a secretary. By the time he became a partner in the Rangers' ownership group he had amassed a personal fortune in the neighborhood of $70 million. He refinanced the franchise's long-term $25 million debt, then renegotiated the team's television contract. Arlington Stadium, however, remained a sore point. Almost half of its 43,508 seats remained in the outfield, priced at just $4, while $10 premium seats numbered only 8,000. To completely renovate the facility was cost prohibitive, so the only solution was to build an entirely new facility, which was estimated to cost $200 million.

Bush and his fellow owners, intent on obtaining public financing for a new facility, hinted that they might move the franchise. The City of Arlington would eventually agree to contribute $135 million to the building of a new stadium, funded by an increase in sales tax. While the Rangers would gain complete control, it would simply pay a modest rent and,

therefore, be exempt from property ownership obligations such as paying school taxes. After 12 years the club would be able to assume ownership at no cost, but it made no economic sense to do so. In fact, later ownership would waive the option. The Rangers contributed $90 million to the deal, but did not have to invest any new capital. The team's stake would come from future commitments of revenues generated by the public largesse, from luxury suites and concessions.

Although a number of critics were upset by the public financing of the new stadium, area landowners were outraged when the city used its power of eminent domain to purchase land at nominal prices for the project that already had enough space, then sold it to the Rangers for commercial development. The heirs of television tycoon Curtis Mathes sued the Rangers and the City of Arlington when their land was seized. According to the *New York Times,* "Confidential memos among the Rangers owners became part of the public record in subsequent litigation, and they paint a picture of the owners casting a proprietary eye over the area and then telling the city what land to seize." After a seven-year court fight, the Mathes family was awarded a settlement, which the Rangers refused to pay, insisting that the City of Arlington bore the legal obligation. It was not until 1999 when, under new ownership, the Rangers agreed to repay the city.

The Rangers' new home, named The Ballpark in Arlington, opened on April 1, 1994. The 49,115-seat stadium was replete with club level seats, luxury suites, and all the other revenue-generating amenities of a modern facility. It was located in a 270-acre complex that would include a four-story office building located within the ballpark, a youth ballpark with seating for 600, a Legends of the Game Baseball Museum, a natural grass amphitheater, and a 12-acre lake and adjoining recreational space. Rangers' attendance soon soared to almost three million, as the team in the mid-1990s also enjoyed its greatest success on the field. Although the Rangers won division championships, however, they failed to advance to the League Championship Series, let alone the World Series.

Bush, meanwhile, relinquished his role with the Rangers to become the governor of Texas. In 1998, when the ownership group decided to sell the team for $250 million, Bush's $606,000 investment netted him $14.9 million, with the possibility of another million or two in later years. With his finances now secure, he was able to freely entertain the possibility of running for the presidency of the United States, which he would eventually win in 2000.

The new ownership group of the Rangers was headed by Thomas O. Hicks, a University of Texas graduate who returned home to become a venture capitalist after learning the trade on Wall Street. He recovered from the 1980s collapse in oil prices that ruined Chiles to make a fortune in soft drinks, which he parlayed into a broadcasting empire. He became involved in professional sports in 1995 when he bought the Dallas Stars National Hockey League franchise. What Hicks recognized was that by buying the Rangers he could control the television rights to two major sports teams and would be in a position to start up his own regional sports network, as well as move the Rangers' over-the-air games to an area television station he owned. In that light, paying $250 million for the Rangers was a smart economic move. It is more likely, however, that the idea of a cable sports channel was more of a threat aimed at Fox Sports Net, which was building a national chain of regional sports channels to rival the established cable sports franchise ESPN. Fox could not do without the country's seventh largest TV market, and securing the rights to both the Stars and Rangers was imperative. In the end, Hicks and his newly formed Southwest Sports Group were able to coerce a 15-year $550 million deal from Fox that included both cable and over-the-air broadcasts. The new deal tripled the money the Stars received and doubled the Rangers' amount.

With this guaranteed money, Hicks was then able in 2000 to broker one of the most controversial free agent player signings in baseball history, when he beat out larger market teams like the New York Mets to secure the services of star shortstop Alex Rodriguez. The ten-year $252 million deal was highly criticized in many quarters as both an exorbitant amount to pay, especially since it was $2 million more than Hicks had paid for the entire franchise, and as a further widening of the breach between the poor and rich teams of baseball. In reality, the Rodriguez deal was shrewdly structured so that much of the money was spread out and the costs remained in line with the Rangers salary structure. Moreover, Rodriguez had marquee value that would be instrumental in the all-important Rangers' television ratings. In his first year with the team, Rodriguez lived up to his end of the bargain, providing the offensive output expected from him, but the team's pitching was so porous that the Rangers languished in last place in its division. It was the second criticism of signing Rodriguez that threatened to have a more lasting effect on the sport and the Rangers' long-term plans. As Jay Weiner assessed the situation in *Business Week:* "For years, there has been building concern about the disparities between big-media-market teams—with fat TV deals and new stadiums—and teams with neither. As the collective bargaining agreement between sports' most unmoving union and sports' most undisciplined owners heads toward expiration after the 2001 season, a civil war between the have and have-nots owners appears to be on the horizon.''

Principal Competitors

Anaheim Angels; Oakland Athletics; Seattle Mariners.

Further Reading

Badenhausen, Kurt, ''Cable Guy,'' *Forbes,* April 16, 2001, p. 146.

DeMarco, Tony, ''Determination Marked Chiles' Life,'' *San Francisco Chronicle,* August 25, 1993, p. D4.

Kaplan, David, ''More Than Most Anything, Hicks Wants to Win,'' *Dallas Business Journal,* February 12, 1999, p. 8.

Kristof, Nicholas D., ''Road to Politics Ran Through a Texas Ballpark,'' *New York Times,* September 24, 2000, p. 1.

McCartney, Scott, ''Why A Baseball Superstar's Megacontract Can Be Less Than It Seems,'' *Wall Street Journal,* December 27, 2000, p. B1.

Nadel, Eric, *The Texas Rangers: The Authorized History,* Dallas: Taylor Publishing Company, 1997.

Rogers, Phil, *The Impossible Dream Takes a Little Longer: The Texas Rangers from Pretenders to Contenders,* Dallas: Taylor Publishing Company, 1990.

Sandomir, Richard, ''How Can the Rangers Afford SO Much? TV,'' *New York Times,* December 12, 2000, p. D5.

Thorn, John, et al., *Total Baseball,* Kingston, N.Y.: Total Sports, 1999.

Weiner, Jay, ''Good for a-Rod, Bad for Baseball,'' *Business Week,* December 25, 2000, p. 59.

—Ed Dinger

'TORAY'

Toray Industries, Inc.

2-1, Nihonbashi-Marunouchi 2-chome
Chuo-ku
Tokyo 103-8666
Japan
Telephone: (03) 3245-5113
Fax: (03) 3245-5459
Web site: http://www.toray.co.jp

Public Company
Incorporated: 1926 as Toyo Rayon Company Ltd.
Employees: 34,910
Sales: ¥1,015.7 billion ($7.65 billion) (2002)
Stock Exchanges: Tokyo Osaka London Luxembourg
Frankfurt Düsseldorf Paris
Ticker Symbol: TRYIY
NAIC: 325211 Plastics Material and Resin Manufactur-
ing; 325222 Noncellulosic Organic Fiber Manufactur-
ing; 325221 Cellulosic Organic Fiber Manufacturing

Toray Industries, Inc. operates as one of Japan's largest fiber
producers. Through a network of over 200 subsidiaries and affiliates, the company manufactures fibers and textiles, plastics and
chemicals, films and resins and circuit materials used in information technology-related products, housing and engineering products, and a host of various other products ranging from artificial
kidneys and catheters to contact lenses. While the company has a
presence in throughout Asia, Europe, and North and South America, operations in Japan account for the majority of Toray's sales.

Early History: 1920s

Toray began as a fiber manufacturer. In the first half of the
1920s, two large rayon manufacturing companies—Teikoku
Jinzo Kenshi Ltd. (Teikoku Jinken) and Asahi Kenshoku Ltd.—
and two smaller companies occupied almost half of the Japanese rayon market, with the other half filled by imported products, mostly from Britain. Courtaulds Limited was the largest
British supplier, and the Japanese trading house Mitsui Bussan
Ltd. had been an exclusive agent for Courtaulds since 1919.

Rayon yarn was a substitute for raw silk, one of the most
important goods Mitsui Bussan handled at that time. Mitsui
Bussan was very interested in the future potential of rayon yarn
and became aware of Courtaulds's good business record. In
addition, the Japanese government was planning a tariff revision, and a rise in the import tariff for rayon yarn was anticipated. In 1923, Mitsui Bussan began to examine the world
rayon industry with a view to importing technology, but attempts to contract licensing with Courtaulds and Du Pont were
unsuccessful. In 1925, a director of Mitsui Bussan in London
reported to headquarters that Mitsui Bussan should buy equipment from a rayon machine manufacturer that would send
chemical and machine engineers to Japan. Mitsui Bussan decided to adopt this method of importing technology and established Toyo Rayon Company Ltd. (Toyo Rayon) in 1926. A
wholly owned subsidiary, its capital amounted to ¥10 million.
In August 1927, Toyo Rayon began to produce rayon yarn at its
Shiga plant. Mitsui Bussan asked the German company Oskar
Kohorn & Company to establish the plant, teach Toyo Rayon
employees to operate the equipment, and send engineers and
skilled workers to Mitsui Bussan. Moreover, Mitsui Bussan sent
a chemical engineer, who had carried out research on viscose at
the University of Tokyo and had joined Mitsui Bussan, to Oskar
Kohorn & Co. in order to learn the technology on the shop floor.

Toyo Rayon made profits in the first half of 1928 but
retained all the profit inside the company until the latter half of
1931. Toyo Rayon began to pay dividends in the first half of
1932 and from 1933 to 1935 its profits grew rapidly. The profit
to sales ratio amounted to about 20 percent during this period.
Toyo Rayon thus became one of Japan's largest rayon manufacturing companies, next to Teikoku Jinken, by the outbreak of
the Sino-Japanese War.

Wartime Production

During World War II, Toyo Rayon's rayon production capacity decreased significantly as a result of mergers in the rayon
industry, which occurred five times at the insistence of the
government after October 1941, and as a result of the removal
and destruction of equipment, to allow scrapped iron to be used
as raw material for weapons. Toyo Rayon's rayon filament

Company Perspectives:

Toray strives to contribute to society through the creation of new value by innovative ideas, technologies, and products. Our mission is to provide new value to our customers through high-quality products and superior services, to provide our employees with opportunities for self-development in a challenging environment, to provide our shareholders with dependable and trustworthy management, and to act as a responsible corporate citizen to build a long-lasting beneficial partnership with the local communities in which we do business.

---

production decreased from a peak of 18,200 tons in 1937 to only 345 tons in 1945, and its rayon staple production from a peak of 12,422 tons in 1941 to 1,840 tons in 1945. After 1943, the company was forced to convert to wartime production. Part of the Shiga plant produced torpedoes and torpedo heads for the Japanese Navy, and part of the Aichi plant produced tanks for airplanes. Toyo Rayon established Sanyo Yushi (Oils and Fats) Ltd. as a joint venture with Mitsui Bussan and produced a high-grade lubricating oil for airplanes. It bought the Rakuto plant from Kyoto Sarashi Senko, which bleached and dyed textiles, mainly silks, and named it Yamashina Denki Kojo (Electric Machinery Plant). This plant produced electric and communication machinery for the Japanese Navy.

Nevertheless, Toyo Rayon also developed a new product during this period. Asahiko Karashima, a president of Toyo Rayon, realized the importance of innovation in the industry and thought that Toyo Rayon should enter the field of new textiles. When Du Pont succeeded in the development of nylon 66 in 1938, he ordered branches of Mitsui Bussan in the United States to collect information on nylon and to send it, together with samples of nylon stockings, to Toyo Rayon's research institute in Japan. In 1939, Toyo Rayon succeeded in analyzing and synthesizing nylon 66 and in spinning it into yarn in both dry and molten form. It also succeeded in developing nylon 6 independently and in spinning multifilament yarn from nylon in 1941. Toyo Rayon established experimental equipment for industrial use that produced ten kilograms of nylon per day by the end of 1942 and sold its product, named Amilan, as fishing yarn. This plant too was converted to wartime production. Toyo Rayon produced nylon chips in the plant and supplied them to the navy as raw material for electrical insulation in airplanes.

After World War II, war production stopped and employees who had been enlisted in the army returned to the company. Materials and chemicals for rayon production were in short supply, however, and restoration of equipment was forbidden immediately after the war by the Allied powers. Toyo Rayon therefore had to undertake conversion work of wartime production facilities for civilian industries other than the rayon industry. It conducted many kinds of business, including manufacturing and repairing railroad passenger and freight wagons, and pot motors and spinning pumps for rayon manufacture. It also produced penicillin, and made ice, salt, and fertilizers and insecticides, utilizing byproducts of nylon production for the latter.

Toyo Rayon's rayon production increased rapidly after the General Headquarters of the Allied Powers permitted Japan to raise its rayon production capacity to 150,000 tons per year on April 4, 1947. Its production volume of rayon yarn increased rapidly from 570 tons in 1946 to 17,305 tons in 1957, and its production of rayon staple, fibers which are spun to make yarn, rose from 1,159 tons in 1946 to 28,560 tons in 1956. The level of rayon yarn production in 1957, the company's postwar peak, was a little lower than the peak level before and during the war, 18,200 tons, while the production level for rayon staple in 1953 already surpassed its 1942 wartime peak of 12,422 tons. The rayon staple production level in 1956, a postwar peak, was more than twice as high as the 1942 level. Profitability was high during this period of recovery, particularly during the Korean War boom period. These profits enabled Toyo Rayon to begin nylon production.

Partnering With Du Pont: 1951

Toyo Rayon planned to change from equipment that produced 1.05 tons of nylon resin, a raw material of rayon yarn, and 0.06 tons of nylon filament for fishing line per day, to equipment which produced one ton of nylon filament per day in the Shiga plant in June 1949. It established a new plan to construct both equipment which produced five tons of nylon filament per day and equipment which produced caprolactam, a raw material of nylon, corresponding to the volume of nylon in October 1949. This plan was launched in response to the government's promotion of a synthetic fiber industry in Japan, and came into effect in 1949. Needless to say, Toyo Rayon's experience of nylon production during World War II enabled it to respond actively to government policy. It was, however, necessary for Toyo Rayon to tie up with Du Pont, which had a nylon patent network all over the world. Shigeki Tashiro, who had become the president of Toyo Rayon in 1945 but had retired because of the Allied powers' purging of leading Japanese industrialists and had later negotiated with the Allied occupation authorities as a spokesman for the Japanese chemical fiber industry, pointed out to Toyo Rayon's management that Toyo Rayon risked accusations of infringing Du Pont's patent rights if the Japanese company exported nylon products in the future. He advised Toyo Rayon to tie up with Du Pont in order to avoid such a possibility. Toyo Rayon's production method differed from Du Pont's as the Allies knew, but Tashiro's fears were based on the fact that Du Pont had a worldwide patent network not only for the nylon production method but for nylon and nylon product manufacturing equipment. In autumn 1948, Toyo Rayon approached a representative of Du Pont's Far East Section to inquire about the possibility of importing nylon production technology, but received no response.

Toyo Rayon had to import the necessary technology in time for the implementation of a full-scale industrial production plan for nylon in the latter half of 1949. Tashiro therefore asked a manager of Mitsui Bussan's New York branch, where Tashiro himself had once worked, to contact Du Pont. This time, Du Pont replied, demanding that Toyo Rayon pay 3 percent of nylon sales as a royalty for use of the patent for 15 years, with $3 million payable in advance. This sum was equivalent to ¥108 billion, which far exceeded Toyo Rayon's capital, ¥759 million yen at that time. Tashiro had become chairman of Toyo Rayon's board of directors in March 1950 and was very much surprised by Du Pont's terms at first, but calculated that if the advance

Key Dates:

1926: Toyo Rayon Company Ltd. is established.
1927: The firm begins to produce rayon yarn at its Shiga plant.
1939: The company succeeds in analyzing and synthesizing nylon 66.
1943: The company is forced to convert to wartime production.
1951: Toyo Rayon signs a technology import contract for nylon with Du Pont.
1957: The firm, along with competitor Teikoku Jinken, import polyester production technology from Imperial Chemical Industries.
1963: The company stops producing rayon yarn.
1970: The firm renames itself Toray Industries Inc. as a result of restructuring changes.
1988: Toray begins international expansion.
1998: Toray Ultrasuede Inc. is established in the United States.
2002: The company launches its ''Project New Toray 21'' program.

payment became ¥500 million yen per year, Toyo Rayon could pay it in two years without great difficulty. He succeeded in persuading Du Pont to agree to these conditions. The technology import contract for nylon was formally signed in June 1951.

At first Toyo Rayon experienced difficulties in its nylon business, even after it had overcome the problems of the nylon production process, as it had no experience in spinning, weaving, knitting, dyeing, or printing nylon. However, these problems were largely resolved by 1953. Toyo Rayon monopolized the nylon market until Nihon Rayon began full operation of its nylon production facilities in December 1956. Even after that, the Japanese nylon industry consisted of only two companies until 1963, when a few latecomers entered the industry. At first, nylon was mainly used for fishing nets, but its uses were extended to women's blouses, knitted underwear, seamless stockings, and tire-cord for use in car tires. In 1959, Toyo Rayon organized spinners, knitters, weavers, dyers, and printers into production teams, and also organized manufacturers of secondary products, trading companies, and wholesalers into sales teams, assisting them technically and financially. In 1951, it organized retailers who stocked clothing made from Toyo Rayon's nylon into the Toray Circle, assisting their research in shop management and educating employees about Toray products, advertisement of new merchandise, and the display of goods. Toyo Rayon's nylon business was highly profitable, and its profits exceeded the combined profits of the other six Japanese chemical fiber manufacturing companies between the first half of 1958 and the first half of 1962—at that time the company adopted the half-yearly accounting system.

Polyester and Synthetic Fibers: Late 1950s–Early 1960s

In January 1957, Toyo Rayon imported polyester production technology from the United Kingdom's Imperial Chemical In-

dustries (ICI) together with rival company Teikoku Jinken, a pioneer in the Japanese chemical fiber industry. ICI sold Toyo Rayon and Teikoku Jinken the exclusive rights to use its patent in Japan, in return for £1.15 million payable in advance by installments. Until September 16, 1968, 5.25 percent of sales was payable for production less than ten million pounds per year and 3 percent of sales for production that surpassed ten million pounds per year in the case of products other than photograph films. Toyo Rayon and Teikoku Jinken monopolized the polyester market until 1964, when several newcomers entered the market. Toyo Rayon started a prize-contest for product brand names jointly with Teikoku Jinken, which resulted in the name of ''Tetoron'' for polyester fiber. The two companies advertised Tetoron jointly. Previous experience in dealing with synthetic fibers and in joint technology import and successful joint marketing with Teikoku Jinken enabled Toyo Rayon to minimize difficulties in starting up its Tetoron business. Tetoron made a significant contribution to Toyo Rayon's profits during this period.

In September 1958, Toyo Rayon established a pilot plant for acrylic fibers at its central research institute and constructed equipment which produced three tons of acrylic fibers per day at its Nagoya plant. In 1954, it constructed equipment which produced 15 tons of acrylic fibers at the Ehime plant. Acrylic fibers found a market in sweaters, undershirts, stockings, and fabrics. Toyo Rayon's acrylic fiber production was based on its own technology. In the middle of the 1960s, the company grew to become the third largest general synthetic fiber manufacturer in the world, next to Du Pont and Monsanto Chemical Co. in the United States.

Rayon was the most important product in terms of sales up to 1954, when it contributed 54.7 percent and nylon contributed 45.2 percent. In 1955, nylon sales surpassed those of rayon, contributing 60.0 percent while rayon contributed 40 percent. In 1960, Tetoron sales surpassed rayon sales when nylon contributed 57.3 percent of sales, Tetoron 24.3 percent, and rayon 18.5 percent. Tetoron sales surpassed nylon and became Toyo Rayon's largest-selling product in 1965, when Tetoron's share was 43.8 percent, nylon's 43.6 percent, and rayon's only 2.3 percent, with the share of Toraylon (an acrylic fiber) at 4.3 percent, plastics at 4.1 percent, and Piren (a polypropylene textile) at 2.0 percent.

In 1973, when the first oil crisis occurred, Toray's sales breakdown was as follows: Tetoron 39.5 percent, nylon 27.9 percent, plastics 10.9 percent, Toraylon 8.5 percent, rayon 0.9 percent, and others 2.4 percent. In the first half of 1973, Toray still ranked first in terms of profit after tax among the seven Japanese chemical fiber manufacturing companies, although the difference in profits diminished between Toray and Teijin (as Teikoku Jinken became known in 1962), which ranked second. Tetoron sales grew faster than nylon, and competition, especially in the nylon and Tetoron businesses, intensified after latecomers entered these industries aggressively. These factors caused Toray's comparative decline in the synthetic fiber industry, especially in comparison with Teijin.

Making Changes: Mid-1960s to the 1990s

Toray made three important changes in the 1960s and 1970s. Firstly, it ceased rayon production, withdrawing from rayon yarn production in 1963 and decreasing the scale of its rayon staple production from 102.6 tons to 40 tons per day in 1968. Rayon staple was used for mixed spinning with Tetoron. Toray ceased rayon staple production in May 1975.

Secondly, Toyo Rayon resumed production of raw materials for synthetic fibers. In 1969, it established the Kawasaki plant, which produced 135,000 tons of cyclohexane (a raw material for nylon), 73,000 tons of paraxylene, and 100,000 tons of orthoxylene (the raw materials for polyester) per year. It cooperated with Nihon Sekiyu Kagaku (Japan Petro-Chemical Ltd.), which produced BTX (benzene, toluene, and xylene) from naphtha and supplied it to Toyo Rayon. Toyo Rayon in turn produced raw materials for nylon and Tetoron from BTX. In 1971, Toray established the Tokai branch factory of the Nagoya plant, which produced 125 tons of lactam and 50 tons of terephthalic acid (the raw materials for nylon and Tetoron) per day. In 1970, it established a joint venture with Mitsui Toatsu Kagaku Ltd., which produced acrylonitrile. Toray thus established a system whereby it could supply its own raw materials for the three major synthetic fibers it produced and moved toward becoming a general chemical manufacturing company.

Thirdly, it developed new high value-added products and diversified into the non-textile field. In the former category, it established in April 1971 a department to explore possible ventures outside the textiles industry and successfully marketed an artificial suede named Ecsaine and a carbon fiber named Torayca in 1970 and 1971 respectively. In the nontextiles field, Toray established a plastics department, and nylon resin, polyester film, ABS resin, and polypropylene film sold well. In particular, Toray's polyester film became popular for use in magnetic tape for tape recorders, chips for Fuji Shashin Film Ltd. (photographic film), and wrapping materials. In January 1970, Toyo Rayon renamed itself Toray Industries, Inc. as a result of these changes.

After the 1973 oil crisis, Toray's business performance deteriorated and its operating profits fell into the red for the second half of 1974 and at its financial year end in 1975 and 1977. Toray endeavored to rationalize production, reducing its work force from 19,108 in 1975 to 10,000 after 1987. It continued to develop and sell new high value-added products outside the textile fields. The ratio of non-textiles to total sales increased from 22.4 percent in 1975 to 44.7 percent in 1990. Among nontextiles, the ratio of chemicals, including plastics, increased from 20 percent to 34.1 percent and the ratio of new businesses and others not elsewhere classified, including carbon fiber, increased from 2.4 percent to 10.6 percent during the same period. It also reexamined investment in and loans to related companies, and the ratio of investment and loans to total assets decreased from 26.1 percent in 1977 to around 20 percent after 1986. As a result of these efforts, Toray's post-tax profits to sales ratio returned to almost the same level as during Japan's rapid economic growth period from 1966 to 1974.

In 1988, Toray began expanding its fibers, textiles, and plastics operations overseas. By the early 1990s, Toray's global network included nearly 60 overseas subsidiaries and affiliates, notably in Southeast Asia, where its first overseas fiber production facilities were established, and in the United States, where Toray Plastics (America), Inc. (TPA) produced polyester and polypropylene films. In France, Toray received the active support of the French government when it formed Société des Fibres de Carbone S.A. for the transfer of PAN-based carbon fiber technology to France. In April 1991, Toray formulated a long-term business plan: to increase its consolidated sales to ¥2 trillion by the year 2000 and to become a general chemicals group.

A Period of Diversification and Expansion: 1990s

As such, the company spent the majority of the 1990s diversifying and expanding its operations. In 1992, it received approval for the Dorner prostacyclin derivative drug as well as Feron, a drug used to detect Hepatitis C. The company also started to manufacture and market ABS resin at subsidiary Toray Plastics in Malaysia. In 1993, the firm established a polyester weaving and dyeing plant in the United Kingdom.

Toray's expansion continued in 1994 with the creation of subsidiaries in both China and Indonesia. That year, the company gained access to the patents for waterless offset printing plates. After the purchasing these patents from 3M, Toray was positioned as the sole supplier of such plates, which were gaining popularity, in North America.

The company's presence in Europe was strengthened in 1996 when Toray acquired the Rhone Poulenc Group's film manufacturing and marketing businesses, which were folded into Toray Plastics Europe S.A. That year the company also created KTP Industries, a Korean subsidiary. In 1997, Toray created subsidiaries in China, the United States, and the Czech Republic.

In order to bolster its U.S. textiles business, Toray acquired the Ultrasuede brand name from Springs Industries Inc. in 1998. The $15 million deal, which created Toray Ultrasuede America Inc., allowed Toray to market the brand in North, Central, and South America. These regions were key in the firm's expansion plans.

A New Plan for the New Century

Toray entered the new century on steady ground. During 2000, profits at the company's textile, plastics, and chemicals divisions grew at a steady clip. Overall, the firm reported operating profits of $415.3 million, a 58 percent increase over the previous year's results. In 2001, the firm partnered with Dow Corning Corp. Under the terms of the deal, Dow would market Toray's photosensitive polymide coatings to the North American semiconductor market. Toray also acquired engineering plastics compounding concern Nippisun Indiana Corp. in a move that strengthened the company's ties to the North American automotive industry.

During 2001, however, Toray's business environment weakened as global economies slowed, demand fell, and competition increased. The firm was forced to make some changes to its operations as both sales and net income faltered. In April 2002, the firm launched ''Project New Toray 21,'' a two-year restructuring program developed to restore both profitability and competitiveness. Led by chairman and CEO Katsunosuke Maeda and president and COO Sadayuki Sakakibara, the plan included projects aimed at divesting poor performing businesses, consolidating manufacturing operations in Japan, and expanding production in China. The program also included new marketing and customer services initiatives as well as labor-related cost-cutting measures.

Toray eyed the information and telecommunications, life sciences, and environmental industries as key to future growth. By developing key patents and brands in these areas and by forming global alliances, the company felt confident that its efforts would leave it well positioned for success. While Toray would indeed face challenges along the way, its strong history and respected reputation would no doubt carry it well into the future.

Principal Subsidiaries

Toray Coatex Co. Ltd.; Marusa Co. Ltd.; Toray Techno Co. Ltd.; Toray Engineering Co. Ltd.; Toray Research Center; Toray International Inc.; Toray Group USA; Toray Ultrasuede (America) Inc.; Toray Plastics (America) Inc.; Toray Textiles Central Europe s.r.o. (Czech Republic); Toray Plastics Europe S.A. (France); Toray Deutschland GmbH (Germany); Taltex Ltd. (China); Société des Fibres de Carbone S.A. (France).

Principal Competitors

Kuraray Co. Ltd.; Teijin Limited; Toyobo Co. Ltd.

Further Reading

"Dow Corning-Toray Deal," *Chemical Week*, July 25, 2001, p. 26.

Furukawa, Tsukasa, "Toray Aims to Expand in China," *WWD*, April 9, 2002, p. 20.

"Japan's Toray Industries Posts 58% Higher FY2000 Group Op Profit," *AsiaPulse News*, May 16, 2001.

Maycumber, S. Gray, and Tsukasa Furukawa, "Toray Buys Ultrasuede From Springs For $15 Mil," *Daily News Record*, July 8, 1998, p. 1A.

Moore, Stephen, "Toray Acquires U.S. Compounder," *Chemical Week*, August 29, 2001, p. 11.

"Toray Buys Dupont's PTFE Fibers Business," *Chemical Week*, August 21, 2002, p. 7.

Toray 50 Nenshi 1926–1976, Tokyo: Toray Industries, 1977.

"Toray Merges Specialties Unit," *Chemical Week*, April 24, 2002, p. 29.

Yamazaki, Hiroaki, *Nihon Kasensangyo Hattatsushi Ron*, Tokyo: University of Tokyo Press, 1975.

—Hiroaki Yamazaki
—updated by Christina M. Stansell

Trans-Lux Corporation

110 Richards Avenue
Norwalk, Connecticut 06856
U.S.A.
Telephone: (203) 853-4321
Fax: (203) 854-6891
Web site: http://www.trans-lux.com

Public Company
Founded: 1920
Employees: 660
Sales: $70 million (2001)
Stock Exchanges: American
Ticker Symbol: TLX
NAIC: 334290 Other Communications Equipment
Manufacturing

Trans-Lux Corporation manufactures, distributes, and markets large-scale, real-time electronic information displays for both indoor and outdoor use. The company's displays provide up-to-the-minute information and promotional messages in graphic, animation, video, and text formats. Listed on the American Stock Exchange since 1925, the company has a history of innovation and financial strength. It is the world leader in displays for financial applications, serving more than 50 stock and financial exchanges and thousands of banks. It also serves the retail, gaming, corporate, transportation, entertainment, and sports markets.

Company Origins

After mining quicksilver and drilling for oil in Mexico, Englishman Percy Norman Furber arrived in the United States in October 1918 and soon delved into another difficult but completely unrelated endeavor. Furber wanted to develop a projection system that could be used in a lighted room. He enlisted the aid of a friend, Arthur Payne, who had worked with Thomas Edison. Payne hit upon the idea of rear projection. But projecting images through a screen would require the invention of a finely wrought translucent material of much higher quality than any in existence.

In 1920, Furber formed American Lux (Latin for "light") Products, and three years later the company used natural silk to create its first successful screen. Initial sales of the screens and the rear projector went mostly to schools and churches. Furber thought about developing a similar system for the stock market after a visit to the New York Stock Exchange. At the time, the brokers crowded around a dome-topped ticker tape. Those who were closest gained an advantage. Furber created a system that projected and enlarged the stock quotations from the ticker tape onto a rear projection screen.

Financing this new operation required more capital. Furber took his company public on August 26, 1925. It was listed on the New York Curb Exchange, which later became the American Stock Exchange. That year, the company had 41 installations throughout the country on stock exchange floors and in brokerage house boardrooms.

Within a few years, the company broke into the entertainment business by creating a much larger screen for movie viewing. By 1927, it began marketing its commercial-sized theater screen, rear projector, and a new wide-angle lens to the motion picture industry. To further penetrate this market, the company created the Trans-Lux Movies Corporation in partnership with a major Hollywood production and theater company, Radio-Keith-Orpheum (RKO). Together the two companies began a theater-building program using Trans-Lux as the trade name.

4,000 Stockholders, $2 Million Value by 1931

In 1931, Percy Furber turned over the company reins to his son, also named Percy. By this time, Trans-Lux had 4,000 stockholders, 100 plus employees, and was valued at $2 million. The first Trans-Lux theater at 58th Street and Madison Avenue in New York City offered newsreels in a setting featuring larger seats, more leg room, and wider aisles than the average theater of the day. Rear projection allowed patrons to read their programs and easily locate their seats. It also eliminated the distraction of a beam of light slicing down through the crowd from an overhead projection booth.

In 1934, the company opened two newsreel theaters in Brooklyn and one in Philadelphia. Three years later, it added

Company Perspectives:

We take great pride in the cutting-edge display solutions we design for clients around the world and the high standard of client service we maintain. And we look forward, moving to take advantage of dynamic new technologies, to our continued leadership in the expanding communication environments of the future.

three more theaters and shortened its name to Trans-Lux Corporation. With newsreels no longer the draw they once were, the company began offering short films and feature movies.

Trans-Lux Enters the Outdoor Sign Business: 1940s

In 1940, Trans-Lux purchased Louis Casper's patent on a remote-control signaling system that enabled small rounded pellets to form letters and numbers and travel around outdoor message signs. The best-known figure in this new moving message sign industry was Jacob Starr. Starr's company, Artkraft Strauss Sign Corporation, first illuminated the "Great White Way" of Broadway. Trans-Lux joined forces with Artkraft Strauss and by 1948 was supplying electrical traveling message signs to advertisers, radio stations, and publishers throughout the country. At the same time, Trans-Lux had 1,400 stock-ticker projectors and 80 news projectors in the United States, plus another 200 in Canada.

When the television industry burst on the scene in the late 1940s, Trans-Lux began developing specialized rear-projection equipment for television studios. The company greatly expanded its engineering capacity and started supplying the studios with "Teleprocess" screens and projectors. When closed-circuit television (CCTV) emerged, Trans-Lux adapted that technology for viewing stock market information. In 1959, the company formed an electronics division to develop and sell CCTV systems. The expanded business required Trans-Lux to move from its Brooklyn headquarters to a larger, five-story building in Long Island City.

Declining Movie Audiences: 1950s

Closely tied to the fate of the movie theater industry, Trans-Lux suffered when theater attendance dropped dramatically from 78.2 million weekly in 1946 to 58 million by 1950. Sitting at home in front of the television began replacing going out to the movies.

The company's movie exhibition business recovered by the late fifties, however, when its theaters became first-run houses for some important domestic and foreign feature films. As the U.S. middle-class began moving from the city to the suburbs, theaters followed. Shopping complexes outside the cities proliferated, and in 1964 Trans-Lux built its first shopping center theater, an 850-seat in Reisterstown Plaza Mall in Baltimore. By 1969, the company had brought large, modern theaters to five more suburban shopping centers, nearly doubling the size of its theater holdings. The next year, Eugene Picker joined Trans-Lux to head up its entertainment division and added 16 theaters to the chain, bringing the total to 37 theaters in ten states.

New Electronics Development: 1960s

Trans-Lux began to see a need for greater investment in electronics. Stock exchanges and brokerage houses were inundated with new, advanced techniques for gathering and projecting information. An anchor on Trans-Lux's fortunes was its system's two-step process. The information Trans-Lux relied on began with prices printed on ticker tape from Western Union. Then, a delay was required as the ticker tape shifted away from the print head to a viewing position for projecting or televising. With an electronic ticker display, Trans-Lux could bypass the printing stage, creating a real-time, immediate information system. Electronics would also eliminate the need for telegraphic data through Western Union.

In 1965, Charles Holloman was brought on board to help the company make the transition to electronics. That year Trans-Lux was shocked by the introduction of a new 45-foot-long electronic display installed on the trading floor of the New York Stock Exchange by a competitor. Even though the Ultronic's Letrascan electronic wall device had been steadily replacing Trans-Lux tickers for several years, the New York Stock Exchange installation created great concern. Trans-Lux had enjoyed a long-standing business relationship with the exchange.

Percy Furber, Richard Brandt, Charles Holloman, and others visited the display's developer, Recognition Equipment Company of Texas, and made a deal. Recognition needed Trans-Lux's knowledge of how to market stock-ticker equipment. Trans-Lux needed Recognition's technology. In a joint effort, Holloman set out to create a much smaller version of the Recognition system.

Two years later, Trans-Lux announced the Trans-Lux Jet, named for the jets of air that controlled character formation in the sign. It was the highest quality, real-time, continuous flow wall display yet produced and a new method of viewing up-to-the-minute stock market sales information. Its ten-foot size made it appropriate for brokerage offices. Perhaps the best news for Trans-Lux was that it no longer needed to rely on the Western Union ticker.

U.S. and Canadian brokerage houses ordered more than 1,000 Trans-Lux Jets in the first six months. To handle overseas orders, Trans-Lux opened an international office in Zurich, Switzerland. By mid-1969, about 3,000 Jets were in use. Shortly after introducing the Jet, Trans-Lux applied the same innovations to a closed-circuit television system.

Relocating to Connecticut: 1970s

The Jet's popularity required Trans-Lux to find a larger production facility. In 1970, the company moved to Norwalk, Connecticut. Demand for Jets continued to grow. Longer versions of 15, 25, and 43 feet were produced. In 1969, Holloman succeeded in reducing the size of the Jet to one-fifth of the original. Ten years later, by developing a powerful miniature microprocessor chip, the company reduced the Jet to a twenty-fifth of its original size.

The other side of Trans-Lux's business, the entertainment industry, began rapidly evolving again in the early 1970s, producing new challenges. The theater building boom of the 1960s ended. The boom had aggravated the traditional industry problem of a shortage of quality movies. Bidding on films became fierce. Many companies split their single theaters into twins. Three screen and four screen theaters began appearing.

Trans-Lux lost money on its theaters in 1973 for the first time in many years. Bud Levy took over the theater department. In 1974, the year Richard Brandt replaced Percy Furber as chairman of the board, the multiplex trend (with as many as 12 screens) was in full force. Levy split some of the company's theaters into two and three screen houses and sold off others. By 1981, Trans-Lux's theater holdings were concentrated in the Northeast, particularly Connecticut, and the company was down to 28 screens.

Selective Stock Read-out Device

As successful as the Jet was, it left out one important segment of the stock market. Large portfolio holders and active traders had no device that would automatically zero in on their individual stock holdings or market objectives. When a Chicago-based company, Quotemaster (later called Extel) developed an experimental prototype for a selective tape read-out device, Trans-Lux expressed interest. The companies reached an agreement and Trans-Lux began further development and manufacturing of the device, naming it the Personal Ticker. Personal Tickers could be programmed to monitor up to 40 stocks on one stock exchange. By 1969, Trans-Lux began installing the product for private investors, portfolio managers, pension fund administrators, investment advisors, and individual brokers. That same year, a strong bull market ended abruptly, sending installations of all types of Trans-Lux equipment on a plunge.

Changes at Trans-Lux

Following the 1969 stock market decline, Trans-Lux management learned that their electronic display sales should not be overly dependent on a single industry. The company therefore decided to diversify and formed an industrial sales department in 1970 under the leadership of Louis Credidio. Credidio went

after the commodities market and in 1971 sold an adaptation of the Personal Ticker, the T-900, to the Chicago Board of Trade. Soon Trans-Lux completed sales to many other commodity exchanges, capturing a small but significant new market.

When Extel's teleprinter terminal sales boomed, it contracted Trans-Lux to manufacture keyboards and way-station selectors. This led to Trans-Lux's entry into the teleprinter market. Credidio studied the telex terminal field and by 1974 Trans-Lux began marketing a telex terminal, the Trans-Lux Teleprinter (TLT), to several industries. More than 700 terminals were installed by 1975.

Entrance into Multimedia Show Business

One of Brandt's dreams was to lead Trans-Lux into the business of multimedia shows. In 1970, the premiere of the ''San Francisco Experience,'' a 29-projector, seven-screen spectacular with 30 special effects wowed Brandt. He hired the creators of that show to develop a nearly $1 million budget multimedia entertainment film on New York City. The September 28, 1973 opening of the 45-projector, 16-screen film was called ''bedazzling and breathtaking'' by *The New York Times*. ''The New York Experience'' became the longest-running commercial multimedia show in history, an attraction in New York City, and the source of inspiration for shows in other cities. In 1986, Trans-Lux operated two multimedia attractions in New York City, ''The New York Experience'' and ''The Seaport Experience.'' That year, the company's net income hit a record high of $4.1 million.

Further Growth and Expansion: 1990s and Beyond

In 1992, Victor Liss took over as CEO. That year annual revenues reached $24.1 million. By the time Liss retired in 2001, the company had experienced a nearly three-fold increase in annual revenues.

Early in 1995, Trans-Lux acquired Integrated Systems Engineering, Inc., a full service electronic sign manufacturing company, to broaden Trans-Lux's outdoor signage capabilities. On November 10 of that year, Trans-Lux and Metropolitan Theatres opened a sophisticated, high-tech, 12-screen cinema complex in Loveland, Colorado. Advanced projection systems, digital sound technologies, and an architecturally elaborate 38,000-square-foot setting helped the complex draw impressive reviews.

Trans-Lux in the mid-1990s had a communications division that designed, produced, leased, sold, and serviced the company's electronic information displays. Another division, the entertainment and real estate division, ran an expanding chain of motion picture theaters and some real estate in both the United States and Canada for corporate and income-producing purposes. From about 1998 to 2001, that division invested in building new theaters in the western states, bringing the company's total to 65 theater screens. In 2000, the company opened a Los Angeles-based film booking office that allowed it to book films for other theater companies.

The company's capacity to produce electronic displays increased in 2000 when it opened a modern outdoor display manufacturing facility in Utah. The facility helped boost the division's bookings by 50 percent the next year. The indoor display division remained a major supplier of communications tools for the financial community, including banks, brokerage houses, and stock exchanges. Theaters, museums, hotels, corporations, and military hospitals were also customers. The division experienced a growth spurt in 2000 when the Australian gaming authorities approved Trans-Lux's serial slot controller for sale in that country. That decision also boosted sales of the LED (light-emitting diode) jackpot meter displays that work hand in hand with the slot controllers.

Trans-Lux also entered the healthcare industry with products designed to help hospitals, pharmacies, and outpatient clinics operate more effectively by delivering critical information displays. By 2002, Trans-Lux products and services were used worldwide. That year the company also operated about a dozen movie theaters with 65 screens in the western mountain states that produced about 20 percent of company sales. Company annual revenues had reached $70.1 million in three divisions: outdoor displays, indoor displays, and entertainment/real estate.

Principal Competitors

Daktroniks Inc.; Display Technologies Inc.; SI Diamond Technology Inc.

Principal Divisions

Outdoor Displays; Indoor Displays; Entertainment/Real Estate.

Further Reading

Grenz, Christine, *Trans-Lux, Biography of a Corporation*, Norwalk, Conn.: Trans-Lux Corporation, 1982.

—Chris John Amorosino

Tully's Coffee Corporation

3100 Airport Way South
Seattle, Washington 98134
U.S.A.
Telephone: (206) 233-2070
Toll Free: (800) 968-8559
Fax: (206) 233-2077
Web site: http://www.tullys.com

Private Company
Incorporated: 1992
Employees: 1,000
Sales: $51.5 million (2002)
NAIC: 722213 Snack and Nonalcoholic Beverage Bars;
312111 Soft Drink Manufacturing; 445299 All Other
Specialty Food Stores

Founded in 1992, Tully's Coffee Corporation is the third largest company-owned specialty coffee retailer in the United States. Tully's Coffee currently has 101 locations in Washington, Oregon, California, Idaho, and the Pacific Rim. Its wholesale division provides Tully's whole bean coffee, related products, and supplies to domestic supermarkets, food services, restaurants, office coffee services, and institutions, as well as to customers through Tully's mail order and Internet sales. The company's international division sells Tully's coffee, related products, and supplies to foreign licensees.

Early 1990s: New Barista on the Block

Tom Tully O'Keefe—head barista, founder, and chairman of Tully's Coffee Corporation—founded the company in 1992 with an initial investment of more than $1 million. O'Keefe first began thinking about opening a gourmet coffee business in 1991, when, as president and chief executive officer of O'Keefe Development Corporation—a real estate development and investment firm he'd founded in 1986—he helped Starbucks and other coffee companies find retail sites for their coffee shops.

Known for his fun loving, but extremely competitive nature, O'Keefe was puzzled by the fact that no company had stepped

forward to challenge Starbucks. "Nobody was competing with Starbucks," he said in the *Seattle Post Intelligencer* in 1999. "It didn't make sense to me. There were a lot of mom-and-pop operations. There were a lot of franchises. But nobody was competing with Starbucks' profile." He decided that he would. O'Keefe named his new company Tully's, using the middle name he shared with his Greek uncle, Tully, a man in his seventies who lived in New Hampshire.

From the start, Tully's aimed to offer a European café culture experience, selling custom-roasted whole bean coffees, specialty coffee beverages, pastries, and, in some locations, magazines and newspapers. Its coffee houses were modeled after Starbucks but featured warmer interiors and targeted customers who wanted to spend time lingering over their espresso. In later years, select stores featured electrical outlets for computers, fireplaces, shoeshine stands, outdoor seating, and a "strictly business" section with local and national newspapers. Tully's further differentiated itself from Starbucks by its lighter roast and by investing its marketing dollars directly in the community instead of advertising. Tully's became and has remained a regular supporter of Northwest AIDS Foundation, DARE, Juvenile Diabetes Foundation, and the Pacific Northwest Ballet.

The company grew at a steady pace. By late 1994, Tully's had close to ten retail outlet stores in the Seattle area ranging in size from 800 to 1,500 square feet and had added Italian-style "Tullini" sandwiches to its offerings. It was also the official coffee of the Seattle Space Needle restaurant. In January 1994, O'Keefe raised another $1 million through a private placement—the first of many—bringing in 35 shareholders and diminishing his share of the company to slightly more than 70 percent. The money raised went toward leasing new corporate headquarters and a roasting plant where Tully's began roasting its own coffee blends. The new roasting plant and corporate offices, which opened in January 1995, had previously been those of Starbucks Coffee Co.

Mid- to Late 1990s: Aggressive Expansion

According to a 1995 *Restaurant Business* article, the United States was in the midst of a coffee café boom by the mid-1990s.

Company Perspectives:

Since we opened our first store in 1992, Tully's has provided a coffee experience that customers eagerly savor and enjoy. Our goal is to continuously build upon the quality of our products, customer service, and store ambience, and to extend that experience to customers outside of stores.

The impetus for this trend emanated from San Francisco, Portland, and Seattle. The National Coffee Association, quoted in *Restaurant Business*, attributed the dramatic increase in the number of coffee houses nationally—from 564 in 1993 to 2,273 in 1994—to an increased interest in coffee among younger as well as older people. As the market for coffee grew, the number of players in the coffee business grew, although with the rapid expansion, smaller companies soon disappeared in corporate mergers and acquisitions.

Tully's had revenues of almost $2 million annually by the mid-1990s. By 1996, its number of stores had increased to 22, and same store sales increases were roughly 15 percent higher than the year before. The company still modeled many of its choices after market groundbreaker Starbucks, often opening stores adjacent to the market leader. According to O'Keefe in a 1996 *Puget Sound Business Journal* article, "Wherever Starbucks is, we want to be right across the street."

Starting in 1997, Tully's formulated an aggressive growth strategy combined with a desire to move into regional markets outside the Pacific Northwest. It also began to sell its coffee overseas: In February, its coffee debuted in Shanghai at an upscale grocery; in August, it opened a store in Tokyo; and in November, it opened three stores in Beijing, becoming the first gourmet coffee retailer to sell in China. The company founded Tully's Coffee Japan Co. as an entirely separate venture in May 1998. By end of 2001, Tully's Coffee Japan had 34 outlets and had become the exclusive wholesaler of Tully's products in Japan.

Also in 1998, Tully's bought Spinelli Coffee Co. of California for $8 million. The acquisition brought with it stores in the Bay Area, Singapore, and Taiwan, which Tully's rebranded, as well as a direct connection to coffee growers. With the acquisition, Tully's stores numbered more than 50. The company began selling its beans in supermarket chains owned by Brown & Cole in October 1998.

Yet the company that boasted of doubling its size annually had yet to turn a profit. There were losses of $2.5 million on sales of $5.4 million for fiscal year 1997. By fiscal year 1998, sales had increased to about $9 million, and by 1999 to $20 million. However, losses continued to climb—from $3.8 million in 1998 to $6.5 million in 1999.

Although Tully's had replaced Starbucks as the "official coffee" of the Mariners, agreeing to pay somewhere between $1 and $2 million to become the only coffee served at Safeco Field ballpark in 1998, Tully's was still far behind Starbucks and the number two national coffee chain, Diedrich Coffee, in both earnings and sales. Another private placement in 1999

brought in more millions, and the company continued to open stores at a fast clip as well as renovating its new headquarters in the old Rainier Brewery. Beginning in 1999, Tully's moved into Europe, signing its first licensing agreement in Scandinavia. By the middle of 2000, there were 114 Tully's internationally (compared to Starbucks' 3,215), and attention was on the company's expansion in San Francisco's East Bay. In 2000, Tully's formed a joint venture, called Tully's Coffee Europe, with Belgium-based Seattle Coffee Factory to rebrand that company's Stockholm retail outlets as Tully's.

Back home, Tully's formed a partnership with Home Grocer.com to sell bagged beans for delivery to online shoppers. It partnered with Briazz to offer sandwiches and salads at its downtown Seattle stores and became the official coffee of the San Francisco Giants at Pac Bell Field. The company also turned attention to its wholesale business both home and abroad. However, despite these efforts, Tully's continued to operate in the red, losing $8 million in 2000.

In part, this deficit was due to Tully's six-month store opening binge. A new Tully's opened every six days in 2000 as the number of employees increased dramatically from 400 to 1,300. In late 2000, the company purchased Portland's Marsee Bakery chain and five stores from Coffee Station in Los Angeles. When, by 2001, its expansion came to an end, it was leaking cash even as its sales grew. It had exhausted its bank credit line and had to turn to its board for emergency funds to keep growing. Losses for fiscal year 2001 were $25 million on sales of $42 million.

2001–02: Two New Management Teams

At this point, O'Keefe recognized that he no longer had the expertise needed to manage a company of more than 100 stores. To prepare Tully's for its long-awaited initial public offering, the company brought in its first president and chief operating officer and later chief executive, Jamie Colbourne. Colbourne, who came from Coca Cola and 7-Up Canada, took over Tully's day-to-day operations in February 2001.

Colbourne brought Tully's rapid expansion to a halt. His first move, focusing on profitability over expansion, was to land a major licensing deal with Japan-based Ueshima Coffee Co. Ltd., making it the exclusive Tully's supplier for all of Asia except Japan. This helped resolve the company's immediate cash crisis. In place of O'Keefe's vision of a Tully's across the street from every Starbuck's, Colbourne substituted the idea of Tully's becoming a niche player. "We need to be a little more selective in our store sites," he was quoted in a 2001 *Portland Business Journal* article. "I want to make sure we've got the business right first." Colbourne also focused on expanding the company's wholesale business beginning in March 2001.

However, in July 2001, Colbourne suddenly resigned, citing differences with the board of directors and saying that the company's finances were in worse shape than he'd been told. Marc Evanger became interim president and chief executive of Tully's and continued to implement Colbourne's profitability plan. Evanger closed some U.S. stores and all stores in Sweden, stopped offering sandwiches and salads in some locations, and cut corporate employees almost 20 percent. He continued to put

Key Dates:

1992: Tom Tully O'Keefe founds Tully's Coffee Corporation in Seattle.
1994: Tully's holds its first of many private placements.
1995: The company opens a new roasting plant and corporate offices.
1997: Tully's begins to sell its coffee overseas.
1998: The company founds Tully's Coffee Japan Co. as an entirely separate venture and buys Spinelli Coffee Co.
2001: Jamie Colbourne becomes president and chief executive officer.
2002: Tony Gioia becomes president and chief executive officer.

expansion plans on hold while increasing the company's wholesale and grocery business. Through the remainder of 2001 and into 2002, the emphasis on the company's wholesale business continued, and by January 2002 Tully's had signed on four supermarkets: Rosauers Supermarkets, Albertson's, Safeway, and Quality Food Centers in the Pacific Northwest. By the middle of 2002, Tully's coffee was selling in 650 grocery stores.

Despite Tully's losses in 2001, it closed the year debt free because of the cash it received from Ueshima Coffee and Tully's Coffee Japan. Tully's Coffee Japan turned a profit of $758,000 on sales of $8.6 million in 2001, and in fiscal 2002 brought in nearly $2 million to the company. In fiscal 2002, Tully's lost $11.2 million on increased revenues of $51.5 million, despite the fact that sales fell 6 percent at established stores.

Tony Gioia, former president of Southwest Supermarkets and before that of Baskin-Robbins, as well as co-founder of Wolfgang Puck Food, assumed the roles of chief executive officer and president of Tully's in June 2002. To pit Tully's against its competition and prepare it for going public, Gioia focused attention on improving the company's financial performance and strengthening its market position, saving costs and increasing sales at its 103 stores.

With $700,000 left in cash in late 2002, Gioia hired an investment firm to pursue additional short-term and long-term financing for Tully's. Yet he insisted that he had not "lost one minute of sleep over our cash position" in a 2002 *Puget Sound Business Journal* article. "We decided it was important to focus on our existing assets and make them generate more cash flow for the company." It was also important to continue to expand Tully's international licensees.

Gioia had high hopes for the company's new gourmet, soft-serve ice creams, free samples of which were bringing in new customers. With the introduction of the ice cream, as a separate item and as a part of a drink, Tully's was finally moving in a direction entirely different than Starbuck's. Despite the fact that same store sales were down 6 percent in 2002 and the company continued to close stores, management firmly believed that strong revenue growth and slower increases in expenses would pay off for Tully's in the end.

Principal Competitors

Diedrich Coffee, Inc.; Starbucks Corporation.

Further Reading

Flores, Michele Matassa, "Batter Up," *Seattle Post-Intelligencer*, April 4, 1999.
"Grounds for Expansion," *Restaurant Business*, May 20, 1995, p. 112.
Lalwani, Sheila, "Ready for the Race: CEO Aims to Power Up Tully's Competitive Position," *Seattle Times*, July 4, 2002, p. 2F.
Lim, Paul, "Brewing a Good Fight," *Dallas Morning News*, March 2, 1996, p. 2F.
Mulady, Kathy, "Leaner and More Focused, Tully's Ready to Perk in 2002," *Seattle Post-Intelligencer*, December 20, 2001, p. D6.
Tice, Carol, "Extra-hot Outlook: Tully's CEO Brims With Confidence," *Puget Sound Business Journal*, August 30, 2002, p. 1.
——, "Tully's New CEO Moves Quickly to Shift Stratify," *Portland Business Journal*, May 4, 2001, p. 14.
——, "Tully's Short on Cash, Long on Plans," *Puget Sound Business Journal*, February 23, 2001, p. 1.

—Carrie Rothburd

 UNION FENOSA

Unión Fenosa, S.A.

Capitán Haya, 53
28020 Madrid
Spain
Telephone: (+34) 91-567-60-00
Fax: (+34) 91-567-63-29
Web site: http://www.uef.es

Public Company
Incorporated: 1982 as Unión Electrica Fenosa
Employees: 24,772
Sales: EUR 5.42 billion ($5.32 billion) (2001)
Stock Exchanges: Mercado Continuo
Ticker Symbol: UNF
NAIC: 324110 Petroleum Refineries; 221122 Electric
Power Generation, Transmission and Distribution;
221210 Natural Gas Distribution; 513310 Wired
Telecommunications Carriers; 513322 Cellular and
Other Wireless Telecommunications; 531210 Offices
of Real Estate Agents and Brokers; 541211 Offices of
Certified Public Accountants; 541330 Engineering
Services; 541611 Administrative Management and
General Management Consulting Services; 541710
Research and Development in the Physical,
Engineering, and Life Sciences

Unión Fenosa, S.A. is powering ahead with its plans to redevelop itself into a diversified, international conglomerate. Known as Unión Electrica Fenosa until 2001, the company's electric power generation and distribution business remains at the core of its operations. Unión Fenosa is Spain's third-largest electrical power supplier, with a diversified power-generation infrastructure—including windmill farms and other alternative sources—capable of generating more than 5,500 megawatts in Spain. The company's Spanish power generation operations are centered in Madrid, Castilla y Léon, Galicia, and Castilla-La Mancha. Thwarted by its attempt to gain size after the Spanish government vetoed its agreed-upon takeover of number four electricity company Hidrocantrabrico, Fenosa has stepped up its

international investments, exporting its power generation expertise, especially to the Latin American market, with holdings in Colombia, Guatemala, Mexico, Costa Rica, Ecuador, Nicaragua, Uruguay, the Dominican Republic, and Panama. Elsewhere, the company has holdings in the Philippines, Moldova, and Morocco. A primary focus of Fenosa's diversification strategy has been the building up of a strong position in the international gas industry by acquiring and developing operations covering gas production, transportation, marketing, and distribution. The company has scored a number of major concessions, such as the construction of a natural gas liquefaction plant in Damietta, Egypt, and the acquisition of a 20 percent share of the Algerian natural gas pipeline, which has enabled Fenosa to begin providing natural gas to the Spanish industrial market. Elsewhere, Fenosa's power and utility interests included the UK's Cambridge Water, a water and electrical power utility. Another key division of the company is Fenosa Soluciones, an engineering and consulting unit dedicated to developing new technologies and services. The company also has holdings in the telecommunications sector, including a share in Auna, Spain's second-largest telecommunications provider (Fenosa planned to put that share up for sale as early as 2003). However, Fenosa's heavy investment program has come at a cost. By the end of the 2002, the company, which had built up a debt load of nearly EUR 7 billion, was forced to put up for sale half of its profitable gas division.

A Leading Electric Power Company in the 1980s

Unión Fenosa was formed from the merger of Unión Eléctrica and Fuerzas Eléctricas del Noroeste (Fenosa), in 1982. Both companies operated in Spain's electrical power generation and distribution market, with Fenosa's presence in Galicia and elsewhere in northern Spain complementing Unión Eléctrica's chiefly Madrid- and central Spain-based operations. The newly merged company inherited its predecessors' crushing debt load—which had reached some $6 billion by the early 1980s—brought on by the Franco regime's efforts to develop Spain's electrical power infrastructure and particularly by the country's decision to add nuclear power generating capacity in the 1960s.

Spain's electrical industry had started out in the private sector at the turn of the 20th century. Between 1890 and the

---

Company Perspectives:

''Drawing value from our expertise'' is one of the mainstays of our business success. It encourages us to innovate and to set and enforce best practice standards to the benefit of our customers. We invest 27 million Euros in Professional Development every year to ensure ongoing improvement of our knowledge and quality competencies.

---

beginning of World War I, most of the country's electrical power industry was controlled by a few groups. Among these was Unión Eléctrica, originally known as Unión Eléctrica Madrilena, which emerged in 1912 when three small electrical power companies joined together to capture the Madrid power market. As with much of Spain's electrical power industry, Unión Eléctrica Madrilena's development was hampered by the unsettled political and economic situation surrounding the Spanish Civil War.

The arrival of Francisco Franco to power took control of the country's electrical power industry out of the private sector. In 1941, the Franco regime created the Instituto Nacional de Industria (INI, or National Industrial Institute), which became the holding company for much of the country's industry, particularly the components of its infrastructure. The INI's role was to act as a bridge between the government and industry with the aim of stimulating the country's industrial development.

The electrical industry was brought under the INI's control, and the period that followed saw the establishment of many of the country's leading power companies, including later leaders Endesa and Iberdrola. In 1942, Fuerzas Eléctricas del Noroeste was formed to cover the northern and eastern parts of the country. The INI instituted a variety of changes in the Spain's power industry, including a single rate structure. The INI also forced the country's power companies to take the lead in building up a self-reliant infrastructure for the country. As a result, power companies were expected to invest heavily in redeveloping the country's electrical network and to adopt new power-generation technologies, especially nuclear power generating capacity. Unión Eléctrica Madrilena's entry into nuclear power came during the 1960s, with its first nuclear power plant coming online in 1968. Two years later, the company, which by then had expanded beyond Madrid to include operations throughout much of central Spain, changed its name to Unión Eléctrica.

By the end of the 1970s, the Spanish electrical industry was capable of producing far more electricity than the country needed, while the race to expand had burdened the markets many and relatively small utility companies with massive debts. This situation sparked a round of consolidation at the beginning of the 1980s, including the merger between Fenosa and Unión Éléctrica, which created the country's third-largest power supplier, Unión Eléctrica Fenosa. Taking the lead of the newly enlarged company was Julián Trincado, who had been named general manager of Fuerzas Eléctricas del Noroeste in 1971 before becoming the company's managing director, a position he retained after the merger. In 1983, Trincado was appointed chairman of the new company.

Over the next ten years, Trincado not only led Fenosa back into the black but was also credited as being the chief architect of Fenosa's transformation from a relatively minor power supplier to becoming a player on the international stage. By the beginning of the 1990s, Fenosa had managed to cut out a large part of its debt, trim down its payroll, and increase sales. A key part of the company's success was its early decision to diversify its operations in preparation for the coming deregulation of the European electricity market slated for the late 1990s.

A Diversified International Company in the 21st Century

Fenosa's diversification took two different tracks. The company began expanding its core electrical power generation operations by moving into new and alternative technologies, including the building of windmill farms in the early 1990s. But Fenosa also began developing interests and holdings outside of its core business, diversifying into a variety of industries, such as construction and building materials, mining, and telecommunications. This effort was in part a response to the growing strength of state-owned utility Endesa, which had begun buying stakes in a number of Spain's smaller, private-sector utilities. In 1991, for example, Endesa bought up nearly 10 percent of Fenosa in what was seen as part of the Spanish government's effort to encourage the consolidation of the Spanish energy sector.

Fenosa remained independent, however, and continued to build up its diversified operations. International operations came to play an increasingly important role in the company's growth during the 1990s. Fenosa's successful turnaround had inspired a number of other utility operators around the world, and the company now found itself with a thriving consulting business, later brought under business unit Fenosa Soluciones. By the mid-1990s, Fenosa was present in more than 20 countries worldwide, particularly in the Asian and Latin American markets. Among the company's investments made during the time was a stake in Argentina's Emersa ni 1995 (sold off in 1999) and the purchase of a share in Iberafrica, based in Kenya, in 1996.

Fenosa also was quick to enter the growing telecommunications arena, including an early investment in mobile telephone operator Airtel. By 1996, Fenosa controlled more than 8 percent of Airtel's shares. In 1998, Fenosa joined a consortium that included Telecom Italia and Endesa to acquire television broadcaster Retevision, formerly owned by the Spanish government. Then, in 2000, Fenosa and its partners bundled their various telecommunications and related operations into a new company, Auna, which was slated for a public offering in the first half of 2000.

In 1997, the Spanish government passed legislation deregulating parts the country's electricity system in preparation for the European-wide deregulation scheduled to begin in 1999. The new system separated the electrical power industry into two systems—Transmission and Distribution, which remained regulated by the Spanish government, and Generation and Retailing, which was deregulated and thus opened to competition, both within Spain and, later, across European borders. The new system freed up Fenosa and other Spanish operators to begin constructing new power generation facilities and gave them full access to the country's distribution grid, which in turn enabled

Key Dates:

1912: Unión Electrica Madrilena is established through the merger of three small electric companies.

1942: Fuerzas Electricas del Noroeste (Fenosa) is established. 1970: Unión Electrica Madrilena changes its name to Unión Electrica.

1982: Unión Eléctrica and Fuerzas Eléctricas del Noroeste merge to form Unión Electrica Fenosa.

1998: Fenosa divides its generation and distribution facilities into two separate subsidiaries.

2000: The company attempts a takeover of the number four Spanish electric company, Hidrocantabrico, but is blocked by the Spanish government.

2001: Unión Electrica Fenosa changes its name to Unión Fenosa, S.A. as it enters into the production, transportation, and distribution of liquefied natural gas.

2002: Fenosa announces its intention to sell off half of its LNG subsidiary in order to pay down debt.

companies to compete against each other for consumer, corporate, and industrial customers.

As a result of the new legislation, Fenosa began restructuring its operations, creating a separate subsidiary for its generation operations. In 1998, Fenosa went a step further, forming a new company, Unión Fenosa Generacion (UFG) in partnership with the United Kingdom's National Power, which paid the equivalent of nearly EUR 600 million for a 25 percent stake in UFG. Fenosa, which had begun developing a new power station for Spain's Basque region, also began preparing to sell off its Airtel holding, as it built up a war chest of nearly EUR 2 billion to continue its investment and expansion drive.

The company stepped up its international expansion in the late 1990s with a series of purchases which made it a key figure in the utilities sector in a number of countries. Fenosa's investments included a stake in the Philippines' Meralco I in 1997 and Meralco II in 1999 as well as in Bolivia's TDE. Latin America in particular attracted Fenosa's attention, with the purchases of Mexico's Hermosillo and Panama's Edemet-Edechi in 1998, then Edenmorte-Edesur in the Dominican Republic, Deocsa-Deorasa in Guatemala, and GAP in Mexico in 1999. The company also moved into the United Kingdom, buying up smallish water and electricity provider Cambridge Water that same year.

Fenosa's Spanish operations suffered a setback in 2000, when the company launched a EUR 2.6 billion takeover of the country's number four electrical company, Hidrocatabrico, outbidding the United States' Texas Utilities. Yet the Spanish government, in a move to protect the competitiveness of the Spanish market, vetoed the purchase. The company's failure to expand in its domestic market encouraged it to step up its international purchases—by the end of 2000, Fenosa had picked up new operations in Colombia, Costa Rica, Nicaragua, and Uruguay, while boosting its presence in the Dominican Republic. In Mexico, meanwhile, the company won a contract to build its third electrical power generation plant, which, when completed, was expected to make the company the largest

private electricity producer in that country. The company also entered the eastern European market through the purchase of Moldova's Red Chisinau-Centro-Sur.

At this time, Fenosa was also preparing to enter a new market, that of the production, transportation, and distribution of liquid natural gas. The company scored its first success in that field with the award in 2000 of a contract from the Egyptian government to build a new natural gas liquefaction and export facility. Fenosa continued the expansion of its gas subsidiary, winning a contract to build regasification plants in Valentia and Ferrol, as well as its bid for a 20 percent share of the Algerian LNG pipeline. Fenosa also gained full control of its gas subsidiary when it bought back the 25 percent held by International Power, the successor company to National Power. At the end of 2001, the company began to supply industrial customers in Spain for the first time.

The diversified nature of Fenosa's operations led it to shorten its name to Unión Fenosa in 2001. The company continued to develop its expansion plans, particularly in Mexico, where it announced its intention to spend more than EUR 1 billion to build three new power plants in that country. Yet the company was also preparing a massive investment campaign to build up its position at home, with plans to earmark as much as two-thirds of its investment budget on the Spanish market. Fenosa was especially keen to expand its share of the natural gas market in Spain, setting itself the goal of a 25 percent share of the market by 2005. By the end of 2002, however, the company appeared forced to take a breather: with its debt nearing EUR 7 billion, Fenosa was said to be looking for a new strategic partner and offered to sell 50 percent of its Fenosa Gas subsidiary for some EUR 1.6 billion.

Principal Subsidiaries

Cambridge Water (U.K.); Deocsa (Guatemala) (85%); Deorsa (Guatemala) (85%); Disnorte (Nicaragua) (95%); Dissur (Nicaragua) (95%); Edechi (Panama) (51%); Edemet (Panama) (51%); Edesur (Dominican Republic) (50%); Edenorte (Dominican Republic) (50%); Electricaribe (Colombia) (69.2%); Electricity Transmission And Distribution Tde (Bolivia) (68.69%); Electrocosta (Colombia) (70.3%); Epsa (Colombia) (64.2%); Hermosillo (Mexico); Iberáfrica Power (Kenya) (71.67%); La Joya (Costa Rica); La Vega (Dominican Rep.); Naco-Nogales (Mexico); Omegaport (Ecuador) (75%); Palamara (Dominican Republic); Red Chisinau (Moldova); Red Centru (Moldova); Red Sud (Moldova); Tuxpan (Mexico).

Principal Competitors

Royal Dutch Petroleum Co; Electricité de France; E.ON AG; RWE AG; Duke Energy Corp.; American Electric Power Company Inc.; Tokyo Electric Power Company Inc.; State Power Corporation of China; TXU Corp.; Southern Co.; Hydro-Quebec; FirstEnergy Corp.; Edison International; AES Corp.; Dominion Resources Inc.; Mirant Corp.; Reliant Energy Inc.; Entergy Corp.; Alcatel; Centrais Eletricas Brasileiras S.A.; TRACTEBEL S.A.; E.ON Energie AG; FPL Group Inc. (FPL); TRACTEBEL SA Bruxelles; Edison SpA; RAG AG; National Grid Group PLC; Montedison SpA; Electrabel NV.

Further Reading

''Fenosa to Invest US$1.1 Billion in Mexican Electricity Sector,'' *Infolatina*, April 4, 2002.

Kremer, Victor, and Will Ainger, ''Unión Fenosa Focuses on Domestic Market,'' *Power, Finance and Risk*, February 25, 2002, p. 7.

''Spain's Fenosa Set To Become No. 1 Electricity Company In Mexico,'' *InfoLatina*, October 5, 2000.

''Unión Fenosa Alliance Sealed,'' *Wall Street Journal. Europe*, September 4, 1997, p. 4.

''Uruguay: Unión Fenosa Outlines Plans,''*South American Business Information*, January 5, 2000.

—M. L. Cohen

Variflex, Inc.

5152 North Commerce Avenue
Moorpark, California 93021
U.S.A.
Telephone: (805) 523-0322
Toll Free: (800) 327-0821
Fax: (805) 523-7384
Web site: http://www.variflex.com

Public Company
Incorporated: 1977
Employees: 93
Sales: $59.2 million
Stock Exchanges: NASDAQ
Ticker Symbol: VFLX
NAIC: 339920 Sporting and Athletic Good
    Manufacturing

Variflex, Inc. is a distributor and wholesaler of sporting goods, including in-line skates, recreational protective equipment, springless trampolines, portable canopies, skateboards, scooters, and safety helmets. Variflex designs and develops its products, but outsources production to contracted manufacturers. The company markets its products through independent sales representatives and marketing organizations, selling its brand name goods to national and regional mass merchandisers, sporting goods chains, mail-order businesses, and home improvement chains. Los Angeles investment firm REMY Capital Partners IV LP holds a 41 percent stake in Variflex.

Origins

Variflex began as a family affair, a sporting goods company founded by Raymond H. Losi and his son, Raymond H. Losi II, in California in August 1977. Upon Variflex's inception, Raymond Losi served as the company's board chairman and president. His 25-year-old son was given the task of heading the company's product development. Losi's wife, Barbara Losi, served as chief financial officer.

Variflex registered its greatest success as a designer and developer of in-line skates, which featured wheels mounted in a straight line, functioning much like the blade on an ice skate. The company did not manufacture its highly popular in-line skates, preferring instead to outsource the production of its products to independent contractors located in Taiwan, mainland China, and South Korea. The height of the company's success occurred during the mid-1990s, when in-line skate sales in the United States fanned excitement throughout the sporting goods industry. The company's peak years of financial performance occurred not long after Variflex completed its initial public offering (IPO) of stock, which also coincided with company's fall from its historic highs. Variflex's June 17, 1994 conversion to public ownership cast its performance in the spotlight, enabling industry observers to scrutinize the company's struggle to wean itself from a product that had once delivered rousing success.

The market for in-line skates in the United States peaked between late 1994 and early 1995, when industry-wide sales reached approximately 17 million units. Variflex, which derived nearly 90 percent of its business from marketing in-line skates, rode the crest of the popularity wave, enjoying substantial gains in revenue and net income. From $58 million in 1992, the company's annual sales soared to $100 million in 1995. The company's net income swelled during the three-year period as well, jumping from $1.6 million to nearly $7 million. Unfortunately for the Losi family, the financial figures posted in 1995 would be the last year-end totals it could look at with unmitigated enthusiasm. For the remainder of the 1990s, waning financial strength would become the norm, as the Losis struggled to add new revenue streams to replace the once powerful river of profits supplied by in-line skate sales.

To their credit, the Losis recognized the decline in in-line skates and began to diversify to offset the losses rather than remaining obdurately steadfast to in-line skates as the company's nearly exclusive source of financial sustenance. When in-line skate sales began to falter, Variflex was involved in marketing several other products, including skateboards and athletic protective equipment such as knee pads, elbow pads, wrist guards, and bicycle and recreational safety helmets. (As with in-line skates, Variflex did not manufacture any of the products it developed and marketed.) In 1994, the sales generated from marketing these secondary products accounted for 10 percent of Variflex's business. The Losis intended to augment these product offerings to invigorate sales and profits by delving into other areas of the sporting goods industry. At the time of the strategic switch, Raymond Losi, by then a septuagenarian, had added the title of chief executive officer in addition to his post as board chairman. His son Raymond Losi II, then in his mid-40s, continued to serve as the director of product development, having added the titles of president and chief operating officer in 1992. Barbara Losi relinquished her title as chief financial officer in 1991 but continued to serve as Variflex's secretary and as one of its directors when the diversification program began in 1995.

Search for New Business Begins in 1995

The first new addition to the company broke with Variflex tradition, moving it into manufacturing for the first time. In April 1995, the company formed a new subsidiary named Static Snowboards, Inc. to acquire an existing snowboard manufacturer named Plunkett Snowboards, Inc. Completed in May 1995, the acquisition cost Variflex the equivalent of $400,000, giving it a manufacturing facility in Huntington Beach in Southern California. The snowboards were manufactured under the Static brand name. Also in 1995, Variflex began marketing Scoot Skates, which were skateboards with an upright handle that replicated the experience of riding a scooter.

The financial figures released in July 1996 for the previous fiscal year delivered the first indication of a company on decline. From $100 million the year before, sales plummeted 28 percent to $72 million. The company's in-line skate product line, comprising 30 models that retailed for between $29 and $169, suffered a 31 percent decline in revenue, as sales dropped by 1.2 million units to 2.6 million units. The decline in in-line skate sales was compounded by losses suffered by the company's other product lines, including a 32 percent drop in athletic protective equipment sales and a 51 percent decrease in safety helmet sales. Skateboard sales represented the one area of financial growth for the company, as sales leaped 300 percent to $7.3 million, but this surge was not enough to offset the other losses. For the year, the company's net income shriveled from $6.9 million to $564,000.

Searching to remedy its financial woes, Variflex turned to its nascent snowboard manufacturing business. In September 1996, the company announced a joint manufacturing agreement with Barfoot Snoboards, one of the first companies to produce snowboards. Under the terms of the agreement, Variflex, through its subsidiary Static Snowboards, agreed to manufac-

ture, market, and distribute all Barfoot snowboards for an initial one-year term. The agreement with Barfoot was not enough, however, to compensate for further distressing financial news. When the next annual financial figures were released in July 1997, a net loss of $1.8 million triggered alarms at the company's Moorpark, California, headquarters. Hobbled by declining in-line skate sales, which led to a drop in annual sales to $51 million, the company exited the upper end of this market.

Several months after the results for 1997 were announced, help arrived in the form of an investment partner. In November 1997, a Los Angeles investment firm named REMY Capital Partners IV LP acquired 28 percent of Variflex, purchasing the stock from Raymond Losi, who stepped aside as Variflex's board chairman, remaining a director of the company. Losi's son, Raymond Losi II, was elected chief executive officer, while Mark S. Siegel, a REMY executive, assumed the post of board chairman. Losi II, who controlled 22 percent of Variflex stock, welcomed the arrival of REMY, remarking in a December 2, 1997 interview with the *Los Angeles Times:* "We are extremely pleased that REMY has recognized the inherent value in Variflex. We believe that REMY's knowledge of the consumer products market and their financial expertise, coupled with Variflex's existing strengths, will enable us to move forward and take advantage of the growth opportunities in this industry."

Late 1990s Diversification

In the wake of the REMY investment and the subsequent boardroom shakeup, Variflex turned to the task of developing new products. Two new additions to the company's stable of products were a line of safety helmets featuring textured, three-dimensional graphics, which debuted at roughly the same time REMY purchased its stake in Variflex, and a more promising product called Quik-Shade. Marketed as an instant canopy that could be erected in less than a minute, Quik-Shade was introduced in the spring of 1997, designated by the company as a principal product. By the end of 1997, 45,000 units of Quik-Shade canopies were sold, accounting for 1 percent of Variflex's total sales. In 1998, to accelerate the growth of the Quik-Shade line, Variflex doubled the distribution network established for the sale of the portable canopies, which led to an increase in revenue that represented 8 percent of total sales in 1998.

In a November 3, 1998 interview with the *Los Angeles Times,* chairman Siegel attempted to quell the reaction to the company's financial results for fiscal 1998. "This has been a year of rebuilding for Variflex," he said, "as we focused on taking the steps we believe necessary to position the company for long-term growth and profitability." The totals were discouraging, reflective of a worrisome pattern that had begun more than two years earlier. For the year, the company lost $3.5 million on sales of $43.1 million. Industry-wide sales of in-line skates were expected to fall to 9.5 million units in 1998, far below the 17 million units sold three years earlier. Variflex management believed the unit volume sales would plateau at 1998 levels, and remain there for the next several years, but the prospect that sales would cease their downward slide offered little solace. Despite the efforts to find additional revenue streams, the company's annual sales totals had plunged from $100 million in 1995 to $43 million during the following three-year period.

At this point in the company's struggles, another change in senior management was made. In September 1998, Steven L. Muellner was named president of the company, replacing Losi II, who continued to serve as chief executive officer. Under the new leadership combination of Siegel, Losi II, and Muellner, the company added another link to its chain of new product introductions, moving from snowboards to portable canopies to trampolines. In December 1998, Variflex announced that it was introducing a springless trampoline. The company had signed an exclusive license agreement with Product Resource and Development, which had a patent pending on a springless trampoline system that used a series of elastic straps to connect the mat to the frame. Purported to provide increased bounce, lift, and safety, the springless trampoline was slated for limited distribution before Christmas, with full-scale distribution scheduled for the first quarter of 1999. Retailing for between $200 and $229, the trampoline, called Ultra-Flex, was available initially in a 14-foot model, with smaller sizes planned for later introduction.

For the first time in years, the announcement of annual financial totals for 1999 could be greeted with a modicum of satisfaction. Although revenues continued to shrink, falling from $43 million to $37 million, the pattern of annual net losses was interrupted. Variflex earned $803,000 for the year, but the relief proved only temporary. The following year the company registered a net loss of $2 million as it became embroiled in a patent infringement lawsuit and felt the sting of a product recall. In October 2000, Variflex announced it was voluntarily recalling 150,000 of its X-Games safety helmets. Manufactured by a third-party contractor, the X-Games helmets did not comply with federal safety standards. Variflex also spent a considerable amount of money to settle a lawsuit filed by International E-Z Up, which claimed that the portable canopies marketed by Variflex infringed on E-Z Up's patent.

As Variflex prepared for its 25th anniversary and the years beyond, its financial condition began to improve. Sales increased to $59 million as profits climbed, reaching $1.3 million in 2001. Variflex completed its helmet recall in 2001, concurrent with the expansion of its international marketing efforts. In 1987, the company had established a subsidiary named Oketa Ltd., through which Variflex conducted sales and shipping agreements with international customers. In 2001, the company closed Oketa, opting instead to conduct its international expansion directly through Variflex.

Principal Subsidiaries

Static Snowboards, Inc.

Principal Competitors

Bell Sports Corp.; K2 Inc.; Rollerblade, Inc.

Further Reading

"Firm Hopes for Jump-Start; Variflex Sees Sales in New Trampoline," *Daily News,* December 8, 1998, p. B2.

"Lawsuit Lowers Variflex Profits," *Daily News,* October 31, 2000, p. B1.

McNary, Dave, "Variflex Patents Canopy Product," *Daily News,* January 14, 1998, p. B2.

Murphy, Barbara, "Variflex Suffers Losses, Continues to Rebuild," *Los Angeles Times,* November 3, 1998, p. 1.

——, "Variflex, Inc. to Manufacture, Distribute Barfoot Snowboards for 1 Year," *Los Angeles Times,* September 3, 1996, p. 4.

——, "Skateboard Maker Variflex Predicts Profit Resurgence," *Los Angeles Times,* June 18, 1996, p. 4.

"Quarterly Earnings Fall at Skate Manufacturer," *Daily News,* June 1, 1996, p. B1.

"Sports Gear Maker Seeks Helmet Recall," *Daily News,* October 7, 2000, p. B1.

Rivero, Enrique, "Stock Buy-In Brings Overhaul to Variflex," *Daily News,* November 20, 1997, p. B1.

—Jeffrey L. Covell

Vermont Pure Holdings, Ltd.

Catamount Industrial Park, Route 66
Randolph, Vermont 05060
U.S.A.
Telephone: (802) 728-3600
Toll Free: (800) 939-9119
Fax: (802) 728-4614
Web site: http://www.vermontpure.com

Public Company
Incorporated: 1990
Employees: 384
Sales: $67.17 million (2001)
Stock Exchanges: American
Ticker Symbol: VPS
NAIC: 422490 Other Grocery and Related Product
    Wholesalers; 339999 All Other Miscellaneous
    Manufacturing; 551112 Offices of Other Holding
    Companies

Vermont Pure Holdings, Ltd. (VPH) is the largest independent bottled water company in the United States, marketing its bottled water under the brands Vermont Pure Natural Spring Water, Hidden Spring, and Crystal Rock. VPH sells its branded and private label water to retail outlets but derives the majority of its sales from distributing water and coffee to home and office customers. The company's products are sold in northeastern, mid-Atlantic, and midwestern states. VHP ranks as the eighth-largest bottled water company in the United States and as the fourth-largest in the home and office sector. The company owns two springs, located in Randolph and Tinmouth, Vermont, that serve as its primary sources of water.

Origins

After incorporating as a Delaware corporation in 1990, VPH acquired a bottled water company named Vermont's Hidden Spring, Inc. The purchase was completed in July 1991, giving VPH control over one spring on 1.7 acres of land, a 10,000-square-foot office facility and bottling plant, and the rights to a

brand marketed as Vermont's Hidden Spring. The acquisition positioned the company as a competitor in the non-sparkling bottled water market, a sector responsible for more than 90 percent of all bottled water sales and, as it would happen, the source of 99 percent of the industry's growth during the 1990s. Vermont's Hidden Spring was not the brand that marked the company's entry into the bottled water market, however. Immediately after the acquisition of the Randolph, Vermont-based company, VPH developed a new brand marketed under the label Vermont Pure Natural Spring Water.

Positioned as a premium brand for the general consumer market, Vermont Pure was distributed to supermarkets, convenience stores, and a variety of retail outlets, as well as to home and office markets. From the start, VPH distributed Vermont Pure to locations in the New England, New York, New Jersey, and mid-Atlantic regions.

For a company that celebrated its tenth anniversary as a nearly $70-million-in-sales concern, growth was slow to come for VPH, its annual sales volume failing to reach $10 million in sales by its fifth anniversary. The energetic growth of the company during the latter half of the 1990s was largely attributable to a strategy adopted by VPH's leadership during the mid-1990s, not long after Timothy Fallon assumed control over operations. A vice-president for the New York subsidiary of the Pepsi Cola Bottling Company throughout much of the 1980s, Fallon held a similar post at Canada Dry USA between 1989 and 1991, before being named the senior vice-president of sales and marketing for Cadbury Beverages, Inc., the owner of Canada Dry USA. Fallon joined VPH after his two-year stint at Cadbury Beverages, becoming president and chief executive officer of the bottled water company in November 1994.

Acquisition Campaign Begins in 1996

The strategy developed by Fallon and his management team drew its impetus from a desire for independence. Large companies controlled the distribution of VPH's bottled water, putting the small company at the mercy of others, a dependence Fallon sought to reduce. The solution was to emphasize the company's involvement in servicing home and office customers, a strategy

Company Perspectives:

Vermont Pure Holdings, Ltd. believes that consumers perceive bottled water as a healthy and refreshing beverage alternative to beer, liquor, wine, soft drinks, coffee, and tea. The Company anticipates that sales of bottled water will continue to grow as consumers focus on health and fitness, alcohol moderation, and the avoidance of both caffeine and sodium. Bottled water has become a mainstream beverage as the centerpiece of consumers' healthy living lifestyles. In addition, the Company believes that the development and continued growth of the bottled water industry since the early 1980s reflects growing public awareness of the potential contamination and unreliability of municipal water supplies.

put to action in 1996, one year after Fallon re-introduced the Vermont's Hidden Spring brand. The home and office market offered other advantages as well, including higher gross margins than the traditional retail market, roughly 70 percent higher. The home and office market was also less vulnerable to seasonal influences. At the time, Fallon began re-orienting VPH's business focus. Previously, the company had derived 90 percent of its sales from retail business, a percentage that would drop markedly as Fallon embarked on an acquisition campaign and shaped VPH into a different type of company.

Fallon pursued his objective primarily by acquiring distribution businesses involved in serving the home and office markets, a strategy that also broadened VPH's geographic base. The acquisition spree began May 1996, when Vermont Pure Springs, Inc., a wholly owned subsidiary of VPH, acquired certain assets belonging to Happy Ice Corp., a Buffalo, New York-based company serving 18 counties in Buffalo, Syracuse, and Rochester. The assets acquired by VPH were part of Happy Ice Corp.'s spring water division and included property used to bottle, sell, and distribute spring water in three and five gallon bottles, as well as the rental of water coolers and coffee dispensers and coffee supplies for home and office customers. Through Vermont Pure Springs, VPH paid approximately $1.6 million for the Happy Ice assets.

Less than a year later, in March 1997, the company struck again, acquiring home and office assets belonging to Greatwater Refreshment Services, Inc., which bolstered VPH's presence in upstate New York. In July 1997, Fallon purchased A.M. Fridays, Inc., a home and office distributor of bottled water, coffee, and vending services, with warehouse and distribution facilities located in Manchester, New Hampshire, and Shelton, Connecticut. The following month, VPH acquired a bottled water and coffee distributor named Excelsior Springs Water Company. Based in Saratoga, New York, Excelsior Springs drew the bulk of its business from home and commercial accounts in Albany, New York, but also conducted business in parts of southern Vermont and western Massachusetts. Before the end of the year, Fallon completed one more acquisition, purchasing the worldwide trademark and distribution rights for AKVA Icelandic bottled spring water.

By the end of 1997, the effect of the ongoing acquisition campaign was evident in the company's financial growth. From

$8.5 million in 1995, annual sales more than doubled in 1997, swelling to $17.6 million. Equally important to Fallon, considerable gains were being made in the growth of the company's home and office distribution business. Fallon showed no signs of slackening his pace in 1998, resuming his acquisitive ways in January with the purchase of certain assets of Vermont Coffee Time, Inc., a $1.5 million-in-sales company based in Williston, Vermont. Vermont Coffee distributed Green Mountain Coffee and spring water to homes and offices in Vermont, New Hampshire, and upstate New York. In May 1998, the company acquired the home and office delivery assets of Perrier Group of America. VPH's acquisition was limited to Perrier Group's business in Albany, New York, where the company's 4,000 customers accounted for roughly $2 million of business in 1997. Before the end of the year, Fallon acquired four additional home and office businesses. Combined, the four small firms generated $500,000 in annual revenue.

By the end of 1998, VPH was generating nearly $30 million in sales, its financial growth fueled by Fallon's acquisition campaign and by the growth of the bottled water industry. In looking at studies prepared by the Beverage Marketing Corporation, Fallon, who was named chairman in 1998, found further incentive to pursue expansion. The industry was recording sustained, robust growth, underpinned by growing public suspicion about municipal water supplies and the possible presence of bacterial contamination, lead, and carcinogenic chemicals caused by over-chlorination. An increasingly health-conscious public turned to the bottled water industry as an alternative, causing total bottled water consumption to more than quadruple between 1980 and 1998. On an individual basis, annual consumption increased from 2.8 gallons in 1980 to 13.9 gallons in 1998, by which time the industry was generating $4.3 billion in sales.

The historical growth of the industry and the equally promising growth projections for bottled water consumption encouraged Fallon to press ahead with expansion. The company's acquisition campaign began in 1999 with the purchase of Adirondack Coffee Services, Inc., a $1.5-million-in-sales company with home and office accounts in Albany, New York, and Rutland, Vermont. An additional $800,000 in annual revenue was realized before the end of the year with the acquisition of eight small companies that served home and office customers. The company's next move would represent the defining moment in its history of growth. During VPH's tenth anniversary year, the company proposed a merger with Crystal Rock Water Co., a business combination that would nearly double the size of VHP and make it the eighth-largest bottled water company in the nation.

1998 Merger with Crystal Rock

When the merger was announced, Crystal Rock was stewarded by the third generation of a family named Baker. The company was founded in 1914 by Henry Baker, Sr., who used a horse-drawn wagon to deliver water in half-gallon bottles to customers in Stamford, Connecticut. Baker drew the majority of his business from neighborhoods occupied by European immigrants, creating a lasting enterprise that would employ his family for the rest of the century. Baker's son, Henry Baker, Jr., joined the company in 1947 and became its president in 1965. Under his leadership, growth was pursued aggressively. A bottling plant was built in Stamford to aid in Baker's expansion in the office coffee and refreshment services market. During the mid-1970s, Baker was joined by his two sons, Peter and Jack. Company headquarters were moved to Watertown, Connecticut, in 1988, when a new office building and a 72,000-square-foot bottling facility were constructed. Peter and Jack Baker were named co-presidents in 1993.

The effect of the October 2000 merger was profound, giving VPH ownership of the largest provider of office refreshment services in Connecticut. The union of the oldest bottled water company in Connecticut and Vermont's fast-rising, relatively young, home and office refreshment services provider created the country's fourth-largest company in the home and office market, with projected combined revenues of more than $60 million. After the merger, VHP drew 75 percent of its sales from home and office business, up considerably from the 10 percent derived from such business before Fallon initiated his acquisition campaign in 1996. Fallon was enthused, remarking in the December 2000 issue of *The Vermont Business Magazine*, "The combined strengths of Vermont Pure and Crystal Rock position us to take advantage of the anticipated continued boom in the bottled water industry. In the next decade," he continued, "we expect U.S. bottled water consumption to go the way of Europe, where sales of bottled water lead all beverage categories."

The Baker family received the equivalent of $64.2 million to join VPH's fold. Both Henry, Jr. and Peter Baker continued their tenure in the bottled water industry. Henry Baker was named chairman emeritus of VHP, while Peter Baker was named president of the company, heading its home and office division. Fallon retained his titles as chief executive officer and chairman, posts from which he would continue to orchestrate VPH's acquisition campaign, with the Bakers at his side.

After achieving considerable strides in the development of VPH's home and office business, Fallon turned his attention to bolstering the company's retail business. In March 2001, he signed an agreement with Hannaford Bros. Co. to supply the supermarket chain with private label bottled water. Based in

Scarborough, Maine, Hannaford Bros. operated 108 stores in Maine, New Hampshire, Vermont, Massachusetts, and New York. The day after the agreement with Hannaford Bros. was signed, Fallon signed another supply agreement, inking a deal with the retail division of Ahold USA, the operator of five retail companies in the eastern part of United States. According to the terms of the multi-year agreement, VHP agreed to supply bottled spring water to supermarkets operating under the banners Tops Markets, Stop & Shop, and Giant Food Stores, Inc. In September 2001, the company's retail business received an additional boost with another signed agreement, one that would significantly increase the geographic scope of VPH. The company entered into a distribution agreement with The Royal Crown Bottling Company of Chicago that ensured the distribution Vermont Pure bottled water to retail outlets in Chicago, Richmond and Norfolk, Virginia, and Columbus, Georgia.

After strengthening the company's position in the retail sector, Fallon returned to expanding VPH's home and office business. In October 2001, VHP acquired Norwalk, Connecticut-based Iceberg Springs Water Company. Iceberg, with $3 million in annual sales, served roughly 4,500 home and office customers in Connecticut and New York. On the heels of this acquisition, the company announced its financial results for 2001, the first full year reflecting the impact of the Crystal Rock merger. The results were record totals, including $67 million posted in sales and a 57 percent increase in net income to $1.1 million. With these figures providing encouragement to keep expanding, Fallon pressed ahead, hoping bottled water sales would "go the way of Europe."

Principal Subsidiaries

Vermont Pure Springs, Inc.; Crystal Rock Water Co.

Principal Competitors

Nestlé S.A.; Suntory Limited; The Perrier Group of America, Inc.

Further Reading

Hedbor, Eloise Roberts, "Familiar Names Come from the Upper Valley," *The Vermont Business Magazine*, December 2000, p. 68.
"Pure Agreement," *Beverage World*, October 15, 1998, p. 32.
"Vermont Pure Holdings Acquires Iceberg Springs," *The Vermont Business Magazine*, November 2001, p. 65.
"Vermont Pure Holdings," *Private Label Buyer*, June 2002, p. 10.
"Vermont Pure May Get Siphoned Off," *Business Week*, November 12, 2001, p. 163.

—Jeffrey L. Covell

INDEX TO COMPANIES

Index to Companies

Listings in this index are arranged in alphabetical order under the company name. Company names beginning with a letter or proper name such as Eli Lilly & Co. will be found under the first letter of the company name. Definite articles (The, Le, La) are ignored for alphabetical purposes as are forms of incorporation that precede the company name (AB, NV). Company names printed in bold type have full, historical essays on the page numbers appearing in bold. Updates to entries that appeared in earlier volumes are signified by the notation **(upd.)**. Company names in light type are references within an essay to that company, not full historical essays. This index is cumulative with volume numbers printed in bold type.

Almanij NV, 44 15–18. *See also* Algemeene Maatschappij voor Nijverheidskrediet.

Almay, Inc., III 54

Almeida Banking House. *See* Banco Bradesco S.A.

Almours Security Co., IV 311; 19 266

Almys, 24 461

Aloe Vera of America, 17 187

Aloha Airlines, Incorporated, I 97; 9 271–72; 21 142; 22 251; 24 20–22

ALP. *See* Associated London Properties.

Alp Sport Sandals, 22 173

Alpen-Elektrowerke Aktiengesellschaft, IV 230

Alpex Computer Corp., III 157

Alpex, S.A. de C.V., 19 12

Alpha Beta Co., II 605, 625, 653; 17 559

Alpha Engineering Group, Inc., 16 259–60

Alpha Healthcare Ltd., 25 455

Alpha Processor Inc., 41 349

Alpha Technical Systems, 19 279

Alphaform, 40 214–15

Alphanumeric Publication Systems, Inc., 26 518

Alpharma Inc., 35 22–26 (upd.)

Alphonse Allard Inc., II 652; 51 303

Alpina Versicherungs-Aktiengesellschaft, III 412

Alpine, IV 234

Alpine Electronics, Inc., II 5; 13 30–31

Alpine Lace Brands, Inc., 18 14–16

Alpine Securities Corporation, 22 5

Alpre, 19 192

Alps Electric Co., Ltd., II 5–6; 13 30; 44 19–21 (upd.)

Alric Packing, II 466

Alsen-Breitenbury, III 702

ALSO Holding AG, 29 419, 422

Alsons Corp., III 571; 20 362

Alsthom, II 12

Alsthom-Atlantique, 9 9

Alta Dena, 25 83, 85

Alta Electric Company, 25 15

Alta Gold Co., IV 76

ALTA Health Strategies, Inc., 11 113

Alta Holidays Ltd., I 95

Alta Vista Company, 50 228

Altamil Corp., IV 137

Altana AG, 23 498

AltaSteel Ltd., 51 352

AltaVista Company, 43 11–13

Alte Leipziger, III 242

Altec Electronics, I 489–90

ALTEC International, 21 107–09

Altenburg & Gooding, 22 428

Altera Corporation, 18 17–20; 43 14–18 (upd.); 47 384

Alternate Postal Delivery, 6 14

Alternative Living Services. *See* Alterra Healthcare Corporation.

Alternative Youth Services, Inc., 29 399–400

Alterra Healthcare Corporation, 42 3–5

Altex, 19 192–93

Althoff KG, V 101

Althouse Chemical Company, 9 153

Althus Corp., I 361

Altman Weil Pensa, 29 237

Alton & Eastern Railroad Company, 6 504

Alton Box Board Co., IV 295; 19 225

Altos Computer Systems, 6 279; 10 362

Altos Hornos de México, S.A. de C.V., 13 144; 19 220; 39 188; 42 6–8

Altran Technologies, 51 15–18

Altron Incorporated, 20 8–10

Altura Energy Ltd., 41 359

Aluar. *See* Aluminios Argentinos.

Aluma Systems Corp., 9 512; 22 14

Alumax Inc., I 508; III 758; IV 18–19; 8 505–06; 22 286

Alumina Partners of Jamaica, IV 123

Aluminate Sales Corp, I 373

Aluminio de Galicia, IV 174

Aluminios Argentinos, 26 433

Aluminium Co. of London, IV 69

L'Aluminium Francais, IV 173

Aluminium Ltd., IV 9–11, 14, 153

Aluminium-Oxid Stade GmbH, IV 231

Aluminium Plant and Vessel Co., III 419

Aluminum Can Co., I 607

Aluminum Company of America, I 373, 599; II 315, 402, 422; III 490–91, 613; IV 9–12, 14–16, 56, 59, 121–22, 131, 173, 703; 6 39; 12 346; 19 240, 292; 20 11–14 (upd.); 22 455; 42 438

Aluminum Company of Canada Ltd., II 345; IV 10–12, 154

Aluminum Cooking Utensil Co., IV 14

Aluminum Forge Co., IV 137

Aluminum Norf GmbH, IV 231

Aluminum of Korea, III 516

Aluminum Rolling Mills, 17 280

Aluminum Sales Corporation, 12 346

Aluminum Seating Corp., I 201

Alun Cathcart, 6 357

Alup-Kompressoren Pressorun, III 570; 20 361

Alupak, A.G., 12 377

Alusaf, IV 92

Alusuisse Lonza Group Ltd., IV 12; 31 11

Alva Jams Pty., I 437

Alvic Group, 20 363

Alvis Plc, 47 7–9

Alyeska Pipeline Service Co., IV 522, 571; 14 542; 24 521; 40 356

Alyeska Seafoods Co., II 578

ALZA Corporation, 10 53–55; 36 36–39 (upd.); 40 11; 41 200–01

Alzwerke GmbH, IV 230

AM Acquisition Inc., 8 559–60

AM Cosmetics, Inc., 31 89

Am-Par Records, II 129

Am-Safe, Inc., 16 357

AM-TEX Corp., Inc., 12 443

Amagasaki Co., I 492; 24 325

Amagasaki Spinners Co., V 387

Amagasaki Steel Co., Ltd., IV 130

Amalgamaize Co., 14 18

Amalgamated Chemicals, Ltd., IV 401

Amalgamated Dental International, 10 271–72

Amalgamated Distilled Products, II 609

Amalgamated Press, IV 666; 7 244, 342; 17 397

Amalgamated Roadstone Corp., III 752; 28 449

Amalgamated Sugar Co., 14 18; 19 467–68

Amalgamated Weatherware, IV 696

Amana Refrigeration Company, II 86; 11 413; 18 226; 38 374; 42 159

Amaray International Corporation, 12 264

Amarillo Gas Company. *See* Atmos Energy Corporation.

Amarillo Railcar Services, 6 580

Amarin Plastics, IV 290

Amax Gold, 36 316

AMAX Inc., I 508; III 687; IV 17–19, 46, 139, 171, 239, 387; 6 148; 12 244; 22 106, 286

Amazon.com, Inc., 25 17–19

Amazôna Mineracao SA, IV 56

AMB Generali Holding AG, 51 19–23

Ambac Industries, I 85

AmBase Corp., III 264

Amber's Stores, Inc., 17 360

Amberg Hospach AG, 49 436

Amblin Entertainment, 21 23–27; 33 431

AMBRA, Inc., 48 209

Ambrose Shardlow, III 494

AMC Entertainment Inc., 12 12–14; 14 87; 21 362; 23 126; 35 27–29 (upd.)

AMCA International Corporation, 7 513; 8 545; 10 329; 23 299

AMCC. *See* Applied Micro Circuits Corporation.

Amcell. *See* American Cellular Network.

Amchem Products Inc., I 666

AMCO, Inc., 13 159

Amcor Limited, IV 248–50; 19 13–16 (upd.)

AMCORE Financial Inc., 44 22–26

Amcraft Building Products Co., Inc., 22 15

AMD. *See* Advanced Micro Devices, Inc.

Amdahl Corporation, III 109–11, 140; 6 272; 12 238; 13 202; 14 13–16 (upd.); 16 194, 225–26; 22 293; 25 87; 40 20–25 (upd.); 42 147. *See also* Fujitsu Limited.

Amdocs Ltd., 47 10–12

AME Finanziaria, IV 587; 19 19

AMEC plc, I 568; 36 322; 49 65

Amedco, 6 295

Amer Group plc, 24 530; 41 14–16

Amer Sport, 22 202

Amerada Hess Corporation, IV 365–67, 400, 454, 522, 571, 658; 11 353; 21 28–31 (upd.); 24 521

Amerco, 6 351–52

AmerGen Energy LLC, 49 65, 67

Ameri-Kart Corp., 19 277, 279

America Japan Sheet Glass Co., III 714

America Latina Companhia de Seguros, III 289

America Online, Inc., 10 56–58, 237; 13 147; 15 54, 265, 321; 18 24; 19 41; 22 52, 519, 522; 26 16–20 (upd.); 27 20, 106, 301, 430, 517–18; 29 143, 227; 32 163; 33 254; 34 361; 35 304, 306; 38 269–71; 49 311–12. *See also* CompuServe Interactive Services, Inc.

America Publishing Company, 18 213

America Today, 13 545

America Unplugged, 18 77

America West Airlines, 6 72–74, 121

America West Express, 32 334

America West Holdings Corporation, 34 22–26 (upd.)

America's Favorite Chicken Company, Inc., 7 26–28. *See also* AFC Enterprises, Inc.

American & Efird, Inc., 12 501; 23 260

American Acquisitions, Inc., 49 279

American Agricultural Chemical Co., IV 401

American Air Conditioning, 25 15

American Air Filter, 26 3–4

American Airlines, I 30–31, 48, 71, 89–91, 97, 106, 115, 118, 124–26, 130, 132, 512, 530; III 102; 6 60, 81, 75–77 (upd.), 121, 129–31; 9 271–72; 10 163;

First National Bank of Raleigh, **II** 336

First National Bank of Salt Lake, **11** 118

First National Bank of Seattle, **8** 469–70

First National Bank of York, **II** 317

First National Bankshares, Inc., **21** 524

First National Boston Corp., **II** 208

First National Casualty Co., **III** 203

First National City Bank, **9** 124; **16** 13

First National City Bank of New York, **II** 254; **9** 124

First National City Corp., **III** 220–21

First National Holding Corporation, **16** 522

First National Insurance Co., **III** 352

First National Life Insurance Co., **III** 218

First National Supermarkets, Inc., **II** 641–42; **9** 452

First Nations Gaming, Ltd., **44** 334

First Nationwide Bank, **8** 30; **14** 191–93

First Nationwide Financial Corp., **I** 167; **11** 139

First Nationwide Holdings Inc., **28** 246

First New England Bankshares Corp., **13** 467

First Nitrogen, Inc., **8** 184

First Nuclear Corporation, **49** 411

First of America Bank Corporation, **8** 187–89

First of America Bank-Monroe, **9** 476

First of Boston, **II** 402–03

First Omni Bank NA, **16** 14; **18** 518; **43** 8

First Options of Chicago, Inc., **51** 148

First Pacific Company Limited, **18** 180–82

First Penn-Pacific Life Insurance Co., **III** 276

First Physician Care, Inc., **36** 367

First Pick Stores, **12** 458

First Railroad and Banking Company, **11** 111

First Republic Bank of Texas, **II** 336

First Republic Corp., **III** 383; **14** 483

First RepublicBank Corporation, **II** 337; **10** 425–26

First Savings and Loan, **10** 339

First Seattle Dexter Horton National Bank, **8** 470

First Security Bank of Missoula, **35** 197–99

First Security Corporation, **11** 117–19; **38** 491

First Signature Bank and Trust Co., **III** 268

First Sport Ltd., **39** 60

1st State Bank & Trust, **9** 474

First State Bank Southwest Indiana, **41** 178–79

First SunAmerican Life Insurance Company, **11** 482

First Team Sports, Inc., **15** 396–97; **22** 202–04

First Tennessee National Corporation, **11** 120–21; **48** 176–79 (upd.)

First Texas Pharmaceuticals, **I** 678

First Trust and Savings Bank, **II** 284

First Trust Bank, **16** 14

First Union Corporation, **10** 298–300; **24** 482; **37** 148. See also Wachovia Corporation.

First Union Trust and Savings Bank, **II** 284–85; **11** 126; **22** 52

First United Financial Services Inc., **II** 286

First USA, Inc., **11** 122–24

First USA Paymentech, **24** 393

First Virginia Banks, Inc., **11** 125–26

First Westchester National Bank of New Rochelle, **II** 236

First Western Bank and Trust Co., **II** 289

First Women's Bank of New York, **23** 3

First Worth Corporation, **19** 232

The First Years Inc., **46** 191–94

FirstAir Inc., **48** 113

Firstamerica Bancorporation, **II** 288–89

Firstar Corporation, **11** 127–29; **33** 152–55 (upd.)

FirstBancorp., **13** 467

FirstGroup plc, **38** 321

FirstMiss, Inc., **8** 185

FirstPage USA Inc., **41** 265

Firth Carpet, **19** 275

Fischbach & Moore, **III** 535

Fischbach Corp., **III** 198; **8** 536–37

FISCOT, **10** 337

Fiserv Inc., **11** 130–32; **33** 156–60 (upd.)

Fisher & Company, **9** 16

Fisher Body Company, **I** 171; **10** 325

Fisher Broadcasting Co., **15** 164

Fisher-Camuto Corp., **14** 441

Fisher Companies, Inc., **15** 164–66

Fisher Controls International, Inc., **13** 224–26; **15** 405, 407; **29** 330; **46** 171

Fisher Foods, Inc., **II** 602; **9** 451, 452; **13** 237; **41** 11, 13

Fisher Marine, **III** 444; **22** 116

Fisher Nut, **14** 275

Fisher-Price Inc., **II** 559–60; **12** 167–69, 410–11; **13** 317; **25** 314, 380; **32** 190–94 (upd.); **34** 365

Fisher Scientific International Inc., **III** 511–12; **24** 162–66; **25** 260

Fishers Agricultural Holdings, **II** 466

Fishers Nutrition, **II** 466

Fishers Seed and Grain, **II** 466

Fishery Department of Tamura Kisen Co., **II** 552

Fisk Telephone Systems, **6** 313

Fiskars Corporation, **33** 161–64

Fiskeby Board AB, **48** 344

Fisons plc, **9** 224–27; **23** 194–97 (upd.)

Fitch IBCA Inc., **37** 143, 145

Fitch Lovell PLC, **13** 103

Fitchburg Daily News Co., **IV** 581

Fitchburg Gas and Electric Light, **37** 406

Fitchell and Sachs, **III** 495

Fitel, **III** 491

Fitzsimmons Stores Inc., **16** 452

Fitzwilton Public Limited Company, **12** 529; **34** 496

Five Bros. Inc., **19** 456

Five Star Entertainment Inc., **28** 241

546274 Alberta Ltd., **48** 97

FKM Advertising, **27** 280

FL Industries Holdings, Inc., **11** 516

Flachglass A.G., **II** 474

Flagship Resources, **22** 495

Flagstar Companies, Inc., **10** 301–03; **29** 150. See also Advantica Restaurant Group, Inc.

Flair Corporation, **18** 467

Flair Fold, **25** 11

Flanagan McAdam Resources Inc., **IV** 76

Flapdoodles, **15** 291

Flashes Publishers, Inc., **36** 341

Flatbush Gas Co., **6** 455–56

Flatiron Mandolin Company, **16** 239

Flatow, Moore, Bryan, and Fairburn, **21** 33

Flavors Holdings Inc., **38** 294

Fleck Controls, Inc., **26** 361, 363

Fleer Corporation, **10** 402; **13** 519; **15** 167–69; **19** 386; **34** 447; **37** 295

Fleet Aerospace Corporation. See Magellan Aerospace Corporation.

Fleet Call, Inc., **10** 431–32

Fleet Financial Group, Inc., **IV** 687; **9** 228–30; **12** 31; **13** 468; **18** 535; **38** 13, 393

Fleet Holdings, **28** 503

FleetBoston Financial Corporation, **36** 206–14 (upd.)

Fleetway, **7** 244

Fleetwood Enterprises, Inc., **III** 484–85; **13** 155; **17** 83; **21** 153; **22** 205–08 (upd.); **33** 399

Fleischmann Co., **II** 544; **7** 367

Fleischmann Malting Co., **I** 420–21; **11** 22

Fleming Chinese Restaurants Inc., **37** 297

Fleming Companies, Inc., **II** 624–25, 671; **7** 450; **12** 107, 125; **13** 335–37; **17** 178–81 (upd.); **18** 506–07; **23** 407; **24** 529; **26** 449; **28** 152, 154; **31** 25; **34** 198; **50** 457

Fleming Foodservice, **26** 504

Fleming Machine Co., **III** 435

Fleming-Wilson Co., **II** 624

Fletcher Challenge Ltd., **III** 687; **IV** 250, 278–80; **19** 153–57 (upd.); **25** 12

Fleury Michon S.A., **39** 159–61

Fleuve Noir, **IV** 614

Flex Elektrowerkzeuge GmbH, **26** 363

Flex Interim, **16** 421; **43** 308

Flex-O-Lite, **14** 325

Flexi-Van Corporations, **II** 492; **20** 118

Flexible Packaging, **I** 605

Flexsteel Industries Inc., **15** 170–72; **41** 159–62 (upd.)

Flextronics International Ltd., **12** 451; **38** 186–89

Flexys, **16** 462

FLGI Holding Company, **10** 321

Flick Industrial Group, **II** 280, 283; **III** 692–95

Flight One Logistics, Inc., **22** 311

Flight Refuelling Limited. See Cobham plc.

Flight Transportation Co., **II** 408

FlightSafety International, Inc., **9** 231–33; **29** 189–92 (upd.)

Flint and Walling Water Systems, **III** 570; **20** 362

Flint Eaton & Co., **I** 627

Flint Ink Corporation, **13** 227–29; **41** 163–66 (upd.)

Flip Chip Technologies, LLC, **33** 248

Florafax International, Inc., **37** 162

Floral City Furniture Company, **14** 302–03; **50** 309–10

Flori Roberts, Inc., **11** 208

Florida Crystals Inc., **35** 176–78

Florida Cypress Gardens, Inc., **IV** 623

Florida Distillers Company, **27** 479

Florida East Coast Railway Company, **8** 486–87; **12** 278

Florida Flavors, **44** 137

Florida Frozen Foods, **13** 244

Florida Gaming Corporation, **47** 130–33

Florida Gas Co., **15** 129

Florida Gas Transmission Company, **6** 578

Florida National Banks of Florida, Inc., **II** 252

Florida Panthers Hockey Club, Ltd., **37** 33, 35

Florida Power & Light Company. See FPL Group, Inc.

Gilman & Co., **III** 523
Gilman Fanfold Corp., Ltd., **IV** 644
Gilman Paper Co., **37** 178
Gilmore Brother's, **I** 707
Gilmore Steel Corporation. *See* Oregon
    Steel Mills, Inc.
Gilroy Foods, **27** 299
Giltspur, **II** 587
Gimbel Brothers, Inc. *See* Saks Holdings,
    Inc.
Gimbel's Department Store, **I** 426–27; **8**
    59; **22** 72; **50** 117–18
Gindick Productions, **6** 28
Ginn & Co., **IV** 672; **19** 405
Ginnie Mae. *See* Government National
    Mortgage Association.
Gino's, **III** 103
Gino's East, **21** 362
Ginsber Beer Group, **15** 47; **38** 77
Giorgio Armani S.p.A., 45 180–83
Giorgio Beverly Hills, Inc., **26** 384
Giorgio, Inc., **III** 16; **19** 28
Girard Bank, **II** 315–16; **44** 280
Girbaud, **17** 513; **31** 261
Girl Scouts of the USA, 35 193–96
Giro Sport Designs International Inc., **16**
    53; **44** 53–54
Girod, **19** 50
Girsa S.A., **23** 170
Girvin, Inc., **16** 297
Gist-Brocades Co., **III** 53; **26** 384
The Gitano Group, Inc., 8 219–21; 20
    136 **25** 167; **37** 81
Givaudan SA, 43 190–93
GJM International Ltd., **25** 121–22
GK Technologies Incorporated, **10** 547
GKH Partners, **29** 295
GKN plc, III 493–96, 554, 556; **38**
    208–13 (upd.); 42 47; **47** 7, 9, 279–80
Glaceries de Saint-Roch, **III** 677; **16** 121
Glaces de Boussois, **II** 474–75
Glacier Bancorp, Inc., 35 197–200
Glacier Park Co., **10** 191
Glacier Water Services, Inc., 47 155–58
Gladieux Corp., **III** 103
Glamar Group plc, **14** 224
Glamor Shops, Inc., **14** 93
Glanbia Group, **38** 196, 198
Glasrock Home Health Care, **I** 316; **25** 81
Glass Containers Corp., **I** 609–10
Glass Fibres Ltd., **III** 726
Glasstite, Inc., **33** 360–61
GlasTec, **II** 420
Glastron. *See* Genmar Holdings, Inc.
Glatfelter Wood Pulp Company, **8** 413
Glaverbel, **III** 667
Glaxo Holdings plc, I 639–41, 643, 668,
    675, 693; **III** 66; **6** 346; **9** 263–65
    (upd.); 10 551; **11** 173; **20** 39; **26** 31;
    34 284; **38** 365; **50** 56
GlaxoSmithKline plc, 46 201–08 (upd.)
Gleason Corporation, 24 184–87
Glen & Co, **I** 453
Glen Alden Corp., **15** 247
Glen Cove Mutual Insurance Co., **III** 269
Glen-Gery Corporation, **14** 249
Glen Iris Bricks, **III** 673
Glen Line, **6** 416
Glencairn Ltd., **25** 418
Glendale Federal Savings, **IV** 29
The Glenlyte Group, **29** 469
Glenlyte Thomas Group LLC, **29** 466
Glenn Advertising Agency, **25** 90

Glenn Pleass Holdings Pty. Ltd., **21** 339
Glens Falls Insurance Co., **III** 242
GLF-Eastern States Association, **7** 17
The Glidden Company, I 353; 8 222–24;
    21 545
Glimcher Co., **26** 262
Glitsch International, Inc., **6** 146; **23** 206,
    208
Global Access, **31** 469
Global Apparel Sourcing Ltd., **22** 223
Global Communications of New York,
    Inc., **45** 261
Global Crossing Ltd., 32 216–19
Global Energy Group, **II** 345
Global Engineering Company, **9** 266
Global Health Care Partners, **42** 68
Global Industries, Ltd., 37 168–72
Global Information Solutions, **34** 257
Global Interactive Communications
    Corporation, **28** 242
Global Marine Inc., 9 266–67; 11 87
Global Natural Resources, **II** 401; **10** 145
Global Outdoors, Inc., 49 173–76
Global Telesystems Ltd. *See* Global
    Crossing Ltd.
Global Transport Organization, **6** 383
Global Vacations Group. *See* Classic
    Vacation Group, Inc.
Global Van Lines. *See* Allied Worldwide,
    Inc.
GlobalCom Telecommunications, Inc., **24**
    122
GlobaLex, **28** 141
GlobalSantaFe Corporation, 48 187–92
    (upd.)
Globe & Rutgers Insurance Co., **III**
    195–96
Globe Business Furniture, **39** 207
Globe Co. **I** 201
Globe Electric Co., **III** 536
Globe Feather & Down, **19** 304
Globe Files Co., **I** 201
Globe Grain and Milling Co., **II** 555
Globe Industries, **I** 540
Globe Insurance Co., **III** 350
Globe Life Insurance Co., **III** 187; **10** 28;
    38 15
Globe National Bank, **II** 261
Globe Newspaper Co., **7** 15
Globe Pequot Press, **36** 339, 341
Globe Petroleum Ltd., **IV** 401
Globe Steel Abrasive Co., **17** 371
Globe Telegraph and Trust Company, **25**
    99
Globe-Union, **III** 536; **26** 229
Globe-Wernicke Co., **I** 201
Globelle Corp., **43** 368
Globetrotter Communications, **7** 199
Globo, **18** 211
Glock Ges.m.b.H., 42 154–56
Gloria Jean's Gourmet Coffees, **20** 83
La Gloria Oil and Gas Company, **7** 102
Gloria Separator GmbH Berlin, **III** 418
Glosser Brothers, **13** 394
Gloster Aircraft, **I** 50; **III** 508; **24** 85
Gloucester Cold Storage and Warehouse
    Company, **13** 243
Glovatorium, **III** 152; **6** 266; **30** 339
Glowlite Corporation, **48** 359
Glycomed Inc., **13** 241; **47** 222
Glyn, Mills and Co., **II** 308; **12** 422
GM. *See* General Motors Corporation.

GM Hughes Electronics Corporation, II
    32–36; 10 325. *See also* Hughes
    Electronics Corporation.
GMARA, **II** 608
GMFanuc Robotics, **III** 482–83
GMR Properties, **21** 257
GNB International Battery Group, **10** 445
GND Holdings Corp., **7** 204; **28** 164
GNMA. *See* Government National
    Mortgage Association.
Gnôme & Rhône, **46** 369
The Go-Ahead Group Plc, 28 155–57
Go Fly Ltd., **39** 128
Go-Gro Industries, Ltd., **43** 99
Go Sport. *See* Groupe Go Sport S.A.
Go-Video, Inc. *See* Sensory Science
    Corporation.
Goal Systems International Inc., **10** 394
Godfather's Pizza Incorporated, II
    556–57; 11 50; **12** 123; **14** 351; **17** 86;
    25 179–81
Godfrey Co., **II** 625
Godfrey L. Cabot, Inc., **8** 77
Godiva Chocolatier, **II** 480; **26** 56
Godo Shusei, **III** 42
Godsell, **10** 277
Godtfred Kristiansen, **13** 310–11
Goebel & Wetterau Grocery Co., **II** 681
Goelitz Confectionary. *See* Herman
    Goelitz, Inc.
Goering Werke, **II** 282
Göhner AG, **6** 491
Gokey Company, **10** 216; **28** 339
Gold Bond Stamp Company, **6** 363–64; **22**
    125
Gold Crust Bakeries, **II** 465
Gold Dust Corp., **II** 497
Gold Exploration and Mining Co. Limited
    Partnership, **13** 503
Gold Fields of South Africa Ltd., I 423;
    IV 91, **94–97**
Gold Kist Inc., 7 432; **17 207–09; 26**
    166–68
Gold Lance Inc., **19** 451–52
Gold Lion, **20** 263
Gold Prospectors' Association of America,
    49 173
Gold Seal, **II** 567
Gold Star Foods Co., **IV** 410
Gold's Gym Enterprises, **25** 450
Goldblatt Bros., **IV** 135
Goldblatt's Department Stores, **15** 240–42
Golden Bear International, **33** 103; **42** 433;
    45 300
Golden Belt Manufacturing Co., 16
    241–43
Golden Books Family Entertainment,
    Inc., 28 158–61
Golden Circle Financial Services, **15** 328
Golden Corral Corporation, 10 331–33
Golden Eagle Exploration, **IV** 566–67
Golden Enterprises, Inc., 26 163–65
Golden Gate Airlines, **25** 421
Golden Grain Macaroni Co., **II** 560; **12**
    411; **30** 219; **34** 366
Golden Hope Rubber Estate, **III** 697, 699
Golden Moores Finance Company, **48** 286
Golden Nugget, Inc. *See* Mirage Resorts,
    Incorporated.
Golden Ocean Group, **45** 164
Golden Partners, **10** 333
Golden Peanut Company, **17** 207
Golden Poultry Company, **26** 168
Golden Press, Inc., **13** 559–61

INDEX TO INDUSTRIES

Index to Industries

ACCOUNTING

American Institute of Certified Public
  Accountants (AICPA), 44
Andersen Worldwide, 29 (upd.)
Automatic Data Processing, Inc., 47 (upd.)
Deloitte & Touche, 9
Deloitte Touche Tohmatsu International, 29
  (upd.)
Ernst & Young, 9; 29 (upd.)
KPMG International, 33 (upd.)
L.S. Starrett Co., 13
McLane Company, Inc., 13
NCO Group, Inc., 42
Paychex, Inc., 46 (upd.)
Price Waterhouse, 9
PricewaterhouseCoopers, 29 (upd.)
Robert Wood Johnson Foundation, 35
Univision Communications Inc., 24

ADVERTISING & OTHER BUSINESS SERVICES

A.C. Nielsen Company, 13
ABM Industries Incorporated, 25 (upd.)
Ackerley Communications, Inc., 9
ACNielsen Corporation, 38 (upd.)
Acsys, Inc., 44
Adecco S.A., 36 (upd.)
Adia S.A., 6
Advo, Inc., 6
Aegis Group plc, 6
AHL Services, Inc., 27
Amdocs Ltd., 47
American Building Maintenance Industries,
  Inc., 6
The American Society of Composers,
  Authors and Publishers (ASCAP), 29
Amey Plc, 47
Analysts International Corporation, 36
The Arbitron Company, 38
Armor Holdings, Inc., 27
Ashtead Group plc, 34
The Associated Press, 13
Barrett Business Services, Inc., 16
Bates Worldwide, Inc., 14; 33 (upd.)
Bearings, Inc., 13
Berlitz International, Inc., 13
Big Flower Press Holdings, Inc., 21
Boron, LePore & Associates, Inc., 45
Bozell Worldwide Inc., 25
Bright Horizons Family Solutions, Inc., 31
Broadcast Music Inc., 23
Burns International Services Corporation,
  13; 41 (upd.)
Cambridge Technology Partners, Inc., 36
Campbell-Mithun-Esty, Inc., 16
Career Education Corporation, 45
Carmichael Lynch Inc., 28
Central Parking Corporation, 18
ChartHouse International Learning
  Corporation, 49
Chiat/Day Inc. Advertising, 11
Chicago Board of Trade, 41
Chisholm-Mingo Group, Inc., 41
Christie's International plc, 15; 39 (upd.)

Cintas Corporation, 21
COMFORCE Corporation, 40
Computer Learning Centers, Inc., 26
Corporate Express, Inc., 47 (upd.)
CORT Business Services Corporation, 26
Cox Enterprises, Inc., 22 (upd.)
Creative Artists Agency LLC, 38
Cyrk Inc., 19
Dale Carnegie Training, Inc., 28
D'Arcy Masius Benton & Bowles, Inc., 6;
  32 (upd.)
Dawson Holdings PLC, 43
DDB Needham Worldwide, 14
Deluxe Corporation, 22 (upd.)
Dentsu Inc., I; 16 (upd.); 40 (upd.)
Deutsch, Inc., 42
Deutsche Post AG, 29
DoubleClick Inc., 46
Drake Beam Morin, Inc., 44
Earl Scheib, Inc., 32
EBSCO Industries, Inc., 17
Ecology and Environment, Inc., 39
Edison Schools Inc., 37
Education Management Corporation, 35
Employee Solutions, Inc., 18
Ennis Business Forms, Inc., 21
Equifax Inc., 6; 28 (upd.)
Equity Marketing, Inc., 26
ERLY Industries Inc., 17
Euro RSCG Worldwide S.A., 13
Fallon McElligott Inc., 22
Fiserv, Inc., 33 (upd.)
FlightSafety International, Inc., 29 (upd.)
Florists' Transworld Delivery, Inc., 28
Foote, Cone & Belding Communications,
  Inc., I
Frankel & Co., 39
Franklin Covey Company, 37 (upd.)
Gage Marketing Group, 26
The Gallup Organization, 37
GfK Aktiengesellschaft, 49
Grey Advertising, Inc., 6
Group 4 Falck A/S, 42
Groupe Jean-Claude Darmon, 44
GSD&M Advertising, 44
Gwathmey Siegel & Associates Architects
  LLC, 26
Ha-Lo Industries, Inc., 27
Hakuhodo, Inc., 6; 42 (upd.)
Handleman Company, 15
Havas SA, 33 (upd.)
Hays Plc, 27
Headway Corporate Resources, Inc., 40
Heidrick & Struggles International, Inc., 28
Hildebrandt International, 29
IKON Office Solutions, Inc., 50
Interep National Radio Sales Inc., 35
International Brotherhood of Teamsters, 37
International Management Group, 18
International Total Services, Inc., 37
The Interpublic Group of Companies, Inc.,
  I; 22 (upd.)
Ipsos SA, 48
Iron Mountain, Inc., 33
ITT Educational Services, Inc., 33

J.D. Power and Associates, 32
Jackson Hewitt, Inc., 48
Japan Leasing Corporation, 8
Jostens, Inc., 25 (upd.)
JWT Group Inc., I
Katz Communications, Inc., 6
Katz Media Group, Inc., 35
Kelly Services Inc., 6; 26 (upd.)
Ketchum Communications Inc., 6
Kinko's, Inc., 16; 43 (upd.)
Korn/Ferry International, 34
Labor Ready, Inc., 29
Lamar Advertising Company, 27
Learning Tree International Inc., 24
Leo Burnett Company Inc., I; 20 (upd.)
Lintas: Worldwide, 14
Mail Boxes Etc., 18; 41 (upd.)
Manpower, Inc., 30
marchFIRST, Inc., 34
Maritz Inc., 38
MAXIMUS, Inc., 43
Mediaset SpA, 50
MPS Group, Inc., 49
Mullen Advertising Inc., 51
National Media Corporation, 27
New England Business Services, Inc., 18
New Valley Corporation, 17
NFO Worldwide, Inc., 24
Nobel Learning Communities, Inc., 37
Norrell Corporation, 25
Norwood Promotional Products, Inc., 26
The Ogilvy Group, Inc., I
Olsten Corporation, 6; 29 (upd.)
Omnicom Group, I; 22 (upd.)
On Assignment, Inc., 20
1-800-FLOWERS, Inc., 26
Opinion Research Corporation, 46
Outdoor Systems, Inc., 25
Paris Corporation, 22
Paychex, Inc., 15
Penauille Polyservices SA, 49
Phillips, de Pury & Luxembourg, 49
Pierce Leahy Corporation, 24
Pinkerton's Inc., 9
PMT Services, Inc., 24
Publicis S.A., 19
Publishers Clearing House, 23
Randstad Holding n.v., 16; 43 (upd.)
RemedyTemp, Inc., 20
Rental Service Corporation, 28
Rentokil Initial Plc, 47
Right Management Consultants, Inc., 42
Ritchie Bros. Auctioneers Inc., 41
Robert Half International Inc., 18
Roland Berger & Partner GmbH, 37
Ronco, Inc., 15
Russell Reynolds Associates Inc., 38
Saatchi & Saatchi, I; 42 (upd.)
Securitas AB, 42
ServiceMaster Limited Partnership, 6
Shared Medical Systems Corporation, 14
Sir Speedy, Inc., 16
Skidmore, Owings & Merrill, 13
SmartForce PLC, 43
SOS Staffing Services, 25

ELECTRICAL & ELECTRONICS

FINANCIAL SERVICES: NON-BANKS

HEALTH & PERSONAL CARE PRODUCTS

HEALTH CARE SERVICES

INSURANCE

MANUFACTURING

REAL ESTATE

RETAIL & WHOLESALE

TEXTILES & APPAREL

UTILITIES

GEOGRAPHIC INDEX

Geographic Index

NOTES ON CONTRIBUTORS

Notes on Contributors

AMOROSINO, Chris. Connecticut-based freelance writer.

BIANCO, David. Freelance writer, editor, and publishing consultant.

BRENNAN, Gerald E. Freelance writer based in California.

BRYNILDSSEN, Shawna. Freelance writer and editor based in Bloomington, Indiana.

CAMPBELL, June. Freelance writer and Internet marketer living in Vancouver, Canada.

COHEN, M. L. Novelist and freelance writer living in Paris.

COVELL, Jeffrey L. Seattle-based freelance writer.

DINGER, Ed. Brooklyn-based freelance writer and editor.

FIERO, John W. Freelance writer, researcher, and consultant.

GREENLAND, Paul R. Illinois-based writer and researcher; author of two books and former senior editor of a national business magazine; contributor to *The Encyclopedia of Chicago History* (University of Chicago Press) and *Company Profiles for Students.*

HALASZ, Robert. Former editor in chief of *World Progress* and *Funk & Wagnalls New Encyclopedia Yearbook;* author, *The U.S. Marines* (Millbrook Press, 1993).

HAUSER, Evelyn. Researcher, writer and marketing specialist based in Arcata, California; expertise includes historical and trend research in such topics as globalization, emerging industries and lifestyles, future scenarios, biographies, and the history of organizations.

INGRAM, Frederick C. Utah-based business writer who has contributed to *GSA Business, Appalachian Trailway News,* the *Encyclopedia of Business,* the *Encyclopedia of Global Industries,* the *Encyclopedia of Consumer Brands,* and other regional and trade publications.

KARL, Lisa Musolf. Freelance editor, writer, and columnist living in the Chicago area.

LEMIEUX, Gloria A. Freelance writer and editor living in Nashua, New Hampshire.

LORENZ, Sarah Ruth. Minnesota-based freelance writer.

MONTGOMERY, Bruce P. Curator and director of historical collection, University of Colorado at Boulder.

ROTHBURD, Carrie. Freelance writer and editor specializing in corporate profiles, academic texts, and academic journal articles.

STANSELL, Christina M. Freelance writer and editor based in Farmington Hills, Michigan.

TRADII, Mary. Freelance writer based in Denver, Colorado.

UHLE, Frank. Ann Arbor-based freelance writer; movie projectionist, disc jockey, and staff member of *Psychotronic Video* magazine.

WALDEN, David M. Freelance writer and historian in Salt Lake City; adjunct history instructor at Salt Lake City Community College.

WOODWARD, A. Freelance writer.